KB084284

문제집

해커스 토익

실전 1200제

READING RC

베스트셀러 1위

"내가 틀릴만한 문제만 골라서 공부한다!"

해커스토익 빅플

본 교재
모든 문제
**취약 유형
심층 분석**
무료 제공

물토익부터 불토익까지!

최근 12개월
실제 시험 난이도
반영된 문제로

**토익
졸업**

맞춤 과외식
해설로

**추가
자료** 해커스인강 HackersIngang.com 본 교재 인강, 무료 단어암기장 및 단어암기 MP3, 무료 정답녹음 MP3
해커스토익 Hackers.co.kr 스타강사 무료 적중 예상특강, 무료 실시간 토익시험 정답확인/해설강의, 무료 매일 실전 RC/LC 문제

[최근 12개월] 2019.03.31~2020.03.31까지의 토익 시험 난이도 분석 및 반영
알라딘 외국어 베스트셀러 토익 종합 분야 1위[2020년 8월 1주 주간 베스트 기준]

해커스 어학연구소

대한민국 토익커

평 균 응 시 횟 수	9 회
평 균 점 수	6 7 8 점

난
토익졸업
언제하지 ?

해커스 토익 _{실전}1200제 로
바로 **졸업**할 수 있습니다

실제 시험과 똑같은 난이도의 문제로 대비하니까!

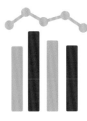

최근 12개월 실제 시험과
동일한 난이도의
실전 문제 풀이

정답 찾는 방법을 콕 짚어주는 해설이 있으니까!

오답의 이유까지
꼼꼼하게 알려주는
맞춤 과외식 해설로 실력 상승

내 약점을 정확하게 찾아서 보완해주니까!

해커스 인공지능 시스템
"빅플"로
취약 유형 문제 반복 학습

해커스 토익 실전 1200제 READING RC

300% 활용법

단어암기장 및 단어암기 MP3

정답 PDF 및 정답 녹음 MP3

이용방법 **해커스인강** HackersIngang.com 접속 후 로그인 ≫
상단 메뉴 [토익 → MP3/자료 → 무료 MP3/자료] 클릭하여 이용하기

무료 매일 실전 RC/LC 문제

이용방법 **해커스토익** Hackers.co.kr 접속 ≫
상단 메뉴 [토익 → 토익 무료학습 → 매일 실전 RC/LC 풀기] 클릭하여 이용하기

빅플 약점집중학습 이용권

이용방법 **해커스인강** HackersIngang.com 접속 후 로그인 ≫
[마이클래스 → 결제관리 → 내 쿠폰 확인하기] 클릭 ≫
위 쿠폰번호 입력 후 빅플 어플에서 이용권 확인하기

* 이용기한: 2025년 12월 31일(등록 후 14일간 사용 가능)

함께 학습하면 좋은 **해커스토익 빅플 APP**

해커스토익 빅플

본 교재 모든 문제

취약 유형 심층 분석

무료 제공

· 어플을 통해 언제 어디서나 편리하게 토익 문제풀이 학습
· 문제풀이에 대한 학습결과 분석 자료로 취약점 파악 및 약점 보완

≫ 구글 플레이스토어/애플 앱스토어에서 '빅플'을 검색하세요.

▲ 빅플 다운 받기

이용방법 [해커스토익 빅플] 어플 접속 ≫ 상단 [교재풀이] 클릭 후 본 교재 OMR 답안 입력 및 제출 ≫
[분석레포트] 클릭 ≫ 교재 풀이 분석 결과보기

해커스 토익

문제집

실전 **1200**제

READING RC

해커스 어학연구소

최신 토익 경향과 난이도를 완벽하게 반영한
해커스 토익
실전 1200제 READING을 내면서

대한민국 토익커 평균 응시 횟수 9회, 평균 점수 678점..

많은 토익커들의 토익 졸업을 앞당길 수 있도록, 최신 토익 경향과 난이도를 완벽 반영한 ≪**해커스 토익 실전 1200제 READING**≫을 출간하였습니다.

최근 12개월 실제 토익 난이도와 출제 경향을 완벽 반영한 문제집으로 실전 대비!

물토익부터 불토익까지 종잡을 수 없이 들쑥날쑥하게 출제되는 토익 시험의 난이도를 철저히 분석하여, 최근 12개월의 토익 시험 출제 경향 및 기출 유형이 완벽 반영된 12회분의 테스트를 수록하였습니다. 12회분의 테스트 안에서도 파트마다 난이도가 다르게 출제되는 경향까지 완벽하게 반영하여, 실제 시험과 동일한 난이도의 문제로 연습하며 실전 감각을 최대로 끌어올릴 수 있습니다.

오답의 이유까지 상세하게 설명해주는 맞춤 과외식 해설 제공!

각 문제에 대한 스크립트와 해석, 정답에 대한 해설은 물론, 오답의 이유까지 상세하게 설명해주는 맞춤 과외식 해설을 제공하여 모든 문제를 확실하게 이해하고 문제풀이 노하우까지 익힐 수 있도록 하였습니다. 또한, 모든 문제에 난이도와 세분화된 문제 유형을 제공하여 자신의 실력과 학습 목표에 따라 학습할 수 있도록 하였습니다.

인공지능 토익어플 '해커스토익 빅플'로 내 약점을 정확하게 찾아서 집중 공략!

문제를 풀고 답안을 입력하기만 하면, 인공지능 어플 '해커스토익 빅플'이 자동 채점은 물론 성적분석표와 취약 유형 심층 분석까지 제공합니다. 이를 통해, 자신이 가장 많이 틀리는 취약 유형이 무엇인지 확인하고, 관련 문제들을 추가로 학습하며 취약 유형을 집중 공략하여 약점을 보완할 수 있습니다.

≪**해커스 토익 실전 1200제 READING**≫이 여러분의 토익 목표 점수 달성에 확실한 해결책이 되고, 여러분의 꿈을 향한 길에 믿음직한 동반자가 되기를 소망합니다.

CONTENTS

오답의 이유까지 설명해 주는 맞춤 과외식
해설집

 인공지능 토익튜터 빅플

 단어암기장 및 단어암기 MP3

해커스 토익 실전 1200제 READING

실제 시험과 똑같은 난이도로 실전 감각을 최대로 끌어올리는 12회분 문제

실전과 동일한 난이도와 경향 반영

<해커스 토익 실전 1200제 READING>은 최근 12개월 간 출제된 토익 시험을 철저하게 분석하여 실제 시험의 들쑥날쑥한 난이도와 출제 경향을 완벽하게 반영한 12회분 문제를 수록하였습니다. 또한, 실제 시험처럼 한 테스트 안에서도 파트별 난이도를 서로 다르게 출제하여, 실전과 가장 비슷한 12회분 문제로 토익 시험에 대비할 수 있습니다.

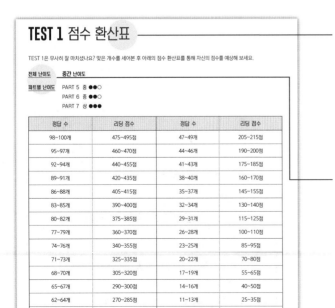

점수 환산표

각 테스트의 마지막에 테스트별 난이도에 따라 다르게 구성된 점수 환산표가 수록되어 있습니다. 이를 통해 자신의 토익 리딩 점수를 보다 정확하게 예상할 수 있습니다.

점수 환산표에 수록된 테스트별 난이도와 파트별 난이도를 통해, 방금 풀어 본 테스트의 종합적인 난이도와 각 파트의 난이도를 한눈에 확인할 수 있습니다.

오답의 이유까지 설명하여 모든 궁금증을 완벽히 해결해 주는 맞춤 과외식 해설집

문제 유형 및 난이도

세부 문제 유형을 통해 자주 틀리는 유형을 쉽게 파악할 수 있고, 문제별 난이도를 확인하여 자신의 실력에 따라 학습할 수 있습니다.

상세한 해설과 오답의 이유 설명

문제 유형별로 가장 효과적인 풀이 방법을 제시하고, 정답은 물론 오답의 이유까지 상세하게 설명하여 틀린 문제의 원인을 파악하고 보완할 수 있습니다.

패러프레이징 및 어휘

지문의 내용이 문제에서 패러프레이징된 경우, 이를 [지문의 표현 → 문제의 표현] 또는 [질문의 표현 → 지문의 표현]으로 정리하여 한눈에 확인할 수 있도록 하였습니다. 또한, 지문 및 문제에서 등장한 표현 및 어휘를 제공하여 문제를 복습할 때 사전을 찾는 불편을 덜 수 있습니다.

취약 유형을 콕 집어 집중 공략하는 인공지능 1:1 토익어플 '빅플'

자동 채점 및 분석 레포트

교재의 문제를 풀고 난 후, '해커스토익 빅플' 어플에 정답을 입력해 자동으로 채점 및 취약 유형 분석을 진행할 수 있습니다.

[성적분석] 탭에서는 나의 총점, 석차백분율, 상위권 10%와 비교했을 때 나의 점수 등을 확인하고, 각 PART별로 맞은 개수를 한 눈에 볼 수 있습니다. 또한, [난이도]와 [심층분석] 탭에서 문제별 난이도와 맞은 개수, 각 문제별 실제 유저들의 정답률을 확인하여, 방금 풀었던 문제의 난이도를 상세하게 파악할 수 있습니다.

취약점 분석

[취약점] 탭에서 지금까지 풀어 본 문제 중 가장 오답률이 높은 취약 유형 3가지를 한눈에 확인할 수 있습니다. 해당 유형의 총 문제 수 대비 맞힌 문제 수와 응시생 정답률을 통해 취약점을 구체적인 수치로 확인한 후, 오답 문제 번호들을 보고 교재로 돌아가 약점 유형 문제들만을 골라 다시 복습해 볼 수 있습니다.

약점 집중 학습

[취약 유형] 탭에서는 분석 레포트를 통해 확인한 취약 유형 문제들만을 집중적으로 풀어보며 약점을 효율적으로 보완할 수 있습니다. 또한, [도전 유형] 탭에서는 취약 유형 다음으로 오답률이 높은 문제 유형까지 확인하고 집중 학습하여, 점수를 더 빠르게 올릴 수 있습니다.

맞춤 집중 학습

각각의 유형 문제를 클릭하여 해당 유형의 문제들을 한 번에 모아서 풀어 볼 수 있습니다. 이를 통해, 시험장에 갔을 때 틀릴 가능성이 높은 문제들만을 집중적으로 학습해 효율적으로 점수를 올릴 수 있습니다.

토익 졸업의 가능성을 한 단계 더 높이는 다양한 부가물

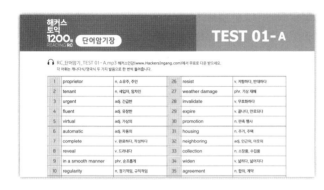

단어암기자료 PDF & MP3

해커스인강(HackersIngang.com) 사이트에서 단어암기 PDF 와 MP3를 무료로 제공하여, 교재에 수록된 테스트의 중요 단어를 쉽고 편리하게 복습하고 암기할 수 있도록 하였습니다.

방대한 무료 학습자료[Hackers.co.kr] / 동영상 강의[HackersIngang.com]

해커스토익(Hackers.co.kr) 사이트에서는 토익 적중 예상 특강을 비롯한 방대하고 유용한 토익 학습 자료를 무료로 이용 할 수 있습니다. 또한 온라인 교육 포털 사이트인 해커스인강 (HackersIngang.com) 사이트에서 교재 동영상 강의를 수강 하면, 보다 깊이 있는 학습이 가능합니다.

PART 5

101 (C)	102 (D)	103 (B)	104 (C)	105 (C)
106 (B)	107 (C)	108 (A)	109 (B)	110 (C)
111 (D)	112 (C)	113 (D)	114 (B)	115 (C)
116 (C)	117 (D)	118 (D)	119 (D)	120 (B)
121 (C)	122 (A)	123 (C)	124 (C)	125 (A)
126 (C)	127 (B)	128 (B)	129 (C)	130 (D)

PART 6

131 (C)	132 (A)	133 (A)	134 (D)	135 (A)
136 (B)	137 (B)	138 (A)	139 (C)	140 (D)

정답지 PDF & 정답 녹음 MP3

해커스인강(HackersIngang.com) 사이트에서 정답지 PDF 와 정답 녹음 MP3를 무료로 제공하여 학습자들이 보다 편리하 게 채점할 수 있도록 하였습니다.

토익 소개 및 시험장 Tips

토익이란 무엇인가?

TOEIC은 Test of English for International Communication의 약자로 영어가 모국어가 아닌 사람들을 대상으로 언어 본래의 기능인 '커뮤니케이션' 능력에 중점을 두고 일상생활 또는 국제 업무 등에 필요한 실용영어 능력을 평가하는 시험입니다. 토익은 일상생활 및 비즈니스 현장에서 필요로 하는 내용을 평가하기 위해 개발되었고 다음과 같은 실용적인 주제들을 주로 다룹니다.

- 협력 개발: 연구, 제품 개발
- 재무 회계: 대출, 투자, 세금, 회계, 은행 업무
- 일반 업무: 계약, 협상. 마케팅, 판매
- 기술 영역: 전기, 공업 기술, 컴퓨터, 실험실
- 사무 영역: 회의, 서류 업무
- 물품 구입: 쇼핑, 물건 주문, 대금 지불

- 식사: 레스토랑, 회식, 만찬
- 문화: 극장, 스포츠, 피크닉
- 건강: 의료 보험, 병원 진료, 치과
- 제조: 생산 조립 라인, 공장 경영
- 직원: 채용, 은퇴, 급여, 진급, 고용 기회
- 주택: 부동산, 이사, 기업 부지

토익의 파트별 구성

구성		내용	문항수	시간	배점
Listening Test	Part 1	사진 묘사	6문항 (1번-6번)	45분	495점
	Part 2	질의 응답	25문항 (7번-31번)		
	Part 3	짧은 대화	39문항, 13지문 (32번-70번)		
	Part 4	짧은 담화	30문항, 10지문 (71번-100번)		
Reading Test	Part 5	단문 빈칸 채우기	30문항 (101번-130번)	75분	495점
	Part 6	장문 빈칸 채우기	16문항, 4지문 (131번-146번)		
	Part 7	지문 읽고 문제 풀기(독해) -단일 지문 (Single Passage) -이중 지문 (Double Passages) -삼중 지문 (Triple Passages)	54문항, 15지문 (147번-200번) -29문항, 10지문 (147번-175번) -10문항, 2지문 (176번-185번) -15문항, 3지문 (186번-200번)		
Total		**7 Parts**	**200문항**	**120분**	**990점**

토익 접수 방법 및 성적 확인

1. 접수 방법
· 접수 기간을 TOEIC위원회 인터넷 사이트(www.toeic.co.kr) 혹은 공식 애플리케이션에서 확인하고 접수합니다.
· 접수 시 jpg형식의 사진 파일이 필요하므로 미리 준비합니다.

2. 성적 확인
· 시험일로부터 약 10일 이후 TOEIC위원회 인터넷 사이트(www.toeic.co.kr) 혹은 공식 애플리케이션에서 확인합니다. (성적 발표 기간은 회차마다 상이함)
· 시험 접수 시, 우편 수령과 온라인 출력 중 성적 수령 방법을 선택할 수 있습니다.
  *온라인 출력은 성적 발표 즉시 발급 가능하나, 우편 수령은 약 7일가량의 발송 기간이 소요될 수 있습니다.

시험 당일 준비물

| 신분증 | 연필&지우개 | 시계 | 수험번호를 적어둔 메모 | 오답노트&단어암기장 |

* 시험 당일 신분증이 없으면 시험에 응시할 수 없으므로, 반드시 ETS에서 요구하는 신분증(주민등록증, 운전면허증, 공무원증 등)을 지참해야 합니다.
  ETS에서 인정하는 신분증 종류는 TOEIC위원회 인터넷 사이트(www.toeic.co.kr)에서 확인 가능합니다.

시험 진행 순서

정기시험/추가시험(오전)	추가시험(오후)	진행내용	유의사항
AM 9:30-9:45	PM 2:30-2:45	답안지 작성 오리엔테이션	10분 전에 고사장에 도착하여, 이름과 수험번호로 고사실을 확인합니다.
AM 9:45-9:50	PM 2:45-2:50	쉬는 시간	준비해 간 오답노트나 단어암기장으로 최종 정리를 합니다. 시험 중간에는 쉬는 시간이 없으므로 화장실에 꼭 다녀오도록 합니다.
AM 9:50-10:10	PM 2:50-3:10	신분 확인 및 문제지 배부	
AM 10:10-10:55	PM 3:10-3:55	Listening Test	Part 1과 Part 2는 문제를 풀면서 정답을 바로 답안지에 마킹합니다. Part 3와 Part 4는 문제의 정답 보기 옆에 살짝 표시해두고, READING Test가 끝난 후 한꺼번에 마킹합니다.
AM 10:55-12:10	PM 3:55-5:10	Reading Test	각 문제를 풀 때 바로 정답을 마킹합니다.

파트별 형태 및 전략

Part 5 단문 빈칸 채우기 (30문제)

· 한 문장의 빈칸에 알맞은 문법 사항이나 어휘를 4개의 보기 중에서 고르는 유형
· 권장 소요 시간: 11분 (문제당 풀이 시간: 20초~22초)

문제 형태

1 문법

101. Mr. Monroe announced his ------- to retire from the firm at a meeting last week.
(A) decides
(B) decisively
(C) decision
(D) decisive

해설 **101.** 빈칸 앞에 형용사 역할을 하는 소유격 인칭대명사(his)가 왔으므로 형용사의 꾸밈을 받을 수 있는 명사 (C)가 정답이다.

2 어휘

102. Effective on Monday, employees must start ------- a new procedure for ordering office supplies.
(A) causing
(B) following
(C) excluding
(D) informing

해설 **102.** '직원들은 새로운 절차를 ____ 하기 시작해야 한다'라는 문맥에 가장 잘 어울리는 단어는 동사 follow의 동명사 (B)이다.

문제 풀이 전략

1. 보기를 보고 문법 문제인지, 어휘 문제인지 유형을 파악합니다.

네 개의 보기를 보고 문법 사항을 묻는 문제인지, 어휘의 의미를 묻는 문제인지를 파악합니다. 보기가 첫 번째 예제의 decides, decisively, decision, decisive처럼 품사가 다른 단어들로 구성되어 있으면 문법 문제이고, 두 번째 예제의 causing, following, excluding, informing처럼 품사는 같지만 의미가 다른 단어들로 구성되어 있으면 어휘 문제입니다.

2. 문제 유형에 따라 빈칸 주변이나 문장 구조 또는 문맥을 통해 정답을 선택합니다.

문법 문제는 빈칸 주변이나 문장 구조를 통해 빈칸에 적합한 문법적 요소를 정답으로 선택합니다. 어휘 문제의 경우 문맥을 확인하여 문맥에 가장 적합한 단어를 정답으로 선택합니다.

* 실제 시험을 볼 때, Part 1과 Part 2의 디렉션이 나오는 동안 Part 5 문제를 최대한 많이 풀면 전체 시험 시간 조절에 도움이 됩니다.

Part 6 장문 빈칸 채우기 [16문제]

· 한 지문 내의 4개의 빈칸에 알맞은 문법 사항이나 어휘, 문장을 고르는 유형. 총 4개의 지문 출제.
· 권장 소요 시간: 8분 (문제당 풀이 시간: 25초~30초)

문제 형태

Questions 131-134 refer to the following e-mail.

Dear Ms. Swerter,

It was a treat to see your group ------- its music at the community event in Morristown. Do you think you could do the
                                    131.
same for us at a private gathering next month? My company ------- a welcoming celebration for some clients. -------.
                                                            132.   **133.**
We are planning a special dinner and are hoping your group can provide the accompanying entertainment. We'd

also like to book the dancers who were with you at the concert. Their performance was quite ------- to watch. Our
                                                                                            134.
guests would surely enjoy seeing both acts together. Please let me know.

Shannon Lemmick

어휘 **131.** (A) act
(B) explain
(C) perform
(D) observe

문법 **132.** (A) will be hosting
(B) hosted
(C) hosts
(D) to host

문장 **133.** (A) I'd like to buy tickets for the afternoon show.
고르기 (B) You may request their services for an additional charge.
(C) It will be their first time meeting with my company's staff.
(D) We approve of the schedule you have proposed.

어휘 **134.** (A) tough
(B) thrilling
(C) content
(D) punctual

해설 **131.** '당신의 그룹이 지역 사회 행사에서 곡을 연주하는 것을 보게 되어 좋았다'라는 문맥이므로 동사 (C)가 정답이다.

132. 앞 문장에서 다음 달에 같은 공연을 해줄 수 있는지 물었으므로 행사가 미래에 열린다는 것을 알 수 있다. 따라서 미래 시제 (A)가 정답이다.

133. 앞 문장에서 '회사는 몇몇 고객들을 위한 환영 행사를 개최할 것이다'라고 했으므로 빈칸에는 고객들과의 만남에 대한 추가적인 내용이 들어가
야 함을 알 수 있다. 따라서 (C)가 정답이다.

134. '그들의 공연은 관람하기에 꽤 황홀했다'라는 문맥이므로 형용사 (B)가 정답이다.

문제 풀이 전략

1. 보기를 보고 문제 유형을 파악합니다.

보기를 먼저 보고 문법 문제, 어휘 문제, 문장 고르기 문제 가운데 어떤 유형의 문제인지를 파악합니다.

2. 문제 유형에 따라 빈칸이 포함된 문장이나, 앞뒤 문장, 또는 전체 지문의 문맥을 통해 정답을 선택합니다.

Part 6에서는 빈칸이 포함된 문장뿐만 아니라 앞뒤 문장, 전체 지문의 문맥을 통해 정답을 파악해야 하는 문제도 출제됩니다.
그러므로 빈칸이 포함된 문장의 구조 및 문맥만으로 정답 선택이 어려울 경우 앞뒤 문맥이나 전체 문맥을 통해 정답을 선택합니다.

Part 7 지문 읽고 문제 풀기 [54문제]

· 지문을 읽고 지문과 관련된 질문들에 대해 가장 적절한 보기를 정답으로 고르는 유형
· 구성: Single Passage에서 29문제, Double Passages에서 10문제, Triple Passages에서 15문제 출제
· 권장 소요 시간: 54분 (문제당 풀이 시간: 1분)

문제 형태

1 단일 지문 (Single Passage)

Questions 164-167 refer to the following advertisement.

AVALON WINDOWS
The window professionals

For over 30 years, homeowners have trusted Avalon Windows for expert window installation and repair. We offer quick and efficient service no matter what the job is. — [1] —. We ensure total customer satisfaction for a reasonable price. — [2] —. We provide accurate measurements, a complete project estimate with no hidden fees, and a 10-year warranty on all installations. We also offer a selection of window styles and sizes for you to choose from. — [3] —. Simply call us at 555-2092 to receive a free catalog in the mail or to schedule a consultation. Mention this advertisement when you call and receive 15 percent off your next window installation. — [4] —.

164. For whom is the advertisement intended?

(A) Real estate consultants
(B) Proprietors of residences
(C) Construction contractors
(D) Building supply retailers

165. What is true about Avalon Windows?

(A) It offers guarantees on installations.
(B) It also offers construction services.
(C) It plans to expand style selections.
(D) It charges a small fee for job estimates.

166. How can customers obtain discounts on a service?

(A) By ordering a specific number of windows
(B) By signing up on a Web site
(C) By mailing in a special coupon
(D) By mentioning an advertisement

167. In which of the positions marked [1], [2], [3], and [4] does the following sentence best belong?

"In fact, if you aren't pleased with our work, you'll get your money back."

(A) [1]
(B) [2]
(C) [3]
(D) [4]

해설 **164.** 주택 소유자들이 Avalon Windows사에 전문적인 창문 설치와 수리를 믿고 맡겨왔다고 했으므로 (B)가 정답이다.

165. Avalon Windows사가 모든 설치에 대해 10년의 보증을 제공한다고 했으므로 (A)가 정답이다.

166. 전화해서 이 광고를 언급하면 다음 창문 설치 시 15퍼센트 할인을 받는다고 했으므로 (D)가 정답이다.

167. 제시된 문장이 실제로 작업에 만족하지 않을 시에는 돈을 돌려받을 것이라고 했으므로, [2]에 제시된 문장이 들어가면 Avalon Windows사는 전면적인 고객 만족을 보장하므로 실제로 작업에 만족하지 않을 시에는 돈을 돌려받을 것이라는 자연스러운 문맥이 된다는 것을 알 수 있다. 따라서 (B)가 정답이다.

2 이중 지문 (Double Passages)

Questions 176-180 refer to the following e-mails.

To: Natalie Mercer <n.mercer@silverfield.com>
From: Robert Altieri <r.altieri@silverfield.com>
Subject: Digital Creators Conference (DCC)
Date: October 9
Attachment: DCC passes

Natalie,

I have attached four passes for you and your team to the upcoming DCC in San Francisco and would now like to go ahead and book your accommodations there. I know you stayed at the Gordon Suites and the Grand Burgess Hotel in previous years, but I think I have found some better options. Please indicate which of the following hotels you wish to stay at in response to this e-mail.

The Bismarck Hotel is close to the convention center but unfortunately does not offer access to Wi-Fi. Those who need to work from the hotel may thus be interested in the Newburg Plaza, which provides free Internet use. However, staying at this location would require the reservation of a car service, as it is a 20-minute drive from the conference venue.

Let me know which one you prefer when you have a moment. Also, please note that the passes I have attached allow entry to the event halls on all four days. Meals are not included, but there are places to purchase food at nearby restaurants. Thank you.

Robert

To: Robert Altieri <r.altieri@silverfield.com>
From: Natalie Mercer <n.mercer@silverfield.com>
Subject: Re: Digital Creators Conference (DCC)
Date: October 9

Robert,

I think it's best for us to have access to the Internet at the hotel. Some of my team members will be convening on evenings following the conference events and may want to reference information online. As for the car service, I believe we can have expenses reimbursed for that. Everyone agrees that a 20-minute ride doesn't sound like a major inconvenience.

But before you make the reservation, could you check what the rates are for parking at the hotel? Francine will be taking her own vehicle to San Francisco and will need to leave it in a lot for the duration of the conference. Thanks in advance.

Natalie

176. Why did Mr. Altieri write the e-mail?

(A) To invite a guest to speak at a conference
(B) To ask about a preference for a trip
(C) To explain a travel expense policy
(D) To ask for airline recommendations

177. What is NOT mentioned about the Digital Creators Conference?

(A) It lasts for four days.
(B) It is a short drive from the airport.
(C) It is close to dining establishments.
(D) It is being held in San Francisco.

178. In the second e-mail, the word "reference" in paragraph 1, line 2, is closest in meaning to

(A) mention
(B) supply
(C) search
(D) adapt

179. Which hotel will Mr. Altieri most likely book?

(A) The Gordon Suites
(B) The Grand Burgess Hotel
(C) The Bismarck Hotel
(D) The Newburg Plaza

180. What is indicated about Ms. Mercer?

(A) She has a team member who will bring her own car.
(B) She might change her mind about attending the DCC.
(C) She has an issue with Mr. Altieri's proposals.
(D) She is busy preparing for a series of presentations.

해설 **176.** 선택할 수 있는 2가지 숙박 시설 중 어느 것을 더 선호하는지 알려달라고 했으므로 (B)가 정답이다.

177 공항에서 차로 가까운 거리에 있다는 내용은 지문에 언급되지 않았으므로 (B)가 정답이다.

178. reference를 포함하고 있는 구절 'will be convening ~ and may want to reference information online'에서 reference가 '찾아보다, 참고하다'라는 뜻으로 사용되었다. 따라서 '찾다'라는 의미의 (C)가 정답이다.

179. 두 번째 이메일에서 호텔에 인터넷 이용이 가능한 것이 좋을 것 같다고 했고, 첫 번째 이메일에서 Newburg Plaza가 무료 인터넷 이용을 제공한다고 했으므로 (D)가 정답이다.

180. 같이 회의에 가는 Francine이 자신의 차량을 샌프란시스코에 가져올 것이라고 했으므로 (A)가 정답이다.

3 삼중 지문 (Triple Passages)

Questions 186-190 refer to the following e-mail, schedule, and article.

TO: Ben Finch <ben.finch@mymail.com>
FROM: Taylor Gray <t.gray@streetmag.com>
SUBJECT: Welcome to *Street Magazine*
DATE: June 12

Hi Ben,

Congratulations on being selected as an intern for *Street Magazine*. For 25 years, the citizens of Seattle have looked to us weekly for the latest fashion, art, and music news.

Your internship will be from July 1 to December 31. You will report to me five days a week from 9:00 A.M. to 6:00 P.M. As an intern, you will not be a salaried employee, but we will provide an allowance for some expenses. If you do well, there may be a place for you here after your internship ends.

Please note that although you will have to do office work for various departments as the need arises, your responsibilities will be to research, take notes, and fact check content for me.

Taylor Gray

Personal Work Schedule: Taylor Gray
Thursday, August 7

Time	Activities	To do
09:30	Discuss budget with Mr. Robinson	
11:30	Leave for lunch appointment with photographer Stacy Larson	
13:00	Review photo submissions for "People" section	
14:30	Proofread articles for print version of lifestyle section	Send final list to Ms. McKee
16:00	Cover photo shoot at West Town Music Club	Assign to Ryan Oakley
16:30	Fact check music section for Web site	
17:30	Pick up laundry at Van's Cleaners	
18:00	Interview owner of Contempo Art Space	

Street Magazine

"Fusion In Fusion"
Opening Reception, Contempo Art Space
Thursday, August 7, 6:00 P.M. – 8:00 P.M.

This exhibit of artwork expresses an appreciation for all creative art forms, such as visual art, music, dance, film, and more. Works are representational or abstract, in 2D or 3D. All pieces exhibited in the main gallery will be for sale. This exhibit will be on display until November 6. For details, please contact gallery owner Mischa Michaels at 555-3941.

186. What is NOT true about the internship position at *Street Magazine*?

(A) It does not pay a regular salary.
(B) It involves working with different departments.
(C) It can lead to offers of a permanent job.
(D) It is available only during the summer.

187. What is suggested about *Street Magazine* in the e-mail?

(A) It is planning to relocate its office.
(B) It is published on a weekly basis.
(C) It is mainly devoted to fashion news.
(D) It has subscribers in many cities.

188. What task will Mr. Finch most likely be assigned on August 7?

(A) Proofreading lifestyle section material
(B) Collecting items from a laundry facility
(C) Reviewing photographic submissions
(D) Fact checking music section content

189. What can be inferred about Ms. Gray?

(A) She will be interviewing Ms. Michaels.
(B) She is unable to make her lunch appointment.
(C) She will be supervising a photo shoot.
(D) She is responsible for approving a budget.

190. What is mentioned about the exhibit at Contempo Art Space?

(A) It is a collection of past works by a group.
(B) Some of the artworks may be purchased on-site.
(C) It will run in conjunction with another event.
(D) Most of the participants are known artists.

해설 **186.** 이메일에서 *Street*지에서의 인턴직이 7월 1일부터 12월 31일까지라고 했으므로 (D)가 정답이다.

187. 지역 독자들이 *Street*지가 주간 단위로 최신 사건들을 알려줄 것이라고 기대해왔다고 했으므로 (B)가 정답이다.

188. 이메일에서 Ms. Finch가 맡을 일 중 Ms. Gray를 위해 온라인 기사의 사실 확인을 하는 것이 있다고 했고, 일정표에서 Ms. Gray의 8월 7일 일정에 웹사이트의 음악 부문에 대한 사실 확인이 포함되어 있으므로 (D)가 정답이다.

189. 일정표에서 Ms. Gray의 일정에 Contempo Art Space의 소유주와의 인터뷰가 있고, 기사에서 Contempo Art Space의 소유주가 Mischa Michaels라고 했으므로 (A)가 정답이다.

190. 기사에서 Contempo Art Space의 주요 갤러리에 전시된 모든 작품들은 판매될 것이라고 했으므로 (B)가 정답이다.

문제 풀이 전략

아래 전략 선택 TIP을 참고하여 <문제 먼저 읽고 지문 읽기> 또는 <지문 먼저 읽고 문제 읽기> 중 자신에게 맞는 전략을 택하여 빠르고 정확하게 문제를 풀 수 있도록 합니다.

전략 선택 TIP

1) 다음 주어진 글의 내용을 이해하며 읽는 데 몇 초가 걸리는지 기록해 둡니다.

Come join the annual office party on Friday, December 20th! Be sure to stop by Mr. Maschino's desk to inform him of your participation as well as the attendance of any accompanying family members. We hope to see you all there!

2) 아래 문제를 풀어봅니다.

What should employees tell Mr. Maschino about?
(A) Bringing family members to a party   (B) Planning for a celebration
(C) Catering for company events   (D) Giving cash to a charity

정답: (A)

글을 읽는 데 10초 이상이 걸렸거나 문제를 풀면서 다시 글의 내용을 확인했다면 → **전략 1**
글을 읽는 데 10초 미만이 걸렸고, 문제를 한번에 풀었다면 → **전략 2**

전략 1 문제 먼저 읽고 지문 읽기

1. **질문들을 빠르게 읽고 지문에서 확인할 내용을 파악합니다.**
   지문을 읽기 전 먼저 질문들을 빠르게 읽어서, 어떤 내용을 지문에서 중점적으로 읽어야 하는지 확인합니다.

2. **지문을 읽으며, 미리 읽어 두었던 질문과 관련된 내용이 언급된 부분에서 정답의 단서를 확인합니다.**
   미리 읽어 두었던 질문의 핵심 어구와 관련된 내용이 언급된 부분을 지문에서 찾아 정답의 단서를 확인합니다.

3. **정답의 단서를 그대로 언급했거나, 다른 말로 바꾸어 표현한 보기를 정답으로 선택합니다.**

전략 2 지문 먼저 읽고 문제 읽기

1. **지문의 종류나 글의 제목을 확인하여 지문의 전반적인 내용을 추측합니다.**

2. **지문을 읽으며 문제로 나올 것 같은 부분을 특히 꼼꼼히 확인합니다.**
   중심 내용, 특정 인물 및 사건, 예외 및 변동 등의 사항은 문제로 나올 가능성이 크므로 이러한 부분들을 집중적으로 확인하며 지문을 읽습니다.

3. **정답의 단서를 그대로 언급했거나, 다른 말로 바꾸어 표현한 보기를 정답으로 선택합니다.**

토익커 성향에 맞춰 학습하는
1200제 케바케 활용법

CASE 1
쉬운 테스트부터 차근차근 공부해서
토익 시험을 졸업하고 싶어요!

* **추천 학습자:** 토익 무경험자, 토익 600-700점대 학습자, 단계별로 실력을 올리고 싶은 학습자

1 난이도가 쉬운 테스트부터 차근차근 풀어보세요.
매일매일 토익 실력이 쌓이는 것을 확인할 수 있을 거예요.

※ 제시된 테스트 번호 순서대로 풀어 보세요. (쉬운 테스트 → 어려운 테스트 순)

2 아래의 4주 완성 맞춤 학습 플랜에 맞춰 교재를 학습하세요.

	Day 1	Day 2	Day 3	Day 4	Day 5	Day 6
Week 1	□ TEST 6 풀기 □ 빅플로 취약 유형 학습	□ TEST 6 해설 리뷰 □ TEST 6 단어장 암기	□ TEST 8 풀기 □ 빅플로 취약 유형 학습	□ TEST 8 해설 리뷰 □ TEST 8 단어장 암기	□ TEST 2 풀기 □ 빅플로 취약 유형 학습	□ TEST 2 해설 리뷰 □ TEST 2 단어장 암기
Week 2	□ TEST 7 풀기 □ 빅플로 취약 유형 학습	□ TEST 7 해설 리뷰 □ TEST 7 단어장 암기	□ TEST 12 풀기 □ 빅플로 취약 유형 학습	□ TEST 12 해설 리뷰 □ TEST 12 단어장 암기	□ TEST 5 풀기 □ 빅플로 취약 유형 학습	□ TEST 5 해설 리뷰 □ TEST 5 단어장 암기
Week 3	□ TEST 1 풀기 □ 빅플로 취약 유형 학습	□ TEST 1 해설 리뷰 □ TEST 1 단어장 암기	□ TEST 3 풀기 □ 빅플로 취약 유형 학습	□ TEST 3 해설 리뷰 □ TEST 3 단어장 암기	□ TEST 11 풀기 □ 빅플로 취약 유형 학습	□ TEST 11 해설 리뷰 □ TEST 11 단어장 암기
Week 4	□ TEST 9 풀기 □ 빅플로 취약 유형 학습	□ TEST 9 해설 리뷰 □ TEST 9 단어장 암기	□ TEST 10 풀기 □ 빅플로 취약 유형 학습	□ TEST 10 해설 리뷰 □ TEST 10 단어장 암기	□ TEST 4 풀기 □ 빅플로 취약 유형 학습	□ TEST 4 해설 리뷰 □ TEST 4 단어장 암기

*2주 동안에 단기간 교재를 학습하고 싶으시면 이틀 분량을 하루 동안에 학습하면 됩니다.

4주만에
토익 졸업!!

 실제 토익을 치는 것처럼 학습해서 실전 경험치를 높여,
빨리 토익시험을 졸업하고 싶어요!

＊추천 학습자: 토익 800-900점대 학습자, 토익 실전 감각을 빠르게 익히고 싶은 학습자

1 테스트 1부터 12까지 순서대로 풀어보세요.

실제 시험을 치듯 들쑥날쑥한 난이도로 학습하면 토익에서 어떤 난이도를 만나도 대비할 수 있어요.

2 아래의 2주 완성 맞춤 학습 플랜에 맞춰 교재를 학습하세요.

	Day 1	Day 2	Day 3	Day 4	Day 5	Day 6
Week 1	☐ TEST 1 풀기 ☐ 빅플로 취약 유형 학습 ☐ 최고난도 문제 복습	☐ TEST 2 풀기 ☐ 빅플로 취약 유형 학습 ☐ 최고난도 문제 복습	☐ TEST 3 풀기 ☐ 빅플로 취약 유형 학습 ☐ 최고난도 문제 복습	☐ TEST 4 풀기 ☐ 빅플로 취약 유형 학습 ☐ 최고난도 문제 복습	☐ TEST 5 풀기 ☐ 빅플로 취약 유형 학습 ☐ 최고난도 문제 복습	☐ TEST 6 풀기 ☐ 빅플로 취약 유형 학습 ☐ 최고난도 문제 복습
Week 2	☐ TEST 7 풀기 ☐ 빅플로 취약 유형 학습 ☐ 최고난도 문제 복습	☐ TEST 8 풀기 ☐ 빅플로 취약 유형 학습 ☐ 최고난도 문제 복습	☐ TEST 9 풀기 ☐ 빅플로 취약 유형 학습 ☐ 최고난도 문제 복습	☐ TEST 10 풀기 ☐ 빅플로 취약 유형 학습 ☐ 최고난도 문제 복습	☐ TEST 11 풀기 ☐ 빅플로 취약 유형 학습 ☐ 최고난도 문제 복습	☐ TEST 12 풀기 ☐ 빅플로 취약 유형 학습 ☐ 최고난도 문제 복습

*4주 동안 교재를 학습하고 싶으시면 하루 분량을 이틀에 나누어 학습하면 됩니다.

TEST 1

✕

PART 5
PART 6
PART 7
점수 환산표

잠깐! 테스트 전 확인사항

1. 문제 풀이에 방해가 되는 물건을 모두 치우셨나요?   예 □
2. Answer Sheet, 연필, 지우개를 준비하셨나요?   예 □
3. 시계를 준비하셨나요?   예 □

모든 준비가 완료되었으면 목표 점수를 떠올린 후 테스트를 시작합니다.

문제 풀이를 마치는 시간은 지금부터 **75분 후인** _____시 _____분입니다.
테스트 시간은 **총 75분**이며, 시험 종료 전 2~3분은 정답 검토 및 답안지 마킹을 위해 사용합니다.

READING TEST

In this section, you must demonstrate your ability to read and comprehend English. You will be given a variety of texts and asked to answer questions about these texts. This section is divided into three parts and will take 75 minutes to complete.

Do not mark the answers in your test book. Use the answer sheet that is separately provided.

PART 5

Directions: In each question, you will be asked to review a statement that is missing a word or phrase. Four answer choices will be provided for each statement. Select the best answer and mark the corresponding letter (A), (B), (C), or (D) on the answer sheet.

---

101. Ms. Hunter will be relocating to Iowa, ------- she can supervise the company's project there.

(A) such as
(B) by
(C) so
(D) that

102. The buyer and seller ------- negotiations, and all they need to do now is to sign the final contract.

(A) ending
(B) to end
(C) will end
(D) have ended

103. At her retirement party, Ms. McClatchy said she hoped to be ------- for her contributions to the company.

(A) remembering
(B) remembered
(C) remember
(D) remembers

104. Branson Pictures produced several low-budget ------- successful films.

(A) nor
(B) as
(C) but
(D) for

105. The bookcase is designed to be ------- attached to the wall with a set of special screws.

(A) secure
(B) security
(C) securely
(D) secured

106. Ms. Claiborne believes it is ------- job as a marketing consultant to find out what consumers want.

(A) our
(B) her
(C) its
(D) their

107. Gasmark International agreed to a five-year contract with a possible ------- of five more years.

(A) extend
(B) extensive
(C) extension
(D) extended

108. Mr. Cory called a meeting to address employees' concerns ------- the revised policy on work hours.

(A) regarding
(B) around
(C) among
(D) throughout

109. The executives of Windsor Food Service ------- to opening additional store branches.

(A) objects
(B) object
(C) objections
(D) objecting

110. Garnet Mobile's ------- offer for new customers promises 30 percent off the first three months of service.

(A) specializing
(B) specializes
(C) special
(D) specially

111. The newsletter is mailed to subscribers weekly, ------- recent trends in the media industry.

(A) admitting
(B) implementing
(C) relieving
(D) summarizing

112. Though the main actors performed their roles -------, the musicians were not good.

(A) equally
(B) occasionally
(C) perfectly
(D) simply

113. All required forms should be filled out as ------- as possible.

(A) completed
(B) completion
(C) completing
(D) completely

114. Veran Tech announced a new ------- in computer software that prevents hacking.

(A) destination
(B) advancement
(C) moderation
(D) qualification

115. In addition to providing the model number, customers requesting a refund must ------- the date of purchase.

(A) accept
(B) propose
(C) specify
(D) insist

116. The Bridgerton Group has lent ------- funds to small businesses over the past 30 years.

(A) consider
(B) considerate
(C) considerable
(D) consideration

117. Residents of the Hillside area consist ------- of students from the nearby Morgan College.

(A) namely
(B) frequently
(C) publicly
(D) mostly

118. Kenneth Publishing will give a bonus to ------- in the firm who suggests an effective way to reduce operating costs.

(A) those
(B) all
(C) none
(D) anyone

119. The electric company immediately sends out a repair crew ------- a major problem is reported.

(A) as if
(B) whereas
(C) during
(D) whenever

120. The project's ------- goal is to lower manufacturing costs, although the board hopes to increase productivity as well.

(A) adverse
(B) primary
(C) fluent
(D) neutral

GO ON TO THE NEXT PAGE

121. Howell Corporation's decision to replace its CEO is ------- as a sign of positive change by many investors.

(A) charged
(B) determined
(C) perceived
(D) instructed

122. Since Mr. Weiss has ------- booked tables at Sandro's Italian, there is no need to look further for a party venue.

(A) already
(B) still
(C) later
(D) forward

123. Engineers were able to limit the car's emissions to ------- levels by creating a more efficient engine design.

(A) tolerate
(B) tolerating
(C) tolerable
(D) tolerably

124. A seminar could help the staff ------- demands placed on them by their work.

(A) managers
(B) management
(C) manage
(D) manageable

125. The news that producer Joel Manning had resigned from Harper Studios spread quickly ------- the entertainment industry.

(A) across
(B) above
(C) onto
(D) between

126. Many of the building's structural details were ------- to their original state.

(A) restorers
(B) restoring
(C) restored
(D) restore

127. Mr. Thorne convinced the committee to adopt his strategy by making a ------- argument about its potential advantages.

(A) fortunate
(B) compelling
(C) reputable
(D) talented

128. ------- Greg Larson pays for his unpaid charges, his phone service cannot be reconnected.

(A) Despite
(B) Until
(C) From
(D) Because

129. Some passengers may be asked to empty the ------- of their luggage if airport employees detect a security risk.

(A) assets
(B) subjects
(C) contents
(D) matters

130. Mr. Fisher will take ------- look at the final draft of the report before submission.

(A) more
(B) little
(C) some
(D) another

PART 6

Directions: In this part, you will be asked to read four English texts. Each text is missing a word, phrase, or sentence. Select the answer choice that correctly completes the text and mark the corresponding letter (A), (B), (C), or (D) on the answer sheet.

Questions 131-134 refer to the following memo.

TO: All staff
FROM: Olivia Cabral, Office Manager
SUBJECT: Photographer visit
DATE: August 26

A photographer will be visiting our office on August 30 to take photos of all ------- . The photos
                                                                              131.
taken on this day will replace the old ones in our online employee directory. They will also be used

for press releases and various other purposes. ------- , you are expected to wear formal business
                                                132.
clothes for this occasion. You may get your picture taken ------- between 9 A.M. and 2 P.M. ------- .
                                                          133.   **134.**
The process will take less than 10 minutes.

131. (A) equipment
     (B) vehicles
     (C) personnel
     (D) facilities

132. (A) Therefore
     (B) On the contrary
     (C) Regardless
     (D) However

133. (A) anytime
     (B) less
     (C) previously
     (D) near

134. (A) You can choose a day that suits your
         schedule.
     (B) Another example is our employee
         identification badges.
     (C) The photographer will not be available at
         that time.
     (D) This will be done in the main conference
         room.

GO ON TO THE NEXT PAGE

Questions 135-138 refer to the following e-mail.

To: Dennis Craig <d.craig@quickmail.com>
From: Caroline Peel <c.peel@lbistro.com>
Date: February 21
Subject: Comment Card
Attachment: Voucher

Dear Mr. Craig,

I am writing in response to the comment card you ------- on February 19. I appreciate you doing
                                                    135.
this while visiting our establishment. Although I am glad that you enjoyed your food, I regret that

you found the service -------. Your meals should have been brought to you 20 minutes after you
                      136.
ordered -------.
        137.

-------. The next time you eat at Lochlane Bistro on a Friday night, there will be two more servers
138.
on duty than last time.

To make up for your inconvenience, I have attached a voucher for €20 off your next dinner.

We look forward to seeing you again.

Caroline Peel
Manager, Lochlane Bistro

135. (A) completed
     (B) misplaced
     (C) printed
     (D) announced

136. (A) rare
     (B) disappointing
     (C) encouraging
     (D) admirable

137. (A) either
     (B) them
     (C) it
     (D) whichever

138. (A) Thanks to your feedback, our staff
         schedule has been adjusted.
     (B) This is one of the reasons why
         reservations are required.
     (C) I hope you can let me know when your
         article will be printed.
     (D) Our new branch will be just a couple of
         blocks away.

Hamlin International Airport Celebrates New Terminal

Hamlin International Airport has unveiled its second terminal ------- years of construction. The new
139.

terminal will open on May 2.

"The additional terminal has many amenities," stated airport spokesperson Kurt Vogel. -------.
140.

There are dozens of comfortable sofas and free drinks are provided.

-------, travelers arriving at one terminal and departing from the other may be inconvenienced due
141.

to the distance between them. To solve this issue, a shuttle bus will run between the terminals.

The new terminal is exclusively for SeaCrescent Air and Blue Fin. All other airlines will continue

operating at the ------- terminal.
142.

---

139. (A) beside
(B) since
(C) after
(D) into

140. (A) Then the group of reporters was shown the security gates.
(B) Flight attendants have complained about the facilities.
(C) The cost of admission was discounted to mark the anniversary.
(D) Passengers will surely like the executive lounge.

141. (A) Once
(B) In addition
(C) On the other hand
(D) Instead

142. (A) original
(B) private
(C) temporary
(D) standard

GO ON TO THE NEXT PAGE

DOBRY YOGURT CO.
May 21

Amin Patel
CEO, Renowned Processed Foods
52 Sunder Lane
Mumbai, India 400070

Dear Mr. Patel,

Your company was selected as a candidate to be one of our future suppliers. We may now

proceed with the -------. This review is to ensure that your company meets our quality standards.
143.

It will be conducted by our preferred contractor, HDI International. -------. For now, I can only tell
144.

you that it will involve an evaluation of your production facility. The process will take two months.

At the end, HDI ------- a report containing specific recommendations. We must confirm that you
145.

have complied with all recommendations before ------- you as a supplier. I can discuss this with
146.

you on my next visit to Mumbai.

Sincerely,

Stephanie Moravec
Regional Director for South Asia
Dobry Yogurt Co.

143. (A) registration
(B) contract
(C) invoice
(D) inspection

144. (A) Exact details will be forthcoming.
(B) The terms of our contract are clear.
(C) I await further instructions from you.
(D) Please describe the problem you are having.

145. (A) issued
(B) will issue
(C) was issued
(D) would have issued

146. (A) approve
(B) approved
(C) approving
(D) to approve

해커스 토익 실전 1200제 READING

PART 7

Directions: In this part, you will be asked to read several texts, such as advertisements, articles, instant messages, or examples of business correspondence. Each text is followed by several questions. Select the best answer and mark the corresponding letter (A), (B), (C), or (D) on your answer sheet.

Questions 147-148 refer to the following notice.

Updated Schedule for Street Improvements
May 10

The work on Wilkinson Road that was originally scheduled to take place in April will be carried out next week. It was postponed at the request of the Sudbury Summer Arts Fair organizers. They were concerned that the project would create difficulties for people going to Grove Park to see exhibits by local artists.

Please note the following schedule:
• May 15, 9:00 A.M. – 12:00 P.M. (filling in potholes)
• May 16, 12:00 P.M. – 3:00 P.M. (painting centerlines)
• May 17, 1:00 P.M. – 6:00 P.M. (repairing sidewalks)
• May 18, 11:00 A.M. – 4:00 P.M. (installing traffic lights)

Parking on Wilkinson Road will be prohibited while the painting crew is at work. Residents are advised to leave their vehicles on Patterson Street during this period.

---

147. Why was a work schedule changed?

(A) To ensure access to a government facility
(B) To comply with a municipal regulation
(C) To avoid inconveniencing event attendees
(D) To address a worker safety issue

148. When will residents be unable to park on Wilkinson Road?

(A) On May 15 at 9:00 A.M.
(B) On May 16 at 2:00 P.M.
(C) On May 17 at 1:00 P.M.
(D) On May 18 at 12:00 P.M.

GO ON TO THE NEXT PAGE

Questions 149-150 refer to the following e-mail.

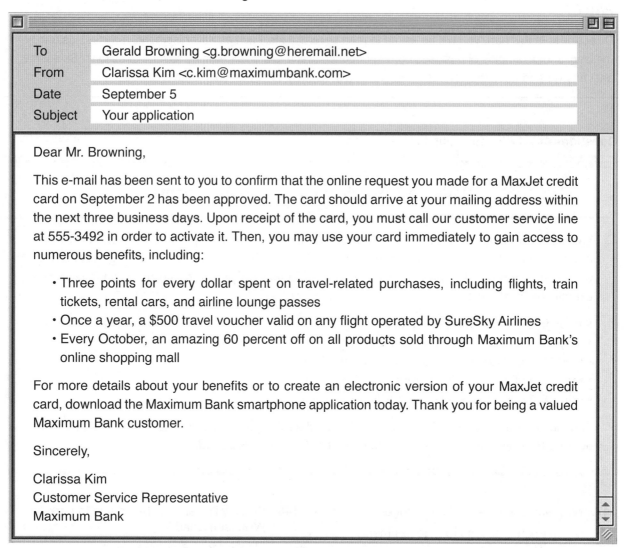

To	Gerald Browning <g.browning@heremail.net>
From	Clarissa Kim <c.kim@maximumbank.com>
Date	September 5
Subject	Your application

Dear Mr. Browning,

This e-mail has been sent to you to confirm that the online request you made for a MaxJet credit card on September 2 has been approved. The card should arrive at your mailing address within the next three business days. Upon receipt of the card, you must call our customer service line at 555-3492 in order to activate it. Then, you may use your card immediately to gain access to numerous benefits, including:

- Three points for every dollar spent on travel-related purchases, including flights, train tickets, rental cars, and airline lounge passes
- Once a year, a $500 travel voucher valid on any flight operated by SureSky Airlines
- Every October, an amazing 60 percent off on all products sold through Maximum Bank's online shopping mall

For more details about your benefits or to create an electronic version of your MaxJet credit card, download the Maximum Bank smartphone application today. Thank you for being a valued Maximum Bank customer.

Sincerely,

Clarissa Kim
Customer Service Representative
Maximum Bank

149. What did Mr. Browning most likely do on September 2?

(A) Met with Ms. Kim at an information desk
(B) Set up a personal savings account
(C) Submitted an application form
(D) Made a credit card payment

150. What can Mr. Browning do next month?

(A) Use a voucher to purchase train tickets
(B) Attend an event sponsored by Maximum Bank
(C) Receive a reduced price on some items
(D) Earn extra points by referring a friend

Course Evaluation Form for Participants

The Leadership Training Center (LTC) appreciates your feedback. Please fill out this form and submit it to your instructor upon completing your final class.

Name: <u>Sandra Mohan</u>　　　　**Company**: <u>Clorinda Consulting</u>
Instructor Name: <u>Raymond Shaw</u>　　**Program Name**: <u>Preparing for Leadership</u>

Instructions: Please rate your satisfaction with each listed item.

	Very Poor	Poor	Average	Good	Excellent
1. Overall impression			✓		
2. Value for money		✓			
3. Lecturer			✓		
4. Training facility				✓	
5. Training topics			✓		
6. Training materials		✓			

Comments: While certain aspects of this class were helpful, I honestly expected more. At the beginning of the two-week course, we were provided with an outline of the topics that would be covered, and I was glad to see that we would be learning how to identify our management styles. However, I found that most of the course was about how to motivate employees and handle workplace conflicts, and neither of these topics was mentioned in the syllabus. Also, there was much less class participation compared to the Critical Thinking at Work seminar that I took last year. I think the instructor could have come up with better activities.

---

151. What is the purpose of the form?

(A) To gather ideas for a future activity
(B) To take note of a client's preferences
(C) To rate the quality of a course
(D) To assess a student's performance

152. What is true about Mr. Shaw?

(A) He provided students with an accurate syllabus.
(B) He was unable to answer participant questions.
(C) He helped to resolve a conflict in class.
(D) He collected the form at the end of a session.

153. What is suggested about Ms. Mohan?

(A) She was recently promoted to a management role.
(B) She was required by her company to take a course.
(C) She gave some ideas for in-class activities.
(D) She has taken other professional development classes.

GO ON TO THE NEXT PAGE

Questions 154-155 refer to the following text-message chain.

Agnes Beecroft [5:45 P.M.]
Bart, thanks for helping me with my accounting report. Would you be interested in going to a basketball game on Thursday night? Ms. Farrow from Hart Technologies gave me two tickets.

Bart Kreps [5:48 P.M.]
I can't make it. I have to go to a parent-teacher conference at my son's high school.

Agnes Beecroft [5:49 P.M.]
That's all right. Who else do you think I could ask?

Bart Kreps [5:51 P.M.]
What about Tina Rodriguez? I worked with her on the last advertising campaign we did for Hart Technologies. I always thought she did a great job and deserved some kind of reward.

Agnes Beecroft [5:54 P.M.]
OK, thanks! I'll ask Tina then.

154. At 5:48 P.M., what does Mr. Kreps mean when he writes, "I can't make it"?

(A) He is too busy to help with a task.
(B) He will not be able to attend an event.
(C) He has to leave work early on Thursday.
(D) He is not planning to join a conference.

155. What is indicated about Ms. Rodriguez?

(A) She was employed by Hart Technologies.
(B) She is being considered for a promotion.
(C) She worked with Mr. Kreps on a project.
(D) She belongs to the accounting team.

Questions 156-157 refer to the following advertisement.

Pixel Pro

 Equipped with two offset presses, a high-speed copier, and three digital color printers, we can fulfill all of your needs quickly and reliably. Whether you need brochures, business cards, envelopes, or party invitations, simply bring in your image or text, and we will produce a high-quality product that you can be proud of. If you do not have material ready, consult with our full-time graphic artists to come up with a design that works for you. Examples of their work can be found at www.pixelpro.com. We are open Monday through Saturday from 8:30 A.M. to 4:30 P.M. Visit us today.

156. What type of business is being advertised?

(A) An electronics manufacturer
(B) A stationery store
(C) A photography studio
(D) A print shop

157. According to the advertisement, why should customers visit a Web site?

(A) To download a price list
(B) To place an order
(C) To view samples
(D) To make appointments

GO ON TO THE NEXT PAGE

Questions 158-160 refer to the following information.

The City of Rochester is introducing our Corliss Gardens mobile application. Now, visitors can get convenient access to information about Corliss Gardens from any mobile device. Use it to explore the park's facilities, to plan a visit, or simply to obtain news on events and activities at Corliss Gardens.

Aside from having access to a detailed and interactive map of the park grounds, users can get directions to the nearest available parking spaces, receive notifications on the latest weather forecast, and even book any of the park's four event venues for a private function. Users who sign up on the application also become instantly eligible to receive special offers from local businesses.

To find out any information about Corliss Gardens, visit the city Web site, www.rochestercity.gov.

158. What is the purpose of the information?

(A) To announce a public event
(B) To describe a park's attractions
(C) To promote a software program
(D) To offer directions around a city

159. How can people qualify for special offers?

(A) By completing a survey
(B) By visiting local businesses
(C) By registering online
(D) By making a donation

160. What is suggested about Corliss Gardens?

(A) It underwent some renovations recently.
(B) It was chosen as the site for a trade event.
(C) It charges visitors an admission fee.
(D) It is managed by a city government.

Questions 161-164 refer to the following online chat discussion.

Jerry Miller	**[2:10 P.M.]**	Are there any questions about Basket Burger's upcoming summertime promotion? I just sent each of your franchises new promotional materials.
Lois Denver	**[2:11 P.M.]**	The seasonal menu will be the same as last year's, right? If so, I can start showing my staff how to make everything now.
Jerry Miller	**[2:13 P.M.]**	Correct. We're keeping all the ice cream treats, burgers, and side dishes. However, we're discontinuing the frozen coffee beverages.
Kiel Bronson	**[2:14 P.M.]**	Really? There have been many diners asking about them recently. I have leftover syrups for them as well. Can I sell the drinks until my supply runs out?
Jerry Miller	**[2:15 P.M.]**	OK, but don't advertise them because headquarters will not provide any more stock. Instead, promote our tornado pops and the half-off milkshake.
Lois Denver	**[2:18 P.M.]**	Will the money from tornado pop sales go to charity again this year?
Jerry Miller	**[2:20 P.M.]**	That's right. I also sent you donation boxes for extra contributions. Is there anything else?
Kim Patton	**[2:21 P.M.]**	Yes. I'm worried that my Beauville staff won't be able to handle this promotion. We just opened, and many are still training.
Jerry Miller	**[2:24 P.M.]**	I see. I can send a couple of experienced employees to help you for the duration of the promotion. Let's talk more about this in a private message.

Send

161. At 2:13 P.M., what does Mr. Miller mean when he writes, "Correct"?

(A) Seasonal items generate a significant percentage of profits.
(B) Franchise staff should begin training as soon as possible.
(C) A chain's summer menu will remain largely unchanged.
(D) An establishment's desserts are popular with the public.

162. Why does Mr. Bronson want to continue selling frozen coffee drinks?

(A) They appear in some promotional materials.
(B) They require little time for staff to prepare.
(C) They are made with inexpensive ingredients.
(D) They are in demand by customers already.

163. Who most likely operates the newest franchise?

(A) Jerry Miller
(B) Lois Denver
(C) Kiel Bronson
(D) Kim Patton

164. What does Mr. Miller offer to do?

(A) Promote a menu item
(B) Supply temporary staff
(C) Hire a new manager
(D) Send a copy of a manual

GO ON TO THE NEXT PAGE

TEST 1 **37**

Questions 165-167 refer to the following article.

Pan-African Film Festival Moved to Cape Town

August 18—Organizers of the Pan-African Film Festival have moved this year's event from Johannesburg to Cape Town. — [1] —. Currently in its 11th year, the festival has grown in size each year. However, despite Johannesburg being the bigger city, the organizers chose Cape Town as the festival's new permanent site because it offers other benefits. — [2] —. "Being located along the coast means it attracts a large number of visitors each year, particularly during the summer," said organizer Joma Nkosi. — [3] —. Overseas visitors who have already made flight and hotel arrangements for the coming festival will be assisted with changing their reservations. — [4] —. They are asked to contact the festival's organizers through www.paff.com.

---

165. What most likely prompted the festival's organizers to relocate?

(A) They were offered tax incentives to move.
(B) They find Cape Town's weather more agreeable.
(C) They want the festival to be in an area with many summer visitors.
(D) They need a bigger venue than Johannesburg can provide.

166. What are some festivalgoers asked to do?

(A) Go to a Web site for help
(B) Make a hotel reservation
(C) Call an event venue
(D) Book a flight for February

167. In which of the positions marked [1], [2], [3], and [4] does the following sentence best belong?

"Mainly, it is more popular with tourists."

(A) [1]
(B) [2]
(C) [3]
(D) [4]

BRONMAN HARDWARE

To: Store managers
From: Steven Tisdale, CEO
Subject: Some news
Date: September 6

As you know, I was at the 44th Annual Building Industries Trade Fair in Columbus, Ohio. I'd like to take this opportunity to tell you about a recent trend in construction materials that I observed during this event. — [1] —. It seems that among homeowners there is a growing demand for locally sourced building supplies.

In light of this news, I asked the marketing division to do some research. — [2] —. They drew up a list of local products that could potentially do well in our stores, including items such as floor tiles, wall panels, garden supplies, and more. Next month, we will ask each store manager to hold a special promotion on a different selection of products. We will then look at the sales figures from each branch. — [3] —.

Naturally, these changes will affect our purchasing and transportation costs. — [4] —. However, the finance department has done its calculations and determined that expected revenues make this move worthwhile. Indeed, we will probably see some savings. Having suppliers nearby allows us to reduce a number of items we keep in our warehouses.

In closing, I hope that you will welcome these changes. I believe they will help to ensure that Bronman Hardware remains competitive in the future.

---

168. Why did Mr. Tisdale write the memo?

(A) To describe how a company has been performing
(B) To inform employees about a new development
(C) To confirm his attendance at an upcoming event
(D) To remind supervisors about their responsibilities

169. What will store managers be expected to do?

(A) Hire new staff members
(B) Conduct customer surveys
(C) Promote specific products
(D) Prepare budget estimates

170. What is suggested about Bronman Hardware?

(A) It maintains its own fleet of delivery trucks.
(B) It has been losing customers to competitors.
(C) It will expand its network of stores in the coming years.
(D) It spends a lot of money storing large inventories.

171. In which of the positions marked [1], [2], [3], and [4] does the following sentence best belong?

"Based on this, we will decide which locally made items to begin offering regularly."

(A) [1]
(B) [2]
(C) [3]
(D) [4]

GO ON TO THE NEXT PAGE

Questions 172-175 refer to the following e-mail.

TO: Jason Briar <jbriar@postnet.com>
FROM: Jack Gray <grayjack@gilhoolytech.com>
SUBJECT: Application
DATE: April 27

Dear Mr. Briar,

Thank you for applying for Gilhooly Tech's summer student internship program. We received your résumé and application form a few days ago, and we will be scheduling interviews shortly. Should you meet our eligibility requirements, you will be contacted by phone at some point to set up an appointment at our office in Richmond.

Please note that this is a full-time, unpaid position that will last for a period of eight weeks. However, Gilhooly Tech will provide $3,000 to your educational institution, Maryland Academy, to help pay for your tuition fees if you are selected. This amount will be sent at the successful conclusion of your internship. Gilhooly Tech is also prepared to offer a housing allowance of $100 per week for interns who are from out of town.

Once again, thanks for taking an interest in our program, and we will be in touch soon.

Sincerely yours,

Jack Gray
Associate Recruitment Director, Gilhooly Tech

172. What has Mr. Briar recently done?

(A) Sent in documents for a summer position
(B) Completed a study program with a company
(C) Spoken to a recruiter on the telephone
(D) Requested information on his grade

173. The word "point" in paragraph 1, line 3, is closest in meaning to

(A) time
(B) location
(C) score
(D) direction

174. What is implied about Mr. Briar?

(A) He recently relocated to Richmond.
(B) He will have to do an interview over the Internet.
(C) He may have to work for over a month.
(D) He is currently attending a university on scholarship.

175. What can be inferred about Gilhooly Tech?

(A) It is preparing to launch a new product.
(B) It provides a dormitory for regular staff.
(C) It compensates employees based on performance.
(D) It will consider candidates from outside of Richmond.

GO ON TO THE NEXT PAGE

To	All Warehouse Staff <warehousestaff@crystalfashions.com>
From	Victor Mariscal <v.mariscal@crystalfashions.com>
Subject	A Concern
Date	August 4

Dear Staff,

I have a concern to share with all of you. One of our top clients, nationwide retail chain Kerrington Apparel, recently received a shipment over a week later than expected. The shipment(number 5883A) arrived on July 30, but the client had selected the express delivery option, meaning that it should have arrived on July 25. Clearly, an error was made in our shipping cycle.

To address this issue, I've asked Francesca Leach from our head office to lead several training sessions, starting on August 15. Everyone who works in the warehouse must attend all three one-hour sessions. I will leave a copy of the training schedule at each of your workstations before the end of the day.

Sincerely,

Victor Mariscal
Warehouse Manager
Crystal Fashions

Crystal Fashions INVOICE

Bill to:

Kerrington Apparel, Denver branch
100 Westside Road
Denver, CO 80222
(**Customer ID:** 7737)

Invoice Number: 1023526E
Invoice Date: August 3
Shipment Number: 5883A

Item	Units	Per Unit Charge	Total Charge
Cardigan sweaters, gray	50	$8	$400
Dress shirts, sky blue	100	$6	$600
Winter boots, brown	25	$10	$250
		Discount (late delivery)	($200)
		Total Amount Due	$1,050

Note:
You can now pay your total amount due using our newly launched mobile application, CrystalPay. Simply download the application from your mobile store and enter your customer ID to get started. For questions about our application, please call an agent at our customer service center on 555-9323.

176. Why did Mr. Mariscal write the e-mail?

(A) To remind staff about following a company policy
(B) To correct a misunderstanding from an earlier message
(C) To report on the results of an employee evaluation
(D) To announce some measures that will be taken

177. What is mentioned about Kerrington Apparel?

(A) It opened several new stores nationwide last year.
(B) It has never received a delayed shipment before.
(C) It is an important customer for Crystal Fashions.
(D) It will send an employee to work with Ms. Leach.

178. In the e-mail, the word "issue" in paragraph 2, line 1, is closest in meaning to

(A) idea
(B) problem
(C) reason
(D) document

179. What is indicated about Kerrington Apparel's Denver branch?

(A) It received a rate reduction for a shipment sent in July.
(B) It will undergo some renovation work in early August.
(C) It will relocate to a more central location.
(D) It forgot to make a payment for an order of clothing.

180. What is true about Crystal Fashion's customers?

(A) They are required to wait one month for deliveries.
(B) They can receive discounts when ordering online.
(C) They may make payments using a mobile device.
(D) They should submit complaints through a Web site.

GO ON TO THE NEXT PAGE

To	Ellen Georgiou <e.georgiou@australbc.edu>
From	Marianne Andino <m.andino@australbc.edu>
Subject	Schedule
Date	August 21

Dear Ellen,

I'd like to request a change to my course schedule. I have been invited to speak at a symposium in Athens on Wednesday, September 5. Consequently, I will not be able to teach any of my classes that day. Mr. Bakir, who teaches several marketing courses at our college, agreed to take my place in the morning, but he prefers to hold the class in the room where I teach on Tuesdays and Thursdays. As for the afternoon class, I would like to recommend a former colleague. His name is Myron Katsaros, and he and I worked closely together at Pallas Digital around five years ago, just before I was hired here. He now runs his own advertising agency and is respected in the industry. He has also taught advanced marketing classes on occasion at Kallithea School of Management. I would suggest that you reach out to him through e-mail at m.katsaros@agora.com.

Thank you,

Marianne Andino
Professor of Marketing
Austral Business College

Austral Business College, Penteli Campus

Instructor schedule for Marianne Andino
Semester 2 (July 15 to November 30)

Course name	Days	Time	Location
Introduction to Marketing	Mon/Wed/Fri	10:00 to 11:30 A.M.	East Hall 302A
Advanced Marketing Management	Tues/Thu	1:00 to 2:30 P.M.	West Hall 402B
Advanced Advertising and Promotions	Mon	3:00 to 4:30 P.M.	East Hall 612
Ethics in Marketing	Wed	3:00 to 4:30 P.M.	West Hall 415

181. What is NOT mentioned about Mr. Katsaros?

(A) He is admired by other professionals.
(B) He has experience as an instructor.
(C) He began his career in advertising.
(D) He started a company of his own.

182. What is indicated about Ms. Andino?

(A) She is hosting an academic conference.
(B) She needs approval from her department head.
(C) She has been teaching for nearly five years.
(D) She works at two different institutions.

183. What does Ms. Andino suggest that Ms. Georgiou do?

(A) Contact an industry expert
(B) Call an advertising agency
(C) Reschedule an advanced class
(D) Meet with a department head

184. What is suggested about Mr. Bakir?

(A) He was hired to become a substitute teacher.
(B) He is also attending a symposium in Athens.
(C) He can teach an introductory course in marketing.
(D) He is leaving the school's faculty in September.

185. Where does Mr. Bakir prefer to hold a class?

(A) In East Hall 302A
(B) In West Hall 402B
(C) In East Hall 612
(D) In West Hall 415

GO ON TO THE NEXT PAGE

Soaring Skies Academy
Flight Attendant Training Program

Soaring Skies Academy offers comprehensive training to individuals wishing to become flight attendants. Our next program starts on June 1 and ends on July 31. It will cover a variety of topics, ranging from how to provide excellent customer service to what to do in situations that threaten the safety of our passengers.

Prospective participants must fill out the application form on our Web site at www.soaringskies.com/trainingapp. The completed form, along with one letter of recommendation from a previous supervisor or teacher, can be submitted online. Applicants may also print it out and mail their application to our head office at 55 Westwood Avenue, San Francisco, CA 94125.

Upon completion of the training program, graduates will receive one-on-one counseling from our instructors regarding the most effective methods to obtain a flight attendant position with a major airline.

Soaring Skies Academy
55 Westwood Avenue
San Francisco, CA 94125

April 28

Dear Sir or Madam,

I am writing to provide my recommendation for Linda Sykes as a potential trainee in your flight attendant training program that begins on June 1. Having come to know Ms. Sykes from the Harper Hotel in Sacramento, I can say with confidence that she is a diligent employee who is dedicated to customer service.

Additionally, I'm aware that Ms. Sykes has completed several courses in flight attendant training from Redmond Online Vocational Academy. Thus, it is clear that her true passion lies in becoming a professional in the airline industry.

Should you have any queries regarding this letter of reference, please contact me at 555-2329.

Sincerely,

Simon Chung

Soaring Skies Academy
Flight Attendant Training Program
Online Application Form

Full Name: Linda Sykes
Address: 120 Norwell Street, Sacramento, CA 94240
Phone Number: 555-1287

Have you received any airline attendant training in the past?
☑ Yes ☐ No

Please be sure to attach a letter of recommendation by clicking <u>here</u> if submitting this form electronically.

Application Fee Payment
Amount Due: $50
Payment Method: Credit card number XXXX-XXXX-7382-1281

*Tuition payment will be due by June 9 if accepted for the program. A 10 percent discount will be applied if you have past work experience at one of our academy's partner companies listed below:

- Graytown Rental Vehicles
- Pristine Travel Agency
- Harper Hotels

SUBMIT ONLINE	PRINTOUT

---

186. What is true about the program?

(A) It will take place over the course of a year.
(B) It is conducted entirely using an online system.
(C) It will deal with emergency procedures.
(D) It is designed for current airline employees.

187. What will happen at the end of the program?

(A) Trainees will participate in a social event.
(B) A written test will be administered by an instructor.
(C) Staff members will give advice to participants.
(D) A ceremony will be held for course graduates.

188. How does Mr. Chung know Ms. Sykes?

(A) He was her supervisor at a previous job.
(B) He took classes with her at an online school.
(C) He was a guest at a hotel where she worked.
(D) He was her instructor at university.

189. What information does the application form ask for?

(A) Prior education experience
(B) Partner branch locations
(C) A financial document
(D) An e-mail address

190. What is Ms. Sykes eligible to receive?

(A) A guided tour of a training facility
(B) A free textbook for a course
(C) A membership in a rewards program
(D) A reduced rate on a tuition fee

GO ON TO THE NEXT PAGE

Bonaventura Systems
Parking Policy

Effective November 10, all 50 spaces in Parking Lot A will be reserved for participants in the company's carpool program. If it becomes necessary, Parking Lot B will be set aside as well. Employees who do not carpool are not permitted to use the reserved spaces. They should also keep in mind that the parking spots near the main entrance of the office complex are for the exclusive use of our clients.

Bonaventura Systems Carpool Program

Registration Process (updated December 12):

1. Log in to our office network, proceed to "Staff Services," and click on "Carpooling."
2. Confirm that the home address associated with your name in our personnel files is correct. This may be edited at any time.
3. The system will present all compatible carpool groups based on your home address. Select the one you wish to become a member of and click "Join." Each group may have up to five members.
4. Select "Register Vehicle" and enter your license plate number. Note that only employees who own a vehicle may participate in this program.

Notes:
- Employees canceling a commute, whether as a driver or passenger, are required to notify program coordinator Lilia Parry by 5 P.M. the previous day.
- Drivers must ensure that they only use their group's assigned space in Parking Lot A or Parking Lot B.

From: Lilia Parry (555-0393)

To: Brendan Sanz (555-9383)

Ms. Marcos notified me at 5:45 P.M. this evening that she will not be able to drive your carpooling group to work tomorrow morning because she has to travel to Barcelona with Elena Hernandez to assist a client having technical problems. She said that she spoke to Javier Rubio and has arranged for him to take over driving duties for the day. She apologizes for the short notice.

191. What is the purpose of the policy page?

(A) To encourage employees to use public transportation

(B) To notify employees about a change in a reservation process

(C) To explain the proper use of parking facilities

(D) To announce preparations for an upcoming client visit

192. What is suggested about the carpool program?

(A) It includes employees from only one department.

(B) It was proposed by a staff member.

(C) It was established on December 12.

(D) It involves more than 50 vehicles.

193. What is NOT part of the carpool program registration process?

(A) Verifying the location of a residence

(B) Selecting a group to join

(C) Submitting a copy of a driver's license

(D) Providing information about a vehicle

194. Why did Ms. Marcos apologize?

(A) She did not meet a requirement.

(B) She forgot about a previous obligation.

(C) She made a mistake while programming a device.

(D) She could not finish her part of a presentation.

195. Who will Ms. Marcos go on a business trip with?

(A) Lilia Parry

(B) Brendan Sanz

(C) Elena Hernandez

(D) Javier Rubio

GO ON TO THE NEXT PAGE

Questions 196-200 refer to the following article and e-mails.

May 15—During a press conference on Monday, Jacob Laurence, a representative of the Department of Public Works, announced that the municipal government has secured funding for the construction of approximately 23 kilometers of additional bike paths. This project was a campaign promise of Mayor David Ellis, and with his reelection on April 25, the project has become a reality. Paths will be constructed along Harborview Road, Center Boulevard, and Oak Way—major roads in the downtown business district. One will also be built along Kensington Avenue, which runs through the Bradford Heights neighborhood. This is the only residential area to get a new bike path under the current plan. Mr. Laurence specified that parking along these streets will be prohibited while the construction is underway. The project will begin June 8 and is scheduled to finish on June 22.

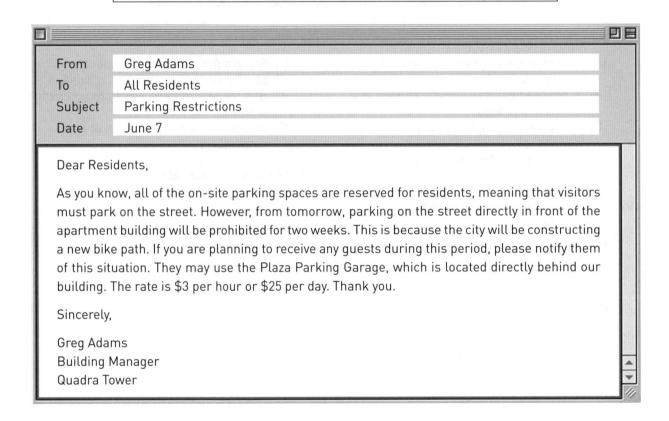

From	Greg Adams
To	All Residents
Subject	Parking Restrictions
Date	June 7

Dear Residents,

As you know, all of the on-site parking spaces are reserved for residents, meaning that visitors must park on the street. However, from tomorrow, parking on the street directly in front of the apartment building will be prohibited for two weeks. This is because the city will be constructing a new bike path. If you are planning to receive any guests during this period, please notify them of this situation. They may use the Plaza Parking Garage, which is located directly behind our building. The rate is $3 per hour or $25 per day. Thank you.

Sincerely,

Greg Adams
Building Manager
Quadra Tower

From	Vince Carter <v.carter@greenville.gov.com>
To	Debra Lawson <d.lawson@pal.com>
Subject	Complaint
Date	June 20

Dear Ms. Lawson,

I am writing in response to the e-mail you sent to my department on June 18, in which you expressed frustration about the construction of the new bike path. You specified that the work is making it difficult for customers to locate a parking spot near your store and that this is having a negative impact on your sales revenue. I would like to apologize for this situation and assure you that we will wrap up this project shortly. The construction work will be completed by June 26. Once again, please accept my sincere apologies for this inconvenience.

Sincerely,

Vince Carter
Greenville Public Works Department

196. According to the article, what happened on Monday?

(A) A marketing campaign was launched.
(B) A fund-raiser was announced.
(C) A parking facility was opened.
(D) A media event was held.

197. What did Mr. Ellis do recently?

(A) He approved a tax increase.
(B) He won a city election.
(C) He hired a new spokesperson.
(D) He attended an opening ceremony.

198. Where is Quadra Tower located?

(A) On Harborview Road
(B) On Center Boulevard
(C) On Oak Way
(D) On Kensington Avenue

199. What is indicated about the bike path project?

(A) It was not sufficiently funded.
(B) It will be debated by the city council.
(C) It was not approved by the mayor.
(D) It will be finished later than planned.

200. What did Ms. Lawson complain about?

(A) Her parking facility is under construction.
(B) Her store is inaccessible to customers.
(C) Her business is generating less profit.
(D) Her building entrance is blocked by equipment.

This is the end of the test. You may review Parts 5, 6, and 7 if you finish the test early.

정답 p.384 / 해석·해설 [별권] 해설집 p.2 / 해커스 토익 빅플로 자동 채점 및 취약 유형 분석하기
* 다음 페이지에 있는 TEST 1 점수 환산표를 확인해 자신의 토익 리딩 점수를 예상해 보세요.

TEST 1 점수 환산표

TEST 1은 무사히 잘 마치셨나요? 맞은 개수를 세어본 후 아래의 점수 환산표를 통해 자신의 점수를 예상해 보세요.

전체 난이도   중간 난이도

파트별 난이도   PART 5 중 ●●○
                 PART 6 중 ●●○
                 PART 7 상 ●●●

정답 수	리딩 점수	정답 수	리딩 점수
98~100개	475~495점	47~49개	205~215점
95~97개	460~470점	44~46개	190~200점
92~94개	440~455점	41~43개	175~185점
89~91개	420~435점	38~40개	160~170점
86~88개	405~415점	35~37개	145~155점
83~85개	390~400점	32~34개	130~140점
80~82개	375~385점	29~31개	115~125점
77~79개	360~370점	26~28개	100~110점
74~76개	340~355점	23~25개	85~95점
71~73개	325~335점	20~22개	70~80점
68~70개	305~320점	17~19개	55~65점
65~67개	290~300점	14~16개	40~50점
62~64개	270~285점	11~13개	25~35점
59~61개	260~270점	8~10개	10~20점
56~58개	245~255점	5~7개	5~10점
53~55개	235~240점	2~4개	5~10점
50~52개	220~230점	0~1개	0~5점

* 점수 환산표는 해커스토익 사이트 유저 데이터를 근거로 제작되었으며, 주기적으로 업데이트되고 있습니다. 해커스토익 사이트
 (Hackers.co.kr)에서 최신 경향을 반영하여 업데이트된 점수환산기를 이용하실 수 있습니다. (토익 > 토익게시판 > 토익점수환산기)

TEST 2

×

PART 5
PART 6
PART 7
점수 환산표

잠깐! 테스트 전 확인사항

1. 문제 풀이에 방해가 되는 물건을 모두 치우셨나요?　　　예 ☐
2. Answer Sheet, 연필, 지우개를 준비하셨나요?　　　　예 ☐
3. 시계를 준비하셨나요?　　　　　　　　　　　　　　　예 ☐

모든 준비가 완료되었으면 목표 점수를 떠올린 후 테스트를 시작합니다.

문제 풀이를 마치는 시간은 지금부터 **75분 후인** _____시 _____분입니다.

테스트 시간은 **총 75분**이며, 시험 종료 전 2~3분은 정답 검토 및 답안지 마킹을 위해 사용합니다.

READING TEST

In this section, you must demonstrate your ability to read and comprehend English. You will be given a variety of texts and asked to answer questions about these texts. This section is divided into three parts and will take 75 minutes to complete.

Do not mark the answers in your test book. Use the answer sheet that is separately provided.

PART 5

Directions: In each question, you will be asked to review a statement that is missing a word or phrase. Four answer choices will be provided for each statement. Select the best answer and mark the corresponding letter (A), (B), (C), or (D) on the answer sheet.

---

101. Mr. Chase ------- declined the invitation to lead the workshop and suggested a substitute.

(A) kind
(B) kinder
(C) kindly
(D) kindliness

102. Jackson City has transformed ------- into a vibrant city by spending more on recreational facilities.

(A) it
(B) themselves
(C) itself
(D) their

103. Once viewers ------- about a lack of original content, the Spotlight Network introduced new programs that fall.

(A) complain
(B) complained
(C) complaining
(D) having complained

104. The effectiveness of the advertising campaign depends on a well-coordinated ------- carried out by all team members.

(A) perform
(B) performed
(C) performance
(D) performer

105. ------- crafted out of wood, Mark Escher's furniture pieces are as attractive as they are functional.

(A) Exactly
(B) Finely
(C) Relatively
(D) Possibly

106. Oakland's city council held meetings to hear from residents ------- changes to public transit.

(A) including
(B) concluding
(C) proposing
(D) persuading

107. Participants in the blind taste test found no ------- difference between the two leading brands of soda.

(A) appreciate
(B) appreciable
(C) appreciably
(D) appreciation

108. ------- the small crowd, the opening was considered a big success for Dew Coffee.

(A) In spite of
(B) As in
(C) Although
(D) With respect to

109. The auditorium where the seminar is going to be held has the maximum ------- of 300 people.

(A) occupied
(B) occupy
(C) occupancy
(D) occupant

110. Mr. Rolland's job performance will gradually improve ------- time and continual training.

(A) on
(B) with
(C) above
(D) among

111. The two firms finally came to a compromise after years of intensive ------- over their merger.

(A) experiments
(B) transactions
(C) acquisitions
(D) negotiations

112. The ------- economic growth of the country was facilitated by investments in its infrastructure.

(A) sustained
(B) sustaining
(C) sustain
(D) sustainment

113. The event hall will be decorated by ------- expert event planners.

(A) us
(B) we
(C) ourselves
(D) our

114. Following a schedule can keep employees ------- on group projects.

(A) productive
(B) productivity
(C) produce
(D) produced

115. ------- manufactured for athletes, the smart watch has many functions.

(A) Excluding
(B) Exclusive
(C) Exclusively
(D) Exclusion

116. Mr. Davis ------- full price for his tickets before YHW Rails announced its special half-price offer.

(A) is paying
(B) had paid
(C) was paid
(D) has paid

117. Some cities are switching to renewable energy sources rather than relying on ------- ones such as coal and gas.

(A) endless
(B) latest
(C) conventional
(D) instructional

118. Arqua Inc. advised users to install a security update ------- to prevent potential attacks.

(A) justly
(B) promptly
(C) substantially
(D) abundantly

119. A copy of the employee manual has been posted online ------- people want to review it.

(A) if not
(B) in case
(C) on behalf of
(D) aside from

120. Street vendors must carry the ------- permits with them while working.

(A) capable
(B) convenient
(C) profitable
(D) appropriate

GO ON TO THE NEXT PAGE

121. The funding will help researchers achieve their goal of ------- the causes of various illnesses.

(A) determination
(B) determined
(C) determining
(D) determines

122. ------- compensation for the delay, the airline offered passengers a free night's stay at a nearby hotel.

(A) Except for
(B) Provided that
(C) By way of
(D) As soon as

123. The presentation will finish ahead of schedule ------- people have a lot of questions.

(A) besides
(B) despite
(C) since
(D) unless

124. Ms. Dreyfuss remains ------- active at tourism industry events even though she has retired.

(A) notice
(B) noticed
(C) noticeable
(D) noticeably

125. ------- of services may occur if account holders have not settled an outstanding balance for longer than 30 days.

(A) Suspension
(B) Exchange
(C) Dismissal
(D) Distraction

126. ------- used the stapler last is requested to return it to the mail room.

(A) Whoever
(B) Whatever
(C) Everyone
(D) Anyone

127. Unlike her competitors, Ms. Lewiston was ------- her business through creative marketing.

(A) publishing
(B) growing
(C) measuring
(D) associating

128. Registration for annual school event is discounted for current students ------- individuals enrolled in the alumni association.

(A) based on
(B) so that
(C) above all
(D) as well as

129. Customers had to type information into the online form ------- because of errors with the Web site.

(A) sharply
(B) instantly
(C) collectively
(D) repetitively

130. The new product is made from rare materials and is, ------- quite expensive.

(A) yet
(B) more
(C) therefore
(D) nevertheless

Directions: In this part, you will be asked to read four English texts. Each text is missing a word, phrase, or sentence. Select the answer choice that correctly completes the text and mark the corresponding letter (A), (B), (C), or (D) on the answer sheet.

Questions 131-134 refer to the following advertisement.

Kelli Corporation is proud to introduce its newly ------- Hava-Go hair dryer. The company's most
131.

portable model, the Hava-Go is cordless and weighs only 500 grams. These ------- make it very
132.

easy to use. -------. When fully charged, its battery lasts for up to 100 minutes.
133.

------- a Hava-Go now. They're sold at electronics stores such as Ciao Mall and online retailers,
134.

including GoodsSupply.com.

131. (A) releasable
(B) releasing
(C) released
(D) release

132. (A) containers
(B) machines
(C) accessories
(D) features

133. (A) The device is also ideal for traveling.
(B) The design will be updated later this month.
(C) A model name hasn't yet been chosen.
(D) They're only being supplied to major hotel chains.

134. (A) Lend
(B) Connect
(C) Estimate
(D) Purchase

GO ON TO THE NEXT PAGE

Announcement for Cliffdale Ridge Manor Residents

This is to inform you that the new ------- permits for this apartment complex will be issued on
135.

August 26. These new permits will include a bar code that can be ------- scanned. To receive one,
136.

turn in your old pass at Cliffdale Ridge Manor's maintenance office. ------- you receive your new
137.

permit, stick it to the interior of your vehicle's front windshield. -------.
138.

135. (A) parking
(B) renovation
(C) residence
(D) storage

136. (A) easy
(B) easily
(C) ease
(D) easiest

137. (A) Even if
(B) By the time
(C) Before
(D) As soon as

138. (A) This will speed up the checkout process.
(B) The safety inspection will be similar to last year's.
(C) Vehicles should be kept in good repair.
(D) Be sure to check that it is clearly visible from outside.

Questions 139-142 refer to the following press release.

NEW YORK (January 28)—An advertisement for TymTech's newest laptop was named Best TV Ad at this year's Worldwide Marketing Awards. The ------- advertisement was made by Telerana
139.
Associates.

------- the world-famous athlete Wanda Vilanova, the 30-second advertisement was broadcast on
140.
stations across North America. English, Spanish, and French versions were created. "We -------
141.
considered cultural differences. Thus, we ensured that all three versions were effective," said

Harold Martel, the director of Telerana Associates.

According to TymTech, the advertisement has resulted in record sales for the company. -------.
142.

139. (A) controversial
(B) sample
(C) winning
(D) final

140. (A) Starred
(B) Star
(C) Starring
(D) Stars

141. (A) carefully
(B) barely
(C) roughly
(D) randomly

142. (A) Vouchers were sent to all contestants of the competition.
(B) The Worldwide Marketing Awards will make a decision soon.
(C) It plans to hire Telerana Associates again for future campaigns.
(D) This record was later broken by one of its main competitors.

GO ON TO THE NEXT PAGE

Questions 143-146 refer to the following e-mail.

To: Blair McKay <b.mckay@rdedental.com>
From: Nancy Tang <n.tang@goldhotel.com>
Subject: Business luncheon
Date: December 12

Dear Mr. McKay,

I have just received your e-mail. -------. The room you are renting for your event can fit up to 50
143.

people. Adding 10 more to the guest list will not be a problem. Because you chose our

buffet-style menu, it is simple for us to increase the ------- of food. Regarding the flowers, I think
144.

it is a wonderful idea to match the colors with your company logo. I ------- with our florist that this
145.

is possible. He will use a combination of blue and orange flowers. If there are ------- remaining
146.

issues, I am ready to prepare a final draft of the agreement. This can be faxed to your office today.

Sincerely,

Nancy Tang
Gold Hotel

143. (A) We sincerely value your feedback.
(B) There have been changes to the room
you rented.
(C) We can certainly accommodate your
request.
(D) Our manager will contact you regarding
your concerns.

144. (A) quantity
(B) sale
(C) flavor
(D) freshness

145. (A) will confirm
(B) am confirming
(C) have confirmed
(D) had confirmed

146. (A) none
(B) some
(C) any
(D) no

PART 7

Directions: In this part, you will be asked to read several texts, such as advertisements, articles, instant messages, or examples of business correspondence. Each text is followed by several questions. Select the best answer and mark the corresponding letter (A), (B), (C), or (D) on your answer sheet.

Questions 147-148 refer to the following notice.

Customer Advisory

Victory Bank would like to advise its customers that the following electronic banking services will be suspended on Sunday, July 8, from 12 A.M. to 8 A.M.

- Automated teller machines (ATMs)
- Online fund transfers and bill payments
- Online usage of credit and debit cards

During this time, clients may continue to check their account balances online. We regret any inconvenience this may cause, but it is necessary to facilitate vital maintenance tasks that ensure the utmost integrity of our electronic banking system.

---

147. What is the purpose of the notice?

(A) To explain a recent policy change
(B) To provide information about weekend hours
(C) To request updates of personal information
(D) To announce a temporary service interruption

148. According to the notice, what can customers continue to do?

(A) Review account information
(B) Obtain cash from machines
(C) Transfer money between accounts
(D) Purchase items online

GO ON TO THE NEXT PAGE

Questions 149-150 refer to the following text-message chain.

Daniel Miller [3:40 P.M.]

Hey, are you going to Ms. Downing's farewell party? Apparently, the whole office is invited to meet up at Finlay's Bar & Grill tonight after work.

Elaine Larue [3:43 P.M.]

I don't know. I'm feeling pretty tired today. Plus, you are the only person I've gotten to know since starting here. I'd feel uncomfortable going to the party alone.

Daniel Miller [3:44 P.M.]

Why don't we go together? It'll be a good opportunity for you to meet people. I've got a few things to finish up but should be ready to go by 7:00 P.M.

Elaine Larue [3:45 P.M.]

That sounds good. Let's meet in the lobby at 7:00 P.M.

149. At 3:43 P.M., what does Ms. Larue mean when she writes, "I don't know"?

(A) She was not sent an invitation.
(B) She does not plan to attend an event.
(C) She will leave a staff gathering early.
(D) She needs directions to a venue.

150. What is suggested about the party?

(A) It will occur close to a place of work.
(B) It will help Ms. Larue meet coworkers.
(C) It will celebrate a colleague's promotion.
(D) It will be a surprise for Ms. Downing.

Questions 151-152 refer to the following Web page.

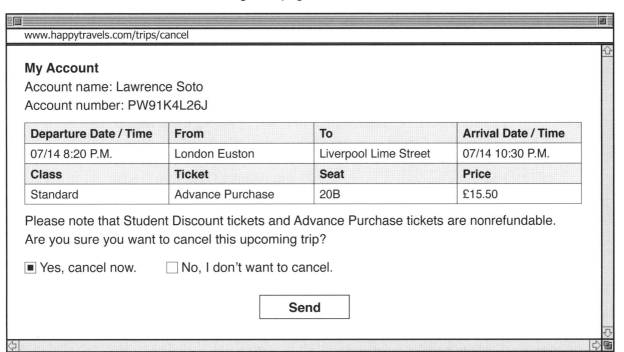

www.happytravels.com/trips/cancel

My Account

Account name: Lawrence Soto

Account number: PW91K4L26J

Departure Date / Time	From	To	Arrival Date / Time
07/14 8:20 P.M.	London Euston	Liverpool Lime Street	07/14 10:30 P.M.
Class	**Ticket**	**Seat**	**Price**
Standard	Advance Purchase	20B	£15.50

Please note that Student Discount tickets and Advance Purchase tickets are nonrefundable.
Are you sure you want to cancel this upcoming trip?

■ Yes, cancel now.   ☐ No, I don't want to cancel.

Send

151. What information is NOT included on the Web page?

(A) The location of a seat
(B) The destination point
(C) The cost of a journey
(D) The ticket number

152. What is suggested about Mr. Soto?

(A) He has two days to confirm a cancellation.
(B) He will not get his money back.
(C) He paid for a trip with a credit card.
(D) He is not able to upgrade his seat.

GO ON TO THE NEXT PAGE

Questions 153-154 refer to the following advertisement.

 SheerYou—Dewdrop Skincare's Newest Product

Dewdrop Skincare is the country's top provider of cosmetic products. We are proud to unveil SheerYou, our latest moisturizer. It is scientifically proven to restore the natural moisture of your skin, making it look brighter and healthier. Created by dermatologists using only natural ingredients, SheerYou is our gentlest yet most powerful moisturizer. To celebrate its release, we are offering a special deal for the month of June. Anyone who purchases SheerYou will receive a complimentary three-ounce bottle of Floria. This is the signature perfume of Jenna Harvel, star of the popular TV drama *Broken Hearts*. For a list of stores that sell Dewdrop's merchandise, please visit www.dewdropskin.com/vendors.

153. What is mentioned about SheerYou?

(A) It is available in a variety of scents.
(B) It does not include artificial substances.
(C) It does not provide health benefits to users.
(D) It is only sold on Dewdrop Skincare's Web site.

154. Who is Jenna Harvel?

(A) A movie producer
(B) A television actor
(C) A company president
(D) A medical professional

Questions 155-157 refer to the following information.

 Chesterfield Park REGULATIONS

In all park areas, please do not:

- Make loud noise that might disturb other visitors
- Litter or put trash anywhere other than in designated waste bins

Camping Zones are located throughout the park for overnight visitors. Staying anywhere other than in these designated areas is prohibited. For safety reasons, campfires are not allowed, but cooking is permitted at the barbecue grills situated next to the snack bar.

Pets are allowed in the park but must be kept on a leash at all times. However, we advise you not to bring pets on the third Wednesday of each month as park grass is sprayed to control insects on those days and the chemicals can be harmful if consumed by animals.

If you feel unsafe while at our facilities, you are welcome to call our security hot line, which will be dialed instantly upon picking up one of the red phone receivers in the booths scattered throughout the park. Emergency response personnel are available to assist you on this hot line 24 hours a day, 7 days a week.

155. What are park visitors instructed to avoid?

(A) Walking their pets late at night
(B) Bringing their own camping equipment
(C) Cooking food in the park
(D) Throwing garbage on the ground

156. According to the information, what happens every month?

(A) Membership fees are collected.
(B) Some community events are held.
(C) Parking lots are closed off to visitors.
(D) Some chemicals are applied to plants.

157. What has been placed in several locations in the park?

(A) Fire extinguishers
(B) Snack bars
(C) Phone booths
(D) Barbecue grills

GO ON TO THE NEXT PAGE

Questions 158-160 refer to the following form.

Thank you, Nadia Abdulhak, for choosing Frontward Car Rental. We want to know how satisfied you are with your experience of renting a Gallapot Mini from May 7 to 13. After completing this form, please click SUBMIT.

1) The variety of available rental options was suitable.	● Agree	○ Disagree
2) The reservation system was convenient.	○ Agree	● Disagree
3) The quality of service when picking up the vehicle was satisfactory.	● Agree	○ Disagree
4) The vehicle performed reliably.	○ Agree	● Disagree
5) The quality of service when returning the vehicle was satisfactory.	○ Agree	● Disagree

Additional Comments

I decided to use Frontward Car Rental after seeing its Web site advertisement. Upon picking up the car from your Fairfield location, Derek, the staff member on duty, did a good job of answering my questions. However, when the vehicle broke down on Highway 99 two days later, your company took about three hours to resolve the situation. I was also disappointed that no refund was offered at your Danbury location when I returned the automobile.

SUBMIT

158. What is the purpose of the form?

(A) To determine interest in a product
(B) To grant a refund for a payment
(C) To request feedback on a service
(D) To confirm a reservation for an event

159. What aspect of the business was Ms. Abdulhak pleased with?

(A) The simplicity of the booking process
(B) The customer service skills of an employee
(C) The fuel efficiency of the Gallapot Mini
(D) The conditions of a contract

160. What is indicated about Frontward Car Rental?

(A) It allows patrons to pick up and return vehicles at different branches.
(B) It has established a team of automobile mechanics in Danbury.
(C) It has rented some advertising space along Highway 99.
(D) It requires that a report be filled out before offering reimbursements.

Jen Kim (9:40 A.M.)	I just wanted to remind everyone that our monthly managers' meeting will not be held this Friday as scheduled due to the national holiday. But we cannot just cancel it because we need to make a final decision about the company's new logo. Would it be all right with everyone to have it on Monday at 11 A.M. next week instead?
Richard Smythe (9:43 A.M.)	That's fine with me. I don't have anything else scheduled.
Kelly Leech (9:45 A.M.)	Actually, I am taking Monday off. But I am free to meet at the same time on Tuesday or Thursday.
Hassan Sadat (9:48 A.M.)	I won't be here Monday either. I've got an appointment at that time on Friday though.
Jen Kim (9:49 A.M.)	OK, so can I schedule the meeting for Tuesday?
Richard Smythe (9:51 A.M.)	I am free Tuesday morning, but I have to leave before noon to meet with a supplier.
Jen Kim (9:52 A.M.)	That won't work. I am leading a workshop for our new interns. It starts at 9:00 A.M. and ends just before 12:00 P.M. What about Thursday at about 1:00 P.M.?
Richard Smythe (9:54 A.M.)	All right. Fine by me.
Hassan Sadat (9:55 A.M.)	I don't have a problem with that. Another option is to get some food delivered and have the meeting at noon.
Kelly Leech (9:57 A.M.)	I like that idea.
Richard Smythe (9:58 A.M.)	Yes. Let's do that.
Jen Kim (10:02 A.M.)	Good. It's all settled now. If there are any changes, I'll let you know. Thanks everyone!

Send

161. What are the writers discussing?

(A) Rescheduling an upcoming meeting
(B) Closing an office for extra days off
(C) Changing policies related to leave
(D) Scheduling work shifts for management staff

162. When will the managers select a logo?

(A) On Monday
(B) On Tuesday
(C) On Thursday
(D) On Friday

163. At 9:52 A.M., what does Ms. Kim mean when she writes, "That won't work"?

(A) She has a problem with a supplier's product quality.
(B) She thinks that it is impossible to add topics to an agenda.
(C) She is conducting a training session in the morning.
(D) She feels that interns need additional assignments.

164. What does Mr. Sadat recommend?

(A) Contacting another manager
(B) Ordering some meals
(C) Extending a project deadline
(D) Bringing lunches from home

GO ON TO THE NEXT PAGE

Questions 165-167 refer to the following article.

Former Automotive Parts Factory Finds New Life
By Gregory McKenna

May 15—Following extensive renovations, the abandoned automotive parts factory formerly operated by XLT Industries has been converted into a 3,000-square-meter complex. The new Grand Prairie Cultural Center will feature an open-air performing arts stage with seating for 1,500 people. — [1] —. In addition, it will house art galleries, studios, and teaching spaces. Commercial areas for cafés, bookstores, and similar ventures have also been made available for lease. — [2] —.

The Grand Prairie Cultural Center is the end result of a prolonged effort by the Grand Prairie Arts Council to develop a public space centered on the arts. Council chairperson Belinda Blair credited Mayor Wilma Brown with helping to realize the project. — [3] —. She also recognized the contributions of firms like Keystone Bank, which helped to keep project costs manageable. — [4] —. The Center took just two years to build and opens to the public on August 5.

---

165. What is the article mainly about?

(A) A property developer's latest project
(B) The newest photo exhibit at a gallery
(C) A city's efforts to promote green energy
(D) The construction of a public arts complex

166. What is suggested about Ms. Blair's project?

(A) It was first proposed by the mayor of Grand Prairie.
(B) It was completed approximately two years ago.
(C) It would have been finished sooner if not for some delays.
(D) It received funding from private companies.

167. In which of the positions marked [1], [2], [3], and [4] does the following sentence best belong?

"Many local business owners have already expressed an interest in renting a space."

(A) [1]
(B) [2]
(C) [3]
(D) [4]

March 12

Nelly Garrison
493 22nd Street
Portland, OR 97246

Dear Ms. Garrison,

Thank you for coming in last Friday to interview for the associate curator position here at the Weston Archeological Institute (WAI). We were impressed with your performance and would like to offer you the position.

Enclosed is an employment contract. It includes the salary discussed during the interview and the benefits package I mentioned. Also included are forms from our medical insurance provider. Should you agree to our offer, please sign the contract and complete the forms before submitting them to our personnel department.

Your starting day would be April 1. You will go through an orientation with another one of the museum's curators, Arnold Hazelton. The training period will last one week, during which time Mr. Hazelton will direct you to do specific tasks. You will assume your regular responsibilities the week after. Mr. Hazelton will give you more details on your first day.

We would appreciate receiving a response by March 15. You may call me at 555-3029.

Sincerely yours,

Marsha Kent
WAI Head of Personnel

168. What did Ms. Garrison do last week?

(A) Signed a new employment contract
(B) Called a number to inquire about a job
(C) Participated in an orientation session
(D) Attended a job interview at an institute

169. What is indicated about the Weston Archeological Institute?

(A) It provides medical coverage for staff.
(B) It outsources recruitment to an agency.
(C) It recently promoted one of its staff members.
(D) It only offers benefits to full-time employees.

170. The word "direct" in paragraph 3, line 3, is closest in meaning to

(A) apply
(B) order
(C) operate
(D) demonstrate

171. What will Mr. Hazelton do on April 1?

(A) Interview several job applicants
(B) Begin training an employee
(C) Resign from his duties at the institute
(D) Hand in some forms at a human resources office

GO ON TO THE NEXT PAGE

Questions 172-175 refer to the following e-mail.

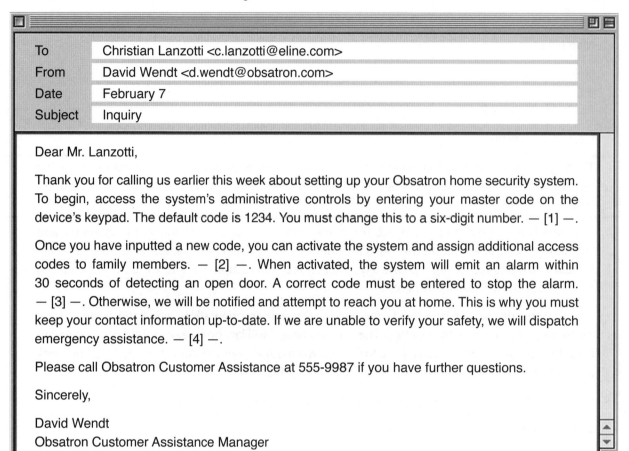

To   Christian Lanzotti <c.lanzotti@eline.com>

From   David Wendt <d.wendt@obsatron.com>

Date   February 7

Subject   Inquiry

Dear Mr. Lanzotti,

Thank you for calling us earlier this week about setting up your Obsatron home security system. To begin, access the system's administrative controls by entering your master code on the device's keypad. The default code is 1234. You must change this to a six-digit number. — [1] —.

Once you have inputted a new code, you can activate the system and assign additional access codes to family members. — [2] —. When activated, the system will emit an alarm within 30 seconds of detecting an open door. A correct code must be entered to stop the alarm. — [3] —. Otherwise, we will be notified and attempt to reach you at home. This is why you must keep your contact information up-to-date. If we are unable to verify your safety, we will dispatch emergency assistance. — [4] —.

Please call Obsatron Customer Assistance at 555-9987 if you have further questions.

Sincerely,

David Wendt
Obsatron Customer Assistance Manager

172. What is indicated about Obsatron?

(A) It replaced the software for some of its systems.

(B) It was recently contacted by Mr. Lanzotti.

(C) It specializes in security for corporate clients.

(D) It changed its telephone number for customer assistance.

173. What is mentioned about the alarm?

(A) It will wait one minute before triggering a loud sound.

(B) It can be modified to reduce the volume.

(C) It will stay on until confirmation is provided.

(D) It is located next to the control panel.

174. What is Mr. Lanzotti advised to do?

(A) Update his contact information as needed

(B) Call an emergency number immediately

(C) Replace the keypad of a security system

(D) Learn some important safety procedures

175. In which of the positions marked [1], [2], [3], and [4] does the following sentence best belong?

"Avoid one that is easy for others to guess."

(A) [1]

(B) [2]

(C) [3]

(D) [4]

GO ON TO THE NEXT PAGE

Questions 176-180 refer to the following schedule and online review.

Upcoming Performances by Geocrab

August 27	Carson City, Nevada — Lakeview Music Hall	Buy Tickets (CANCELED)
August 29	Folsom, California — Drake Auditorium	Buy Tickets
August 30	Stockton, California — Terry Benson Concert Center	Buy Tickets (SOLD OUT)
September-October	*The band will take some time off from touring to record its fifth studio album*	
November 15	Fairfield, California — Mooncastle Lounge	Private Party for Invited Guests
November 20	Santa Rosa, California — Whiteout Record Shop	Free Admittance for First 100 People Who Arrive

www.newmusicreviews.com

Band name: Geocrab
Album title: *Indelible Ink*

In its latest effort, the rock band Geocrab has gone back to its familiar sound—simple keyboard melodies and loud drums. Fans of the group's first three albums are sure to like *Indelible Ink*, but those expecting something like Geocrab's experimental fourth album may be let down.

Indelible Ink is the band's first release to feature Donna Redmond, who replaced Ellen Banbury as the lead singer. Redmond's singing throughout the album is terrific, and she also wrote five of the seventeen songs. Keyboardist Michael Wilkinson and drummer Wendy Palmer composed the others. With a length of 65 minutes, *Indelible Ink* feels a bit too long—several of the tracks could have been omitted.

While its fifth album is not especially adventurous musically, Geocrab has decided to try something new in terms of marketing, making *Indelible Ink* available on the Takashi Online Store. Those who purchase the digital version of the album can enjoy a bonus track that was recorded live at the Terry Benson Concert Center in Stockton.

By Veronica Meyberg

176. What is indicated about Geocrab?

(A) It will not charge some performance attendees.
(B) It will release a music video in November.
(C) It sells merchandise at its concerts.
(D) It accepts song requests from fans.

177. According to the schedule, which venue will host an invitation-only event?

(A) Drake Auditorium
(B) Terry Benson Concert Center
(C) Mooncastle Lounge
(D) Whiteout Record Shop

178. In the online review, the word "expecting" in paragraph 1, line 2, is closest in meaning to

(A) presenting
(B) deliberating
(C) considering
(D) anticipating

179. Who is NOT currently a member of Geocrab?

(A) Donna Redmond
(B) Ellen Banbury
(C) Michael Wilkinson
(D) Wendy Palmer

180. What can be inferred about the digital version of *Indelible Ink*?

(A) It features the work of guest artists.
(B) It is sold by multiple music services.
(C) It will be given for free to concertgoers.
(D) It contains a song recorded on August 30.

GO ON TO THE NEXT PAGE

Glisten Plan Pricing

Stream hours of high-quality background music at multiple retail locations, all fully licensed for public playback! Choose easy monthly payments or a one-time annual fee for greater savings.

Glisten Beat	Glisten Rhythm	Glisten Harmony
$9.99 a month or $100 a year per location Includes a 5-day free trial	$15.99 a month or $150 a year per location Includes a 15-day free trial	$24.99 a month or $250 a year per location Includes a 30-day free trial
• Choose from several custom radio stations or create your own playlists • Control the listening experience from your mobile device	• All features of the Glisten Beat package • The ability to create audio advertisements to support your marketing activities • Customize music per region or store	• All features of the Glisten Rhythm package • Access to music experts who create playlists in support of your brand • Allow your guests to request music using our smartphone application

If you operate 5 or more locations, please contact us at 555-3092 to develop a customized plan.

GLISTEN
www.glisten.com

Company: Coax Clothing
Address: 1228 Willow Wood Drive
           Hubbard, OH 44425
Contact: Andy Lewis
E-mail: a.lewis@mailbot.com

Web site (optional): www.coaxclothing.com
Title: Marketing director
Phone: 555-9946

Preferred Plan:

☒ Glisten Beat   ☐ Glisten Rhythm   ☐ Glisten Harmony

Your trial period begins upon completion of the application process.

Payment Scheme:

☐ One-time charge   ☒ Monthly

Clicking on SUBMIT will take you to a payment page. Please have your credit card ready.

Please check your e-mail for a confirmation message. To view our refund policy and other terms and conditions, click here.

RESET	SUBMIT

181. For whom is the advertisement most likely intended?

(A) Professional musicians
(B) Software programmers
(C) Recording technicians
(D) Store owners

182. What is NOT included with every payment plan?

(A) Free trials
(B) Radio stations
(C) Custom playlists
(D) Guest access

183. What can users on the highest payment plan do?

(A) Broadcast video advertisements
(B) Send messages through social media
(C) Get expert help with music selections
(D) Take advantage of additional discounts

184. What is indicated about Coax Clothing?

(A) It will pay $100 dollars a year.
(B) It has fewer than five locations.
(C) Its trial period expires in a month.
(D) Its first payment is due in five days.

185. Why should Mr. Lewis check his e-mail?

(A) To read the terms and conditions
(B) To verify his registration
(C) To receive his monthly invoice
(D) To obtain a copy of a receipt

GO ON TO THE NEXT PAGE

Questions 186-190 refer to the following e-mail, Web page, and invoice.

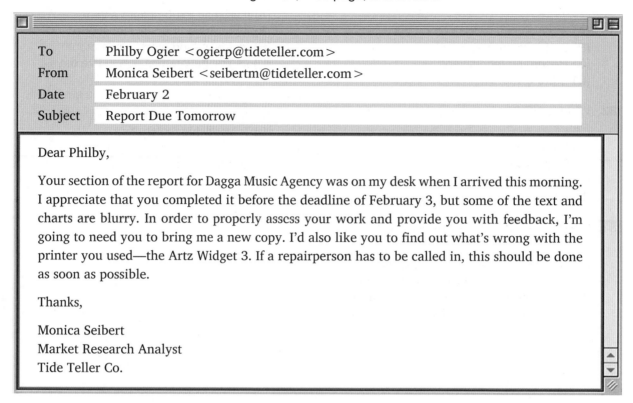

To	Philby Ogier <ogierp@tideteller.com>
From	Monica Seibert <seibertm@tideteller.com>
Date	February 2
Subject	Report Due Tomorrow

Dear Philby,

Your section of the report for Dagga Music Agency was on my desk when I arrived this morning. I appreciate that you completed it before the deadline of February 3, but some of the text and charts are blurry. In order to properly assess your work and provide you with feedback, I'm going to need you to bring me a new copy. I'd also like you to find out what's wrong with the printer you used—the Artz Widget 3. If a repairperson has to be called in, this should be done as soon as possible.

Thanks,

Monica Seibert
Market Research Analyst
Tide Teller Co.

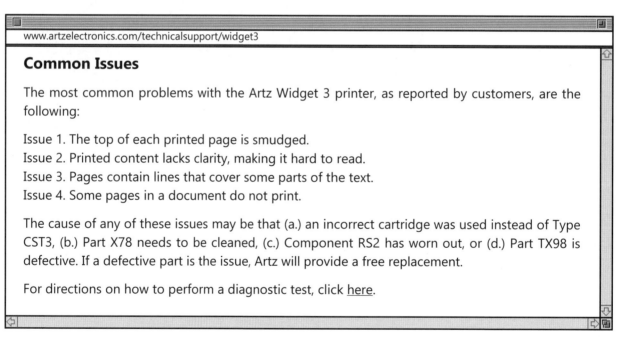

www.artzelectronics.com/technicalsupport/widget3

Common Issues

The most common problems with the Artz Widget 3 printer, as reported by customers, are the following:

Issue 1. The top of each printed page is smudged.
Issue 2. Printed content lacks clarity, making it hard to read.
Issue 3. Pages contain lines that cover some parts of the text.
Issue 4. Some pages in a document do not print.

The cause of any of these issues may be that (a.) an incorrect cartridge was used instead of Type CST3, (b.) Part X78 needs to be cleaned, (c.) Component RS2 has worn out, or (d.) Part TX98 is defective. If a defective part is the issue, Artz will provide a free replacement.

For directions on how to perform a diagnostic test, click here.

From:	To:	
Artz Electronics	Beth Kaczka	
2020 Eastern Industrial Zone,	81 Tyler Hill Road, Blean,	
Kardzhali, Bulgaria 6600	Canterbury, United Kingdom CT2 9HP	

Number of Units	Description	Cost
1	Replacement part	€0.00
	Subtotal:	€0.00
	Shipping and Handling:	€15.22
	Total:	€15.22*
	Amount Due:	**€00.00**

* Paid by Artz Electronics

Because our products are fragile, we use Foam-It-All packing wrap to protect each item we mail. If, however, your order does not arrive fully intact, call our customer service department at 555-4578. One of our agents will tell you how to proceed.

186. What is mentioned about Mr. Ogier?

(A) He works for a music agency.
(B) He completed a task early.
(C) He ordered a new device.
(D) He contacted an important client.

187. What problem did Mr. Ogier encounter?

(A) Issue 1
(B) Issue 2
(C) Issue 3
(D) Issue 4

188. According to the Web Page, what is true about the Artz Widget 3 printer?

(A) It is compatible with only one type of cartridge.
(B) It has more technical problems than other models.
(C) It is sold with several replacement components.
(D) It requires cleaning on a monthly basis.

189. Which item did Ms. Kaczka most likely receive?

(A) Type CST3
(B) Part X78
(C) Component RS2
(D) Part TX98

190. According to the invoice, why might someone call the customer service department?

(A) To change a delivery preference
(B) To sign up for a membership plan
(C) To report some shipping damage
(D) To request an instruction manual

GO ON TO THE NEXT PAGE

Innovations in Job Training
Thursday, September 8
Randolph Hall, Otis University

4:00 P.M. Networking event for participants

4:30 P.M. Introductory remarks by Diane Riggs, Ellis Institute Director of Education

4:45 P.M. Feature presentation by Dr. Samuel Limanto, Professor of Psychology at Austria's Graz University and author of *Open Pathways to Learning*

5:30 P.M. Half-hour break for refreshments

6:00 P.M. One-hour forum with our main speakers Dr. Harriet Keach of Melbourne College and Dr. Lawrence Hillburger of Amsterdam School of Technology

Signed copies of *Open Pathways to Learning* will be distributed free to participants at the event. Reserve your tickets for $25 by contacting Joan Adams of the Ellis Institute at 555-0231. Limited seating available.

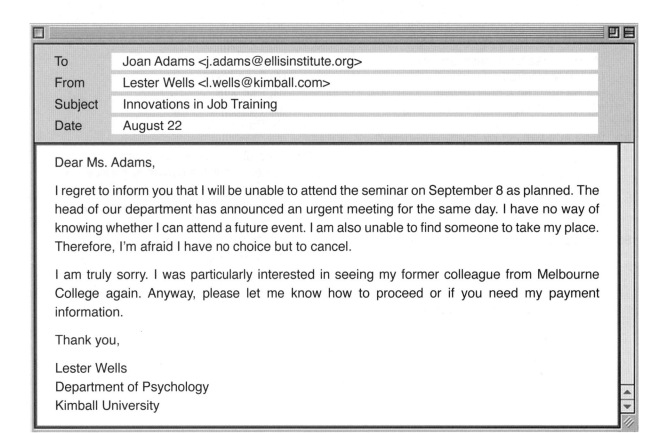

To	Joan Adams <j.adams@ellisinstitute.org>
From	Lester Wells <l.wells@kimball.com>
Subject	Innovations in Job Training
Date	August 22

Dear Ms. Adams,

I regret to inform you that I will be unable to attend the seminar on September 8 as planned. The head of our department has announced an urgent meeting for the same day. I have no way of knowing whether I can attend a future event. I am also unable to find someone to take my place. Therefore, I'm afraid I have no choice but to cancel.

I am truly sorry. I was particularly interested in seeing my former colleague from Melbourne College again. Anyway, please let me know how to proceed or if you need my payment information.

Thank you,

Lester Wells
Department of Psychology
Kimball University

Refund and Cancellation Policy

- The Ellis Institute reserves the right to cancel events due to low enrollment, speaker cancellations, and other circumstances.

- Should a seminar be canceled, you will be offered a full refund. Should it be postponed, you will have the option of receiving a refund or transferring your registration to the future event.

- If you wish to cancel attendance, notify us in writing at least five days before the event and you will be refunded the cost of your ticket. Please note that there is a $10 cancellation fee. Alternatively, you may nominate someone in writing to replace you or use the same ticket at another event up to six months after the event you have chosen to cancel.

- Send cancellation requests by letter, fax, or e-mail only. Credit cards used for payment will be refunded within 15 working days of the scheduled event date.

191. What is mentioned about "Innovations in Job Training"?

(A) It will include time for social interaction.
(B) It will feature several published authors.
(C) It will take place over a two-day period.
(D) It will have an hour-long meal break.

192. Who does Mr. Wells say he was eager to see?

(A) Diane Riggs
(B) Harriet Keach
(C) Samuel Limanto
(D) Lawrence Hillburger

193. What can be inferred about Mr. Wells?

(A) He used to teach at Otis University.
(B) He will be going away for six months.
(C) He can expect repayment in September.
(D) He was invited to speak by the Ellis Institute.

194. According to the refund policy, when can event participants use tickets for a future event?

(A) When speakers become unavailable
(B) When the organizer delays an event
(C) When retracting last-minute withdrawals
(D) When lack of interest causes a cancellation

195. What is suggested about the Ellis Institute?

(A) It holds multiple events each year.
(B) It sells discounted tickets for groups.
(C) It will make a seminar available online.
(D) It accepts recommendations for speakers.

GO ON TO THE NEXT PAGE

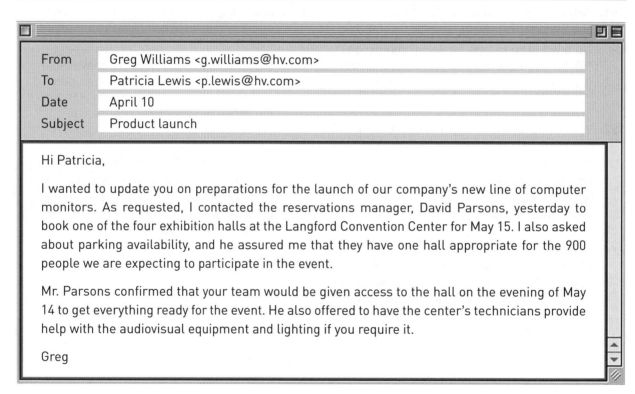

Langford Convention Center

About	Upcoming Events	Facility Map	Contact

Located in downtown San Diego, the Langford Convention Center is a state-of-the-art facility with friendly and professional staff members. Whatever type of event you are planning, we have the ideal venue.

Exhibition Halls

Name	Capacity	Size	Location
Hall A	1,000	10,800 Square Feet	First Floor, West Wing
Hall B	800	7,900 Square Feet	Second Floor, East Wing
Hall C	600	5,600 Square Feet	First Floor, South Wing
Hall D	400	4,100 Square Feet	Second Floor, North Wing

We also have smaller meeting rooms available. Click here for more information or call 555-0393 to book a space.

From	Greg Williams <g.williams@hv.com>
To	Patricia Lewis <p.lewis@hv.com>
Date	April 10
Subject	Product launch

Hi Patricia,

I wanted to update you on preparations for the launch of our company's new line of computer monitors. As requested, I contacted the reservations manager, David Parsons, yesterday to book one of the four exhibition halls at the Langford Convention Center for May 15. I also asked about parking availability, and he assured me that they have one hall appropriate for the 900 people we are expecting to participate in the event.

Mr. Parsons confirmed that your team would be given access to the hall on the evening of May 14 to get everything ready for the event. He also offered to have the center's technicians provide help with the audiovisual equipment and lighting if you require it.

Greg

Langford Convention Center to close temporarily

June 25—Wendy Lee, the director of the Langford Convention Center, announced that the facility will be closed from August 15 to September 30 to undergo renovations. The planned multimillion-dollar project has generated a great deal of excitement among local residents and business owners as it is expected to bring thousands of additional visitors to the city annually.

Brett Hanson, the new reservations manager at the Langford Convention Center, stated that the goal is to attract more international events. "At present, the capacity of our four halls is limited," he said. "Building two new ones capable of accommodating 5,000 visitors each will make the Langford Convention Center more popular with organizers of international conferences and trade shows."

196. Where does Mr. Williams most likely work?

(A) At a public relations firm
(B) At a media company
(C) At an electronics manufacturer
(D) At a software developer

197. Which exhibition hall did Mr. Williams reserve?

(A) Hall A
(B) Hall B
(C) Hall C
(D) Hall D

198. According to the e-mail, what will happen on May 14?

(A) A venue will be prepared for an upcoming occasion.
(B) Some equipment will be delivered to a branch office.
(C) Some information will be distributed to event attendees.
(D) An audiovisual technician will be hired by a company.

199. What is suggested about Mr. Hanson?

(A) He will attend an international conference in August.
(B) He submitted a proposal to Ms. Lee recently.
(C) He will meet soon with local business leaders.
(D) He took over the position of Mr. Parsons.

200. What is NOT mentioned in the article?

(A) Additional event areas are going to be constructed.
(B) The center will be closed for a period of over a month.
(C) Few people are aware of the planned expansion.
(D) The renovation work will be very expensive.

This is the end of the test. You may review Parts 5, 6, and 7 if you finish the test early.

TEST 2 점수 환산표

TEST 2는 무사히 잘 마치셨나요? 맞은 개수를 세어본 후 아래의 점수 환산표를 통해 자신의 점수를 예상해 보세요.

전체 난이도 **쉬운 난이도**

파트별 난이도 PART 5 중 ●●○
　　　　　　　　　PART 6 하 ●○○
　　　　　　　　　PART 7 중 ●●○

정답 수	리딩 점수	정답 수	리딩 점수
98~100개	465~495점	47~49개	200~210점
95~97개	445~460점	44~46개	185~195점
92~94개	425~440점	41~43개	170~180점
89~91개	405~420점	38~40개	155~165점
86~88개	390~400점	35~37개	140~150점
83~85개	375~385점	32~34개	125~135점
80~82개	360~370점	29~31개	110~120점
77~79개	340~355점	26~28개	95~105점
74~76개	325~335점	23~25개	80~90점
71~73개	305~320점	20~22개	65~75점
68~70개	290~300점	17~19개	50~60점
65~67개	275~285점	14~16개	35~45점
62~64개	260~270점	11~13개	20~30점
59~61개	245~255점	8~10개	10~20점
56~58개	235~240점	5~7개	5~10점
53~55개	225~230점	2~4개	5~10점
50~52개	215~220점	0~1개	0~5점

* 점수 환산표는 해커스토익 사이트 유저 데이터를 근거로 제작되었으며, 주기적으로 업데이트되고 있습니다. 해커스토익 사이트
  (Hackers.co.kr)에서 최신 경향을 반영하여 업데이트된 점수환산기를 이용하실 수 있습니다. (토익 > 토익게시판 > 토익점수환산기)

TEST 3

PART 5
PART 6
PART 7
점수 환산표

잠깐! 테스트 전 확인사항

1. 문제 풀이에 방해가 되는 물건을 모두 치우셨나요?   예 □
2. Answer Sheet, 연필, 지우개를 준비하셨나요?   예 □
3. 시계를 준비하셨나요?   예 □

모든 준비가 완료되었으면 목표 점수를 떠올린 후 테스트를 시작합니다.

문제 풀이를 마치는 시간은 지금부터 **75분 후인** _____시 _____분입니다.

테스트 시간은 **총 75분**이며, 시험 종료 전 2~3분은 정답 검토 및 답안지 마킹을 위해 사용합니다.

READING TEST

In this section, you must demonstrate your ability to read and comprehend English. You will be given a variety of texts and asked to answer questions about these texts. This section is divided into three parts and will take 75 minutes to complete.

Do not mark the answers in your test book. Use the answer sheet that is separately provided.

PART 5

Directions: In each question, you will be asked to review a statement that is missing a word or phrase. Four answer choices will be provided for each statement. Select the best answer and mark the corresponding letter (A), (B), (C), or (D) on the answer sheet.

101. Many residents are not happy about the city's ------- to shut down the highway.

(A) decide
(B) decision
(C) decisive
(D) decided

102. If ------- need to make an appointment, please call the receptionist.

(A) yours
(B) you
(C) your
(D) yourself

103. Customers who ------- a prompt reply to their problem can start an online chat with a specialist.

(A) constrain
(B) release
(C) provide
(D) require

104. Mr. Robertson sought the advice of financial experts ------- choosing which stocks to purchase.

(A) according to
(B) before
(C) beyond
(D) far from

105. The flight was canceled because of ------- weather, so passengers waited six hours to depart.

(A) immense
(B) striking
(C) nervous
(D) severe

106. Ms. Adrian had to prepare ------- for the visitors from Novart Group.

(A) entertains
(B) entertained
(C) entertainment
(D) entertain

107. Ms. Valdez, the legal assistant, works ------- with lawyers and clients.

(A) close
(B) closer
(C) closely
(D) closure

108. CE Inc. has promoted numerous brands ------- its founding a decade ago.

(A) since
(B) throughout
(C) except for
(D) even though

109. At the construction site, workers will be ------- monitored by an on-site safety inspector.

(A) regular
(B) regularly
(C) regularity
(D) regulation

110. Directwork Solutions has gained ------- recognition than its competitors in the mobile advertising industry.

(A) great
(B) greater
(C) greatly
(D) greatest

111. Mirado Bakery raised the prices of some goods ------- an increase in the cost of ingredients.

(A) as of
(B) due to
(C) such as
(D) besides

112. Survey respondents prefer listening to ------- audiobooks or podcasts while they drive to work.

(A) either
(B) both
(C) every
(D) neither

113. Dr. Cruz showed some ------- when invited to speak at the conference, but ultimately consented.

(A) hesitate
(B) hesitant
(C) hesitation
(D) hesitated

114. Beemz Cable will ------- stop the service of any customer whose bill is overdue.

(A) instinctively
(B) patiently
(C) mutually
(D) immediately

115. The instruction manual explains how to ------- the photocopier in several languages.

(A) print
(B) operate
(C) reveal
(D) overlook

116. The ------- of the old hotel were successful and it now looks quite modern.

(A) locations
(B) advantages
(C) renovations
(D) productions

117. In addition to restaurants, points earned on the Aviato Card are ------- at certain retail establishments.

(A) redeeming
(B) redeemable
(C) redeem
(D) redeems

118. ------- considered the leader in computing innovation, Frye Systems has not had a new product in years.

(A) Necessarily
(B) Formerly
(C) Eventually
(D) Wisely

119. Staff members at Fasheng Industries are entitled to discounts ------- online Chinese language courses.

(A) of
(B) on
(C) into
(D) like

120. Mr. Mattson began the presentation by passing out a ------- outline of his speech topic.

(A) constant
(B) brief
(C) talented
(D) potential

GO ON TO THE NEXT PAGE

121. Users of Era Bank ------- to change their passwords after their data was accessed by hackers.

(A) instruct
(B) will instruct
(C) was instructed
(D) are being instructed

122. The decorator recommends making ------- use of white paint to lower expenses.

(A) extensive
(B) extension
(C) extensively
(D) extend

123. All details about the new product have been ------- concealed to prevent information from leaking.

(A) lastly
(B) publicly
(C) remotely
(D) thoroughly

124. The marketing team has developed a solid ------- plan just in case the original one proves inadequate.

(A) authority
(B) opportunity
(C) contingency
(D) coincidence

125. When working from home, some employees find it difficult to perform their tasks -------.

(A) effects
(B) effecting
(C) effective
(D) effectively

126. *Starlight Fractals* by Mr. Kazuka will be distributed to all major bookstores ------- Barton to Fort Bend.

(A) among
(B) when
(C) between
(D) from

127. Apex Gas agreed to ------- its rate increase at the request of the Fairfax city council.

(A) obtain
(B) delay
(C) compare
(D) recognize

128. VoyageX Holdings consulted a ------- of steel manufacturers prior to awarding a contract.

(A) vary
(B) various
(C) varied
(D) variety

129. The finance committee allocates ------- of the budget to each department.

(A) objects
(B) salaries
(C) portions
(D) patterns

130. The measure will ------- sugar consumption by placing a higher tax on sweetened beverages.

(A) adopt
(B) declare
(C) stimulate
(D) reduce

PART 6

Directions: In this part, you will be asked to read four English texts. Each text is missing a word, phrase, or sentence. Select the answer choice that correctly completes the text and mark the corresponding letter (A), (B), (C), or (D) on the answer sheet.

Questions 131-134 refer to the following advertisement.

STAFF REQUIRED
Job Code: Y51633

A design agency that consists of -------, highly competitive staff is seeking individuals to join its
          131.

team in Bangkok. Successful candidates will develop original packaging ideas for their clients.

Required qualifications include two years of relevant professional experience, a bachelor's degree

in a related field, and knowledge of illustration software. -------.
           132.

Please apply ------- sending an e-mail to staff@bkrecruit.com. Attach your résumé and enclose a
        133.

link to an online portfolio.

IMPORTANT: Enter the job code for this posting in the subject line of your e-mail. -------, we will
           134.

send you a notification to let you know that your application was received.

---

131. (A) creative
(B) creativity
(C) create
(D) creatively

132. (A) Computer software has advanced to a
high degree.
(B) Ability to drive a vehicle is crucial to the
job.
(C) Candidates with design certifications are
preferred.
(D) You have been invited to an online
interview.

133. (A) to
(B) for
(C) by
(D) in

134. (A) In the meantime
(B) Immediately afterward
(C) On the whole
(D) Nevertheless

GO ON TO THE NEXT PAGE

Questions 135-138 refer to the following letter.

November 19

Theodore Arum
99 West Wooley Road
California 93035

Dear Mr. Arum,

Thank you for visiting Silver Shore Community Center to give a talk on 20th century inventions earlier this month. I especially appreciate that you went into a more detailed ------- compared to last time. This made the event particularly enjoyable for audience members who ------- your presentation the year before. Though you agreed to give your time to Silver Shore Community Center on a voluntary basis, we would like to offer you -------. I am sending you a $50 gift voucher for the coffee chain Better Beans. -------.

Best regards,

Valery Miranda
Event Coordinator, Silver Shore Community Center

Enclosure: Better Beans gift voucher

135. (A) procedure
(B) statement
(C) discussion
(D) characteristic

136. (A) had attended
(B) attending
(C) were attending
(D) have attended

137. (A) convenience
(B) redemption
(C) occupation
(D) compensation

138. (A) Complete your registration over the phone.
(B) We hope you return again to give another speech.
(C) Once again, I apologize for the problem with the microphone.
(D) Your article is appearing in this month's issue.

Questions 139-142 refer to the following advertisement.

Save Big at O'Toole's Gym!

Winter has arrived, but don't let that stop you from getting fit! Sign up at O'Toole's Gym by the end

of December, and you ------- with discounts of up to 50 percent off the regular price.
                        139.

Our monthly and three-month passes are just $55 and $135, respectively. In addition, you

can receive even bigger discounts if you invite your friends. The more people -------, the more
                                                                              140.

discounts you get.

All members receive full access to our workout equipment during normal hours of operation. -------.
                                                                                            141.

Fees must be paid per session for personal training and classes. Register in person today.

------- our location at 81 Juniper Road.
142.

---

139. (A) rewarded
(B) are rewarded
(C) will be rewarding
(D) will be rewarded

140. (A) join
(B) joins
(C) joined
(D) joining

141. (A) Keep in mind that some services cost extra, though.
(B) Present the card to the front desk staff at any of our branches.
(C) You'd better act fast because we will be closing soon.
(D) Many people take advantage of these savings in the summer.

142. (A) Drop by
(B) Stay at
(C) Drive through
(D) Work out

GO ON TO THE NEXT PAGE →

Questions 143-146 refer to the following information.

Hong Kong Automotive Expo
How to receive your entrance pass

All ------- of this year's Hong Kong Automotive Expo must have a pass to enter the exhibition hall.
　　143.

Guests will receive their pass by mail during the last week of August. If yours has not arrived by

August 31, please notify us. -------.
　　　　　　　　　　　　144.

Registration for the event is now closed. -------, those who would like to sign up for late registration
　　　　　　　　　　　　　　145.

will have to pay a higher fee. They may pick up their passes at the event -------. Passes will be
　　　　　　　　　　　　　　　　　　146.

distributed before the expo starts and throughout the day.

---

143. (A) reviewers
(B) lecturers
(C) attendees
(D) organizers

144. (A) We apologize for our late response to
your inquiries.
(B) A maximum of three guests can be
brought along.
(C) You can inform us by calling 555-2801.
(D) We will then help you assemble your
booth.

145. (A) Specifically
(B) At that time
(C) Overall
(D) Accordingly

146. (A) system
(B) scheme
(C) page
(D) venue

Directions: In this part, you will be asked to read several texts, such as advertisements, articles, instant messages, or examples of business correspondence. Each text is followed by several questions. Select the best answer and mark the corresponding letter (A), (B), (C), or (D) on your answer sheet.

Questions 147-148 refer to the following invitation.

> You are cordially invited to the inauguration of the
> ## *West Hobart Performing Arts Center*
> April 9 at 7:30 P.M.
>
> To commemorate this occasion, the Hobart Symphony orchestra will perform a 30-minute concert at 8:30 P.M. This will be followed by a performance by opera singer Kelly Tekanawa.
>
> Dress code for the event is formal. Complimentary beverages and appetizers will be served before and after the performances. Confirmation of attendance is required. This invitation is valid for the invited guest and one other person.
>
> This event is made possible through generous contributions from our sponsors, Tasmania Savings Bank and Barkley Investors Group.
>
> The center is located at 67 Mount Stuart Road, and valet parking will be available.

147. Why is an event being held at the West Hobart Performing Arts Center?

(A) To introduce a group of musicians
(B) To celebrate a facility's opening
(C) To raise funds for a charity organization
(D) To honor a company's accomplishments

148. What is indicated about invited guests?

(A) They must be seated 30 minutes before a performance.
(B) They can purchase food and drinks at the event.
(C) They are members of an organization.
(D) They can bring an additional person.

GO ON TO THE NEXT PAGE

MEMO

To: All Forrester Communications staff
From: Judie Tomlinson
Subject: Media Conference
Date: August 21

The annual Peabody Media Conference will be held at the Arlington Hotel in Seattle from September 3 to 7. Management would like four representatives from our company to attend. If you are interested, please notify me by August 25 as that is the deadline for companies to purchase passes for their employees.

The company will reimburse conference participants for all travel expenses. However, please keep the following policies in mind when planning your trip. First, the maximum amount that can be claimed for a hotel room is $125 per night. Second, employees will only receive reimbursement for airfare if they book economy-class seats.

If you have questions about this event or the company's reimbursement policy, please feel free to contact me.

149. What is NOT stated about the conference?

(A) It will be held at an accommodation facility.
(B) It takes place once every year.
(C) It is organized by a Seattle-based company.
(D) It will last for a period of multiple days.

150. What can be inferred about some Forrester Communications employees?

(A) They will pay for their own admission passes.
(B) They will share a hotel room with a coworker.
(C) They will make their own travel arrangements.
(D) They will purchase business-class airline tickets.

Questions 151-153 refer to the following letter.

Picica Insurance

Lavi Steinem
4304 Cordova Street
Vancouver, BC
V6B 1E1

February 2

Dear Mr. Steinem,

We have gone over the documents you submitted, and I regret to inform you that we cannot satisfy your claim for repairs to your automobile. The terms of your policy state that, in the event of an accident, you are required to contact Picica Insurance as soon as possible. If you had done this, one of our agents would have been able to assess the damage and determine how much of it is covered by your policy. Because you chose to have repairs carried out on your vehicle before submitting your claim, it is impossible for us to know who was at fault or the true extent of the damage, even if you did enclose a photo of the damaged area of your car.

Please review your policy carefully. If you fail to adhere to the agreement, there is little we can do. Should you require further clarification or wish to raise an objection, please visit your nearest Picica Insurance office or call 1-800-555-8899.

Regards,

Lou Mortimer

Lou Mortimer
Picica Insurance Agent

---

151. What is mentioned about Mr. Steinem?

(A) He will have to pay a higher insurance fee.
(B) He did not meet a contractual requirement.
(C) He was in an accident with another driver.
(D) He is no longer eligible for coverage by Picica.

152. The word "satisfy" in paragraph 1, line 1, is closest in meaning to

(A) convince
(B) reward
(C) please
(D) fulfill

153. What did Mr. Steinem send to Mr. Mortimer?

(A) A request for car repairs
(B) A photograph of a vehicle
(C) A record of a transaction
(D) A rejection of a compensation offer

GO ON TO THE NEXT PAGE

Questions 154-155 refer to the following text-message chain.

Joseph Donahue [10:46 A.M.]
Hi, Lesley. I received an assignment that requires me to compare data, so I was wondering if it would be possible to get a second computer monitor. Otherwise, it'll take longer to get the work done.

Lesley Roussell [10:47 A.M.]
I see. You can send a request to the IT department. They're in charge of allocating computer equipment to staff. It might take several days, though. They're busy getting new staff set up in the accounting department.

Joseph Donahue [10:48 A.M.]
Isn't there another way? The assignment needs to be done by Friday. Besides, I won't need the extra monitor after that.

Lesley Roussell [10:50 A.M.]
In that case, I have a laptop you can use until then. I can help you set it up after lunch.

154. At 10:48 A.M., what does Mr. Donahue mean when he writes, "Isn't there another way"?

(A) He requires more data to complete an assignment.
(B) He cannot help new staff set up computers.
(C) He does not think a project schedule is reasonable.
(D) He is unable to wait for a response to a request.

155. What is suggested about Ms. Roussell?

(A) She is a project manager for the accounting department.
(B) She will let a colleague borrow a device until Friday.
(C) She should go out to lunch with some associates.
(D) She must get a laptop from an office equipment cabinet.

Magic Moments Photography

Our photographers specialize in capturing the magic moments of special events, such as weddings, anniversaries, and graduations. We offer the following package options:

~**Silver Package**~ $1,500
One photographer will cover two hours of your special event.
You will receive 250 edited high-resolution prints on a DVD.

~**Gold Package**~ $2,500
Two photographers will cover four hours of your special event.
You will receive 500 edited high-resolution prints on a DVD, plus a 5-minute video.

~**Platinum Package**~ $3,500
Two photographers will cover your entire special event.
You will receive a minimum of 1,000 edited high-resolution prints on a DVD as well as a 10-minute video and photos specifically formatted for online use.

Please allow up to three weeks for all items to be delivered.

156. What is indicated about Magic Moments Photography?

(A) It books clients a minimum of three weeks in advance.
(B) It sends multiple photographers to all events.
(C) It can expedite image delivery for an extra fee.
(D) It provides photo modification in all of its packages.

157. What is true about the Platinum Package?

(A) It is the only package that includes a video.
(B) It comes with a Web page to share photos.
(C) It includes pictures customized for the Internet.
(D) It offers a choice of custom-made DVDs.

GO ON TO THE NEXT PAGE

Questions 158-161 refer to the following job announcement.

Job Opening at Hamasaki Corporation

Hamasaki Corporation is a global corporation involved in the manufacture and supply of automotive parts. We are currently seeking a warehouse supervisor to perform duties at our main production plant in Chicago, Illinois.

Primary functions:
• Supervise deliveries of raw materials from suppliers
• Coordinate shipment of finished goods to clients
• Maintain a safe and productive work environment
• Recommend the hiring, disciplinary action, rewarding, and termination of employees
• Evaluate work processes and recommend improvements

Essential qualifications include:
• Completion of at least a two-year college degree
• At least five years of experience in a related role, preferably in the automotive industry
• Ability to work with database programs
• Being highly organized and detail oriented

This is a full-time role offering a competitive salary and benefits package. To apply, send your résumé to jobs@hamasakicorp.com. If you do not receive a confirmation e-mail, please contact our HR manager at 555-3090. Applications will not be accepted in person.

158. Which company posted the job announcement?

(A) A car dealership
(B) A shipping provider
(C) A parts manufacturer
(D) A transport services firm

159. What is NOT mentioned about the position?

(A) It includes supervisory duties.
(B) It may involve hiring and dismissing staff.
(C) It demands attention to detail.
(D) It is available to part-time workers.

160. What is required of applicants for the position?

(A) Possession of a four-year degree
(B) Completion of a training program
(C) Ability in more than one language
(D) Familiarity with a job type

161. How should people apply?

(A) By contacting a manager
(B) By mailing an application letter
(C) By using e-mail
(D) By visiting a Web site

Questions 162-164 refer to the following press release.

Zoet Foods to launch new product lines

March 21—Responding to current trends in the ice cream market, Switzerland's Zoet Foods has announced that it will be releasing a new line of products later this year. James Farnham, a marketing manager at Zoet, credits changing tastes for this development. — [1] —. "We have seen a clear shift in consumer preferences in the last couple of years," he said. "Consumers are eating less ice cream because of its high sugar content and now prefer healthier alternatives like yogurt." The market is being further eroded by demand for premium products like gelato, and ice creams made with organic or non-dairy ingredients. — [2] —.

While Zoet has recently gained strength in emerging markets like China, Brazil, and India, the majority of its sales still come from Europe and the US. — [3] —. "We have plenty of room for growth in emerging markets," Farnham added, "but our biggest challenge is maintaining our leading position in Europe and the US." — [4] —. With Zoet's innovative new product lines encompassing yogurts and gelatos as well as organic and non-dairy ingredients, the company appears ready to take on this challenge.

---

162. What does the press release mainly discuss?

(A) Innovations in food production
(B) Market conditions for a product
(C) Consumer behaviors in some countries
(D) Strategies of major food producers

163. How most likely does Zoet plan to maintain its position?

(A) By reducing the scale of its operations
(B) By developing lower-cost ingredients
(C) By introducing new products in Europe
(D) By marketing more aggressively in Asia

164. In which of the positions marked [1], [2], [3] and [4] does the following sentence best belong?

"These categories are typically dominated by local specialty companies rather than global ones."

(A) [1]
(B) [2]
(C) [3]
(D) [4]

GO ON TO THE NEXT PAGE

Questions 165-167 refer to the following e-mail.

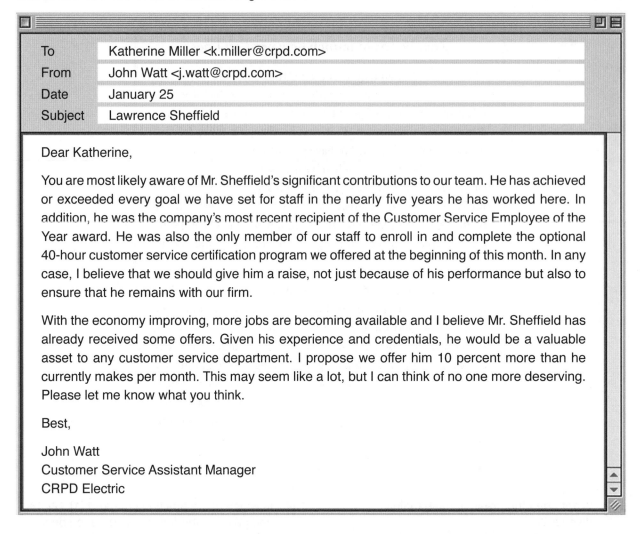

To	Katherine Miller <k.miller@crpd.com>
From	John Watt <j.watt@crpd.com>
Date	January 25
Subject	Lawrence Sheffield

Dear Katherine,

You are most likely aware of Mr. Sheffield's significant contributions to our team. He has achieved or exceeded every goal we have set for staff in the nearly five years he has worked here. In addition, he was the company's most recent recipient of the Customer Service Employee of the Year award. He was also the only member of our staff to enroll in and complete the optional 40-hour customer service certification program we offered at the beginning of this month. In any case, I believe that we should give him a raise, not just because of his performance but also to ensure that he remains with our firm.

With the economy improving, more jobs are becoming available and I believe Mr. Sheffield has already received some offers. Given his experience and credentials, he would be a valuable asset to any customer service department. I propose we offer him 10 percent more than he currently makes per month. This may seem like a lot, but I can think of no one more deserving. Please let me know what you think.

Best,

John Watt
Customer Service Assistant Manager
CRPD Electric

165. Why was the e-mail written?

(A) To recommend a suitable candidate for a management position
(B) To announce the recipient of an annual award
(C) To suggest increasing the compensation of an employee
(D) To justify the recent promotion of a staff member

166. What is suggested about Mr. Sheffield?

(A) He has been promoted more than once.
(B) He is well liked by his fellow workers.
(C) He earned a certification in under a month.
(D) He met with Mr. Watt to make a request.

167. What is Mr. Watt's concern?

(A) A training program had a low participation rate.
(B) A weak economy is threatening an industry.
(C) A company lacks the funds to provide incentives.
(D) A department will lose an employee to another firm.

Adriana Scorsese [10:10 A.M.] — As I mentioned in the e-mail I sent to both of you on May 14, my department will begin looking for applicants next month. I'd like to confirm the hiring requirements for each of your departments. Kathy, the accounting team needs two new members, right?

Kathy Chiu [10:14 A.M.] — Three, actually. Jack Wallace, one of my senior accountants, announced his retirement last month. He'll be leaving us on May 31.

Adriana Scorsese [10:14 A.M.] — Got it. Charles, what about you? Do you still require six new employees for marketing?

Charles Jones [10:15 A.M.] — That's right. We are planning several campaigns to boost sales of the company's newest product, so we'll need a lot of staff. And they should have experience with social media promotions. Maybe this could be specified in the job advertisement.

Adriana Scorsese [10:18 A.M.] — I'll take care of that. My assistant, Judith Harper, is in charge of writing the advertisements, and I'll make sure she includes that requirement. I'll send the advertisements to each of you on May 18 to review.

Kathy Chiu [10:19 A.M.] — I'm going to be attending a seminar in Chicago that day. Would it be alright if I provide you with my feedback on May 20?

Adriana Scorsese [10:19 A.M.] — No problem. There's one more thing. As I mentioned before, I'd like to review your training plans in advance. I've already received Kathy's, but I am still waiting for yours, Charles.

Charles Jones [10:21 A.M.] — Sorry about that. I can e-mail it to you on Friday afternoon. Will that work for you?

Adriana Scorsese [10:22 A.M.] — Perfect. Thanks.

[Send]

---

168. In which department does Ms. Scorsese most likely work?

(A) Accounting
(B) Marketing
(C) Personnel
(D) Sales

169. At 10:18 A.M., what does Ms. Scorsese mean when she writes "I'll take care of that"?

(A) She will ask an applicant to complete a form.
(B) She will assign a task to another employee.
(C) She will have a manager attend a meeting.
(D) She will conduct an interview with a client.

170. On which date will Ms. Chiu be absent from work?

(A) May 14
(B) May 18
(C) May 20
(D) May 31

171. What does Mr. Jones say he will do?

(A) Organize a training seminar for staff
(B) Review a post on a social media platform
(C) Provide some information to a colleague
(D) Update some data in the company records

GO ON TO THE NEXT PAGE

Bishop Advisors to offer artwork

By Blaine Webster

October 10 — The finance corporation Bishop Advisors announced on Thursday that it will be disposing of its extensive collection of paintings and sculptures. The works were purchased over several decades by former Bishop Advisors CEO Aileen MacIntyre and are estimated to be worth over €3 million in total. — [1] —.

Current Bishop Advisors CEO Gavin Brodie admits that he is not interested in art, but this was not the main reason for his choice. Rather, he pointed to the need to raise funds and the recent transfer of Bishop Advisors' headquarters. — [2] —. "While there was plenty of space in Ledmore Tower for wall and floor decorations, we have considerably less of that here in the Seascape Building," Brodie commented.

Prominent figures in the art world are excited by the news. — [3] —. "The paintings include some priceless landscapes by Tessa Menzies," said art expert Jennifer Harper. "For my part, I hope to bid on some of the sculptures by Bret Kennedy." The sale, to be held on October 14, will be handled by Avidia Auctions. — [4] —.

172. What does the article mainly discuss?

(A) The appointment of a new executive
(B) A proposed set of financial regulations
(C) An upcoming sale of artworks
(D) The discovery of a valuable piece of art

173. What is NOT a reason for Mr. Brodie's decision?

(A) Monetary requirements
(B) Space limitations
(C) Lack of interest
(D) Employee preferences

174. Who most likely will attend an event on October 14?

(A) Aileen MacIntyre
(B) Tessa Menzies
(C) Jennifer Harper
(D) Bret Kennedy

175. In which of the positions marked [1], [2], [3], and [4] does the following sentence best belong?

"Most are currently on display in the company's headquarters."

(A) [1]
(B) [2]
(C) [3]
(D) [4]

GO ON TO THE NEXT PAGE

To	Frida Gertner <f.gertner@essenplatz.com>
From	Cecilia Okumu <c.okumu@kitamutea.com>
Subject	New teas
Date	November 18

Dear Ms. Gertner,

By early next March, our company will be ready to harvest commercial quantities of the new teas we have developed. I thought you should know in case you wished to place an order. We expect to sell out our entire inventory by December 31, so I would recommend that you order soon. Prices are listed below for your reference.

Because you are one of our preferred customers, we are prepared to offer you the new green and yellow teas at a discounted rate. However, the terms are that you must place the minimum order of 1,000 kilos before December 1 and settle any unpaid balances before placing a new order.

Variety	Price per 1,000 kilos	Discounted rate
Black	$3,080	$2,926
White	$2,980	$2,831
Green	$2,840	$2,698
Yellow	$2,720	$2,584

Sincerely,

Cecilia Okumu
Client Services, Kitamu Tea Company

February 24

Cecilia Okumu
Kitamu Tea Company
414 Magongo Road
Mombasa, Kenya

Dear Ms. Okumu,

I am writing to inform you that the Halten Corporation has acquired Essen Platz. Consequently, there may be some changes with respect to our arrangements with Kitamu Tea. For one thing, starting on March 15, all future communications with your company will be handled by my replacement, Ms. Diana Schneider, whose contact details I will be sending to you. Moreover, the new management will place a hold on all further orders effective immediately, pending a review of our supplier contracts. That said, I have been assured that unpaid invoices will be settled in accordance with current agreements. So, I believe a payment of $2,698 should be forthcoming to cover our last shipment.

In closing, I'd like to say it was a pleasure working with you and I wish you all the best.

Frida Gertner, Chief Department Supervisor, Essen Platz

176. What is the main purpose of the e-mail?

(A) To encourage the purchase of new products
(B) To confirm the delivery of a recent order
(C) To explain an ordering process
(D) To report some research results

177. In the e-mail, the word "terms" in paragraph 2, line 2, is closest in meaning to

(A) words
(B) periods
(C) relations
(D) conditions

178. Who most likely is Ms. Schneider?

(A) A senior accountant
(B) A customer service representative
(C) A department supervisor
(D) A communications manager

179. What does Halten Corporation plan to do?

(A) Evaluate existing agreements
(B) Delay all payments until March
(C) Reduce the size of its workforce
(D) Offer shipping contracts to a new supplier

180. What is implied about Essen Platz?

(A) It is transferring some personnel to a new office.
(B) It placed an order of green tea in November.
(C) It is changing its main line of business.
(D) It owes several companies for past purchases.

GO ON TO THE NEXT PAGE

Questions 181-185 refer to the following Web page and form.

www.crawfordoffice.com

| Home | About | Shop | Accounts | Customer Service |

About Crawford Office Supply

Find everything your office needs!

Crawford Office Supply has been meeting the needs of businesses in Dallas for over 30 years now. As a locally owned and operated company, we take pride in providing great customer service and low prices to area residents. And we are pleased to announce that we will be opening our second branch at 321 Victor Street on the south side of the city on June 15.

To celebrate, both of our stores will be offering customers a free tote bag with the company logo for every purchase of office furniture from June 15 to 30. So, whatever you need for your workspace, be sure to visit Crawford Office Supply. We are open from 9:00 A.M. until 10:00 P.M. seven days a week. See you soon!

Crawford Office Supply
Order Form

Customer Name: Yvonne Murphy   **Date:** June 20
Company: Stanford Accounting   **Phone Number:** 555-0396
Delivery Address: 789 Harbor Road, Seattle, WA 98250

Item #	Product	Quantity	Price
2837	EZ Write Pen	10	$15
5839	Harris Notebook	15	$60
6934	RX350 Printer Cartridge	2	$50
7135	Sylex Chair	4	$300

Notes:		
I would like my order to be delivered by June 23. Please call me back today to let me know if this is possible. Workers will be replacing the flooring in our lobby from June 24 to 27, and visitors making deliveries will not be allowed in the building during this period. Thank you.	Subtotal	$425
	Tax	$34
	Shipping	$48
	Total	$507

181. What is mentioned about Crawford Office Supply?

(A) It will open a new location in June.
(B) It will relocate staff to its Dallas store.
(C) It will establish branches in several cities.
(D) It will change its current operating hours.

182. What must customers do to take advantage of an offer?

(A) Select a certain brand
(B) Order within a specified period
(C) Make a minimum purchase
(D) Visit a particular branch

183. For which product did Ms. Murphy receive a free item?

(A) EZ Write Pen
(B) Harris Notebook
(C) RX350 Printer Cartridge
(D) Sylex Chair

184. What does Ms. Murphy request?

(A) Verification of a price
(B) Information about a service
(C) Confirmation regarding a request
(D) Cancellation of a purchase

185. What problem does Ms. Murphy mention?

(A) Products are currently out of stock.
(B) A parking lot will be closed for several days.
(C) Elevators in the lobby are under repair.
(D) An area of a building will be inaccessible.

GO ON TO THE NEXT PAGE

Marcus Dodd
91 Webber Row
London SE1 8XH

July 24

Dear Mr. Dodd,

We are looking forward to your arrival at Seafair Resort on August 18. As you and the two other guests in your group will be staying for four days, you may want to take part in some of our offered activities. For instance, our tennis courts and lawn for bowling are available to anyone who wants to use them during daylight hours. We also have windsurfing equipment that can be used on a first-come, first-served basis. However, if you would like to join one of our popular hikes on Grand Soeur Island, it is recommended that you register at our front desk or on our Web site at least one day in advance. This is also the case for kayaking trips to Petite Soeur Island and Reynolds Island, as well as snorkeling and scuba diving excursions. Participants from both groups will enjoy lunch together on the beach at Coco Island. To join any of these activities, visit www.seafairer.com/activities.

Sincerely,

Keisha Joubert
Activity Manager
Seafair Resort

Seafair Resort—Sign-Up Form * Snorkeling

Name of Guest	Marcus Dodd		
Room Number	723		
Today's Date	August 19		
Desired Date of Activity	August 20		
Equipment Needed (Check All that Apply)	☐ Fins	☐ Mask	☐ Snorkel
Ability Level	☐ Inexperienced	☐ Competent	☑ Expert

Important Considerations
1. We are unable to loan, rent, or sell bathing suits. Participants must have their own.
2. This activity is limited to 15 people per day.
3. If less than 5 people have enrolled in the scuba diving excursion planned for the same day, they will join your group on the boat, the Waveroller.
4. If weather conditions are unsuitable, this activity will be canceled.
5. Participants with health conditions must provide relevant medical information to the guide.

Plan for August 20 Snorkeling Excursion Guide: Terry Haide, Bluewater License holder		
Activities	Time	Notes
Meet at Seafair Resort's Leisure Hut	➡ 9:00 A.M.	
Departure from Seafair Dock	➡ 9:10 A.M.	*Scuba diving groups will take the same transport.*
Arrival at Site 1	➡ 9:30 A.M.	
Safety briefing	➡ 9:40 A.M.	
Instructions on using equipment	➡ 10:00 A.M.	
Snorkeling around Ombre Reef	➡ 10:15 A.M.	*Participants will be led on an underwater tour.*
Break	➡ 11:00 A.M.	
Snorkeling around Urchin Cove	➡ 11:15 A.M.	*Participants will be able to explore on their own.*
Lunch	➡ 12:00 P.M.	*Meal will be served at a picnic area.*
Return to Seafair Resort	➡ 1:00 P.M.	

186. Why did Ms. Joubert contact Mr. Dodd?

(A) To inform him about leisure options
(B) To convince him to change a booking
(C) To ask about accommodation preferences
(D) To offer an incentive for joining a club

187. What is NOT indicated about Mr. Dodd?

(A) He has brought his own gear with him.
(B) He has submitted a medical document.
(C) He has decided to register early.
(D) He has gone snorkeling in the past.

188. What is indicated about the scuba diving participants on August 20?

(A) They are composed of fewer than five individuals.
(B) They are attempting to obtain the Bluewater License.
(C) They will have to pay extra fees upon checking out.
(D) They will return to Seafair Resort in the evening.

189. According to the schedule, when will an independent session take place?

(A) 9:40 A.M.
(B) 10:00 A.M.
(C) 10:15 A.M.
(D) 11:15 A.M.

190. Which island will the group led by Mr. Haide visit on August 20?

(A) Grand Soeur Island
(B) Petite Soeur Island
(C) Reynolds Island
(D) Coco Island

GO ON TO THE NEXT PAGE

Questions 191-195 refer to the following online form, schedule, and e-mail.

Linwood Bank

Home >> Online Forms >> Home Loan Application

Application Date: February 5

Applicant's Name: William Tanaka
Current Address: 18 Ridgeway Lane, Boston, MA 02115
Address of Home to Purchase: 250 Chestnut Drive, Providence, RI 02907

Company Name: Creston Software Development
Job Title: Computer Programmer

Do you have a savings account at our institution?
☑ Yes   ☐ No
If so, enter your account number: 3467-999-2551

Please register for a mandatory initial consultation with one of our financial advisors to discuss the details of your loan.

Selected Advisor: Nadine Frye
Preferred Initial Appointment Days/Times: Monday, Tuesday, or Thursday mornings and Friday afternoons

Thank you! Your application has been submitted. We will contact you to confirm your initial consultation date.

Linwood Bank
Financial Advisor Schedule

NOTE: Submit vacation and time off requests for approval by administrative manager Marcie Welford. We are closed for the national holiday on Monday, February 8.

Last Updated: February 4

	Tuesday, February 9	Wednesday, February 10	Thursday, February 11	Friday, February 12
Harold Marks	10 A.M. - 2 P.M. Free	Vacation day: approved	Vacation day: approved	10 A.M. - 12 P.M. Free 12 P.M. - 2 P.M. Appointment
Kelly Wong	Vacation day: approved	9 A.M. - 11 A.M. Appointment 11 A.M. - 1 P.M. Appointment	9 A.M. - 12 P.M. Free 12 P.M. - 1P.M. Appointment	Vacation day: approved
Nadine Frye	Vacation day: approved	Vacation day: approved	11 A.M. - 1 P.M. Appointment 1 P.M. - 3 P.M. Appointment	9 A.M. - 11 A.M. Appointment 12 P.M. - 3 P.M. Free

To	William Tanaka <w.tanaka@upmail.net>
From	Nadine Frye <n.frye@linwoodbank.com>
Date	February 15
Subject	Our Meeting
Attachment	Documents list

Dear Mr. Tanaka,

Thank you for coming to see me for your initial home loan consultation at Linwood Bank last week. I have attached a list containing documents that you will need to provide in order to be approved for your loan. Please upload those documents to our online system by February 28. Once submitted, our bank's associates will review them and contact you by March 5 to let you know whether your application has been approved or rejected.

Additionally, I know that you had a question about how to make automatic loan payments from your account. I will provide you with instructions on that in a separate e-mail. I should also point out that current account holders are entitled to receive a 1 percent discount on their home loan interest rates.

Sincerely,

Nadine Frye

191. When did Mr. Tanaka most likely meet with Ms. Frye?

(A) On February 9
(B) On February 10
(C) On February 11
(D) On February 12

192. What is indicated about Mr. Marks?

(A) He was recently hired as a consultant at Linwood Bank.
(B) He was unable to cover Ms. Wong's Monday appointments.
(C) He sent out an approval letter to a prospective loan applicant.
(D) He received permission from Ms. Welford for some time off.

193. According to the e-mail, what will Linwood Bank's associates do?

(A) Apply some updates to forms on the company's Web site
(B) Modify the advisors' schedules to create more availability
(C) Authorize the opening of an account without an initial deposit
(D) Look over some documents to determine financial assistance

194. Why will Ms. Frye send another e-mail to Mr. Tanaka?

(A) To schedule a follow-up meeting
(B) To update him on the status of his loan application
(C) To give directions concerning his savings account
(D) To explain the conditions of an agreement

195. What is stated about Mr. Tanaka?

(A) He is eligible for a rate reduction.
(B) He made a loan payment in February.
(C) He started a new position recently.
(D) He will withdraw cash from a machine.

GO ON TO THE NEXT PAGE

To   All marketing staff <marketingteam@fizzlespark.com>
From   Irina Sokolov <i.sokolov@fizzlespark.com>
Date   April 4
Subject Congratulations

Hello all,

I want to thank everyone for their hard work last month finishing up our advertising campaign for the company's newly launched line of organic juices — Whole Renew. The CEO has reviewed the finalized ads and is delighted with what we've put together, so congratulations to all of you.

As a reminder, the advertisements will be posted on our homepage as follows:

May — Buy one, get one free offer
June — 20 percent off promotion
July — Coupon for $5 off a future purchase

Finally, I encourage you all to sample the line using your employee discount. Having tried the products a few times myself, I can guarantee that they are incredibly tasty!

Regards,

Irina Sokolov
Marketing Department Head, FizzleSpark National

FizzleSpark National Whole Renew

Are the summer months leaving you feeling dehydrated? Then reach for a bottle of Whole Renew—a line of delicious juices made with 100 percent organic ingredients. Choose from a wide selection of drinks to suit your taste, from beet and apple to mango and ginger. Plus, all of these refreshing choices are two for the price of one this month.

The deals don't end there! Pick up Whole Renew at any Victoria Café location on June 10 from 11 A.M. to 3 P.M. and receive a free organic snack. Download the Victoria Café smartphone application for additional details.

To	Owen Collins <o.collins@victioriacafedenver.com>
From	Sarah Klein <sklein488@parkmail.net>
Subject	Your café
Date	June 15

Dear Mr. Collins,

As your neighbor in the Shearmont Shopping Plaza, I want to say that the renovation work that you recently completed at Victoria Café was wonderfully done. Having owned my gift shop in this plaza for many years, I've seen several businesses come and go. And I'm glad to see that you've made some nice improvements at your location.

Also, when I visited your café on June 10 at noon, I tried one of the Whole Renew juices that you were selling and took part in the special promotion that day—what a pleasant surprise! I'm interested in developing partnerships with major food corporations like the one that makes Whole Renew. Would you be able to share their contact information so that I can reach out to them? I'd really appreciate your help.

Sarah Klein, Owner, Brightstar Gifts

196. What type of company most likely is FizzleSpark National?

(A) A coffee shop
(B) A drink producer
(C) A gift store
(D) A supermarket chain

197. What is NOT mentioned about the marketing staff?

(A) They will be evaluated by an executive.
(B) They worked on some advertisements last month.
(C) They have been congratulated by a department head.
(D) They can receive a lower price on some products.

198. What is indicated about the deal in the advertisement?

(A) It is only offered to customers enrolled in a membership program.
(B) It was rejected by the president of a corporation.
(C) It is limited to purchases made at one location.
(D) It was posted on a Web site in May.

199. What is one feature of Whole Renew?

(A) A variety of flavors
(B) A sugar-free ingredient
(C) Colorful packaging
(D) Extra vitamins

200. What did Ms. Klein most likely do at the Victoria Café?

(A) Tried a food item free of charge
(B) Assisted with some renovation work
(C) Spoke with a facility manager
(D) Picked up a limited-time coupon

This is the end of the test. You may review Parts 5, 6, and 7 if you finish the test early.

TEST 3 점수 환산표

TEST 3은 무사히 잘 마치셨나요? 맞은 개수를 세어본 후 아래의 점수 환산표를 통해 자신의 점수를 예상해 보세요.

전체 난이도　　**중간 난이도**

파트별 난이도　　PART 5　중　●●○
　　　　　　　　　PART 6　상　●●●
　　　　　　　　　PART 7　상　●●●

정답 수	리딩 점수	정답 수	리딩 점수
98~100개	475~495점	47~49개	205~215점
95~97개	460~470점	44~46개	190~200점
92~94개	440~455점	41~43개	175~185점
89~91개	420~435점	38~40개	160~170점
86~88개	405~415점	35~37개	145~155점
83~85개	390~400점	32~34개	130~140점
80~82개	375~385점	29~31개	115~125점
77~79개	360~370점	26~28개	100~110점
74~76개	340~355점	23~25개	85~95점
71~73개	325~335점	20~22개	70~80점
68~70개	305~320점	17~19개	55~65점
65~67개	290~300점	14~16개	40~50점
62~64개	270~285점	11~13개	25~35점
59~61개	260~270점	8~10개	10~20점
56~58개	245~255점	5~7개	5~10점
53~55개	235~240점	2~4개	5~10점
50~52개	220~230점	0~1개	0~5점

* 점수 환산표는 해커스토익 사이트 유저 데이터를 근거로 제작되었으며, 주기적으로 업데이트되고 있습니다. 해커스토익 사이트
  (Hackers.co.kr)에서 최신 경향을 반영하여 업데이트된 점수환산기를 이용하실 수 있습니다. (토익 > 토익게시판 > 토익점수환산기)

TEST 4

×

PART 5
PART 6
PART 7
점수 환산표

잠깐! 테스트 전 확인사항

1. 문제 풀이에 방해가 되는 물건을 모두 치우셨나요?   예 □
2. Answer Sheet, 연필, 지우개를 준비하셨나요?   예 □
3. 시계를 준비하셨나요?   예 □

모든 준비가 완료되었으면 목표 점수를 떠올린 후 테스트를 시작합니다.

문제 풀이를 마치는 시간은 지금부터 **75분 후인** _____시 _____분입니다.

테스트 시간은 **총 75분**이며, 시험 종료 전 2~3분은 정답 검토 및 답안지 마킹을 위해 사용합니다.

READING TEST

In this section, you must demonstrate your ability to read and comprehend English. You will be given a variety of texts and asked to answer questions about these texts. This section is divided into three parts and will take 75 minutes to complete.

Do not mark the answers in your test book. Use the answer sheet that is separately provided.

PART 5

Directions: In each question, you will be asked to review a statement that is missing a word or phrase. Four answer choices will be provided for each statement. Select the best answer and mark the corresponding letter (A), (B), (C), or (D) on the answer sheet.

101. Vintron Labs employees have been working ------- to ensure the final product is perfect.

(A) deliberate
(B) deliberated
(C) deliberately
(D) deliberation

102. The machine ------- the parking garage will dispense a receipt and change for cash payments.

(A) among
(B) from
(C) in
(D) onto

103. Should the bill be paid ------- the next 15 days, the utility company will not apply a penalty.

(A) upon
(B) within
(C) behind
(D) toward

104. LightTrek's video-editing software did not sell well ------- having some impressive features.

(A) for
(B) despite
(C) than
(D) since

105. The accidentally deleted files could have been retrieved if the user had contacted customer support -------.

(A) thoroughly
(B) fairly
(C) nearly
(D) rapidly

106. The police officer was ------- that she had spoken to every witness involved.

(A) attentive
(B) sharp
(C) certain
(D) unique

107. The well-made appliance has functioned for 20 years without much ------- required.

(A) convenience
(B) maintenance
(C) protection
(D) resistance

108. The company plans to hire ------- to handle Ms. Kovac's duties during her vacation.

(A) other
(B) one another
(C) anything
(D) someone

109. It is illegal to use a copyrighted photo without obtaining ------- from its owner.

(A) certification
(B) declaration
(C) discipline
(D) consent

110. If you are interested in a personalized program, please ------- your preferences on the gym's membership registration form.

(A) authorize
(B) initiate
(C) state
(D) tolerate

111. Ms. Ebbets has been responsible for ------- the legal department for over a decade.

(A) manager
(B) manage
(C) managing
(D) managed

112. Ms. Olsen ------- caffeine from her diet until next week based on her doctor's recommendations.

(A) was removed
(B) removing
(C) has removed
(D) will be removing

113. After successfully completing a major construction project, Goldfield Land aims to become one of Asia's ------- land developers.

(A) led
(B) leads
(C) leading
(D) leaders

114. Though it has yet to be confirmed, news reports ------- that Braxco and Haskill are considering a merger.

(A) implement
(B) respond
(C) acquire
(D) indicate

115. At Donald's Doughnuts anniversary event, ------- have bought a coffee to obtain a free muffin.

(A) many
(B) either
(C) little
(D) anyone

116. Red Pail Hardware offers products at reasonable prices, but the goods of Jerry's Home Supplies are more -------.

(A) afforded
(B) affords
(C) affording
(D) affordable

117. Those who wish to ------- the local art festival must purchase tickets at the town hall.

(A) engage
(B) attend
(C) participate
(D) perform

118. Following the meeting, Mr. Hoffman appeared ------- in his team's ability to meet the deadline.

(A) confidence
(B) confide
(C) confidential
(D) confident

119. Each employee must join the workshop ------- his or her position at the company.

(A) regardless of
(B) other than
(C) such as
(D) except for

120. The company's Web site included some ------- information concerning the job application process.

(A) contradictable
(B) contradiction
(C) contradictory
(D) contradict

GO ON TO THE NEXT PAGE

121. Customers who place orders for the XP290 at least one month ------- will receive a special gift.

(A) beforehand
(B) anytime
(C) instantly
(D) nowadays

122. Mr. Turner is regarded as an ------- fashion designer for his innovative creations.

(A) available
(B) ingenious
(C) appreciative
(D) inactive

123. Producing a standard employee orientation manual would be of ------- help to staff.

(A) customary
(B) extravagant
(C) intelligent
(D) immense

124. By taking physical therapy classes and stretching frequently, the patient ------- recovered from her injury.

(A) progressive
(B) progress
(C) progressively
(D) progression

125. Ms. Lee showed her athletic ------- by qualifying for the prestigious Valley River Running Competition.

(A) potential
(B) authority
(C) property
(D) acquisition

126. The large project that Wassco is bidding for is ------- competitive due to its profitability.

(A) extremely
(B) efficiently
(C) unanimously
(D) promptly

127. The salary paid to the top ------- at CK Logistics is one of the highest in the industry.

(A) execute
(B) execution
(C) executive
(D) executing

128. The product was taken from store shelves ------- concerns that it might be defective.

(A) along with
(B) because of
(C) whenever
(D) in observance of

129. A purchase request form must be signed by a supervisor, ------- it will not receive approval.

(A) or
(B) nevertheless
(C) and
(D) yet

130. Lyon Incorporated's staff will receive an annual salary increase that is ------- to revenue growth.

(A) complimentary
(B) counting
(C) complex
(D) proportional

PART 6

Directions: In this part, you will be asked to read four English texts. Each text is missing a word, phrase, or sentence. Select the answer choice that correctly completes the text and mark the corresponding letter (A), (B), (C), or (D) on the answer sheet.

Questions 131-134 refer to the following flyer.

Help Us Preserve Landmark Park!
Join Dothan City Youth League's Annual Cleanup Event
May 15 I 10 A.M. to 4 P.M.

Activities include picking up litter and planting trees. Volunteers will be provided ------- equipment.
131.
Since supplies may be limited, we encourage you to bring your own gear.

Participants ------- into groups and assigned specific areas to clean. Remember to dress -------.
132. **133.**
Wear long pants and appropriate shoes.

If you are considering providing aid to the Dothan City Youth League, your contributions will be

used for this and future events. -------. However, we recommend taking them to the Dothan City
134.
Homeless Shelter. Register for the cleanup event at www.dothanyouth.org.

131. (A) with
(B) of
(C) for
(D) to

132. (A) separated
(B) were separated
(C) have been separated
(D) will be separated

133. (A) proper
(B) propriety
(C) more proper
(D) properly

134. (A) Sign up to be notified by e-mail.
(B) We do not accept donations of items.
(C) Attendance was higher than anticipated.
(D) The park may be rented for private events.

GO ON TO THE NEXT PAGE

Questions 135-138 refer to the following notice.

Dear customers,

Banerjee Roof Tiles will be upgrading its computer system. This is expected to affect our order and e-mail handling, as well as customer service. Our online ordering system will be disabled between May 20 and May 31. -------. Our personnel will be glad to assist you. Provided everything
135.
------- smoothly, normal operations should resume by June 1.
136.

During the last week of May, we will also focus on training staff, ------- familiarizing employees with
137.
the new system. Consequently, we may be slow to respond to inquiries and will be unable to offer

our ------- service and support.
138.

We apologize for the inconvenience and thank you for your patience.

135. (A) Directions for alternative routes are available on our Web site.
(B) If you'd like to place an order, please call us during business hours.
(C) Therefore, some items will not be in stock for the duration of this issue.
(D) We will accept product returns under our terms and conditions.

136. (A) will be advanced
(B) advances
(C) advance
(D) has been advanced

137. (A) otherwise
(B) in case
(C) thereby
(D) as a result of

138. (A) public
(B) approved
(C) usual
(D) selective

Eric Frears
6633 7th Street
Sacramento, CA 95673

Dear Mr. Frears,

Thank you for considering The Aldrich at Shasta Lake. ------- that quality of life has always been
139.
our priority, it is no surprise that we have satisfied hundreds of residents.

As a member of our community, you will have ------- to around-the-clock medical care and
140.
assistance with cooking and cleaning. There are also frequent get-togethers and volunteering

opportunities at local events. We hope to make every day as ------- as it can be.
141.

Come for a visit, take a look around, and experience a taste of retirement living in The Aldrich. -------.
142.

I look forward to welcoming you!

Mona Sorenstein
Executive Director
The Aldrich Retirement Community

139. (A) Whether
(B) Especially
(C) Although
(D) Given

140. (A) access
(B) accessed
(C) accessing
(D) accessible

141. (A) consistent
(B) fulfilling
(C) influential
(D) fortunate

142. (A) Call before our peak season begins.
(B) We treat our employees here like they are family.
(C) We are confident you will find it worthy of calling home.
(D) I will clean and prepare your room when you get here.

GO ON TO THE NEXT PAGE

Questions 143-146 refer to the following e-mail.

To: Alison Jackson <ajackson@champleather.com>
From: Victoria Green <vgreen@champleather.com>
Subject: New policy
Date: 15 June

Hi, Alison,

Please distribute the following information. I want to make sure ------- in the company are aware of
143.
our new policy. Effective November 1, the company will require periodic medical checks of certain

groups of employees. This is in accordance with regulations enacted by the National Labor Board.

-------. Specifically, the policy covers personnel who ------- to hazardous conditions at work, such as
144.   145.
workers who handle chemicals. The policy also affects employees whose health is crucial to the

safe performance of his or her job. -------, our delivery truck drivers must undergo health checks to
146.
make sure that they are fit to operate heavy vehicles. We will discuss this in more detail over the

coming days.

Sincerely,

Victoria Green
Champ Leather

---

143. (A) all
(B) them
(C) every
(D) these

144. (A) A detailed proposal has been left on
your desk.
(B) The regulatory body is composed of
legal experts.
(C) The commission approved the measure
last week.
(D) Management values the safety of its
staff.

145. (A) has been exposing
(B) exposes
(C) have exposed
(D) are exposed

146. (A) Conversely
(B) Rather than
(C) In particular
(D) Continuously

Directions: In this part, you will be asked to read several texts, such as advertisements, articles, instant messages, or examples of business correspondence. Each text is followed by several questions. Select the best answer and mark the corresponding letter (A), (B), (C), or (D) on your answer sheet.

Questions 147-148 refer to the following advertisement.

Spaces for Rent

Located at 57 Buckwold Drive, this recently renovated commercial property is in the heart of Renuville and is within walking distance of many cafes and shops. It is also just two blocks from Renfrew Park. Each of its 11 floors provides 10,500 square feet of office space. There is also a large underground garage. Tenants and their visitors may leave their vehicles there at no charge. All floors in the building are ready for immediate occupancy. Call 555-9982 for more information or to request a viewing.

147. What is a feature of 57 Buckwold Drive?

(A) It contains residential units.
(B) It has a central location.
(C) It has a view of a park.
(D) It includes furnished offices.

148. What are tenants able to do?

(A) Obtain a discount on larger offices
(B) Request partially furnished rooms
(C) Use a parking facility for free
(D) Delay payment on the initial rent

GO ON TO THE NEXT PAGE

Questions 149-150 refer to the following e-mail.

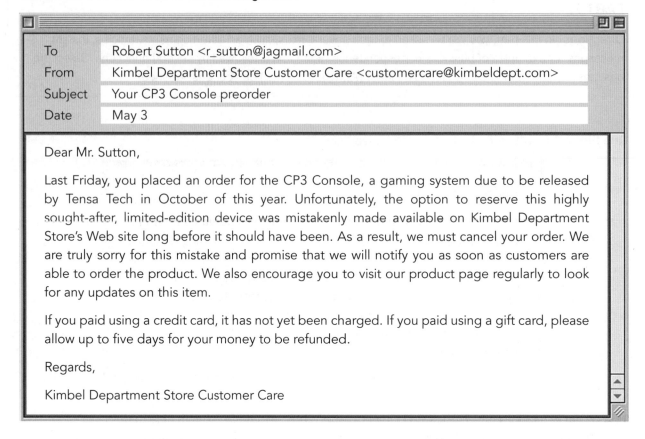

To   Robert Sutton <r_sutton@jagmail.com>

From   Kimbel Department Store Customer Care <customercare@kimbeldept.com>

Subject   Your CP3 Console preorder

Date   May 3

Dear Mr. Sutton,

Last Friday, you placed an order for the CP3 Console, a gaming system due to be released by Tensa Tech in October of this year. Unfortunately, the option to reserve this highly sought-after, limited-edition device was mistakenly made available on Kimbel Department Store's Web site long before it should have been. As a result, we must cancel your order. We are truly sorry for this mistake and promise that we will notify you as soon as customers are able to order the product. We also encourage you to visit our product page regularly to look for any updates on this item.

If you paid using a credit card, it has not yet been charged. If you paid using a gift card, please allow up to five days for your money to be refunded.

Regards,

Kimbel Department Store Customer Care

---

149. What is suggested about Mr. Sutton?

(A) He will purchase a device after its release.
(B) He canceled an order due to a mistake.
(C) He will have to wait to receive a refund.
(D) He submitted a payment online last Friday.

150. When will Kimbel Department Store contact Mr. Sutton again?

(A) After a refund request has been approved
(B) When an item is available to purchase
(C) After a store's inventory has been restocked
(D) When the location of a product launch is revealed

Talk of the Town   *Hamilton Enquirer*

Hamilton Native Wins Award
By Troy Cheung

January 6—Vino Kiwi CEO Gloria Wilson accepted a Company of the Year award from the National Business Forum (NBF) last week. Her company, which offers holiday packages in New Zealand's wine country, beat several competitors in the category for tourism.

Each year, a wide range of professional organizations nominate companies for consideration. The NBF then evaluates these firms on criteria such as service standards and customer satisfaction to determine the best company in each field. During this process, Vino Kiwi received 4.5 points out of a possible 5.

When asked to comment, Ms. Wilson said, "This is a great honor that validates years of hard work." She thanked family, friends, and coworkers for their support and invited the public to try her services. Further information about Vino Kiwi may be found at www.vinokiwi.com.

151. What does the article mainly discuss?

(A) The government regulations for a local industry
(B) A business group's charitable contributions
(C) The criteria for membership in an organization
(D) A business's recent accomplishment

152. According to the article, what is one of the tasks of the National Business Forum?

(A) Promoting businesses in international markets
(B) Managing a fund that supports local companies
(C) Assessing recommendations from other organizations
(D) Selecting entrepreneurs to represent the country

Chic Life Magazine

Marilyn DuBois's Spring Farewell

(20 December)—Next month, famed designer Marilyn DuBois will put on a show for her spring collection, which will be the last line of clothing she will ever produce. The fashion world was shocked in November when Ms. DuBois made the unexpected announcement about her plans to retire next February. Although only 45 years old, Ms. DuBois has had an illustrious career in the apparel design industry, opening nearly 200 boutiques worldwide.

In an exclusive interview with our magazine, Ms. DuBois enlightened us with some details about her retirement. "I've had a wonderful career designing clothes," she said, "but the constant expectation from the public for me to create innovative work has been stressful." Ms. DuBois further explained that her daughter Janelle will take over as CEO of DuBois Corporation beginning in February. "She is more passionate about the job than I ever was," Ms. DuBois joked.

With Ms. DuBois at a high point in her career, fashion professionals are sad to see her move on. At the same time, they eagerly anticipate what the future may bring after February.

153. According to the article, what will happen next year?

(A) A garment designer will come to the end of her career.
(B) An announcement about an industry event will be made.
(C) A photo shoot for a clothing line will take place.
(D) A fashion show will be held at a boutique.

154. What has been a cause of concern for Marilyn DuBois?

(A) Reduced sales in her stores
(B) Declining passion for her work
(C) Pressure to be creative
(D) Changing public opinion

155. What can be inferred about Janelle DuBois?

(A) She has plans of hiring new fashion models.
(B) Her promotion to CEO has been well received.
(C) She majored in fashion design in college.
(D) Her designs have attracted more attention than her mother's.

Frank Danes (7:40 P.M.)
Sorry to bother you, but I was wondering whether I could get off early tomorrow. I'm going to Denver for the weekend and was hoping to catch a 4 P.M. flight. Would it be OK to leave work after lunch?

Maria Faubert (7:42 P.M.)
Sure. I don't expect the bank will be too busy at that time anyway.

Frank Danes (7:43 P.M.)
Thanks!

Maria Faubert (7:45 P.M.)
I'll adjust your work schedule first thing tomorrow morning.

Frank Danes (7:48 P.M.)
Great! Oh, do I need to fill out a leave request form for this?

Maria Faubert (7:50 P.M.)
No, because it isn't a full day.

Frank Danes (7:51 P.M.)
Understood. Thanks, and have a good evening.

156. At 7:42 P.M., what does Ms. Faubert most likely mean when she writes, "Sure"?

(A) She can help Mr. Danes book a flight.
(B) She will convey a request to her supervisor.
(C) She is willing to let Mr. Danes leave the office early.
(D) She will retrieve a form on a coworker's behalf.

157. What is suggested about the bank?

(A) It requires staff to complete forms for full-day absences.
(B) It usually closes at four in the afternoon.
(C) It organizes weekly staff training sessions.
(D) It makes travel arrangements for staff business trips.

GO ON TO THE NEXT PAGE

Peele, Knowles, and Associates

TO: Secretarial Staff
FROM: Marjorie Dodds, Office Manager

I am pleased to inform the law firm's secretarial staff that office policies regarding lunch hour have been changed. After feedback from you during our staff meeting last week, management has decided to implement the following changes:

Lunchtime will be extended from 12:00 P.M. until 1:30 P.M. every Friday. During this time, the offices will be closed to the public, so make sure to switch your telephones to our answering service. Be sure to notify our regular clients of this change as well. The administrative staff will take care of recording a new message for the machine.

Staff who are requested to work through the lunch hour by their superiors have the option of doing so for overtime pay. That means you will receive double pay for working through the noon hour. However, staff may turn down such requests.

Those with questions regarding these changes may speak with me directly or send me an e-mail at marjdodds@peeleknowlesassoc.com.

---

158. The word "implement" in paragraph 1, line 3, is closest in meaning to

(A) account for
(B) carry out
(C) dispose of
(D) attend to

159. What are the administrative staff probably going to do?

(A) Monitor the number of breaks taken by staff
(B) Gather comments and suggestions about policies
(C) Create a recorded message
(D) Take over the reception desk during breaks

160. What is mentioned about secretarial staff?

(A) They will receive extra pay for working during their lunch hour.
(B) They must get permission from supervisors to do overtime.
(C) They are obligated to work through the noon hour if requested.
(D) They need to e-mail their break schedules to a manager.

Why You Should Join a Business Association

By Jan de Vries

Joining a business association provides many benefits to business owners, such as visibility, networking opportunities, and training. These and other advantages could be just the things your business needs to grow and thrive. — [1] —.

For instance, when Martha Yancey first opened her specialty shoe store Walking on Air a decade ago, finding customers was difficult because she was not well-known in the local community. By joining a business association, she was able to introduce herself to potential customers and receive multiple client referrals. — [2] —. "Additionally," she said, "my interactions led me to other business owners who could give me essential services and advice, like my current electrician and accountant."

Similarly, when Lucas Smitt was starting out, he knew plenty about furniture repair but almost nothing about operating a business. "Through my membership in a business association, I was able to get access to free and discounted seminars, workshops, and online classes. — [3] —. From these, I learned how to run a company properly." This November, Smitt Restoration will be celebrating its 10th successful year.

Naturally, benefits like those mentioned do not always come free. Most associations charge an annual membership fee, and expect regular participation in official functions and events. — [4] —.

161. What is suggested about Ms. Yancey?

(A) She joined a group at first to meet new friends.
(B) Her first store was in a difficult location to access.
(C) She got her product idea from another member.
(D) Her accountant is in a business association.

162. What can be inferred about Mr. Smitt?

(A) He was still in school when he started his firm.
(B) He joined the same organization that Ms. Yancey did.
(C) He and Ms. Yancey opened their companies at about the same time.
(D) He teaches other young entrepreneurs how to run their businesses.

163. In which of the positions marked [1], [2], [3], and [4] does the following sentence best belong?

"However, the cost is small compared to the value offered in return."

(A) [1]
(B) [2]
(C) [3]
(D) [4]

GO ON TO THE NEXT PAGE

Questions 164-167 refer to the following online chat discussion.

🧑 **Travis Coleman** [12:00 P.M.]		Someone named James Vine called to ask whether the hotel will be purchasing any new equipment.
Sheila Leblanc [12:03 P.M.]		Right. I talked to him last week and asked him to send us a catalog. I left it with you at the front desk, Travis.
Gabby Ross [12:04 P.M.]		If possible, I think we should get larger buffet tables for the dining area now that it's been expanded. By the way, how are the other renovations going?
Sheila Leblanc [12:04 P.M.]		They've been a challenge. The contractors we hired say the pool won't be ready in time. We may have to delay reopening the hotel for two weeks longer than we thought.
Sheila Leblanc [12:04 P.M.]		As for the buffet tables, I agree. I bookmarked two in the catalog. Travis, can you find them and describe them for Gabby?
🧑 **Travis Coleman** [12:07 P.M.]		No problem. The first one is black and has a glass sneeze guard and under-the-counter refrigeration. The second is maple, has heat lamps above the food pans, and trays for ice. Which one do you prefer?
Gabby Ross [12:10 P.M.]		I'll go check out the catalog in a moment to see what they look like, but the first one sounds better. It's not easy to keep food cool just with ice.
Sheila Leblanc [12:11 P.M.]		OK, let me know. I'm finishing up the recreation room today, so I'll be down in the basement if you need me.

Send

164. Who did Mr. Coleman speak to recently?

(A) A hotel manager
(B) An event organizer
(C) A real estate agent
(D) An equipment salesperson

165. At 12:04 P.M., what does Ms. Leblanc mean when she writes, "They've been a challenge"?

(A) Progress is slow on a remodeling project.
(B) Product descriptions are difficult to understand.
(C) Some service providers refused to do a job.
(D) Some appliances did not come with instructions.

166. What buffet table feature will most likely affect Ms. Ross's decision?

(A) The hanging heating elements
(B) The hardwood exterior
(C) The built-in refrigerators
(D) The glass sneeze guard

167. Where does Ms. Ross plan to go shortly?

(A) The swimming pool
(B) The front desk
(C) The dining area
(D) The recreation room

Questions 168-171 refer to the following e-mail.

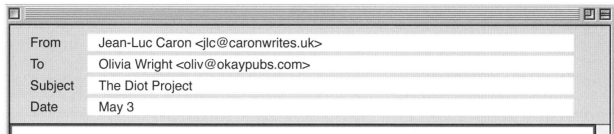

From   Jean-Luc Caron <jlc@caronwrites.uk>

To   Olivia Wright <oliv@okaypubs.com>

Subject   The Diot Project

Date   May 3

Dear Ms. Wright,

When I checked my bank balance today, I saw that $10,770 had been transferred into my account by Okay Publications. While I appreciate your company's timely payment, according to my calculations, this sum is short by $232. Before I signed the contract to translate *The Thoughts of Anne Diot* from French to English, the rate was agreed upon at $0.15 per word. Further, my records indicate that the main text of the book totaled 71,800 words, which was the exact amount for which I was paid. I'm not sure you're aware, though, that last week, Mr. Stuart sent me his newly written footnotes, which also needed to be translated. It seems that these footnotes, consisting of 1,547 words, were not taken into account when my fee was calculated.

Please double-check the total word count for the project, and let me know if there was indeed a mistake. I understand that your projects are usually only handled by in-house staff members, and perhaps this led to some confusion about the payment.

Sincerely,

Jean-Luc Caron

168. Why did Mr. Caron write the e-mail?

(A) To clear up a billing error
(B) To clarify some writing instructions
(C) To suggest corrections to a manuscript
(D) To follow up on overdue work

169. Who is Mr. Stuart?

(A) A book author
(B) A publishing manager
(C) A document translator
(D) A magazine editor

170. The phrase "taken into account" in paragraph 1, line 8, is closest in meaning to

(A) stored
(B) allowed
(C) questioned
(D) considered

171. What is indicated about Ms. Wright?

(A) She rarely works with outside contractors.
(B) She did not check the current exchange rate.
(C) She is the director of a finance department.
(D) She will have to revise a previous contract.

GO ON TO THE NEXT PAGE

OAKPORT COMPUTING
Job Training Program

Oakport Computing regularly offers employees the opportunity to enhance their skills and knowledge through its job training program. — [1] —.

The list of courses shown below has been gathered based on a survey of all employees. Except where indicated, each course has been designed to be completed in half a day. Nevertheless, due to budget restrictions, we can only offer three at a time. — [2] —. The company will present a final selection of courses based on everyone's choices and announce the course dates on June 6. To confirm your attendance, submit the attached form to the human resources manager by June 3. — [3] —.

Please choose the three courses that you are most interested in attending:

....

Employee Name: Kevin Montoya   **Date:** June 1

- General Job Skills
  ___ Time Management
  ___ Presentation Skills
  ___ Problem Solving*
  ✓ Working with Teams

  * One-day course

- Technical Skills
  ___ Advanced Programming*
  ✓ Big Data Analysis*
  ✓ Network Security*
  ___ User Interface Design

To find out which courses will be offered, go to www.oakport.com/training on June 6. There will also be information on how to register. Participants are responsible for securing leave from their supervisors. — [4] —.

172. What is one purpose of the form?

(A) To invite volunteers to join an activity
(B) To reduce the number of options
(C) To gather feedback on a course
(D) To announce classes for new employees

173. Which course can be completed in half a day?

(A) Problem Solving
(B) Working with Teams
(C) Advanced Programming
(D) Network Security

174. What is suggested about Mr. Montoya?

(A) He submitted his application form late.
(B) His supervisor may not approve some leave.
(C) He may not take all the courses he chose.
(D) His main job is in information technology.

175. In which of the positions marked [1], [2], [3], and [4] does the following sentence best belong?

"This must be done at least two weeks prior to the start of the courses."

(A) [1]
(B) [2]
(C) [3]
(D) [4]

GO ON TO THE NEXT PAGE

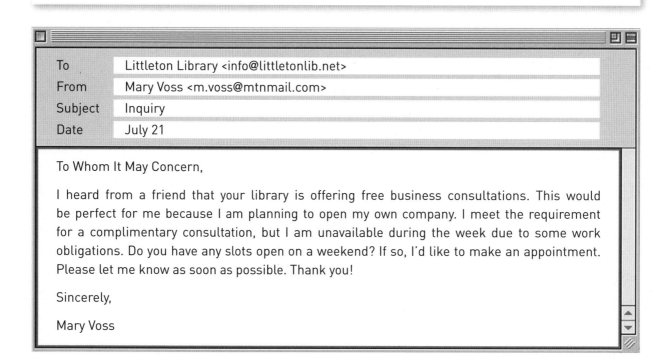

Join the Littleton Library Community Learning Series

The Littleton Library's Community Learning Series is back by popular demand. Book a 30-minute consultation with an expert and get advice on matters related to business registration, accounting, sales, and more. Be sure to book this soon as this program has always been popular. Adamant Consulting will offer assistance to current and prospective small-business owners during scheduled hours at the library. Adamant Consulting operates a business center for entrepreneurs. Further details about Adamant Consulting are available at www.adamant.com.

Consultations are free for residents and will take place from 10:00 A.M. to 1:00 P.M. on the dates shown below. To register for an appointment, call the library at 555-7184 or e-mail info@littletonlib.net. Proof of residence will be required to confirm your place.

Consultation dates:
- Tuesday, July 18
- Wednesday, August 2
- Thursday, August 17
- Saturday, September 2
- Tuesday, September 12

Please note that dates are subject to change. In the event of cancellation or delay, a notice will be posted on www.littletonlib.net.

To	Littleton Library <info@littletonlib.net>
From	Mary Voss <m.voss@mtnmail.com>
Subject	Inquiry
Date	July 21

To Whom It May Concern,

I heard from a friend that your library is offering free business consultations. This would be perfect for me because I am planning to open my own company. I meet the requirement for a complimentary consultation, but I am unavailable during the week due to some work obligations. Do you have any slots open on a weekend? If so, I'd like to make an appointment. Please let me know as soon as possible. Thank you!

Sincerely,

Mary Voss

176. What is suggested about the Littleton Library?

(A) It opens at 10 o'clock in the morning.
(B) It has hosted consultations in the past.
(C) It recently introduced some business courses.
(D) It has a center available for entrepreneurs.

177. According to the advertisement, what will be posted on a Web site?

(A) Profiles of course instructors
(B) Details regarding discussion topics
(C) Announcements about schedule changes
(D) Directions to a venue

178. What is true about Ms. Voss?

(A) She recently started a business.
(B) Her friend is a consultant.
(C) She is a resident of Littleton.
(D) Her library membership expired.

179. Which date is Ms. Voss available to attend a consultation?

(A) August 2
(B) August 17
(C) September 2
(D) September 12

180. In the e-mail, the word "meet" in paragraph 1, line 2, is closest in meaning to

(A) encounter
(B) join
(C) contact
(D) fulfill

GO ON TO THE NEXT PAGE

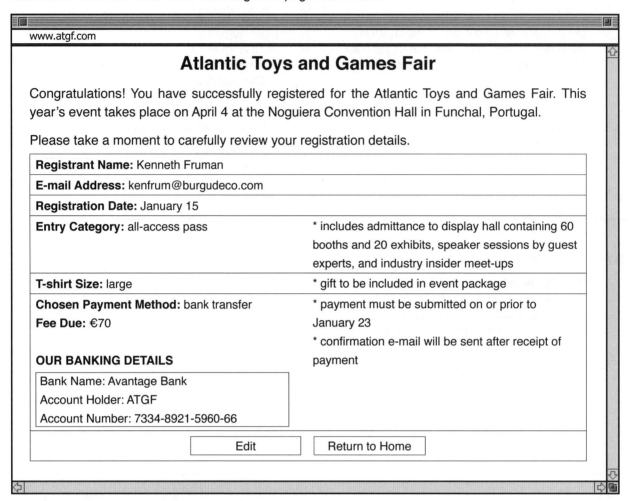

www.atgf.com

Atlantic Toys and Games Fair

Congratulations! You have successfully registered for the Atlantic Toys and Games Fair. This year's event takes place on April 4 at the Noguiera Convention Hall in Funchal, Portugal.

Please take a moment to carefully review your registration details.

Registrant Name: Kenneth Fruman	
E-mail Address: kenfrum@burgudeco.com	
Registration Date: January 15	
Entry Category: all-access pass	* includes admittance to display hall containing 60 booths and 20 exhibits, speaker sessions by guest experts, and industry insider meet-ups
T-shirt Size: large	* gift to be included in event package
Chosen Payment Method: bank transfer **Fee Due:** €70 **OUR BANKING DETAILS** Bank Name: Avantage Bank Account Holder: ATGF Account Number: 7334-8921-5960-66	* payment must be submitted on or prior to January 23 * confirmation e-mail will be sent after receipt of payment

Edit	Return to Home

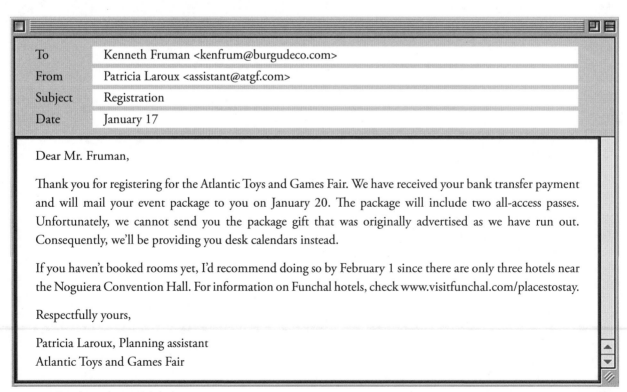

To	Kenneth Fruman <kenfrum@burgudeco.com>
From	Patricia Laroux <assistant@atgf.com>
Subject	Registration
Date	January 17

Dear Mr. Fruman,

Thank you for registering for the Atlantic Toys and Games Fair. We have received your bank transfer payment and will mail your event package to you on January 20. The package will include two all-access passes. Unfortunately, we cannot send you the package gift that was originally advertised as we have run out. Consequently, we'll be providing you desk calendars instead.

If you haven't booked rooms yet, I'd recommend doing so by February 1 since there are only three hotels near the Noguiera Convention Hall. For information on Funchal hotels, check www.visitfunchal.com/placestostay.

Respectfully yours,

Patricia Laroux, Planning assistant
Atlantic Toys and Games Fair

181. What is one purpose of the Web page?

(A) To inform association members about an event
(B) To confirm a reservation for a booth space
(C) To provide instructions for sending money
(D) To register a participant in a workshop activity

182. What will NOT be available to all-access pass holders?

(A) Talks by specialists
(B) Product demonstrations
(C) Display spaces
(D) Networking sessions

183. What is indicated about Mr. Fruman?

(A) He has an office located in Funchal, Portugal.
(B) He received a confirmation e-mail with an attached receipt.
(C) He paid a total of €70 for a pair of tickets.
(D) He is renting an exhibition space in the display hall.

184. What can be inferred about the Atlantic Toys and Games Fair?

(A) It does not plan to invite guest speakers this year.
(B) It takes place in a different country each time.
(C) It provides ticket refunds only until January 23.
(D) It does not have T-shirts to offer attendees.

185. What is mentioned about Noguiera Convention Hall?

(A) It is adjacent to the city's airport.
(B) It has been the venue for the fair in the past.
(C) It is holding two events at the same time.
(D) It is located close to accommodation facilities.

GO ON TO THE NEXT PAGE

Dyna Flooring
Clearance Sale

Throughout this August, Dyna Flooring will be holding a clearance sale to make way for new inventory. Enjoy great deals on a variety of merchandise for home and office use, including products by top-rated brands like Disena, Molik, Maitland, and more.

✓ 10 percent general discount on every product
✓ 20 percent off merchandise increasing in price next month
✓ 30 percent off bulk purchases of discontinued products

The sale extends to items sold online and in stores across the Midwest. Additional special discounts of 10 percent apply to customers who purchase items at a store and 20 percent to Dyna Club rewards program members.

Free delivery on all orders worth $500 or more!
For additional information, go to www.dynaflooring.com or
visit your nearest Dyna Flooring location.

Dyna Flooring
www.dynaflooring.com

Sold to: Danielle Welch
Company: Westwood Accounting
Payment method: Verifian credit card

Transaction date: August 29
Dyna Club member? Yes

Product code	Item	Quantity	Price
MKT1431Y	Molik ceramic kitchen tile (10% off)	24	$388.80
CTJN9091G	Johnson grey carpet tile (10% off)	16	$264.00
CTLS3816B	Laster blue carpet tile (30% off)	58	$740.95
FTIN643RW	Intone wood-finish floor tile (20% off)	12	$787.20

Terms: All sales are final. Payments may not be refunded except for store credit. Exchanges may be accepted on merchandise of equal or lesser value for as long as supplies last. Exchanges are not possible for new items.	Subtotal	$2,180.95
	Less 10%	($218.10)
	Tax	$130.86
	Shipping	$0.00
	TOTAL	$2,093.71

Thank you for your business!

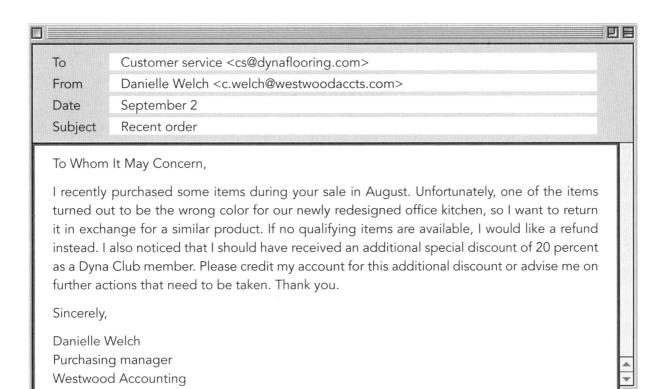

To   Customer service <cs@dynaflooring.com>
From   Danielle Welch <c.welch@westwoodaccts.com>
Date   September 2
Subject   Recent order

To Whom It May Concern,

I recently purchased some items during your sale in August. Unfortunately, one of the items turned out to be the wrong color for our newly redesigned office kitchen, so I want to return it in exchange for a similar product. If no qualifying items are available, I would like a refund instead. I also noticed that I should have received an additional special discount of 20 percent as a Dyna Club member. Please credit my account for this additional discount or advise me on further actions that need to be taken. Thank you.

Sincerely,

Danielle Welch
Purchasing manager
Westwood Accounting

186. What is the purpose of the advertisement?

(A) To promote the launch of an online shopping service
(B) To encourage customers to join a membership program
(C) To introduce a cost-saving opportunity
(D) To advertise a product made out of new materials

187. What is NOT mentioned about Dyna Flooring?

(A) It has stores throughout a region.
(B) It only carries items for office use.
(C) It is offering free shipping for qualifying orders.
(D) It will no longer be selling some products.

188. What is indicated on the invoice?

(A) Ms. Welch attended the final day of a sale.
(B) Some items are currently out of stock.
(C) Johnson's tiles were delivered ahead of schedule.
(D) Intone's tiles will increase in price next month.

189. What does Ms. Welch want Dyna Flooring to do?

(A) Sign her up to a membership program
(B) Refund the cost of shipping
(C) Send her installation instructions
(D) Apply an additional price reduction

190. What is suggested about Ms. Welch?

(A) She purchased some of her items online.
(B) She may be given store credit of over $300.
(C) She was in charge of redesigning an office.
(D) She used rewards points to pay for a purchase.

GO ON TO THE NEXT PAGE

**Elfman Home Cooling
Warranty Claims**

Elfman is committed to serving the needs of its customers. All equipment we sell comes with a six-month parts and labor warranty. If you experience problems during the warranty period, a technician will visit your home or business and perform all necessary repairs free of charge. In addition, if your unit malfunctions within one month of purchase, we will replace it at our expense.

To submit a warranty claim, go to www.elfmanequip.com/customers. You will be asked to enter your username and password. Then, click the CLAIMS button at the bottom of the screen to access the online form. To ensure timely processing, fill out the claim form as completely as possible.

Elfman Home Cooling Claim Form

Claim number: EC1081626
Date: August 3
Customer name: Larry Regan
Address: 219 Duncan Street, Forsyth, GA 31029
Tel.: 555-4086
E-mail: l.regan@pellstone.com
Product: Elfman central air conditioner
Model: AU-0951   **Serial number:** P118946QJ

Problem Description:
The unit is fine for the first 30 minutes after it starts, but then it begins to make a strange noise that becomes progressively louder. It is very difficult for the staff in my office to work. This is the first problem I have had since I purchased the unit about seven months ago.

Elfman Home Cooling Claim Form

Claim number: EK0194114
Date: August 15
Customer name: Michelle Bowman
Address: 176 King Boulevard, High Springs, FL 32643
Tel.: 555-7182
E-mail: m.bowman@springmail.com
Product: Elfman ventilation system
Model: PK-4317   **Serial number:** T27386HX

Problem Description:
This morning, I noticed that very little air was coming out of the vents. I turned the unit off to check for any blockages but did not see anything out of ordinary. Given that it was installed less than two weeks ago, this is unacceptable.

TEST 4

191. How can customers submit a warranty claim?

(A) By visiting a service center
(B) By mailing a written request
(C) By accessing an online account
(D) By installing a mobile application

192. What is suggested about Mr. Regan?

(A) He will have to wait several days for a technician to visit.
(B) He contacted a company representative by e-mail.
(C) He requested a discount on an air conditioner.
(D) He will have to pay for the cost of repairs.

193. What is mentioned in the form completed by Mr. Regan?

(A) He ordered the latest model of an appliance.
(B) His office will be closed until repairs are performed.
(C) His unit functions properly when first turned on.
(D) He purchased an Elfman product on August 3.

194. What can be inferred about Ms. Bowman?

(A) She failed to fill out a form completely.
(B) She will receive a replacement product.
(C) She installed some equipment incorrectly.
(D) She ordered extra parts for a ventilation system.

195. What is indicated on the form completed by Ms. Bowman?

(A) She will receive a full refund for a purchase.
(B) She did not register on a company Web site.
(C) She tried to determine the cause of a problem.
(D) She does not know the serial number of a device.

GO ON TO THE NEXT PAGE

Arizona Medical Professionals Association (AMPA)
We are pleased to announce the release of our Spring Events Calendar for this year.

April 16 – NEW MEMBERS WELCOME
Welcome reception for new members at the Desert Hotel in downtown Phoenix from 4:00 to 6:00 P.M. Includes light refreshments.

April 19 – PRESENTATION
The country's most popular journal, *Modern Journal of Medicine*, will be hosting a special presentation for members from 6:00 to 7:00 P.M. at the AMPA Conference Center in downtown Phoenix.

April 23 – LECTURE AND BOOK SIGNING
AMPA will be hosting a lecture and book-signing event with esteemed medical author and leading expert on health-care issues Dr. Katherine Bradley, from 9:00 to 11:00 A.M. at the Book Stop bookstore in Glendale, Arizona.

May 2 to 4 – ANNUAL CONFERENCE
The 51st Annual AMPA Conference will be held in Las Vegas, Nevada this year. Please visit the Web site for more details.

All events are exclusively for registered AMPA members. To join, please visit www.ampa.org.

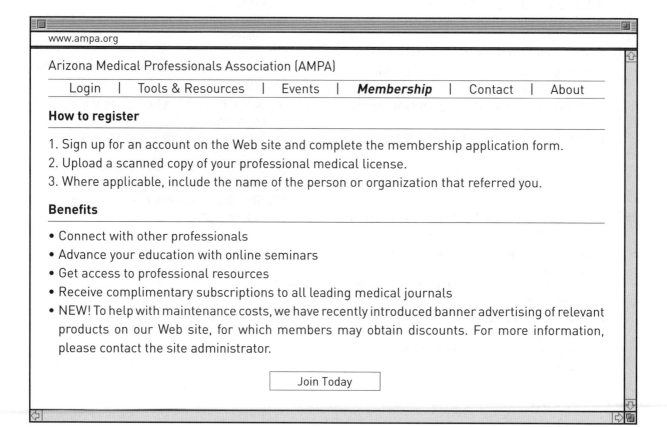

www.ampa.org

Arizona Medical Professionals Association (AMPA)

Login | Tools & Resources | Events | **Membership** | Contact | About

How to register

1. Sign up for an account on the Web site and complete the membership application form.
2. Upload a scanned copy of your professional medical license.
3. Where applicable, include the name of the person or organization that referred you.

Benefits

• Connect with other professionals
• Advance your education with online seminars
• Get access to professional resources
• Receive complimentary subscriptions to all leading medical journals
• NEW! To help with maintenance costs, we have recently introduced banner advertising of relevant products on our Web site, for which members may obtain discounts. For more information, please contact the site administrator.

Join Today

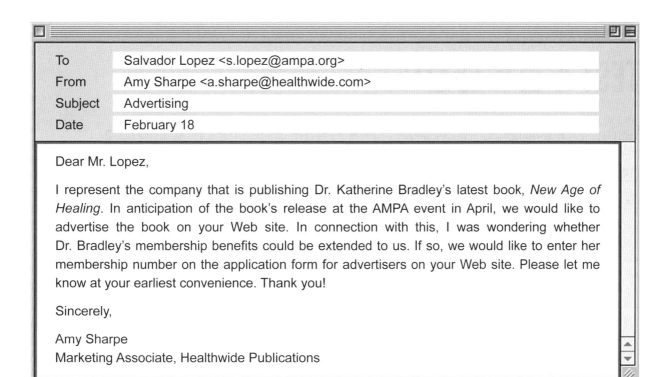

To   Salvador Lopez <s.lopez@ampa.org>

From   Amy Sharpe <a.sharpe@healthwide.com>

Subject Advertising

Date   February 18

Dear Mr. Lopez,

I represent the company that is publishing Dr. Katherine Bradley's latest book, *New Age of Healing*. In anticipation of the book's release at the AMPA event in April, we would like to advertise the book on your Web site. In connection with this, I was wondering whether Dr. Bradley's membership benefits could be extended to us. If so, we would like to enter her membership number on the application form for advertisers on your Web site. Please let me know at your earliest convenience. Thank you!

Sincerely,

Amy Sharpe
Marketing Associate, Healthwide Publications

---

196. What is implied about AMPA members?

(A) They completed their medical training at the same institution.
(B) They can subscribe for free to *Modern Journal of Medicine*.
(C) They are encouraged to volunteer their services.
(D) They form the country's largest professional association.

197. What are prospective members asked to provide?

(A) A payment for an annual fee
(B) Details about their place of employment
(C) An electronic copy of a certificate
(D) Preferences for communications

198. What has the AMPA recently done?

(A) Changed the date of an annual event
(B) Increased a fee for members
(C) Established a partner organization
(D) Added advertising to its Web site

199. In the e-mail, the word "enter" in paragraph 1, line 4, is closest in meaning to

(A) describe
(B) admit
(C) begin
(D) submit

200. Who most likely is Mr. Lopez?

(A) A marketing consultant
(B) A commercial director
(C) An event planner
(D) A Web site manager

This is the end of the test. You may review Parts 5, 6, and 7 if you finish the test early.

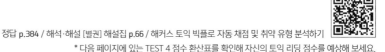

TEST 4 점수 환산표

TEST 4는 무사히 잘 마치셨나요? 맞은 개수를 세어본 후 아래의 점수 환산표를 통해 자신의 점수를 예상해 보세요.

전체 난이도　　**어려운 난이도**

파트별 난이도　PART 5　중　●●○
　　　　　　　　　PART 6　상　●●●
　　　　　　　　　PART 7　상　●●●

정답 수	리딩 점수	정답 수	리딩 점수
98~100개	480~495점	47~49개	210~225점
95~97개	470~475점	44~46개	195~205점
92~94개	455~465점	41~43개	180~190점
89~91개	440~450점	38~40개	165~175점
86~88개	425~435점	35~37개	150~160점
83~85개	410~420점	32~34개	135~145점
80~82개	395~405점	29~31개	120~130점
77~79개	380~390점	26~28개	105~115점
74~76개	365~375점	23~25개	90~100점
71~73개	350~360점	20~22개	75~85점
68~70개	330~345점	17~19개	60~70점
65~67개	315~325점	14~16개	45~55점
62~64개	295~310점	11~13개	30~40점
59~61개	275~290점	8~10개	15~25점
56~58개	260~270점	5~7개	10~15점
53~55개	245~255점	2~4개	5~10점
50~52개	230~240점	0~1개	0~5점

* 점수 환산표는 해커스토익 사이트 유저 데이터를 근거로 제작되었으며, 주기적으로 업데이트되고 있습니다. 해커스토익 사이트
　(Hackers.co.kr)에서 최신 경향을 반영하여 업데이트된 점수환산기를 이용하실 수 있습니다. (토익 > 토익게시판 > 토익점수환산기)

TEST 5

×

PART 5
PART 6
PART 7
점수 환산표

잠깐! 테스트 전 확인사항

1. 문제 풀이에 방해가 되는 물건을 모두 치우셨나요?   예 □
2. Answer Sheet, 연필, 지우개를 준비하셨나요?   예 □
3. 시계를 준비하셨나요?   예 □

모든 준비가 완료되었으면 목표 점수를 떠올린 후 테스트를 시작합니다.

문제 풀이를 마치는 시간은 지금부터 **75분 후인** _____시 _____분입니다.

테스트 시간은 **총 75분**이며, 시험 종료 전 2~3분은 정답 검토 및 답안지 마킹을 위해 사용합니다.

READING TEST

In this section, you must demonstrate your ability to read and comprehend English. You will be given a variety of texts and asked to answer questions about these texts. This section is divided into three parts and will take 75 minutes to complete.

Do not mark the answers in your test book. Use the answer sheet that is separately provided.

PART 5

Directions: In each question, you will be asked to review a statement that is missing a word or phrase. Four answer choices will be provided for each statement. Select the best answer and mark the corresponding letter (A), (B), (C), or (D) on the answer sheet.

101. Lod Net Corp. ------- responds to clients' inquiries all the time.
    (A) very
    (B) quickly
    (C) ago
    (D) so

102. According to a recent report, NineEast Mall ------- to a new location next month.
    (A) has moved
    (B) moving
    (C) moved
    (D) will move

103. Relivium is ------- more effective at reducing headache symptoms than other brands.
    (A) signify
    (B) signifier
    (C) significant
    (D) significantly

104. Mr. Jones was awarded a bonus for ------- contributions to the company.
    (A) he
    (B) his
    (C) him
    (D) himself

105. Ms. Potter works at Wallace's Used Books every day ------- Sunday.
    (A) around
    (B) except
    (C) across
    (D) within

106. Before registering for online classes, be sure ------- our terms and conditions.
    (A) to read
    (B) read
    (C) reading
    (D) reads

107. The economy of the island nation is ------- on tourism.
    (A) exclusive
    (B) dependent
    (C) necessary
    (D) interested

108. All participants must pay a $500 deposit that will be returned at the end ------- the four-day trade show.
    (A) into
    (B) in
    (C) for
    (D) of

109. All roads ------- to flooding will be closed to motorists during the storm.

(A) attainable
(B) responsible
(C) vulnerable
(D) preventable

110. One of the factory's conveyor belts malfunctioned, resulting in a ------- in daily output.

(A) permit
(B) shortfall
(C) routine
(D) contract

111. ------- demand for the new bag is high, most retailers will soon run out of stock.

(A) Even if
(B) Unless
(C) Although
(D) Because

112. Customers can only be ------- with store credit if they don't have a purchase receipt.

(A) refunds
(B) refunded
(C) refunding
(D) refundable

113. Management concluded ------- the feedback that customers can afford to pay more for the products.

(A) at
(B) from
(C) during
(D) below

114. Citizens are required to wear masks while the spread of the disease is not ------- contained.

(A) more current
(B) current
(C) currently
(D) most current

115. The government used the money that it received in a ------- with Habro Chemical to restore polluted waterways.

(A) settle
(B) settled
(C) settleable
(D) settlement

116. Due to a computer virus, some of the files ------- on the department's computers have been corrupted.

(A) stored
(B) announced
(C) attached
(D) reminded

117. The report outlines several important ------- why the company should change the way it manages data.

(A) reason
(B) reasoned
(C) reasons
(D) reasoning

118. Sparta Foundation's mentoring program has proven to be ------- to students.

(A) inform
(B) informs
(C) informative
(D) information

119. This ------- precaution causes users to lose access to online accounts if they enter the wrong password three times.

(A) secured
(B) securely
(C) secures
(D) security

120. The manager ------- must approve all purchases, but exceptions can be made for items less than $50.

(A) relatively
(B) greatly
(C) normally
(D) patiently

GO ON TO THE NEXT PAGE

121. Shoppers can get a 30 percent discount on all items ------- the promotional period.

(A) among
(B) throughout
(C) between
(D) to

122. The city council converted parts of the waterfront district into a commercial and residential -------.

(A) design
(B) standard
(C) complex
(D) matter

123. News of the oil spill got ------- attention before videos about it were spread on the internet.

(A) few
(B) little
(C) many
(D) each

124. Students who wish to prepare for tomorrow's quiz should ------- to Chapter 9 of the textbook.

(A) refer
(B) apply
(C) regard
(D) assign

125. Please ------- that the elevator will be closed for repairs on Wednesday morning.

(A) be advised
(B) advice
(C) advised
(D) advising

126. Expecting a small group, Ms. Madsen was surprised ------- 100 people arrived at her gardening tutorial.

(A) about
(B) whereas
(C) as if
(D) when

127. As the mayor of a tourist town, Mr. Venturi must ------- the needs of locals and those of visitors.

(A) balance
(B) waive
(C) overcome
(D) expose

128. The online questionnaire allows prospective car buyers to determine ------- vehicle might suit them best.

(A) that
(B) which
(C) their
(D) another

129. Ms. Hansen is often strict about rules but is willing to exercise ------- with new staff members.

(A) flexibly
(B) flexible
(C) flex
(D) flexibility

130. The CEO tried to keep the majority of shareholders ------- about the financial situation.

(A) knowledgeable
(B) knowledge
(C) know
(D) known

PART 6

Directions: In this part, you will be asked to read four English texts. Each text is missing a word, phrase, or sentence. Select the answer choice that correctly completes the text and mark the corresponding letter (A), (B), (C), or (D) on the answer sheet.

Questions 131-134 refer to the following e-mail.

To: Amira Yaziri <amira72@goodtidings.tn>
From: Ernie Vollmer <e.vollmer@mahalsuites.com>
Date: December 9
Subject: Special arrangements

Dear Ms. Yaziri,

Firstly, thank you for ------- Mahal Suites for your accommodation while in Jamesville. As you will
       131.

be staying in one of our deluxe rooms, you are entitled to our free ------- transportation. However,
                 132.

your reservation form indicates that your flight will be arriving at 1:26 A.M., and the shuttle runs

only from 6 A.M. to 11 P.M. -------. I would be happy to contact a private transfer service for you.
              133.

-------, the driver would meet you at your arrival gate.
134.

Sincere regards,

Ernie Vollmer
Guest Services Agent
Mahal Suites

131. (A) acquiring
    (B) choosing
    (C) reviewing
    (D) preparing

132. (A) city
    (B) tour
    (C) train
    (D) airport

133. (A) Do you need somewhere to park your car?
    (B) The travel agency used to have an office in our lobby.
    (C) So feel free to order room service at any time of the day.
    (D) Are you able to make alternative arrangements?

134. (A) Until then
    (B) Elsewhere
    (C) In this case
    (D) Likewise

GO ON TO THE NEXT PAGE

Questions 135-138 refer to the following article.

The travel agency Alexis Journeys recently announced that it is ------- its selection of tours. On
                                                                        135.
August 1, Alexis Journeys will introduce trips to Colombia, El Salvador, and Belize. These are in

addition to the 12 travel packages it already offers for Latin America.

Alexis Journeys is known for its -------. Its new Mayan Discovery tour, for example, is only $1,050
                                    136.
for one week, with all transportation and accommodations included. -------.
                                                                     137.

"With our new packages, Alexis Journeys is attempting ------- travelers who have found trips to
                                                        138.
Latin America too expensive," said Marketing Director Hal Clive.

135. (A) combining
     (B) expanding
     (C) withholding
     (D) reducing

136. (A) suitability
     (B) flexibility
     (C) diversity
     (D) affordability

137. (A) Some people have expressed their
         dissatisfaction with the tour.
     (B) It also has great reviews on all of its tour
         packages.
     (C) This rumor has not yet been confirmed
         by the company.
     (D) Guests may pay extra to take advantage
         of in-room Wi-Fi as well.

138. (A) targets
     (B) targeted
     (C) target
     (D) to target

Questions 139-142 refer to the following information.

Important Registration Information

Ryder College asks for payment of fees at least a month before a course start date. When registering, a non-refundable deposit of $75 is required to secure your place. ------- . Therefore, we
                                                                                                                                                             139.
try to make sure that the limited spaces go to students with ------- intentions of attending.
                                                                                              140.

If the university is unable to provide the course for which you have paid, you will get a full refund of your deposit along with your course fees. The same holds true if students ------- 20 days before
                                                                                                                       141.
the start date. In any other cases, the deposit will not be refunded. Also, students may not cancel a course ------- begun.
              142.

139. (A) Consult the classroom seating chart.
     (B) This amount will be returned in two weeks.
     (C) There's usually high demand for most courses.
     (D) The school ranks highly among state colleges.

140. (A) qualified
     (B) serious
     (C) courteous
     (D) promising

141. (A) depart
     (B) enroll
     (C) separate
     (D) withdraw

142. (A) since
     (B) before
     (C) after
     (D) once

Questions 143-146 refer to the following announcement.

Gavin Hackett is coming to Waco!

The acclaimed writer Gavin Hackett will be delivering a ------- talk at Waco's Central Auditorium at
143.
8 P.M. on Tuesday, September 13. In his talk, Mr. Hackett will explore the science of memory. He

will reveal several techniques for boosting one's ability to retain and recall information.

Mr. Hackett's ------- here is part of a promotional tour for his upcoming book *Remember Harder*.
144.
He ------- several other books over the past 20 years of his career.
145.

An entry fee of $15 will be charged at the door. -------.
146.

143. (A) motivator
(B) motivational
(C) motivates
(D) motivationally

144. (A) acceptance
(B) conclusion
(C) appearance
(D) approach

145. (A) has authored
(B) authors
(C) will author
(D) is authoring

146. (A) Finally, Hackett's discovery will be
recognized.
(B) The winning entries will be announced
after the event.
(C) Download the coupon code from our
Web site.
(D) The first 50 people to enter will receive a
free book.

Directions: In this part, you will be asked to read several texts, such as advertisements, articles, instant messages, or examples of business correspondence. Each text is followed by several questions. Select the best answer and mark the corresponding letter (A), (B), (C), or (D) on your answer sheet.

Questions 147-148 refer to the following article.

Hurlimann to Open at Gilford Shopping Center
By Fred Sharpe

OWENSBURG—Swiss premium chocolate maker Hurlimann is opening its first shop in Owensburg. It has scheduled a ribbon-cutting ceremony for January 8 at the Gilford Shopping Center.

According to store manager Joanne Lutz, the first 100 customers who purchase its chocolate will receive a free box of candy. Otherwise, customers can get 50 percent off purchases of selected items in the shop for the first two weeks.

Founded over 100 years ago, Hurlimann has long exported its delicate chocolate products to vendors worldwide. "Now that we are finally opening our own branches overseas, we are excited to see what the future holds." said CEO David Carle.

147. What is indicated about Hurlimann?

(A) It has just appointed David Carle as its new CEO.
(B) It was founded in Owensburg a hundred years ago.
(C) It has recently started to open shops internationally.
(D) It is expanding its line of signature delicacies.

148. How can customers receive a complimentary product?

(A) By answering some survey questions
(B) By being among a store's first 100 buyers
(C) By purchasing specially selected items
(D) By returning within two weeks

Questions 149-150 refer to the following Web page.

Canbury Hospital Intranet

Home >> Patient Management >> Dr. Hatch >> Patient Information

Patient Name: Charlotte Reed
Phone Number: 555-4839

Medical History

Patient has experienced past symptoms of:

☐ chest pain	☑ stomach pain	☐ headaches
☑ ear aches	☑ seasonal allergies	☑ skin irritation
☑ throat irritation	☐ back pain	☐ stress or anxiety

Appointment Center

Patient's next appointment with Dr. Michael Hatch is scheduled for
Monday, April 22 at 11:30 A.M.

Reschedule Appointment?   ● Yes   ○ No
Click here to enter a new appointment time.

Notes:

Dr. Hatch will be traveling to London to give a lecture on heart health from April 21 to 24, and thus Ms. Reed's checkup must be rescheduled.

---

149. What has Ms. Reed experienced in the past?

(A) Heart problems
(B) Back trouble
(C) Allergic reactions
(D) Work stress

150. Why does Ms. Reed's checkup have to be rescheduled?

(A) Canbury Hospital will be closing for a day.
(B) She did not submit her insurance details.
(C) Her physician is leaving on a trip.
(D) Some test results have not come in.

Pam Gordon [9:10 A.M.]
I just e-mailed you the travel expense reimbursement form for the trip you took last week. Could you turn it in by the end of the month? Otherwise, your money won't be repaid to you with your next paycheck.

Hadassah Aboud [9:12 A.M.]
Absolutely. I printed out the form from the intranet as soon as I got back and took it to the accounting department office right away.

Pam Gordon [9:13 A.M.]
Great! I wasn't sure if you knew where to take it.

151. What is suggested about the form?

(A) Ms. Aboud usually picked it up at the accounting office.
(B) It must be signed by a department's supervisor.
(C) It must be submitted within a set amount of time.
(D) Ms. Gordon recently downloaded it from the intranet.

152. At 9:12 A.M., what does Ms. Aboud mean when she writes, "Absolutely"?

(A) She is ahead of a coworker on some work.
(B) She has been repaid for the cost of a trip.
(C) She is on her way to hand in a form.
(D) She has completed a task already.

GO ON TO THE NEXT PAGE

Questions 153-154 refer to the following announcement.

Halliston Theater

Visitors should be aware that our facility will be closed next week to accommodate renovation work. Specifically, we will be installing new equipment that will allow movie-goers to enter the theater using electronic tickets on their mobile devices without the assistance of an employee. For more information on the new process for using e-tickets, visit our Web site. Additionally, we are pleased to announce that five of our screens will be updated to provide 3-D film capabilities. This is an effort to address the most commonly noted suggestion in our recently conducted customer questionnaire on our homepage. Lastly, cinema fans can now check out the newly added movie review section on www.hallistontheater.com. Thank you for your understanding during this remodeling period.

153. According to the announcement, what will take place next week?

(A) A premiere for the sequel to a popular film
(B) An autograph event with a movie star
(C) The replacement of some seats in a theater
(D) The setup of some devices for customer use

154. What is suggested about Halliston Theater?

(A) It has updated the pricing information available online.
(B) It did not use to have reviews on its Web site.
(C) It has published customer survey results in a newsletter.
(D) It did not offer mobile tickets until the remodeling.

Drew Shields to become a host on *Mornings on 7*

PNW Channel 7 has announced that Drew Shields will be replacing Gail Figgis as a presenter on the 6 A.M. to 9 A.M. weekday morning talk show, *Mornings on 7.* — [1] —. His first day on the air will be on Monday, August 19. "I'll miss working with Gail, but I think the station made a good choice. Drew is a passionate and versatile speaker, so we're bound to work well together." said Wallace Jeffers, who has been Ms. Figgis's co-host on the show for nearly 20 years now.

— [2] —. Mr. Shields is an award-winning presenter who has covered numerous breaking stories for PNW Channel 7 since joining the station as a general assignment reporter eight years ago. — [3] —. "I am really grateful for the opportunity to try something new, but I realize that I am taking the place of someone who has been very popular. Gail Figgis is a living legend," he said.

Retiring after nearly 35 years on the air, Ms. Figgis plans to devote her time to writing a memoir about her career. — [4] —. She will also work as an occasional correspondent for PNW Channel 7's evening news.

155. What is NOT mentioned about Mr. Shields?

(A) He will be taking over for a longtime presenter.
(B) Mr. Jeffers selected him for a position on a show.
(C) He has been awarded for his broadcasting work.
(D) PNW Channel 7 hired him eight years earlier.

156. What does Ms. Figgis plan to do?

(A) Apply to another station
(B) Work as a host
(C) Contribute to a program
(D) Start a talk show

157. In which of the positions marked [1], [2], [3], and [4] does the following sentence best belong?

"Prior to this, he worked as a features reporter and appeared on URS Channel 12's *Nightly News*."

(A) [1]
(B) [2]
(C) [3]
(D) [4]

Questions 158-160 refer to the following information.

Astrapia Air — Using Rewards Points for Domestic Seat Upgrades

To use your points to fly in a higher class, select the "Rewards Points Upgrade" option on our Web site when you reserve a ticket. After a ticket has been purchased, upgrades can be requested in one of three ways. First, you may call the Astrapia Air Call Center. Second, you may modify your booking on our Web site. And third, you may speak with one of our airport agents at a check-in counter. Regardless of which method you choose, be sure to make your request at least 24 hours before your flight. The chart below indicates how many points are required to upgrade from one class to another within the various regions we fly to. Please note that upgrades may not be possible on some flights.

	From Economy Class to Premium Economy Class	From Premium Economy Class to Business Class	From Business Class to First Class
Europe	20,000 points	35,000 points	50,000 points
North America	20,000 points	35,000 points	
Central Asia	20,000 points	35,000 points	50,000 points
South East Asia	20,000 points		

Note: 1 point = 1 mile flown

158. What is true about Astrapia Air?

(A) It has different policies for each seat class.
(B) It maintains a partner program with other airlines.
(C) It does not allow upgrades within 24 hours of a flight.
(D) It requires the most points for flights to Central Asia.

159. The word "reserve" in paragraph 1, line 2, is closest in meaning to

(A) stack up
(B) put aside
(C) hold back
(D) arrange to use

160. What can be inferred about flights within North America?

(A) Full ticket refunds are not provided.
(B) They can only be booked using an airline Web site.
(C) They do not earn passengers reward points.
(D) Upgrades are not available for all seat classes.

Questions 161-163 refer to the following article.

Where Has All the Money Gone?
By Jackson McGuire

Lindow City—When Beanzo Café announced it was going cashless on August 1, it was hardly a surprise. It is not the first local business to give up cash for electronic payment systems.

In fact, a growing number of businesses are making the switch. For instance, shop owner Marie Ramirez, whose boutique Blondah stopped accepting coins and paper bills in May, is pleased with the arrangement. "I no longer worry about counting bills, keeping change, or losing money from the register," she said.

Other businesses have their own reasons for going cashless. For jeweler Rajit Banga, being able to avoid making cash deposits at the bank saves him the trouble of traveling with large amounts of cash. Meanwhile, for convenience store manager Anna Mellor, processing transactions more quickly with card payments creates a better experience for her customers. "People are in a hurry," she said, "and want things done right away."

What do consumers think? According to a survey, nearly 20 percent of Lindow City residents no longer use any cash, and 50 percent plan to stop entirely. If this pattern continues, everyone will have to face the reality that physical currency is becoming obsolete.

161. What is the article mainly about?

(A) The rise of technologies that facilitate making payments
(B) An issue that has resulted from changing a system
(C) An event that led to a café eliminating cash transactions
(D) The reasons businesses are embracing a trend

162. What can be inferred about Lindow City?

(A) It is attracting a large number of upscale businesses.
(B) Its citizens voted to support cashless programs.
(C) It is offering incentives to consumers who accept a policy.
(D) Its residents may soon stop carrying money.

163. What problem is Ms. Mellor most likely concerned about?

(A) Counterfeit bills
(B) Long wait times
(C) Store security
(D) Missing money

Kelsey Chase [1:50 P.M.] Could someone recommend a supplier of office chairs? Mine broke down earlier.

Miles Dunphy [1:52 P.M.] Have you checked the stockroom? We might have some extra ones in there.

Kelsey Chase [1:53 P.M.] Yes, but it seems we're all out.

Megan Contreras [1:55 P.M.] Our office chairs aren't very durable. How much can you spend on a new one?

Kelsey Chase [1:55 P.M.] As far as I know, less than $30.

Megan Contreras [1:56 P.M.] I was going to head out to Fastmax this afternoon for some printer ink. I could get one for you. I just need to finish a presentation I'm working on.

Kelsey Chase [1:57 P.M.] Take your time. I'm using a plastic chair for now. But let me know if you go. I'd like to come along if I'm not too busy.

Miles Dunphy [1:59 P.M.] I found one online if you're willing to wait a few days. It's on www.everyoffice.com and costs just $24.

Kelsey Chase [2:00 P.M.] Thanks, Miles! I'll be sure to check it out if Megan and I don't go this afternoon.

Miles Dunphy [2:01 P.M.] No problem. I'd better get back to work. I have a report due in an hour.

Send

---

164. What does Mr. Chase want to do?

(A) Conduct a product survey
(B) Have an office computer repaired
(C) Replace a piece of furniture
(D) Count items in the stockroom

165. What is indicated about Ms. Contreras?

(A) She is responsible for an office budget.
(B) She is willing to pick up an item.
(C) She has just returned from a print shop.
(D) She can spend up to $30 on printer ink.

166. At 1:57 P.M., what does Mr. Chase mean when he writes, "Take your time"?

(A) Ms. Contreras should finish a report.
(B) He has made an alternative arrangement.
(C) Ms. Contreras should request overtime hours.
(D) He has plenty of work to do in the meantime.

167. Why does Mr. Dunphy need to get back to work?

(A) He is preparing for a presentation.
(B) He made plans to meet a coworker.
(C) He has an imminent deadline to meet.
(D) He is heading to a store in the next hour.

Questions 168-171 refer to the following e-mail.

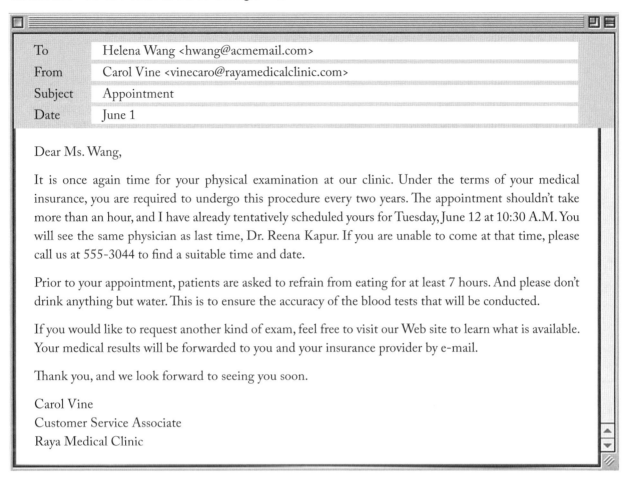

To: Helena Wang <hwang@acmemail.com>

From: Carol Vine <vinecaro@rayamedicalclinic.com>

Subject: Appointment

Date: June 1

Dear Ms. Wang,

It is once again time for your physical examination at our clinic. Under the terms of your medical insurance, you are required to undergo this procedure every two years. The appointment shouldn't take more than an hour, and I have already tentatively scheduled yours for Tuesday, June 12 at 10:30 A.M. You will see the same physician as last time, Dr. Reena Kapur. If you are unable to come at that time, please call us at 555-3044 to find a suitable time and date.

Prior to your appointment, patients are asked to refrain from eating for at least 7 hours. And please don't drink anything but water. This is to ensure the accuracy of the blood tests that will be conducted.

If you would like to request another kind of exam, feel free to visit our Web site to learn what is available. Your medical results will be forwarded to you and your insurance provider by e-mail.

Thank you, and we look forward to seeing you soon.

Carol Vine
Customer Service Associate
Raya Medical Clinic

168. Why did Ms. Vine write the e-mail?

(A) To explain the terms of an agreement
(B) To organize a time for an interview
(C) To remind a client about an engagement
(D) To give medical advice to a patient

169. What is suggested about Ms. Wang?

(A) She reported having a medical problem.
(B) She last saw Dr. Kapur two years before.
(C) She is unavailable on June 12.
(D) She had a physical exam last year.

170. What is Ms. Wang asked to do?

(A) Restrict her intake to water
(B) Have a surgical procedure
(C) Avoid foods that are high in fat
(D) Forward a copy of a document

171. How can Ms. Wang obtain her results?

(A) By contacting an insurance firm
(B) By waiting for an e-mail
(C) By returning at a later date
(D) By logging onto a Web site

GO ON TO THE NEXT PAGE

Electronics Monthly

SleekEffects Striving to Change

March 2—Electrical appliance manufacturer SleekEffects is making an attempt to recover from its poor sales results last year. — [1] —. SleekEffects suffered a massive recall of its Cavalier line of electronic shavers for men last November. According to hundreds of complaints submitted by customers, the shavers had a tendency to overheat and may pose a fire hazard. — [2] —.

To turn things around, SleekEffects CEO Leonard Martin announced major alterations to its production processes. — [3] —. In a press release, Mr. Martin said that the firm has addressed the shortcomings that resulted in the recall and is preparing to launch a new line of products designed to attract a wider range of customers. "The line, called SleekSmooth, consists of electronic foot, neck, and back massagers that will appeal to both men and women," he said.

Mr. Martin also mentioned that movie stars Jacqueline Amano and Rene Bisset will endorse the new product line. The two stars are well known throughout Europe and Asia for their appearances in the blockbuster film, *Hide and Go*. SleekSmooth will be available in stores in June. — [4] —.

172. What is the article mainly about?

(A) A firm's poor performance last year
(B) The appointment of a new CEO
(C) A company's efforts to improve
(D) The conditions in an industry

173. The word "shortcomings", in paragraph 2, line 5 is closest in meaning to

(A) losses
(B) expenses
(C) mistakes
(D) obstacles

174. What can be inferred about SleekEffects?

(A) It contributed to the production of a film.
(B) It operates a chain of stores around the world.
(C) It created a device based on customer feedback.
(D) It made items that were solely for men.

175. In which of the positions marked [1], [2], [3], and [4] does the following sentence best belong?

"As a result, nearly 1 million units of the products were removed from retailers' shelves."

(A) [1]
(B) [2]
(C) [3]
(D) [4]

GO ON TO THE NEXT PAGE

Questions 176-180 refer to the following e-mail and notice.

To   Dan Maris <d.maris@shopgoodman.com>
From   Amber Gonzalez <a.gonzalez@shopgoodman.com>
Subject   Update
Date   October 28

Dear Mr. Maris,

As you were unable to participate in the meeting with the other store managers on October 25, I thought I would send you a summary of what was discussed. The focus of the meeting was the promotions we have planned for the Goodman Supermarkets chain early next year. My department manager, Mr. Barnhart, was not in attendance, but he has approved the following initiatives:

- Customers will not be charged for their first use of the home delivery service that we will be introducing in January. Banners promoting this service will be sent to each store next week. Please have your employees put these up in prominent locations.

- Cooking classes will be offered at each store branch to attract new customers. Branch managers will be responsible for organizing these events. Let me know who you would like to teach the classes at your Bedford branch.

Feel free to call me at 555-0393 if you have any questions or concerns about these plans.

Sincerely,

Amber Gonzalez
Marketing Associate
Goodman Supermarkets

Goodman Supermarkets — Bedford Branch
NOTICE TO CUSTOMERS

We are pleased to announce our new home delivery service. It will be available from February 18 onwards. Visit www.shopgoodman.com/delivery for more details.

In addition, we will be hosting cooking classes here on Saturday, February 12. We've invited Chef Shelly Burch to teach participants a few of her favorite recipes using fresh ingredients from our store. Ms. Burch is the host of *Cooking with Shelly*, which is presented daily from 2 P.M. to 4 P.M. on Channel 21.

There will be a morning class and an afternoon class. Due to space limitations, we can only accommodate 30 people in each session. Please stop by our service desk to sign up.

176. What is suggested about Mr. Barnhart?

(A) He participated in the meeting on October 25.
(B) He is the manager of a supermarket branch.
(C) He requested that an e-mail be sent to Mr. Maris.
(D) He is the head of the marketing department.

177. What is Goodman Supermarkets planning to do next week?

(A) Release a mobile application
(B) Hire additional employees
(C) Distribute promotional materials
(D) Update a Web site

178. What can be inferred about the delivery service?

(A) It was not launched on schedule.
(B) It is not popular with customers.
(C) It is offered at a limited number of stores.
(D) It was first proposed by Ms. Gonzalez.

179. What is true about Ms. Burch?

(A) She will be doing a live broadcast on February 18.
(B) She is a frequent shopper at Goodman Supermarkets.
(C) She runs a popular restaurant near a grocery store.
(D) She will be teaching two different groups on February 12.

180. According to the notice, why should customers visit the service desk?

(A) To sign up for membership
(B) To make a complaint
(C) To register for an event
(D) To ask for directions

GO ON TO THE NEXT PAGE

Newshine Flooring

www.newshineflooring.com

| HOME | | PRODUCT & SERVICES | | CONTACT US |

For over 30 years, Newshine Flooring has supplied a wide range of high-quality hardwood flooring to customers. We serve homeowners nationwide and can provide you with the perfect solution for your home remodeling project. Please refer to the options below.

Flooring Material	Room Size	Estimated Cost
cedar	0-250 square feet	$1,000
cedar	250+ square feet	$1,750
oak	0-250 square feet	$1,750
oak	250+ square feet	$2,500
bamboo	0-250 square feet	$2,500
bamboo	250+ square feet	$4,000

Estimated costs are for materials only. If you require a quote for labor costs, one of our installation specialists will need to visit your home and examine the area you plan to remodel. Please contact us here for inquiries.

To	Newshine Flooring Customer Service <service@newshineflooring.com>
From	David Wescott <dwest78@realmail.net>
Subject	Interest in your services
Date	May 4

Hello,

I am interested in some of the products that you offer on your Web site. I just moved into my current home one month ago, and I am in the process of updating my kitchen. I finished setting up the lights yesterday, but I think the flooring needs some work. Specifically, I'd like to remove the current floor and replace it with your bamboo option. The space is just under 150 square feet, so I don't think much intensive labor will be required.

I would like the work to be done on May 10, if possible. However, I need to know the cost of labor before making a final decision about this project. Could you provide me with an estimate?

Thank you,

David Wescott

181. What is the purpose of the Web page?

   (A) To announce a store opening
   (B) To report on a firm's performance
   (C) To promote company's products
   (D) To request feedback on some services

182. What is indicated about Newshine Flooring?

   (A) It was established a decade ago.
   (B) It has recently uploaded images to a
       Web site.
   (C) It will change its product line next month.
   (D) It supplies three types of materials.

183. According to the e-mail, what did
    Mr. Wescott do yesterday?

   (A) Installed some equipment
   (B) Downloaded a brochure
   (C) Signed a rental contract
   (D) Transported some furniture

184. How much will Mr. Wescott most likely pay
    for materials?

   (A) $1,000
   (B) $1,750
   (C) $2,500
   (D) $4,000

185. What will Newshine Flooring most likely do
    before May 10?

   (A) Order some supplies
   (B) Schedule an inspection
   (C) Remove some lighting
   (D) Obtain a work authorization

GO ON TO THE NEXT PAGE

Spirant Energy Canada Wind Power Project Announced

January 3—Spirant Energy Canada has announced plans to partner with the Netherland's TWC Energy to build a wind farm with four towers near Lake Ontario. Each tower will generate enough electricity to supply approximately 6,000 homes.

According to Spirant Energy Canada spokesperson Oscar Lee, the Lake Ontario Wind Power Project could open the door to larger-scale wind power projects throughout Canada. Development work is expected to begin immediately, with installation targeted for this December.

If completed, this will be Spirant Energy Canada's third wind farm in six years. Its last project was abandoned following protests from wildlife conservation groups. Netherland's TWC Energy will provide technical assistance. Funding will come from the local governments of Ontario and Toronto, with additional support from the Canadian Wind Power Association.

To   Tom Hiltern <t.hiltern@torontonianobserver.com>
From   Linda Castillo <l.castillo@spirantenergy.com>
Subject Article on Spirant Energy Canada
Date   January 6

Dear Mr. Hiltern,

I am writing to point out some inaccuracies in your article on the Lake Ontario Wind Power Project. First, it suggests that each tower can produce enough electricity for 6,000 homes. Rather, it will take all four towers combined to serve 6,000 homes in total.

Second, our Hudson Bay project was not abandoned. It was put on hold so we could conduct further studies. Since that time, we have determined that it will be possible to resume the project soon by moving the wind farm away from critical routes followed by migrating birds. Details will be released next month.

In the meantime, please print the necessary corrections. Thank you.

Sincerely,

Linda Castillo
Head of Public Relations
Spirant Energy Canada

You are invited to the opening of the
Lake Ontario Wind Farm

Presented by Spirant Energy Canada and TWC Energy
in cooperation with Ontario State Government and Toronto City Government
Sponsored by the Canadian Wind Power Association

WHEN: Friday, November 22, 4:30 P.M. to 7:00 P.M.
WHERE: Toronto Ferry Building

Special guests include Premier Roy Brown, Mayor Edwina Smythe, and Harold Bennett, host of Canadian television's longest-running nature program, *Wildlife Crossing*. The event will include a half-hour sunset cruise aboard a Toronto ferry to visit the finished wind farm. This will be followed by a social function at which complimentary refreshments will be served.

Please be on time as the boat leaves promptly at 5 P.M. from Harbor B. For more information, call 555-4182.

186. What is the article mainly about?

(A) A merger between two competing firms
(B) A project to construct a bridge
(C) An energy company's development plans
(D) An expansion of an existing power facility

187. What does Ms. Castillo suggest about the Hudson Bay project?

(A) It was halted due to a lack of funding.
(B) It may be developed with the help of TWC Energy.
(C) It could become Spirant Energy Canada's last wind farm.
(D) It might be approved by environmental groups.

188. In the e-mail, the word "critical" in paragraph 2, line 3, is closest in meaning to

(A) exclusive
(B) demanding
(C) dangerous
(D) important

189. According to the invitation, what are guests of the event asked to do?

(A) Present an invitation at the door
(B) Reserve spaces by calling a number
(C) Arrive at a transportation facility at a given time
(D) Indicate meal preferences to the organizer

190. What is true about the Lake Ontario wind farm?

(A) It is a half hour from Toronto by boat.
(B) It is opening ahead of schedule.
(C) It was moved from its original location.
(D) It will be inspected by a government official.

GO ON TO THE NEXT PAGE ➡

| Home | **About Us** | Find a Part | Contact Us |

www.rusticrevival.com

Rustic Revival specializes in rare and hard-to-find parts for vintage furniture. Our warehouse contains thousands of items, many of which are no longer manufactured.

If you need a replacement part for a residential, commercial, or industrial item, we offer several options for tracking it down within our huge inventory. If you happen to know brand and model names, you may use our search function. If you only know the brand name, you may browse our online catalog to identify exactly what you are looking for. Even if you are unaware of either, you may send us a picture or description of what you need, and we will try to locate it.

From	Elspeth Panter <reception@chiringshoals.org>
To	Rustic Revival <admin@rusticrevival.com>
Subject	Urgent business-related inquiry
Date	July 3

Dear Rustic Revival,

I'm the proprietor of the boutique hotel Chiring Shoals Bed & Breakfast. Unfortunately, an accident took place in one of my guest rooms, and the handle of a bathtub faucet was broken. Because the part is an antique, I've been unable to find it here in Wilmington. When I used the search on www.rusticrevival.com, I found that you do have it in stock. But I need to know whether you can have it sent to me by July 5. It's the high season, and, because my establishment is fully booked for the weekend, the repairs must be done as soon as possible. If you are unable to meet my shipping requirements, I will find other options.

Regards,

Elspeth Panter

Wellsworth Plumbing
Servicing New Hanover County for over 10 years

Shinn Point, Wilmington
555-0001

Job Location
Chiring Shoals Bed & Breakfast
773 Wind Chase Lane
Wilmington, NC 28409

LABOR Serviceperson

Yvonne Severin

Date	Hours	Rate	Total
July 4	1.5	$60 per hour	$90

Guarantee: Repairs and replacements are free within three months of work date.

PARTS

Quantity	Description	Price	Total
1	Goutte Magnalift X-T	$45	$45

Recommendation: Take care not to lift new faucet handle forcefully. I will conduct a second visit in a week to check that there are no problems.

Total Cost (Parts and Labor)	
	$135

191. What is mentioned about Rustic Revival?

(A) It accepts contracts for home renovations.
(B) It sells items that are unavailable in most stores.
(C) It specializes in products made for hotels.
(D) It carries merchandise under its own brand name.

192. What is suggested about Ms. Panter?

(A) She owns a collection of antique decorations.
(B) She had to visit a medical clinic for treatment.
(C) She knew the model name of a broken part.
(D) She runs a place of accommodation with a partner.

193. Why is an item needed at Chiring Shoals Bed & Breakfast?

(A) A room must be made suitable for arriving visitors.
(B) Customers made several complaints about its facilities.
(C) A large event has been planned for the coming days.
(D) The hotel has to comply with a new set of regulations.

194. What did Ms. Severin offer to do?

(A) Refund a portion of the charges
(B) Check for parts from another supplier
(C) Return to perform an inspection
(D) Increase a home's water pressure

195. What can be inferred about Rustic Revival?

(A) It made some alterations to the Goutte Magnalift X-T.
(B) It was unable to meet Ms. Panter's shipping deadline.
(C) It manufactures most of its products in house.
(D) It will provide a complimentary service next month.

GO ON TO THE NEXT PAGE

---

www.magnumcruises.com

Magnum Cruises

HOME	ABOUT	PRESS	**JOBS**

We are currently taking applicants for the following positions on regional cruises operating throughout the year.

Southern Africa

As a Guest Relations Officer, work aboard the Magnum Explorer from October through March welcoming guests, organizing activities, and addressing customer concerns. See more

Australia & the Pacific

As an Entertainment Specialist, work aboard the Magnum Endeavor from November through February as a creative performer under the supervision of the entertainment director. See more

India & Sri Lanka

As a Ship's Nurse, work aboard the Magnum Adventure from April through July caring for the day-to-day health of passengers. See more

Southeast Asia

As an Assistant Restaurant Manager, work aboard the Magnum Pacifica from May through September ensuring the smooth delivery of dining services to guests. See more

To apply, send your résumé, together with a cover letter, to our head office at Suite 100, Capital Building, 65 Canal Road, Singapore 049513. Only applicants who make it through the initial screening process will be contacted. They will be invited to interview online. When applying, please state your desired position.

October 22
1245 Miller Street
North Sydney, NSW 2060

Dear Sir or Madam,

I am interested in the position of assistant restaurant manager. I am confident that I can meet all of the requirements. I have a degree in food and beverage management, recent and related work experience, and I have worked on cruise ships before. I also speak three languages, have a certificate of good health from a licensed physician, and have all of my travel documents in order. I hope that given these qualifications, you will seriously consider me for a position with Magnum Cruises.

Sincerely,

Leo Manresa

To	Leo Manresa <l.manresa@hypemail.com>
From	Jessica Lewen <j.lewen@magnumcruises.com>
Subject	Interview
Date	November 11

Dear Mr. Manresa,

Thank you for applying for a position with Magnum Cruises. We believe that you are sufficiently qualified to proceed with your application. In connection with this, we would like to invite you to attend an online interview on November 15 at 10:00 A.M. Detailed instructions will be provided once you have confirmed your availability. If successful, you will travel to our head office to undergo two months' training before officially starting your job at the beginning of the season.

Sincerely,

Jessica Lewen
Recruitment Manager
Magnum Cruises

196. What is true about Magnum Cruises?

(A) It has just introduced a new cruise itinerary.
(B) It has some openings at its head office.
(C) It provides services all year long.
(D) It travels to cities in Europe and North America.

197. What is suggested about the advertised jobs?

(A) Not all applicants will receive replies.
(B) Candidates must be licensed professionals.
(C) They require previous cruise experience.
(D) All involve supervising others.

198. On which ship is Mr. Manresa applying to work?

(A) Magnum Explorer
(B) Magnum Endeavor
(C) Magnum Adventure
(D) Magnum Pacifica

199. What will Ms. Lewen be providing to Mr. Manresa?

(A) A list of job duties
(B) A training plan
(C) A plane ticket
(D) A set of instructions

200. What can be inferred about Mr. Manresa?

(A) He may be departing in November.
(B) He might have to travel to Singapore.
(C) He was referred by a former employer.
(D) He worked on a ship near India and Sri Lanka.

This is the end of the test. You may review Parts 5, 6, and 7 if you finish the test early.

정답 p.385 / 해석·해설 [별권] 해설집 p.88 / 해커스 토익 빅플로 자동 채점 및 취약 유형 분석하기
* 다음 페이지에 있는 TEST 5 점수 환산표를 확인해 자신의 토익 리딩 점수를 예상해 보세요.

TEST 5 171

TEST 5 점수 환산표

TEST 5는 무사히 잘 마치셨나요? 맞은 개수를 세어본 후 아래의 점수 환산표를 통해 자신의 점수를 예상해 보세요.

전체 난이도   **중간 난이도**

파트별 난이도   PART 5 중 ●●○
             PART 6 중 ●●○
             PART 7 중 ●●○

정답 수	리딩 점수	정답 수	리딩 점수
98~100개	475~495점	47~49개	205~215점
95~97개	460~470점	44~46개	190~200점
92~94개	440~455점	41~43개	175~185점
89~91개	420~435점	38~40개	160~170점
86~88개	405~415점	35~37개	145~155점
83~85개	390~400점	32~34개	130~140점
80~82개	375~385점	29~31개	115~125점
77~79개	360~370점	26~28개	100~110점
74~76개	340~355점	23~25개	85~95점
71~73개	325~335점	20~22개	70~80점
68~70개	305~320점	17~19개	55~65점
65~67개	290~300점	14~16개	40~50점
62~64개	270~285점	11~13개	25~35점
59~61개	260~270점	8~10개	10~20점
56~58개	245~255점	5~7개	5~10점
53~55개	235~240점	2~4개	5~10점
50~52개	220~230점	0~1개	0~5점

* 점수 환산표는 해커스토익 사이트 유저 데이터를 근거로 제작되었으며, 주기적으로 업데이트되고 있습니다. 해커스토익 사이트
  (Hackers.co.kr)에서 최신 경향을 반영하여 업데이트된 점수환산기를 이용하실 수 있습니다. (토익 > 토익게시판 > 토익점수환산기)

TEST 6

PART 5
PART 6
PART 7
점수 환산표

잠깐! 테스트 전 확인사항

1. 문제 풀이에 방해가 되는 물건을 모두 치우셨나요?   예 □
2. Answer Sheet, 연필, 지우개를 준비하셨나요?   예 □
3. 시계를 준비하셨나요?   예 □

모든 준비가 완료되었으면 목표 점수를 떠올린 후 테스트를 시작합니다.

문제 풀이를 마치는 시간은 지금부터 **75분 후인** _____시 _____분입니다.

테스트 시간은 **총 75분**이며, 시험 종료 전 2~3분은 정답 검토 및 답안지 마킹을 위해 사용합니다.

READING TEST

In this section, you must demonstrate your ability to read and comprehend English. You will be given a variety of texts and asked to answer questions about these texts. This section is divided into three parts and will take 75 minutes to complete.

Do not mark the answers in your test book. Use the answer sheet that is separately provided.

PART 5

Directions: In each question, you will be asked to review a statement that is missing a word or phrase. Four answer choices will be provided for each statement. Select the best answer and mark the corresponding letter (A), (B), (C), or (D) on the answer sheet.

---

101. If it rains, ------- outdoor events will be substituted with indoor activities.

(A) every
(B) these
(C) others
(D) another

102. Monthly meetings are attended by each team's -------, who gives a rundown of the latest developments.

(A) supervised
(B) supervision
(C) supervise
(D) supervisor

103. The job market became ------- as many recent graduates started looking for work.

(A) competes
(B) competitively
(C) compete
(D) competitive

104. The residents had to ------- for three hours while technicians were restoring power.

(A) wait
(B) practice
(C) grant
(D) agree

105. Politicians have praised the president's economic plan, especially where job ------- and security are concerned.

(A) create
(B) creative
(C) creation
(D) creator

106. The Tuscaloosa Airport provides wheelchair assistance to passengers who ------- it.

(A) touch
(B) request
(C) begin
(D) leave

107. A number of hotels consider the ------- changes in demand when pricing their rooms.

(A) seasons
(B) seasonally
(C) seasonal
(D) seasoned

108. The factory equipment will operate ------- for a period of several weeks.

(A) continuation
(B) continued
(C) continuously
(D) continuous

109. ------- including only the important facts, analysts can make concise research reports.

(A) By
(B) To
(C) At
(D) Beyond

110. The CEO spoke frankly ------- the company's problems to make sure there was no misunderstanding.

(A) about
(B) with
(C) for
(D) in

111. Following government health guidelines can ------- reduce the risk of food poisoning.

(A) optionally
(B) carefully
(C) unexpectedly
(D) substantially

112. The marketing department spent too much on last year's ------- and is looking to make cutbacks this year.

(A) promotion
(B) promote
(C) promotional
(D) promoted

113. Laurent Software's new mobile application earned a ------- review score than the developers anticipated.

(A) high
(B) highly
(C) higher
(D) highest

114. The one-month ------- period is designed to equip new employees with the necessary skills.

(A) training
(B) enrollment
(C) innovation
(D) manufacturing

115. Westgate Subway Station opened just last month, but it is ------- one of the city's busiest subway stops.

(A) though
(B) instead
(C) therefore
(D) nonetheless

116. Many aspiring interpreters find our language courses ------- for their career.

(A) ambitious
(B) conservative
(C) subtle
(D) helpful

117. Sandy's Cantina ------- dominates the country's fast food industry these days.

(A) complete
(B) more complete
(C) completely
(D) completing

118. Trinity Tablemates ------- for under a year, but already ranks as the best restaurant in town.

(A) operates
(B) has operated
(C) will operate
(D) to operate

119. Mr. Abrams hired a consulting firm ------- he could get some advice on dealing with suppliers.

(A) so that
(B) in the event that
(C) even if
(D) regarding

120. Organizers are still searching for a venue ------- they can hold an event for 200 guests.

(A) who
(B) what
(C) when
(D) where

GO ON TO THE NEXT PAGE

121. The visa application must be submitted ------- to avoid delays.

(A) punctual
(B) punctuating
(C) punctuation
(D) punctually

122. Investing in new machinery is expensive, but it is ------- in the long run.

(A) fortunate
(B) memorable
(C) beneficial
(D) sudden

123. ------- in business class will be allowed to board the plane first.

(A) They
(B) This
(C) Those
(D) Either

124. Two weeks -------, Prendit Corp. will hold a press conference to announce its business expansion.

(A) next
(B) later
(C) usually
(D) still

125. As a personnel manager, Ms. Goldfinch is in charge of ------- staff.

(A) indicating
(B) compiling
(C) manipulating
(D) recruiting

126. The quarterly bonus is divided -------, with all members of the sales team getting a share.

(A) equally
(B) equal
(C) equality
(D) more equal

127. The software conference encourages sharing ideas ------- developers in the field.

(A) above
(B) among
(C) into
(D) plus

128. The building's central location makes it extremely -------, and its high rental prices reflect this.

(A) attractive
(B) actual
(C) attentive
(D) complimentary

129. Mr. Calderon had a business partner but now runs the company by -------.

(A) himself
(B) his
(C) him
(D) he

130. Mr. Parker decided to remove the old brown sofa and place it in -------.

(A) storage
(B) solutions
(C) absence
(D) procedure

Directions: In this part, you will be asked to read four English texts. Each text is missing a word, phrase, or sentence. Select the answer choice that correctly completes the text and mark the corresponding letter (A), (B), (C), or (D) on the answer sheet.

Questions 131-134 refer to the following e-mail.

To: Derrian Enterprises <info@derrianenterprises.com>
From: Carlos Juarez <cjuar@jadeair.com>
Date: 9 May
Subject: Inquiry

To Whom It May Concern:

I am writing on the recommendation of a colleague who has used your services before. I work in the marketing department for Jade Air and we are running a promotional campaign ------- our
131.
20th anniversary. As part of the campaign, we will be giving away complimentary T-shirts to all passengers.

I am hoping you can give me a price -------. I want to know how much it will cost to get 4,000 shirts
132.
in red material with our logo printed on the front. -------, could you send me a sample for this item?
133.
-------. Should the sample meet our standards, we will proceed with an order.
134.

Thank you,

Carlos Juarez
Jade Air

131. (A) to celebrate
(B) celebrated
(C) celebrations
(D) celebrate

132. (A) benefit
(B) draft
(C) analysis
(D) estimate

133. (A) Furthermore
(B) For instance
(C) Otherwise
(D) After all

134. (A) It satisfied all of my specifications.
(B) It wasn't exactly what I requested.
(C) I will notify you when it will be sent.
(D) I want to be sure it's comfortable to wear.

GO ON TO THE NEXT PAGE

Questions 135-138 refer to the following letter.

January 18

Lucinda Botello
Owner, Condesa Textiles
920 Cuevas Avenue
Mexico City, Mexico 03100

Dear Ms. Botello,

We would like to invite you to be a judge in our community's annual entrepreneurship contest.

Every year, local residents can present their business ideas to a panel of experienced ------- .
135.

As one of these experts, you would evaluate the ideas based on selected criteria. ------- .
136.

Each ------- gets only 15 minutes to share their proposal.
137.

Should you be willing to accept, please return the enclosed form by mail. The contest will be held

at our community center on Friday, March 6, from 10:00 A.M. to 11:30 A.M. It ------- by a casual
138.

lunch.

Further details may be found on our Web site.

Sincerely,

Rafael Pedragon
Chair, Community Entrepreneurship Program

135. (A) specially
(B) specialize
(C) specialists
(D) special

136. (A) We have a wide selection to offer.
(B) The presentations will be brief.
(C) Suggestions for topics are welcome.
(D) All contestants will receive a prize.

137. (A) partner
(B) representative
(C) spectator
(D) participant

138. (A) follows
(B) following
(C) followed
(D) will be followed

Questions 139-142 refer to the following information.

As of September 1, the *Canberra Post* will stop publishing the Saturday edition of its newspaper.

This decision was made in response ------- a decline in the number of weekend readers. These
                                     139.

numbers ------- from about 500,000 to 100,000 over the past three years. By discontinuing our
             140.

Saturday edition, we will be able to focus on our weekday readership. We will also be adding

several new ------- to our weekday edition. These will include Travel, Health, Gardening and more.
            141.

-------.
142.

139. (A) to
(B) of
(C) by
(D) on

140. (A) are decreasing
(B) have decreased
(C) were decreased
(D) decrease

141. (A) methods
(B) machines
(C) sections
(D) positions

142. (A) They will begin appearing in our Friday issues.
(B) There were many inquiries about refunds.
(C) We wish our editor the best of luck in the future.
(D) It can only be delivered within the city limits, though.

GO ON TO THE NEXT PAGE ▶

Questions 143-146 refer to the following memo.

To: All call center workers
From: John Dooley, Customer support specialist
Subject: Collecting information
Date: June 22

In the last six months, the amount of time that callers have waited in order to speak to one of our representatives has almost doubled. ------- time was 7 minutes in May, and now it is 13 minutes.
143.

-------. Thus, I will add a new page to our Web site. It will be labeled "frequently asked questions"
144.

and will contain ------- answers. I would like each of you to send me a list of the 10 most common
145.

questions you ------- each day about our software programs.
146.

143. (A) This
     (B) Our
     (C) These
     (D) Theirs

144. (A) Customers need other means for solving their problems.
     (B) The new overtime policy will take effect in a few days.
     (C) Our company had to delay the launch due to the added time.
     (D) Our phone service has been temporarily disconnected.

145. (A) comprehensive
     (B) comprehending
     (C) comprehensively
     (D) comprehension

146. (A) receiving
     (B) will receive
     (C) receive
     (D) are received

PART 7

Directions: In this part, you will be asked to read several texts, such as advertisements, articles, instant messages, or examples of business correspondence. Each text is followed by several questions. Select the best answer and mark the corresponding letter (A), (B), (C), or (D) on your answer sheet.

Questions 147-148 refer to the following notice.

City Hall Snow Removal Services Needed

Brannethville is seeking bids for the removal of snow and ice on paved areas surrounding City Hall. Before submitting a proposal, please take note of the requirements:

1. All snow and ice must be removed by 7:00 A.M. every day.
2. The contractor must be available from 7:00 A.M. to 5:00 P.M. on days when snowfall is moderate to heavy.
3. The contractor must supply all equipment.
4. The contract will last for six months from December 3 to May 3, regardless of whether snow removal services are needed.

If interested, please mail your proposal to Brannethville City Hall. Bids must be received by December 1 to qualify.

147. What is the purpose of the notice?

(A) To announce a new regulation
(B) To request applications for a seasonal job
(C) To provide helpful snow removal advice
(D) To remind residents to prepare for winter

148. What are contractors required to do?

(A) Register on a Web site
(B) Provide their own equipment
(C) Work only at night
(D) Complete a job by December

GO ON TO THE NEXT PAGE

Questions 149-150 refer to the following e-mail.

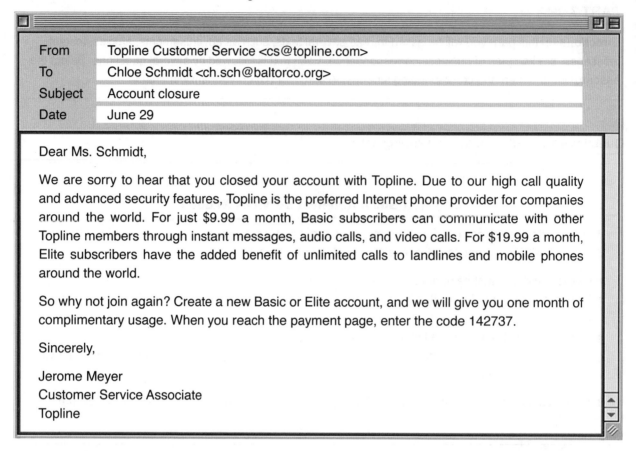

From：Topline Customer Service <cs@topline.com>

To：Chloe Schmidt <ch.sch@baltorco.org>

Subject：Account closure

Date：June 29

Dear Ms. Schmidt,

We are sorry to hear that you closed your account with Topline. Due to our high call quality and advanced security features, Topline is the preferred Internet phone provider for companies around the world. For just $9.99 a month, Basic subscribers can communicate with other Topline members through instant messages, audio calls, and video calls. For $19.99 a month, Elite subscribers have the added benefit of unlimited calls to landlines and mobile phones around the world.

So why not join again? Create a new Basic or Elite account, and we will give you one month of complimentary usage. When you reach the payment page, enter the code 142737.

Sincerely,

Jerome Meyer
Customer Service Associate
Topline

149. Why was the e-mail written?

(A) To apologize for a service problem
(B) To request payment of a bill
(C) To advertise a new product
(D) To persuade a customer to return

150. How can Ms. Schmidt obtain a free service?

(A) By upgrading a subscription
(B) By redeeming points
(C) By entering certain numbers
(D) By referring a friend

Questions 151-152 refer to the following text-message chain.

Leo Henderson   10:48 A.M.

My flight from San Diego has been delayed for five hours. I won't arrive in Chicago until 6:30 P.M. So I'll miss the regional managers' meeting scheduled for four o'clock this afternoon.

Shelly Summers   10:52 A.M.

I'll call the director right now and inform him. He may want to reschedule. Let me check.

Shelly Summers   10:59 A.M.

Yes, he wants to reschedule for tomorrow morning at 8:30 A.M. He would like all regional managers in attendance. Will that work for you?

Leo Henderson   11:02 A.M.

Don't I have a meeting with the financial director at 9:30 A.M.?

Shelly Summers   11:04 A.M.

Yes, but we can put that off until the afternoon. You don't have anything scheduled after 3 P.M. I'll let you know the time once I've confirmed with the financial director. Have a good flight!

151. At 10:52 A.M., what does Ms. Summers mean when she writes, "Let me check"?

(A) She will determine when a flight arrives.
(B) She will consult a company director.
(C) She will see if a car and driver are available.
(D) She will contact the regional managers.

152. When will Mr. Henderson attend the regional managers' meeting tomorrow?

(A) At 8:30 A.M.
(B) At 9:30 A.M.
(C) At 3:00 P.M.
(D) At 6:30 P.M.

GO ON TO THE NEXT PAGE

Ascott Foods to Say Goodbye to Plastic Bags
By Nicole Chase

March 20—Supermarket chain Ascott Foods has announced that it will no longer be providing single-use plastic shopping bags, which are bad for the environment. It will become the second chain to do so after Golden Supermarket. However, Ascott's ban will not come into effect immediately. According to a company representative, each store will keep using plastic bags for as long as supplies last.

In the coming weeks, all 166 Ascott Foods locations across the country will begin offering reusable canvas bags. They will come at no cost for three months to encourage customers to use them. The company is also looking for ways to avoid using plastic in its produce packaging.

153. The word "keep" in paragraph 1, line 8, is closest in meaning to

(A) secure
(B) continue
(C) withhold
(D) reserve

154. What is NOT true about Ascott Foods?

(A) It will be providing free shopping bags for three months.
(B) It may extend a policy to include fruit and vegetable products.
(C) It will be the first supermarket to stop using single-use bags.
(D) It has multiple store locations throughout the country.

Cadigan Industries Expense Report

Employee Name: Cole Bradley
Department: Sales
Purpose of Expense: Trip to visit client
Today's Date: March 28

Date of Expense	Description	Expense Category	Total
March 4	Gateway Air —Toronto to Fort Lauderdale, economy class, one-way	Travel	$126.25
March 4-6	Julbee Car Rental, compact car, $50/day	Travel	$150.00
March 4-5	Bonneville Hotel, single room, $90/night	Accommodation	$180.00
March 5	Cowbell Grill, 4 people	Business meal	$270.00
March 6	Natura Air — Fort Lauderdale to Toronto, business class, one-way	Travel	$316.10
		Total	$1,042.35

General Guidelines:

- All purchases must have occurred within the last 30 days.
- Original receipts for all business-related expenses must be attached or reimbursement to the employee will be denied.
- Economy-class travel expenses will be fully refunded, as well as the cost of single hotel rooms and compact car rentals. Business-class travel tickets should only be purchased when there are no available seats in economy class, and expenses may not be paid back in full depending on the situation. Any personal insurance purchased for a trip is not reimbursable.

155. Why did Mr. Bradley fill out the form?

(A) To reveal sales figures
(B) To provide an estimate
(C) To suggest an itinerary
(D) To request compensation

156. What can be inferred about Mr. Bradley?

(A) He used a corporate credit card on a trip.
(B) He may not be fully repaid for a flight.
(C) He did not meet the deadline to submit a report.
(D) He exceeded the acceptable limit on meal expenses.

157. What is true about Cadigan Industries?

(A) It recently changed its policy regarding business trips.
(B) It requires payment records from some employees.
(C) It relocated its headquarters to Toronto.
(D) It provides full refunds to some customers.

GO ON TO THE NEXT PAGE

Questions 158-160 refer to the following e-mail.

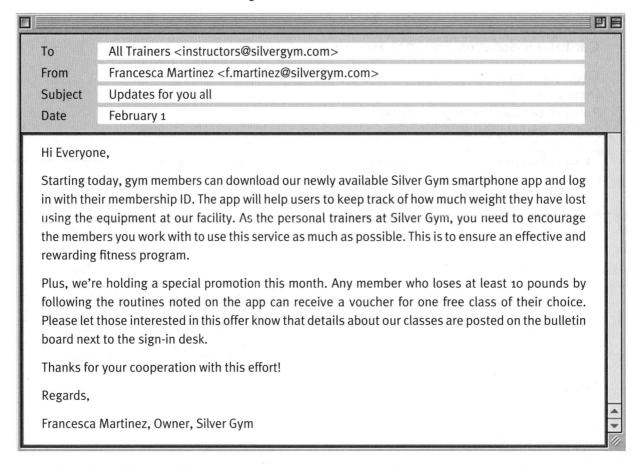

To	All Trainers <instructors@silvergym.com>
From	Francesca Martinez <f.martinez@silvergym.com>
Subject	Updates for you all
Date	February 1

Hi Everyone,

Starting today, gym members can download our newly available Silver Gym smartphone app and log in with their membership ID. The app will help users to keep track of how much weight they have lost using the equipment at our facility. As the personal trainers at Silver Gym, you need to encourage the members you work with to use this service as much as possible. This is to ensure an effective and rewarding fitness program.

Plus, we're holding a special promotion this month. Any member who loses at least 10 pounds by following the routines noted on the app can receive a voucher for one free class of their choice. Please let those interested in this offer know that details about our classes are posted on the bulletin board next to the sign-in desk.

Thanks for your cooperation with this effort!

Regards,

Francesca Martinez, Owner, Silver Gym

---

158. What is one purpose of the e-mail?

(A) To notify gym members of a price change
(B) To remind customers about a policy
(C) To inform employees about a program
(D) To encourage users to join a class

159. What is NOT indicated about gym members?

(A) They are eligible to receive a complimentary session.
(B) They can monitor weight loss using an application.
(C) They can exercise using equipment in the gym.
(D) They will receive a notice about benefits in the mail.

160. Where can information about classes be found?

(A) On a notice board
(B) On a Web site
(C) In an e-mail
(D) In the locker room

Questions 161-163 refer to the following information.

Gleason's Grill Server Training Guide

Step 1

Approach customers as soon as they have been seated, greeting them in a friendly manner. Bring enough menus and cutlery for each member of the party and fill their water glasses. If you are busy serving a table when new customers walk in, acknowledge them loudly. — [1] —.

Step 2

Give customers a moment to go over the menu. — [2] —. Inform them of our daily special and answer any questions they have about menu items. In the event that a customer inquires as to whether a dish has a specific ingredient because they are allergic to it, excuse yourself to find out from the kitchen staff if you are unsure. — [3] —. When the customers are ready to order, make sure to write everything down on your pad, taking note of who ordered what. Next, repeat their orders back to them to be certain that no mistakes have been made.

Step 3

Check back with customers several minutes after bringing the food out to see whether everything is satisfactory. Once they have finished eating, suggest dessert or coffee before bringing the bill. — [4] —.

161. According to the information, why do servers need to speak with kitchen staff?

(A) To complain about how slow the food is being prepared
(B) To request smaller meal portions for children
(C) To inform them of newly added menu items
(D) To inquire about the contents of a dish

162. What should servers do immediately after taking customers' orders?

(A) Bring a notepad to a counter
(B) Recommend additional items
(C) Confirm some selections
(D) Add each item to the bill

163. In which of the positions marked [1], [2], [3], and [4] does the following sentence best belong?

"This will alert other staff members that they have entered the restaurant."

(A) [1]
(B) [2]
(C) [3]
(D) [4]

GO ON TO THE NEXT PAGE

Questions 164-167 refer to the following online chat discussion.

Mimi Pearson	**[3:45 P.M.]**	Anyone else having trouble with the new word processing software?
Donald Platt	**[3:45 P.M.]**	I am. Each time I try to install it, my screen freezes. I've been waiting for someone from IT.
Grace Helmsley	**[3:46 P.M.]**	An IT employee told me that that they are working on the problem. They just finished here on the second floor. Louis and some others were having problems, too.
Louis Jones	**[3:46 P.M.]**	Right. My software is working fine now. You just have to update your operating system for the installation to work.
Mimi Pearson	**[3:47 P.M.]**	That's not the problem. I was able to install it just fine. I'm having trouble figuring out how to use the software.
Donald Platt	**[3:48 P.M.]**	Mimi, there's a user manual on the company Intranet. I can send you a link if you want me to.
Grace Helmsley	**[3:48 P.M.]**	You can also click on the Help button in the toolbar for detailed explanations.
Mimi Pearson	**[3:49 P.M.]**	I didn't know there were instructions. I'll look at them later. I'll try Grace's suggestion first as it might be faster, and I need to print a file right away.
Louis Jones	**[3:50 P.M.]**	The company should really provide us with training. I'll talk to Mr. West. But first I'll ask around to see who feels they need it.

Send

164. What is mentioned about Ms. Helmsley?

(A) She spoke to a member of the IT department.
(B) She works on the third floor of a building.
(C) She required an operating system update.
(D) She finds the software complicated.

165. At 3:47 P.M., what does Ms. Pearson mean when she writes, "That's not the problem"?

(A) She did not understand an explanation.
(B) She was able to install the new software.
(C) She thinks an issue has been resolved.
(D) She was not able to contact an employee from IT.

166. Why does Ms. Pearson decide not to look at the software instructions right away?

(A) She can't turn her computer on.
(B) She can't find them.
(C) She works far from Mr. Platt.
(D) She is in a hurry.

167. What most likely will Mr. Jones do next?

(A) Print a document for a coworker
(B) Inquire about some second-floor employees
(C) Have a conversation with Mr. West
(D) Find out if staff are interested in training

GALAXIS MAGAZINE

January 7

Dr. Frederick Simons
492 Lerner Drive, Apt. 901
Bloomfield Township, MI 48401

Dear Dr. Simons,

We found your proposal for a story on the mountains of Pluto to be quite promising. We feel that it would appeal to our readers and would like you to write an article of 2,500 to 3,000 words. — [1] —. Ideally, we'd like the article to focus on the events leading up to the discovery of landforms on Pluto and to emphasize how unexpected this was for the scientific community. — [2] —.

We can offer you $2,500 for the article. However, take note that unlike in the past, we will not be able to compensate you fully if we decide not to use your work for any reason. — [3] —. That said, we will pay you $500 for your time. We intend to publish the article in our May issue, so we'd like you to submit your first draft by March 5. I have enclosed two contracts with this letter stating these terms. — [4] —. If you agree to them, please sign and return one of the contracts to us using the magazine's postal address. Please keep the other one for your records.

If you have any questions or concerns, don't hesitate to contact me by e-mail. We look forward to working with you again.

Molly Hamilton
Senior Editor, *Galaxis Magazine*

TEST 6

해커스 토익 실전 1200제 READING

168. What information about the article does Ms. Hamilton NOT mention?

(A) The word length
(B) The due date
(C) The publication issue
(D) The revision process

169. What has Dr. Simons been asked to do?

(A) Mail back an agreement
(B) Negotiate some terms
(C) Save some e-mail messages
(D) Rewrite an article

170. What is suggested about *Galaxis Magazine*?

(A) Subscribers can choose to receive online content.
(B) It is available for purchase in several countries.
(C) Dr. Simons has contributed an article to it before.
(D) It pays its freelance writers less than regular staff.

171. In which of the following positions marked [1], [2], [3], and [4] does the following sentence best belong?

"Please note that if it exceeds this amount, we will not be able to publish it."

(A) [1]
(B) [2]
(C) [3]
(D) [4]

GO ON TO THE NEXT PAGE →

Visit the Vallarta-Nayarit Region of Mexico with Galenus Travel for an Unforgettable Experience

The Vallarta-Nayarit region has so much to offer, and when you book a trip using Galenus Travel, you'll have full support for the duration of your trip. Not only will representatives from our local branch be there to greet you when you land, but they'll also help arrange any activities you might be interested in. Some areas not to be missed include:

Downtown Puerto Vallarta

With a boardwalk closed to vehicles, the downtown area is a perfect place to take in the sights as you shop, dine, and visit local contemporary art galleries. It's a must if you're traveling with children as the main square is always full of street performers and artists at work.

Mismaloya

Within walking distance of downtown, this area is full of affordable accommodations. The relaxed atmosphere of Mismaloya is ideal for travelers who want to be closer to the beach without spending too much money. Nearby attractions include the Puerto Vallarta Zoo, the Vallarta Botanical Gardens, and Las Animas Adventure Park.

Punta Mita

Looking for a romantic getaway? Popular among honeymooners, celebrities, and tourists, this village is an oasis of white-sand beaches, isolated retreats, and picturesque sunsets.

Riviera Nayarit

Famous for its spectacular beaches, Riviera Nayarit is the place to go for golf courses, amusement parks, and all-inclusive five-star luxury resorts. Beach restaurants serving up fish tacos and other authentic delicacies can be found throughout this 200-mile stretch of land.

172. What can be inferred about Galenus Travel?

(A) It is currently offering discounts on trips to Mexico.
(B) It has a location in the Vallarta-Nayarit region.
(C) It specializes in arranging tours for families.
(D) It provides travel insurance for all destinations.

173. According to the advertisement, why is Downtown Puerto Vallarta a good place to bring children?

(A) Vehicles are not allowed on the roads there.
(B) It includes many inexpensive restaurants.
(C) Public entertainment can be found there.
(D) It is within walking distance of a beach.

174. Which group would Mismaloya probably appeal to the most?

(A) Museum lovers
(B) Budget travelers
(C) Landscape photographers
(D) Professional artists

175. What is suggested about Riviera Nayarit?

(A) It has very costly accommodation options.
(B) It is becoming famous for its local contemporary art scene.
(C) It is a popular destination for newly married couples.
(D) It has developed significantly in the past decade.

GO ON TO THE NEXT PAGE

Questions 176-180 refer to the following memo and e-mail.

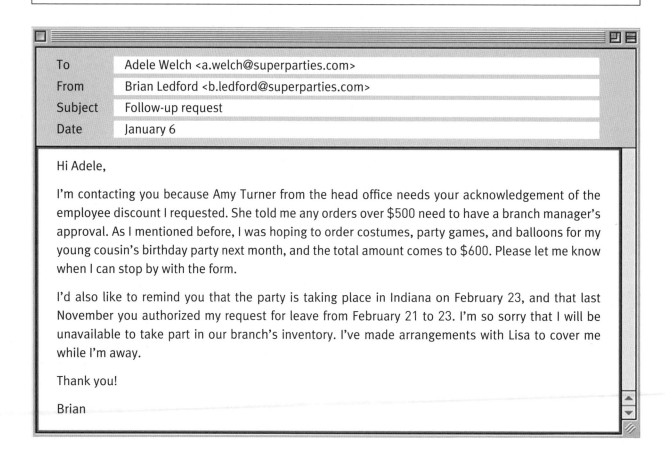

MEMO

To: All branch managers
From: Lori Morrison
Subject: Inventory
Date: January 5

Be reminded that we have scheduled one-day closures at all Super Parties branches in order to undertake our yearly inventory. During this time, all products must be counted by hand and verified against our computer records. Details are below.

Branch	Date
Chicago, Illinois	Tuesday, February 12
Fort Wayne, Indiana	Wednesday, February 13
Milwaukee, Wisconsin	Wednesday, February 20
St. Louis, Missouri	Friday, February 22

Make sure that all of your staff members are aware of these closures and that they may be asked to help out. In addition, advise your customers that orders scheduled for delivery on any of the above dates will not be affected. Also, they can still purchase products through our Web site during this period.

To	Adele Welch <a.welch@superparties.com>
From	Brian Ledford <b.ledford@superparties.com>
Subject	Follow-up request
Date	January 6

Hi Adele,

I'm contacting you because Amy Turner from the head office needs your acknowledgement of the employee discount I requested. She told me any orders over $500 need to have a branch manager's approval. As I mentioned before, I was hoping to order costumes, party games, and balloons for my young cousin's birthday party next month, and the total amount comes to $600. Please let me know when I can stop by with the form.

I'd also like to remind you that the party is taking place in Indiana on February 23, and that last November you authorized my request for leave from February 21 to 23. I'm so sorry that I will be unavailable to take part in our branch's inventory. I've made arrangements with Lisa to cover me while I'm away.

Thank you!

Brian

176. Why is Super Parties closing its branches?

(A) To reduce financial losses
(B) To count merchandise
(C) To address market changes
(D) To undertake renovations

177. What is NOT indicated about Super Parties?

(A) Its items may be rented.
(B) It has stores in four locations.
(C) Its merchandise is available online.
(D) It ships products to customers.

178. Who most likely is Ms. Welch?

(A) A chief executive
(B) A travel agent
(C) A branch supervisor
(D) A head accountant

179. What is Mr. Ledford planning to do?

(A) Move to a new city
(B) Join a company seminar
(C) Attend a training workshop
(D) Visit family members

180. Where most likely does Mr. Ledford work?

(A) In Chicago
(B) In Fort Wayne
(C) In Milwaukee
(D) In St. Louis

GO ON TO THE NEXT PAGE

TEST 6

해커스 토익 실전 1200제 READING

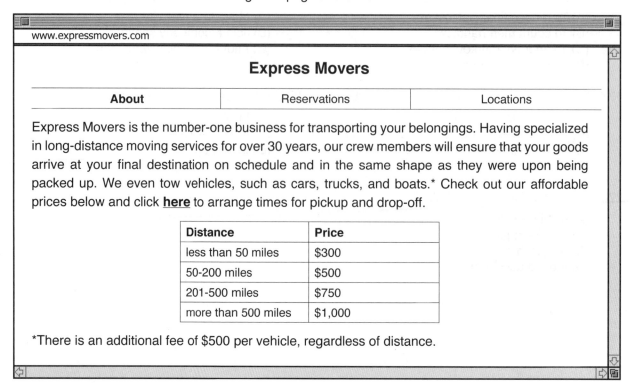

www.expressmovers.com

Express Movers

| **About** | Reservations | Locations |

Express Movers is the number-one business for transporting your belongings. Having specialized in long-distance moving services for over 30 years, our crew members will ensure that your goods arrive at your final destination on schedule and in the same shape as they were upon being packed up. We even tow vehicles, such as cars, trucks, and boats.* Check out our affordable prices below and click **here** to arrange times for pickup and drop-off.

Distance	Price
less than 50 miles	$300
50-200 miles	$500
201-500 miles	$750
more than 500 miles	$1,000

*There is an additional fee of $500 per vehicle, regardless of distance.

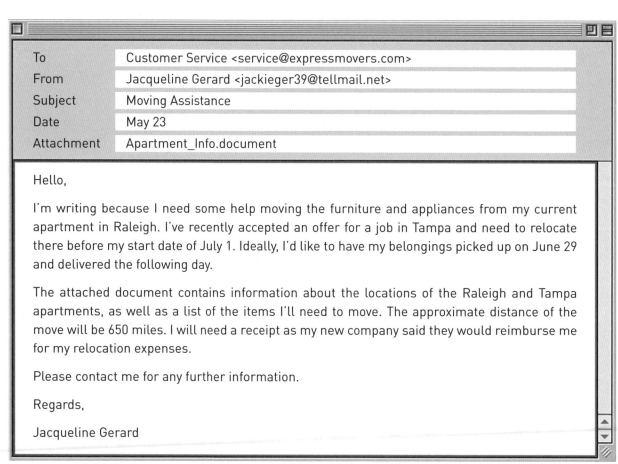

To	Customer Service <service@expressmovers.com>
From	Jacqueline Gerard <jackieger39@tellmail.net>
Subject	Moving Assistance
Date	May 23
Attachment	Apartment_Info.document

Hello,

I'm writing because I need some help moving the furniture and appliances from my current apartment in Raleigh. I've recently accepted an offer for a job in Tampa and need to relocate there before my start date of July 1. Ideally, I'd like to have my belongings picked up on June 29 and delivered the following day.

The attached document contains information about the locations of the Raleigh and Tampa apartments, as well as a list of the items I'll need to move. The approximate distance of the move will be 650 miles. I will need a receipt as my new company said they would reimburse me for my relocation expenses.

Please contact me for any further information.

Regards,

Jacqueline Gerard

181. According to the Web page, what will crew members do?

(A) Clean items at the destination
(B) Ensure delivery of items in good condition
(C) Use a navigation system to locate a residence
(D) Collect payment in advance

182. What is stated about Express Movers?

(A) It will transport automobiles for an extra charge.
(B) It has recently opened a new drop-off center.
(C) It offers an online chat service for customers.
(D) It was established a decade ago.

183. Why is Ms. Gerard relocating?

(A) To live close to some relatives
(B) To enroll in a university program
(C) To take up a new project
(D) To begin work in a new location

184. What can be inferred about Ms. Gerard?

(A) She is moving into a small apartment.
(B) She will be promoted soon.
(C) She is leaving some furniture in storage.
(D) She will pay at least $1,000 for a service.

185. What did Ms. Gerard request?

(A) A delivery schedule
(B) A transaction record
(C) A feedback form
(D) A contract copy

GO ON TO THE NEXT PAGE

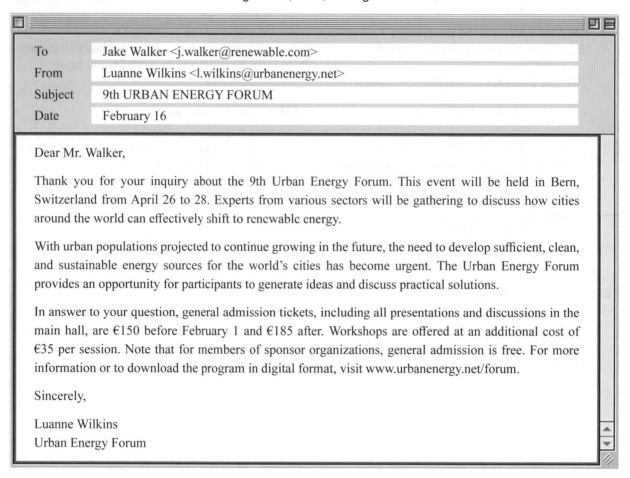

To   Jake Walker <j.walker@renewable.com>

From   Luanne Wilkins <l.wilkins@urbanenergy.net>

Subject 9th URBAN ENERGY FORUM

Date   February 16

Dear Mr. Walker,

Thank you for your inquiry about the 9th Urban Energy Forum. This event will be held in Bern, Switzerland from April 26 to 28. Experts from various sectors will be gathering to discuss how cities around the world can effectively shift to renewable energy.

With urban populations projected to continue growing in the future, the need to develop sufficient, clean, and sustainable energy sources for the world's cities has become urgent. The Urban Energy Forum provides an opportunity for participants to generate ideas and discuss practical solutions.

In answer to your question, general admission tickets, including all presentations and discussions in the main hall, are €150 before February 1 and €185 after. Workshops are offered at an additional cost of €35 per session. Note that for members of sponsor organizations, general admission is free. For more information or to download the program in digital format, visit www.urbanenergy.net/forum.

Sincerely,

Luanne Wilkins
Urban Energy Forum

9th URBAN ENERGY FORUM
Bern, Switzerland · April 26-28

Thank you! Your payment has been received. Please retain a copy of this form for your records. If you require any changes, contact us at forum@urbanenergy.net.

ORDER DETAILS

Name: Irwin Patel
Company (optional): Solar India
Address: 75 Murti Lane, New Delhi, India 110011
Telephone: 555-2390
E-mail: i.patel@solarindia.com
Number of tickets: One(1)
Total amount paid: €35.00
   - Admission fees: €0.00
   - Workshop fees: €35.00

To obtain a full refund, please contact us at least three days before the start of the event.

9th URBAN ENERGY FORUM

Bern, Switzerland · April 26-28

Agenda for Day 2

10:00-11:00 A.M.   Opening presentation
Main hall: Urban Energy Forum president Kurt Bollinger will talk about accelerating the transition to renewable energy.

11:00 A.M.-12:00 P.M.   Morning workshops
Hall B: "Financing Green Energy"
presented by Eloisa Davide, CEO, Global Energy Investment Bank

Hall C: "How Governments Can Lead the Way"
presented by Alan Holm, Chair, UK Energy Initiative

12:00-2:00 P.M.   Lunch break

2:00-3:30 P.M.   Afternoon workshops
Hall B: "Using the Power of the Sun"
presented by Lester Agarwal, Founder, South Asian Energy Consortium (CEO, Solar India)

Hall C: "Advancements in Battery Technology"
presented by Richard Liu, Professor of Engineering, Queensland University

3:30-4:30 P.M.   Roundtable discussion
Main hall: Urban Energy Forum member Stephanie Bernard will lead a discussion on promoting renewable energy in the media.

---

186. According to the e-mail, what is true about cities?

(A) They will each host future forums.
(B) They need better transportation systems.
(C) They will become more crowded.
(D) They could suffer more frequent power outages.

187. What is available on the Urban Energy Forum's Web site?

(A) Sponsorship applications
(B) Copies of a program
(C) Refund request forms
(D) Transcripts of lectures

188. What is true about Mr. Patel?

(A) He purchased a ticket before February 1.
(B) His ticket grants him entry only to the main hall.
(C) He will be participating in more than one workshop.
(D) His firm is a sponsor of the 9th Urban Energy Forum.

189. Which workshop leader does Mr. Patel have a professional relationship with?

(A) Alan Holm
(B) Richard Liu
(C) Eloisa Davide
(D) Lester Agarwal

190. What is indicated about Day 2 of the forum?

(A) Some speakers will give a presentation more than one time.
(B) All participants will be provided with one hour for lunch.
(C) A televised debate on renewable energy will take place.
(D) A presentation on battery technology will be given.

GO ON TO THE NEXT PAGE

Gumbo Grocers Rewards Program
APPLICATION FORM

Drop off the completed form at your local Gumbo's customer service counter or mail to Gumbo Grocers Rewards Program, 104 Jefferson St., Richmond, VA 23284. If you have an online account, you may also sign up at www.shopgumbo.com.

Name: _____

Address: _____

Phone: _____

E-mail: _____

Check <u>here</u> to receive our weekly newsletter and get discount coupons sent to your e-mail inbox.

Program details:

- Earn 1 point for every dollar you spend in our store or online. Earn points on groceries, medical prescriptions, magazines, and more!

- Every 200 points you earn can be used toward bigger discounts on your grocery bill.

- Instantly earn 100 points by referring a friend who signs up.

Good News for Our Customers!

Customers who earn rewards points by shopping at their local Gumbo Grocers and Tiptop Appliance stores will now be able to use their rewards points when filling up at Fullerton gas stations. Every 100 points can be redeemed for $1 in savings on your fuel purchase.

This expansion of rewards promises to deliver greater value and savings to Fullerton's customers, as well as both Gumbo and Tiptop shoppers.

Fullerton's Gas Rewards Program is available at over 25 retail firms across the country and may be used at thousands of gas stations nationwide. Learn more at www.fullertongas.com or ask about registering for gas rewards at your local Gumbo or Tiptop.

To   Dale Wilson <d.wilson@okmail.com>

From   Karen Sirling <k.sirling@shopgumbo.com>

Subject   Rewards points

Date   April 24

Dear Mr. Wilson,

Thank you for contacting us. I double-checked your account information as requested. It seems that we neglected to credit you for the 64 points that you earned on your trip to the grocery store last week. I have corrected your information just now. As for the other question, I can confirm that your account has been updated to reflect the referral that you made last month. Altogether, since becoming a member last February, you have earned 350 points.

I encourage you to sign up for an online account on our Web site so that you can keep track of your points and get access to other products and services, such as our recipe collection, budgeting tool, and more.

Thank you for your business!

Sincerely,

Karen Sirling
Customer Service Representative
Gumbo Grocers

---

191. What is true about the Gumbo Grocers' Rewards Program?

(A) A referral earns enough points for a discount on gas.
(B) Online purchases qualify for the largest number of points.
(C) A coupon will be provided for each 200 points earned.
(D) Prescriptions are worth less points than groceries.

192. What is suggested about Fullerton Gas Company?

(A) It is going to supply automotive services at some retail stores.
(B) It has negotiated deals with more than 25 different companies.
(C) It is currently in the process of increasing its gas station locations.
(D) It has its head office in the same building as Gumbo Grocers.

193. In the announcement, the word "deliver" in paragraph 2, line 1, is closest in meaning to

(A) pass on
(B) take in
(C) carry on
(D) drop out

194. Why did Ms. Sirling write the e-mail?

(A) To verify a recent order
(B) To extend a special offer
(C) To request payment of a bill
(D) To address a couple of inquiries

195. What does Ms. Sirling indicate about Mr. Wilson?

(A) He has not redeemed any points.
(B) His membership is expiring very soon.
(C) He earned at least 100 points last month.
(D) His online password was recently changed.

GO ON TO THE NEXT PAGE

Plumtree Nutritional Advice

HOME	BLOG	Q&A	LOG IN

Tips for Healthy Living

Posted by: Brad Shear, Head Nutritionist

Staying fit can be challenging, but I have compiled the lists below to help my clients keep on track:

Be sure to
- Drink at least three glasses of water per day
- Exercise for 20 to 30 minutes, three times per week
- Get seven hours of sleep every night

Be careful not to
- Eat dinner within one hour of going to bed
- Sit down for more than three hours at a time

To learn more, click on one of the diet and exercise plans below and e-mail me to set up an initial consultation.

Plan	Prices
FreshStart	$30
FreshUp	$35
FreshPlus	$40
FreshPremium	$45

To	Brad Shear <bshear@plumtreenutrition.com>
From	Madison Costa <maddiecosta77@rentmail.net>
Date	April 28
Subject	Consultation

Dear Mr. Shear,

I'm writing because I'd like to set up an initial appointment with you to discuss the plans on your Web site. You came highly recommended to me by one of my coworkers, Kerry Franklin. She follows your FreshPlus plan and says that it has greatly improved her health. I'm excited to be a new client of yours, but I don't want to pay as much as she does and I also don't want the cheapest plan.

My main problem is that I have recently switched to working a later shift than I previously had at my office, and I've been having trouble adjusting my sleep and meal schedule. I'm hoping to meet with you either in the morning on May 2 or in the afternoon of May 3, since I have to travel for a training activity with my company on May 4.

Madison Costa

Plumtree Nutritional Advice Employee Timesheet

Please enter the number of hours that you have worked for each day of the week.

Employee name: <u>Brad Shear</u>

	May 1	May 2	May 3	May 4	May 5
Client consultation	4h	6h	0h	6h	4h
Administration	0h	1h	0h	1h	2h
Training	0h	0h	6h	0h	0h
TOTAL HOURS	**4h**	**7h**	**6h**	**7h**	**6h**

196. What advice does Mr. Shear give to his clients?

(A) Consume at least three meals a day
(B) Protect the skin from sunlight
(C) Participate in athletic competitions
(D) Engage in regular physical activities

197. What is mentioned about the FreshPlus plan?

(A) It will be updated on Plumtree's Web site.
(B) It will be discussed at an upcoming conference.
(C) It has been used by Ms. Costa's colleague.
(D) It has been discounted for a limited time.

198. How much is Ms. Costa willing to pay for a plan?

(A) $30
(B) $35
(C) $40
(D) $45

199. What will Ms. Costa do in May?

(A) Attend a corporate event
(B) Apply for health insurance
(C) Change the time of an appointment
(D) Take a day off for vacation

200. When did Ms. Costa most likely meet with Mr. Shear?

(A) On May 2
(B) On May 3
(C) On May 4
(D) On May 5

This is the end of the test. You may review Parts 5, 6, and 7 if you finish the test early.

TEST 6 점수 환산표

TEST 6은 무사히 잘 마치셨나요? 맞은 개수를 세어본 후 아래의 점수 환산표를 통해 자신의 점수를 예상해 보세요.

전체 난이도　　**쉬운 난이도**

파트별 난이도　PART 5　하 ●○○
　　　　　　　　　PART 6　하 ●○○
　　　　　　　　　PART 7　중 ●●○

정답 수	리딩 점수	정답 수	리딩 점수
98~100개	465~495점	47~49개	200~210점
95~97개	445~460점	44~46개	185~195점
92~94개	425~440점	41~43개	170~180점
89~91개	405~420점	38~40개	155~165점
86~88개	390~400점	35~37개	140~150점
83~85개	375~385점	32~34개	125~135점
80~82개	360~370점	29~31개	110~120점
77~79개	340~355점	26~28개	95~105점
74~76개	325~335점	23~25개	80~90점
71~73개	305~320점	20~22개	65~75점
68~70개	290~300점	17~19개	50~60점
65~67개	275~285점	14~16개	35~45점
62~64개	260~270점	11~13개	20~30점
59~61개	245~255점	8~10개	10~20점
56~58개	235~240점	5~7개	5~10점
53~55개	225~230점	2~4개	5~10점
50~52개	215~220점	0~1개	0~5점

* 점수 환산표는 해커스토익 사이트 유저 데이터를 근거로 제작되었으며, 주기적으로 업데이트되고 있습니다. 해커스토익 사이트
　(Hackers.co.kr)에서 최신 경향을 반영하여 업데이트된 점수환산기를 이용하실 수 있습니다. (토익 > 토익게시판 > 토익점수환산기)

TEST 7

PART 5
PART 6
PART 7
점수 환산표

잠깐! 테스트 전 확인사항

1. 문제 풀이에 방해가 되는 물건을 모두 치우셨나요?   예 ☐
2. Answer Sheet, 연필, 지우개를 준비하셨나요?   예 ☐
3. 시계를 준비하셨나요?   예 ☐

모든 준비가 완료되었으면 목표 점수를 떠올린 후 테스트를 시작합니다.

문제 풀이를 마치는 시간은 지금부터 **75분 후인** _____**시** _____**분입니다.**

테스트 시간은 **총 75분**이며, 시험 종료 전 2~3분은 정답 검토 및 답안지 마킹을 위해 사용합니다.

READING TEST

In this section, you must demonstrate your ability to read and comprehend English. You will be given a variety of texts and asked to answer questions about these texts. This section is divided into three parts and will take 75 minutes to complete.

Do not mark the answers in your test book. Use the answer sheet that is separately provided.

PART 5

Directions: In each question, you will be asked to review a statement that is missing a word or phrase. Four answer choices will be provided for each statement. Select the best answer and mark the corresponding letter (A), (B), (C), or (D) on the answer sheet.

---

101. It is ------- than before for small companies to attain profitability due to the tax increase.

(A) hard
(B) hardly
(C) harder
(D) hardest

102. Power tools should be handled ------- to minimize the risk of serious injury.

(A) cautious
(B) caution
(C) cautiously
(D) more cautious

103. The gift card may be used 24 hours ------- the cardholder has activated it online.

(A) later
(B) after
(C) while
(D) sometimes

104. A number of the firm's problems were ------- to a lack of proper leadership.

(A) attributed
(B) relied
(C) mentioned
(D) determined

105. ------- the request of residents, the council installed street lamps around Tyler Park.

(A) At
(B) From
(C) Under
(D) Among

106. Automated features of the new factory equipment eliminate the need for personnel to monitor it -------.

(A) overly
(B) abruptly
(C) constantly
(D) immensely

107. Mr. Zendaya is a competent employee with an individual ------- in marketing.

(A) interested
(B) interests
(C) interest
(D) interesting

108. The old bridge has become structurally ------- and needs to be fixed.

(A) innovative
(B) temporary
(C) unstable
(D) precise

109. The members of the Help-A-Neighbor Organization ------- a variety of local charitable groups.

(A) supportive
(B) supports
(C) supporting
(D) support

110. Young people are drawn to big cities by the promise of ------- and opportunity.

(A) excite
(B) excited
(C) excitement
(D) excitable

111. Ms. Lawrence is in ------- of training new employees for three weeks as she thinks this will give them enough time to adjust.

(A) response
(B) favor
(C) advance
(D) order

112. Every month, the National Forest Society provides contributors with updates on its ongoing conservation -------.

(A) notice
(B) efforts
(C) facility
(D) contacts

113. BT Industries organized a dinner banquet in honor ------- its newly appointed CEO.

(A) to
(B) toward
(C) of
(D) following

114. After a year of construction, the housing development is ------- a long way from being completed.

(A) still
(B) behind
(C) so
(D) far

115. The country's stock market achieved gains, ------- other nations suffered losses.

(A) thus
(B) besides
(C) whereas
(D) concerning

116. The manager wants to know ------- might be willing to work over the weekend.

(A) who
(B) whom
(C) how
(D) those

117. Over the past few months, Ms. Saer ------- colleagues with her deep knowledge of computer engineering.

(A) impresses
(B) impressing
(C) impressive
(D) has impressed

118. Attracting new customers costs more than retaining ------- ones.

(A) existing
(B) existed
(C) exist
(D) existence

119. Financial experts have not seen ------- indications that the global economy has come out of recession.

(A) firm
(B) firmly
(C) firms
(D) firmness

120. Manufacturers are looking for ways to ------- lower operating costs.

(A) considering
(B) considerate
(C) considerable
(D) considerably

GO ON TO THE NEXT PAGE

121. The house is in good condition for its age, but some floor tiles and lighting fixtures may need to be -------.

(A) filled
(B) compared
(C) replaced
(D) initiated

122. Capable leaders are ------- to the ideas of other people.

(A) informative
(B) successful
(C) attractive
(D) receptive

123. The photographer ------- image is selected for this year's magazine cover will be given a cash prize of $10,000.

(A) that
(B) when
(C) whose
(D) whoever

124. Interns are expected to make an exclusive ------- to the company.

(A) property
(B) commitment
(C) negotiation
(D) appreciation

125. Mercura Auto decided that it will move its production plant to Mexico, ------- costly that is.

(A) once
(B) however
(C) very
(D) just as

126. Shutting down Web servers for ------- maintenance is vital as it can prevent system errors.

(A) periods
(B) periodic
(C) periodically
(D) periodicals

127. Mr. Tsai receives a 10 percent commission for ------- sale he makes.

(A) some
(B) each
(C) all
(D) few

128. The positive results of a recent visitor survey ------- Scottsdale's reputation as an excellent tourist destination.

(A) contradict
(B) consult
(C) reinforce
(D) permit

129. Thornton & Jones settled its disagreement with the client ------- to avoid negative publicity.

(A) wishfully
(B) confidentially
(C) extensively
(D) incrementally

130. Students are encouraged to participate in a sport that offers a ------- from the everyday stress of school work.

(A) releasable
(B) released
(C) releasing
(D) release

PART 6

Directions: In this part, you will be asked to read four English texts. Each text is missing a word, phrase, or sentence. Select the answer choice that correctly completes the text and mark the corresponding letter (A), (B), (C), or (D) on the answer sheet.

Questions 131-134 refer to the following notice.

Notice to all Diego Corporation employees

The staff lunchroom will be inaccessible ------- June 4 and June 7 to allow for some minor
                                                131.
renovations to be done. The primary improvement will be the addition of a window to one of the

walls to let in more sunlight. Moreover, old appliances will be substituted with modern ones.

-------, a much larger stainless-steel refrigerator will be installed. In the meantime, -------
132.   133.
Conference Rooms 1 and 2 during your lunch breaks. -------. We appreciate your patience and
                                                        134.
understanding in this matter.

131. (A) since
(B) with
(C) into
(D) between

132. (A) In case
(B) By all means
(C) For example
(D) On the whole

133. (A) utilizes
(B) utilizing
(C) utilization
(D) utilize

134. (A) Those schedules have been posted on the doors as well.
(B) Both spaces are reserved for that specific purpose.
(C) Some staff members have asked for more time.
(D) The breaks were supposed to last less than an hour.

GO ON TO THE NEXT PAGE

Kendra Sampson
338 West Elm Drive
Burlington, Vermont 05402

Dear Ms. Sampson,

We are writing to notify you that your subscription to *Literature Now* ------- on June 1. If you do
135.

not take any action to prevent your membership from ending before then, no further charges will

be ------- to your credit card. However, if you wish to continue your subscription, you can do so by
136.

contacting us at 555-3922.

-------. For starters, you will be able to enjoy more short stories and essays from some of today's
137.

leading writers. You can also save $24 over the ------- of the year with our May renewal discount.
138.

We hope you continue to subscribe to *Literature Now*.

Sincerely,

Literature Now Team

---

135. (A) expired
(B) expiring
(C) will expire
(D) is expired

136. (A) applying
(B) applied
(C) applies
(D) apply

137. (A) Trial subscriptions typically run for a
six-month period.
(B) You can expect to receive the latest
edition within just a few weeks.
(C) Our records indicate that you have been
a reader of *Literature Now* for two years.
(D) There are plenty of reasons to subscribe
to our award-winning publication again.

138. (A) course
(B) limit
(C) piece
(D) width

Questions 139-142 refer to the following article.

ALICE SPRINGS (August 26)— Owler Inc. was selected for an upcoming ------- project by Alice
139.

Springs City Hall. It will install solar panels at all local public schools. -------. The project begins
140.

on October 1 at Gillen High School, ------- will be equipped with 225 panels. Next, Owler Inc. will
141.

move on to East Side Elementary and Braitling Middle schools. When completed, the panels are

expected to result in thousands of dollars in annual ------- for the school board. "We chose Owler
142.

Inc. because of its low cost and wealth of experience," said Alice Springs Mayor Tanya McCrindle.

139. (A) energetic
(B) energy
(C) energized
(D) energetically

140. (A) Several environmental groups have indicated their support for the project.
(B) Local residents have volunteered to perform the installation work.
(C) They apologized to parents for the additional delay.
(D) The winner of the contract will remain anonymous.

141. (A) where
(B) whenever
(C) which
(D) what

142. (A) subsidies
(B) estimates
(C) revenues
(D) savings

GO ON TO THE NEXT PAGE

Questions 143-146 refer to the following e-mail.

TO　　　　: Andrea Stinton <stinton.a@kuvarik.com>
FROM　　　: Leroy Wauters <wauters.l@kuvarik.com>
SUBJECT : Recent inspection
DATE　　　: November 17

Dear Ms. Stinton,

Yesterday, I ------- a mandatory inspection of the Kuvarik production plant in Donetsk. Though
　　　　　　143.

most items on the checklist were satisfactory, I discovered two potential ------- issues. First of
　　　　　　　　　　　　　　　　　　　　　　　　　　　　144.

all, we need to add three more fire extinguishers due to a change in regulations last year. -------.
　　145.

Secondly, I saw that some handrails are missing along one stairway, and ------- would be essential
　　　　　　　　　　　　　　　　　　　　　　　　　　　　　　　　　　　146.

in the event of an emergency. Before I place an order for new handrails, I would like to discuss the

various options with you. When you are available today, please drop by my office.

Regards,

Leroy Wauters
Facility Manager

143. (A) scheduled
(B) postponed
(C) canceled
(D) conducted

144. (A) service
(B) safety
(C) security
(D) personnel

145. (A) If this isn't done promptly, we will be
issued a fine.
(B) The new regulations require that we
update our employee handbook.
(C) New employees were trained to use the
fire extinguishers.
(D) As expected, we met our production
quota last year.

146. (A) it
(B) that
(C) theirs
(D) they

PART 7

Directions: In this part, you will be asked to read several texts, such as advertisements, articles, instant messages, or examples of business correspondence. Each text is followed by several questions. Select the best answer and mark the corresponding letter (A), (B), (C), or (D) on your answer sheet.

Questions 147-148 refer to the following coupon.

BENISON HILLS $9.99 for each admission ticket
It's Our First Day of the Season!   Valid from 11 A.M. to 8 P.M. on March 31 only

- Can be used for all rides, including the famous Cliffdrop Roller Coaster
- Not valid for the Rocket Ship Simulation Theater
- Valid for up to five people
- Cannot be used with any other offer

www.benisonhills.com / 555-6616
7554 Grand Ledge Highway, Sunfield, MI 48890

147. Where most likely can the coupon be used?

(A) At a train station
(B) At a fitness center
(C) At a music hall
(D) At an amusement park

148. What is mentioned about Benison Hills?

(A) It has a special entrance for groups.
(B) It is famous for its restaurant selection.
(C) It has an attraction that is well-known.
(D) It offers discounts throughout March.

GO ON TO THE NEXT PAGE

Questions 149-150 refer to the following online chat discussion.

Bastian Guthrie	[4:35 P.M.]	I don't think it's in our best interest to keep working with JEPN Manufacturing.
Marie Holcomb	[4:38 P.M.]	Why? Is there a problem?
Bastian Guthrie	[4:43 P.M.]	Their last order had to be returned because many of the components were faulty.
Marie Holcomb	[4:44 P.M.]	I see. Should we break the contract? It doesn't end for a couple of months.
Bastian Guthrie	[4:46 P.M.]	No. But I don't think we should sign a new one. I'd like you to find a replacement supplier.
Marie Holcomb	[4:48 P.M.]	I will see to it. I have a list of manufacturers on my computer. They will probably charge more than JEPN, though.
Bastian Guthrie	[4:49 P.M.]	That's all right. We should see fewer production delays, which will save us money in the long run.

Send

149. Why does Mr. Guthrie want to replace JEPN Manufacturing?

(A) It has increased its prices.
(B) It sent some defective parts.
(C) It delays retailing its products.
(D) It uses outdated technology.

150. At 4:48 P.M., what does Ms. Holcomb most likely mean when she writes, "I will see to it"?

(A) She will meet with a manufacturer.
(B) She will download some files to her computer.
(C) She will search for alternative suppliers.
(D) She will make sure to meet a production deadline.

Questions 151-152 refer to the following e-mail.

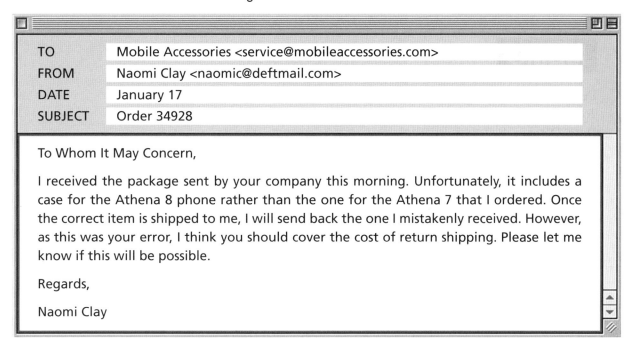

TO   Mobile Accessories <service@mobileaccessories.com>

FROM   Naomi Clay <naomic@deftmail.com>

DATE   January 17

SUBJECT   Order 34928

To Whom It May Concern,

I received the package sent by your company this morning. Unfortunately, it includes a case for the Athena 8 phone rather than the one for the Athena 7 that I ordered. Once the correct item is shipped to me, I will send back the one I mistakenly received. However, as this was your error, I think you should cover the cost of return shipping. Please let me know if this will be possible.

Regards,

Naomi Clay

151. Why did Ms. Clay send the e-mail?

(A) She did not receive a package.
(B) She was overcharged for a service.
(C) She was sent the wrong product.
(D) She did not select the right model.

152. What does Ms. Clay want Mobile Accessories to do?

(A) Confirm an address
(B) Provide a refund
(C) Cancel an order
(D) Cover a cost

GO ON TO THE NEXT PAGE

MEMO

From: Spencer Buffone, Building Services Officer
To: Tenants of Hylox Tower
Date: October 4
Subject: Annual Window Cleaning Schedule

I have arranged for workers to clean the exterior windows of Hylox Tower next week, from October 10 to 12. Long-term tenants of Hylox Tower are already familiar with the process. However, businesses that have moved in within the past year, including Razor Lee Entertainment and Wheatstock Publishing, should note that windows must be fully closed on the day of cleaning. Occupants are also advised to close their blinds to ensure their privacy when the workers are cleaning the windows.

The window cleaning schedule is as follows:

North side of building	October 10 / 10 A.M.-5 P.M.
Southeast side of building	October 11 / 8 A.M.-3 P.M.
Southwest side of building	October 12 / 12 P.M.-7 P.M.

153. Who will receive the memo?

(A) Parking attendants
(B) Building occupants
(C) Construction workers
(D) Tour members

154. What are the recipients told to do?

(A) Close the coverings of some windows
(B) Welcome Wheatstock Publishing staff
(C) State a preference before October 12
(D) Call a front desk for janitorial assistance

155. What is NOT suggested about Hylox Tower?

(A) Its exterior is cleaned once a year.
(B) Its maintenance is handled by Mr. Buffone.
(C) It currently has some space left for rent.
(D) It is occupied by multiple businesses.

We're Moving!

After 25 years at the same location, Nickel Books will be moving to 3408 Polson Street.* The reason is that the storeroom of our current building does not have enough space for our growing inventory. The new store will open on April 30. To celebrate, we're offering a 15 percent discount on all books and magazines from May 1 to 15. In addition, anyone making a purchase of $25 and over will receive a free tote bag with our logo.

*From Exit 5 of Panhurst Station, walk straight for about two blocks. We're located above a restaurant called Color Kitchen and occupy the second and third floors of the building.

156. Why will Nickel Books move to a new location?

(A) A storage area is insufficient.
(B) Property rent rose significantly.
(C) A parking facility is closed.
(D) Increased competition reduced sales.

157. What is indicated about Nickel Books?

(A) It will sell both new and used reading materials.
(B) It will offer clients a choice of free gifts.
(C) It will have fewer employees than before.
(D) It will share a building with another business.

GO ON TO THE NEXT PAGE

Questions 158-160 refer to the following article.

Casa Bella Announces Plans to Launch in India
By Reena Singh

Casa Bella, the Italian furniture retailer, has announced plans to open its first branch in India. The company plans to construct the store in Mumbai, with the opening tentatively scheduled for March. — [1] —. The store will cost Casa Bella $18 million to build and will offer the same products and services as its other global branches.

In addition to the Mumbai outlet, stores in other Indian cities are planned. According to company representative Daniella Fieri, the growth of the Indian economy has made the country an attractive target. — [2] —. Ms. Fieri also indicated that because the company already operates a production plant for some of its product lines in India, the shipping costs for stores will be low. Furniture industry experts have high expectations, and the value of the company's stock has gone up by nearly 10 percent since the store launch was announced. — [3] —.

Should the retail outlets in India be successful, Casa Bella will likely expand into Southeast Asia. The retailer is already a market leader in Europe and North America. — [4] —.

158. What is the article mainly about?

(A) An opportunity for investment in a business
(B) An expansion plan of a retail company
(C) A merger between two companies in India
(D) A decision to discontinue underperforming product lines

159. What is NOT indicated about Casa Bella?

(A) It aims to open retail outlets in multiple Indian cities.
(B) It manufactures some goods in India.
(C) It launched operations in Southeast Asia.
(D) It went up in value on the stock market.

160. In which of the positions marked [1], [2], [3], and [4] does the following sentence best belong?

"Consumers now have more income to spend on items for the home."

(A) [1]
(B) [2]
(C) [3]
(D) [4]

Questions 161-164 refer to the following e-mail.

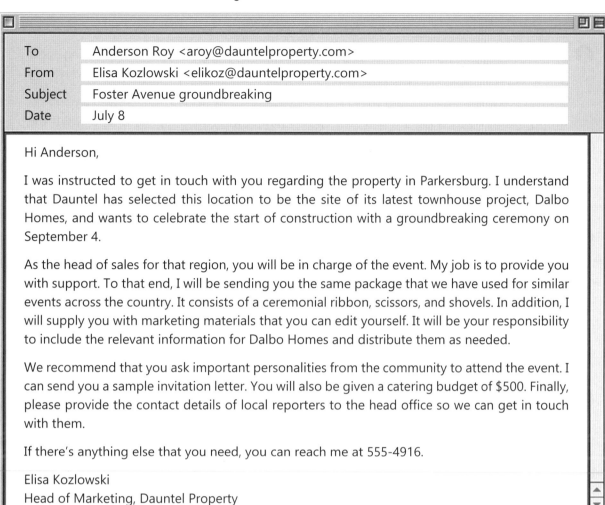

To	Anderson Roy <aroy@dauntelproperty.com>
From	Elisa Kozlowski <elikoz@dauntelproperty.com>
Subject	Foster Avenue groundbreaking
Date	July 8

Hi Anderson,

I was instructed to get in touch with you regarding the property in Parkersburg. I understand that Dauntel has selected this location to be the site of its latest townhouse project, Dalbo Homes, and wants to celebrate the start of construction with a groundbreaking ceremony on September 4.

As the head of sales for that region, you will be in charge of the event. My job is to provide you with support. To that end, I will be sending you the same package that we have used for similar events across the country. It consists of a ceremonial ribbon, scissors, and shovels. In addition, I will supply you with marketing materials that you can edit yourself. It will be your responsibility to include the relevant information for Dalbo Homes and distribute them as needed.

We recommend that you ask important personalities from the community to attend the event. I can send you a sample invitation letter. You will also be given a catering budget of $500. Finally, please provide the contact details of local reporters to the head office so we can get in touch with them.

If there's anything else that you need, you can reach me at 555-4916.

Elisa Kozlowski
Head of Marketing, Dauntel Property

---

161. Why was the e-mail sent?

(A) To inquire about a property
(B) To inform a colleague about a plan
(C) To congratulate a client
(D) To confirm the agenda of a meeting

162. What is suggested about Dauntel Property?

(A) It builds structures around the country.
(B) It specializes in managing commercial properties.
(C) It plans to construct affordable housing.
(D) It beat several competitors to win a contract.

163. What will Mr. Roy be responsible for?

(A) Hiring staff for a special event
(B) Supervising a construction project
(C) Revising some promotional materials
(D) Drafting a service contract

164. Who does Ms. Kozlowski recommend that Mr. Roy contact?

(A) A printing shop
(B) Local reporters
(C) A catering company
(D) Community representatives

GO ON TO THE NEXT PAGE

Questions 165-168 refer to the following online chat discussion.

Aria Torrez [2:16 P.M.] Do any of you have a problem with your new parking spot? I was assigned one all the way in Lot G, which is a very long walk from the office.

Mindy Summers [2:17 P.M.] My new spot is farther away than my old one, too. But the company needs the closer spaces for clients, so I understand why it was assigned to me.

Raymond Wells [2:17 P.M.] Aria, have you brought this up with our manager? Maybe the company can find you a more reasonable location.

Aria Torrez [2:20 P.M.] I tried earlier. She said that the best she can do is to put me on a waiting list.

Carmen Salgado [2:20 P.M.] Why don't you just take the bus? I get dropped off at Harrison Avenue, and it's a short walk to the building entrance from there. Several other buses stop there as well.

Raymond Wells [2:23 P.M.] Or maybe you can carpool with me, Aria. I park right in front of the building's rear entrance.

Aria Torrez [2:24 P.M.] I'm not sure that carpooling will work since I've been taking a lot of extra shifts lately. I'm going to check the bus option, though. Thank you all!

Send

---

165. What problem does Ms. Torrez have?

(A) She has been assigned extra shifts.
(B) She needs a larger parking space.
(C) She has to walk too far to the office.
(D) She arrives to work later than before.

166. Why most likely were parking spaces reassigned?

(A) To allow employees to get to their car quicker
(B) To improve visitor access to the building
(C) To make room for major construction work
(D) To reserve more spaces for management

167. At 2:20 P.M., what does Ms. Torrez most likely mean when she writes, "I tried earlier"?

(A) She discussed an issue with a manager.
(B) She has not tried another method of transportation.
(C) She brought up a problem in a team meeting.
(D) She was not able to get to a bus station on time.

168. What is suggested about Ms. Salgado?

(A) She is satisfied with her new assignment.
(B) She takes public transportation to work.
(C) She handles travel arrangements for a firm.
(D) She is willing to trade parking spots.

무료 토익 학습자료·취업정보 제공 Hackers.co.kr

Questions 169-171 refer to the following notice.

Before entering the **Iceland Heritage Gallery**, please review our basic regulations. These apply to all ticket holders. Complying with these will ensure that all visitors have an enjoyable experience. — [1] —.

- You may bring a camera inside any of the display halls, but be aware that some items may not be photographed. — [2] —. These objects are marked accordingly.
- Large bags may not be brought beyond the lobby. You may store baggage and other belongings in one of our lockers, which are located across from the gift shop.
- Gallery visitors may stroll around our garden during the summer months of June through August. Note that it is closed to the public on July 10 as our annual fund-raiser is scheduled for that day. — [3] —.
- We ask that you begin proceeding to the gallery's exit 30 minutes before closing time. — [4] —. An announcement will be made at this time.

169. Where would the notice most likely be found?

(A) Next to a ticket counter
(B) Outside a film screening room
(C) Beside an administrative office
(D) Inside a souvenir store

170. Why is access to the garden restricted on July 10?

(A) A government inspection is scheduled.
(B) A maintenance task is performed.
(C) A special exhibit is arranged.
(D) A charity event is held.

171. In which of the positions marked [1], [2], [3], and [4] does the following sentence best belong?

"This is upon the request of the individuals who lent us the pieces."

(A) [1]
(B) [2]
(C) [3]
(D) [4]

GO ON TO THE NEXT PAGE

Try Using Jade Airlines' Easy Board Check-in Service

Your January 25 flight from Muscat to Istanbul is just one week away. To avoid having to wait in line to receive your boarding pass, why not use our Easy Board check-in service? When you enter the departure section of Khalid International Airport, head to Area K. Our check-in machines are conveniently located there, adjacent to a screen listing departures and arrivals. To begin, enter your reservation number. The next step is to scan the picture page of your passport. After this, the machine will supply your boarding pass. At this stage, proceed with any check-in luggage to Desk 7.

If you prefer not to use our Easy Board check-in service, you may proceed directly to our regular check-in counters. Do note, though, that we will be completely switching to a digital check-in service on April 15.

172. What is the main purpose of the information?

(A) To recommend that a deal be taken advantage of
(B) To make it known that a facility's layout has changed
(C) To announce that a flight has arrived
(D) To suggest that an electronic service be used

173. Where can Jade Airlines' check-in machines be found?

(A) Next to a display
(B) Within a lounge
(C) At an entrance
(D) Beside an elevator

174. What can passengers do at Desk 7?

(A) Have a boarding pass examined
(B) Pick up a set of guidelines
(C) Receive an Internet password
(D) Leave some baggage

175. What will change starting from April 15?

(A) Departure times
(B) Luggage restrictions
(C) Check-in procedures
(D) Refund policies

GO ON TO THE NEXT PAGE

Greenfield City to Introduce New Community Center Hours

August 10—In a press release issued on August 4, Greenfield City Council announced plans to extend the operating hours of the community centers run by the municipal government. This decision is based on responses in questionnaires distributed in May to solicit feedback from residents on city services. The press release specified that the Oakwood and Selma community centers will remain open until 8:30 P.M., while the Belleville and Blanchard centers will close at 8:00 and 9:00 P.M., respectively. The new schedules will start on August 15. Wilma Gomez, head of the Department of Public Services, stated in an interview on August 8 that the changes in community center hours are part of an ongoing effort by the city government to make life more convenient for residents.

August 12

Wilma Gomez
Department of Public Services
387 Paterson Street
Greenfield, MA 02125

Dear Ms. Gomez,

I am contacting you regarding the recently announced changes to the hours of operation for our city's community centers. In general, I am in favor of the plan because I have signed up for a number of programs since I retired last year. However, I was disappointed to learn that the community center nearest to my apartment building would only be staying open for an additional 30 minutes—until 8:00 P.M. This strikes me as unfair because the other three facilities will close an hour later than they used to. I would like to ask that your department reconsider this decision and ensure that all of the community centers have their operating hours extended by the same amount of time. Thank you.

Sincerely,

Adam Ferris

Adam Ferris

176. According to the article, what happened in May?

(A) An election was held.
(B) A survey was conducted.
(C) An announcement was made.
(D) A service was introduced.

177. When will community center operating hours be extended?

(A) On August 4
(B) On August 8
(C) On August 10
(D) On August 15

178. What is suggested about Mr. Ferris?

(A) He is currently unemployed.
(B) He completed a questionnaire.
(C) He recently moved to Greenfield.
(D) He is a volunteer at a city facility.

179. Which community center is closest to Mr. Ferris's residence?

(A) Oakwood Community Center
(B) Selma Community Center
(C) Belleville Community Center
(D) Blanchard Community Center

180. What does Mr. Ferris request?

(A) A modification to a plan
(B) A meeting with an official
(C) A decision about a proposal
(D) A copy of a schedule

GO ON TO THE NEXT PAGE

National Space Museum
Special Exhibit Schedule — Summer

Name	Description	Dates
The Apollo Program	Learn about the space program that resulted in humans visiting the moon.	May 26-June 15
Communicating by Satellite	Explore the different roles of modern communication satellites and how they function.	June 16-July 5
Exploring the Solar System	Examine exhibits on the various spacecraft sent from Earth to other planets in our Solar System.	July 6-July 25
Journey to Mars	Discover the proposed manned missions to Mars and learn about the various challenges that must be overcome to make them a reality.	July 26-August 15

All special exhibits will be set up in Bergman Hall. Access to these exhibits is not included in the regular admission price. The additional fee is $11 for adults and $8 for students.

Attention All Museum Visitors

Due to a problem with a fire sprinkler on the second floor of the museum, water damage has occurred in Bergman Hall. Fortunately, none of the items on display were damaged as a result of this incident. However, the hall will be closed from June 25 to July 2 while repairs are being made. The exhibit in this hall will be temporarily moved to Sanderson Hall on the main floor during this period. We apologize for any inconvenience this may cause. Visitors who are unable to find the relocated exhibit should ask one of our employees for assistance. Thank you.

181. In the schedule, the phrase "set up" in paragraph 1, line 1, is closest in meaning to

(A) adapted
(B) developed
(C) arranged
(D) operated

182. What is true about the National Space Museum?

(A) It closes for part of the year.
(B) It charges extra for some displays.
(C) It hosts several special exhibits at once.
(D) It features items borrowed from other institutions.

183. According to the notice, what problem has occurred?

(A) An item was misplaced.
(B) A device malfunctioned.
(C) An exhibit was lost.
(D) A case was damaged.

184. Which exhibit has been moved to the Sanderson Hall?

(A) The Apollo Program
(B) Communicating by Satellite
(C) Exploring the Solar System
(D) Journey to Mars

185. What are some museum visitors instructed to do?

(A) Talk to a staff member
(B) Visit a different branch
(C) Request a ticket refund
(D) Fill out a questionnaire

GO ON TO THE NEXT PAGE

Questions 186-190 refer to the following memo, advertisement, and notice.

MEYERHOFFER INSURANCE

MEMO

To: All staff
From: James Loris, Human Resources Manager
Subject: Company outing
Date: January 11

If you haven't let me know whether you plan to come along on next month's company outing, don't forget that this must be done by the end of the week. It will be a one-day trip, and the company will cover all food, transportation, and entertainment costs. Each of you may bring along one companion. The outing will take place on Saturday, February 22. We will use the Brunswick Ferry to travel to Simon island and return to the mainland. Simon Island is a lovely place, and I would recommend visiting all of the local attractions. You can learn more at www.visitsimonisland.com. Anyway, please tell me if you plan to attend by Friday. Thank you.

Come to the Windward Inn

Located on Georgia's Simon Island, the Windward Inn sits on a magnificent property with a view of the Atlantic Ocean. Our comfortable rooms feature flat-screen TVs and Wi-Fi. Beach cabins are also available to rent by the day. Guests will enjoy access to a world-class golf course, a fitness center, a swimming pool, and meeting rooms. Dining options include a seafood restaurant and a steakhouse. Popular local attractions include the historic Fort Frederick Museum and the Simon Island Lighthouse Museum. For reservations, call 555-4081 or go to www.windwardinn.com.

The Brunswick Ferry
NOTICE TO PASSENGERS

Please note that the spring schedule will take effect next month.

RATES (roundtrip fare plus tax)

Adults:	$32
Seniors 65 and over:	$30
Children 15 and under:	$22

WINTER SCHEDULE
December 1 – February 28 (5 days a week, Thursday to Monday)

Leave Brunswick	Arrive Simon Island	Leave Simon Island	Arrive Brunswick
8:30 A.M.	9:15 A.M.	9:45 A.M.	10:30 A.M.
11:00 A.M.	11:45 A.M.	4:15 P.M.	5:00 P.M.

SPRING SCHEDULE
March 1 – May 31 (7 days a week)

Leave Brunswick	Arrive Simon Island	Leave Simon Island	Arrive Brunswick
9:00 A.M.	9:45 A.M.	10:15 A.M.	11:00 A.M.
11:30 A.M.	12:15 P.M.	12:45 P.M.	1:30 P.M.
2:00 P.M.	2:15 P.M.	5:00 P.M.	5:45 P.M.

Passengers leaving for Simon Island must check in at the Visitor Center at least 45 minutes before departure. Refunds will not be provided for missed departures.

186. What is the purpose of the memo?

(A) To notify staff about an important meeting
(B) To ask for suggestions for an annual outing
(C) To verify participation in an employee survey
(D) To remind employees of a confirmation deadline

187. What does Mr. Loris recommend that some employees do?

(A) Visit a museum
(B) Pack a light lunch
(C) Organize transportation
(D) Invite their relatives

188. What is stated about the Windward Inn?

(A) It requires a two-night minimum stay.
(B) It offers views of the ocean.
(C) It has rooms for groups of four or more.
(D) It provides a complimentary breakfast.

189. What is true about the Brunswick Ferry?

(A) It operates multiple vessels simultaneously.
(B) It makes fewer trips in the winter.
(C) It stops briefly on the way to Simon Island.
(D) It allows vehicles aboard its ships.

190. What is suggested about employees attending the company outing?

(A) They will have to buy their own ferry tickets.
(B) They need to check in by 8:30 in the morning.
(C) They can obtain refunds if they miss a departure.
(D) They will be back in Brunswick by 5 o'clock.

GO ON TO THE NEXT PAGE

Questions 191-195 refer to the following information, form, and e-mail.

How does Buzzchain work?

Buzzchain is a network of consumers who review products and provide assistance with online marketing. To join, sign up and let us know what kinds of products you are interested in. We will notify you when a product is available for review. You will be sent either a free sample or a voucher that can be exchanged at a store near you.

As a member, you will earn points for every review you complete. The more activities you do, the more points you earn for each review. Redeem your points for products and services on our partner Web site, www.linkchange.com.

ACTIVITY	POINTS EARNED
Answer a survey	10
Write a 50-word-minimum review	30
Upload photos or videos with your review	50
Share your review on social media	60
Receive 25 or more "likes" on your shared content	100
Total possible points per product	250

Note: All submissions must meet our guidelines and are subject to evaluation.

Buzzchain Reviewer: Sean Morgan
Product name: Limba Air
Attachment: Product_Photo.jpg

Buzzchain Reviewer ID: M90746
Category: Household products

Is this your first time using the product?
Yes.

Do you use a similar product in your daily life?
No, not regularly. But I buy air fresheners on occasion.

Did the product perform as advertised?
I thought it smelled nice at first, but the scent didn't last long.

What is your overall opinion of the product?
I received a package of two scents, Berry Fresh and Crisp Sheets. I didn't like the first one, but I might buy the second. Apart from the scents, I found the packaging attractive.

Would you recommend this product to friends?
I would if somebody asked me my opinion. Otherwise, I'm not sure.

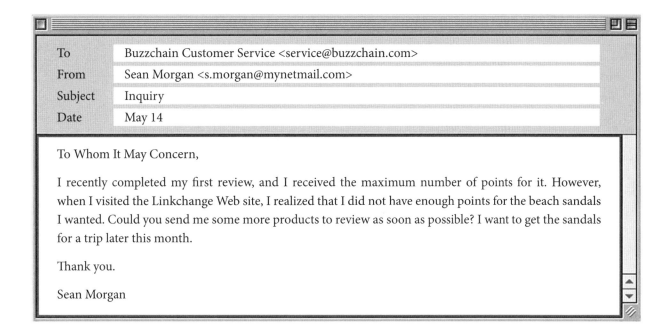

To	Buzzchain Customer Service <service@buzzchain.com>
From	Sean Morgan <s.morgan@mynetmail.com>
Subject	Inquiry
Date	May 14

To Whom It May Concern,

I recently completed my first review, and I received the maximum number of points for it. However, when I visited the Linkchange Web site, I realized that I did not have enough points for the beach sandals I wanted. Could you send me some more products to review as soon as possible? I want to get the sandals for a trip later this month.

Thank you.

Sean Morgan

191. What is indicated about Buzzchain?

(A) It helps companies sell their products.
(B) It gets paid for sending customers to Linkchange.
(C) It pays cash for online activities.
(D) It maintains offices across the country.

192. What is true about Mr. Morgan?

(A) He is a frequent user of air fresheners.
(B) He expressed an interest in household items.
(C) He is unqualified to perform a review.
(D) He designs product packaging.

193. What is mentioned about Limba Air?

(A) It can be delivered in one day.
(B) It leaves a scent that lasts for weeks.
(C) It comes in at least two varieties.
(D) It can be purchased on a Web site.

194. Why did Mr. Morgan write the e-mail?

(A) To confirm his current point total
(B) To update his account information
(C) To complain about a product's quality
(D) To ask about doing more reviews

195. Why was Mr. Morgan probably unable to obtain the item he wanted?

(A) He provided some incorrect information
(B) The item received a negative review.
(C) He submitted a review past a deadline.
(D) The item cost more than 250 points.

GO ON TO THE NEXT PAGE

Questions 196-200 refer to the following e-mail, online form, and newsletter.

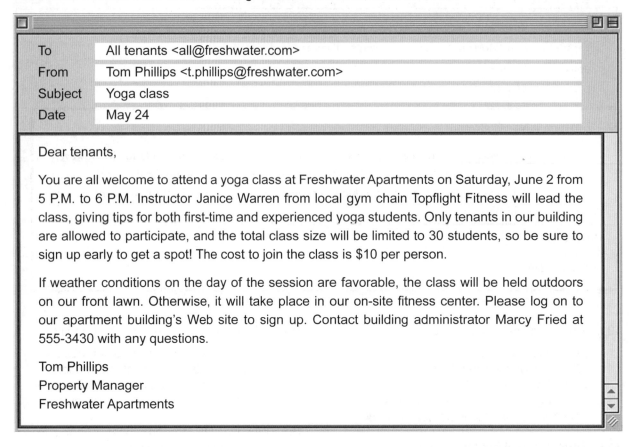

To	All tenants <all@freshwater.com>
From	Tom Phillips <t.phillips@freshwater.com>
Subject	Yoga class
Date	May 24

Dear tenants,

You are all welcome to attend a yoga class at Freshwater Apartments on Saturday, June 2 from 5 P.M. to 6 P.M. Instructor Janice Warren from local gym chain Topflight Fitness will lead the class, giving tips for both first-time and experienced yoga students. Only tenants in our building are allowed to participate, and the total class size will be limited to 30 students, so be sure to sign up early to get a spot! The cost to join the class is $10 per person.

If weather conditions on the day of the session are favorable, the class will be held outdoors on our front lawn. Otherwise, it will take place in our on-site fitness center. Please log on to our apartment building's Web site to sign up. Contact building administrator Marcy Fried at 555-3430 with any questions.

Tom Phillips
Property Manager
Freshwater Apartments

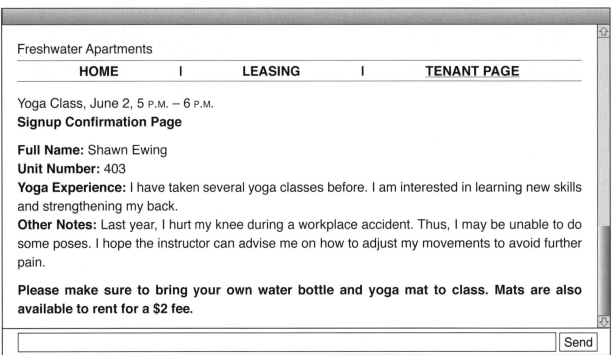

Freshwater Apartments

| **HOME** | I | **LEASING** | I | **TENANT PAGE** |

Yoga Class, June 2, 5 P.M. – 6 P.M.
Signup Confirmation Page

Full Name: Shawn Ewing
Unit Number: 403
Yoga Experience: I have taken several yoga classes before. I am interested in learning new skills and strengthening my back.
Other Notes: Last year, I hurt my knee during a workplace accident. Thus, I may be unable to do some poses. I hope the instructor can advise me on how to adjust my movements to avoid further pain.

Please make sure to bring your own water bottle and yoga mat to class. Mats are also available to rent for a $2 fee.

| | Send |

Freshwater Apartments Monthly Newsletter

July

This month, all tenants should be aware of some renovation work that will be taking place in our lobby. The work is expected to occur from July 20 to July 31. During this period, the front entrance to our building will be blocked off, and residents should use the door near Grove Street instead.

On July 23, our regular monthly gathering will be held in the third-floor lounge. This will be a great opportunity to socialize with the other tenants in the building. In addition, we will be showing photos from our yoga class, which happened last month in our on-site gym.

196. Who is Janice Warren?

(A) A building manager
(B) A new tenant
(C) A fitness instructor
(D) A construction worker

197. What must Mr. Ewing do?

(A) Sign up for a gym membership
(B) Speak to Ms. Fried in person
(C) Make a payment for a $10 fee
(D) Fill out a photo release form

198. What Is NOT mentloned about Mr. Ewlng?

(A) He has participated in a yoga class before.
(B) He was injured within the past few years.
(C) He will rent a mat for the session.
(D) He wants to improve strength in his back.

199. What are tenants instructed to do during the renovation period?

(A) Avoid using an elevator on the third floor
(B) Be careful of equipment left on the front lawn
(C) Park their cars in a lot on Grove Street
(D) Access the building through an alternate entryway

200. What is indicated about Freshwater Apartments' yoga class?

(A) It followed a social gathering in the lounge.
(B) Its organizer demonstrated some techniques.
(C) Its instructor rescheduled the first session.
(D) It took place indoors due to poor weather.

This is the end of the test. You may review Parts 5, 6, and 7 if you finish the test early.

TEST 7 점수 환산표

TEST 7은 무사히 잘 마치셨나요? 맞은 개수를 세어본 후 아래의 점수 환산표를 통해 자신의 점수를 예상해 보세요.

전체 난이도   중간 난이도

파트별 난이도   PART 5 중 ●●○
PART 6 중 ●●○
PART 7 중 ●●○

정답 수	리딩 점수	정답 수	리딩 점수
98~100개	475~495점	47~49개	205~215점
95~97개	460~470점	44~46개	190~200점
92~94개	440~455점	41~43개	175~185점
89~91개	420~435점	38~40개	160~170점
86~88개	405~415점	35~37개	145~155점
83~85개	390~400점	32~34개	130~140점
80~82개	375~385점	29~31개	115~125점
77~79개	360~370점	26~28개	100~110점
74~76개	340~355점	23~25개	85~95점
71~73개	325~335점	20~22개	70~80점
68~70개	305~320점	17~19개	55~65점
65~67개	290~300점	14~16개	40~50점
62~64개	270~285점	11~13개	25~35점
59~61개	260~270점	8~10개	10~20점
56~58개	245~255점	5~7개	5~10점
53~55개	235~240점	2~4개	5~10점
50~52개	220~230점	0~1개	0~5점

* 점수 환산표는 해커스토익 사이트 유저 데이터를 근거로 제작되었으며, 주기적으로 업데이트되고 있습니다. 해커스토익 사이트
(Hackers.co.kr)에서 최신 경향을 반영하여 업데이트된 점수환산기를 이용하실 수 있습니다. (토익 > 토익게시판 > 토익점수환산기)

TEST 8

PART 5
PART 6
PART 7
점수 환산표

잠깐! 테스트 전 확인사항

1. 문제 풀이에 방해가 되는 물건을 모두 치우셨나요?   예 ☐
2. Answer Sheet, 연필, 지우개를 준비하셨나요?   예 ☐
3. 시계를 준비히 셨나요?   예 ☐

모든 준비가 완료되었으면 목표 점수를 떠올린 후 테스트를 시작합니다.

문제 풀이를 마치는 시간은 지금부터 **75분 후인** _____시 _____분입니다.

테스트 시간은 **총 75분**이며, 시험 종료 전 2~3분은 정답 검토 및 답안지 마킹을 위해 사용합니다.

READING TEST

In this section, you must demonstrate your ability to read and comprehend English. You will be given a variety of texts and asked to answer questions about these texts. This section is divided into three parts and will take 75 minutes to complete.

Do not mark the answers in your test book. Use the answer sheet that is separately provided.

PART 5

Directions: In each question, you will be asked to review a statement that is missing a word or phrase. Four answer choices will be provided for each statement. Select the best answer and mark the corresponding letter (A), (B), (C), or (D) on the answer sheet.

---

101. Ms. Adams volunteered ------- to assist Calterna Technology's representatives from Korea.

(A) she
(B) her
(C) hers
(D) herself

102. The design team had a ------- discussion that produced many useful ideas.

(A) uncertain
(B) valuable
(C) redundant
(D) generous

103. The movie differs from the book in some ways, but it ------- tells the same story.

(A) eagerly
(B) previously
(C) nearly
(D) rarely

104. Thurmond Rail has enough capital for an ------- of its services.

(A) expand
(B) expanded
(C) expandable
(D) expansion

105. Whereas many retailers ship items ------- without additional costs, they charge high fees for overseas orders.

(A) domesticates
(B) domesticating
(C) domestic
(D) domestically

106. Fital Electronics is receiving more inquiries ------- its advertisements have begun appealing to more consumers.

(A) which
(B) although
(C) as
(D) gradually

107. Ms. Goodman drove to Pasadena ------- visit the store where she purchased a blender.

(A) by
(B) to
(C) on
(D) due to

108. Metrix's 3D scanning software can identify objects in photos more ------- than competing products.

(A) accurately
(B) originally
(C) outwardly
(D) silently

109. While Rexval Technologies does collect user data, the company will never ------- this information.

(A) refuse
(B) oversee
(C) disclose
(D) exclude

110. The presentation will be more effective ------- it includes more charts.

(A) if
(B) unlike
(C) else
(D) just

111. Coster Securities does not permit the use of phones for personal reasons ------- working hours.

(A) at
(B) during
(C) around
(D) since

112. The textile is made of a substance that is ------- to heat.

(A) resist
(B) resists
(C) resistant
(D) resistance

113. The research assistant ------- the customer survey data next week.

(A) reviewer
(B) will review
(C) reviewing
(D) reviewed

114. The studio audience reacted ------- to the new TV show, laughing frequently.

(A) suddenly
(B) positively
(C) mutually
(D) slowly

115. Kractal Solutions requires all employees to complete each assigned job, ------- it is.

(A) everything
(B) or
(C) anyone
(D) whatever

116. This project for Suntair Venture will be ------- difficult compared to the Fitan Enterprises task.

(A) moderate
(B) moderated
(C) moderately
(D) moderation

117. Lawyers have presented evidence ------- Blade Lawncare's unfair trade practices.

(A) along
(B) concerning
(C) through
(D) onto

118. The sports training facility is ------- with the latest fitness machines.

(A) equipped
(B) targeted
(C) composed
(D) obtained

119. People may indicate their ------- of participating in the event by registering their names on a list.

(A) intend
(B) intended
(C) intends
(D) intention

120. The management committee has ------- a strategic plan to guide the firm's actions in South America.

(A) recruited
(B) nominated
(C) formulated
(D) prevented

해커스토익 실전 1200제 READING

GO ON TO THE NEXT PAGE

121. As a result of a potato shortage, Burger Bix will increase prices by 20 percent for a single ------- of French fries.

    (A) service
    (B) server
    (C) serving
    (D) serve

122. The installation of the audio system is finished, but the ------- for the work has not yet been sent.

    (A) draft
    (B) invoice
    (C) proposal
    (D) booking

123. Gishwa Music is a very popular music streaming program that allows users ------- its collection for free.

    (A) browsed
    (B) browses
    (C) browse
    (D) to browse

124. All staff, without exception, will participate in a ------- of development seminars.

    (A) kind
    (B) range
    (C) member
    (D) lack

125. Ms. Thompkins had been a ------- reporter before she accepted a faculty position at Baird University.

    (A) distinguished
    (B) distinguish
    (C) distinguishing
    (D) distinguishes

126. With the advent of social networking sites, most companies made changes in ------- they advertise.

    (A) about
    (B) so
    (C) thus
    (D) how

127. The error causing processing delays for applications should be ------- immediately.

    (A) address
    (B) addressed
    (C) addressing
    (D) addresses

128. No payments can be made to the insurance subscriber, ------- a claim has been examined by the department.

    (A) otherwise
    (B) besides
    (C) until
    (D) despite

129. Salads sold in TotalMarket ------- with dressings and recyclable forks.

    (A) contain
    (B) present
    (C) provide
    (D) come

130. Failure to give ------- information to our technicians could result in an inaccurate assessment.

    (A) corrects
    (B) correct
    (C) correctly
    (D) corrector

Directions: In this part, you will be asked to read four English texts. Each text is missing a word, phrase, or sentence. Select the answer choice that correctly completes the text and mark the corresponding letter (A), (B), (C), or (D) on the answer sheet.

Questions 131-134 refer to the following article.

September 9, Mexico City—Compensa Solutions has announced the ------- of Valeria Gomez as
131.
its chief marketing officer. -------. Speaking to reporters, spokesperson Thomas Walden described
132.
Ms. Gomez as a terrific addition to the senior management of the firm. "We are ------- to welcome
133.
Ms. Gomez and hope that she can help us enter new markets with her extensive knowledge and

years of experience," he said. ------- Ms. Gomez has not held an executive position previously, she
134.
gave assurances that she is prepared for the coming challenge.

131. (A) retirement
(B) appointment
(C) investment
(D) accomplishment

132. (A) They offer superior products and
services.
(B) The company's sales have climbed
steadily for over a year.
(C) A list of open positions at the firm is
accessible through the Web site.
(D) The statement was made at a press
conference yesterday.

133. (A) please
(B) pleased
(C) pleases
(D) pleasing

134. (A) While
(B) In spite of
(C) During
(D) Because of

GO ON TO THE NEXT PAGE

Questions 135-138 refer to the following information.

Sign up for the Middletown Photography Exhibition!

Middletown's 8th Annual Photography Exhibition will be held from August 1 to 14. Local photographers

are ------- to participate. The event will feature artwork from numerous artists. Art will be on ------- at
    135.   136.

Emerson Gallery and city hall. All artworks will be returned to the artists after this two-week event.

In order to join the event, visit www.middletown.gov/photoexhibit and submit your application.

We will notify those ------- for the event by January 13. For further details on requirements, visit our
                     137.

Web site. -------.
          138.

---

135. (A) invite
     (B) inviting
     (C) invited
     (D) invites

136. (A) duty
     (B) display
     (C) sale
     (D) time

137. (A) advised
     (B) selected
     (C) divided
     (D) replaced

138. (A) Or you can drop by the Middletown Arts
         Council office.
     (B) They must follow all of our necessary
         specifications.
     (C) The announcement will be made in
         a few days.
     (D) Only a small number of entries are
         permitted.

Questions 139-142 refer to the advertisement.

This fall, upgrade your wardrobe with a Winchester casual jacket by Edward Dormer! This jacket

revives the brand's iconic look, ------- was popular in the 1940s. Each jacket is handcrafted from
                                139.

durable -------. These include high-quality leather and aluminum zippers. Designed for use in the
        140.

UK's cold and wet climate, a special coating ------- to make each jacket durable and waterproof.
                                            141.

-------. Find it online or at our stores around the country.
142.

139. (A) that
     (B) who
     (C) which
     (D) when

140. (A) cases
     (B) equipment
     (C) shapes
     (D) materials

141. (A) applying
     (B) is applied
     (C) will be applied
     (D) to apply

142. (A) Therefore, it will keep your body warm
         and dry.
     (B) However, the jacket can be quite heavy
         to some people.
     (C) The first leather jackets appeared in
         the early 20th century.
     (D) Mr. Dormer has owned the same jacket
         for years.

GO ON TO THE NEXT PAGE

Questions 143-146 refer to the following announcement.

Sortix Digital Security Consultancy
URGENT ANNOUNCEMENT

Alephnet, makers of the Zeno operating system, will stop providing support for older versions of its

platform. ------, the company will not provide software upgrades for Zeno-10 anymore. So, please
     143.

update to Zeno-11 soon. ------ this advice could leave your computers vulnerable to security
              144.

threats. In general, Zeno-11 provides better security compared to Zeno-10, the ------ platform. To
                                                                          145.

ensure the stability of your systems, we strongly urge you to update immediately. ------. In case
                                                                              146.

you have any additional questions, please contact us at cs@sortix.com.

---

143. (A) As a result
(B) Instead
(C) Once
(D) However

144. (A) Accepting
(B) Obtaining
(C) Ignoring
(D) Avoiding

145. (A) previous
(B) clear
(C) standard
(D) popular

146. (A) Act now before this special promotion expires.
(B) We will send you a reminder as soon as one is available.
(C) Modern business operations depend on computer technology.
(D) For installation instructions and support, refer to our Web site.

Directions: In this part, you will be asked to read several texts, such as advertisements, articles, instant messages, or examples of business correspondence. Each text is followed by several questions. Select the best answer and mark the corresponding letter (A), (B), (C), or (D) on your answer sheet.

Questions 147-148 refer to the following receipt.

Ronson Home Supplies

167 Caldwell Boulevard, Twin Lakes, NM 86515

555-8863

–Date: 08/08 –Time: 5:26 P.M.

A refund or exchange may only be issued upon presentation of this receipt.

93432-B	Electric Fan	$34.99
88822-F	HDMI Cable	$18.50
	Subtotal	$53.49
	5% Sales Tax	$2.67
	Total	$56.16
	Cash	$60.00
	Change	$3.84

Thank you for visiting Ronson Home Supplies. Please tell us what you thought of your shopping experience today by completing our online survey at www.ronsonhome.com or by calling our customer center at 555-9933. You'll be automatically entered into a draw to win a free tablet computer.

147. What is indicated about Ronson Home Supplies?

(A) It is open until late at night.
(B) It is currently holding a sale on appliances.
(C) It does not take credit or debit cards.
(D) It accepts returned merchandise.

148. What are customers asked to do?

(A) Sign up as members on a Web site
(B) Provide feedback about a store
(C) Call a service center for coupons
(D) Buy raffle tickets for a free device

GO ON TO THE NEXT PAGE

Questions 149-150 refer to the following online customer service chat.

Robert Patton [1:03 P.M.] Hi. I moved two months ago, but I haven't received any bank statements at my new address.

RMF Bank [1:05 P.M.] I see, Mr. Patton. You probably need to update your contact information using our online banking service. After you do this, a code will be sent to your phone to confirm your identity. You'll have to type it in within 20 seconds for the changes to take effect.

Robert Patton [1:06 P.M.] Actually, I already did that.

RMF Bank [1:07 P.M.] Well, then check the Communication Preferences setting at our Web site. If you had chosen the Electronic option, your statements would have been e-mailed to you. You need to select the Paper option to get hard copies sent to you.

Robert Patton [1:10 P.M.] Hold on . . . OK, done. Thank you for your help.

`                                                              ` [Send]

---

149. What is indicated about the code?

(A) It will be selected by Mr. Patton.
(B) It must be given to an employee.
(C) It must be entered right away.
(D) It will be based on a name.

150. At 1:10 P.M., what does Mr. Patton most likely mean when he writes, "OK, done"?

(A) He updated his contact information.
(B) He changed an online setting.
(C) He completed a bank transaction.
(D) He printed a financial document.

Questions 151-153 refer to the following e-mail.

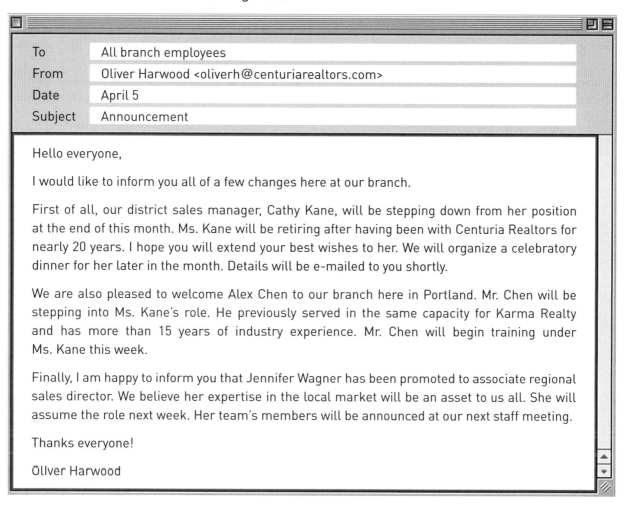

To	All branch employees
From	Oliver Harwood <oliverh@centuriarealtors.com>
Date	April 5
Subject	Announcement

Hello everyone,

I would like to inform you all of a few changes here at our branch.

First of all, our district sales manager, Cathy Kane, will be stepping down from her position at the end of this month. Ms. Kane will be retiring after having been with Centuria Realtors for nearly 20 years. I hope you will extend your best wishes to her. We will organize a celebratory dinner for her later in the month. Details will be e-mailed to you shortly.

We are also pleased to welcome Alex Chen to our branch here in Portland. Mr. Chen will be stepping into Ms. Kane's role. He previously served in the same capacity for Karma Realty and has more than 15 years of industry experience. Mr. Chen will begin training under Ms. Kane this week.

Finally, I am happy to inform you that Jennifer Wagner has been promoted to associate regional sales director. We believe her expertise in the local market will be an asset to us all. She will assume the role next week. Her team's members will be announced at our next staff meeting.

Thanks everyone!

Oliver Harwood

151. What is the purpose of the e-mail?

(A) To request opinions regarding a policy
(B) To inform employees of staffing changes
(C) To announce available job positions
(D) To describe modifications to hiring procedures

152. What is indicated about Mr. Chen?

(A) He has been asked to train Jennifer Wagner.
(B) He worked as a district sales manager before.
(C) He will be temporarily taking over Ms. Kane's position.
(D) He will arrive at the agency office at the end of April.

153. What will take place at the next employee meeting?

(A) Ms. Wagner's team members will be announced.
(B) A gift will be given to celebrate a retirement.
(C) New employees will be introduced.
(D) A training session with Mr. Harwood will be conducted.

GO ON TO THE NEXT PAGE

Questions 154-157 refer to the following e-mail.

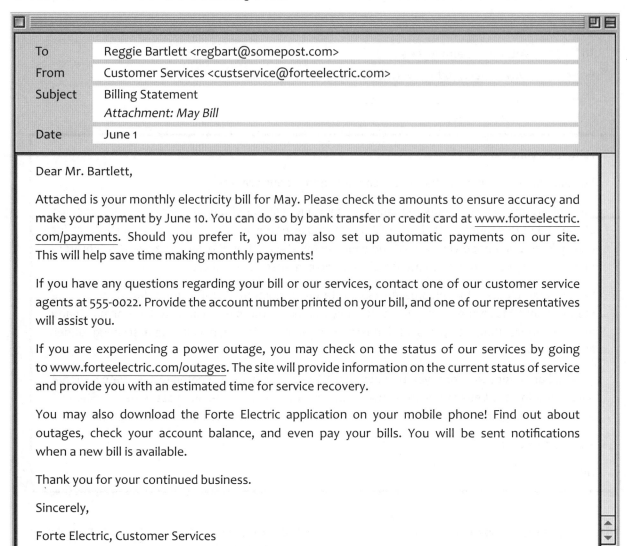

To	Reggie Bartlett <regbart@somepost.com>
From	Customer Services <custservice@forteelectric.com>
Subject	Billing Statement
	Attachment: May Bill
Date	June 1

Dear Mr. Bartlett,

Attached is your monthly electricity bill for May. Please check the amounts to ensure accuracy and make your payment by June 10. You can do so by bank transfer or credit card at www.forteelectric. com/payments. Should you prefer it, you may also set up automatic payments on our site. This will help save time making monthly payments!

If you have any questions regarding your bill or our services, contact one of our customer service agents at 555-0022. Provide the account number printed on your bill, and one of our representatives will assist you.

If you are experiencing a power outage, you may check on the status of our services by going to www.forteelectric.com/outages. The site will provide information on the current status of service and provide you with an estimated time for service recovery.

You may also download the Forte Electric application on your mobile phone! Find out about outages, check your account balance, and even pay your bills. You will be sent notifications when a new bill is available.

Thank you for your continued business.

Sincerely,

Forte Electric, Customer Services

---

154. What is the main purpose of the e-mail?

(A) To request reactivation of a service
(B) To provide a bill for utility fees
(C) To announce a new application service
(D) To report an inaccurate charge

155. What can clients do on Forte Electric's Web site?

(A) Set up automatic payments
(B) Track their usage over time
(C) Cancel a service
(D) Report a change of address

156. According to the e-mail, what is included on billing statements?

(A) A preferred payment method
(B) A customer account number
(C) A banking institution name
(D) A customer service telephone number

157. What is NOT stated as a method for checking the electrical service?

(A) Calling a company representative
(B) Reviewing updates on a Web site
(C) Opening a mobile phone application
(D) Sending a text message notification

Questions 158-159 refer to the following advertisement.

The 35th Annual Western Canada Vintage Auto Show
Friday and Saturday, July 7-8, 10 A.M.-9 P.M.

Visit downtown Vernon for this year's vintage auto show, with over 400 vehicles on view!

Admission is free, and souvenirs will be available for purchase from numerous vendors. Check out the snack and beverage booths for hot-dogs, burgers, fries, soft drinks, and much more!

Paid parking is available downtown on Friday, but is free to the public on weekends. And don't forget to enter our raffle to win a vintage sports car! Sign up for the draw at the fair's help desk on both days. For further information, visit www.wcvintageautoshow.com.

158. What is NOT indicated about the auto show?

(A) It will take place over a two-day period.
(B) It is held once every twelve months.
(C) It is hosted in a venue in the suburbs.
(D) It does not charge fees for attendance.

159. What is available to visitors only on Saturday?

(A) Complimentary parking
(B) Food and beverage samples
(C) Participation in a draw for a prize
(D) Access to public transport

GO ON TO THE NEXT PAGE

Questions 160-162 refer to the following article.

July 14—The St. Louis Restaurant Association will begin offering a monthly subscription plan on August 1. — [1] —. The goal is to promote the city's little-known restaurants. "Many of the establishments that belong to our organization opened in the past six months, so they do not have many regular customers yet," said Martha Hale, the current head of the association. — [2] —.

When people sign up, they will be asked to indicate their preferred types of foods. — [3] —. They can change this at any time by logging in to the St. Louis Restaurant Association's Web site and updating their information. Subscribers will receive a voucher for two entrées at a different restaurant each month and will be billed a monthly fee of only $20. — [4] —. The St. Louis Restaurant Association is optimistic that the subscription model will lead to an overall increase in customers for its members.

160. What is the article mainly about?

(A) An event to celebrate regional cooking styles
(B) A service to promote local businesses
(C) A business that will open in August
(D) A product that will be used in restaurants

161. How can subscribers change their food preferences?

(A) By sending an e-mail to an association
(B) By renewing a monthly subscription
(C) By mailing a form to a customer center
(D) By accessing an online account

162. In which of the positions marked [1], [2], [3], and [4] does the following sentence best belong?

"This amount is significantly less than the regular price of a meal for two."

(A) [1]
(B) [2]
(C) [3]
(D) [4]

Questions 163-166 refer to the following text-message chain.

May 3 Friday

Allan McDonald [1:35 P.M.] Last week we talked about improving the leadership skills of the team managers here at BYR Incorporated. I've found a company called Rework Pro that specializes in this type of corporate training.

Julianne Nash [1:37 P.M.] Great. The results from our monthly employee survey show that our workers want more effective guidance from their immediate supervisors. I think we need to address this issue immediately to ensure we don't lose staff to other companies.

Mallory Smithers [1:38 P.M.] What sort of services does Rework Pro offer?

Allan McDonald [1:41 P.M.] They will design custom workshops for us. These will be conducted by a Rework Pro instructor.

Julianne Nash [1:42 P.M.] Will that be sufficient? We regularly hold workshops ourselves, but we still have this issue.

Allan McDonald [1:45 P.M.] Having a qualified instructor will make a big difference.

Mallory Smithers [1:46 P.M.] I agree. But, I'm concerned about scheduling. We have several project deadlines in June, and many of our employees take their summer vacation in August.

Allan McDonald [1:46 P.M.] I already checked that. The Rework Pro representative said that the workshops could be done in July.

Julianne Nash [1:48 P.M.] Then I guess the only issue remaining is whether this program would fit within our budget.

Allan McDonald [1:49 P.M.] Rework Pro is sending me a quote in three days. I'll e-mail a copy to both of you so that we can discuss it in our meeting on Wednesday.

163. What is suggested about BYR Incorporated?

(A) It promoted several employees to management positions.
(B) It provides benefits to supervisors.
(C) It requests periodic feedback from staff members.
(D) It lost workers to other companies last year.

164. At 1:42 P.M., what does Ms. Nash most likely mean when she writes, "Will that be sufficient"?

(A) A workshop can be organized quickly.
(B) A staffing issue will remain unresolved.
(C) Managers require a longer training period.
(D) An instructional method is ineffective.

165. What does Mr. McDonald say he has already done?

(A) Checked dates of staff vacations
(B) Requested schedule information
(C) Provided names of workshop attendees
(D) Confirmed venue availability

166. What will most likely happen next week?

(A) Rework Pro will submit a price estimate.
(B) Mr. McDonald will meet with an instructor.
(C) Ms. Smithers will present a budget proposal.
(D) BYR Incorporated will change a project deadline.

GO ON TO THE NEXT PAGE

Book Donations

From July 20 to August 20, Willpoint Public Library will be collecting book donations from the public and we are now seeking volunteers to help with the sorting of donated items. If you are 18 years old or above, please apply at the library in person. You will need to make yourself available for a minimum of two hours per day.

Those who want to donate their books can visit our library. Books may be brought to the library during our regular operating hours of 9:00 A.M. to 11:00 P.M. on weekdays and from 9:00 A.M. to 6:00 P.M. on weekends. You can also leave them in our donation box at City Hall, which is open from 9:00 A.M. to 5:00 P.M., Monday to Friday.

167. According to the notice, what will the volunteers do?

(A) Organize items given to the library
(B) Assist with supervising children
(C) Help visitors apply for services
(D) Prepare books for shipment

168. What is true about Willpoint Public Library?

(A) It closes later on Saturdays and Sundays.
(B) It accepts donations at multiple locations.
(C) It will extend its operating hours in August.
(D) It is renovating some of its facilities.

Questions 169-171 refer to the following e-mail.

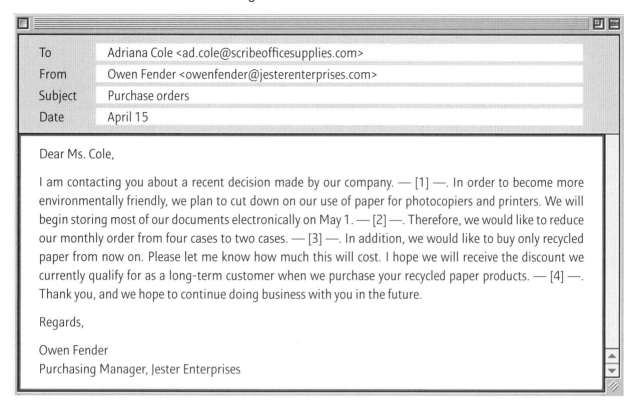

To   Adriana Cole <ad.cole@scribeofficesupplies.com>

From   Owen Fender <owenfender@jesterenterprises.com>

Subject   Purchase orders

Date   April 15

Dear Ms. Cole,

I am contacting you about a recent decision made by our company. — [1] —. In order to become more environmentally friendly, we plan to cut down on our use of paper for photocopiers and printers. We will begin storing most of our documents electronically on May 1. — [2] —. Therefore, we would like to reduce our monthly order from four cases to two cases. — [3] —. In addition, we would like to buy only recycled paper from now on. Please let me know how much this will cost. I hope we will receive the discount we currently qualify for as a long-term customer when we purchase your recycled paper products. — [4] —. Thank you, and we hope to continue doing business with you in the future.

Regards,

Owen Fender
Purchasing Manager, Jester Enterprises

---

169. Why was the e-mail written?

(A) To inform a supplier of an order adjustment
(B) To inquire about new products
(C) To submit a complaint about a policy
(D) To request a higher discount rate

170. What is suggested about Jester Enterprises?

(A) Its manager has decided to reduce operating expenses.
(B) It will not keep its current photocopiers and printers.
(C) Its environmental efforts have received positive publicity.
(D) It has not been paying the regular price for paper.

171. In which of the positions marked [1], [2], [3], and [4] does the following sentence best belong?

"However, we will still require a supply of paper for various purposes."

(A) [1]
(B) [2]
(C) [3]
(D) [4]

GO ON TO THE NEXT PAGE

LiteraLegends Offers New Authors Opportunity for Publication

There is hope for authors trying to get their works published! Founded just five years ago, LiteraLegends is a Web site that offers writers a chance to publish their novels, short stories, poetry, and non-fiction works. Authors simply upload their works to the site, and members can download them for their reading pleasure.

LiteraLegends CEO Sam Ashoka said, "First-time writers usually offer their work for free. If members like what they read, they leave a positive review." Should a work become popular, the author then has the option of charging members for downloads. The price can be as low as $2.99 or as high as $35.99. LiteraLegends charges a 20 percent commission fee on all sales and also helps promote authors to mainstream publishing companies.

Well-known author of *The Belivers*, Meridiana Chase was discovered by a publishing house after developing a significant readership for her works on LiteraLegends. "Some works have been downloaded over a million times," Ashoka also stated. "LiteraLegends hopes to bring the same level of success to authors as famous video content sites have brought to performers."

172. In paragraph 1, line 1, the word "Founded" is closest in meaning to

(A) Discovered
(B) Established
(C) Searched
(D) Revealed

173. What is mentioned about LiteraLegends?

(A) It offers services on other Web sites.
(B) It requires customers to pay in advance.
(C) It forms partnership with other companies.
(D) It allows users to provide feedback.

174. How does LiteraLegends generate revenue?

(A) By charging for memberships
(B) By taking a sales commission
(C) By collecting subscription fees
(D) By running advertisements

175. Who is Meridiana Chase?

(A) A publishing company spokesperson
(B) A literary critic
(C) A popular author
(D) A marketing expert

GO ON TO THE NEXT PAGE

Questions 176-180 refer to the following Web page and letter.

www.csjobsglobal.com

CS JOBS GLOBAL

HOME | Job Listings | Sign in | Contact Us | Help

Talle Centrum Contact Center

With offices in India, Sri Lanka, and Bangladesh, we have been a leading provider of contact center services for global companies for over 20 years. We are seeking individuals interested in joining our team of customer service agents.

RESPONSIBILITIES
- Handling customer service calls for corporate clients
- Gathering and maintaining customer information
- Recommending solutions and services as required
- Participating in periodic training workshops and meetings

QUALIFICATIONS
- A minimum of two years of college is required
- Must be willing to work flexible hours
- Previous experience preferred
- Excellent written and verbal communication skills in English, German, or French

COMPENSATION
- $12.50 per hour plus performance bonuses
- Health insurance
- Subsidy for housing and transportation

The application deadline is July 10.

Talle Centrum Contact Center

www.tallecentrum.com

August 16

Angela Lakmal
22 Weerangula Road
Morenna, Sri Lanka

Dear Ms. Lakmal,

Thank you for stopping by on August 10 to discuss your employment. As agreed, you will be taking on the role of a full-time customer service agent here at our center in Colombo. You will be working at least 40 hours per week. Compensation will be as advertised. Your start date, unless you specify otherwise, will be on September 15. We look forward to having you on our team!

If you have any concerns that have not been addressed, please call me at 555-2795. Otherwise, I look forward to seeing you on your first day of work.

Sincerely,

Dennis Carlsen
Human Resources Manager

176. What is suggested about Talle Centrum Contact Center?

(A) It originated in Sri Lanka.
(B) It is opening a new branch office.
(C) It is currently developing a software product.
(D) It provides services in multiple languages.

177. What is stated about the advertised position?

(A) It includes a fixed work schedule.
(B) It provides overseas travel opportunities.
(C) It involves regular training sessions.
(D) It requires prior work experience.

178. What is indicated about Ms. Lakmal?

(A) She will earn a bonus for every sale.
(B) She will receive extra pay for good work.
(C) She will have to earn a professional certificate.
(D) She will be working mostly at night.

179. In the letter, the word "addressed" in paragraph 2, line 1, is closest in meaning to

(A) delivered
(B) proposed
(C) written down
(D) dealt with

180. When most likely will Ms. Lakmal begin her employment?

(A) On August 10
(B) On August 17
(C) On September 1
(D) On September 15

GO ON TO THE NEXT PAGE

Dawn Taylor
42 Coote Road
Bluff Hill, Napier 4110
New Zealand

Dear Ms. Taylor,

I am honored by your request that I speak at the event in February marking the 100th year of the New Zealand Sailing Society (NZSS). As a former NZSS president, I am well acquainted with the club's history. And it has been a pleasure to watch it evolve in the years since I stepped down from my leadership post.

Regrettably, I am unable to join because I will be taking part in a sailing race on the same day. In my place, I would like to recommend Brenda Wilson, a yachting enthusiast and accomplished public speaker. Another good choice would be Ling Zhang, who has broken some world records for solo sailing. Alison Scott also comes to mind. Her grandfather was an original member of the NZSS, so she has some interesting stories about the society's early days. Let me know if one of these people seems suitable to speak at the event. Then I will provide you with that person's e-mail address.

Kind regards,

Patrick Patel

Schedule of Events for 100 Years of Smooth Sailing:
An Anniversary Celebration of the New Zealand Sailing Society

<u>Location</u>: Walter Donahue Clubhouse
<u>Date</u>: February 28

Time	Event	Speaker
5:00-5:20 P.M.	Opening speech - "Welcome Fellow Sailors"	Dominika Gladstone
5:20-5:50 P.M.	Main address - "Why Sailing Matters"	Ling Zhang
6:00-7:30 P.M.	Dinner banquet in the Ketch Room	
7:30-8:00 P.M.	Slideshow - "The NZSS Over the Years"	Winny Baxter
8:00-8:30 P.M.	NZSS trivia quiz with prizes for the winners	David Young
8:40-9:00 P.M.	Fireworks display over Breakwater Harbor	

181. What is the main purpose of the letter?

(A) To suggest holding an event
(B) To turn down an invitation
(C) To review some qualifications
(D) To ask for a change in date

182. According to the letter, what will Mr. Patel be occupied with in February?

(A) Creating a membership directory
(B) Participating in a competition
(C) Organizing an exhibition
(D) Running in a local election

183. What did Mr. Patel probably do?

(A) Sent Mr. Zhang's contact details to an event organizer
(B) Provided Ms. Taylor with a suitable topic for a lecture
(C) Gave a speech about Ms. Scott's background
(D) Taught Mr. Zhang how to sail

184. According to the schedule, when will attendees play a game?

(A) 5:00 P.M.
(B) 6:00 P.M.
(C) 8:00 P.M.
(D) 8:40 P.M.

185. What will NOT take place at 100 Years of Smooth Sailing?

(A) An outdoor show
(B) A product demonstration
(C) A visual presentation
(D) An opening talk

GO ON TO THE NEXT PAGE

Questions 186-190 refer to the following e-mail, invoice, and letter.

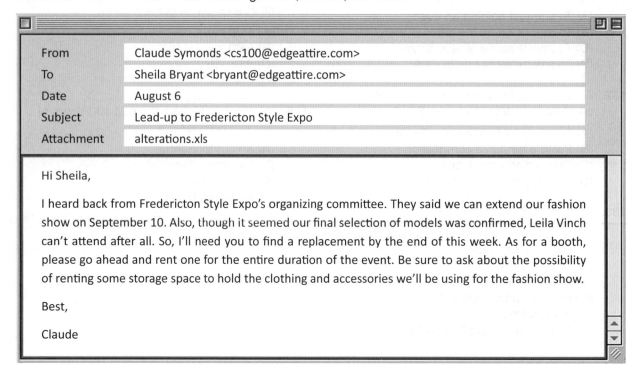

From	Claude Symonds <cs100@edgeattire.com>
To	Sheila Bryant <bryant@edgeattire.com>
Date	August 6
Subject	Lead-up to Fredericton Style Expo
Attachment	alterations.xls

Hi Sheila,

I heard back from Fredericton Style Expo's organizing committee. They said we can extend our fashion show on September 10. Also, though it seemed our final selection of models was confirmed, Leila Vinch can't attend after all. So, I'll need you to find a replacement by the end of this week. As for a booth, please go ahead and rent one for the entire duration of the event. Be sure to ask about the possibility of renting some storage space to hold the clothing and accessories we'll be using for the fashion show.

Best,

Claude

Fredericton Style Expo

Renter: Edge Attire
Contact: Sheila Bryant, 555-4096

Booth size: 4 x 4 (square meters)
Rental charge: $320 ($80 daily rental x 4 days)
Deposit: $45

Terms: Booth rentals include four event tickets, one table, two chairs, one electrical outlet, one set of lighting, and one standard sign. The following are available for an extra fee:

Additional outlets, tables, chairs: $20 per day
Custom sign: $50 installation fee
Wi-Fi access: $10 per day
Storage rental: $15 per day

September 27

Fredericton Style Expo
5 Bulkley Street
Shelburne, NS B0T 1W0

Dear Fredericton Style Expo,

Our company participated in your recent event as an exhibitor. We requested a standard booth and a storage locker for the items used in our fashion show. However, when I checked our final bill, I noticed that we were also charged for access to the Internet. Please refund me the amount we were mistakenly charged as soon as possible. I would also like someone to let me know when this has been done. You can reach me at 555-3938. Thank you.

Yours truly,

Claude Symonds
Edge Attire

186. What is the purpose of the e-mail?

(A) To assign some tasks
(B) To request a price estimate
(C) To make some complaints
(D) To postpone an upcoming event

187. What can be inferred about the Fredericton Style Expo?

(A) It lasted for a total of four days.
(B) It charges a penalty for exhibitors who open late.
(C) It helps models find jobs in the fashion industry.
(D) It promoted exhibitors' products on its Web site.

188. What is NOT included with every booth rental?

(A) Expo Tickets
(B) Furniture
(C) Lights
(D) Storage space

189. How much was Mr. Symonds most likely overcharged for each day of the event?

(A) $10
(B) $15
(C) $20
(D) $50

190. Why does Mr. Symonds ask that a Fredericton Style Expo representative contact him?

(A) To explain why a bill was inaccurate
(B) To inform him that a refund has been completed
(C) To describe how to request a refund
(D) To tell him where a payment can be submitted

GO ON TO THE NEXT PAGE

Questions 191-195 refer to the following review, e-mail, and property list.

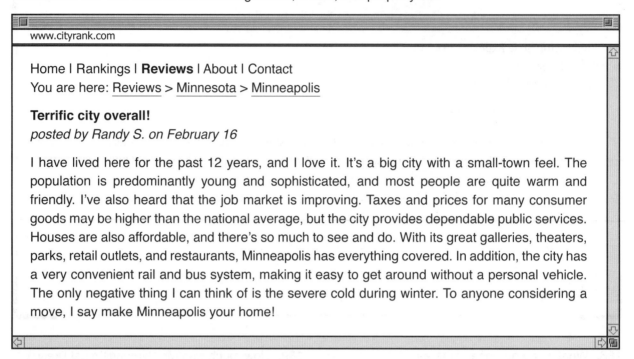

www.cityrank.com

Home I Rankings I **Reviews** I About I Contact
You are here: Reviews > Minnesota > Minneapolis

Terrific city overall!
posted by Randy S. on February 16

I have lived here for the past 12 years, and I love it. It's a big city with a small-town feel. The population is predominantly young and sophisticated, and most people are quite warm and friendly. I've also heard that the job market is improving. Taxes and prices for many consumer goods may be higher than the national average, but the city provides dependable public services. Houses are also affordable, and there's so much to see and do. With its great galleries, theaters, parks, retail outlets, and restaurants, Minneapolis has everything covered. In addition, the city has a very convenient rail and bus system, making it easy to get around without a personal vehicle. The only negative thing I can think of is the severe cold during winter. To anyone considering a move, I say make Minneapolis your home!

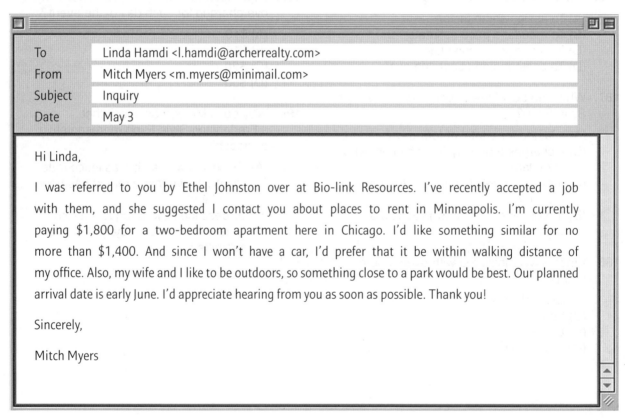

To	Linda Hamdi <l.hamdi@archerrealty.com>
From	Mitch Myers <m.myers@minimail.com>
Subject	Inquiry
Date	May 3

Hi Linda,

I was referred to you by Ethel Johnston over at Bio-link Resources. I've recently accepted a job with them, and she suggested I contact you about places to rent in Minneapolis. I'm currently paying $1,800 for a two-bedroom apartment here in Chicago. I'd like something similar for no more than $1,400. And since I won't have a car, I'd prefer that it be within walking distance of my office. Also, my wife and I like to be outdoors, so something close to a park would be best. Our planned arrival date is early June. I'd appreciate hearing from you as soon as possible. Thank you!

Sincerely,

Mitch Myers

Archer Realty

www.archerrealty.com

Property listings
Prepared on May 4 by Linda Hamdi

Client name: Mr. Mitch Myers
Contact number: 555-2934
E-mail: m.myers@minimail.com
Expected move-in: June 3

2615 Logan Avenue — $1,350

• Features hardwood floors, gym, business center, two bedrooms

• Minimum two-year lease

1611 Plymouth Avenue — $1,050

• Pets OK, reserved parking, near Plymouth Shopping Center, two bedrooms

• Minimum six-month lease

1311 N 17th Avenue — $1,220

• Ample parking, convenient to North Commons Park, two bedrooms

• Minimum one-year lease

2020 Golden Valley Road — $1,300

• Near Golden Valley train station and Sacred Heart Hospital, two bedrooms

• Minimum one-year lease

---

191. In the review, the word "covered" in paragraph 1, line 6 is closest in meaning to

(A) accounted for
(B) reported on
(C) taken care of
(D) looked forward to

192. What is mentioned about Minneapolis?

(A) It has lower taxes than other cities.
(B) It has few options for public transportation.
(C) It has high unemployment.
(D) It has extremely cold weather.

193. Which aspect of Minneapolis will most likely appeal to Mr. Myers?

(A) Luxury houses
(B) Convenient public transportation
(C) Improving job market
(D) Trendy retail outlets

194. What is NOT suggested about the properties listed by Ms. Hamdi?

(A) They will be available in early June.
(B) They require a lease agreement.
(C) They have more than one bedroom.
(D) They are located south of the city.

195. Which location would Mr. Myers most likely be interested in?

(A) 2615 Logan Avenue
(B) 1611 Plymouth Avenue
(C) 1311 N 17th Avenue
(D) 2020 Golden Valley Road

GO ON TO THE NEXT PAGE

Questions 196-200 refer to the following Web page, e-mail, and review.

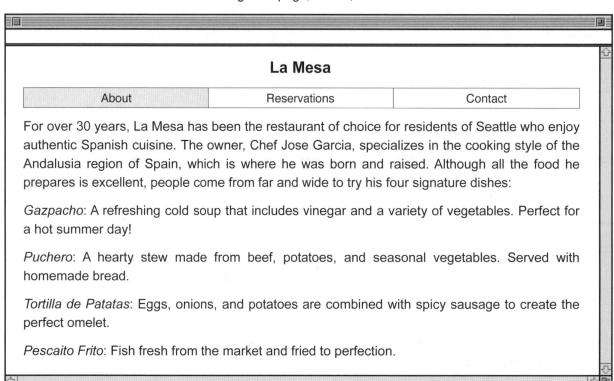

La Mesa

About	Reservations	Contact

For over 30 years, La Mesa has been the restaurant of choice for residents of Seattle who enjoy authentic Spanish cuisine. The owner, Chef Jose Garcia, specializes in the cooking style of the Andalusia region of Spain, which is where he was born and raised. Although all the food he prepares is excellent, people come from far and wide to try his four signature dishes:

Gazpacho: A refreshing cold soup that includes vinegar and a variety of vegetables. Perfect for a hot summer day!

Puchero: A hearty stew made from beef, potatoes, and seasonal vegetables. Served with homemade bread.

Tortilla de Patatas: Eggs, onions, and potatoes are combined with spicy sausage to create the perfect omelet.

Pescaito Frito: Fish fresh from the market and fried to perfection.

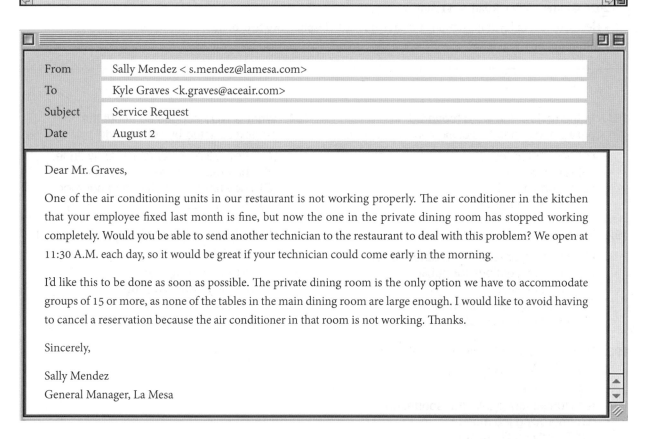

From	Sally Mendez < s.mendez@lamesa.com>
To	Kyle Graves <k.graves@aceair.com>
Subject	Service Request
Date	August 2

Dear Mr. Graves,

One of the air conditioning units in our restaurant is not working properly. The air conditioner in the kitchen that your employee fixed last month is fine, but now the one in the private dining room has stopped working completely. Would you be able to send another technician to the restaurant to deal with this problem? We open at 11:30 A.M. each day, so it would be great if your technician could come early in the morning.

I'd like this to be done as soon as possible. The private dining room is the only option we have to accommodate groups of 15 or more, as none of the tables in the main dining room are large enough. I would like to avoid having to cancel a reservation because the air conditioner in that room is not working. Thanks.

Sincerely,

Sally Mendez
General Manager, La Mesa

Restaurant: La Mesa
Reviewer: David Porter
Date: August 5
Score: 4/5

I arranged for La Mesa to host the retirement party of my company's CEO on August 4. Overall, everyone was very impressed with this restaurant. The dining area was clean and comfortable, and the decor created a very relaxing atmosphere. In addition, the service was excellent — especially considering that there were 18 people in our party. The waiter assigned to us was friendly and efficient. With regard to the food, most of us were very happy with the dishes we ordered. I especially liked that the chef obviously tried to use authentic Spanish cooking methods and seasonings. However, I had the seafood dish, one of the chef's signature dish, and it was a little overcooked.

196. What is mentioned about Mr. Garcia?

(A) He operates several restaurants.
(B) He was born in Spain.
(C) He recently relocated to Seattle.
(D) He has attended culinary school.

197. According to the e-mail, what happened last month?

(A) A kitchen was remodeled.
(B) An employee was promoted.
(C) An appliance was repaired.
(D) A menu was updated.

198. What does Ms. Mendez ask Mr. Graves to do?

(A) Order some equipment
(B) Send a worker
(C) Repair some furniture
(D) Confirm a reservation

199. What is suggested about Mr. Porter?

(A) He is organizing another event with his coworkers.
(B) He has decided not to eat a meal at La Mesa again.
(C) He will be retiring from his company in the near future.
(D) He was not seated in the main area of the restaurant.

200. Which dish did Mr. Porter most likely order?

(A) *Gazpacho*
(B) *Puchero*
(C) *Tortilla de Patatas*
(D) *Pescaito Frito*

This is the end of the test. You may review Parts 5, 6, and 7 if you finish the test early.

TEST 8 점수 환산표

TEST 8은 무사히 잘 마치셨나요? 맞은 개수를 세어본 후 아래의 점수 환산표를 통해 자신의 점수를 예상해 보세요.

전체 난이도   **쉬운 난이도**

파트별 난이도   PART 5 중 ●●○

                  PART 6 하 ●○○

                  PART 7 중 ●●○

정답 수	리딩 점수	정답 수	리딩 점수
98~100개	465~495점	47~49개	200~210점
95~97개	445~460점	44~46개	185~195점
92~94개	425~440점	41~43개	170~180점
89~91개	405~420점	38~40개	155~165점
86~88개	390~400점	35~37개	140~150점
83~85개	375~385점	32~34개	125~135점
80~82개	360~370점	29~31개	110~120점
77~79개	340~355점	26~28개	95~105점
74~76개	325~335점	23~25개	80~90점
71~73개	305~320점	20~22개	65~75점
68~70개	290~300점	17~19개	50~60점
65~67개	275~285점	14~16개	35~45점
62~64개	260~270점	11~13개	20~30점
59~61개	245~255점	8~10개	10~20점
56~58개	235~240점	5~7개	5~10점
53~55개	225~230점	2~4개	5~10점
50~52개	215~220점	0~1개	0~5점

* 점수 환산표는 해커스토익 사이트 유저 데이터를 근거로 제작되었으며, 주기적으로 업데이트되고 있습니다. 해커스토익 사이트
(Hackers.co.kr)에서 최신 경향을 반영하여 업데이트된 점수환산기를 이용하실 수 있습니다. (토익 > 토익게시판 > 토익점수환산기)

TEST 9

×

PART 5
PART 6
PART 7
점수 환산표

잠깐! 테스트 전 확인사항

1. 문제 풀이에 방해가 되는 물건을 모두 치우셨나요?　　　　예 □
2. Answer Sheet, 연필, 지우개를 준비하셨나요?　　　　예 □
3. 시계를 준비하셨나요?　　　　예 □

모든 준비가 완료되었으면 목표 점수를 떠올린 후 테스트를 시작합니다.

문제 풀이를 마치는 시간은 지금부터 **75분 후인** _____시 _____분입니다.

테스트 시간은 총 **75분**이며, 시험 종료 전 2~3분은 정답 검토 및 답안지 마킹을 위해 사용합니다.

READING TEST

In this section, you must demonstrate your ability to read and comprehend English. You will be given a variety of texts and asked to answer questions about these texts. This section is divided into three parts and will take 75 minutes to complete.

Do not mark the answers in your test book. Use the answer sheet that is separately provided.

PART 5

Directions: In each question, you will be asked to review a statement that is missing a word or phrase. Four answer choices will be provided for each statement. Select the best answer and mark the corresponding letter (A), (B), (C), or (D) on the answer sheet.

101. Agricultural products imported from overseas are ------- sold at high prices.

(A) general
(B) generally
(C) generalized
(D) generality

102. Erin Costa ------- head of Biogant's research department in Germany and will be moving there in the fall.

(A) name
(B) named
(C) will name
(D) has been named

103. The reception will take place at 6 o'clock, ------- the speaker finishes the lecture on time.

(A) so that
(B) provided
(C) as if
(D) otherwise

104. The owners of Quora Café posted ------- advertising their new menu around town.

(A) notices
(B) measures
(C) records
(D) contracts

105. All of the conference attendees ------- satisfaction about learning so much useful information.

(A) are expressed
(B) expressed
(C) expressing
(D) expresses

106. Elevai Cruise Lines' newest ships feature a large ------- of dining and entertainment options.

(A) selected
(B) selective
(C) selection
(D) select

107. According to experts, air pollution could worsen unless ------- regulations are enforced.

(A) curious
(B) strict
(C) equal
(D) hazardous

108. The book can give you tips on how to care for ------- plants you have.

(A) where
(B) which
(C) whichever
(D) whoever

109. Piercent Cosmetics is looking for a sales ------- who will deal with foreign customers.

(A) character
(B) associate
(C) proprietor
(D) attribute

110. The restaurant ------- offers a 20 percent discount in addition to free dessert.

(A) yet
(B) quite
(C) even
(D) far

111. The administration's goal is to create an atmosphere that is conducive to innovation, ------- collaboration.

(A) either
(B) despite
(C) above all
(D) as well as

112. Hiring managers will review applications for several ------- in the marketing department.

(A) documents
(B) descriptions
(C) openings
(D) issues

113. The meeting was held on Thursday ------- Friday to save on costs.

(A) such as
(B) due to
(C) instead of
(D) regardless of

114. The workshop teaches aspiring entrepreneurs how to ------- various essential business functions.

(A) impress
(B) convene
(C) perform
(D) affect

115. Mr. Branson ------- left to pick up his luggage after a representative of Turnbull International Airport contacted him.

(A) firstly
(B) closely
(C) instantly
(D) expertly

116. Prior to developing the unused land, Kinsport Property must ------- an agreement with the city.

(A) occupy
(B) reach
(C) reserve
(D) alert

117. Employees should ------- the proposals by Friday to get the supervisor's approval.

(A) resign
(B) submit
(C) compel
(D) command

118. The amount of taxes the town has collected has grown ------- since it adopted the new policies.

(A) reliable
(B) reliance
(C) reliably
(D) rellabllIty

119. Ms. Orville always tries hard to make her clients ------- with her work.

(A) satisfaction
(B) satisfied
(C) satisfying
(D) satisfy

120. The Phoenix Foundation will give a presentation about ------- nature on Wednesday.

(A) protect
(B) protection
(C) protecting
(D) protective

GO ON TO THE NEXT PAGE

121. In his podcast, *Money Talk*, Sam Park provides regular ------- on financial markets.

(A) commenter
(B) commented
(C) commentary
(D) commentator

122. In order to focus on her work, Ms. Heinz does not use her cell phone ------- on duty.

(A) conducting
(B) while
(C) scarcely
(D) after

123. The staff objected to ------- for factory automation because it could lead to job losses.

(A) proposals
(B) proposed
(C) propose
(D) proposes

124. Customers may ------- any complaints they have to our service desk.

(A) demand
(B) accept
(C) direct
(D) engage

125. Glenmark Band postponed its ------- concert after one of its members fell ill.

(A) instinctive
(B) former
(C) eventful
(D) impending

126. If Mr. Vines had known the delivery usually takes more than a week, he ------- his order.

(A) has been canceled
(B) has canceled
(C) would have canceled
(D) will cancel

127. Ski resorts were open ------- late November to mid-April last season.

(A) into
(B) when
(C) from
(D) within

128. The library's Web site did not mention ------- about its changed operating hours.

(A) some
(B) anything
(C) someone
(D) both

129. The new employees will be assigned to different teams ------- their experience and abilities.

(A) dependable
(B) depended
(C) depend
(D) depending on

130. Mr. Cruise was not able to complete his task on time ------- he had all day.

(A) in spite of
(B) even though
(C) as soon as
(D) besides

PART 6

Directions: In this part, you will be asked to read four English texts. Each text is missing a word, phrase, or sentence. Select the answer choice that correctly completes the text and mark the corresponding letter (A), (B), (C), or (D) on the answer sheet.

Questions 131-134 refer to the following e-mail.

To: Raymond Ashburn <ray.ash@insta-flux.com>
From: Gail Stromboli <stromboli@insta-flux.com>
Date: November 13
Subject: Senior Program Analyst

Dear Raymond,

You may have heard that Heidi Birt, our senior program analyst, will be leaving Insta-Flux in five

weeks. I'm in charge of hiring her replacement and would like to ask you for some -------. Firstly,
                                                                                          131.
do you think that any of the programmers here at our Phoenix branch are ------- enough to fill the
                                                                          132.
position? -------. If no suitable internal candidate can be found, I must advertise the job. I would
          133.
prefer ------- this process, though.
       134.

I'm looking forward to hearing back from you.

Sincerely,

Gail Stromboli
Hiring Manager

131. (A) reports
     (B) suggestions
     (C) explanations
     (D) assurances

132. (A) experience
     (B) experiencing
     (C) experiences
     (D) experienced

133. (A) I think she would make an excellent
         department head.
     (B) Furthermore, you will be receiving a
         retirement bonus.
     (C) The employment agency was helpful in
         this regard.
     (D) If not, please recommend someone from
         another location.

134. (A) avoiding
     (B) to avoiding
     (C) avoid
     (D) avoided

GO ON TO THE NEXT PAGE

Questions 135-138 refer to the following notice.

Attention Hotel Guests:

We recently completed renovations at our facility and are pleased to introduce the hotel's new features!

First, our swimming pool facilities -------, and now include a new area for children. -------.
                  135.   **136.**
Furthermore, our reception desk was redecorated to have a tropical look. You can check out the artwork in our public areas ------- relax on the new sofas in the lobby.
                                       137.

When you're feeling hungry, try our newest restaurant! There you can find a variety of popular barbecue dishes, ------- a list of beverages. The restaurant is located next to our reception desk.
                     138.

---

135. (A) will be expanded
    (B) are expanding
    (C) have been expanded
    (D) have been expanding

136. (A) Please keep such items out of the swimming areas.
    (B) You can request them from staff in the lobby.
    (C) The lessons were taught by a well-known instructor.
    (D) We also installed new changing rooms for your convenience.

137. (A) until
    (B) yet
    (C) so
    (D) and

138. (A) along with
    (B) between
    (C) towards
    (D) such as

To: Ludwig Flooring Employees
From: Sylvia Kerry, Head of Human Resources
Subject: Annual performance review
Date: June 10

It is time once again for our annual performance evaluations. Your supervisor will contact you

------- to schedule a meeting.
139.

The evaluations will allow you to discuss your expectations and concerns with your manager. They

also provide the ------- to review your strengths and weaknesses. If improvement is needed, you
140.

will be asked to participate in staff development courses. -------.
141.

Before the evaluations can begin, you must complete a self-assessment of your performance

by June 13. Doing this prior to the discussion ------- better results in the last evaluation. All
142.

performance evaluations need to be completed by July 1.

139. (A) shortly
(B) rarely
(C) typically
(D) hopefully

140. (A) rehearsal
(B) authority
(C) opportunity
(D) designation

141. (A) Innovative product development is crucial to our success.
(B) Keep in mind that training will be obligatory in these cases.
(C) An orientation for new employees is scheduled for Monday.
(D) Top sales performers are rewarded with a bonus.

142. (A) produced
(B) to produce
(C) produces
(D) will produce

GO ON TO THE NEXT PAGE

Questions 143-146 refer to the following article.

(June 3)—The bottled water company IcyBrook plans to change its name to Juniper Food & Bev,

according to recent news -------. The decision was made after the company's acquisition of the
143.

juice company Berry Crush in March. -------.
144.

"We will be selling a wider range of products now. Our original name no longer ------- represents
145.

our brand," said CEO Charles Shah. There will be ------- changes as a result. One of these will be
146.

a new logo. Details will be announced over the coming weeks.

---

143. (A) coverage
(B) covers
(C) coverable
(D) cover

144. (A) It took over the business after a year of
negotiations.
(B) Therefore, the drink was not popular
among consumers.
(C) Another job appointment is set to be
announced soon.
(D) All employees are encouraged to take
part in the contest.

145. (A) full
(B) fullest
(C) fullness
(D) fully

146. (A) further
(B) regulatory
(C) slow
(D) confidential

PART 7

Directions: In this part, you will be asked to read several texts, such as advertisements, articles, instant messages, or examples of business correspondence. Each text is followed by several questions. Select the best answer and mark the corresponding letter (A), (B), (C), or (D) on your answer sheet.

Questions 147-148 refer to the following notice.

Attention Senior Passengers

Passengers of the Harrisburg Mass Transit System (HMTS) are informed that senior passes are available for purchase at any location where bus tickets are sold. To get your senior pass, simply complete the following steps:

- Visit any ticketing location and present a valid piece of photo identification showing that you are 65 or older.
- Fill out a registration form, including your current address and phone number.
- Pay a monthly fee of $46 or an annual fee (for 12 full months) of just $420.

Your card will be processed while you wait. After that, simply present the card when boarding any HMTS bus. If your card is lost, a replacement will cost $5.

---

147. What is the notice mainly about?

(A) Locations for the purchase of transportation cards
(B) Regulations for bus operators
(C) Instructions for getting a transit pass
(D) Increases in fees for use of a system

148. Why might passengers need to pay a $5 fee?

(A) To extend card validity by a month
(B) To register for the first time
(C) To buy a daily pass
(D) To replace a missing item

GO ON TO THE NEXT PAGE

Questions 149-150 refer to the following text-message chain.

Ellen Greenburg [5:14 P.M.]
I really like the script for Cromwell Electronics' upcoming commercial. Our writers did a superb job.

Kelsey Chenoweth [5:15 P.M.]
I agree. There is one thing, though. Marian Ellis wasn't very lively during the rehearsal today. Cromwell Electronics isn't going to be happy if she sounds like that when we record the advertisement next week. Maybe we should consider looking for another voice actor. We have enough left in the budget to hire someone else.

Ellen Greenburg [5:18 P.M.]
I noticed that, too. We need a person who is enthusiastic and expressive. Otherwise, the commercial will not capture the attention of consumers when it is played over the radio. Let's give her one more chance. If she doesn't improve, we will search for a replacement.

149. At 5:15 P.M., what does Mr. Chenoweth most likely mean when he writes, "There is one thing, though"?

(A) He believes that a writer needs to make changes to a script.
(B) He is concerned about the budget for an advertising project.
(C) He has identified a problem with an individual's performance.
(D) He feels that a commercial's release date should be postponed.

150. What is indicated about Cromwell Electronics?

(A) It is expanding its range of electronics.
(B) It is planning to hire more marketing staff.
(C) It will promote its goods on the radio.
(D) It has employed Marian Ellis in the past.

Questions 151-152 refer to the following Web page.

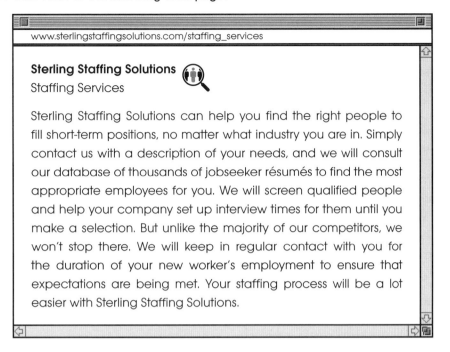

www.sterlingstaffingsolutions.com/staffing_services

Sterling Staffing Solutions
Staffing Services

Sterling Staffing Solutions can help you find the right people to fill short-term positions, no matter what industry you are in. Simply contact us with a description of your needs, and we will consult our database of thousands of jobseeker résumés to find the most appropriate employees for you. We will screen qualified people and help your company set up interview times for them until you make a selection. But unlike the majority of our competitors, we won't stop there. We will keep in regular contact with you for the duration of your new worker's employment to ensure that expectations are being met. Your staffing process will be a lot easier with Sterling Staffing Solutions.

151. What is mentioned about Sterling Staffing Solutions?

(A) It helps companies train workers for promotion.
(B) It makes the final decision on employee placements.
(C) It recruits temporary staff members for businesses.
(D) It has numerous offices located throughout the nation.

152. What is suggested about Sterling Staffing Solutions' business rivals?

(A) They have a limited pool of jobseekers.
(B) They do not thoroughly evaluate candidates.
(C) They charge more for their services.
(D) They do not provide ongoing support.

GO ON TO THE NEXT PAGE

Questions 153-154 refer to the following e-mail.

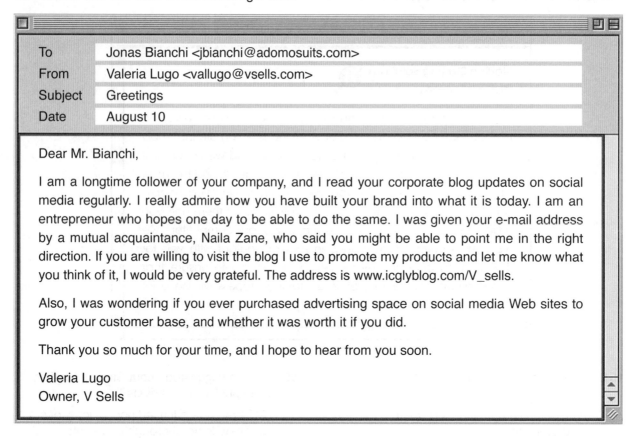

To	Jonas Bianchi <jbianchi@adomosuits.com>
From	Valeria Lugo <vallugo@vsells.com>
Subject	Greetings
Date	August 10

Dear Mr. Bianchi,

I am a longtime follower of your company, and I read your corporate blog updates on social media regularly. I really admire how you have built your brand into what it is today. I am an entrepreneur who hopes one day to be able to do the same. I was given your e-mail address by a mutual acquaintance, Naila Zane, who said you might be able to point me in the right direction. If you are willing to visit the blog I use to promote my products and let me know what you think of it, I would be very grateful. The address is www.icglyblog.com/V_sells.

Also, I was wondering if you ever purchased advertising space on social media Web sites to grow your customer base, and whether it was worth it if you did.

Thank you so much for your time, and I hope to hear from you soon.

Valeria Lugo
Owner, V Sells

153. What is the purpose of the e-mail?

(A) To inquire about a post on a blog
(B) To seek feedback on a Web page
(C) To apply for a position at a corporation
(D) To express admiration for a product

154. What most likely is Ms. Lugo considering?

(A) Launching a new Web site
(B) Hiring a marketing assistant
(C) Promoting goods online
(D) Offering membership discounts

Questions 155-157 refer to the following memo.

To: All Sales Staff, Battista Department Store
From: Andreas Nielsen, Store Manager
Date: October 22

Dear Sales Staff,

Based on your feedback during recent staff meetings, management has decided to eliminate the requirement to wear a uniform. However, it is still important that we present a professional image to our customers. In that regard, sales staff will be required to follow the store's new dress code, which is described below. These changes go into effect at the beginning of next month.

For female staff members, you can wear a black skirt or pair of pants with a white top. Shoes no longer have to be high-heeled, but all footwear must be black leather and cannot be open-toed. Modest jewelry is permitted. Hairstyles are at the discretion of staff, but unnatural colors are not allowed.

For male employees, you have to wear black trousers with a white, collared shirt. Shoes must be black leather. Modest jewelry is also acceptable for men. You may select your own hairstyle, and beards and moustaches are permitted as long as they are kept tidy.

Should you require any further information on the store's dress code, speak with the manager of your department.

---

155. What will take place at the start of November?

(A) New uniforms will be distributed to staff.
(B) A meeting to discuss dress codes will be held.
(C) Managers will hand out lists of new regulations.
(D) A new policy will go into effect.

156. What is suggested about Battista Department Store's female sales staff?

(A) They are currently required to wear high-heeled shoes.
(B) They have guidelines regarding styles of hair.
(C) They wear uniforms that are black in color.
(D) They are asked to refrain from wearing any jewelry.

157. What is NOT part of the dress code for male employees?

(A) Leather footwear must be worn.
(B) Facial hair is not allowed.
(C) Collared shirts are required.
(D) Jewelry is permitted.

GO ON TO THE NEXT PAGE

A Play of Shire Theater Company

By Andrew Craft

Shire Theater Company, situated in London's entertainment district, announced that its current play, *The West Wind*, will not end its run in July as originally planned. — [1] —. Instead, it will continue for at least one more season. — [2] —. This comes as great news to the theater fans who have been unable to buy tickets for the play's sold-out performances. — [3] —. Written by Julie Fielding, *The West Wind* currently stars Noah Wilson. — [4] —. Shire Theater has not yet disclosed whether he will continue with the production. However, the company has confirmed the return of Fiona O'Rourke as the female lead. Her acting skills have been acclaimed by critics. The theater said it would be taking a two-month break to upgrade the set and costumes. The next season of the show is expected to premiere in September.

158. What is the article mainly about?

(A) A new play written by a famous author
(B) An opinion of a theater critic
(C) A former cast member of a play
(D) An extension of a production

159. In which of the positions marked [1], [2], [3], and [4] does the following sentence best belong?

"Many of them were concerned that they would not get a chance to see this play."

(A) [1]
(B) [2]
(C) [3]
(D) [4]

160. What is indicated about Fiona O'Rourke?

(A) She will not continue to play the same role.
(B) She has received positive reviews.
(C) She has not worked with Noah Wilson before.
(D) She will take time off during September.

Boyle Regency Hotel

Lost and Found Items

Please read through the following information regarding lost and found items.

Items found in the hotel lobby, event halls, restrooms, and lounges will be turned in to the main reception desk. Go to the desk and speak with the on-duty manager if you lost something in those areas.

Belongings found in our restaurant, café, and buffet dining area will be turned in to the secondary reception desk at the hotel's rear entrance on Bates Street. Ask the manager on duty about items lost in those areas.

If you forget something at our gym, spa, or swimming facilities, go to the spa's front desk. One of our receptionists will assist you.

Should you forget something in the room you stayed in, check at the main reception desk. If you have already departed, call 555-3009. One of our housekeeping staff will check if your item has been turned in.

Lost items of significant value are stored for 90 days, after which they are auctioned off for local charities. Less valuable items are kept for a period of one month and then discarded.

---

161. For whom is the notice most likely intended?

(A) Reception desk staff members
(B) Guests at an accommodation facility
(C) Managers working at a hotel
(D) Event organizers booking halls

162. Who should visitors speak to if they lose an item in the buffet area?

(A) The manager at the secondary reception desk
(B) A staff member at the hotel's main entrance
(C) The manager of a restaurant
(D) A member of staff in housekeeping

163. What happens to some belongings that are unclaimed after 90 days?

(A) They are distributed to employees.
(B) They are sold for charity groups.
(C) They are donated to used-goods stores.
(D) They are sent to a storage facility.

GO ON TO THE NEXT PAGE

Questions 164-167 refer to the following newsletter article.

Lundus Incorporated Newsletter
December Edition

Lundus Finishes the Year Confidently

As of November, the stock price of Lundus Incorporated was at an all-time high thanks to the Erco Plaza venture and a promising lineup of future projects. "For Erco Plaza," said company CEO Mia Jenkins, "we were able to purchase an affordable plot of land just outside of Johannesburg. And we correctly predicted that there would be high demand for a mall there." All the commercial units in the shopping mall sold by the end of August—the same month they became available.

"Two employees especially deserving of praise for their roles in the Erco Plaza project are Senior Land Acquisition Manager Declan Chetty and Construction Project Manager Aimee Joubert," Ms. Jenkins pointed out.

Next on the company's agenda is the redevelopment of Brakpan Glade, an aging housing complex that will be replaced with modern apartment towers. Next year, Lundus Incorporated hopes to acquire a large plot in Redruth Industrial Park. If all goes smoothly, it will then build a production facility there on behalf of Basin Rock Components.

---

164. Who most likely is Ms. Jenkins?

(A) A member of a municipal committee
(B) The head of a development company
(C) The founder of an investment firm
(D) An executive at a design agency

165. In paragraph 1, line 3, the word "predicted" is closest in meaning to

(A) deliberated
(B) investigated
(C) forecasted
(D) accepted

166. What is suggested about Ms. Joubert?

(A) She participated in the Erco Plaza project.
(B) She received professional training in Johannesburg.
(C) She began running a business enterprise in August.
(D) She followed instructions delivered by Mr. Chetty.

167. What is NOT a goal of Lundus Incorporated?

(A) To carry out a project for a client
(B) To manufacture its own products
(C) To replace some old structures
(D) To gain possession of some land

Questions 168-171 refer to the following text-message chain.

Fatima Shiraz (7:40 P.M.)
Are you planning to go to the textile fair in Bangkok in May?

Stefano Alto (7:43 P.M.)
Yes. I'll probably go for three days.

Fatima Shiraz (7:43 P.M.)
Have you booked a flight yet? I thought we could travel together.

Stefano Alto (7:45 P.M.)
I'd enjoy that. I booked a ticket on Royal Siam Airlines for May 12 at 8:20 A.M. I just got the ticket a few days ago, and there were lots of seats left.

Fatima Shiraz (7:46 P.M.)
Great! Let me check some travel Web sites, and I'll let you know if we can go together.

Fatima Shiraz (7:59 P.M.)
All set!

Stefano Alto (8:04 P.M.)
Fantastic. I'll pick you up at 5:30 A.M. I plan on leaving my vehicle at the long-term parking lot at the airport.

Fatima Shiraz (8:05 P.M.)
Thanks! Sounds good. Anyway, I need to go now. My team manager wants me to stop by his office to talk about Dresden Fashion. They have a problem with the fabric we shipped them last month.

---

168. What is mainly discussed?

(A) Opening a branch
(B) Touring a production facility
(C) Attending a trade fair
(D) Taking a vacation

169. At 7:59 P.M., what does Ms. Shiraz mean when she writes, "All set"?

(A) She submitted a three-day leave request.
(B) She will catch the same flight as Mr. Alto.
(C) She purchased an airline ticket for Mr. Alto.
(D) She will send an updated travel itinerary.

170. What does Mr. Alto offer to do for Ms. Shiraz?

(A) Make a reservation for a hotel
(B) Give her a ride to an airport
(C) Contact a travel agent
(D) Pick up a parcel

171. Why will Ms. Shiraz meet with her supervisor?

(A) She will explain why a shipment was late.
(B) She will discuss a customer complaint.
(C) She will request an office transfer.
(D) She will confirm that a task was completed.

GO ON TO THE NEXT PAGE

Questions 172-175 refer to the following article.

May 15

Westwood Lodge—an international hotel chain that operates in 17 countries—has announced the upcoming availability of Gold Rewards. Guests who sign up for a membership will be able to accumulate points at any Westwood Lodge location. — [1] —.

The new initiative is credited to Dianna Keyes, who was promoted to CEO of Westwood Lodge just two months ago. "Retention of existing customers must be a key part of our business strategy," she said in a recent interview with *Travel Magazine*. — [2] —. "Our competitors have developed this type of system, so we need to provide our guests with access to one as well."

Individuals with a Gold Rewards account will be able to use their points in lieu of paying for a room. — [3] —. The points can also be applied to a wide range of other services. For example, guests staying at the Westwood Lodge here in Miami will be able to book a candlelight dinner on the patio overlooking the beach or a private session with one of the trainers at the state-of-the-art gym. — [4] —. They can even purchase souvenirs at the store in the lobby. And once the hotel completes construction of its spa, guests will be able to redeem points for massages and beauty treatments.

172. What is the main topic of the article?

(A) The expansion of a company overseas
(B) The launch of a membership program
(C) The opening of a new hotel location
(D) The construction of a recreation facility

173. What is indicated about Ms. Keyes?

(A) She implemented a policy change two months ago.
(B) She was employed by a Westwood Lodge competitor.
(C) She took on a leadership role in a company recently.
(D) She was interviewed on a local television show.

174. What is NOT currently a feature of the Westwood Lodge in Miami?

(A) A fitness center
(B) A gift shop
(C) A spa
(D) An outdoor restaurant

175. In which of the following positions marked [1], [2], [3], and [4] does the following sentence best belong?

"However, there will be some limitations with regard to complimentary accommodations during the peak travel season."

(A) [1]
(B) [2]
(C) [3]
(D) [4]

GO ON TO THE NEXT PAGE

Questions 176-180 refer to the following e-mails.

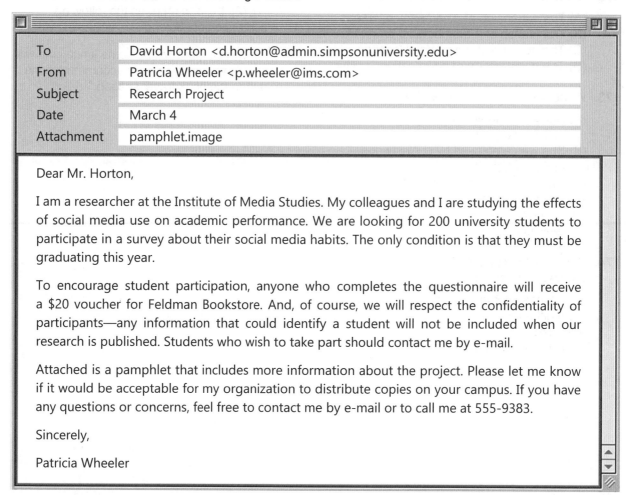

To	David Horton <d.horton@admin.simpsonuniversity.edu>
From	Patricia Wheeler <p.wheeler@ims.com>
Subject	Research Project
Date	March 4
Attachment	pamphlet.image

Dear Mr. Horton,

I am a researcher at the Institute of Media Studies. My colleagues and I are studying the effects of social media use on academic performance. We are looking for 200 university students to participate in a survey about their social media habits. The only condition is that they must be graduating this year.

To encourage student participation, anyone who completes the questionnaire will receive a $20 voucher for Feldman Bookstore. And, of course, we will respect the confidentiality of participants—any information that could identify a student will not be included when our research is published. Students who wish to take part should contact me by e-mail.

Attached is a pamphlet that includes more information about the project. Please let me know if it would be acceptable for my organization to distribute copies on your campus. If you have any questions or concerns, feel free to contact me by e-mail or to call me at 555-9383.

Sincerely,

Patricia Wheeler

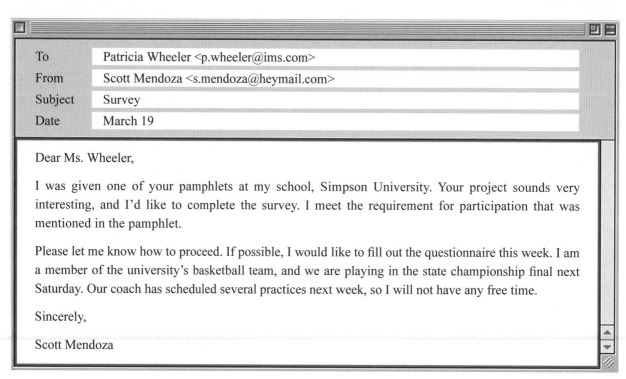

To	Patricia Wheeler <p.wheeler@ims.com>
From	Scott Mendoza <s.mendoza@heymail.com>
Subject	Survey
Date	March 19

Dear Ms. Wheeler,

I was given one of your pamphlets at my school, Simpson University. Your project sounds very interesting, and I'd like to complete the survey. I meet the requirement for participation that was mentioned in the pamphlet.

Please let me know how to proceed. If possible, I would like to fill out the questionnaire this week. I am a member of the university's basketball team, and we are playing in the state championship final next Saturday. Our coach has scheduled several practices next week, so I will not have any free time.

Sincerely,

Scott Mendoza

176. What is indicated about Ms. Wheeler?

(A) She is the head of a student organization.
(B) She is a professor at an educational institution.
(C) She is developing a social media application.
(D) She is working on a project with associates.

177. What will participants in the survey receive?

(A) A cash payment of $20
(B) A coupon for a retail outlet
(C) A ticket for a university event
(D) A book by a popular author

178. What did Mr. Horton most likely do?

(A) He requested a copy of the survey in advance.
(B) He called Ms. Wheeler with some follow-up questions.
(C) He gave permission for a document to be handed out.
(D) He selected students to take part in a research project.

179. What is suggested about Mr. Mendoza?

(A) He is in his final year of university.
(B) He recently transferred to Simpson College.
(C) He has contacted Ms. Wheeler previously.
(D) He works part-time at a school library.

180. Why will Mr. Mendoza be unavailable next week?

(A) He will be traveling to another state.
(B) He will be preparing for a sports event.
(C) He will be studying for a final exam.
(D) He will be trying out for a professional team.

GO ON TO THE NEXT PAGE

Questions 181-185 refer to the following e-mail and article.

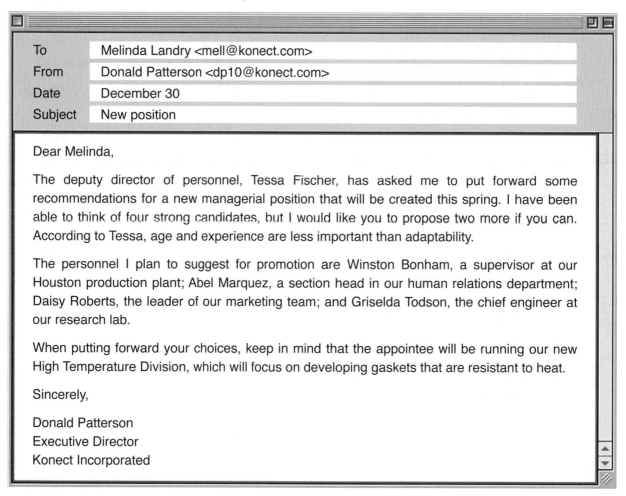

To: Melinda Landry <mell@konect.com>
From: Donald Patterson <dp10@konect.com>
Date: December 30
Subject: New position

Dear Melinda,

The deputy director of personnel, Tessa Fischer, has asked me to put forward some recommendations for a new managerial position that will be created this spring. I have been able to think of four strong candidates, but I would like you to propose two more if you can. According to Tessa, age and experience are less important than adaptability.

The personnel I plan to suggest for promotion are Winston Bonham, a supervisor at our Houston production plant; Abel Marquez, a section head in our human relations department; Daisy Roberts, the leader of our marketing team; and Griselda Todson, the chief engineer at our research lab.

When putting forward your choices, keep in mind that the appointee will be running our new High Temperature Division, which will focus on developing gaskets that are resistant to heat.

Sincerely,

Donald Patterson
Executive Director
Konect Incorporated

Konect Expands Operations, Regains Market Share

Austin (March 17)—The Texas-based company Konect has captured more than half of the market share for gaskets in North America for the first time in over a decade. Its recent success is a result of a set of new products—gaskets made of a synthetic material that can withstand extreme heat.

While Konect has long been a leading producer of rubber and metal gaskets, it has struggled in recent years to compete here against the Indian company Suraja Industries, according to Executive Director Donald Patterson. "We've become more competitive, though, with the launch of our High Temperature Division," said Patterson. "And much of the credit can be given to the head of that division, whose manufacturing background has led to the achievement of high-quality standards."

Konect's stock price increased by 15 percent last quarter, and analyst Benedict Tink predicts that it will rise steadily in the near future.

181. Why did Mr. Patterson contact Ms. Landry?

(A) To praise her contributions to a company
(B) To encourage her to submit an application
(C) To put her in touch with some coworkers
(D) To ask her to provide some suggestions

182. What did Ms. Fischer focus on while selecting an employee?

(A) The ability to meet important deadlines
(B) Familiarity with technological advances
(C) The capability to deal with changes
(D) Knowledge of organizational strategies

183. Which employee most likely received a promotion?

(A) Winston Bonham
(B) Abel Marquez
(C) Daisy Roberts
(D) Griselda Todson

184. What can be inferred about Suraja Industries?

(A) It is attempting to set up a production plant in Austin.
(B) It signed an agreement with another company.
(C) It sells goods in the North American market.
(D) It purchased patents for a wide assortment of gaskets.

185. According to the article, what does Mr. Tink believe will happen?

(A) An invention will be used to improve environmental safety.
(B) A business executive will propose a merger.
(C) A manufacturer will be granted a commercial loan.
(D) A company's stock will increase in value.

GO ON TO THE NEXT PAGE

Questions 186-190 refer to the following e-mail, review, and text message.

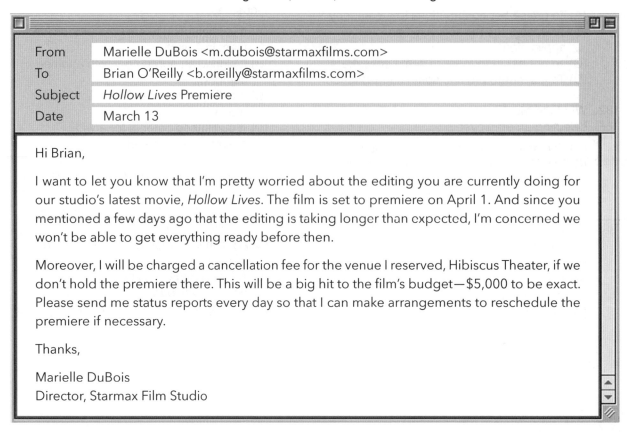

From: Marielle DuBois <m.dubois@starmaxfilms.com>
To: Brian O'Reilly <b.oreilly@starmaxfilms.com>
Subject: *Hollow Lives* Premiere
Date: March 13

Hi Brian,

I want to let you know that I'm pretty worried about the editing you are currently doing for our studio's latest movie, *Hollow Lives*. The film is set to premiere on April 1. And since you mentioned a few days ago that the editing is taking longer than expected, I'm concerned we won't be able to get everything ready before then.

Moreover, I will be charged a cancellation fee for the venue I reserved, Hibiscus Theater, if we don't hold the premiere there. This will be a big hit to the film's budget—$5,000 to be exact. Please send me status reports every day so that I can make arrangements to reschedule the premiere if necessary.

Thanks,

Marielle DuBois
Director, Starmax Film Studio

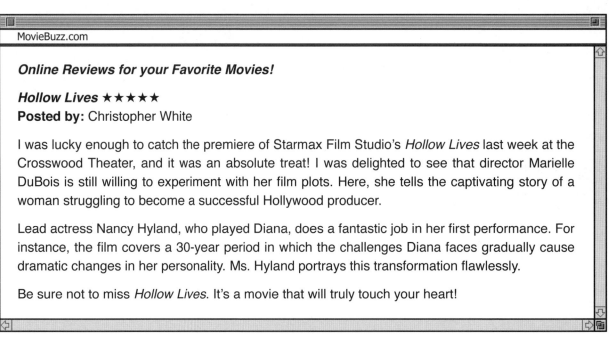

MovieBuzz.com

Online Reviews for your Favorite Movies!

Hollow Lives ★★★★★
Posted by: Christopher White

I was lucky enough to catch the premiere of Starmax Film Studio's *Hollow Lives* last week at the Crosswood Theater, and it was an absolute treat! I was delighted to see that director Marielle DuBois is still willing to experiment with her film plots. Here, she tells the captivating story of a woman struggling to become a successful Hollywood producer.

Lead actress Nancy Hyland, who played Diana, does a fantastic job in her first performance. For instance, the film covers a 30-year period in which the challenges Diana faces gradually cause dramatic changes in her personality. Ms. Hyland portrays this transformation flawlessly.

Be sure not to miss *Hollow Lives*. It's a movie that will truly touch your heart!

Date Received: September 4
Time Received: 10:02 A.M.

Hi, Marielle. As you know, I have been nominated for the Greenfield Film Festival's Best Actress Award for my role as Diana in *Hollow Lives*. I have received three invitations to the festival's awards ceremony on October 1. However, I will only need to use two of them. If you would like to bring an additional guest, just let me know and I will give you my extra invitation. I look forward to seeing you there.

186. Who most likely is Mr. O'Reilly?

(A) A producer
(B) An actor
(C) An editor
(D) A director

187. What does Ms. DuBois ask Mr. O'Reilly to provide?

(A) Scripts for newly hired stars
(B) Budget reports for a production
(C) Résumés for prospective talent
(D) Updates on daily progress

188. What did Ms. DuBois have to do prior to *Hollow Lives*' premiere?

(A) Check on the transitions between scenes
(B) Make a payment in the amount of $5,000
(C) Recruit additional assistants for the studio
(D) Arrange for a celebratory ceremony

189. What is indicated about *Hollow Lives*?

(A) It was the creation of an inexperienced director.
(B) It takes place over a period of several decades.
(C) It was criticized in a popular movie magazine.
(D) It includes scenes shot in various major cities.

190. What is mentioned about Ms. Hyland?

(A) She has been contracted to appear in an upcoming film.
(B) She will meet with Ms. Dubois in person on September 4.
(C) She has scheduled a dinner with one of her colleagues.
(D) She might receive an award for her very first performance.

GO ON TO THE NEXT PAGE

Hilltop AC

Serving Scottsdale for over 25 years!

Prepared for: Brent Accounting

Date: May 21

Contact: Jeremy Watson
Tel: 555-7264
E-mail: j.watson@brentacc.com

Address:
Flanders Building
1509 Greene Circle
Scottsdale, AZ 85254

Description	Amount
Install one Becool Glacier air conditioner	$150.00
Repair one Becool Alpine air conditioner	$300.00
Repair one Becool Frost air conditioner	$400.00
Clean one Becool Frost air conditioner	$125.00
	Total $975.00

To book an appointment, please call 555-3209 or send an e-mail to service@ hilltop.com. Our customer service manager, Judith Hawkins, will be happy to assist you. Hilltop AC technicians are available to perform service calls Monday to Saturday, 8 A.M. to 5 P.M.

To	Judith Hawkins <service@hilltop.com>
From	Jeremy Watson <j.watson@brentacc.com>
Subject	Billing error
Date	June 3

Dear Ms. Hawkins,

I received the bill for the work your technician did in my office last week. Unfortunately, it includes an error. As we discussed after you sent me the initial estimate, the maintenance manager in my building was able to resolve the issue with the Becool Alpine air conditioner. Therefore, the technician from your company did not need to do any work on it. Could you send me a revised bill? Once you do this, I will make full payment. I will be out of the office all afternoon today as I am attending a tax seminar hosted by the National Revenue Agency. However, you can contact me by phone tomorrow if you have any questions. Thank you.

Sincerely,

Jeremy Watson
General Manager
Brent Accounting

Posted by J. Watson on June 7

Overall, I had a very positive experience with Hilltop AC. The technician arrived promptly at 6 P.M. as I requested, and he was very polite and efficient. I also appreciated that he took the time to show me the various functions of the new air conditioner he installed. My only complaint is that there was an error in my bill, but the customer service manager dealt with this issue quickly. I would strongly recommend Hilltop AC to anyone.

191. What is indicated about Hilltop AC?

(A) It provides services seven days a week.
(B) It is located in the Flanders Building.
(C) It opened a second location in Scottsdale.
(D) It was established over two decades ago.

192. Which amount was Mr. Watson not required to pay?

(A) $150
(B) $300
(C) $400
(D) $125

193. Why was Mr. Watson unavailable to take a call on June 3?

(A) He was visiting his company's other branch office.
(B) He was submitting a complaint to a government agency.
(C) He was reviewing his client's tax documents.
(D) He was participating in an informational session.

194. What did Hilltop AC agree to do?

(A) Change an appointment at the last minute
(B) Replace an appliance damaged during cleaning
(C) Provide a discount for an additional charge
(D) Send a worker outside of regular hours

195. What does Mr. Watson say about the technician who visited his office?

(A) He consulted with a maintenance manager.
(B) He explained the operation of a device.
(C) He recommended an inexpensive model.
(D) He arrived after the scheduled time.

GO ON TO THE NEXT PAGE

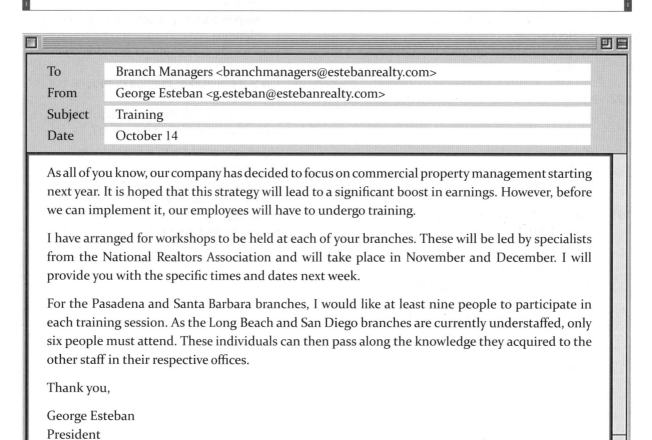

ESTEBAN REALTY — Training Plan

To facilitate our transition from residential to commercial real estate rentals, our employees will need to understand the following:

– **City Zoning Laws** (some businesses are not permitted to operate in certain areas of the city)
– **Commercial Lease Agreements** (leases for commercial tenants are more complex than ones for residential tenants)
– **Building Security** (businesses tend to have many items of value, making it important to properly secure the building)

Training sessions to address these issues and more will be scheduled for the end of the year.

*Slide prepared by Sandra Williams

To	Branch Managers <branchmanagers@estebanrealty.com>
From	George Esteban <g.esteban@estebanrealty.com>
Subject	Training
Date	October 14

As all of you know, our company has decided to focus on commercial property management starting next year. It is hoped that this strategy will lead to a significant boost in earnings. However, before we can implement it, our employees will have to undergo training.

I have arranged for workshops to be held at each of your branches. These will be led by specialists from the National Realtors Association and will take place in November and December. I will provide you with the specific times and dates next week.

For the Pasadena and Santa Barbara branches, I would like at least nine people to participate in each training session. As the Long Beach and San Diego branches are currently understaffed, only six people must attend. These individuals can then pass along the knowledge they acquired to the other staff in their respective offices.

Thank you,

George Esteban
President
Esteban Realty

To	George Esteban <g.esteban@estebanrealty.com>
From	Sandra Williams <s.williams@estebanrealty.com>
Subject	Training Update
Date	November 2

Dear Mr. Esteban,

I just wanted to provide you with an update on the training. The first round of workshops will begin tomorrow. There was one minor issue at the Long Beach Branch—the fire sprinkler system malfunctioned yesterday, so the conference room is not available. However, one of the team leaders, Sam Weber, arranged a meeting room at a nearby conference center, so the workshop will proceed on schedule. As you requested, here is the number of employees who will be attending the first session at each branch:

- Santa Barbara: 10 staff members
- Pasadena: 8 staff members
- Long Beach: 6 staff members
- San Diego: 6 staff members

Let me know if you have any questions or concerns.

Sandra Williams, Human Resources Manager, Esteban Realty

196. According to the presentation slide, what will Esteban Realty employees NOT receive training in?

(A) Municipal regulations
(B) Legal contracts
(C) Building maintenance
(D) Property protection

197. What does Mr. Esteban hope to accomplish with the new strategy?

(A) Reduced customer complaints
(B) Improved employee benefits
(C) Increased company profits
(D) Decreased operating expenses

198. What is indicated about the workshops?

(A) They will be conducted by outside experts.
(B) They will be held at a corporate headquarters.
(C) They will take place for more than two months.
(D) They will include a test for all participants.

199. Who prepared the presentation slide?

(A) A company president
(B) A real estate agent
(C) A department head
(D) A branch manager

200. Which office did not meet Mr. Esteban's requirement?

(A) Santa Barbara
(B) Pasadena
(C) Long Beach
(D) San Diego

This is the end of the test. You may review Parts 5, 6, and 7 if you finish the test early.

TEST 9 점수 환산표

TEST 9는 무사히 잘 마치셨나요? 맞은 개수를 세어본 후 아래의 점수 환산표를 통해 자신의 점수를 예상해 보세요.

전체 난이도   **어려운 난이도**

파트별 난이도   PART 5 상 ●●●
                    PART 6 중 ●●○
                    PART 7 상 ●●●

정답 수	리딩 점수	정답 수	리딩 점수
98~100개	480~495점	47~49개	210~225점
95~97개	470~475점	44~46개	195~205점
92~94개	455~465점	41~43개	180~190점
89~91개	440~450점	38~40개	165~175점
86~88개	425~435점	35~37개	150~160점
83~85개	410~420점	32~34개	135~145점
80~82개	395~405점	29~31개	120~130점
77~79개	380~390점	26~28개	105~115점
74~76개	365~375점	23~25개	90~100점
71~73개	350~360점	20~22개	75~85점
68~70개	330~345점	17~19개	60~70점
65~67개	315~325점	14~16개	45~55점
62~64개	295~310점	11~13개	30~40점
59~61개	275~290점	8~10개	15~25점
56~58개	260~270점	5~7개	10~15점
53~55개	245~255점	2~4개	5~10점
50~52개	230~240점	0~1개	0~5점

* 점수 환산표는 해커스토익 사이트 유저 데이터를 근거로 제작되었으며, 주기적으로 업데이트되고 있습니다. 해커스토익 사이트 (Hackers.co.kr)에서 최신 경향을 반영하여 업데이트된 점수환산기를 이용하실 수 있습니다. (토익 > 토익게시판 > 토익점수환산기)

TEST 10

×

PART 5
PART 6
PART 7
점수 환산표

잠깐! 테스트 전 확인사항

1. 문제 풀이에 방해가 되는 물건을 모두 치우셨나요?   예 □
2. Answer Sheet, 연필, 지우개를 준비하셨나요?   예 □
3. 시계를 준비하셨나요?   예 □

모든 준비가 완료되었으면 목표 점수를 떠올린 후 테스트를 시작합니다.

문제 풀이를 마치는 시간은 지금부터 **75분 후인** _____시 _____분입니다.

테스트 시간은 **총 75분**이며, 시험 종료 전 2~3분은 정답 검토 및 답안지 마킹을 위해 사용합니다.

READING TEST

In this section, you must demonstrate your ability to read and comprehend English. You will be given a variety of texts and asked to answer questions about these texts. This section is divided into three parts and will take 75 minutes to complete.

Do not mark the answers in your test book. Use the answer sheet that is separately provided.

PART 5

Directions: In each question, you will be asked to review a statement that is missing a word or phrase. Four answer choices will be provided for each statement. Select the best answer and mark the corresponding letter (A), (B), (C), or (D) on the answer sheet.

101. There are no seats left in economy class, ------- several remain in business.

(A) but
(B) that
(C) than
(D) nor

102. Mr. Gaviria asked Mr. Horne's staff for assistance as none of ------- were available.

(A) he
(B) him
(C) his
(D) himself

103. Brinity Electronics' latest refrigerator shows a significant ------- in energy use compared to its predecessor.

(A) reduction
(B) reduced
(C) reduce
(D) reduces

104. During delivery, packages that contain delicate items must be handled -------.

(A) caution
(B) cautious
(C) cautions
(D) cautiously

105. ------- on the company's financial difficulties, Mr. Sawyer asked all department managers to cut expenses.

(A) Remarking
(B) Remarks
(C) Remarked
(D) Remark

106. The service centers of Terta Corporation ------- specialized software to track customer complaints.

(A) employ
(B) employs
(C) employing
(D) has employed

107. Board members hope to gain more affordable labor by ------- manufacturing to Asian countries.

(A) inverting
(B) substituting
(C) shifting
(D) transforming

108. -------, Godsal Appliances holds seminars for employees, which have proved to be effective training programs.

(A) Potentially
(B) Questionably
(C) Occasionally
(D) Unanimously

109. New York City will impose a $25 fine on
------- drivers caught in violation of the
parking policy.

(A) any
(B) few
(C) each
(D) much

110. ------- push the reset button whenever the
Internet disconnects, and the problem will
be fixed immediately.

(A) Simple
(B) Simply
(C) Simplicity
(D) Simplify

111. ------- the yearly marketing plan has been
the responsibility of Ms. Hurley and her
team.

(A) Produce
(B) Produced
(C) Producing
(D) Production

112. HynaCorp's newest chemical plant will be
fully ------- by the end of the quarter.

(A) function
(B) functional
(C) functionally
(D) functions

113. Travelers can customize trips easily
because most vacation packages include
------- tours.

(A) scheduled
(B) optional
(C) affluent
(D) reliable

114. The café located ------- the lobby of the
building offers discounts to all tenants.

(A) among
(B) from
(C) on
(D) in

115. Once the committee had reviewed
Mr. Souko's business proposal, it ------- him
a considerable subsidy.

(A) charged
(B) awarded
(C) accessed
(D) donated

116. Hightower Bank's West Covina branch -------
to El Monte at the beginning of last month.

(A) moves
(B) moved
(C) has moved
(D) will move

117. The Kerner Foundation is supported by the
government and also receives funding -------
corporate sponsors.

(A) over
(B) along
(C) through
(D) across

118. Although Hamada's SUV ranks higher than
Sunza's in most surveys, ------- vehicles are
known to be dependable.

(A) and
(B) both
(C) either
(D) several

119. Now retired from public life, Ms. Hicks was a
------- figure during her term as the mayor of
Houston.

(A) previous
(B) private
(C) numerous
(D) prominent

120. Due to budget cuts, from now on city
health inspectors will make ------- visits to
restaurants only twice a year.

(A) frequent
(B) impressive
(C) industrious
(D) routine

GO ON TO THE NEXT PAGE

121. Please check the article thoroughly before ------- it on the Web site to prevent the publication of serious errors.

(A) upload
(B) uploaded
(C) uploading
(D) to upload

122. ------- the charity auction, local bands will hold a free concert in Brighton Hall.

(A) Toward
(B) Upon
(C) Whereas
(D) Following

123. Even though airline miles usually expire after a given period, ------- offered by Leisure Plans do not.

(A) they
(B) them
(C) those
(D) there

124. Employees may refer to the ------- on the intranet for the different project deadlines.

(A) catalog
(B) category
(C) formation
(D) timetable

125. The trade agreement between Japan and India facilitated ------- economic growth in the retail sector.

(A) except
(B) exception
(C) excepts
(D) exceptional

126. The factory workers at Qartman Enterprises were hoping for sizable pay ------- as well as better benefits.

(A) raise
(B) raises
(C) raised
(D) raising

127. The candidate made ------- a positive impression at the interview that he was hired immediately.

(A) so
(B) too
(C) very
(D) such

128. Venus Fashion was unsuccessful with its television campaign and turned to social media to ------- its products.

(A) generate
(B) exchange
(C) market
(D) contribute

129. Members of staff will ensure that customers line up outside the store in an ------- manner.

(A) order
(B) orders
(C) orderly
(D) ordering

130. Since ------- Jonas Meier as CEO of Electa, Ms. Harris has expressed optimism about the future of the company.

(A) replacing
(B) replaced
(C) replace
(D) replacement

PART 6

Directions: In this part, you will be asked to read four English texts. Each text is missing a word, phrase, or sentence. Select the answer choice that correctly completes the text and mark the corresponding letter (A), (B), (C), or (D) on the answer sheet.

Questions 131-134 refer to the following flyer.

The Forge is Open!

Lodz Technological Institute (LTI) proudly introduces the Forge. The Forge is a ------- run by a
131.

community of creators. It is a place where amateur inventors can develop their projects. ------- your
132.

interest lies in electronics, carpentry, or metalworking, the Forge can help you realize your creative

vision. It offers ------- access to a range of facilities such as 3D printers, laser cutters, and more. All
133.

LTI students are welcome to use the equipment during regular university hours. Machinery may be

used for free, and materials are provided at a low cost when required. -------. Stop by the Kaminski
134.

Building, or visit www.lodz.edu/forge for more information.

---

131. (A) group
(B) course
(C) workspace
(D) discussion

132. (A) Whether
(B) Unless
(C) Although
(D) Whereas

133. (A) paid
(B) shared
(C) supervised
(D) finished

134. (A) We offer free shipping for all users.
(B) Items for donation may be dropped off at the office.
(C) We can even help you order whatever you may need.
(D) Membership fees must be paid in advance each month.

Questions 135-138 refer to the following article.

Stelly's Latest Work Sells Out

NEW ORLEANS (April 24)— Local writer Maria Stelly spent almost a decade ------- her novel
135.

Mystery Street. But when the book was finally released on Monday, it sold out in just two hours.

It was ------- to 17 bookstores throughout New Orleans.
136.

"Even though my first publication was moderately successful, I'm surprised by the popularity

of *Mystery Street*, and I'm thankful for all my fans," said Stelly. She believes that innovative

marketing is partially responsible for the book's popularity. -------. Additional copies of Stelly's new
137.

book ------- available by April 30.
138.

---

135. (A) wrote
(B) had written
(C) to write
(D) writer

136. (A) distributed
(B) reported
(C) connected
(D) compared

137. (A) This involved targeting readers who are active on social media.
(B) New Orleans has never hosted the ceremony before.
(C) Yet Stelly only began writing fiction a year ago.
(D) Stelly's first novel was about a young girl who grew up on a farm.

138. (A) became
(B) have become
(C) were becoming
(D) will become

Questions 139-142 refer to the following e-mail.

TO: Joe Hamlin <joe.ham@homeready.com>
FROM: Caroline Quigley <car.qui@homeready.com>
SUBJECT: Sales manager
DATE: August 9

Dear Mr. Hamlin,

I'm writing to let you know that Deborah Watson, one of our sales managers, will be ------- our
                                                                                          139.
manufacturing facility on August 16. Ms. Watson is new to our company. -------, it is important for
                                                                          140.
her to tour the factory and learn how our cleaning appliances are made.

As the assistant supervisor of the factory, I would like you to take Ms. Watson to the assembly

lines. Please ------- her around the manufacturing facility so that she can become familiar with how
              141.
we produce our merchandise. -------. Also, encourage her to ask questions and talk to some of our
                             142.
workers.

Sincerely,

Caroline Quigley
Chief Supervisor, Home Ready Production Plant

---

139. (A) evaluating
(B) leaving
(C) visiting
(D) suspending

140. (A) That is
(B) In contrast
(C) Unusually
(D) Accordingly

141. (A) promote
(B) accompany
(C) recruit
(D) demonstrate

142. (A) Let me know if you think she should be hired after the visit.
(B) It may be possible to eliminate this defect before production.
(C) All the expenses of your trip will be reimbursed by August.
(D) Give special attention to our newest model line at the same time.

Questions 143-146 refer to the following memo.

To: All staff of Brentwood Corp.
From: Dale Rosen, Human Relations Chief
Date: February 26
Subject: Mobile phones in the office

Over the past month, several department managers have expressed concerns about the use of

mobile phones. In particular, the ------- of meetings has decreased significantly. Thus, Brentwood
143.

Corp. ------- to launch a new policy. From now on, mobile phones must be left on employees'
144.

desks instead of being brought inside conference rooms. This is to prevent -------. It is our hope
145.

that staff will be able to better concentrate on the topics being discussed. -------. If an urgent call
146.

or message is expected, a phone may be brought inside on silent mode.

---

143. (A) duration
(B) attendance
(C) productivity
(D) number

144. (A) deciding
(B) was deciding
(C) decides
(D) has decided

145. (A) errors
(B) charges
(C) regulations
(D) interruptions

146. (A) Personal devices will be provided by the company.
(B) You can access the Internet on your phone as needed.
(C) The audiovisual system must be reserved in advance.
(D) We will allow one exception to this office rule.

PART 7

Directions: In this part, you will be asked to read several texts, such as advertisements, articles, instant messages, or examples of business correspondence. Each text is followed by several questions. Select the best answer and mark the corresponding letter (A), (B), (C), or (D) on your answer sheet.

Questions 147-148 refer to the following instructions.

Deena Water Filtration System Maintenance Instructions

To ensure your new Deena Water Filtration System lasts for years, be sure to follow these simple maintenance instructions:

- After installing a filter, turn on any faucet and allow water to flow through it for at least two minutes to wash out any dust and prepare the filter for use.
- Change the filter in each device every six months. A buildup of the substances removed from the water can cause blockages. Do not attempt to use a cleanser as this will damage the filter and prevent it from functioning properly.
- Keep in mind that during the rainy season, filters may need to be changed more frequently.

147. What is the purpose of the instructions?

(A) To explain the process for selecting a suitable model
(B) To illustrate the benefits of a system
(C) To train technicians in a repair procedure
(D) To help customers extend the life of a product

148. What should users do on a regular basis?

(A) Schedule an inspection
(B) Replace a component
(C) Check water quality
(D) Apply a filter cleanser

GO ON TO THE NEXT PAGE

Questions 149-150 refer to the following e-mail.

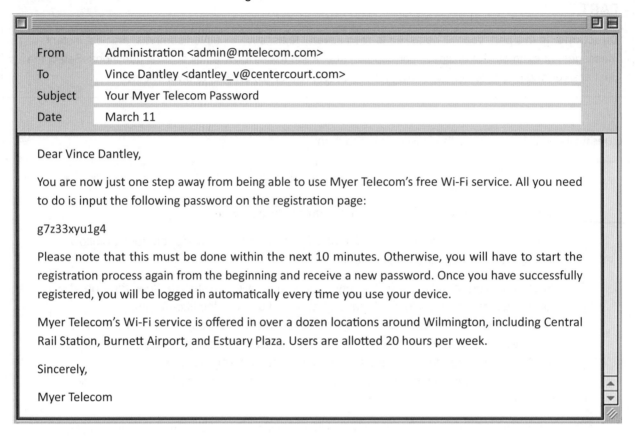

From | Administration <admin@mtelecom.com>
To | Vince Dantley <dantley_v@centercourt.com>
Subject | Your Myer Telecom Password
Date | March 11

Dear Vince Dantley,

You are now just one step away from being able to use Myer Telecom's free Wi-Fi service. All you need to do is input the following password on the registration page:

g7z33xyu1g4

Please note that this must be done within the next 10 minutes. Otherwise, you will have to start the registration process again from the beginning and receive a new password. Once you have successfully registered, you will be logged in automatically every time you use your device.

Myer Telecom's Wi-Fi service is offered in over a dozen locations around Wilmington, including Central Rail Station, Burnett Airport, and Estuary Plaza. Users are allotted 20 hours per week.

Sincerely,

Myer Telecom

---

149. What can be inferred about Mr. Dantley?

(A) He has not completed a registration process.
(B) He was not able to remember a password.
(C) He paid for a mobile phone application.
(D) He relocated to Wilmington recently.

150. What is NOT true about Myer Telecom's Wi-Fi service?

(A) It can be used for a limited amount of time.
(B) It is available in some transportation facilities.
(C) It was launched less than a year ago.
(D) It connects automatically for registered users.

Questions 151-153 refer to the following article.

Renovations Completed at Faber Medical and Dental

June 24—Wallberg Health Group will be reopening its newly renovated third floor at Faber Medical and Dental in Doeville tomorrow. The space, which now features 14 examination rooms, is expected to help reduce patient waiting periods while allowing medical staff to spend more time on consultations. According to Wallberg Health Group representative Joan Bronson, visits to Faber Medical and Dental rose nearly 22 percent last year alone. "The residents of Doeville are getting older, which has resulted in more patients needing to see a doctor. Until now, Faber Medical and Dental has lacked the resources to give these patients the attention they deserve."

To keep up with the growing demand, Faber Medical and Dental has also hired nine additional registered nurses and two full-time general practitioners. The 25 staff that formerly occupied the floor when it was used as an administrative office will return there to resume their former duties. They were sent to Wallberg Health Group's Sharaton and McCollough locations when the six-month, nearly $1.4 million, reconstruction began.

---

151. What is the purpose of the article?

(A) To announce a management change at a clinic
(B) To complain about the lack of available medical staff
(C) To report that a facility will soon be accessible
(D) To describe a process for hiring doctors

152. What caused demand to increase at Faber Medical and Dental?

(A) Improved services
(B) A hospital closure
(C) An aging population
(D) Free consultations

153. What is indicated about the administrative staff?

(A) They will receive training for their new positions.
(B) They were temporarily reassigned to other locations.
(C) They were asked to take a short-term leave of absence.
(D) They were relocated to a newly constructed building.

GO ON TO THE NEXT PAGE

Questions 154-155 refer to the following text-message chain.

Dan Hummel (8:19 P.M.)
I've got some bad news about Natalia Manco's European tour. We're going to have to postpone the rest of her concerts until further notice.

Phoebe Fiscella (8:21 P.M.)
Are you serious? We've already sold a lot of tickets for those shows.

Dan Hummel (8:24 P.M.)
I know, but she is very ill, so there is no chance that she will be able to sing any time soon. I will start working on a statement for the media. We also need to let the halls where she was scheduled to perform know about the situation. Could you do that now?

Phoebe Fiscella (8:25 P.M.)
Possibly. It's pretty late in the evening, so I don't know if all of the managers will be available. But I will definitely be able to do this tomorrow.

154. Why has part of a tour been delayed?

(A) Shows have not received good reviews.
(B) A performer has a schedule conflict.
(C) A singer has a health issue.
(D) Tickets have not been selling well.

155. At 8:25 P.M., what does Ms. Fiscella mean when she writes, "Possibly"?

(A) She cannot confirm that Ms. Manco's concerts will sell out.
(B) She might meet with a representative of the media tomorrow.
(C) She will likely provide refunds to people who purchased tickets.
(D) She may not be able to fulfill Mr. Hummel's request immediately.

Questions 156-157 refer to the following announcement.

Annenberg County Community Job Fair

Tuesday, June 15, 1:00 P.M. to 5:00 P.M.
At Annenberg Convention Center — Seaview Ballroom, 2nd Floor

Need a job?
Come meet representatives of various local companies including:
- Wender Hotel Services
- Porter Medical Center
- Gelec Inc.
- Renew Manufacturing
- Annenberg Transportation
- Oarfield Technical

The event is free to attend, but space is limited. Therefore, participants must register in advance at www.annenbergcounty.com/events. The deadline for registration is June 5. On the day of the job fair, bring copies of your résumé and cover letter to hand out, dress professionally, and be prepared for on-the-spot interviews. Annenberg Convention Center is a two-minute walk from Exit 6 of Gibbs Station, and convention center parking is available at a cost of $10 per hour.

156. What must those interested in attending the job fair do by June 5?

(A) Make a payment online
(B) Visit a registration booth
(C) Sign up on a Web page
(D) Provide proof of residency

157. What is indicated about Annenberg Convention Center?

(A) It is accessible by public transportation.
(B) It has a small number of parking spaces.
(C) It is closed on weekday mornings.
(D) It is adjacent to a well-known hotel.

GO ON TO THE NEXT PAGE

Questions 158-161 refer to the following online chat discussion.

Neil Webb [4:20 P.M.]
Hi, everyone. I met with our department manager, Mr. Tate, this morning, and he asked me to organize a team to make a commercial for the national supermarket chain Vatusi Foods. Elsa, are you available?

Elsa Moss [4:23 P.M.]
I'd like to help out, but I am currently working on the Dresden Apparel campaign. I won't be able to do both projects at the same time.

Neil Webb [4:23 P.M.]
I forgot about that. Courtney, you're the team leader for that campaign. Could you spare Elsa for a few weeks? She worked on the Vatusi Foods advertisement we produced last year, so she should be involved in this one.

Courtney McGuire [4:24 P.M.]
If it's absolutely necessary, I can transfer her to your team. But that's going to make it difficult to meet my deadline.

Neil Webb [4:25 P.M.]
Why don't I ask Mr. Tate to assign two of the junior marketing staff to your project to make up for the loss of Elsa?

Courtney McGuire [4:26 P.M.]
I'd appreciate that. Otherwise, I might have to ask Dresden Apparel for an extension. Elsa, you can start on the Vatusi Foods campaign at the end of the week.

Elsa Moss [4:27 P.M.]
Got it. Neil, do you know when the team will get together to discuss this project?

Neil Webb [4:30 P.M.]
Friday morning. We will meet in the conference room on the second floor at 10 A.M. I'll send you an e-mail with the agenda.

Send

158. What did Mr. Tate do this morning?

(A) Introduced a new team member
(B) Assigned a task to a subordinate
(C) Talked to a department head
(D) Provided feedback on an advertisement

159. What is indicated about Vatusi Foods?

(A) It hired additional staff recently.
(B) It is a locally owned company.
(C) It disliked a commercial idea.
(D) It has worked with Ms. Moss before.

160. At 4:26 P.M., what does Ms. McGuire most likely mean when she writes, "I'd appreciate that"?

(A) She feels that a worker should not be reassigned.
(B) She needs an extension of a project deadline.
(C) She thinks that a campaign should not be released.
(D) She wants more employees added to her team.

161. What most likely will Ms. Moss do on Friday?

(A) Evaluate the performance of some employees
(B) Participate in a meeting with new team members
(C) Send an email to a former client of the company
(D) Give a presentation about Dresden Apparel

GO ON TO THE NEXT PAGE

QUEENSBORO PIZZA

We deliver free to all neighborhoods in Hartford!*

From now until June 30, order a **$19.99 Queen's Combo** consisting of **any three** of the following items:

1 medium cheese pizza
1 spaghetti with meat sauce
1 Caesar salad with grilled chicken
6 buttered breadsticks
10 spicy chicken wings

Plus, all summer long, buy any large pizza with premium toppings and receive a large cheese pizza **absolutely free!**

Premium toppings include:
Artichokes
Sun-dried tomatoes
Roasted red peppers

Ordering is quick and easy using our new smartphone application! Simply download the application and register your personal and payment information to get started. Enter the promotional code 4SUMR on checkout to get 20 percent off on your first order.

*For areas up to two kilometers outside of the Hartford city limits, there is an additional charge of $5.

162. What is NOT true about Queensboro Pizza?

(A) It charges a fee for all deliveries.
(B) It serves other items besides pizza.
(C) It makes pizzas in at least two sizes.
(D) It receives orders through a mobile application.

163. What is indicated about the Queen's Combo?

(A) It includes a complimentary side salad.
(B) Its price has recently been reduced.
(C) Its options will be changed next month.
(D) It is available for a limited time only.

164. How can customers receive a free pizza?

(A) By using a credit card to pay
(B) By entering a summer prize draw
(C) By ordering an item with special ingredients
(D) By presenting a voucher at a restaurant

MEMO

TO: All staff
FROM: Patricia Diaz, CEO, BestSnack Inc.
SUBJECT: Exciting news
DATE: March 18

I'm delighted to announce to everyone that our BestSnack Vending Machine will be launched in 1,000 test locations nationwide starting next Monday. As you all know, the BestSnack is our vending machine with touch-screen technology. — [1] —. It allows users to choose beverages and snacks tailored to their nutritional needs by selecting items based on categories. There are zero-calorie, low-carbohydrate, and sugar-free options. — [2] —. The marketing team is currently in the process of creating press releases informing national news outlets about the BestSnack. — [3] —. As employees, you are invited to participate in the testing process by buying items from these machines. — [4] —. Details about machine locations and item prices will be provided to you this week.

165. What is one purpose of the memo?

(A) To announce a company policy change
(B) To provide information about a product release
(C) To report an addition to the company cafeteria
(D) To introduce a new benefit available to employees

166. What does Ms. Diaz say that the marketing staff is doing?

(A) Completing a survey on people's eating habits
(B) Developing official statements for media companies
(C) Arranging a meeting with the company's suppliers
(D) Planning a campaign event for the near future

167. In which of the positions marked [1], [2], [3], and [4] does the following sentence best belong?

"We will also be posting a message on our Web site."

(A) [1]
(B) [2]
(C) [3]
(D) [4]

GO ON TO THE NEXT PAGE

Questions 168-171 refer to the following advertisement.

Freewater Lavender Farm

Looking for a unique experience this summer? Visit the Freewater Lavender Farm at 821 Corkscrew Road just outside of Lewiston City! The farm's picturesque location and beautiful landscape make it an ideal place to relax.

Stroll among our fields of fragrant lavender or sample homemade delights such as lemonade, teas, cakes, and cookies at the Freewater Café—all perfectly flavored with the farm's finest lavender! Stop by our gift shop for products containing lavender, including soap, lotion, and essential oils. We also carry handicrafts from local artisans and jams, honey, pickles, and cheeses from local farmers.

The café features an outdoor sitting area with views of the river and mountains. Freewater Lavender Farm also welcomes picnic groups and has a beautiful outdoor dining area with tables and benches.

And naturally, a trip to the farm wouldn't be complete without a purchase of beautiful and fragrant lavender blossoms! Drop by our harvest booth and pick up a bunch of dried or fresh lavender for only $12. For further details on our operations and services, visit www.freewaterlavender.com today!

168. What is the advertisement mainly about?

(A) Attractions at an agricultural facility
(B) New products at a local farm
(C) The health benefits of natural foods
(D) A regional crafts fair for artisans

169. The word "finest" in paragraph 2, line 2, is closest in meaning to

(A) best
(B) smoothest
(C) most common
(D) most expensive

170. What is NOT a feature of Freewater Lavender Farm?

(A) A dining establishment serving homemade goods
(B) An area for having outdoor meals
(C) A store selling a variety of local items
(D) A gallery featuring the work of regional artists

171. What can visitors do at the farm's booth?

(A) Register to host a special function
(B) Buy some flowers
(C) Try samples of products
(D) Purchase admission tickets

https://www.clearyfoods.com

Cleary Foods

Home | Shop | Locations | Rewards Program | News | Contact Us

Dear Shoppers:

Cleary Foods has a lot more to offer than just high-quality grocery products and household necessities.

1. The butchers in our fresh meat section are happy to cut your meat into pieces and trim away fat. They will also sharpen your cooking knives for you. — (1) —. If they are busy taking orders, just drop your knives off at the designated knife station and retrieve them when you're done shopping.

2. When the weather is warm, remember to ask our staff to package frozen items with dry ice so they don't melt on the way home. — (2) —. Also, try our brand new rapid beverage chiller in the wine section if you're purchasing unrefrigerated drinks.

3. We will order special products for you that the store doesn't stock as long as our vendors carry them. Just fill out a request form at the checkout counter and give it to the cashier. — (3) —.

Make sure to take advantage of these services on your next visit to Cleary Foods. — (4) —. Click here for a complete list of participating stores.

---

172. What is suggested about butchers at Cleary Foods?

(A) They are glad to flavor purchases with special seasonings.
(B) They provide customers with tips on meat preparation.
(C) They offer daily discounts on a variety of products.
(D) They may be unable to perform a service right away.

173. What is true about special orders?

(A) They are only available to members of a program.
(B) Customers are required to make payment in advance.
(C) They may be delivered to a home address for an extra charge.
(D) Requests may be placed at a store's checkout counter.

174. What is mentioned about Cleary Foods' new piece of equipment?

(A) It is located in the flower aisle.
(B) It cools beverages quickly.
(C) It processes special requests.
(D) It produces dry ice for grocery bags.

175. In which of the positions marked [1], [2], [3], and [4] does the following sentence best belong?

"They are currently available at select locations around the country."

(A) [1]
(B) [2]
(C) [3]
(D) [4]

GO ON TO THE NEXT PAGE

Charity Car Auction
June 25 at Metropolitan Park

The 21st Annual Charity Car Auction will be held on June 25 at Metropolitan Park. This yearly activity is sponsored by several major automobile manufacturers and raises money for children's charities around the state.

The park will open to the public at 10 A.M. The auction starts at 1 P.M. and ends at 6 P.M. or when all cars have been sold. Find great deals on cars and trucks, including commercial vehicles. Bring the family and enjoy a fun day outside. In addition to the auction, there will be a vintage car exhibit, food booths, play areas, and vendors selling various car-related products. Tickets for this event are $5 per person.

For inquiries, call 555-3403 or visit www.charitycarauction.org to get a preview of the cars for sale.

MEMO

June 15

To: All Metropolitan Park staff
From: Joel Gage, Park services director
Subject: Event preparations

In preparation for the 21st Annual Charity Car Auction, I'd like to give everyone some reminders. One day before the event, we will be receiving deliveries of vehicles for the auction and the planned display. The cars for sale will stay in our secure parking lot while the rest will be brought inside through the north entrance.

On the day of the event, the south entrance will be opened to pedestrians, the east entrance will be reserved for park and event staff, and the west entrance will be for emergency personnel. Assistance with traffic and crowd management will be provided by the city's police department.

If you have any questions, do not hesitate to call or stop by my office on the park grounds. Note that I will be unavailable next week as I will be traveling to Chicago to attend a conference. I will see all of you on the day of the deliveries.

176. What is the notice mainly about?

(A) A product launch
(B) An outdoor concert
(C) A fund-raising activity
(D) A sports event

177. Why should readers visit a Web site?

(A) To reserve a booth space
(B) To submit proposals for future events
(C) To see some offerings in advance
(D) To purchase tickets for a group

178. What is suggested about the vintage cars?

(A) They will be offered as prizes in a draw.
(B) They will be sold on the last day of the event.
(C) They will be driven through the north gate.
(D) They will be parked in a secure parking lot.

179. What can be inferred about Mr. Gage?

(A) He will return from a business trip before June 25.
(B) He is seeking volunteer workers to assist emergency crews.
(C) He will move to a new office at the end of the month.
(D) He is planning to take a vacation in Chicago next week.

180. In the memo, the word "management" in paragraph 2, line 3, is closest in meaning to

(A) control
(B) authority
(C) executive
(D) operation

GO ON TO THE NEXT PAGE ➤

Questions 181-185 refer to the following press release and e-mail.

February 14—Larcorn Development is pleased to announce two new residential properties in the Portland area. City View Apartments will be completed on May 10 of this year and will include 30 units. Its convenient location in the business district is sure to make it popular among young professionals. The building will also feature amenities such as a fitness center and entertainment lounge that can be used without charge by residents. Larcorn will also be finishing Star Condominiums on Park Drive. This 20-story building will include 40 luxury apartments and an assortment of high-end shops and restaurants. The completion date for this project is July 28. For more information about both of these properties, visit www.larcorn.com.

To	Sheila Bridges <s.bridges@mailranger.com>
From	Victor Marino <v.marino@topspeedmovers.com>
Subject	Move
Date	July 22
Attachment	invoice.doc

Dear Ms. Bridges,

I just wanted to confirm the schedule for next week. Our movers will arrive at your current residence on August 1 at 7:30 A.M. We estimate that it will take approximately three hours to pack your belongings and load them onto the truck, which means that we should arrive at City View Apartments by 11:30 A.M. Please remind the residence manager to grant us access to the unit at that time.

I also wanted to let you know that there is an error in the invoice you received on July 14. You were mistakenly charged $980 when you should have been billed $883. The coupon you presented qualifies you for a 10 percent price deduction, but this was not included. I have attached a corrected invoice to this e-mail. I apologize for any inconvenience our mistake may have caused.

Sincerely,

Victor Marino
Assistant Manager, Topspeed Movers

181. What is true about Larcorn Development?

(A) It won a competitive bid to construct an office tower.
(B) It has a celebration planned for a specific date.
(C) It is in the process of completing two projects.
(D) It has model units available for buyers to see.

182. What is mentioned about Star Condominiums?

(A) It will be finished on May 10.
(B) It will include commercial spaces.
(C) It will be located in a business area.
(D) It will overlook a city park.

183. What is suggested about Ms. Bridges?

(A) She will pay a monthly maintenance fee.
(B) She will have free access to a gym.
(C) She will receive a partial refund.
(D) She will visit the moving company's office.

184. What is Ms. Bridges asked to do?

(A) Confirm a delivery time
(B) Contact a building manager
(C) Submit an additional payment
(D) Reply to a previous e-mail

185. What problem does Mr. Marino mention?

(A) An invoice was not sent.
(B) An apartment cannot be accessed.
(C) An appointment cannot be changed.
(D) A discount was not applied.

GO ON TO THE NEXT PAGE

To	Maureen Chapman <maureen@lovetts.com>
From	Rodney Tucker <rt77@exchanger.com>
Subject	Request for more hours
Date	April 10

Dear Ms. Chapman,

Thank you for the offer of full-time work at Lovett's Department Store. I feel like I'm doing a good job as a checkout clerk and have enjoyed working with my colleagues. Unfortunately, I must turn down the offer. I'm currently being considered for a summer work program at my school's Department of Computing that would allow me to earn course credits while employed at a software company. The program runs from June through August. If I'm admitted into the program, I will not even have time for a part-time position. Otherwise, I would be happy to keep working for Lovett's Department Store until I graduate in December of this year. After that, I plan to work at the insurance firm my uncle owns.

Thanks,

Rodney Tucker

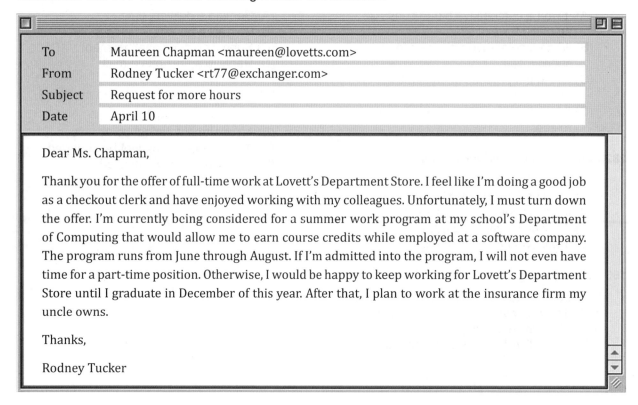

Electronics Section, Lovett's Department Store

Schedule for the second week of June

	June 9	June 10	June 11	June 12	June 13
8:00 A.M.-12:00 P.M.	• Hazel Gates • Annie Montrose	• Dion Kirk • Hazel Gates	• Annie Montrose • Chico Benavidez	• Hazel Gates • Rodney Tucker	• Chico Benavidez • Rodney Tucker
12:00 P.M.-3:00 P.M.	• Annie Montrose	• Hazel Gates	• Chico Benavidez	• Rodney Tucker	• Dion Kirk
3:00 P.M.-7:00 P.M.	• Rodney Tucker	• Chico Benavidez • Rodney Tucker	• Chico Benavidez • Rodney Tucker	• Chico Benavidez	• Annie Montrose • Dion Kirk

Full-time staff: Chico Benavidez (23 hours), Rodney Tucker (23 hours)
Part-time staff: Hazel Gates (12 hours), Dion Kirk (11 hours), Annie Montrose (15 hours)

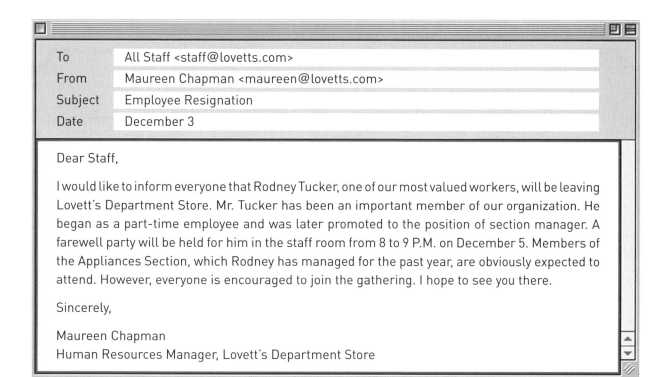

To   All Staff <staff@lovetts.com>

From   Maureen Chapman <maureen@lovetts.com>

Subject Employee Resignation

Date   December 3

Dear Staff,

I would like to inform everyone that Rodney Tucker, one of our most valued workers, will be leaving Lovett's Department Store. Mr. Tucker has been an important member of our organization. He began as a part-time employee and was later promoted to the position of section manager. A farewell party will be held for him in the staff room from 8 to 9 P.M. on December 5. Members of the Appliances Section, which Rodney has managed for the past year, are obviously expected to attend. However, everyone is encouraged to join the gathering. I hope to see you there.

Sincerely,

Maureen Chapman
Human Resources Manager, Lovett's Department Store

---

186. What is suggested about Mr. Tucker?

(A) He did not get a job that he wanted.
(B) He designed a computer program for a retail store.
(C) He usually travels during the summer holidays.
(D) He was not given an opportunity to earn overtime pay.

187. When did some part-timers work together in the evening?

(A) June 8
(B) June 10
(C) June 12
(D) June 13

188. What can be inferred about Lovett's Department Store?

(A) Its branches all have the same hours of operation.
(B) Its full-time employees work 23 hours per week.
(C) It runs a management training program for staff.
(D) It only recently began to sell computers.

189. According to the second e-mail, who is invited to the goodbye party?

(A) Members of a rewards program
(B) Contributors to an organization's fund-raiser
(C) Suppliers to an appliances section
(D) Staff stationed in a certain area

190. Why most likely is Mr. Tucker leaving Lovett's Department Store?

(A) He failed to satisfy some requirements.
(B) He plans to expand his family's business.
(C) He is preparing to relocate to a different city.
(D) He will take a position at a relative's company.

GO ON TO THE NEXT PAGE

Questions 191-195 refer to the following map and e-mails.

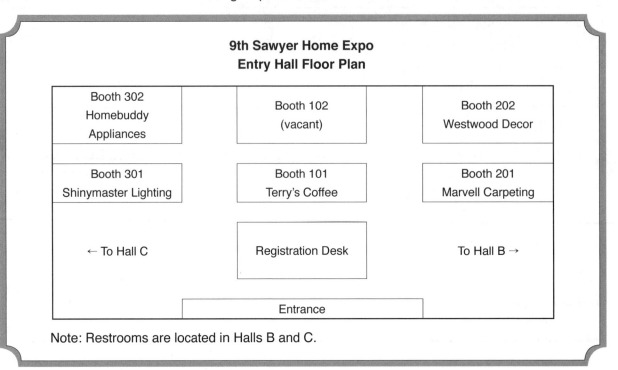

9th Sawyer Home Expo
Entry Hall Floor Plan

Booth 302 Homebuddy Appliances	Booth 102 (vacant)	Booth 202 Westwood Decor
Booth 301 Shinymaster Lighting	Booth 101 Terry's Coffee	Booth 201 Marvell Carpeting
← To Hall C	Registration Desk	To Hall B →
	Entrance	

Note: Restrooms are located in Halls B and C.

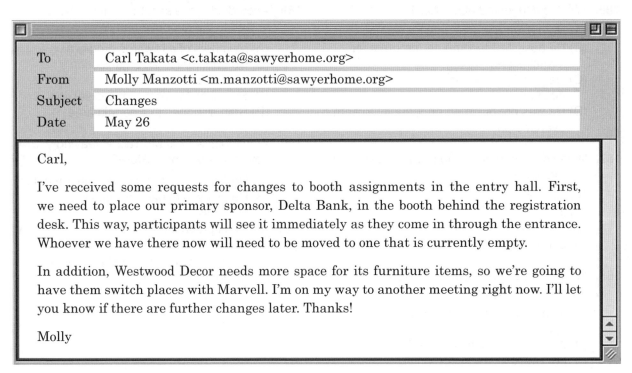

To	Carl Takata <c.takata@sawyerhome.org>
From	Molly Manzotti <m.manzotti@sawyerhome.org>
Subject	Changes
Date	May 26

Carl,

I've received some requests for changes to booth assignments in the entry hall. First, we need to place our primary sponsor, Delta Bank, in the booth behind the registration desk. This way, participants will see it immediately as they come in through the entrance. Whoever we have there now will need to be moved to one that is currently empty.

In addition, Westwood Decor needs more space for its furniture items, so we're going to have them switch places with Marvell. I'm on my way to another meeting right now. I'll let you know if there are further changes later. Thanks!

Molly

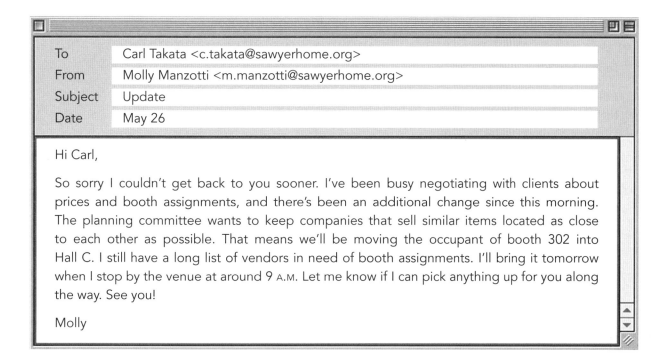

To   Carl Takata <c.takata@sawyerhome.org>

From   Molly Manzotti <m.manzotti@sawyerhome.org>

Subject   Update

Date   May 26

Hi Carl,

So sorry I couldn't get back to you sooner. I've been busy negotiating with clients about prices and booth assignments, and there's been an additional change since this morning. The planning committee wants to keep companies that sell similar items located as close to each other as possible. That means we'll be moving the occupant of booth 302 into Hall C. I still have a long list of vendors in need of booth assignments. I'll bring it tomorrow when I stop by the venue at around 9 A.M. Let me know if I can pick anything up for you along the way. See you!

Molly

191. Where might customers find light fixtures?

(A) Booth 101
(B) Booth 201
(C) Booth 301
(D) Booth 302

192. What is indicated about Westwood Decor?

(A) It is a primary event sponsor.
(B) It is being moved into a different hall.
(C) It needs more space for its merchandise.
(D) It requested a booth behind Marvell Carpeting.

193. Whose booth is Delta Bank replacing?

(A) Marvell Carpeting
(B) Westwood Decor
(C) Terry's Coffee
(D) Shinymaster Lighting

194. What can be inferred about Hall C?

(A) It has lower-priced booths.
(B) It does not have any restrooms.
(C) It will hold all of the appliance sellers.
(D) It was added to accommodate more vendors.

195. What does Ms. Manzotti say she is going to bring to Mr. Takata?

(A) A floor plan
(B) A food order
(C) A list of vendors
(D) An event calendar

GO ON TO THE NEXT PAGE

Questions 196-200 refer to the following letter, brochure, and information.

September 20

Arapali Express
Nichi Building, Lalmati
Jabalpur, Madhya Pradesh 482002

To Whom It May Concern,

I wish to tell you about my experience as a passenger on Arapali Express Flight AE010 on September 7. Overall, it was satisfactory. I appreciated being able to board before some of the others and that our flight departed on time. However, I almost immediately had trouble with my video monitor and, despite the flight crew's assistance, never got it to work. Additionally, I could not get online access because of a problem with my credit card. Thankfully, the flight wasn't too long. Otherwise, I would have become extremely frustrated. I hope you will take steps to ensure that all onboard devices are working properly in the future.

Yours truly,

Sandra Bulsara

Arapali Express Cabin Classes and Amenities

First Class
- Increased baggage allowance
- Complimentary Wi-Fi
- Gourmet meal service with free premium snacks and drinks
- Extra-large seatback monitor with handheld device
- Complimentary luxury skin care kit
- Priority check-in and boarding

Business Class
- Increased baggage allowance
- Complimentary Wi-Fi
- Scheduled meal service with free premium snacks and drinks
- Large seatback monitor with touch-screen access
- Priority check-in and boarding

Premium Economy Class (international flights only)
- Increased baggage allowance
- Paid Wi-Fi access
- Scheduled meal service
- Regular seatback monitor
- Priority boarding

Economy Class
- Scheduled meal service
- Paid Wi-Fi access
- Regular seatback monitor

Arapali Express In-Flight Magazine

New movies this month:

To watch a movie, switch on your video monitor and use the available controls to navigate the screen. Headphones are provided free of charge. For assistance, please call the attention of an in-flight crew member.

Route:	Movie:	Genre:	Length:
Within India	*Mr. Matchbox*	biopic	83 minutes
India to Africa	*Tabla in Heaven*	drama	112 minutes
India to Southeast Asia	*Boman Verma's Fantastic Adventures*	comedy	98 minutes
India to the Middle East	*Bride from Nagpur*	romance	121 minutes
India to Europe	*Tiger that Roams the City*	thriller	105 minutes

Notes:

1. Only P360 and P380 aircraft are equipped with touch screens and handheld devices.
2. Wi-Fi is available on all aircraft except P110s and P120s.
3. Some films may be unavailable on domestic flights.

196. Why was the letter written?

(A) To apply for compensation
(B) To cancel a flight itinerary
(C) To report a policy violation
(D) To convey some feedback

197. In which class was Ms. Bulsara probably seated?

(A) First Class
(B) Business Class
(C) Premium Economy Class
(D) Economy Class

198. What is available exclusively to passengers in first class?

(A) Bonus airline miles
(B) Larger baggage allowance
(C) Early boarding privileges
(D) Skin care products

199. What is indicated about the video controls in business class?

(A) They are not provided on international flights.
(B) They must be specifically requested ahead of time.
(C) They are not installed on some models of airplanes.
(D) They cost a small additional charge to use.

200. What is suggested about the movie, *Mr. Matchbox*?

(A) It is the only one provided free of charge to all classes.
(B) It might not be viewed by Premium Economy Passengers.
(C) It is the latest movie to be added to the airline's selections.
(D) It may not be shown on international routes at a later date.

This is the end of the test. You may review Parts 5, 6, and 7 if you finish the test early.

TEST 10

해커스 토익 실전 1200제 READING

TEST 10 점수 환산표

TEST 10은 무사히 잘 마치셨나요? 맞은 개수를 세어본 후 아래의 점수 환산표를 통해 자신의 점수를 예상해 보세요.

전체 난이도   **어려운 난이도**

파트별 난이도   PART 5 상 ●●●
　　　　　　　　PART 6 상 ●●●
　　　　　　　　PART 7 상 ●●●

정답 수	리딩 점수	정답 수	리딩 점수
98~100개	480~495점	47~49개	210~225점
95~97개	470~475점	44~46개	195~205점
92~94개	455~465점	41~43개	180~190점
89~91개	440~450점	38~40개	165~175점
86~88개	425~435점	35~37개	150~160점
83~85개	410~420점	32~34개	135~145점
80~82개	395~405점	29~31개	120~130점
77~79개	380~390점	26~28개	105~115점
74~76개	365~375점	23~25개	90~100점
71~73개	350~360점	20~22개	75~85점
68~70개	330~345점	17~19개	60~70점
65~67개	315~325점	14~16개	45~55점
62~64개	295~310점	11~13개	30~40점
59~61개	275~290점	8~10개	15~25점
56~58개	260~270점	5~7개	10~15점
53~55개	245~255점	2~4개	5~10점
50~52개	230~240점	0~1개	0~5점

* 점수 환산표는 해커스토익 사이트 유저 데이터를 근거로 제작되었으며, 주기적으로 업데이트되고 있습니다. 해커스토익 사이트
　(Hackers.co.kr)에서 최신 경향을 반영하여 업데이트된 점수환산기를 이용하실 수 있습니다. (토익 > 토익게시판 > 토익점수환산기)

TEST 11

PART 5
PART 6
PART 7
점수 환산표

잠깐! 테스트 전 확인사항

1. 문제 풀이에 방해가 되는 물건을 모두 치우셨나요?   예 □
2. Answer Sheet, 연필, 지우개를 준비하셨나요?   예 □
3. 시계를 준비하셨나요?   예 □

모든 준비가 완료되었으면 목표 점수를 떠올린 후 테스트를 시작합니다.

문제 풀이를 마치는 시간은 지금부터 **75분 후인** _____시 _____분입니다.

테스트 시간은 **총 75분**이며, 시험 종료 전 2~3분은 정답 검토 및 답안지 마킹을 위해 사용합니다.

READING TEST

In this section, you must demonstrate your ability to read and comprehend English. You will be given a variety of texts and asked to answer questions about these texts. This section is divided into three parts and will take 75 minutes to complete.

Do not mark the answers in your test book. Use the answer sheet that is separately provided.

PART 5

Directions: In each question, you will be asked to review a statement that is missing a word or phrase. Four answer choices will be provided for each statement. Select the best answer and mark the corresponding letter (A), (B), (C), or (D) on the answer sheet.

---

101. It has become ------- that the business will improve its profitability by the end of the year.

(A) attractive
(B) honest
(C) obvious
(D) inclusive

102. If a payment deadline is -------, gym members must settle their accounts in person.

(A) miss
(B) misses
(C) missing
(D) missed

103. The employees came ------- the office just as the manager was leaving.

(A) above
(B) into
(C) throughout
(D) often

104. The possibility of a salary increase provided Ms. Farina with adequate financial ------- to improve her performance.

(A) contribution
(B) discussion
(C) decision
(D) motivation

105. Primordial Technologies spent $50,000 in four months, which is half of its ------- advertising budget for the year.

(A) eager
(B) entire
(C) reliant
(D) adjacent

106. Ms. Brooks was recognized by the director ------- being able to handle customer complaints.

(A) for
(B) about
(C) within
(D) between

107. A lack of affordable housing and high unemployment are some of the problems of ------- populated cities.

(A) solely
(B) evenly
(C) heavily
(D) nearly

108. The assistant administrator was given ------- to oversee one of the Greene Foundation's projects.

(A) authoritatively
(B) authority
(C) authorize
(D) authoritative

109. The loan officer has developed a strong ------- with the bank's regular clients.

(A) conversion
(B) knowledge
(C) connection
(D) agreement

110. The employee manual ------- describes the process for requesting an extended leave of absence.

(A) extremely
(B) immediately
(C) specifically
(D) accidentally

111. Engineers ------- that the breakdown in the main pump was caused by damaged electrical wiring.

(A) admire
(B) suspect
(C) resume
(D) implement

112. When giving presentations, researchers have to ------- a thorough understanding of the subject matter.

(A) arrange
(B) demonstrate
(C) initiate
(D) substitute

113. Volunteers ------- refreshments to all attendees at the conclusion of the upcoming seminar.

(A) will be served
(B) is serving
(C) will be serving
(D) had been served

114. The firm has a backup server containing a duplicate set of records ------- the main server should ever fail.

(A) because of
(B) in the event that
(C) as long as
(D) now that

115. Nimble Dynamics is willing to reduce the ------- shipping price if Falconia increases the size of its order.

(A) contractibility
(B) contraction
(C) contracted
(D) contractually

116. The city council favors ------- subsidies so that entrepreneurs will be encouraged to start small businesses.

(A) enveloping
(B) enlarging
(C) relieving
(D) constraining

117. The X300 laptop was not Magnet's most popular model last year, ------- was it the least.

(A) but
(B) nor
(C) and
(D) yet

118. Guests are asked to pay with checks ------- are made out to Enterprise Seminars.

(A) what
(B) whose
(C) that
(D) who

119. Under the revised policy, all foreign workers will be issued permits with three-year ------- dates.

(A) productivity
(B) partnership
(C) validity
(D) symbol

120. Participants must observe the rules of the contest at all times to remain ------- to win a prize.

(A) compatible
(B) responsive
(C) eligible
(D) privileged

GO ON TO THE NEXT PAGE

121. The antibiotic created by BioPharmin has proven to be an ------- treatment for infectious diseases.

(A) assembled
(B) eternal
(C) effective
(D) intimate

122. Due to the fires, some agricultural products became ------- hard to find in stores.

(A) relate
(B) relatively
(C) relative
(D) relativity

123. The organizer recommends that presenters ------- their speeches to 15 minutes or less.

(A) keep
(B) keeps
(C) will keep
(D) is keeping

124. Queensland Holdings has satisfied its investors by ------- generating positive returns over the last decade.

(A) automatically
(B) hopefully
(C) consistently
(D) temporarily

125. Analysts found a ------- amount of evidence suggesting the country's economy was on the path to recovery.

(A) suffice
(B) sufficiency
(C) sufficient
(D) sufficiently

126. Drivers should renew their automobile insurance to ensure that ------- are protected in an accident.

(A) themselves
(B) them
(C) their
(D) they

127. Sanjay Medhi became the head of Deacon Medical College's alumni association as ------- September 1.

(A) on
(B) until
(C) upon
(D) of

128. The laboratory has a significant ------- in its funding for the advancement of life-changing innovations.

(A) allocate
(B) allocator
(C) allocating
(D) allocation

129. During the meeting, the supervisor reminded employees ------- that any violations of policies would have negative consequences.

(A) repeats
(B) repeatedly
(C) repeated
(D) repetition

130. Numerous fans have been engaging in lively online debates since the new game *Battle Planet* -------.

(A) releases
(B) had released
(C) is releasing
(D) was released

Directions: In this part, you will be asked to read four English texts. Each text is missing a word, phrase, or sentence. Select the answer choice that correctly completes the text and mark the corresponding letter (A), (B), (C), or (D) on the answer sheet.

Questions 131-134 refer to the following review.

CAMPFIRE STARLIGHT DREAM 2

We once called Campfire's original Starlight Dream "the best digital reader that money can buy."

Many of you evidently agreed. Because of its dazzling display, slim design, and long battery life,

it was ------- at the time it was released. Well, the all-new Starlight Dream 2 goes further, but is it
    131.

worth buying? Although cheaper overall than the initial -------, the base unit still sells for $250. Let's
                                                      132.

compare the standard features on both. -------. The Dream 2 is thinner, and fits more comfortably
                                       133.

in your hand. The slightly larger screen displays 30 percent more words, but it is 60 grams heavier.

And the new ------- exhibits a sturdy yet elegant aluminum body.
          134.

131. (A) popular
     (B) predictable
     (C) unavailable
     (D) durable

132. (A) it
     (B) that
     (C) one
     (D) all

133. (A) The previous model surpasses all others
         in every way.
     (B) A premium version offers mobile Internet
         connectivity.
     (C) There are a few subtle but important
         differences.
     (D) Campfire is taking pre-orders ahead of
         the item's launch.

134. (A) device
     (B) service
     (C) order
     (D) bundle

GO ON TO THE NEXT PAGE

Questions 135-138 refer to the following notice.

Notice to Shareholders

Orbitall Inc. has changed the venue of its planned shareholder meeting. It ------- at 4:30 P.M. on
135.
December 5 at Rudalle Hotel's banquet hall instead of the JadeLink Center.

In addition, we have made another change. -------. You will have received the Shareholder
136.
Statement form with this year's report by now. Please fill it out and return it by October 31. We will

send an e-mail ------- once your name has been added to the guest list.
137.

Please be reminded that you do not have to be ------- to vote on the resolutions. It is also possible
138.
to vote through Orbitall Inc.'s Web site, www.orbitall.com/vote.

---

135. (A) will take place
(B) has taken place
(C) took place
(D) had taken place

136. (A) However, the gathering will certainly
happen next year.
(B) The board has appointed a new
company director.
(C) The announcements are usually made
at press conferences.
(D) We now require advance registration
in order to attend.

137. (A) confirm
(B) confirmable
(C) confirmation
(D) confirms

138. (A) licensed
(B) selective
(C) present
(D) knowledgeable

To: Ron Winkle <r.winkle@gotmail.com>
From: TG Metro Customer Service <cs@tgmetro.com>
Subject: Reported issue
Date: March 19
Attachment: $10 pass

Dear Mr. Winkle,

TG Metro would like to apologize for the problem you faced on March 14. -------. Even a short
139.

delay is enough to upset a busy schedule. Be assured that our goal is to make sure passengers

always reach their destinations on time. Unfortunately, in this case, a tree branch ------- on one
140.

of our routes, causing the delay. It took less than an hour to resolve this situation. Still, we are

working to avoid a ------- in the future. Branches that overhang the rail lines will be trimmed over
141.

the coming weeks. Please accept the attached electronic pass worth $10. You may consider it

------- a token of our apology. If you need more assistance, you may e-mail us at any time.
142.

Sincerely,

Shane Costa
Customer Service Representative

139. (A) Your complaint has been addressed
         by a customer service agent.
     (B) Our workers were unaware that this
         problem had occurred.
     (C) We would be willing to reschedule your
         appointment.
     (D) We can certainly understand your
         frustration.

140. (A) falls
     (B) fell
     (C) will fall
     (D) has been falling

141. (A) recurrence
     (B) malfunction
     (C) violation
     (D) termination

142. (A) as
     (B) to
     (C) along
     (D) with

GO ON TO THE NEXT PAGE

Questions 143-146 refer to the following announcement.

Demair International Is Becoming Greener

Demair International recently joined the Green Stay Network (GSN), a group of hotels and

guesthouses that work to engage in ------- sustainable practices. To fulfill its obligations as a GSN
                                    143.

member, Demair International places ------- brochures in every suite. These explain in simple
                                   144.

terms how to conserve water and energy while staying at our hotel. In addition, Demair International

now requires that all staff ------- a training video on sustainable practices in the accommodation
                            145.

industry. Bigger improvements are planned as well. -------.
                                                   146.

---

143. (A) environmental
     (B) environmentally
     (C) environment
     (D) environmentalist

144. (A) controversial
     (B) difficult
     (C) instructional
     (D) entertaining

145. (A) watch
     (B) watching
     (C) watches
     (D) to watch

146. (A) Future measures will include the
         installation of solar panels.
     (B) To sign up for a tour, talk to the staff
         at the front desk.
     (C) It will be filmed at various locations
         later this week.
     (D) Reward points can be redeemed for
         room upgrades.

PART 7

Directions: In this part, you will be asked to read several texts, such as advertisements, articles, instant messages, or examples of business correspondence. Each text is followed by several questions. Select the best answer and mark the corresponding letter (A), (B), (C), or (D) on your answer sheet.

Questions 147-148 refer to the following text-message chain.

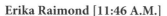

Erika Raimond [11:46 A.M.]
The custom pens we ordered last month were just delivered. Unfortunately, our firm's name is spelled incorrectly. I called the company that made them for us, but it will take at least three days for them to resolve this situation.

Jayce Vills [11:48 A.M.]
Uh-oh. We won't have anything to hand out at tomorrow's seminar.

Erika Raimond [11:50 A.M.]
Actually, we have some notepads with our logo on them in storage. I don't think anyone will mind if we use them.

Jayce Vills [11:55 A.M.]
You have a point. Let's use those for now, but we should also send back the pens to have them corrected.

147. What did Ms. Raimond do this morning?

(A) Attended a seminar
(B) Made an appointment
(C) Mailed a package
(D) Contacted a supplier

148. At 11:55 A.M., what does Mr. Vills most likely mean when he writes, "You have a point"?

(A) An order needs to be refunded.
(B) An activity should be postponed.
(C) Some stationery may be used for an cvcnt.
(D) Some products should be placed in storage.

GO ON TO THE NEXT PAGE

TEST 11

해커스 토익 실전 1200제 READING

Questions 149-150 refer to the following notice.

NOTICE

Be advised that elevator 4, which is normally used as a service elevator to transport workers and equipment, will be briefly unavailable from June 27 to 29 next week. Technicians will be performing routine maintenance. In the meantime, elevator 3 will be used as a service elevator. Tenants' pass cards will not function in that elevator, so please use either elevators 1 or 2. We apologize for any inconvenience this may cause. Please feel free to contact the building's administrative office should you have further questions.

Parker Residential Tower Management

149. What is the purpose of the notice?

(A) To announce planned renovations of a lobby
(B) To inform residents of a temporary change
(C) To notify tenants of a new building policy
(D) To provide guidelines for technicians

150. What is suggested about building tenants?

(A) They have complained about visitor policies.
(B) They will need to visit the administrative office.
(C) They will share all elevators with workers.
(D) They need pass cards to use the elevators.

Questions 151-154 refer to the following article.

Announcements Boost Tatkraft Share Price

June 13—Shares in German electric car manufacturer Tatkraft increased sharply following CEO Johannes Schneider's announcement of the company's performance. Last week, Mr. Schneider announced that Tatkraft made a profit of $212 million the year before and expects to sell over half a million new cars this year. The company's stock price subsequently rose from $567 to $601 a share, revealing strong investor confidence in Tatkraft's ability to continue delivering positive financial results. Prior to last year, the company struggled to convince investors of its capacity for growth with production consistently failing to keep up with demand. Thanks to improvements implemented after the hiring of Elias Muller, an automotive industry veteran, the company simplified its manufacturing process and is producing cars more efficiently. Today, Tatkraft is valued at over $100 billion.

151. The word "performance" in paragraph 1, line 2, is closest in meaning to

(A) routine
(B) appearance
(C) presentation
(D) achievement

152. What did Mr. Schneider do the week before?

(A) He purchased a commercial property.
(B) He appointed a new top executive.
(C) He provided information on anticipated sales.
(D) He distributed profits among shareholders.

153. What is implied about Tatkraft's investors?

(A) They placed orders for vehicles in the new year.
(B) They had doubts about the company's potential.
(C) They increased their investments two years before.
(D) They believe the firm was valued unfairly.

154. What most likely is Mr. Muller mainly responsible for?

(A) Meeting production goals
(B) Developing sales strategies
(C) Analyzing financial results
(D) Resolving customer complaints

GO ON TO THE NEXT PAGE

Questions 155-156 refer to the following Web page.

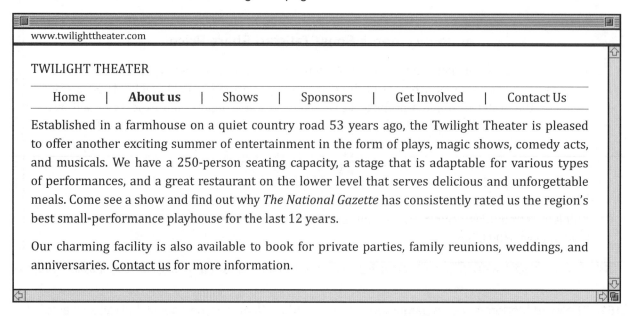

www.twilighttheater.com

TWILIGHT THEATER

Home | **About us** | Shows | Sponsors | Get Involved | Contact Us

Established in a farmhouse on a quiet country road 53 years ago, the Twilight Theater is pleased to offer another exciting summer of entertainment in the form of plays, magic shows, comedy acts, and musicals. We have a 250-person seating capacity, a stage that is adaptable for various types of performances, and a great restaurant on the lower level that serves delicious and unforgettable meals. Come see a show and find out why *The National Gazette* has consistently rated us the region's best small-performance playhouse for the last 12 years.

Our charming facility is also available to book for private parties, family reunions, weddings, and anniversaries. Contact us for more information.

155. What is NOT mentioned about the Twilight Theater?

(A) It occupies a former farm building.
(B) It offers a variety of shows.
(C) It expanded its seating capacity.
(D) It can be reserved for special events.

156. What is indicated about *The National Gazette*?

(A) It supports the Twilight Theater as a sponsor.
(B) It published its first issue on regional playhouses.
(C) It has repeatedly commended the Twilight Theater.
(D) It recently celebrated its 12-year anniversary.

Advertising Sales Executive

Emerald Publications, a leading publisher of daily and weekly newspapers in the UK, is seeking a candidate to work out of its London office. The role involves promoting the company's portfolio of publications over the phone to companies within assigned sectors.

Primary responsibilities:
- Responding to inquiries
- Booking advertising space
- Maintaining customer records
- Meeting revenue targets

Qualifications:
- Ability to negotiate with clients
- Excellent telephone communication skills
- At least one year of media sales experience preferred
- Familiarity with office software

This is a full-time position offering annual base compensation of £20,000 to £24,000 (relative to experience), and benefits such as health insurance, retirement savings, and paid time off.

Click here to apply.

157. What is suggested about Emerald Publications?

(A) It owns newspapers in several countries.
(B) It recently moved to a new office.
(C) It sets financial goals for its staff.
(D) It maintains several different Web sites.

158. What is stated about the advertised position?

(A) It requires a candidate with a degree.
(B) It will pay a salary based on work history.
(C) It will involve occasional business travel.
(D) It provides training in the use of software.

GO ON TO THE NEXT PAGE

Questions 159-161 refer to the following letter.

August 24

Leanna Murillo
111 Fort Street, Basseterre
St. Kitts & Nevis, KN 1201

Dear Ms. Murillo,

Carpenters United has begun planning its fifth symposium, which will bring together members from around the world at a venue in Singapore from February 20 to 23. As with previous events, the aim will be to discuss the latest technological developments in our field. — [1] —. It will also be an opportunity for members to form connections.

This time, we will have the additional task of planning a publicity campaign about sustainable building materials. — [2] —. The campaign will spread awareness about the role that new materials can play in carpentry as well as the environmental benefits of switching to them. We will need to decide whether to carry out this campaign through social media, public events, or traditional advertising. — [3] —.

The symposium will conclude with a vote to determine the members of our leadership committee for the next three years.

We hope that, as a valued member of our association, you will be able to attend. — [4] —.

Danton Spritz
President, Carpenters United

---

159. What is the purpose of the letter?

(A) To confirm attendance at an event
(B) To report a change in leadership
(C) To announce a regular gathering
(D) To emphasize a set of rules

160. According to the letter, what are participants NOT going to do?

(A) Reward successful firms
(B) Talk about industry innovations
(C) Engage in internal networking
(D) Plan a public awareness activity

161. In which of the positions marked [1], [2], [3], and [4] does the following sentence best belong?

"Our choice will probably depend on available funding at the time."

(A) [1]
(B) [2]
(C) [3]
(D) [4]

FINTRAD INC.

Meeting Minutes of July 8

<u>Participants</u>: Sherilyn Mitchell, Dan Gregory, Marva Jackson
<u>Absent</u>: Harvey Fleck
<u>Summary</u>

• Mr. Fleck did not participate because he is representing our store chain at the Fashion Industry Fair in Shanghai and will not be returning until July 15.

• The previous quarter's promotional event was discussed, including its effect on sales, which rose 3 percent compared to the quarter before.

• Ms. Jackson asked about the launch of Fintrad's new clothing line for men at September's Milan Fashion Week event. Ms. Mitchell agreed to contact Fintrad's global head of marketing for detailed plans.

• Items to be finalized at the next meeting on July 16 include team members' roles. Mr. Gregory and Ms. Jackson volunteered to handle press releases and Internet promotions, respectively, while Mr. Fleck's role will be determined later.

162. What most likely is Fintrad?

(A) A conference organizer
(B) A clothing retailer
(C) A financial services firm
(D) A marketing agency

163. What is mentioned about Mr. Fleck?

(A) He is currently away on business.
(B) He recently concluded a major deal.
(C) He was responsible for a sales increase.
(D) He normally works at a head office.

164. Who will probably be placed in charge of online activities?

(A) Sherilyn Mitchell
(B) Dan Gregory
(C) Marva Jackson
(D) Harvey Fleck

GO ON TO THE NEXT PAGE

TEST 11

해커스 토익 실전 1200제 READING

Questions 165-167 refer to the following e-mail.

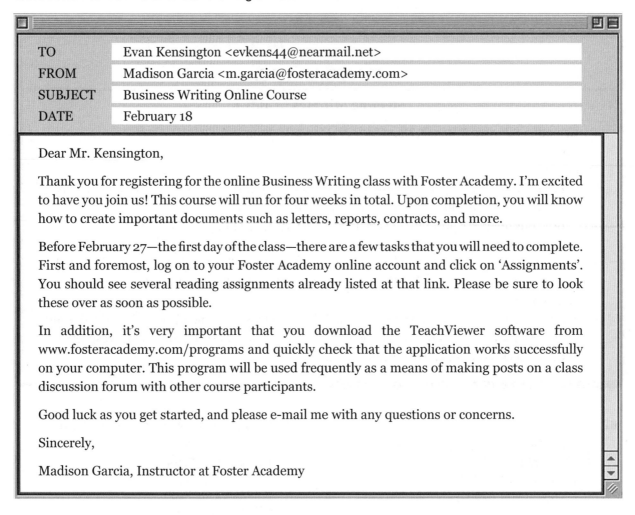

TO   Evan Kensington <evkens44@nearmail.net>

FROM   Madison Garcia <m.garcia@fosteracademy.com>

SUBJECT   Business Writing Online Course

DATE   February 18

Dear Mr. Kensington,

Thank you for registering for the online Business Writing class with Foster Academy. I'm excited to have you join us! This course will run for four weeks in total. Upon completion, you will know how to create important documents such as letters, reports, contracts, and more.

Before February 27—the first day of the class—there are a few tasks that you will need to complete. First and foremost, log on to your Foster Academy online account and click on 'Assignments'. You should see several reading assignments already listed at that link. Please be sure to look these over as soon as possible.

In addition, it's very important that you download the TeachViewer software from www.fosteracademy.com/programs and quickly check that the application works successfully on your computer. This program will be used frequently as a means of making posts on a class discussion forum with other course participants.

Good luck as you get started, and please e-mail me with any questions or concerns.

Sincerely,

Madison Garcia, Instructor at Foster Academy

---

165. What is the main purpose of the e-mail?

(A) To request submission of some documents
(B) To explain a registration process
(C) To get a student ready for a class
(D) To provide a completion certificate

166. What is Mr. Kensington asked to do before February 27?

(A) Navigate to an online page
(B) Post a comment on a Web site
(C) Print out a course schedule
(D) Download some publications

167. What is NOT mentioned about the Business Writing course?

(A) It will take place over several weeks.
(B) It requires the use of some software.
(C) It will end with a graded writing assignment.
(D) It involves communication among classmates.

Questions 168-171 refer to the following online chat discussion.

Fran Jenkins [11:40 A.M.] Hi, team. There's something I'd like to discuss. I know you're all busy, but we need to figure out what to do for the office's social activity this summer. I thought about a beach trip. Does anyone else have ideas?

Harriet Tibbs [11:43 A.M.] Don't you think the water will be too cold for swimming? What about the pool at the sports center?

Gary Franklin [11:43 A.M.] Or a picnic at a local park? We haven't had one in a while.

Fran Jenkins [11:45 A.M.] I agree with you, Harriet. And I'm not sure the sports facility allows food at the pool, but I like the idea of a picnic.

Gary Franklin [11:47 A.M.] Henderson Park has a nice picnic area. There's a big playground and lots of parking.

Harriet Tibbs [11:48 A.M.] It's nice there, but it can get crowded. Gold Ridge Park might be better because it doesn't usually have as many people and we could even do a barbecue.

Fran Jenkins [11:49 A.M.] A barbecue would be perfect, with salads, watermelon, and lots of drinks. Our food budget is higher this year at $1,200.

Gary Franklin [11:50 A.M.] Fantastic! We could even hire a caterer with that amount. I know a good one named Ruth Bernard. She catered my brother's wedding. I could get an estimate from her.

Fran Jenkins [11:52 A.M.] Please do. Find out how much she charges for about 60 people. Then let's meet again on Friday to finalize our plans.

Send

---

168. What does Ms. Jenkins want to discuss with her team?

(A) Finalizing a meeting agenda
(B) Confirming a travel itinerary
(C) Gathering volunteers for an event
(D) Developing ideas for an outing

169. What is indicated about Henderson Park?

(A) It is the nearest one to an office.
(B) It allows visitors to bring their pets.
(C) It tends to attract large crowds.
(D) It has indoor spaces for rent.

170. At 11:50 A.M., what does Mr. Franklin mean when he writes "Fantastic"?

(A) He is pleased that so many people are coming.
(B) A budget was more than he realized.
(C) He is surprised at the high cost of catering.
(D) A venue rental fee is more expensive than he thought.

171. What does Mr. Franklin recommend?

(A) Limiting an event to employees
(B) Hosting an outdoor barbecue
(C) Serving salads and fruit
(D) Hiring Ruth Bernard

GO ON TO THE NEXT PAGE

Questions 172-175 refer to the following e-mail.

To	Lauren Bisson <laurenb@junomail.com>
From	Jaleela Attar <j_attar@geladatech.com>
Subject	RE: Questions
Date	February 8

Dear Ms. Bisson,

I understand that you may be feeling a bit nervous about starting work at Gelada Technologies and am glad that you want to be as prepared as possible. In response to your question about what to do once you get to our building, please stop at the front desk on the first floor. — [1] —. The staff there will be expecting you. Although your normal workday begins at 9:00 A.M., you and some other new staff members will be participating in orientation sessions on the first two days. Make sure you arrive at 8:00 A.M. on these days. — [2] —.

The orientation sessions will cover your day-to-day responsibilities and Gelada Technologies' policies. You will also be issued a laptop with several software applications installed that you must familiarize yourself with. — [3] —. There is no need to bring lunch as it will be provided on the days you are training. Finally, we maintain a casual dress code policy so that employees feel comfortable as they work, so please dress accordingly. — [4] —.

I hope this information addresses your questions. I'll see you next week.

Jaleela Attar
Human Resources Coordinator, Gelada Technologies

172. Why did Ms. Attar write the e-mail?

(A) To remind a trainee to submit some documents
(B) To reply to a question about a job interview
(C) To request feedback on an instructional workshop
(D) To prepare an employee for the first days of work

173. What is true about the training sessions?

(A) They will begin immediately after a tour.
(B) They require participants to arrive earlier than normal.
(C) They will be held separately for two different groups.
(D) They usually take place on the first floor of the building.

174. What is suggested about Gelada Technologies?

(A) It allows some employees to work from home.
(B) It updated the software used by employees.
(C) It will arrange two meals for new staff members.
(D) It recently changed its office dress code policy.

175. In which of the positions marked [1], [2], [3] and [4] does the following sentence best belong?

"Detailed instructions regarding these are included in the training materials."

(A) [1]
(B) [2]
(C) [3]
(D) [4]

GO ON TO THE NEXT PAGE

Migoi Air

Report of Lost Baggage

To be completed at the baggage services desk in the arrivals area

We will do our utmost to locate and return your piece of luggage. If, however, it has not been found after 15 days, it will be officially declared lost, and reimbursement will be issued.

Passenger name	Jane Rubenstein
Telephone number	555-6090
E-mail address	rube@otomail.net
Address during the next month	Snow Treasure Resort, Yuksom, Sikkim 737113, India
Duration of stay	11 days
Permanent address	47570 East Harry Street, Wichita, Kansas 67230, USA
Airport of departure	Kansas City Airport
Airport of arrival	Gangtok Airport
Flight number	MA882

Lost baggage Information

Type	Suitcase
Color	Pink
Brand	Regem
Description	Made of aluminum; square-shaped; one handle on the side and one on the top; Jamaican flag sticker on front
Baggage claim number	AJ8727TP

I declare that the above details are complete and correct to the best of my knowledge.

Signature *Jane Rubenstein*   Date: November 28

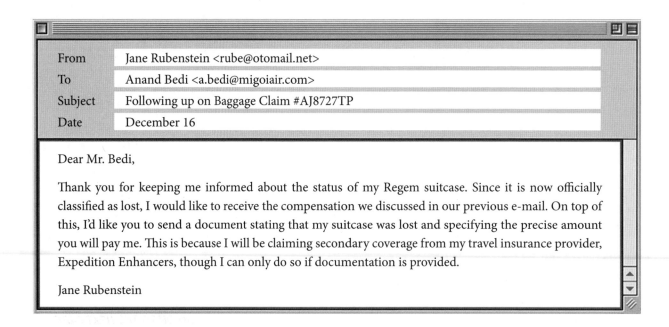

From	Jane Rubenstein <rube@otomail.net>
To	Anand Bedi <a.bedi@migoiair.com>
Subject	Following up on Baggage Claim #AJ8727TP
Date	December 16

Dear Mr. Bedi,

Thank you for keeping me informed about the status of my Regem suitcase. Since it is now officially classified as lost, I would like to receive the compensation we discussed in our previous e-mail. On top of this, I'd like you to send a document stating that my suitcase was lost and specifying the precise amount you will pay me. This is because I will be claiming secondary coverage from my travel insurance provider, Expedition Enhancers, though I can only do so if documentation is provided.

Jane Rubenstein

176. Where will Ms. Rubenstein stay during her trip?

(A) In Yuksom
(B) In Wichita
(C) In Kansas City
(D) In Gangtok

177. What is NOT true about Ms. Rubenstein?

(A) She received a baggage claim code.
(B) She was a passenger on Flight MA882.
(C) She resides on East Harry Street.
(D) She earns reward miles from an airline.

178. What is suggested about Ms. Rubenstein's suitcase?

(A) It was left at the departure airport.
(B) It contains product samples.
(C) It has been missing for over 15 days.
(D) It has a name tag with personal details.

179. According to the e-mail, what did Migoi Air provide?

(A) Regular status updates
(B) Entry to an exclusive lounge
(C) Scanned financial documents
(D) Accommodation vouchers

180. What does Ms. Rubenstein say she will do?

(A) Ask for payment from another company
(B) Provide a list of items that were lost
(C) Submit a complaint to a government official
(D) Send a description of a suitcase

GO ON TO THE NEXT PAGE

Questions 181-185 refer to the following e-mail and receipt.

To	Andrew Quintanar <a.quintanar@baudmail.com>
From	Lynn Choi <l.choi@makerfoods.com>
Subject	Complaint
Date	May 1
Attachment	voucher a592900g

Dear Mr. Quintanar,

I was concerned to read the complaint you submitted using Maker Foods' mobile application. We have a dependable packaging process, and cases like yours, where a purchased bag of snacks is found to be almost entirely full of air, are quite unusual. This problem was likely caused by a machine error.

To compensate you, I would like to send a package containing a selection of our company's products. Please provide an address where we can send it. Moreover, I have attached a voucher that may be redeemed for the product you bought, Curly Chips. It is also good for several other products of ours, including Fruit Chunks, Diet Puffs, and Galaxy Munchies. Though there is no expiration date on the voucher, it will only be accepted by a store that belongs to the retail network Shop Rich Group.

Kind regards,

Lynn Choi
Customer Service Agent

Gordon's Grocers
Stock your kitchen affordably.
Lot 99, Bessell Drive
Baudin Beach, SA 5222
+61 8 5553 6885

Chicken wings (2 kg)	$5.78
Avocados (680 g)	$6.40
Curly Chips (1 bag)	*no charge* **voucher a592900g**
Canned tuna (set of 4)	$3.79
Normal price:	*$3.99*
You save:	*$0.20*
Subtotal:	$15.97
Tax:	$1.76
Total:	$17.73

May 7   7:48 P.M.
Visit www.gordonsgrocers.au to use
our grocery drop-off service.
Enjoy the rest of your day!

0 36000 29145 2

181. What is Ms. Choi concerned about?

(A) A customer's experience with a product
(B) The popularity of a shopping application
(C) The supervision of a manufacturing process
(D) An expiration date printed on a package

182. How most likely did Mr. Quintanar report an issue?

(A) By calling a customer service center
(B) By completing an online form
(C) By submitting a comment card
(D) By visiting an information desk

183. What is indicated about Gordon's Grocers?

(A) It has established multiple branches.
(B) It is part of the Shop Rich Group.
(C) It closes at 8:00 P.M. on weekends.
(D) It is promoting Maker Foods' snacks.

184. What took place during the transaction?

(A) A voucher was exchanged for a beverage.
(B) A credit card was used to make a payment.
(C) A discount was applied to an item.
(D) A sales tax was calculated incorrectly.

185. According to the receipt, what can shoppers do on the Gordon's Grocers Web site?

(A) Learn about a store's history
(B) Search for job vacancies
(C) Schedule a home delivery
(D) Browse promotional items

GO ON TO THE NEXT PAGE

Questions 186-190 refer to the following Web site, e-mail, and memo.

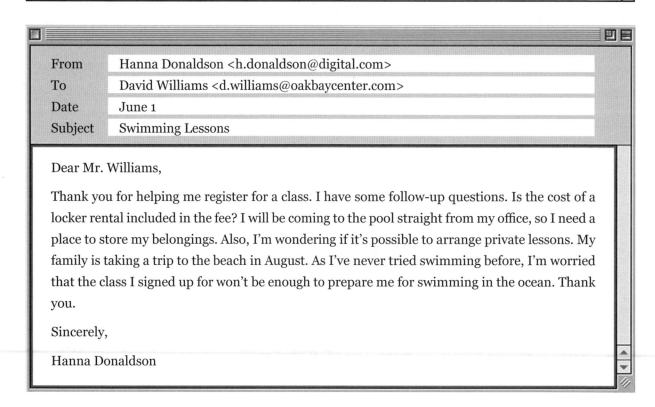

www.oakbaycenter.com

Oak Bay Recreation Center

Home | About | Facilities | **Classes** | Reservations

From June 15 to July 20, we are offering swimming lessons for students of all skill levels.

Class	Description	Instructor	Schedule
Blue	Complete beginners will learn basic swimming skills.	Beth Park	Tuesdays / Thursdays 6:00 P.M. – 7:00 P.M.
Green	Low-intermediate swimmers will work on front and back crawls.	Brett Harford	Saturdays / Sundays 9:00 A.M. – 10:00 A.M.
Yellow	High-intermediate techniques such as the breaststroke will be taught.	Denise Porter	Mondays / Wednesdays 3:00 P.M. – 4:00 P.M.
Red	An opportunity for skilled swimmers to improve their skills	Carl Hong	Saturdays / Sundays 6:30 P.M. – 7:30 P.M.

To sign up, stop by the reception desk and fill out a registration form. For inquiries, you may contact the program coordinator, David Williams, at 555-0398 or e-mail d.williams@oakbaycenter.com.

From	Hanna Donaldson <h.donaldson@digital.com>
To	David Williams <d.williams@oakbaycenter.com>
Date	June 1
Subject	Swimming Lessons

Dear Mr. Williams,

Thank you for helping me register for a class. I have some follow-up questions. Is the cost of a locker rental included in the fee? I will be coming to the pool straight from my office, so I need a place to store my belongings. Also, I'm wondering if it's possible to arrange private lessons. My family is taking a trip to the beach in August. As I've never tried swimming before, I'm worried that the class I signed up for won't be enough to prepare me for swimming in the ocean. Thank you.

Sincerely,

Hanna Donaldson

MEMO

To   All employees
From   Maria Gomez
Date   May 25
Subject Operating hours

Oak Bay Recreation Center's hours of operation will be extended for the summer. From June 10 to August 31, we will close one hour later each day:

Monday to Thursday: 8:30 A.M. – 8:00 P.M.
Friday: 8:30 A.M. – 9:30 P.M.
Saturday: 8:00 A.M. – 10:00 P.M.
Sunday: 8:00 A.M. – 9:00 P.M.

For national holidays that occur during this period, we will follow the Sunday schedule. Also, note that classes on Saturday and Sunday evenings will start one hour later than originally planned. An e-mail will be sent to all registered students next Monday notifying them of this change.

---

186. What is suggested about Ms. Donaldson?

(A) She lives near a beach.
(B) She is currently employed.
(C) She has rented a locker.
(D) She is going to call Mr. Williams.

187. Which class did Ms. Donaldson most likely sign up for?

(A) Blue
(B) Green
(C) Yellow
(D) Red

188. What time will the pool close on national holidays during the summer?

(A) At 8:00 P.M.
(B) At 9:00 P.M.
(C) At 9:30 P.M.
(D) At 10:00 P.M.

189. Which instructor's class has been rescheduled?

(A) Beth Park's
(B) Brett Harford's
(C) Denise Porter's
(D) Carl Hong's

190. According to the memo, what will happen next week?

(A) A schedule will be updated.
(B) Instructors will be assigned.
(C) Students will be contacted.
(D) A facility will be inspected.

GO ON TO THE NEXT PAGE

Questions 191-195 refer to the following e-mails and announcement.

TO: Windfield Art Gallery Staff <staff@windfieldart.com>
FROM: Martina Klancy <m.klancy@windfieldart.com>
SUBJECT: Handling Sculptures
DATE: November 23

Hi, Everyone.

As our gallery will be exhibiting a large number of sculptures next month, it is important that everyone knows how to handle this type of artwork. Please take note of the following guidelines:

1. Put on protective cloth gloves prior to handling any sculptures.
2. Wipe down the base of a sculpted work using the cleaning spray stored in the maintenance closet. This must be done on Thursday afternoons. Please notify gallery visitors that the artwork cannot be viewed while it is being cleaned or dusted.
3. Any pieces weighing more than 15 kilograms must be placed on a cart before being transported through the gallery. Lighter artwork may be relocated by hand as long as gloves are worn.
4. Highly valuable pieces, such as *Fragile Hands*, need to be enclosed in glass cases. These cases must be dusted on Thursday mornings, when the gallery is least busy.

If you have any questions, please feel free to stop by my office.

Sincerely,

Martina Klancy
Owner, Windfield Art Gallery

Windfield Art Gallery

Gallery visitors should be aware that our building will be closed starting tomorrow, November 25, through Friday, November 29. This closure is happening to accommodate the installation of sculptures created by Kali Adisa that recently arrived at our facility from Nigeria. We appreciate your patience while we complete these arrangements.

During this period, we encourage our patrons to view information about Ms. Adisa's December exhibition on our mobile application. Advance tickets are available at a discounted rate exclusively through the application. Pamphlets about our gallery's winter exhibitions can also be picked up from the slot attached to our gallery's front door.

Martina Klancy
Owner, Windfield Art Gallery

TO: Martina Klancy <m.klancy@windfieldart.com>
FROM: Joshua Nero <j.nero@brexfordmuseum.org>
SUBJECT: Last week's visit
DATE: December 16

Dear Ms. Klancy,

I want to congratulate you on the success of last week's Kali Adisa exhibition at your gallery. I was delighted that I took your recommendation to purchase tickets for the exhibition at a reduced price. Overall, I was impressed by Ms. Adisa's work. They were excellent representations of contemporary Nigerian art.

I was disappointed, however, that one piece I had heard about from critics — *Fragile Hands* — was not available on the day I visited because its case was being dusted off. Luckily, the ticket I bought includes admission for multiple days, so I'll plan to come back and see that piece later.

Congratulations again, and I look forward to seeing you at our fund-raiser next Friday.

Regards,

Joshua Nero
Curator, Brexford Art Museum

191. What should staff do with sculptures that weigh over 15 kilograms?

(A) Place them on the floor of the gallery
(B) Use a piece of equipment to move them
(C) Apply a cleaning spray to them twice a week
(D) Wear gloves when lifting them by hand

192. According to the announcement, what happened recently?

(A) Some features were added to a mobile application.
(B) A sculptor gave a series of lectures about an exhibit.
(C) Some works were delivered from another country.
(D) A gallery informed patrons of a permanent closure.

193. What is available at Windfield Art Gallery's front entrance?

(A) Discount coupons
(B) Informational booklets
(C) Artwork prints
(D) Advance tickets

194. What recommendation did Ms. Klancy make to Mr. Nero?

(A) Visiting a facility on a day with fewer people
(B) Taking some photographs of a popular sculpture
(C) Speaking to some art critics about an exhibition
(D) Using a mobile application to get passes

195. When most likely did Mr. Nero see the Kali Adisa exhibition?

(A) On a Thursday morning
(B) On a Thursday afternoon
(C) On a Friday morning
(D) On a Friday afternoon

GO ON TO THE NEXT PAGE

Questions 196-200 refer to the following e-mails and newsletter article.

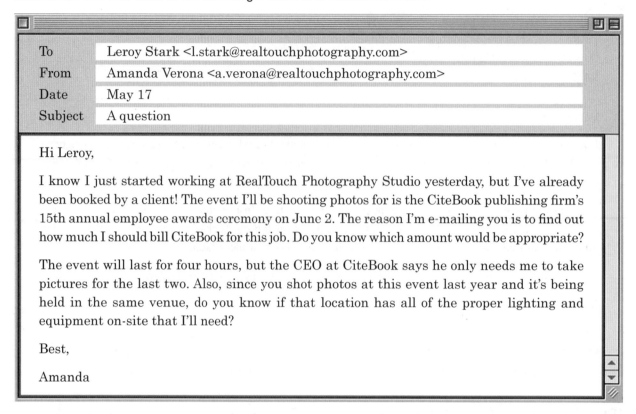

To: Leroy Stark <l.stark@realtouchphotography.com>
From: Amanda Verona <a.verona@realtouchphotography.com>
Date: May 17
Subject: A question

Hi Leroy,

I know I just started working at RealTouch Photography Studio yesterday, but I've already been booked by a client! The event I'll be shooting photos for is the CiteBook publishing firm's 15th annual employee awards ceremony on June 2. The reason I'm e-mailing you is to find out how much I should bill CiteBook for this job. Do you know which amount would be appropriate?

The event will last for four hours, but the CEO at CiteBook says he only needs me to take pictures for the last two. Also, since you shot photos at this event last year and it's being held in the same venue, do you know if that location has all of the proper lighting and equipment on-site that I'll need?

Best,

Amanda

TO: Amanda Verona <a.verona@realtouchphotography.com>
FROM: Patrick Chen <pat_chen@citebook.com>
SUBJECT: Next week's event
DATE: May 25

Dear Ms. Verona,

Thank you for agreeing to take some photographs at our upcoming staff awards ceremony. I just want to remind you of a few things. First, please make sure to show up and start preparing the space reserved for picture-taking at 6 P.M. I know that you'll only be shooting from 7 P.M. to 9 P.M., but I want to ensure you'll be there ahead of time because we would like to get shots of our executives promptly at 7 P.M.

Also, the lighting and equipment you'll need should be all set up in Rosewood Hall. Please don't worry about bringing anything extra. Should you have any questions throughout the ceremony, please text my cell phone at 555-9233, as I am in charge of overseeing everything for this event.

I look forward to seeing you on June 2.

Sincerely,

Patrick Chen
Event Planner
CiteBook

CiteBook Company Newsletter

Employee Awards Ceremony a Success
by Fiona Walsh

July 1—Last month's yearly employee awards ceremony was a huge success. Countless awards were presented, with the CEO distributing medals to several staff members for their work on last winter's e-book social media campaign.

Event planner Patrick Chen did an excellent job as well, finding a replacement photographer at the last minute because the one he had originally booked back in May was sick. The photographer took excellent shots of our executive team as well as workers from each department. To view photos from the event, follow the link to our company network here.

---

196. What is suggested about RealTouch Photography Studio?

(A) It has launched a social media page.
(B) It will hold an anniversary event this year.
(C) It hired a new staff member in May.
(D) It provides discounts for returning customers.

197. How long will the CiteBook ceremony last?

(A) For two hours
(B) For three hours
(C) For four hours
(D) For five hours

198. What is suggested about Mr. Stark?

(A) He will bring some lighting equipment to a venue.
(B) He took some pictures at Rosewood Hall last year.
(C) He is responsible for Ms. Verona's training.
(D) He is familiar with CiteBook's e-book products.

199. In the second e-mail, the phrase "show up" in paragraph 1, line 2, is closest in meaning to

(A) guide
(B) display
(C) arrive
(D) impress

200. According to the article, what happened on June 2?

(A) Ms. Verona was unable to work due to illness.
(B) Marketing employees unveiled a future campaign.
(C) Mr. Chen took a photo with the executives at 7 P.M.
(D) CiteBook's CEO gave out some cash prizes to staff.

This is the end of the test. You may review Parts 5, 6, and 7 if you finish the test early.

정답 p.386 / 해석·해설 [별권] 해설집 p.214 / 해커스 토익 빅플로 자동 채점 및 취약 유형 분석하기

* 다음 페이지에 있는 TEST 11 점수 환산표를 확인해 자신의 토익 리딩 점수를 예상해 보세요.

TEST 11

해커스 토익 실전 1200제 READING

TEST 11 점수 환산표

TEST 11은 무사히 잘 마치셨나요? 맞은 개수를 세어본 후 아래의 점수 환산표를 통해 자신의 점수를 예상해 보세요.

전체 난이도   **어려운 난이도**

파트별 난이도   PART 5 중 ●●○
                        PART 6 중 ●●○
                        PART 7 상 ●●●

정답 수	리딩 점수	정답 수	리딩 점수
98~100개	480~495점	47~49개	210~225점
95~97개	470~475점	44~46개	195~205점
92~94개	455~465점	41~43개	180~190점
89~91개	440~450점	38~40개	165~175점
86~88개	425~435점	35~37개	150~160점
83~85개	410~420점	32~34개	135~145점
80~82개	395~405점	29~31개	120~130점
77~79개	380~390점	26~28개	105~115점
74~76개	365~375점	23~25개	90~100점
71~73개	350~360점	20~22개	75~85점
68~70개	330~345점	17~19개	60~70점
65~67개	315~325점	14~16개	45~55점
62~64개	295~310점	11~13개	30~40점
59~61개	275~290점	8~10개	15~25점
56~58개	260~270점	5~7개	10~15점
53~55개	245~255점	2~4개	5~10점
50~52개	230~240점	0~1개	0~5점

* 점수 환산표는 해커스토익 사이트 유저 데이터를 근거로 제작되었으며, 주기적으로 업데이트되고 있습니다. 해커스토익 사이트
  (Hackers.co.kr)에서 최신 경향을 반영하여 업데이트된 점수환산기를 이용하실 수 있습니다. (토익 > 토익게시판 > 토익점수환산기)

TEST 12

PART 5
PART 6
PART 7
점수 환산표

잠깐! 테스트 전 확인사항

1. 문제 풀이에 방해가 되는 물건을 모두 치우셨나요?   예 □
2. Answer Sheet, 연필, 지우개를 준비하셨나요?   예 □
3. 시계를 준비하셨나요?   예 □

모든 준비가 완료되었으면 목표 점수를 떠올린 후 테스트를 시작합니다.

문제 풀이를 마치는 시간은 지금부터 **75분 후인** _____시 _____분입니다.

테스트 시간은 **총 75분**이며, 시험 종료 전 2~3분은 정답 검토 및 답안지 마킹을 위해 사용합니다.

READING TEST

In this section, you must demonstrate your ability to read and comprehend English. You will be given a variety of texts and asked to answer questions about these texts. This section is divided into three parts and will take 75 minutes to complete.

Do not mark the answers in your test book. Use the answer sheet that is separately provided.

PART 5

Directions: In each question, you will be asked to review a statement that is missing a word or phrase. Four answer choices will be provided for each statement. Select the best answer and mark the corresponding letter (A), (B), (C), or (D) on the answer sheet.

101. Good speakers can usually ------- people's moods and change their tone accordingly.

(A) sense
(B) sensed
(C) sensing
(D) sensibly

102. Ms. Paget's flight doesn't arrive until Monday night, so ------- asked the meeting to be moved.

(A) her
(B) herself
(C) hers
(D) she

103. Hartman Motors lowered its prices significantly ------- stay competitive.

(A) now that
(B) on account of
(C) in order to
(D) in spite of

104. The freezer maintains ------- storage conditions that preserve the freshness of meat.

(A) low
(B) ideal
(C) visible
(D) sincere

105. The merger ------- under negotiation for the past two years, but is close to being concluded.

(A) to be
(B) has been
(C) will be
(D) is being

106. Many of Greenvale Hospital's charitable programs ------- with generous grants.

(A) supports
(B) to support
(C) supporting
(D) are being supported

107. The shipment is being examined ------- warehouse personnel to check its quality.

(A) in
(B) by
(C) at
(D) over

108. Fit Trend's fitness tracker is without ------- the most capable device of its kind on the market.

(A) trust
(B) means
(C) question
(D) value

109. Each branch manager should report customers' complaints ------- to the regional supervisor and other branch managers.

(A) lately
(B) directly
(C) upwardly
(D) abruptly

110. A committee ensured a smooth ------- when Haxpa Corp. took control of Brava Holdings.

(A) transiting
(B) transitory
(C) transition
(D) transitional

111. The marketing trainees were given a few minutes to decide on ------- partners for the team project.

(A) they
(B) them
(C) their
(D) themselves

112. For a film with so much promotion, *Origin of Hope* did ------- poorly during the weekend box office.

(A) surprise
(B) surprised
(C) surprising
(D) surprisingly

113. Laura Baker is in charge of instructing the new intern, ------- will be employed this summer.

(A) which
(B) who
(C) one
(D) that

114. *The Manchester Post* attracted readers by offering a one-month trial ------- for free.

(A) introductlon
(B) subscription
(C) section
(D) information

115. All salaries ------- those of part-time employees will be paid on the 10th of every month.

(A) while
(B) into
(C) throughout
(D) including

116. A fine of $115 ------- on vehicle owners leaving their cars parked on the sidewalk.

(A) imposed
(B) is imposed
(C) will impose
(D) was imposing

117. Dr. Chauncey's previous work experience was discussed ------- his interview.

(A) about
(B) aside
(C) along
(D) during

118. Adopting ------- approaches to product design allowed Hyde Enterprises to succeed.

(A) thought
(B) thoughtful
(C) thoughtfulness
(D) thoughtfully

119. Tyne Apparel could better attract new shoppers by holding promotions ------- throughout the year.

(A) frequent
(B) frequency
(C) frequenting
(D) frequently

120. Ms. Nielsen has agreed to lead the presentation ------- she needs help with preparations.

(A) after
(B) since
(C) unless
(D) although

GO ON TO THE NEXT PAGE

121. Those in entry-level positions thrive under the ------- of experienced coworkers.

(A) familiarity
(B) guidance
(C) confirmation
(D) invitation

122. Ms. Wyman resigned three years ago, but still stops by ------- to catch up with former colleagues.

(A) jointly
(B) recently
(C) gradually
(D) occasionally

123. The trade show promises to connect vendors with ------- buyers from around the world.

(A) prospect
(B) prospected
(C) prospector
(D) prospective

124. Transport officials sent out extra buses to ------- the impact of the subway line's closure.

(A) assess
(B) diminish
(C) intensify
(D) dismiss

125. ------- with the right tools, the repair crew can finish the job in days rather than weeks.

(A) Suppliers
(B) Supplies
(C) Supplied
(D) Supplying

126. ------- the movie is well received by fans, a sequel could start production as early as next year.

(A) Providing
(B) Likewise
(C) Due to
(D) Even if

127. The internship program allowed students ------- what it is like to work different jobs.

(A) explore
(B) explored
(C) to explore
(D) exploratory

128. Puff Bakery sells cupcake boxes filled with an ------- of flavors.

(A) acquisition
(B) amount
(C) assortment
(D) availability

129. Baxter Corporation is looking for ------- that will oversee its professional training courses.

(A) facilitate
(B) facilitates
(C) facilitators
(D) facilitation

130. The firm's data ------- on an alternate server while technicians check the main one for errors.

(A) has stored
(B) will store
(C) to store
(D) will be stored

PART 6

Directions: In this part, you will be asked to read four English texts. Each text is missing a word, phrase, or sentence. Select the answer choice that correctly completes the text and mark the corresponding letter (A), (B), (C), or (D) on the answer sheet.

Questions 131-134 refer to the following e-mail.

From: Gail Rossey <g.rossey@quailcooling.com>
To: Peter Edmonds <pe880@tmail.net>
Subject: Re: Product complaint
Date: March 22

Dear Mr. Edmonds,

Your e-mail of March 21 indicated that your Quail Cooling air conditioner ------- a loud noise
                                                                            131.
every time you turn it on. -------.
                            132.

You asked whether you should take the product back to the shop where you purchased it. -------,
                                                                                        133.
I recommend that you bring it to a Quail Cooling service center. The one closest to your house is

at 147 Field Street. To avoid having to wait, you may make an appointment in advance by calling

555-2827.

The technician will fix your air conditioner on the spot. No ------- fee will be charged.
                                                             134.

Gail Rossey
Customer Service Agent, Quail Cooling

---

131. (A) made
(B) making
(C) to make
(D) makes

132. (A) This problem is likely caused by a faulty
part.
(B) A repairperson is scheduled to visit your
home.
(C) I can help you as long as you present
your receipt.
(D) Please follow the directions in the user
manual.

133. (A) Instead
(B) Furthermore
(C) Nonetheless
(D) Therefore

134. (A) shipping
(B) monthly
(C) service
(D) transfer

GO ON TO THE NEXT PAGE

Questions 135-138 refer to the following invitation.

The Blackpool Chamber Music Society
proudly presents its spring concert
on May 3

You are cordially invited to attend the Blackpool Chamber Music Society's spring concert, which

will be held ------- at Greenfield Auditorium. This venue, which was first used last year, can seat
      135.

up to 300 people. The concert will include performances by a string quartet and a piano trio. The

evening of entertainment will start at 7 P.M. and ------- until 9 P.M.
          136.

On the night of the concert, tickets will be sold at the entrance for $20. Those with a season pass

will not only be able to enter the building for free, but will also be able to attend the final rehearsal

and after-party. These will ------- on May 2 and 4, respectively. -------. For further details, please
          137.   **138.**

visit our Web site.

---

135. (A) weekly
    (B) effectively
    (C) last
    (D) again

136. (A) continuation
    (B) continually
    (C) continuing
    (D) continue

137. (A) resume
    (B) broadcast
    (C) expire
    (D) occur

138. (A) The reservation was confirmed on
        April 20.
    (B) Both will be held at 5 o'clock in the
        afternoon.
    (C) Your donation will be put to good use.
    (D) It was a suitable venue for the banquet.

Emerald Island Resort, Australia ★★★★★
Review posted February 12 by Agatha Henriksen

My husband and I were looking for a ------- getaway to end our month-long holiday. Emerald Island
                                         139.

Resort seemed like the most suitable place for this. Situated in a remote marine park, the resort

features detached villas with their own swimming pools. This resort also has a reputation for

top-notch service. This is why it can also be expensive. -------, we secured a deal at an affordable
                                                          140.

price. Apart from a free night's stay, the offer included wine tastings and massages. From the

impressive surroundings to the superb customer service, Emerald Island Resort surpassed -------
                                                                                          141.

expectation. For those wishing to go, the resort is 90 minutes by plane from Cairns. -------.
                                                                                      142.

---

139. (A) traditional
　　　(B) bargain
　　　(C) private
　　　(D) popular

140. (A) Once
　　　(B) Nearly
　　　(C) Fortunately
　　　(D) Additionally

141. (A) these
　　　(B) no
　　　(C) every
　　　(D) many

142. (A) The city is great for outdoor enthusiasts.
　　　(B) I would be happy to make your
　　　　　reservation.
　　　(C) It is also possible to reach it by boat.
　　　(D) Our return flight to Denmark was
　　　　　delayed.

GO ON TO THE NEXT PAGE

Questions 143-146 refer to the following instructions.

Before making your first cup of coffee with the Delux Home Brewer(DHB), the device needs to be

-------. This eliminates any residue in the machine. Start by opening the lid on the top and pouring
143.

water inside. The amount should reach but not exceed the line marked FULL. -------, close the lid
144.

and plug the DHB in to an electrical outlet. Make sure that the coffeepot is resting on the inner

tray. Now, simply press the Clean button and wait until all the water has circulated through the

DHB. -------.
145.

You are now ready to make your first batch of coffee. Refer to Page 7 of this manual for -------
146.

directions about the process.

---

143. (A) taken
(B) checked
(C) washed
(D) shaken

144. (A) Alternatively
(B) Likewise
(C) Eventually
(D) Next

145. (A) The filter was not made for such a
purpose.
(B) Up to four different options can be
selected.
(C) A standard serving consists of
10 ounces.
(D) This water should be poured down
the drain.

146. (A) precise
(B) precisely
(C) precision
(D) preciseness

Directions: In this part, you will be asked to read several texts, such as advertisements, articles, instant messages, or examples of business correspondence. Each text is followed by several questions. Select the best answer and mark the corresponding letter (A), (B), (C), or (D) on your answer sheet.

Questions 147-148 refer to the following advertisement.

Fiona's Garden!

Visit Fiona's Garden for all of your flower and plant needs! Choose from a wide variety!

• *Customized floral arrangements of any size for weddings and other special occasions.*
• *A range of indoor plants and trees.*
• *Delivery services to all locations within the city limits. Free for orders of $100 or more.*

Call us at 555-3049 to discuss prices and products. Fiona's Garden is located at 938 Colonial Drive in downtown Orlando. Our hours of operation are from 10 A.M. to 7 P.M., Monday through Friday.

147. What type of business is Fiona's Garden?

(A) A planner of events for special occasions
(B) A venue for private or business functions
(C) A supplier of plants and flowers
(D) A landscaper for homes and businesses

148. How can customers become eligible for free delivery?

(A) By ordering a new product
(B) By spending a specific amount
(C) By placing an order by phone
(D) By having an address in the downtown area

GO ON TO THE NEXT PAGE

Questions 149-150 refer to the following memo.

Memorandum

To: Plant operation division, Cready Power Company
From: Millie Wickens, Assistant Plant Manager
Date: Monday, September 14
Subject: Access system

This Wednesday, the system for gaining entry to the plant operations room will be changed. This is because the plastic cards we currently use often need to be reissued on account of loss or damage. Instead of a card reader, we will begin using a fingerprint scanner. However, you still should bring your access card on Wednesday because the serviceperson will not arrive until around 11 A.M. Please return from lunch before 1 P.M. because all of you will be required to register your fingerprints at that time.

149. Why will the current security system be changed?

(A) Sensitive information needs to be protected.
(B) Some machinery has been damaged.
(C) Some additional employees have been hired.
(D) Some items must be replaced frequently.

150. What will members of the plant operation division do at 1 P.M. on Wednesday?

(A) Meet a client
(B) Fill out a questionnaire
(C) Conduct some training
(D) Provide some data

Questions 151-152 refer to the following text-message chain.

Marcus Jones	**10:03 A.M.**

Hello, Ms. Girard. This is Marcus from Assure Technology. I've just arrived with a package for you. I tried the intercom system, but I didn't get a reply. Could you please let me in so that I can bring it up to your apartment unit?

Helen Girard	**10:04 A.M.**

Oh, I'm sorry, but I'm at my office right now. Please leave it with the building manager instead. Just enter 101 on the intercom to call him.

Marcus Jones	**10:05 A.M.**

I wish I could. But you must be here to sign for this package, as it contains valuable computer parts.

Helen Girard	**10:05 A.M.**

I see. In that case, would you be able to come back to the apartment at 5:30 P.M.? I should be home by then.

151. What can be inferred about Mr. Jones?

(A) He brought a package to an office.
(B) He cannot locate a residence.
(C) He requested assistance from a manager.
(D) He cannot enter a building.

152. At 10:05 A.M., what does Mr. Jones mean when he writes, "I wish I could"?

(A) Some equipment is too heavy to be carried.
(B) The company cannot rush an upcoming shipment.
(C) Some items must be given directly to a customer.
(D) The management office is not currently open.

GO ON TO THE NEXT PAGE ➤

To   Galina Kusnetsov <galinakus@postamail.com>
From   Jovin Medical Center <admin@jmc.com>
Subject Our new mobile application
Date   September 18

Dear Ms. Kusnetsov,

You may be interested to know that Jovin Medical Center launched a mobile application last week that patients can use to manage appointments and make inquiries. We recognize that having to call clinic staff during working hours can be inconvenient since our phone lines are often busy. — [1] —. We therefore hope that most of our patients will use the application, which is accessible at all times, and free up our phone lines for those who urgently need to reach us.

Once you have downloaded the Jovin Medical Center application, sign in using your medical center ID number. — [2] —. Your patient profile will list your upcoming appointments and provide the option of requesting cancellations or modifications. A chat system also allows you to get answers to your questions about clinic procedures. — [3] —. While the application is currently limited to these functions, we plan to make it possible for patients to access other information, such as the results of medical tests. If you have any questions about the application, please respond to this e-mail or read the updated FAQ page on our Web site. — [4] —.

Jovin Medical Center

---

153. According to the e-mail, what is the purpose of the application?

(A) To provide follow-up advice to regular patients
(B) To reduce the volume of calls to the clinic
(C) To lower the number of appointment cancellations
(D) To allow patients to locate nearby clinics

154. What is true about the Jovin Medical Center application?

(A) It can be used to reach doctors and nurses directly.
(B) It may be updated to display medical records.
(C) It can be installed after paying a small fee.
(D) It has been functional for approximately a month now.

155. In which of the positions marked [1], [2], [3], and [4] does the following sentence best belong?

"You can use this feature to make new appointments and to ask any questions you might have."

(A) [1]
(B) [2]
(C) [3]
(D) [4]

www.organifresh.com

Organi Fresh – Making Mealtime Easier

| About Us | | Menu | | Order | | FAQ | | Contact Us |

Organi Fresh takes the hassle out of shopping for food and preparing healthy meals by doing the work for you. When you order an Organi Fresh meal delivery, you'll get a week's worth of delicious food prepared by our highly skilled professional chefs. All of our food is made using seasonal organic produce and natural ingredients. We never use preservatives, and we keep the use of oil, sugar, and salt to a minimum.

Simply take a look at our menu, which includes a mix of Asian, Mediterranean, and South American cuisine, then choose the meals you want for the week. With our Standard Plan, you'll get three meals a day for a week at a cost of $28 per day. Or, order our Lunch & Dinner Plan to receive two meals a day for a week at a cost of just $22.50 per day. All of these prices include the cost of shipping!

Finally, all of our meals are packed in containers that are both microwavable and ovenproof. Your order for the week will be shipped fresh in a cooler packed with ice every Friday. Try us once, and we're certain you'll be back for more!

156. What is the topic of the Web page?

(A) An organic restaurant
(B) A pre-packed meal service
(C) A catering business
(D) A new diet program

157. What information is NOT mentioned on the Web page?

(A) Cuisine types
(B) Ordering options
(C) Delivery costs
(D) Storage suggestions

158. What is true about meal orders?

(A) They must be consumed immediately.
(B) They can be placed over the phone.
(C) They are delivered on the same day each week.
(D) They come with reusable containers.

GO ON TO THE NEXT PAGE

Questions 159-161 refer to the following article.

Wave Technologies Finalizes Uptron Acquisition

December 8—Electronics company Wave Technologies has acquired appliance manufacturer Uptron. The move is seen as a demonstration of Wave Technologies' commitment to increasing its presence in the lucrative kitchen appliance market. Having already established itself as a leading producer of household electronics such as televisions, Wave Technologies entered into an agreement with the Bolton Department Store chain two years ago to provide dishwashers and refrigerators.

"The acquisition of Uptron will allow us to expand our product range and better serve our existing clients" said Karen Fowler, Wave Technologies' chief business strategist. The purchase provides Wave Technologies with access to Uptron's 12,000-square-meter Ohio plant, which meets international standards for product safety. However, Wave Technologies will continue to be based in Indiana.

159. Why did Wave Technologies acquire Uptron?

(A) To prevent a competitor from releasing a product
(B) To further expand its share of a market
(C) To sign a contract with a major client
(D) To open its stores in another country

160. What is indicated about Bolton Department Store?

(A) It will widen its product line in December.
(B) It had a business partnership with Uptron.
(C) It was established approximately two years ago.
(D) It sells products made by Wave Technologies.

161. What is suggested about Wave Technologies?

(A) It changed its product safety standards recently.
(B) It will be moving manufacturing equipment to Ohio.
(C) It increased its production capacity significantly.
(D) It has reduced the size of its workforce in Indiana.

Joyful Home Housekeeping Services

3948 Beechnut Street, Lethbridge, AB T1H-0L6

INVOICE NUMBER: 394827

DATE OF INVOICE: February 28

CLIENT: Severson Accounting Firm
583 South Parkside Drive, Office #12
Lethbridge, AB T1H-0L4

SERVICES PROVIDED:

February 18	Floor cleaning and vacuuming	$380.00
February 21	Interior and exterior window washing	$260.00
February 22	Steam-cleaning of sofa and chairs	$130.00

SUBTOTAL: $770.00

TAX: $92.40

TOTAL AMOUNT DUE: $862.40   **PAYMENT DUE BY:** March 7

---

162. What most likely took place on February 28?

(A) An exterior office window was washed.
(B) A customer made a complaint about a worker.
(C) A billing statement was prepared for a client.
(D) A worker vacuumed a carpet in a building.

163. How much will Severson Accounting Firm have to pay for furniture cleaning services?

(A) $130.00
(B) $260.00
(C) $380.00
(D) $770.00

GO ON TO THE NEXT PAGE

Questions 164-167 refer to the following online chat discussion.

🧑 **Zelda Coe**	3:15 P.M.	I've been considering allowing my staff to work remotely. It's just an idea. What do you think?
Stuart Ojeda	3:15 P.M.	Well, it could be ideal for employees who live far away, but some might not have the necessary equipment.
Libby Schuster	3:16 P.M.	Right. Their home computers might not be powerful enough to run the graphic design software we use.
🧑 **Zelda Coe**	3:16 P.M.	I see. What if I just offered this option to anyone who has a suitable computer and prefers to telecommute then?
Stuart Ojeda	3:17 P.M.	I don't know. At my old job, I found that employees who worked from home contributed less during meetings.
Libby Schuster	3:17 P.M.	Plus, they may feel excluded if they don't see their coworkers regularly. In any case, coming into the office puts employees in the right state of mind to work.
🧑 **Zelda Coe**	3:18 P.M.	Thank you all for your thoughts. I'm going to do some research and look into this more thoroughly.

Send

164. At 3:15 P.M., what does Ms. Coe mean when she writes, "It's just an idea"?

(A) A decision has not yet been made.
(B) She wants a specific answer.
(C) A problem has been resolved.
(D) She had no time to develop a plan.

165. What do Mr. Ojeda and Ms. Schuster agree on?

(A) Those who work from home do not feel like part of a team.
(B) Employees commuting to the office are often late.
(C) Workers may not have what is needed to work remotely.
(D) Those who work outside the office are unreliable.

166. What is suggested about Mr. Ojeda?

(A) He thinks it is necessary to conduct performance evaluations.
(B) He has worked in an office where telecommuting was an option.
(C) He believes that some workers should receive salary increases.
(D) He has recently been promoted to a management position.

167. What does Ms. Coe indicate she will do?

(A) Create a presentation
(B) Request feedback from employees
(C) Submit a request to a superior
(D) Consider a matter carefully

Dear Cost Smart Customers,

As you may have heard, several other large retail stores across the country were targeted by cyber criminals earlier this week. This may have resulted in the theft of customer information, including personal and payment details. — [1] —. Because we value you and know how much of a threat unauthorized access to your information can be, we promise to do everything we can to safeguard Cost Smart's system against similar attacks.

We have already upgraded our security and encryption software. — [2] —. We also plan to provide additional training to staff to make them aware of precautions they should take. While we believe that our actions will be effective in deterring cybercriminals, as a Cost Smart customer, we ask you to be cautious as well.

Please note that we will never contact you over the phone to ask for personal information. — [3] —. If you receive text messages from senders representing themselves as Cost Smart customer service associates, delete them immediately. — [4] —. Also, always visit our Web site directly rather than clicking on links in e-mails. The Web sites you are directed to may be designed to look exactly like ours. This is to trick you into entering your password, thereby revealing it to the operator of the site.

Thank you for your loyalty. If you have any questions, please call us at 555-8897.

Florence Stoddard
Cost Smart President

168. What is the purpose of the letter?

(A) To suggest that online shopping should be avoided
(B) To describe some preventive measures
(C) To explain how criminals use stolen data
(D) To apologize for the loss of customer information

169. What is suggested about the text messages mentioned in the letter?

(A) They allow customers to confirm orders.
(B) They advertise upcoming sales events.
(C) They are not received during regular business hours.
(D) They are not sent by store employees.

170. According to the letter, why should customers not click on an e-mail link?

(A) It may infect a computer with a virus.
(B) It will disable security programs.
(C) It may lead to a fake Web page.
(D) It will delete important data.

171. In which of the positions marked [1], [2], [3], and [4] does the following sentence best belong?

"We are confident that these improvements will help prevent your data from being transferred out of our systems illegally."

(A) [1]
(B) [2]
(C) [3]
(D) [4]

GO ON TO THE NEXT PAGE

Questions 172-175 refer to the following e-mail.

To   Christina Meister <chrismeister@gomail.com>
From   Martin Jedlika <mjedlikakey@translations.com>
Subject Re: Document translation
Date   July 8

Dear Ms. Meister,

Thank you for contacting Key Translations about your need for an English-to-Greek document translation. We have reviewed the file you sent and estimate that it will take us approximately 10 hours to complete the work. You can find our initial quote below:

Pages	4 pages priced at $40 per page
Duration	10 hours
Translation	$160
10% first-time customer discount	-$16
Total	$144

We can also provide a certified hard copy of the translation. This will include the translator's name and signature, as well as a statement that affirms the accuracy of the translation. We can send it to you by courier at the following rates:

Domestic Standard (2-3 days)	$16
Domestic Express (1 day)	$22
International Standard (5-8 days)	$25
International Express (3-4 days)	$33

If you require a certified copy, please send a reply stating which courier option you prefer, and I will adjust the estimate accordingly. Otherwise, simply make a bank transfer using the account information on our Web site. Once your payment has been received, we will proceed with the project.

We look forward to your reply!

Sincerely,

Martin Jedlika
Project Manager, Key Translations

172. Why was the e-mail written?

(A) To verify that a project is in progress
(B) To request a document translation
(C) To explain a project delay
(D) To specify a price for a potential client

173. What is indicated about Ms. Meister?

(A) She has never done business with Key Translations.
(B) She is comparing quotes from a number of companies.
(C) She will travel to Greece in July.
(D) She did not include the correct file in her e-mail.

174. How much does it cost for a one-day delivery of a document?

(A) $16
(B) $22
(C) $25
(D) $33

175. According to Mr. Jedlika, why should Ms. Meister reply to the e-mail?

(A) To confirm that a translation is accurate
(B) To make use of an additional service
(C) To provide information about a bank account
(D) To approve a revision to a file

GO ON TO THE NEXT PAGE

Questions 176-180 refer to the following e-mail and online form.

TO	Contigo Tours <service@contigotours.com>
FROM	Jason Lambert <jlamb63@howmail.net>
SUBJECT	Montevideo Tours
DATE	March 20

Hello,

I'm writing because I'm interested in booking one of the tours to Montevideo that was posted on your travel agency's Web page earlier this week. I understand that you have both three-night and five-night hotel stay options for your tours. However, other than that the five-night stay includes an additional trip to Punta del Este, I'm not entirely sure what the difference is between the two options. Could you please send me some in-depth information about each tour?

Also, I would like to rent a car to do a bit of exploring on my own. I was hoping you could help me arrange this. If I go with the five-night tour, I'd prefer to drop off the car on June 15. This is because I need to go back to Chicago for a conference I'm attending there on June 16. Otherwise, I'll return the car earlier.

Regards,

Jason Lambert

---

http://www.sunwaycarrentals.com/confirmation

Sunway Car Rentals
Confirmation Page

Jason Lambert, please review the booking details for your rental vehicle below.

Car Model: Trekker V70 Convertible
This model comes with built-in touch-screen GPS on its dashboard that is able to connect to any mobile device.

Rental Period: June 10 – June 13
Please be sure to drop off your vehicle at Sunway's 16 Maria Way office—not our airport location.

Payment Amount: $350
This amount includes a $50 insurance deposit.

Paid by: Surefire Credit Card Number 4553-1002-2023-9099

176. What is mentioned about Contigo Tours?

(A) It opened an office in Chicago.
(B) It updated its Web site recently.
(C) It canceled a planned weekend trip.
(D) It changed a payment process.

177. What does Mr. Lambert request?

(A) Details about trip choices
(B) Dates of flight departures
(C) Contact information for a supervisor
(D) Recommendations for lodging options

178. In the form, the word "connect" in paragraph 2, line 2, is closest in meaning to

(A) converse
(B) fasten
(C) assign
(D) link

179. What is suggested about Mr. Lambert?

(A) He will be late for his appointment in Chicago.
(B) He will stay in Montevideo for three nights.
(C) He will receive a refund on June 10.
(D) He will visit a friend in Punta del Este.

180. What can be inferred about Sunway Car Rentals?

(A) It has purchased additional vehicles lately.
(B) It was featured in a travel magazine.
(C) It will be closed for business on June 15.
(D) It operates more than one branch.

GO ON TO THE NEXT PAGE

TEST 12

해커스 토익 실전 1200제 READING

DesignChic Magazine

The Best Patio Furniture for the Summer

By: Darrell Cruz

May 10—Nothing beats spending the warm summer nights relaxing on your patio. Finding the right furniture for your patio is the key to making the outdoor space at your house your own. Numerous furniture retailers have popular patio sets for this season, but none are better regarded than Diamond Home.

With constantly high consumer ratings since its founding, Diamond Home has an impressive patio collection this summer. Filled with modern chairs, tables, and other items, the Diamond Home summer outdoor line is made entirely of organic materials that do not harm the environment. CEO of the company, Nina Roman, even said in an interview this month with our publication that the collection has already received rave reviews from the company's loyal customers. To take a look at some of the pieces in this line, click on the link <u>here</u>.

Diamond Home's Baltimore Branch
Grand Opening Sale!

Are you looking for a way to freshen up the design of your home? Then don't miss the grand opening sale at Diamond Home's brand-new Baltimore branch this weekend, from June 10 to 11. Founded over 10 years ago, Diamond Home is committed to bringing quality furniture to its customers. And now you can buy some of these amazing pieces and receive extra benefits! Be sure to check out the amazing deals below at this weekend's sale.

Item	Deal
Patio chairs	Buy one, get one free
Kitchen tables	Free set of plates with purchase
Computer desks	50 percent off coupon for your next purchase

More details about the specific items included in the sale can be found on www.diamondhome.com/baltimorestore.

181. For whom most likely is the article intended?

(A) Company executives
(B) Furniture manufacturers
(C) Web designers
(D) House owners

182. What is stated about Diamond Home's summer collection?

(A) It was photographed in a celebrity's residence.
(B) It was created with environmentally friendly materials.
(C) It was produced in a factory located overseas.
(D) It was featured in an advertising campaign on television.

183. What did Ms. Roman do in May?

(A) Conducted a customer satisfaction survey
(B) Launched her own lifestyle magazine
(C) Answered some questions for a publication
(D) Attended an industry trade fair

184. What is indicated about Diamond Home?

(A) It has been highly rated for more than a decade.
(B) It sells its products in department stores.
(C) It specializes in the production of outdoor furniture.
(D) It will open several new stores this summer.

185. What deal is being offered for outdoor furniture?

(A) Complimentary product samples
(B) A coupon for half off an item
(C) A set of free kitchenware
(D) Two items for the price of one

GO ON TO THE NEXT PAGE

Multiple Positions Available — Quadra Realty

Are you interested in working for the largest commercial real estate agency in Los Angeles? Quadra Realty is a growing company that offers a generous compensation and benefits package to all of its employees. We are currently looking for people to fill the following positions:

Accountant / Fairfax Branch
Requirements: Bachelor's degree in accounting and three years' related experience

Real Estate Agent / Huntington Branch
Requirements: Realtor's license and four years' related experience

Receptionist / San Pedro Branch
Requirements: High school diploma and two years' related experience

Assistant Manager / Forest Grove Branch
Requirements: Bachelor's degree in business administration and six years' related experience

Please go to our homepage, www.quadrarealty.com, for more information about these positions and instructions on how to apply.

July 15
David Reynolds Quadra Realty
1602 Delta Avenue
Los Angeles, CA 90293

Dear Mr. Reynolds,

I would like to express my interest in becoming an employee of Quadra Realty. I believe that I am well suited for the listed position. Although I have not worked for a real estate agency previously, I majored in accounting in university. In addition, I have spent the last four years in the accounting department of Blackwood Construction. I am looking for a new employment opportunity at this time because my company is planning to relocate to Oakland, and I wish to remain in the Los Angeles area.

You can reach me by phone at 555-0393 or by e-mail at j.quayle@digiquest.com if you have any questions. Unfortunately, I am only available to interview on weekday mornings because of my current work schedule. Thank you for considering my application.

Sincerely,

Jenna Quayle

To	Doug Stevens <d.stevens@quadra.com>, Laura Meyers <l.meyers@quadra.com>, Jeff Kim <j.kim@quadra.com>, Pauline Greer <p.greer@quadra.com>
From	Brett Reynolds <b.reynolds@quadra.com>
Subject	Hiring status
Date	September 8

Hi everyone,

I just wanted to update all of the branch managers on the hiring process. At this point, we have several promising candidates for the open positions. The interviews will take place on the following days:

Monday, September 15 (2 P.M.)
Wednesday, September 17 (10 A.M.)
Thursday, September 18 (4 P.M.)
Saturday, September 20 (11 A.M.)

If you have any specific questions you would like me to ask the applicants, please send them to me. I'll need this information by September 10 so that I will have time to prepare for my first meetings with the candidates. Once the interviews are completed, I will create summary reports on the most suitable applicants. These will be e-mailed on September 24 for you to review.

Sincerely,

Brett Reynolds
Human Resources Manager, Quadra Realty

186. How can applicants find out more about the available jobs?

(A) By e-mailing a recruitment agency
(B) By stopping by a local office
(C) By calling a branch manager
(D) By going to a company Web site

187. Which branch is Ms. Quayle applying for a position at?

(A) The Fairfax branch
(B) The Huntington branch
(C) The San Pedro branch
(D) The Forest Grove branch

188. What is mentioned about Blackwood Construction?

(A) It will close some offices.
(B) It will begin a new building project.
(C) It will hire more staff members.
(D) It will move to a different city.

189. When will Ms. Quayle most likely be interviewed?

(A) On September 15
(B) On September 17
(C) On September 18
(D) On September 20

190. What is implied about Mr. Reynolds?

(A) He will conduct the interviews personally.
(B) He has already made an offer to a candidate.
(C) He is uncertain if a position is still available.
(D) He is in charge of training new employees.

GO ON TO THE NEXT PAGE

TEST 12 해커스 토익 실전 1200제 READING

Bath Vitals Employee Newsletter
March 9

Customers to Win Prizes for Doing Survey

By Vincent Heidecker

Earlier this year, the Bath Vitals executive board concluded that in order to improve customer satisfaction, shoppers need to be surveyed. To encourage customers to visit our Web site and complete the survey, they will be offered a chance to win a $200 gift certificate. Each month, we will award a gift certificate that is redeemable at any of our locations to two customers who complete the online survey. Marketing Director Cassandra Jo is responsible for designing the survey, while Information Analyst Joshua Gooding will be in charge of processing the responses.

Bath Vitals

89 West Sinto Avenue
Spokane, Washington
(509) 555 9889

Monday, May 12, 12:30 P.M.

Quantity	Item	Price
1	Charmy soap (six-pack)	$6.89
1	Brilliant Fiber hand towel	$12.19
1	Mayor's Choice shampoo	$3.49
1	Grandi & Corto shower curtain	$34.99

Subtotal	$57.56
Tax	$4.03
Total	$61.59
Cash	$65.00
Change	$3.41

Frequent Shopper Cardholder	Lindsey Brant
New Points Accumulated	17
Total Points	211

You can win a $200 gift certificate redeemable at any of our stores. To qualify, visit www.bathvitals.com/feedback and complete a short survey about your shopping experience today or simply fill out a questionnaire by hand at our customer service counter.

After answering the following questions, push the "NEXT" button to proceed.

Your name: Lindsey Brant   *Branch visited:* Spokane   *Date of visit:* May 12

How was our customer service?
A sales clerk asked if there was anything I needed but couldn't tell me which bathroom slippers were the most comfortable.

How would you rate our selection?
I was glad to have lots of brands and products to choose from.

Were you satisfied with our pricing?
Yes. Your prices are 5 to 10 percent cheaper than those at Ted's Toiletries.

Did you find the store layout convenient?
Not really. I expected to find the soap made by Charmy in Aisle 7, but it was in Aisle 4 between the air fresheners and showerheads.

NEXT ▷

---

191. What is the main topic of the newsletter article?

(A) The expansion of a company
(B) An incentive for customers
(C) The results of a survey
(D) An excursion for executives

192. What did Bath Vitals most likely decide to do after publishing the newsletter?

(A) Use another method to gather feedback
(B) Request assistance from a consulting firm
(C) Change the content of its Website
(D) Renovate some of its branches

193. According to the receipt, what is true about Bath Vitals?

(A) It plans to open a new location.
(B) It runs a customer rewards program.
(C) It remains open on weekday evenings.
(D) It intends to hire additional staff members.

194. What did Ms. Brant ask an employee for?

(A) A low-price guarantee
(B) A store layout map
(C) A product recommendation
(D) A gift-wrapping service

195. What was the cost of Ms. Brant's purchase from Aisle 4?

(A) $6.89
(B) $12.19
(C) $3.49
(D) $34.99

Park Hotel

About	Reservations	Location	Contact

Conveniently located next to the Dawson Convention Center in downtown Olympia, the Park Hotel is ideal for business travelers and tourists alike. Our recently renovated building includes a state-of-the-art fitness center, a gift shop, and a five-star restaurant. And we have a variety of special rates for guests this summer:

- Group Rate: Traveling with friends or colleagues? Pay only $110 per night when your party books four or more rooms.
- Weekday Rate: If your stay does not include a Friday, Saturday, or Sunday, you will be charged only $130 per night.
- Extended Stay Rate: If you plan to stay with us for seven days or more, you can reserve a room for $115 per night.
- Member Rate: Members of our Park Hotel Rewards Program are charged only $120 per night.

These rates are valid until August 31 and apply only to deluxe rooms.
Payment must be made in full at the time of booking.

To	Park Hotel Customer Service <customerservice@parkhotel.com>
From	Beth Davidson <b.davidson@westmail.com>
Subject	Booking 83478
Date	June 15

I am contacting you about a booking I made on June 12. I happened to check my online credit card statement this morning, and I noticed that I had been overcharged. I should have qualified for the Extended Stay Rate. I would appreciate it if someone from your hotel would contact me as soon as possible to resolve this issue. Also, when does your shuttle bus stop running each night? I'm asking because my flight arrives at 11:30 P.M. If your shuttle bus does not operate this late, I will just catch a taxi.

Thanks,

Beth Davidson

To	Beth Davidson <b.davidson@westmail.com>
From	Joseph Hong <j.hong@parkhotel.com>
Subject	Booking 83478
Date	June 16
Attachment	Shuttle_schedule.doc

Dear Ms. Davidson,

I would like to apologize for the mistake made with your reservation. It appears that you were billed the Weekday Rate as a result of an error with our online booking system. The amount you overpaid will be charged back to your credit card by June 18 at the latest. With regard to your question, our shuttle service is available until 1:00 A.M. each day, so you will not have any problems. I have included a schedule with this e-mail. Please let me know if there is any other assistance you require.

Sincerely,

Joseph Hong

196. What is mentioned about the Park Hotel?

(A) It will be refurbished in the summer.
(B) It is situated near an event venue.
(C) It will be hosting a convention.
(D) It is introducing a new room type.

197. What is NOT available at the Park Hotel?

(A) A store
(B) A business center
(C) A gym
(D) A dining area

198. What is indicated about Ms. Davidson?

(A) She will stay at the hotel for at least a week.
(B) She will receive a refund for a tour.
(C) She will pay for her room at check-in.
(D) She will travel with some of her coworkers.

199. Why does Ms. Davidson inquire about the shuttle service?

(A) She is uncertain whether a taxi will be available.
(B) She will arrive at the airport late at night.
(C) She thinks the online schedule includes an error.
(D) She was told that it was no longer offered.

200. How much was Ms. Davidson originally billed per night?

(A) $110
(B) $115
(C) $120
(D) $130

This is the end of the test. You may review Parts 5, 6, and 7 if you finish the test early.

TEST 12 점수 환산표

TEST 12는 무사히 잘 마치셨나요? 맞은 개수를 세어본 후 아래의 점수 환산표를 통해 자신의 점수를 예상해 보세요.

전체 난이도   **중간 난이도**

파트별 난이도   PART 5 중 ●●○
　　　　　　　　PART 6 중 ●●○
　　　　　　　　PART 7 중 ●●○

정답 수	리딩 점수	정답 수	리딩 점수
98~100개	475~495점	47~49개	205~215점
95~97개	460~470점	44~46개	190~200점
92~94개	440~455점	41~43개	175~185점
89~91개	420~435점	38~40개	160~170점
86~88개	405~415점	35~37개	145~155점
83~85개	390~400점	32~34개	130~140점
80~82개	375~385점	29~31개	115~125점
77~79개	360~370점	26~28개	100~110점
74~76개	340~355점	23~25개	85~95점
71~73개	325~335점	20~22개	70~80점
68~70개	305~320점	17~19개	55~65점
65~67개	290~300점	14~16개	40~50점
62~64개	270~285점	11~13개	25~35점
59~61개	260~270점	8~10개	10~20점
56~58개	245~255점	5~7개	5~10점
53~55개	235~240점	2~4개	5~10점
50~52개	220~230점	0~1개	0~5점

* 점수 환산표는 해커스토익 사이트 유저 데이터를 근거로 제작되었으며, 주기적으로 업데이트되고 있습니다. 해커스토익 사이트
　(Hackers.co.kr)에서 최신 경향을 반영하여 업데이트된 점수환산기를 이용하실 수 있습니다. (토익 > 토익게시판 > 토익점수환산기)

정답

&

ANSWER SHEET

정답

TEST 1
p.23

PART 5
101 (C)	102 (D)	103 (B)	104 (C)	105 (C)
106 (B)	107 (C)	108 (A)	109 (B)	110 (C)
111 (D)	112 (C)	113 (D)	114 (B)	115 (C)
116 (C)	117 (D)	118 (D)	119 (D)	120 (B)
121 (C)	122 (A)	123 (C)	124 (C)	125 (A)
126 (C)	127 (B)	128 (B)	129 (C)	130 (D)

PART 6
131 (C)	132 (A)	133 (A)	134 (D)	135 (A)
136 (B)	137 (B)	138 (A)	139 (C)	140 (D)
141 (C)	142 (A)	143 (D)	144 (A)	145 (B)
146 (C)				

PART 7
147 (C)	148 (B)	149 (C)	150 (C)	151 (C)
152 (D)	153 (D)	154 (B)	155 (C)	156 (D)
157 (C)	158 (C)	159 (C)	160 (D)	161 (C)
162 (D)	163 (D)	164 (B)	165 (C)	166 (A)
167 (B)	168 (B)	169 (C)	170 (D)	171 (C)
172 (A)	173 (A)	174 (C)	175 (D)	176 (D)
177 (C)	178 (B)	179 (A)	180 (C)	181 (C)
182 (C)	183 (A)	184 (C)	185 (B)	186 (C)
187 (C)	188 (A)	189 (A)	190 (D)	191 (C)
192 (D)	193 (C)	194 (A)	195 (C)	196 (D)
197 (B)	198 (D)	199 (D)	200 (C)	

TEST 2
p.53

PART 5
101 (C)	102 (C)	103 (B)	104 (C)	105 (B)
106 (C)	107 (B)	108 (A)	109 (C)	110 (B)
111 (D)	112 (A)	113 (D)	114 (A)	115 (C)
116 (B)	117 (C)	118 (B)	119 (B)	120 (D)
121 (C)	122 (C)	123 (D)	124 (D)	125 (A)
126 (A)	127 (B)	128 (D)	129 (D)	130 (C)

PART 6
131 (C)	132 (D)	133 (A)	134 (D)	135 (A)
136 (B)	137 (D)	138 (D)	139 (C)	140 (C)
141 (A)	142 (C)	143 (C)	144 (A)	145 (C)
146 (D)				

PART 7
147 (D)	148 (A)	149 (B)	150 (B)	151 (D)
152 (B)	153 (B)	154 (B)	155 (D)	156 (D)
157 (C)	158 (C)	159 (B)	160 (A)	161 (A)
162 (C)	163 (D)	164 (B)	165 (D)	166 (D)
167 (B)	168 (D)	169 (A)	170 (B)	171 (B)
172 (B)	173 (C)	174 (A)	175 (A)	176 (A)
177 (C)	178 (D)	179 (B)	180 (D)	181 (D)
182 (D)	183 (A)	184 (B)	185 (B)	186 (B)
187 (B)	188 (A)	189 (D)	190 (C)	191 (A)
192 (B)	193 (C)	194 (B)	195 (A)	196 (C)
197 (A)	198 (A)	199 (D)	200 (C)	

TEST 3
p.83

PART 5
101 (B)	102 (B)	103 (D)	104 (B)	105 (D)
106 (C)	107 (C)	108 (A)	109 (B)	110 (B)
111 (B)	112 (A)	113 (C)	114 (D)	115 (B)
116 (C)	117 (B)	118 (B)	119 (B)	120 (B)
121 (D)	122 (A)	123 (D)	124 (C)	125 (D)
126 (D)	127 (B)	128 (D)	129 (C)	130 (D)

PART 6
131 (A)	132 (C)	133 (C)	134 (B)	135 (C)
136 (A)	137 (D)	138 (B)	139 (D)	140 (A)
141 (A)	142 (A)	143 (C)	144 (C)	145 (D)
146 (D)				

PART 7
147 (B)	148 (D)	149 (C)	150 (C)	151 (B)
152 (D)	153 (B)	154 (D)	155 (B)	156 (D)
157 (C)	158 (C)	159 (D)	160 (D)	161 (C)
162 (B)	163 (C)	164 (B)	165 (C)	166 (C)
167 (D)	168 (C)	169 (B)	170 (B)	171 (C)
172 (C)	173 (D)	174 (C)	175 (A)	176 (A)
177 (D)	178 (C)	179 (A)	180 (B)	181 (A)
182 (B)	183 (D)	184 (C)	185 (D)	186 (A)
187 (B)	188 (A)	189 (D)	190 (C)	191 (D)
192 (D)	193 (D)	194 (C)	195 (A)	196 (B)
197 (A)	198 (D)	199 (A)	200 (A)	

TEST 4
p.113

PART 5
101 (C)	102 (C)	103 (B)	104 (B)	105 (D)
106 (C)	107 (B)	108 (D)	109 (D)	110 (C)
111 (C)	112 (D)	113 (C)	114 (D)	115 (A)
116 (D)	117 (B)	118 (D)	119 (A)	120 (C)
121 (A)	122 (B)	123 (D)	124 (C)	125 (A)
126 (A)	127 (C)	128 (B)	129 (A)	130 (D)

PART 6
131 (A)	132 (D)	133 (D)	134 (B)	135 (B)
136 (B)	137 (C)	138 (C)	139 (D)	140 (A)
141 (B)	142 (C)	143 (A)	144 (C)	145 (D)
146 (C)				

PART 7
147 (B)	148 (C)	149 (D)	150 (B)	151 (D)
152 (C)	153 (A)	154 (C)	155 (B)	156 (C)
157 (A)	158 (B)	159 (C)	160 (A)	161 (D)
162 (C)	163 (D)	164 (D)	165 (A)	166 (C)
167 (B)	168 (A)	169 (A)	170 (D)	171 (A)
172 (B)	173 (B)	174 (C)	175 (D)	176 (B)
177 (C)	178 (C)	179 (C)	180 (D)	181 (C)
182 (B)	183 (C)	184 (D)	185 (D)	186 (C)
187 (B)	188 (D)	189 (D)	190 (B)	191 (C)
192 (D)	193 (C)	194 (B)	195 (C)	196 (B)
197 (C)	198 (D)	199 (D)	200 (D)	

TEST 5

PART 5

101 (B)	102 (D)	103 (D)	104 (B)	105 (B)
106 (A)	107 (B)	108 (D)	109 (C)	110 (B)
111 (D)	112 (B)	113 (B)	114 (C)	115 (D)
116 (A)	117 (C)	118 (C)	119 (D)	120 (C)
121 (B)	122 (C)	123 (B)	124 (A)	125 (A)
126 (D)	127 (A)	128 (B)	129 (D)	130 (A)

PART 6

131 (B)	132 (D)	133 (D)	134 (C)	135 (B)
136 (D)	137 (B)	138 (D)	139 (C)	140 (B)
141 (D)	142 (D)	143 (B)	144 (C)	145 (A)
146 (D)				

PART 7

147 (C)	148 (B)	149 (C)	150 (C)	151 (C)
152 (D)	153 (D)	154 (B)	155 (B)	156 (C)
157 (C)	158 (C)	159 (D)	160 (D)	161 (D)
162 (D)	163 (B)	164 (C)	165 (B)	166 (B)
167 (C)	168 (C)	169 (B)	170 (A)	171 (B)
172 (C)	173 (C)	174 (D)	175 (B)	176 (D)
177 (C)	178 (A)	179 (D)	180 (C)	181 (C)
182 (D)	183 (A)	184 (C)	185 (B)	186 (C)
187 (D)	188 (D)	189 (C)	190 (B)	191 (B)
192 (C)	193 (A)	194 (C)	195 (B)	196 (C)
197 (A)	198 (D)	199 (D)	200 (B)	

TEST 6
p.173

PART 5

101 (B)	102 (D)	103 (D)	104 (A)	105 (C)
106 (B)	107 (C)	108 (C)	109 (A)	110 (A)
111 (D)	112 (A)	113 (C)	114 (A)	115 (D)
116 (D)	117 (C)	118 (B)	119 (A)	120 (D)
121 (D)	122 (C)	123 (C)	124 (B)	125 (D)
126 (A)	127 (B)	128 (A)	129 (A)	130 (A)

PART 6

131 (A)	132 (D)	133 (A)	134 (D)	135 (C)
136 (B)	137 (D)	138 (D)	139 (A)	140 (B)
141 (C)	142 (A)	143 (A)	144 (A)	145 (A)
146 (C)				

PART 7

147 (B)	148 (B)	149 (D)	150 (C)	151 (B)
152 (A)	153 (B)	154 (C)	155 (D)	156 (B)
157 (B)	158 (C)	159 (B)	160 (A)	161 (D)
162 (B)	163 (A)	164 (A)	165 (B)	166 (D)
167 (D)	168 (D)	169 (A)	170 (C)	171 (A)
172 (B)	173 (C)	174 (B)	175 (A)	176 (B)
177 (A)	178 (C)	179 (D)	180 (D)	181 (B)
182 (A)	183 (D)	184 (D)	185 (B)	186 (C)
187 (B)	188 (D)	189 (D)	190 (D)	191 (A)
192 (B)	193 (A)	194 (D)	195 (C)	196 (D)
197 (C)	198 (B)	199 (A)	200 (A)	

TEST 7
p.203

PART 5

101 (C)	102 (C)	103 (B)	104 (A)	105 (A)
106 (C)	107 (C)	108 (C)	109 (D)	110 (C)
111 (B)	112 (B)	113 (C)	114 (A)	115 (C)
116 (A)	117 (D)	118 (A)	119 (A)	120 (D)
121 (C)	122 (D)	123 (C)	124 (B)	125 (B)
126 (B)	127 (B)	128 (C)	129 (B)	130 (D)

PART 6

131 (D)	132 (C)	133 (D)	134 (B)	135 (C)
136 (B)	137 (D)	138 (A)	139 (B)	140 (A)
141 (C)	142 (D)	143 (D)	144 (B)	145 (A)
146 (D)				

PART 7

147 (D)	148 (C)	149 (B)	150 (C)	151 (C)
152 (D)	153 (B)	154 (A)	155 (C)	156 (A)
157 (D)	158 (B)	159 (C)	160 (B)	161 (B)
162 (A)	163 (C)	164 (D)	165 (C)	166 (B)
167 (A)	168 (B)	169 (A)	170 (D)	171 (B)
172 (D)	173 (A)	174 (D)	175 (C)	176 (B)
177 (D)	178 (A)	179 (C)	180 (A)	181 (C)
182 (B)	183 (B)	184 (B)	185 (A)	186 (D)
187 (A)	188 (B)	189 (B)	190 (D)	191 (A)
192 (B)	193 (C)	194 (B)	195 (D)	196 (C)
197 (C)	198 (C)	199 (D)	200 (D)	

TEST 8
p.233

PART 5

101 (D)	102 (B)	103 (C)	104 (D)	105 (D)
106 (C)	107 (B)	108 (A)	109 (C)	110 (A)
111 (B)	112 (C)	113 (B)	114 (B)	115 (D)
116 (C)	117 (B)	118 (A)	119 (D)	120 (C)
121 (C)	122 (B)	123 (D)	124 (B)	125 (A)
126 (D)	127 (B)	128 (C)	129 (D)	130 (B)

PART 6

131 (B)	132 (D)	133 (B)	134 (A)	135 (C)
136 (B)	137 (B)	138 (A)	139 (C)	140 (D)
141 (B)	142 (A)	143 (A)	144 (C)	145 (A)
146 (D)				

PART 7

147 (D)	148 (B)	149 (C)	150 (B)	151 (B)
152 (B)	153 (A)	154 (B)	155 (A)	156 (B)
157 (D)	158 (C)	159 (A)	160 (B)	161 (D)
162 (D)	163 (C)	164 (D)	165 (B)	166 (A)
167 (A)	168 (B)	169 (A)	170 (D)	171 (B)
172 (B)	173 (D)	174 (B)	175 (C)	176 (D)
177 (C)	178 (B)	179 (D)	180 (D)	181 (B)
182 (B)	183 (A)	184 (C)	185 (B)	186 (A)
187 (A)	188 (D)	189 (A)	190 (B)	191 (C)
192 (D)	193 (B)	194 (D)	195 (C)	196 (B)
197 (C)	198 (B)	199 (D)	200 (D)	

TEST 9
p.263

PART 5

101 (B)	102 (D)	103 (B)	104 (A)	105 (B)
106 (C)	107 (B)	108 (C)	109 (B)	110 (C)
111 (D)	112 (C)	113 (C)	114 (C)	115 (C)
116 (B)	117 (B)	118 (C)	119 (B)	120 (C)
121 (C)	122 (B)	123 (A)	124 (C)	125 (D)
126 (C)	127 (C)	128 (B)	129 (D)	130 (B)

PART 6

131 (B)	132 (D)	133 (D)	134 (A)	135 (C)
136 (D)	137 (D)	138 (A)	139 (A)	140 (C)
141 (B)	142 (A)	143 (A)	144 (A)	145 (D)
146 (A)				

PART 7

147 (C)	148 (D)	149 (C)	150 (C)	151 (C)
152 (D)	153 (B)	154 (C)	155 (D)	156 (A)
157 (B)	158 (D)	159 (C)	160 (B)	161 (B)
162 (A)	163 (B)	164 (B)	165 (C)	166 (A)
167 (B)	168 (C)	169 (B)	170 (B)	171 (B)
172 (B)	173 (C)	174 (D)	175 (D)	176 (D)
177 (B)	178 (C)	179 (A)	180 (B)	181 (D)
182 (C)	183 (A)	184 (C)	185 (D)	186 (C)
187 (D)	188 (B)	189 (B)	190 (D)	191 (D)
192 (B)	193 (D)	194 (D)	195 (B)	196 (C)
197 (C)	198 (A)	199 (C)	200 (B)	

TEST 10
p.293

PART 5

101 (A)	102 (C)	103 (A)	104 (D)	105 (A)
106 (A)	107 (C)	108 (C)	109 (A)	110 (B)
111 (C)	112 (B)	113 (B)	114 (D)	115 (B)
116 (B)	117 (C)	118 (B)	119 (D)	120 (D)
121 (C)	122 (D)	123 (C)	124 (D)	125 (D)
126 (B)	127 (D)	128 (C)	129 (C)	130 (A)

PART 6

131 (C)	132 (A)	133 (B)	134 (C)	135 (C)
136 (A)	137 (A)	138 (D)	139 (C)	140 (D)
141 (B)	142 (D)	143 (C)	144 (D)	145 (D)
146 (D)				

PART 7

147 (D)	148 (B)	149 (A)	150 (C)	151 (C)
152 (C)	153 (B)	154 (C)	155 (D)	156 (C)
157 (A)	158 (B)	159 (D)	160 (D)	161 (B)
162 (A)	163 (C)	164 (C)	165 (B)	166 (B)
167 (C)	168 (A)	169 (A)	170 (D)	171 (B)
172 (D)	173 (C)	174 (B)	175 (D)	176 (C)
177 (C)	178 (C)	179 (A)	180 (A)	181 (C)
182 (C)	183 (B)	184 (B)	185 (D)	186 (A)
187 (C)	188 (B)	189 (D)	190 (D)	191 (C)
192 (C)	193 (C)	194 (C)	195 (C)	196 (D)
197 (C)	198 (D)	199 (C)	200 (B)	

TEST 11
p.323

PART 5

101 (C)	102 (D)	103 (B)	104 (D)	105 (B)
106 (A)	107 (C)	108 (B)	109 (C)	110 (C)
111 (B)	112 (B)	113 (C)	114 (B)	115 (C)
116 (B)	117 (B)	118 (C)	119 (C)	120 (C)
121 (C)	122 (B)	123 (A)	124 (C)	125 (C)
126 (D)	127 (D)	128 (D)	129 (B)	130 (D)

PART 6

131 (A)	132 (C)	133 (C)	134 (A)	135 (A)
136 (D)	137 (C)	138 (C)	139 (D)	140 (B)
141 (A)	142 (A)	143 (B)	144 (C)	145 (A)
146 (A)				

PART 7

147 (D)	148 (C)	149 (B)	150 (D)	151 (D)
152 (C)	153 (B)	154 (A)	155 (C)	156 (C)
157 (C)	158 (B)	159 (C)	160 (A)	161 (C)
162 (B)	163 (A)	164 (C)	165 (C)	166 (A)
167 (C)	168 (D)	169 (C)	170 (B)	171 (D)
172 (D)	173 (B)	174 (C)	175 (C)	176 (A)
177 (D)	178 (C)	179 (A)	180 (A)	181 (A)
182 (B)	183 (B)	184 (C)	185 (C)	186 (B)
187 (A)	188 (B)	189 (D)	190 (C)	191 (B)
192 (C)	193 (B)	194 (D)	195 (A)	196 (C)
197 (C)	198 (B)	199 (C)	200 (A)	

TEST 12
p.353

PART 5

101 (A)	102 (D)	103 (C)	104 (B)	105 (B)
106 (D)	107 (B)	108 (C)	109 (B)	110 (C)
111 (C)	112 (D)	113 (B)	114 (B)	115 (D)
116 (B)	117 (D)	118 (B)	119 (D)	120 (D)
121 (B)	122 (D)	123 (D)	124 (B)	125 (C)
126 (A)	127 (C)	128 (C)	129 (C)	130 (D)

PART 6

131 (D)	132 (A)	133 (A)	134 (C)	135 (D)
136 (D)	137 (D)	138 (B)	139 (C)	140 (C)
141 (C)	142 (C)	143 (C)	144 (D)	145 (D)
146 (A)				

PART 7

147 (C)	148 (B)	149 (D)	150 (D)	151 (D)
152 (C)	153 (B)	154 (B)	155 (C)	156 (B)
157 (C)	158 (C)	159 (B)	160 (D)	161 (C)
162 (C)	163 (A)	164 (A)	165 (C)	166 (B)
167 (D)	168 (B)	169 (D)	170 (C)	171 (B)
172 (D)	173 (A)	174 (B)	175 (B)	176 (B)
177 (A)	178 (D)	179 (B)	180 (D)	181 (D)
182 (B)	183 (C)	184 (A)	185 (D)	186 (D)
187 (A)	188 (D)	189 (B)	190 (A)	191 (B)
192 (A)	193 (B)	194 (C)	195 (A)	196 (B)
197 (B)	198 (A)	199 (B)	200 (D)	

Answer Sheet

TEST 2

READING (Part V~VII)

101	102	103	104	105	106	107	108	109	110	111	112	113	114	115	116	117	118	119	120
121	122	123	124	125	126	127	128	129	130	131	132	133	134	135	136	137	138	139	140
141	142	143	144	145	146	147	148	149	150	151	152	153	154	155	156	157	158	159	160
161	162	163	164	165	166	167	168	169	170	171	172	173	174	175	176	177	178	179	180
181	182	183	184	185	186	187	188	189	190	191	192	193	194	195	196	197	198	199	200

맞은 문제 개수: ___/100

자르는 선 ✂

Answer Sheet

TEST 1

READING (Part V~VII)

101	102	103	104	105	106	107	108	109	110	111	112	113	114	115	116	117	118	119	120
121	122	123	124	125	126	127	128	129	130	131	132	133	134	135	136	137	138	139	140
141	142	143	144	145	146	147	148	149	150	151	152	153	154	155	156	157	158	159	160
161	162	163	164	165	166	167	168	169	170	171	172	173	174	175	176	177	178	179	180
181	182	183	184	185	186	187	188	189	190	191	192	193	194	195	196	197	198	199	200

맞은 문제 개수: ___/100

자르는 선 ✂

무료 토익 · 토스 · 오픽 · 취업 자료 제공

Hackers.co.kr

Answer Sheet

TEST 4

READING (Part V~VII)

#					#					#					#				
101	Ⓐ	Ⓑ	Ⓒ	Ⓓ	121	Ⓐ	Ⓑ	Ⓒ	Ⓓ	141	Ⓐ	Ⓑ	Ⓒ	Ⓓ	161	Ⓐ	Ⓑ	Ⓒ	Ⓓ
102	Ⓐ	Ⓑ	Ⓒ	Ⓓ	122	Ⓐ	Ⓑ	Ⓒ	Ⓓ	142	Ⓐ	Ⓑ	Ⓒ	Ⓓ	162	Ⓐ	Ⓑ	Ⓒ	Ⓓ
103	Ⓐ	Ⓑ	Ⓒ	Ⓓ	123	Ⓐ	Ⓑ	Ⓒ	Ⓓ	143	Ⓐ	Ⓑ	Ⓒ	Ⓓ	163	Ⓐ	Ⓑ	Ⓒ	Ⓓ
104	Ⓐ	Ⓑ	Ⓒ	Ⓓ	124	Ⓐ	Ⓑ	Ⓒ	Ⓓ	144	Ⓐ	Ⓑ	Ⓒ	Ⓓ	164	Ⓐ	Ⓑ	Ⓒ	Ⓓ
105	Ⓐ	Ⓑ	Ⓒ	Ⓓ	125	Ⓐ	Ⓑ	Ⓒ	Ⓓ	145	Ⓐ	Ⓑ	Ⓒ	Ⓓ	165	Ⓐ	Ⓑ	Ⓒ	Ⓓ
106	Ⓐ	Ⓑ	Ⓒ	Ⓓ	126	Ⓐ	Ⓑ	Ⓒ	Ⓓ	146	Ⓐ	Ⓑ	Ⓒ	Ⓓ	166	Ⓐ	Ⓑ	Ⓒ	Ⓓ
107	Ⓐ	Ⓑ	Ⓒ	Ⓓ	127	Ⓐ	Ⓑ	Ⓒ	Ⓓ	147	Ⓐ	Ⓑ	Ⓒ	Ⓓ	167	Ⓐ	Ⓑ	Ⓒ	Ⓓ
108	Ⓐ	Ⓑ	Ⓒ	Ⓓ	128	Ⓐ	Ⓑ	Ⓒ	Ⓓ	148	Ⓐ	Ⓑ	Ⓒ	Ⓓ	168	Ⓐ	Ⓑ	Ⓒ	Ⓓ
109	Ⓐ	Ⓑ	Ⓒ	Ⓓ	129	Ⓐ	Ⓑ	Ⓒ	Ⓓ	149	Ⓐ	Ⓑ	Ⓒ	Ⓓ	169	Ⓐ	Ⓑ	Ⓒ	Ⓓ
110	Ⓐ	Ⓑ	Ⓒ	Ⓓ	130	Ⓐ	Ⓑ	Ⓒ	Ⓓ	150	Ⓐ	Ⓑ	Ⓒ	Ⓓ	170	Ⓐ	Ⓑ	Ⓒ	Ⓓ
111	Ⓐ	Ⓑ	Ⓒ	Ⓓ	131	Ⓐ	Ⓑ	Ⓒ	Ⓓ	151	Ⓐ	Ⓑ	Ⓒ	Ⓓ	171	Ⓐ	Ⓑ	Ⓒ	Ⓓ
112	Ⓐ	Ⓑ	Ⓒ	Ⓓ	132	Ⓐ	Ⓑ	Ⓒ	Ⓓ	152	Ⓐ	Ⓑ	Ⓒ	Ⓓ	172	Ⓐ	Ⓑ	Ⓒ	Ⓓ
113	Ⓐ	Ⓑ	Ⓒ	Ⓓ	133	Ⓐ	Ⓑ	Ⓒ	Ⓓ	153	Ⓐ	Ⓑ	Ⓒ	Ⓓ	173	Ⓐ	Ⓑ	Ⓒ	Ⓓ
114	Ⓐ	Ⓑ	Ⓒ	Ⓓ	134	Ⓐ	Ⓑ	Ⓒ	Ⓓ	154	Ⓐ	Ⓑ	Ⓒ	Ⓓ	174	Ⓐ	Ⓑ	Ⓒ	Ⓓ
115	Ⓐ	Ⓑ	Ⓒ	Ⓓ	135	Ⓐ	Ⓑ	Ⓒ	Ⓓ	155	Ⓐ	Ⓑ	Ⓒ	Ⓓ	175	Ⓐ	Ⓑ	Ⓒ	Ⓓ
116	Ⓐ	Ⓑ	Ⓒ	Ⓓ	136	Ⓐ	Ⓑ	Ⓒ	Ⓓ	156	Ⓐ	Ⓑ	Ⓒ	Ⓓ	176	Ⓐ	Ⓑ	Ⓒ	Ⓓ
117	Ⓐ	Ⓑ	Ⓒ	Ⓓ	137	Ⓐ	Ⓑ	Ⓒ	Ⓓ	157	Ⓐ	Ⓑ	Ⓒ	Ⓓ	177	Ⓐ	Ⓑ	Ⓒ	Ⓓ
118	Ⓐ	Ⓑ	Ⓒ	Ⓓ	138	Ⓐ	Ⓑ	Ⓒ	Ⓓ	158	Ⓐ	Ⓑ	Ⓒ	Ⓓ	178	Ⓐ	Ⓑ	Ⓒ	Ⓓ
119	Ⓐ	Ⓑ	Ⓒ	Ⓓ	139	Ⓐ	Ⓑ	Ⓒ	Ⓓ	159	Ⓐ	Ⓑ	Ⓒ	Ⓓ	179	Ⓐ	Ⓑ	Ⓒ	Ⓓ
120	Ⓐ	Ⓑ	Ⓒ	Ⓓ	140	Ⓐ	Ⓑ	Ⓒ	Ⓓ	160	Ⓐ	Ⓑ	Ⓒ	Ⓓ	180	Ⓐ	Ⓑ	Ⓒ	Ⓓ
															181	Ⓐ	Ⓑ	Ⓒ	Ⓓ
															182	Ⓐ	Ⓑ	Ⓒ	Ⓓ
															183	Ⓐ	Ⓑ	Ⓒ	Ⓓ
															184	Ⓐ	Ⓑ	Ⓒ	Ⓓ
															185	Ⓐ	Ⓑ	Ⓒ	Ⓓ
															186	Ⓐ	Ⓑ	Ⓒ	Ⓓ
															187	Ⓐ	Ⓑ	Ⓒ	Ⓓ
															188	Ⓐ	Ⓑ	Ⓒ	Ⓓ
															189	Ⓐ	Ⓑ	Ⓒ	Ⓓ
															190	Ⓐ	Ⓑ	Ⓒ	Ⓓ
															191	Ⓐ	Ⓑ	Ⓒ	Ⓓ
															192	Ⓐ	Ⓑ	Ⓒ	Ⓓ
															193	Ⓐ	Ⓑ	Ⓒ	Ⓓ
															194	Ⓐ	Ⓑ	Ⓒ	Ⓓ
															195	Ⓐ	Ⓑ	Ⓒ	Ⓓ
															196	Ⓐ	Ⓑ	Ⓒ	Ⓓ
															197	Ⓐ	Ⓑ	Ⓒ	Ⓓ
															198	Ⓐ	Ⓑ	Ⓒ	Ⓓ
															199	Ⓐ	Ⓑ	Ⓒ	Ⓓ
															200	Ⓐ	Ⓑ	Ⓒ	Ⓓ

맞은 문제 개수: ___ / 100

자르는 선 ✂

Answer Sheet

TEST 3

READING (Part V~VII)

#					#					#					#				
101	Ⓐ	Ⓑ	Ⓒ	Ⓓ	121	Ⓐ	Ⓑ	Ⓒ	Ⓓ	141	Ⓐ	Ⓑ	Ⓒ	Ⓓ	161	Ⓐ	Ⓑ	Ⓒ	Ⓓ
102	Ⓐ	Ⓑ	Ⓒ	Ⓓ	122	Ⓐ	Ⓑ	Ⓒ	Ⓓ	142	Ⓐ	Ⓑ	Ⓒ	Ⓓ	162	Ⓐ	Ⓑ	Ⓒ	Ⓓ
103	Ⓐ	Ⓑ	Ⓒ	Ⓓ	123	Ⓐ	Ⓑ	Ⓒ	Ⓓ	143	Ⓐ	Ⓑ	Ⓒ	Ⓓ	163	Ⓐ	Ⓑ	Ⓒ	Ⓓ
104	Ⓐ	Ⓑ	Ⓒ	Ⓓ	124	Ⓐ	Ⓑ	Ⓒ	Ⓓ	144	Ⓐ	Ⓑ	Ⓒ	Ⓓ	164	Ⓐ	Ⓑ	Ⓒ	Ⓓ
105	Ⓐ	Ⓑ	Ⓒ	Ⓓ	125	Ⓐ	Ⓑ	Ⓒ	Ⓓ	145	Ⓐ	Ⓑ	Ⓒ	Ⓓ	165	Ⓐ	Ⓑ	Ⓒ	Ⓓ
106	Ⓐ	Ⓑ	Ⓒ	Ⓓ	126	Ⓐ	Ⓑ	Ⓒ	Ⓓ	146	Ⓐ	Ⓑ	Ⓒ	Ⓓ	166	Ⓐ	Ⓑ	Ⓒ	Ⓓ
107	Ⓐ	Ⓑ	Ⓒ	Ⓓ	127	Ⓐ	Ⓑ	Ⓒ	Ⓓ	147	Ⓐ	Ⓑ	Ⓒ	Ⓓ	167	Ⓐ	Ⓑ	Ⓒ	Ⓓ
108	Ⓐ	Ⓑ	Ⓒ	Ⓓ	128	Ⓐ	Ⓑ	Ⓒ	Ⓓ	148	Ⓐ	Ⓑ	Ⓒ	Ⓓ	168	Ⓐ	Ⓑ	Ⓒ	Ⓓ
109	Ⓐ	Ⓑ	Ⓒ	Ⓓ	129	Ⓐ	Ⓑ	Ⓒ	Ⓓ	149	Ⓐ	Ⓑ	Ⓒ	Ⓓ	169	Ⓐ	Ⓑ	Ⓒ	Ⓓ
110	Ⓐ	Ⓑ	Ⓒ	Ⓓ	130	Ⓐ	Ⓑ	Ⓒ	Ⓓ	150	Ⓐ	Ⓑ	Ⓒ	Ⓓ	170	Ⓐ	Ⓑ	Ⓒ	Ⓓ
111	Ⓐ	Ⓑ	Ⓒ	Ⓓ	131	Ⓐ	Ⓑ	Ⓒ	Ⓓ	151	Ⓐ	Ⓑ	Ⓒ	Ⓓ	171	Ⓐ	Ⓑ	Ⓒ	Ⓓ
112	Ⓐ	Ⓑ	Ⓒ	Ⓓ	132	Ⓐ	Ⓑ	Ⓒ	Ⓓ	152	Ⓐ	Ⓑ	Ⓒ	Ⓓ	172	Ⓐ	Ⓑ	Ⓒ	Ⓓ
113	Ⓐ	Ⓑ	Ⓒ	Ⓓ	133	Ⓐ	Ⓑ	Ⓒ	Ⓓ	153	Ⓐ	Ⓑ	Ⓒ	Ⓓ	173	Ⓐ	Ⓑ	Ⓒ	Ⓓ
114	Ⓐ	Ⓑ	Ⓒ	Ⓓ	134	Ⓐ	Ⓑ	Ⓒ	Ⓓ	154	Ⓐ	Ⓑ	Ⓒ	Ⓓ	174	Ⓐ	Ⓑ	Ⓒ	Ⓓ
115	Ⓐ	Ⓑ	Ⓒ	Ⓓ	135	Ⓐ	Ⓑ	Ⓒ	Ⓓ	155	Ⓐ	Ⓑ	Ⓒ	Ⓓ	175	Ⓐ	Ⓑ	Ⓒ	Ⓓ
116	Ⓐ	Ⓑ	Ⓒ	Ⓓ	136	Ⓐ	Ⓑ	Ⓒ	Ⓓ	156	Ⓐ	Ⓑ	Ⓒ	Ⓓ	176	Ⓐ	Ⓑ	Ⓒ	Ⓓ
117	Ⓐ	Ⓑ	Ⓒ	Ⓓ	137	Ⓐ	Ⓑ	Ⓒ	Ⓓ	157	Ⓐ	Ⓑ	Ⓒ	Ⓓ	177	Ⓐ	Ⓑ	Ⓒ	Ⓓ
118	Ⓐ	Ⓑ	Ⓒ	Ⓓ	138	Ⓐ	Ⓑ	Ⓒ	Ⓓ	158	Ⓐ	Ⓑ	Ⓒ	Ⓓ	178	Ⓐ	Ⓑ	Ⓒ	Ⓓ
119	Ⓐ	Ⓑ	Ⓒ	Ⓓ	139	Ⓐ	Ⓑ	Ⓒ	Ⓓ	159	Ⓐ	Ⓑ	Ⓒ	Ⓓ	179	Ⓐ	Ⓑ	Ⓒ	Ⓓ
120	Ⓐ	Ⓑ	Ⓒ	Ⓓ	140	Ⓐ	Ⓑ	Ⓒ	Ⓓ	160	Ⓐ	Ⓑ	Ⓒ	Ⓓ	180	Ⓐ	Ⓑ	Ⓒ	Ⓓ
															181	Ⓐ	Ⓑ	Ⓒ	Ⓓ
															182	Ⓐ	Ⓑ	Ⓒ	Ⓓ
															183	Ⓐ	Ⓑ	Ⓒ	Ⓓ
															184	Ⓐ	Ⓑ	Ⓒ	Ⓓ
															185	Ⓐ	Ⓑ	Ⓒ	Ⓓ
															186	Ⓐ	Ⓑ	Ⓒ	Ⓓ
															187	Ⓐ	Ⓑ	Ⓒ	Ⓓ
															188	Ⓐ	Ⓑ	Ⓒ	Ⓓ
															189	Ⓐ	Ⓑ	Ⓒ	Ⓓ
															190	Ⓐ	Ⓑ	Ⓒ	Ⓓ
															191	Ⓐ	Ⓑ	Ⓒ	Ⓓ
															192	Ⓐ	Ⓑ	Ⓒ	Ⓓ
															193	Ⓐ	Ⓑ	Ⓒ	Ⓓ
															194	Ⓐ	Ⓑ	Ⓒ	Ⓓ
															195	Ⓐ	Ⓑ	Ⓒ	Ⓓ
															196	Ⓐ	Ⓑ	Ⓒ	Ⓓ
															197	Ⓐ	Ⓑ	Ⓒ	Ⓓ
															198	Ⓐ	Ⓑ	Ⓒ	Ⓓ
															199	Ⓐ	Ⓑ	Ⓒ	Ⓓ
															200	Ⓐ	Ⓑ	Ⓒ	Ⓓ

맞은 문제 개수: ___ / 100

✂ 자르는 선

무료 토익 · 토스 · 오픽 · 취업 자료 제공

Hackers.co.kr

Answer Sheet

TEST 6

READING (Part V~VII)

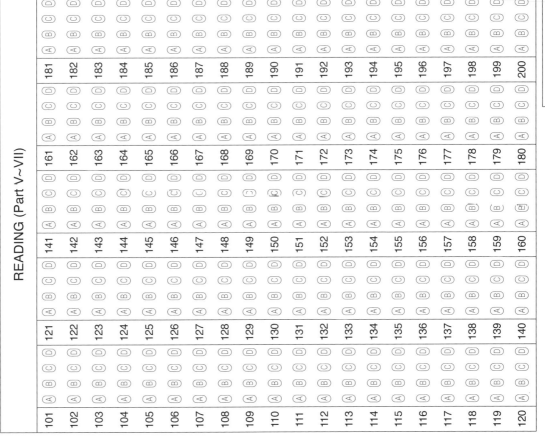

Answer Sheet

TEST 5

READING (Part V~VII)

무료 토익 · 토스 · 오픽 · 취업 자료 제공

Hackers.co.kr

Answer Sheet
TEST 8

READING (Part V~VII)

맞은 문제 개수: ___ /100

Answer Sheet
TEST 7

READING (Part V~VII)

맞은 문제 개수: ___ /100

자르는 선 ✂

무료 토익 · 토스 · 오픽 · 취업 자료 제공

Hackers.co.kr

Answer Sheet

TEST 10

READING (Part V~VII)

#					#					#					#				
101	Ⓐ	Ⓑ	Ⓒ	Ⓓ	121	Ⓐ	Ⓑ	Ⓒ	Ⓓ	141	Ⓐ	Ⓑ	Ⓒ	Ⓓ	161	Ⓐ	Ⓑ	Ⓒ	Ⓓ	181	Ⓐ	Ⓑ	Ⓒ	Ⓓ
102	Ⓐ	Ⓑ	Ⓒ	Ⓓ	122	Ⓐ	Ⓑ	Ⓒ	Ⓓ	142	Ⓐ	Ⓑ	Ⓒ	Ⓓ	162	Ⓐ	Ⓑ	Ⓒ	Ⓓ	182	Ⓐ	Ⓑ	Ⓒ	Ⓓ
103	Ⓐ	Ⓑ	Ⓒ	Ⓓ	123	Ⓐ	Ⓑ	Ⓒ	Ⓓ	143	Ⓐ	Ⓑ	Ⓒ	Ⓓ	163	Ⓐ	Ⓑ	Ⓒ	Ⓓ	183	Ⓐ	Ⓑ	Ⓒ	Ⓓ
104	Ⓐ	Ⓑ	Ⓒ	Ⓓ	124	Ⓐ	Ⓑ	Ⓒ	Ⓓ	144	Ⓐ	Ⓑ	Ⓒ	Ⓓ	164	Ⓐ	Ⓑ	Ⓒ	Ⓓ	184	Ⓐ	Ⓑ	Ⓒ	Ⓓ
105	Ⓐ	Ⓑ	Ⓒ	Ⓓ	125	Ⓐ	Ⓑ	Ⓒ	Ⓓ	145	Ⓐ	Ⓑ	Ⓒ	Ⓓ	165	Ⓐ	Ⓑ	Ⓒ	Ⓓ	185	Ⓐ	Ⓑ	Ⓒ	Ⓓ
106	Ⓐ	Ⓑ	Ⓒ	Ⓓ	126	Ⓐ	Ⓑ	Ⓒ	Ⓓ	146	Ⓐ	Ⓑ	Ⓒ	Ⓓ	166	Ⓐ	Ⓑ	Ⓒ	Ⓓ	186	Ⓐ	Ⓑ	Ⓒ	Ⓓ
107	Ⓐ	Ⓑ	Ⓒ	Ⓓ	127	Ⓐ	Ⓑ	Ⓒ	Ⓓ	147	Ⓐ	Ⓑ	Ⓒ	Ⓓ	167	Ⓐ	Ⓑ	Ⓒ	Ⓓ	187	Ⓐ	Ⓑ	Ⓒ	Ⓓ
108	Ⓐ	Ⓑ	Ⓒ	Ⓓ	128	Ⓐ	Ⓑ	Ⓒ	Ⓓ	148	Ⓐ	Ⓑ	Ⓒ	Ⓓ	168	Ⓐ	Ⓑ	Ⓒ	Ⓓ	188	Ⓐ	Ⓑ	Ⓒ	Ⓓ
109	Ⓐ	Ⓑ	Ⓒ	Ⓓ	129	Ⓐ	Ⓑ	Ⓒ	Ⓓ	149	Ⓐ	Ⓑ	Ⓒ	Ⓓ	169	Ⓐ	Ⓑ	Ⓒ	Ⓓ	189	Ⓐ	Ⓑ	Ⓒ	Ⓓ
110	Ⓐ	Ⓑ	Ⓒ	Ⓓ	130	Ⓐ	Ⓑ	Ⓒ	Ⓓ	150	Ⓐ	Ⓑ	Ⓒ	Ⓓ	170	Ⓐ	Ⓑ	Ⓒ	Ⓓ	190	Ⓐ	Ⓑ	Ⓒ	Ⓓ
111	Ⓐ	Ⓑ	Ⓒ	Ⓓ	131	Ⓐ	Ⓑ	Ⓒ	Ⓓ	151	Ⓐ	Ⓑ	Ⓒ	Ⓓ	171	Ⓐ	Ⓑ	Ⓒ	Ⓓ	191	Ⓐ	Ⓑ	Ⓒ	Ⓓ
112	Ⓐ	Ⓑ	Ⓒ	Ⓓ	132	Ⓐ	Ⓑ	Ⓒ	Ⓓ	152	Ⓐ	Ⓑ	Ⓒ	Ⓓ	172	Ⓐ	Ⓑ	Ⓒ	Ⓓ	192	Ⓐ	Ⓑ	Ⓒ	Ⓓ
113	Ⓐ	Ⓑ	Ⓒ	Ⓓ	133	Ⓐ	Ⓑ	Ⓒ	Ⓓ	153	Ⓐ	Ⓑ	Ⓒ	Ⓓ	173	Ⓐ	Ⓑ	Ⓒ	Ⓓ	193	Ⓐ	Ⓑ	Ⓒ	Ⓓ
114	Ⓐ	Ⓑ	Ⓒ	Ⓓ	134	Ⓐ	Ⓑ	Ⓒ	Ⓓ	154	Ⓐ	Ⓑ	Ⓒ	Ⓓ	174	Ⓐ	Ⓑ	Ⓒ	Ⓓ	194	Ⓐ	Ⓑ	Ⓒ	Ⓓ
115	Ⓐ	Ⓑ	Ⓒ	Ⓓ	135	Ⓐ	Ⓑ	Ⓒ	Ⓓ	155	Ⓐ	Ⓑ	Ⓒ	Ⓓ	175	Ⓐ	Ⓑ	Ⓒ	Ⓓ	195	Ⓐ	Ⓑ	Ⓒ	Ⓓ
116	Ⓐ	Ⓑ	Ⓒ	Ⓓ	136	Ⓐ	Ⓑ	Ⓒ	Ⓓ	156	Ⓐ	Ⓑ	Ⓒ	Ⓓ	176	Ⓐ	Ⓑ	Ⓒ	Ⓓ	196	Ⓐ	Ⓑ	Ⓒ	Ⓓ
117	Ⓐ	Ⓑ	Ⓒ	Ⓓ	137	Ⓐ	Ⓑ	Ⓒ	Ⓓ	157	Ⓐ	Ⓑ	Ⓒ	Ⓓ	177	Ⓐ	Ⓑ	Ⓒ	Ⓓ	197	Ⓐ	Ⓑ	Ⓒ	Ⓓ
118	Ⓐ	Ⓑ	Ⓒ	Ⓓ	138	Ⓐ	Ⓑ	Ⓒ	Ⓓ	158	Ⓐ	Ⓑ	Ⓒ	Ⓓ	178	Ⓐ	Ⓑ	Ⓒ	Ⓓ	198	Ⓐ	Ⓑ	Ⓒ	Ⓓ
119	Ⓐ	Ⓑ	Ⓒ	Ⓓ	139	Ⓐ	Ⓑ	Ⓒ	Ⓓ	159	Ⓐ	Ⓑ	Ⓒ	Ⓓ	179	Ⓐ	Ⓑ	Ⓒ	Ⓓ	199	Ⓐ	Ⓑ	Ⓒ	Ⓓ
120	Ⓐ	Ⓑ	Ⓒ	Ⓓ	140	Ⓐ	Ⓑ	Ⓒ	Ⓓ	160	Ⓐ	Ⓑ	Ⓒ	Ⓓ	180	Ⓐ	Ⓑ	Ⓒ	Ⓓ	200	Ⓐ	Ⓑ	Ⓒ	Ⓓ

맞은 문제 개수: ＿＿ / 100

자르는 선 ✂

Answer Sheet

TEST 9

READING (Part V~VII)

#					#					#					#				
101	Ⓐ	Ⓑ	Ⓒ	Ⓓ	121	Ⓐ	Ⓑ	Ⓒ	Ⓓ	141	Ⓐ	Ⓑ	Ⓒ	Ⓓ	161	Ⓐ	Ⓑ	Ⓒ	Ⓓ	181	Ⓐ	Ⓑ	Ⓒ	Ⓓ
102	Ⓐ	Ⓑ	Ⓒ	Ⓓ	122	Ⓐ	Ⓑ	Ⓒ	Ⓓ	142	Ⓐ	Ⓑ	Ⓒ	Ⓓ	162	Ⓐ	Ⓑ	Ⓒ	Ⓓ	182	Ⓐ	Ⓑ	Ⓒ	Ⓓ
103	Ⓐ	Ⓑ	Ⓒ	Ⓓ	123	Ⓐ	Ⓑ	Ⓒ	Ⓓ	143	Ⓐ	Ⓑ	Ⓒ	Ⓓ	163	Ⓐ	Ⓑ	Ⓒ	Ⓓ	183	Ⓐ	Ⓑ	Ⓒ	Ⓓ
104	Ⓐ	Ⓑ	Ⓒ	Ⓓ	124	Ⓐ	Ⓑ	Ⓒ	Ⓓ	144	Ⓐ	Ⓑ	Ⓒ	Ⓓ	164	Ⓐ	Ⓑ	Ⓒ	Ⓓ	184	Ⓐ	Ⓑ	Ⓒ	Ⓓ
105	Ⓐ	Ⓑ	Ⓒ	Ⓓ	125	Ⓐ	Ⓑ	Ⓒ	Ⓓ	145	Ⓐ	Ⓑ	Ⓒ	Ⓓ	165	Ⓐ	Ⓑ	Ⓒ	Ⓓ	185	Ⓐ	Ⓑ	Ⓒ	Ⓓ
106	Ⓐ	Ⓑ	Ⓒ	Ⓓ	126	Ⓐ	Ⓑ	Ⓒ	Ⓓ	146	Ⓐ	Ⓑ	Ⓒ	Ⓓ	166	Ⓐ	Ⓑ	Ⓒ	Ⓓ	186	Ⓐ	Ⓑ	Ⓒ	Ⓓ
107	Ⓐ	Ⓑ	Ⓒ	Ⓓ	127	Ⓐ	Ⓑ	Ⓒ	Ⓓ	147	Ⓐ	Ⓑ	Ⓒ	Ⓓ	167	Ⓐ	Ⓑ	Ⓒ	Ⓓ	187	Ⓐ	Ⓑ	Ⓒ	Ⓓ
108	Ⓐ	Ⓑ	Ⓒ	Ⓓ	128	Ⓐ	Ⓑ	Ⓒ	Ⓓ	148	Ⓐ	Ⓑ	Ⓒ	Ⓓ	168	Ⓐ	Ⓑ	Ⓒ	Ⓓ	188	Ⓐ	Ⓑ	Ⓒ	Ⓓ
109	Ⓐ	Ⓑ	Ⓒ	Ⓓ	129	Ⓐ	Ⓑ	Ⓒ	Ⓓ	149	Ⓐ	Ⓑ	Ⓒ	Ⓓ	169	Ⓐ	Ⓑ	Ⓒ	Ⓓ	189	Ⓐ	Ⓑ	Ⓒ	Ⓓ
110	Ⓐ	Ⓑ	Ⓒ	Ⓓ	130	Ⓐ	Ⓑ	Ⓒ	Ⓓ	150	Ⓐ	Ⓑ	Ⓒ	Ⓓ	170	Ⓐ	Ⓑ	Ⓒ	Ⓓ	190	Ⓐ	Ⓑ	Ⓒ	Ⓓ
111	Ⓐ	Ⓑ	Ⓒ	Ⓓ	131	Ⓐ	Ⓑ	Ⓒ	Ⓓ	151	Ⓐ	Ⓑ	Ⓒ	Ⓓ	171	Ⓐ	Ⓑ	Ⓒ	Ⓓ	191	Ⓐ	Ⓑ	Ⓒ	Ⓓ
112	Ⓐ	Ⓑ	Ⓒ	Ⓓ	132	Ⓐ	Ⓑ	Ⓒ	Ⓓ	152	Ⓐ	Ⓑ	Ⓒ	Ⓓ	172	Ⓐ	Ⓑ	Ⓒ	Ⓓ	192	Ⓐ	Ⓑ	Ⓒ	Ⓓ
113	Ⓐ	Ⓑ	Ⓒ	Ⓓ	133	Ⓐ	Ⓑ	Ⓒ	Ⓓ	153	Ⓐ	Ⓑ	Ⓒ	Ⓓ	173	Ⓐ	Ⓑ	Ⓒ	Ⓓ	193	Ⓐ	Ⓑ	Ⓒ	Ⓓ
114	Ⓐ	Ⓑ	Ⓒ	Ⓓ	134	Ⓐ	Ⓑ	Ⓒ	Ⓓ	154	Ⓐ	Ⓑ	Ⓒ	Ⓓ	174	Ⓐ	Ⓑ	Ⓒ	Ⓓ	194	Ⓐ	Ⓑ	Ⓒ	Ⓓ
115	Ⓐ	Ⓑ	Ⓒ	Ⓓ	135	Ⓐ	Ⓑ	Ⓒ	Ⓓ	155	Ⓐ	Ⓑ	Ⓒ	Ⓓ	175	Ⓐ	Ⓑ	Ⓒ	Ⓓ	195	Ⓐ	Ⓑ	Ⓒ	Ⓓ
116	Ⓐ	Ⓑ	Ⓒ	Ⓓ	136	Ⓐ	Ⓑ	Ⓒ	Ⓓ	156	Ⓐ	Ⓑ	Ⓒ	Ⓓ	176	Ⓐ	Ⓑ	Ⓒ	Ⓓ	196	Ⓐ	Ⓑ	Ⓒ	Ⓓ
117	Ⓐ	Ⓑ	Ⓒ	Ⓓ	137	Ⓐ	Ⓑ	Ⓒ	Ⓓ	157	Ⓐ	Ⓑ	Ⓒ	Ⓓ	177	Ⓐ	Ⓑ	Ⓒ	Ⓓ	197	Ⓐ	Ⓑ	Ⓒ	Ⓓ
118	Ⓐ	Ⓑ	Ⓒ	Ⓓ	138	Ⓐ	Ⓑ	Ⓒ	Ⓓ	158	Ⓐ	Ⓑ	Ⓒ	Ⓓ	178	Ⓐ	Ⓑ	Ⓒ	Ⓓ	198	Ⓐ	Ⓑ	Ⓒ	Ⓓ
119	Ⓐ	Ⓑ	Ⓒ	Ⓓ	139	Ⓐ	Ⓑ	Ⓒ	Ⓓ	159	Ⓐ	Ⓑ	Ⓒ	Ⓓ	179	Ⓐ	Ⓑ	Ⓒ	Ⓓ	199	Ⓐ	Ⓑ	Ⓒ	Ⓓ
120	Ⓐ	Ⓑ	Ⓒ	Ⓓ	140	Ⓐ	Ⓑ	Ⓒ	Ⓓ	160	Ⓐ	Ⓑ	Ⓒ	Ⓓ	180	Ⓐ	Ⓑ	Ⓒ	Ⓓ	200	Ⓐ	Ⓑ	Ⓒ	Ⓓ

맞은 문제 개수: ＿＿ / 100

무료 토익 · 토스 · 오픽 · 취업 자료 제공

Hackers.co.kr

Answer Sheet

TEST 12

READING (Part V~VII)

맞은 문제 개수: ___ / 100

자르는 선

Answer Sheet

TEST 11

READING (Part V~VII)

맞은 문제 개수: ___ / 100

자르는 선

물토익부터 **불토익**까지, **1200제**로 토익 졸업!

해커스 토익

실전 1200제
READING RC

초판 8쇄 발행 2024년 7월 22일
초판 1쇄 발행   2020년 7월 1일

지은이	해커스 어학연구소
펴낸곳	(주)해커스 어학연구소
펴낸이	해커스 어학연구소 출판팀

주소	서울특별시 서초구 강남대로61길 23 (주)해커스 어학연구소
고객센터	02-537-5000
교재 관련 문의	publishing@hackers.com
동영상강의	HackersIngang.com

ISBN	978-89-6542-373-7 (13740)
Serial Number	01-08-01

영어 전문 포털, 해커스토익
Hackers.co.kr

해커스토익

· 매일 실전 RC/LC 문제 및 토익 보카 TEST 등 **다양한 무료 학습 컨텐츠**
· 매월 무료 적중예상특강 및 실시간 토익시험 정답확인/해설강의

외국어인강 1위, 해커스인강
HackersIngang.com

해커스인강

· 취약 문제 유형을 분석해주는 인공지능 시스템 **해커스토익 '빅플' 어플**(교재 내 이용권 수록)
· 무료 단어암기장&단어암기 MP3 및 정답녹음 MP3
· 토익 스타강사의 고득점 전략이 담긴 **본 교재 인강**

5천 개가 넘는
해커스토익 무료 자료!

대한민국에서 공짜로 토익 공부하고 싶으면   해커스영어 Hackers.co.kr ▾   검색

RC 정수진

RC 이상길

토익 강의 무료

베스트셀러 1위 토익 강의 150강 무료 서비스,
누적 시청 1,900만 돌파!

Q1
Thousands of park visitors came for the free
concert, but _____ simply wanted a quiet place to
sit and watch people walk by.

A some   B any
C other   D these

토익 실전 문제 무료

토익 RC/LC 풀기, 모의토익 등
실전토익 대비 문제 제공!

LC 한승태   RC 김동영

최신 특강 무료

2,400만뷰 스타강사의
압도적 적중예상특강 매달 업데이트!

고득점 달성 비법 무료

토익 고득점 달성팁, 파트별 비법,
점수대별 공부법 무료 확인

전원
무료
*미션 달성 시

가장 빠른 정답까지!

615만이 선택한 해커스 토익 정답!
시험 직후 가장 빠른 정답 확인

더 많은
토익 무료자료 보기 ▶

"1분 레벨테스트"로
바로 확인하는 내 토익 레벨 ▶

I 토익 교재 시리즈

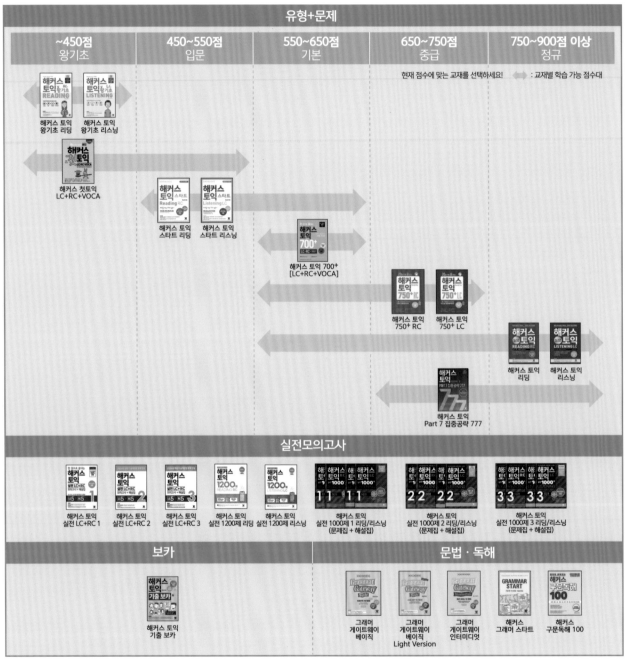

유형+문제				
~450점 왕기초	450~550점 입문	550~650점 기본	650~750점 중급	750~900점 이상 정규

현재 점수에 맞는 교재를 선택하세요! ▶ : 교재별 학습 가능 점수대

해커스 토익
왕기초 리딩 · 해커스 토익 왕기초 리스닝

해커스 첫토익
LC+RC+VOCA

해커스 토익
스타트 리딩 · 해커스 토익 스타트 리스닝

해커스 토익 700+
[LC+RC+VOCA]

해커스 토익 750+ RC · 해커스 토익 750+ LC

해커스 토익 리딩 · 해커스 토익 리스닝

해커스 토익
Part 7 집중공략 777

실전모의고사

해커스 토익 실전 LC+RC 1 · 해커스 토익 실전 LC+RC 2 · 해커스 토익 실전 LC+RC 3 · 해커스 토익 실전 1200제 리딩 · 해커스 토익 실전 1200제 리스닝 · 해커스 토익 실전 1000제 1 리딩/리스닝 (문제집 + 해설집) · 해커스 토익 실전 1000제 2 리딩/리스닝 (문제집 + 해설집) · 해커스 토익 실전 1000제 3 리딩/리스닝 (문제집 + 해설집)

보카

해커스 토익 기출 보카

문법 · 독해

그래머 게이트웨이 베이직 · 그래머 게이트웨이 베이직 Light Version · 그래머 게이트웨이 인터미디엇 · 해커스 그래머 스타트 · 해커스 구문독해 100

I 토익스피킹 교재 시리즈

해커스 토익스피킹 스타트 · 만능 템플릿과 위기탈출 표현으로 해커스 토익스피킹 5일 완성 · 해커스 토익스피킹 · 해커스 토익스피킹 실전모의고사 15회

I 오픽 교재 시리즈

해커스 오픽 스타트 [Intermediate 공략] · 서베이부터 실전까지 해커스 오픽 매뉴얼 · 해커스 오픽 [Advanced 공략]

13740

9 788965 423737

ISBN 978-89-6542-373-7

해설집

해커스
토익

실전 **1200**제

READING RC

베스트셀러
1위

"내가 틀릴만한 문제만
골라서 공부한다!"

해커스토익 빅플

본 교재
모든 문제
취약 유형
심층 분석
무료 제공

물 토 익 부 터 불 토 익 까 지 !

| 최근 12개월
실제 시험 난이도
반영된 문제로 | **토익
졸업** | **맞춤 과외식**
해설로 |

**추가
자료** 해커스인강 HackersIngang.com 본 교재 인강, 무료 단어암기장 및 단어암기 MP3, 무료 정답녹음 MP3
해커스토익 Hackers.co.kr 스타강사 무료 적중 예상특강, 무료 실시간 토익시험 정답확인/해설강의, 무료 매일 실전 RC/LC 문제

[최근 12개월] 2019.03.31~2020.03.31까지의 토익 시험 난이도 분석 및 반영
알라딘 외국어 베스트셀러 토익 종합 분야 1위(2020년 8월 1주 주간 베스트 기준)

해커스 어학연구소

대한민국 토익커

| 평 균 응 시 횟 수 | 9 회 |
| 평 균 점 수 | 6 7 8 점 |

난
토익졸업
언제하지 ?

해커스 토익 실전 1200제 로
바로 **졸업**할 수 있습니다

실제 시험과 똑같은 난이도의 문제로 대비하니까!

최근 12개월 실제 시험과
동일한 난이도의
실전 문제 풀이

정답 찾는 방법을 콕 짚어주는 해설이 있으니까!

오답의 이유까지
꼼꼼하게 알려주는
맞춤 과외식 해설로 실력 상승

내 약점을 정확하게 찾아서 보완해주니까!

해커스 인공지능 시스템
"빅플"로
취약 유형 문제 반복 학습

해커스 토익
실전 1200제
READING RC

300% 활용법

단어암기장 및
단어암기 MP3

정답 PDF 및
정답 녹음 MP3

이용방법 **해커스인강** HackersIngang.com 접속 후 로그인 >>
상단 메뉴 [토익 → MP3/자료 → 무료 MP3/자료] 클릭하여 이용하기

무료 매일
실전 RC/LC 문제

이용방법 **해커스토익** Hackers.co.kr 접속 >>
상단 메뉴 [토익 → 토익 무료학습 → 매일 실전 RC/LC 풀기] 클릭하여 이용하기

빅플
약점집중학습
이용권

87BEDC5375AB577C

이용방법 **해커스인강** HackersIngang.com 접속 후 로그인 >>
[마이클래스 → 결제관리 → 내 쿠폰 확인하기] 클릭 >>
위 쿠폰번호 입력 후 빅플 어플에서 이용권 확인하기

* 이용기한: 2025년 12월 31일(등록 후 14일간 사용 가능)

해커스토익 빅플⁶

본 교재
모든 문제

취약 유형
심층 분석

무료 제공

함께 학습하면 좋은 **해커스토익 빅플 APP**

· 어플을 통해 언제 어디서나 편리하게 토익 문제풀이 학습
· 문제풀이에 대한 학습결과 분석 자료로 취약점 파악 및 약점 보완

▲ 빅플 다운 받기

>> 구글 플레이스토어/애플 앱스토어에서 '빅플'을 검색하세요.

이용방법 [해커스토익 빅플] 어플 접속 >> 상단 [교재풀이] 클릭 후 본 교재 OMR 답안 입력 및 제출 >>
[분석레포트] 클릭 >> 교재 풀이 분석 결과보기

최신기출유형 **100%** 반영

해커스 토익

해설집

실전 **1200** 제

READING RC

해커스 어학연구소

PART 5

101 (C)	102 (D)	103 (B)	104 (C)	105 (C)
106 (B)	107 (C)	108 (A)	109 (B)	110 (C)
111 (D)	112 (C)	113 (D)	114 (B)	115 (C)
116 (C)	117 (D)	118 (D)	119 (D)	120 (B)
121 (C)	122 (A)	123 (C)	124 (C)	125 (A)
126 (C)	127 (B)	128 (B)	129 (C)	130 (D)

PART 6

131 (C)	132 (A)	133 (A)	134 (D)	135 (A)
136 (B)	137 (B)	138 (A)	139 (C)	140 (D)
141 (C)	142 (A)	143 (D)	144 (A)	145 (B)
146 (C)				

PART 7

147 (C)	148 (B)	149 (C)	150 (C)	151 (C)
152 (D)	153 (D)	154 (B)	155 (C)	156 (D)
157 (C)	158 (C)	159 (C)	160 (C)	161 (C)
162 (B)	163 (D)	164 (B)	165 (C)	166 (A)
167 (B)	168 (B)	169 (C)	170 (D)	171 (C)
172 (A)	173 (A)	174 (C)	175 (D)	176 (D)
177 (C)	178 (B)	179 (A)	180 (C)	181 (C)
182 (C)	183 (A)	184 (C)	185 (B)	186 (C)
187 (C)	188 (A)	189 (A)	190 (D)	191 (C)
192 (D)	193 (C)	194 (A)	195 (C)	196 (D)
197 (B)	198 (D)	199 (D)	200 (C)	

PART 5

101 등위접속사 채우기   하 ●○○

해석 Ms. Hunter는 아이오와로 이주할 것이므로, 그녀는 그곳에서 회사의 프로젝트를 감독할 수 있다.

해설 절(Ms. Hunter will be relocating to Iowa)과 절(she can supervise ~ there)을 연결하면서 콤마 바로 뒤에 올 수 있는 접속사가 필요하므로 등위접속사 (C) so(그래서)가 정답이다. 전치사 (A)와 (B)는 절과 절을 연결할 수 없다. 관계대명사 또는 명사절 접속사 (D)는 콤마 바로 뒤에 올 수 없다.

어휘 relocate v. 이주하다, 이동하다   supervise v. 감독하다
such as phr. ~과 같은

102 올바른 시제의 동사 채우기   중 ●●○

해석 구매자와 판매자는 협상을 끝냈고, 이제 그들이 해야 하는 것은 최종 계약을 맺는 것이다.

해설 첫 번째 절(The buyer ~ negotiations)에 동사가 없으므로 동사 (C)와 (D)가 정답의 후보이다. '구매자와 판매자는 협상을 끝냈고, 이제 그들이 해야 하는 것은 최종 계약을 맺는 것이다'라는 의미가 되어야 하므로 과거에 시작되어 방금 완료된 일을 나타낼 때 사용되는 현재 완료 시제 (D) have ended가 정답이다. 참고로, 현재 완료 시제는 과거에 발생한 일이 현재까지 영향을 미칠 때도 사용된다. 미래 시제 (C)는 아직 일어나지 않은 미래의 일을 나타낸다. 동명사 또는 현재분사 (A)와 to 부정사 (B)는 동사 자리에 올 수 없다.

어휘 seller n. 판매자   negotiation n. 협상   sign a contract phr. 계약을 맺다

103 'be동사 + p.p.' 채우기   중 ●●○

해석 그녀의 퇴직 기념 파티에서, Ms. McClatchy는 그녀가 회사에 대한 그녀의 공헌들로 기억되길 원한다고 말했다.

해설 빈칸이 be동사(be) 다음에 왔으므로 진행형을 만드는 -ing형 (A)와 수동태를 만드는 p.p.형 (B)가 정답의 후보이다. '회사에 대한 그녀의 공헌들로 기억되다'라는 수동의 의미가 되어야 하므로 수동태를 만드는 p.p.형 (B) remembered가 정답이다. -ing형 (A)는 능동태가 되어 '그녀의 은퇴 기념 파티에서, Ms. McClatchy는 그녀가 회사에 대한 그녀의 공헌들로 기억하고 싶다고 말했다'라는 어색한 문맥을 만든다. 동사 (C)와 (D)는 be동사 다음에 올 수 없다.

어휘 retirement n. 퇴직, 은퇴   contribution n. 공헌, 기여, 기부금

104 등위접속사 채우기   하 ●○○

해석 Branson 영화사는 몇몇 저예산이지만 성공적인 영화들을 제작했다.

해설 명사(films)를 꾸미는 형용사(low-budget)와 형용사(successful)를 동등하게 연결해주는 등위접속사가 필요하고 '저예산이지만 성공적인 영화들'이라는 의미가 되어야 하므로 등위접속사 (C) but(하지만)이 정답이다. 참고로, but은 상반되는 내용의 단어와 단어, 구와 구, 절과 절을 연결한다는 것을 알아둔다. (A)는 neither와 함께 neither A nor B(A도 B도 아닌)의 상관접속사 형태로 쓰인다. 부사절 접속사 또는 전치사 (B) as는 단어와 단어를 동등하게 연결할 수 없으며, 부사절 접속사일 때 '~하고 있을 때, ~이므로'라는 의미로 시간이나 이유를 나타내고 전치사일 때는 '~으로서, ~과 같은'이라는 의미로 쓰인다. (D) for는 '왜냐하면'이라는 의미의 등위접속사로 쓰일 수 있지만 오직 절과 절을 연결할 수 있으며, 단어나 구는 연결할 수 없다.

어휘 produce v. 제작하다   low-budget adj. 저예산의

105 부사 자리 채우기   중 ●●○

해석 그 책장은 특수 나사 세트로 안전하게 벽에 붙어 있도록 설계되었다.

해설 to 부정사(to be attached)를 꾸밀 수 있는 것은 부사이므로 부사 (C) securely(안전하게, 튼튼하게)가 정답이다. 형용사 또는 동사 (A), 명사 (B), 동사 또는 과거분사 (D)는 to 부정사를 꾸밀 수 없다. 명사 (B)를 be동사의 보어로 보고 빈칸 뒤의 분사(attached)가 명사를 수식하는 것으로 본다

해도, '그 책장은 붙여진 안정성으로 설계되었다'라는 어색한 문맥을 만든다.

어휘 attach v. 붙이다, 연결하다 screw n. 나사
secure adj. 안심하는, 안전한; v. 확보하다 security n. 안정성, 경비

106 명사와 수/인칭 일치하는 대명사 채우기 　　　하 ●○○

해석 Ms. Claiborne은 마케팅 컨설턴트로서 소비자들이 무엇을 원하는지 알아내는 것이 그녀의 일이라고 생각한다.

해설 빈칸 뒤의 명사(job)를 꾸밀 수 있고, Ms. Claiborne을 가리킬 수 있는 3인칭 단수 소유격 인칭대명사 (B) her가 정답이다. (C)도 3인칭 단수 소유격 인칭대명사이지만, 사물을 가리키기 때문에 답이 될 수 없다. (A)와 (D)는 각각 1인칭/3인칭 복수 소유격 인칭대명사이다.

어휘 find out phr. 알아내다, 알게 되다 consumer n. 소비자

107 명사 자리 채우기 　　　하 ●○○

해석 Gasmark International사는 5년 더 연장이 가능한 5년 계약에 동의했다.

해설 부정관사(a) 다음에 오면서 빈칸 앞의 형용사(possible)의 꾸밈을 받을 수 있는 것은 명사이므로 명사 (C) extension(연장)이 정답이다. 동사 (A), 형용사 (B), 동사 또는 과거분사 (D)는 명사 자리에 올 수 없다.

어휘 extend v. 연장하다, 확대하다 extensive adj. 대규모의, 광범위한

108 전치사 채우기 　　　중 ●●○

해석 Mr. Cory는 업무 시간 관련 변경된 정책에 대한 직원들의 우려를 해결하기 위해 회의를 소집했다.

해설 빈칸은 뒤에 명사구(the revised policy on work hours)를 목적어로 취하는 전치사 자리이다. '변경된 정책에 대한 직원들의 우려'라는 의미가 되어야 하므로 (A) regarding(~에 대한)이 정답이다.

어휘 call a meeting phr. 회의를 소집하다 address v. 해결하다, 다루다
concern n. 우려, 걱정 revised adj. 변경된, 수정된
around prep. ~의 주위에 among prep. (셋 이상의) 사이에
throughout prep. ~동안, 도처에

109 주어와 수 일치하는 동사 채우기 　　　하 ●○○

해석 Windsor Food Service사의 임원들은 추가적인 상점 지점을 여는 것에 반대한다.

해설 문장에 동사가 없으므로 동사 (A)와 (B)가 정답의 후보이다. 주어(The executives)가 복수이므로 복수 동사 (B) object가 정답이다. 참고로, 주어(The executives)와 동사 사이의 전치사구(of Windsor Food Service)는 수식어 거품이므로 동사의 수 결정에 아무런 영향을 주지 않는다. 단수 동사 (A)는 복수 주어와 함께 쓰일 수 없다. 명사 (C)와 동명사 또는 현재분사 (D)는 동사 자리에 올 수 없다.

어휘 executive n. 임원 object v. 반대하다; n. 물건 objection n. 이의, 반대

110 형용사 자리 채우기 　　　중 ●●○

해석 Garnet 통신사의 신규 고객들을 위한 특별 할인은 첫 3개월의 서비스에 대해 30퍼센트 할인을 약속한다.

해설 빈칸 뒤의 명사(offer)를 꾸밀 수 있는 것은 형용사이므로 현재분사 (A)와 형용사 (C)가 정답의 후보이다. '신규 고객들을 위한 특별 할인'이라는 의미가 되어야 하므로 형용사 (C) special(특별한)이 정답이다. 현재분사 (A)를 쓸 경우 '신규 고객들을 위한 전문으로 하는 할인'이라는 어색한 문맥을 만든다. 동사 (B)와 부사 (D)는 명사를 꾸밀 수 없다.

어휘 offer n. 할인, 제공; v. 제공하다, 제안하다
specialize v. ~을 전문으로 하다, 전공하다 specially adv. 특히, 특별히

111 동사 어휘 고르기 　　　상 ●●●

해석 미디어 산업의 최신 동향을 요약하는 그 소식지는 구독자들에게 매주 발송된다.

해설 빈칸은 수식어 거품(___ ~ industry)을 이끌 수 있고, 주절의 주어(The newsletter)와 능동 관계를 이루는 현재분사 자리이다. '그 소식지는 미디어 산업의 최신 동향을 요약한다'라는 문맥이므로 동사 summarize(요약하다)의 현재분사 (D) summarizing이 정답이다. (B)의 admit(인정하다, 시인하다)도 해석상 그럴듯해 보이지만, 무언가를 사실이라고 마지못해 인정하는 것을 나타낸다.

어휘 newsletter n. 소식지, 회보 subscriber n. 구독자, 가입자
implement v. 시행하다, 이행하다 relieve v. 안도하게 하다, 완화하다

112 부사 어휘 고르기 　　　하 ●○○

해석 비록 주연 배우들은 그들의 배역을 완벽하게 연기했지만, 음악가들은 잘하지 못했다.

해설 빈칸은 동사(performed)를 꾸미는 부사 자리이다. '주연 배우들은 그들의 배역을 완벽하게 연기했지만, 음악가들은 잘하지 못했다'라는 문맥이므로 (C) perfectly(완벽하게)가 정답이다.

어휘 perform v. 연기하다 role n. 배역 equally adv. 동일하게
occasionally adv. 때때로 simply adv. 간단히

113 원급 표현 채우기 　　　중 ●●○

해석 모든 필수 양식들은 가능한 한 완벽하게 작성되어야 한다.

해설 빈칸 앞뒤에 as가 왔으므로 원급 표현(as + 형용사/부사 + as)을 만들 수 있는 형용사 역할을 하는 과거분사 (A)와 현재분사 (C), 부사 (D)가 정답의 후보이다. 빈칸 앞의 동사(should be filled out)를 꾸밀 수 있는 것은 부사이므로 부사 (D) completely(완벽하게)가 정답이다. 과거분사 (A)와 현재분사 (C)는 동사를 꾸밀 수 없다. 명사 (B)가 as ~ as 사이에 오려면 'as + many/much/few/little + 명사 + as'의 형태가 되어야 한다.

어휘 fill out phr. 작성하다, 기재하다

114 명사 어휘 고르기 　　　중 ●●○

해석 Veran Tech사는 해킹을 예방하는 컴퓨터 소프트웨어의 새로운 발전을 발표했다.

해설 빈칸은 형용사(new)의 꾸밈을 받는 명사 자리이다. '해킹을 예방하는 컴퓨터 소프트웨어의 새로운 발전을 발표했다'라는 문맥이므로 (B) advancement(발전, 진보)가 정답이다.

어휘 prevent v. 예방하다, 막다 destination n. (여행의) 목적지, 도착지
moderation n. 적당함 qualification n. 자질, 자격

115 동사 어휘 고르기 　　　상 ●●●

해석 모델 번호를 제공하는 것에 더하여, 환불을 요구하는 고객들은 구매 날짜를 반드시 명시해야 한다.

해설 빈칸은 조동사(must) 다음에 오는 동사원형 자리이다. '환불을 요구하는 고객들은 구매 날짜를 반드시 명시해야 한다'라는 문맥이므로 (C) specify(명시하다, 구체적으로 작성하다)가 정답이다. (B) propose(제시하다, 제안하다)도 해석상 그럴듯해 보이지만, 제안이나 의견 등을 제시하는 것을 나타낸다.

어휘 accept v. 받아들이다, 수락하다 insist v. 주장하다

116 혼동하기 쉬운 형용사 채우기 　　　중 ●●○

해석 Bridgerton Group사는 지난 30년 동안 소기업에 많은 자금을 제공했다.

해설 빈칸 뒤의 명사(funds)를 꾸밀 수 있는 것은 형용사이므로 형용사 (B)와 (C)가 정답의 후보이다. '많은 자금을 제공했다'라는 의미가 되어야 하므로 형용사 (C) considerable(많은, 상당한)이 정답이다. (B) considerate(이해심이 있는)를 쓸 경우 '이해심이 있는 자금을 제공했다'라는 어색한 문맥이 된다. 동사 (A)와 명사 (D)는 명사를 꾸밀 수 없다.

어휘 lend v. 제공하다, 빌려주다 small business phr. 소기업
consider v. 고려하다 consideration n. 고려

117 부사 어휘 고르기 　　　하 ●○○

해석 Hillside 지역의 주민들은 대부분 근처 Morgan 대학의 학생들로 구성된다.

해설 빈칸은 동사구(consist of)를 꾸미는 부사 자리이다. '주민들은 대부분 근처 Morgan 대학의 학생들로 구성된다'라는 문맥이므로 부사 (D) mostly(대부분, 주로)가 정답이다.

어휘 resident n. 주민, 거주민 consist of phr. ~으로 구성되다
namely adv. 즉, 다시 말해 frequently adv. 자주
publicly adv. 공개적으로, 여론에 의해

최고난도 문제

118 부정대명사/형용사 채우기 　　　상 ●●●

해석 Kenneth 출판사는 운영비를 줄이는 효과적인 방법을 제안하는 회사의 누구에게든 상여금을 줄 것이다.

해설 빈칸은 주격 관계절(who suggests ~ costs)의 선행사인데, 선행사와 수 일치하는 관계절의 동사(suggests)가 단수 동사이므로 단수 취급되는 부정대명사 (D) anyone(누구나)이 정답이다. 지시대명사 (A)는 '~한 사람들'이라는 의미로, 복수 취급되므로 복수 동사와 쓰여야 한다. (B)는 대명사로 쓰일 때 가리키는 대상에 따라 단수 취급될 수도, 복수로 취급될 수도 있는데, 이 문맥에서처럼 '모든 사람들'이라는 의미일 때에는 복수 취급된다. 참고로, all이 불가산 명사를 지칭하거나 전체를 하나의 대상이나 개념으로 지칭할 때는 단수 취급됨을 알아둔다. 부정대명사 (C)를 쓸 경우 '효과적인 방법을 제안하는 회사의 누구에게도 상여금을 제공하지 않을 것이다'라는 어색한 문맥이 된다.

어휘 effective adj. 효과적인, 시행되는, 유효한 reduce v. 줄이다
operating cost phr. 운영비, 경영비

119 부사절 접속사 채우기 　　　중 ●●○

해석 그 전기 회사는 중대한 문제가 보고될 때마다 즉시 수리 직원을 보낸다.

해설 이 문장은 주어(The electric company), 동사(sends out), 목적어(a repair crew)를 갖춘 완전한 절이므로, ___ ~ reported는 수식어 거품으로 보아야 한다. 이 수식어 거품은 동사(is reported)가 있는 거품절이므로, 거품절을 이끌 수 있는 부사절 접속사 (A), (B), (D)가 정답의 후보이다. '그 회사는 중대한 문제가 보고될 때마다 즉시 수리 직원을 보낸다'라는 의미가 되어야 하므로 시간을 나타내는 부사절 접속사 (D) whenever(~할 때마다)가 정답이다. 부사절 접속사 (A)와 (B)를 쓸 경우 각각 '그 회사는 마치 중대한 문제가 보고된 것처럼/보고되는 반면에 즉시 수리 직원을 보낸다'라는 어색한 문맥이 된다. 전치사 (C)는 거품절이 아닌 거품구를 이끈다.

어휘 send out phr. 보내다 repair n. 수리; v. 수리하다 crew n. 직원, 팀

120 형용사 어휘 고르기 　　　중 ●●●

해석 비록 이사회는 생산성도 높이기를 바라지만, 그 프로젝트의 주된 목표는 제조비용을 줄이는 것이다.

해설 빈칸은 명사(goal)를 꾸미는 형용사 자리이다. '생산성도 높이기를 바라지만, 그 프로젝트의 주된 목표는 제조비용을 줄이는 것이다'라는 문맥이므로 (B) primary(주된, 주요한)가 정답이다.

어휘 lower v. 줄이다 manufacturing cost phr. 제조비용
board n. 이사회, 위원회 productivity n. 생산성
adverse adj. 부정적인, 불리한 fluent adj. 능숙한, 유창한
neutral adj. 중립의

121 동사 어휘 고르기 　　　중 ●●●

해석 최고경영자를 교체하기로 한 Howell사의 결정은 많은 투자자들로부터 긍정적인 변화의 신호로 여겨진다.

해설 빈칸은 be동사(is)와 함께 수동태 동사를 만드는 p.p.형 자리이다. 'Howell사의 결정은 많은 투자자들로부터 긍정적인 변화의 신호로 여겨진다'라는 문맥이므로 동사 perceive(~을 -으로 여기다)의 p.p.형 (C) perceived가 정답이다.

어휘 replace v. 교체하다 investor n. 투자자 charge v. 청구하다
determine v. 결정하다, 알아내다 instruct v. 지시하다

122 시간 부사 채우기 　　　중 ●●○

해석 Mr. Weiss가 이미 Sandro's Italian에 자리를 예약했기 때문에, 파티 장소를 더 찾아볼 필요가 없다.

해설 빈칸은 동사(has booked)를 꾸미는 부사 자리이다. 'Mr. Weiss가 이미 자리를 예약했다'라는 의미가 되어야 하므로 시간을 나타내는 부사 (A) already(이미, 벌써)가 정답이다.

어휘 book a table phr. 자리를 예약하다 venue n. 장소 still adv. 아직, 여전히
later adv. 나중에 forward adv. (위치상·시간상) 앞으로

123 형용사 자리 채우기 　　　중 ●●○

해석 기술자들은 더 효율적인 엔진 설계를 만들어냄으로써 자동차 배기가스를 허용할 수 있는 수준으로 제한할 수 있었다.

해설 빈칸 뒤의 명사(levels)를 꾸밀 수 있는 것은 형용사이므로 현재분사 (B)와 형용사 (C)가 정답의 후보이다. '자동차 배기가스를 허용할 수 있는 수준으로 제한할 수 있었다'라는 의미가 되어야 하므로 형용사 (C) tolerable(허용할 수 있는, 견딜 만한)이 정답이다. 현재분사 (B)는 '자동차 배기가스를 견디는 수준으로 제한할 수 있었다(수준이 견디고 있다)'라는 어색한 문맥을 만든다. 동사 (A)와 부사 (D)는 형용사 자리에 올 수 없다. 동사 (A)를 빈칸 앞의 to와 함께 to 부정사를 만드는 것으로 본다 해도, '수준을 참기 위해 자동차 배기가스를 제한할 수 있었다'라는 어색한 문맥이 된다. 참고로, limit A to B(A를 B로 제한하다)를 관용구로 알아둔다.

어휘 emission n. 배기가스 efficient adj. 효율적인, 유효한
tolerate v. 참다, 용인하다 tolerably adv. 참을 수 있을 만큼, 완만하게

124 원형 부정사 채우기 　　　상 ●●●

해석 세미나는 직원들이 그들의 업무에 의해 그들에게 놓인 요구들을 관리하도록 도울 수 있다.

해설 준 사역동사 help의 목적격 보어 자리에는 원형 부정사나 to 부정사가 올 수 있으므로 원형 부정사 (C) manage(관리하다)가 정답이다. 명사 (A)와 (B),

4 무료 단어암기장 및 단어암기 MP3 HackersIngang.com

형용사 (D)는 준 사역동사 help의 목적격 보어 자리에 올 수 없다. 명사 (A) 와 (B)를 빈칸 앞의 명사 staff와 함께 쓰인 복합 명사로 본다 해도, 특별한 연결어 없이 빈칸 뒤에 있는 명사(demands)와 나란히 올 수 없으므로 답이 될 수 없다.

어휘 demand n. 요구, 수요 place v. 놓다, 두다 manager n. 관리자, 경영자
management n. 관리, 경영진 manageable adj. 관리할 수 있는

125 전치사 채우기 상 ●●●

해석 제작자 Joel Manning이 Harper Studios사에서 사임했다는 소식은 연예계 전체에 걸쳐 빠르게 퍼졌다.

해설 빈칸은 명사구(the entertainment industry)를 목적어로 취하는 전치사 자리이다. '소식은 연예계 전체에 걸쳐 빠르게 퍼졌다'라는 의미가 되어야 하므로 전치사 (A) across(~의 전체에 걸쳐, ~의 건너에)가 정답이다. (D) between(~ 사이에)도 해석상 그럴듯해 보이지만, 두 개의 대상 사이의 위치나 관계, 또는 시간을 나타내며, 주로 between A and B의 형태로 쓰이므로 답이 될 수 없다.

어휘 resign v. 사임하다, 퇴직하다 spread v. 퍼지다, 확산되다
above prep. ~ 위에 onto prep. ~ 위에

126 'be동사 + p.p.' 채우기 중 ●●○

해석 건물의 많은 건축 세부 사항들이 그것들의 원래 상태로 복원되었다.

해설 be동사(were) 다음에 올 수 있는 명사 (A), 진행형을 만드는 -ing형 (B), 수동태를 만드는 p.p.형 (C)가 정답의 후보이다. '건물의 많은 건축 세부 사항들이 그것들의 원래 상태로 복원되다'라는 수동의 의미가 되어야 하므로 p.p.형 (C) restored가 정답이다. 명사 (A)는 보어로서 주어와 동격 관계가 되어 '건물의 많은 건축 세부 사항들은 복원 전문가들이다'라는 어색한 문맥을 만든다. -ing형 (B)는 '건물의 많은 건축 세부 사항들이 복원하는 중이다'라는 어색한 문맥을 만든다. 동사 (D)는 be동사 다음에 올 수 없다.

어휘 structural adj. 건축의, 구조상의 detail n. 세부 사항
state n. 상태, 국가; v. 말하다 restorer n. 복원 전문가

127 형용사 어휘 고르기 상 ●●●

해석 Mr. Thorne은 그것의 잠재적 이점들에 관해 설득력 있는 주장을 함으로써 그의 전략을 채택하도록 위원회를 납득시켰다.

해설 빈칸은 명사(argument)를 꾸미는 형용사 자리이다. 'Mr. Thorne은 설득력 있는 주장을 함으로써 위원회를 납득시켰다'라는 문맥이므로 (B) compelling(설득력 있는)이 정답이다.

어휘 convince v. 납득시키다, 확신시키다 adopt v. 채택하다
argument n. 주장, 논쟁 potential adj. 잠재적인, 가능성이 있는
fortunate adj. 운 좋은 reputable adj. 평판이 좋은
talented adj. 재능이 있는

128 부사절 접속사 채우기 중 ●●○

해석 Greg Larson이 그의 미지불된 요금을 지불할 때까지, 그의 전화 서비스는 다시 연결될 수 없다.

해설 이 문장은 주어(his phone service)와 동사(cannot be reconnected)를 갖춘 완전한 절이므로, ___ ~ charges는 수식어 거품으로 보아야 한다. 이 수식어 거품은 동사구(pays for)가 있는 거품절이므로 거품절을 이끌 수 있는 부사절 접속사 (B)와 (D)가 정답의 후보이다. 'Greg Larson이 그의 미지불된 요금을 지불할 때까지, 그의 전화 서비스는 다시 연결될 수 없다'라는 의미가 되어야 하므로 시점을 나타내는 부사절 접속사 (B) Until(~할 때까지)이 정답이다. 부사절 접속사 (D)를 쓸 경우 'Greg Larson이 그의 미지불된

요금을 지불하기 때문에, 그의 전화 서비스는 다시 연결될 수 없다'라는 어색한 문맥이 된다. 전치사 (A)와 (C)는 거품절이 아닌 거품구를 이끈다.

어휘 unpaid adj. 미지불된 charge n. 요금; v. 청구하다, 부과하다
despite prep. ~에도 불구하고 from prep. ~에서부터

129 유사 의미 명사 어휘 고르기 상 ●●●

해석 공항 직원이 보안상 위험을 감지하면 몇몇 승객들은 그들의 수하물 속에 든 것들을 비우도록 요구될 수 있다.

해설 빈칸은 정관사(the)와 전치사(of) 사이에 올 수 있는 명사 자리이다. '몇몇 승객들은 그들의 수하물 속에 든 것들을 비우도록 요구될 수 있다'라는 문맥이므로 (C) contents(속에 든 것들, 내용물)가 정답이다.

어휘 empty v. 비우다; adj. 비어 있는 luggage n. 수하물, 여행 가방
detect v. 감지하다, 발견하다 asset n. 재산, 자산 subject n. 대상, 주제
matter n. 사안, 문제

130 부정대명사/형용사 채우기 상 ●●●

해석 Mr. Fisher는 제출 전에 보고서의 최종본을 또 한 번 볼 것이다.

해설 빈칸 뒤의 단수 가산 명사(look)를 꾸밀 수 있는 부정형용사 (D) another (또 한 번)가 정답이다. 수량 표현 (A)와 (C)는 복수 가산 명사나 불가산 명사 앞에 오며, 수량 표현 (B)는 불가산 명사 앞에 온다. 참고로, take a look at (~을 보다)을 관용구로 알아두며, 이때 look은 '보기, 쳐다봄'이라는 의미의 단수 가산 명사라는 것을 알아둔다.

어휘 final draft phr. 최종본 submission n. 제출

PART 6

131-134번은 다음 회람에 관한 문제입니다.

수신: 전 직원
발신: Olivia Cabral, 사무장
제목: 사진작가 방문
날짜: 8월 26일

사진작가가 8월 30일에 모든 [131]직원들의 사진을 찍기 위해 우리 사무실을 방문할 것입니다. 이날 찍힌 사진들은 우리의 온라인 직원 주소 성명록에 있는 오래된 사진들을 교체할 것입니다. 그것들은 또한 보도 자료들과 다양한 다른 목적들을 위해 사용될 것입니다. [132]따라서, 이때를 위해 여러분은 격식을 차린 정장을 입도록 요구됩니다. 당신은 오전 9시부터 오후 2시 사이에 [133]언제든 당신의 사진을 찍을 수 있습니다. [134]이것은 주 회의실에서 이루어질 것입니다. 이 과정은 10분보다 더 적게 걸릴 것입니다.

replace v. 교체하다 directory n. 주소 성명록, (이름 등이 나열된) 안내 책자
press release phr. 보도 자료, 공식 발표 formal adj. 격식을 차린, 공식적인
business clothes phr. 정장

131 명사 어휘 고르기 주변 문맥 파악 중 ●●○

해석 빈칸은 전치사(of)의 목적어 역할을 하는 명사 자리이다. '사진작가가 모든 ___의 사진을 찍기 위해 우리 사무실을 방문할 것이다'라는 문맥이므로 모든 보기가 정답의 후보이다. 뒤 문장에서 이날 찍힌 사진들은 우리의 온라인 직

해커스 토익 실전 1200제 READING

원 주소 성명록에 있는 오래된 사진들을 교체할 것이라고 했으므로 사진작가가 직원들의 사진을 찍을 것임을 알 수 있다. 따라서 (C) personnel(직원들)이 정답이다.

어휘 **equipment** n. 장비, 용품 **vehicle** n. 차량, 탈것 **facility** n. 시설, 설비

132 접속부사 채우기 주변 문맥 파악 중 ●●○

해설 앞 문장에서 그것들 즉, 이날 찍힌 사진들은 또한 보도 자료들과 다양한 다른 목적들을 위해 사용될 것이라고 했고, 빈칸이 있는 문장에서는 이때를 위해 여러분은 격식을 차린 정장을 입도록 요구된다고 했으므로 앞 문장과 이어지는 결과 등의 내용을 나타낼 때 사용되는 접속부사 (A) Therefore(따라서)가 정답이다.

어휘 **on the contrary** phr. 그와는 반대로 **regardless** adv. 그럼에도 불구하고 **however** adv. 그러나; conj. 어떤 방법으로라도

133 시간 부사 채우기 중 ●●○

해설 빈칸은 전치사구(between 9 A.M. and 2 P.M.)를 꾸미는 부사 자리이다. '오전 9시부터 오후 2시 사이에 언제든 당신의 사진을 찍을 수 있다'라는 의미가 되어야 하므로 시간을 나타내는 부사 (A) anytime(언제든)이 정답이다.

어휘 **less** adv. 더 적게 **previously** adv. 이전에 **near** adv. 가까이

134 알맞은 문장 고르기 중 ●●○

해석 (A) 당신은 당신의 일정에 맞는 날을 선택할 수 있습니다.
(B) 또 다른 예시는 우리의 직원 신분 확인 명찰입니다.
(C) 사진작가는 그때 가능하지 않을 것입니다.
(D) 이것은 주 회의실에서 이루어질 것입니다.

해설 뒤 문장 'The process will take less than 10 minutes.'에서 이 과정은 10분보다 더 적게 걸릴 것이라고 하며 사진을 찍는 데 소요되는 시간에 대해 언급했고, 앞 문장 'You may get your picture taken (anytime) between 9 A.M. and 2 P.M.'에서 오전 9시와 오후 2시 사이에 언제든 사진을 찍을 수 있다고 하며 사진을 찍는 시간에 대해 말했으므로 빈칸에는 이 과정이 이루어질 장소에 관한 내용이 들어가야 함을 알 수 있다. 따라서 (D)가 정답이다.

어휘 **suit** v. 맞다, 어울리다 **identification badge** phr. 신분 확인 명찰

135-138번은 다음 이메일에 관한 문제입니다.

수신: Dennis Craig <d.craig@quickmail.com>
발신: Caroline Peel <c.peel@lbistro.com>
날짜: 2월 21일
제목: 의견 카드
첨부: 상품권

Mr. Craig께,

저는 당신이 2월 19일에 135**작성한** 의견 카드에 응하여 이메일을 씁니다. 저희 점포를 방문하는 동안 당신이 이것을 해주신 것에 감사합니다. 저는 당신이 당신의 음식을 즐기셨다고 해서 기쁘지만, 당신이 서비스가 136**실망스럽다고** 느끼신 것에 대해 유감스럽게 생각합니다. 당신의 식사들은 당신이 137**그것들을** 주문한 지 20분 후에 당신에게 가져와졌어야 했습니다.

138**당신의 의견 덕분에, 저희의 직원 일정이 조정되었습니다.** 다음번에 당신이 금요일 밤에 Lochlane Bistro에서 식사할 때는, 지난번보다 두 명 더 많은 종업원들이 근무 중일 것입니다.

당신의 불편에 대해 보상하기 위해, 저는 당신의 다음 저녁 식사에 20유로로 할인을 위한 상품권을 첨부했습니다.

저희는 당신을 다시 만나기를 기대합니다.

Caroline Peel 드림
관리자, Lochlane Bistro

voucher n. 상품권, 할인권 **in response to** phr. ~에 응하여, 따라 **establishment** n. 점포, 설립 **on duty** phr. 근무 중인, 당번인 **inconvenience** n. 불편, 애로 **make up** phr. 보상하다, 만회하다

135 동사 어휘 고르기 전체 문맥 파악 하 ●○○

해설 빈칸은 목적격 관계대명사 which 또는 that이 생략된 절(you ~ on February 19)의 동사 자리이다. '당신이 2월 19일에 ___한 의견 카드에 응하여 이메일을 쓴다'라는 문맥이므로 모든 보기가 정답의 후보이다. 뒤 문장에서 점포를 방문하는 동안 이것을 해 준 것에 감사하다고 한 후, 뒷부분에서 당신, 즉 Mr. Craig의 음식과 서비스에 대해 남긴 의견에 대해 답변하고 있으므로 Mr. Craig가 2월 19일에 의견 카드를 작성했다는 것을 알 수 있다. 따라서 동사 complete(작성하다)의 과거형 (A) completed가 정답이다.

어휘 **misplace** v. 잘못 두다 **print** v. 인쇄하다 **announce** v. 발표하다, 알리다

136 형용사 어휘 고르기 하 ●○○

해설 빈칸은 5형식 동사 find(found)의 목적격 보어 역할을 하는 형용사 자리이다. '저는 당신이 당신의 음식을 즐겼다고 해서 기쁘지만, 당신이 서비스가 실망스럽다고 느낀 것에 대해 유감스럽게 생각한다'라는 문맥이므로 (B) disappointing(실망스러운)이 정답이다.

어휘 **rare** adj. 희귀한 **encouraging** adj. 격려의 **admirable** adj. 감탄스러운

137 명사와 수/인칭 일치하는 대명사 채우기 하 ●○○

해설 동사(ordered)의 목적어 자리에 올 수 있는 것은 명사이므로 모든 보기가 정답의 후보이다. '당신의 식사들은 당신이 ___을 주문한 지 20분 후에 가져와져야 했다'라는 의미가 되어야 하므로 빈칸에 들어갈 대명사가 가리키는 것은 Your meals(당신의 식사들)이다. 따라서 복수 사물명사(Your meals)를 가리키는 대명사 (B) them(그것들)이 정답이다. 한정사 (A)는 두 가지 대상 중 하나를 지칭하는 경우에 쓰인다. 인칭대명사 (C)는 단수 명사를 가리킨다. 복합관계대명사 (D)는 단독으로 쓰일 수 없고 뒤에 절이 와야 한다.

138 알맞은 문장 고르기 상 ●●●

해석 **(A) 당신의 의견 덕분에, 저희의 직원 일정이 조정되었습니다.**
(B) 이것은 왜 예약이 요구되는지에 대한 이유들 중 하나입니다.
(C) 당신의 기사가 언제 발행될 것인지 당신이 제게 알려줄 수 있길 바랍니다.
(D) 저희의 새로운 지점은 단지 몇 블록 떨어져 있을 것입니다.

해설 뒤 문장 'The next time you eat at Lochlane Bistro on a Friday night, there will be two more servers on duty than last time.'에서 다음번에 당신이 금요일 밤에 Lochlane Bistro에서 식사할 때는 지난번보다 두 명 더 많은 종업원들이 근무 중일 것이라고 했으므로, 빈칸에는 직원 근무 일정과 관련된 내용이 들어가야 함을 알 수 있다. 따라서 (A)가 정답이다.

어휘 **feedback** n. 의견, 피드백 **adjust** v. 조정하다, 적응하다

139-142번은 다음 기사에 관한 문제입니다.

Hamlin 국제 공항이 새로운 터미널을 기념하다

Hamlin 국제 공항이 몇 년 동안의 건설 ¹³⁹후에 이것의 두 번째 터미널을 공개했다. 새로운 터미널은 5월 2일에 개장할 것이다.

"추가 터미널은 많은 편의 시설들을 가지고 있습니다."라고 공항 대변인 Kurt Vogel이 말했다. ¹⁴⁰승객들은 분명히 이 고급 라운지를 좋아할 것이다. 그곳에는 많은 편한 소파들이 있으며 무료 음료들이 제공된다.

¹⁴¹한편, 한 터미널에 도착한 뒤 다른 터미널에서 출발하는 여행객들은 그것들 사이의 거리로 인해 불편을 겪을 수도 있다. 이 문제를 해결하기 위해, 셔틀버스가 터미널들 사이를 운행할 것이다.

새로운 터미널은 오로지 SeaCrescent 항공사와 Blue Fin사만을 위한 것이다. 모든 다른 항공사들은 계속해서 ¹⁴²기존 터미널에서 운영할 것이다.

celebrate v. 기념하다, 축하하다 unveil v. 공개하다, 발표하다
amenity n. 편의 시설 spokesperson n. 대변인 dozens of phr. 많은
solve v. 해결하다 exclusively adv. 오로지 ~만, 독점적으로

139 전치사 채우기 중 ●●○

해설 빈칸은 명사구(years of construction)를 목적어로 취하는 전치사 자리이다. 'Hamlin 국제 공항이 몇 년 동안의 건설 후에 이것의 두 번째 터미널을 공개했다'라는 의미가 되어야 하므로 시점을 나타내는 전치사 (C) after(~ 후에)가 정답이다. (B) since(~ 이래로)도 해석상 그럴듯해 보이지만, 특정 시점 이후 계속되는 일을 나타내어 'Hamlin 국제 공항이 몇 년 동안의 건설 이래로 계속해서 두 번째 터미널을 공개했다'라는 어색한 문맥을 만든다.

어휘 beside prep. 옆에 into prep. ~안으로

140 알맞은 문장 고르기 중 ●●○

해석 (A) 그 다음에 한 무리의 기자들은 보안 출입구를 안내받았다.
(B) 공무원들은 시설들에 대해 불평해왔다.
(C) 입장 요금은 기념일을 축하하기 위해 할인되었다.
(D) 승객들은 분명히 이 고급 라운지를 좋아할 것이다.

해설 앞 문장 'The additional terminal has many amenities'에서 추가 터미널은 많은 편의 시설들을 가지고 있다고 했고, 뒤 문장 'There are dozens of comfortable sofas and free drinks are provided.'에서 그곳에는 많은 편한 소파들이 있으며 무료 음료들이 제공된다고 했으므로 빈칸에는 편의 시설들 중 하나이면서 소파와 음료가 있는 고급 라운지에 관한 내용이 들어가야 함을 알 수 있다. 따라서 (D)가 정답이다.

어휘 flight attendant phr. 승무원 admission n. 입장
mark v. 축하하다, 기념하다 surely adv. 분명히 executive adj. 고급의

141 접속부사 채우기 전체 문맥 파악 중 ●●○

해설 앞부분에서 추가 터미널은 많은 편의 시설들을 가지고 있으며 승객들이 이 고급 라운지를 좋아할 것이라고 했고, 빈칸이 있는 문장에서는 한 터미널에 도착한 뒤 다른 터미널에서 출발하는 여행객들은 그것들 사이의 거리로 인해 불편을 겪을 수도 있다고 했으므로, 앞에서 말한 내용과 다른 내용으로 전환되는 문장을 언급할 때 사용되는 (C) On the other hand(한편)가 정답이다. (D) Instead(대신에)도 해석상 그럴듯해 보이지만, instead는 선택이나 행동의 결과로, 앞서 언급된 내용이 아니라 instead 뒤에 언급된 내용이 일어난다는 의미를 나타낸다.

어휘 once adv. 한동안, 한때, 언젠가 in addition phr. 게다가

142 형용사 어휘 고르기 주변 문맥 파악 상 ●●●

해설 빈칸은 명사(terminal)를 꾸미는 형용사 자리이다. '모든 다른 항공사들은 계속해서 ___ 터미널에서 운영할 것이다'라는 문맥이므로 모든 보기가 정답의 후보이다. 앞 문장에서 새로운 터미널은 오로지 SeaCrescent 항공사와 Blue Fin사만을 위한 것이라고 했으므로 다른 항공사들은 계속해서 기존 터미널에서 운영할 것임을 알 수 있다. 따라서 (A) original(기존의)이 정답이다.

어휘 private adj. 전용의, 사적인 temporary adj. 임시의, 일시적인
standard adj. 표준의, 모범적인

143-146번은 다음 편지에 관한 문제입니다.

DOBRY YOGURT사
5월 21일

Amin Patel
최고경영자, Renowned 가공식품회사
52번지 Sunder로
뭄바이시, 인도 400070

Mr. Patel께,

당신의 회사가 저희의 미래 공급업체들 중 하나가 될 후보로 선정되었습니다. 저희는 이제 ¹⁴³점검을 진행할 것입니다. 이 조사는 당신의 회사가 저희의 품질 기준을 충족한다는 것을 확실하게 하기 위함입니다. 이것은 저희의 발탁된 계약자인 HDI International사에 의해 실시될 것입니다. ¹⁴⁴정확한 세부사항은 곧 나올 것입니다. 현재로서, 저는 당신에게 이것이 당신의 생산 시설에 대한 평가를 수반할 것이라고만 말씀드릴 수 있습니다. 이 과정은 2개월이 걸릴 것입니다. 마지막에, HDI사가 구체적인 권장사항들을 포함한 보고서를 ¹⁴⁵발표할 것입니다. 저는 당신을 공급업체로 ¹⁴⁶승인하기 전에 당신이 모든 권장사항들을 준수했는지 확인해야만 합니다. 저는 제 다음 뭄바이 방문에서 당신과 이것에 대해 논의할 수 있습니다.

Stephanie Moravec 드림
남아시아 지사장
Dobry Yogurt사

supplier n. 공급업체, 공급자 proceed with phr. ~을 진행하다
review n. 조사, 검토 ensure v. 확실하게 하다, 보장하다
standard n. 기준, 표준 conduct v. 실시하다, 안내하다
preferred adj. 발탁된, 우선의 contractor n. 계약자, 도급업자
involve v. 수반하다, 포함하다 recommendation n. 권장사항
comply with phr. 준수하다, 순응하다 regional director phr. 지사장

143 명사 어휘 고르기 주변 문맥 파악 상 ●●●

해설 빈칸은 관사(the)와 함께 전치사(with)의 목적어 역할을 하는 명사 자리이다. '우리는 이제 ___을 진행할 것이다'라는 문맥이므로 모든 보기가 정답의 후보이다. 뒤 문장에서 이 조사는 당신의 회사가 우리의 품질 기준을 충족한다는 것을 확실하게 하기 위함이라고 했으므로 점검을 진행할 것임을 알 수 있다. 따라서 (D) inspection(점검, 검사)이 정답이다.

어휘 registration n. 등록, 신고 contract n. 계약 invoice n. 송장, 청구서

144 알맞은 문장 고르기 상 ●●●

해석 (A) 정확한 세부사항은 곧 나올 것입니다.

(B) 저희 계약서의 조건들은 명확합니다.
(C) 저는 당신으로부터 추가적인 지시를 기다리고 있습니다.
(D) 당신이 가지고 있는 문제를 설명해주십시오.

해설 앞부분에서 이 조사는 당신의 회사가 우리의 품질 기준을 충족한다는 것을 확실하게 하기 위함이라고 한 후, 뒤 문장 'For now, I can only tell you that it will involve an evaluation of your production facility.'에서 현재로서, 이것이 당신의 생산 시설에 대한 평가를 수반할 것이라고만 말할 수 있다고 했으므로, 빈칸에는 조사에 대한 정확한 세부사항이 곧 나올 것이라는 내용이 들어가야 함을 알 수 있다. 따라서 (A)가 정답이다.

어휘 **exact** adj. 정확한, 꼼꼼한 **forthcoming** adj. 곧 나오는, 다가오는
await v. 기다리고 있다, 기대하다 **instruction** n. 지시
describe v. 설명하다, 묘사하다

145 올바른 시제의 동사 채우기 주변 문맥 파악 중 ●●●○

해설 문장에 동사가 없으므로 동사인 모든 보기가 정답의 후보이다. '마지막에, HDI사가 보고서를 발표하다'라는 문맥인데, 앞 문장에서 미래 시제(will take)를 사용해서 이 과정, 즉 조사에 2개월이 걸릴 것이라고 했으므로 HDI사가 조사 마지막에 보고서를 발표하는 시점이 미래임을 알 수 있다. 따라서 특정한 미래 시점에 진행될 일을 표현하는 미래 시제 (B) will issue가 정답이다. 과거 시제 (A)와 (C)는 미래의 일을 나타낼 수 없다. would have p.p. 형태인 (D)는 과거 사실의 반대를 가정하는 가정법 과거 완료 구문에서 주로 쓰인다.

어휘 **issue** v. 발표하다, 발행하다

146 동명사 채우기 중 ●●●○

해설 전치사(before)의 목적어 자리에 올 수 있고 명사(you)를 목적어로 취할 수 있는 동명사 (C) approving(승인하는 것)이 정답이다. 동사 (A), 동사 또는 과거분사 (B), to 부정사 (D)는 전치사의 목적어 자리에 올 수 없다.

PART 7

147-148번은 다음 공고에 관한 문제입니다.

도로 개량 공사 최신 일정
5월 10일

원래 4월에 이루어질 것으로 예정되었던 Wilkinson가의 작업이 다음 주에 실행될 것입니다. [147]이것은 Sudbury 여름 미술 박람회 주최자들의 요청으로 연기되었습니다. 그들은 그 프로젝트가 지역 예술가들의 전시회를 보러 Grove 공원에 가는 사람들에게 어려움을 초래할 것이라고 우려했습니다.

다음 일정에 유의해 주시기 바랍니다:
· 5월 15일, 오전 9시 – 오후 12시 (움푹 팬 곳 채우기)
· [148]5월 16일, 오후 12시 – 오후 3시 (중앙선 페인트칠하기)
· 5월 17일, 오후 1시 – 오후 6시 (인도 고치기)
· 5월 18일, 오전 11시 – 오후 4시 (신호등 설치하기)

[148]페인팅 팀이 일하는 동안 Wilkinson가에 주차하는 것은 금지됩니다. 주민들은 이 기간 동안 그들의 차량을 Patterson가에 두도록 권고됩니다.

improvement n. 개량 공사, 개선 **postpone** v. 연기하다
request n. 요청, 신청; v. 요청하다 **exhibit** n. 전시회
pothole n. (도로에) 움푹 팬 곳 **centerline** n. 중앙선

traffic light phr. 신호등 **prohibit** v. 금지하다, 방해하다 **crew** n. 팀, 조
resident n. 주민, 거주자 **advise** v. 권고하다, 조언하다
vehicle n. 차량, 이동 수단 **municipal** adj. 지방 자치의, 시의

147 육하원칙 문제 중 ●●●○

해석 작업 일정은 왜 변경되었는가?
(A) 정부 시설에 대한 접근 권한을 보장하기 위해
(B) 시의 규정을 따르기 위해
(C) 행사 참석자들을 불편하게 하는 것을 막기 위해
(D) 근로자의 안전 문제를 해결하기 위해

해설 지문의 'It was postponed at the request of the Sudbury Summer Arts Fair organizers. They were concerned that the project would create difficulties for people going to Grove Park to see exhibits'에서 이것, 즉 Wilkinson가의 작업은 Sudbury 여름 미술 박람회 주최자들의 요청으로 연기되었으며 그들은 그 프로젝트가 전시회를 보러 Grove 공원에 가는 사람들에게 어려움을 초래할 것이라고 우려했다고 했으므로 (C)가 정답이다.

어휘 **ensure** v. 보장하다 **comply with** phr. ~을 따르다, 준수하다
regulation n. 규정, 규제, 제한 **inconvenience** v. 불편하게 하다; n. 불편
attendee n. 참석자 **address** v. 해결하다; n. 주소

148 육하원칙 문제 중 ●●●○

해석 주민들은 언제 Wilkinson가에 주차할 수 없을 것인가?
(A) 5월 15일, 오전 9시에
(B) 5월 16일, 오후 2시에
(C) 5월 17일, 오후 1시에
(D) 5월 18일, 오후 12시에

해설 지문의 'May 16, 12:00 P.M. – 3:00 P.M. (painting centerlines)'에서 5월 16일 오후 12시부터 오후 3시까지 중앙선을 페인트칠한다고 했고, 'Parking on Wilkinson Road will be prohibited while the painting crew is at work.'에서 페인팅 팀이 일하는 동안 Wilkinson가에 주차하는 것이 금지된다고 했으므로 (B)가 정답이다.

149-150번은 다음 이메일에 관한 문제입니다.

수신: Gerald Browning <g.browning@heremail.net>
발신: Clarissa Kim <c.kim@maximumbank.com>
[150]날짜: 9월 5일
제목: 당신의 신청

Mr. Browning께,

[149]이 이메일은 당신이 9월 2일에 했던 MaxJet 신용카드에 대한 온라인 신청이 승인되었다는 것을 확정하기 위해 당신에게 발송되었습니다. 카드는 당신의 우편 주소로 영업일 3일 내에 도착할 것입니다. 카드 수령과 동시에, 당신은 그것을 활성화하기 위해 555-3492로 저희의 고객 서비스 전화에 전화해야 합니다. 그러고 나서, 당신은 다양한 혜택에 대한 접근 권한을 얻기 위해 당신의 카드를 즉시 사용할 수 있으며, 다음을 포함합니다:

· 항공권, 기차표, 렌터카, 그리고 항공사 라운지 입장권을 포함하는 여행 관련 구매에 사용된 모든 금액에 대한 포인트 3점
· 일 년에 한 번, SureSky 항공사에 의해 운영되는 모든 항공편에 유효한 500달러 여행 상품권
· [150]매 10월, Maximum 은행의 온라인 쇼핑몰을 통해 판매되는 모든 제품들에 대한 놀라운 60퍼센트 할인

당신의 혜택에 대한 세부 사항을 원하거나 당신의 MaxJet 신용카드의 전자 버전을 만들고 싶다면, Maximum 은행의 스마트폰 애플리케이션을 오늘 다운로드하세요. Maximum 은행의 소중한 고객이 되어주셔서 감사드립니다.

Clarissa Kim 드림
고객 서비스 직원
Maximum 은행

---

confirm v. 확정하다, 확인하다 **receipt** n. 수령, 인수
activate v. 활성화하다, 작동시키다 **voucher** n. 상품권, 할인권
valid adj. 유효한, 정당한 **valued** adj. 소중한, 귀중한

149 추론 문제　　　　　　　　　　　　　　중 ●●○

해석　Mr. Browning은 9월 2일에 무엇을 했을 것 같은가?
(A) 안내소에서 Ms. Kim과 만났다
(B) 개인 보통 예금 계좌를 만들었다
(C) 신청서를 제출했다
(D) 신용카드 대금을 지불했다

해설　지문의 'This e-mail has been sent to you to confirm that the online request you made ~ on September 2 has been approved.'에서 이 이메일은 당신, 즉 Mr. Browning이 9월 2일에 했던 온라인 신청이 승인되었다는 것을 확정하기 위해 당신에게 발송되었다고 했으므로 Mr. Browning이 9월 2일에 신청서를 제출했다는 사실을 추론할 수 있다. 따라서 (C)가 정답이다.

어휘　**information desk** phr. 안내소 **set up** phr. 만들다, 준비하다
savings account phr. 보통 예금 계좌

150 육하원칙 문제　　　　　　　　　　　중 ●●○

해석　Mr. Browning은 다음 달에 무엇을 할 수 있는가?
(A) 기차표를 구매하기 위해 상품권을 사용한다
(B) Maximum 은행에 의해 후원되는 행사에 참석한다
(C) 몇몇 상품들에 대해 할인된 가격을 받는다
(D) 친구를 소개함으로써 추가 포인트를 얻는다

해설　지문의 'Date: September 5'에서 이메일이 9월 5일에 작성되었다고 했고, 'Every October, an amazing 60 percent off on all products sold through Maximum Bank's online shopping mall'에서 매 10월에 Maximum 은행의 온라인 쇼핑몰을 통해 판매되는 모든 제품들에 대한 놀라운 60퍼센트 할인 혜택을 받을 수 있다고 했으므로 (C)가 정답이다.

어휘　**refer** v. 소개하다, 보내다

패러프레이징

60 percent off on ~ products 제품들에 대한 60퍼센트 할인 → reduced price on ~ items 상품들에 대한 할인된 가격

151-153번은 양식에 관한 문제입니다.

¹⁵¹참가자들을 위한 강의 평가서

리더십 교육 센터(LTC)는 당신의 의견에 감사합니다. ¹⁵²⁻ᴰ당신의 마지막 수업을 완료한 후에 이 양식을 작성하여 이것을 당신의 강사에게 제출해주십시오.

이름: Sandra Mohan　　　　**회사:** Clorinda Consulting사
¹⁵²⁻ᴰ**강사 이름:** Raymond Shaw　　**프로그램 이름:** 리더십 준비하기

¹⁵¹**지시 사항:** 각 나열된 항목에 대한 **당신의 만족도를 평가해주십시오.**

	매우 나쁨	나쁨	평균	좋음	훌륭함
1. 전체적인 인상			✓		
2. 돈에 합당한 가치		✓			
3. 강사			✓		
4. 교육 시설				✓	
5. 교육 주제			✓		
6. 교육 자료		✓			

의견: 이 수업의 특정 측면은 도움이 되긴 했지만, 저는 솔직히 더 기대했습니다. 2주 강의를 시작할 때, 저희는 다뤄질 주제들의 개요를 제공 받았고, 저는 저희가 저희의 관리 방식을 찾는 방법을 배울 것이라는 것을 보게 되어 기뻤습니다. 하지만, 저는 ¹⁵²⁻ᴬ강의의 대부분이 직원들에게 동기를 부여하고 직장 갈등을 다루는 방법에 대한 것임을 알게 되었고, 이것들 중 어느 것도 개요에 언급되어 있지 않았습니다. 또한, ¹⁵³제가 작년에 들었던 직장에서의 비판적인 사고 세미나와 비교하면 훨씬 더 적은 수업 참여가 있었습니다. 저는 강사가 더 나은 활동들을 생각해낼 수 있었다고 생각합니다.

---

course n. 강의, 강좌 **evaluation** n. 평가, 사정
appreciate v. 감사하다, 이해하다 **submit** v. 제출하다
rate v. 평가하다 **satisfaction** n. 만족, 충족 **aspect** n. 측면, 관점
identify v. 찾다, 발견하다 **motivate** v. 동기를 부여하다, 자극하다
handle v. 다루다, 처리하다 **conflict** n. 갈등, 충동
syllabus n. (강연·강의 등의) 개요 **come up with** phr. 생각해내다, 제기하다

151 목적 찾기 문제　　　　　　　　　　하 ●○○

해석　양식의 목적은 무엇인가?
(A) 앞으로의 활동을 위한 아이디어를 수집하기 위해
(B) 고객의 선호에 대해 기록하기 위해
(C) 강의의 질을 평가하기 위해
(D) 학생의 성취를 평가하기 위해

해설　지문의 'Course Evaluation Form for Participants'에서 이 양식이 참가자들을 위한 강의 평가서라고 했고 'Instructions: Please rate your satisfaction'에서 지시사항으로 강의에 대한 당신, 즉 참가자의 만족도를 평가해달라고 했으므로 (C)가 정답이다.

어휘　**gather** v. 수집하다, 모으다 **take note** phr. 기록하다, 메모하다
preference n. 선호, 희망하는 것 **assess** v. 평가하다, 가늠하다

152 Not/True 문제　　　　　　　　　　중 ●●○

해석　Mr. Shaw에 대해 사실인 것은?
(A) 학생들에게 정확한 개요를 제공했다.
(B) 참가자들의 질문에 대답하지 못했다.
(C) 교실 내 갈등을 해결하는 데 도움을 주었다.
(D) 수업의 마지막에 양식을 모았다.

해설　지문의 'Please fill out this form and submit it to your instructor upon completing your final class.'와 'Instructor Name: Raymond Shaw'에서 당신의 마지막 수업을 완료한 후에 이 양식을 작성하여 이것을 당신의 강사인 Raymond Shaw에게 제출하라고 했으므로 (D)는 지문의 내용과 일치한다. 따라서 (D)가 정답이다. (A)는 'most of the course was about how to motivate employees and handle workplace conflicts, and neither of these topics was mentioned in the syllabus'에서 강의의 대부분이 직원들에게 동기를 부여하고 직장 갈등을 다루는 방법에 대한 것이었고, 이것들 중 어느 것도 개요에 언급되어 있지 않았다고 했으므로 지문의 내용과 일치하지 않는다. (B)와 (C)는 지문에 언급되지 않은 내용이다.

어휘　**resolve** v. 해결하다 **session** n. 수업

153 추론 문제   중 ●●○

해석 Ms. Mohan에 대해 암시되는 것은?
(A) 최근에 관리직으로 승진되었다.
(B) 그녀의 회사로부터 수업을 듣도록 요구되었다.
(C) 수업 중 활동들에 대해 몇 가지 아이디어를 주었다.
(D) 다른 직업 개발 과정을 들은 적이 있다.

해설 지문의 'Critical Thinking at Work seminar that I took last year'에서 Ms. Mohan이 작년에 자신이 들었던 직장에서의 비판적인 사고 세미나를 언급했으므로 Ms. Mohan이 다른 직업 개발 과정을 들은 적이 있다는 사실을 추론할 수 있다. 따라서 (D)가 정답이다.

어휘 promote v. 승진시키다, 홍보하다   professional adj. 직업의; n. 전문가

154-155번은 다음 메시지 대화문에 관한 문제입니다.

Agnes Beecroft [오후 5시 45분]
Bart, 저의 회계 보고서와 관련해 저를 도와줘서 고마워요. ¹⁵⁴당신은 목요일 밤 농구 게임을 보러 가는 것에 관심이 있나요? Hart Technologies사의 Ms. Farrow가 저에게 티켓 2장을 줬어요.

Bart Kreps [오후 5시 48분]
저는 참석할 수 없어요. 저는 제 아들의 고등학교에서의 학부모-교사 회의에 가야 해요.

Agnes Beecroft [오후 5시 49분]
괜찮아요. 당신이 생각하기에 제가 물어볼 수 있는 다른 사람은 누구인가요?

Bart Kreps [오후 5시 51분]
Tina Rodriguez는 어때요? ¹⁵⁵⁻ᶜ/ᴰ우리가 Hart Technologies사를 위해 진행했던 지난 광고 캠페인에서 저는 그녀와 같이 일했어요. 저는 항상 그녀가 잘해냈고 어떤 종류의 보상을 받을 자격이 있다고 생각했어요.

Agnes Beecroft [오후 5시 54분]
알겠어요, 고마워요! 그럼 제가 Tina에게 물어볼게요.

---

accounting n. 회계   make it phr. (모임 등에) 참석하다
deserve v. ~을 받을 자격이 있다   reward n. 보상

154 의도 파악 문제   중 ●●●

해석 오후 5시 48분에, Mr. Kreps가 "I can't make it"이라고 썼을 때 그가 의도한 것은?
(A) 업무를 돕기에는 너무 바쁘다.
(B) 행사에 참석할 수 없을 것이다.
(C) 목요일에 일찍 퇴근해야 한다.
(D) 회의에 참석할 계획이 없다.

해설 지문의 'Would you be interested in going to a basketball game on Thursday night?'에서 Ms. Beecroft가 목요일 밤 농구 게임을 보러 가는 것에 관심이 있는지 묻자, Mr. Kreps가 'I can't make it.'(저는 참석할 수 없어요)이라고 한 것을 통해, Mr. Kreps는 농구 게임에 참석할 수 없을 것이라는 것을 알 수 있다. 따라서 (B)가 정답이다.

어휘 task n. 업무, 과제

155 Not/True 문제   상 ●●●

해석 Ms. Rodriguez에 대해 언급된 것은?
(A) Hart Technologies사에 의해 고용되었다.
(B) 승진이 고려되고 있다.

(C) 프로젝트에서 Mr. Kreps와 함께 일했다.
(D) 회계팀에 속해 있다.

해설 지문의 'I worked with her on the last advertising campaign we did for Hart Technologies.'에서 저, 즉 Mr. Kreps가 Hart Technologies사를 위해 진행했던 지난 광고 캠페인에서 그녀, 즉 Ms. Rodriguez와 같이 일했다고 했으므로 (C)는 지문의 내용과 일치한다. 따라서 (C)가 정답이다. (A)와 (B)는 지문에 언급되지 않은 내용이다. (D)는 'I worked with her on the last advertising campaign ~.'에서 Mr. Kreps가 지난 광고 캠페인에서 Ms. Rodriguez와 같이 일했다고 했으므로 지문의 내용과 일치하지 않는다.

어휘 employ v. 고용하다, 사용하다   consider v. 고려하다
belong v. (~에) 속해 있다, (~의) 소유물이다

156-157번은 다음 광고에 관한 문제입니다.

Pixel Pro

¹⁵⁶두 대의 오프셋 인쇄기들, 한 대의 고속 복사기, 세 대의 디지털 컬러 인쇄기들이 갖춰진 저희는 당신의 요구를 빠르고 확실하게 만족시킬 수 있습니다. ¹⁵⁶당신이 브로슈어, 명함, 봉투, 혹은 파티 초대장이 필요하든, 당신의 이미지 또는 글을 가져오시기만 하면, 저희는 당신이 자랑스러워할 수 있는 높은 품질의 상품을 제작할 것입니다. 만약 당신이 준비가 된 자료를 가지고 있지 않으시다면, 당신에게 필요한 디자인을 생각해내기 위해 저희의 정규직 그래픽 디자이너들과 상의하세요. ¹⁵⁷그들의 작품 견본은 www.pixelpro.com에서 확인될 수 있습니다. 저희는 월요일부터 토요일 오전 8시 30분부터 오후 4시 30분까지 영업합니다. 오늘 저희를 방문하세요.

---

equip with phr. ~을 갖추다   offset press phr. 오프셋 인쇄기
fulfill v. 만족시키다, 실현하다   reliably adv. 확실하게, 믿을 수 있게
consult v. 상의하다, 참고하다   full-time adj. 정규직의
come up with phr. ~을 생각해내다, ~을 떠올리다

156 육하원칙 문제   중 ●●●

해석 어떤 종류의 사업체가 광고되고 있는가?
(A) 전자 기기 제조업체
(B) 문구류 상점
(C) 사진 스튜디오
(D) 인쇄소

해설 지문의 'Equipped with two offset presses, a high-speed copier, and three digital color printers'와 'Whether you need brochures, business cards, envelopes, or party invitations, ~ we will produce a high-quality product'에서 두 대의 오프셋 인쇄기들, 한 대의 고속 복사기, 세 대의 디지털 컬러 인쇄기들을 갖추고 있고, 브로슈어, 명함, 봉투, 혹은 파티 초대장이 필요하든, 저희, 즉 Pixel Pro사는 높은 품질의 상품을 제작할 것이라고 했으므로 Pixel Pro사가 인쇄소임을 알 수 있다. 따라서 (D)가 정답이다.

어휘 electronics n. 전자 기기, 전자 기술   stationery n. 문구류, 문구

157 육하원칙 문제   하 ●○○

해석 광고에 따르면, 고객들은 왜 웹사이트를 방문해야 하는가?
(A) 가격표를 다운로드하기 위해
(B) 주문하기 위해
(C) 견본을 보기 위해
(D) 약속을 잡기 위해

해설 지문의 'Examples of their work can be found at www.pixelpro.com.'에서 그들, 즉 정규직 그래픽 디자이너들의 작품 견본은 웹사이트인 www.pixelpro.com에서 확인될 수 있다고 했으므로 (C)가 정답이다.

어휘 place an order phr. 주문하다 make an appointment phr. 약속을 잡다

158-160번은 다음 안내문에 관한 문제입니다.

158/160로체스터시는 저희의 Corliss Gardens 모바일 애플리케이션을 소개합니다. 이제, 방문객들은 어떤 모바일 기기에서도 Corliss Gardens에 대한 정보로의 편리한 접근을 가질 수 있습니다. 공원의 시설들을 살펴보거나, 방문을 계획하거나, 또는 단지 Corliss Gardens에서의 행사 및 활동에 관한 소식을 얻기 위해 이것을 사용하세요.

상세하고 쌍방향의 공원 내 지도에 대한 접근권을 갖는 것 이외에도, 사용자들은 가장 가까운 이용 가능한 주차 공간으로 찾아가는 길을 얻고, 최신 기상 예보에 대한 알림을 받고, 심지어 개인적인 행사를 위해 공원의 네 개 행사 장소 중 어디든 예약도 할 수 있습니다. 159애플리케이션에서 가입하는 사용자들 또한 즉시 지역 사업체들로부터 특별 할인을 받을 자격이 있게 됩니다.

160Corliss Gardens에 대한 모든 정보를 알기 위해서는, 시 웹사이트 www.rochestercity.gov를 방문하세요.

access n. 접근, 접속 facility n. 시설, 기관 explore v. 살펴보다, 탐험하다
obtain v. 얻다, 획득하다 aside from phr. ~ 이외에도, ~을 제외하고
interactive adj. 쌍방향의, 상호적인 notification n. 알림, 공지
venue n. 장소, 개최지 function n. 행사, 기능 instantly adv. 즉시
eligible adj. ~할 자격이 있는, ~을 할 수 있는 offer n. 할인

158 목적 찾기 문제

중 ●●○

해석 안내문의 목적은 무엇인가?
(A) 공공 행사를 발표하기 위해
(B) 공원의 명소를 설명하기 위해
(C) 소프트웨어 프로그램을 홍보하기 위해
(D) 도시 주변 길 안내를 제공하기 위해

해설 지문의 'The City of Rochester is introducing our Corliss Gardens mobile application.'에서 로체스터시는 그들의 Corliss Gardens 모바일 애플리케이션을 소개한다고 한 후, 애플리케이션의 기능들을 설명하고 있으므로 (C)가 정답이다.

어휘 attraction n. 명소, 명물 promote v. 홍보하다

159 육하원칙 문제

하 ●○○

해석 사람들은 어떻게 특별 할인에 대한 자격을 얻을 수 있는가?
(A) 설문조사를 작성함으로써
(B) 지역 사업체를 방문함으로써
(C) 온라인으로 등록함으로써
(D) 기부를 함으로써

해설 지문의 'Users who sign up on the application ~ become ~ eligible to receive special offers'에서 애플리케이션에서 가입하는 사용자들은 특

별 할인을 받을 자격이 있게 된다고 했으므로 (C)가 정답이다.

어휘 qualify for phr. ~할 자격을 얻다 donation n. 기부

160 추론 문제

중 ●●○

해석 Corliss Gardens에 대해 암시되는 것은?
(A) 최근 몇 가지 보수를 진행했다.
(B) 무역 행사를 위한 장소로 선정되었다.
(C) 방문객들에게 입장료를 청구한다.
(D) 시 정부에 의해 관리된다.

해설 지문의 'The City of Rochester is introducing our Corliss Gardens mobile application.'에서 로체스터시는 그들의 Corliss Gardens 모바일 애플리케이션을 소개한다고 했고, 'To find out any information about Corliss Gardens, visit the city Web site'에서 Corliss Gardens에 대한 모든 정보를 알기 위해서는 시 웹사이트를 방문하라고 했으므로 Corliss Gardens가 로체스터시에 의해 관리된다는 사실을 추론할 수 있다. 따라서 (D)가 정답이다.

어휘 undergo v. 진행하다, 겪다 renovation n. 보수, 수리
admission fee phr. 입장료

161-164번은 다음 온라인 채팅 대화문에 관한 문제입니다.

Jerry Miller [오후 2시 10분]
161Basket Burger의 다가오는 여름철 판촉에 대해 질문이 있나요? 저는 방금 새로운 홍보 자료들을 여러분 각각의 체인점으로 발송했습니다.

Lois Denver [오후 2시 11분]
161계절 메뉴는 작년의 것과 같을 것이죠, 그렇죠? 만약 그렇다면, 저는 지금부터 제 직원들에게 모든 것을 어떻게 만드는지 보여주는 것을 시작할 수 있어요.

Jerry Miller [오후 2시 13분]
맞아요. 161우리는 모든 아이스크림 간식들, 버거들, 그리고 곁들임 요리들을 유지합니다. 하지만, 161/162얼린 커피 음료들은 중단합니다.

Kiel Bronson [오후 2시 14분]
정말요? 162최근에 그것들에 대해 물어보는 많은 손님들이 있었어요. 또한 저는 그것들을 위한 남은 시럽들도 있어요. 제 재고가 떨어질 때까지 음료를 팔아도 될까요?

Jerry Miller [오후 2시 15분]
알겠어요, 하지만 본사가 더 이상의 재고를 제공하지 않을 것이기 때문에 그것들을 광고하지는 마세요. 대신에, 우리의 토네이도 막대 아이스크림과 반값 밀크셰이크를 홍보하세요.

Lois Denver [오후 2시 18분]
토네이도 막대 아이스크림의 매출액은 올해에도 자선 단체에 전달될 것인가요?

Jerry Miller [오후 2시 20분]
맞아요. 저는 또한 추가적인 기부를 위한 기부함들을 당신에게 보냈어요. 다른 것이 더 있나요?

Kim Patton [오후 2시 21분]
네. ¹⁶³저는 저의 Beauville 지점 직원들이 이 판촉을 처리하지 못할 것 같아서 걱정스럽네요. 저희는 막 문을 열었고, 많은 사람들이 아직 교육 중이에요.

Jerry Miller [오후 2시 24분]
그렇군요. ¹⁶⁴제가 판촉 기간 동안 당신을 도와줄 두어 명의 경험 있는 직원들을 보낼 수 있어요. 개인 메시지로 이것에 대해 더 얘기해요.

- -

upcoming adj. 다가오는 promotion n. 판촉, 홍보
side dish phr. 곁들임 요리 discontinue v. 중단하다, 그만두다
diner n. 손님, 식사하는 사람 leftover adj. 남은 stock n. 재고
charity n. 자선 단체 contribution n. 기부, 기여
handle v. 처리하다, 다루다 duration n. 기간

161 의도 파악 문제   중 ●●○

해석   오후 2시 13분에, Mr. Miller가 "Correct"라고 썼을 때 그가 의도한 것은?
(A) 계절 제품들은 수익의 상당한 비율을 만들어낸다.
(B) 가맹점 직원은 가능한 빨리 교육을 시작해야 한다.
(C) 체인점의 여름 메뉴는 대체로 바뀌지 않을 것이다.
(D) 상점의 디저트들은 대중에게 인기가 있다.

해설   지문의 'Are there any questions about ~ summertime promotion?'에서 Mr. Miller가 여름철 판촉에 대해 질문이 있는지 묻자, 'The seasonal menu will be the same as last year's, right?'에서 Ms. Denver가 계절 메뉴는 작년의 것과 같을 것인지 물었고, Mr. Miller가 'Correct.'(맞아요)라고 한 후, 'We're keeping all the ice cream treats, burgers, and side dishes. However, we're discontinuing the frozen coffee beverages.'에서 모든 아이스크림 간식들, 버거들, 그리고 곁들임 요리들을 유지하지만, 얼린 커피 음료들은 중단한다고 한 것을 통해 체인점의 여름 메뉴는 대체로 바뀌지 않을 것임을 알 수 있다. 따라서 (C)가 정답이다.

어휘   generate v. 만들어내다, 발생시키다 significant adj. 상당한, 중요한
profit n. 수익, 이윤 largely adv. 대체로, 주로 establishment n. 상점, 기관

162 육하원칙 문제   중 ●●○

해석   Mr. Bronson은 왜 얼린 커피 음료들을 계속해서 팔고 싶어 하는가?
(A) 몇몇 홍보 자료들에 나온다.
(B) 직원들이 준비하는 데 적은 시간을 필요로 한다.
(C) 저렴한 재료들로 만들어진다.
(D) 이미 고객들에게 수요가 많다.

해설   지문의 'we're discontinuing the frozen coffee beverages'에서 Mr. Miller가 얼린 커피 음료들은 중단한다고 하자, 'There have been many diners asking about them recently.'에서 Mr. Bronson이 최근에 그것들, 즉 얼린 커피 음료들에 대해 물어보는 많은 손님들이 있었다고 했으므로 (D)가 정답이다.

어휘   appear v. 나오다, 나타나다 inexpensive adj. 저렴한, 비싸지 않은
in demand phr. 수요가 많은

163 추론 문제   상 ●●●

해석   누가 가장 최근에 생긴 가맹점을 운영할 것 같은가?
(A) Jerry Miller
(B) Lois Denver
(C) Kiel Bronson
(D) Kim Patton

해설   지문의 'I'm worried that my Beauville staff won't be able to handle this promotion. We just opened, and many are still training.'에서 Ms. Patton이 저희, 즉 Beauville 지점이 막 문을 열었고, 많은 사람들이 아직 교육 중이기 때문에 자신의 Beauville 지점 직원들이 이 판촉을 처리하지 못할 것 같아서 걱정스럽다고 했으므로 가장 최근에 생긴 가맹점을 Kim Patton이 운영한다는 사실을 추론할 수 있다. 따라서 (D)가 정답이다.

어휘   operate v. 운영하다

164 육하원칙 문제   중 ●●●

해석   Mr. Miller는 무엇을 하겠다고 제안하는가?
(A) 메뉴 항목을 홍보한다
(B) 임시 직원을 제공한다
(C) 새로운 관리자를 고용한다
(D) 설명시 한 부를 보낸다

해설   지문의 'I can send a couple of experienced employees to help you for the duration of the promotion.'에서 Mr. Miller가 판촉 기간 동안 당신, 즉 Ms. Patton을 도와줄 두어 명의 경험 있는 직원들을 보낼 수 있다고 했으므로, Mr. Miller가 임시 직원을 제공하겠다고 제안한 것을 알 수 있다. 따라서 (B)가 정답이다.

165-167번은 다음 기사에 관한 문제입니다.

범아프리카 영화제가 케이프타운으로 옮겨지다

8월 18일―범아프리카 영화제의 주최자들이 올해 행사를 요하네스버그에서 케이프타운으로 옮겼다. ― [1] ―. 현재 이것의 11년째인 이 축제는 매년 규모가 커져왔다. ¹⁶⁷하지만, 요하네스버그가 더 큰 도시임에도 불구하고, ^{165/167}주최자들은 케이프타운이 다른 이점들을 제공하기 때문에 이곳을 축제의 새로운 영구적인 장소로 선정했다. ― [2] ―. "¹⁶⁷해안을 따라 위치해 있다는 것은 ^{165/167}이곳이 특히 여름 동안 매년 많은 수의 방문객들을 끌어모은다는 것을 의미합니다."라고 주최자 Joma Nkosi가 말했다. ― [3] ―. ¹⁶⁶다가오는 축제를 위해 이미 항공편과 호텔 준비를 한 해외 방문객들은 그들의 예약을 변경하는 것에 도움을 받을 것이다. ― [4] ―. ¹⁶⁶그들은 www.paff.com을 통해 축제 주최자들에게 연락하도록 요청된다.

- -

organizer n. 주최자, 창설자 permanent adj. 영구적인, 불변의
benefit n. 이점, 혜택, 이득 coast n. 해안 attract v. 끌어모으다, 유치하다
particularly adv. 특히 overseas adj. 해외의 arrangement n. 준비
assist v. 돕다, 보조하다

165 추론 문제   중 ●●○

해석   축제 주최자들이 이전하도록 무엇이 유도했을 것 같은가?
(A) 옮기는 데 세금 혜택을 제공 받았다.
(B) 케이프타운의 날씨가 더 쾌적하다고 생각한다.
(C) 축제가 많은 여름 방문객들이 있는 지역에 있기를 원한다.
(D) 요하네스버그가 제공할 수 있는 것보다 더 큰 장소가 필요하다.

해설   지문의 'the organizers chose Cape Town as the festival's new permanent site because it offers other benefits'와 'it attracts a large number of visitors ~, particularly during the summer'에서 주최자들은 케이프타운이 다른 이점들을 제공하기 때문에 이곳을 축제의 새로운 영구적인 장소로 선정했고, 이곳, 즉 케이프타운은 특히 여름 동안 많은 수의 방문객들을 끌어모은다고 했으므로 축제 주최자들이 축제가 많은 여름 방문객들이 있는 지역에 있기를 원한 것이 이전하도록 유도했다는 사실을 추론할 수 있다. 따라서 (C)가 정답이다.

어휘   prompt v. 유도하다, 촉구하다 relocate v. 이전하다, 옮기다

agreeable adj. 쾌적한, 기분 좋은   venue n. 장소, 개최지

166 육하원칙 문제   중 ●●○

해석 몇몇 축제에 가는 사람들은 무엇을 하도록 요청받는가?
(A) 도움을 위해 웹사이트를 방문한다
(B) 호텔을 예약한다
(C) 행사 장소에 전화한다
(D) 2월의 항공편을 예약한다

해설 지문의 'Overseas visitors who have already made flight and hotel arrangements for the ~ festival will be assisted with changing their reservations.'와 'They are asked to contact the festival's organizers through www.paff.com.'에서 축제를 위해 이미 항공편과 호텔 준비를 한 해외 방문객들은 그들의 예약을 변경하는 것에 도움을 받을 것이고 그들은 www.paff.com을 통해 축제 주최자들에게 연락하도록 요청된다고 했으므로 (A)가 정답이다.

어휘 festivalgoer n. 축제에 가는 사람

167 문장 위치 찾기 문제   중 ●●○

해석 [1], [2], [3], [4]로 표시된 위치 중, 다음 문장이 들어갈 곳으로 가장 적절한 것은?
"주로, 이곳은 관광객들에게 더 유명하다."
(A) [1]
(B) [2]
(C) [3]
(D) [4]

해설 주어진 문장에서 주로, 이곳은 관광객들에게 더 유명하다고 했으므로, 이 문장이 관광객들과 관련된 내용이 나오는 부분에 들어가야 함을 알 수 있다. [2]의 앞 문장인 'However, despite Johannesburg being the bigger city, the organizers chose Cape Town as the festival's new permanent site because it offers other benefits.'에서 하지만, 요하네스버그가 더 큰 도시에도 불구하고 주최자들은 케이프타운이 다른 이점들을 제공하기 때문에 이곳을 축제의 새로운 영구적인 장소로 선정했다고 했고, 뒤 문장인 'Being located along the coast means it attracts a large number of visitors each year, particularly during the summer'에서 해안을 따라 위치해 있다는 것은 이곳이 특히 여름 동안 매년 많은 수의 방문객들을 끌어모은다는 것을 의미한다고 했으므로 [2]에 제시된 문장이 들어가면 케이프타운의 다른 이점들은 관광객들에게 더 유명하다는 것과 해안을 따라 위치해 여름 동안 매년 많은 수의 방문객들을 끌어모은다는 것이라는 자연스러운 문맥이 된다는 것을 알 수 있다. 따라서 (B)가 정답이다.

168-171번은 다음 회람에 관한 문제입니다.

BRONMAN HARDWARE사

수신: 상점 관리자들
발신: Steven Tisdale, 최고경영자
제목: 몇 가지 소식들
날짜: 9월 6일

여러분도 아시다시피, 저는 오하이오 콜럼버스에서의 제44회 연례 건축 산업 무역 박람회에 참석했습니다. ¹⁶⁸**저는 이 기회를 통해 제가 이 행사 동안 관찰했던 건축 자재들의 최신 동향에 관련하여 여러분들에게 말하고자 합니다.** — [1] —. 주택소유주들 사이에서 지역에서 얻어진 건축 물자에 대해 증가하는 수요가 있는 것으로 보입니다.

이 소식을 고려하여, 저는 마케팅 부서에 몇 가지 조사를 할 것을 요청했습니다. — [2] —. 그들은 바닥 타일, 벽 패널, 그리고 정원 용품 등과 같은 제품들을 포함하여, 우리 상점에서 잠재적으로 잘 팔릴 것 같은 지역 제품들의 목록을 작성하였습니다. ^{169/171}**다음 달, 우리는 각 상점 관리자에게 다른 종류의 제품들의 특별 판촉 활동을 할 것을 요청할 것입니다.** ¹⁷¹우리는 그다음에 각 지점의 매출액을 살펴볼 것입니다. — [3] —.

자연스럽게, 이 변화들은 우리의 구매와 운송 비용에 영향을 줄 것입니다. — [4] —. 하지만, 재무 부서가 이것의 계산을 했고 예상되는 수익이 이 변화를 가치 있게 만든다는 것을 알아냈습니다. ¹⁷⁰**확실히, 우리는 아마도 일부 절감을 볼 것입니다. 근처에 공급업체들을 가지는 것은 우리가 창고에 보관하는 많은 물품들을 줄이는 것이 가능하도록 합니다.**

마지막으로, 저는 여러분들이 이런 변화들을 환영하기를 바랍니다. 저는 그것들이 미래에 Bronman Hardware사가 경쟁력을 유지하는 것을 보장하도록 도울 것이라고 생각합니다.

trend n. 동향, 추세   observe v. 관찰하다, 준수하다
demand n. 수요, 요구; v. 요구하다   source v. 얻다; n. 근원
supply n. 물자, 용품; v. 공급하다   in light of phr. ~을 고려하여, ~에 비추어
draw up phr. 작성하다, 만들다   potentially adv. 잠재적으로, 어쩌면
sales figure phr. 매출액   calculation n. 계산, 셈
determine v. 알아내다, 결정하다   revenue n. 수익, 이윤
worthwhile adj. 가치 있는, 훌륭한   saving n. 절감, 절약
nearby adv. 근처에; adj. 인근의   warehouse n. 창고
competitive adj. 경쟁력 있는

┃최고난도 문제┃

168 목적 찾기 문제   상 ●●●

해석 Mr. Tisdale은 왜 회람을 썼는가?
(A) 어떻게 회사가 수행해오고 있는지 설명하기 위해
(B) 직원들에게 새로운 사실에 대해 알리기 위해
(C) 다가오는 행사에 대한 그의 참석을 확정하기 위해
(D) 관리자들에게 그들의 책임에 대해 상기시키기 위해

해설 지문의 'I'd like to ~ tell you about a recent trend in construction materials that I observed during this event.'에서 저, 즉 Mr. Tisdale이 행사, 즉 건축 산업 무역 박람회 동안 관찰했던 건축 자재들의 최신 동향에 관해 말하고자 한다고 한 후, 지역에서 얻는 건축 물자에 대해 증가하는 수요가 있는 것으로 보이며 이에 따라 상점에도 변화를 주려고 한다는 새로운 사실에 대해 설명하고 있으므로 (B)가 정답이다.

어휘 inform v. 알리다, 통보하다   development n. 새로운 사실, 현상, 발전
remind v. 상기시키다, 생각나게 하다   supervisor n. 관리자, 감독관

169 육하원칙 문제   중 ●●○

해석 상점 관리자들은 무엇을 할 것으로 예상되는가?
(A) 새로운 직원들을 고용한다
(B) 고객 설문조사를 실시한다
(C) 특정 제품들을 홍보한다
(D) 예산 견적을 준비한다

해설 지문의 'Next month, we will ask each store manager to hold a special promotion on a different selection of products.'에서 다음 달, 우리는 각 상점 관리자에게 다른 종류의 제품들의 특별 판촉 활동을 할 것을 요청할 것이라고 했으므로 (C)가 정답이다.

어휘 conduct v. 실시하다, 하다   promote v. 홍보하다   estimate n. 견적, 견적서

hold a ~ promotion 판촉 활동을 하다 → promote 홍보하다

170 추론 문제　　　　　　　　중 ●●○

해석　Bronman Hardware사에 대해 암시되는 것은?
(A) 그것의 자체 배송 트럭의 전체 차량을 유지한다.
(B) 경쟁사에 고객들을 빼앗겨왔다.
(C) 다가오는 해에 점포망을 확장할 것이다.
(D) 대량의 재고들을 저장하는 것에 많은 돈을 쓰고 있다.

해설　지문의 'Indeed, we will probably see some savings. Having suppliers nearby allows us to reduce a number of items we keep in our warehouses.'에서 확실히, 우리, 즉 Bronman Hardware사는 아마도 일부 절감을 볼 것이며, 근처에 공급업체들을 가지는 것은 우리가 창고에 보관하는 많은 물품들을 줄이는 것이 가능하도록 한다고 했으므로 대량의 재고를 저장하는 것에 많은 돈을 쓰고 있다는 사실을 추론할 수 있다. 따라서 (D)가 정답이다.

어휘　**maintain** v. 유지하다　**fleet** n. (한 기관이 소유한) 전체 차량
competitor n. 경쟁사, 경쟁 상대　**inventory** n. 재고, 물품

171 문장 위치 찾기 문제　　　　　중 ●●○

해석　[1], [2], [3], [4]로 표시된 위치 중, 다음 문장이 들어갈 곳으로 가장 적절한 것은?

"이것에 근거하여, 우리는 어느 지역적으로 생산된 제품들을 정기적으로 제공하기 시작할지 결정할 것입니다."

(A) [1]
(B) [2]
(C) [3]
(D) [4]

해설　주어진 문장에서 이것에 근거하여, 우리는 어느 지역적으로 생산된 제품들을 정기적으로 제공하기 시작할지 결정할 것이라고 했으므로, 이 문장이 정기적으로 제공할 제품들을 선정하는 근거와 관련된 내용이 나오는 부분에 들어가야 함을 알 수 있다. [3]의 앞부분인 'Next month, we will ask each store manager to hold a special promotion on a different selection of products.'에서 다음 달, 우리는 각 상점 관리자에게 다른 종류의 제품들의 특별 판촉 활동을 할 것을 요청할 것이라고 했으며, 앞 문장인 'We will then look at the sales figures from each branch.'에서 우리는 그 다음에 각 지점의 매출액들을 살펴볼 것이라고 했으므로, [3]에 제시된 문장이 들어가면 우리는 각 상점에 다른 종류의 제품들의 특별 판촉 활동을 요청하고, 그 다음에 각 지점의 매출액들을 살펴볼 것이며, 이것에 근거하여 어느 지역적으로 생산된 제품들을 제공할지 결정할 것이라는 자연스러운 문맥이 된다는 것을 알 수 있다. 따라서 (C)가 정답이다.

어휘　**based on** phr. ~에 근거하여　**regularly** adv. 정기적으로

172-175번은 다음 이메일에 관한 문제입니다.

수신: Jason Briar <jbriar@postnet.com>
발신: Jack Gray <grayjack@gilhoolytech.com>
제목: 지원
날짜: 4월 27일

Mr. Briar께,

¹⁷²/¹⁷⁴Gilhooly Tech사의 여름 학생 인턴십 프로그램에 지원해주셔서 🔘

감사드립니다. ¹⁷²저희는 며칠 전에 당신의 이력서와 지원서를 받았고, 저희는 곧 면접 일정을 잡을 것입니다. 만약 당신이 저희의 적격 요건을 충족한다면, ¹⁷⁵리치먼드에 있는 저희의 사무실에서의 ¹⁷³당신은 약속을 잡기 위해 어느 시점에 전화로 연락받을 것입니다.

이것이 ¹⁷⁴8주 동안 지속될 전일제, 무보수 일자리라는 점에 유의해 주시기 바랍니다. 하지만, 당신이 선정된다면 당신의 등록금 지불을 돕기 위해 Gilhooly Tech사는 당신의 학교인 Maryland 학교에 3,000달러를 제공할 것입니다. 이 금액은 당신의 인턴십의 성공적인 마무리에 보내질 것입니다. ¹⁷⁵Gilhooly Tech사는 또한 시외에서 온 인턴들에게 매주 100달러의 주택 수당을 제공할 준비가 되어 있습니다.

다시 한 번, 저희의 프로그램에 관심을 가져주셔서 감사드리며, 곧 연락드리겠습니다.

Jack Gray 드림
직원 채용 관리자, Gilhooly Tech사

eligibility n. 적격, 적격성　**résumé** n. 이력서　**position** n. 일자리, 위치
tuition n. 등록금, 수업료　**conclusion** n. 마무리, 결론
housing n. 주택, 주택 공급　**allowance** n. 수당, 비용
be in touch phr. 연락하다　**associate** n. 직원, 동료
recruitment n. 채용, 모집

172 육하원칙 문제　　　　　　중 ●●○

해석　Mr. Briar는 최근에 무엇을 했는가?
(A) 여름 일자리를 위해 서류를 제출했다
(B) 회사와 연구 프로그램을 완료했다
(C) 채용담당자와 전화로 통화했다
(D) 그의 성적에 대한 정보를 요청했다

해설　지문의 'Thank you for applying for Gilhooly Tech's summer student internship program. We received your résumé and application form a few days ago'에서 Gilhooly Tech사의 여름 학생 인턴십 프로그램에 지원해주셔서 감사하다고 하며, 며칠 전에 당신, 즉 Mr. Briar의 이력서와 지원서를 받았다고 했으므로 (A)가 정답이다.

어휘　**send in** phr. ~을 제출하다　**recruiter** n. 채용담당자, 모집자
grade n. 성적, 품질

recently 최근에 → a few days ago 며칠 전에

최고난도 문제

173 동의어 찾기 문제　　　　　상 ●●●

해석　1문단 세 번째 줄의 단어 "point"는 의미상 –와 가장 가깝다.
(A) 시점
(B) 장소
(C) 점수
(D) 방향

해설　point를 포함한 구절 'you will be contacted by phone at some point to set up an appointment'에서 당신은 약속을 잡기 위해 어느 시점에 전화로 연락받을 것이라고 했으므로 point는 '시점'이라는 뜻으로 사용되었다. 따라서 '시점'이라는 뜻을 가진 (A) time이 정답이다. point가 각각 '장소', '점수'라는 의미도 가지기 때문에 (B)와 (C)도 해석상 그럴듯해 보이지만, 이 문장에서는 '약속을 잡기 위해 어느 장소/점수에 전화로 연락받을 것이다'라는 어색한 문맥을 만든다.

174 추론 문제

중 ●●○

해석 Mr. Briar에 대해 암시되는 것은?
(A) 최근에 리치먼드로 이사했다.
(B) 인터넷으로 면접을 봐야 할 것이다.
(C) 한 달 넘게 일을 해야 할 수도 있다.
(D) 현재 장학생으로 대학을 다니고 있다.

해설 지문의 'Thank you for applying for Gilhooly Tech's summer student internship program.'과 'a ~ position that ~ will last for a period of eight weeks'에서 Gilhooly Tech사의 여름 학생 인턴십 프로그램에 지원해서 감사하다고 했고, 8주 동안 지속될 일자리라고 했으므로 Mr. Briar가 이 프로그램에 합격하면 한 달 넘게 일을 해야 할 수도 있다는 사실을 추론할 수 있다. 따라서 (C)가 정답이다.

어휘 relocate v. 이사하다, 이동하다 scholarship n. 장학생 (신분), 장학금

175 추론 문제

중 ●●○

해석 Gilhooly Tech사에 대해 추론될 수 있는 것은?
(A) 새로운 제품을 출시하려고 준비하고 있다.
(B) 정규 직원에게 기숙사를 제공한다.
(C) 성과에 따라 직원들에게 급료를 지불한다.
(D) 리치먼드 외부의 지원자들을 고려할 것이다.

해설 지문의 'our office in Richmond'에서 리치먼드에 있는 저희, 즉 Gilhooly Tech사의 사무실이라고 했고 'Gilhooly Tech is ~ prepared to offer a housing allowance ~ for interns who are from out of town.'에서 Gilhooly Tech사는 시외에서 온 인턴들에게 주택 수당을 제공할 준비가 되어 있다고 했으므로 Gilhooly Tech사는 리치먼드 외부의 지원자들을 고려할 것이라는 사실을 추론할 수 있다. 따라서 (D)가 정답이다.

어휘 launch v. 출시하다, 시작하다 dormitory n. 기숙사
compensate v. ~에게 급료를 지불하다 candidate n. 지원자, 후보자

176-180번은 다음 이메일과 송장에 관한 문제입니다.

수신: 모든 창고 직원 <warehousestaff@crystalfashions.com>
발신: Victor Mariscal <v.mariscal@crystalfashions.com>
제목: 우려 사항
날짜: 8월 4일

직원들께,

저는 여러분 모두와 공유할 우려 사항이 있습니다. [177-C]우리의 주요 고객들 중 하나인 전국적인 소매점 체인 [177-C/179-A]Kerrington 의류사가 최근에 예상보다 일주일 더 늦게 배송품을 받았습니다. [179-A]배송품(번호 5883A)은 7월 30일에 도착했지만, 고객은 급송 배송 옵션을 선택했으며, 이는 이것이 7월 25일에 도착했어야 한다는 것을 의미합니다. 분명히, [176]우리 배송 주기에 오류가 발생되었습니다.

[176/178]이 문제를 다루기 위해, 저는 본사의 Francesca Leach에게 8월 15일부터 시작하는 **여러 교육 수업들을 이끌어줄 것을 요청했습니다.** 창고에서 근무하는 모든 사람들은 반드시 3개의 한 시간 짜리 수업들에 모두 참석해야 합니다. 저는 하루가 끝나기 전에 여러분 각각의 작업 장소들에 교육 일정표 한 부를 놓아둘 것입니다.

Victor Mariscal 드림
창고 관리자
Crystal Fashions사

warehouse n. 창고 concern n. 우려, 걱정 nationwide adj. 전국적인 ○

retail n. 소매점 express adj. 급송의, 신속한 cycle n. 주기
address v. 다루다, 처리하다 workstation n. 작업 장소
session n. 수업, 시간

| Crystal Fashions사 | | | 송장 |

청구서 수신:
[179-A]Kerrington 의류사, 덴버 지점
100번지 Westside로
덴버시, 콜로라도주 80222
(고객 ID: 7737)

송장 번호: 1023526E
송장 날짜: 8월 3일
[179-A]배송품 번호: 5883A

물품	개수	개당 요금	총 요금
카디건 스웨터, 회색	50	8달러	400달러
와이셔츠, 하늘색	100	6달러	600달러
겨울 부츠, 갈색	25	10달러	250달러
		[179-A]할인 (늦은 배송)	[179-A](200달러)
		총 정산액	1,050달러

유의 사항:
[180-C]당신은 이제 당신의 총 정산액을 저희의 새롭게 출시된 모바일 애플리케이션인 CrystalPay를 사용하여 지불하실 수 있습니다. 그저 당신의 모바일 상점에서 애플리케이션을 다운로드하시고 시작하기 위해 당신의 고객 ID를 입력하십시오. 저희 애플리케이션에 대한 질문이 있으시면, 저희 고객 서비스 센터의 직원에게 555-9323으로 전화해주십시오.

amount due phr. 정산액, 지불해야 할 금액

최고난도 문제

176 목적 찾기 문제

상 ●●●

해석 Mr. Mariscal은 왜 이메일을 썼는가?
(A) 회사 정책을 따르는 것에 대해 직원들에게 상기시키기 위해
(B) 이전 메시지에 의한 오해를 바로잡기 위해
(C) 직원 평가의 결과를 보고하기 위해
(D) 취해질 몇몇 조치들에 대해 알리기 위해

해설 이메일의 'an error was made in our shipping cycle'에서 우리 배송 주기에 오류가 발생되었다고 했고, 'To address this issue, I've asked Francesca Leach ~ to lead several training sessions'에서 이 문제를 다루기 위해, 지, 즉 Mr. Mariscal은 Francesca Leach에게 여러 교육 수업들을 이끌어줄 것을 요청했다고 한 후, 앞으로 진행될 교육 수업들에 참석해야 한다는 것을 알리고 있으므로 (D)가 정답이다.

어휘 remind v. 상기시키다, 다시 알려주다 correct v. 바로잡다, 정정하다
misunderstanding n. 오해, 불화 evaluation n. 평가, 사정
measure n. 조치, 대책

177 Not/True 문제

중 ●●○

해석 Kerrington 의류사에 대해 언급된 것은?
(A) 작년에 전국적으로 여러 새로운 상점들을 열었다.
(B) 이전에 지연된 배송품을 받아본 적이 없다.
(C) Crystal Fashions사의 중요한 고객이다.
(D) Ms. Leach와 함께 일할 직원을 보낼 것이다.

해설 이메일의 'One of our top clients, ~ Kerrington Apparel'에서 우리의 주요 고객들 중 하나인 Kerrington 의류사라고 했으므로 (C)는 지문의 내용과 일치한다. 따라서 (C)가 정답이다. (A), (B), (D)는 지문에 언급되지 않은 내용이다.

어휘 delay v. 지연시키다, 연기하다

패러프레이징

One of our top clients 주요 고객들 중 하나 → an important customer 중요한 고객

178 동의어 찾기 문제   하 ●○○

해석 이메일에서, 2문단 첫 번째 줄의 단어 "issue"는 의미상 -와 가장 가깝다.
(A) 아이디어
(B) 문제
(C) 이유
(D) 문서

해설 이메일의 issue를 포함한 구절 'To address this issue, I've asked Francesca Leach ~ to lead several training sessions'에서 이 문제를 다루기 위해, 저는 Francesca Leach에게 여러 교육 수업들을 이끌어줄 것을 요청했다고 했으므로 issue는 '문제'라는 뜻으로 사용되었다. 따라서 '문제'라는 뜻을 가진 (B) problem이 정답이다.

179 Not/True 문제 연계   중 ●●●

해석 Kerrington 의류사의 덴버 지점에 대해 언급된 것은?
(A) 7월에 보내진 배송품에 대해 요금 할인을 받았다.
(B) 8월 초에 일부 보수 작업을 진행할 것이다.
(C) 더 중심가인 위치로 이전할 것이다.
(D) 의류 주문에 대해 비용을 지불하는 것을 잊어버렸다.

해설 송장의 'Kerrington Apparel, Denver branch', 'Shipment Number: 5883A', 'Discount (late delivery)', '($200)'에서 Kerrington 의류사의 덴버 지점이 5883A번 배송품의 늦은 배송으로 인해 200달러 할인을 받았다고 했다. 또한, 이메일의 'Kerrington Apparel, recently received a shipment over a week later than expected. The shipment(number 5883A) arrived on July 30, but ~ it should have arrived on July 25.'에서는 Kerrington 의류사가 최근에 예상했던 것보다 일주일 더 늦게 배송품을 받았고 배송품(번호 5883A)은 7월 30일에 도착했지만, 이것은 7월 25일에 도착했어야 한다는 사실을 확인할 수 있다.
두 단서를 종합할 때, Kerrington 의류사의 덴버 지점은 7월에 보내진 5883A번 배송품에 대해 요금 할인을 받았다는 것을 알 수 있다. 따라서 (A)가 정답이다. (B), (C), (D)는 지문에 언급되지 않은 내용이다.

어휘 undergo v. 진행하다, 받다   renovation n. 보수, 수리

패러프레이징

Discount 할인 → rate reduction 요금 할인

180 Not/True 문제   중 ●●○

해석 Crystal Fashions사의 고객들에 대해 사실인 것은?
(A) 배송을 한 달 기다리도록 요구된다.
(B) 온라인 주문 시 할인을 받을 수 있다.
(C) 모바일 기기를 사용해서 비용을 지불할 수 있다.
(D) 웹사이트를 통해 불만 사항을 제출해야 한다.

해설 송장의 'You can now pay your total amount due using our newly launched mobile application, CrystalPay.'에서 당신, 즉 Crystal

---

Fashions사의 고객들은 이제 총 정산액을 저희, 즉 Crystal Fashions사의 새롭게 출시된 모바일 애플리케이션인 CrystalPay를 사용하여 지불할 수 있다고 했으므로 (C)는 지문의 내용과 일치한다. 따라서 (C)가 정답이다. (A), (B), (D)는 지문에 언급되지 않은 내용이다.

어휘 submit v. 제출하다   complaint n. 불만 사항

패러프레이징

pay 지불하다 → make payments 비용을 지불하다

181-185번은 다음 이메일과 일정표에 관한 문제입니다.

수신: Ellen Georgiou <e.georgiou@australbc.edu>
발신: Marianne Andino <m.andino@australbc.edu>
제목: 일정표
날짜: 8월 21일

Ellen께,

저는 제 강의 일정표에 변경을 요청하고자 합니다. [182-A]저는 9월 5일 수요일에 아테네의 학술 토론회에서 연설하도록 초청되었습니다. [184]결과적으로, 저는 그날 제 수업들 중 어떤 것도 가르칠 수 없을 것입니다. 우리 대학에서 여러 마케팅 수업들을 가르치는 Mr. Bakir가 오전에 저를 대신해주기로 동의했지만, [185]그는 제가 화요일과 목요일에 가르치는 장소에서 수업을 하기를 선호합니다. 오후 수업에 관해서라면, 저는 제 이전 동료를 추천하고 싶습니다. 그의 이름은 Myron Katsaros이고, [182-C]제가 이곳에 고용되기 바로 전인 약 5년 전에 그와 저는 Pallas Digital사에서 함께 긴밀히 일했습니다. [181-A/D][183]그는 현재 자신의 광고 대행사를 운영하고 있고 업계에서 존경받습니다. [181-B]그는 또한 때때로 Kallithea 경영 대학에서 상급 마케팅 수업들을 가르쳐왔습니다. [183]저는 당신이 그에게 m.katsaros@agora.com으로 이메일을 통해 연락을 취할 것을 제안드립니다.
감사합니다.

Marianne Andino 드림
마케팅 교수
Austral 경영 대학

symposium n. 학술 토론회, 심포지엄   prefer v. 선호하다, 택하다
recommend v. 추천하다, 권하다   former adj. 이전의   colleague n. 동료
run v. 운영하다   respect v. 존경하다   reach out phr. 연락을 취하다

Austral 경영 대학, Penteli 캠퍼스
[184/185]**Marianne Andino의 강사 일정표**
2학기 (7월 15일부터 11월 30일)

수업 명	요일	시간	장소
[184]마케팅 입문	월/수/금	[184]오전 10시부터 11시 30분	동쪽 홀 302A호
상급 마케팅 관리	[185]화/목	오후 1시부터 2시 30분	[185]서쪽 홀 402B호
상급 광고와 홍보	월	오후 3시부터 4시 30분	동쪽 홀 612호
마케팅 윤리학	수	오후 3시부터 4시 30분	서쪽 홀 415호

semester n. 학기   promotion n. 홍보, 승진   ethics n. 윤리학, 도덕

최고난도 문제

181 Not/True 문제   상 ●●●

해석 Mr. Katsaros에 대해 언급되지 않은 것은?

(A) 다른 전문가들에 의해 존경받는다.

(B) 강사로서의 경험이 있다.

(C) 광고업에서 그의 직장 생활을 시작했다.

(D) 그 자신의 회사를 시작했다.

해설 질문의 Mr. Katsaros와 관련된 내용이 언급된 이메일에서 (C)는 언급되지 않은 내용이다. 따라서 (C)가 정답이다. (A)와 (D)는 'He now runs his own advertising agency and is respected in the industry.'에서 그는 현재 자신의 광고 대행사를 운영하고 있고 업계에서 존경받는다고 했으므로 지문의 내용과 일치한다. (B)는 'He has also taught advanced marketing classes'에서 그는 또한 상급 마케팅 수업들을 가르쳐왔다고 했으므로 지문의 내용과 일치한다.

어휘 admire v. 존경하다, 칭찬하다 professional n. 전문가
career n. 직장 생활, 경력

패러프레이징

runs his own advertising agency 자신의 광고 대행사를 운영하다 → started a company of his own 그 자신의 회사를 시작했다

respected in the industry 업계에서 존경받다 → admired by other professionals 다른 전문가들에 의해 존경받다

taught ~ classes 수업들을 가르쳤다 → has experience as an instructor 강사로서의 경험이 있다

182 Not/True 문제   상 ●●●

해석 Ms. Andino에 대해 언급된 것은?

(A) 학술 회의를 주최하고 있다.

(B) 그녀의 학과장으로부터 승인이 필요하다.

(C) 거의 5년 동안 가르쳐왔다.

(D) 두 개의 다른 기관들에서 근무한다.

해설 이메일의 'he and I worked closely together at Pallas Digital around five years ago, just before I was hired here'에서 그와 저, 즉 Mr. Katsaros와 Ms. Andino는 Ms. Andino가 이곳, 즉 Austral 경영 대학에 고용되기 전인 약 5년 전에 Pallas Digital사에서 가깝게 일했다고 했으므로 (C)는 지문의 내용과 일치한다. 따라서 (C)가 정답이다. (A)는 이메일의 'I have been invited to speak at a symposium'에서 학술 토론회에서 연설하도록 초청되었다고 했으므로 지문의 내용과 일치하지 않는다. (B)와 (D)는 지문에 언급되지 않은 내용이다.

어휘 host v. 주최하다 approval n. 승인, 인정

183 육하원칙 문제   중 ●●○

해석 Ms. Andino는 Ms. Georgiou가 무엇을 하기를 제안하는가?

(A) 업계 전문가에게 연락한다

(B) 광고 대행사에 전화한다

(C) 상급 수업 일정을 변경한다

(D) 학과장과 만난다

해설 이메일의 'He now runs his own advertising agency and is respected in the industry.'에서 그, 즉 Mr. Katsaros가 현재 자신의 광고 대행사를 운영하고 있고 업계에서 존경받는다고 했고 'I would suggest that you reach out to him through e-mail'에서 저, 즉 Ms. Andino는 당신, 즉 Ms. Georgiou가 그, 즉 광고 업계 전문가인 Mr. Katsaros에게 이메일을 통해 연락을 취하는 것을 제안한다고 했으므로 (A)가 정답이다.

어휘 expert n. 전문가 reschedule v. 일정을 변경하다
department head phr. 학과장

184 추론 문제 연계   중 ●●○

해석 Mr. Bakir에 대해 암시되는 것은?

(A) 대리 선생님으로 고용되었다.

(B) 아테네에서 학술 토론회에도 참석한다.

(C) 마케팅 개론 강의를 가르칠 수 있다.

(D) 9월에 학교의 교수진을 떠난다.

해설 이메일의 'Consequently, I will not be able to teach any of my classes that day. Mr. Bakir, who teaches several marketing courses at our college, agreed to take my place in the morning'에서 Ms. Andino가 그날 수업들 중 어떤 것도 가르칠 수 없을 것이며, 우리 대학에서 여러 마케팅 수업들을 가르치는 Mr. Bakir가 오전에 자신, 즉 Ms. Andino를 대신해주기로 동의했다고 했다. 또한, 일정표의 'Instructor schedule for Marianne Andino', 'Introduction to Marketing', '10:00 to 11:30 A.M.'에서는 Ms. Andino의 유일한 오전 수업이 마케팅 입문이라는 사실을 확인할 수 있다.

두 단서를 종합할 때, Mr. Bakir는 Ms. Andino를 대신해 마케팅 개론 강의를 가르칠 수 있다는 사실을 추론할 수 있다. 따라서 (C)가 정답이다.

어휘 substitute adj. 대리의 introductory course phr. 개론 강의, 입문 강좌
faculty n. 교수진, 교직원

패러프레이징

Introduction to Marketing 마케팅 입문 → an introductory course in marketing 마케팅 개론 강의

최고난도 문제

185 육하원칙 문제 연계   상 ●●●

해석 Mr. Bakir는 어디에서 수업을 하기를 선호하는가?

(A) 동쪽 홀 302A호에서

(B) 서쪽 홀 402B호에서

(C) 동쪽 홀 612호에서

(D) 서쪽 홀 415호에서

해설 이메일의 'he prefers to hold the class in the room where I teach on Tuesdays and Thursdays'에서 그, 즉 Mr. Bakir는 저, 즉 Ms. Andino가 화요일과 목요일에 가르치는 장소에서 수업을 하길 선호한다고 했다. 또한, 일정표의 'Instructor schedule for Marianne Andino', 'Tues/Thu', 'West Hall 402B'에서는 Ms. Andino가 화요일과 목요일에는 서쪽 홀 402B호에서 수업을 한다는 사실을 확인할 수 있다.

두 단서를 종합할 때, Mr. Bakir는 서쪽 홀 402B호에서 수업하기를 선호한다는 것을 알 수 있다. 따라서 (B)가 정답이다.

186-190번은 다음 공고, 편지, 신청서에 관한 문제입니다.

Soaring Skies 아카데미
승무원 교육 프로그램

186-DSoaring Skies 아카데미는 승무원이 되기를 원하는 사람들에게 종합적인 교육을 제공합니다. 186-A저희의 다음 프로그램은 6월 1일에 시작해서 7월 31일에 종료합니다. 186-C이것은 훌륭한 고객 서비스를 제공하는 방법에서부터 승객들의 안전을 위협하는 상황에서 무엇을 해야 하는지까지에 이르는 다양한 주제들을 다룰 것입니다.

예비 참가자들은 저희의 웹사이트 www.soaringskies.com/trainingapp에서 신청서를 작성해야 합니다. 작성된 양식은 188이전 상관 또는 선생님의 추천서 한 장과 함께 온라인으로 제출될 수 있습니다. 지원자들은 또한

이것을 출력해서 그들의 지원서를 55번지 Westwood가, 샌프란시스코, 캘리포니아주 94125에 있는 저희 본사로 우편 발송할 수 있습니다.

[187]교육 프로그램 종료와 동시에, 졸업자들은 대형 항공사의 승무원 직책을 얻기 위한 가장 효과적인 방법에 관해 저희 강사들로부터 일대일 상담을 받을 것입니다.

---

flight attendant phr. 승무원 comprehensive adj. 종합적인, 포괄적인
threaten v. 위협하다, 협박하다 prospective adj. 예비의, 장래의
recommendation n. 추천, 권고 supervisor n. 상관, 감독관
submit n. 제출하다, 항복하다 applicant n. 지원자, 후보자
completion n. 종료, 수료 one-on-one adj. 일대일의
counseling n. 상담, 조언 obtain v. 받다, 얻다

Soaring Skies 아카데미
55번지 Westwood가
샌프란시스코, 캘리포니아주 94125

4월 28일

관계자분께,

[188]저는 6월 1일부터 시작하는 귀사의 승무원 교육 프로그램의 잠재적인 교육생으로서 Linda Sykes에 대한 저의 추천서를 제공하고자 편지를 씁니다. [188/190]새크라멘토의 Harper 호텔에서 Ms. Sykes를 알게 된 저는 [190]그녀가 고객 서비스에 전념하는 근면한 직원이라는 것을 자신 있게 말할 수 있습니다.

또한, 저는 Ms. Sykes가 Redmond 온라인 직업 교육 아카데미에서 승무원 교육의 여러 수업들을 수료했다는 것을 알고 있습니다. 따라서, 그녀의 진정한 열정이 항공 업계에서 전문가가 되는 것에 있다는 것은 확실합니다.

이 추천서와 관련하여 어떤 질문이라도 있으시면, 저에게 555-2329로 연락해주십시오.

Simon Chung 드림

---

potential adj. 잠재적인, 가능성이 있는; n. 가능성 trainee n. 교육생
confidence n. 자신(감), 확신 diligent adj. 근면한, 성실한
dedicate v. 전념하다, 헌신하다, 중점으로 하다 aware adj. 알고 있는
vocational adj. 직업 교육의, 직업상의 passion n. 열정, 흥미
query n. 질문, 의문; v. 질문하다 reference n. 추천서, 참고

Soaring Skies 아카데미
승무원 교육 프로그램
온라인 신청서

성명: Linda Sykes
주소: 120번지 Norwell가, 새크라멘토, 캘리포니아주 94240
전화번호: 555-1287

[189]당신은 과거에 어떤 항공사 승무원 훈련을 받은 적이 있습니까?
☑ 네 ☐ 아니요

만약 이 추천서를 전자상으로 제출한다면 여기를 클릭하여 이 양식을 반드시 첨부하십시오.

신청비 지불

지불 금액: 50달러
지불 방법: 신용카드 번호 XXXX-XXXX-7382-1281

*프로그램에 합격된다면 수업료 지불은 6월 9일까지입니다. [190]만약 아래 나열된 저희 아카데미의 파트너 회사들 중 한 곳에서 과거 업무 경험이

있다면 10퍼센트 할인이 적용될 것입니다:
· Graytown Rental Vehicles사
· Pristine 여행 대행사
· [190]Harper 호텔

| 온라인 제출 | 인쇄 |

---

tuition n. 수업료, 등록금 printout n. 인쇄

---

186 Not/True 문제   중 ●●○

해석 이 프로그램에 대해 사실인 것은?
(A) 일 년에 걸쳐 이루어질 것이다.
(B) 전적으로 온라인 시스템을 사용해서 실시된다.
(C) 위급 상황 조치를 다룰 것이다.
(D) 현재 항공사 직원들을 위해 설계되었다.

해설 공고의 'It will cover ~ what to do in situations that threaten the safety of our passengers.'에서 이것, 즉 승무원 교육 프로그램은 승객들의 안전을 위협하는 상황에서 무엇을 해야 하는지 다룰 것이라고 했으므로 (C)는 지문의 내용과 일치한다. 따라서 (C)가 정답이다. (A)는 'Our next program starts on June 1 and ends on July 31.'에서 저희의 다음 프로그램은 6월 1일에 시작해서 7월 31일에 종료한다고 했으므로 지문의 내용과 일치하지 않는다. (B)는 지문에 언급되지 않은 내용이다. (D)는 'Soaring Skies Academy offers comprehensive training to individuals wishing to become flight attendants.'에서 Soaring Skies 아카데미는 승무원이 되기를 바라는 사람들에게 종합적인 교육을 제공한다고 했으므로 지문의 내용과 일치하지 않는다.

어휘 take place phr. 이루어지다 conduct v. 실시하다; n. 행동
deal with phr. ~을 다루다, 처리하다 design v. 설계하다, 디자인하다
current adj. 현재의

---

187 육하원칙 문제   중 ●●○

해석 프로그램이 끝날 때 무슨 일이 일어날 것인가?
(A) 교육생들은 사교 행사에 참여할 것이다.
(B) 강사에 의해 필기시험이 실시될 것이다.
(C) 직원들이 참가자들에게 조언을 해줄 것이다.
(D) 수업 졸업자들을 위해 기념식이 열릴 것이다.

해설 공고의 'Upon completion of the training program, graduates will receive one-on-one counseling from our instructors'에서 교육 프로그램 수료와 동시에, 졸업자들은 저희, 즉 Soaring Skies 아카데미의 강사들로부터 일대일 상담을 받을 것이라고 했으므로 (C)가 정답이다.

어휘 trainee n. 교육생, 훈련생 administer v. 실시하다, 관리하다
graduate n. 졸업자; v. 졸업하다

패러프레이징

at the end of the program 프로그램이 끝날 때 → Upon completion of the ~ program 프로그램의 종료와 동시에

---

188 육하원칙 문제 연계   중 ●●○

해석 Mr. Chung은 어떻게 Ms. Sykes를 아는가?
(A) 이전 직장에서 그녀의 상관이었다.
(B) 온라인 학교에서 그녀와 함께 수업을 들었다.
(C) 그녀가 일했던 호텔에서 손님이었다.

(D) 대학교에서 그녀의 선생님이었다.

해설 편지의 'I am writing to provide my recommendation for Linda Sykes'와 'Having come to know Ms. Sykes from the Harper Hotel in Sacramento'에서는 저, 즉 Mr. Chung이 Linda Sykes를 추천하고자 편지를 작성했고 새크라멘토의 Harper 호텔에서 Ms. Sykes를 알게 되었다고 했다. 또한, 공고의 'one letter of recommendation from a previous supervisor or teacher, can be submitted'에서는 이전 상관 또는 선생님의 추천서 한 장이 제출될 수 있다는 사실을 확인할 수 있다.
두 단서를 종합할 때, Mr. Chung은 이전 직장에서 Ms. Sykes의 상관이었다는 것을 알 수 있다. 따라서 (A)가 정답이다.

189 육하원칙 문제   중 ●●○

해석 신청서는 어떤 정보를 요구하는가?
(A) 이전의 교육 경험
(B) 파트너사 지점 위치
(C) 재정 문서
(D) 이메일 주소

해설 신청서의 'Have you received any airline attendant training in the past?'에서 과거에 어떤 항공사 승무원 훈련을 받은 적이 있는지 물었으므로 (A)가 정답이다.

어휘 prior adj. 이전의, 과거의

패러프레이징

received ~ training in the past 과거에 훈련을 받았다 → Prior education experience 이전의 교육 경험

190 육하원칙 문제 연계   중 ●●○

해석 Ms. Sykes는 무엇을 받을 자격이 있는가?
(A) 교육 시설의 가이드 투어
(B) 수업을 위한 무료 교과서
(C) 보상 프로그램의 회원권
(D) 수업료에 대한 할인된 금액

해설 신청서의 'A 10 percent discount will be applied if you have past work experience at one of our academy's partner companies listed below:'와 'Harper Hotels'에서 만약 아래 나열된 아카데미의 파트너 회사들 중 한 곳에서 과거 업무 경험이 있다면 10퍼센트 할인이 적용될 것이라고 했고 이 파트너 회사들에 Harper 호텔이 포함된다고 했다. 또한, 편지의 'Having come to know Ms. Sykes from the Harper Hotel in Sacramento'와 'she is a diligent employee'에서는 새크라멘토의 Harper 호텔에서 Ms. Sykes를 알게 되었으며 그녀가 근면한 직원이라고 했으므로 Ms. Sykes가 Harper 호텔에서 근무했다는 사실을 확인할 수 있다.
두 단서를 종합할 때, Ms. Sykes는 Harper 호텔에서 근무한 과거 경험으로 수업료의 10퍼센트 할인을 받을 자격이 있다는 것을 알 수 있다. 따라서 (D)가 정답이다.

어휘 eligible adj. ~할 자격이 있는, 적격의

191-195번은 다음 정책 페이지, 안내문, 문자 메시지에 관한 문제입니다.

Bonaventura Systems사
[191]주차 정책

11월 10일부터 시행되어, [191/192]A 주차장의 모든 50개 공간들은 회사의 카풀 프로그램 참가자들을 위해 지정될 것입니다. [192]필요할 경우, B 주차장 또한 확보될 것입니다. 카풀을 하지 않는 직원들은 지정된 공간들을 사용하

는 것이 허용되지 않습니다. 그들은 또한 사무실 복합 건물 정문 가까이의 주차 공간들은 고객의 독점적인 사용을 위한 것임을 명심해야 합니다.

effective adj. 시행되는, 효과적인   reserve v. 지정하다, 예약하다
carpool v. 카풀[승용차 함께 타기]을 하다   set aside phr. 확보하다
permit v. 허용하다, 허락하다   keep in mind phr. 명심하다
exclusive adj. 독점적인, 배타적인

[192]Bonaventura Systems사 카풀 프로그램

등록 절차(12월 12일 업데이트됨):
1. 우리의 회사 네트워크에 로그인하고, "직원 서비스"로 이동하여, "카풀 하기"를 클릭하세요.
2. [193-A]우리의 직원 파일 내 당신의 이름과 관련된 자택 주소가 올바른지 확인하세요. 이것은 언제든 수정될 수 있습니다.
3. 시스템은 당신의 자택 주소를 기반으로 모든 적합한 카풀 그룹들을 제시할 것입니다. [193-B]당신이 멤버가 되고 싶은 그룹을 선택하고 "참여"를 클릭하세요. 각 그룹은 최대 5명의 멤버들을 가질 수 있습니다.
4. "차량 등록"을 선택하고 [193-D]당신의 차량 등록 번호를 입력하세요. 차량을 소유하고 있는 직원들만 이 프로그램에 참여할 수 있다는 점에 유의하세요.

유의 사항:
- [194]운전자로서든 승객으로서든, 통근을 취소하는 직원들은 그 전날 오후 5시까지 프로그램 담당자 Lilia Parry에게 알리도록 요구됩니다.
- [192]운전자들은 A 주차장 또는 B 주차장에 있는 그들의 그룹에 할당된 공간만 사용한다는 것을 확실히 해야 합니다.

proceed v. 나아가다, 진행하다   confirm v. 확인하다, 확정하다
associate v. 관련시키다   personnel n. 직원   compatible adj. 적합한
license plate number phr. 차량 등록 번호
commute n. 통근; v. 통근하다   coordinator n. 담당자, 조정자
ensure v. 확실히 하다, 반드시 ~이게 하다   assigned adj. 할당된

발신: Lilia Parry (555-0393)
수신: Brendan Sanz (555-9383)

[194/195]Ms. Marcos는 오늘 저녁 5시 45분에 그녀가 기술적인 문제들을 겪고 있는 고객을 돕기 위해 Elena Hernandez와 바르셀로나로 출장을 가야 하기 때문에 내일 아침에 당신의 카풀 그룹을 태워다 줄 수 없을 것이라고 저에게 알려주었습니다. 그녀는 그녀가 Javier Rubio와 이야기했고 그가 하루 동안 운전 임무를 대신하기로 조정했다고 말했습니다. [194]그녀는 촉박한 통보에 대해 사과했습니다.

take over phr. 대신하다, 양도받다   duty n. 임무, 의무

191 목적 찾기 문제   중 ●●○

해석 정책 페이지의 목적은 무엇인가?
(A) 직원들이 대중교통을 이용하도록 장려하기 위해
(B) 예약 절차의 변화에 관해 직원들에게 알리기 위해
(C) 주차 시설의 올바른 이용을 설명하기 위해
(D) 다가오는 고객 방문을 위한 준비를 공지하기 위해

해설 정책 페이지의 'Parking Policy'와 'all 50 spaces in Parking Lot A will be reserved for participants in the company's carpool program'에서 정책 페이지가 주차 정책에 관한 것이며, A 주차장의 모든 50개 공간들이 회사의 카풀 프로그램 참가자들을 위해 지정될 것이라고 한 후, 주차장 공간

의 올바른 이용을 설명하고 있으므로 (C)가 정답이다.

어휘 **proper** adj. 올바른, 적절한 **preparation** n. 준비, 대비
upcoming adj. 다가오는

192 추론 문제 연계 상 ●●●

해석 카풀 프로그램에 대해 암시되는 것은?
(A) 오직 한 부서의 직원들만 포함한다.
(B) 한 직원에 의해 제안되었다.
(C) 12월 12일에 확정되었다.
(D) 50대보다 많은 차량을 수반한다.

해설 정책 페이지의 'all 50 spaces in Parking Lot A will be reserved for participants in the company's carpool program. If it becomes necessary, Parking Lot B will be set aside as well.'에서 A 주차장의 모든 50개 공간들이 회사의 카풀 프로그램 참가자들을 위해 지정될 것이고, 필요할 경우, B 주차장 또한 확보될 것이라고 했다. 또한, 안내문의 'Bonaventura Systems Carpool Program'과 'Drivers must ~ use their group's assigned space in Parking Lot A or Parking Lot B.'에서는 카풀 프로그램의 운전자들은 A 주차장 또는 B 주차장 내 그들의 그룹에 할당된 공간만 사용해야 한다고 했으므로, 카풀 참가자들이 A와 B 주차장을 모두 사용 중이라는 사실을 확인할 수 있다.
두 단서를 종합할 때, 카풀 프로그램은 주차장 A와 B를 모두 사용하므로 50대보다 많은 차량을 수반한다는 사실을 추론할 수 있다. 따라서 (D)가 정답이다.

어휘 **propose** v. 제안하다 **establish** v. 확정하다, 설립하다
involve v. 수반하다, 포함하다, 참가시키다

193 Not/True 문제 중 ●●●

해석 카풀 프로그램 등록 절차의 일부가 아닌 것은?
(A) 거주지의 위치를 확인하는 것
(B) 함께할 그룹을 선택하는 것
(C) 운전 면허증 복사본을 제출하는 것
(D) 차량에 대한 정보를 제공하는 것

해설 질문의 the carpool program registration process와 관련된 내용이 언급된 안내문에서 (C)는 언급되지 않은 내용이다. 따라서 (C)가 정답이다. (A)는 'Confirm that the home address associated with your name in our personnel files is correct.'에서 우리의 직원 파일 내 당신의 이름과 관련된 자택 주소가 올바른지 확인하라고 했으므로 지문의 내용과 일치한다. (B)는 'Select the one you wish to become a member of'에서 당신이 멤버가 되고 싶은 그룹을 선택하라고 했으므로 지문의 내용과 일치한다. (D)는 'enter your license plate number'에서 당신의 차량 등록 번호를 입력하라고 했으므로 지문의 내용과 일치한다.

어휘 **verify** v. 확인하다, 증명하다 **residence** n. 거주지, 주택

패러프레이징

Confirm that the home address ~ is correct 자택 주소가 올바른지 확인하다 → Verifying the location of a residence 거주지의 위치를 확인하는 것
Select the one you wish to become a member of 멤버가 되고 싶은 그룹을 선택하다 → Selecting group to join 함께할 그룹을 선택하는 것
enter ~ license plate number 차량 등록 번호를 입력하다 → Providing information about a vehicle 차량에 대한 정보를 제공하는 것

194 육하원칙 문제 연계 중 ●●●

해석 Ms. Marcos는 왜 사과했는가?
(A) 요구사항을 충족하지 않았다.
(B) 이전 의무에 대해 잊어버렸다.
(C) 기기를 프로그래밍하는 동안 실수를 했다.
(D) 발표에서 그녀의 부분을 끝내지 못했다.

해설 문자 메시지의 'Ms. Marcos notified me at 5:45 P.M. this evening that she will not be able to drive your carpooling group to work tomorrow morning ~.'과 'She apologizes for the short notice.'에서 Ms. Marcos가 내일 아침에 당신, 즉 Mr. Sanz의 카풀 그룹을 태워다 줄 수 없을 것이라고 저, 즉 Ms. Parry에게 오늘 저녁 5시 45분에 알려주었으며 촉박한 통보에 대해 사과했다고 했다. 또한, 안내문의 'Employees canceling a commute ~ are required to notify program coordinator Lilla Parry by 5 P.M. the previous day.'에서는 통근을 취소하는 직원들은 그 전날 오후 5시까지 프로그램 담당자 Lilia Parry에게 알리도록 요구된다는 사실을 확인할 수 있다.
두 단서를 종합할 때, Ms. Marcos는 전날 오후 5시보다 늦게 Ms. Parry에게 통근 취소 사실을 알렸기 때문에 요구사항을 충족하지 않았다는 것을 알 수 있다. 따라서 (A)가 정답이다.

어휘 **requirement** n. 요구사항 **obligation** n. 의무, 책무

195 육하원칙 문제 중 ●●●○

해석 Ms. Marcos는 누구와 함께 출장을 갈 것인가?
(A) Lilia Parry
(B) Brendan Sanz
(C) Elena Hernandez
(D) Javier Rubio

해설 문자 메시지의 'Ms. Marcos ~ has to travel to Barcelona with Elena Hernandez to assist a client having technical problems.'에서 Ms. Marcos는 기술적인 문제를 겪고 있는 고객을 돕기 위해 Elena Hernandez와 바르셀로나로 출장을 가야 한다고 했다. 따라서 (C)가 정답이다.

196-200번은 다음 기사와 두 이메일에 관한 문제입니다.

[197]5월 15일—[196]월요일 기자 회견 동안, 공공 공사 부서장인 Jacob Laurence는 시 정부가 대략 23킬로미터의 추가적인 자전거 도로의 건설을 위한 자금을 확보했다고 발표했다. [199-C]이 프로젝트는 시장 David Ellis의 선거 공약이었고, [197]4월 25일 그의 재선과 함께 이 프로젝트는 현실이 되었다. 도로는 도심 상업 지역의 주요 도로들인 Harborview로, Center대로, 그리고 Oak로를 따라 건설될 것이다. [198]하나는 또한 Bradford Heights 부근을 관통하는 Kensington가를 따라 건설될 것이다. 현재 계획에 따르면 이곳은 새로운 자전거 도로를 가지는 유일한 주거 지역이다. Mr. Laurence는 공사가 진행 중인 동안 이 도로들을 따라 주차하는 것은 금지된다고 명시했다. [199-D]프로젝트는 6월 8일에 시작할 것이고 6월 22일에 끝날 계획이다.

press conference phr. 기자 회견 **public works** phr. 공공 공사
municipal government phr. 시 정부 **secure** v. 확보하다
funding n. 자금, 재정 지원 **campaign promise** phr. 선거 공약
reelection n. 재선 **reality** n. 현실, 진실 **residential** adj. 주거의
prohibit v. 금지하다, 방해하다 **underway** adj. 진행 중인

발신: Greg Adams
198수신: 모든 거주자들
제목: 주차 제한
날짜: 6월 7일

거주자들께,

아시다시피, 모든 현장 주차 공간들은 거주자들을 위해 지정되어 있으며, 이는 방문객들은 도로에 주차해야만 한다는 것을 의미합니다. 하지만, 198**내일부터, 아파트 건물 바로 앞 도로에 주차하는 것이 2주 동안 금지될 것입니다. 이것은 도시가 새로운 자전거 도로를 건설할 것이기 때문입니다.** 만약 당신이 이 기간 동안 어떤 손님들을 받을 계획을 하고 있다면, 그들에게 이 상황에 대해 알려주십시오. 그들은 우리 건물 바로 뒤에 위치한 Plaza 주차장을 사용할 수 있습니다. 요금은 한 시간에 3달러 또는 하루에 25달러입니다. 감사합니다.

Greg Adams 드림
건물 관리자
Quadra 타워

---

restriction n. 제한, 규제, 구속 **on-site** adj. 현장의, 현지의
notify v. 알려주다, 공지하다

발신: Vince Carter <v.carter@greenville.gov.com>
수신: Debra Lawson <d.lawson@pal.com>
제목: 불만
날짜: 6월 20일

Ms. Lawson께,

저는 당신이 새로운 자전거 도로의 건설에 관해 불만을 표했던, 6월 18일에 제 부서로 보낸 이메일에 응하여 작성합니다. 당신은 200**그 작업이 고객들이 당신의 가게 근처 주차 장소를 찾기 어렵게 만들고 있고 이것이 당신의 매출액에 부정적인 영향을 미치고 있다**고 명시했습니다. 저는 이 상황에 대해 사과드리고자 하며 당신에게 저희가 이 프로젝트를 곧 마무리할 것이라고 장담합니다. 199-D**건설 작업은 6월 26일에 완료될 것입니다.** 다시 한 번, 이 불편에 대해 저의 진심 어린 사과를 받아주시기 바랍니다.

Vince Carter 드림
Greenville 공공 공사 부서

---

in response to phr. ~에 응하여, 대응하여 **frustration** n. 불만
specify v. 명시하다, 구체적으로 말하다 **impact** n. 영향, 충격
assure v. 장담하다, 안심시키다 **wrap up** phr. 마무리하다
sincere adj. 진심 어린, 진실된

---

196 육하원칙 문제 중 ●●○

해석 기사에 따르면, 월요일에 무슨 일이 있었는가?
(A) 마케팅 캠페인이 시작되었다.
(B) 기금 모금 행사가 발표되었다.
(C) 주차 시설이 문을 열었다.
(D) 언론 행사가 열렸다.

해설 기사의 'a press conference on Monday'에서 월요일 기자 회견이라고 했으므로 (D)가 정답이다.

어휘 **fund-raiser** n. 기금 모금 행사 **media** n. 언론, 대중 매체

패러프레이징

a press conference 기자 회견 → A media event 언론 행사

---

197 육하원칙 문제 중 ●●○

해석 Mr. Ellis는 최근에 무엇을 했는가?
(A) 세금 인상을 승인했다.
(B) 시 선거에서 이겼다.
(C) 새로운 대변인을 고용했다.
(D) 개회식에 참석했다.

해설 기사의 'May 15'에서 기사가 5월 15일에 쓰였다고 했고 'his reelection on April 25'에서 4월 25일에 그, 즉 Mr. Ellis의 재선이 있었다고 했으므로 (B)가 정답이다.

어휘 **spokesperson** n. 대변인

---

198 육하원칙 문제 연계 상 ●●●

해석 Quadra 타워는 어디에 위치해 있는가?
(A) Harborview로에
(B) Center대로에
(C) Oak로에
(D) Kensington가에

해설 이메일1의 'To All Residents'에서 수신인이 모든 거주자들이라고 했으므로 Quadra 타워가 주거지역임을 알 수 있고, 'from tomorrow, parking on the street directly in front of the apartment building will be prohibited for two weeks. This is because the city will be constructing a new bike path.'에서 시에서 새로운 자전거 도로를 건설할 것이기 때문에 내일부터 2주 동안 아파트 건물, 즉 Quadra 타워 바로 앞의 도로에 주차를 하는 것이 금지될 것이라고 했다. 또한, 기사의 'One will ~ be built along Kensington Avenue. This is the only residential area to get a new bike path under the current plan.'에서는 하나는 Kensington가를 따라 건설될 것이고, 현재 계획에 따르면 이곳, 즉 Kensington가가 새로운 자전거 도로를 가지는 유일한 주거 지역이라는 사실을 확인할 수 있다.
두 단서를 종합할 때, Quadra 타워는 주거 지역인 Kensington가에 있다는 것을 알 수 있다. 따라서 (D)가 정답이다.

---

199 Not/True 문제 연계 상 ●●●

해석 자전거 도로 프로젝트에 관해 언급된 것은?
(A) 자금이 충분히 조달되지 않았다.
(B) 시의회에서 논의될 것이다.
(C) 시장으로부터 승인되지 않았다.
(D) 계획했던 것보다 늦게 완료될 것이다.

해설 기사의 'The project ~ is scheduled to finish on June 22.'에서 프로젝트, 즉 자전거 도로 프로젝트가 6월 22일에 끝날 계획이라고 했다. 또한, 이메일2의 'The construction work will be completed by June 26.'에서는 건설 작업이 6월 26일에 완료될 것이라는 사실을 확인할 수 있다.
두 단서를 종합할 때, 자전거 도로 프로젝트는 계획했던 완공일인 6월 22일보다 늦은 6월 26일에 완료될 것이라는 것을 알 수 있다. 따라서 (D)가 정답이다. (A)와 (B)는 지문에 언급되지 않은 내용이다. (C)는 기사의 'This project was a campaign promise of Mayor David Ellis'에서 이 프로젝트는 시장 David Ellis의 선거 공약이었다고 했으므로 지문의 내용과 일치하지 않는다.

어휘 **sufficiently** adv. 충분히 **fund** v. 자금을 조달하다; n. 자금
debate v. 논의하다, 토론하다 **approve** v. 승인하다, 찬성하다

해석   Ms. Lawson은 무엇에 대해 불평했는가?

(A) 그녀의 주차 시설이 공사 중이다.

(B) 그녀의 상점은 고객들이 접근할 수 없다.

(C) 그녀의 사업체가 더 적은 이익을 만들어내고 있다.

(D) 그녀의 건물 입구가 장비로 막혀있다.

해설   이메일2의 'the work is making it difficult for customers to locate a parking spot near your store and that this is having a negative impact on your sales revenue'에서 그 작업이 고객들이 당신, 즉 Ms. Lawson의 가게 근처 주차 장소를 찾기 어렵게 만들고 있고 이것이 Ms. Lawson의 매출액에 부정적인 영향을 미치고 있다고 했으므로 (C)가 정답이다.

어휘   **inaccessible** adj. 접근할 수 없는   **generate** v. 만들어내다, 발생시키다   **profit** n. 이익   **block** v. 막다   **equipment** n. 장비, 용품

패러프레이징

a negative impact on ~ sales revenue 매출액에 대한 부정적인 영향   → generating less profit 더 적은 이익을 만들어내다

PART 5

101 (C)	102 (C)	103 (B)	104 (C)	105 (B)
106 (C)	107 (B)	108 (A)	109 (C)	110 (B)
111 (D)	112 (A)	113 (D)	114 (A)	115 (C)
116 (B)	117 (C)	118 (B)	119 (B)	120 (D)
121 (C)	122 (C)	123 (D)	124 (C)	125 (A)
126 (A)	127 (C)	128 (D)	129 (C)	130 (C)

PART 6

131 (C)	132 (D)	133 (A)	134 (D)	135 (A)
136 (B)	137 (D)	138 (D)	139 (C)	140 (C)
141 (A)	142 (C)	143 (C)	144 (A)	145 (C)
146 (D)				

PART 7

147 (D)	148 (A)	149 (B)	150 (B)	151 (D)
152 (B)	153 (B)	154 (B)	155 (C)	156 (D)
157 (C)	158 (C)	159 (D)	160 (C)	161 (A)
162 (C)	163 (C)	164 (B)	165 (D)	166 (D)
167 (B)	168 (D)	169 (A)	170 (B)	171 (B)
172 (B)	173 (C)	174 (B)	175 (A)	176 (B)
177 (C)	178 (D)	179 (B)	180 (D)	181 (D)
182 (D)	183 (C)	184 (B)	185 (B)	186 (B)
187 (B)	188 (B)	189 (B)	190 (C)	191 (A)
192 (B)	193 (C)	194 (B)	195 (A)	196 (C)
197 (A)	198 (A)	199 (D)	200 (C)	

PART 5

101 부사 자리 채우기 하 ●○○

해석 Mr. Chase는 워크숍을 이끌어 달라는 초청을 정중히 거절하고 대리인을 제안했다.

해설 동사(declined)를 꾸밀 수 있는 것은 부사이므로 부사 (C) kindly(정중히)가 정답이다. 명사 또는 형용사 (A), 형용사의 비교급 (B), 명사 (D)는 동사를 꾸밀 수 없다.

어휘 decline v. 거절하다 invitation n. 초청, 초대 suggest v. 제안하다
substitute n. 대리인 kind n. 종류; adj. 친절한 kindliness n. 친절, 온정

102 재귀대명사 채우기 하 ●○○

해석 Jackson시는 오락 시설에 돈을 더 들임으로써 그 자체를 활기찬 도시로 변화

시켰다.

해설 동사(has transformed)의 목적어 자리에 올 수 있는 목적격 인칭대명사 (A), 재귀대명사 (B)와 (C)가 정답의 후보이다. 'Jackson시가 그 자체를 활기찬 도시로 변화시켰다'라는 의미가 되어야 하므로 주어(Jackson City)와 목적어가 동일한 대상을 가리킬 때 목적어 자리에 올 수 있는 재귀대명사 중 단수 주어인 Jackson City와 함께 쓰일 수 있는 (C) itself가 정답이다. 재귀대명사 (B)는 주어가 복수일 때 쓰인다. 목적격 인칭대명사 (A)는 'Jackson시는 오락 시설에 돈을 더 들임으로써 그것(Jackson시가 아닌 다른 시)을 활기찬 도시로 변화시켰다'라는 어색한 문맥을 만든다. (A)를 주격 인칭대명사로 본다 해도, 주격 인칭대명사는 목적어 자리에 올 수 없으므로 답이 될 수 없다. 소유격 인칭대명사 (D)는 목적어 자리에 올 수 없다.

어휘 transform v. 변화시키다 vibrant adj. 활기찬
spend v. (돈을) 들이다, 소비하다 recreational adj. 오락의

103 올바른 시제의 동사 채우기 상 ●●●

해석 시청자들이 참신한 콘텐츠의 부족에 대해 불평하자마자, Spotlight Network 사는 그해 가을에 새로운 프로그램들을 도입했다.

해설 Once로 시작하는 종속절(Once ~ content)에 동사가 없으므로 동사 (A)와 (B)가 정답의 후보이다. 주절(the Spotlight Network ~ that fall)의 동사(introduced)가 과거 시제이고 '시청자들이 참신한 콘텐츠의 부족에 대해 불평하자마자, 새로운 프로그램들을 도입했다'라는 의미가 되어야 하므로 시청자들이 불평을 한 것도 이미 과거에 일어난 일이다. 따라서 이미 끝난 과거의 동작이나 상태를 나타내는 과거 시제 (B) complained(불평했다)가 정답이다. 현재 시제 (A)는 현재의 상태나 반복되는 동작, 일반적인 사실을 나타낸다. 동명사 또는 현재분사 (C)와 (D)는 동사 자리에 올 수 없다.

어휘 viewer n. 시청자 lack n. 부족 original adj. 참신한
content n. 콘텐츠, 내용 introduce v. 도입하다

104 사람명사 추상명사 구별하여 채우기 중 ●●○

해석 광고 캠페인의 효과는 모든 팀원들에 의해 이행되는 잘 조직화된 실행에 달려 있다.

해설 전치사(on)의 목적어 자리에 올 수 있으면서 형용사(well-coordinated)의 꾸밈을 받을 수 있는 것은 명사이므로 명사 (C)와 (D)가 정답의 후보이다. '모든 팀원들에 의해 이행되는 실행'이라는 의미가 되어야 하므로 추상명사 (C) performance(실행)가 정답이다. 사람명사 (D) performer(연기자)는 '모든 팀원들에 의해 이행되는 연기자'라는 어색한 문맥을 만든다. 동사 (A)와 동사 또는 과거분사 (B)는 명사 자리에 올 수 없다.

어휘 effectiveness n. 효과(성) depend on phr. ~에 달려있다, ~에 의존하다
carry out phr. ~을 이행하다

105 부사 어휘 고르기 중 ●●○

해석 나무로 섬세하게 만들어진 Mark Escher의 가구들은 그것들이 실용적인 것만큼이나 멋지다.

해설 빈칸은 과거분사(crafted)를 꾸미는 부사 자리이다. '나무로 섬세하게 만들어진 가구들은 멋지다'라는 문맥이므로 (B) Finely(섬세하게, 정교하게)가 정답이다. (A) Exactly(정확히)도 해석상 그럴듯해 보이지만, 주로 수를 나타내는 표현이나 전치사, 부사 앞에 와서 수량, 숫자, 위치 등이 정확한 것을 의미

하거나, 무언가와 정확히 부합해서 '바로 그대로'라는 뜻으로 사용된다.

어휘 **craft** v. (공예품을) 만들다 **out of** phr. ~으로, ~에 의해 **furniture** n. 가구
attractive adj. 멋진 **functional** adj. 실용적인 **relatively** adv. 비교적
possibly adv. 아마

106 동사 어휘 고르기 상 ●●●

해석 오클랜드의 시의회는 대중교통의 변화를 제안하는 주민들의 의견을 듣기 위해 회의를 개최하였다.

해설 빈칸은 명사(residents)를 뒤에서 꾸미면서 목적어(changes)를 갖는 현재분사 자리이다. '시의회가 대중교통의 변화를 제안하는 주민들의 의견을 듣다'라는 문맥이므로 (C) proposing(제안하는)이 정답이다. (D)의 persuade(설득하다)도 해석상 그럴듯해 보이지만, 동사 바로 뒤 목적어 자리에 설득을 당하는 대상인 사람명사가 와야 하므로 답이 될 수 없다.

어휘 **council** n. 의회 **meeting** n. 회의, 만남 **resident** n. 주민
include v. 포함하다 **conclude** v. ~이라고 결론을 내리다, 끝내다

107 형용사 자리 채우기 하 ●○○

해석 블라인드 시음회의 참가자들은 두 선도적인 브랜드들의 탄산음료 사이에서 주목할만한 차이를 발견하지 못했다.

해설 명사(difference)를 꾸밀 수 있는 것은 형용사이므로 형용사 (B) appreciable(주목할만한)이 정답이다. 동사 (A), 부사 (C), 명사 (D)는 형용사 자리에 올 수 없다.

어휘 **participant** n. 참가자 **taste test** phr. 시음회, 시식회
leading adj. 선도적인, 최고의 **appreciate** v. 인식하다, 인정하다
appreciably adv. 눈에 띄게 **appreciation** n. 감사, 감상

108 전치사 채우기 중 ●●○

해석 소수의 사람들에도 불구하고, 그 개업식은 Dew Coffee에게 큰 성공으로 여겨졌다.

해설 이 문장은 주어(the opening), 동사(was considered), 보어(a ~ success)를 갖춘 완전한 절이므로, ___ ~ crowd는 수식어 거품으로 보아야 한다. 이 수식어 거품은 동사가 없는 거품구이므로, 거품구를 이끌 수 있는 전치사 (A), (B), (D)가 정답의 후보이다. '소수의 사람들에도 불구하고, 그 개업식은 큰 성공으로 여겨졌다'라는 의미이므로 양보를 나타내는 전치사 (A) In spite of(~에도 불구하고)가 정답이다. 부사절 접속사 (C) Although(~에도 불구하고)는 거품구가 아닌 거품절을 이끈다.

어휘 **crowd** n. 사람들, 군중 **opening** n. 개업식, 개관식
consider v. 여기다, 간주하다 **as in** phr. ~과 같이
with respect to phr. ~에 관하여

109 사람명사 추상명사 구별하여 채우기 중 ●●○

해석 세미나가 열릴 예정인 강당은 최대 300명의 사람들의 수용 능력을 가진다.

해설 동사(has)의 목적어 자리에 올 수 있으면서 형용사(maximum)의 꾸밈을 받을 수 있는 것은 명사이므로 명사 (C)와 (D)가 정답의 후보이다. '강당은 최대 300명의 사람들의 수용 능력을 가진다'라는 의미이므로 추상명사 (C) occupancy(수용 능력, 점유)가 정답이다. 사람명사 (D) occupant (사용자)는 '강당은 300명의 사람들의 최대 사용자를 가진다'라는 어색한 의미를 만든다. 동사 또는 과거분사 (A)와 동사 (B)는 명사 자리에 올 수 없다. maximum을 명사로 보고, (A) occupied가 과거분사로 쓰여 maximum을 수식하는 구조로 본다 해도, '세미나가 열릴 강당은 300명의 사람들의 점유된 최대를 가진다'라는 어색한 문맥이 된다.

어휘 **auditorium** n. 강당 **hold** v. 열다, 개최하다
maximum adj. 최대의; n. 최대 **occupy** v. 차지하다, 사용하다

110 전치사 채우기 중 ●●○

해석 Mr. Rolland의 업무 능력은 시간 및 계속적인 교육과 함께 점차 나아질 것이다.

해설 빈칸은 명사구(time ~ training)를 목적어로 취하는 전치사 자리이다. '업무 능력은 시간 및 계속적인 교육과 함께 점차 나아질 것이다'라는 의미가 되어야 하므로 (B) with(~과 함께)가 정답이다. 전치사 (D) among(~ 사이에, ~ 중에)도 해석상 그럴듯해 보이지만, 셋 이상의 사람이나 사물 사이를 나타낼 때 쓰인다. 참고로, 전치사 (A) on은 명사 time과 함께 '정각에'라는 의미의 어구인 on time을 만들며, '업무 능력은 정각에 서서히 나아질 것이다'라는 어색한 문맥을 만든다.

어휘 **job performance** phr. 업무 능력 **gradually** adv. 점차, 서서히
improve v. 나아지다, 개선되다 **continual** adj. 계속적인, 자주 일어나는
training n. 교육, 훈련 **above** prep. ~보다 위에

111 명사 어휘 고르기 중 ●●○

해석 두 회사는 그들의 합병에 대한 수년간의 철두철미한 협상 후에 마침내 타협에 이르렀다.

해설 빈칸은 형용사(intensive)의 꾸밈을 받는 명사 자리이다. '합병에 대한 수년간의 철두철미한 협상 후에 마침내 타협에 이르렀다'라는 문맥이므로 (D) negotiations(협상)이 정답이다. (A) experiments(실험)도 합병과 관련하여 실험을 했다는 의미에서 그럴듯해 보이지만, experiment는 in, on, with와 같은 전치사와 함께 쓰인다.

어휘 **firm** n. 회사 **come to a compromise** phr. 타협에 이르다
intensive adj. 철두철미한, 집중적인 **merger** n. 합병
transaction n. 거래 **acquisition** n. 습득

112 현재분사와 과거분사 구별하여 채우기 상 ●●●

해석 나라의 계속된 경제 성장은 그것의 사회 기반 시설에 대한 투자에 의해 가능하게 되었다.

해설 빈칸 뒤의 명사구(economic growth)를 꾸밀 수 있는 것은 형용사이므로 과거분사 (A)와 현재분사 (B)가 정답의 후보이다. 꾸밈을 받는 명사구 (economic growth)와 분사가 '계속된 경제 성장'이라는 수동의 의미이므로 과거분사 (A) sustained(계속된)가 정답이다. 현재분사 (B)를 쓸 경우 '계속시키는 경제 성장'이라는 어색한 문맥이 된다. 동사 (C)와 명사 (D)는 형용사 자리에 올 수 없다. 참고로, 동사 sustain은 '~을 계속시키다, 지속시키다'라는 의미로 타동사로만 쓰임을 알아둔다.

어휘 **economic** adj. 경제의, 경제적인 **facilitate** v. 가능하게 하다
investment n. 투자 **infrastructure** n. 사회 기반 시설
sustainment n. 떠받침, 지탱

113 격에 맞는 인칭대명사 채우기 하 ●○○

해석 행사장은 우리의 전문적인 이벤트 기획자들에 의해 장식될 것이다.

해설 명사구(expert ~ planners) 앞에서 형용사처럼 명사를 꾸밀 수 있는 인칭대명사는 소유격이므로 소유격 인칭대명사 (D) our가 정답이다. 전치사 (by) 다음의 목적어 자리로 생각하여 목적격인 (A) us와 재귀대명사 (C) ourselves를 선택하지 않도록 주의한다. 참고로, by oneself(혼자, 혼자 힘으로)를 관용구로 알아둔다. 주격 인칭대명사 (B)는 형용사 자리에 올 수 없다. 참고로, 주격 인칭대명사는 주어 역할을 하므로 형용사가 아닌 명사 자리

에서 쓰임을 알아둔다.

어휘 decorate v. 장식하다, 꾸미다 expert adj. 전문적인; n. 전문가

114 형용사 자리 채우기 중 ●●○

해석 일정을 따르는 것은 그룹 프로젝트들에서 직원들을 생산적으로 유지시킬 수 있다.

해설 5형식 동사 keep의 목적격 보어 자리에 올 수 있는 것은 형용사이므로 형용사 (A)와 과거분사 (D)가 정답의 후보이다. '직원들을 생산적으로 유지시킬 수 있다'라는 의미가 되어야 하므로 형용사 (A) productive(생산적인)가 정답이다. 과거분사 (D) produced(생산된)를 쓸 경우 '직원들이 생산되도록 유지시킬 수 있다'라는 어색한 의미가 되므로 정답이 될 수 없다. 명사 (B)와 명사 또는 동사 (C)는 동사 keep의 목적격 보어 자리에 올 수 없다. 동사 keep을 3형식 동사로 보고, 명사 (B)를 employees와 함께 목적어로 본다고 해도, 명사(employees) 바로 뒤에 명사가 올 수 없으므로 employees' productivity와 같은 형태로 쓰여야 하고, keep의 경우 다음에 명사가 2개가 와서 'keep A+B'의 형태로 쓰이면 'A를 위해 B를 남겨놓다'라는 다른 의미를 나타낸다. 또한, employees 뒤에 productivity가 와서 복합 명사(employee productivity)를 만든다고 해도 복합 명사의 첫 번째 단어는 단수형이어야 하므로 -(e)s가 붙을 수 없다.

어휘 employee n. 직원 productivity n. 생산성
produce n. 농산물; v. 생산하다

115 부사 자리 채우기 중 ●●○

해석 전적으로 운동선수들을 위해 생산된 스마트 시계는 많은 기능들을 가지고 있다.

해설 과거분사(manufactured)를 꾸밀 수 있는 것은 부사이므로 부사 (C) Exclusively(전적으로, 오직 ~만)가 정답이다. 동명사, 현재분사, 전치사 (A), 형용사 (B), 명사 (D)는 과거분사를 꾸밀 수 없다. 참고로, (D)를 꾸밈을 받는 명사로 보고 manufactured를 명사를 뒤에서 꾸미는 과거분사로 본다 해도, 문장이 '운동선수들을 위해 전적으로 생산된 제외된 것'이라는 어색한 문맥이 된다.

어휘 manufacture v. 생산하다, 제조하다 function n. 기능
exclusively adv. 독점적으로 exclusion n. 제외, 배제

116 시간 표현과 일치하는 시제의 동사 채우기 중 ●●○

해석 Mr. Davis는 YHW Rails사가 특별 반값 할인을 발표하기 전에 그의 티켓에 대해 전액을 지불했다.

해설 주절(Mr. Davis ~ tickets)에서 나타내는 사건, 즉 Mr. Davis가 티켓에 대해 전액을 지불한 사건은 before가 이끄는 절(before ~ offer)에서 나타내는 사건, 즉 YHW Rails사가 특별 반값 할인을 발표한 시점보다 먼저 일어난 일이다. before가 이끄는 절에 과거 시제(announced)가 쓰였으므로 과거의 특정 시점 이전에 발생한 일을 표현할 수 있는 과거 완료 시제 (B) had paid가 정답이다. 현재 진행 시제 (A), 과거 시제 (C), 현재 완료 시제 (D)는 과거의 특정 시점 이전에 발생한 일을 나타낼 수 없다.

어휘 announce v. 발표하다, 알리다 half-price adj. 반값의
offer n. 할인, 제안

117 형용사 어휘 고르기 중 ●●○

해석 몇몇 도시들은 석탄과 가스와 같은 전통적인 것들에 의존하는 것 대신에 재생 가능한 에너지원들로 전환하고 있다.

해설 빈칸은 명사(ones)를 꾸미는 형용사 자리이다. '몇몇 도시들은 석탄과 가스

와 같은 전통적인 것들에 의존하는 것 대신에 재생 가능한 에너지원들로 전환하고 있다'라는 문맥이므로 (C) conventional(전통적인)이 정답이다.

어휘 switch v. 전환하다, 바꾸다 renewable adj. 재생 가능한
energy source phr. 에너지원 rather than phr. ~ 대신에, ~보다
rely on phr. ~에 의존하다 coal n. 석탄 endless adj. 무한한
latest adj. 최신의 instructional adj. 교육용의

118 부사 어휘 고르기 중 ●●○

해석 Arqua사는 잠재적인 공격을 예방하기 위해 사용자들에게 보안 업데이트를 신속히 설치하라고 조언했다.

해설 빈칸은 to 부정사(to install)를 꾸미는 부사 자리이다. '잠재적인 공격을 예방하기 위해 업데이트를 신속히 설치하라고 조언했다'라는 문맥이므로 (B) promptly(신속히)가 정답이다.

어휘 advise v. 조언하다, 충고하다 install v. 설치하다 security n. 보안
prevent v. 예방하다, 막다 potential adj. 잠재적인 justly adv. 정당하게
substantially adv. 상당히 abundantly adv. 풍부하게

119 부사절 접속사 채우기 중 ●●○

해석 직원 수칙의 사본은 사람들이 그것을 재검토하기를 원할 경우에 대비하여 온라인에 게시되었다.

해설 이 문장은 주어(A copy ~ manual)와 동사(has been posted)를 갖춘 완전한 절이므로, ___ ~ it은 수식어 거품으로 보아야 한다. 이 수식어 거품은 동사(want)가 있는 거품절이므로, 거품절을 이끌 수 있는 부사절 접속사 (B) in case(~에 대비하여)가 정답이다. 접속부사 (A)는 수식어 거품을 이끌 수 없다. 전치사 (C)와 (D)는 거품절이 아닌 거품구를 이끈다.

어휘 copy n. 사본 manual n. 수칙, 설명서 post v. 게시하다
review v. 재검토하다, 평가하다 if not phr. 그렇지 않다면
on behalf of phr. ~을 대표하여 aside from phr. ~ 이외에

120 형용사 어휘 고르기 중 ●●○

해석 노점 상인들은 일하는 동안 적절한 허가증을 소지해야 한다.

해설 빈칸은 명사(permits)를 꾸미는 형용사 자리이다. '노점 상인들은 일하는 동안 적절한 허가증을 소지해야 한다'라는 문맥이므로 (D) appropriate(적절한)가 정답이다.

어휘 street vendor phr. 노점 상인 permit n. 허가증; v. 허가하다
capable adj. 유능한, 능력 있는 convenient adj. 편리한
profitable adj. 수익성 있는

121 동명사와 명사 구별하여 채우기 중 ●●○

해석 그 자금은 연구자들이 다양한 병들의 원인들을 알아내는 그들의 목표를 달성하도록 도울 것이다.

해설 전치사(of)의 목적어 자리에 올 수 있는 것은 명사이므로 명사 (A)와 명사 역할을 하는 동명사 (C)가 정답의 후보이다. 빈칸 다음에 온 목적어(the causes)를 가질 수 있는 것은 동명사이므로 (C) determining(알아내는 것)이 정답이다. 명사 (A)는 목적어를 가질 수 없다. 동사 또는 과거분사 (B)와 동사 (D)는 전치사의 목적어 자리에 올 수 없다.

어휘 funding n. 자금 researcher n. 연구자 achieve v. 달성하다
cause n. 원인 various adj. 다양한 illness n. 병
determination n. 결정, 투지 determine v. 알아내다, 밝히다

122 전치사 표현 채우기　　　　　中 ●●○

해석　지연에 대한 보상으로, 항공사는 승객들에게 인근 호텔에서의 무료 숙박을 제공했다.

해설　이 문장은 주어(the airline), 동사(offered), 간접 목적어(passengers), 직접 목적어(a free ~ stay)를 갖춘 완전한 절이므로, ___ ~ delay는 수식어 거품으로 보아야 한다. 이 수식어 거품은 동사가 없는 거품구이므로, 거품구를 이끌 수 있는 전치사 (A)와 (C)가 정답의 후보이다. '지연에 대한 보상으로 무료 숙박을 제공했다'라는 의미가 되어야 하므로 (C) By way of(~로, ~의 형태로)가 정답이다. (A) Except for(~을 제외하고)는 '지연에 대한 보상을 제외하고 항공사는 무료 숙박을 제공했다'라는 어색한 문맥을 만든다. 접속사 (B)와 (D)는 거품구가 아닌 거품절을 이끈다.

어휘　compensation n. 보상　delay n. 지연　airline n. 항공사
offer v. 제공하다　passenger n. 승객　stay n. 숙박, 머무름
nearby adj. 인근의　provided that phr. 만일 ~이라면
as soon as phr. ~하자마자

123 부사절 접속사 채우기　　　　　中 ●●○

해석　사람들이 많은 질문들을 가지고 있지 않는 한 발표는 일정보다 일찍 끝날 것이다.

해설　이 문장은 주어(The presentation)와 동사(will finish)를 갖춘 완전한 절이므로, ___ ~ questions는 수식어 거품으로 보아야 한다. 이 수식어 거품은 동사(have)가 있는 거품절이므로, 거품절을 이끌 수 있는 부사절 접속사 (C)와 (D)가 정답의 후보이다. '많은 질문들을 가지고 있지 않는 한 일찍 끝날 것이다'라는 의미가 되어야 하므로 (D) unless(~하지 않는 한)가 정답이다. 전치사 (A)와 (B)는 거품절이 아닌 거품구를 이끌며, (A)가 부사일 경우 수식어 거품을 이끌 수 없다.

어휘　presentation n. 발표　ahead of phr. ~보다 일찍
besides prep. ~외에; adv. ~뿐만 아니라　despite prep. ~에도 불구하고
since conj. ~ 이후로, ~때문에; prep. ~ 이후로

124 부사 자리 채우기　　　　　下 ●○○

해석　Ms. Dreyfuss가 은퇴했음에도 불구하고 그녀는 관광 산업 행사들에서 여전히 두드러지게 활동 중이다.

해설　2형식 동사 remain의 보어 자리에 온 형용사(active)를 꾸밀 수 있는 것은 부사이므로 부사 (D) noticeably(두드러지게)가 정답이다. 명사 또는 동사 (A), 동사 또는 과거분사 (B), 형용사 (C)는 형용사를 꾸밀 수 없다.

어휘　remain v. 여전히 ~이다　active adj. 활동 중의, 활발한
tourism industry phr. 관광 산업　retire v. 은퇴하다
notice n. 알림; v. ~에게 알리다, 알아차리다
noticeable adj. 두드러지는, 뚜렷한

[최고난도 문제]

125 명사 어휘 고르기　　　　　上 ●●●

해석　만약 예금주가 미지불액을 30일 이상 동안 지불하지 않는다면 서비스의 중단이 일어날 수도 있다.

해설　빈칸은 동사(may occur)의 주어 역할을 하는 명사 자리이다. '예금주가 미지불액을 30일 이상 동안 지불하지 않는다면 서비스의 중단이 일어날 수도 있다'라는 문맥이므로 (A) Suspension(중단)이 정답이다.

어휘　occur v. 일어나다, 발생하다　account holder phr. 예금주
settle v. 지불하다, 해결하다　outstanding adj. 미지불된, 뛰어난
balance n. 잔액, 균형　exchange n. 교환　dismissal n. 해고, 해산

distraction n. 집중을 방해하는 것

126 명사절 접속사 채우기　　　　　上 ●●●

해석　스테이플러를 마지막으로 사용한 사람이 누구든 간에 그것을 우편실로 반납하도록 요구된다.

해설　동사(is requested)의 주어 자리에 온 절(___ ~ last)의 맨 앞에 올 수 있는 것은 명사절 접속사이므로 복합관계대명사 (A)와 (B)가 정답의 후보이다. '스테이플러를 마지막으로 사용한 사람이 누구든 간에 우편실로 반납하도록 요구된다'라는 의미가 되어야 하므로 (A) Whoever(누구든 간에)가 정답이다. 복합관계대명사 (B) Whatever(무엇이든 간에)는 사물을 지칭할 때 쓰이므로 답이 될 수 없다. 대명사 (C)와 (D)는 절을 이끌 수 없다. 참고로, (C)와 (D)가 used the stapler last의 꾸밈을 받는 것으로 착각할 수 있지만, 과거분사인 used 뒤에는 목적어가 올 수 없을 뿐만 아니라 대명사 everyone/anyone과 동사 use는 '스테이플러를 사용하는 사람'이라는 의미의 능동 관계이므로 현재분사 using이 쓰여야 함을 알아둔다.

어휘　stapler n. 스테이플러　last adv. 마지막으로　return v. 반납하다
mail room phr. 우편실　anyone n. 누구든, 아무도

127 동사 어휘 고르기　　　　　下 ●○○

해석　그녀의 경쟁자들과는 달리, Ms. Lewiston은 창의적인 마케팅을 통해 그녀의 사업을 키우고 있었다.

해설　빈칸은 be동사(was)와 함께 주어(Ms. Lewiston)의 동사 역할을 하는 -ing형의 자리이다. '그녀의 경쟁자들과 달리, 창의적인 마케팅을 통해 사업을 키우고 있다'라는 문맥이므로 동사 grow(키우다, 자라다)의 -ing형 (B) growing이 정답이다. 참고로, (D)의 associate(연관시키다, 결합시키다)는 associate A with B(A를 B와 연관/결합시키다)의 형태로 자주 쓰임을 알아둔다.

어휘　unlike prep. ~와 달리　competitor n. 경쟁자　through prep. ~을 통해
creative adj. 창의적인　publish v. 출판하다　measure v. 측정하다

128 상관접속사 채우기　　　　　上 ●●●

해석　연례 학교 행사에 대한 등록은 동창회에 등록된 사람들뿐만 아니라 현재 학생들에게도 할인이 된다.

해설　이 문장은 주어(Registration ~ event)와 동사(is discounted)를 갖춘 완전한 절이므로, ___ ~ association은 수식어 거품으로 보아야 한다. 이 수식어 거품은 동사가 없는 거품구이므로, 거품구를 이끌 수 있는 전치사 (A)와 상관접속사 (D)가 정답의 후보이다. '동창회에 등록된 사람들뿐만 아니라 현재 학생들에게도 할인이 된다'라는 의미이므로, 상관접속사 (D) as well as(~뿐만 아니라)가 정답이다. 참고로, 상관접속사 as well as는 전치사(for) 다음의 두 개의 구(current students, individuals ~ association)를 대등하게 연결하고 있음을 알아둔다. 전치사 (A)는 '동창회에 등록된 개인들에 근거하여 현재 학생들에게 접수가 할인이 된다'라는 어색한 문맥을 만든다. 접속사 (B)와 접속부사 (C)는 구와 구를 연결할 수 없다. 빈칸 뒤의 individuals를 주어, enrolled를 동사로 보고, 접속사 (B)를 절과 절을 이어주는 구조로 본다 해도, '사람들이 동창회에 등록했을 수 있도록, 행사에 대한 등록은 현재 학생들에게 할인이 된다'라는 어색한 문맥이 된다.

어휘　registration n. 등록　annual adj. 연례의, 연간의　current adj. 현재의
individual n. 사람, 개인　enroll v. 등록하다
alumni association phr. 동창회　based on phr. ~에 근거하여
so that phr. ~할 수 있도록　above all phr. 무엇보다도

최고난도 문제

129 부사 어휘 고르기 　　　　　상 ●●●

해석　고객들은 웹사이트의 오류들 때문에 온라인 양식에 정보를 되풀이하여 입력해야 했다.

해설　빈칸은 동사(had to type)를 꾸미는 부사 자리이다. '웹사이트의 오류들 때문에 정보를 되풀이하여 입력해야 했다'라는 문맥이므로 (D) repetitively (되풀이하여)가 정답이다. (B) instantly(순간적으로, 즉시)도 해석상 그럴듯해 보이지만, 매우 짧은 순간을 의미하여 정보를 입력하는 데 시간이 소요되므로 답이 될 수 없다. (C) collectively(집단으로, 공동으로)도 해석상 그럴듯해 보이지만, 단체가 동시에 함께하는 것을 의미하므로 답이 될 수 없다.

어휘　type v. 입력하다　sharply adv. 날카롭게, 급격히

130 부사 어휘 고르기 　　　　　중 ●●○

해석　신제품은 희귀한 재료들로 만들어져 있고, 따라서 꽤 비싸다.

해설　빈칸은 문장 전체를 꾸미는 부사 자리이다. '신제품은 희귀한 재료들로 만들어져 있고, 따라서 비싸다'라는 문맥이므로 부사 (C) therefore(따라서)가 정답이다. 참고로, quite는 비교급이 아닌 최상급을 강조하는 부사이고, 강조 부사는 비교급의 more와 형용사/부사 사이가 아니라 more 앞에서 쓰임을 알아둔다.

어휘　be made from phr. ~으로 만들어지다　rare adj. 희귀한
material n. 재료, 물질　quite adv. 꽤　yet adv. 아직; conj. 하지만
more adv. 더　nevertheless adv. 그럼에도 불구하고

PART 6

131-134번은 다음 광고에 관한 문제입니다.

Kelli사는 새롭게 ¹³¹**출시된** Hava-Go 헤어 드라이기를 소개하게 되어 자랑스럽습니다. 당사에서 가장 휴대가 쉬운 모델인 Hava-Go는 무선이며 무게가 단 500그램입니다. 이러한 ¹³²**특징들**은 그것을 매우 사용하기 쉽게 만들어 줍니다. ¹³³**이 기기는 또한 여행에도 이상적입니다.** 완전히 충전되면, 그것의 배터리는 100분까지 지속됩니다.

지금 Hava-Go를 ¹³⁴**구입하세요.** 그것들은 Ciao 쇼핑몰과 같은 전자제품 매장들이나 GoodsSupply.com을 포함한 온라인 상점들에서 판매됩니다.

introduce v. 소개하다　portable adj. 휴대가 쉬운　cordless adj. 무선인
weigh v. 무게가 ~이다　charge v. 충전하다　last v. 지속되다

131 현재분사와 과거분사 구별하여 채우기 　　중 ●●○

해설　빈칸 뒤의 명사(Hava-Go hair dryer)를 꾸미면서 빈칸 앞의 부사(newly)의 꾸밈을 받을 수 있는 것은 형용사이므로 형용사 (A), 현재분사 (B)와 과거분사 (C)가 정답의 후보이다. 수식을 받는 명사(Hava-Go hair dryer)와 형용사 또는 분사가 '출시된 Hava-Go 헤어 드라이기'라는 의미의 수동 관계이므로 과거분사 (C) released(출시된)가 정답이다. 형용사 (A)와 현재분사 (B)를 쓸 경우 각각 '포기할 수 있는/출시하는 Hava-Go 헤어 드라이기(헤어 드라이기가 출시하다)'라는 어색한 의미를 만든다. 동사 또는 명사 (D)는 형용사 자리에 올 수 없다.

어휘　releasable adj. 포기할 수 있는, 양도할 수 있는

132 명사 어휘 고르기 　주변 문맥 파악　　　중 ●●○

해설　빈칸은 지시형용사(These)의 꾸밈을 받으면서 동사(make)의 주어 역할을 하는 명사 자리이다. '이러한 ___은 그것을 매우 사용하기 쉽게 만들어 준다'라는 문맥이므로 모든 보기가 정답의 후보이다. 앞 문장에서 Hava-Go는 무선이며 무게가 단 500그램이라고 했으므로 Hava-Go의 이러한 특징들이 Hava-Go를 매우 사용하기 쉽게 만들어 준다는 것을 알 수 있다. 따라서 (D) features(특징들)가 정답이다.

어휘　container n. 용기　machine n. 기계　accessory n. 액세서리, 부품

133 알맞은 문장 고르기 　　　　　중 ●●●

해석　(A) 그 기기는 또한 여행에도 이상적입니다.
(B) 그 디자인은 이번 달 후반에 업데이트될 것입니다.
(C) 모델명은 아직 정해지지 않았습니다.
(D) 그것들은 대형 호텔 체인들에만 공급되고 있습니다.

해설　앞부분에서 Hava-Go가 휴대 및 사용이 쉬운 기기라고 한 후, 뒤 문장 'When fully charged, its battery lasts for up to 100 minutes.'에서 완전히 충전되면, 그것의 배터리는 100분까지 지속된다고 했으므로 빈칸에는 이 기기가 휴대가 쉬우며 장시간 사용할 수 있다는 장점과 관련된 내용이 들어가야 함을 알 수 있다. 따라서 (A)가 정답이다.

어휘　ideal adj. 이상적인　supply v. 공급하다

134 동사 어휘 고르기 　주변 문맥 파악　　　하 ●○○

해설　빈칸은 명령문의 동사 자리이다. '지금 Hava-Go를 ___하라'라는 문맥이므로 모든 보기가 정답의 후보이다. 뒤 문장에서 그것들은 전자제품 매장이나 온라인 상점에서 판매된다고 했으므로 지금 Hava-Go를 구입하라는 것임을 알 수 있다. 따라서 (D) Purchase(구입하다)가 정답이다.

어휘　lend v. 빌려주다　connect v. 연결하다　estimate v. 추정하다

135-138번은 다음 공고에 관한 문제입니다.

Cliffdale Ridge Manor 주민들에 대한 공고

이 공고는 여러분에게 이 아파트 단지의 새로운 ¹³⁵**주차** 허가증이 8월 26일에 발행될 것임을 알려드리기 위함입니다. 이 새로운 허가증은 ¹³⁶**쉽게** 스캔될 수 있는 바코드를 포함할 것입니다. 하나를 받기 위해서는, Cliffdale Ridge Manor의 관리 사무실에서 여러분의 이전 출입증을 반납하십시오. 여러분의 새로운 허가증을 ¹³⁷**받자마자**, 여러분 차량의 앞쪽 전면유리창 내부에 그것을 부착하십시오. ¹³⁸**바깥쪽에서 그것이 명확히 보이는지 반드시 확인하십시오.**

permit n. 허가증; v. 허용하다　complex n. (복합) 단지
issue v. 발행하다, 발표하다; n. 발행물, 쟁점
turn in phr. ~을 반납하다, 제출하다　interior n. 내부; adj. 내부의
vehicle n. 차량　windshield n. 전면유리창

135 명사 관련 어구 채우기 　전체 문맥 파악　　　중 ●●○

해설　빈칸은 동사(will be issued)의 주어이면서 형용사(new)의 꾸밈을 받는 명사 자리로, 빈칸 뒤의 명사(permits)와 함께 복합 명사를 이룬다. '아파트 단지의 새로운 ___ 허가증이 발행될 것이다'라는 문맥이므로 모든 보기가 정답의 후보이다. 뒷부분에서 차량의 앞쪽 전면유리창 내부에 새로운 허가증을 부착하라고 했으므로 아파트 단지의 새로운 주차 허가증이 발행될 것임을 알 수 있다. 따라서 (A) parking(주차)이 정답이다. (C) residence(거주)도 해석상 그럴듯해 보이지만 빈칸 뒤의 명사(permits)와 함께 쓰일 경우 특정한 국가에서 체류할 수 있는 허가증을 의미하므로 답이 될 수 없다.

어휘 renovation n. 개조 storage n. 보관

136 부사 자리 채우기   하 ●○○

해설 동사(can be scanned)를 꾸밀 수 있는 것은 부사이므로 부사 (B) easily (쉽게)가 정답이다. 형용사 (A), 명사 또는 동사 (C), 형용사의 최상급 (D)는 부사 자리에 올 수 없다.

어휘 easy adj. 쉬운 ease n. 쉬움; v. 수월하게 하다, 편하게 해주다

137 부사절 접속사 채우기   중 ●●○

해설 이 문장은 주절(stick it ~ windshield)이 주어가 없는 명령문으로 동사(stick)와 목적어(it)를 갖추고 있으므로, ___ ~ permit은 수식어 거품으로 보아야 한다. 이 수식어 거품은 동사(receive)가 있는 거품절이므로, 거품절을 이끌 수 있는 부사절 접속사인 모든 보기가 성답의 후보이나. 새로운 허가증을 받자마자 여러분 차량의 앞쪽 전면유리창 내부에 그것을 부착하라'라는 의미가 되어야 하므로 시간을 나타내는 부사절 접속사 (D) As soon as(~하자마자)가 정답이다. 시간을 나타내는 부사절 접속사 (B) By the time(~할 때까지)과 (C) Before(~하기 전에)를 쓸 경우 각각 '새로운 허가증을 받을 때까지/받기 전에, 전면유리창 내부에 그것(새로운 허가증)을 부착하라'라는 어색한 문맥이 된다.

어휘 even if phr. 비록 ~일지라도

138 알맞은 문장 고르기   중 ●●○

해석 (A) 이것은 체크아웃 과정의 속도를 더 높일 것입니다.
(B) 안전 점검은 지난해의 것과 유사할 것입니다.
(C) 차량들은 수리가 잘 되어 있어야 합니다.
(D) 바깥쪽에서 그것이 명확히 보이는지 반드시 확인하십시오.

해설 앞 문장 '(As soon as) you receive your new permit, stick it to the interior of your vehicle's front windshield.'에서 여러분의 새로운 허가증을 받자마자, 여러분 차량의 앞쪽 전면유리창 내부에 그것을 부착하라고 했으므로, 빈칸에는 허가증 부착과 관련된 내용이 들어가야 함을 알 수 있다. 따라서 (D)가 정답이다.

어휘 speed up phr. 속도를 더 높이다 checkout n. (호텔에서의) 체크아웃 inspection n. 점검 in good repair phr. 수리가 잘 되어 있는, 상태가 좋은 visible adj. 보이는

139-142번은 다음 보도 자료에 관한 문제입니다.

뉴욕 (1월 28일)—TymTech사의 최신 노트북에 대한 광고가 올해 전 세계 마케팅 시상식에서 최고의 TV 광고로 선정되었다. 이 ¹³⁹**우승한** 광고는 Telerana Associates사에 의해 제작되었다.

세계적으로 유명한 운동선수 Wanda Vilanova에게 ¹⁴⁰**주연을 맡긴** 그 30초짜리 광고는 북미 전역의 방송국들에서 방송되었다. 영어, 스페인어, 그리고 프랑스어 버전들이 만들어졌다. "저희는 문화적 차이들을 ¹⁴¹**세심하게** 고려했습니다. 따라서, 저희는 세 가지 버전이 모두 확실히 효과적이도록 했습니다."라고 Telerana Associates사의 감독인 Harold Martel은 말했다.

TymTech사에 따르면, 그 광고는 회사에 최고 기록의 매출을 내었다. ¹⁴²**그것은 향후 캠페인들을 위해 Telerana Associates사를 다시 고용할 계획이다.**

laptop n. 노트북 world-famous adj. 세계적으로 유명한
broadcast v. 방송하다 station n. 방송국 ensure v. 확실히 ~하게 하다 ⟳

---

effective adj. 효과적인 result in phr. (어떠한 결과를) 내다, 낳다
record adj. 최고 기록의, 기록적인

139 형용사 어휘 고르기 주변 문맥 파악   하 ●○○

해설 빈칸은 명사(advertisement)를 꾸미는 형용사 자리이다. '이 ___ 광고는 Telerana Associates사에 의해 제작되었다'라는 문맥이므로 모든 보기가 정답의 후보이다. 앞 문장에서 'TymTech사의 최신 노트북에 대한 광고가 올해 전 세계 마케팅 시상식에서 최고의 TV 광고로 선정되었다'라고 했으므로 이 우승한 광고가 Telerana Associates사에 의해 제작된 것을 알 수 있다. 따라서 (C) winning(우승한)이 정답이다.

어휘 controversial adj. 논란이 많은 sample adj. 견본의; n. 견본, 샘플
final adj. 최종의

140 현재분사와 과거분사 구별하여 채우기   중 ●●○

해설 이 문장은 주어(the 30-second advertisement), 동사(was broadcast)를 갖춘 완전한 절이므로, ___ ~ Wanda Vilanova는 수식어 거품으로 보아야 한다. 따라서 수식어 거품이 될 수 있는 과거분사 (A)와 현재분사 (C)가 정답의 후보이다. 빈칸 다음에 목적어(the world-famous ~ Wanda Vilanova)가 있고, 주절의 주어(the 30-second advertisement)와 분사구문이 'Wanda Vilanova에게 주연을 맡긴 30초짜리 광고'라는 의미의 능동 관계이므로 현재분사 (C) Starring이 정답이다. 과거분사 (A)는 수동의 의미를 나타내므로 정답이 될 수 없다. 동사 또는 명사 (B)와 (D)는 수식어 거품을 이끌 수 없다.

어휘 star v. 주연을 맡기다; n. 인기인, 스타

141 부사 어휘 고르기 주변 문맥 파악   하 ●○○

해설 빈칸은 동사(considered)를 꾸미는 부사 자리이다. '우리는 문화적 차이를 ___ 고려했다'라는 문맥이므로 모든 보기가 정답의 후보이다. 앞 문장에서 영어, 스페인어, 그리고 프랑스어 버전들이 만들어졌다고 했고, 뒤 문장에서 세 가지 버전이 모두 확실히 효과적이도록 했다고 했으므로 문화적 차이들을 세심하게 고려했다는 것을 알 수 있다. 따라서 (A) carefully(세심하게)가 정답이다.

어휘 barely adv. 거의 ~아니게 roughly adv. 대충, 거칠게
randomly adv. 무작위로

142 알맞은 문장 고르기   중 ●●○

해석 (A) 대회의 모든 참가자들에게 상품권이 발송되었다.
(B) 전 세계 마케팅 시상식은 곧 결정을 내릴 것이다.
(C) 그것은 향후 캠페인들을 위해 Telerana Associates사를 다시 고용할 계획이다.
(D) 이 기록은 나중에 그것의 주요 경쟁사들 중 하나에 의해 깨졌다.

해설 앞 문장 'According to TymTech, the advertisement has resulted in record sales for the company.'에서 TymTech사에 따르면, 그 광고, 즉 Telerana Associates사에 의해 만들어진 광고가 회사에 최고 기록의 매출을 내었다고 했으므로, 빈칸에는 추후 캠페인을 위해 TymTech사가 다시 Telerana Associates사를 고용할 것이라는 내용이 들어가야 함을 알 수 있다. 따라서 (C)가 정답이다. (D)가 This record(이 기록)를 언급해서 언뜻 보기에 정답인 것으로 착각할 수 있지만, TymTech사가 최고 기록의 매출을 냈다는 것과 그 기록을 나중에 다른 회사가 깼다는 것은 전체 문맥상 어울리지 않으므로 답이 될 수 없다.

어휘 voucher n. 상품권 contestant n. 참가자 competition n. 대회, 경쟁

competitor n. 경쟁사

143-146번은 다음 이메일에 관한 문제입니다.

수신: Blair McKay <b.mckay@rdedental.com>
발신: Nancy Tang <n.tang@goldhotel.com>
제목: 비즈니스 오찬
날짜: 12월 12일

Mr. McKay께,

저는 방금 귀하의 이메일을 받았습니다. 143저희는 귀하의 요청사항을 확실히 수용할 수 있습니다. 귀하가 행사를 위해 빌리시는 방은 50명까지 수용할 수 있습니다. 초대자 명단에 10명을 더 추가하는 것은 문제가 되지 않을 것입니다. 귀하가 저희의 뷔페 형식 메뉴를 선택하셨기 때문에, 음식의 144양을 늘리는 것은 저희에게 간단합니다. 꽃에 관련하여, 저는 귀사의 로고와 색을 맞추는 것이 멋진 아이디어라고 생각합니다. 저는 저희의 플로리스트와 이것이 가능하다는 것을 145확인했습니다. 그는 파란색과 주황색 꽃의 조합을 사용할 것입니다. 남아 있는 사안146이 없다면, 저는 계약서의 최종안을 마련할 준비가 되어 있습니다. 이것은 오늘 귀하의 사무실에 팩스로 보내질 수 있습니다.

Nancy Tang 드림
Gold 호텔

rent v. 빌리다   list n. 명단   simple adj. 간단한   match v. 맞추다
florist n. 플로리스트, 꽃집 주인   combination n. 조합
final draft phr. 최종안   agreement n. 계약서, 합의

143 알맞은 문장 고르기   상 ●●●

해석   (A) 저희는 진심으로 귀하의 피드백을 소중하게 여깁니다.
(B) 귀하께서 빌리신 방에 변경사항들이 생겼습니다.
(C) 저희는 귀하의 요청사항을 확실히 수용할 수 있습니다.
(D) 저희 매니저가 귀하의 우려와 관련하여 귀하께 연락할 것입니다.

해설   뒷부분에서 초대자 명단에 10명을 더 추가하는 것은 문제가 되지 않을 것이라고 했으므로, 빈칸에는 명단에 10명을 추가해달라는 요청사항을 수용할 수 있다는 것과 관련된 내용이 들어가야 함을 알 수 있다. 따라서 (C)가 정답이다.

어휘   value v. 소중하게 여기다   accommodate v. 수용하다

144 명사 어휘 고르기   주변 문맥 파악   상 ●●●

해설   빈칸은 동사(increase)의 목적어 역할을 하는 명사 자리이다. '음식의 ____을 늘리는 것은 간단하다'라는 문맥이므로 모든 보기가 정답의 후보이다. 앞 문장에서 초대자 명단에 10명을 더 추가하는 것은 문제가 되지 않을 것이라고 했으므로 음식의 양을 늘리는 것이 간단하다는 것을 알 수 있다. 따라서 (A) quantity(양)가 정답이다.

어휘   sale n. 판매   flavor n. 맛   freshness n. 신선함

145 올바른 시제의 동사 채우기   주변 문맥 파악   중 ●●○

해설   '플로리스트와 이것이 가능하다는 것을 확인하다'라는 문맥이며, 뒤 문장에서 그, 즉 플로리스트는 파란색과 주황색 꽃의 조합을 사용할 것이라고 했으므로 플로리스트와 이것, 즉 회사의 로고와 꽃의 색을 맞추는 것이 가능하다는 것을 이미 확인했음을 알 수 있다. 따라서 과거에 발생한 일이 현재까지 영향을 미치거나 방금 완료된 것을 표현할 때 사용되는 현재 완료 시제 (C) have confirmed가 정답이다. 미래 시제 (A)는 미래에 일어날 일, 현재 진행 시제

(B)는 현재 진행되고 있는 일, 과거 완료 시제 (D)는 과거의 특정 시점 이전에 발생한 일을 나타낸다.

어휘   confirm v. 확인하다

146 부정대명사/형용사 채우기   상 ●●●

해설   명사구(remaining issues)를 꾸밀 수 있는 것은 형용사이므로 부정형용사 (B), (C), (D)가 정답의 후보이다. '남아 있는 사안이 없다면, 나는 계약서의 최종안을 마련할 준비가 되어 있다'라는 의미가 되어야 하므로 (D) no(~이 없는)가 정답이다. (B) some과 (C) any는 각각 '몇몇/어떤 남아있는 사안이 있다면, 계약서의 최종안을 마련할 준비가 되어 있다'라는 어색한 문맥이 된다. 참고로, some은 주로 긍정문에서, any는 주로 부정문, 의문문, if절에서 사용됨을 알아둔다. 또한, any가 긍정문에서 쓰일 경우 '아무것, 무엇이든지'라는 의미를 가지며, '아무것도 없다'라는 의미로 쓰이기 위해서는 not과 함께 쓰여 If there are not any remaining issues와 같은 형태로 쓰여야 함을 알아둔다. 부정대명사 또는 부사 (A)는 형용사 자리에 올 수 없다.

어휘   none n. 아무도; adv. 전혀 ~ 아니다

PART 7

147-148번은 다음 공고에 관한 문제입니다.

고객 발표

147Victory 은행은 다음의 인터넷 뱅킹 서비스들이 7월 8일 일요일 오전 12시부터 오전 8시까지 중단될 것임을 고객들에게 알리고자 합니다.

· 현금 자동 입출금기(ATM기)
· 온라인 자금 송금 및 청구서 납부
· 신용 및 직불카드의 온라인 사용

이 기간 동안, 148고객들은 온라인으로 그들의 계좌 잔액을 계속해서 확인할 수 있습니다. 저희는 이것이 야기할 수 있는 모든 불편에 대해 유감스럽게 생각하지만, 이것은 저희 인터넷 뱅킹 시스템의 최대한 온전한 상태를 확보하는 중요한 유지 관리 업무들을 가능하게 하기 위해 필수적입니다.

advise v. 알리다   suspend v. 중단하다
automated teller machine phr. 현금 자동 입출금기(ATM)
fund n. 자금, 돈   transfer n. 송금; v. 송금하다, 옮기다   bill n. 청구서
debit card phr. 직불카드   account balance phr. 계좌 잔액
regret v. 유감스럽게 생각하다   inconvenience n. 불편
facilitate v. 가능하게 하다, 용이하게 하다   vital adj. 중요한, 필수적인
maintenance n. 유지 관리, 보수   ensure v. 확보하다, 보장하다
utmost adj. 최대한   integrity n. 온전한 상태, 무결성

147 목적 찾기 문제   하 ●○○

해석   공고의 목적은 무엇인가?
(A) 최근의 정책 변화를 설명하기 위해
(B) 주말 영업시간에 관한 정보를 제공하기 위해
(C) 개인 정보의 업데이트를 요청하기 위해
(D) 일시적인 서비스 중단을 알리기 위해

해설   지문의 'Victory Bank would like to advise ~ services will be suspended on Sunday, July 8, from 12 A.M. to 8 A.M.'에서 Victory 은행은 서비스들이 7월 8일 일요일 오전 12시부터 오전 8시까지 중단될 것임을 알리고자 한다고 했으므로 (D)가 정답이다.

어휘 request v. 요청하다; n. 요청

148 육하원칙 문제　　중 ●●●

해석 공고에 따르면, 고객들은 계속해서 무엇을 할 수 있는가?
(A) 계좌 정보를 확인한다
(B) 기계로부터 현금을 얻는다
(C) 계좌 간 돈을 송금한다
(D) 온라인으로 물품을 구매한다

해설 지문의 'clients may continue to check their account balances
online'에서 고객들은 온라인으로 그들의 계좌 잔액을 계속해서 확인할 수
있다고 했으므로 (A)가 정답이다.

어휘 obtain v. 얻다, 획득하다

149-150번은 다음 메시지 대화문에 관한 문제입니다.

Daniel Miller [오후 3시 40분]
안녕하세요. 149당신은 Ms. Downing의 송별회에 가나요? 보아하니, 사무
실 전체가 오늘 밤 퇴근 후에 Finlay's Bar & Grill에서 만나도록 초대된 것
같아요.

Elaine Larue [오후 3시 43분]
저는 모르겠어요. 149저는 오늘 꽤 피곤해요. 게다가, 여기서 일을 시작한 후
로 당신이 제가 알게 된 유일한 사람이에요. 149저는 혼자 파티에 가면 불편
할 거예요.

Daniel Miller [오후 3시 44분]
우리 같이 가는 게 어때요? 150그것은 당신이 사람들을 만날 수 있는 좋은 기
회가 될 거예요. 저는 끝내야 할 몇 가지 일들이 있지만 오후 7시까지는 갈 준
비가 되어 있을 거예요.

Elaine Larue [오후 3시 45분]
좋아요. 오후 7시에 로비에서 만나요.

farewell party phr. 송별회　apparently adv. 보아하니, 분명히
opportunity n. 기회

149 의도 파악 문제　　중 ●●●

해석 오후 3시 43분에, Ms. Larue가 "I don't know"라고 썼을 때 그녀가 의도한
것은?
(A) 초대장을 받지 않았다.
(B) 행사에 참석할 계획이 없다.
(C) 직원 모임을 일찍 떠날 것이다.
(D) 장소로 가는 길 안내를 필요로 한다.

해설 지문의 'are you going to Ms. Downing's farewell party?'에서
Mr. Miller가 Ms. Downing의 송별회에 갈 것인지 묻자, Ms. Larue가

'I don't know.'(저는 모르겠어요)라고 한 후 'I'm feeling pretty tired
today.'와 'I'd feel uncomfortable going to the party alone.'에서
자신은 오늘 꽤 피곤하고 혼자 파티에 가면 불편할 것이라고 한 것을 통해
Ms. Larue가 송별회에 갈 계획이 없다는 것을 알 수 있다. 따라서 (B)가 정
답이다.

어휘 attend v. 참석하다　gathering n. 모임　venue n. 장소

150 추론 문제　　중 ●●●

해석 파티에 대해 암시되는 것은?
(A) 직장 가까이에서 일어날 것이다.
(B) Ms. Larue가 동료들을 만나는데 도움이 될 것이다.
(C) 동료의 승진을 축하할 것이다.
(D) Ms. Downing을 위한 깜짝 파티일 것이다.

해설 지문의 'It'll be a good opportunity for you to meet people.'에서 그것
은 당신, 즉 Ms. Larue에게 사람들, 즉 사무실 사람들을 만날 수 있는 좋은
기회가 될 것이라고 했으므로, 파티를 통해 Ms. Larue가 동료들을 만날 수
있을 것이라는 사실을 추론할 수 있다. 따라서 (B)가 정답이다.

어휘 occur v. 일어나다　coworker n. 동료
celebrate v. 축하하다, 기념하다　colleague n. 동료

151-152번은 다음 웹페이지에 관한 문제입니다.

www.happytravels.com/trips/cancel

내 계정
계정명: Lawrence Soto
계정 번호: PW91K4L26J

출발 일자 / 시간	출발지	151-B도착지	도착 일자 / 시간
7월 14일 오후 8시 20분	런던 Euston	151-B리버풀 Lime가	7월 14일 오후 10시 30분
등급	152**티켓**	151-A**좌석**	151-C**가격**
일반석	152사전 구매	151-A20B	151-C15.50파운드

학생 할인 티켓과 152사전 구매 티켓은 환불되지 않는다는 점에 유의하십시오.
곧 있을 이 여행을 취소하고 싶은 것이 확실합니까?

☑ 네, 152지금 취소하겠습니다.　　☐ 아니요, 취소하지 않겠습니다.

보내기

departure n. 출발　arrival n. 도착　advance adj. 사전의
purchase n. 구매　upcoming adj. 곧 있을

151 Not/True 문제　　중 ●●●

해석 웹페이지에 포함되지 않은 정보는?
(A) 좌석의 위치
(B) 목적지
(C) 이동 경비
(D) 티켓 번호

해설 지문에서 (D)는 언급되지 않은 내용이다. 따라서 (D)가 정답이다. (A)는
'Seat', '20B'에서 좌석의 위치가 20B라고 했으므로 지문의 내용과 일치한
다. (B)는 'To', 'Liverpool Lime Street'에서 도착지가 리버풀 Lime가라
고 했으므로 지문의 내용과 일치한다. (C)는 'Price', '£15.50'에서 가격이
15.50파운드라고 했으므로 지문의 내용과 일치한다.

어휘 destination n. (여행) 목적지　journey n. 이동; v. 이동하다

152 추론 문제
상 ●●●

해석 Mr. Soto에 대해 암시되는 것은?
(A) 취소를 확정할 이틀의 시간이 있다.
(B) 그의 돈을 돌려받지 못할 것이다.
(C) 신용카드로 여행 경비를 지불했다.
(D) 그의 좌석 등급을 높일 수 없다.

해설 지문의 'Ticket', 'Advance Purchase'에서 Mr. Soto가 티켓을 사전 구매한 것을 알 수 있으며, 'Advance Purchase tickets are nonrefundable'과 'cancel now'에서 사전 구매 티켓은 환불되지 않고 Mr. Soto가 여행 취소를 선택한다고 했으므로 Mr. Soto는 사전 구매한 티켓의 비용을 돌려받지 못할 것임을 추론할 수 있다. 따라서 (B)가 정답이다.

어휘 confirm v. 확정하다 cancellation n. (예약) 취소

패러프레이징

tickets are nonrefundable 티켓은 환불되지 않는다 → will not get ~ money back 돈을 돌려받지 못할 것이다

153-154번은 다음 광고에 관한 문제입니다.

SheerYou—Dewdrop Skincare사의 최신 제품

Dewdrop Skincare사는 국내 최고의 화장품 제공업체입니다. 저희는 저희의 최신 보습제 SheerYou를 공개하게 되어 자랑스럽습니다. 이것은 당신 피부의 천연 수분을 회복시켜 피부가 더 밝고 건강하게 보이도록 한다고 과학적으로 증명되었습니다. ¹⁵³⁻ᴮ**천연 재료만을 사용해 피부과 전문의들에 의해 만들어진** SheerYou는 저희의 가장 순하면서도 가장 강력한 보습제입니다. 이것의 출시를 기념하기 위해, 저희는 6월 동안 특가 상품을 제공하고 있습니다. SheerYou를 구매하는 사람은 누구든지 무료 Floria 3온스 한 병을 받을 것입니다. 이것은 ¹⁵⁴**인기 TV 드라마** Broken Hearts**의 주연, Jenna Harvel의** 대표적인 향수입니다. ¹⁵³⁻ᴰ**Dewdrop사의 상품을 판매하는 상점들의 목록을 위해서는, www.dewdropskin.com/vendors를 방문하십시오.**

provider n. 제공업체 cosmetic product phr. 화장품
unveil v. 공개하다, 발표하다 latest adj. 최신의 moisturizer n. 보습제
restore v. 회복시키다, 복원하다 dermatologist n. 피부과 전문의
ingredient n. 재료 gentle adj. 순한, 온화한
release n. 출시, 석방; v. 방출하다, 석방하다 special deal phr. 특가 상품
complimentary adj. 무료의 signature adj. 대표적인, 전형적인

153 Not/True 문제
중 ●●○

해석 SheerYou에 대해 언급된 것은?
(A) 나양한 향기들로 이용 가능하다.
(B) 인공적인 물질들을 포함하지 않는다.
(C) 사용자들에게 건강상의 혜택을 제공하지 않는다.
(D) Dewdrop Skincare사의 웹사이트에서만 판매된다.

해설 지문의 'Created by ~ using only natural ingredients'에서 SheerYou는 천연 재료만을 사용해 만들어졌다고 했으므로 (B)는 지문의 내용과 일치한다. 따라서 (B)가 정답이다. (A)와 (C)는 지문에 언급되지 않은 내용이다. (D)는 'For a list of stores that sell Dewdrop's merchandise, please visit www.dewdropskin.com/vendors.'에서 Dewdrop사의 상품을 판매하는 상점들의 목록을 위해서는, 웹사이트를 방문하라고 했으므로 지문의 내용과 일치하지 않는다.

어휘 a variety of phr. 다양한, 많은 scent n. 향기 artificial adj. 인공적인
substance n. 물질, 본질

154 육하원칙 문제
하 ●○○

해석 Jenna Harvel은 누구인가?
(A) 영화 제작자
(B) 텔레비전 배우
(C) 회사 사장
(D) 의료 전문가

해설 지문의 'Jenna Harvel, star of the ~ TV drama Broken Hearts'에서 Jenna Harvel이 TV 드라마 Broken Hearts의 주연이라고 했으므로 (B)가 정답이다.

어휘 producer n. 제작자, 생산자 medical adj. 의료의

패러프레이징

star of the ~ TV drama TV 드라마의 주연 → A television actor 텔레비전 배우

155-157번은 다음 안내문에 관한 문제입니다.

Chesterfield 공원 규정들

¹⁵⁵**모든 공원 구역들에서, 다음을 하지 마십시오:**

· 다른 방문객들을 방해할 수 있는 큰 소음을 낸다
· ¹⁵⁵**지정된 쓰레기통들이 아닌 아무 곳에 쓰레기를 버리거나 둔다**

캠핑 구역들은 하룻밤 묵는 방문객들을 위해 공원 전체에 위치해 있습니다. 이러한 지정된 구역들이 아닌 아무 곳에 머무는 것은 금지되어 있습니다. 안전상의 이유로, 캠프파이어는 허용되지 않지만, 스낵바 옆에 위치한 바비큐 그릴에서 요리하는 것은 허용됩니다.

애완동물들은 공원 내에서 허용되지만, 항상 줄로 묶여 있어야 합니다. 하지만, ¹⁵⁶**매달 셋째 주 수요일에는 벌레들을 관리하기 위해 공원 잔디에 살충제가 살포되고 이 화학 약품들이 동물에 의해 섭취될 경우 해로울 수 있기 때문에** 저희는 당신에게 그날들에 애완동물을 데려오지 않을 것을 권고합니다.

만약 당신이 저희 시설들에 있는 동안 안전하지 않다고 느낀다면, 당신은 보안 직통 전화로 자유롭게 전화하실 수 있는데, 이것은 ¹⁵⁷**공원 전체에 흩어져 있는 부스들 안의 빨간 전화 수화기** 중 하나를 들면 즉시 전화가 걸어질 것입니다. 긴급 대응 요원들은 하루 24시간, 주 7일 동안 이 직통 전화로 당신을 도울 수 있습니다.

regulation n. 규정 disturb v. 방해하다 litter v. (쓰레기를) 버리다
designated adj. 지정된 prohibit v. 금지하다 permit v. 허용하다
situated adj. 위치한 leash n. 줄 spray v. (살충제를) 살포하다
scatter v. 흩어지다 personnel n. 요원, 직원

155 육하원칙 문제
중 ●●○

해석 공원 방문객들은 무엇을 하지 않도록 안내되는가?
(A) 늦은 밤에 그들의 애완동물을 산책시키는 것
(B) 그들 소유의 캠핑 장비를 가져오는 것
(C) 공원에서 요리를 하는 것
(D) 바닥에 쓰레기를 버리는 것

해설 지문의 'In all park areas, please do not:'과 'Litter or put trash anywhere other than in designated waste bins'에서 모든 공원 구역들에서 지정된 쓰레기통들이 아닌 아무 곳에 쓰레기를 버리거나 두지 말라고 했으므로 (D)가 정답이다.

어휘 avoid v. ~하지 않도록 하다, 피하다

Litter or put trash anywhere other than in designated waste bins 지정된 쓰레기통들이 아닌 아무 곳에 쓰레기를 버리거나 둔다 → Throwing garbage on the ground 바닥에 쓰레기를 버리는 것

156 육하원칙 문제 중 ●●●○

해석 안내문에 따르면, 매달 무슨 일이 일어나는가?
(A) 회원권 요금이 거두어진다.
(B) 몇몇 지역 행사들이 개최된다.
(C) 주차장이 방문객들에게 폐쇄된다.
(D) 몇몇 화학 약품들이 식물들에 발라진다.

해설 지문의 'we advise you not to bring pets on the third Wednesday of each month as park grass is sprayed ~ and the chemicals can be harmful'에서 매달 셋째 주 수요일에 공원 잔디에 살충제가 살포되고 이 화학 약품들이 해로울 수 있어 애완동물들을 데려오지 않을 것을 권고했으므로 (D)가 정답이다.

어휘 fee n. 요금 collect v. 거두다, 수금하다 hold v. 개최하다, 열다 parking lot phr. 주차장 close off phr. 폐쇄하다

패러프레이징

park grass is sprayed 공원 잔디에 살충제가 살포되다 → Some chemicals are applied to plants 몇몇 화학 약품들이 식물들에게 발라진다

157 육하원칙 문제 중 ●●●○

해석 공원 내 몇몇 장소들에 무엇이 놓여 있는가?
(A) 소화기
(B) 스낵바
(C) 전화 부스
(D) 바비큐 그릴

해설 지문의 'the red phone receivers in the booths scattered throughout the park'에서 공원 전체에 흩어져 있는 부스들 안의 빨간 전화 수화기라고 했으므로 (C)가 정답이다.

어휘 fire extinguisher phr. 소화기

158-160번은 다음 양식에 관한 문제입니다.

Frontward Car Rental사를 선택해주셔서 감사합니다, Nadia Abdulhak님. 저희는 5월 7일부터 13일까지 Gallapot Mini를 대여한 ¹⁵⁸/¹⁶⁰⁻ᴰ귀하의 경험에 대해 귀하가 얼마나 만족스러웠는지 알고 싶습니다. ¹⁶⁰⁻ᴰ이 양식을 작성한 후, 제출을 클릭하십시오.

1) 여러 가지 이용 가능한 대여 선택권들이 적절했다.	● 동의	○비동의
2) 예약 시스템은 편리했다.	○동의	●비동의
3) 차량을 찾아올 때 서비스의 품질은 만족스러웠다.	●동의	○비동의
4) 차량이 확실하게 작동했다.	○동의	●비동의
5) 차량을 반납할 때 서비스의 품질은 만족스러웠다.	○동의	●비동의

추가적인 의견
저는 웹사이트 광고를 본 후 Frontward Car Rental사를 이용하기로 결정했습니다. ¹⁶⁰⁻ᴬ귀사의 Fairfield 지점에서 차량을 찾아올 때 ¹⁵⁹근무 중이었던 직원 Derek은 저의 질문들에 잘 대답해 주었습니다. 하지만, 이틀 뒤 차량이 99번 고속도로에서 고장 났을 때, 귀사는 상황을 해결하는 데에 약 세 시간이 걸렸습니다. ¹⁶⁰⁻ᴬ저는 또한 귀사의 Danbury 지점에서 차량을 반납할 때 환불이 제공되지 않은 것에 실망했습니다.

제출하기

experience n. 경험 available adj. 이용 가능한 rental n. 대여, 대여료 suitable adj. 적절한 reservation n. 예약 convenient adj. 편리한 vehicle n. 차량 satisfactory adj. 만족스러운 reliably adv. 확실하게 upon -ing phr. ~할 때, ~하자마자 on duty phr. 근무 중인, 당직의 resolve v. 해결하다 disappointed adj. 실망한 refund n. 환불; v. 환불하다

158 목적 찾기 문제 중 ●●●○

해석 양식의 목적은 무엇인가?
(A) 제품에 대한 관심을 알아내기 위해
(B) 지불금에 대한 환불을 승인하기 위해
(C) 서비스에 대한 피드백을 요청하기 위해
(D) 행사에 대한 예약을 확인하기 위해

해설 지문의 'We want to know how satisfied you are with your experience'에서 귀하의 경험에 대해 귀하가 얼마나 만족스러웠는지 알고 싶다고 했으므로 (C)가 정답이다.

어휘 determine v. 알아내다, 결정하다 grant v. 승인하다 confirm v. 확인하다

159 육하원칙 문제 중 ●●●○

해석 Ms. Abdulhak은 이 회사의 어떤 측면에 만족했는가?
(A) 예약 과정의 간단함
(B) 직원의 고객 서비스 기술
(C) Gallapot Mini의 연비
(D) 계약의 조건

해설 지문의 'Derek, the staff member on duty, did a good job of answering my questions'에서 근무 중이었던 직원 Derek이 자신의 질문들에 잘 대답해 주었다고 했으므로 (B)가 정답이다.

어휘 business n. 회사 booking n. 예약 fuel efficiency phr. 연비

160 Not/True 문제 중 ●●●○

해석 Frontward Car Rental사에 대해 언급된 것은?
(A) 고객들이 다른 지점들에서 차량을 찾아오고 반납하는 것을 허용한다.
(B) Danbury에 자동차 정비공들의 팀을 만들었다.
(C) 99번 고속도로를 따라 일부 광고 공간을 임대했다.
(D) 환급을 제공하기 전 보고서가 작성되어야 함을 요구한다.

해설 지문의 'picking up the car from your Fairfield location'과 'at your Danbury location when I returned the automobile'에서 귀사의 Fairfield 지점에서 차량을 찾아왔고, Danbury 지점에서 차량을 반납했다고 했으므로 (A)는 지문의 내용과 일치한다. 따라서 (A)가 정답이다. (B)와 (C)는 지문에 언급되지 않은 내용이다. (D)는 'We want to know how satisfied you are with your experience'와 'After completing this form, please click SUBMIT.'에서 귀하의 경험에 대해 귀하가 얼마나 만족스러웠는지 알고 싶으며 이 양식을 작성한 후, 제출을 클릭하라고 했다. 즉, 환급이 아닌 차량 대여에 대한 피드백을 제공하기 위한 양식이므로 지문의 내용과 일치하지 않는다.

어휘 patron n. 고객 branch n. 지점 automobile n. 자동차 mechanic n. 정비공 reimbursement n. 환급, 상환

161-164번은 다음 온라인 채팅 대화문에 관한 문제입니다.

Jen Kim (오전 9시 40분)

저는 모든 사람에게 우리의 월별 관리자 회의가 국경일로 인해 이번 주 금요일에 예정대로 열리지 않을 것임을 상기시키고 싶었어요. 하지만 162우리는 회사의 새로운 로고에 대한 최종 결정을 해야 하기 때문에 161/162그냥 그것을 취소할 수는 없어요. 161대신 다음 주 월요일 오전 11시에 이것을 해도 여러분 모두 괜찮을까요?

Richard Smythe (오전 9시 43분)

저는 좋아요. 저는 다른 어떤 것도 예정된 것이 없어요.

Kelly Leech (오전 9시 45분)

사실, 저는 월요일에 휴가예요. 하지만 저는 같은 시간으로 화요일 또는 목요일에는 마음껏 만날 수 있어요.

Hassan Sadat (오전 9시 48분)

저도 월요일에 여기에 없을 거예요. 하지만 저는 금요일 그 시간에 약속이 있어요.

Jen Kim (오전 9시 49분)

좋아요, 그럼 제가 화요일에 회의 일정을 잡아도 될까요?

Richard Smythe (오전 9시 51분)

163저는 화요일 아침에는 되지만, 공급업체와 만나기 위해 정오 전에 떠나야 해요.

Jen Kim (오전 9시 52분)

그건 안 될 거예요. 163저는 우리의 새로운 인턴들을 대상으로 워크숍을 진행하고 있어요. 이것은 오전 9시에 시작하고 오후 12시 직전에 끝나요. 162목요일 오후 1시쯤은 어떨까요?

Richard Smythe (오전 9시 54분)

알겠어요. 저는 괜찮아요.

Hassan Sadat (오전 9시 55분)

저는 그것에 문제가 없어요. 162/164또 다른 옵션은 음식을 배달되도록 하고 정오에 회의를 하는 거예요.

Kelly Leech (오전 9시 57분)

저는 그 아이디어가 마음에 들어요.

Richard Smythe (오전 9시3 58분)

네. 그렇게 해요.

Jen Kim (오전 10시 02분)

좋아요. 162이제 다 결정되었네요. 만약 어떤 변경사항이라도 생긴다면, 제가 여러분에게 알려줄게요. 모두 감사해요!

---

remind v. 상기시키다 **as scheduled** phr. 예정대로 **appointment** n. 약속
supplier n. 공급업체 **settle** v. 결정하다, 합의를 보다

---

161 주제 찾기 문제   중 ●●○

해석 작성자들은 무엇에 대해 논의하고 있는가?
(A) 다가오는 회의 일정을 변경하는 것
(B) 추가 휴일들을 위해 사무실 문을 닫는 것
(C) 휴가에 관련된 정책들을 변경하는 것
(D) 관리진 직원들의 근무 교대 일정을 정하는 것

해설 지문의 'we cannot just cancel it'과 'Would it be all right with everyone to have it on Monday ~ instead?'에서 Ms. Kim이 그것, 즉 회의를 그냥 취소할 수는 없다고 하며 대신 다음 주 월요일에 회의를 해도 모

두가 괜찮을지 물었으므로 (A)가 정답이다.

어휘 **reschedule** v. 일정을 변경하다 **upcoming** adj. 다가오는
policy n. 정책 **leave** n. 휴가; v. 떠나다 **work shift** phr. 근무 교대(제)

---

162 육하원칙 문제   중 ●●○

해석 관리자들은 언제 로고를 선정할 것인가?
(A) 월요일에
(B) 화요일에
(C) 목요일에
(D) 금요일에

해설 지문의 'we cannot just cancel it because we need to make a final decision about the company's new logo'에서 Ms. Kim이 우리, 즉 관리자들은 회사의 새로운 로고에 대한 최종 결정을 해야 하기 때문에 그것, 즉 회의를 취소할 수 없다고 했고 'What about Thursday at about 1:00 P.M.?'에서 목요일 오후 1시쯤 회의할 것을 제안하였다. 그 후 'Another option is to get some food delivered and have the meeting at noon.'에서 Mr. Sadat이 또 다른 옵션은 음식을 주문하고 정오에 회의를 하는 것이라고 한 후, 'It's all settled now.'에서 Ms. Kim이 이제 다 결정되었다고 했으므로 (C)가 정답이다.

어휘 **select** v. 선정하다, 선택하다

패러프레이징

> select a logo 로고를 선정하다 → make a final decision about the company's new logo 회사의 새로운 로고에 대한 최종 결정을 하다

---

163 의도 파악 문제   하 ●○○

해석 오전 9시 52분에, Ms. Kim이 "That won't work"라고 썼을 때 그녀가 의도한 것은?
(A) 공급업체의 제품 품질에 문제가 있다.
(B) 안건에 의제들을 추가하는 것은 불가능하다고 생각한다.
(C) 아침에 교육을 실시하고 있다.
(D) 인턴들에게 추가적인 과제가 필요하다고 느낀다.

해설 지문의 'I am free Tuesday morning, but I have to leave before noon'에서 Mr. Smythe가 화요일 아침에는 되지만 정오 전에 떠나야 한다고 하자, Ms. Kim이 'That won't work.'(그건 안 될 거예요)라고 한 후, 'I am leading a workshop for our new interns. It starts at 9:00 A.M. and ends just before 12:00 P.M.'에서 자신이 새로운 인턴들을 대상으로 워크숍을 진행하고 있으며 이것은 오전 9시에 시작하고 오후 12시 직전에 끝난다고 한 것을 통해, Ms. Kim이 아침에 교육을 실시하고 있어 화요일 아침에 회의를 할 수 없다는 것을 알 수 있다. 따라서 (C)가 정답이다.

어휘 **topic** n. 의제, 주제 **agenda** n. 안건 **conduct** v. 실시하다, 시행하다
training session phr. 교육(과정) **assignment** n. 과제, 배정

패러프레이징

> leading a workshop 워크숍을 진행하는 것 → conducting a training session 교육을 실시하는 것

---

164 육하원칙 문제   하 ●○○

해석 Mr. Sadat은 무엇을 추천하는가?
(A) 또 다른 관리자에게 연락하는 것
(B) 식사를 주문하는 것
(C) 프로젝트 마감기한을 늘리는 것

(D) 집에서 점심을 가져오는 것

해설 지문의 'Another option is to get some food delivered'에서 Mr. Sadat이 또 다른 옵션은 음식을 배달되도록 하는 것이라고 했으므로 (B)가 정답이다.

어휘 contact v. 연락하다 meal n. 식사 extend v. 늘리다, 연장하다

패러프레이징

get some food delivered 음식을 배달되도록 하다 → Ordering some meals 식사를 주문하는 것

165-167번은 다음 기사에 관한 문제입니다.

과거의 자동차 부품 공장이 새로운 삶을 찾다
Gregory McKenna 작성

5월 15일—광범위한 보수 공사 후에, ¹⁶⁵이전에 XLT Industries사에 의해 운영되었던 버려진 자동차 부품 공장이 3,000제곱미터의 복합 단지로 개조되었다. ¹⁶⁵새로운 Grand Prairie 문화 센터는 1,500명을 위한 좌석을 가진 야외 공연 예술 무대를 특별히 포함할 것이다. — [1] —. 또한, 그것은 미술관, 스튜디오, 그리고 교육 공간을 제공할 것이다. ¹⁶⁷카페, 서점, 그리고 유사한 사업들을 위한 상업 지역들도 임대할 수 있게 되었다. — [2] —.

Grand Prairie 문화 센터는 Grand Prairie 예술 위원회의 예술 중심의 공공장소를 개발하기 위한 장기적인 노력의 최종 결과이다. Belinda Blair 위원장은 이 프로젝트를 실현하도록 도와준 것에 대해 Wilma Brown 시장에게 공을 돌렸다. — [3] —. ¹⁶⁶그녀는 또한 프로젝트 비용을 계속 감당할 수 있게 도와준 Keystone 은행과 같은 기업들의 기부금에도 감사를 전했다. — [4] —. 이 센터는 건설하는 데 단 2년이 걸렸으며 8월 5일에 대중에게 개방한다.

former adj. 과거의 automotive adj. 자동차의 extensive adj. 광범위한
renovation n. 보수 공사, 개조 abandon v. 버리다 convert v. 개조하다
complex n. 복합 단지 feature v. 특별히 포함하다
open-air adj. 야외의, 옥외의 house v. (장소를) 제공하다, 수용하다
commercial adj. 상업의 venture n. 사업, 모험 lease n. 임대
prolonged adj. 장기적인 council n. 위원회
credit v. (공적·명예를) ~에게 돌리다 realize v. 실현하다, 인식하다
recognize v. (남의 공로에) 감사하다, 인정하다
contribution n. 기부금, 기여 manageable adj. 감당할 수 있는

165 주제 찾기 문제 중 ●●○

해석 기사는 주로 무엇에 대한 것인가?
(A) 부동산 개발 회사의 최근 프로젝트
(B) 미술관의 가장 최근 사진 전시회
(C) 청정 에너지를 홍보하기 위한 도시의 노력
(D) 공공 예술 복합 단지의 건설

해설 지문의 'the abandoned automotive parts factory ~ has been converted into a 3,000-square-meter complex'와 'The new ~ Cultural Center will feature an open-air performing arts stage'에서 버려진 자동차 부품 공장이 3,000제곱미터의 복합 단지로 개조되었고, 그 새로운 문화 센터는 야외 공연 예술 무대를 특별히 포함할 것이라고 했으므로 (D)가 정답이다.

어휘 property developer phr. 부동산 개발 회사 latest adj. 최근의, 최신의
exhibit n. 전시회, 전시품 effort n. 노력 promote v. 홍보하다
construction n. 건설

166 추론 문제 중 ●●○

해석 Ms. Blair의 프로젝트에 대해 암시되는 것은?
(A) Grand Prairie의 시장에 의해 처음 제안되었다.
(B) 대략 2년 전에 완공되었다.
(C) 몇몇 지연들이 없었다면 더 빨리 끝났을 것이다.
(D) 사기업들로부터 자금을 받았다.

해설 지문의 'She also recognized the contributions of firms like Keystone Bank, which helped to keep project costs manageable.'에서 그녀는 또한 프로젝트 비용을 계속 감당할 수 있게 도와준 Keystone 은행과 같은 기업들의 기부금에 감사를 전했다고 했으므로 Keystone 은행을 비롯해 사기업들로부터 자금을 받았다는 것을 추론할 수 있다. 따라서 (D)가 정답이다.

어휘 propose v. 제안하다 mayor n. 시장 approximately adv. 대략, 거의
delay n. 지연, 지체 funding n. 자금, 기금

패러프레이징

the contributions of firms 기업들의 기부금 → funding from private companies 사기업들로부터의 자금

167 문장 위치 찾기 문제 중 ●●○

해석 [1], [2], [3], [4]로 표시된 위치 중, 다음 문장이 들어갈 곳으로 가장 적절한 것은?
"많은 지역 사업주들이 이미 공간을 임대하는 것에 관심을 표했다."
(A) [1]
(B) [2]
(C) [3]
(D) [4]

해설 주어진 문장에서 많은 지역 사업주들은 이미 공간을 임대하는 것에 관심을 표했다고 했으므로, 이 문장이 사업을 위해 공간을 임대할 수 있다는 내용이 나오는 부분에 들어가야 함을 알 수 있다. [2]의 앞 문장인 'Commercial areas ~ have also been made available for lease.'에서 상업 지역들도 임대할 수 있게 되었다고 했으므로, [2]에 제시된 문장이 들어가면 상업 지역들을 임대할 수 있게 되었으며 많은 지역 사업주들이 이 공간에 이미 관심을 표했다는 자연스러운 문맥이 된다는 것을 알 수 있다. 따라서 (B)가 정답이다.

어휘 rent v. ~을 임대하다

168-171번은 다음 편지에 관한 문제입니다.

3월 12일

Nelly Garrison
493번지 22번가
포틀랜드, 오리건주 97246

¹⁶⁸Ms. Garrison께,

¹⁶⁸지난 금요일에 여기 Weston 고고학 연구소(WAI)의 부 큐레이터 직책을 위한 면접에 와주셔서 감사합니다. 저희는 당신의 성과에 깊은 인상을 받았고 이 자리를 당신에게 제안하고자 합니다.

^{169-A}동봉된 것은 고용 계약서입니다. ^{169-D}그것은 면접에서 논의된 임금과 제가 언급했던 복지 혜택을 포함합니다. ^{169-A}또한 포함된 것은 저희 의료보험 제공업체의 양식들입니다. 저희의 제안에 동의하신다면, 그것들을 저희 인사부에 제출하시기 전에 계약서에 서명해주시고 양식을 작성해주십시오.

¹⁷¹당신의 시작일은 4월 1일일 것입니다. 박물관의 큐레이터들 중 또 다른 한 명인 Arnold Hazelton과 함께 당신은 오리엔테이션을 거칠 것입니다. 교육 기간은 일주일 동안 계속될 것이고, 이 기간 동안 ¹⁷⁰/¹⁷¹**Mr. Hazelton이 당신이 특정 업무들을 하도록 지시할** 것입니다. 일주일 후 당신은 당신의 정규 책무를 맡게 될 것입니다. Mr. Hazelton이 당신의 첫날에 더 많은 세부 사항을 알려줄 것입니다.

3월 15일까지 답변을 받을 수 있다면 감사하겠습니다. 당신은 제게 555-3029로 전화 주실 수 있습니다.

Marsha Kent 드림
WAI 인사부장

associate adj. 부, 준 impressed adj. 깊은 인상을 받은
enclosed adj. 동봉된 employment n. 고용, 직직 contract n. 계약서
benefits package phr. 복지 혜택 insurance n. 보험
provider n. 제공업체 last v. 계속되다 direct v. 지시하다
assume v. 맡다

168 육하원칙 문제   중 ●●○

해석 Ms. Garrison은 지난주에 무엇을 했는가?
(A) 새로운 고용 계약서에 서명했다
(B) 일자리에 대해 문의하기 위해 번호로 전화했다
(C) 오리엔테이션에 참여했다
(D) 연구소에서의 구직 면접에 참석했다

해설 지문의 'Dear Ms. Garrison', 'Thank you for coming in last Friday to interview for the associate curator position here at the Weston Archeological Institute (WAI).'에서 Ms. Garrison에게 지난 금요일에 여기 Weston 고고학 연구소(WAI)의 부 큐레이터 직책을 위한 면접에 와주셔서 감사하다고 했으므로 (D)가 정답이다.

어휘 inquire v. 문의하다 attend v. 참석하다 institute n. 연구소, 기관

169 Not/True 문제   중 ●●○

해석 Weston 고고학 연구소에 대해 언급된 것은?
(A) 직원들에게 의료 혜택을 제공한다.
(B) 대행사에 채용을 위탁한다.
(C) 직원들 중 한 명을 최근에 승진시켰다.
(D) 정규직 직원들에게만 복리후생을 제공한다.

해설 지문의 'Enclosed is an employment contract.'와 'Also included are forms from our medical insurance provider.'에서 동봉된 것은 고용 계약서이며, 또한 포함된 것은 자신들, 즉 Weston 고고학 연구소의 의료보험 제공업체의 양식들이라고 했으므로 (A)는 지문의 내용과 일치한다. 따라서 (A)가 정답이다. (B)와 (C)는 지문에 언급되지 않은 내용이다. (D)는 'It includes ~ the benefits package I mentioned.'에서 그것, 즉 고용 계약서가 자신, 즉 Ms. Kent가 언급했던 복지 혜택을 포함한다고 했지 정규직 직원들에게만 복리후생을 제공하는지에 대해서는 알 수 없으므로 지문의 내용과 일치하지 않는다.

어휘 medical coverage phr. 의료 혜택
outsource v. (외부에) 위탁하다, (외부에서) 조달하다
recruitment n. 채용, 신규 모집 agency n. 대행사
promote v. 승진시키다, 홍보하다 full-time adj. 정규직의

170 동의어 찾기 문제   중 ●●○

해석 3문단 세 번째 줄의 단어 "direct"는 의미상 ~와 가장 가깝다.
(A) 적용하다
(B) 지시하다
(C) 운영하다
(D) 입증하다

해설 direct를 포함하는 구절 'Mr. Hazelton will direct you to do specific tasks'에서 Mr. Hazelton이 당신이 특정 업무들을 하도록 지시할 것이라고 했으므로 direct는 '지시하다'라는 뜻으로 사용되었다. 따라서 '지시하다'라는 뜻을 가진 (B) order가 정답이다.

171 육하원칙 문제   중 ●●○

해석 Mr. Hazelton은 4월 1일에 무엇을 할 것인가?
(A) 몇몇 구직자들을 면접 본다
(B) 직원을 교육하는 것을 시작한다
(C) 연구소의 그의 직무에서 사임한다
(D) 인사부에 몇몇 양식들을 제출한다

해설 지문의 'Your starting day would be April 1. You will go through an orientation with ~ Arnold Hazelton.'에서 당신, 즉 Mr. Garrison이 일을 시작하는 날은 4월 1일이며 Mr. Hazelton과 함께 오리엔테이션을 거칠 것이라고 했고, 'Mr. Hazelton will direct ~ to do specific tasks'에서 Mr. Hazelton이 특정 업무들을 하도록 지시할 것이라고 했으므로 교육 담당자 Mr. Hazelton이 4월 1일부터 직원을 대상으로 오리엔테이션 교육을 시작할 것임을 알 수 있다. 따라서 (B)가 정답이다.

어휘 job applicant phr. 구직자 resign v. 사임하다, 그만두다
duty n. 직무, 의무 hand in phr. 제출하다

172-175번은 다음 이메일에 관한 문제입니다.

수신: Christian Lanzotti <c.lanzotti@eline.com>
발신: David Wendt <d.wendt@obsatron.com>
날짜: 2월 7일
제목: 문의

¹⁷²⁻ᴰMr. Lanzotti께,

¹⁷²⁻ᶜ당신의 Obsatron 가정 보안 시스템을 설치하는 것에 대해 ¹⁷²⁻ᴰ이번 주 초에 저희에게 연락해 주셔서 감사합니다. 우선, 상치의 키패드에 당신의 마스터 코드를 입력하여 시스템의 관리 제어에 접속하십시오. 초기 설정 코드는 1234입니다. ¹⁷⁵당신은 이것을 6자리 숫자로 변경해야 합니다. ─ [1] ─.

당신이 새로운 코드를 입력하고 나면, 당신은 시스템을 활성화할 수 있고 가족 구성원들에게 추가적인 접근 권한을 배정할 수 있습니다. ─ [2] ─. 활성화되었을 때, ¹⁷³⁻ᴬ시스템은 열린 문을 감지하면 30초 이내에 경보음을 낼 것입니다. ¹⁷³⁻ᶜ경보음을 멈추기 위해서는 올바른 코드가 입력되어야 합니다. ─ [3] ─. 그렇지 않으면, 저희는 통지를 받을 것이고 집에 있는 당신에게 연락하려고 시도할 것입니다. 이것이 ¹⁷⁴당신이 당신의 연락처 정보를 최신으로 유지해야 하는 이유입니다. 만약 저희가 당신의 안전을 확인할 수 없다면, 저희는 긴급 지원을 보낼 것입니다. ─ [4] ─.

추가적인 질문이 있으시면 Obsatron사 고객 지원팀에 555-9987로 전화해 주십시오.

David Wendt 드림
Obsatron사 고객 지원 관리자

---

set up phr. 설치하다 access v. 접속하다, 접근하다; n. 접근 권한
administrative adj. 관리의 default n. 초기 설정, 채무 불이행
input v. 입력하다 activate v. 활성화하다 emit v. (소리를) 내다
detect v. 감지하다, 발견하다 attempt v. 시도하다
reach v. 연락하다, 도달하다 up-to-date adj. 최신의
verify v. 확인하다, 입증하다 dispatch v. 보내다, 파견하다

172 Not/True 문제 중 ●●○

해석 Obsatron사에 대해 언급된 것은?
(A) 그것의 시스템 중 일부를 위해 소프트웨어를 교체했다.
(B) 최근에 Mr. Lanzotti로부터 연락을 받았다.
(C) 기업 고객들을 위한 보안을 전문으로 한다.
(D) 고객 지원을 위한 전화번호를 바꿨다.

해설 지문의 'Dear Mr. Lanzotti', 'Thank you for calling us earlier this week'에서 Mr. Lanzotti에게 이번 주 초에 연락해 주어서 감사하다고 했으므로 (B)는 지문의 내용과 일치한다. 따라서 (B)가 정답이다. (A)와 (D)는 지문에 언급되지 않은 내용이다. (C)는 'setting up your Obsatron home security system'에서 Obsatron사 가정 보안 시스템을 설치하는 것이라고 했으므로 지문의 내용과 일치하지 않는다.

어휘 replace v. 교체하다, 대체하다 specialize v. 전문으로 하다
corporate adj. 기업의

173 Not/True 문제 중 ●●○

해석 경보음에 대해 언급된 것은?
(A) 큰 소리를 일으키기 전에 1분 동안 대기할 것이다.
(B) 음량을 줄이도록 조정될 수 있다.
(C) 확인이 제공되기 전까지 계속 켜져 있을 것이다.
(D) 제어판 옆에 위치해 있다.

해설 지문의 'A correct code must be entered to stop the alarm.'에서 경보음을 멈추기 위해서는 올바른 코드가 입력되어야 한다고 했으므로 (C)는 지문의 내용과 일치한다. 따라서 (C)가 정답이다. (A)는 'the system will emit an alarm within 30 seconds of detecting an open door'에서 시스템은 열린 문을 감지하면 30초 이내에 경보음을 낼 것이라고 했으므로 지문의 내용과 일치하지 않는다. (B)와 (D)는 지문에 언급되지 않은 내용이다.

어휘 trigger v. 일으키다, 촉발하다; n. 계기 modify v. 조정하다
reduce v. 줄이다, 낮추다 stay on phr. 계속 켜져 있다, 계속 하다

패러프레이징

A correct code must be entered to stop 멈추기 위해서는 올바른 코드가 입력되어야 한다 → stay on until confirmation is provided 확인이 제공되기 전까지 계속 켜져 있다

174 육하원칙 문제 중 ●●○

해석 Mr. Lanzotti는 무엇을 하라고 권고되는가?
(A) 필요한 경우 그의 연락처 정보를 업데이트한다
(B) 긴급 전화번호로 즉시 전화한다
(C) 보안 시스템의 키패드를 교체한다
(D) 몇몇 중요한 보안 절차를 익힌다

해설 지문의 'you must keep your contact information up-to-date'에서 당신이 당신의 연락처 정보를 최신으로 유지해야 한다고 했으므로 (A)가 정답이다.

어휘 immediately adv. 즉시, 즉각적으로 procedure n. 절차

패러프레이징

keep ~ contact information up-to-date 연락처 정보를 최신으로 유지하다
→ Update ~ contact information 연락처 정보를 업데이트하다

175 문장 위치 찾기 문제 중 ●●○

해석 [1], [2], [3], [4]로 표시된 위치 중, 다음 문장이 들어갈 곳으로 가장 적절한 것은?

"다른 이들이 추측하기 쉬운 것은 피하십시오."

(A) [1]
(B) [2]
(C) [3]
(D) [4]

해설 주어진 문장에서 다른 이들이 추측하기 쉬운 것은 피하라고 했으므로, 이 문장이 다른 이들이 추측하기 어려운 것을 설정하는 것과 관련된 내용이 나오는 부분에 들어가야 함을 알 수 있다. [1]의 앞 문장인 'You must change this to a six-digit number.'에서 당신은 이것, 즉 초기 설정 코드를 6자리 숫자로 변경해야 한다고 했으므로, [1]에 제시된 문장이 들어가면 초기 설정 코드를 6자리 숫자로 변경해야 하며, 다른 이들이 추측하기 쉬운 것은 피해야 한다는 자연스러운 문맥이 된다는 것을 알 수 있다. 따라서 (A)가 정답이다.

어휘 avoid v. 피하다, 방지하다 guess v. 추측하다, 짐작하다

176-180번은 다음 일정표와 온라인 후기에 관한 문제입니다.

Geocrab의 다가오는 공연들

8월 27일	Carson City, 네바다	– Lakeview 음악홀	티켓 구매 (취소됨)
8월 29일	Folsom, 캘리포니아	– Drake 강당	티켓 구매
180 8월 30일	180 Stockton, 캘리포니아	180 Terry Benson 콘서트 센터	티켓 구매 (매진)
9월-10월	*밴드는 다섯 번째 스튜디오 앨범을 녹음하기 위해 투어로부터 휴식을 가질 것임.*		
11월 15일	Fairfield, 캘리포니아	– 177 Mooncastle 라운지	177 초대된 손님들을 위한 비공개 파티
176-A 11월 20일	Santa Rosa, 캘리포니아	– Whiteout 음반 가게	176-A 선착순 100명 무료입장

upcoming adj. 다가오는, 곧 있을 auditorium n. 강당
take some time off phr. 휴식을 갖다 admittance n. 입장, 허가

---

www.newmusicreviews.com

밴드 이름: Geocrab
앨범 제목: *Indelible Ink*

최근 활동에서, 록 밴드 Geocrab은 단순한 키보드 멜로디와 시끄러운 드럼과 같은 그것의 친숙한 소리로 돌아갔습니다. 그룹의 처음 세 앨범들의 팬들은 확실히 *Indelible Ink*를 좋아할 것이지만, 178 Geocrab의 실험적인 네 번째 앨범과 같은 것을 기대하는 사람들은 실망할 수도 있습니다.

*Indelible Ink*는 179-A/B 리드 보컬로서 Ellen Banbury를 대신한 Donna Redmond를 포함하는 밴드의 첫 번째 발매 음반입니다. 앨범 전반에 걸쳐 Redmond의 노래는 훌륭하며, 그녀는 또한 17곡의 노래 중 5곡을 작곡했습니다. 179-C/D 키보드 연주자 Michael Wilkinson과 드럼 연주자 Wendy

Palmer가 나머지 곡들을 작곡했습니다. 65분의 길이를 가진 *Indelible Ink*는 조금 많이 길게 느껴집니다. 몇몇 곡들은 생략될 수도 있었을 것입니다.

다섯 번째 앨범은 음악적으로 특별히 모험적이지 않지만, Geocrab은 *Indelible Ink*를 Takashi 온라인 상점에서 구매할 수 있게 하면서, 마케팅에 관해 새로운 것을 시도하기로 결정했습니다. ¹⁸⁰앨범의 디지털 버전을 구매하는 사람들은 Stockton의 Terry Benson 콘서트 센터에서 라이브로 녹음된 보너스 곡을 즐길 수 있습니다.

Veronica Meyberg 작성

---

effort n. 활동, 노력 **let down** phr. 실망시키다 **release** n. 발매 음반, 발표 **terrific** adj. 훌륭한, 좋은 **track** n. (음반테이프에 녹음된 음악) 한 곡 **omit** v. 생략하다, 빼다 **especially** adv. 특별히, 유난히 **adventurous** adj. 모험적인 **in terms of** phr. ~에 관하여

176 Not/True 문제   상 ●●●

해석 Geocrab에 대해 언급된 것은?
(A) 몇몇 공연 참석자들에게 요금을 청구하지 않을 것이다.
(B) 11월에 뮤직비디오를 공개할 것이다.
(C) 콘서트들에서 물품을 판매한다.
(D) 팬들로부터 노래 요청을 받는다.

해설 일정표의 'November 20', 'Free Admittance for First 100 People Who Arrive'에서 11월 20일 공연은 선착순 100명이 무료입장이라고 했으므로 (A)는 지문의 내용과 일치한다. 따라서 (A)가 정답이다. (B), (C), (D)는 지문에 언급되지 않은 내용이다.

어휘 **charge** v. (요금·값을) 청구하다 **attendee** n. 참석자
merchandise n. 물품, 상품

패러프레이징

Free admittance 무료입장 → will not charge ~ attendees 참석자들에게 요금을 청구하지 않을 것이다

177 육하원칙 문제   중 ●●○

해석 일정표에 따르면, 어떤 장소가 초청객 전용 행사를 열 것인가?
(A) Drake 강당
(B) Terry Benson 콘서트 센터
(C) Mooncastle 라운지
(D) Whiteout 음반 가게

해설 일정표의 'Mooncastle Lounge', 'Private Party for Invited Guests'에서 Mooncastle 라운지의 공연은 초대된 손님들을 위한 비공개 파티라고 했으므로 초청객 전용 행사가 Mooncastle 라운지에서 열린다는 것을 알 수 있다. 따라서 (C)가 정답이다.

어휘 **venue** n. 장소 **host** v. 열다, 주최하다

178 동의어 찾기 문제   중 ●●○

해석 온라인 후기에서, 1문단 두 번째 줄의 단어 "expecting"은 의미상 –와 가장 가깝다.
(A) 제시하는
(B) 심사숙고하는
(C) 고려하는
(D) 기대하는

해설 후기의 expecting을 포함한 구절 'those expecting something like

Geocrab's experimental fourth album'에서 Geocrab의 실험적인 네 번째 앨범과 같은 것을 기대하는 사람들이라고 했으므로 expecting은 '기대하다'라는 뜻으로 사용되었다. 따라서 '기대하다'라는 뜻을 가진 (D) anticipating이 정답이다.

179 Not/True 문제   중 ●●○

해석 누가 현재 Geocrab의 멤버가 아닌가?
(A) Donna Redmond
(B) Ellen Banbury
(C) Michael Wilkinson
(D) Wendy Palmer

해설 질문의 member of Geocrab과 관련된 내용이 언급된 온라인 후기의 'Donna Redmond, who replaced Ellen Banbury as the lead singer'에서 리드 보컬로서 Ellen Banbury를 Donna Redmond가 대신했다고 했으므로 (B)는 지문의 내용과 일치하지 않는다. 따라서 (B)가 정답이다. (A)는 'Donna Redmond, who replaced ~ as the lead singer'에서 Donna Redmond가 리드 보컬로서 대신했다고 했으므로 지문의 내용과 일치한다. (C)와 (D)는 'Keyboardist Michael Wilkinson and drummer Wendy Palmer'에서 Michael Wilkinson이 키보드 연주자이고 Wendy Palmer가 드럼 연주자라고 했으므로 지문의 내용과 일치한다.

최고난도 문제

180 추론 문제 연계   상 ●●●

해석 *Indelible Ink*의 디지털 버전에 대해 추론될 수 있는 것은?
(A) 초대 예술가들의 작품들을 포함한다.
(B) 여러 음악 서비스들에 의해 판매된다.
(C) 음악회에 자주 가는 사람들에게 무료로 주어질 것이다.
(D) 8월 30일에 녹음된 곡을 포함한다.

해설 온라인 후기의 'Those who purchase the digital version of the album can enjoy a bonus track that was recorded live at the Terry Benson Concert Center in Stockton.'에서 앨범의 디지털 버전을 구매하는 사람들은 Stockton의 Terry Benson 콘서트 센터에서 라이브로 녹음된 보너스 곡을 즐길 수 있다고 했다. 또한, 일정표의 'August 30', 'Stockton, California', 'Terry Benson Concert Center'에서는 캘리포니아 Stockton의 Terry Benson 콘서트 센터에서 8월 30일에 공연이 있었다는 사실을 확인할 수 있다.
두 단서를 종합할 때, *Indelible Ink*의 디지털 버전은 8월 30일에 녹음된 곡을 포함한다는 사실을 추론할 수 있다. 따라서 (D)가 정답이다.

어휘 **feature** v. (특별히) 포함하다 **multiple** adj. 여러, 다양한
concertgoer n. 음악회에 자주 가는 사람

181-185번은 다음 광고와 양식에 관한 문제입니다.

Glisten 요금제 가격 책정

모두 완전히 공공의 재생이 허가된 ¹⁸¹높은 품질의 배경 음악을 몇 시간에 걸쳐 다수의 소매점에서 스트리밍하세요! 용이한 월간 결제 또는 더 큰 절약된 금액을 위한 일시불의 연회비를 선택하세요.

^{182-B/C/184-A/C}Glisten 비트	^{182-D}Glisten 리듬	^{182-D/183}Glisten 하모니
장소당 ^{184-A}한 달에 9.99달러 또는 일 년에 100달러	장소당 한 달에 15.99달러 또는 일 년에 150달러 ^{182-A}15일 무료 체험 포함	장소당 ¹⁸³한 달에 24.99달러 또는 일 년에 250달러 ^{182-A}30일 무료 체험 포함

| 182-A/184-C 5일 무료 체험 포함

· 182-B여러 맞춤 라디오 방송국들 중에서 선택하거나 182-C당신만의 재생 목록을 만드세요

· 당신의 모바일 기기에서 청취 경험을 관리하세요 | 182-DGlisten 비트 패키지의 모든 특징들

· 당신의 마케팅 활동을 지원하기 위한 오디오 광고를 제작할 수 있음

· 각 지역 또는 상점마다 음악을 주문 제작하세요 | 182-DGlisten 리듬 패키지의 모든 특징들

· 183당신의 브랜드를 홍보하는 재생 목록을 제작하는 음악 전문가 이용

· 182-D당신의 손님들이 저희의 스마트폰 애플리케이션을 사용해 음악을 신청하게 할 수 있도록 하세요 |

181/184-B만약 당신이 다섯 지점들 이상 운영한다면, 맞춤형 요금제를 만들어내기 위해 555-3092로 저희에게 연락해 주십시오.

plan n. 요금제 pricing n. 가격 책정 license v. 허가하다
playback n. (녹음한 테이프·레코드 따위의) 재생 savings n. 절약된 금액
trial n. 체험, 시험 custom adj. 맞춤의 customize v. 주문 제작하다
access n. 이용, 접근 in support of phr. ~을 홍보하는, 지지하여
operate v. 운영하다, 작동하다

GLISTEN
www.glisten.com

184-B회사: Coax 의류사	웹사이트 (선택적):
주소: 1228번지 Willow Wood로 허바드, 오하이오주 44425	www.coaxclothing.com 직책: 마케팅부장
185연락처: Andy Lewis 이메일: a.lewis@mailbot.com	전화: 555-9946

184-A/B/C선호하는 요금제:

☒ 184-A/B/CGlisten 비트   ☐ Glisten 리듬   ☐ Glisten 하모니

185당신의 체험 기간은 신청 절차 완료 시 시작됩니다.

184-A지불 계획:

☐ 일시불   ☒ 184-A매월

제출을 클릭하면 결제 화면으로 이동합니다. 당신의 신용카드를 준비하십시오.

185당신의 이메일에서 확정 메시지를 확인하세요. 저희의 환불 정책 및 다른 약관을 보시려면, 여기를 클릭하세요.   [재설정]   [제출]

completion n. 완료, 성취 scheme n. 계획, 책략
confirmation n. 확정, 확인 terms and conditions phr. 약관, 조건

---

181 추론 문제   중 ●●●○

해석 광고는 누구를 대상으로 하는 것 같은가?
(A) 전문 음악가들
(B) 소프트웨어 프로그래머들
(C) 녹음 기술자들
(D) 상점 소유주들

해설 광고의 'Stream hours of high-quality background music at multiple retail locations'에서 높은 품질의 배경 음악을 몇 시간에 걸쳐 다수의 소매점에서 스트리밍하라고 했고, 'If you operate more than 5 locations, please contact us ~ to develop a customized plan.'에서 만약 다섯 지점들 이상 운영한다면, 맞춤형 요금제를 만들어내기 위해 연락해 달라고 했으므로 상점 소유주들을 대상으로 하는 광고임을 추론할 수 있다. 따라서 (D)가 정답이다.

어휘 technician n. 기술자 owner n. 소유주

182 Not/True 문제   중 ●●●○

해석 모든 요금제에 포함되지 않은 것은?
(A) 무료 체험
(B) 라디오 방송국
(C) 맞춤형 재생 목록
(D) 손님 접속

해설 질문의 payment plan과 관련된 내용이 언급된 광고의 'Glisten Rhythm', 'All features of the Glisten Beat package', 'Glisten Harmony', 'All features of the Glisten Rhythm package'에서 Glisten 리듬은 Glisten 비트 패키지의 모든 특징을 포함하며 Glisten 하모니는 Glisten 리듬 패키지의 모든 특징을 포함한다고 했다. 또한 'Glisten Harmony', 'Allow your guests to request music using our smartphone application'에서 Glisten 하모니 요금제만 손님들이 스마트폰 애플리케이션을 사용해서 음악을 신청하게 할 수 있다고 했으므로 (D)는 지문의 내용과 일치하지 않는다. 따라서 (D)가 정답이다. (A)는 '5-day free trial', '15-day free trial', '30-day free trial'에서 모든 요금제에 무료 체험이 포함된다는 것을 알 수 있으므로 지문의 내용과 일치한다. (B)는 'Glisten Beat', 'Choose from several custom radio stations'에서 Glisten 비트 요금제에 여러 맞춤 라디오 방송국들 중에서 선택하는 것이 포함되어 있으므로 지문의 내용과 일치한다. (C)는 'Glisten Beat', 'create your own playlists'에서 Glisten 비트 요금제에 당신만의 재생 목록을 만드는 것이 포함되어 있으므로 지문의 내용과 일치한다.

패러프레이징

your own playlists 당신만의 재생 목록 → Custom playlists 맞춤형 재생 목록

183 육하원칙 문제   중 ●●●○

해석 가장 비싼 지불 요금제의 사용자들은 무엇을 할 수 있는가?
(A) 영상 광고를 방송한다
(B) 소셜 미디어를 통해 메시지를 보낸다
(C) 음악 선정에 전문가의 도움을 받는다
(D) 추가적인 할인을 이용한다

해설 광고의 'Glisten Harmony', '$24.99 a month or $250 a year', 'Access to music experts who create playlists in support of your brand'에서 Glisten 하모니가 한 달에 24.99달러 혹은 일 년에 250달러를 지불하는 가장 비싼 지불 요금제이며 당신의 브랜드를 홍보하는 재생 목록을 제작하는 음악 전문가를 이용할 수 있다고 했으므로 음악 선정에 전문가의 도움을 받을 수 있다는 것을 알 수 있다. 따라서 (C)가 정답이다.

어휘 broadcast v. 방송하다, 광고하다
take advantage of phr. ~을 이용하다, 활용하다

184 Not/True 문제 연계   상 ●●●

해석 Coax 의류사에 대해 언급된 것은?
(A) 일 년에 100달러를 지불할 것이다.
(B) 다섯 지점들보다 적다.
(C) 그것의 체험 기간은 한 달 후에 만료된다.
(D) 그것의 첫 지불은 5일 이내로 해야 한다.

해설 양식의 'Company: Coax Clothing', 'Preferred Plan: Glisten Beat'에서 Coax 의류사가 선호하는 요금제는 Glisten 비트임을 알 수 있다. 또한, 광고의 'If you operate 5 or more locations, please contact us ~ to develop a customized plan.'에서는 만약 당신이 다섯 지점들 이상을

운영한다면, 맞춤형 요금제를 만들어 내기 위해 연락해 달라고 한 사실을 확인할 수 있다.

두 단서를 종합할 때, Coax 의류사는 맞춤형 요금제가 아닌 Glisten 비트를 선택했기 때문에 다섯 지점보다 적은 곳을 운영한다는 것을 알 수 있으므로 (B)가 정답이다. (A)는 양식의 'Preferred Plan: Glisten Beat', 'Payment Scheme: Monthly'와 광고의 'Glisten Beat', '$9.99 a month'에서 Coax 의류사가 선호하는 요금제인 Glisten 비트를 매월 9.99 달러를 지불하여 사용할 것임을 알 수 있으므로 지문의 내용과 일치하지 않는다. (C)는 양식의 'Preferred Plan: Glisten Beat'와 광고의 'Glisten Beat', 'Includes a 5-day free trial'에서 Coax 의류사가 선호하는 요금제인 Glisten 비트는 무료 체험 기간이 5일이므로 지문의 내용과 일치하지 않는다. (D)는 지문에 언급되지 않은 내용이다.

어휘 expire v. 만료되다, 끝나다 due adj. (돈을) 지불해야 하는, ~하기로 예정된

185 육하원칙 문제 　　　　中 ●●○

해석 Mr. Lewis는 왜 그의 이메일을 확인해야 하는가?
(A) 약관을 읽기 위해
(B) 그의 신청을 확인하기 위해
(C) 그의 월별 청구서를 받기 위해
(D) 영수증 사본을 받기 위해

해설 양식의 'Contact: Andy Lewis', 'Your trial period begins upon completion of the application process.'와 'Please check your e-mail for a confirmation message.'에서 Mr. Lewis에게 당신의 체험 기간은 신청 절차 완료시 시작되며 이메일에서 확정 메시지를 확인하라고 했으므로 Mr. Lewis는 신청을 확인하기 위해서 그의 이메일을 확인해야 한다는 것을 알 수 있다. 따라서 (B)가 정답이다.

어휘 verify v. 확인하다, 증명하다 registration n. 신청(서), 등록
invoice n. 청구서, 송장 obtain v. 받다, 얻다

186-190번은 다음 이메일, 웹페이지, 송장에 관한 문제입니다.

수신: Philby Ogier <ogierp@tideteller.com>
발신: Monica Seibert <seibertm@tideteller.com>
날짜: 2월 2일
제목: 내일 마감인 보고서

Philby께,

186-ADagga 음반 회사 보고서 중 당신의 부분이 제가 오늘 아침에 도착했을 때 제 책상 위에 있었습니다. 186-B저는 당신이 마감기한인 2월 3일 전에 그것을 완료한 것은 높이 평가하지만, 187일부 글과 도표들이 흐릿합니다. 당신의 작업물을 제대로 평가하고 당신에게 피드백을 제공하기 위해서, 저는 당신이 제게 새로운 한 부를 가져오길 바랍니다. 188저는 또한 당신이 사용한 Artz Widget 3 프린터에 무슨 문제가 있는지 파악해주면 좋겠습니다. 만약 수리공을 불러야 한다면, 이것은 최대한 빨리 이뤄져야 합니다.

감사합니다,

Monica Seibert 드림
시장 조사 분석가
Tide Teller사

due adj. 마감인 appreciate v. 높이 평가하다, 감사하다
deadline n. 마감기한 blurry adj. 흐릿한, 모호한 assess v. 평가하다
repairperson n. 수리공 call in phr. (전문가를) 부르다, 전화를 하다
analyst n. 분석가

---

www.artzelectronics.com/technicalsupport/widget3

공통적인 문제들

고객들에 의해 보고된 바와 같이, 187/188-AArtz Widget 3 프린터의 가장 흔한 문제들은 다음과 같습니다:

문제 1. 각 출력된 페이지의 상단이 번진다.
187문제 2. 출력된 내용이 선명도가 부족하여, 그것을 읽기 어렵게 만든다.
문제 3. 페이지들에 문서의 몇몇 부분들을 가리는 선들이 포함되어 있다.
문제 4. 문서의 몇몇 페이지들이 출력되지 않는다.

188-A이러한 모든 문제들의 원인은 (a.) CST3 타입이 아닌 잘못된 카트리지가 사용된 것, (b.) X78 부품이 청소되어야 하는 것, (c.) RS2 부품이 닳은 것, 또는 (d.) 189TX98 부품에 결함이 있는 것일 수 있습니다. 188-C/189결함이 있는 부품이 문제라면, Artz사는 무료 교체품을 제공할 것입니다.

진단 테스트를 수행하는 방법에 대한 안내를 위해서는, 여기를 클릭하세요.

issue n. 문제 smudge v. 번지다, 더러워지다 lack v. 부족하다
clarity n. 선명도 cause n. 원인, 이유 component n. 부품, 요소
wear out phr. 닳다, 낡게 하다 defective adj. 결함이 있는
replacement n. 교체(품), 후임자 diagnostic adj. 진단의

발신:		수신:
Artz Electronics사		189Beth Kaczka
2020번지 동부 산업단지,		81번지 Tyler Hill로, Blean,
커르잘리, 불가리아 6600		캔터베리, 영국 CT2 9HP

개수	설명	비용
1	189교체 부품	0.00유로
	소계:	0.00유로
	배송과 취급 수수료:	15.22유로
	총액:	15.22유로*
	189지불 금액:	00.00유로

*Artz Electronics사에 의해 지불됨

저희 제품들은 깨지기 쉽기 때문에, 저희는 저희가 보내는 각 물품을 보호하기 위해 Foam-It-All 포장용 포장지를 사용합니다. 하지만, 190만약 당신의 주문이 완전히 온전하게 도착하지 않는다면, 저희 고객 서비스 부서에 555-4578로 전화하세요. 저희의 직원들 중 한 명이 당신에게 처리 방법을 알려드릴 것입니다.

unit n. (제품 등의) 개수, 단위 description n. 설명, 묘사
subtotal n. 소계 handling n. 취급 수수료, 조작
fragile adj. 깨시기 쉬운, 약한 intact adj. 본선안, 손상되지 않은
proceed v. 처리하다, 진행하다

186 Not/True 문제 　　　　中 ●●○

해석 Mr. Ogier에 대해 언급된 것은?
(A) 음반 회사에 근무한다.
(B) 업무를 일찍 완료했다.
(C) 새로운 기기를 주문했다.
(D) 중요한 고객에게 연락했다.

해설 이메일의 'I appreciate that you completed it before the deadline of February 3'에서 저는 당신이 마감기한인 2월 3일 전에 그것, 즉 보고서를 완료한 것은 높이 평가한다고 했으므로 (B)는 지문의 내용과 일치한다. 따라서 (B)가 정답이다. (A)는 'Your section of the report for Dagga Music

Agency'에서 당신, 즉 Mr. Ogier가 Tide Teller사에서 일하며 Dagga 음반 회사에 관한 보고서를 작성했다고는 했으나 음반 회사에서 근무한다는 것은 언급되지 않았으므로 지문의 내용과 일치하지 않는다. (C)와 (D)는 지문에 언급되지 않은 내용이다.

어휘　task n. 업무, 작업　client n. 고객

패러프레이징

completed ~ before the deadline 마감 기한 전에 완료했다 → completed ~ early 일찍 완료했다

187　육하원칙 문제 연계　　　상 ●●●

해석　Mr. Ogier는 어떤 문제에 부딪혔는가?
(A) 문제 1
(B) 문제 2
(C) 문제 3
(D) 문제 4

해설　이메일의 'some of the text and charts are blurry', 'I'd ~ like you to find out what's wrong with the printer you used—the Artz Widget 3'에서 일부 글과 도표들이 흐릿하며 당신, 즉 Mr. Ogier가 사용한 Artz Widget 3 프린터에 무슨 문제가 있는지 파악해달라고 했다. 또한, 웹페이지의 'The ~ problems with the Artz Widget 3 printer', 'Issue 2. Printed content lacks clarity, making it hard to read.'에서는 Artz Widget 3 프린터의 문제 중 문제 2가 출력된 내용이 선명도가 부족하여 읽기 어렵게 만든다는 것임을 확인할 수 있다.
두 단서를 종합할 때, Mr. Ogier가 사용한 Artz Widget 3 프린터에 일부 글과 차트들이 흐릿하여 읽기 어려운 문제 2가 발생했다는 것을 알 수 있다. 따라서 (B)가 정답이다.

어휘　encounter v. 부딪히다, 마주하다

최고난도 문제

188　Not/True 문제　　　상 ●●●

해석　웹페이지에 따르면, Artz Widget 3 프린터에 대해 사실인 것은?
(A) 단 한 가지 타입의 카트리지와 호환된다.
(B) 다른 모델들보다 더 많은 기술적인 문제들을 갖고 있다.
(C) 여러 교체 부품들과 함께 판매된다.
(D) 월 단위로 청소를 필요로 한다.

해설　웹페이지의 'The most common problems with the Artz Widget 3 printer'와 'The cause of any of these issues may be that an incorrect cartridge was used instead of Type CST3'에서 Artz Widget 3 프린터의 가장 흔한 문제들의 원인 중 하나로 CST3 타입이 아닌 잘못된 카트리지가 사용된 경우가 있다고 했으므로 (A)는 지문의 내용과 일치한다. 따라서 (A)가 정답이다. (B)와 (D)는 지문에 언급되지 않은 내용이다. (C)는 'If a defective part is the issue, Artz will provide a free replacement.'에서 결함이 있는 부품이 문제라면, Artz사는 무료 교체품을 제공할 것이라고 했으므로 지문의 내용과 일치하지 않는다.

어휘　be compatible with phr. ~과 호환되다　basis n. 단위, 기초

최고난도 문제

189　추론 문제 연계　　　상 ●●●

해석　Ms. Kaczka는 어떤 제품을 받았을 것 같은가?
(A) CST3 타입

(B) X78 부품
(C) RS2 부품
(D) TX98 부품

해설　송장의 'Beth Kaczka', 'Replacement part', 'Amount Due', '€00.00'에서 Ms. Kaczka가 교체 부품을 무료로 받았다는 것을 알 수 있다. 또한, 웹페이지의 'Part TX98 is defective. If a defective part is the issue, Artz will provide a free replacement.'에서는 TX98 부품에 결함이 있는 경우, Artz사에서 무료 교체품을 제공할 것이라는 사실을 확인할 수 있다. 두 단서를 종합할 때, Ms. Kaczka는 TX98 부품을 받았다는 사실을 추론할 수 있다. 따라서 (D)가 정답이다.

190　추론 문제　　　중 ●●○

해석　송장에 따르면, 누군가는 왜 고객 서비스 부서에 전화할 것 같은가?
(A) 배달 선호도를 변경하기 위해
(B) 회원제에 등록하기 위해
(C) 몇몇 배송 손상을 알리기 위해
(D) 사용 설명서를 요청하기 위해

해설　송장의 'If ~ your order does not arrive fully intact, call our customer service department'에서 만약 당신의 주문이 완전히 온전하게 도착하지 않는다면, 자신들의 고객 서비스 부서에 전화하라고 했으므로 누군가는 배송 손상을 알리기 위해 고객 서비스 부서에 전화할 것이라는 사실을 추론할 수 있다. 따라서 (C)가 정답이다.

어휘　preference n. 선호(도), 애호　sign up for phr. ~에 등록하다
instruction manual phr. 사용 설명서

191-195번은 다음 프로그램, 이메일, 환불 정책에 관한 문제입니다.

191-C직무 교육에서의 혁신
목요일, 191-C9월 8일
Randolph홀, Otis 대학교

오후 4시	191-A참가자들을 위한 인적 네트워크 형성 행사
오후 4시 30분	Ellis 연구소의 교육 책임자 Diane Riggs의 소개 연설
오후 4시 45분	191-B오스트리아 Graz 대학교의 심리학 교수이자 *Open Pathways to Learning*의 저자 Dr. Samuel Limanto의 특별 발표
오후 5시 30분	191-D다과를 위한 30분 휴식 시간
오후 6시	192우리의 주요 연사들인 Melbourne 대학의 Dr. Harriet Keach와 Amsterdam 기술 대학의 Dr. Lawrence Hillburger의 한 시간짜리 포럼

*Open Pathways to Learning*의 자필 서명본이 행사에서 참가자들에게 무료로 배부될 것입니다. Ellis 연구소의 Joan Adams에게 555-0231로 연락하여 25달러에 당신의 티켓을 예약하세요. 한정된 좌석이 이용 가능합니다.

innovation n. 혁신　networking n. 인적 네트워크 형성
participant n. 참가자　introductory adj. 소개의, 서두의
remark n. 연설, 말　feature n. 특별, 특집 ; v. 특별히 포함하다
psychology n. 심리학　refreshment n. 다과　distribute v. 배부하다

수신: Joan Adams <j.adams@ellisinstitute.org>
발신: Lester Wells <l.wells@kimball.com>
제목: 직무 교육에서의 혁신

날짜: 8월 22일

Ms. Adams께,

저는 ¹⁹³제가 9월 8일의 세미나에 예정대로 **참석할 수 없을 것임**을 당신에게 알려드리게 되어 유감입니다. 저희 부서의 책임자가 같은 날에 긴급회의를 공지하였습니다. 추후의 행사에 제가 참석할 수 있을지 알 수 없습니다. 저는 또한 제 자리를 대신할 누군가를 찾을 수 없습니다. 따라서, 안타깝게도 저는 취소할 수밖에 없을 것 같습니다.

정말 유감입니다. ¹⁹²저는 Melbourne 대학의 제 예전 동료를 다시 보는 것에 특히 관심이 있었습니다. 어쨌든, 어떻게 진행하면 되는지 또는 당신이 제 지불 정보가 필요한지 제게 알려주십시오.

감사합니다,

Lester Wells 드림
심리학부
Kimball 대학교

inform v. 알리다 attend v. 참석하다 head n. 책임자
department n. 부서, 학과 announce v. 알리다 urgent adj. 긴급한
colleague n. 동료 proceed v. 진행하다

환불 및 취소 정책

· Ellis 연구소는 저조한 등록, 연사 취소, 그리고 다른 상황들로 인해 행사를 취소할 권리가 있습니다.

· 세미나가 취소되는 경우, 당신은 전액 환불을 받을 것입니다. ¹⁹⁴그것이 연기되는 경우, 당신은 환불을 받는 것 또는 추후 행사로 당신의 등록을 변경하는 것의 선택권을 가질 것입니다.

· 만약 당신이 참석을 취소하기를 원할 경우, 최소한 행사 5일 전에 서면으로 저희에게 알리면 당신은 당신의 티켓 비용을 환불받게 될 것입니다. 10달러의 취소 수수료가 있다는 것을 유의하기 바랍니다. ¹⁹⁵아니면 그 대신에, 당신은 당신을 대신할 사람을 서면으로 지명하거나 취소하기로 선택한 행사의 6개월 후까지 동일한 티켓을 또 다른 행사에 사용할 수 있습니다.

· 오직 편지, 팩스, 또는 이메일으로만 ¹⁹³취소 요청을 보내세요. ¹⁹³지불에 사용된 신용카드는 예정된 행사 날짜로부터 영업일 기준 15일 이내에 환불될 것입니다.

refund n. 환불 cancellation n. 취소 policy n. 정책
reserve v. (어떤 권한 등이) 있다, 예약하다 enrollment n. 등록
circumstance n. 상황, 환경 postpone v. 연기하다 registration n. 등록
attendance n. 참석 notify v. 알리다 fee n. 수수료
alternatively adv. 아니면 그 대신에 nominate v. 지명하다, 임명하다

191 Not/True 문제   중 ●●○

해석 "직무 교육에서의 혁신"에 대해 언급된 것은?
(A) 사회적 교류를 위한 시간을 포함할 것이다.
(B) 책을 출간한 여러 작가들을 특별히 포함할 것이다.
(C) 이틀의 기간 동안 개최될 것이다.
(D) 한 시간의 식사 시간을 가질 것이다.

해설 프로그램의 'Networking event for participants'에서 참가자들을 위한 인적 네트워크 형성 행사가 있다고 했으므로 (A)는 지문의 내용과 일치한다. 따라서 (A)가 정답이다. (B)는 'Feature presentation by Dr. Samuel Limanto, ~ author of *Open Pathways to Learning*'에서 *Open Pathways to Learning*의 저자 Dr. Samuel Limanto 단 한 명의 특별

발표가 있다는 것을 알 수 있으므로 지문의 내용과 일치하지 않는다. (C)는 'Innovations in Job Training', 'September 8'에서 직무교육에서의 혁신이 9월 8일에 개최된다고 했으므로 지문의 내용과 일치하지 않는다. (D)는 'Half-hour break for refreshments'에서 다과를 위한 30분 휴식 시간이 있다고 했으므로 지문의 내용과 일치하지 않는다.

어휘 social adj. 사회적인 interaction n. 교류, 상호작용
publish v. 출간하다, 출판하다 take place phr. 개최되다, 일어나다

패러프레이징

Networking event 인적 네트워크 형성 행사 → social interaction 사회적 교류

192 육하원칙 문제 연계   상 ●●●

해석 Mr. Wells은 그가 누구를 보고 싶어 했다고 말하는가?
(A) Diane Riggs
(B) Harriet Keach
(C) Samuel Limanto
(D) Lawrence Hillburger

해설 이메일의 'I was ~ interested in seeing my former colleague from Melbourne College again.'에서 저, 즉 Mr. Wells는 Melbourne 대학의 자신의 예전 동료를 다시 보는 것에 관심이 있었다고 했다. 또한, 프로그램의 'our main speakers Dr. Harriet Keach of Melbourne College'에서는 Melbourne 대학에서 온 연사가 Dr. Harriet Keach라는 사실을 확인할 수 있다.
두 단서를 종합할 때, Mr. Wells의 예전 동료는 Melbourne 대학에서 온 Harriet Keach라는 것을 알 수 있다. 따라서 (B)가 정답이다.

어휘 eager adj. (몹시) ~하고 싶어 하는

패러프레이징

was eager to see ~를 보고 싶어 했다 → was ~ interested in seeing ~을 보는 것에 관심이 있었다

193 추론 문제 연계   상 ●●●

해석 Mr. Wells에 대해 추론될 수 있는 것은?
(A) Otis 대학교에서 학생들을 가르쳤었다.
(B) 6개월 동안 떠나 있을 것이다.
(C) 9월에 환급을 기대할 수 있다.
(D) Ellis 연구소에 의해 연설하도록 초청받았다.

해설 이메일의 'I will be unable to attend the seminar on September 8'에서 저, 즉 Mr. Wells가 9월 8일에 열리는 세미나에 참석할 수 없다고 했다. 또한, 환불 정책의 'Send cancellation requests'와 'Credit cards ~ will be refunded within 15 working days of the scheduled event date.'에서는 취소 요청을 보내면 신용카드가 예정된 행사 날짜로부터 영업일 기준 15일 이내에 환불이 될 것이라는 것을 알 수 있다.
두 단서를 종합할 때, Mr. Wells가 9월에 환급을 기대할 수 있다는 것을 추론할 수 있다. 따라서 (C)가 정답이다.

어휘 expect v. 기대하다, 예상하다 repayment n. 환급, 상환

패러프레이징

Credit cards ~ will be refunded 신용카드가 환불될 것이다 → repayment 환급

194 육하원칙 문제   상 ●●●

해석 환불 정책에 따르면, 행사 참가자들은 티켓을 언제 추후 행사에 사용할 수 있는가?

(A) 연사들이 가능하지 않게 될 때
(B) 주최자가 행사를 연기할 때
(C) 막바지에 한 취소를 철회할 때
(D) 관심의 부족이 취소를 야기했을 때

해설 환불 정책의 'Should it be postponed, you will have the option of ~ transferring your registration to the future event.'에서 그것, 즉 세미나가 연기되는 경우, 당신은 추후 행사로 당신의 등록을 변경하는 것의 선택권을 가질 것이라고 했으므로 (B)가 정답이다. 참고로, 연사들이 가능하지 않은 경우나 관심 부족이 취소를 야기할 경우는 전액 환불이 된다고 했으므로 답이 될 수 없다.

어휘 organizer n. 주최자   delay v. 연기하다   retract v. 철회하다
last-minute adj. 막바지의   withdrawal n. 취소, 철회

패러프레이징

use tickets for a future event 티켓을 추후 행사에 사용하다 → transferring your registration to the future event 추후 행사로 등록을 변경하는 것
be postponed 연기되다 → delay 연기하다

195 추론 문제   상 ●●●

해석 Ellis 연구소에 대해 암시되는 것은?
(A) 매년 다수의 행사들을 개최한다.
(B) 단체에 할인된 티켓을 판매한다.
(C) 온라인에서 이용 가능한 세미나를 만들 것이다.
(D) 연사들에 대한 추천을 받는다.

해설 환불 정책의 'Alternatively, you may ~ use the same ticket at another event up to six months after the event you have chosen to cancel.'에서 아니면 그 대신에, 당신은 취소하기로 선택한 행사의 6개월 후까지 동일한 티켓을 또 다른 행사에 사용할 수 있다고 했으므로 Ellis 연구소는 매년 다수의 행사들을 개최한다는 것을 추론할 수 있다. 따라서 (A)가 정답이다.

어휘 multiple adj. 다수의   recommendation n. 추천

196-200번은 다음 웹페이지, 이메일, 기사에 관한 문제입니다.

Langford 컨벤션 센터

소개	다가오는 행사들	시설 지도	연락
샌디에이고 시내에 위치한, Langford 컨벤션 센터는 친절하고 전문적인 직원들이 있는 최첨단 시설입니다. 당신이 무슨 종류의 행사를 계획하고 있든, 저희는 이상적인 장소를 가지고 있습니다.			

전시회장들

이름	¹⁹⁷수용 인원	크기	장소
¹⁹⁷A홀	¹⁹⁷1,000	10,800제곱 피트	1층, 서쪽 별관
B홀	800	7,900제곱 피트	2층, 동쪽 별관
C홀	600	5,600제곱 피트	1층, 남쪽 별관
D홀	400	4,100제곱 피트	2층, 북쪽 별관

저희는 또한 이용할 수 있는 더 작은 회의실들도 있습니다. 더 많은 정보를 위해서 여기를 클릭하거나 공간을 예약하기 위해 555-0393으로 전화해 주십시오.

---

upcoming adj. 다가오는   facility n. 시설   state-of-the-art adj. 최첨단의
ideal adj. 이상적인   venue n. 장소   exhibition hall phr. 전시회장
capacity n. 수용 인원   book v. 예약하다

발신: Greg Williams <g.williams@hv.com>
수신: Patricia Lewis <p.lewis@hv.com>
¹⁹⁹날짜: 4월 10일
제목: 제품 출시

안녕하세요 Patricia,

¹⁹⁶저는 우리 회사의 새로운 컴퓨터 모니터 라인의 출시 준비에 관하여 당신에게 최신정보를 알려드리고 싶습니다. 요청받은 대로, 5월 15일에 ¹⁹⁹Langford 컨벤션 센터의 네 개의 전시회장들 중 하나를 예약하기 위해서는 예약 관리사 David Parsons에게 어제 연락하였습니다. 저는 또한 수차 가능 여부에 대해 물어보았고, 그는 ¹⁹⁷우리가 행사에 참석할 것이라고 예상하고 있는 900명의 사람들에게 적합한 하나의 홀을 그들이 가지고 있다고 제게 장담했습니다.

Mr. Parsons는 ¹⁹⁸행사를 위한 모든 것이 준비되도록 하기 위해 5월 14일 저녁에 당신의 팀이 홀에 대한 접근 권한을 받게 될 것이라고 확인해주었습니다. 그는 또한 당신이 필요하다면 센터의 기술자들이 시청각 장비와 조명에 관련된 도움을 제공하도록 하겠다고 제안하였습니다.

Greg

launch n. 출시   preparation n. 준비   reservation n. 예약
availability n. 가능 여부, 가능성   assure v. 장담하다
participate v. 참석하다, 참여하다   confirm v. 확인하다
access n. 접근 권한, 접근   technician n. 기술자
audiovisual adj. 시청각의   equipment n. 장비   lighting n. 조명

Langford 컨벤션 센터가 일시적으로 문을 닫다

¹⁹⁶6월 25일—Langford 컨벤션 센터의 이사 Wendy Lee는 ²⁰⁰⁻ᴮ8월 15일부터 9월 30일까지 수리를 받기 위해 시설이 폐쇄될 것이라고 발표했다. 그것이 도시에 매년 수천 명의 추가적인 방문객들을 데려올 것이라고 예상되어 ²⁰⁰⁻ᶜ이 계획된 수백만 달러의 프로젝트는 지역 주민들과 사업주들 사이에 상당한 흥분을 일으켰다.

¹⁹⁹Langford 컨벤션 센터의 새로운 예약 관리자 Brett Hanson은 더 많은 국제적인 행사들을 유치하는 것이 목표라고 말했다. "현재, ¹⁹⁹저희 네 개 홀들의 수용 인원은 제한적입니다."라고 그는 말했다. "²⁰⁰⁻ᴬ각각 5,000명의 방문객들을 수용할 수 있는 두 개의 새로운 것들을 건설하는 것은 Langford 컨벤션 센터를 국제회의와 무역 박람회의 개최자들에게 더욱 인기 있게 만들 것입니다."

director n. 이사   undergo v. 받다, 겪다   renovation n. 수리
resident n. 주민   annually adv. 매년   state v. 말하다
accommodate v. 수용하다   conference n. 회의
trade show phr. 무역 박람회

196 추론 문제   중 ●●○

해석 Mr. Williams는 어디에서 일하는 것 같은가?
(A) 홍보 회사에서
(B) 미디어 회사에서
(C) 전자제품 제조회사에서
(D) 소프트웨어 개발 업체에서

해설 이메일의 'I wanted to update ~ on preparations for the launch of our company's new line of computer monitors.'에서 자신, 즉 Mr. Williams가 자신들의 회사의 새로운 컴퓨터 모니터 라인의 출시 준비에 관하여 최신정보를 알려주고 싶다고 했다고 했으므로, Mr. Williams는 전자 제품 제조회사에서 일하고 있음을 추론할 수 있다. 따라서 (C)가 정답이다.

어휘 public relation phr. 홍보
electronics manufacturer phr. 전자제품 제조회사
developer n. 개발 업체, 개발자

197 육하원칙 문제 연계   중 ●●○

해석 Mr. Williams는 어느 전시회장을 예약했는가?

(A) A홀
(B) B홀
(C) C홀
(D) D홀

해설 이메일의 'they have one hall appropriate for the 900 people we are expecting to participate in the event'에서 행사에 참석할 것으로 예상하고 있는 900명의 사람들에게 적합한 하나의 홀을 그들, 즉 Langford 컨벤션 센터가 가지고 있다고 Mr. Williams가 언급했다. 또한, 웹페이지의 'Hall A', 'Capacity', '1000'에서는 A홀의 수용 인원이 1000명이므로 홀들 중에서 유일하게 900명의 사람들을 수용할 수 있다는 사실을 확인할 수 있다. 두 단서를 종합할 때, Mr. Williams가 A홀을 예약했다는 것을 알 수 있다. 따라서 (A)가 정답이다.

198 육하원칙 문제   하 ●○○

해석 이메일에 따르면, 5월 14일에는 무슨 일이 일어날 것인가?

(A) 다가오는 행사를 위해 장소가 준비될 것이다.
(B) 몇몇 장비가 지점으로 배달될 것이다.
(C) 몇몇 정보가 행사 참석자들에게 배부될 것이다.
(D) 시청각 기술자가 회사에 의해 고용될 것이다.

해설 이메일의 'your team would be given access to the hall on the evening of May 14 to get everything ready for the event'에서 행사를 위한 모든 것이 준비되도록 하기 위해 5월 14일 저녁에 당신의 팀이 홀에 대한 접근 권한을 받게 될 것이라고 했으므로 (A)가 정답이다.

어휘 occasion n. 행사 branch office phr. 지점 attendee n. 참석자

패러프레이징

get everything ready for the event 행사를 위한 모든 것이 준비되도록 하다
→ will be prepared for an ~ occasion 행사를 위해 준비될 것이다

199 추론 문제 연계   상 ●●●

해석 Mr. Hanson에 대해 암시되는 것은?

(A) 8월에 국제회의에 참석할 것이다.
(B) 최근에 Ms. Lee에게 제안서를 제출했다.
(C) 지역 기업가들과 곧 만날 것이다.
(D) Mr. Parsons의 자리를 인계받았다.

해설 기사의 'June 25'에서 해당 기사가 6월 25일 자 기사이고, 'Brett Hanson, the new reservations manager at the Langford Convention Center'와 'the capacity of our four halls is limited'에서 Langford 컨벤션 센터의 새로운 예약 관리자가 Brett Hanson이며 네 개의 홀들의 수용 인원이 제한적이라고 했다. 또한, 이메일의 'Date: April 10'에서 이메일이 4월 10일에 작성되었고, 'I contacted the reservations manager,

David Parsons, yesterday to book one of the four exhibition halls at the Langford Convention Center'에서는 Langford 컨벤션 센터의 네 개의 전시회장들 중 하나를 예약하기 위해 예약 관리자 David Parsons 에게 어제 연락했다고 했으므로 Mr. Parsons가 4월 9일에 예약 관리자로 근무했다는 사실을 확인할 수 있다.

두 단서를 종합할 때, Mr. Hanson이 Mr. Parsons의 자리를 인계받았음을 추론할 수 있다. 따라서 (D)가 정답이다.

어휘 submit v. 제출하다 proposal n. 제안서, 제안
business leader phr. 기업가, 경영자 take over phr. 인계받다

200 Not/True 문제   중 ●●○

해석 기사에서 언급되지 않은 것은?

(A) 추가적인 행사 장소들이 건설될 것이다.
(B) 센터는 한 달이 넘는 기간 동안 폐쇄될 것이다.
(C) 계획된 확장에 대해 알고 있는 사람이 거의 없다.
(D) 수리 작업은 매우 비쌀 것이다.

해설 기사의 'The planned ~ project has generated a great deal of excitement among local residents and business owners'에서 계 획된 프로젝트가 지역 주민들과 사업주들 사이에서 상당한 흥분을 일으켰다고 했으므로 (C)는 지문의 내용과 일치하지 않는다. 따라서 (C)가 정답이다. (A)는 'Building two new ones capable of accommodating 5,000 visitors each'에서 각각 5,000명의 방문객들을 수용할 수 있는 두 개의 새로운 것들, 즉 홀들을 건설한다고 했으므로 지문의 내용과 일치한다. (B) 는 'the facility will be closed from August 15 to September 30 to undergo renovations'에서 8월 15일부터 9월 30일까지 수리를 받기 위 해 시설이 폐쇄될 것이라고 했으므로 지문의 내용과 일치한다. (D)는 'The planned multimillion-dollar project'에서 계획된 수백만 달러의 프로젝 트, 즉 계획된 수리가 수백만 달러라고 했으므로 지문의 내용과 일치한다.

어휘 construct v. 건설하다 expansion n. 확장

패러프레이징

Building two new ones 두 개의 새로운 것들을 건설하는 것 → Additional ~ areas are going to be constructed 추가적인 장소들이 건설될 것이다
from August 15 to September 30 8월 15일부터 9월 30일까지 → for a period of over a month 한 달이 넘는 기간 동안
multimillion-dollar 수백만 달러 → very expensive 매우 비싼

PART 5

101 (B)	102 (B)	103 (D)	104 (B)	105 (D)
106 (C)	107 (C)	108 (A)	109 (B)	110 (B)
111 (B)	112 (A)	113 (C)	114 (D)	115 (B)
116 (C)	117 (B)	118 (B)	119 (B)	120 (B)
121 (D)	122 (A)	123 (D)	124 (C)	125 (D)
126 (D)	127 (B)	128 (D)	129 (C)	130 (D)

PART 6

131 (A)	132 (C)	133 (C)	134 (B)	135 (C)
136 (A)	137 (D)	138 (B)	139 (D)	140 (A)
141 (A)	142 (A)	143 (C)	144 (C)	145 (D)
146 (D)				

PART 7

147 (B)	148 (D)	149 (C)	150 (C)	151 (B)
152 (D)	153 (B)	154 (D)	155 (B)	156 (D)
157 (C)	158 (C)	159 (D)	160 (D)	161 (C)
162 (B)	163 (C)	164 (B)	165 (C)	166 (C)
167 (D)	168 (C)	169 (D)	170 (B)	171 (C)
172 (C)	173 (D)	174 (C)	175 (A)	176 (A)
177 (D)	178 (C)	179 (A)	180 (B)	181 (A)
182 (B)	183 (D)	184 (C)	185 (D)	186 (A)
187 (B)	188 (A)	189 (D)	190 (D)	191 (D)
192 (D)	193 (D)	194 (C)	195 (A)	196 (B)
197 (A)	198 (D)	199 (A)	200 (A)	

PART 5

101 명사 자리 채우기　　하 ●○○

해석 많은 주민들은 고속도로를 폐쇄하겠다는 시의 결정에 대해 만족하지 않는다.

해설 소유격(the city's) 다음에 올 수 있는 것은 명사이므로 명사 (B) decision (결정)이 정답이다. 동사 (A), 형용사 (C), 동사 또는 과거분사 (D)는 명사 자리에 올 수 없다.

어휘 resident n. 주민, 거주자　highway n. 고속도로
decide v. 결정하다　decisive adj. 결정적인

102 격에 맞는 인칭대명사 채우기　　하 ●○○

해석 만약 당신이 예약을 해야 한다면, 접수 담당자에게 전화해주십시오.

해설 If절에 동사(need)만 있고, 주어가 없으므로 주어 역할을 할 수 있는 소유대명사 (A)와 주격 인칭대명사 (B)가 정답의 후보이다. '만약 당신이 예약을 해야 한다면, 접수 담당자에게 전화하라'라는 의미가 되어야 하므로 주격 인칭대명사 (B) you(당신이)가 정답이다. 소유대명사 (A)를 쓸 경우 '만약 당신의 것이 예약을 해야 한다면'이라는 어색한 문맥을 만든다. 소유격 인칭대명사 (C)는 주어 역할을 할 수 없다. 재귀대명사 (D)는 목적어가 주어와 같은 사람이나 사물을 지칭할 때나, 주어나 목적어를 강조할 때 쓰인다.

어휘 make an appointment phr. 예약을 하다, 약속을 잡다
receptionist n. 접수 담당자

103 동사 어휘 고르기　　중 ●●○

해석 그들의 문제에 신속한 답변이 필요한 고객들은 전문가와의 온라인 채팅을 시작할 수 있다.

해설 빈칸은 주격 관계절(who ~ problem)의 동사 자리이다. '신속한 답변이 필요한 고객들은 온라인 채팅을 시작할 수 있다'라는 문맥이므로 (D) require (필요하다)가 정답이다. (A) constrain(강요하다, 억제하다)도 해석상 그럴듯해 보이지만, 복종 등을 강요하거나 무언가를 억지로 하게 하는 것을 나타내므로 답이 될 수 없다.

어휘 prompt adj. 신속한　specialist n. 전문가　release v. 출시하다
provide v. 제공하다

104 전치사 채우기　　중 ●●○

해석 Mr. Robertson은 어떤 주식을 구매할 것인지 선택하기 전에 재정 전문가들의 조언을 구했다.

해설 빈칸은 동명사(choosing)를 목적어로 취하는 전치사 자리이다. '어떤 주식을 구매할 것인지 선택하기 전에 재정 전문가들의 조언을 구했다'라는 의미가 되어야 하므로 (B) before(~전에)가 정답이다.

어휘 seek v. 구하다, 찾다　advice n. 조언　financial expert phr. 재정 전문가
stock n. 주식　according to phr. ~에 따르면　beyond prep. ~을 넘어서
far from phr. 전혀 ~이 아닌

105 형용사 어휘 고르기　　중 ●●○

해석 험한 날씨 때문에 항공편이 취소되어서, 승객들은 출발하기 위해 6시간을 기다렸다.

해설 빈칸은 명사(weather)를 꾸미는 형용사 자리이다. '험한 날씨 때문에 항공편이 취소되었다'라는 문맥이므로 (D) severe(험한)가 정답이다. (A) immense(엄청난, 거대한)도 해석상 그럴듯해 보이지만, 수, 양, 크기가 엄청난 것을 의미한다. (B) striking(눈에 띄는, 치는)도 해석상 그럴듯해 보이지만, 시선을 끄는 방식에 있어서 특이하거나 정도가 심한 것을 의미하므로 답이 될 수 없다.

어휘 flight n. 항공편　passenger n. 승객　depart v. 출발하다
nervous adj. 초조한

106 명사 자리 채우기　　하 ●○○

해석 Ms. Adrian은 Novart Group사에서 온 방문객들을 위해 환영회를 준비해야 했다.

해설 타동사(prepare)의 목적어 자리에 올 수 있는 것은 명사이므로 명사 (C) entertainment(환영회, 파티)가 정답이다. 동사 (A)와 (D), 동사 또는 과거분사 (B)는 명사 자리에 올 수 없다.

어휘 prepare v. 준비하다　visitor n. 방문객　entertain v. 즐겁게 해주다, 접대하다

107 의미 구별하여 부사 채우기　중 ●●○

해석 법률 사무소 직원인 Ms. Valdez는 변호사들 및 고객들과 긴밀하게 일한다.

해설 동사(works)를 꾸밀 수 있는 것은 부사이므로 부사 (A), (B), (C)가 정답의 후보이다. '변호사들 및 고객들과 긴밀하게 일한다'라는 의미가 되어야 하므로 부사 (C) closely(긴밀하게, 밀접하게)가 정답이다. 부사 (A) close(가까이)와 (B) closer(더 가까이)를 쓸 경우 물리적인 거리의 가까움을 의미하기 때문에 어색한 문맥이 되며, '~와 가깝게'라는 의미를 가지기 위해서는 전치사 with가 아닌 to와 함께 쓰여야 한다. 명사 (D)는 동사를 꾸밀 수 없다. 동사 work를 '~을 작동시키다, ~을 일으키다'라는 의미의 타동사로 보고 명사 (D)를 목적어로 본다 해도, '변호사들 및 고객들과의 폐쇄를 작동시킨다/일으킨다'라는 어색한 문맥을 만든다.

어휘 legal assistant phr. 법률 사무소 직원

108 전치사 채우기　중 ●●○

해석 CE사는 10년 전 이것의 설립 이후 수많은 브랜드들을 홍보해왔다.

해설 이 문장은 주어(CE Inc.), 동사(has promoted), 목적어(numerous brands)를 갖춘 완전한 절이므로, ____ ~ ago는 수식어 거품이다. 이 수식어 거품은 동사가 없는 거품구이므로 거품구를 이끌 수 있는 전치사 (A), (B), (C)가 정답의 후보이다. '설립 이후 수많은 브랜드들을 홍보해왔다'라는 의미가 되어야 하므로 시점을 나타내는 전치사 (A) since(~ 이후)가 정답이다. 참고로, since는 '~이기 때문에'라는 의미의 이유를 나타내는 부사절 접속사로도 쓰일 수 있음을 알아둔다. (B) throughout(~ 동안, ~ 내내)은 기간을 나타내므로 빈칸 뒤에 특정 시점이 아닌 기간을 나타내는 표현이 와야 한다. (C) except for(~을 제외하고)도 설립 당시에는 홍보를 하지 않았다는 의미로 해석상 그럴듯해 보이지만, 특정한 하나를 제외하고 나머지는 다 그러하다는 의미를 나타내므로 이 문장의 경우에는 빈칸 뒤에 홍보하지 않은 특정 브랜드를 언급해야 한다. 부사절 접속사 (D)는 거품구가 아닌 거품절을 이끈다.

어휘 promote v. 홍보하다　numerous adj. 수많은　founding n. 설립

109 부사 자리 채우기　하 ●○○

해석 건축 현장에서, 노동자들은 현장 안전 감독관에 의해 정기적으로 관리될 것이다.

해설 동사(will be monitored)를 꾸밀 수 있는 것은 부사이므로 부사 (B) regularly(정기적으로)가 정답이다. 형용사 또는 명사 (A), 명사 (C)와 (D)는 동사를 꾸밀 수 없다. 명사 (A), (C), (D)를 be동사(will be)의 보어로 본다 해도, 각각 '노동자들은 감독관에 의해 관리되는 단골손님/규칙적임/규정이다'라는 어색한 문맥을 만든다.

어휘 construction site phr. 건축 현장　monitor v. 관리하다, 감시하다
on-site adj. 현장의　inspector n. 감독관

110 비교급 표현 채우기　하 ●○○

해석 Directwork Solutions사는 모바일 광고 업계에서 그것의 경쟁사들보다 더 큰 인정을 받았다.

해설 명사(recognition)를 꾸밀 수 있는 것은 형용사이므로 형용사 (A), (B), (D)가 정답의 후보이다. 빈칸 뒤에 than(~보다)이 왔으므로 함께 비교급 표현을 만드는 형용사의 비교급 (B) greater(더 큰)가 정답이다. 형용사의 원급 (A)

와 최상급 (D)는 비교급 표현과 함께 쓰일 수 없다. 부사 (C)는 형용사 자리에 올 수 없다.

어휘 gain v. 받다, 얻다　recognition n. 인정, 인식
competitor n. 경쟁사, 경쟁자　greatly adv. 대단히, 크게

111 전치사 채우기　중 ●●○

해석 Mirado 제과점은 재료들의 가격 상승 때문에 몇몇 제품들의 가격을 인상했다.

해설 빈칸은 명사구(an increase ~ ingredients)를 목적어로 취하는 전치사 자리이다. '재료들의 가격 상승 때문에 제품들의 가격을 인상했다'라는 의미가 되어야 하므로 이유를 나타내는 전치사 (B) due to(~ 때문에)가 정답이다.

어휘 ingredient n. 재료　as of phr. ~일자로, ~ 현재로
such as phr. ~과 같은　besides prep. ~ 외에

112 상관접속사 채우기　하 ●○○

해석 설문조사 응답자들은 그들이 차로 출근하는 동안 오디오북 또는 팟캐스트들 중 하나를 듣는 것을 선호한다.

해설 등위접속사 or와 맞는 짝인 (A) either(둘 중 하나의)가 정답이다. 참고로, either A or B가 명사(audiobooks)와 명사(podcasts)를 연결하고 있음을 알아둔다. (B)는 and와 함께 상관접속사 both A and B(A와 B 둘 다)의 형태로 쓰이며, (D)는 nor와 함께 상관접속사 neither A nor B(A도 B도 아닌)의 형태로 쓰인다. 수량 형용사 (C)는 두 단어를 연결할 수 없고, 복수 명사가 아닌 단수 명사 앞에 와야 한다.

어휘 respondent n. 응답자　prefer v. 선호하다

113 명사 자리 채우기　하 ●○○

해석 Dr. Cruz는 회의에서 연설하도록 요청받았을 때 약간의 망설임을 보였지만, 결국 동의하였다.

해설 타동사(showed)의 목적어 자리에 올 수 있으면서 빈칸 앞의 한정사(some)의 꾸밈을 받을 수 있는 것은 명사이므로 명사 (C) hesitation(망설임)이 정답이다. 동사 (A), 형용사 (B), 동사 또는 과거분사 (D)는 명사 자리에 올 수 없다.

어휘 invite v. 요청하다, 초대하다　ultimately adv. 결국, 궁극적으로
consent v. 동의하다　hesitate v. 망설이다, 주저하다
hesitant adj. 망설이는, 주저하는

114 부사 어휘 고르기　하 ●○○

해석 Beemz Cable사는 그들이 청구서 지불 기한이 지난 모든 고객들에게 서비스를 즉시 중단할 것이다.

해설 빈칸은 동사(will stop)를 꾸미는 부사 자리이다. '청구서 지불 기한이 지난 모든 고객들의 서비스를 즉시 중단할 것이다'라는 문맥이 되어야 하므로 (D) immediately(즉시)가 정답이다.

어휘 bill n. 청구서　overdue adj. (지불) 기한이 지난
instinctively adv. 본능적으로　patiently adv. 끈기 있게
mutually adv. 서로

115 동사 어휘 고르기　중 ●●○

해석 사용 설명서는 복사기를 작동하는 방법을 몇 가지 언어로 설명한다.

해설 빈칸은 의문사 how 뒤의 to와 함께 to 부정사를 만드는 동사원형 자리이다. '사용 설명서는 복사기를 작동하는 방법을 설명한다'라는 문맥이므로

(B) operate(작동하다)가 정답이다.

어휘   instruction manual phr. 사용 설명서   photocopier n. 복사기
print v. 인쇄하다   reveal v. 드러내다, 밝히다   overlook v. 간과하다

116 명사 어휘 고르기   중 ●●○

해석   오래된 호텔의 보수공사는 성공적이었으며 그것은 이제 꽤 현대적으로 보인다.

해설   빈칸은 be동사(were)의 주어이면서 전치사구(of the old hotel)의 꾸밈을 받는 명사 자리이다. '오래된 호텔의 보수공사는 성공적이었으며 그것은 이제 꽤 현대적으로 보인다'라는 문맥이므로 (C) renovations(보수공사, 개조)가 정답이다. (D) productions(생산, 제조)도 무언가를 만든다는 의미로 해석상 그럴듯해 보이지만, 식품, 상품, 자재 등을 대량으로 생산하는 것을 의미한다.

어휘   quite adv. 꽤   modern adj. 현대적인   location n. 위치
advantage n. 이점, 장점

117 형용사 자리 채우기   중 ●●○

해석   식당에 더하여, Aviato 카드에 적립된 포인트들은 특정 소매업체에서 교환할 수 있다.

해설   빈칸이 be동사(are) 다음에 왔으므로 진행형을 만드는 -ing형 (A)와 be동사의 보어 자리에 올 수 있는 형용사 (B)가 정답의 후보이다. '적립된 포인트들은 특정 소매업체에서 교환할 수 있다'라는 의미가 되어야 하므로 형용사 (B) redeemable(교환할 수 있는)이 정답이다. -ing형 (A)를 쓸 경우 '포인트들은 교환하는 중이다'라는 어색한 문맥이 된다. 동사 (C)와 (D)는 be동사 다음에 올 수 없다.

어휘   earn v. 얻다   redeem v. 교환하다, 보완하다

118 부사 어휘 고르기   중 ●●○

해석   이전에 컴퓨터 사용 혁신에서의 선두 주자로 여겨졌던, Frye Systems사는 몇 년 동안 신제품을 가지고 있지 않았다.

해설   빈칸은 과거분사(considered)를 꾸미는 부사 자리이다. '이전에 선두 주자로 여겨졌던, Frye Systems사는 몇 년 동안 신제품을 가지고 있지 않았다'라는 문맥이므로 (B) Formerly(이전에)가 정답이다.

어휘   consider v. 여기다   computing n. 컴퓨터 사용   innovation n. 혁신
necessarily adv. 필연적으로   eventually adv. 결국
wisely adv. 현명하게

119 전치사 표현 채우기   중 ●●○

해석   Fasheng Industries사의 직원들은 온라인 중국어 강좌에 대한 할인을 받을 자격이 있다.

해설   빈칸은 명사구(online Chinese language courses)를 목적어로 취하는 전치사 자리이다. '온라인 중국어 강좌에 대한 할인'이라는 의미가 되어야 하므로 빈칸 앞의 명사 discounts(할인)와 함께 '~에 대한 할인'이라는 의미의 어구인 discounts on을 만드는 전치사 (B) on(~에 대한)이 정답이다. (A) of(~의)도 해석상 그럴듯해 보이지만, discount of 다음에는 할인되는 금액이 와야 한다.

어휘   be entitled to phr. ~을 받을 자격이 있다   discount n. 할인
into prep. ~ 안으로   like prep. ~처럼, ~같은

120 형용사 어휘 고르기   중 ●●○

해석   Mr. Mattson은 그의 발표 주제에 대한 간단한 개요를 나누어줌으로써 발표

를 시작했다.

해설   빈칸은 명사(outline)를 꾸미는 형용사 자리이다. '발표 주제에 대한 간단한 개요를 나누어줌으로써 발표를 시작했다'라는 문맥이므로 (B) brief(간단한)가 정답이다.

어휘   pass out phr. 나누어 주다   outline n. 개요
constant adj. 끊임없는, 거듭되는   talented adj. 재능이 있는
potential adj. 가능성 있는, 잠재적인

121 수, 태, 시제에 맞는 동사 채우기   상 ●●●

해석   Era 은행의 사용자들은 그들의 정보가 해커들에 의해 접근된 후에 그들의 암호를 변경하도록 지시받고 있다.

해설   주어(Users of Era Bank)가 복수이고, 동사 instruct가 '지시하다'라는 의미의 타동사인데 빈칸 뒤에 목적어가 없으므로 복수 동사이면서 수동태인 현재 진행 시제 수동태 (D) are being instructed가 정답이다. 능동태 (A)와 (B)는 각각 '은행 사용자들이 그들의 암호를 변경하도록 지시한다/지시할 것이다'라는 어색한 문맥을 만든다. 단수 동사 (C)는 단수 주어와 함께 쓰여야 한다.

어휘   access v. 접근하다

122 형용사 자리 채우기   중 ●●○

해석   실내 장식가는 비용을 줄이기 위해 흰색 페인트의 광범위한 사용을 추천했다.

해설   동명사(making)의 목적어 자리에 온 명사(use)를 꾸밀 수 있는 것은 형용사이므로 형용사 (A) extensive(광범위한, 아주 많은)가 정답이다. 명사 (B), 부사 (C), 동사 (D)는 명사를 꾸밀 수 없다.

어휘   decorator n. 실내 장식가   recommend v. 추천하다
make use of phr. ~을 사용하다   lower v. 줄이다   expense n. 비용
extension n. 확대   extensively adv. 광범위하게, 널리
extend v. 확대하다

123 부사 어휘 고르기   상 ●●●

해석   정보가 유출되는 것을 방지하기 위해 신제품에 대한 모든 세부 사항들이 철저히 숨겨졌다.

해설   빈칸은 동사(have been concealed)를 꾸미는 부사 자리이다. '정보가 유출되는 것을 방지하기 위해 세부 사항들이 철저히 숨겨졌다'라는 문맥이므로 (D) thoroughly(철저히)가 정답이다.

어휘   detail n. 세부 사항   conceal v. 숨기다, 감추다
prevent v. 방지하다, 막다   leak v. 유출되다   lastly adv. 마지막으로
publicly adv. 공개적으로   remotely adv. 원격으로, 멀리서

124 명사 관련 어구 완성하기   상 ●●●

해석   마케팅팀은 원래의 계획이 불충분하다고 판명될 경우를 대비하여 철저한 비상 대책을 개발했다.

해설   빈칸은 명사(plan)와 복합 명사를 이루어 동사(has developed)의 목적어 역할을 하는 명사 자리이다. '원래의 계획이 불충분하다고 판명될 경우를 대비하여 비상 대책을 개발했다'라는 문맥이므로 빈칸 뒤의 명사 plan(대책, 계획)과 함께 '비상 대책'이라는 의미의 어구인 contingency plan을 만드는 (C) contingency(비상, 만일의 사태)가 정답이다.

어휘 **solid** adj. 철저한, 견고한 **in case** phr. ~의 경우를 대비하여
original adj. 원래의 **prove** v. 판명되다, 입증되다
inadequate adj. 불충분한 **authority** n. 권위 **opportunity** n. 기회
coincidence n. 우연의 일치

125 부사 자리 채우기   중 ●●○

해석 집에서 일할 때, 몇몇 직원들은 그들의 업무를 효과적으로 수행하는 것이 어렵다고 생각한다.

해설 to 부정사(to perform)를 꾸밀 수 있는 것은 부사이므로 부사 (D) effectively(효과적으로)가 정답이다. 명사 또는 동사 (A), 동명사 또는 현재분사 (B), 형용사 (C)는 to 부정사를 꾸밀 수 없다.

어휘 **perform** v. 수행하다 **task** n. 업무
effect n. 효과, 영향; v. (어떤 결과물을) 가져오다 **effective** adj. 효과적인

126 전치사 채우기   하 ●○○

해석 Mr. Kazuka의 *Starlight Fractals*가 Barton에서 Fort Bend까지 모든 주요 서점들에 배부될 것이다.

해설 이 문장은 주어(*Starlight Fractals*)와 동사(will be distributed)를 갖춘 완전한 절이므로, ___ ~ Fort Bend는 수식어 거품으로 보아야 한다. 이 수식어 거품은 동사가 없는 거품구이므로 거품구를 이끌 수 있는 전치사 (A), (C), (D)가 정답의 후보이다. '*Starlight Fractals*가 Barton에서 Fort Bend까지 주요 서점들에 배부될 것이다'라는 의미가 되어야 하므로 빈칸 뒤의 to와 함께 from A to B(A에서 B까지)를 만드는 (D) from(~부터)이 정답이다. 전치사 (A) among(~간에, ~ 사이에)와 (C) between(~의 사이에)도 해석상 그럴듯해 보이지만, (A)는 셋 이상의 사람이나 사물 사이를 나타내고, (C)는 두 개의 대상 사이의 관계나 위치, 또는 시간을 나타내며 보통 between A and B(A와 B 사이에)의 형태로 쓰이기 때문에 답이 될 수 없다. 부사절 접속사 (B)는 거품구가 아닌 거품절을 이끈다.

어휘 **distribute** v. 배부하다 **major** adj. 주요한

127 동사 어휘 고르기   중 ●●○

해석 Apex Gas사는 Fairfax시 의회의 요청에 따라 그것의 요금 인상을 연기하는 것에 동의했다.

해설 빈칸은 동사(agreed) 뒤의 to와 함께 to 부정사를 만드는 동사원형 자리이다. '시 의회의 요청에 따라 요금 인상을 연기하는 것에 동의했다'라는 문맥이므로 (B) delay(연기하다)가 정답이다. (C) compare(비교하다)도 해석상 그럴듯해 보이지만, 주로 compare A with/to B의 형태로 비교하는 대상과 함께 쓰이기 때문에 답이 될 수 없다.

어휘 **rate** n. 요금 **request** n. 요청 **city council** phr. 시 의회 **obtain** v. 얻다
recognize v. 인식하다, 인정하다

128 명사 자리 채우기   중 ●●○

해석 VoyageX Holdings사는 계약을 체결하기 전에 다양한 철강 제조업체들과 상담을 했다.

해설 동사(consulted)의 목적어 자리에 올 수 있으면서 관사(a) 뒤에 올 수 있는 것은 명사이므로 명사 (D) variety(다양성)가 정답이다. 참고로, a variety of(다양한)를 관용구로 알아둔다. 동사 (A), 형용사 (B), 동사 또는 과거분사 (C)는 명사 자리에 올 수 없다.

어휘 **consult** v. 상담하다 **manufacturer** n. 제조업체
award a contract phr. 계약을 체결하다 **vary** v. 서로 다르다
various adj. 다양한 **varied** adj. 다양한

129 명사 어휘 고르기   상 ●●●

해석 재정 위원회는 각 부서에 예산의 일부를 배분한다.

해설 빈칸은 타동사(allocates)의 목적어이면서 전치사구(of the budget)의 꾸밈을 받는 명사 자리이다. '각 부서에 예산의 일부를 배분한다'라는 문맥이므로 (C) portions(일부, 부분)가 정답이다.

어휘 **finance committee** phr. 재정 위원회 **allocate** v. 배분하다, 할당하다
budget n. 예산 **object** n. 물건, 대상, 목표 **salary** n. 봉급, 월급
pattern n. 양식, 패턴

130 동사 어휘 고르기   중 ●●○

해석 그 정책은 설탕이 함유된 음료들에 더 높은 세금을 부과함으로써 설탕 소비를 줄일 것이다.

해설 빈칸은 조동사(will) 뒤에 오는 동사원형 자리이다. '설탕이 함유된 음료들에 세금을 부과함으로써 설탕 소비를 줄일 ·것이다'라는 문맥이므로 (D) reduce(줄이다)가 정답이다.

어휘 **measure** n. 정책 **consumption** n. 소비 **sweetened** adj. 설탕이 함유된
beverage n. 음료 **adopt** v. 채택하다 **declare** v. 선언하다
stimulate v. 자극하다

PART 6

131-134번은 다음 광고에 관한 문제입니다.

직원 필요
직업 코드: Y51633

[131]창의적이고, 매우 경쟁력 있는 직원들로 구성된 한 디자인 대행사가 방콕에 있는 이것의 팀에 합류할 사람을 찾고 있습니다. 합격자들은 그들의 고객들을 위해 독창적인 포장 아이디어들을 개발할 것입니다.

필수 자격요건은 2년의 관련된 직무 경험, 관련 분야의 학사 학위, 그리고 일러스트레이션 소프트웨어에 대한 지식을 포함합니다. [132]디자인 자격증이 있는 지원자가 선호됩니다.

staff@bkrecruit.com으로 이메일을 보냄[133]으로써 지원해주십시오. 귀하의 이력서를 첨부하고 온라인 포트폴리오로의 링크를 첨부하십시오.

중요: 귀하의 이메일의 제목란에 이 게시글의 직업 코드를 입력하십시오. [134]직후에, 저희는 귀하의 지원서가 수신되었다는 것을 귀하께 알려드리기 위해 알림을 보낼 것입니다.

consist of phr. ~으로 구성되다 **competitive** adj. 경쟁력 있는
individual n. 사람, 개인 **successful candidate** phr. 합격자
original adj. 독창적인 **qualification** n. 자격요건 **relevant** adj. 관련된
professional experience phr. 직무 경험
bachelor's degree phr. 학사 학위 **enclose** v. 첨부하다, 동봉하다
posting n. 게시글 **subject line** phr. 제목란 **notification** n. 알림

최고난도 문제

131 형용사 자리 채우기   상 ●●●

해설 형용사(competitive)와 함께 전치사(of)의 목적어인 명사(staff)를 꾸밀 수 있는 것은 형용사이므로 형용사 (A) creative(창의적인)가 정답이다. 참고로, 이 문장은 콤마로 연결된 두 개의 형용사(creative, ~ competitive)가 명사

(staff)를 꾸미는 구조로, 명사 앞에 형용사를 두 개만 사용할 경우 접속사 없이 콤마로 연결될 수 있음을 알아둔다. 명사 (B)도 전치사(of)의 목적어 자리에 올 수는 있지만, 명사(staff)와 연결해주는 등위접속사가 없으므로 답이 될 수 없다. 동사 (C)와 부사 (D)는 형용사 자리에 올 수 없다.

어휘 **creativity** n. 창의성 **creatively** adv. 창의적으로

132 알맞은 문장 고르기
중 ●●○

해석 (A) 컴퓨터 소프트웨어가 고도로 발전했습니다.
(B) 자동차를 운전할 수 있는 능력이 이 직업에 매우 중요합니다.
(C) 디자인 자격증이 있는 지원자가 선호됩니다.
(D) 귀하는 온라인 면접에 초청받았습니다.

해설 앞 문장 'Required qualifications include two years of relevant professional experience, ~, and knowledge of illustration software.'에서 필수 자격요건은 2년의 관련된 직무 경험과 일러스트레이션 소프트웨어에 대한 지식을 포함한다고 했으므로, 빈칸에는 디자인 자격증이 있는 지원자가 선호된다는 내용이 들어가야 함을 알 수 있다. 따라서 (C)가 정답이다.

어휘 **vehicle** n. 자동차 **crucial** adj. 매우 중요한

133 전치사 채우기
상 ●●●

해설 빈칸은 동명사구(sending an e-mail)를 목적어로 취하는 전치사 자리이다. '이메일을 보냄으로써 지원하라'라는 의미가 되어야 하므로 전치사 (C) by (~함으로써)가 정답이다. 참고로, 전치사 (A) to, (B) for, (D) in을 쓸 경우 각각 '이메일을 보내는 것에 적용되어라/이메일을 보내는 것에 지원하라/이메일을 보냄에 있어서 지원하라'라는 어색한 문맥이 된다.

어휘 **apply to** phr. ~에 적용되다 **apply for** phr. ~에 지원하다
in -ing phr. ~함에 있어서

134 접속부사 채우기 주변 문맥 파악
중 ●●○

해설 앞 문장에서 당신의 이메일의 제목란에 이 게시글에 있는 직업 코드를 입력하라고 했고, 빈칸이 있는 문장에서는 당신의 지원서가 수신되었다는 것을 알려주기 위해 알림을 보낼 것이라고 했으므로 시간 순서대로 일어나는 순차적인 두 사건을 연결할 때 사용되는 접속부사 (B) Immediately afterward(직후에)가 정답이다.

어휘 **in the meantime** phr. 그동안에 **on the whole** phr. 대체로
nevertheless adv. 그럼에도 불구하고

135-138번은 다음 편지에 관한 문제입니다.

11월 19일

Theodore Arum
99번지 West Wooley로
캘리포니아주 93035

Mr. Arum께,

이번 달 초에 20세기의 발명품들에 대한 강연을 하기 위해 Silver Shore 시민 문화회관을 방문해주셔서 감사합니다. 저는 특히 지난번과 비교하여 당신이 더욱 상세한 ¹³⁵해설을 논해주신 것에 대해 감사드립니다. 이것은 지난해에 당신의 강연에 ¹³⁶참석했었던 청중들에게 행사를 특히 즐겁게 만들어주었습니다. 비록 당신이 자원 봉사로 Silver Shore 시민 문화회관에 시간을 내주시는 것에 동의하셨지만, 저희는 당신에게 ¹³⁷보상을 제공해드리고 싶습니다. 저는 당신에게 커피 체인점 Better Beans의 50달러 상품권을 보냅니다.

¹³⁸저희는 당신이 다시 방문하여 또 다른 강연을 해주시기를 바랍니다.

Valery Miranda 드림
행사진행자, Silver Shore 시민 문화회관

동봉물: Better Beans 상품권

talk n. 강연 **invention** n. 발명품 **appreciate** v. 감사하다
go into phr. ~을 (상세히) 논하다 **detailed** adj. 상세한
particularly adv. 특히 **enjoyable** adj. 즐거운
audience member phr. 청중 **gift voucher** phr. 상품권
coordinator n. 진행자

135 명사 어휘 고르기 주변 문맥 파악
상 ●●●

해설 빈칸은 형용사(more detailed)의 꾸밈을 받는 명사 자리이다 '지난번과 비교하여 더욱 상세한 ___을 논해주신 것에 대해 특히 감사드린다'라는 문맥이므로 모든 보기가 정답의 후보이다. 앞 문장에서 발명품들에 대한 강연을 하기 위해 방문해줘서 감사하다고 했으므로 (C) discussion(해설)이 정답이다. (B) statement(성명, 진술, 발표)도 해석상 그럴듯해 보이지만, 주로 공식적인 성명, 진술, 발표를 의미하므로 답이 될 수 없다.

어휘 **procedure** n. 절차 **characteristic** n. 특징

136 올바른 시제의 동사 채우기
상 ●●●

해설 빈칸은 주격 관계절(who ~ before)의 동사 자리이므로 동사 (A), (C), (D)가 정답의 후보이다. 관계절(who ~ before)에서 나타내는 사건, 즉 지난해에 청중들이 당신, 즉 Mr. Arum의 강연에 참석한 과거의 일은 주절(This ~ members)에서 나타내는 사건, 즉 이번 달 초에 Mr. Arum이 강연을 했을 때 지난번과 비교하여 더욱 상세한 해설을 논해준 것이 청중들에게 행사를 특히 즐겁게 만든 시점보다 먼저 일어난 일이다. 따라서, 과거의 특정 시점 이전에 발생한 일을 표현할 수 있는 과거 완료 시제 (A) had attended가 정답이다. 과거 진행 시제 (C)와 현재 완료 시제 (D)는 과거의 특정 시점 이전에 발생한 일을 표현할 수 없다. 동명사 또는 현재분사 (B)는 동사 자리에 올 수 없다.

어휘 **attend** v. 참석하다

137 명사 어휘 고르기 주변 문맥 파악
중 ●●○

해설 빈칸은 타동사(offer)의 간접 목적어 역할을 하는 명사 자리이다. '비록 당신이 자원 봉사로 시간을 내주는 것에 동의했지만, 당신에게 ___을 제공하고 싶다'라는 문맥이므로 모든 보기가 정답의 후보이다. 뒤 문장에서 커피 체인점의 50달러 상품권을 보낸다고 했으므로 (D) compensation(보상)이 정답이다. 참고로, 이 문장에서 타동사 offer가 2개의 목적어, 즉 직접 목적어와 간접 목적어를 갖는 4형식 동사로 쓰였음을 알아둔다.

어휘 **convenience** n. 편리 **redemption** n. 상환, 변제 **occupation** n. 직업

138 알맞은 문장 고르기
중 ●●○

해석 (A) 휴대폰으로 당신의 등록을 완료해주십시오.
(B) 저희는 당신이 다시 방문하여 또 다른 강연을 해주시기를 바랍니다.
(C) 다시 한 번, 저는 마이크로 인한 문제에 대해 사과드립니다.
(D) 당신의 기사가 이번 달 호에 나올 것입니다.

해설 앞부분에서 이번 달 초에 Mr. Arum이 강연을 한 것에 대해 감사드린다고 했고, 앞 문장 'I am sending you a $50 gift voucher'에서 50달러 상품권을 보낸다고 했으므로, 빈칸에는 Mr. Arum이 다시 방문하여 강연을 해주기를 바란다는 내용이 들어가야 함을 알 수 있다. 따라서 (B)가 정답이다.

어휘 complete v. 완료하다 registration n. 등록 apologize v. 사과하다
appear v. 나오다

139-142번은 다음 광고에 관한 문제입니다.

O'Toole's 체육관에서 크게 절약하세요!

겨울이 왔지만, 그것이 당신이 건강해지는 것을 막도록 두지 마세요! 12월 말까지 O'Toole's 체육관에서 가입하시면, 당신은 정가의 50퍼센트까지 할인을 ¹³⁹보상받으실 것입니다.

저희의 1개월과 3개월의 정기권은 각각 단 55달러와 135달러입니다. 게다가, 만약 당신의 친구들을 초대한다면 당신은 훨씬 더 큰 할인을 받을 수 있습니다. 더 많은 사람들이 ¹⁴⁰가입할수록, 당신은 더 많은 할인을 받습니다.

모든 회원들은 정상 운영 시간 동안 저희의 운동 기구에 대한 전체 이용 권한을 받습니다. ¹⁴¹그러나, 몇몇 서비스들은 추가 비용이 든다는 것을 명심하세요. 요금은 개인 지도와 수업들의 세션마다 지불되어야 합니다. 오늘 직접 등록하세요. 81번지 Juniper로에 있는 저희 지점¹⁴²에 들르세요.

fit adj. 건강한 up to phr. ~까지 regular price phr. 정가
access n. 이용 권한 fee n. 요금 session n. 세션, 강의 시간

139 수, 태, 시제에 맞는 동사 채우기 중 ●●○

해설 12월 말까지 체육관에 가입하면, 할인을 보상받을 것이라는 미래의 상황이고, 주어(you)와 동사(reward)가 '당신은 보상받다'라는 수동의 의미를 가지므로 미래 시제 수동태 (D) will be rewarded가 정답이다. 과거 시제 (A)는 이미 끝난 과거의 동작이나 상태를 나타내고, 현재 시제 (B)는 현재의 상태나 반복되는 동작, 일반적인 사실을 나타낸다. 미래 진행 시제 (C)는 특정한 미래 시점에 진행되고 있을 일을 표현할 때 쓰이며 능동태이므로 답이 될 수 없다.

140 비교급 표현 채우기 중 ●●○

해설 'the + 비교급 + 주어 + 동사 ~, the + 비교급 + 주어 + 동사 -'(~할수록 점점 더 -하다) 형태가 온 것으로 보아, 빈칸은 첫 번째 복수 주어(people)의 동사 자리이므로 복수 동사 (A)와 (C)가 정답의 후보이다. 두 번째 절의 동사가 현재 시제(get)이므로 현재 시제 복수 동사 (A) join이 정답이다. 과거 시제 (C)는 현재 시제와 함께 쓰일 수 없고, 단수 동사 (B)는 단수 주어와 함께 쓰여야 한다. 동명사 또는 현재분사 (D)는 동사 자리에 올 수 없다.

141 알맞은 문장 고르기 중 ●●○

해석 (A) 그러나, 몇몇 서비스들은 추가 비용이 든다는 것을 명심하세요.
(B) 저희의 어느 지점에서든지 프런트의 직원에게 카드를 보여주세요.
(C) 저희는 곧 종료할 것이기 때문에 신속하게 행동하는 것이 좋을 것입니다.
(D) 많은 사람들이 여름에 이 절약을 이용합니다.

해설 앞 문장 'All members receive full access to our workout equipment during normal hours of operation.'에서 모든 회원들은 정상 운영 시간 동안 운동 기구에 대한 전체 이용 권한을 받는다고 했고, 뒤 문장 'Fees must be paid per session for personal training and classes.'에서 요금은 개인 지도와 수업들의 세션마다 지불되어야 한다고 했으므로, 빈칸에는 그러나 몇몇 서비스들은 추가 비용을 부과한다는 내용이 들어가야 함을 알 수 있다. 따라서 (A)가 정답이다.

어휘 keep in mind phr. ~을 명심하다 present v. 보여주다
take advantage of phr. ~을 이용하다 saving n. 절약

142 동사 어휘 고르기 주변 문맥 파악 상 ●●●

해설 문장이 주어 없이 시작되는 명령문이므로 빈칸은 명령문의 동사원형 자리이다. '우리 지점에 ___하라'라는 문맥이므로 모든 보기가 정답의 후보이다. 앞 문장에서 오늘 직접 등록하라고 했으므로 (A) Drop by(~에 들르다)가 정답이다. (D) Work out(운동하다)도 해석상 그럴듯해 보이지만, '~에서 운동하다'라는 의미를 가지기 위해서는 위치를 나타내는 전치사 in, at 등과 함께 work out at/in의 형태로 쓰여야 하며, 전치사 없이 바로 목적어가 올 경우 '~을 해결하다, ~을 산출하다'라는 의미가 되어 '우리 지점을 해결하라/산출하라'라는 어색한 문맥을 만든다.

어휘 stay at phr. ~에 머무르다 drive through phr. 차로 지나가다

143-146번은 다음 안내문에 관한 문제입니다.

홍콩 자동차 박람회
당신의 입장권을 수령하는 방법

올해 홍콩 자동차 박람회의 모든 ¹⁴³참석자들은 전시회장에 입장하기 위해 입장권을 가지고 있어야 합니다. 손님들은 8월의 마지막 주 동안 우편으로 그들의 입장권을 받을 것입니다. 만약 당신의 것이 8월 31일까지 도착하지 않는다면, 저희에게 알려주십시오. ¹⁴⁴당신은 555-2801로 전화하셔서 저희에게 알려주실 수 있습니다.

행사 등록은 현재 종료되었습니다. ¹⁴⁵따라서, 추가 등록을 신청하고자 하는 사람들은 더 높은 요금을 내야 할 것입니다. 그들은 행사 ¹⁴⁶장소에서 그들의 티켓을 찾을 수 있을 것입니다. 입장권은 박람회가 시작하기 전에 하루 종일 배부될 것입니다.

receive v. 수령하다, 받다 pass n. 입장권 exhibition hall phr. 전시회장
sign up phr. 신청하다 late registration phr. 추가 등록
distribute v. 배부하다, 나누어주다

143 명사 어휘 고르기 전체 문맥 파악 중 ●●○

해설 빈칸은 수량 형용사(All)의 꾸밈을 받는 명사 자리이다. '자동차 박람회의 모든 ___은 전시회장에 입장하기 위해 입장권을 가지고 있어야 한다'라는 문맥이므로 모든 보기가 정답의 후보이다. 뒤 문장에서 손님들은 우편으로 입장권을 받을 것이라고 했고, 뒷부분에서 추가 등록을 신청하고자 하는 사람들은 더 높은 요금을 내고 티켓을 찾을 수 있다고 했으므로 (C) attendees(참석자들)가 정답이다.

어휘 reviewer n. 비평가 lecturer n. 강연자 organizer n. 주최자

144 알맞은 문장 고르기 중 ●●○

해석 (A) 귀하의 질문에 대한 저희의 늦은 응답에 대해 사과드립니다.
(B) 최대 3명의 손님들을 함께 데려올 수 있습니다.
(C) 당신은 555-2801로 전화하셔서 저희에게 알려주실 수 있습니다.
(D) 그럼 저희가 당신의 부스를 조립하는 것을 도와드리겠습니다.

해설 앞 문장 'If yours has not arrived by August 31, please notify us.'에서 만약 당신의 것, 즉 입장권이 8월 31일까지 도착하지 않는다면 저희에게 알려달라고 했으므로, 빈칸에는 555-2801로 전화해서 저희에게 알려줄 수 있다는 내용이 들어가야 함을 알 수 있다. 따라서 (C)가 정답이다.

어휘 apologize v. 사과하다 response n. 응답 inquiry n. 질문
maximum n. 최대 inform v. 알리다 assemble v. 조립하다

145 접속부사 채우기 주변 문맥 파악 상 ●●●

해설 앞 문장에서 행사 등록은 현재 종료되었다고 했고, 빈칸이 있는 문장에서는 추가 등록을 신청하고자 하는 사람들은 더 높은 요금을 내야 한다고 했으므로, 앞 문장의 내용에 대한 결과를 언급할 때 사용되는 접속부사 (D) Accordingly (따라서)가 정답이다. (B) At that time(그때에)도 해석상 그럴듯해 보이지만, 앞서 언급된 특정한 시간을 의미하므로 답이 될 수 없다.

어휘 specifically adv. 구체적으로 overall adv. 종합적으로, 전반적인

146 명사 관련 어구 완성하기 주변 문맥 파악 중 ●●○

해설 빈칸은 명사(event)와 복합 명사를 이루어 전치사(at)의 목적어 역할을 하는 명사 자리이다. '그들은 행사 ___에/에서 티켓을 찾을 수 있다'라는 문맥이며, 뒤 문장에서 입장권은 박람회가 시작하기 전부터 하루 종일 배부될 것이라고 했으므로, 행사 장소에서 티켓을 찾을 수 있음을 알 수 있다. 따라서 빈칸 앞의 명사 event(행사)와 함께 '행사 장소'라는 의미의 어구인 event venue를 만드는 (D) venue(장소)가 정답이다.

어휘 system n. 시스템 scheme n. 계획 page n. 화면, 페이지

PART 7

147-148번은 다음 초대장에 관한 문제입니다.

> ¹⁴⁷West Hobart 공연예술센터의
> 준공식에 귀하는 정중히 초대되었습니다
> 4월 9일 오후 7시 30분
>
> ¹⁴⁷이 행사를 기념하기 위해, ¹⁴⁸⁻ᴬHobart 교향악단은 오후 8시 30분에 30분짜리 콘서트를 공연할 것입니다. 오페라 가수 Kelly Tekanawa의 공연이 이후에 이어질 것입니다.
>
> 행사의 복장 규정은 격식을 갖춘 것입니다. ¹⁴⁸⁻ᴮ무료 음료와 전채 요리가 공연 전과 후에 제공될 것입니다. 참석 확정이 요구됩니다. ¹⁴⁸⁻ᴰ이 초대장은 초대된 손님과 다른 한 명에 유효합니다.
>
> 이 행사는 저희의 후원자인 Tasmania Savings 은행과 Barkley Investors Group사의 후한 기부를 통해 가능해졌습니다.
>
> 센터는 67번지 Mount Stuart로에 위치해 있으며, 대리 주차가 이용 가능할 것입니다.
>
> ---
>
> cordially adv. 정중히, 다정하게 inauguration n. 준공식
> commemorate v. 기념하다 occasion n. 행사
> dress code phr. 복장 규정 formal adj. 격식을 갖춘
> complimentary adj. 무료의 beverage n. 음료 appetizer n. 전채 요리
> confirmation n. 확정, 확인 attendance n. 참석 valid adj. 유효한
> generous adj. 후한 contribution n. 기부

147 육하원칙 문제 중 ●●○

해석 행사는 왜 West Hobart 공연예술센터에서 열리는가?
(A) 음악가들의 집단을 소개하기 위해
(B) 시설의 개관식을 축하하기 위해
(C) 자선 단체를 위한 기금을 모금하기 위해
(D) 회사의 성과를 기리기 위해

해설 지문의 'You are ~ invited to the inauguration of the West Hobart Performing Arts Center'에서 West Hobart 공연예술센터의 준공식에

초대되었다고 했고, 'To commemorate this occasion'에서 이 행사, 즉 센터의 준공식을 기념하기 위해라고 했으므로 (B)가 정답이다.

어휘 opening n. 개관식 raise v. 모금하다 fund n. 기금
charity organization phr. 자선 단체 honor v. 기리다
accomplishment n. 성과, 성취

패러프레이징

> inauguration 준공식 → opening 개관식
> commemorate 기념하다 → celebrate 축하하다

148 Not/True 문제 중 ●●●

해석 초대된 손님들에 대해 언급된 것은?
(A) 공연 30분 전에 착석해야 한다.
(B) 행사에서 음식과 음료를 구매할 수 있다.
(C) 단체의 구성원들이다.
(D) 추가 인원을 데려올 수 있다.

해설 지문의 'This invitation is valid for the invited guest and one other person.'에서 초대장은 초대된 손님과 다른 한 명에 유효하다고 했으므로 (D)는 지문의 내용과 일치한다. 따라서 (D)가 정답이다. (A)는 'the Hobart Symphony orchestra will perform a 30-minute concert'에서 Hobart 교향악단이 30분짜리 콘서트를 공연할 것이라고는 했으나 공연 30분 전에 착석해야 하는지는 언급되지 않았으므로 지문의 내용과 일치하지 않는다. (B)는 'Complimentary beverages and appetizers will be served'에서 무료 음료와 전채 요리가 제공될 것이라고 했으므로 지문의 내용과 일치하지 않는다. (C)는 지문에 언급되지 않은 내용이다.

어휘 additional adj. 추가의

패러프레이징

> one other person 다른 한 명 → an additional person 추가 인원

149-150번은 다음 회람에 관한 문제입니다.

> 회람
>
> 수신: 모든 Forrester Communications사 직원
> 발신: Judie Tomlinson
> 제목: 대중매체 회의
> 날짜: 8월 21일
>
> ---
>
> ¹⁴⁹⁻ᴬ/ᴮ/ᴰ연례 Peabody 대중매체 회의가 9월 3일부터 7일까지 시애틀의 Arlington 호텔에서 열릴 것입니다. 경영진은 우리 회사에서 네 명의 대표자들이 참석하기를 원합니다. 만약 관심이 있으시다면, 8월 25일이 회사가 그들의 직원들을 위해 출입증을 구매하기 위한 마감일이기 때문에 그 때까지 저에게 알려주십시오.
>
> 회사는 회의 참석자들에게 모든 출장비용을 환급해줄 것입니다. 그러나, ¹⁵⁰여러분의 출장을 계획할 때 다음의 규정들을 명심해 주십시오. 첫째로, 호텔 객실에 청구될 수 있는 최대 금액은 1박에 125달러 입니다. 둘째로, 직원들은 그들이 이코노미 좌석을 예약할 때만 항공 요금에 대한 환급을 받을 수 있을 것입니다.
>
> 만약 이 행사 또는 회사의 환급 정책에 대해 문의 사항이 있으시면, 언제든지 저에게 연락해 주십시오.
>
> ---
>
> representative n. 대표자 notify v. 알리다 deadline n. 마감일
> pass n. 출입증 reimburse v. 환급하다, 상환하다 participant n. 참석자
> expense n. 비용 policy n. 규정, 정책 maximum adj. 최대의

claim v. 청구하다, 주장하다 reimbursement n. 환급 airfare n. 항공 요금

149 Not/True 문제

해석 회의에 대해 언급되지 않은 것은?
(A) 숙박 시설에서 열릴 것이다.
(B) 매년 한 번 열린다.
(C) 시애틀에 근거지를 둔 회사에 의해 개최된다.
(D) 며칠의 기간 동안 지속될 것이다.

해설 지문에서 (C)는 언급되지 않은 내용이다. 따라서 (C)가 정답이다. (A), (B), (D)는 'The annual Peabody Media Conference will be held at the Arlington Hotel in Seattle from September 3 to 7.'에서 연례 Peabody 대중매체 회의가 9월 3일부터 7일까지 시애틀의 Arlington 호텔에서 열릴 것이라고 했으므로 지문의 내용과 일치한다.

어휘 accommodation facility phr. 숙박 시설
take place phr. 열리다, 일어나다 organize v. 개최하다

패러프레이징

annual 연례의 → once every year 매년 한 번
be held 열리다 → take place 열리다
Hotel 호텔 → an accommodation facility 숙박 시설
from September 3 to 7 9월 3일부터 7일까지 → a period of multiple days 며칠의 기간

150 추론 문제
중 ●●○

해석 몇몇 Forrester Communications사 직원들에 대해 추론될 수 있는 것은?
(A) 그들 자신의 입장권에 대해 돈을 지불해야 할 것이다.
(B) 동료와 호텔 객실을 함께 사용할 것이다.
(C) 그들 자신의 출장 준비를 할 것이다.
(D) 비즈니스 좌석 항공권을 구매할 것이다.

해설 지문의 'please keep the following policies in mind when planning your trip'에서 여러분, 즉 Forrester Communications사 직원들이 그들의 출장을 계획할 때 다음의 규정들을 명심하라고 했으므로 직원들이 그들 자신의 출장 준비를 할 것이라는 사실을 추론할 수 있다. 따라서 (C)가 정답이다.

어휘 admission pass phr. 입장권 coworker n. 동료
arrangement n. 준비

패러프레이징

planning ~ trip 출장을 계획하다 → make ~ travel arrangements 출장 준비를 하다

151-153번은 다음 편지에 관한 문제입니다.

Picica 보험사

Lavi Steinem
4304번지 Cordova가
밴쿠버시, 브리티시 콜롬비아주
V6B 1E1

2월 2일

Mr. Steinem께,

저희는 귀하가 제출하신 서류들을 검토했으며, 저는 ¹⁵²**저희가 귀하의**

자동차 수리에 대한 귀하의 청구를 이행할 수 없다는 것을 알려드리게 되어 유감입니다. ^{151-B}귀하의 보험증서의 조건은 사고의 경우에, 귀하가 Picica 보험사에 가능한 한 빨리 연락하도록 요구된다고 명시합니다. 만약 귀하가 이것을 하셨다면, 우리 직원들 중 한 명이 손해를 평가하고 귀하의 보험증서에 의해 얼마가 보장되는지 산정할 수 있었을 것입니다. ^{151-B}귀하가 청구서를 제출하시기 전에 귀하의 자동차에 수리가 이행되는 것을 선택하셨기 때문에, 비록 ¹⁵³귀하가 귀하의 자동차의 손상 입은 부분의 사진을 동봉하셨을지라도, 누구에게 과실이 있는지 또는 손상의 실제 정도에 대해 저희가 아는 것은 불가능합니다.

귀하의 보험증서를 꼼꼼하게 검토해 주십시오. 만약 귀하가 계약을 지키시지 못하신다면, 저희가 할 수 있는 것은 거의 없습니다. 만약 추가 설명이 필요하시거나 이의를 제기하고자 하신다면, 귀하의 가장 가까운 Picica 보험사 사무실을 방문하시거나 1-800-555-8899로 전화해주십시오.

Lou Mortimer 드림
Picica 보험사 직원

go over phr. 검토하다 submit v. 제출하다 inform v. 알리다
claim n. 청구, 요구 term n. 조건 policy n. 보험증서, 정책
state v. 명시하다 agent n. 직원 assess v. 평가하다
determine v. 산정하다, 결정하다 carry out phr. 이행하다
enclose v. 동봉하다 adhere to phr. 지키다, 고수하다
agreement n. 계약 clarification n. 설명 objection n. 이의

151 Not/True 문제
상 ●●●

해석 Mr. Steinem에 대해 언급된 것은?
(A) 더 높은 보험료를 지불해야 할 것이다.
(B) 계약상의 요건을 충족하지 않았다.
(C) 다른 운전자와 사고가 났다.
(D) Picica사의 보험 보상에 대한 자격이 더 이상 없다.

해설 지문의 'The terms of your policy state that, in the event of an accident, you are required to contact Picica Insurance as soon as possible.'에서 보험증서의 조건은 사고의 경우에, 귀하, 즉 Mr. Steinem이 Picica 보험사에 가능한 한 빨리 연락하도록 요구된다고 명시한다고 했고, 'you chose to have repairs carried out ~ before submitting your claim'에서 Mr. Steinem이 청구서를 제출하기 전에 수리가 이행되는 것을 선택했다고 했으므로 (B)는 지문의 내용과 일치한다. 따라서 (B)가 정답이다. (A), (C), (D)는 지문에 언급되지 않은 내용이다.

어휘 insurance fee phr. 보험료 requirement n. 요건, 조건
eligible adj. 자격이 있는 coverage n. (보험의) 보상, 보장

152 동의어 찾기 문제
중 ●●○

해석 1문단 첫 번째 줄의 단어 "satisfy"는 의미상 -와 가장 가깝다.
(A) 설득하다
(B) 보상하다
(C) 만족시키다
(D) 이행하다

해설 satisfy를 포함한 구절 'we cannot satisfy your claim for repairs to your automobile'에서 저희가 귀하의 자동차 수리에 대한 청구를 이행할 수 없다고 했으므로 satisfy는 '이행하다'라는 뜻으로 사용되었다. 따라서 '이행하다, 실행하다'라는 뜻을 가진 (D) fulfill이 정답이다.

해커스 토익 실전 1200제 READING

해석   Mr. Steinem은 Mr. Mortimer에게 무엇을 보냈는가?
(A) 자동차 수리에 대한 요청서
(B) 차량 사진
(C) 거래 기록
(D) 보상 제공에 대한 거절

해설   지문의 'you did enclose a photo of the damaged area of your car'에서 귀하, 즉 Mr. Steinem이 자동차의 손상 입은 부분의 사진을 동봉하였다고 했으므로 (B)가 정답이다.

어휘   transaction n. 거래   rejection n. 거절   compensation n. 보상

패러프레이징

> a photo of ~ car 자동차의 사진 → A photograph of a vehicle 차량 사진

154-155번은 다음 메시지 대화문에 관한 문제입니다.

Joseph Donahue [오전 10시 46분]
안녕하세요, Lesley. 저는 제가 자료를 비교하도록 요구하는 업무를 받아서, 또 하나의 컴퓨터 모니터를 받는 것이 가능할지 궁금해요. 그렇지 않다면, 업무를 끝내는 것이 더 오래 걸릴 거예요.

Lesley Roussell [오전 10시 47분]
그렇군요. ¹⁵⁴당신은 IT 부서에 요청서를 보낼 수 있어요. 그들이 직원들에게 컴퓨터 장비를 할당하는 것을 담당해요. ¹⁵⁴하지만, 이것은 며칠이 걸릴 수도 있어요. 그들은 회계부서의 새로운 직원들에게 설치해주느라 바빠서요.

Joseph Donahue [오전 10시 48분]
다른 방법은 없을까요? ¹⁵⁴/¹⁵⁵이 업무는 금요일까지 완료되어야 해요. ¹⁵⁵게다가, 저는 그 이후에는 추가 모니터가 필요 없을 거예요.

Lesley Roussell [오전 10시 50분]
그런 경우에는, ¹⁵⁵제가 당신이 그때까지 사용할 수 있는 노트북 컴퓨터를 가지고 있어요. 점심 이후에 당신이 그것을 설치하는 것을 제가 도와줄 수 있어요.

---

assignment n. 업무   compare v. 비교하다   wonder v. 궁금하다
a second phr. 또 하나의   in charge of phr. ~을 담당하다
allocate v. 할당하다, 배분하다

해석   오전 10시 48분에, Mr. Donahue가 "Isn't there another way"라고 썼을 때 그가 의도한 것은?
(A) 업무를 완료하기 위해 더 많은 자료를 필요로 한다.
(B) 새로운 직원이 컴퓨터를 설치하는 것을 도울 수 없다.
(C) 프로젝트 일정이 합당하다고 생각하지 않는다.
(D) 요청에 대한 응답을 기다릴 수 없다.

해설   지문의 'You can send a request to the IT department.'와 'It might take several days, though.'에서 Ms. Roussell이 당신, 즉 Mr. Donahue가 IT 부서에 요청서를 보낼 수 있지만 이것은 며칠이 걸릴 수도 있다고 하자, Mr. Donahue가 'Isn't there another way?'(다른 방법은 없을까요?)라고 한 후, 'The assignment needs to be done by Friday.'에서 이 업무가 금요일까지 완료되어야 한다고 한 것을 통해, Mr. Donahue는 요청에 대한 응답을 기다릴 수 없음을 알 수 있다. 따라서 (D)가 정답이다.

어휘   reasonable adj. 합당한, 합리적인   response n. 응답

해석   Ms. Roussell에 대해 암시되는 것은?
(A) 회계부서의 프로젝트 관리자이다.
(B) 금요일까지 동료가 장비를 빌리는 것을 허락할 것이다.
(C) 몇몇 직원들과 점심을 먹으러 나가야 한다.
(D) 사무실 장비 보관함에서 노트북을 구해야 한다.

해설   지문의 'The assignment needs to be done by Friday. Besides, I won't need the extra monitor after that.'에서 Mr. Donahue는 이 업무가 금요일까지 완료되어야 하고, 그 이후에는 추가 모니터가 필요 없을 것이라고 하자, 'I have a laptop you can use until then'에서 Ms. Roussell이 당신, 즉 Mr. Donahue가 그때, 즉 금요일까지 사용할 수 있는 노트북 컴퓨터를 가지고 있다고 했으므로 금요일까지 동료가 장비를 빌리는 것을 허락할 것이라는 사실을 추론할 수 있다. 따라서 (B)가 정답이다.

어휘   colleague n. 동료   device n. 장비, 장치   associate n. 직원

패러프레이징

> laptop 노트북 컴퓨터 → device 장비

156-157번은 다음 브로슈어에 관한 문제입니다.

> *Magic Moments* 사진 촬영
>
> 저희의 사진작가들은 결혼식, 기념일, 그리고 졸업식과 같은 특별한 행사들의 마법 같은 순간들을 포착하는 것을 전문으로 합니다. 저희는 다음과 같은 패키지 옵션들을 제공합니다:
>
> ~¹⁵⁶⁻ᴮ/ᴰ**실버 패키지**~ 1,500달러
> ¹⁵⁶⁻ᴮ한 명의 사진작가가 당신의 특별한 행사의 2시간을 담당할 것입니다. 당신은 DVD에 ¹⁵⁶⁻ᴰ**편집된** 250개의 **고해상도 사진들**을 받을 것입니다.
>
> ~¹⁵⁶⁻ᴰ/¹⁵⁷⁻ᴬ**골드 패키지**~ 2,500달러
> 두 명의 사진작가들이 당신의 특별한 행사의 4시간을 담당할 것입니다. 당신은 DVD에 ¹⁵⁶⁻ᴰ**편집된** 500개의 **고해상도 사진들**과 ¹⁵⁷⁻ᴬ5분짜리 영상을 받을 것입니다.
>
> ~¹⁵⁶⁻ᴰ/¹⁵⁷⁻ᶜ**플래티넘 패키지**~ 3,500달러
> 두 명의 사진작가들이 당신의 특별한 행사의 전체를 담당할 것입니다. 당신은 DVD에 10분짜리 영상과 ¹⁵⁷⁻ᶜ**온라인 사용을 위해 특별히 구성된 사진들** 뿐만 아니라 ¹⁵⁶⁻ᴰ**편집된** 최소 1,000개의 **고해상도 사진들**을 받을 것입니다.
>
> 모든 물품들이 배송되는 것에 대해 3주까지 감안하여 주십시오.

---

specialize in phr. ~을 전문으로 하다   capture v. 포착하다
anniversary n. 기념일   cover v. 담당하다
high-resolution adj. 고해상도의   minimum adj. 최소의
as well as phr. ~뿐만 아니라   specifically adv. 특별히
format v. 구성하다   up to phr. ~까지

해석   Magic Moments 사진 촬영에 대해 언급된 것은?
(A) 최소 3주 전에 고객들을 예약한다.
(B) 모든 행사에 여러 명의 사진사들을 보낸다.
(C) 추가 요금으로 사진 배송을 더 신속히 처리할 수 있다.
(D) 그것의 모든 패키지에 사진 수정을 제공한다.

해설   지문의 'Silver Package', 'Gold Package', 'Platinum Package', 'edited high-resolution prints'에서 실버, 골드, 플래티넘 패키지 모두 편

집된 고해상도 사진들을 포함하고 있으므로 (D)는 지문의 내용과 일치한다. 따라서 (D)가 정답이다. (A)와 (C)는 지문에 언급되지 않은 내용이다. (B)는 'Silver Package'와 'One photographer'에서 실버 패키지에는 한 명의 사진작가가 있다고 했으므로 지문의 내용과 일치하지 않는다.

어휘 **book** v. 예약하다 **in advance** phr. ~전에, 미리
expedite v. 더 신속히 처리하다 **modification** n. 수정

패러프레이징

edited ~ prints 편집된 사진들 → photo modification 사진 수정

157 Not/True 문제   중 ●●○

해석 플래티넘 패키지에 대해 사실인 것은?
(A) 영상을 포함하는 유일한 패키지이다.
(B) 사진들을 공유하기 위한 웹페이지가 딸려 있다.
(C) 인터넷을 위해 맞춤 제작된 사진들을 포함한다.
(D) 주문 제작한 DVD 선택권을 제공한다.

해설 지문의 'Platinum Package'와 'photos specifically formatted for online use'에서 플래티넘 패키지에는 온라인 사용을 위해 특별히 구성된 사진들이 있다는 것을 알 수 있으므로 (C)는 지문의 내용과 일치한다. 따라서 (C)가 정답이다. (A)는 'Gold Package', 'a 5-minute video'에서 골드 패키지에도 5분짜리 영상이 있다는 것을 알 수 있으므로 지문의 내용과 일치하지 않는다. (B)와 (D)는 지문에 언급되지 않은 내용이다.

어휘 **come with** phr. ~이 딸려 있다 **customized** adj. 맞춤 제작된
custom-made adj. 주문 제작한

패러프레이징

specifically formatted for online use 온라인 사용을 위해 특별히 구성된
→ customized for the Internet 인터넷을 위해 맞춤 제작된

158-161번은 다음 취업 공고에 관한 문제입니다.

Hamasaki사의 채용 공고

¹⁵⁸Hamasaki사는 자동차 부품들의 제조와 공급에 관련된 세계적인 기업입니다. 저희는 현재 일리노이 시카고에 있는 저희의 주요 생산 공장에서 직무를 수행할 창고 관리자를 찾고 있습니다.

주된 역할들:
· 공급업체들로부터의 ¹⁵⁹⁻ᴬ원자재 배달을 관리한다
· 고객들에 대한 완제품 배송을 조정한다
· 안전하고 생산적인 작업 환경을 유지한다
· ¹⁵⁹⁻ᴮ직원들의 고용, 징계 조치, 보상, 해고를 제안한다
· 작업 절차를 평가하고 개선을 제안한다

¹⁶⁰필수적인 자격요건들은 포함합니다:
· 최소 2년제 대학 학위 수료
· 되도록이면 자동차 산업에서의 ¹⁶⁰최소 5년의 관련 직무 경험
· 데이터베이스 프로그램 작업 능력
· ¹⁵⁹⁻ᶜ매우 체계적이며 꼼꼼한 것

¹⁵⁹⁻ᴰ이것은 경쟁력 있는 연봉과 복리후생제도를 제공하는 **정규직입니다.**
¹⁶¹지원하기 위해서는, 당신의 이력서를 jobs@hamasakicorp.com으로 보내주십시오. 만약 당신이 확인 이메일을 받지 못한다면, 저희의 인사담당자에게 555-3090으로 연락해주십시오. 지원서는 직접 받아지지 않을 것입니다.

automotive adj. 자동차의 **warehouse** n. 창고

---

supervisor n. 관리자 **primary** adj. 주된, 주요한
raw material phr. 원자재 **supplier** n. 공급업체 **coordinate** v. 조정하다
finished goods phr. 완제품 **productive** adj. 생산적인
disciplinary action phr. 징계 조치 **rewarding** n. 보상
termination n. 해고, 종료 **evaluate** v. 평가하다 **improvement** n. 개선
qualification n. 자격요건 **preferably** adv. 되도록이면
organized adj. 체계적인 **detail oriented** phr. 꼼꼼한
benefits package phr. 복리후생제도 **résumé** n. 이력서
confirmation n. 확인 **in person** phr. 직접, 몸소

158 육하원칙 문제   중 ●●○

해석 어떤 회사가 취업 공고를 게시했는가?
(A) 자동차 대리점
(B) 배송 업체
(C) 부품 제조사
(D) 운송 서비스 회사

해설 지문의 'Hamasaki Corporation is a ~ corporation involved in the manufacture ~ of automotive parts.'에서 Hamasaki사는 자동차 부품들의 제조에 관련된 기업이라고 했으므로 (C)가 정답이다.

어휘 **dealership** n. 대리점 **firm** n. 회사

패러프레이징

a ~ corporation involved in the manufacture ~ of automotive parts
자동차 부품들의 제조에 관련된 기업 → A parts manufacturer 부품 제조사

159 Not/True 문제   중 ●●○

해석 일자리에 대해 언급되지 않은 것은?
(A) 관리 임무를 포함한다.
(B) 직원을 고용하고 해고하는 것을 수반할 수 있다.
(C) 세부 사항에 대한 주의력을 요구한다.
(D) 시간제 근로자에게 유효하다.

해설 지문의 'This is a full-time role'에서 이것은 정규직이라고 했으므로 (D)는 지문의 내용과 일치하지 않는다. 따라서 (D)가 정답이다. (A)는 'Supervise deliveries of raw materials'에서 원자재 배달을 관리한다고 했으므로 지문의 내용과 일치한다. (B)는 'Recommend the hiring ~ and termination of employees'에서 직원들의 고용과 해고를 제안한다고 했으므로 지문의 내용과 일치한다. (C)는 'Being ~ detail oriented'에서 꼼꼼한 것이라고 했으므로 지문의 내용과 일치한다.

어휘 **supervisory** adj. 관리의 **dismiss** v. 해고하다
attention n. 주의력 **available** adj. 유효한, 이용 가능한
part-time worker phr. 시간제 근로자

패러프레이징

Supervise 관리하다 → supervisory 관리의
termination of employees 직원들의 해고 → dismissing staff 직원들을 해고하는 것
Being ~ detail oriented 꼼꼼한 것 → attention to detail 세부 사항에 대한 주의력

160 육하원칙 문제   중 ●●○

해석 일자리의 지원자들에게 무엇이 요구되는가?
(A) 4년제 학위 소유
(B) 교육 프로그램 수료

(C) 한 개 이상의 언어 구사 능력

(D) 직무 형태에 대한 숙지

해설 지문의 'Essential qualifications include:', 'At least five years of experience in a related role'에서 최소 5년의 관련 직무 경험이 필수적인 자격요건이라고 했으므로 (D)가 정답이다.

어휘 possession n. 소유 completion n. 수료 familiarity n. 숙지, 잘 앎

패러프레이징

experience in a related role 관련 직무 경험 → Familiarity with a job type 직무 형태에 대한 숙지

---

161 육하원칙 문제   하 ●○○

해석 사람들은 어떻게 지원해야 하는가?
(A) 관리자에게 연락함으로써
(B) 지원서를 우편 발송함으로써
(C) 이메일을 사용함으로써
(D) 웹사이트를 방문함으로써

해설 지문의 'To apply, send your résumé to jobs@hamasakicorp.com.'에서 지원하기 위해서는, 당신의 이력서를 jobs@hamasakicorp.com으로 보내라고 했으므로 (C)가 정답이다.

어휘 application letter phr. 지원서

패러프레이징

send ~ résumé to jobs@hamasakicorp.com 이력서를 jobs@hamasakicorp.com으로 보내다 → using e-mail 이메일을 사용하는 것

162-164번은 다음 보도 자료에 관한 문제입니다.

Zoet 식품사가 새로운 제품라인을 출시한다

3월 21일—¹⁶²아이스크림 시장의 최근 경향에 대응하여, 스위스의 Zoet 식품사는 올해 말에 새로운 제품라인을 출시할 것이라고 밝혔다. Zoet사의 마케팅 관리자 James Farnham은 이러한 개발에 대해 변화하는 입맛을 원인으로 돌렸다. — [1] —. ¹⁶²**"우리는 지난 몇 년 동안 고객 선호도의 분명한 변화를 봐왔습니다."**라고 그는 말했다. "고객들은 아이스크림의 높은 설탕 함유량 때문에 이것을 덜 먹고 있으며 이제 요거트 같은 더 건강한 대체재들을 선호합니다." ¹⁶⁴**젤라또와 유기농 또는 유제품이 아닌 재료들로 만들어진 아이스크림들 같은 고급 제품들에 대한 수요에 의해 이 시장은 더욱 약화되고 있다.** — [2] —.

Zoet사가 최근 중국, 브라질, 그리고 인도와 같은 신흥 시장들에서 영향력을 늘리긴 했지만, 이것의 매출의 대부분은 여전히 유럽과 미국에서 나온다. — [3] —. Farnham은 "우리는 신흥 시장들에서 많은 성장의 여지를 가지고 있지만, ¹⁶³**우리의 가장 큰 어려움은 유럽과 미국에서 우리의 선두적인 입지를 유지하는 것입니다.**"라고 덧붙였다. — [4] —. ¹⁶³Zoet사의 유기농과 유제품이 아닌 재료들뿐만 아니라 요거트와 젤라또를 아우르는 혁신적인 새로운 제품 라인과 함께, 회사는 이러한 어려움에 맞설 준비가 된 것으로 보인다.

respond v. 대응하다 release v. 출시하다 shift n. 변화
preference n. 선호도 content n. 함유량 alternative n. 대체재
erode v. 약화시키다 non-dairy adj. 유제품이 아닌 ingredient n. 재료
emerging adj. 신흥의 majority n. 대부분 plenty of phr. 많은
room n. 여지 challenge n. 어려움 leading adj. 선두적인
encompassing adj. 아우르는 take on phr. 맞서다

---

162 주제 찾기 문제   상 ●●●

해석 보도 자료는 주로 무엇에 대한 것인가?
(A) 음식 생산에서의 혁신
(B) 제품에 대한 시장 상황
(C) 몇몇 국가들에서의 소비자 행동
(D) 주요 음식 생산업체들의 전략

해설 지문의 'current trends in the ice cream market'에서 아이스크림 시장의 최근 경향이라고 했고 'We have seen a clear shift in consumer preferences in the last couple of years'에서 지난 몇 년 동안 고객들의 선호도 변화를 봐왔다고 한 후, 아이스크림 시장의 최근 경향에 대해 설명하고 있으므로 (B)가 정답이다.

어휘 innovation n. 혁신 condition n. 상황 strategy n. 전략

패러프레이징

trends in the ~ market 시장의 경향 → Market conditions 시장 상황

---

163 추론 문제   상 ●●●

해석 Zoet사는 어떻게 그것의 입지를 유지할 계획인 것 같은가?
(A) 그것의 운영 규모를 감소시킴으로써
(B) 더 낮은 가격의 재료를 개발함으로써
(C) 유럽에 신제품들을 소개함으로써
(D) 아시아에서 더욱 공격적으로 광고함으로써

해설 지문의 'our biggest challenge is maintaining our leading position in Europe and the US'에서 우리, 즉 Zoet사의 가장 큰 어려움은 유럽과 미국에서 선두적인 입지를 유지하는 것이라고 했고, 'With Zoet's innovative new product lines ~, the company appears ready to take on this challenge.'에서 Zoet사의 혁신적인 새로운 제품 라인과 함께, 회사는 이러한 어려움 즉, 유럽과 미국에서 선두적인 입지를 유지하는 어려움에 맞설 준비가 된 것으로 보인다고 했으므로 유럽과 미국에 신제품들을 소개함으로써 입지를 유지할 계획이라는 사실을 추론할 수 있다. 따라서 (C)가 정답이다.

어휘 scale n. 규모 operation n. 운영 aggressively adv. 공격적으로

---

164 문장 위치 찾기 문제   중 ●●○

해석 [1], [2], [3], [4]로 표시된 위치 중, 다음 문장이 들어갈 곳으로 가장 적절한 것은?

"이러한 종류들은 일반적으로 세계적인 회사보다 지역 전문 회사들에 의해 지배된다."

(A) [1]
(B) [2]
(C) [3]
(D) [4]

해설 주어진 문장에서 이러한 종류들은 일반적으로 세계적인 회사들보다 지역 전문 회사들에 의해 지배된다고 했으므로, 주어진 문장 앞에 이러한 종류들과 관련된 내용이 있을 것임을 예상할 수 있다. [2]의 앞 문장인 'The market is being further eroded by demand for premium products like gelato, and ice creams made with organic or non-dairy ingredients.'에서 젤라또와 유기농 또는 유제품이 아닌 재료들로 만들어진 아이스크림들 같은 고급 제품들에 대한 수요에 의해 시장은 더욱 약화되고 있다고 했으므로, [2]에 주어진 문장이 들어가면 이러한 종류의 고급 제품들은 일반적으로 세계적인 회사들보다 지역 전문 회사들에 의해 지배된다는 자연스러운 문맥이 된다는 것을 알 수 있다. 따라서 (B)가 정답이다.

어휘 category n. 종류 typically adv. 일반적으로
dominate v. 지배하다, 우세하다 specialty n. 전문, 본업

165-167번은 다음 이메일에 관한 문제입니다.

수신: Katherine Miller <k.miller@crpd.com>
발신: John Watt <j.watt@crpd.com>
날짜: 1월 25일
제목: Lawrence Sheffield

Katherine께,

당신은 우리 팀에 대한 Mr. Sheffield의 상당한 공헌을 아마 알고 있을 것입니다. 그는 그가 여기서 일한 거의 5년 동안 우리가 직원들에 대해 정했던 모든 목표들을 성취하거나 능가해 왔습니다. 게다가, 그는 회사의 올해 고객 서비스 직원상의 가장 최근 수상자였습니다. ¹⁶⁶그는 또한 우리 직원들 중 이달 초 우리가 제공했던 선택적인 40시간 고객 서비스 자격증 프로그램에 등록하고 수료한 유일한 직원입니다. 어쨌든, ¹⁶⁷저는 단지 그의 성과 때문만 아니라 그가 계속 우리 회사와 함께하는 것을 보장하기 위해 ¹⁶⁵/¹⁶⁷우리가 그에게 임금 인상을 해주어야 한다고 생각합니다.

경제가 나아짐에 따라, 더 많은 일자리들을 구할 수 있게 되어서 ¹⁶⁷저는 Mr. Sheffield가 이미 몇몇 제안들을 받았을 것으로 생각합니다. 그의 경력과 자격을 고려해볼 때, 그는 어느 고객 서비스 부서에서든지 귀중한 자산이 될 것입니다. 저는 현재 그가 매달 받는 것보다 그에게 10퍼센트를 더 제공할 것을 제안 드립니다. 이것은 많아 보일 수도 있으나, 저는 더 자격이 있는 사람은 없다고 생각합니다. 당신이 어떻게 생각하는지 제게 알려주십시오.

John Watt 드림
고객 서비스 부팀장
CRPD Electric사

be aware of phr. ~을 알다 significant adj. 상당한
contribution n. 공헌 exceed v. 능가하다, 넘다 recipient n. 수상자
enroll v. 등록하다 optional adj. 선택적인 certification n. 자격증
offer v. 제공하다; n. 제안 raise n. 임금 인상, 상승 performance n. 성과
ensure v. 보장하다 credentials n. 자격 valuable adj. 귀중한
asset n. 자산 propose v. 제안하다 deserving adj. 자격이 있는, 받을 만한

165 목적 찾기 문제
상 ●●●

해석 이메일은 왜 쓰였는가?
(A) 관리직에 적합한 지원자를 추천하기 위해
(B) 연례 상의 수상자를 발표하기 위해
(C) 직원의 보상을 늘리는 것을 제안하기 위해
(D) 직원의 최근 승진을 정당화하기 위해

해설 지문의 'I believe that we should give him a raise'에서 우리가 그, 즉 Mr. Sheffield에게 임금 인상을 해주어야 한다고 생각한다고 한 후, 해당 직원의 보상을 늘리는 것을 제안하는 이유를 설명하고 있으므로 (C)가 정답이다.

어휘 suitable adj. 적합한, 알맞은 position n. 직, 직책
compensation n. 보상 justify v. 정당화하다

패러프레이징

give ~ a raise 임금을 인상하다 → increasing the compensation 보상을 늘리는 것

166 추론 문제
상 ●●●

해석 Mr. Sheffield에 대해 암시되는 것은?
(A) 한 번 이상 승진했다.
(B) 그의 동료 직원들에게 인기가 많다.
(C) 한 달 이내에 자격증을 받았다.
(D) 한 가지 요청을 하기 위해 Mr. Watt을 만났다.

해설 지문의 'He was also the only member ~ to enroll in and complete the ~ certification program ~ offered at the beginning of this month.'에서 그, 즉 Mr. Sheffield는 또한 이달 초에 제공했던 자격증 프로그램에 등록하고 수료한 유일한 직원이라고 했으므로 Mr. Sheffield가 한 달 이내에 자격증을 받았다는 사실을 추론할 수 있다. 따라서 (C)가 정답이다.

어휘 fellow n. 동료

패러프레이징

complete the ~ certification program ~ offered at the beginning of this month 이달 초 제공했던 자격증 프로그램을 수료하다 → earned a certification in under a month 한 달 이내에 자격증을 받았다

167 육하원칙 문제
중 ●●○

해석 Mr. Watt의 걱정은 무엇인가?
(A) 교육 프로그램이 낮은 참여율을 가졌다.
(B) 경기 침체가 산업을 위협하고 있다.
(C) 회사는 장려금을 제공할 자금이 부족하다.
(D) 부서가 다른 회사에 직원을 빼앗길 것이다.

해설 지문의 'I believe that we should give him a raise, ~ to ensure that he remains with our firm'에서 저, 즉 Mr. Watt는 그, 즉 Mr. Sheffield가 계속 회사와 함께하는 것을 보장하기 위해 임금 인상을 해줘야 한다고 생각한다고 했고, 'I believe Mr. Sheffield has already received some offers'에서 Mr. Sheffield가 이미 몇몇 제안들을 받았을 것으로 생각한다고 했으므로 (D)가 정답이다.

어휘 participation rate phr. 참여율 weak economy phr. 경기 침체
threat v. 위협하다 incentive n. 장려금 firm n. 회사

168-171번은 다음 온라인 채팅 대화문에 관한 문제입니다.

Adriana Scorsese [오전 10시 10분]
5월 14일에 제가 두 분 모두에게 보냈던 이메일에서 언급했듯이, ¹⁶⁸저의 부서가 다음 달에 지원자들을 찾기 시작할 거예요. ¹⁶⁸저는 당신 부서 각각의 채용 요구 사항들을 확인하고 싶어요. Kathy, 회계팀은 두 명의 새로운 직원들이 필요한 것이 맞죠?

Kathy Chiu [오전 10시 14분]
사실, 3명이에요. 제 선임 회계사들 중 한 명인 Jack Wallace가 지난달 그의 은퇴를 발표했어요. 그는 5월 31일에 떠날 거예요.

Adriana Scorsese [오전 10시 14분]
알겠습니다. Charles, 당신은 어때요? 마케팅에 여전히 6명의 신입 사원들이 필요하나요?

Charles Jones [오전 10시 15분]
맞아요. 저희는 회사의 최신 제품 판매를 증가시키기 위해 몇 개의 캠페인을 계획하고 있기 때문에, 저희는 많은 직원이 필요할 거예요. 그리고 그들은 소셜 미디어 홍보에 경험이 있어야 해요. ¹⁶⁹아마도 이것은 구인광고에 명시될 수 있을 거예요.

Adriana Scorsese [오전 10시 18분]

제가 그것을 맡을게요. ¹⁶⁹제 비서인 Judith Harper가 광고 쓰는 것을 담당하고 있고, 그녀가 그 요구 사항을 포함하도록 제가 확실히 할 거예요. ¹⁷⁰5월 18일에 검토를 위해 여러분 각자에게 제가 광고를 보낼게요.

Kathy Chiu [오전 10시 19분]

¹⁷⁰저는 그날 시카고의 세미나에 참석할 예정이에요. 5월 20일에 제가 저의 의견을 드려도 괜찮을까요?

Adriana Scorsese [오전 10시 19분]

문제없어요. 한 가지가 더 있어요. 이전에 제가 언급했듯이, ¹⁷¹저는 여러분의 교육 계획을 미리 검토하고 싶어요. 저는 Kathy의 것은 이미 받았지만, ¹⁷¹Charles 당신의 것은 여전히 기다리고 있어요.

Charles Jones [오전 10시 21분]

죄송합니다. ¹⁷¹저는 금요일 오후에 당신에게 이메일로 그것을 보내드릴 수 있어요. 그때 괜찮을까요?

Adriana Scorsese [오전 10시 22분]

완벽해요. 고마워요.

---

applicant n. 지원자 **confirm** v. 확인하다 **requirement** n. 요구 사항 **accounting team** phr. 회계팀 **senior** adj. 선임의 **accountant** n. 회계사 **retirement** n. 은퇴 **boost** v. 증가시키다 **promotion** n. 홍보 **specify** v. 명시하다 **assistant** n. 비서 **in charge of** phr. ~을 담당하는 **make sure** phr. 확실히 하다, 확인하다 **in advance** phr. 미리

168 추론 문제 중 ●●●○

해석 Ms. Scorsese는 어느 부서에서 일할 것 같은가?

(A) 회계
(B) 마케팅
(C) 인사
(D) 판매

해설 지문의 'my department will begin looking for applicants'와 'I'd like to confirm the hiring requirements ~ of your departments.'에서 Ms. Scorsese가 본인의 부서가 지원자들을 찾기 시작할 것이며 당신 부서들, 즉 회계팀과 마케팅팀의 채용 요구 사항들을 확인하고 싶다고 했으므로 Ms. Scorsese는 인사 부서에서 일하고 있다는 사실을 추론할 수 있다. 따라서 (C)가 정답이다.

169 의도 파악 문제 중 ●●●○

해석 오전 10시 18분에, Ms. Scorsese가 "I'll take care of that"이라고 썼을 때 그녀가 의도한 것은?

(A) 지원자에게 양식을 작성하라고 요청할 것이다.
(B) 다른 직원에게 업무를 할당할 것이다.
(C) 관리자가 회의에 참석하게 할 것이다.
(D) 고객과의 인터뷰를 실시할 것이다.

해설 지문의 'Maybe this could be specified in the job advertisement.'에서 Mr. Jones가 아마도 이것, 즉 앞서 언급된 내용이 구인광고에 명시될 수 있을 것이라고 하자, Ms. Scorsese가 'I'll take care of that.'(제가 그것을 맡을게요)이라고 한 후, 'My assistant, Judith Harper, is ~ writing the advertisements, and I'll make sure she includes that requirement.'에서 본인의 비서인 Ms. Harper가 광고를 쓰고 있고, 그녀가 그 요구 사항을 포함하도록 확실히 할 것이라고 했으므로 다른 직원에게 업무를 할당할 것임을 알 수 있다. 따라서 (B)가 정답이다.

어휘 **assign** v. 할당하다 **task** n. 임무 **conduct** v. 실시하다

패러프레이징

make sure she includes that requirement 그녀가 요구 사항을 포함하도록 확실히 하다 → assign a task to another employee 다른 직원에게 업무를 할당하다

170 육하원칙 문제 중 ●●●○

해석 Ms. Chiu는 어느 날짜에 결근할 것인가?

(A) 5월 14일
(B) 5월 18일
(C) 5월 20일
(D) 5월 31일

해설 지문의 'I'll send the advertisements ~ on May 18 to review.'에서 Ms. Scorsese가 5월 18일에 검토를 위해 광고를 보낼 것이라고 하자, 'I'm going to be attending a seminar in Chicago that day.'에서 Ms. Chiu가 그날 시카고의 세미나에 참석할 예정이라고 했으므로 (B)가 정답이다.

패러프레이징

be absent from work 결근하다 → attending a seminar 세미나에 참석하는 것

171 육하원칙 문제 중 ●●●○

해석 Mr. Jones는 그가 무엇을 할 것이라고 말하는가?

(A) 직원들을 위한 교육 세미나를 준비한다
(B) 소셜 미디어 플랫폼의 게시물을 검토한다
(C) 동료에게 몇 가지 정보를 제공한다
(D) 회사 기록에서 몇 가지 정보를 갱신한다

해설 지문의 'I'd like to review your training plans'와 'I am still waiting for yours, Charles'에서 저, 즉 Ms. Scorsese는 여러분의 교육 계획을 검토하고 싶으며 Charles, 즉 Mr. Jones의 것을 여전히 기다리고 있다고 하자, 'I can e-mail it to you on Friday afternoon.'에서 Mr. Jones가 금요일 오후에 당신, 즉 Ms. Scorsese에게 이메일로 그것, 즉 그의 교육 계획을 보낼 수 있다고 했으므로 (C)가 정답이다.

어휘 **organize** v. 준비하다 **colleague** n. 동료

172-175번은 다음 기사에 관한 문제입니다.

미술품을 내놓은 Bishop Advisors사
Blaine Webster 작성

¹⁷²10월 10일—금융 회사 Bishop Advisors사는 목요일에 자사의 아주 많은 그림들과 조각들의 수집품을 처리할 것이라고 밝혔다. ¹⁷⁵이 작품들은 이전 Bishop Advisors사의 최고경영자 Aileen MacIntyre에 의해 수십 년에 걸쳐 구매되었으며 총 3백만 유로 이상의 가치가 있다고 추산된다. — [1] —.

현재 Bishop Advisors사의 최고경영자 ^{173-C}Gavin Brodie는 자신이 예술에 관심이 없다고 인정했지만, 이것이 그의 선택의 주요한 이유는 아니라고 했다. 오히려, ^{173-A}그는 자금을 모을 필요성과 최근 Bishop Advisors사의 본사 이전을 이유로 들었다. — [2] —. "^{173-B}Ledmore 타워에는 벽과 바닥 장식을 위한 공간이 많이 있었던 반면, 여기 Seascape 건물에는 그것보다 상당히 더 적은 공간을 가지고 있습니다."라고 Brodie는 언급했다.

예술계의 저명한 인사들은 이 소식에 들떠 있다. — [3] —. "그 그림들은 Tessa Menzies의 몇몇 값을 매길 수 없는 풍경화들을 포함합니다."라고 예술 전문가 Jennifer Harper는 말했다. "¹⁷⁴저로서는, 제가 Bret Kennedy의 **몇몇 조각품들을 입찰하기를 희망합니다.**" ^{172/174}**10월 14일에 열리는 판매는** Avidia Auctions에 의해 다루어질 것이다. — [4] —.

- - -

dispose of phr. ~을 처리하다 extensive adj. 아주 많은, 광범위한
collection n. 수집품 sculpture n. 조각 former adj. 이전의
estimate v. 추산하다 worth adj. ~의 가치가 있는 admit v. 인정하다
rather adv. 오히려 point to phr. (이유로) ~을 들다 transfer n. 이전, 이동
headquarters n. 본사 considerably adv. 상당히
comment v. 언급하다 prominent adj. 저명한 figure n. 인사
priceless adj. 값을 매길 수 없는 landscape n. 풍경화
bid on phr. ~에 입찰하다 handle v. 다루다, 맡다

172 주제 찾기 문제

중 ●●○

해석 기사는 주로 무엇에 대한 것인가?
(A) 새로운 경영진의 임명
(B) 제안된 일련의 재무 규정
(C) 다가오는 예술품 판매
(D) 가치 있는 예술품의 발견

해설 지문의 'October 10 ~ Bishop Advisors announced ~ that it will be disposing of its extensive collection of paintings and sculptures'에서 10월 10일에 기사가 쓰였고 Bishop Advisors사가 자사의 아주 많은 그림들과 조각들의 수집품을 처리할 것임을 밝혔다고 했고, 'The sale, to be held on October 14'에서 판매가 10월 14일에 열린다고 했으므로 (C)가 정답이다.

어휘 appointment n. 임명 executive n. 경영진 proposed adj. 제안된
a set of phr. 일련의 regulation n. 규정 upcoming adj. 다가오는
discovery n. 발견

173 Not/True 문제

중 ●●○

해석 Mr. Brodie의 결정에 대한 이유가 아닌 것은?
(A) 재정적 필요
(B) 공간 제약
(C) 흥미의 부족
(D) 직원의 기호

해설 지문에서 (D)는 언급되지 않은 내용이다. 따라서 (D)가 정답이다. (A)는 'he pointed to the need to raise funds'에서 그, 즉 Mr. Brodie는 자금을 모을 필요성을 이유로 들었다고 했으므로 지문의 내용과 일치한다. (B)는 'While there was plenty of space in Ledmore Tower for wall and floor decorations, we have ~ less of that here in the Seascape Building'에서 Ledmore 타워에는 벽과 바닥 장식을 위한 공간이 많이 있었던 반면, 여기 Seascape 건물에는 그것보다 더 적은 공간을 가지고 있다고 했으므로 지문의 내용과 일치한다. (C)는 'Gavin Brodie ~ is not interested in art'에서 Gavin Brodie는 예술에 관심이 없다고 했으므로 지문의 내용과 일치한다.

어휘 monetary adj. 재정적 requirement n. 필요 limitation n. 제약
preference n. 기호, 선호

패러프레이징

the need to raise funds 자금을 모을 필요성 → Monetary requirements 재정적 필요
is not interested 관심이 없다 → Lack of interest 흥미의 부족

174 추론 문제

중 ●●○

해석 누가 10월 14일 행사에 참석할 것 같은가?
(A) Aileen MacIntyre
(B) Tessa Menzies
(C) Jennifer Harper
(D) Bret Kennedy

해설 지문의 'For my part, I hope to bid on ~ the sculptures'에서 저, 즉 Jennifer Harper는 자신이 조각품들을 입찰하기를 희망한다고 했고, 'The sale, to be held on October 14'에서 판매, 즉 경매 행사가 10월 14일에 열린다고 했으므로 Jennifer Harper가 10월 14일 행사에 참석할 것이라는 사실을 추론할 수 있다. 따라서 (C)가 정답이다.

175 문장 위치 찾기 문제

중 ●●○

해석 [1], [2], [3], [4]로 표시된 위치 중, 다음 문장이 들어갈 곳으로 가장 적절한 것은?

"대부분은 현재 회사의 본사에 전시되어 있다."

(A) [1]
(B) [2]
(C) [3]
(D) [4]

해설 주어진 문장에서 대부분은 현재 회사의 본사에 전시되어 있다고 했으므로, 주어진 문장 앞에 작품에 관련된 내용이 있을 것임을 예상할 수 있다. [1]의 앞 문장인 'The works ~ are estimated to be worth over €3 million in total.'에서 이 작품들, 즉 Bishop Advisors사가 가지고 있는 수집품들은 총 3백만 유로 이상의 가치가 있다고 추산된다고 했으므로, [1]에 주어진 문장이 들어가면 총 3백만 유로 이상의 가치가 있다고 추산되는 수집품들의 대부분은 현재 회사의 본사에 전시되어 있다는 자연스러운 문맥이 된다는 것을 알 수 있다. 따라서 (A)가 정답이다.

어휘 currently adv. 현재 on display phr. 전시된

176-180번은 다음 이메일과 편지에 관한 문제입니다.

수신: Frida Gertner <f.gertner@essenplatz.com>
발신: Cecilia Okumu <c.okumu@kitamutea.com>
제목: 새로운 차들
¹⁸⁰**날짜: 11월 18일**

Ms. Gertner께,

내년 3월 초까지, ¹⁷⁶**저희 회사는** 저희가 개발한 **새로운 차들의 판매용 수량을 수확할 준비가 될 것입니다.** 저는 귀하가 주문하고 싶은 경우를 대비하여 귀하가 알아야 한다고 생각했습니다. 저희는 12월 31일까지 저희의 전체 재고가 다 팔릴 것이라고 예상하기 때문에, ¹⁷⁶**저는 귀하가 곧 주문할 것을 추천해 드립니다.** 귀하의 참고를 위해 가격은 아래에 기재되어 있습니다.

귀하는 저희의 우수 고객들 중 한 명이기 때문에, ¹⁸⁰**저희는 귀하에게 새로운 녹차와 황차를 할인된 가격에 제공할 준비가 되어있습니다.** 그러나, ^{177/180}**조건은 귀하가 12월 1일 이전에 최소한 1,000킬로그램의 주문을 하고 새로운 주문을 하기 전에 모든 미납금을 지불해야 한다는 것입니다.**

종류	1,000킬로그램당 가격	할인가
홍차	3,080달러	2,926달러
백차	2,980달러	2,831달러
¹⁸⁰녹차	2,840달러	¹⁸⁰2,698달러
황차	2,720달러	2,584달러

Cecilia Okumu 드림
고객 서비스, Kitamu Tea사

harvest v. 수확하다 commercial adj. 판매용의, 상업적인
quantity n. 양 sell out phr. 다 팔리다, 매진되다 inventory n. 재고, 물품
list v. 기재하다, 열거하다 reference n. 참고, 언급
preferred customer phr. 우수 고객 rate n. 가격, 요금
minimum adj. 최소한의 settle v. 지불하다, 정산하다
unpaid balance phr. 미납금

2월 24일

Cecilia Okumu
Kitamu Tea사
414번지 Magongo로
몸바사시, 케냐

Ms. Okumu께,

저는 Halten사가 Essen Platz사를 인수했다는 것을 알리고자 편지를 씁니다. 따라서, Kitamu Tea사와의 계약에 관하여 몇 가지 변화가 있을 수도 있습니다. 우선 한 가지는, 3월 15일부터, 귀사와의 앞으로의 모든 의사소통들은 ¹⁷⁸저의 후임자 Ms. Diana Schneider에 의해 처리될 것이며, 그녀의 연락처는 제가 귀하께 보내드릴 것입니다. 또한, ¹⁷⁹새로운 경영진은 저희의 공급업체 계약들에 대한 검토를 하는 동안, 즉시 모든 추가적인 주문을 보류할 것입니다. 그렇긴 하지만, 저는 미지불된 송장들이 현재 계약에 따라 정산될 것이라고 장담합니다. 그러니, ¹⁸⁰저는 저희의 지난 배송을 부담하기 위해 2,698달러의 지불이 곧 있을 것이라고 생각합니다.

끝으로, 저는 귀사와 일할 수 있어서 영광이었다는 것을 말씀 드리고 싶으며 저는 귀사에 행운이 있기를 바랍니다.

¹⁷⁸Frida Gertner, 최고 부서장, Essen Platz사

acquire v. 인수하다, 획득하다 consequently adv. 따라서, 결과적으로
with respect to phr. ~에 관하여 arrangement n. 계약, 조정
replacement n. 후임자 contact details phr. 연락처
pending prep. ~을 하는 동안, 있을 때까지 that said phr. 그렇긴 하지만
assure v. 장담하다 in accordance with phr. ~에 따라
forthcoming adj. 곧 있을 cover v. 부담하다, 덜다

176 목적 찾기 문제 중 ●●○

해석 이메일의 주 목적은 무엇인가?
(A) 새로운 제품의 구매를 장려하기 위해
(B) 최근 주문의 배송을 확인하기 위해
(C) 주문 절차에 대해 설명하기 위해
(D) 몇몇 연구 결과를 보고하기 위해

해설 이메일의 'our company will be ready to harvest ~ the new teas'에서 회사는 새로운 차들을 수확할 준비가 될 것이라고 한 후, 'I would recommend that you order soon'에서 귀하가 곧 주문할 것을 추천한다고 했으므로 (A)가 정답이다.

어휘 encourage v. 장려하다 confirm v. 확인하다 report v. 보고하다

패러프레이징

recommend 추천하다 → encourage 장려하다
order 주문하다 → purchase 구매

177 동의어 찾기 문제 상 ●●●

해석 이메일에서, 2문단 두 번째 줄의 단어 "terms"는 의미상 –와 가장 가깝다.
(A) 단어
(B) 기간
(C) 관계
(D) 조건

해설 이메일의 terms를 포함한 구절 'the terms are that you must place the minimum order of 1,000 kilos'에서 조건은 최소한 1,000킬로그램의 주문을 하는 것이라고 했으므로 terms는 '조건'이라는 뜻으로 사용되었다. 따라서 '조건'이라는 뜻을 가진 (D) conditions가 정답이다.

178 추론 문제 중 ●●○

해석 Ms. Schneider는 누구일 것 같은가?
(A) 선임 회계사
(B) 고객 서비스 상담원
(C) 부서장
(D) 커뮤니케이션 관리자

해설 편지의 'my replacement, Ms. Diana Schneider'에서 Ms. Schneider가 자신, 즉 Frida Gertner의 후임자라고 했고, 'Frida Gertner, Chief Department Supervisor'에서 Frida Gertner가 최고 부서장이라는 것을 알 수 있으므로 Ms. Schneider가 부서장일 것이라는 사실을 추론할 수 있다. 따라서 (C)가 정답이다.

어휘 senior adj. 선임의, 고위의 representative n. 상담원, 직원

179 육하원칙 문제 상 ●●●

해석 Halten사는 무엇을 할 계획인가?
(A) 기존의 계약들을 검토한다
(B) 3월까지 모든 지불을 연기한다
(C) 직원 규모를 줄인다
(D) 새로운 공급업체에 배송 계약을 제안한다

해설 편지의 'the new management will place a hold on all further orders ~, pending a review of our supplier contracts'에서 새로운 경영진, 즉 Halten사의 새로운 경영진은 공급업체 계약들에 대한 검토를 하는 동안, 모든 추가적인 주문을 보류할 것이라고 했으므로 (A)가 정답이다.

어휘 evaluate v. 검토하다, 평가하다 existing adj. 기존의
delay v. 연기하다 workforce n. 직원

패러프레이징

a review of ~ contracts 계약들에 대한 검토 → Evaluate ~ agreements 계약들을 검토한다

최고난도 문제

180 추론 문제 연계 상 ●●●

해석 Essen Platz사에 대해 암시되는 것은?
(A) 몇몇 직원들을 새로운 사무실로 이동시키고 있다.
(B) 11월에 녹차를 주문했다.
(C) 주요 사업 분야를 바꾸고 있다.
(D) 이전 구매에 대해 여러 회사들에 빚을 지고 있다.

해설 편지의 'I believe a payment of $2,698 should be forthcoming to cover our last shipment'에서 저, 즉 Essen Platz사의 Ms. Gertner는 지난 배송을 부담하기 위해 2,698달러의 지불이 곧 있을 것이라고 생각

한다고 했다. 또한, 이메일의 'Date: November 18'에서는 이메일이 11월 18일에 쓰인 것을 알 수 있고, 'we are prepared to offer you the new green and yellow teas at a discounted rate', 'the terms are that you must place the minimum order of 1,000 kilos before December 1'에서 새로운 녹차와 황차를 12월 1일 이전에 최소한 1,000킬로를 주문하는 조건으로 할인된 가격에 제공한다고 하였고, 'Green', '$2,698'에서 녹차의 할인가가 2,698달러라는 사실을 확인할 수 있다.

두 단서를 종합할 때, Essen Platz사가 11월 18일과 12월 1일 사이인 11월에 녹차를 주문했다는 사실을 추론할 수 있다. 따라서 (B)가 정답이다.

어휘 transfer v. 이동시키다 personnel n. 직원
line of business phr. 사업 분야 owe v. 빚을 지다

패러프레이징

before December 1 12월 1일 이전 → November 11월

181-185번은 다음 웹페이지와 양식에 관한 문제입니다.

www.crawfordoffice.com

홈 | 소개 | 가게 | 계정 | 고객 서비스

Crawford Office Supply사 소개
당신의 사무실에 필요한 모든 것들을 찾아보세요!

Crawford Office Supply사는 댈러스에서 현재 30년 이상 동안 사업체들의 필요를 충족시켜오고 있습니다. 지역적으로 소유되고 운영되는 회사로서, 저희는 지역 주민들에게 훌륭한 고객 서비스와 낮은 가격을 제공하는 것에 자부심이 있습니다. 그리고 181-A/C저희가 저희의 두 번째 지점을 6월 15일 도시 남쪽의 Victor가 321번지에 개점할 것임을 알리게 되어 저희는 기쁩니다.

기념하기 위해, 182/183저희 두 가게 모두가 6월 15일부터 30일까지의 모든 사무용 가구 구매에 대해 회사의 로고가 있는 무료 손가방을 고객들에게 제공할 것입니다. 그러니, 당신이 당신의 사무실에 무엇이 필요하든, 꼭 Crawford Office Supply사를 방문해보세요. 저희는 일주일 내내 오전 9시부터 오후 10시까지 운영합니다. 곧 뵙겠습니다!

locally adv. 지역적으로 own v. 소유하다 operate v. 운영하다
take pride in phr. ~에 자부심을 갖다 workspace n. 사무실

Crawford Office Supply사
주문 양식

고객명: 183Yvonne Murphy 183날짜: 6월 20일
회사: Stanford Accounting사 전화번호: 555-0396
배송 주소: 789번지 Harbor로, 시애틀시, 워싱턴주 98250

품목 번호	세품	수량	가격
2837	EZ Write 펜	10	15달러
5839	Harris 공책	15	60달러
6934	RX350 프린터 카트리지	2	50달러
7135	183Sylex 의자	4	300달러
참고: 184저는 제 주문이 6월 23일까지 배송되기를 원합니다. 이것이 가능한지 오늘 회신하여 제게 알려주십시오. 185직원들이 6월 24일부터 27일까지 로비의 바닥재를 교체하고 있을 것이며, 배달을 하는 방문객들은 이 기간 동안 건물에 들어올 수 없을 것입니다. 감사합니다.	소계		425달러
	세금		34달러
	배송		48달러
	합계		507달러

replace v. 교체하다 flooring n. 바닥재

---

181 Not/True 문제 중 ●●○

해석 Crawford Office Supply사에 대해 언급된 것은?
(A) 6월에 새로운 지점을 열 것이다.
(B) 직원들을 댈러스 매장으로 이동시킬 것이다.
(C) 여러 도시에 지점들을 설립할 것이다.
(D) 현재 운영 시간을 변경할 것이다.

해설 웹페이지의 'we will be opening our second branch ~ on June 15'에서 저희, 즉 Crawford Office Supply사가 그것의 두 번째 지점을 6월 15일에 개점한다고 하였으므로 (A)는 지문의 내용과 일치한다. 따라서 (A)가 정답이다. (B)와 (D)는 지문에 언급되지 않은 내용이다. (C)는 'we will be opening our second branch ~ on the south side of the city'에서 두 번째 지점을 도시 남쪽에 개점한다고 했으므로 지문의 내용과 일치하지 않는다.

어휘 location n. 지점, 장소 relocate v. 이동시키다

패러프레이징

will be opening ~ second branch 두 번째 지점을 개점할 것이다 → will open a new location 새로운 지점을 열 것이다

---

182 육하원칙 문제 중 ●●○

해석 고객들은 물건 제공의 기회를 이용하기 위해 무엇을 해야 하는가?
(A) 특정한 브랜드를 선택한다
(B) 명시된 기간 내에 주문한다
(C) 최소한의 구매를 한다
(D) 특정 지점을 방문한다

해설 웹페이지의 'both of our stores will be offering customers a free tote bag ~ for every purchase of office furniture from June 15 to 30'에서 두 가게 모두가 6월 15일부터 30일까지의 모든 사무용 가구 구매에 대해 무료 손가방을 고객들에게 제공할 것이라고 했으므로 (B)가 정답이다.

어휘 offer n. (물건) 제공 certain adj. 특정한 specified adj. 명시된
particular adj. 특정한

패러프레이징

purchase ~ from June 15 to 30 6월 15일부터 30일까지의 구매
→ Order within a specified period 명시된 기간 내에 주문하다

---

183 육하원칙 문제 연계 중 ●●○

해석 Ms. Murphy는 어떤 제품 때문에 무료 물품을 받았는가?
(A) EZ Write 펜
(B) Harris 공책
(C) RX350 프린터 카트리지
(D) Sylex 의자

해설 양식의 'Yvonne Murphy', 'Date: June 20', 'Sylex Chair'에서 Yvonne Murphy가 6월 20일에 Sylex 의자를 구매했다고 했다. 또한, 웹페이지의 'both of our stores will be offering customers a free tote bag ~ for every purchase of office furniture from June 15 to 30'에서는 두 가게 모두가 6월 15일부터 30일까지의 모든 사무용 가구 구매에 대해 무료 손가방을 고객들에게 제공할 것이라고 한 사실을 확인할 수 있다.

두 단서를 종합할 때, Ms. Murphy는 사무용 가구인 Sylex 의자 때문에 손가방, 즉 무료 물품을 받았다는 것을 알 수 있다. 따라서 (D)가 정답이다.

패러프레이징

a free item 무료 물품 → a free tote bag 무료 손가방

184 육하원칙 문제   중 ●●●○

해석 Ms. Murphy는 무엇을 요청하는가?
(A) 가격 확인
(B) 서비스에 대한 정보
(C) 요청에 대한 확인
(D) 구매의 취소

해설 양식의 'I would like my order to be delivered by June 23. Please call me back today to let me know if this is possible.'에서 저, 즉 Ms. Murphy가 주문이 6월 23일까지 배송되기를 원하고, 이것이 가능한지 오늘 회신하여 자신에게 알려달라고 했으므로 (C)가 정답이다.

어휘 verification n. 확인, 조회   confirmation n. 확인

186 육하원칙 문제   중 ●●●○

해석 Ms. Murphy는 어떤 문제를 언급하는가?
(A) 제품들이 현재 재고가 없다.
(B) 주차장이 며칠 동안 문을 닫을 것이다.
(C) 로비의 엘리베이터가 수리 중이다.
(D) 건물의 한 구역이 접근할 수 없을 것이다.

해설 양식의 'Workers will be replacing the flooring in our lobby ~, and visitors making deliveries will not be allowed in the building during this period.'에서 직원들이 로비의 바닥재를 교체하고 있을 것이며, 배달을 하는 방문객들은 이 기간 동안 건물에 들어올 수 없을 것이라고 했으므로 (D)가 정답이다.

어휘 out of stock phr. 재고가 없는   inaccessible adj. 접근할 수 없는

패러프레이징

will not be allowed 들어올 수 없을 것이다 → will be inaccessible 접근할 수 없을 것이다

186-190번은 다음 편지, 양식, 일정표에 관한 문제입니다.

Marcus Dodd
91번지 Webber가
런던시 SE1 8XH

7월 24일

Mr. Dodd께,

저희는 8월 18일에 Seafair 리조트에서의 귀하의 도착을 기대하고 있습니다. 귀하와 귀하 그룹의 다른 두 명의 손님들이 4일 동안 머무를 예정이기 때문에, 186귀하는 저희의 몇몇 제공되는 활동들에 참여하고 싶을 수 있습니다. 예를 들어, 저희의 테니스 코트들과 볼링을 위한 잔디 구장은 낮 동안 그것들을 사용하기를 원하는 누구든지 이용 가능 합니다. 저희는 또한 선착순으로 이용될 수 있는 윈드서핑 장비를 구비하고 있습니다. 그러나, 만약 Grand Soeur섬에서의 인기 있는 하이킹들 중 하나에 참여하고 싶으시다면, 최소한 하루 전에 미리 안내 데스크 또는 저희의 웹사이트에서 등록하시는 것이 권장됩니다. 이것은 또한 190스노클링과 스쿠버다이빙 여행뿐만 아니라 Petite Soeur섬과 Reynolds섬 카약 여행에도 해당합니다. 190두 그룹의 참가자들은 모두 Coco섬의 해변에서 함께 점심을 즐길 것입니다. 이 활동들 중 어떠한 것이라도 참여하시려면, www.seafairer.com/activities를 방문하십시오.

Keisha Joubert 드림
활동 관리자
Seafair 리조트

---

look forward to phr. ~을 기대하다   take part in phr. ~에 참여하다
lawn n. 잔디 구장   daylight n. 낮, 일광
first-come, first-served phr. 선착순   at least phr. 최소한
in advance phr. 미리, 이전에   excursion n. 여행

Seafair 리조트 — 신청 양식 * 스노클링

손님 이름	187-AMarcus Dodd		
객실 번호	723		
187-C오늘의 날짜	187-C8월 19일		
187-D원하는 활동 날짜	187-D8월 20일		
187-A필요한 장비 (해당하는 것 모두 체크하세요!)	187-A☐ 물갈퀴	☐ 마스크	☐ 스노클
187-D능력 수준	☐ 미숙	☐ 능숙	187-D☑ 전문가

중요한 고려 사항
1. 저희는 수영복을 빌려주거나, 빌리거나, 또는 판매할 수 없습니다. 참가자들은 자신의 것을 가지고 있어야 합니다.
2. 이 활동은 하루에 15명으로 제한됩니다.
3. 188-A만약 같은 날 예정된 스쿠버 다이빙 여행에 5명 이하의 사람이 등록한다면, 그들은 Waveroller 배에서 귀하의 그룹에 합류할 것입니다.
4. 만약 기상 상태가 적합하지 않다면, 이 활동은 취소될 것입니다.
5. 건강상 문제가 있는 참가자들은 가이드에게 관련된 의료 정보를 제공해야 합니다.

---

fin n. 물갈퀴, 지느러미   snorkel n. 스노클, 잠수용 호흡 기구
inexperienced adj. 미숙한   competent adj. 능숙한
expert adj. 전문가의   consideration n. 고려사항   loan v. 빌려주다
rent v. 빌리다   enroll v. 등록하다   unsuitable adj. 적합하지 않은
health condition phr. 건강상 문제   relevant adj. 관련된

188-A/1908월 20일 스노클링 여행 계획
190가이드: Terry Haide, Bluewater 자격증 소유자

활동	시간	참고
Seafair 리조트의 Leisure Hut에서 만남	▶ 오전 9시	
Seafair 부두에서 출발	▶ 오전 9시 10분	188-A스쿠버 다이빙 그룹들이 같은 이동수단을 이용할 것입니다.
장소 1에 도착	▶ 오전 9시 30분	
안전 브리핑	▶ 오전 9시 40분	
장비 사용에 대한 설명	▶ 오전 10시	
Ombre Reef 주위에서 스노클링	▶ 오전 10시 15분	참가자들은 수중 투어로 인솔될 것입니다.
휴식	▶ 오전 11시	
Urchin Cove 주위에서 스노클링	▶189오전11시15분	189참가자들은 혼자서 탐험할 수 있을 것입니다.
190점심	▶ 오후 12시	190식사는 피크닉 구역에서 제공될 것입니다.
188-DSeafair 리조트로 돌아옴	▶188-D오후 1시	

---

holder n. 소유자   departure n. 출발   transport n. 이동수단
on one's own phr. 혼자서, 스스로   serve v. 제공하다

186 목적 찾기 문제 　중 ●●○

해석　Ms. Joubert는 왜 Mr. Dodd에게 연락했는가?

(A) 그에게 여가 선택 사항들을 알리기 위해
(B) 그가 예약을 변경하도록 설득하기 위해
(C) 숙소 선호사항에 관해 묻기 위해
(D) 동호회에 가입하는 것에 대한 혜택을 제공하기 위해

해설　편지의 'you may want to take part in ~ offered activities'에서 귀하, 즉 Mr. Dodd가 제공되는 활동들에 참여하고 싶을 수 있다고 한 후, 활동들에 대한 정보를 제공하고 있으므로 (A)가 정답이다.

어휘　leisure n. 여가, 자유시간　option n. 선택 사항　booking n. 예약
accommodation n. 숙소, 숙박　preference n. 선호사항, 선호
incentive n. 혜택

패러프레이징

offered activities 제공되는 활동들 → leisure options 여가 선택 사항들

187 Not/True 문제 　상 ●●●

해석　Mr. Dodd에 대해 언급되지 않은 것은?
(A) 그의 장비를 직접 가져왔다.
(B) 의료 문서를 제출하였다.
(C) 일찍 등록하기로 결정했다.
(D) 이전에 스노클링을 간 적이 있다.

해설　질문의 Mr. Dodd와 관련된 내용이 언급된 양식에서 (B)는 언급되지 않은 내용이다. 따라서 (B)가 정답이다. (A)는 양식의 'Marcus Dodd', 'Equipment Needed (Check All that Apply)', '☑ Fins ☐ Mask ☐ Snorkel'에서 Mr. Dodd가 필요한 장비들에 체크하지 않았으므로 지문의 내용과 일치한다. (C)는 'Today's Date', 'August 19', 'Desired Date of Activity', 'August 20'에서 오늘의 날짜, 즉 등록한 날짜인 8월 19일이 원하는 활동 날짜인 8월 20일보다 하루 전이므로 지문의 내용과 일치한다. (D)는 'Ability Level', '☑ Expert'에서 Mr. Dodd가 능력 수준으로 전문가에 체크했으므로 지문의 내용과 일치한다.

어휘　gear n. 장비　submit v. 제출하다

패러프레이징

Equipment 장비 → gear 장비 Expert 전문가 → has gone ~ in the past 과거에 간 적이 있다

188 Not/True 문제 연계 　상 ●●●

해석　8월 20일의 스쿠버 다이빙 참가자들에 대해 언급된 것은?
(A) 다섯 명의 사람보다 더 적게 구성되어 있다.
(B) Bluewater 자격증을 취득하려고 있다.
(C) 체크아웃을 한 후에 추가 요금을 지불할 것이다.
(D) Seafair 리조트로 저녁에 돌아올 것이다.

해설　양식의 'If less than 5 people have enrolled in the scuba diving excursion ~ for the same day, they will join your group on the boat, the Waveroller.'에서 만약 같은 날 스쿠버 다이빙 여행에 5명 이하의 사람이 등록한다면, 그들, 즉 스쿠버 다이빙 참가자들은 Waveroller 배에서 귀하의 그룹에 합류할 것이라고 했다. 또한, 일정표의 'Plan for August 20 Snorkeling Excursion', 'Scuba diving groups will take the same transport.'에서는 8월 20일의 스노클링 여행에서 스쿠버 다이빙 그룹들이 같은 이동수단을 이용할 것이라고 한 사실을 확인할 수 있다.
두 단서를 종합할 때, 스노클링 여행에서 스쿠버 다이빙 그룹과 같은 이동수단을 이용할 것이라고 했으므로 5명 이하의 사람이 스쿠버 다이빙을 신청했

음을 알 수 있다. 따라서 (A)가 정답이다. (B)와 (C)는 지문에 언급되지 않은 내용이다. (D)는 일정표의 'Return to Seafair Resort', '1:00 P.M.'에서 Seafair 리조트로 오후 1시에 돌아온다고 했으므로 지문의 내용과 일치하지 않는다.

어휘　composed of phr. ~으로 구성된　individual n. 사람, 개인
attempt v. ~하려 하다, 시도하다　obtain a license phr. 자격증을 취득하다

패러프레이징

less than 5 people 다섯 명 보다 더 적은 → fewer than five individuals 다섯 명 보다 더 적은

189 육하원칙 문제 　중 ●●○

해석　일정표에 따르면, 자유 시간은 언제 일어날 것인가?
(A) 오전 9시 40분
(B) 오전 10시
(C) 오전 10시 15분
(D) 오전 11시 15분

해설　일정표의 '11:15 A.M.', 'Participants will be able to explore on their own.'에서 오전 11시 15분에 참가자들이 혼자서 탐험할 수 있을 것이라고 했으므로 (D)가 정답이다.

어휘　take place phr. 일어나다, 이루어지다

패러프레이징

independent 자유의, 독립된 → on their own 혼자서, 스스로

최고난도 문제

190 육하원칙 문제 연계 　상 ●●●

해석　8월 20일에 Mr. Haide에 의해 인솔되는 단체는 어느 섬을 방문할 것인가?
(A) Grand Soeur섬
(B) Petite Soeur섬
(C) Reynolds섬
(D) Coco섬

해설　일정표의 'Plan for August 20 Snorkeling Excursion', 'Guide: Terry Haide', 'Lunch', 'Meal will be served at a picnic area.'에서 8월 20일 스노클링 여행의 가이드가 Terry Haide이며 피크닉 구역에서 점심 식사를 할 것이라고 했다. 또한, 편지의 'snorkeling and scuba diving excursions', 'Participants from both groups will enjoy lunch together ~ at Coco Island.'에서는 두 그룹, 즉 스노클링과 스쿠버 다이빙 참가자들은 모두 Coco섬에서 함께 점심을 즐길 것이라고 한 사실을 확인할 수 있다.
두 단서를 종합할 때, 8월 20일에 Mr. Haide에 의해 인솔되는 단체, 즉 스노클링 참가자들은 점심 식사를 위해 Coco섬을 방문할 것임을 알 수 있다. 따라서 (D)가 정답이다.

191-195번은 다음 온라인 양식, 일정표, 이메일에 관한 문제입니다.

Linwood 은행

홈 >> 온라인 양식들>> 주택 대출 신청서

¹⁹¹신청 날짜: 2월 5일

신청자의 이름: ¹⁹¹/¹⁹⁵⁻ᴬWilliam Tanaka

현재 주소: 18번지 Ridgeway로, 보스턴시, 매사추세츠주 02115

구입할 집의 주소: 250번지 Chestnut로, 프로비던스, 로드아일랜드주 02907

회사 이름: Creston 소프트웨어 개발사

직책: 컴퓨터 프로그래머

[195-A]당신은 우리 기관의 저축 계좌를 가지고 있습니까?

[195-A]☑ 예 ☐ 아니오

만약 그렇다면, 계좌 번호를 입력하십시오: 3467-999-2551

당신의 대출에 관해 세부사항을 논의하기 위해 우리의 재정 자문위원들 중 한 명과의 필수적인 첫 상담을 등록하십시오.

[191]**선택된 자문위원:** Nadine Frye
[191]**선호하는 첫 예약 날짜/시간:** 월요일, 화요일, 또는 목요일 아침 그리고 금요일 오후

감사합니다! 당신의 신청서가 제출되었습니다. 당신의 첫 번째 상담 날짜를 확정하기 위해 당신에게 저희가 연락 드릴 것입니다.

loan n. 대출 application n. 신청(서) applicant n. 신청자
savings account phr. 저축 계좌 institution n. 기관 register v. 등록하다
mandatory adj. 필수의, 의무적인 initial adj. 첫, 처음의
consultation n. 상담

Linwood 은행
재정 자문위원 일정표

참고: [192-D]휴가 및 결근 승인 요청은 행정 관리자 Marcie Welford에게 제출하십시오. 2월 8일 월요일에 우리는 국가 공휴일로 문을 닫습니다.

[191]**마지막 업데이트: 2월 4일**

	2월 9일, 화요일	[192-D]2월 10일, 수요일	[192-D]2월 11일, 목요일	[191]2월 12일, 금요일
[192-D]Harold Marks	오전 10시 - 오후 2시 예약 없음	[192-D]휴가: 승인됨	[192-D]휴가: 승인됨	오전 10시 - 오후 2시 예약 없음 오후 12시 - 오후 2시 예약
Kelly Wong	휴가: 승인됨	오전 9시 - 오전 11시 예약 오전 11시 - 오후 1시 예약	오전 9시 - 오후 12시 예약 없음 오후 12시 - 오후 1시 예약	휴가: 승인됨
[191]Nadine Frye	휴가: 승인됨	휴가: 승인됨	오전 11시 - 오후 1시 예약 오후 1시 - 오후 3시 예약	오전 9시 - 오전 11시 예약 [191]오후 12시 - 오후 3시 예약 없음

approve v. 승인하다

수신: William Tanaka <w.tanaka@upmail.net>
발신: Nadine Frye <n.frye@linwoodbank.com>
날짜: 2월 15일
제목: 저희의 만남

첨부파일: 서류 목록

Mr. Tanaka께,

지난주 Linwood 은행에 당신의 첫 번째 주택 대출 상담을 위해 저를 보러 와 주신 것에 감사드립니다. 저는 귀하의 대출을 승인받기 위해 귀하가 제공하셔야 할 서류들을 포함하는 목록을 첨부하였습니다. 2월 28일까지 저희의 온라인 시스템에 그 문서들을 업로드해주십시오. 제출되고 나면, [193]저희 은행의 직원들이 그것들을 검토한 후 3월 5일까지 귀하의 신청이 승인되었는지 거절되었는지에 대해 알려드리기 위해 연락을 드릴 것입니다.

추가적으로, [194]저는 귀하가 계좌에서 어떻게 자동 대출 납입을 하는지에 대한 궁금증이 있다고 알고 있습니다. [194]별도의 이메일로 그것에 대한 설명을 제공해드리겠습니다. 저는 [195-A]현재 예금주들은 그들의 주택 대출 이자율에 대해 1퍼센트 할인을 받을 자격이 있다는 점도 알려드려야 합니다.

Nadine Frye 드림

attach v. 첨부하다, 붙이다 associate n. 직원 reject v. 거절하다
additionally adv. 추가적으로 automatic adj. 자동의
account holder phr. 예금주 be entitled to phr. ~할 자격이 있다
interest rate phr. 이자율

최고난도 문제

191 추론 문제 연계 상 ●●●

해석 Mr. Tanaka는 Ms. Frye를 언제 만났을 것 같은가?
(A) 2월 9일에
(B) 2월 10일에
(C) 2월 11일에
(D) 2월 12일에

해설 온라인 양식의 'Application Date: February 5', 'William Tanaka', 'Selected Advisor: Nadine Frye'에서 Mr. Tanaka가 2월 5일에 신청했으며 선택된 자문위원이 Ms. Frye라고 했고, 'Preferred Initial Appointment Days/Times: Monday, Tuesday, or Thursday mornings and Friday afternoons'에서 Mr. Tanaka가 선호하는 시간이 월요일, 화요일, 또는 목요일 아침 그리고 금요일 오후라고 했다. 또한, 일정표의 'Last Updated: February 4', 'Nadine Frye', 'Friday, February 12', '12 P.M. – 3 P.M. Free'에서는 일정표가 2월 4일에 마지막으로 업데이트되었고 Ms. Frye가 2월 12일 금요일에 오후 12시부터 오후 3시까지 예약이 없다는 사실을 확인할 수 있다.
두 단서를 종합할 때, Mr. Tanaka가 Ms. Frye를 2월 12일에 만났다는 사실을 추론할 수 있다. 따라서 (D)가 정답이다

192 Not/True 문제 상 ●●●

해석 Mr. Marks에 대해 언급된 것은?
(A) 최근에 Linwood 은행의 자문위원으로 고용되었다.
(B) Ms. Wong의 월요일 예약을 대신할 수 없었다.
(C) 예비 대출 신청자에게 승인서를 보냈다.
(D) Ms. Welford로부터 휴가에 대한 허가를 받았다.

해설 일정표의 'Submit vacation ~ requests for approval by administrative manager Marcie Welford.'에서 휴가 승인 요청은 행정 관리자 Marcie Welford에게 제출하라고 했고, 'Harold Marks', 'Wednesday, February 10', 'Vacation day: approved', 'Thursday, February 11', 'Vacation day: approved'에서 Mr. Marks의 2월 10일과 11일 휴가가 승인되었다고 했으므로 (D)는 지문의 내용과 일치한다. 따라서 (D)가 정답이다. (A), (B), (C)는 지문에 언급되지 않은 내용이다.

어휘 recently adv. 최근에 prospective adj. 예비의, 장래의

패러프레이징

approval 승인 → permission 허가

[최고난도 문제]

193 육하원칙 문제   상 ●●●

해석 이메일에 따르면, Linwood 은행의 직원들은 무엇을 할 것인가?
(A) 회사 웹사이트의 양식들에 몇 가지 업데이트들을 적용한다
(B) 이용가능성을 더 만들기 위해 자문위원들의 일정을 수정한다
(C) 초기 예금 없이 계좌 개설을 승인한다
(D) 재정적 지원을 결정하기 위해 몇몇 서류들을 검토한다

해설 이메일의 'our bank's associates will review them and ~ let you know whether your application has been approved or rejected'에서 은행의 직원들이 그것들, 즉 문서들을 검토한 후 귀하의 신청이 승인되었는지 거절되었는지에 대해 알려줄 것이라고 했으므로 (D)가 정답이다.

어휘 apply v. 적용하다 modify v. 수정하다 availability n. 이용가능성
authorize v. 승인하다 opening n. 개설 deposit n. 예금, 보증금
look over phr. 검토하다 assistance n. 지원

패러프레이징

review 검토하다 → look over 검토하다

[최고난도 문제]

194 육하원칙 문제   상 ●●●

해석 Ms. Frye는 왜 Mr. Tanaka에게 또 하나의 이메일을 보낼 것인가?
(A) 다음의 만남 일정을 잡기 위해서
(B) 그의 대출 신청의 진행 상황에 대해 알려주기 위해서
(C) 그의 저축 계좌에 관하여 안내를 제공하기 위해서
(D) 계약 조건들에 관해 설명하기 위해서

해설 이메일의 'I know that you had a question about ~ your account'와 'I will provide you with instructions on that in a separate e-mail.'에서 저, 즉 Ms. Frye는 귀하, 즉 Mr. Tanaka가 계좌와 관련하여 궁금증이 있다고 알고 있으며, 별도의 이메일로 그것에 대한 설명을 제공하겠다고 했으므로 (C)가 정답이다.

어휘 follow-up adj. 다음의, 후속의 update v. 알려주다
status n. (진행 과정상의) 상황 concerning prep. ~에 관하여
condition n. 조건 agreement n. 계약, 동의

패러프레이징

provide ~ with instructions ~에게 설명을 제공하다 → give directions 안내를 제공하다

195 Not/True 문제   상 ●●●

해석 Mr. Tanaka에 대해 언급된 것은?
(A) 요금 할인을 받을 자격이 있다.
(B) 2월에 대출금을 갚았다.
(C) 최근에 새로운 직책을 시작하였다.
(D) 기계에서 현금을 인출할 것이다.

해설 [온라인 양식]의 'William Tanaka', 'Do you have a savings account at our institution?', '☑ Yes'에서 William Tanaka가 우리 기관, 즉

Linwood 은행의 저축 계좌를 가지고 있다고 했다. 또한, [이메일]의 'current account holders are entitled to receive a 1 percent discount'에서 현재 예금주들은 1퍼센트 할인을 받을 자격이 있다고 한 사실을 확인할 수 있다.
두 단서를 종합할 때, Mr. Tanaka는 요금 할인을 받을 자격이 있다는 것을 알 수 있다. 따라서 (A)가 정답이다. (B), (C), (D)는 지문에 언급되지 않은 내용이다.

어휘 be eligible for phr. ~을 받을 자격이 있다 withdraw v. 인출하다

패러프레이징

discount 할인 → reduction 할인
are entitled to ~할 자격이 있다 → is eligible for ~을 받을 자격이 있다

196-200번은 다음 두 이메일과 광고에 관한 문제입니다.

수신: 모든 마케팅 직원 <marketingteam@fizzlespark.com>
발신: Irina Sokolov <i.sokolov@fizzlespark.com>
날짜: 4월 4일
제목: 축하드립니다

모두들 안녕하세요,

[196]회사의 새롭게 출시된 유기농 주스 라인인 Whole Renew를 위한 [197-B]광고 캠페인을 지난달 마무리한 모두의 노고에 감사드리고 싶습니다. 최고경영자가 완료된 광고들을 검토하고 우리가 만들어낸 것에 기뻐했으므로, [197-C]여러분 모두에게 축하를 드립니다.

상기시켜드리자면, [198-D]광고들은 우리 홈페이지에 다음과 같이 게시될 것입니다:

[198-D]5월 — 하나 구매 시 하나를 무료로 제공
6월 — 20퍼센트 할인 판촉
7월 — 향후 구매의 5달러 할인 쿠폰

마지막으로, [197-D]저는 여러분 모두에게 여러분의 직원 할인을 이용해 그 라인을 시음해볼 것을 권장합니다. 저 자신도 직접 여러 제품들을 시음해보았기 때문에, 저는 그것들이 엄청나게 맛있다고 보장할 수 있습니다!

Irina Sokolov 드림
[196/197-C]마케팅부장, [196]FizzleSpark National사

launch v. 출시하다 finalize v. 마무리하다 delighted adj. 기쁜
put together phr. 만들다, 준비하다 post v. 게시하다
promotion n. 판촉, 홍보 encourage v. 권장하다 sample v. 시음하다
guarantee v. 보장하다 incredibly adv. 엄청나게

FizzleSpark National사
Whole Renew

여름철이 당신이 탈수 상태가 되었다고 느끼게 하고 있나요? 그렇다면 100퍼센트 유기농 재료들로 만들어진 맛있는 주스 제품인 Whole Renew 한 병에 손을 뻗어 보세요. 비트와 사과부터 망고와 생강까지, [199]다양한 종류의 음료들 중에 당신의 입맛에 맞는 것을 고르세요. 또한, [198-D]이번 달에는 이 모든 신선한 선택지들은 하나의 가격에 두 개입니다.

특가는 여기서 끝나지 않습니다! [198-C/200]6월 10일 오전 11시부터 오후 3시까지 어느 Victoria 카페 지점에서든 Whole Renew를 사고 무료 유기농 간식을 받으세요. 추가적인 세부사항에 대해서는 Victoria 카페 스마트폰 애플리케이션을 다운받으세요.

summary months phr. 여름철 dehydrate v. 탈수 상태가 되다
reach v. 뻗다 ingredient n. 재료 suit v. 맞다, 어울리다
refreshing adj. 신선한, 상쾌한 deal n. 특가, 거래 pick up phr. ~을 사다

수신: Owen Collins <o.collins@victioriacafedenver.com>
발신: Sarah Klein <sklein488@parkmail.net>
제목: 당신의 카페
날짜: 6월 15일

Mr. Collins께,

Shearmont Shopping Plaza에서 당신의 이웃으로서, 당신이 최근 Victoria 카페에 완공한 개조작업이 훌륭하게 끝났다고 말하고 싶습니다. 몇 년 동안 이 쇼핑센터에서 선물 가게를 소유하면서, 저는 여러 사업체들이 잠깐 있다가 없어지는 것을 보아왔습니다. 그리고 당신이 당신의 지점에 멋진 개량공사를 한 것을 보아 기쁩니다.

또한, ²⁰⁰6월 10일 정오에 당신의 카페에 제가 방문했을 때, 당신이 팔고 있었던 Whole Renew 주스들 중 하나를 시음하였고 그날의 특별한 홍보에 참여했었는데, 정말 뜻밖의 기쁨이었습니다! 저는 Whole Renew를 만든 회사와 같은 주요 식품 회사들과 협력관계를 발전시키는 것에 관심이 있습니다. 제가 그들에게 연락을 취할 수 있도록 그들의 연락처를 공유해주실 수 있으신가요? 당신의 도움을 주신다면 정말 감사할 것입니다.

Sarah Klein 드림, 소유주, Brightstar Gifts

renovation n. 개조 come and go phr. 잠깐 있다가 없어지다
improvement n. 개량공사 take part in phr. 참여하다
partnership n. 협력관계 corporation n. 회사
reach out phr. 연락을 취하다 appreciate v. 고마워하다

196 추론 문제   중 ●●○

해석 FizzleSpark National사는 어떤 종류의 회사일 것 같은가?
(A) 커피숍
(B) 음료 생산 회사
(C) 선물 가게
(D) 슈퍼마켓 체인

해설 이메일1의 'the company's newly launched line of organic juices'에서 회사가 새롭게 유기농 주스의 라인을 출시했다고 했고, 'Marketing Department Head, FizzleSpark National'에서 FizzleSpark National사의 마케팅부장이 작성하였다고 했으므로 FizzleSpark National사가 음료 생산 회사라는 사실을 추론할 수 있다. 따라서 정답은 (B)이다.

어휘 producer n. 생산 회사, 생산자

패러프레이징
juice 주스 → drink 음료

197 Not/True 문제   중 ●●○

해석 마케팅 직원들에 대해 언급되지 않은 것은?
(A) 임원에 의해 평가될 것이다.
(B) 지난달에 몇몇 광고들을 작업하였다.
(C) 부서장으로부터 축하를 받았다.
(D) 몇몇 상품들에 더 낮은 가격을 받을 수 있다.

해설 질문의 마케팅 직원들과 관련된 내용이 언급된 이메일1에서 (A)는 언급되지 않은 내용이다. 따라서 (A)가 정답이다. (B)는 'I want to thank everyone

for ~ hard work last month finishing up our advertising campaign'에서 광고 캠페인을 지난달 마무리한 노고에 감사한다고 했으므로 지문의 내용과 일치한다. (C)는 'congratulations to all of you', 'Marketing Department Head'에서 마케팅부장이 여러분 모두에게 축하한다고 했으므로 지문의 내용과 일치한다. (D)는 'I encourage you all to sample the line using your employee discount'에서 여러분 모두에게 직원 할인을 이용해 그 라인을 시음해볼 것을 권장한다고 했으므로 지문의 내용과 일치한다.

어휘 evaluate v. 평가하다 executive n. 임원, 간부

패러프레이징
discount 할인 → a lower price 더 낮은 가격

198 Not/True 문제 연계   상 ●●●

해석 광고의 특가에 대해 언급된 것은?
(A) 멤버십 프로그램에 등록된 고객들에게만 제공된다.
(B) 회사의 회장에 의해 거절되었다.
(C) 한 지점에서의 구매로 제한된다.
(D) 5월에 웹사이트에 게시되었다.

해설 광고의 'all of these refreshing choices are two for the price of one this month'에서 이번 달에는 이 모든 신선한 선택지들은 하나의 가격에 두 개라고 했다. 또한, 이메일1의 'the advertisements will be posted on our homepage', 'May — Buy one, get one free offer'에서는 5월에 하나를 구매하면 하나를 무료로 제공한다는 광고가 홈페이지에 게시될 것이라고 한 사실을 확인할 수 있다.
두 단서를 종합할 때, 광고가 5월에 웹사이트에 게시되었음을 알 수 있다. 따라서 (D)가 정답이다. (A)와 (B)는 지문에 언급되지 않은 내용이다. (C)는 광고의 'Pick up Whole Renew at any Victoria Café location ~.'에서 어느 Victoria 카페 지점에서든 Whole Renew를 사라고 했으므로 지문의 내용과 일치하지 않는다.

어휘 enroll in phr. ~에 등록하다 reject v. 거절하다 limit v. 제한하다
post v. 게시하다

패러프레이징
homepage 홈페이지 → Web site 웹사이트

199 육하원칙 문제   하 ●○○

해석 Whole Renew의 한 가지 특징은 무엇인가?
(A) 다양한 맛
(B) 무설탕 성분
(C) 다채로운 포장
(D) 추가적인 비타민

해설 광고의 'Choose from a wide selection of drinks to suit your taste'에서 다양한 종류의 음료들 중에 당신의 입맛에 맞는 것을 고르라고 했으므로 (A)가 정답이다.

어휘 packaging n. 포장

패러프레이징
a wide selection of 다양한 종류의 → a variety of 다양한

200 추론 문제 연계   상 ●●●

해석 Ms. Klein은 Victoria 카페에서 무엇을 했을 것 같은가?

(A) 무료로 식품을 시식했다

(B) 몇몇 개조작업을 도왔다

(C) 시설 관리자와 이야기했다

(D) 기간이 한정된 쿠폰을 가져왔다

해설 이메일2의 'when I visited your café on June 10 at noon, I tried one of the Whole Renew juices ~ and took part in the special promotion that day'에서 Ms. Klein이 6월 10일 정오에 카페에 방문하여 음료를 시음했고 그날의 특별한 홍보, 즉 무료 유기농 간식을 준 홍보에 참여했다고 했다. 또한, 광고의 'Pick up Whole Renew at any Victoria Café location on June 10 from 11 A.M. to 3 P.M. and receive a free organic snack.'에서는 6월 10일 오전 11시부터 오후 3시까지 어느 Victoria 카페 지점에서든 Whole Renew를 사고 무료 유기농 간식을 받으라고 한 사실을 확인할 수 있다.

두 단서를 종합할 때, Ms. Klein이 Victoria 카페에서 무료로 식품을 시식했다는 사실을 추론할 수 있다. 따라서 (A)가 정답이다.

어휘 **free of charge** phr. 무료의   **assist with** phr. ~을 돕다

PART 5

101 (C)	**102** (C)	**103** (B)	**104** (B)	**105** (D)
106 (C)	**107** (B)	**108** (D)	**109** (D)	**110** (C)
111 (C)	**112** (D)	**113** (C)	**114** (D)	**115** (A)
116 (D)	**117** (B)	**118** (D)	**119** (A)	**120** (C)
121 (A)	**122** (B)	**123** (B)	**124** (C)	**125** (A)
126 (A)	**127** (C)	**128** (B)	**129** (A)	**130** (D)

PART 6

131 (A)	**132** (D)	**133** (D)	**134** (B)	**135** (B)
136 (B)	**137** (C)	**138** (C)	**139** (D)	**140** (A)
141 (B)	**142** (C)	**143** (A)	**144** (C)	**145** (D)
146 (C)				

PART 7

147 (B)	**148** (C)	**149** (D)	**150** (B)	**151** (D)
152 (C)	**153** (A)	**154** (C)	**155** (B)	**156** (C)
157 (A)	**158** (B)	**159** (D)	**160** (A)	**161** (D)
162 (C)	**163** (D)	**164** (D)	**165** (A)	**166** (C)
167 (B)	**168** (A)	**169** (A)	**170** (D)	**171** (A)
172 (B)	**173** (B)	**174** (B)	**175** (D)	**176** (B)
177 (C)	**178** (C)	**179** (C)	**180** (D)	**181** (C)
182 (B)	**183** (C)	**184** (D)	**185** (D)	**186** (C)
187 (B)	**188** (D)	**189** (D)	**190** (B)	**191** (C)
192 (D)	**193** (C)	**194** (B)	**195** (C)	**196** (B)
197 (C)	**198** (D)	**199** (D)	**200** (D)	

PART 5

101 부사 자리 채우기　　　　중 ●●○

해석　Vintron 연구소 직원들은 최종 상품이 반드시 완벽하도록 하기 위해 신중하게 일해 오고 있다.

해설　동사(have been working)를 꾸밀 수 있는 것은 부사이므로 부사 (C) deliberately(신중하게)가 정답이다. 형용사 또는 동사 (A), 동사 또는 과거분사 (B), 명사 (D)는 동사를 꾸밀 수 없다. 참고로, 동사 work를 '사용하다, 운용하다'라는 의미의 타동사로 보고 명사 (D)를 타동사의 목적어로 본다 해도, '숙고를 사용해오고 있다'라는 어색한 문맥을 만든다.

어휘　deliberate adj. 고의적인, 신중한; v. 심사숙고하다
　　　deliberation n. 숙고, 신중함

102 전치사 채우기　　　　중 ●●○

해석　주차장에 있는 기계는 현금 지불에 대해 영수증과 거스름돈을 제공할 것이다.

해설　빈칸은 명사구(the parking garage)를 목적어로 취하는 전치사 자리이다. '주차장에 있는 기계'라는 의미가 되어야 하므로 장소를 나타내는 전치사 (C) in(~에 있는)이 정답이다. 전치사 (B) from(~에서부터, ~으로부터)은 방향 또는 시점을 나타내는 데 쓰이며, '주차장에서부터 기계'라는 어색한 의미를 만든다. 전치사 (D) onto(~위에, ~위로)도 해석상 그럴듯해 보이지만, 이동을 나타내는 동사와 함께 쓰이므로 답이 될 수 없다.

어휘　parking garage phr. (실내) 주차장, 주차장 건물
　　　dispense v. 제공하다, 베풀다　receipt n. 영수증　change n. 거스름돈
　　　among prep. ~사이에

103 전치사 채우기　　　　상 ●●●

해석　만약 다음 15일 이내에 고지서가 지불된다면 공익기업은 벌금을 적용하지 않을 것이다.

해설　빈칸은 명사구(the next 15 days)를 목적어로 취하는 전치사 자리이다. '다음 15일 이내에'라는 의미가 되어야 하므로 (B) within(~이내에)이 정답이다. (C) behind(~뒤에)도 해석상 그럴듯해 보이지만 장소 또는 위치 뒤를 의미하며, 시간과 관련된 의미로 쓸 경우 '뒤떨어진, 늦은'이라는 의미를 가지므로 문맥상 어울리지 않는다. 참고로, 이 문장은 가정법 미래에서 if절의 if가 생략되어 주어와 조동사가 도치된 형태임을 알아둔다.

어휘　bill n. 고지서　utility company phr. 공익기업　apply v. 적용하다, 신청하다
　　　penalty n. 벌금, 위약금　upon prep. ~위에　toward prep. ~쪽으로

104 전치사 채우기　　　　중 ●●○

해석　LightTrek사의 영상 편집 소프트웨어는 몇몇 인상적인 특징들을 가지고 있음에도 불구하고 잘 팔리지 못했다.

해설　빈칸은 동명사(having)를 목적어로 취하는 전치사 자리이다. '인상적인 특징들을 가지고 있음에도 불구하고 잘 팔리지 못했다'라는 의미가 되어야 하므로 양보를 나타내는 전치사 (B) despite(~에도 불구하고)가 정답이다. 전치사 또는 접속사 (C) than(~보다)은 비교의 대상이 되는 구 또는 절을 이끌 때 사용되는데, 이 문장에서 거품구(___ ~ features)가 주절과 비교되는 대상이 아니므로 답이 될 수 없다.

어휘　video-editing n. 영상 편집　impressive adj. 인상적인, 멋진
　　　feature n. 특징, 특색; v. 특별히 포함하다　for prep. ~을 위해
　　　since prep. ~이후로, ~때문에

105 부사 어휘 고르기　　　　중 ●●○

해석　만약 사용자가 고객지원 서비스에 신속히 연락했더라면 뜻하지 않게 삭제되었던 파일들은 되찾아질 수 있었을 것이다.

해설　빈칸은 if로 시작되는 종속절(if ~ ___)의 동사(had contacted)를 꾸미는 부사 자리이다. '사용자가 신속히 고객지원 서비스에 연락했다'라는 문맥이므로 (D) rapidly(신속히)가 정답이다.

어휘　accidentally adv. 뜻하지 않게, 우연히　retrieve v. 되찾다, 회수하다
　　　customer support phr. 고객지원(서비스)

thoroughly adv. 철저히, 대단히 fairly adv. 상당히, 공정하게
nearly adv. 거의

106 형용사 어휘 고르기 상 ●●●

해석 경찰관은 그녀가 관련된 모든 목격자와 이야기해보았다고 확신했다.

해설 빈칸은 be동사(was)의 보어 역할을 하는 형용사 자리이다. '그녀가 관련된 모든 목격자와 이야기해보았다고 확신했다'라는 문맥이므로 (C) certain(확신하는)이 정답이다. 참고로, 형용사 certain은 뒤에 that절을 취할 수 있는 형용사로, 이러한 형용사에는 aware(~을 알고 있는), confident(~라고 확신하는), sorry(~해서 유감인) 등이 있다. (A)와 (B)도 해석상 그럴듯해 보이지만 뒤에 that절을 취할 수 없다.

어휘 witness n. 목격자 involved adj. 관련된, 연루된
attentive adj. 주의를 기울이는 sharp adj. 예리한
unique adj. 독특한, 특별한

107 명사 어휘 고르기 중 ●●○

해석 그 잘 만들어진 기기는 유지보수에 대한 많은 필요 없이 20년 동안 작동해왔다.

해설 빈칸은 전치사(without)의 목적어 역할을 하며 수량 형용사(much)와 과거분사(required)의 꾸밈을 받는 명사 자리이다. '기기는 유지보수에 대한 많은 필요 없이 작동해왔다'라는 문맥이므로 (B) maintenance(유지보수)가 정답이다.

어휘 well-made adj. 잘 만들어진 appliance n. 기기
function v. 작동하다, 기능하다 convenience n. 편의, 편리
protection n. 보호 resistance n. 저항, 반대

108 부정대명사/형용사 채우기 중 ●●○

해석 그 회사는 Ms. Kovac의 휴가동안 그녀의 업무를 처리할 누군가를 고용할 계획이다.

해설 동사(hire)의 목적어 자리에 올 수 있는 부정대명사 (B), (C), (D)가 정답의 후보이다. 'Ms. Kovac의 업무를 처리할 누군가를 고용하다'라는 의미가 되어야 하므로, 부정대명사 (D) someone(누군가, 어떤 사람)이 정답이다. 부정대명사 (B)와 (C)는 각각 'Ms. Kovac의 업무를 처리할 서로서로를/무엇이든 고용하다'라는 어색한 문맥을 만든다. 부정 형용사 (A)는 목적어 자리에 올 수 없다.

어휘 handle v. 처리하다 duty n. 업무 other adj. 다른

최고난도 문제

109 명사 어휘 고르기 상 ●●●

해석 저작권으로 보호된 사진을 그것의 소유주로부터 동의를 구하지 않고 사용하는 것은 불법이다.

해설 빈칸은 동명사(obtaining)의 목적어 역할을 하는 명사 자리이다. '저작권으로 보호된 사진을 소유주로부터 동의를 구하지 않고 사용하는 것은 불법이다'라는 문맥이므로 (D) consent(동의, 합의)가 정답이다.

어휘 illegal adj. 불법의 copyright v. 저작권으로 보호하다; n. 저작권
certification n. 증명, 증명서 declaration n. 선언(문), 공표
discipline n. 규율, 훈육

110 동사 어휘 고르기 중 ●●○

해석 만약 당신이 개인에게 맞춤화된 프로그램에 관심이 있다면, 당신이 선호하는 것들을 체육관의 회원 신청서에 쓰십시오.

해설 please로 시작하는 절(please ~ registration form)은 주어 없이 시작되는 명령문이므로 빈칸은 명령문의 동사로 사용되는 동사원형 자리이다. '당신이 선호하는 것들을 신청서에 써라'라는 문맥이므로 (C) state(쓰다, 말하다)가 정답이다.

어휘 personalized adj. 개인에게 맞춤화된 preference n. 선호하는 것
registration form phr. 신청서 authorize v. 권한을 부여하다
initiate v. 착수시키다 tolerate v. 용인하다, 참다

111 동명사와 명사 구별하여 채우기 중 ●●○

해석 Ms. Ebbets는 10년 넘게 법무부를 관리하는 것을 맡아왔다.

해설 전치사(for)의 목적어 자리에 올 수 있는 것은 명사이므로 명사 (A)와 동명사 (C)가 정답의 후보이다. 빈칸 다음에 온 목적어(the ~ department)를 가질 수 있는 것은 동명사이므로 동명사 (C) managing(관리하는 것)이 정답이다. 동사 (B)와 동사 또는 과거분사 (D)는 명사 자리에 올 수 없다.

어휘 responsible for phr. ~을 맡은 decade n. 10년
manager n. 관리자, 경영자 manage v. 관리하다, 처리하다

112 수, 태, 시제에 맞는 동사 채우기 중 ●●○

해석 Ms. Olsen은 그녀의 의사의 권고 사항들에 근거하여 다음 주까지 그녀의 식단에서 카페인을 없앨 것이다.

해설 문장에 동사가 없으므로 동사 (A), (C), (D) 중 빈칸 뒤의 목적어 (caffeine)를 가질 수 있는 능동태 (C)와 (D)가 정답의 후보이다. 미래를 나타내는 시간 표현(until next week)이 있으므로 특정한 미래 시점에 진행되고 있을 일을 표현하는 미래 진행 시제 (D) will be removing이 정답이다. 과거 시제 (A)와 현재 완료 시제 (C)는 미래를 나타내는 시간 표현과 함께 쓰일 수 없다. 동명사 또는 현재분사 (B)는 동사 자리에 올 수 없다.

어휘 based on phr. ~에 근거하여 recommendation n. 권고 (사항)
remove v. 없애다, 제거하다

113 현재분사와 과거분사 구별하여 채우기 중 ●●○

해석 주요 건설 사업을 성공적으로 완료한 후에, Goldfield Land사는 아시아의 선두적인 토지 개발회사들 중 하나가 되는 것을 목표로 한다.

해설 명사구(land developers)를 꾸밀 수 있는 것은 형용사이므로 과거분사 (A)와 현재분사 (C)가 정답의 후보이다. 꾸밈을 받는 명사와 분사가 '선두적인 토지 개발회사들'이라는 의미의 능동 관계이므로 현재분사 (C) leading(선두적인)이 정답이다. 과거분사 (A)를 쓸 경우 '이끌어진 토지 개발 회사들'이라는 어색한 문맥이 된다. 명사 또는 동사 (B)와 명사 (D)는 명사구를 꾸밀 수 없다. 참고로, (D) leaders를 '선두, 지도자'라는 의미의 명사로서 빈칸 뒤의 land developers와 함께 복합 명사를 만드는 것으로 본다 해도, 복합 명사의 첫 번째 단어인 leaders는 단수형이어야 하므로 답이 될 수 없다.

어휘 construction n. 건설 aim v. 목표로 하다; n. 목적, 겨냥
land developer phr. 토지 개발 회사 lead n. 선두, 우세; v. 선도하다, 이끌다

114 동사 어휘 고르기 중 ●●○

해석 비록 아직 확정된 것은 아니지만, 신문 기사들은 Braxco사와 Haskill사가 합병을 고려하고 있다는 것을 시사한다.

해설 빈칸은 주절(news reports ~ merger)의 동사 자리이다. '신문 기사들은 Braxco사와 Haskill사가 합병을 고려하고 있다는 것을 시사한다'라는 문맥이므로 (D) indicate(시사하다, 나타내다)가 정답이다.

어휘 confirm v. 확정하다, 공식화하다 merger n. 합병
implement v. 시행하다 respond v. 응답하다
acquire v. 취득하다, 매입하다

115 부정대명사/형용사 채우기   중 ●●○

해석 Donald's Doughnuts의 기념행사에서, 많은 사람들이 무료 머핀을 받기 위해 커피를 샀다.

해설 주절(___ ~ muffin)의 동사(have bought)가 복수 동사이므로 복수 취급되는 부정대명사 (A) many(많은 사람들)가 정답이다. (B) either(어느 하나), (C) little(거의 없는 것), (D) anyone(누구나)은 단수 동사와 함께 쓰이므로 답이 될 수 없다.

어휘 anniversary adj. 기념의, 기념일의; n. 기념일 obtain v. 받다

116 형용사 자리 채우기   중 ●●○

해석 Red Pail Hardware사는 합리적인 가격에 제품들을 제공하지만, Jerry's Home Supplies사의 제품들이 더 저렴하다.

해설 be동사(are) 뒤의 보어 자리에 올 수 있는 것은 형용사이므로 과거분사 (A), 현재분사 (C), 형용사 (D)가 정답의 후보이다. '제품들이 더 저렴하다'라는 문맥이므로 형용사 (D) affordable(저렴한)이 정답이다. 과거분사 (A)와 현재분사 (C)를 쓸 경우 각각 'Red Pail Hardware사는 합리적인 가격에 제품들을 제공하지만, Jerry's Home Supplies사의 제품들이 더 제공된다/제공하고 있다'라는 어색한 문맥이 된다. 참고로, (C)가 동명사로 쓰인 경우 주어(the goods of ~ Supplies)와 동격이 되어 'Jerry's Home Supplies사의 제품들은 더 제공하는 것이다'라는 어색한 문맥이 되며 동사 afford(제공하다, ~할 여유가 되다)가 타동사이므로 뒤에 목적어가 와야 한다. 동사 (B)는 보어 자리에 올 수 없다.

어휘 reasonable adj. 합리적인

117 유사의미 동사 고르기   상 ●●●

해석 지역의 예술 축제에 참여하고 싶은 사람들은 시청에서 티켓을 구매해야 한다.

해설 빈칸은 to 부정사를 만드는 동사원형 자리이다. '축제에 참여하고 싶은 사람들은 티켓을 구매해야 한다'라는 문맥이므로 (B) attend(참여하다)가 정답이다. (A) engage(참여하다), (C) participate(참가하다)도 해석상 그럴듯해 보이지만, 자동사이므로 뒤에 목적어(the ~ festival)가 올 수 없다. 참고로, engage와 participate는 전치사 in과 함께 각각 engage in(~에 참여하다)/participate in(~에 참가하다)의 형태로 쓰임을 알아둔다. (D) perform(공연하다)도 해석상 그럴듯해 보이지만 다음에 song(노래)과 같이 공연되는 것이 오거나 perform at the festival과 같은 형태로 쓰인다.

어휘 local adj. 지역의; n. 주민, 현지인 purchase v. 구매하다
town hall phr. 시청, 읍사무소

최고난도 문제

118 명사 보어와 형용사 보어 구별하여 채우기   상 ●●●

해석 회의 후에, Mr. Hoffman은 마감일을 지킬 수 있는 그의 팀의 능력에 대해 자신감 있어 보였다.

해설 2형식 동사 appear의 보어 자리에 올 수 있는 명사 (A), 형용사 (C)와 (D)가 정답의 후보이다. '그는 팀의 능력에 대해 자신감 있어 보였다'라는 의미

로 보어가 주어(Mr. Hoffman)의 상태를 설명하고 있으므로 형용사 (D) confident(자신감 있는)가 정답이다. 명사 (A)는 보어로서 주어와 동격 관계가 되어 '그는 팀의 능력에 대해 자신감처럼 보였다'라는 어색한 문맥을 만든다. 형용사 (C)는 '그는 팀의 능력에 대해 은밀해 보였다'라는 어색한 문맥을 만든다. 동사 (B)는 보어 자리에 올 수 없다.

어휘 appear v. (~처럼) 보이다 meet v. (기한 등을) 지키다, 만나다
confide v. 털어놓다

119 전치사 표현 채우기   중 ●●●

해석 각 직원들은 회사 내에서 그 또는 그녀의 직책에 관계없이 그 워크숍에 참가해야 한다.

해설 빈칸은 명사구(his ~ position)를 목적어로 취하는 전치사 자리이다. '각 직원들은 그 또는 그녀의 직책에 관계없이 워크숍에 참가해야 한다'라는 의미가 되어야 하므로 선치사 (A) regardless of(~에 관계없이)가 정답이다.

어휘 join v. 참가하다, 가입하다 position n. 직책, 직무 other than phr. ~외에
such as phr. ~과 같은 except for phr. ~을 제외하고

120 형용사 자리 채우기   상 ●●●

해석 그 회사의 웹사이트는 직무 지원 과정에 관한 일부 모순되는 정보를 포함했다.

해설 명사(information)를 꾸밀 수 있는 것은 형용사이므로 형용사 (A)와 (C)가 정답의 후보이다. '웹사이트는 직무 지원 과정에 관한 일부 모순되는 정보를 포함했다'라는 문맥이므로 형용사 (C) contradictory(모순되는)가 정답이다. 형용사 (A)를 쓸 경우 '웹사이트는 직무 지원 과정에 관한 반박할 수 있는 정보를 포함했다'라는 어색한 문맥이 된다. 명사 (B)와 동사 (D)는 형용사 자리에 올 수 없다.

어휘 concerning prep. ~에 관한 contradiction n. 모순, 반박
contradict v. 모순되다, 반박하다

121 부사 어휘 고르기   중 ●●○

해석 적어도 한 달 전에 미리 XP290을 주문한 고객들은 특별 선물을 받을 것이다.

해설 빈칸은 기간 표현(one month)과 함께 동사구(place orders)를 꾸미는 부사 자리이다. '적어도 한 달 전에 미리 주문한 고객들'이라는 문맥이므로 (A) beforehand(~전에 미리, 사전에)가 정답이다. 참고로, 부사 beforehand는 기간 표현(three days/two weeks 등)과 함께 쓰여 '~ 전에'라는 의미를 나타내며, 이러한 부사들에는 earlier, ahead, before 등이 있음을 알아둔다.

어휘 place an order phr. 주문하다 anytime adv. 언제나, 반드시
instantly adv. 즉시 nowadays adv. 요즘에는

122 형용사 어휘 고르기   상 ●●●

해석 Mr. Turner는 그의 혁신적인 창작품들로 인해 독창적인 패션 디자이너로 여겨진다.

해설 빈칸은 명사구(fashion designer)를 꾸미는 형용사 자리이다. 'Mr. Turner는 혁신적인 창작품들로 인해 독창적인 패션 디자이너로 여겨진다'라는 문맥이므로 (B) ingenious(독창적인, 기발한)가 정답이다.

어휘 regard v. 여기다, 간주하다 innovative adj. 혁신적인, 획기적인
creation n. 창작품, 창조 available adj. 이용할 수 있는
appreciative adj. 고마워하는, 감탄하는
inactive adj. 활동하지 않는, 활발하지 않은

123 형용사 어휘 고르기　　상 ●●●

해석　표준이 되는 직원 오리엔테이션 안내서를 제작하는 것은 직원들에게 엄청난 도움이 될 것이다.

해설　빈칸은 전치사(of)의 목적어로 쓰인 명사(help)를 꾸미는 형용사 자리이다. '안내서를 제작하는 것은 직원들에게 엄청난 도움이 될 것이다'라는 문맥이므로 (D) immense(엄청난)가 정답이다.

어휘　standard adj. 표준이 되는　be of help to phr. ~에게 도움이 되다
customary adj. 습관적인, 관례적인　extravagant adj. 낭비하는
intelligent adj. 총명한, 똑똑한

124 부사 자리 채우기　　중 ●●○

해석　물리 치료 수업들에 참석하고 자주 스트레칭을 함으로써, 그 환자는 그녀의 부상에서 점차 회복했다.

해설　동사(recovered)를 꾸밀 수 있는 것은 부사이므로 부사 (C) progressively (점차, 점진적으로)가 정답이다. 형용사 (A), 명사 또는 동사 (B), 명사 (D)는 동사를 꾸밀 수 없다. 명사 (B)와 (D)를 patient와 함께 복합 명사를 만드는 것으로 본다 해도, 각각 '환자 진전/진행이 부상으로부터 회복했다'라는 어색한 문맥을 만든다.

어휘　physical therapy phr. 물리 치료　frequently adv. 자주, 흔히
recover v. 회복하다, 되찾다　injury n. 부상
progressive adj. 진보적인, 점진적인
progress n. 진전; v. 진전을 보이다, 진행하다　progression n. 진행, 진전

125 명사 어휘 고르기　　상 ●●●

해석　Ms. Lee는 명성 있는 Valley River 달리기 대회에 대한 자격을 얻음으로써 그녀의 운동선수다운 잠재력을 보여주었다.

해설　빈칸은 동사(showed)의 목적어 역할을 하면서 형용사(athletic)의 꾸밈을 받는 명사 자리이다. '명성 있는 달리기 대회에 대한 자격을 얻음으로써 그녀의 운동선수다운 잠재력을 보여주었다'라는 문맥이므로 (A) potential(잠재력, 가능성)이 정답이다. 참고로, (C) property(속성, 특성)도 해석상 그럴듯해 보이지만 사물이나 물질 고유의 속성과 특성을 의미함을 알아둔다.

어휘　athletic adj. 운동선수다운, 육상 경기의　qualify v. 자격을 얻다
prestigious adj. 명성 있는, 일류의　authority n. 지휘권, 권한
acquisition n. 습득, 매입

126 부사 어휘 고르기　　중 ●●○

해석　Wassco사에서 입찰하고 있는 대형 프로젝트는 그것의 수익성 때문에 매우 경쟁적이다.

해설　빈칸은 형용사(competitive)를 꾸미는 부사 자리이다. '대형 프로젝트는 수익성 때문에 매우 경쟁적이다'라는 문맥이므로 (A) extremely(매우, 극도로)가 정답이다.

어휘　bid v. 입찰하다, 명령하다　competitive adj. 경쟁적인　due to phr. ~때문에
profitability n. 수익성　efficiently adv. 효율적으로, 유효하게
unanimously adv. 만장일치로　promptly adv. 즉시

127 사람명사와 추상명사 구별하여 채우기　　상 ●●●

해석　CK 물류회사의 고위 간부에게 지급되는 급여는 업계에서 가장 높은 것들 중 하나이다.

해설　전치사(to)의 목적어 자리에 오면서 형용사(top)의 꾸밈을 받을 수 있는 것은 명사이므로 명사 (B)와 (C)가 정답의 후보이다. '고위 간부에게 지급되는 급여'라는 의미가 되어야 하므로 사람 명사 (C) executive(간부, 임원)가 정답이다. 추상명사 (B) execution(실행, 수행)을 쓸 경우 '고위 실행에 지급되는 급여'라는 어색한 문맥이 된다. 동사 (A)는 명사 자리에 올 수 없다. 동명사 또는 현재분사 (D)는 동명사로 볼 경우, 형용사(top)의 꾸밈을 받을 수 없고, 부사의 꾸밈을 받을 수 있으므로 답이 될 수 없다. (D)를 현재분사로 보고, '최고, 정상'이라는 의미를 가지는 명사 top을 꾸미는 것으로 볼 경우, 'CK 물류회사에서 수행하는 최고'라는 의미로 해석상 그럴듯해 보이지만 execute는 타동사이므로 빈칸 다음에 목적어가 와야 한다.

어휘　salary n. 급여, 월급　top adj. 고위의, 높은; n. 최고　logistics n. 물류(회사)
execute v. 실행하다, 수행하다

128 전치사 채우기　　중 ●●○

해석　그 제품은 그것이 결함이 있을 수도 있다는 우려 때문에 가게 선반들에서 치워졌다.

해설　주절(The product ~ shelves)이 주어(The product)와 동사(was taken)를 갖춘 완전한 절이므로, ___ ~ defective는 수식어 거품으로 보아야 한다. 이 수식어 거품은 명사절 접속사(that)가 이끄는 절의 수식을 받는 명사(concerns)만 있고 동사가 없는 거품구이므로, 거품구를 이끌 수 있는 전치사 (A), (B), (D)가 정답의 후보이다. '우려 때문에'라는 의미가 되어야 하므로 (B) because of(~때문에)가 정답이다. 참고로, (A) along with (~와 함께)도 해석상 그럴듯해 보이지만 우려로 인해 제품이 치워진 것이 아니라, 우려와 제품이 함께 선반에서 치워졌다는 것을 의미하므로 답이 될 수 없다. 접속사 또는 부사 (C)는 거품구를 이끌 수 없다.

어휘　concern n. 우려, 걱정　defective adj. 결함이 있는
whenever conj. ~할 때는 언제든지　in observance of phr. ~을 준수하여

129 등위접속사 채우기　　상 ●●●

해석　구매 신청서는 관리자에 의해 서명되어야 하며, 그렇지 않으면 그것은 승인을 받지 못할 것이다.

해설　절(A purchase ~ supervisor)과 절(it ~ approval)을 연결할 수 있는 것은 접속사이므로 등위접속사 (A), (C), (D)가 정답의 후보이다. '구매 신청서는 관리자에 의해 서명되어야 하며, 그렇지 않으면 그것은 승인을 받지 못할 것이다'라는 의미가 되어야 하므로 등위접속사 (A) or(그렇지 않으면)가 정답이다. 등위접속사 (C)와 (D)를 쓸 경우 각각 '구매 신청서는 관리자에 의해 서명되어야 하고, 그것은 승인을 받지 못할 것이다/구매 신청서는 관리자에 의해 서명되어야 하지만 그것은 승인을 받지 못할 것이다'라는 어색한 문맥이 된다. 부사 (B)는 절과 절을 연결할 수 없다.

어휘　request n. 신청(서)　supervisor n. 관리자　approval n. 승인
nevertheless adv. 그럼에도 불구하고

130 형용사 어휘 고르기　　상 ●●●

해석　Lyon사의 직원들은 수익 성장에 비례하는 연봉 인상을 받을 것이다.

해설　빈칸은 be동사(is)의 보어 역할을 하는 형용사 자리이다. '직원들은 수익 성장에 비례하는 연봉 인상을 받을 것이다'라는 문맥이므로 (D) proportional (비례하는)이 정답이다. 현재분사 또는 동명사 (B) counting(수를 세는; 수를 세는 것)도 숫자와 관련된 의미로 그럴듯해 보이지만, 각각 '연봉 인상이 수를 센다/연봉 인상은 수를 세는 것이다'라는 어색한 문맥을 만든다.

어휘　revenue n. 수익　growth n. 성장
complimentary adj. 무료의, 칭찬하는　complex adj. 복잡한

PART 6

131-134번은 다음 광고지에 관한 문제입니다.

저희가 Landmark 공원을 보존할 수 있도록 도와주세요!
Dothan시 청년 동맹의 연례 대청소 행사에 함께하세요
5월 15일 | 오전 10시에서 오후 4시

활동에는 쓰레기를 줍는 것과 나무를 심는 것이 포함됩니다. 자원봉사자들에게 장비¹³¹가 제공될 것입니다. 공급품들이 부족할 수 있기 때문에, 저희는 여러분이 여러분 소유의 장비를 가지고 오는 것을 권장합니다.

참가자들은 그룹들로 ¹³²나누어질 것이고 청소할 구체적인 구역들이 배정될 것입니다. 옷을 ¹³³적절하게 입는 것을 명심하세요. 긴 바지와 알맞은 신발을 신으세요.

만약 당신이 Dothan시 청년 동맹에 도움을 제공하는 것을 고려하고 있다면, 당신의 기부금들은 이것과 향후 행사들에 사용될 것입니다. ¹³⁴저희는 물품 기증은 받지 않습니다. 하지만, 저희는 Dothan시 노숙자 보호시설에 그것들을 가져갈 것을 권해 드립니다. www.dothanyouth.org에서 대청소 행사를 신청하세요.

preserve v. 보존하다, 지키다 cleanup n. 대청소 litter n. 쓰레기
supply n. 공급품 limited adj. (시간이나 수가) 부족한, 한정된
assign v. 배정하다 specific adj. 구체적인 appropriate adj. 알맞은
aid n. 도움, 지원 contribution n. 기부금, 공헌 homeless n. 노숙자
shelter n. 보호시설 register v. 신청하다, 등록하다

131 전치사 표현 채우기 중 ●●○

해설 빈칸은 명사(equipment)를 목적어로 취하는 전치사 자리이다. '자원봉사자들에게 장비가 제공될 것이다'라는 의미가 되어야 하므로 빈칸 앞의 동사 provide와 함께 provide A with B(A에게 B를 제공하다)의 수동형 A be provided with B의 형태를 완성하는 전치사 (A) with가 정답이다. (C) for와 (D) to도 provide와 쓰이기는 하지만 'provide (something) for/to (someone)'의 형태로 쓰이므로 for/to 다음에는 제공받은 대상인 사람이나 기관 등을 나타내는 표현이 와야 한다.

어휘 of prep. ~의 for prep. ~을 위한 to prep. ~로, ~에

132 수, 태, 시제에 맞는 동사 채우기 전체 문맥 파악 상 ●●●

해설 문장에 동사가 없고 '참가자들이 그룹들로 나누어지다'라는 수동의 의미가 되어야 하므로 수동태 (B), (C), (D)가 정답의 후보이다. 앞부분에서 행사가 5월 15일에 있을 것이고 자원봉사자들은 장비를 제공받을 것이라고 했으므로 봉사활동이 아직 일어나지 않은 미래의 상황임을 알 수 있다. 따라서 미래 시제 수동태 (D) will be separated가 정답이다. 과거 시제 (B)와 현재 완료 시제 (C)는 미래의 일을 나타낼 수 없다. (A)는 능동태이므로 답이 될 수 없다.

어휘 separate v. 나누다, 분리하다

133 부사 자리 채우기 하 ●○○

해설 동사(dress)를 꾸밀 수 있는 것은 부사이므로 부사 (D) properly(적절하게)가 정답이다. 형용사 (A)와 형용사의 비교급 (C), 명사 (B)는 동사를 꾸밀 수 없다. 참고로, 동사 dress를 '(옷을) 입히다'라는 의미의 타동사로 보고, (B) propriety(적절성, 예절)를 목적어로 본다 해도 '적절성을 입는 것을 명심하라'라는 어색한 문맥이 되므로 답이 될 수 없다.

어휘 proper adj. 적절한

134 알맞은 문장 고르기 중 ●●●

해석 (A) 이메일로 알림을 받기 위해 가입하세요.
(B) 저희는 물품 기증은 받지 않습니다.
(C) 참석률이 예상했던 것보다 더 높았습니다.
(D) 공원은 개인적인 행사들을 위해 임대될 수 있습니다.

해설 앞 문장 'your contributions will be used for this and future events'에서 당신의 기부금들은 이것과 향후 행사들에 사용될 것이라고 했고, 뒤 문장 'However, we recommend taking them to the Dothan City Homeless Shelter.'에서 하지만, Dothan시 노숙자 보호시설에 그것들을 가져갈 것을 권한다고 했으므로 빈칸에는 물품의 기부와 관련된 내용이 들어가야 함을 알 수 있다. 따라서 (B)가 정답이다.

어휘 sign up phr. 가입하다, 등록하다 notify v. 알리다, 통지하다
accept v. 받다, 수락하다 donation n. 기증, 기부
attendance n. 참석률, 출석 anticipate v. 예상하나, 기대하나
rent v. 임대하다

135-138번은 다음 공고에 관한 문제입니다.

고객님들께,

Banerjee Roof Tiles사가 그것의 컴퓨터 시스템을 업그레이드할 것입니다. 이것은 고객 서비스뿐만 아니라, 저희의 주문과 이메일 처리에도 영향을 미칠 것으로 예상됩니다. 저희의 온라인 주문 시스템이 5월 20일과 5월 31일 사이에 사용할 수 없게 될 것입니다. ¹³⁵만약 여러분이 주문하고자 한다면, 영업시간 중 저희에게 전화해주십시오. 저희 직원들이 기꺼이 여러분을 도와드릴 것입니다. 모든 것이 순조롭게 ¹³⁶나아간다면, 6월 1일까지는 정상적인 운영이 재개될 것입니다.

5월의 마지막 주 동안, 저희는 직원 교육에도 집중할 예정인데, ¹³⁷그렇게 함으로써 직원들이 새로운 시스템에 익숙해질 것입니다. 따라서, 저희는 문의들에 응답하는 것이 느릴 수 있으며 저희의 ¹³⁸평상시의 서비스 및 지원을 제공할 수 없을 것입니다.

불편에 사과드리며, 귀하의 인내심에 감사드립니다.

affect v. ~에 영향을 미치다 handling n. 처리, 조작
disable v. 사용할 수 없게 하다 assist v. 돕다, 도움이 되다
provided conj. ~라면 smoothly adv. 순조롭게, 부드럽게
normal adj. 정상적인, 보통의 resume v. 재개되다
consequently adv. 따라서 respond v. 응답하다, 대답하다
inquiry n. 문의, 질의 inconvenience n. 불편
patience n. 인내심, 참을성

최고난도 문제

135 알맞은 문장 고르기 상 ●●●

해석 (A) 대체 경로들에 대한 길 안내는 저희의 웹사이트에서 이용 가능합니다.
(B) 만약 여러분이 주문하고자 한다면, 영업시간 중 저희에게 전화해주십시오.
(C) 따라서, 이 문제의 지속기간 동안 몇몇 제품들은 재고가 없을 수도 있습니다.
(D) 저희는 저희의 조건들에 따라 반품들을 받을 것입니다.

해설 앞 문장 'Our online ordering system will be disabled between May 20 and May 31.'에서 자신들의 온라인 주문 시스템이 5월 20일과 5월 31일 사이에 사용할 수 없게 될 것이라고 했고, 뒤 문장 'Our personnel will be glad to assist you.'에서 직원들이 기꺼이 여러분, 즉 고객들을 도와줄 것이라고 했으므로 빈칸에는 온라인 주문 외에 다른 방법으로 직원들이 고객

들의 주문을 도와주는 것과 관련된 내용이 들어가야 함을 알 수 있다. 따라서 (B)가 정답이다.

어휘 directions n. 길 안내 alternative adj. 대체의, 대체 가능한
place an order phr. 주문하다 in stock phr. 재고가 있는
duration n. 지속기간 under prep. ~에 따라, 아래에
terms and conditions phr. (계약이나 지불 등의) 조건

136 수, 태, 시제에 맞는 동사 채우기   상 ●●●

해설 Provided로 시작하는 종속절(Provided ~ smoothly)에 단수 주어 (everything)만 있고 동사가 없으므로 단수 동사 (A), (B), (D)가 정답의 후보이다. 주절(normal ~ June 1)에 미래를 나타내는 시간 표현(by June 1)이 있고, 6월 1일까지는 운영이 재개될 것이라는 의미가 되어야 하므로 Provided로 시작하는 종속절도 미래를 나타내야 한다. 조건의 부사절에서는 미래를 나타내기 위해 미래 시제 대신 현재 시제를 사용해야 하므로 현재 시제 (B) advances가 정답이다. 미래 시제 (A)와 현재 완료 시제 (D)는 조건의 부사절에서 미래를 나타낼 수 없다.복수 동사 (C)는 단수 주어와 함께 쓰일 수 없다.

어휘 advance v. 나아가다, 진전되다

137 접속부사 채우기   상 ●●●

해설 이 문장은 주어(we)와 동사(will focus)를 갖춘 완전한 절이므로, ___ ~ system은 수식어 거품으로 보아야 한다. 이 수식어 거품은 분사구문이므로, 절과 분사구문의 의미를 연결할 수 있는 접속부사 (A)와 (C)가 정답의 후보이다. '저희는 직원 교육에도 집중할 예정인데, 그렇게 함으로써 직원들이 새로운 시스템에 익숙해질 것이다'라는 의미가 되어야 하므로 (C) thereby(그렇게 함으로써)가 정답이다. 부사절 접속사 (B)는 거품절을 이끈다. 전치사 (D)는 분사구문을 이끌 수 없으며, 현재분사 familiarizing을 전치사의 목적어 자리에 온 동명사로 본다고 하더라도 '새로운 시스템에 직원들을 익숙하게 하는 것의 결과로서, 직원 교육에도 집중할 예정이다'라는 어색한 의미를 만든다.

어휘 otherwise adv. 그렇지 않으면 in case phr. ~에 대비하여

138 형용사 어휘 고르기   전체 문맥 파악   상 ●●●

해설 빈칸은 명사구(service and support)를 꾸미는 형용사 자리이다. '문의들에 응답하는 것이 느릴 수 있으며 우리의 ___ 서비스 및 지원을 제공할 수 없을 것이다'라는 문맥이므로 모든 보기가 정답의 후보이다. 앞부분에서 컴퓨터 시스템 업그레이드로 인해 고객 서비스, 주문 및 이메일 처리에 영향이 있을 것이고, 6월 1일에 정상적인 운영을 재개할 것이라고 했으므로, 평소와 같은 서비스 및 지원을 제공할 수 없을 것임을 알 수 있다. 따라서 (C) usual(평상시의, 보통의)이 정답이다

어휘 public adj. 공공의 approved adj. 인가된, 승인된
selective adj. 선택적인

139-142번은 다음 편지에 관한 문제입니다.

Eric Frears
6633번지 7번가
새크라멘토, 캘리포니아주 95673

Mr. Frears께,

Shasta Lake에 있는 The Aldrich를 고려해주셔서 감사합니다. 삶의 질이 항상 저희의 우선 사항이었던 것을 139고려하면, 저희가 수백 명의 주민들을 만족시킨 것은 놀랍지 않습니다.

저희 지역사회의 구성원으로서, 당신은 24시간 계속되는 의료 서비스 및 요리와 청소에 대한 지원을 140이용할 것입니다. 또한, 빈번한 모임들과 지역 행사들에서의 자원봉사 기회들이 있습니다. 저희는 매일을 될 수 있는 한 141만족스럽게 만들기를 바랍니다.

방문해서, 주위를 둘러보고, 그리고 The Aldrich에서의 은퇴 생활의 맛보기를 경험해보세요. 142저희는 당신이 이곳을 집이라고 부를 가치가 있음을 알게 되리라 확신합니다. 저는 당신을 맞이하기를 기다리겠습니다!

Mona Sorenstein 드림
전무 이사
The Aldrich 노인 주택 지구

quality n. 질 priority n. 우선 (사항)
around-the-clock adj. 24시간 계속되는 assistance n. 지원, 원조
frequent adj. 빈번한 get-together n. 모임 retirement n. 은퇴

139 부사절 접속사 채우기   상 ●●●

해설 이 문장은 주어(it), 동사(is), 보어(no surprise)를 갖춘 완전한 절이므로, ___ ~ priority는 수식어 거품으로 보아야 한다. 이 수식어 거품은 동사(has been)가 있는 거품절이므로, 거품절을 이끌 수 있는 부사절 접속사인 (A), (C), (D)가 정답의 후보이다. '삶의 질이 항상 우리의 우선 사항이었던 것을 고려하면 우리가 수백 명의 주민들을 만족시킨 것은 놀랍지 않다'라는 의미가 되어야 하므로 (D) Given(~을 고려하면)이 정답이다. 부사 (B)는 수식어 거품을 이끌 수 없다.

어휘 whether conj. ~이든 (아니든) especially adv. 특히
although conj. 비록 ~이지만

140 동명사와 명사 구별하여 채우기   상 ●●●

해설 타동사(have)의 목적어 역할을 할 수 있는 것은 명사이므로 명사 (A)와 동명사 (C)가 정답의 후보이다. '의료 서비스 및 요리와 청소에 대한 지원을 이용할 것이다'라는 의미가 되어야 하므로 빈칸 앞의 동사 have와 빈칸 뒤의 전치사 to와 함께 '~을 이용하다'라는 의미의 어구 have access to를 만드는 명사 (A) access(이용, 접근)가 정답이다. 동명사 (C)는 '이용하는 것을 가지다'라는 문맥을 만드는 것으로 본다 해도, access는 타동사이므로 빈칸 뒤에 목적어가 와야 한다. 동사 또는 과거분사 (B)와 형용사 (D)는 명사 자리에 올 수 없다.

어휘 accessible adj. 접근 가능한

141 형용사 어휘 고르기   전체 문맥 파악   상 ●●●

해설 빈칸은 5형식 동사 make의 목적격 보어 역할을 하는 형용사 자리이다. '매일을 될 수 있는 한 ___게 만들기를 바란다'라는 문맥이므로 모든 보기가 정답의 후보이다. 앞부분에서 수백 명의 주민들을 만족시켰다고 한 후, 주민들에게 제공되는 다양한 서비스들에 대해 말하고 있으므로 The Aldrich가 주민들을 만족시키기 위해 노력한다는 것을 알 수 있다. 따라서 (B) fulfilling (만족스러운)이 정답이다.

어휘 consistent adj. 한결같은 influential adj. 영향력 있는
fortunate adj. 운 좋은

142 알맞은 문장 고르기   중 ●●○

해석 (A) 저희의 성수기가 시작되기 전에 전화하세요.
(B) 저희는 여기 저희 직원들을 그들이 가족인 것처럼 대우합니다.

(C) 저희는 당신이 이곳을 집이라고 부를 가치가 있음을 알게 되리라 확신합니다.

(D) 당신이 이곳에 도착할 때 저는 당신의 방을 청소하고 준비할 것입니다.

해설 앞 문장 'Come for a visit, ~ and experience a taste of retirement living in The Aldrich.'에서 The Aldrich를 방문해서 은퇴 생활의 맛보기를 경험해보라고 했으므로 빈칸에는 당신, 즉 잠재적 고객이 The Aldrich를 방문한 후에 어떻게 느끼게 될지와 관련된 내용이 들어가야 함을 알 수 있다. 따라서 (C)가 정답이다.

어휘 peak season phr. 성수기　treat v. 대우하다, 다루다
confident adj. 확신하는, 자신감이 있는　worthy adj. 가치가 있는, 적합한

143-146번은 다음 이메일에 관한 문제입니다.

수신: Alison Jackson <ajackson@champleather.com>
발신: Victoria Green <vgreen@champleather.com>
제목: 새로운 정책
날짜: 6월 15일

안녕하세요, Alison,

다음의 정보를 배포해주십시오. 저는 회사의 ¹⁴³**모두**가 우리의 새로운 정책에 대해 알고 있다는 것을 확실히 하고 싶습니다. 11월 1일부터 시행되어, 회사는 특정 집단의 직원들의 정기적인 건강검진을 요구할 것입니다. 이것은 국가 노동 위원회에 의해 제정된 규제들에 따른 것입니다. ¹⁴⁴**위원회는 지난주에 이 정책을 승인했습니다.** 구체적으로 말하자면, 이 정책은 화학 물질들을 다루는 근로자들과 같이, 직장에서 위험한 환경에 ¹⁴⁵**노출되는** 직원들에게 적용됩니다. 이 정책은 또한 그 또는 그녀의 업무의 안전한 수행에 그들의 건강이 중요한 직원들에게도 작용합니다. ¹⁴⁶**특히**, 우리의 배달 트럭 운전기사들은 그들이 대형 차량들을 운전하기에 적합한지를 확실히 하기 위해 건강검진을 받아야 합니다. 우리는 앞으로 며칠간 이것에 대해 더 자세히 논의할 것입니다.

Victoria Green 드림
Champ Leather사

aware adj. 알고 있는, 인지한　effective adj. ~부터 시행되는, 효과적인
periodic adj. 정기적인　in accordance with phr. ~에 따라서
regulation n. 규제, 규정　enact v. (법을) 제정하다, 일어나다
specifically adv. 구체적으로 말하자면, 분명히
cover v. (규칙 등이) 적용되다　personnel n. 직원들
hazardous adj. 위험한　condition n. 환경, 조건　handle v. 다루다
affect v. ~에 작용하다, 영향을 미치다　crucial adj. 중요한
undergo v. ~을 받다, 겪다　fit adj. 적합한; v. 맞다
operate v. (기계 등을) 운전하다, 조작하다

143 부정대명사/형용사 채우기　　상 ●●●

해설 동사구(make sure)의 목적어 자리에 온 명사절(___ ~ policy)에서 복수 동사(are)의 주어가 될 수 있는 부정대명사 (A)와 지시대명사 (D)가 정답의 후보이다. '회사의 모두가 알고 있다는 것을 확실히 하고 싶다'라는 의미가 되어야 하므로 부정대명사 (A) all(모두)이 정답이다. 참고로, (D) these는 '이들, 이것들'이라는 의미로 이미 앞에서 명시되었거나, 시간, 공간, 심리적으로 가까이에 있는 사람이나 사물을 가리킬 때 사용됨을 알아둔다. 목적격 인칭대명사 (B)는 주어 자리에 올 수 없다. 수량 형용사 (C)는 단수 가산명사 앞에 오거나 단수 동사와 함께 쓰인다.

144 알맞은 문장 고르기　　상 ●●●

해석 (A) 세부 제안서는 당신의 책상 위에 놓여 있습니다.

(B) 규제기관은 법률 전문가들로 구성되었습니다.

(C) 위원회는 지난주에 이 정책을 승인했습니다.

(D) 경영진은 직원들의 안전을 소중히 여깁니다.

해설 앞 문장 'This is in accordance with regulations enacted by the National Labor Board.'에서 이것, 즉 새로운 정책은 국가 노동 위원회에 의해 제정된 규제들에 따른 것이라고 했고, 뒤 문장 'Specifically, the policy covers personnel'에서 구체적으로 말하자면 이 정책이 직원들에게 적용된다고 했으므로 빈칸에는 정책과 관련된 내용이 들어가야 함을 알 수 있다. 따라서 (C)가 정답이다.

어휘 proposal n. 제안서, 제의　regulatory body phr. 규제기관
be compose of phr. ~으로 구성되다　legal adj. 법률의
expert n. 전문가　commission n. 위원회, 수수료　approve v. 승인하다
measure n. 정책, 조치　value v. 소중히 여기다　safety n. 안전

145 태에 맞는 동사 채우기　　중 ●●○

해설 주격 관계절(who ~ at work)에 동사가 없으므로 동사인 모든 보기가 정답의 후보이다. expose(노출시키다)가 타동사인데, 빈칸 뒤에 목적어가 없고, 주격 관계대명사(who)의 선행사(personnel)와 동사(expose)가 '직원들이 노출되다'라는 의미의 수동 관계이므로 수동태 (D) are exposed가 정답이다. 능동태 (A), (B), (C)는 답이 될 수 없다.

146 접속부사 채우기　주변 문맥 파악　　중 ●●○

해설 앞 문장에서 이 정책은 업무의 안전한 수행에 건강이 중요한 직원들에게도 작용한다고 했고, 빈칸이 있는 문장에서는 배달 트럭 운전기사들이 건강검진을 받아야 한다고 했으므로, 앞 문장과 관련하여 구체적인 사항을 추가할 때 사용되는 접속부사 (C) In particular(특히)가 정답이다.

어휘 conversely adv. 정반대로　rather than phr. 대신에, ~보다는
continuously adv. 계속해서

PART 7

147-148번은 다음 광고에 관한 문제입니다.

대여를 위한 공간

¹⁴⁷번지 Buckwold로에 위치한, 최근에 개조된 이 상업 용지는 Renuville의 중심부에 있으며 많은 카페들과 가게들의 도보 거리 내에 있습니다. 또한, 그것은 Renfrew 공원으로부터 단 두 블록이 떨어져 있습니다. 그것의 11층 각각은 10,500제곱피트의 사무실 공간을 제공합니다. ¹⁴⁸**큰 지하 주차장도 있습니다.** 입주자들과 그들의 방문객들은 그들의 자동차들을 그곳에 무료로 둘 수 있습니다. 건물의 모든 층들은 즉시 사용할 준비가 되어 있습니다. 더 많은 정보를 원하시거나 둘러보는 것을 요청하시려면 555-9982로 전화해 주십시오.

renovate v. 개조하다　commercial property phr. 상업 용지
heart n. 중심부, 핵심　distance n. 거리
underground garage phr. 지하 주차장　tenant n. 입주자
vehicle n. 자동차　at no charge phr. 무료로　immediate adj. 즉시의
occupancy n. 사용, 이용　viewing n. 둘러보는 것

147 육하원칙 문제　　중 ●●○

해석 57번지 Buckwold로의 특징은 무엇인가?
(A) 주거 공간을 포함한다.

(B) 중심가에 위치한다.

(C) 공원의 경치가 보인다.

(D) 가구가 비치된 사무실들을 포함한다.

해설 지문의 'Located at 57 Buckwold Drive, ~ commercial property is in the heart of Renuville'에서 57번지 Buckwold로에 위치한 상업 용지가 Renuville의 중심부에 있다고 했으므로 (B)가 정답이다.

어휘 feature n. 특징 contain v. 포함하다, 가지다 residential adj. 주거의
central adj. 중심가의 view n. 경치 furnished adj. 기구가 비치된

패러프레이징

is in the heart 중심부에 있다 → has a central location 중심가에 위치한다

148 육하원칙 문제 　　　　　　　　중 ●●○

해석 입주자들은 무엇을 할 수 있는가?

(A) 더 큰 사무실에 대해 할인을 받는다

(B) 부분적으로 가구가 비치된 방을 요청한다

(C) 주차 시설을 무료로 이용한다

(D) 첫 임대료의 지불을 연기한다

해설 지문의 'There is ~ underground garage. Tenants ~ may leave their vehicles there at no charge.'에서 지하 주차장이 있으며, 입주자들은 그들의 자동차를 그곳에 무료로 둘 수 있다고 했으므로 (C)가 정답이다.

어휘 obtain v. 받다, 얻다 discount n. 할인 partially adv. 부분적으로
facility n. 시설 delay v. 연기하다 initial adj. 첫, 처음의

패러프레이징

underground garage 지하 주차장 → parking facility 주차 시설
at no charge 무료로 → for free 무료로

149-150번은 다음 이메일에 관한 문제입니다.

수신: Robert Sutton <r_sutton@jagmail.com>

발신: Kimbel 백화점 고객 서비스 <customercare@kimbeldept.com>

제목: 귀하의 CP3 Console 선주문

날짜: 5월 3일

Mr. Sutton께,

149지난 금요일, 귀하께서는 올해 10월에 Tensa Tech사에 의해 출시될 예정인 게임 시스템 CP3 Console을 주문하셨습니다. 유감스럽게도, 이 매우 인기 있는 한정판 149기기를 예약할 수 있는 선택권은 그것이 이용할 수 있었어야 하는 것보다 훨씬 이전에 실수로 Kimbel 백화점의 웹사이트에서 이용할 수 있게 되었습니다. 결과적으로, 저희는 귀하의 주문을 취소해야 합니다. 저희는 이번 실수에 대해 정말 죄송하게 생각하며 150고객분들이 상품을 주문할 수 있게 되자마자 귀하께 알려드릴 것을 약속드립니다. 저희는 또한 귀하께서 이 상품에 대한 어떠한 최신 정보이든지 찾기 위해 저희의 상품 페이지를 정기적으로 방문하시길 권장합니다.

149귀하께서 신용카드로 지불하셨다면, 그것은 아직 청구되지 않았을 것입니다. 상품권으로 지불하셨다면, 귀하의 돈이 환불되기 위해 5일까지 감안해주시기 바랍니다.

Kimbel 백화점 고객 서비스 드림

place an order phr. 주문하다 due adj. ~할 예정인
unfortunately adv. 유감스럽게도 option n. 선택권 reserve v. 예약하다
highly adv. 매우, 몹시 sought-after adj. 인기 있는
mistakenly adv. 실수로, 잘못하여 available adj. 이용할 수 있는

---

notify v. 알리다 as soon as phr. ~하자마자 regularly adv. 정기적으로
charge v. 청구하다 refund v. 환불하다

149 추론 문제 　　　　　　　　중 ●●○

해석 Mr. Sutton에 대해 암시되는 것은?

(A) 출시 후에 기기를 구매할 것이다.

(B) 실수 때문에 주문을 취소했다.

(C) 환불을 받기 위해 기다려야 할 것이다.

(D) 지난 금요일에 온라인으로 비용을 지불했다.

해설 지문의 'Last Friday, you placed an order for the CP3 Console, a gaming system'과 'device was mistakenly made available on Kimbel Department Store's Web site'에서 귀하, 즉 Mr. Sutton이 지난 금요일에 게임 시스템 CP3 Console을 주문했으며, 기기가 실수로 Kimbel 백화점의 웹사이트에서 이용할 수 있게 되었다고 했고, 'If you paid using a credit card, ~. If you paid using a gift card, ~.'에서 신용카드와 상품권으로 돈을 지불한 경우에 대한 환불 처리에 대해 설명하고 있으므로 Mr. Sutton이 지난 금요일에 웹사이트에서 주문하며 온라인으로 비용을 지불했음을 추론할 수 있다. 따라서 (D)가 정답이다.

어휘 due to phr. ~ 때문에 submit a payment phr. 비용을 지불하다

150 육하원칙 문제 　　　　　　　　중 ●●○

해석 Kimbel 백화점은 언제 Mr. Sutton에게 다시 연락할 것인가?

(A) 환불 요청이 승인된 후에

(B) 상품이 구매할 수 있을 때

(C) 가게 재고가 다시 채워진 후에

(D) 상품 출시 장소가 알려질 때

해설 지문의 'we will notify you as soon as customers are able to order the product'에서 고객들이 상품을 주문할 수 있게 되자마자 알려주겠다고 했으므로 (B)가 정답이다.

어휘 request n. 요청 approve v. 승인하다 inventory n. 재고
restock v. 다시 채우다 reveal v. 알리다, 드러내다

패러프레이징

able to order 주문할 수 있는 → available to purchase 구매할 수 있는

151-152번은 다음 기사에 관한 문제입니다.

도시 이야기 　　　　　　　　　　　　　　　　　Hamilton Enquirer

Hamilton 출신이 상을 받다

Troy Cheung 작성

1월 6일—151Vino Kiwi사의 최고 경영자 Gloria Wilson이 지난주 전국 비즈니스 포럼(NBF)으로부터 올해의 회사 상을 받았다. 뉴질랜드의 와인 고장에서의 여행 상품들을 제공하는 그녀의 회사는 관광업 부문에서 몇몇 경쟁사들을 이겼다.

매년, 다양한 152전문가 단체들이 고려할 회사들을 후보로 추천한다. NBF는 그다음에 각 분야에서 최고의 회사를 결정하기 위해 서비스 수준 및 고객 만족과 같은 기준들로 이 회사들을 평가한다. 이 과정에서 Vino Kiwi사는 5점 만점에 4.5점을 받았다.

의견을 말해달라는 요청을 받았을 때, Ms. Wilson은 "이것은 수년간의 노력이 옳았음을 입증해주는 대단한 영광입니다."라고 말했다. 그녀는 가족, 친구들, 그리고 동료들에게 그들의 지지에 대해 감사를 표현했으며, 대중들에게는

그녀의 서비스를 이용해볼 것을 요청했다. Vino Kiwi사에 관한 더 많은 정보는 www.vinokiwi.com에서 찾을 수 있다.

151 주제 찾기 문제 　　　　　　　　 중 ●●●○

해석　기사는 주로 무엇에 대한 것인가?
　　　(A) 지역 산업에 대한 정부 규제들
　　　(B) 한 사업 단체의 자선 기부금
　　　(C) 단체의 회원 기준
　　　(D) 한 사업체의 최근 성취

해설　지문의 'Vino Kiwi CEO ~ accepted a Company of the Year award ~ last week.'에서 Vino Kiwi사의 최고 경영자가 지난주 올해의 회사 상을 받았다고 한 후, 회사의 수상 내용에 대해 설명하고 있으므로 (D)가 정답이다.

어휘　regulation n. 규제 local adj. 지역의 charitable adj. 자선의
　　　contribution n. 기부금, 기여 criteria n. 기준
　　　accomplishment n. 성취

152 육하원칙 문제 　　　　　　　　 중 ●●○

해석　기사에 따르면, 전국 비즈니스 포럼의 임무들 중 하나는 무엇인가?
　　　(A) 세계 시장에서 사업체들을 홍보하는 것
　　　(B) 지역 회사들을 지원하는 자금을 관리하는 것
　　　(C) 다른 기관들로부터의 추천을 평가하는 것
　　　(D) 국가를 대표할 기업가들을 선정하는 것

해설　지문의 'professional organizations nominate companies for consideration. The NBF then evaluates these firms on criteria ~ to determine the best company'에서 전문가 단체들이 고려할 회사들을 후보로 추천하면, NBF는 그다음에 최고의 회사를 결정하기 위해 기준들로 이 회사들을 평가한다고 했으므로 (C)가 정답이다.

어휘　promote v. 홍보하다 manage v. 관리하다 fund n. 자금
　　　assess v. 평가하다 recommendation n. 추천
　　　entrepreneur n. 기업가 represent v. 대표하다

패러프레이징

evaluates 평가하다 → Assessing 평가하는 것

153-155번은 다음 기사에 관한 문제입니다.

Chic Life 잡지
Marilyn DuBois의 봄 작별 인사

(12월 20일)—다음 달, 유명 디자이너 Marilyn DuBois는 그녀의 봄 컬렉션 공연을 할 것인데, 이것은 그녀가 제작할 마지막 의류 라인이 될 것이다. 11월에 패션 업계는 ¹⁵³Ms. DuBois가 내년 2월에 은퇴하는 그녀의 계획에 관해 **예상치 못한 발표를 했을 때** 충격을 받았다. 45세밖에 되지 않았음에도 불구하고, Ms. DuBois는 전 세계적으로 거의 200개의 부티크를 열며, 의류 디자인 업계에서 저명한 경력을 가졌다.

우리 잡지와의 독점 인터뷰에서, Ms. DuBois는 그녀의 은퇴에 관한 몇 가지 세부 사항들로 우리를 이해시켜 주었다. "저는 옷을 디자인하는 아주 멋진 직업을 가졌습니다."라고 그녀가 말했다. "하지만 ¹⁵⁴제가 획기적인 작품을 만들 것이라는 대중들로부터의 끊임없는 기대는 부담이 되었습니다." Ms. DuBois는 게다가 그녀의 딸 ¹⁵⁵Janelle가 2월부터 DuBois사의 최고 경영자 자리를 맡을 것이라고 설명했다. "그녀는 제가 그랬던 것보다 이 직업에 더 열정적입니다."라고 Ms. DuBois는 농담을 했다.

Ms. DuBois가 그녀의 경력에서 최고의 시점에 있어서 패션 전문가들은 그녀가 자리를 떠나는 것을 보게 되어 슬퍼하고 있다. 동시에, ¹⁵⁵그들은 2월 이후부터 미래가 어떻게 될 것인지에 대해 열렬히 기대하고 있다.

153 육하원칙 문제 　　　　　　　　 중 ●●●○

해석　기사에 따르면, 내년에 무슨 일이 일어날 것인가?
　　　(A) 의류 디자이너는 그녀의 경력을 끝마칠 것이다.
　　　(B) 업계 행사에 대한 발표가 있을 것이다.
　　　(C) 의류 라인에 대한 사진 촬영이 있을 것이다.
　　　(D) 패션쇼가 부티크에서 열릴 것이다.

해설　지문의 'Ms. DuBois made the ~ announcement about her plans to retire next February'에서 Ms. DuBois가 내년 2월에 은퇴하는 그녀의 계획에 관해 발표를 했다고 했으므로 (A)가 정답이다.

어휘　garment n. 의류 photo shoot phr. 사진 촬영
　　　take place phr. 있다, 일어나다

패러프레이징

retire 은퇴하다 → come to the end of ~ career 경력을 끝마치다

154 육하원칙 문제 　　　　　　　　 중 ●●●○

해석　Marilyn DuBois의 걱정의 원인은 무엇이었는가?
　　　(A) 그녀의 가게의 줄어든 판매량
　　　(B) 그녀의 일에 대해 줄어드는 열정
　　　(C) 창의적이어야 한다는 압박
　　　(D) 대중의 생각을 바꾸는 것

해설　지문의 'the constant expectation ~ for me to create innovative work has been stressful'에서 자신, 즉 Marilyn DuBois가 획기적인 작품을 만들 것이라는 끊임없는 기대가 부담이 되었다고 했으므로 (C)가 정답이다.

어휘　decline v. 줄어들다, 감소하다 passion n. 열정
　　　opinion n. 생각, 의견

패러프레이징

create innovative work 획기적인 작품을 만들다 → creative 창의적인
stressful 부담이 되는 → Pressure 압박

155 추론 문제 중 ●●○

해석 Janelle DuBois에 대해 추론될 수 있는 것은?
(A) 새로운 패션모델들을 고용할 계획이 있다.
(B) 최고 경영자로의 그녀의 승진이 좋은 반응을 얻었다.
(C) 대학에서 패션 디자인을 전공했다.
(D) 그녀의 디자인들은 그녀의 어머니의 것들보다 더 많은 이목을 끌었다.

해설 지문의 'Janelle will take over as CEO ~ beginning in February'에서 Janelle DuBois가 2월부터 최고 경영자 자리를 맡을 것이라고 했고, 'they eagerly anticipate what the future may bring after February'에서 그들, 즉 패션 전문가들이 2월 이후부터 미래가 어떻게 될 것인지에 대해 열렬히 기대하고 있다고 했으므로 Janelle DuBois의 승진이 좋은 반응을 얻었음을 추론할 수 있다. 따라서 (B)가 정답이다.

어휘 promotion n. 승진 attract v. 끌다 attention n. 이목

156-157번은 다음 메시지 대화문에 관한 문제입니다.

Frank Danes (오후 7시 40분)
귀찮게 해드려서 죄송하지만, ¹⁵⁶제가 내일 일찍 퇴근할 수 있을지 궁금해서요. 제가 주말 동안 덴버에 갈 예정인데 오후 4시 비행기를 타고 싶어요. ¹⁵⁶점심 식사 후에 퇴근해도 될까요?

Maria Faubert (오후 7시 42분)
물론이죠. 어차피 그때 은행이 그렇게 바쁠 것 같지 않아요.

Frank Danes (오후 7시 43분)
감사해요!

Maria Faubert (오후 7시 45분)
내일 아침에 무엇보다도 먼저 당신의 근무 일정을 조정할게요.

Frank Danes (오후 7시 48분)
좋아요! 아, ¹⁵⁷제가 이것에 대해 휴가 신청서를 작성해야 할까요?

Maria Faubert (오후 7시 50분)
¹⁵⁷아니요, 전일이 아니라서요.

Frank Danes (오후 7시 51분)
이해했어요. 감사해요, 그리고 좋은 저녁 보내세요.

bother v. 귀찮게 하다, 괴롭히다 wonder v. 궁금하다
get off phr. 퇴근하다 adjust v. 조정하다 fill out phr. 작성하다
request n. 신청(서)

156 의도 파악 문제 하 ●○○

해석 오후 7시 42분에, Ms. Faubert가 "Sure"라고 썼을 때 그녀가 의도한 것 같은 것은?
(A) Mr. Danes가 항공편을 예약하는 것을 도와줄 수 있다.
(B) 그녀의 관리자에게 신청서를 전달할 것이다.
(C) Mr. Danes가 일찍 퇴근하는 것을 기꺼이 허락한다.
(D) 동료를 대신해서 양식을 회수할 것이다.

해설 지문의 'I was wondering whether I could get off early tomorrow'에서 Mr. Danes가 내일 일찍 퇴근할 수 있을지 궁금하다고 했고, 'Would it be OK to leave work after lunch?'에서 점심 식사 후에 퇴근해도 되는지 묻자, Ms. Faubert가 'Sure.'(물론이죠)라고 한 것을 통해 Ms. Faubert는 Mr. Danes가 일찍 퇴근하는 것을 기꺼이 허락함을 알 수 있다. 따라서 (C)가 정답이다.

어휘 convey v. 전달하다 supervisor n. 관리자 willing to phr. 기꺼이~하는

---

retrieve v. 회수하다 on one's behalf phr. ~을 대신(대표)해서

패러프레이징
get off early 일찍 퇴근하다 → leave the office early 일찍 퇴근하다

157 추론 문제 중 ●●○

해석 은행에 대해 암시되는 것은?
(A) 전일 부재에 대해서는 직원들에게 양식 작성을 요구한다.
(B) 보통 오후 4시에 문을 닫는다.
(C) 매주 직원 교육 시간을 준비한다.
(D) 직원 출장을 위해 여행 준비를 한다.

해설 지문의 'do I need to fill out a leave request form for this?'에서 Mr. Danes가 이것, 즉 내일 일찍 퇴근하는 것에 대해 휴가 신청서를 작성해야 할지 묻자, Ms. Faubert가 'No, because it isn't a full day.'에서 전일이 아니라서 그럴 필요가 없다고 했으므로 전일 부재에 대해 직원들에게 양식 작성을 요구함을 추론할 수 있다. 따라서 (A)가 정답이다.

어휘 absence n. 부재, 결근 organize v. 준비하다 arrangement n. 준비
business trip phr. 출장

패러프레이징
fill out a ~ request form 신청서를 작성하다 → complete forms 양식을 작성하다

158-160번은 다음 회람에 관한 문제입니다.

Peele, Knowles, and Associates사

¹⁶⁰⁻ᴬ수신: 비서진
발신: Marjorie Dodds, 사무실 관리자

저는 법률 사무소의 비서진에게 점심시간 관련 회사 규정이 변경되었음을 알려드리게 되어 기쁩니다. 지난주 우리의 직원회의 동안 여러분의 의견을 받은 후, ¹⁵⁸경영진은 다음의 변경을 이행하기로 결정했습니다:

점심시간은 매주 금요일 오후 12시에서 오후 1시 30분까지로 연장될 것입니다. 이 시간 동안, 사무실은 대중에게 개방되지 않을 것이므로, 귀하의 전화들을 저희의 자동 응답 서비스로 반드시 변경해주십시오. 저희의 단골 고객들에게도 꼭 이 변경사항에 대해 알려주십시오. ¹⁵⁹행정 직원들이 기계에 새로운 메시지를 기록하는 것을 맡을 것입니다.

상사로부터 점심시간 동안 일하는 것을 요청받은 직원들은 초과 근무 수당을 위해 그렇게 할 것인지에 대해 선택권을 가집니다. 그것은 ¹⁶⁰⁻ᴬ여러분이 점심시간 동안 일하는 것에 대해 두 배의 급류를 받을 것임을 의미합니다. 그러나, ¹⁶⁰⁻ᶜ직원들은 이러한 요청들을 거부할 수 있습니다.

이러한 변경들에 관하여 질문이 있으신 분들은 저에게 바로 이야기하시거나 marjdodds@peeleknowlesassoc.com으로 제게 이메일을 보내실 수 있습니다.

secretarial staff phr. 비서진 implement v. 이행하다
extend v. 연장하다 switch v. 변경하다 notify v. 알리다, 공지하다
as well phr. 또한 administrative adj. 행정의
record v. 기록하다, 적어 두다 take care of phr. ~을 맡다
superior n. 상사 option n. 선택권 overtime n. 초과 근무
turn down phr. 거부하다, 거절하다

158 동의어 찾기 문제　　　　　　　상 ●●●

해석　1문단 세 번째 줄의 단어 "implement"는 의미상 ~와 가장 가깝다.
(A) ~을 설명하다
(B) ~을 이행하다
(C) ~을 처리하다
(D) ~을 돌보다

해설　implement를 포함한 구절 'management has decided to implement the following changes'에서 경영진은 다음의 변경을 이행하기로 결정했다고 했으므로 implement는 '이행하다'라는 뜻으로 사용되었다. 따라서 '~을 이행하다'라는 뜻을 가진 (B) carry out이 정답이다. (C) dispose of도 '~을 처리하다'라는 의미로 해석상 그럴듯해 보이지만, 어떠한 문제, 질문, 협박 등을 처리하는 것을 나타낸다.

159 추론 문제　　　　　　　하 ●○○

해석　행정 직원은 무엇을 할 예정인 것 같은가?
(A) 직원들에 의해 사용되는 휴가의 개수를 관리한다
(B) 규정에 대한 의견과 제안들을 모은다
(C) 기록된 메시지를 만들어 낸다
(D) 휴식 시간 동안 프런트를 인계받는다

해설　지문의 'The administrative staff will take care of recording a new message for the machine.'에서 행정 직원들이 기계에 새로운 메시지를 기록하는 것을 맡을 것이라고 했으므로 행정 직원들이 기록된 메시지를 만들어낼 것임을 추론할 수 있다. 따라서 (C)가 정답이다.

어휘　monitor v. 관리하다　gather v. 모으다, 수집하다　comment n. 의견

160 Not/True 문제　　　　　　　중 ●●○

해석　비서진에 대해 언급된 것은?
(A) 그들의 점심시간 동안 근무하는 것에 대해 추가 급여를 받을 것이다.
(B) 초과 근무를 하기 위해서 관리자들로부터 허가를 받아야 한다.
(C) 요청받는다면, 점심시간 동안 근무해야 할 의무가 있다.
(D) 관리자에게 그들의 휴식 일정표를 이메일로 보내야 한다.

해설　지문의 'To: Secretarial Staff', 'you will receive double pay for working through the noon hour'에서 회람의 수신자인 비서진에게 점심시간 동안 일하는 것에 대해 두 배의 급료를 받을 것이라고 했으므로 (A)는 지문의 내용과 일치한다. 따라서 (A)가 정답이다. (B)와 (D)는 지문에 언급되지 않은 내용이다. (C)는 'staff may turn down such requests'에서 직원들은 이러한 요청들, 즉 점심시간 동안 일하는 것에 대한 요청을 거부할 수 있다고 했으므로 지문의 내용과 일치하지 않는다.

어휘　extra adj. 추가의　permission n. 허가　supervisor n. 관리자
obligated to phr. ~할 의무가 있는

패러프레이징

> double pay 두 배의 급료 → extra pay 추가 급여

161-163번은 다음 기사에 관한 문제입니다.

> **당신이 사업체 협회에 가입해야 하는 이유**
> Jan de Vries 작성
>
> 하나의 사업체 협회에 가입하는 것은 사업주들에게 지명도, 인적 교류 기회, 그리고 교육과 같은 많은 혜택들을 제공한다. 이러한 것들 및 다른 이점들은 당

신의 사업이 성장하고 번창하기 위해 필요한 안성맞춤의 것일 수 있다. — [1] —.

예를 들어, [162]Martha Yancey가 그녀의 신발 전문점 Walking on Air를 10년 전에 처음 열었을 때, 그녀가 지역 사회에서 잘 알려져 있지 않았기 때문에 고객들을 찾는 것이 어려웠다. [161]한 사업체 협회에 가입함으로써, 그녀는 자신을 잠재적인 고객들에게 소개하고 많은 고객 소개를 받을 수 있었다. — [2] —. "또한," 그녀는 말했다. "[161]저의 교류들은 저를 저의 현재 전기 기사와 회계사처럼, 제게 필수적인 서비스 및 조언을 줄 수 있는 다른 사업주들에게로 이끌었어요."

마찬가지로, [162]Lucas Smitt이 사업을 시작했을 때, 그는 가구 수리에 대해서는 많은 것을 알고 있었지만, 사업체를 운영하는 것에 대해서는 거의 아무것도 알지 못했다. "사업체 협회의 회원임을 통해, 저는 무료 및 할인된 세미나, 워크숍, 그리고 온라인 수업들에 대한 이용 권한을 얻을 수 있었습니다 — [3] — 이것들로부터, 저는 회사를 올바르게 운영하는 방법에 대해 배웠습니다." [162]이번 11월, Smitt Restoration은 그것의 성공적인 10주년을 기념할 예정이다.

물론, 언급된 것과 같은 혜택들이 항상 무료인 것은 아니다. [163]대부분의 협회들은 연간 회비를 청구하며, 공식적인 행사들과 일들에 정기적인 참여를 요구한다. — [4] —.

association n. 협회　business owner phr. 사업주　visibility n. 지명도
networking n. 인적 교류　advantage n. 이점
just the thing phr. 안성맞춤의 것　thrive v. 번창하다
specialty store phr. 전문점　potential adj. 잠재적인
referral n. 소개, 추천　interaction n. 교류, 상호작용
essential adj. 필수적인　electrician n. 전기 기사　accountant n. 회계사
similarly adv. 마찬가지로　start out phr. 사업을 시작하다
operate v. 운영하다　access n. 이용 권한; v. 접근하다
discounted adj. 할인된　properly adv. 올바르게
naturally adv. 물론, 자연스럽게　participation n. 참여　function n. 행사

161 추론 문제　　　　　　　중 ●●○

해석　Ms. Yancey에 대해 암시되는 것은?
(A) 처음에는 새로운 친구들을 만나기 위해 단체에 가입하였다.
(B) 그녀의 첫 번째 가게는 접근하기 어려운 위치에 있었다.
(C) 다른 회원으로부터 그녀의 상품 아이디어를 얻었다.
(D) 그녀의 회계사는 사업체 협회에 소속되어 있다.

해설　지문의 'By joining a business association'에서 Ms. Yancey가 사업체 협회에 가입했다고 했고, 'my interactions led me to other business owners ~ like my current electrician and accountant'에서 Ms. Yancey의 교류들, 즉 사업체 협회를 통한 교류들이 현재 그녀의 전기 기사와 회계사와 같은 다른 사업주들에게 그녀를 이끌었다고 했으므로, Ms. Yancey의 회계사는 그녀가 가입한 사업체 협회에 소속되어 있음을 추론할 수 있다. 따라서 (D)가 정답이다.

162 추론 문제　　　　　　　상 ●●●

해석　Mr. Smitt에 대해 추론될 수 있는 것은?
(A) 그의 회사를 시작했을 때 아직 학교에 다니고 있었다.
(B) Ms. Yancey가 가입했던 같은 단체에 가입했다.
(C) Ms. Yancey와 거의 같은 시기에 회사를 열었다.
(D) 다른 젊은 사업가들에게 그들의 사업체를 운영하는 방법에 대해 가르친다.

해설   지문의 'Martha Yancey first opened her specialty shoe store ~ a decade ago'에서 Ms. Yancey가 그녀의 신발 전문점을 10년 전에 처음 열었다고 했고, 'When Lucas Smitt was starting out'과 'This November, Smitt Restoration will be celebrating its 10th successful year.'에서 Mr. Smitt이 설립한 Smitt Restoration은 이번 11월에 그것의 성공적인 10주년을 기념할 예정이라고 했으므로 Mr. Smitt과 Ms. Yancey는 10년 전 거의 같은 시기에 회사를 열었음을 추론할 수 있다. 따라서 (C)가 정답이다. 참고로, (B)도 Mr. Smitt과 Ms. Yang 모두 사업체 협회에 가입했기 때문에 답이 될 것 같지만, 같은 사업체 협회인지는 언급되지 않았으므로 답이 될 수 없다.

어휘   organization n. 단체   about adv. 거의, 대략   entrepreneur n. 사업가

163 문장 위치 찾기 문제   중 ●●○

해석   [1], [2], [3], [4]로 표시된 위치 중, 다음 문장이 들어갈 곳으로 가장 적절한 것은?

"그러나, 이 비용은 대가로 제공되는 가치에 비해 작습니다."

(A) [1]
(B) [2]
(C) [3]
(D) [4]

해설   주어진 문장에서 그러나, 이 비용은 대가로 제공되는 가치에 비해 작다고 했으므로, 이 문장이 비용과 관련된 내용이 나오는 부분에 들어가야 함을 알 수 있다. [4]의 앞 문장인 'Most associations charge an annual membership fee'에서 대부분의 협회들은 연간 회비를 청구한다고 했으므로, [4]에 제시된 문장이 들어가면 대부분의 협회들이 연간 회비를 청구하지만, 이 비용은 대가로 제공되는 가치에 비해 작다는 자연스러운 문맥이 된다는 것을 알 수 있다. 따라서 (D)가 정답이다.

어휘   compared to phr. ~에 비해, ~와 비교하여   in return phr. 대가로, 보답으로

164-167번은 다음 온라인 채팅 대화문에 관한 문제입니다.

Travis Coleman [오후 12시]
164James Vine이라는 이름의 누군가가 전화하여 호텔이 새로운 장비를 살 것인지 물었어요.

Sheila Leblanc [오후 12시 3분]
맞아요. 164지난주에 제가 그와 대화를 나누었고 우리에게 안내 책자를 보내 달라고 그에게 요청했어요. Travis, 167제가 그것을 안내데스크에 당신에게 맡겼어요.

Gabby Ross [오후 12시 4분]
가능하다면, 저는 이제 식사공간이 확장되었기 때문에 그것을 위해 우리가 더 큰 뷔페 테이블을 구매해야 한다고 생각해요. 그건 그렇고, 165다른 수리들은 어떻게 되어가고 있나요?

Sheila Leblanc [오후 12시 4분]
어려움이 있었어요. 165저희가 고용했던 계약자들이 수영장이 제때 준비되지 않을 것이라고 말해요. 호텔 문을 다시 여는 것을 우리가 생각했던 것보다 2주 더 연기해야 할 수도 있어요.

Sheila Leblanc [오후 12시 4분]
뷔페 테이블에 관해서는, 저도 동의해요. 안내 책자에서 두 개를 표시해 놓았어요. Travis, Gabby를 위해 그것들을 찾아서 설명해줄 수 있나요?

Travis Coleman [오후 12시 7분]
그럼요. 166첫 번째 것은 검은색이며 유리로 된 재채기 막이 및 진열대

아래의 냉장 장치를 갖추고 있어요. 두 번째 것은 단풍나무 재목이고, 음식 팬 위의 열 램프 및 얼음을 담는 통이 있어요. 어느 것을 선호하나요?

Gabby Ross [오후 12시 10분]
저는 그것들이 어떻게 생겼는지 보기 위해 167곧 그 안내 책자를 확인해볼 것이지만, 166첫 번째 것이 더 좋아 보이네요. 단지 얼음으로만 음식을 시원하게 유지하기가 쉽지 않잖아요.

Sheila Leblanc [오후 12시 11분]
알겠어요, 제게 알려주세요. 오늘 오락실을 마무리할 예정이라서, 만약 당신이 제가 필요하다면 저는 지하에 있을 거예요.

어휘   equipment n. 장비   catalog n. 안내 책자   by the way phr. 그건 그렇고   renovation n. 수리, 보수   challenge n. 어려움   contractor n. 계약자   delay v. 연기하다   bookmark v. (나중에 참조할 수 있도록) 표시를 해두다   sneeze guard phr. 재채기 막이(식품의 오염 방지를 위해 덮는 유리판)   counter n. 진열대   refrigeration n. 냉장 (장치)   tray n. 통   in a moment phr. 곧   recreation room phr. 오락실

164 육하원칙 문제   중 ●●○

해석   Mr. Coleman은 최근 누구와 이야기했는가?
(A) 호텔 관리자
(B) 행사 주최자
(C) 부동산 중개인
(D) 장비 판매원

해설   지문의 'Someone ~ called to ask whether the hotel will be purchasing any new equipment.'에서 Mr. Coleman이 누군가가 전화하여 호텔이 새로운 장비를 살 것인지 물었다고 했고, 'I talked to him last week and asked him to send us a catalog.'에서 Ms. Leblanc이 지난주에 그와 대화를 나누었고 자신들에게 안내 책자를 보내 달라고 그에게 요청했다고 했다. 따라서 (D)가 정답이다.

어휘   organizer n. 주최자   salesperson n. 판매원

165 의도 파악 문제   중 ●●○

해석   오후 12시 4분에 Ms. Leblanc이 "They've been a challenge"라고 썼을 때 그녀가 의도한 것은?
(A) 리모델링 프로젝트의 진행이 느리다.
(B) 제품 설명이 이해하기 어렵다.
(C) 몇몇 서비스 제공업체들이 작업하는 것을 거부했다.
(D) 몇몇 기구들에 설명서가 딸려 있지 않았다.

해설   지문의 'how are the other renovations going?'에서 Ms. Ross가 다른 수리들은 어떻게 되어가고 있는지 묻자, Ms. Leblanc이 'They've been a challenge.'(어려움이 있었어요)라고 한 후, 'The contractors ~ say the pool won't be ready in time.'에서 계약자들이 수영장이 제때 준비되지 않을 것이라고 말했다고 한 것을 통해 리모델링 프로젝트의 진행이 느리다는 것을 알 수 있다. 따라서 (A)가 정답이다.

어휘   progress n. 진행   description n. 설명(서)   refuse v. 거부하다   appliance n. 기구   instruction n. 설명(서)   come with phr. ~이 딸려 있다

166 추론 문제   중 ●●○

해석   뷔페 테이블의 어떤 특징이 Ms. Ross의 결정에 영향을 미칠 것 같은가?
(A) 달려 있는 발열체
(B) 견목 외부

(C) 내장된 냉장고

(D) 유리로 된 재채기 막이

해설 지문의 'The first one ~ has a glass sneeze guard and under-the-counter refrigeration.'에서 Mr. Coleman이 첫 번째 것은 유리로 된 재채기 막이 및 진열대 아래의 냉장 장치를 갖추고 있다고 하자, 'the first one sounds better. It's not easy to keep food cool just with ice.'에서 Ms. Ross가 첫 번째 것이 더 좋아 보이며, 단지 얼음으로만 음식을 시원하게 유지하기가 쉽지 않다고 했으므로 내장된 냉장고가 Ms. Ross의 결정에 영향을 미칠 것임을 추론할 수 있다. 따라서 (C)가 정답이다.

어휘 **heating** adj. 발열의 **hardwood** n. 견목 **exterior** n. 외부
built-in adj. 내장된

패러프레이징

under-the-counter refrigeration 진열대 아래의 냉장 장치 → built-in refrigerators 내상된 냉장고

167 육하원칙 문제 중 ●●○

해석 Ms. Ross는 곧 어디에 갈 예정인가?
(A) 수영장
(B) 안내 데스크
(C) 식사 공간
(D) 오락실

해설 지문의 'I left it ~ at the front desk'에서 Ms. Leblanc이 그것, 즉 안내 책자를 안내 데스크에 맡겼다고 했고, 'I'll go check out the catalog in a moment'에서 Ms. Ross가 곧 그 안내 책자를 확인해 볼 것이라고 했으므로 (B)가 정답이다.

패러프레이징

shortly 곧 → in a moment 곧

168-171번은 다음 이메일에 관한 문제입니다.

발신: Jean-Luc Caron <jlc@caronwrites.uk>
171-A수신: Olivia Wright <oliv@okaypubs.com>
제목: Diot 프로젝트
날짜: 5월 3일

Ms. Wright께,

제가 오늘 저의 은행 잔고를 확인하였을 때, Okay 출판사에 의해 10,770달러가 제 계좌로 송금되었음을 확인했습니다. 168저는 귀사의 때맞춘 지급에 감사드리지만, 제 계산에 따르면, 이 액수는 232달러가 부족합니다. 제가 *The Thoughts of Anne Diot*을 프랑스어에서 영어로 번역하는 계약에 서명하기 전에, 급료는 한 단어당 0.15달러로 합의되었습니다. 게다가, 제 기록은 책의 본문이 총 71,800개의 단어였음을 나타내며, 이는 제가 지불받았던 것에 해당하는 정확한 액수입니다. 그러나, 지난주에, 169Mr. Stuart가 그가 새로 쓴 각주들을 제게 보냈다는 것을 당신이 알고 계시는지 잘 모르겠습니다만, 이것들 또한 번역이 필요했습니다. 1701,547개의 단어로 구성된 이 각주들은, 제 보수가 계산되었을 때 고려되지 않았던 것처럼 보입니다.

프로젝트의 총 단어 수를 재확인해주시길 바라며, 만약 정말 실수가 있었다면 제게 알려주십시오. 171-A귀사의 프로젝트들은 보통 내부의 직원들에 의해서만 처리된다고 알고 있으며, 어쩌면 이것이 지불에 대한 혼동으로 이어졌을 것입니다.

Jean-Luc Caron 드림

---

balance n. 잔고 **transfer** v. 송금하다 **account** n. 계좌
appreciate v. 감사하다 **timely** adj. 때맞춘 **payment** n. 지급
calculation n. 계산 **sum** n. 액수, 합계 **short** adj. 부족한, 불충분한
translate v. 번역하다 **rate** n. 급료 **indicate** v. 나타내다, 보여주다
exact adj. 정확한 **footnote** n. 각주(책 페이지 하단에 붙이는 주석)
consist of phr. ~으로 구성되다 **take into account** phr. 고려하다
double-check v. 재확인하다 **indeed** adv. 정말 **handle** v. 처리하다
in-house adj. 내부의 **confusion** n. 혼동

168 목적 찾기 문제 중 ●●●

해석 Mr. Caron은 왜 이메일을 썼는가?
(A) 거래액 오류를 해결하기 위해
(B) 몇몇 글쓰기 지시사항들을 명확하게 하기 위해
(C) 원고에 대해 수정들을 제안하기 위해
(D) 기한이 지난 업무를 끝까지 하기 위해

해설 지문의 'While I appreciate ~ timely payment, ~ this sum is short by $232.'에서 때맞춘 지급에 감사하지만, 액수가 232달러 부족하다고 했으므로 (A)가 정답이다.

어휘 **clear up** phr. 해결하다, 정리하다 **billing** n. 거래액
clarify v. 명확하게 하다 **instruction** n. 지시(사항) **correction** n. 수정
manuscript n. 원고 **follow up on** phr. ~을 끝까지 하다
overdue adj. 기한이 지난

패러프레이징

sum is short 액수가 부족하다 → billing error 거래액 오류

169 육하원칙 문제 상 ●●●

해석 Mr. Stuart는 누구인가?
(A) 책 작가
(B) 출판 관리자
(C) 문서 번역가
(D) 잡지 편집자

해설 지문의 'Mr. Stuart sent ~ his newly written footnotes'에서 Mr. Stuart가 그가 새로 쓴 각주들을 보냈다고 했으므로 (A)가 정답이다.

어휘 **author** n. 작가, 저자 **publishing** n. 출판(사업) **translator** n. 번역가

170 동의어 찾기 문제 중 ●●○

해석 1문단 여덟 번째 줄의 표현 "taken into account"는 의미상 –와 가장 가깝다.
(A) 저장된
(B) 허용된
(C) 질문된
(D) 고려된

해설 taken into account를 포함한 구절 'these footnotes ~ were not taken into account when my fee was calculated'에서 이 각주들이 자신의 보수가 계산되었을 때 고려되지 않았다고 했으므로 'taken into account'는 '고려된'이라는 뜻으로 사용되었다. 따라서 '고려된'이라는 뜻을 가진 (D) considered가 정답이다.

171 Not/True 문제 상 ●●●

해석 Ms. Wright에 대해 언급된 것은?
(A) 외부 계약자들과는 드물게 일을 한다.

(B) 현재 환율을 확인하지 않았다.
(C) 재무부의 관리자이다.
(D) 이전의 계약을 수정해야 할 것이다.

해설 지문의 'To: Oliva Wright'에서 이메일이 Ms. Wright에게 쓰였음을 확인할 수 있고 'your projects are usually only handled by in-house staff members'에서 귀사, 즉 Ms. Wright가 일하는 회사의 프로젝트들은 보통 내부의 직원들에 의해서만 처리된다고 했으므로 (A)는 지문의 내용과 일치한다. 따라서 (A)가 정답이다. (B)와 (C)는 지문에 언급되지 않은 내용이다. (D)는 Ms. Wright가 이전의 잘못된 송금액에 대해 수정해야 하는 것은 맞지만 이전 계약 내용 자체를 수정해야 하는 것은 아니므로 지문의 내용과 일치하지 않는다.

어휘 exchange rate phr. 환율 director n. 관리자 revise v. 수정하다

패러프레이징

projects are usually only handled by in-house staff members 프로젝트들은 보통 내부의 직원들에 의해서만 처리된다 → rarely works with outside contractors 외부 계약자들과 드물게 일을 하다

172-175번은 다음 양식에 관한 문제입니다.

OAKPORT COMPUTING사
직업 교육 프로그램

Oakport Computing사는 직업 교육 프로그램을 통해 직원들에게 그들의 기술과 지식을 향상시킬 수 있는 기회를 정기적으로 제공합니다. ― [1] ―.

아래에 제시된 강좌들의 목록은 전 직원들의 설문조사를 바탕으로 모아졌습니다. ¹⁷³표시된 곳을 제외하고, 각 강좌는 반나절 안에 완료될 수 있도록 계획되었습니다. 그러나, ¹⁷²예산 제한 때문에, 저희는 한 번에 단 3개만 제공할 수 있습니다. ― [2] ―. ¹⁷²/¹⁷⁴회사는 6월 6일에 모두의 선택을 바탕으로 최종 선정된 강좌들을 공개하고 강좌 날짜를 발표할 것입니다. 당신의 참석을 확정하기 위해, 첨부한 양식을 인사부 관리자에게 6월 3일까지 제출하여 주십시오. ― [3] ―.

¹⁷²/¹⁷⁴참석하는 것에 당신이 가장 관심 있는 3개의 강좌를 선택해 주십시오:

직원 이름: Kevin Montoya	날짜: 6월 1일
·일반적인 직무 기술	·전문적인 기술
___ 시간 관리	___ 고급 프로그래밍*
___ 발표 기술	✓ 빅 데이터 분석*
___ 문제 해결*	✓ 네트워크 보안*
✓ ¹⁷³팀과의 협업	___ 사용자 인터페이스 디자인

¹⁷³*일일 강좌

어떤 강좌들이 제공될 것인지 알기 위해서는, 6월 6일에 www.oakport.com/training으로 가십시오. 등록하는 방법에 대한 정보도 있을 것입니다. ¹⁷⁵참석자들은 그들의 관리자로부터 공식적인 허가를 얻어낼 책임이 있습니다. ― [4] ―.

enhance v. 향상시키다 course n. 강좌 gather v. 모으다 indicate v. 표시하다, 가리키다 nevertheless adv. 그러나, 그럼에도 불구하고 restriction n. 제한 at a time phr. 한 번에 present v. 보여주다 announce v. 발표하다 confirm v. 확정하다 attendance n. 참석 human resource phr. 인사부 management n. 관리 advanced adj. 고급의 analysis n. 분석 responsible for phr. ~에 책임이 있는 secure v. 얻어 내다, 확보하다 leave n. (공식적인) 허가, 휴가 supervisor n. 관리자

172 목적 찾기 문제 상 ●●●

해석 양식의 하나의 목적은 무엇인가?
(A) 자원봉사자들에게 활동에 참여할 것을 요청하기 위해
(B) 선택과목들의 수를 줄이기 위해서
(C) 한 강좌에 대한 의견을 수집하기 위해
(D) 신입 직원들을 위한 강좌를 알리기 위해

해설 지문의 'due to budget restrictions, we can only offer three at a time'에서 예산 제한 때문에, 한 번에 단 3개, 즉 3개의 강좌만 제공할 수 있다고 한 후, 'The company will present a final selection of courses based on everyone's choices'에서 회사는 모두의 선택을 바탕으로 최종 선정된 강좌들을 공개할 것이라고 하고, 'Please choose the three courses that you are most interested in attending:'에서 참석하는 것에 당신이 가장 관심 있는 3개의 강좌를 선택해달라고 했으므로 (B)가 정답이다. 참고로, (C)도 지문에 강좌에 관한 설문조사 내용이 있어 답이 될 것 같지만, 하나의 강좌에 대한 의견을 수집하는 것이 아닌 한 프로그램과 관련된 여러 개의 강좌에 대해 의견을 묻고 있으므로 답이 될 수 없다.

어휘 invite v. 요청하다, 초대하다 option n. 선택과목 feedback n. 의견

173 육하원칙 문제 중 ●●○

해석 어떤 강좌가 반나절 안에 완료될 수 있는가?
(A) 문제 해결
(B) 팀과의 협업
(C) 고급 프로그래밍
(D) 네트워크 보안

해설 지문의 'Except where indicated, each course has been designed to be completed in half a day.'에서 표시된 곳을 제외하고, 각 강좌는 반나절 안에 완료될 수 있도록 계획되었다고 했고, 'Working with Teams', '*One-day course'에서 팀과의 협업 강좌에는 일일 강좌에 표시되는 * 표시가 없으므로 (B)가 정답이다.

174 추론 문제 중 ●●○

해석 Mr. Montoya에 대해 암시되는 것은?
(A) 그의 신청서를 늦게 제출했다.
(B) 그의 관리자는 휴가를 승인하지 않을 수도 있다.
(C) 그가 선택했던 모든 강좌를 듣지는 못할 수도 있다.
(D) 그의 주요 직무는 정보 통신 기술이다.

해설 지문의 'The company will present a final selection of courses based on everyone's choices'에서 회사는 모두의 선택을 바탕으로 최종 선택된 강좌들을 공개할 것이라고 했고, 'Please choose the three courses that you are most interested in attending:'에서 참석하는 것에 당신이 가장 관심 있는 3개의 강좌를 선택하라고 했으므로 Mr. Montoya는 그가 선택했던 3개의 모든 강좌들을 듣지는 못할 수도 있음을 추론할 수 있다. 따라서 (C)가 정답이다.

어휘 application form phr. 신청서 approve v. 승인하다 information technology phr. 정보 통신 기술

175 문장 위치 찾기 문제 상 ●●●

해석 [1], [2], [3], [4]로 표시된 위치 중, 다음 문장이 들어갈 곳으로 가장 적절한 것은?

"이것은 강좌들이 시작되기 최소 2주 전에 완료되어야 합니다."

(A) [1]

(B) [2]
(C) [3]
(D) [4]

해설　주어진 문장에서 이것은 강좌들이 시작되기 최소 2주 전에 완료되어야 한다고 했으므로, 이 문장이 강좌들에 참석하기 전에 해야 하는 것과 관련된 내용이 나오는 부분에 들어가야 함을 알 수 있다. [4]의 앞 문장인 'Participants are responsible for securing leave from their supervisors.'에서 참석자들은 그들의 관리자로부터 공식적인 허가를 얻어낼 책임이 있다고 했으므로, [4]에 제시된 문장이 들어가면 참석자들은 그들의 관리자로부터 공식적인 허가를 얻어낼 책임이 있으며, 이것은 강좌들이 시작되기 최소 2주 전에 완료되어야 한다는 자연스러운 문맥이 된다는 것을 알 수 있다. 따라서 (D)가 정답이다. 참고로, (C)에 주어진 문장을 넣으면, 강좌 참석을 확정하기 위해 첨부된 양식, 즉 관심 있는 강좌의 선택 양식을 6월 3일까지 제출하라고 한 뒤 이것, 즉 양식 제출이 강좌들이 시작되기 최소 2주 전에 완료되어야 한다는 문맥이 되어 답이 될 것 같지만, 'The company will ~ announce the course dates on June 6'에서 강좌 날짜는 6월 6일에 발표할 것이라고 했으므로 강좌 시작일을 발표하지 않은 상태에서 강좌 시작 최소 2주 전에 양식을 제출하라고 했으므로 답이 될 수 없다.

어휘　**at least** phr. 최소한　**prior to** phr. ~전에, 앞서

176-180번은 다음 광고와 이메일에 관한 문제입니다.

Littleton 도서관 주민 학습 시리즈에 참여하세요

¹⁷⁶**Littleton 도서관의 주민 학습 시리즈가 많은 사람들의 요청으로 돌아왔습니다.** 전문가와의 30분 상담을 예약하시고 사업 등록, 회계, 판매, 그리고 그 이상에 관련된 사안들에 대해 조언을 얻으십시오. ¹⁷⁶**이 프로그램이 항상 인기 있었기 때문에 빨리 이것을 예약하십시오.** Adamant Consulting사가 현재와 장래의 소규모 사업주들에게 예정된 시간동안 도서관에서 도움을 제공할 것입니다. Adamant Consulting사는 기업가들을 위한 비즈니스 센터를 운영하고 있습니다. Adamant Consulting사에 관한 추가 세부사항들은 www.adamant.com에서 얻을 수 있습니다.

^{178-C}**상담은 주민들에게 무료이며** 오전 10시부터 오후 1시까지 아래 제시된 날짜들에 열릴 예정입니다. 예약을 신청하시려면, 555-7184로 도서관에 전화를 주시거나 info@littletonlib.net으로 이메일을 보내주십시오. ^{178-C}**당신의 자리를 확정하기 위해서는 거주지에 대한 증명이 요구될 것입니다.**

¹⁷⁹**상담 날짜들:**
- 화요일, 7월 18일
- 수요일, 8월 2일
- 목요일, 8월 17일
- ¹⁷⁹**토요일, 9월 2일**
- 화요일, 9월 12일

날짜들은 변경될 수 있다는 점을 유의해주십시오. ¹⁷⁷**취소 또는 지연의 경우에는, www.littletonlib.net에 공고문이 게시될 것입니다.**

---

demand n. 요청　**book** v. 예약하다　**consultation** n. 상담
accounting n. 회계　**assistance** n. 도움　**prospective** adj. 장래의
scheduled adj. 예정된　**maintain** v. 유지하다　**entrepreneur** n. 기업가
available adj. 얻을 수 있는　**resident** n. 주민　**take place** phr. 열리다
register for phr. 신청하다　**appointment** n. 예약　**proof** n. 증명
residence n. 거주　**confirm** v. 확정하다　**subject to** phr. ~될 수 있는
delay n. 지연

수신: Littleton 도서관 <info@littletonlib.net>
^{178-C}**발신: Mary Voss <m.voss@mtnmail.com>**
제목: 문의
날짜: 7월 21일

담당자분께,

저는 친구로부터 당신의 도서관이 무료 사업 상담을 제공하고 있다는 것을 들었습니다. ^{178-A}**저는 제 회사를 열려고 계획 중이기** 때문에, 이것은 저에게 안성맞춤일 것입니다. ^{178-C/180}**저는 무료 상담을 위한 요건들을 충족시키지만,** 업무상 의무들 때문에 주중에는 불가능합니다. ¹⁷⁹**주말에 참여할 수 있는 자리들이 있을까요?** 만약 그렇다면, 저는 예약을 하고 싶습니다. 가능한 한 빨리 제게 알려주십시오. 감사합니다!

Mary Voss 드림

---

requirement n. 요건　**unavailable** adj. 불가능한, (다른 사람과) 만날 수 없는
due to phr. ~ 때문에　**obligation** n. 의무　**slot** n. 자리
appointment n. 예약, 약속

176　추론 문제　상 ●●●

해석　Littleton 도서관에 대해 암시되는 것은?
(A) 오전 10시에 문을 연다.
(B) 과거에 상담들을 주최하였다.
(C) 최근에 몇몇 비즈니스 강좌들을 진행하였다.
(D) 기업가들이 이용할 수 있는 센터가 있다.

해설　광고의 'The Littleton Library's Community Learning Series is back ~. Book a 30-minute consultation with an expert'에서 Littleton 도서관의 주민 학습 시리즈가 돌아왔으며, 전문가와의 30분 상담을 예약하라고 했고, 'Be sure to book this soon as this program has always been popular.'에서 이 프로그램이 항상 인기 있었기 때문에 빨리 이것을 예약하라고 했으므로 Littleton 도서관이 과거에 상담들을 주최하였음을 추론할 수 있다. 따라서 (B)가 정답이다.

어휘　**host** v. 주최하다, 열다　**introduce** v. 진행하다, 소개하다

177　육하원칙 문제　중 ●●○

해석　광고에 따르면, 웹사이트에는 무엇이 게시될 것인가?
(A) 강좌 강사들에 대한 소개
(B) 토론 주제에 대한 세부 사항
(C) 일정 변경에 대한 발표
(D) 장소에 대한 길 안내

해설　광고의 'In the event of cancellation or delay, a notice will be posted on www.littletonlib.net.'에서 취소 또는 지연의 경우에는, 웹사이트에 공고문이 게시될 것이라 했으므로 (C)가 정답이다.

어휘　**profile** n. 소개　**instructor** n. 강사　**regarding** prep. ~에 대한
directions n. 길 안내　**venue** n. 장소

패러프레이징

> **cancellation or delay** 취소 또는 지연 → **schedule changes** 일정 변경
> **a notice** 공고문 → **Announcements** 발표

178　Not/True 문제　연계　중 ●●○

해석　Ms. Voss에 대해 사실인 것은?
(A) 최근에 사업을 시작했다.

(B) 그녀의 친구는 상담가이다.

(C) Littleton의 주민이다.

(D) 그녀의 도서관 회원권이 만료되었다.

해설 이메일의 'From: Mary Voss', 'I meet the requirement for a complimentary consultation'에서 Ms. Voss가 자신이 무료 상담을 위한 요건들을 충족시킨다고 했다. 또한, 광고의 'Consultations are free for residents'에서는 상담은 주민들, 즉 Littleton 주민들에게 무료라고 했고, 'Proof of residence will be required to confirm your place.'에서 당신의 자리, 즉 상담 자리를 확정하기 위해서는 거주지에 대한 증명이 요구될 것이라고 했다.

두 단서를 종합할 때, Ms. Voss가 Littleton의 주민이어야 하는 무료 상담 요건을 충족시킨다는 것을 알 수 있다. 따라서 (C)가 정답이다. (A)는 이메일의 'I am planning to open my own company'에서 Ms. Voss가 그녀의 회사를 열려고 계획 중이라고 했으므로 지문의 내용과 일치하지 않는다. (B)와 (D)는 지문에 언급되지 않은 내용이다.

어휘 expire v. 만료되다

179 육하원칙 문제 연계   중 ●●○

해석 Ms. Voss는 어느 날짜에 상담에 참석할 수 있는가?

(A) 8월 2일

(B) 8월 17일

(C) 9월 2일

(D) 9월 12일

해설 이메일의 'Do you have any slots open on a weekend? If so, I'd like to make an appointment.'에서 Ms. Voss가 주말에 참석할 수 있는 자리들이 있는지 질문한 후, 만약 그렇다면, 예약을 하고 싶다고 했다. 또한, 광고의 'Consultation dates:', 'Saturday, September 2'에서는 9월 2일 토요일이 주말에 있는 유일한 상담 날짜라는 사실을 확인할 수 있다.

두 단서를 종합할 때, Ms. Voss는 주말인 9월 2일의 상담에 참석할 수 있음을 알 수 있다. 따라서 (C)가 정답이다.

어휘 attend v. 참석하다, 다니다

180 동의어 찾기 문제   상 ●●●

해석 이메일에서, 1문단 두 번째 줄의 단어 "meet"은 의미상 ~와 가장 가깝다.

(A) 맞닥뜨리다

(B) 가입하다

(C) 연락하다

(D) 충족시키다

해설 이메일의 meet을 포함한 문장 'I meet the requirement for a complimentary consultation'에서 자신이 무료 상담을 위한 요건들을 충족시킨다고 했으므로 meet은 '충족시키다'라는 뜻으로 사용되었다. 따라서 '충족시키다'라는 뜻을 가진 (D) fulfill이 정답이다.

181-185번은 다음 웹페이지와 이메일에 관한 문제입니다.

www.atgf.com

Atlantic 장난감 및 게임 박람회

축하합니다! 귀하는 성공적으로 Atlantic 장난감 및 게임 박람회에 등록하셨습니다. 올해의 행사는 4월 4일 포르투갈의 풍살에 있는 Noguiera 컨벤션 홀에서 열립니다.

시간을 내어 귀하의 등록 세부사항을 주의 깊게 검토하여 주십시오.

183-C 등록자 이름:	Kenneth Fruman
이메일 주소:	*kenfrum@burgudeco.com*
등록 날짜:	1월 15일
입장 종류: 182-A/C/D자유 입장권	*182-A/C/D60개의 부스들과 20개의 전시들을 포함하는 전시 홀, 초청 전문가들의 연설 시간들, 그리고 업계 내부자 모임들에 대한 입장을 포함함
184티셔츠 사이즈: 대	*184행사 소포에 포함될 선물
선택한 지불 방법: 은행 이체	*181/183-C1월 23일 또는 그 이전에 대금이
183-C지불될 금액: 70유로	지불되어야 함
저희의 은행 세부 정보	*확인 이메일은 대금 수령 후에 발송될 것임

| 은행 이름: Avantage 은행 |
| 예금주: ATGF |
| 계좌 번호: 7334-8921-5960-66 |

[수정하기]   [홈으로 돌아가기]

successfully adv. 성공적으로   register for phr. ~에 등록하다
take place phr. 열리다   carefully adv. 주의 깊게   review v. 검토하다
registration n. 등록   registrant n. 등록자   entry n. 입장
all-access pass phr. 자유 입장권   admittance n. 입장
display hall phr. 전시 홀   exhibit n. 전시   session n. 시간, 기간
insider n. 내부자   meet-up n. 모임   package n. 소포
payment n. 지불, 대금   prior to phr. ~이전에   confirmation n. 확인
receipt n. 수령, 영수증   account holder phr. 예금주
account number phr. 계좌 번호

수신: Kenneth Fruman <kenfrum@burgudeco.com>
발신: Patricia Laroux <assistant@atgf.com>
제목: 등록
날짜: 1월 17일

Mr. Fruman께,

Atlantic 장난감 및 게임 박람회에 등록해주셔서 감사드립니다. 183-C저희는 귀하의 은행 이체 대금을 수령하였으며 1월 20일까지 귀하께 귀하의 행사 소포를 발송할 것입니다. 183-C소포는 두 개의 자유 입장권을 포함할 것입니다. 유감스럽게도, 184저희는 원래 광고되었던 소포 선물이 다 소진되어 귀하께 보내드릴 수 없습니다. 따라서, 저희는 대신 귀하께 탁상 달력을 제공할 예정입니다.

만약 귀하께서 아직 객실을 예약하지 않으셨다면, 185-D Noguiera 컨벤션 홀 가까이에 오직 3개의 호텔들이 있기 때문에 2월 1일까지는 그렇게 하실 것을 권장합니다. 풍살의 호텔들에 내한 정보에 대해서는 www.visitfunchal.com/placestostay를 확인하십시오.

Patricia Laroux 드림, 기획 보조
Atlantic 장난감 및 게임 박람회

bank transfer phr. 은행 이체   run out phr. 소진되다
consequently adv. 따라서   provide v. 제공하다

[최고난도 문제]

181 목적 찾기 문제   상 ●●●

해석 웹페이지의 하나의 목적은 무엇인가?

(A) 협회 회원들에게 행사에 대해 알리기 위해

(B) 부스 공간에 대한 예약을 확정하기 위해

(C) 돈을 보내는 것에 대한 설명을 제공하기 위해

(D) 참가자를 워크숍 활동에 등록하기 위해

해설 웹페이지의 'payment must be submitted on or prior to January 23' 에서 1월 23일 또는 그 이전에 대금이 지불되어야 한다고 한 후, 대금 지불과 관련된 세부 정보를 설명하고 있으므로 (C)가 정답이다. 참고로, (A)도 답이 될 것 같지만 협회 회원이 아닌 행사 등록자들을 대상으로 행사에 대해 알려주고 있으므로 답이 될 수 없다.

어휘 inform v. 알리다   association n. 협회   instruction n. 설명
participant n. 참가자

182 Not/True 문제   중 ●●○

해석 자유 입장권 소지자들은 무엇을 이용할 수 없을 것인가?

(A) 전문가들의 연설들

(B) 제품 시연들

(C) 전시 공간들

(D) 사교활동 시간들

해설 질문의 all-access pass holders와 관련된 내용이 언급된 웹페이지에서 (B)는 언급되지 않은 내용이다. 따라서 (B)가 정답이다. (A), (C), (D)는 웹페이지의 'all-access pass', 'includes admittance to display hall ~, speaker sessions by guest experts, and industry insider meet-ups'에서 자유 입장권은 전시 홀, 초청 전문가들의 연설 시간들, 그리고 업계 내부자 모임들에 대한 입장을 포함한다고 했으므로 지문의 내용과 일치한다.

어휘 demonstration n. 시연

패러프레이징

speaker sessions 연설 시간 → Talks 연설들
experts 전문가들 → specialists 전문가들
display hall 전시 홀 → Display spaces 전시 공간
meet-ups 모임들 → Networking 사교활동

183 Not/True 문제 연계   상 ●●●

해석 Mr. Fruman에 대해 언급된 것은?

(A) 포르투갈의 풍샬에 위치한 사무실을 가지고 있다.

(B) 첨부된 영수증과 함께 확인 이메일을 받았다.

(C) 두 장의 티켓에 총 70유로를 지불하였다.

(D) 전시 홀에 있는 전시 공간을 대여하고 있다.

해설 웹페이지의 'Registrant Name: Kenneth Fruman', 'Fee Due: €70' 에서 Mr. Fruman이 지불할 금액이 70유로라고 했다. 또한, 이메일의 'We have received your ~ payment'와 'The package will include two all-access passes.'에서는 당신, 즉 Mr. Fruman의 대금을 수령했으며 소포가 두 개의 자유 입장권을 포함할 것이라고 했다.

두 단서를 종합할 때, Mr. Fruman은 두 장의 티켓에 총 70유로를 지불하였음을 알 수 있다. 따라서 (C)가 정답이다. (A), (B), (D)는 지문에 언급되지 않은 내용이다.

어휘 located adj. 위치한   attached adj. 첨부된   a pair of phr. 두 개의, 한 쌍의

패러프레이징

two ~ passes 두 개의 입장권 → a pair of tickets 두 장의 티켓

184 추론 문제 연계   중 ●●●

해석 Atlantic 장난감 및 게임 박람회에 대해 추론될 수 있는 것은?

(A) 올해는 초청 연사들을 초대하지 않을 계획이다.

(B) 매번 다른 나라에서 열린다.

(C) 1월 23일까지만 티켓 환불을 제공한다.

(D) 참석자들에게 제공할 티셔츠가 없다.

해설 이메일의 'we cannot send you the package gift that was originally advertised as we have run out'에서 자신들, 즉 Atlantic 장난감 및 게임 박람회는 원래 광고되었던 소포 선물이 다 소진되어 보내줄 수 없다는 사실을 확인할 수 있다. 또한, 웹페이지의 'T-shirt', 'gift to be included in event package'에서는 티셔츠가 행사 소포에 포함될 선물이라고 했다.

두 단서를 종합할 때, Atlantic 장난감 및 게임 박람회는 참석자들에게 제공할 티셔츠가 없음을 추론할 수 있다. 따라서 (D)가 정답이다.

어휘 refund n. 환불   attendee n. 참석자

패러프레이징

run out 소진되다 → does not have 없다

185 Not/True 문제   중 ●●●

해석 Noguiera 컨벤션 홀에 대해 언급된 것은?

(A) 도시의 공항에 인접해있다.

(B) 과거에 박람회를 위한 장소였다.

(C) 동시에 두 개의 행사를 개최하고 있다.

(D) 숙박 시설들 가까이에 위치해있다.

해설 이메일의 'there are ~ three hotels near the Noguiera Convention Hall'에서는 Noguiera 컨벤션 홀 가까이에 3개의 호텔들이 있다고 했으므로 (D)가 지문의 내용과 일치한다. 따라서 (D)가 정답이다. (A), (B), (C)는 지문에서 언급되지 않은 내용이다.

어휘 adjacent adj. 인접한   hold v. 개최하다
accommodation facility phr. 숙박 시설

패러프레이징

hotels 호텔 → accommodation facilities 숙박 시설
near 가까이 → close to 가까이에

186-190번은 다음 광고, 송장, 이메일에 관한 문제입니다.

Dyna Flooring사
재고 정리 할인

이번 8월 내내, [186]Dyna Flooring사는 새로운 물품 목록을 위한 공간을 만들기 위해 재고 정리 할인을 열 예정입니다. Disena, Molik, Maitland와 같은 가장 인기 있는 브랜드들 및 더 많은 브랜드들의 제품들을 포함해 [187-B]집과 사무실에서 쓰이는 [186/187-B]다양한 상품들에 대한 엄청난 혜택들을 누리세요.

✓ 모든 제품에 대한 전반적인 10퍼센트 할인
✓ [188-D]다음 달에 가격이 오르는 상품에 대한 20퍼센트 할인
✓ [187-D]단종된 제품들의 대량 구매에 대한 30퍼센트 할인

할인은 온라인 및 [187-A]중서부 지역 전역의 가게들에서 판매되는 상품들을 포함합니다. 가게에서 상품을 구매하는 고객들에게는 10퍼센트의 추가 특별 할인이, Dyna 클럽 보상 프로그램 회원들에게는 20퍼센트가 적용됩니다.

[187-C]500달러 이상의 모든 주문은 무료 배송입니다!
더 많은 정보를 위해서는, www.dynaflooring.com으로 가시거나

당신의 가장 가까운 Dyna Flooring사 지점을 방문해주십시오.

---

clearance sale phr. 재고 정리 할인 throughout prep. ~내내, 전역에
inventory n. 물품 목록, 재고 a variety of phr. 다양한
merchandise n. 상품 top-rated adj. 가장 인기 있는
general adj. 전반적인, 공통된 bulk adj. 대량의 discontinued adj. 단종된
extend v. 포함하다, 연장하다 additional adj. 추가의
apply to phr. ~에 적용되다 delivery n. 배송

Dyna Flooring사
www.dynaflooring.com

구매자: Danielle Welch **거래 날짜:** 8월 29일
회사: Westwood 회계 사무소 **Dyna 클럽 회원입니까?** 네
지불 방법: Verifian 신용카드

제품 코드	상품	수량	가격
MKT1431Y	¹⁹⁰Molik 도자기 부엌 타일 (10퍼센트 할인)	24	¹⁹⁰388.80달러
CTJN9091G	Johnson 회색 카펫 타일 (10퍼센트 할인)	16	264.00달러
CTLS3816B	Laster 파란색 카펫 타일 (30퍼센트 할인)	58	740.95달러
FTIN643RW	¹⁸⁸⁻ᴰIntone 목재 마감 바닥 타일 (20퍼센트 할인)	12	787.20달러

약관: 모든 구매는 변경될 수 없습니다. ¹⁹⁰지불금은 상점 포인트를 제외하고는 환불될 수 없습니다. 교환은 재고품이 있는 한 같거나 더 적은 가격의 상품에 대해 받아들여질 수 있습니다. 새로운 상품으로의 교환은 가능하지 않습니다.	소계	2,180.95달러
	10퍼센트 할인	(218.10달러)
	세금	130.86달러
	배송료	0.00달러
	총액	2,093.71달러

귀하의 거래에 감사드립니다!

---

refund v. 환불하다; n. 환불 exchange n. 교환 merchandise n. 상품
equal adj. 동일한 value n. 가격, 가치 as long as phr. ~하는 한
supply n. 재고품 shipping n. 배송료

수신: 고객 서비스 <cs@dynaflooring.com>
발신: Danielle Welch <c.welch@westwoodaccts.com>
날짜: 9월 2일
제목: 최근 주문

관계자분께,

지는 최근 8월에 귀사의 할인 판매 동안 몇 가지 상품들을 구매하였습니다. 유감스럽게도, ¹⁹⁰상품들 중 하나가 저희의 새롭게 다시 디자인된 사무실 부엌에 어울리지 않는 색으로 드러나서, 저는 그것을 비슷한 제품으로 교환하기를 원합니다. 만약 알맞은 상품을 구할 수 없다면, 저는 대신 환불을 하고 싶습니다. ¹⁸⁹저는 또한 Dyna 클럽 회원으로서 제가 20퍼센트의 추가 특별 할인을 받았어야 했다는 것을 알아차렸습니다. 이 추가 할인금액을 제 계좌에 입금해 주시거나 취해야 할 앞으로의 조치들에 대해 제게 알려주십시오. 감사합니다.

Danielle Welch 드림
구매 담당자
Westwood 회계사무소

---

turn out phr. ~임이 드러나다 wrong adj. 어울리지 않는

---

newly adv. 새롭게 in exchange for phr. ~의 교환으로
qualifying adj. 알맞은, 자격을 주는 available adj. 구할 수 있는
notice v. 알아차리다, 인지하다 credit v. 입금하다

186 목적 찾기 문제   중 ●●○

해석 광고의 목적은 무엇인가?
(A) 온라인 쇼핑 서비스의 개시를 홍보하기 위해
(B) 고객들이 멤버십 프로그램에 가입하도록 장려하기 위해
(C) 비용 절감 기회를 소개하기 위해
(D) 새로운 소재로 만들어진 제품을 알리기 위해

해설 광고의 'Dyna Flooring will be holding a clearance sale'에서 Dyna Flooring사가 재고 정리 할인을 열 예정이라고 했고, 'Enjoy great deals on a variety of merchandise'에서 다양한 상품들에 대한 엄청난 혜택들을 누리라고 한 후, 할인들에 대해 설명하고 있으므로 (C)가 정답이다.

어휘 promote v. 홍보하다 launch n. 개시 cost-saving adj. 비용 절감의 material n. 소재

패러프레이징

> sale 할인 → cost-saving opportunity 비용 절감 기회

최고난도 문제

187 Not/True 문제   상 ●●●

해석 Dyna Flooring사에 대해 언급되지 않은 것은?
(A) 한 지역의 전체에 걸쳐 매장들이 있다.
(B) 사무실에서 쓰이는 상품들만 취급한다.
(C) 자격을 갖춘 주문들에 대해 무료 배송을 제공하고 있다.
(D) 몇몇 제품들을 더 이상 판매하지 않을 것이다.

해설 질문의 Dyna Flooring과 관련된 내용이 언급된 광고의 'Enjoy ~ deals on a variety of merchandise for home and office use'에서 집과 사무실에서 쓰이는 다양한 상품들에 대한 혜택들을 누리라고 했으므로 (B)는 지문의 내용과 일치하지 않는다. 따라서 (B)가 정답이다. (A)는 'stores across the Midwest'에서 중서부 전역에 가게들이 있다고 했으므로 지문의 내용과 일치한다. (C)는 'Free delivery on all orders worth $500 or more!'에서 500달러 이상의 모든 주문은 무료 배송이라고 했으므로 지문의 내용과 일치한다. (D)는 'discontinued products'에서 단종된 제품들이 있다고 했으므로 지문의 내용과 일치한다.

어휘 carry v. (가게에서 품목을) 취급하다 no longer phr. 더 이상 ~ 않는

패러프레이징

> across 전역에, 전체에 걸쳐 → throughout 전체에 걸쳐
> free delivery 무료 배송 → free shipping 무료 배송
> discontinued 단종된 → no longer be selling 더 이상 판매하지 않다

---

188 Not/True 문제 연계   중 ●●○

해석 송장에서 언급된 것은?
(A) Ms. Welch는 세일 마지막 날에 참석했다.
(B) 몇몇 상품들은 현재 품절되었다.
(C) Johnson의 타일들은 일정보다 빨리 배송되었다.
(D) Intone의 타일들은 다음 달에 가격이 오를 것이다.

해설 송장의 'Intone ~ tile (20% off)'에서 Intone의 타일에 20퍼센트 할인이 적용된다는 사실을 확인할 수 있다. 또한, 광고의 '20 percent off

---

TEST 4 **83**

TEST 4 해커스 토익 실전 1200제 READING

merchandise increasing in price next month'에서는 다음 달에 가격이 오르는 상품에 20퍼센트 할인이 제공된다고 했다.

두 단서를 종합할 때, Intone의 타일은 다음 달에 가격이 오를 것임을 알 수 있다. 따라서 (D)가 정답이다. (A), (B), (C)는 지문에 언급되지 않은 내용이다.

어휘 | **attend** v. 참석하다 **out of stock** phr. 품절된

189 육하원칙 문제   중 ●●○

해석 Ms. Welch는 Dyna Flooring사가 무엇을 하기를 원하는가?
(A) 멤버십 프로그램에 그녀를 가입시킨다
(B) 배송 비용을 환불해 준다
(C) 그녀에게 설치 설명서를 보낸다
(D) 추가 가격 인하를 적용한다

해설 이메일의 'I also noticed that I should have received an additional special discount of 20 percent as a Dyna Club member. Please credit my account for this additional discount'에서 저, 즉 Ms. Welch가 Dyna 클럽 회원으로서 자신이 20퍼센트의 추가 특별 할인을 받았어야 했다는 것을 알아차렸다고 하며 추가 할인금액을 본인의 계좌에 입금해 달라고 했으므로 (D)가 정답이다.

어휘 | **instruction** n. 설명(서)

패러프레이징

additional discount 추가 할인 → additional price reduction 추가 가격 인하

190 추론 문제 연계   상 ●●●

해석 Ms. Welch에 대해 암시되는 것은?
(A) 그녀의 몇몇 상품들을 온라인에서 구매했다.
(B) 300달러 이상의 상점 포인트를 받을 수도 있다.
(C) 사무실을 다시 디자인하는 것을 맡았다.
(D) 구매 대금을 지불하기 위해 보상 포인트를 사용했다.

해설 이메일 의 'one of the items turned out to be the wrong color for ~ kitchen, so I want to return it in exchange for a similar product. If no qualifying items are available, I would like a refund instead.'에서 상품들 중의 하나가 부엌에 어울리지 않는 색으로 드러나서 자신, 즉 Ms. Welch는 그것을 비슷한 제품으로 교환하고 싶다고 한 후, 만약 알맞은 상품을 구할 수 없다면 환불하고 싶다고 하였다. 또한, 송장 의 'Molik ceramic kitchen tile', '$388.80'에서는 Ms. Welch가 구매한 상품들 중 388.80달러의 Molik 도자기 부엌 타일이 유일한 부엌 관련 상품임을 확인할 수 있으며, 'Payments may not be refunded except for store credit.'에서는 지불금은 상점 포인트를 제외하고 환불될 수 없다는 사실을 확인할 수 있다.

두 단서를 종합할 때, Ms. Welch가 비슷한 제품으로 교환을 요청한 부엌 타일에 알맞은 상품이 없을 경우, 환불 대신 388.80달러의 상점 포인트를 받을 수도 있음을 추론할 수 있다. 따라서 (B)가 정답이다. 참고로, (A)는 광고의 'Additional special discounts of 10 percent to customers who purchase at a store'에서 가게에서 상품을 구매하는 고객들에게 10퍼센트의 추가 할인을 해준다고 했고, 송장의 'less 10%'에서 10퍼센트의 추가 할인을 받은 것을 알 수 있으므로 답이 될 수 없다.

어휘 | **in charge of** phr. ~을 맡은

191-195번은 다음 안내문과 두 양식에 관한 문제입니다.

Elfman Home Cooling사
품질 보증 청구

Elfman사는 고객들의 요구를 충족시키는 것에 전념합니다. [192]저희가 판매하는 모든 장비는 6개월짜리 부품 및 인력 보증서가 딸려있습니다. 만약 당신이 품질 보증 기간 동안 문제들을 경험한다면, 기술자가 당신의 자택 혹은 사업체를 방문하여 모든 필요한 수리들을 무료로 수행할 것입니다. 또한, [194]만약 구매 후 한 달 이내에 당신의 장치가 제대로 작동하지 않는다면, 저희는 그것을 저희의 비용으로 교체할 것입니다.

[191]품질 보증 청구를 제출하려면, www.elfmanequip.com/customers로 가십시오. 당신은 당신의 사용자 이름과 비밀번호를 입력하도록 요청될 것입니다. 그 후, 온라인 양식에 접속하기 위해 화면 하단의 청구 버튼을 클릭하십시오. 시기에 맞는 처리를 보장하기 위해, 청구서를 가능한 한 완벽하게 작성하십시오.

warranty n. 품질 보증(서) **claim** n. 청구, 요청; v. 주장하다
be committed to phr. ~에 전념하다 **serve** v. 충족시키다, 제공하다
come with phr. ~이 딸려 있다 **unit** n. 장치, 세트
malfunction v. 제대로 작동하지 않다; n. 오작동 **replace** v. 교체하다
expense n. 비용 **ensure** v. 보장하다 **timely** adj. 시기에 맞는, 때맞춘
processing n. 처리 **completely** adv. 완벽하게

Elfman Home Cooling사 청구서

청구 번호: EC1081626
[193-D]**날짜:** 8월 3일
[192/193-C]**고객 이름:** Larry Regan
주소: 219번지 Duncan가, Forsyth, 조지아주 31029
전화번호: 555-4086
이메일: l.regan@pellstone.com
제품: Elfman사 중앙 에어컨
모델: AU-0951   **일련번호:** P118946QJ

문제 설명:
[193-C]그 장치는 그것이 작동되기 시작한 후 처음 30분 동안은 괜찮지만, 그 후 그것은 서서히 더 커지는 이상한 소음을 내기 시작했습니다. 제 사무실의 직원들이 일하는 것이 매우 어렵습니다. [192]이것은 [192/193-D]제가 장치를 약 7개월 전에 구매한 [192]이후로 제가 겪은 첫 번째 문제입니다.

progressively adv. 서서히, 점차적으로

Elfman Home Cooling사 청구서

청구 번호: EK0194114
날짜: 8월 15일
[194/195-C]**고객 이름:** Michelle Bowman
주소: 176번지 King대로, High Springs, 플로리다주 32643
전화번호: 555-7182
이메일: m.bowman@springmail.com
제품: Elfman사 환기 시스템
모델: PK-4317   [195-D]**일련번호:** T27386HX

문제 설명:
오늘 아침, [195-C]저는 공기가 환기구에서 거의 나오지 않고 있었다는 것을 알아차렸습니다. 저는 어떤 방해물들이라도 있는지 확인하기 위해 장치를 껐지만,

어떤 이상한 것도 보지 못했습니다. [194]그것이 설치된 지 2주가 되지 않았다는 것을 고려했을 때, 이것은 용납할 수 없습니다.

ventilation n. 환기, 통풍 notice v. 알아차리다
blockage n. 방해물, 막힘 out of ordinary phr. 이상한, 색다른
unacceptable adj. 용납할 수 없는, 받아들일 수 없는

191 육하원칙 문제 중 ●●○

해석 고객들은 어떻게 품질 보증 청구를 제출할 수 있는가?
(A) 서비스 센터를 방문함으로써
(B) 서면 요청을 우편으로 보냄으로써
(C) 온라인 계정에 접속함으로써
(D) 모바일 애플리케이션을 설치함으로써

해설 안내문의 'To submit a warranty claim, go to www.elfmanequip. com/customers. You will be asked to enter your username and password.'에서 품질 보증 청구를 제출하려면, 웹사이트로 가서 사용자 이름과 비밀번호를 입력하라고 했으므로 (C)가 정답이다.

어휘 mail v. (우편으로) 보내다

192 추론 문제 연계 중 ●●●

해석 Mr. Regan에 대해 암시되는 것은?
(A) 기술자가 방문하려면 며칠을 기다려야 할 것이다.
(B) 이메일로 회사 직원에게 연락했다.
(C) 에어컨에 대한 할인을 요구했다.
(D) 수리비를 지불해야 할 것이다.

해설 양식1의 'Customer name: Larry Regan', 'This is the first problem ~ since I purchased the unit about seven months ago.'에서 고객인 Mr. Regan이 장치, 즉 에어컨을 약 7개월 전에 구매한 이후로 첫 번째 문제를 겪었다고 했다. 또한, 안내문의 'All equipment we sell comes with a six-month parts and labor warranty. If you experience problems during the warranty period, a technician will ~ perform all necessary repairs free of charge.'에서는 Elfman Home Cooling사가 판매하는 모든 장비는 6개월짜리 부품 및 인력 보증서가 딸려 있으며 만약 고객이 품질 보증 기간 동안 문제들을 경험한다면, 기술자가 모든 필요한 수리들을 무료로 수행할 것이라고 했음을 확인할 수 있다.
두 단서를 종합할 때, Mr. Regan은 품질 보증 기간인 6개월이 지난 후에 문제를 겪었으므로 수리비를 지불해야 할 것임을 추론할 수 있다. 따라서 (D)가 정답이다.

어휘 representative n. 직원, 대표 discount n. 할인 repair n. 수리

193 Not/True 문제 중 ●●○

해석 Mr. Regan에 의해 작성된 양식에서 언급된 것은?
(A) 가전제품의 최신 모델을 주문했다.
(B) 그의 사무실이 수리가 행해질 때까지 폐쇄될 것이다.
(C) 그의 장치가 처음 켜질 때는 제대로 작동한다.
(D) Elfman사의 제품을 8월 3일에 구매했다.

해설 양식1의 'Customer name: Larry Regan', 'The unit is fine for the first 30 minutes after it starts'에서 작성자 Mr. Regan이 그 장치는 그것이 작동되기 시작한 후 처음 30분 동안은 괜찮다고 했으므로 (C)는 지문의 내용과 일치한다. 따라서 (C)가 정답이다. (A)와 (B)는 지문에 언급되지 않은 내용이다. (D)는 'Date: August 3', 'I purchased the unit about seven months ago'에서 8월 3일에 작성된 청구서에 자신, 즉 Mr. Regan이 장치

를 약 7개월 전에 구매했다고 했으므로 지문의 내용과 일치하지 않는다.

어휘 latest adj. 최신의, 최근의 appliance n. 가전제품

194 추론 문제 연계 상 ●●●

해석 Ms. Bowman에 대해 추론될 수 있는 것은?
(A) 양식을 완벽하게 작성하지 못했다.
(B) 교체 제품을 받을 것이다.
(C) 몇몇 장비를 부정확하게 설치했다.
(D) 환기 시스템을 위한 추가 부품들을 주문했다.

해설 양식2의 'Customer name: Michelle Bowman', 'it was installed less than two weeks ago'에서 Ms. Bowman이 그것, 즉 환기 시스템이 설치된 지 2주가 되지 않았다고 했다. 또한, 안내문의 'if your unit malfunctions within one month of purchase, we will replace it at our expense'에서는 만약 구매 후 한 달 이내에 당신, 즉 고객의 장치가 제대로 작동하지 않는다면, 그것을 저희, 즉 Elfman Home Cooling사의 비용으로 교체할 것이라고 했다.
두 단서를 종합할 때, Ms. Bowman의 장치가 구매 후 2주 내에 고장이 났으므로 장치를 무료로 교체 받을 것임을 추론할 수 있다. 따라서 (B)가 정답이다.

어휘 replacement n. 교체 incorrectly adv. 부정확하게 extra adj. 추가의

195 Not/True 문제 상 ●●●

해석 Ms. Bowman에 의해 작성된 양식에서 언급된 것은?
(A) 구매에 대해 전액 환불을 받을 것이다.
(B) 회사 웹사이트에 등록하지 않았다.
(C) 문제의 원인을 알아내려고 노력했다.
(D) 장치의 일련번호를 모른다.

해설 양식2의 'Customer name: Michelle Bowman', 'I noticed that very little air was coming out of vents. I turned the unit off to check for any blockages but did not see anything out of ordinary.'에서 저, 즉 Ms. Bowman은 공기가 환기구에서 거의 나오지 않고 있었다는 것을 알아차렸고 어떤 방해물들이라도 있는지 확인하기 위해 장치를 껐지만, 어떤 이상한 것도 보지 못했다고 했으므로 (C)는 지문의 내용과 일치한다. 따라서 (C)가 정답이다. (A)와 (B)는 지문에 언급되지 않은 내용이다. (D)는 'Serial number: T27386HX'에서 Ms. Bowman이 일련번호를 작성한 것을 알 수 있으므로 지문의 내용과 일치하지 않는다.

어휘 refund n. 환불 register v. 등록하다 determine v. 알아내다, 결정하다 cause n. 원인

196-200번은 다음 공고, 웹페이지, 이메일에 관한 문제입니다.

애리조나 의학 전문가 협회 (AMPA)
저희의 올해 봄 행사 일정표의 공개를 알리게 되어 기쁩니다.

4월 16일 – 새로운 회원 환영

피닉스 시내의 Desert 호텔에서 새로운 회원들을 위한 환영회가 오후 4시에서 6시까지 열립니다. 간단한 다과를 포함합니다.

4월 19일 – 발표
196국내의 가장 인기 있는 학술지, *Modern Journal of Medicine*지가 피닉스 시내의 AMPA 회의 센터에서 오후 6시부터 7시까지 회원들을 위한 특별한 발표를 주최할 예정입니다.

4월 23일– 강연 및 책 사인회
AMPA는 존경받는 의학 저자이자 건강 관리 문제들에서 손꼽히는 전문가인 Dr. Katherine Bradley와 함께 오전 9시부터 11시까지 애리조나의 글렌데일에 있는 Book Stop 서점에서 강연 및 책 사인회 행사를 주최할 예정입니다.

5월 2일에서 4일까지 – 연례 회의
제 51회 AMPA 연례 회의가 올해 네바다의 라스베이거스에서 열릴 예정입니다. 더 많은 세부 사항을 원하시면 웹사이트를 방문해주십시오.

모든 행사들은 오직 등록된 AMPA 회원들만을 위한 것입니다. 참여하시려면, www.ampa.org를 방문해주십시오.

professional n. 전문가; adj. 전문의 association n. 협회
release n. 공개 reception n. 환영회 refreshment n. 다과
journal n. 학술지 host v. 주최하다 lecture n. 강연
book-signing n. 책 사인회 esteemed adj. 존경받는, 호평받는
annual adj. 연례의 exclusively adv. 오직, 독점적으로
registered adj. 등록된

www.ampa.org
애리조나 의학 전문가 협회 (AMPA)

| 로그인 | 도구&자원 | 행사 | **회원** | 연락 | 소개 |

등록하는 방법
1. 웹사이트에서 계정을 등록하고 회원 신청서를 작성하십시오.
2. 197당신의 전문 의료 자격증의 스캔된 복사본을 올리십시오.
3. 해당되는 곳에, 당신을 소개한 사람 또는 기관의 이름을 포함하십시오.

혜택
· 다른 전문가들과 친해진다
· 온라인 세미나를 통해 당신의 소양을 향상시킨다
· 전문 자료들에 접근한다
· 196모든 선두적인 의학 학술지들의 무료 구독권을 받는다
· 새로운 소식! 유지비용에 도움이 되기 위해, 198/200저희는 최근 저희의 웹사이트에 관련 상품들의 배너 광고를 도입하였으며, 이에 대해 회원들은 할인을 받을 수 있습니다. 200더 많은 정보를 원하시면, 사이트 관리자에게 연락해주십시오.

[오늘 가입하기]

sign up for phr. 등록하다 account n. 계정 complete v. 작성하다
application form phr. 신청서 license n. 자격증
applicable adj. 해당되는 organization n. 기관
refer v. 소개하다, 가리키다 maintenance costs phr. 유지비
administrator n. 관리자, 행정인

수신: Salvador Lopez <s.lopez@ampa.org>
발신: Amy Sharpe <a.sharpe@healthwide.com>
제목: 광고
날짜: 2월 18일

200Mr. Lopez께,

저는 Dr. Katherine Bradley의 신간 *New Age of Healing*을 출판하는 회사를 대변합니다. 4월에 AMPA의 행사에서 책의 출간을 예상하여, 200저희는 당신의 웹사이트에서 그 책을 광고하고 싶습니다. 이것과 관련하여, 저는 Dr. Bradley의 회원 혜택이 저희에게 적용될 수 있는지에 대해 궁금합니다. 만약 그렇다면, 199저희는 그녀의 회원 번호를 당신의 웹사이트에 있는 광고주들을 위한 신청서에 입력하고자 합니다. 되도록 빨리 저에게 알려주십시오. 감사합니다!

Amy Sharpe 드림
마케팅 직원, Healthwide 출판사

represent v. 대변하다, 대표하다 in anticipation of phr. ~을 예상하여
in connection with phr. ~와 관련하여 wonder v. 궁금하다, 궁금해하다
advertiser n. 광고주

---

196 추론 문제 연계   중 ●●○

해석 AMPA 회원들에 대해 암시되는 것은?
(A) 같은 기관에서 그들의 의료 수련 과정을 수료했다.
(B) *Modern Journal of Medicine*지를 무료로 구독할 수 있다.
(C) 그들의 도움을 자원하도록 권장된다.
(D) 국내의 가장 큰 전문가 협회를 구성한다.

해설 웹페이지의 'Receive complimentary subscriptions to all leading journals'에서 AMPA 회원들은 모든 선두적인 의학 학술지들에 무료 구독권을 받는다고 했다. 또한, 공고의 'The country's most popular journal, *Modern Journal of Medicine*'에서는 *Modern Journal of Medicine*지가 국내의 가장 인기 있는 학술지라는 사실을 확인할 수 있다.
두 단서를 종합할 때, AMPA 회원은 *Modern Journal of Medicine*지를 무료로 구독할 수 있음을 추론할 수 있다. 따라서 (B)가 정답이다.

어휘 institution n. 기관 subscribe v. 구독하다 form v. 구성하다

197 육하원칙 문제   중 ●●●

해석 장래의 회원들은 무엇을 제공하도록 요청받는가?
(A) 연간 회비에 대한 지불
(B) 그들의 근무 장소에 대한 세부사항
(C) 자격증의 전자 복사본
(D) 연락에 대한 선호

해설 웹페이지의 'Upload a scanned copy of your professional medical license.'에서 당신의 전문 의료 자격증의 스캔된 복사본을 올리라고 했으므로 (C)가 정답이다.

어휘 prospective adj. 장래의, 미래의 employment n. 근무, 고용
electronic adj. 전자의 certificate n. 자격증, 증명서
preference n. 선호

패러프레이징

a scanned copy of ~ license 자격증의 스캔된 복사본 → electronic copy of a certificate 자격증의 전자 복사본

198 육하원칙 문제   중 ●●○

해석 AMPA는 최근에 무엇을 했는가?
(A) 연례행사의 날짜를 변경했다.
(B) 회원들의 회비를 인상했다.

(C) 협력 기관을 설립했다.

(D) 웹사이트에 광고를 추가했다.

해설 웹페이지의 'we have recently introduced banner advertising ~ on our Web site'에서 자신들, 즉 AMPA가 최근 웹사이트에 배너 광고를 도입했다고 했으므로 (D)가 정답이다.

어휘 establish v. 설립하다 partner organization phr. 협력 기관

패러프레이징

introduced 도입했다 → Added 추가했다

199 동의어 찾기 문제   중 ●●○

해석 이메일에서, 1문단 네 번째 줄의 단어 "enter"는 의미상 -와 가장 가깝다.
(A) 설명하다
(B) 인정하다
(C) 시작하다
(D) 제시하다

해설 이메일의 enter를 포함하는 구절 'we would like to enter her membership number on the application form'에서 그녀의 회원 번호를 신청서에 입력하고자 한다고 했으므로 enter는 '입력하다, 기입하다'라는 뜻으로 사용되었다. 따라서 '제시하다, 제출하다'라는 뜻을 가진 (D) submit이 정답이다.

어휘 admit v. 인정하다, 허용하다

200 추론 문제 연계   상 ●●●

해석 Mr. Lopez는 누구일 것 같은가?
(A) 마케팅 컨설턴트
(B) 광고 연출가
(C) 이벤트 기획자
(D) 웹사이트 관리자

해설 이메일의 'Dear Mr. Lopez', 'we would like to advertise ~ on your Web site'에서 이메일 수신자인 Mr. Lopez에게 웹사이트의 광고와 관련하여 연락이 왔다는 사실을 확인할 수 있다. 또한, 웹페이지의 'we ~ introduced banner advertising ~ on our Web site'와 'For more information, please contact the site administrator.'에서는 AMPA가 최근 웹사이트에 배너 광고를 도입했고, 더 많은 정보를 원한다면 사이트 관리자에게 연락하라고 했다.
두 단서를 종합할 때, Mr. Lopez는 웹사이트 관리자임을 추론할 수 있다. 따라서 (D)가 정답이다.

어휘 commercial n. 광고 director n. 연출가, 감독

패러프레이징

site administrator 사이트 관리자 → Web site manager 웹사이트 관리자

PART 5

101 (B)	102 (D)	103 (D)	104 (B)	105 (B)
106 (A)	107 (B)	108 (D)	109 (C)	110 (B)
111 (D)	112 (B)	113 (B)	114 (C)	115 (D)
116 (A)	117 (C)	118 (C)	119 (D)	120 (C)
121 (B)	122 (C)	123 (B)	124 (A)	125 (A)
126 (D)	127 (A)	128 (B)	129 (D)	130 (A)

PART 6

131 (B)	132 (D)	133 (D)	134 (C)	135 (B)
136 (D)	137 (B)	138 (D)	139 (C)	140 (B)
141 (D)	142 (D)	143 (B)	144 (C)	145 (A)
146 (D)				

PART 7

147 (C)	148 (B)	149 (C)	150 (C)	151 (C)
152 (D)	153 (D)	154 (B)	155 (B)	156 (C)
157 (C)	158 (C)	159 (B)	160 (D)	161 (D)
162 (B)	163 (B)	164 (C)	165 (B)	166 (B)
167 (C)	168 (C)	169 (B)	170 (A)	171 (B)
172 (C)	173 (C)	174 (D)	175 (B)	176 (D)
177 (B)	178 (A)	179 (D)	180 (C)	181 (C)
182 (D)	183 (A)	184 (C)	185 (B)	186 (C)
187 (D)	188 (D)	189 (D)	190 (B)	191 (B)
192 (C)	193 (A)	194 (C)	195 (B)	196 (C)
197 (A)	198 (D)	199 (D)	200 (B)	

PART 5

101 부사 자리 채우기

하 ●○○

해석 Lod Net사는 고객의 문의에 항상 빠르게 대응한다.

해설 동사(responds)를 꾸밀 수 있는 것은 부사이고 '고객의 문의에 빠르게 대응하다'라는 의미가 되어야 하므로 부사 (B) quickly(빠르게)가 정답이다. 시간 부사 (C) ago(이전에)는 시간 표현 바로 다음에 와서 현재를 기준으로 그 시간 이전에 일어난 일을 나타낸다. 강조 부사 (A)와 (D)는 동사를 꾸밀 수 없고, 형용사나 부사를 꾸며 그 정도를 강조한다.

어휘 respond v. 대응하다, 반응하다 inquiry n. 문의, 연구 very adv. 매우 so adv. 너무나, 대단히

102 시간 표현과 일치하는 시제의 동사 채우기

하 ●○○

해석 최근 보도에 따르면, NineEast 쇼핑몰은 다음 달에 새로운 장소로 이전할 것이다.

해설 문장에 주어(NineEast Mall)만 있고 동사가 없으므로 동사 (A), (C), (D)가 정답의 후보이다. 미래 시제를 나타내는 시간 표현(next month)이 있으므로 미래 시제 (D) will move가 정답이다. 현재 완료 시제 (A)와 과거 시제 (C)는 미래의 일을 나타낼 수 없다. 동명사 또는 현재분사 (B)는 동사 자리에 올 수 없다.

어휘 report n. 보도; v. 알리다

103 부사 자리 채우기

하 ●○○

해석 Relivium은 다른 브랜드들보다 두통 증상을 감소시키는 데 훨씬 더 효과적이다.

해설 빈칸 뒤의 형용사(more effective)를 꾸밀 수 있는 것은 부사이므로 부사 (D) significantly(훨씬, 매우)가 정답이다. 동사 (A), 명사 (B), 형용사 (C)는 형용사를 꾸밀 수 없다.

어휘 effective adj. 효과적인 headache n. 두통 symptom n. 증상 signify v. 의미하다, 나타내다 signifier n. 기표 significant adj. 상당한

104 격에 맞는 인칭대명사 채우기

하 ●○○

해석 Mr. Jones는 회사에 대한 그의 기여에 대해 상여금을 받았다.

해설 명사(contributions) 앞에서 형용사처럼 명사를 꾸밀 수 있는 인칭대명사는 소유격이므로 소유격 인칭대명사 (B) his가 정답이다. 주격 인칭대명사 (A), 목적격 인칭대명사 (C), 재귀대명사 (D)는 명사를 꾸밀 수 없다.

어휘 award v. 주다, 수여하다 bonus n. 상여금 contribution n. 기여

105 전치사 채우기

하 ●○○

해석 Ms. Potter는 Wallace's 중고 서점에서 일요일을 제외하고 매일 일한다.

해설 빈칸은 명사(Sunday)를 목적어로 취하는 전치사 자리이다. 'Ms. Potter는 일요일 제외하고 매일 일한다'라는 의미가 되어야 하므로 제외를 나타내는 전치사 (B) except(~을 제외하고)가 정답이다.

어휘 around prep. ~ 주위에 across prep. ~을 가로질러 within prep. ~ 이내에, ~의 범위 내에서

106 to 부정사 채우기

하 ●○○

해석 온라인 수업에 등록하기 전에, 저희의 약관을 반드시 읽으십시오.

해설 빈칸 앞에 to 부정사를 취하는 형용사(sure)가 있으므로 to 부정사 (A) to read가 정답이다. 동사원형 (B), 동명사 또는 현재분사 (C), 3인칭 단수 동사 (D)는 to 부정사를 취하는 형용사 다음에 올 수 없다. 참고로, 동명사와 명사는 be sure of(~에 확신을 가지다)의 형태 뒤에 올 수 있다는 것을 알아둔다.

어휘 register v. 등록하다 terms and conditions phr. 약관, 조건

107 형용사 어휘 고르기   중 ●●○

해석 그 섬나라의 경제는 관광업에 의존한다.

해설 빈칸은 be동사(is)의 보어 역할을 하는 형용사 자리이다. '경제는 관광업에 의존한다'라는 문맥이므로 (B) dependent(의존하는, 의지하는)가 정답이다. 참고로, 형용사 dependent는 dependent on(~에 의존하는)의 형태로 자주 쓰임을 알아둔다. (A) exclusive(독점적인, 배타적인)도 해석상 그럴듯해 보이지만, 전치사 to와 함께 쓰여야 한다.

어휘 tourism n. 관광업   necessary adj. 필수의, 필요한
interested adj. 관심 있어 하는

108 전치사 채우기   중 ●●○

해석 모든 참가자들은 4일간의 무역 박람회의 마지막에 반환될 500달러의 보증금을 지불해야 한다.

해설 빈칸은 명사구(the four-day trade show)를 목적어로 취하는 전치사 자리이다. 빈칸 앞의 명사(the end)가 the four-day trade show의 한 부분이므로, 부분을 나타내는 전치사 (D) of(~의)가 정답이다.

어휘 deposit n. 보증금   return v. 반환하다, 돌려주다   into prep. ~안으로
in prep. ~안에, ~에서   for prep. ~에 대해

109 형용사 어휘 고르기   중 ●●○

해석 홍수에 취약한 모든 도로들은 폭풍우 동안 운전자들에게 폐쇄될 것이다.

해설 이 문장은 명사(roads)를 꾸미는 관계절(___ to flooding) 앞에 '주격 관계대명사 + be동사'(which/that are)가 생략된 형태로, 빈칸은 명사(roads)를 꾸미면서 be동사(are) 뒤에 올 수 있는 형용사 자리이다. '홍수에 취약한 모든 도로들은 폐쇄될 것이다'라는 문맥이므로 (C) vulnerable(취약한)이 정답이다. 참고로, vulnerable은 전치사 to와 함께 vulnerable to(~에 취약한)의 형태로 자주 쓰임을 알아둔다.

어휘 flooding n. 홍수, 범람   motorist n. 운전자   storm n. 폭풍우
attainable adj. 이룰 수 있는   responsible adj. 책임이 있는
preventable adj. 예방할 수 있는

110 명사 어휘 고르기   중 ●●○

해석 공장의 컨베이어 벨트 중 하나가 오작동하여, 일일 생산량의 부족을 야기했다.

해설 빈칸은 전치사(in)의 목적어 역할을 하면서 부정관사(a) 다음에 올 수 있는 명사 자리이다. '컨베이어 벨트가 오작동하여, 일일 생산량의 부족을 야기했다'라는 의미가 되어야 하므로 (B) shortfall(부족, 부족분)이 정답이다.

어휘 malfunction v. 오작동하다   result in phr. ~을 야기하다, 낳다
output n. 생산량, 산출   permit n. 허가, 허가증; v. 허락하다
routine n. 일과; adj. 정기적인   contract n. 계약; v. 수축하다

111 부사절 접속사 채우기   중 ●●○

해석 새로운 가방에 대한 수요가 높기 때문에, 대부분의 소매상들은 곧 재고가 없을 것이다.

해설 빈칸은 동사(is)가 있는 거품절(___ ~ high)을 이끄는 부사절 접속사 자리이다. '수요가 높기 때문에, 대부분의 소매상들은 곧 재고가 없을 것이다'라는 문맥이므로 이유를 나타내는 부사절 접속사 (D) Because(~이기 때문에)가 정답이다.

어휘 demand n. 수요, 요구; v. 요구하다   retailer n. 소매상, 소매업자
run out of phr. 재고가 없다, (~이) 없어지다   even if conj. ~에도 불구하고
unless conj. ~하지 않으면   although conj. 비록 ~이지만

112 'be동사 + p.p.' 채우기   중 ●●○

해석 만약 고객들이 구매 영수증을 가지고 있지 않다면 그들은 상점 포인트로만 환불받을 수 있다.

해설 빈칸이 be동사(be) 다음에 왔으므로 모든 보기가 정답의 후보이다. '고객들은 상점 포인트로만 환불받을 수 있다'라는 수동의 의미가 되어야 하므로 빈칸 앞의 be동사와 함께 수동태를 만드는 p.p.형 (B) refunded가 정답이다. 명사 (A)는 보어로서 주어와 동격 관계가 되어 '고객들은 환불들일 수 있다'라는 어색한 문맥을 만든다. 능동태를 만드는 -ing형 (C)는 동사 refund가 '환불하다'라는 의미일 때는 타동사인데 빈칸 뒤에 목적어가 없고, '고객들은 환불하는 중일 수 있다'라는 어색한 문맥을 만든다. 형용사 (D)는 be동사 다음에 와서 보어로서 주어를 설명해줄 수는 있지만, refundable(환불 가능한)의 주체는 사람(customers)이 아닌 사물이어야 한다.

어휘 store credit phr. 상점 포인트   purchase receipt phr. 구매 영수증
refund v. 환불하다; n. 환불, 환불금

113 전치사 채우기   중 ●●○

해석 경영진은 피드백으로부터 고객들이 제품에 더 많이 지불할 수 있다고 결론지었다.

해설 빈칸은 명사(the feedback)를 목적어로 취하는 전치사 자리이다. '경영진은 피드백으로부터 결론지었다'라는 의미가 되어야 하므로 (B) from(~으로부터)이 정답이다. 전치사 (D) below(~ 아래에)도 해석상 그럴듯해 보이지만, 위치나 양·수준, 직위가 아래인 것을 나타내므로 답이 될 수 없다.

어휘 management n. 경영진, 경영   conclude v. 결론을 내리다, 끝내다
can afford to phr. (금전적·시간적으로) ~할 수 있다   at prep. ~에
during prep. ~동안

114 부사 자리 채우기   중 ●●○

해석 병의 확산이 현재 억제되지 않고 있는 동안 시민들은 마스크를 착용하도록 요구된다.

해설 동사(is contained)를 꾸밀 수 있는 것은 부사이므로 부사 (C) currently(현재, 지금)가 정답이다. 형용사의 비교급 (A), 형용사의 원급 또는 명사 (B), 형용사의 최상급 (D)는 부사 자리에 올 수 없다.

어휘 citizen n. 시민   disease n. 병   contain v. 억제하다, 함유하다
current adj. 현재의; n. 흐름, 기류

115 명사 자리 채우기   중 ●●○

해석 정부는 그것이 Habro Chemical사와의 합의에서 받았던 돈을 오염된 수로를 복구하기 위해 사용했다.

해설 전치사(in)의 목적어 역할을 하면서 부정관사(a) 다음에 올 수 있는 것은 명사이므로 명사 (D) settlement(합의, 해결)가 정답이다. 동사 (A), 동사 또는 과거분사 (B), 형용사 (C)는 명사 자리에 올 수 없다.

어휘 government n. 정부   restore v. 복구하다, 회복시키다
polluted adj. 오염된, 더럽혀진   waterway n. 수로
settle v. 해결하다, 합의를 보다   settleable adj. 자리 잡을 수 있는

116 동사 어휘 고르기   중 ●●○

해석 컴퓨터 바이러스 때문에, 그 부서의 컴퓨터에 저장된 몇몇 파일들에 오류가 생겼다.

해설 빈칸은 명사구(some of the files)를 꾸미는 과거분사 자리이다. '그 부서의 컴퓨터에 저장된 몇몇 파일들'이라는 문맥이므로 동사 store(저장하다)의 과

거분사 (A) stored가 정답이다.

어휘 **corrupt** v. 오류를 일으키다 **announce** v. 발표하다, 알리다
attach v. 첨부하다, 붙이다 **remind** v. 상기시키다

117 한정사에 맞는 명사 채우기 　　중 ●●●○

해석 그 보고서는 왜 회사가 정보를 관리하는 방법을 바꿔야 하는지 몇몇 중요한 이유들의 개요를 말한다.

해설 빈칸 앞의 형용사(important)의 꾸밈을 받을 수 있는 것은 명사이므로 명사 (A), (C), (D)가 정답의 후보이다. 빈칸 앞에 복수 명사를 꾸미는 수량 형용사 several(몇몇, 몇 개의)이 있으므로 복수 가산 명사 (C) reasons (이유들)가 정답이다. 단수 가산 명사 (A)와 불가산 명사 (D)는 several과 함께 쓰일 수 없다. 동사 또는 과거분사 (B)는 명사 자리에 올 수 없다.

어휘 **outline** v. ~의 개요를 말하다; n. 개요, 윤곽 **manage** v. 관리하다, 처리하다
reason n. 이유, 이성; v. 추론하다 **reasoning** n. 추리, 추론

118 명사 보어와 형용사 보어 구별하여 채우기 　　중 ●●●○

해석 Sparta 재단의 멘토링 프로그램은 학생들에게 유익하다고 판명되었다.

해설 빈칸은 be동사(be) 다음에 나온 보어 자리이므로 형용사 (C)와 명사 (D)가 정답의 후보이다. 'Sparta 재단의 멘토링 프로그램은 유익하다고 판명되었다'라는 의미로, 보어가 주어(Sparta Foundation's mentoring program)의 상태를 설명하고 있으므로 형용사 (C) informative(유익한)가 정답이다. 명사 (D)를 쓸 경우 주어와 동격이 되어 'Sparta 재단의 멘토링 프로그램은 정보라고 판명되었다'라는 어색한 문맥이 된다. 동사 (A)와 (B)는 보어 자리에 올 수 없다.

어휘 **foundation** n. 재단 **prove** v. 판명되다, 입증하다
inform v. 알리다, 통지하다

119 복합 명사 채우기 　　상 ●●●

해석 이 보안 예방 조치는 고객들이 틀린 비밀번호를 세 번 입력하면 그들이 온라인 계정에 대한 이용 권한을 잃도록 한다.

해설 빈칸이 명사(precaution) 앞에 있으므로 명사를 꾸밀 수 있는 과거분사 (A)와 복합 명사를 만드는 명사 (D)가 정답의 후보이다. '이 보안 예방 조치는 고객들이 이용 권한을 잃도록 한다'라는 문맥이므로 빈칸 뒤의 명사 precaution(예방 조치)과 함께 쓰여 '보안 예방 조치'라는 의미의 복합 명사 security precaution을 만드는 명사 (D) security(보안)가 정답이다. 과거분사 (A)를 쓸 경우 '보호되는 예방 조치'라는 어색한 의미가 된다. 부사 (B)와 동사 (C)는 명사를 꾸밀 수 없다.

어휘 **precaution** n. 예방 조치 **access** n. 이용 권한, 접근권; v. 접근하다
account n. 계정, 계좌 **enter** v. 입력하다, 들어가다
secure v. 보호하다, 보증하다 **securely** adv. 안전하게, 단단히

120 부사 어휘 고르기 　　중 ●●●○

해석 관리자가 일반적으로 모든 구매를 승인해야 하지만, 50달러 이하의 물품들에는 예외가 적용될 수 있다.

해설 빈칸은 동사(must approve)를 꾸미는 부사 자리이다. '관리자는 일반적으로 모든 구매를 승인해야 하지만, 50달러 이하의 물품들에는 예외가 적용될 수 있다'라는 문맥이므로 (C) normally(일반적으로)가 정답이다.

어휘 **approve** v. 승인하다 **exception** n. 예외, 이례 **relatively** adv. 비교적
greatly adv. 대단히, 크게 **patiently** adv. 끈기 있게, 참을성 있게

121 전치사 채우기 　　중 ●●●○

해석 홍보 기간 내내 쇼핑객들은 모든 제품에 대해 30퍼센트 할인을 받을 수 있다.

해설 빈칸은 명사구(the promotional period)를 목적어로 취하는 전치사 자리이다. '홍보 기간 내내 쇼핑객들은 모든 제품에 대해 할인을 받을 수 있다'라는 의미가 되어야 하므로 기간을 나타내는 전치사 (B) throughout(~ 내내, ~ 동안 쪽)이 정답이다. 전치사 (A) among과 (C) between도 '~ 사이에'라는 의미로 해석상 그럴듯해 보이지만, (A)는 세 개 이상, (C)는 두 개의 대상 사이를 나타내고, 뒤에 복수 명사나 between A and B의 형태가 와야 한다.

어휘 **discount** n. 할인 **promotional** adj. 홍보의, 판촉의 **to** prep. ~로, ~쪽으로

122 명사 어휘 고르기 　　상 ●●●

해석 시 의회는 해안가 구역의 일부를 상업 및 주거 복합 단지로 개조했다.

해설 빈칸은 등위접속사(and)로 연결된 형용사(commercial, residential)의 꾸밈을 받는 명사 자리이다. '해안가 구역의 일부를 상업 및 주거 복합 단지로 개조했다'라는 문맥이므로 (C) complex(복합 단지, 복합 건물)가 정답이다.

어휘 **city council** phr. 시 의회 **convert** v. 개조하다, 전환시키다
waterfront n. 해안가 **district** n. 구역, 지역 **commercial** adj. 상업의
residential adj. 주거의, 거주하기 좋은 **design** n. 디자인, 설계
standard n. 기준, 표준 **matter** n. 사안, 문제

123 수량 표현 채우기 　　중 ●●●○

해석 기름 유출에 관한 뉴스는 그것에 관한 영상이 인터넷에서 퍼지기 전에는 거의 주목을 얻지 못했다.

해설 빈칸 뒤의 '주목, 주의'라는 의미의 불가산 명사 attention을 꾸밀 수 있는 수량 표현이 와야 하므로 수량 표현 (B) little(거의 없는, 조금의)이 정답이다. 수량 표현 (A)와 (C)는 복수 가산 명사를 꾸미고, 수량 표현 (D)는 단수 가산 명사를 꾸민다. 참고로, attention은 주로 '주목, 주의, 관심, 보살핌' 등의 의미의 불가산 명사로 쓰이지만, '(관심을 끌기 위한) 행동, 배려'라는 의미일 때는 가산 명사로 쓰인다는 것을 알아둔다.

어휘 **oil spill** phr. 기름 유출 **spread** v. 퍼지다, 확산하다
few adj. 많지 않은, 거의 없는 **many** adj. 많은
any adj. 어떤, 어떤 ~라도, 무엇이든지

124 동사 어휘 고르기 　　중 ●●●○

해석 내일 시험을 준비하고 싶은 학생들은 교과서의 챕터 9를 참고해야 한다.

해설 빈칸은 조동사(should) 다음에 오는 동사원형 자리이다. '학생들은 교과서를 참조해야 한다'라는 문맥이므로 (A) refer(참고하다)가 정답이다. 참고로, 동사 refer는 refer to(~을 참고하다)의 형태로 자주 쓰임을 알아둔다.

어휘 **apply** v. 적용하다, 지원하다 **regard** v. ~으로 여기다, 간주하다
assign v. 배정하다, 할당하다

125 명령문의 동사 자리 채우기 　　중 ●●●○

해석 수요일 아침에 수리를 위해 엘리베이터가 폐쇄될 것이라는 점을 알아두시기 바랍니다.

해설 문장이 주어 없이 시작되는 명령문이므로 명령문의 동사로 쓰이는 동사원형(be)을 포함하는 수동태 동사 (A) be advised가 정답이다. 참고로, be advised(알아두다)와 같은 의미를 갖는 be informed도 함께 알아둔다. 명사 (B), 동사 또는 과거분사 (C), 동명사 또는 현재분사 (D)는 동사원형 자리에 올 수 없다.

어휘 **repair** n. 수리 **advice** n. 조언, 충고

126 부사절 접속사 채우기
중 ●●○

해석 작은 그룹을 예상하여서, Ms. Madsen은 100명의 사람들이 그녀의 원예 개인 지도에 도착했을 때 놀랐다.

해설 이 문장은 주어(Ms. Madsen)와 동사(was surprised)를 갖춘 완전한 절이므로, ___ ~ tutorial은 수식어 거품으로 보아야 한다. 이 수식어 거품은 동사(arrived)가 있는 거품절이므로, 거품절을 이끌 수 있는 부사절 접속사 (B), (C), (D)가 정답의 후보이다. '작은 그룹을 예상하여서, Ms. Madsen은 100명의 사람들이 도착했을 때 놀랐다'라는 의미가 되어야 하므로 시간을 나타내는 부사절 접속사 (D) when(~할 때)이 정답이다. 전치사 (A)는 거품절이 아닌 거품구를 이끈다.

어휘 expect v. 예상하다, 기대하다 surprise v. 놀라게 하다, 기습하다
gardening n. 원예 tutorial n. 개인 지도 (시간), 지도서
whereas conj. ~반면에 as if phr. 마치 ~인 것처럼

127 동사 어휘 고르기
상 ●●●

해석 관광 도시의 시장으로서, Mr. Venturi는 방문객들과 주민들의 요구 사이에서 균형을 유지해야 한다.

해설 빈칸은 조동사(must) 다음에 오는 동사원형 자리이다. '방문객들과 주민들의 요구 사이에서 균형을 유지해야 한다'라는 의미가 되어야 하므로 (A) balance(균형을 유지하다, 균형을 이루다)가 정답이다.

어휘 mayor n. 시장 need n. 요구, 필요 local n. 주민, 거주자; adj. 지역의
waive v. 포기하다 overcome v. (장애·반대 등을) 극복하다, 이기다
expose v. 노출시키다, 드러내다

128 의문형용사 채우기
상 ●●●

해석 온라인 설문지는 장래의 자동차 구매자들이 어떤 자동차가 그들에게 가장 어울릴 것 같은지 결정하도록 해준다.

해설 빈칸이 포함된 절(___ ~ them best)은 to 부정사(to determine)의 목적어 역할을 하고 있으므로 목적어 자리에 올 수 있는 명사절을 이끄는 명사절 접속사 (A)와 의문형용사 (B)가 정답의 후보이다. 빈칸 뒤에 관사 없이 명사(vehicle)가 바로 나왔고, '구매자들이 어떤 자동차가 그들에게 가장 어울릴 것 같은지 결정하도록 해준다'라는 의미가 되어야 하므로 의문형용사 (B) which(어떤)가 정답이다. 명사절 접속사 (A)는 '구매자들이 자동차가 그들에게 어울릴 수도 있다는 것을 결정하도록 해준다'라는 어색한 문맥을 만들며, that 바로 뒤 주어 자리에 가산 명사(vehicle)가 올 경우, 관사와 함께 쓰이거나 복수형으로 쓰여야 한다. 소유격 인칭대명사 (C)와 부정형용사 또는 부정대명사 (D)는 거품절을 이끌 수 없다. to 부정사(to determine) 뒤에 명사절 접속사 that이 생략되었고 (C) their와 (D) another가 명사(vehicle)를 꾸미는 것으로 본다 해도, 각각 '그들의/또 하나의 자동차가 그들에게 어울릴 수도 있다는 것을 결정한다'라는 어색한 문맥을 만든다. 참고로, 이 문장은 to 부정사를 목적격 보어로 취하는 5형식 동사 allow(~가 -하도록 해주다) 뒤에 목적어(prospective car buyers)와 목적격 보어(to determine ~ best)가 온 형태임을 알아둔다.

어휘 questionnaire n. 설문지 prospective adj. 장래의, 가능성 있는, 유망한
determine v. 결정하다, 알아내다 suit v. 어울리다, 만족시키다; n. 정장
another adj. 다른; n. 다른 것

129 명사 자리 채우기
상 ●●●

해석 Ms. Hansen은 보통 규칙에 관해 엄격하지만, 신입 사원들에 대해서는 기꺼이 유연성을 발휘한다.

해설 '발휘하다, 행사하다'라는 의미의 타동사 exercise의 목적어 자리에 올 수 있는 것은 명사이므로 명사 (C)와 (D)가 정답의 후보이다. 'Ms. Hansen은 기꺼이 유연성을 발휘한다'라는 의미가 되어야 하므로 명사 (D) flexibility(유연성)가 정답이다. 명사 (C) flex(굴곡)는 'Ms. Hansen은 기꺼이 굴곡을 발휘한다'라는 어색한 문맥을 만든다. 부사 (A)와 형용사 (B)는 명사 자리에 올 수 없다. 부사 (A) flexibly(유연하게)가 동사 exercise를 꾸미는 것으로 본다 해도, exercise가 목적어 없이 자동사로 쓰일 때는 '운동하다'라는 의미이므로 'Ms. Hansen은 보통 규칙에 엄격하지만, 신입 사원들과 함께 기꺼이 유연하게 운동한다'라는 어색한 문맥을 만든다.

어휘 strict adj. 엄격한 exercise v. 발휘하다, 행사하다
flexible adj. 유연한, 융통성 있는

130 형용사 자리 채우기
상 ●●●

해석 그 최고경영자는 다수의 주주들이 재정 상태에 대해 계속 많이 알고 있도록 하기 위해 노력했다.

해설 5형식 동사 keep은 목적어와 목적격 보어를 가지는 동사이며, 동사(keep) 뒤에 목적어(the ~ shareholders)가 있으므로 빈칸은 목적격 보어 자리이다. 따라서 동사 keep의 목적격 보어 자리에 올 수 있는 형용사 (A)와 과거분사 (D)가 정답의 후보이다. '다수의 주주들이 재정 상태에 대해 계속 많이 알고 있도록 하다'라는 의미가 되어야 하므로 형용사 (A) knowledgeable(많이 알고 있는, 아는 것이 많은)이 정답이다. 과거분사 (D) known(알려진)을 쓸 경우 '재정 상태로 알려진 다수의 주주들'이라는 어색한 문맥이 된다. 명사 (B) knowledge(지식)를 쓸 경우 목적어를 2개 갖는 4형식 동사 keep(~을 위해 -을 남겨 두다)이 되어 '다수의 주주들을 위해 재정 상태의 지식을 남겨 두다'라는 어색한 문맥이 된다. 동사 (C)는 보어 자리에 올 수 없다.

어휘 majority n. 다수 shareholder n. 주주
financial situation phr. 재정 상태

PART 6

131-134번은 다음 이메일에 관한 문제입니다.

수신: Amira Yaziri <amira72@goodtidings.tn>
발신: Ernie Vollmer <e.vollmer@mahalsuites.com>
날짜: 12월 9일
제목: 특별 계획

Ms. Yaziri께,

첫째로, Jamesville에 있는 동안 당신의 숙소로 Mahal Suites를 ¹³¹**선택해주신 것**에 감사드립니다. 당신은 저희의 디럭스 객실 중 하나에 묵게 되실 것이므로, 당신은 저희의 무료 ¹³²**공항** 교통편을 받을 권리가 있습니다. 하지만, 당신의 예약 양식은 당신의 항공편이 오전 1시 26분에 도착한다고 나타내며, 셔틀버스는 오직 오전 6시부터 오후 1시까지 운행합니다. ¹³³**당신은 대안을 마련하실 수 있으신가요?** 저는 당신을 위한 개인 이동 서비스에 기꺼이 연락할 것입니다. ¹³⁴**이 경우에는**, 운전기사가 당신의 도착 게이트에서 당신을 만날 것입니다.

Ernie Vollmer 드림
고객 서비스 직원
Mahal Suites

---

arrangement n. 계획, 준비, 마련 **be entitled to** phr. ~을 받을 권리가 있다
transfer n. 이동, 전근; v. 전근 보내다

---

131 동사 어휘 고르기 주변 문맥 파악 중 ●●○

해설 빈칸은 전치사(for)의 목적어 역할을 하면서 명사(Mahal Suites)를 목적어로 취할 수 있는 동명사 자리이다. '당신의 숙소로 Mahal Suites를 ___에 감사하다'라는 문맥이므로 (B)와 (C)가 정답의 후보이다. 뒤 문장에서 우리의 디럭스 객실 중 하나에 묵게 될 것이라고 했으므로 Mahal Suites를 숙소로 선택했음을 알 수 있다. 따라서 동사 choose(선택하다)의 동명사 (B) choosing이 정답이다.

어휘 **acquire** v. 인수하다, 얻다 **review** v. 논평하다, 재검토하다
prepare v. 준비하다

132 명사 어휘 고르기 전체 문맥 파악 중 ●●○

해설 빈칸은 형용사(free)의 꾸밈을 받는 명사 자리이다. '우리의 무료 ___ 교통편을 받을 권리가 있다'라는 문맥이므로 모든 보기가 정답의 후보이다. 뒤 문장에서 하지만, 당신의 예약 양식은 당신의 항공편이 오전 1시 26분에 도착한다고 나타내며, 셔틀버스는 오직 오전 6시부터 오후 11시까지 운행한다고 한 후, 뒷부분에서 개인 이동 서비스에 연락하겠다고 했으므로 무료 공항 교통편을 받을 권리가 있음을 알 수 있다. 따라서 (D) airport(공항)가 정답이다.

133 알맞은 문장 고르기 중 ●●○

해석 (A) 당신의 차를 주차할 곳이 필요하신가요?
(B) 여행사는 한때 저희 로비에 사무실이 있었습니다.
(C) 그러니 하루 중 어느 때에나 자유롭게 룸서비스를 주문해주십시오.
(D) 당신은 대안을 마련하실 수 있으신가요?

해설 앞 문장 'However, your reservation form indicates that your flight will be arriving at 1:26 A.M., and the shuttle runs only from 6 A.M. to 11 P.M.'에서 하지만, 당신의 예약 양식은 당신의 항공편이 오전 1시 26분에 도착한다고 나타내며, 셔틀버스는 오직 오전 6시부터 오후 1시까지 운행한다고 했고, 뒤 문장 'I would be happy to contact a private transfer service for you.'에서는 당신을 위한 개인 이동 서비스에 기꺼이 연락할 것이라고 했으므로 빈칸에는 셔틀버스가 운행되지 않는 시간의 이동에 대한 대안과 관련된 내용이 들어가야 함을 알 수 있다. 따라서 (D)가 정답이다.

어휘 **alternative** adj. 다른, 대체의

134 접속부사 채우기 주변 문맥 파악 상 ●●●

해설 앞 문장에서 당신을 위한 개인 이동 서비스에 기꺼이 연락할 것이라고 했고, 빈칸이 있는 문장에서는 운전기사가 도착 게이트에서 당신을 만날 것이라고 했으므로 앞 문장과 관련하여 추가적인 내용을 나타낼 때 사용되는 접속부사 (C) In this case(이 경우에는)가 정답이다.

어휘 **until then** phr. 그때까지 **elsewhere** adv. 다른 곳으로
likewise adv. 똑같이, 또한

135-138번은 다음 기사에 관한 문제입니다.

여행사 Alexis Journeys사는 최근에 그것이 그것의 투어 종류를 ¹³⁵**확장할 것**이라고 발표했다. 8월 1일에, Alexis Journeys사는 콜롬비아, 엘살바도르, 그리고 벨리즈로의 여행들을 소개할 것이다. 이것들은 그것이 이미 라틴 아메리카에 대해 제공하고 있는 12개의 여행 패키지들에 추가되는 것이다.

Alexis Journeys사는 그것의 ¹³⁶**적절한 가격으로** 알려져 있다. 예를 들어, 그것의 새로운 Mayan Discovery 투어는 모든 교통과 숙박을 포함하여 일주일에 단 1,050달러이다. ¹³⁷**그것은 또한 그것의 모든 투어 패키지들에 훌륭한 후기를 가지고 있다.**

"저희의 새로운 패키지들과 함께, Alexis Journeys사는 라틴 아메리카로의 여행이 너무 비싸다고 생각했던 여행자들을 ¹³⁸**목표로 하려고** 시도하고 있습니다."라고 마케팅 담당자 Hal Clive가 말했다.

---

be known for phr. ~으로 알려져 있다 **accommodation** n. 숙박, 숙소
attempt v. 시도하다, ~하려고 해보다

---

135 동사 어휘 고르기 전체 문맥 파악 중 ●●○

해설 빈칸은 be동사(is) 뒤에 와서 곧 일어날 미래를 나타내는 진행형을 만드는 -ing형의 자리이다. '여행사 Alexis Journeys사는 최근에 그것의 투어 종류를 ___이라고 발표했다'라는 문맥이므로 모든 보기가 정답의 후보이다. 뒤 문장에서 Alexis Journeys사는 콜롬비아, 엘살바도르, 그리고 벨리즈로의 여행들을 소개할 것이라고 한 후, 뒷부분에서 이것들은 그것이 이미 라틴 아메리카에 대해 제공하고 있는 12개의 여행 패키지에 추가되는 것이라고 했으므로 최근에 투어 종류를 확장할 것이라고 발표했음을 알 수 있다. 따라서 동사 expand(확장하다)의 -ing형 (B) expanding이 정답이다. 참고로, 현재진행형(be동사 + -ing)뿐만 아니라, 'be going to + 동사원형'의 형태도 예정된 일이나 곧 일어나려고 하는 일을 표현하여 미래를 나타낸다는 것을 알아 둔다.

어휘 **combine** v. 결합하다 **withhold** v. 보류하다 **reduce** v. 줄이다, 할인하다

136 명사 어휘 고르기 주변 문맥 파악 중 ●●○

해설 빈칸은 소유격 인칭대명사(its)의 꾸밈을 받는 명사 자리이다. 'Alexis Journeys사는 그것의 ___으로 알려져 있다'라는 문맥이므로 모든 보기가 정답의 후보이다. 뒤 문장에서 새로운 Mayan Discovery 투어는 모든 교통과 숙박을 포함하여 일주일에 단 1,050달러라고 했으므로 Alexis Journeys사가 적절한 가격으로 알려져 있다는 것을 알 수 있다. 따라서 (D) affordability(적절한 가격)가 정답이다.

어휘 **suitability** n. 적합 **flexibility** n. 융통성, 유연성 **diversity** n. 다양성, 변화

137 알맞은 문장 고르기 중 ●●○

해석 (A) 몇몇 사람들은 투어에 대한 그들의 불만을 나타냈다.
(B) 그것은 또한 그것의 모든 투어 패키지들에 훌륭한 후기를 가지고 있다.
(C) 이 소문은 아직 회사에 의해 확인되지 않았다.
(D) 또한 손님들은 객실 내 와이파이를 이용하기 위해서 추가로 돈을 낼 수 있다.

해설 앞부분에서 Alexis Journeys사가 적절한 가격으로 잘 알려져 있다고 했고, 앞 문장 'Its new Mayan Discovery tour ~ is only $1,050 for one week'에서 그것의 새로운 Mayan Discovery 투어는 단 1,050달러라고 했으므로 빈칸에는 Alexis Journeys사 투어의 또 다른 장점인 훌륭한 후기와 관련된 내용이 들어가야 함을 알 수 있다. 따라서 (B)가 정답이다.

어휘 **dissatisfaction** n. 불만 **confirm** v. 확인하다

take advantage of phr. ~을 이용하다

138 to 부정사 채우기   중 ●●○

해설 타동사 attempt의 목적어 자리에는 명사 역할을 하는 것이 올 수 있으므로 빈칸 뒤 명사(travelers)와 함께 명사구를 만드는 과거분사 (B)와 명사 (C), to 부정사구를 만드는 to 부정사 (D)가 정답의 후보이다. 'Alexis Journeys 사는 여행자들을 목표하려고 시도하고 있다'라는 의미가 되어야 하므로 to 부정사 (D) to target이 정답이다. 동사 attempt는 사람 명사(travelers)를 목적어로 취할 수 없으므로 과거분사 (B)와 명사 (C)는 답이 될 수 없다. (A)는 동사일 경우 목적어 자리에 올 수 없고, 명사일 경우 복합 명사의 첫 번째 단어는 단수형이어야 하므로 복수 명사 (A)는 복합 명사를 만들 수 없다.

어휘 target v. 목표하다; n. 목표(물)

139-142번은 다음 안내문에 관한 문제입니다.

중요 등록 안내문

Ryder 대학은 강의 시작일 최소 한 달 전에 수업료 지불을 요청합니다. 등록할 때, 환불되지 않는 보증금 75달러가 당신의 자리를 확보하기 위해 요구됩니다. ¹³⁹보통 대부분의 강의들에 대해 높은 수요가 있습니다. 그러므로, 저희는 한정된 자리가 반드시 ¹⁴⁰진지한 출석 의사가 있는 학생들에게 주어지도록 노력합니다.

만약 대학이 당신이 지불한 강의를 제공할 수 없게 되면, 당신은 수업료와 함께 보증금 전액을 환불받을 것입니다. 시작일 20일 전에 학생들이 ¹⁴¹취소하는 경우 동일하게 유효합니다. 다른 경우에는, 보증금이 환불되지 않을 것입니다. 또한, ¹⁴²일단 강의가 시작되면 학생들은 그것을 취소할 수 없습니다.

payment n. 지불, 지불금   deposit n. 보증금, 착수금
secure v. 확보하다, 보호하다   intention n. 의사, 의도, 목적
hold true phr. (규칙·말 따위가) 유효하다

139 알맞은 문장 고르기   중 ●●○

해석 (A) 교실 좌석 배치도를 참고하십시오.
(B) 이 금액은 2주 안에 환불될 것입니다.
(C) 보통 대부분의 강의들에 대해 높은 수요가 있습니다.
(D) 그 학교는 주립 대학들 사이에서 높이 평가됩니다.

해설 앞 문장 'When registering, a ~ deposit ~ is required to secure your place.'에서 등록할 때, 보증금이 당신의 자리를 확보하기 위해 요구된다고 했고, 뒤 문장 'Therefore, we ~ make sure that the limited spaces go to students with ~ intentions of attending.'에서 그러므로, 우리, 즉 Ryder 대학은 한정된 자리가 반드시 출석 의사가 있는 학생들에게 주어지도록 한다고 했으므로 빈칸에는 보통 대부분의 강의들의 수요가 높다는 내용이 들어가야 함을 알 수 있다. 따라서 (C)가 정답이다.

어휘 consult v. 참고하다, 상의하다   demand n. 수요, 요구
rank v. 평가되다; n. 등급, 계급

최고난도 문제

140 형용사 어휘 고르기   상 ●●●

해설 빈칸은 명사(intentions)를 꾸미는 형용사 자리이다. '___ 출석 의사가 있는 학생들'이라는 문맥이므로 (B) serious(진지한)가 정답이다.

어휘 qualified adj. 적격의, 적임의   courteous adj. 공손한, 정중한
promising adj. 유망한, 기대되는

141 동사 어휘 고르기   주변 문맥 파악   상 ●●●

해설 if절(if ~ date)에 동사가 없으므로 빈칸은 동사 자리이다. '시작일 20일 전에 학생들이 ___하는 경우 동일하게 유효하다'라는 문맥인데, 앞 문장에서 만약 대학이 당신이 지불한 강의를 제공할 수 없게 되면, 당신은 수업료와 함께 보증금 전액을 환불받을 것이라고 했으므로 학생들이 시작일 20일 전에 취소하는 경우 동일하게 환불이 유효하다는 것을 알 수 있다. 따라서 (D) withdraw(취소하다, 철회하다)가 정답이다.

어휘 depart v. 떠나다, 출발하다   enroll v. 등록하다   separate v. 분리하다

최고난도 문제

142 부사절 접속사 채우기   상 ●●●

해설 이 문장은 주어(students), 동사(may not cancel), 목적어(a course)를 갖춘 완전한 절이므로, ___ begun은 수식어 거품으로 보아야 한다. 이 수식어 거품은 주어(a course)와 be동사(is)가 생략된 분사구문이며 동사(begun)가 있는 거품절이므로, 거품절을 이끌 수 있는 부사절 접속사인 모든 보기가 정답의 후보이다. '일단 강의가 시작되면 학생들은 그것을 취소할 수 없다'라는 문맥이 되어야 하므로 부사절 접속사 (D) once(일단 ~하면)가 정답이다. (A) since(~한 이래로)와 (C) after(~한 후)도 해석상 그럴듯해 보이지만, 뒤에 과거분사가 포함된 분사구문이 올 경우, p.p.가 아닌 'being + p.p.(being begun)' 형태가 와야 한다. (B) before(~하기 전에)는 어색한 문맥을 만들며, since와 after처럼 뒤에 과거분사가 올 경우 'being + p.p.' 형태가 와야 한다.

143-146번은 다음 공고에 관한 문제입니다.

Gavin Hackett이 Waco에 옵니다!

호평을 받고 있는 작가 Gavin Hackett이 9월 13일 화요일 오후 8시에 Waco의 중앙 강당에서 ¹⁴³동기를 부여하는 강연을 할 것입니다. 그의 강연에서, Mr. Hackett은 기억의 과학에 대해 살펴볼 것입니다. 그는 정보를 보유하고 기억해 내는 인간의 능력을 증대시키는 것에 대한 여러 기술들을 밝힐 것입니다.

이곳에서의 Mr. Hackett의 ¹⁴⁴등장은 그의 곧 발표될 책 *Remember Harder*의 홍보 투어의 일부입니다. 그는 지난 20년의 경력 동안 다른 여러 책들을 ¹⁴⁵써왔습니다.

입장료 15달러는 출입구에서 부과될 것입니다. ¹⁴⁶처음 입장하는 50명은 무료 책을 받을 것입니다.

acclaimed adj. 호평을 받고 있는   deliver v. (강연 등을) 하다, 배달하다
auditorium n. 강당, 관객석   explore v. 살펴보다, 답험하다
reveal v. 밝히다, 드러내다   boost v. 증대시키다, 촉진하다
retain v. 보유하다, 유지하다   recall v. 기억해 내다, 회수하다
upcoming adj. 곧 발표될, 다가오는   entry fee phr. 입장료

143 형용사 자리 채우기   하 ●○○

해설 명사(talk)를 꾸밀 수 있는 것은 형용사이므로 형용사 (B) motivational(동기를 부여하는)이 정답이다. 명사 (A), 동사 (C), 부사 (D)는 명사를 꾸밀 수 없다.

어휘 motivator n. 동기를 부여하는 사람(것)   motivate v. 동기를 부여하다

144 명사 어휘 고르기 · 전체 문맥 파악 · 상 ●●●

해설 빈칸은 소유격(Mr. Hackett's)의 꾸밈을 받는 명사 자리이다. 'Mr. Hackett 의 ___은 홍보 투어의 일부이다'라는 문맥이므로 모든 보기가 정답의 후 보이다. 앞부분에서 Waco의 중앙 강당에서 강연을 한다고 했으므로 Mr. Hackett이 홍보 투어의 일부로 이곳에 등장함을 확인할 수 있다. 따라서 (C) appearance(등장)가 정답이다.

어휘 acceptance n. 수락, 용인 conclusion n. 마무리, 결론, 체결
approach n. 접근, 학습법; v. 접근하다

145 시간 표현과 일치하는 시제의 동사 채우기 · 중 ●●○

해설 문장에 주어(He)만 있고 동사가 없으므로 동사인 모든 보기가 정답의 후보이 다. 현재 완료를 나타내는 시간 표현(over the past 20 years)이 있으므로 현재 완료 시제 (A) has authored가 정답이다. 현재 시제 (B)는 주로 현재 의 상태, 일반적인 사실, 반복적인 행동이나 습관을 나타내며, 미래 시제 (C) 는 미래에 일어날 일, 미래 상황에 대한 추측이나 의지를 나타낸다. 현재 진행 시제 (D)는 현재 진행되고 있는 일을 나타낸다.

어휘 author v. 쓰다, 저술하다

146 알맞은 문장 고르기 · 중 ●●○

해석 (A) 마침내, Hackett의 발견이 인정될 것입니다.
(B) 수상작들은 행사 이후에 발표될 것입니다.
(C) 저희의 웹사이트에서 쿠폰 코드를 다운받으십시오.
(D) 처음 입장하는 50명은 무료 책을 받을 것입니다.

해설 앞 문장 'An entry fee of $15 will be charged at the door.'에서 입장료 15달러는 출입구에서 부과될 것이라고 했으므로 빈칸에는 입장과 관련된 내 용이 들어가야 함을 알 수 있다. 따라서 (D)가 정답이다.

어휘 discovery n. 발견 recognize v. 인정하다, 알아보다
winning entry phr. 수상작 enter v. 입장하다, 들어가다

PART 7

147-148번은 다음 기사에 관한 문제입니다.

> ### Hurlimann사가 Gilford 쇼핑센터에 문을 열다
> #### Fred Sharpe 작성
>
> OWENSBURG—스위스의 프리미엄 초콜릿 제조업체 Hurlimann사가 Owensburg에 그것의 첫 번째 매장을 연다. 이것은 1월 8일에 Gilford 쇼핑 센터에서의 개관식 일정을 잡아두었다.
>
> 매장 관리자 Joanne Lutz에 따르면, [148]그것의 초콜릿을 구입하는 첫 100 명의 고객들은 무료 사탕 한 박스를 받을 것이다. 그 외에, 고객들은 처음 2주 동안 가게에서 선정된 제품들의 구매에 대해 50퍼센트 할인을 받을 수 있다.
>
> 100년 전에 설립된 Hurlimann사는 오랫동안 그것의 맛있는 초콜릿 제품들 을 전 세계의 판매업자들에게 수출해왔다. "[147-C]저희는 마침내 해외에 자사 지점들을 열고 있는 중이기 때문에 미래가 어떻게 될지 기대됩니다."라고 최 고경영자 David Carle이 말했다.
>
> ribbon-cutting n. 개관식, 준공식 export v. 수출하다
> delicate adj. 맛있는, 섬세한 vendor n. 판매업자, 판매 회사

147 Not/True 문제 · 중 ●●○

해석 Hurlimann사에 대해 언급된 것은?
(A) David Carle을 그것의 새로운 최고경영자로 막 임명했다.
(B) 백 년 전에 Owensburg에 설립되었다.
(C) 최근에 국제적으로 매장들을 열기 시작했다.
(D) 이것의 특색 있는 맛있는 것들의 라인을 확장하고 있다.

해설 지문의 'we are ~ opening our own branches overseas'에서 저희, 즉 Hurlimann사는 해외에 자사 지점들을 열고 있는 중이라고 했으므로 (C)는 지문의 내용과 일치한다. 따라서 (C)가 정답이다. (A), (B), (D)는 지문에 언 급되지 않은 내용이다.

어휘 appoint v. 임명하다, 정하다 delicacy n. 맛있는 것, 별미

패러프레이징

> opening ~ branches overseas 해외에 지점들을 열다 → open shops internationally 국제적으로 매장들을 열다

148 육하원칙 문제 · 중 ●●○

해석 고객들은 어떻게 무료 상품을 받을 수 있는가?
(A) 몇 가지 설문조사 질문들에 답함으로써
(B) 가게의 첫 100명의 구매자들 중에 있음으로써
(C) 특별히 선정된 물품들을 구매함으로써
(D) 2주 내로 재방문함으로써

해설 지문의 'the first 100 customers who purchase its chocolate will receive a free box of candy'에서 그것, 즉 Hurlimann사의 초콜릿을 사 는 첫 100명의 고객들은 무료 사탕 한 박스를 받을 것이라고 했으므로 (B)가 정답이다.

패러프레이징

> a complimentary product 무료 상품 → a free box of candy 무료 사탕 한 박스
> customers who purchase 구매하는 고객들 → buyers 구매자들

149-150번은 다음 웹페이지에 관한 문제입니다.

> ### Canbury 병원 인트라넷
>
> **홈 >> 환자 관리 >> Dr. Hatch >> 환자 정보**
>
> [149]환자 이름: Charlotte Reed
> 전화번호: 555-4839
>
> **의료 기록**
> [149]환자는 다음의 과거 증상들을 경험했습니다:
>
> | | | |
> |---|---|---|
> | ☐ 흉통 | ☑ 복통 | ☐ 두통 |
> | ☑ 귀 통증 | [149]☑ 계절성 알레르기 | ☑ 피부 염증 |
> | ☑ 목 염증 | ☐ 허리 통증 | ☐ 스트레스 또는 불안 |
>
> **예약 센터**
> 환자의 Dr. Michael Hatch와의 다음 예약은
> 4월 22일 월요일, 오전 11시 30분으로 예정되어 있습니다.
>
> **예약 일정을 변경하십니까?** ● 네 ○ 아니요
> 새로운 예약 시간을 입력하시려면 여기를 클릭하십시오.
>
> **참고:**
> [150]Dr. Hatch는 심장 건강에 대한 강연을 하기 위해 4월 21일부터 24일

까지 런던에 출장을 갈 것이며, 이에 따라 Ms. Reed의 건강 검진 일정이 변경되어야 합니다.

patient n. 환자 **symptom** n. 증상, 징후 **ache** n. 통증, 아픔
irritation n. 염증, 자극 **anxiety** n. 불안, 염려 **checkup** n. 건강 검진

---

149 육하원칙 문제 하 ●○○

해석 Ms. Reed는 과거에 무엇을 경험했는가?
(A) 심장 문제
(B) 허리 통증
(C) 알레르기 반응
(D) 업무 스트레스

해설 지문의 'Patient Name: Charlotte Reed', 'Patient has experienced past symptoms of:', '☑ seasonal allergies'에서 Ms. Reed가 과거 계절성 알레르기 증상을 경험했다고 했으므로 (C)가 정답이다.

어휘 **trouble** n. 통증, 병, 문제 **reaction** n. 반응, 반작용

---

150 육하원칙 문제 하 ●○○

해석 Ms. Reed의 건강 검진 일정은 왜 변경되어야 하는가?
(A) Canbury 병원은 하루 동안 문을 닫을 것이다.
(B) 그녀의 보험 세부 사항을 제출하지 않았다.
(C) 그녀의 의사가 출장을 갈 예정이다.
(D) 몇몇 검사 결과들이 들어오지 않았다.

해설 지문의 'Dr. Hatch will be traveling to London ~, and thus Ms. Reed's checkup must be rescheduled.'에서 Dr. Hatch가 런던에 출장을 갈 것이며, 이에 따라 Ms. Reed의 건강 검진 일정이 변경되어야 한다고 했으므로 (C)가 정답이다.

어휘 **physician** n. 의사

패러프레이징

will be traveling 출장을 갈 것이다 → is leaving on a trip 출장을 갈 예정이다

151-152번은 다음 메시지 대화문에 관한 문제입니다.

Pam Gordon [오전 9시 10분]
저는 방금 당신이 지난주에 다녀온 출장에 대한 출장 비용 환급 양식을 당신에게 이메일로 보냈어요. ¹⁵¹/¹⁵²당신은 이번 달 말까지 그것을 제출할 수 있나요? ¹⁵¹그렇지 않으면, 당신의 돈은 당신의 다음 급료와 함께 **상환되지 않을 거예요.**

Hadassah Aboud [오전 9시 12분]
물론이죠. ¹⁵²저는 돌아오자마자 인트라넷에서 양식을 출력해서 그것을 회계 부서 사무실로 바로 가져갔어요.

Pam Gordon [오전 9시 13분]
좋아요! 저는 당신이 그것을 어디로 가져가야 하는지를 알고 있는지 확실하지 않았어요.

expense n. 비용 **reimbursement** n. 환급, 상환
turn in phr. 제출하다, 반납하다 **repay** v. 상환하다, 되돌려주다

---

151 추론 문제 상 ●●●

해석 양식에 대해 암시되는 것은?

(A) Ms. Aboud는 주로 그것을 회계 사무실에서 가지고 온다.
(B) 부서의 상관에 의해 서명되어야 한다.
(C) 정해진 시간 내에 제출되어야 한다.
(D) Ms. Gordon은 최근에 인트라넷에서 그것을 다운받았다.

해설 지문의 'Could you turn it in by the end of the month? Otherwise, your money won't be repaid'에서 Ms. Gordon이 이번 달 말까지 그것, 즉 양식을 제출할 수 있는지 물은 후, 그렇지 않으면, 당신의 돈은 상환되지 않을 것이라고 했으므로 양식이 정해진 시간 이내에 제출되어야 한다는 사실을 추론할 수 있다. 따라서 (C)가 정답이다.

어휘 **pick up** phr. ~을 가지고 오다, ~를 태우러 가다
supervisor n. 상관, 관리자 **submit** v. 제출하다

패러프레이징

turn it in by the end of the month 이번 달 말까지 제출하다 → be submitted within a set amount of time 정해진 시간 내에 제출되다

---

152 의도 파악 문제 중 ●●○

해석 오전 9시 12분에, Ms. Aboud가 "Absolutely"라고 썼을 때 그녀가 의도한 것은?
(A) 몇몇 일에서 동료보다 앞서 있다.
(B) 여행 비용에 대해 되돌려 받았다.
(C) 양식을 제출하러 가는 중이다.
(D) 이미 업무를 완료했다.

해설 지문의 'Could you turn it in by the end of the month?'에서 Ms. Gordon이 이번 달 말까지 그것, 즉 양식을 제출할 수 있는지 묻자, Ms. Aboud가 'Absolutely.'(물론이죠)라고 한 후, 'I printed out the form ~ and took it to the ~ office right away.'에서 양식을 출력해서 그것을 사무실로 바로 가져갔다고 한 것을 통해 Ms. Aboud가 이미 업무를 완료했다는 것을 알 수 있다. 따라서 (D)가 정답이다.

어휘 **on one's way** phr. ~로 가는 중에 **hand in** phr. 제출하다
complete v. 완료하다

153-154번은 다음 공고에 관한 문제입니다.

Halliston 극장

방문객들은 ¹⁵³다음 주에 저희 시설이 보수 작업에 협조하기 위해 폐쇄될 것임을 알아두시기 바랍니다. 구체적으로, ¹⁵³저희는 영화 팬들이 직원의 도움 없이 그들의 모바일 기기의 **전자 티켓을 사용해서 극장에 입장하는 것을 가능하게 하는 새로운 장비를 설치할 것입니다.** 전자 티켓을 사용하는 새로운 과정에 대한 더 많은 정보를 위해 저희 웹사이트를 방문하십시오. 추가적으로, 저희는 저희의 스크린 중 다섯 개가 3-D 영화 성능을 제공하기 위해 업데이트될 것이라는 점을 발표하게 되어 기쁩니다. 이는 저희 홈페이지에서 최근에 실시된 고객 설문 조사에서 가장 공통적으로 언급된 제안사항을 다루려는 노력입니다. 마지막으로, 영화 팬들은 이제 ¹⁵⁴www.hallistontheater.com에 새롭게 추가된 영화 후기란을 확인하실 수 있습니다. 이번 리모델링 기간 동안 여러분의 이해에 감사드립니다.

accommodate v. 협조하다, 맞추다 **renovation** n. 보수, 수리
capability n. 성능, 능력 **address** v. 다루다, 처리하다
conduct v. 실시하다, 하다 **questionnaire** n. 설문 조사

---

153 육하원칙 문제 중 ●●○

해석 공고에 따르면, 다음 주에 무엇이 일어날 것인가?

(A) 인기 있는 영화의 속편 개봉
(B) 영화배우와의 사인 행사
(C) 극장 내 몇몇 좌석들의 교체
(D) 고객 사용을 위한 몇몇 장치들의 설치

해설 지문의 'facility will be closed next week to accommodate renovation work'와 'we will be installing new equipment that will allow movie-goers to enter the theater using electronic tickets'에서 다음 주에 시설이 보수 작업에 협조하기 위해 폐쇄될 것이며, 영화 팬들이 전자 티켓을 사용하여 극장에 입장하는 것을 가능하게 하는 새로운 장비를 설치할 것이라고 했으므로 (D)가 정답이다.

어휘 premiere n. 개봉, 초연 sequel n. 속편, 결과
autograph n. 사인; v. 사인을 해주다

패러프레이징

installing ~ equipment 장비를 설치하다 → setup of ~ devices 상치늘의 설치

154 추론 문제 상 ●●●

해석 Halliston 극장에 대해 암시되는 것은?
(A) 온라인에서 이용 가능한 가격 정보를 업데이트했다.
(B) 그것의 웹사이트에 후기가 없었다.
(C) 고객 설문 조사 결과를 소식지에 게재했다.
(D) 리모델링할 때까지 모바일 티켓을 제공하지 않았다.

해설 지문의 'the newly added movie review section on www.hallistontheater.com'에서 www.hallistontheater.com에 새롭게 추가된 영화 후기란이라고 했으므로 이전에는 웹사이트에 후기를 쓰거나 볼 수 있는 후기란이 없었다는 사실을 추론할 수 있다. 따라서 (B)가 정답이다.

어휘 pricing information phr. 가격 정보 newsletter n. 소식지, 화보

155-157번은 다음 기사에 관한 문제입니다.

Drew Shields가 *Mornings on 7*의 진행자가 되다

PNW 채널 7은 155-ADrew Shields가 오전 6시부터 오전 9시까지 평일 아침 토크쇼인 *Mornings on 7*의 진행자로서 Gail Figgis를 대신할 것이라고 발표했다. ― [1] ―. 그의 방송 첫날은 8월 19일 월요일이 될 것이다. "저는 Gail과 일하는 것을 그리워할 것이지만, 155-B저는 방송국이 좋은 선택을 했다고 생각합니다. Drew는 열정적이고 다재다능한 이야기꾼이라서, 우리는 틀림없이 함께 잘 일할 것입니다."라고 155-A지금까지 거의 20년 동안 쇼에서 Ms. Figgis의 공동 진행자였던 Wallace Jeffers가 말했다.

― [2] ―. 155-C/D/157Mr. Shields는 8년 전에 일반 주제 기자로 방송국에 입사한 이후 PNW 채널 7에서 수많은 뉴스 속보를 다뤄온 수상 경력이 있는 뉴스캐스터이다. ― [3] ―. "저는 새로운 것을 시도할 수 있는 기회에 대해 정말 감사하지만, 제가 매우 유명했던 누군가의 자리를 대신할 것이라는 것을 자각합니다. Gail Figgis는 살아있는 전설입니다."라고 그가 말했다.

거의 35년간의 방송 이후에 은퇴하면서, Ms. Figgis는 그녀의 경력에 대한 회고록을 쓰는 데 시간을 쓸 계획이다. ― [4] ―. 156그녀는 또한 때때로 PNW 채널 7의 저녁 뉴스 특파원으로 활동할 것이다.

air n. 방송 passionate adj. 열정적인 versatile adj. 다재다능한, 다방면의
be bound to phr. 틀림없이 ~할 것이다
award-winning adj. 수상 경력이 있는 presenter n. 뉴스캐스터, 진행자
cover v. 다루다, 포함하다 numerous adj. 수많은
breaking story phr. 뉴스 속보 grateful adj. 감사하는

---

devote v. 쓰다, 바치다 memoir n. 회고록
occasional adj. 때때로의, 가끔의 correspondent n. 특파원, 기자

155 Not/True 문제 상 ●●●

해석 Mr. Shields에 대해 언급되지 않은 것은?
(A) 오랜 진행자를 대신할 것이다.
(B) Mr. Jeffers가 그를 쇼의 한 직책으로 선택했다.
(C) 그의 방송 일에 대해 상을 받았다.
(D) PNW 채널 7이 8년 전에 그를 고용했다.

해설 지문의 'I think the station made a good choice'에서 저, 즉 Mr. Jeffers는 방송국이 좋은 선택, 즉 Mr. Shields를 쇼의 진행자로 선택한 것이 좋은 선택이라고 생각한다고 했으므로 (B)는 지문의 내용과 일치하지 않는다. 따라서 (B)가 정답이다. (A)는 'Drew Shields will be replacing Gail Figgis'와 'Wallace Jeffers, ~ Ms. Figgis's co-host ~ for nearly 20 years now'에서 Mr. Shields가 Ms. Figgis를 대신할 것이며, 지금까지 거의 20년 동안 Mr. Jeffers가 Ms. Figgis의 공동 진행자였다고 했으므로 지문의 내용과 일치한다. (C)와 (D)는 'Mr. Shields is an award-winning presenter who has covered ~ breaking stories for PNW Channel 7 since joining the station ~ eight years ago.'에서 Mr. Shields는 8년 전에 방송국에 입사한 이후 PNW 채널 7에서 뉴스 속보를 다뤄온 수상 경력이 있는 뉴스캐스터라고 했으므로 지문의 내용과 일치한다.

어휘 take over phr. 대신하다, 인계하다 longtime adj. 오랜, 여러 해의

패러프레이징

will be replacing 대신할 것이다 → will be taking over 대신할 것이다
co-host ~ for nearly 20 years 거의 20년 동안의 공동 진행자 → a longtime presenter 오랜 진행자
award-winning 수상 경력이 있는 → has been awarded 상을 받았다
joining the station ~ eight years ago 8년 전에 방송국에 입사하다 → PNW Channel 7 hired ~ eight years earlier PNW 채널 7이 8년 전에 고용했다

156 육하원칙 문제 중 ●●○

해석 Ms. Figgis는 무엇을 할 계획인가?
(A) 다른 방송국에 지원한다
(B) 진행자로 일한다
(C) 프로그램에 기여한다
(D) 토크쇼를 시작한다

해설 지문의 'She will also work as ~ correspondent for ~ evening news.'에서 그녀, 즉 Ms. Figgis는 또한 저녁 뉴스의 특파원으로 활동할 것이라고 했으므로 (C)가 정답이다.

어휘 apply v. 지원하다, 신청하다 contribute v. 기여하다

패러프레이징

work as ~ correspondent for ~ evening news 저녁 뉴스의 특파원으로 활동하다 → Contribute to a program 프로그램에 기여하다

157 문장 위치 찾기 문제 중 ●●○

해석 [1], [2], [3], [4]로 표시된 위치 중, 다음 문장이 들어갈 곳으로 가장 적절한 것은?

"이것 이전에, 그는 특집 기자로 일했고 URS 채널 12의 *Nightly News*에 출연했다."

(A) [1]

(B) [2]

(C) [3]

(D) [4]

해설 주어진 문장에서 이것 이전에 그는 특집 기자로 일했고 URS 채널 12
의 *Nightly News*에 출연했다고 했으므로, 이 문장이 그의 경력 활동과
관련된 내용이 나오는 부분에 들어가야 함을 알 수 있다. [3]의 앞 문장인
'Mr. Shields ~ has covered numerous breaking stories ~ since
joining the station as a general assignment reporter eight years
ago.'에서 Mr. Shields는 8년 전에 일반 주제 기자로 방송국에 입사한 이
후 수많은 뉴스 속보를 다뤘다고 했으므로, [3]에 제시된 문장이 들어가면
Mr. Shields는 일반 주제 기자로 8년 전에 방송국에 입사했고 이것 이전에
특집 기자로 URS 채널 12의 *Nightly News*에 출연했다는 자연스러운 문
맥이 된다는 것을 알 수 있다. 따라서 (C)가 정답이다.

어휘 **prior to** phr. 이전에, 앞서   **feature** n. 특집 (기사)   **appear** v. 출연하다

158-160번은 다음 안내문에 관한 문제입니다.

Astrapia 항공사 ― 보상 포인트를 국내선 좌석 업그레이드에 이용하기

더 높은 등급에서 비행하도록 당신의 포인트를 사용하기 위해서, ¹⁵⁹**당신이 티
켓을 예약할 때** 저희의 웹사이트에서 "보상 포인트 업그레이드" 옵션을 선택
하세요. 티켓이 구매된 이후에, 업그레이드는 세 가지 방법 중 하나로 요청될
수 있습니다. 첫 번째로, 당신은 Astrapia 항공사 콜센터로 전화할 수 있습니
다. 두 번째로, 당신은 저희 웹사이트에서 당신의 예약을 변경할 수 있습니
다. 그리고 세 번째로, 당신은 체크인 카운터에서 저희의 공항 직원 중 한 명과 이
야기할 수 있습니다. 당신이 어떤 방법을 선택하는지에 상관없이, ¹⁵⁸⁻ᶜ**반드시
당신의 비행 최소 24시간 전에 요청을 하십시오.** 아래의 표는 저희가 비행
하는 다양한 지역들 내에서 하나의 등급에서 다른 등급으로 업그레이드하기 위
해 포인트가 얼마나 필요한지를 나타냅니다. ¹⁶⁰**몇몇 항공편들에서는 업그레
이드가 가능하지 않을 수도 있다는 점을 유의해주십시오.**

	이코노미석에서 프리미엄 이코노미석으로	프리미엄 이코노미석에서 비즈니스석으로	¹⁶⁰비즈니스석에서 1등석으로
¹⁵⁸⁻ᴰ유럽	¹⁵⁸⁻ᴰ20,000포인트	¹⁵⁸⁻ᴰ35,000포인트	¹⁵⁸⁻ᴰ50,000포인트
¹⁶⁰북아메리카	20,000포인트	35,000포인트	
¹⁵⁸⁻ᴰ중앙아시아	¹⁵⁸⁻ᴰ20,000포인트	¹⁵⁸⁻ᴰ35,000포인트	¹⁵⁸⁻ᴰ50,000포인트
동남아시아	20,000포인트		

비고: 1포인트 = 비행한 1마일

domestic adj. 국내의   **reserve** v. 예약하다   **modify** v. 수정하다
agent n. 직원   **regardless of** phr. ~에 상관없이   **indicate** v. 나타내다

158 Not/True 문제 　　　　　　　　　　　　중 ●●○

해석 Astrapia 항공사에 대해 사실인 것은?

(A) 각 좌석 등급마다 다른 정책을 가지고 있다.

(B) 다른 항공사들과의 제휴 프로그램을 유지한다.

(C) 비행 24시간 이내에는 업그레이드를 허용하지 않는다.

(D) 중앙아시아 항공편에 가장 많은 포인트를 필요로 한다.

해설 지문의 'be sure to make your request at least 24 hours before
your flight'에서 반드시 당신의 비행 최소 24시간 전에 요청, 즉 좌석 업그
레이드 요청을 하라고 했으므로 (C)는 지문의 내용과 일치한다. 따라서 (C)
가 정답이다. (A)와 (B)는 지문에 언급되지 않은 내용이다. (D)는 'Europe',
'20,000 points', '35,000 points', '50,000 points'와 'Central Asia',
'20,000 points', '35,000 points', '50,000 points'에서 유럽과 중앙아시

아 항공편의 업그레이드에 동일한 포인트를 필요로 하는 것을 알 수 있으므로
지문의 내용과 일치하지 않는다.

어휘 **policy** n. 정책   **maintain** v. 유지하다
partner program phr. 제휴 프로그램

159 동의어 찾기 문제 　　　　　　　　　　중 ●●○

해석 1문단 두 번째 줄의 단어 "reserve"는 의미상 ~와 가장 가깝다.

(A) 모으다

(B) 따로 떼어두다

(C) 저지하다

(D) 사용하기 위해 마련하다

해설 reserve를 포함한 구절 'when you reserve a ticket'에서 당신이 티켓을
예약할 때라고 했으므로 reserve는 '예약하다'라는 뜻으로 사용되었다. 따
라서 '사용하기 위해 마련하다'라는 뜻을 가진 (D) arrange to use가 정답
이다.

160 추론 문제 　　　　　　　　　　　　　중 ●●○

해석 북아메리카 내의 항공편에 대해 추론될 수 있는 것은?

(A) 티켓 전액 환불은 제공되지 않는다.

(B) 항공사 웹사이트를 사용해서만 예약될 수 있다.

(C) 승객 보상 포인트를 받지 못한다.

(D) 모든 좌석 등급에 업그레이드가 가능한 것은 아니다.

해설 지문의 'Please note that upgrades may not be possible on some
flights.'에서 몇몇 항공편에서는 업그레이드가 가능하지 않을 수도 있다는
점을 유의해달라고 했고, 'North America', 'From Business Class to
First Class'에서 북아메리카 항공편의 경우 비즈니스석에서 1등석으로 업
그레이드를 할 때 필요한 포인트가 나와 있지 않으므로 북아메리카 내의 항공
편에서 모든 좌석 등급에 업그레이드가 가능한 것은 아니라는 사실을 추론할
수 있다. 따라서 (D)가 정답이다.

어휘 **earn** v. 받다, 얻다   **available** adj. 가능한, 이용 가능한

패러프레이징

possible 가능한 → available 가능한

161-163번은 다음 기사에 관한 문제입니다.

모든 돈이 다 어디로 갔는가?
Jackson McGuire 작성

Lindow시―¹⁶¹**Beanzo 카페가 그것이 8월 1일에 현금을 없앤다고 발표했
을 때,** 이것은 전혀 놀라운 일이 아니었다. 그것은 전자 결제 시스템을 위해
현금을 포기한 첫 번째 지역 사업체가 아니다.

사실, ¹⁶¹**점점 더 많은 수의 사업체들이 그 변경을 하고 있다.** 예를 들어, 5월
에 동전과 지폐 받는 것을 중단한 Blondah 부티크의 가게 소유주인 Marie
Ramirez는 이 방식에 대해 만족스러워한다. "저는 더 이상 지폐를 세는 것, 잔
돈을 가지고 있는 것, 또는 계산대에서 돈을 잃어버리는 것에 대해 걱정하지 않
습니다."라고 그녀가 말했다.

다른 사업체들은 현금을 없애는 것에 대한 그들만의 이유가 있다. 귀금속 상
인 Rajit Banga에게, 은행에 현금 예금하는 것을 피할 수 있는 것은 그가 많
은 양의 현금을 들고 이동하는 수고를 덜어 준다. 한편, ¹⁶³**편의점 매장 관리자
Anna Mellor에게는 카드 지불로 거래를 더 빨리 처리하는 것이 그녀의 고
객들에게 더 나은 경험을 만든다.** "사람들은 바쁘고 일이 바로 완료되길 원
해요."라고 그녀가 말했다.

소비자들은 어떻게 생각할까? 설문조사에 따르면 ¹⁶²Lindow시 주민들의 대략 20퍼센트는 더 이상 현금을 사용하지 않고, 50퍼센트는 완전히 그만둘 계획이다. 이 패턴이 계속된다면, 모든 사람들은 현금이 더 이상 쓸모가 없는 것이 되어가는 현실을 마주해야 할 것이다.

---

cashless adj. 현금이 없는   hardly adv. 전혀 ~은 아니다
give up phr. 포기하다, 그만두다   switch n. 변경, 전환
arrangement n. 방식, 준비   deposit n. 예금, 보증금; v. 예금하다
transaction n. 거래, 처리   physical currency phr. 현금
obsolete adj. 더 이상 쓸모가 없는, 구식의

161 주제 찾기 문제   중 ●●●○

해석 기사는 주로 무엇에 대한 것인가?
(A) 결제를 용이하게 하는 기술의 향상
(B) 시스템을 변경하는 것에서 생겨난 문제
(C) 카페가 현금 거래를 없애도록 이끈 사건
(D) 사업체들이 추세를 수용하는 이유들

해설 지문의 'When Beanzo Café announced it was going cashless ~, it was hardly a surprise.'에서 Beanzo 카페가 현금을 없앤다고 발표했을 때, 이것은 전혀 놀라운 일이 아니었다고 했고 'a growing number of businesses are making the switch'에서 점점 더 많은 수의 사업체들이 그 변경, 즉 현금을 없애는 변경을 하고 있다고 한 후, 여러 사업체들이 현금을 없애는 추세를 수용하는 이유들에 대해 설명하고 있으므로 (D)가 정답이다.

어휘 facilitate v. 용이하게 하다, 촉진하다   eliminate v. 없애다, 제거하다
transaction n. 거래, 처리   embrace v. 수용하다, 기꺼이 받아들이다
trend n. 추세, 유행

162 추론 문제   중 ●●●○

해석 Lindow시에 대해 추론될 수 있는 것은?
(A) 상류층을 대상으로 한 다수의 사업체들을 끌어들이고 있다.
(B) 시민들이 현금이 없는 프로그램들을 지지하기 위해 투표했다.
(C) 정책을 받아들이는 소비자들에게 장려금을 제공하고 있다.
(D) 주민들은 곧 돈을 가지고 다니는 것을 그만둘 수도 있다.

해설 지문의 'nearly 20 percent of Lindow City residents no longer use any cash, and 50 percent plan to stop entirely'에서 Lindow시 주민들의 대략 20퍼센트는 더 이상 현금을 사용하지 않고, 50퍼센트는 완전히 그만둘 계획이라고 했으므로 주민들은 곧 돈을 가지고 다니는 것을 그만둘 수도 있다는 사실을 추론할 수 있다. 따라서 (D)가 정답이다.

어휘 upscale adj. 상류층을 대상으로 한, 고가의   incentive n. 장려금

패러프레이징

no longer use any cash 더 이상 현금을 사용하지 않다 → stop carrying money 돈을 가지고 다니는 것을 그만두다

163 추론 문제   중 ●●●○

해석 Ms. Mellor는 어떤 문제에 대해 걱정할 것 같은가?
(A) 위조지폐
(B) 긴 대기 시간
(C) 상점 보안
(D) 잃어버린 돈

해설 지문의 'for ~ Anna Mellor, processing transactions more quickly with card payments creates a better experience for her customers'

에서 Ms. Mellor에게는 카드 지불로 거래를 더 빨리 처리하는 것이 그녀의 고객들에게 더 나은 경험을 만들며, 'People are in a hurry ~ and want things done right away.'에서 사람들은 바쁘고 일이 빨리 완료되길 원한다고 했으므로 Ms. Mellor가 일이 바로 완료되는 데 지장을 주고 바쁜 사람들에게 불편함을 줄 수 있는 긴 대기 시간을 걱정할 것이라는 사실을 추론할 수 있다. 따라서 (B)가 정답이다.

어휘 counterfeit adj. 위조의   security n. 보안   missing adj. 잃어버린

164-167번은 다음 온라인 채팅 대화문에 관한 문제입니다.

Kelsey Chase [오후 1시 50분]
¹⁶⁴누가 사무실 의자 공급업체를 추천해줄 수 있나요? 제 것이 아까 고장 났어요.

Miles Dunphy [오후 1시 52분]
창고를 확인해봤나요? 우리는 거기에 몇몇 여분의 것들을 가지고 있을 수도 있어요.

Kelsey Chase [오후 1시 53분]
네, 하지만 다 떨어진 것 같아요.

Megan Contreras [오후 1시 55분]
우리의 사무실 의자들은 그렇게 튼튼하지 않아요. ^{165-D}당신은 새로운 것에 얼마를 쓸 수 있나요?

Kelsey Chase [오후 1시 55분]
제가 알고 있는 바로는, ^{165-D}30달러보다 적게요.

Megan Contreras [오후 1시 56분]
저는 오늘 오후에 몇몇 프린터 잉크 때문에 Fastmax로 향하려고 했어요. ^{165-B/166}제가 당신을 위해 하나 구입해줄 수 있어요. 저는 그저 제가 지금 작업하고 있는 프레젠테이션만 끝내면 되요.

Kelsey Chase [오후 1시 57분]
천천히 하세요. ¹⁶⁶저는 우선 플라스틱 의자를 사용하고 있어요. 하지만 만약 당신이 간다면 제게 알려주세요. 제가 너무 바쁘지 않다면 저는 함께 가고 싶어요.

Miles Dunphy [오후 1시 59분]
당신이 며칠 동안 기다릴 의향이 있다면 제가 온라인에서 하나 찾았어요. 그건 www.everyoffice.com에 있고 24달러밖에 들지 않아요.

Kelsey Chase [오후 2시]
고마워요, Miles! 만약 Megan과 제가 오늘 오후에 가지 않는다면 제가 그것을 꼭 살펴볼게요.

Miles Dunphy [오후 2시 1분]
문제없어요. ¹⁶⁷저는 다시 일하러 가봐야겠어요. 제게 한 시간 후에 마감인 보고서가 있거든요.

---

recommend v. 추천하다   supplier n. 공급업체, 공급자
break down phr. 고장 나다, 실패하다   stockroom n. 창고
durable adj. 튼튼한, 내구성이 있는   head out phr. ~로 향하다
come along phr. 함께 가다, 생기다   due adj. 마감의

164 육하원칙 문제   중 ●●●○

해석 Mr. Chase는 무엇을 하기를 원하는가?
(A) 제품 설문조사를 실시하다
(B) 사무실 컴퓨터를 수리받는다
(C) 가구 한 점을 교체한다

(D) 창고에 있는 물품들의 수를 센다

해설 지문의 'Could someone recommend a supplier of office chairs? Mine broke down earlier.'에서 Mr. Chase가 사무실 의자 공급업체를 추천해달라고 하며 본인의 것이 아까 고장 났다고 했으므로 (C)가 정답이다.

어휘 conduct v. 실시하다, 하다; n. 행동 repair v. 수리하다

패러프레이징

chairs 의자 → furniture 가구

165 Not/True 문제

중 ●●○

해석 Ms. Contreras에 대해 언급된 것은?
(A) 사무실 예산을 담당한다.
(B) 물품을 살 의향이 있다.
(C) 인쇄소에서 방금 돌아왔다.
(D) 프린터 잉크에 30달러까지 쓸 수 있다.

해설 지문의 'I could get one for you.'에서 Ms. Contreras가 하나, 즉 사무실 의자 하나를 구입해줄 수 있다고 했으므로 (B)는 지문의 내용과 일치한다. 따라서 (B)가 정답이다. (A)와 (C)는 지문에 언급되지 않은 내용이다. (D)는 'How much can you spend on a new one?'에서 Ms. Contreras가 새로운 것, 즉 새로운 사무실 의자에 얼마를 쓸 수 있는지 묻자, 'less than $30'에서 Mr. Chase가 30달러보다 적게 쓸 수 있다고는 했으나, 프린터 잉크에 쓸 수 있는 비용에 대해서는 언급되지 않았으므로 지문의 내용과 일치하지 않는다.

어휘 responsible for phr. ~을 담당하는, 책임이 있는 budget n. 예산 up to phr. ~까지

패러프레이징

get one 하나를 구입하다 → pick up an item 물품을 사다

166 의도 파악 문제

중 ●●○

해석 오후 1시 57분에, Mr. Chase가 "Take your time"이라고 썼을 때 그가 의도한 것은?
(A) Ms. Contreras는 보고서를 끝내야 한다.
(B) 대안 마련을 했다.
(C) Ms. Contreras는 초과 근무 시간을 신청해야 한다.
(D) 그 사이에 해야 할 많은 일이 있다.

해설 지문의 'I could get one for you.'에서 Ms. Contreras가 하나를 당신, 즉 Mr. Chase를 위해 구입해줄 수 있다고 하자, Mr. Chase가 'Take your time.'(천천히 하세요)이라고 한 후, 'I'm using a plastic chair for now.'에서 우선은 플라스틱 의자를 사용하고 있다고 한 것을 통해, Mr. Chase가 대안을 마련했다는 것을 알 수 있다. 따라서 (B)가 정답이다.

어휘 alternative n. 대안; adj. 대체의 arrangement n. 마련, 준비, 계획 overtime n. 초과 근무 in the meantime phr. 그 사이(동안)에

167 육하원칙 문제

상 ●●●

해석 Mr. Dunphy는 왜 다시 일하러 가봐야 하는가?
(A) 발표를 준비하고 있다.
(B) 동료와 만날 계획을 세웠다.
(C) 맞춰야 할 임박한 마감 시간이 있다.
(D) 한 시간 후에 가게로 향할 것이다.

해설 지문의 'I'd better get back to work. I have a report due in an hour.'에서 Mr. Dunphy가 한 시간 후에 마감인 보고서가 있어서 다시 일하러 가

봐야겠다고 했으므로 (C)가 정답이다.

어휘 coworker n. 동료, 협력자 imminent adj. 임박한, 촉박한 deadline n. 마감 시간

패러프레이징

due in an hour 한 시간 후에 마감인 → an imminent deadline 임박한 마감 시간

168-171번은 다음 이메일에 관한 문제입니다.

수신: Helena Wang <hwang@acmemail.com>
발신: Carol Vine <vinecaro@rayamedicalclinic.com>
제목: 예약
날짜: 6월 1일

Ms. Wang께,

[168]다시 한 번 저희 병원에서 귀하의 신체검사를 할 때가 되었습니다. 귀하의 의료 보험 조항에 따라, [169]귀하는 이 절차를 2년마다 받아야 합니다. 이 예약은 한 시간 이상 걸리지 않을 것이고, 제가 이미 6월 12일 화요일 오전 10시 30분에 잠정적으로 귀하의 것을 예약 잡았습니다. [169]귀하는 지난번과 같은 의사인 Dr. Reena Kapur를 만날 것입니다. 만약 귀하가 그 시간에 오실 수 없다면, 적절한 시간과 날짜를 찾기 위해 555-3044로 저희에게 전화해 주십시오.

귀하의 예약 전에, 환자들은 적어도 7시간 동안 식사하는 것을 삼가도록 요구됩니다. 그리고 [170]물을 제외하고 아무것도 마시지 마십시오. 이것은 실시될 피검사의 정확도를 보장하기 위함입니다.

귀하가 다른 종류의 검사를 요청하고 싶으시다면, 무엇이 가능한지 알기 위해 저희 웹사이트에 주저 말고 방문해주십시오. [171]귀하의 의료 결과는 귀하와 귀하의 보험 제공 기관에 이메일로 보내질 것입니다.

감사드리며, 저희는 귀하를 곧 뵙기를 바랍니다.

Carol Vine
고객 서비스 직원
Raya 병원

physical examination phr. 신체검사 undergo v. 받다, 겪다
procedure n. 절차, 방법 tentatively adv. 잠정적으로
physician n. 의사 suitable adj. 적절한 prior to phr. 전에, 앞서
refrain from phr. ~을 삼가다 ensure v. 보장하다
accuracy n. 정확도, 정확 conduct v. 실시하다, 안내하다; n. 행동
forward v. 보내다, 전달하다

168 목적 찾기 문제

중 ●●○

해석 Ms. Vine은 왜 이메일을 작성하는가?
(A) 계약서의 조항들을 설명하기 위해
(B) 인터뷰를 위한 시간을 준비하기 위해
(C) 고객에게 예약에 대해 상기시키기 위해
(D) 환자에게 의학적 조언을 제공하기 위해

해설 지문의 'It is ~ time for your physical examination at our clinic.'에서 저희 병원에서 귀하의 신체검사를 할 때가 되었다고 한 후, 예약에 대해 안내하고 있으므로 (C)가 정답이다.

어휘 organize v. 준비하다, 조직하다 engagement n. 예약, 약속

169 추론 문제

상 ●●●

해석 Ms. Wang에 대해 암시되는 것은?

(A) 의료 문제가 있다고 알렸다.
(B) Dr. Kapur를 2년 전에 마지막으로 봤다.
(C) 6월 12일에 시간이 없다.
(D) 신체검사를 작년에 받았다.

해설 지문의 'you are required to undergo this procedure every two years'에서 귀하, 즉 Ms. Wang은 이 절차를 2년마다 받아야 한다고 했고, 'You will see the same physician as last time, Dr. Reena Kapur.' 에서 귀하, 즉 Ms. Wang은 지난번과 같은 의사인 Dr. Reena Kapur를 만날 것이라고 했으므로 Ms. Wang은 Dr. Kapur를 2년 전에 마지막으로 봤다는 사실을 추론할 수 있다. 따라서 (B)가 정답이다.

어휘 **report** v. 알리다, 보고하다 **unavailable** adj. 시간이 없는, 이용할 수 없는

170 육하원칙 문제　　　　하 ●○○

해석 Ms. Wang은 무엇을 해달라고 요청되는가?
(A) 그녀의 섭취물을 물로 제한한다
(B) 수술 절차를 밟는다
(C) 지방함량이 높은 음식들을 피한다
(D) 문서 한 부를 전달한다

해설 지문의 'please don't drink anything but water'에서 물을 제외하고 아무것도 마시지 말라고 했으므로 (A)가 정답이다.

어휘 **restrict** v. 제한하다, 한정하다 **intake** n. 섭취(물)
surgical procedure phr. 수술 절차

패러프레이징

don't drink anything but water 물을 제외하고 아무것도 마시지 마라
→ Restrict ~ intake to water 섭취물을 물로 제한한다

171 육하원칙 문제　　　　하 ●○○

해석 Ms. Wang은 어떻게 그녀의 결과를 받을 수 있는가?
(A) 보험 회사에 연락함으로써
(B) 이메일을 기다림으로써
(C) 나중에 다시 찾아옴으로써
(D) 웹사이트에 로그인함으로써

해설 지문의 'Your medical results will be forwarded to you ~ by e-mail.' 에서 귀하, 즉 Ms. Wang의 의료 결과는 귀하에게 이메일로 보내질 것이라고 했으므로 (B)가 정답이다.

어휘 **obtain** v. 받다, 얻다 **insurance firm** phr. 보험 회사
at a later date phr. 나중에, 후일에

172-175번은 다음 기사에 관한 문제입니다.

*Electronics Monthly*지
[172]**변화하려고 노력하는 SleekEffects사**

3월 2일— 전기 기구 제조업체 [172]SleekEffects사가 그것의 지난해 좋지 못한 영업 실적에서 회복하려고 시도하고 있다. — [1] —. SleekEffects 사는 [174]지난 11월에 그것의 남성을 위한 전기면도기 Cavalier 라인의 대규모 제품 회수를 겪었다. [175]고객들에 의해 제출된 수백 개의 불만에 따르면, 면도기가 과열되는 경향이 있었으며 그것들은 화재 위험을 야기할 수도 있다. — [2] —.

상황을 호전시키기 위해, SleekEffects사 최고경영자 Leonard Martin 은 그것의 생산 과정에 중요한 변화를 발표했다. — [3] —. 보도 자료에서 Mr. Martin은 [173]제품 회수를 야기한 **결점들**을 회사가 해결했으며 더

넓은 범위의 고객들을 끌어들이기 위해 고안된 새로운 라인의 제품들을 출시하기 위해 준비하고 있다고 말했다. "SleekSmooth라는 이름의 이 라인은 남성과 여성 모두의 관심을 이끌 전자 발, 목, 그리고 등 마사지 기계로 구성되어 있습니다."라고 그는 말했다.

Mr. Martin은 또한 영화배우 Jacqueline Amano와 Rene Bisset이 새로운 제품 라인을 홍보할 것이라고 언급했다. 그 두 스타는 블록버스터 영화인 *Hide and Go*에서의 출연으로 유럽과 아시아 전역에서 잘 알려져 있다. SleekSmooth는 6월에 상점에서 구매 가능할 것이다. — [4] —.

strive v. 노력하다, 힘쓰다 **appliance** n. 기구
make an attempt phr. 시도하다 **recover** v. 회복하다, 되찾다
suffer v. 겪다, 타격을 받다 **massive** adj. 대규모의
recall n. (결함이 발견된 제품의) 회수, 리콜 **tendency** n. 경향, 성향
overheat v. 과열되다 **pose** v. 야기하다 **hazard** n. 위험
turn around phr. ~을 호전시키다 **alternation** n. 변화, 교체
address v. 해결하다, 다루다 **endorse** v. 홍보하다, 지지하다

172 주제 찾기 문제　　　　중 ●●●

해석 기사는 주로 무엇에 대한 것인가?
(A) 지난해 회사의 좋지 못한 실적
(B) 새로운 최고경영자의 임명
(C) 회사의 개선하려는 노력
(D) 한 산업의 상황

해설 지문의 'SleekEffects Striving to Change'와 'SleekEffects is making an attempt to recover from its poor sales results last year'에서 SleekEffects사가 변화하려고 노력하고 있으며 그것의 지난해 좋지 못한 영업 실적에서 회복하려고 시도하고 있다고 한 후, 상황을 개선하려는 회사의 노력과 관련된 세부 내용을 전달하고 있으므로 (C)가 정답이다.

어휘 **performance** n. 실적, 수행, 연주 **appointment** n. 임명
condition n. 상황, 상태, 환경

173 동의어 찾기 문제　　　　중 ●●○

해석 2문단 다섯 번째 줄의 단어 "shortcomings"는 의미상 -와 가장 가깝다.
(A) 손실들
(B) 비용들
(C) 오류들
(D) 장애물들

해설 shortcomings를 포함한 구절 'the firm has addressed the shortcomings that resulted in the recall'에서 제품 회수를 야기한 결점들을 회사가 해결했다고 했으므로 shortcomings는 '결점들, 단점들'이라는 뜻으로 사용되었다. 따라서 '오류들, 잘못들'이라는 뜻을 가진 (C) mistakes가 정답이다.

174 추론 문제　　　　중 ●●○

해석 SleekEffects사에 대해 추론될 수 있는 것은?
(A) 영화의 제작에 기여했다.
(B) 전 세계에 체인점을 운영한다.
(C) 고객 의견을 바탕으로 기구를 만들었다.
(D) 오로지 남성만을 위한 것이었던 상품을 만들었다.

해설 지문의 'electronic shavers for men last November'에서 지난 11월에 남성을 위한 전기면도기라고 했으므로 SleekEffects사가 오로지 남성만을 위한 것이었던 상품을 만들었다는 사실을 추론할 수 있다. 따라서 (D)가 정답이다.

어휘 **contribute** v. 기여하다, 이바지하다 **operate** v. 운영하다, 가동하다
based on phr. ~을 바탕으로 **solely** adv. 오지, 단독으로

패러프레이징

electronic shavers for men 남성을 위한 전기면도기 → items ~ solely for men 오직 남성만을 위한 상품

175 문장 위치 찾기 문제 중 ●●○

해석 [1], [2], [3], [4]로 표시된 위치 중, 다음 문장이 들어갈 곳으로 가장 적절한 것은?

"그 결과, 거의 1백만 개의 제품들이 소매업체들의 선반에서 치워졌다."

(A) [1]
(B) [2]
(C) [3]
(D) [4]

해설 주어진 문장에서 그 결과, 거의 1백만 개의 제품들이 소매업체들의 선반에서 치워졌다고 했으므로, 이 문장이 제품들이 소매업체들의 선반에서 치워지게 된 배경과 관련된 내용이 나오는 부분에 들어가야 함을 알 수 있다. [2]의 앞 문장인 'According to hundreds of complaints ~, the shavers ~ may pose a fire hazard.'에서 수백 개의 불만에 따르면, 면도기가 화재 위험을 야기할 수도 있다고 했으므로, [2]에 제시된 문장이 들어가면 면도기가 화재 위험을 야기할 수도 있기 때문에 거의 1백만 개의 제품들이 소매업체들의 선반에서 치워졌다는 자연스러운 문맥이 된다는 것을 알 수 있다. 따라서 (B)가 정답이다.

어휘 **retailer** n. 소매업체, 소매상

176-180번은 다음 이메일과 공고에 관한 문제입니다.

수신: Dan Maris <d.maris@shopgoodman.com>
발신: Amber Gonzalez <a.gonzalez@shopgoodman.com>
제목: 업데이트
날짜: 10월 28일

Mr. Maris께,

당신이 10월 25일에 다른 상점 관리자들과의 회의에 참석할 수 없었기 때문에, 저는 논의된 것들의 요약을 당신께 보내드려야겠다고 생각했습니다. 회의의 중심내용은 저희가 내년 초에 계획했던 Goodman 슈퍼마켓 체인의 홍보였습니다. ¹⁷⁶저의 부서장인 Mr. Barnhart는 참석하지 못했지만, 그는 다음의 계획들을 승인했습니다:

· 고객들은 ¹⁷⁸우리가 1월에 도입할 가정 배달 서비스의 첫 번째 사용에 대해서 비용이 청구되지 않을 것입니다. ¹⁷⁷이 서비스를 홍보하는 현수막들이 다음 주에 각 상점으로 보내질 것입니다. 당신의 직원들이 이것들을 눈에 잘 띄는 장소에 게시하도록 하십시오.

· 새로운 고객들을 유치하기 위해 각 상점 지점에서 요리 교실이 제공될 것입니다. 지점 관리자들은 이런 행사들을 준비하는 것에 책임이 있을 것입니다. 당신의 Bedford 지점에서 당신은 누가 수업을 가르쳤으면 하는지 저에게 알려주세요.

이런 계획들에 대해 어떠한 질문이나 우려가 있으시면 주저하지 말고 저에게 555-0393으로 전화하십시오.

¹⁷⁶Amber Gonzalez 드림
¹⁷⁶마케팅부 직원
Goodman 슈퍼마켓

---

summary n. 요약, 개요 **promotion** n. 홍보, 승진
in attendance phr. 참석한 **approve** v. 승인하다, 찬성하다
initiative n. 계획, 진취성 **charge** v. 청구하다, 부과하다
introduce v. 도입하다, 소개하다 **banner** n. 현수막
promote v. 홍보하다 **put up** phr. 게시하다, 내붙이다
prominent adj. 눈에 잘 띄는, 저명한 **organize** v. 준비하다, 조직하다
associate n. 직원, 동료; v. 연관 짓다, 연상하다

Goodman 슈퍼마켓 ― Bedford 지점
고객들에게 알림

¹⁷⁸저희는 저희의 새로운 가정 배달 서비스를 발표하게 되어 기쁩니다. 이것은 2월 18일부터 계속 이용 가능할 것입니다. 더 많은 세부사항을 위해서는 www.shopgoodman.com/delivery를 방문하십시오.

또한, ^{179-D}저희는 2월 12일 토요일에 이곳에서 요리 교실을 열 것입니다. 저희는 요리사 Shelly Burch가 저희 상점의 신선한 재료들을 사용하여 그녀가 가장 좋아하는 레시피 중 몇 개를 **참가자들에게 가르쳐주도록 초청하였습니다**. Ms. Burch는 채널 21에서 매일 오후 2시부터 오후 4시까지 방송되는 *Cooking with Shelly*의 진행자입니다.

^{179-D}오전 교실과 오후 교실이 있을 것입니다. 공간 제약으로 인해, 저희는 각 수업에 30명만 수용할 수 있습니다. ¹⁸⁰신청하시려면 저희의 서비스 데스크에 들러주십시오.

available adj. 이용할 수 있는 **onwards** adv. (특정 시간부터) 계속
host v. 열다, 주최하다 **present** v. 출연하다, 주다, 나타내다
limitation n. 제약, 한계 **accommodate** v. 수용하다, 공간을 제공하다

176 추론 문제 중 ●●○

해석 Mr. Barnhart에 대해 암시되는 것은?
(A) 10월 25일 회의에 참석했다.
(B) 슈퍼마켓 지점의 관리자이다.
(C) Mr. Maris에게 이메일이 전송되도록 요청했다.
(D) 마케팅 부서장이다.

해설 이메일의 'My department manager, Mr. Barnhart', 'Amber Gonzalez', 'Marketing Associate'에서 마케팅부 직원인 Amber Gonzalez의 부서장이 Mr. Barnhart라고 했으므로 Mr. Barnhart가 마케팅 부서장이라는 사실을 추론할 수 있다. 따라서 (D)가 정답이다.

패러프레이징

department manager 부서장 → the head of the ~ department 부서장

177 육하원칙 문제 중 ●●○

해석 Goodman 슈퍼마켓은 다음 주에 무엇을 하려고 계획하고 있는가?
(A) 모바일 애플리케이션을 출시한다
(B) 추가적인 직원들을 고용한다
(C) 홍보물들을 배부한다
(D) 웹사이트를 업데이트한다

해설 이메일의 'Banners promoting this service will be sent to each store next week.'에서 이 서비스, 즉 배달 서비스를 홍보하는 현수막들이 다음 주에 각 상점으로 보내질 것이라고 했으므로 (C)가 정답이다.

어휘 **release** v. 출시하다

패러프레이징

be sent to ~로 보내지다 → Distribute 배부하다

178 추론 문제 연계   상 ●●●

해석 배달 서비스에 대해 추론될 수 있는 것은?
(A) 예정한 시간에 출시되지 않았다.
(B) 고객들에게 인기 있지 않다.
(C) 한정된 수의 상점들에서 제공된다.
(D) Ms. Gonzalez에 의해 처음 제안되었다.

해설 이메일의 'the home delivery service that we will be introducing in January'에서 1월에 도입할 가정 배달 서비스라고 했다. 또한, 공고의 'We ~ announce our new home delivery service. It will be available from February 18 onwards.'에서는 새로운 가정 배달 서비스를 발표하며 이것이 2월 18일부터 계속 이용 가능할 것임을 확인할 수 있다.
두 단서를 종합할 때, 배달 서비스는 예정한 시간에 출시되지 않았다는 사실을 추론할 수 있다. 따라서 (A)가 정답이다.

어휘 launch v. 시작하다, 출시하다   on schedule phr. 예정한 시간에
limited adj. 한정된, 제한된   propose v. 제안하다, 제의하다

179 Not/True 문제   중 ●●○

해석 Ms. Burch에 대해 사실인 것은?
(A) 2월 18일에 생방송을 할 것이다.
(B) Goodman 슈퍼마켓의 단골 쇼핑객이다.
(C) 식료품점 근처에 유명한 레스토랑을 운영한다.
(D) 2월 12일에 두 개의 다른 그룹들을 가르칠 것이다.

해설 공고의 'we will be hosting cooking classes here on ~, February 12. We've invited Chef Shelly Burch to teach participants'에서 2월 12일에 이곳에서 요리 교실들을 열 것이며 요리사 Shelly Burch가 참가자들을 가르쳐주도록 초청했다고 했고, 'There will be a morning class and an afternoon class.'에서 오전 교실과 오후 교실이 있을 것이라고 했으므로 (D)는 지문의 내용과 일치한다. 따라서 (D)가 정답이다. (A), (B), (C)는 지문에 언급되지 않은 내용이다.

어휘 live broadcast phr. 생방송   frequent adj. 단골의, 잦은   run v. 운영하다

패러프레이징

a morning class and an afternoon class 오전 교실과 오후 교실 → two different groups 두 개의 다른 그룹

180 육하원칙 문제   하 ●○○

해석 공고에 따르면, 고객들은 왜 서비스 데스크를 방문해야 하는가?
(A) 회원권을 신청하기 위해
(B) 항의하기 위해
(C) 행사에 등록하기 위해
(D) 길을 묻기 위해

해설 공고의 'Please stop by our service desk to sign up.'에서 신청, 즉 요리 교실에 신청을 하려면 서비스 데스크에 들러 달라고 했으므로 (C)가 정답이다.

어휘 sign up for phr. ~을 신청하다, 등록하다   make a complaint phr. 항의하다
register v. 등록하다, 신고하다

패러프레이징

sign up 신청하다 → register 등록하다

181-185번은 다음 웹페이지와 이메일에 관한 문제입니다.

Newshine Flooring사
www.newshineflooring.com

| 홈 | 제품 & 서비스 | 연락처 |

182-A30년이 넘도록, Newshine Flooring사는 고객들에게 다양한 고품질의 견목 바닥재를 공급해왔습니다. 181저희는 전국의 주택 소유주들에게 물건을 공급하며 당신의 집 리모델링 계획에 대한 완벽한 해결책을 당신에게 제공할 수 있습니다. 아래의 옵션들을 참고하십시오.

182-D/184바닥재 재료	184방 크기	184견적 비용
182-D삼나무	0-250제곱피트	1,000달러
삼나무	250+제곱피트	1,750달러
182-D참나무	0-250제곱피트	1,750달러
참나무	250+제곱피트	2,500달러
182-D/184대나무	1840-250제곱피트	1842,500달러
대나무	250+제곱피트	4,000달러

184예상 비용은 오직 재료들에 대한 것입니다. 185인건비에 대한 견적이 필요하시면, 저희 설치 전문가 중 한 명이 당신의 집을 방문하여 당신이 개조하려고 계획하는 공간을 검토해야 할 것입니다. 문의가 있으시면 여기로 저희에게 연락 주십시오.

supply v. 공급하다, 제공하다   hardwood n. 견목   flooring n. 바닥재
serve v. (필요한 물건을) 공급하다   solution n. 해결책, 해답
refer v. 참고하다, 지시하다   material n. 재료, 자재   quote n. 견적(가)
labor cost phr. 인건비   installation n. 설치   specialist n. 전문가
examine v. 검토하다   inquiry n. 문의, 연구

수신: Newshine Flooring사 고객 서비스 <service@newshineflooring.com>
발신: David Wescott <dwest78@realmail.net>
제목: 귀사의 서비스에 대한 관심
날짜: 5월 4일

안녕하세요,

저는 귀사가 귀사의 웹사이트에서 제공하는 몇몇 제품들에 관심이 있습니다. 저는 한 달 전에 막 저의 현재 집으로 이사를 왔고, 저는 제 주방을 새롭게 하는 중입니다. 183저는 어제 전등을 설치하는 것을 완료했지만, 바닥재에 몇 가지 작업이 필요하다고 생각합니다. 구체적으로, 184저는 현재 바닥을 제거하고 그것을 귀사의 대나무 옵션으로 교체하고 싶습니다. 184그 공간은 딱 150 제곱피트 아래이기 때문에, 저는 크게 강도 높은 노동이 필요하리라 생각하지 않습니다.

185가능하다면, 저는 5월 10일에 이 작업이 완료되길 원합니다. 하지만, 저는 이 프로젝트에 관한 최종 결정을 내리기 전에 인건비에 대해 알아야 합니다. 제게 견적서를 제공해주실 수 있나요?

감사합니다,

David Wescott

be in the process of phr. ~하는 중이다   set up phr. 설치하다, 준비하다
light n. 전등, 빛; v. 불을 붙이다   specifically adv. 구체적으로
replace v. 교체하다, 대신하다   intensive adj. 강도 높은, 집중적인
estimate n. 견적서, 추정

181 목적 찾기 문제 중 ●●○

해석 웹페이지의 목적은 무엇인가?
(A) 가게 개업을 알리기 위해
(B) 회사의 실적을 보고하기 위해
(C) 회사의 제품들을 홍보하기 위해
(D) 몇몇 서비스들에 대한 의견을 요청하기 위해

해설 웹페이지의 'We ~ can provide you with the perfect solution for your home remodeling project.'에서 저희, 즉 Newshine Flooring사는 당신의 집 리모델링 계획에 대한 완벽한 해결책을 제공할 수 있다고 한 후, 제공하는 제품 종류 및 비용에 관해 소개하고 있으므로 (C)가 정답이다.

어휘 opening n. 개업(식) performance n. 실적, 수행, 공연
promote v. 홍보하다 request v. 요청하다

182 Not/True 문제 중 ●●●

해석 Newshine Flooring사에 대해 언급된 것은?
(A) 10년 전에 설립되었다.
(B) 최근에 웹사이트에 사진들을 업로드했다.
(C) 다음 달에 이것의 제품 라인을 변경할 것이다.
(D) 세 종류의 재료들을 공급한다.

해설 웹페이지의 'Flooring Material', 'cedar', 'oak', 'bamboo'에서 바닥재 재료로 삼나무, 참나무, 대나무를 제공한다고 했으므로 (D)는 지문의 내용과 일치한다. 따라서 (D)가 정답이다. (A)는 'For over 30 years, Newshine Flooring has supplied ~ flooring to customers.'에서 Newshine Flooring사가 30년이 넘도록 바닥재를 공급해왔다고 했으므로 지문의 내용과 일치하지 않는다. (B)와 (C)는 지문에 언급되지 않은 내용이다.

어휘 establish v. 설립하다 decade n. 10년

183 육하원칙 문제 중 ●●●

해석 이메일에 따르면, Mr. Wescott은 어제 무엇을 했는가?
(A) 몇몇 장비를 설치했다
(B) 소책자를 다운로드했다
(C) 임대 계약서에 서명했다
(D) 몇몇 가구를 운반했다

해설 이메일의 'I finished setting up the lights yesterday'에서 저, 즉 Mr. Wescott이 어제 전등을 설치하는 것을 완료했다고 했으므로 (A)가 정답이다.

어휘 equipment n. 장비, 용품 rental contract phr. 임대 계약(서)

패러프레이징

setting up the lights 전등을 설치하다 → Installed ~ equipment 장비를 설치하다

184 추론 문제 연계 중 ●●○

해석 Mr. Wescott은 재료에 얼마를 지불할 것 같은가?
(A) 1,000달러
(B) 1,750달러
(C) 2,500달러
(D) 4,000달러

해설 의 'I'd like to ~ replace it with your bamboo option.'과 'The space is just under 150 square feet'에서 저, 즉 Mr. Wescott은 그것, 즉 바닥을 귀사, 즉 Newshine Flooring사의 대나무 옵션으로 교체하고 싶

으며 그 공간은 딱 150제곱피트 아래라고 했다. 또한, 웹페이지의 'Flooring Material', 'bamboo', 'Room Size', '0-250 square feet', 'Estimated Cost', '$2,500'와 'Estimated costs are for materials only.'에서는 대나무 재료의 0-250제곱피트 방 크기의 견적 비용이 2,500달러이며, 예상 비용은 오직 재료들에 대한 것임을 알 수 있다.

두 단서를 종합할 때, Mr. Wescott은 재료에 2,500달러를 지불할 것이라는 사실을 추론할 수 있다. 따라서 (C)가 정답이다.

185 추론 문제 연계 중 ●●○

해석 Newshine Flooring사는 5월 10일 전에 무엇을 할 것 같은가?
(A) 몇몇 용품들을 주문한다
(B) 검토 일정을 잡는다
(C) 몇몇 조명을 치운다
(D) 작업 승인을 얻는다

해설 의 'I would like the work to be done on May 10, ~. However, I need to know the cost of labor before making a final decision'에서 Mr. Wescott이 5월 10일에 작업이 완료되길 원하지만, 최종 결정을 내리기 전에 인건비에 대해 알아야 한다고 했다. 또한, 웹페이지의 'If you require a quote for labor costs, one of our installation specialists will ~ visit ~ and examine the area'에서는 인건비에 대한 견적이 필요하면, 저희, 즉 Newshine Flooring사의 설치 전문가 중 한 명이 방문하여 공간을 검토할 것이라는 사실을 확인할 수 있다.

두 단서를 종합할 때, Newshine Flooring사는 5월 10일 전에 Mr. Wescott의 공간을 검토하기 위한 일정을 잡을 것이라는 사실을 추론할 수 있다. 따라서 (B)가 정답이다.

어휘 supply n. 용품, 물품 lighting n. 조명 authorization n. 승인, 권한 부여

패러프레이징

examine 검토하다 · inspection 검토

186-190번은 다음 기사, 이메일, 초대장에 관한 문제입니다.

Spirant Energy Canada사 풍력 프로젝트가 발표되다

1월 3일 —[186]Spirant Energy Canada사는 온타리오호 가까이에 네 개의 타워가 있는 **풍력 발전 지역을 짓기 위해** 네덜란드의 TWC Energy사와 협력할 계획을 발표했다. 각 타워는 대략 6,000가구에 공급하기 위한 충분한 전력을 만들어낼 것이다.

Spirant Energy Canada사 대변인 Oscar Lee에 따르면, [190-B]**온타리오호 풍력 프로젝트**는 캐나다 전역에 더 큰 규모의 풍력 프로젝트로의 길을 열어 줄 것이다. [190-B]**개발 사업은 이번 12월 설치를 목표로 즉시 시작될 것으로 예상된다.**

만약 완성되면, 이것은 6년 만에 Spirant Energy Canada사의 세 번째 풍력 발전 지역이 될 것이다. [187]**이것의 지난번 프로젝트는 야생동물 보호 단체의 반대 시위에 따라 포기되었다.** 네덜란드의 TWC Energy사가 기술적인 도움을 제공할 것이다. 자금은 캐나다 풍력 협회의 추가적인 지원과 함께 온타리오와 토론토의 지방 정부로부터 나올 것이다.

partner with phr. ~와 협력하다 wind farm phr. 풍력 발전 지역
generate v. 만들어내다, 발생시키다 spokesperson n. 대변인
target v. 목표하다 abandon v. 포기하다, 그만두다
protest n. 반대 시위; v. 반대하다 wildlife n. 야생동물
conservation n. 보호, 보존 assistance n. 도움, 원조
funding n. 자금, 재정 지원

해설　기사의 'Spirant Energy Canada has announced plans ~ to build a wind farm'에서 Spirant Energy Canada사는 풍력 발전 지역을 짓기 위한 계획을 발표했다고 한 후, Spirant Energy Canada사의 개발 계획을 전달하고 있으므로 (C)가 정답이다.

어휘　merger n. 합병　competing adj. 경쟁의　construct v. 건설하다
expansion n. 확장, 팽창　existing adj. 기존의　facility n. 시설

최고난도 문제

187 추론 문제 연계　　　　　상 ●●●

해석　Ms. Castillo가 Hudson만 프로젝트에 대해 암시하는 것은?
(A) 자금의 부족으로 인해 중단되었다.
(B) TWC Energy사의 도움으로 개발될 수 있다.
(C) Spirant Energy Canada사의 마지막 풍력 발전 지역이 될 수 있다.
(D) 아마 동물 권리 단체들의 승인을 받을 것이다.

해설　이메일의 'I am writing to point out some inaccuracies in your article'에서 저, 즉 Ms. Castillo가 기사에서 몇몇 잘못된 점들을 지적하고자 글을 쓴다고 했고, 'our Hudson Bay project was not abandoned. It was put on hold'와 'it will be possible to resume the project soon by moving the wind farm away from critical routes followed by migrating birds'에서 Hudson만 프로젝트는 포기된 것이 아니라 보류되었으며, 철새들이 따라가는 중요 경로들로부터 풍력 발전 지역을 옮김으로써 프로젝트를 재개하는 것이 가능할 것이라고 했다. 또한, 기사의 'Its last project was abandoned following protests from wildlife conservation groups.'에서는 이것, 즉 Spirant Energy Canada사의 지난번 프로젝트는 야생동물 보호 단체의 반대 시위에 따라 포기되었다고 기사에 언급된 것을 확인할 수 있다.
두 단서를 종합할 때, Spirant Energy Canada사의 지난번 프로젝트인 Hudson만 프로젝트는 야생동물 보호 단체의 반대 시위에 따라 보류되었으나, 철새들이 따라가는 중요 경로들로부터 프로젝트를 옮김으로써 이를 재개하는 것이 가능할 것이므로, Hudson만 프로젝트가 이번에는 아마 동물 권리 단체들의 승인을 받을 것이라는 사실을 추론할 수 있다. 따라서 (D)가 정답이다.

어휘　halt v. 중단시키다; n. 중단　lack n. 부족, 결핍

188 동의어 찾기 문제　　　　　하 ●○○

해석　이메일에서, 2문단 세 번째 줄의 단어 "critical"은 의미상 ~와 가장 가깝다.
(A) 독점적인
(B) 힘든
(C) 위험한
(D) 중요한

해설　이메일의 critical을 포함한 구절 'it will be possible to resume the project soon by moving the wind farm away from critical routes followed by migrating birds'에서 철새들이 따라가는 중요 경로들로부터 풍력 발전 지역을 옮김으로써 프로젝트를 재개하는 것이 가능할 것이라고 했으므로 critical은 '중요한'이라는 뜻으로 사용되었다. 따라서 '중요한'이라는 뜻을 가진 (D) important가 정답이다.

189 육하원칙 문제　　　　　하 ●○○

해석　초대장에 따르면, 행사의 손님들은 무엇을 해달라고 요청받는가?
(A) 출입구에서 초대장을 제시한다
(B) 번호로 전화해서 공간을 예약한다

수신: Tom Hiltern <t.hiltern@torontonianobserver.com>
발신: Linda Castillo <l.castillo@spirantenergy.com>
제목: Spirant Energy Canada사에 관한 기사
날짜: 1월 6일

Mr. Hiltern께,

[187]저는 온타리오호 풍력 프로젝트에 관한 **당신의 기사에서 몇몇 잘못된 점들을 지적하고자 글을 씁니다.** 첫 번째로, 그것은 각 타워가 6,000가구들에 충분한 전력을 생산할 수 있다고 시사합니다. 더 정확히 말하면, 총 6,000가구들에 공급하기 위해 모든 네 개의 타워들을 합한 것이 필요할 것입니다.
두 번째로, [187]**저희의 Hudson만 프로젝트는 포기되지 않았습니다.** 이것은 저희가 추가 연구를 수행할 수 있도록 **보류되었습니다.** 그때 이후로, 저희는 [187/188]**철새들이 따라가는 중요 경로들로부터 풍력 발전 지역을 옮김으로써 프로젝트를 곧 재개하는 것이** 가능할 것임을 알아냈습니다. 세부사항들은 다음 달에 발표될 것입니다.

그 동안에, 필요한 수정 사항들을 실어 주시길 바랍니다. 감사합니다.

Linda Castillo 드림
홍보부장
Spirant Energy Canada사

---

point out phr. 지적하다, 언급하다　put on hold phr. 보류하다, 연기하다
conduct v. 수행하다, 실시하다　determine v. 알아내다, 결정하다
resume v. 재개하다, 다시 시작하다　critical adj. 중요한, 비판적인
route n. 경로　migrating bird phr. 철새　release v. 발표하다, 발매하다
correction n. 수정 사항, 정정

[190-B]**온타리오호 풍력 발전 지역의**
개관식에 당신은 초대되었습니다!

온타리오주 정부와 토론토시 정부와 협력하여
Spirant Energy Canada사와 TWC Energy사에 의해 소개됩니다
캐나다 풍력 협회에 의해 후원됩니다

언제: 금요일, [190-B]**11월 22일,** 오후 4시 30분에서 오후 7시까지
어디서: 토론토 여객선 건물

특별 손님들은 Roy Brown 주지사, Edwina Smythe 시장, 그리고 캐나다 TV의 최장수 자연 프로그램 *Wildlife Crossing*의 진행자인 Harold Bennett을 포함합니다. 이 행사는 완성된 풍력 발전 지역을 방문하기 위해 토론토 여객선에 탑승하는 30분의 일몰 유람선 여행을 포함할 것입니다. 무료 다과가 제공될 사교 행사가 그 뒤에 이어질 것입니다.

[189]**B항구에서 오후 5시에 즉시 배가 출발할 것이므로 제시간에 와주십시오.**
더 많은 정보를 위해서는, 555-4182로 전화하십시오.

---

opening n. 개관식, 틈, 빈자리　present v. 소개하다, 제시하다
in cooperation with phr. ~와 협력하여
premier n. (캐나다) 주지사; adj. 최고의　aboard prep. 탑승한, 탄
function n. 행사　complimentary adj. 무료의
refreshment n. 다과, 가벼운 식사　promptly adv. 즉시

186 주제 찾기 문제　　　　　중 ●●○

해석　기사는 주로 무엇에 대한 것인가?
(A) 두 경쟁 회사의 합병
(B) 다리를 건설하기 위한 프로젝트
(C) 에너지 회사의 개발 계획

(C) 정해진 시간에 운송 수단 시설에 도착한다

(D) 주최자에게 식사 선호사항을 알린다

해설 초대장의 'Please be on time as the boat leaves promptly at 5 P.M. from Harbor B.'에서 B항구에서 오후 5시에 즉시 배가 출발할 것이므로 제시간에 와달라고 했으므로 (C)가 정답이다.

어휘 **present** v. 제시하다, 보여주다 **indicate** v. 알리다, 나타내다
preference n. 선호사항, 선호 **organizer** n. 주최자

패러프레이징

on time 제시간에 → at a given time 정해진 시간에

Harbor B B항구 → a transportation facility 교통 시설

190 Not/True 문제 연계 상 ●●●

해석 온타리오호 풍력 발전 지역에 대해 사실인 것은?

(A) 토론토에서 배로 30분 걸린다.

(B) 일정보다 일찍 열고 있다.

(C) 그것의 기존 장소에서 옮겨졌다.

(D) 국가 공무원에 의해 점검될 것이다.

해설 기사의 'the Lake Ontario Wind Power Project'와 'Development work is expected to begin ~, with installation targeted for this December.'에서 온타리오호 풍력 프로젝트의 개발 사업은 이번 12월 설치를 목표로 시작될 것으로 예상된다고 했다. 또한, 초대장의 'the opening of the Lake Ontario Wind Farm'과 'November 22'에서는 온타리오호 풍력 발전 지역의 개관식이 11월 22일이라고 한 사실을 확인할 수 있다.
두 단서를 종합할 때, 온타리오호 풍력 발전 지역은 일정보다 일찍 열고 있다는 것을 알 수 있다. 따라서 (B)가 정답이다. (A), (C), (D)는 지문에 언급되지 않은 내용이다.

191-195번은 다음 웹페이지, 이메일, 송장에 관한 문제입니다.

www.rusticrevival.com

홈	소개	부품 찾기	연락

191-B**Rustic Revival사는 빈티지 가구의 희귀하고 찾기 어려운 부품들을 전문으로 합니다.** 저희 창고는 수천 개의 물품들을 가지고 있으며, 이들 중 많은 것들이 더 이상 생산되지 않습니다.

만약 당신이 주거, 상업, 또는 산업용 제품을 위한 교체 부품을 필요로 한다면, 저희는 저희의 엄청난 수의 물품 목록 내에서 그것을 찾아낼 수 있는 몇 가지 옵션들을 제공합니다. 192혹시 브랜드와 모델명을 알게 된다면, 당신은 저희의 검색 기능을 사용할 수 있습니다. 만약 당신이 브랜드명만 알고 있다면, 당신이 찾는 것이 무엇인지 정확하게 확인하기 위해 당신은 지회의 온라인 카탈로그를 둘러볼 수 있습니다. 비록 당신이 둘 다 모른다고 해도, 당신이 필요한 것의 사진이나 설명을 저희에게 보낼 수 있으며, 저희는 그것을 찾아내기 위해 노력할 것입니다.

specialize in phr. ~을 전문으로 하다 **rare** adj. 희귀한, 드문
warehouse n. 창고 **manufacture** v. 생산하다, 제조하다
residential adj. 주거의, 주택의 **commercial** adj. 상업의, 상업용의
industrial adj. 산업의, 공업의 **track down** phr. ~을 찾아내다, 추적하다
inventory n. 물품 목록, 재고 **function** n. 기능, 행사
unaware adj. 모르는, 알지 못하는 **description** n. 설명, 묘사
locate v. 찾아내다, ~에 두다

발신: Elspeth Panter <reception@chiringshoals.org>
수신: Rustic Revival사 <admin@rusticrevival.com>
제목: 긴급한 사업 관련 문의
날짜: 7월 3일

Rustic Revival사께,

195저는 부티크 호텔 Chiring Shoals Bed & Breakfast의 소유주입니다. 유감스럽게도, 제 객실 중 하나에서 사고가 일어났고 192/195욕조 수도꼭지의 손잡이가 부러졌습니다. 그 부품이 골동품이기 때문에 저는 이곳 월밍턴에서 그것을 찾을 수 없었습니다. 192제가 www.rusticrevival.com에서 검색을 사용했을 때, 귀사가 그것을 재고로 가지고 있다는 것을 발견했습니다. 하지만 195저는 당신이 그것을 저에게 7월 5일까지 보내줄 수 있는지 알아야 합니다. 성수기이고, 193제 시설이 주말 동안 모두 예약되어 있기 때문에 수리는 가능한 빨리 이뤄져야 합니다. 195만약 당신이 제 배송 요구사항을 맞출 수 없다면, 저는 다른 선택지를 찾을 것입니다.

Elspeth Panter 드림

urgent adj. 긴급한, 시급한 **inquiry** n. 문의 **proprietor** n. 소유주, 경영자
faucet n. 수도꼭지 **stock** n. 재고, 매입품 **high season** phr. 성수기
establishment n. 시설, 기관 **requirement** n. 요구사항, 요건

193Wellsworth Plumbing사
Shinn Point, 윌밍턴시
555-0001

New Hanover 카운티에 10년 넘게 서비스하고 있습니다

작업 장소		노동	194정비공	
195Chiring Shoals Bed & Breakfast 773번지 Wind Chase로 윌밍턴시, 노스캐롤라이나주 28409			194Yvonne Severin	

날짜	시간	요금	총계
1957월 4일	1.5	1시간당 60달러	90달러

보증: 수리와 교체는 작업 일로부터 3개월 이내에 무료입니다.

부품			
수량	설명	가격	총계
1	Goutte Magnalift X-T	45달러	45달러

권고: 195새로운 수도꼭지를 힘차게 들어 올리지 않도록 주의하세요. 194일주일 후에 문제가 없는지 확인하기 위해 제가 두 번째 방문을 실시할 것입니다.

총비용 (부품과 작업료)
135달러

serviceperson n. 정비공, 수리원 **replacement** n. 교체, 대체
lift v. 들어올리다 **forcefully** adv. 힘차게, 효과적으로

191 Not/True 문제 상 ●●●

해석 Rustic Revival사에 대해 언급된 것은?

(A) 집수리에 대한 계약을 승낙한다.

(B) 대부분의 상점에서 구할 수 없는 제품들을 판매한다.

(C) 호텔을 위해 만들어진 제품들을 전문으로 한다.

(D) 자사의 상표명으로 제품을 취급한다.

해설 웹페이지의 'Rustic Revival specializes in rare and hard-to-find parts'에서 Rustic Revival사는 희귀하고 찾기 어려운 부품들을 전문으로

한다고 했으므로 (B)는 지문의 내용과 일치한다. 따라서 (B)가 정답이다. (A), (C), (D)는 지문에 언급되지 않은 내용이다.

어휘 renovation n. 수리, 보수 carry v. 취급하다, 나르다
merchandise n. 제품, 물품

192 추론 문제 연계 중 ●●○

해석 Ms. Panter에 대해 암시되는 것은?
(A) 골동품 장식들의 모음을 소유하고 있다.
(B) 치료를 위해 병원을 방문해야 했다.
(C) 부러진 부품의 모델명을 알았다.
(D) 동업자와 함께 숙박 시설을 운영한다.

해설 이메일의 'the handle of a bathtub faucet was broken'에서는 욕조 수도꼭지의 손잡이가 부러졌다고 했고 'When I used the search ~, I found that you do have it in stock.'에서 제가, 즉 Ms. Panter가 검색을 사용했을 때, 귀사가 그것, 즉 부러진 욕조 수도꼭지의 손잡이를 재고로 가지고 있다는 것을 발견했다고 했다. 또한, 웹페이지의 'If you happen to know brand and model names, you may use our search function.'에서는 브랜드와 모델명을 알게 된다면, 검색 기능을 사용할 수 있음을 확인할 수 있다.
두 단서를 종합할 때, Ms. Panter는 부러진 욕조 수도꼭지의 손잡이의 모델명을 알았다는 사실을 추론할 수 있다. 따라서 (C)가 정답이다.

어휘 decoration n. 장식 treatment n. 치료, 대우 run v. 운영하다, 관리하다

193 육하원칙 문제 중 ●●○

해석 Chiring Shoals Bed & Breakfast에 왜 물품이 필요한가?
(A) 도착하는 방문객들을 위해 객실이 적합하게 되어야 한다.
(B) 고객들이 이것의 시설에 대해 여러 불평을 했다.
(C) 다가오는 날들에 큰 행사가 계획되었다.
(D) 호텔은 새로운 일련의 규정들을 따라야 한다.

해설 이메일의 'because my establishment is fully booked for the weekend, the repairs must be done as soon as possible'에서 제 시설, 즉 Chiring Shoals Bed & Breakfast가 주말 동안 모두 예약되어 있기 때문에 수리는 가능한 빨리 이뤄져야 한다고 했으므로 도착하는 방문객들을 위해 객실이 적합하게 되어야 한다는 것을 알 수 있다. 따라서 (A)가 정답이다.

어휘 suitable adj. 적합한, 알맞은 comply with phr. ~을 따르다, 준수하다

194 육하원칙 문제 중 ●●●

해석 Ms. Severin은 무엇을 할 것을 제안했는가?
(A) 요금의 일부를 환불한다
(B) 다른 공급업체의 부품에 대해 확인한다
(C) 점검을 하기 위해 다시 방문한다
(D) 집의 수압을 높인다

해설 송장의 'Serviceperson', 'Yvonne Severin', 'I will conduct a second visit ~ to check that there are no problems.'에서 문제가 없는지 확인하기 위해 저, 즉 정비공인 Ms. Severin이 두 번째 방문을 실시할 것이라고 했으므로 (C)가 정답이다.

어휘 refund v. 환불하다; n. 환불 portion n. 일부, 부분
supplier n. 공급업체, 공급자 inspection n. 점검, 검사

최고난도 문제

195 추론 문제 연계 상 ●●●

해석 Rustic Revival사에 대해 추론될 수 있는 것은?
(A) Goutte Magnalift X-T에 몇 가지 수정을 했다.
(B) Ms. Panter의 배송 기한을 맞추지 못했다.
(C) 이것의 제품들 대부분을 집에서 생산한다.
(D) 다음 달에 무료 서비스를 제공할 것이다.

해설 이메일의 'I'm the proprietor of the boutique hotel Chiring Shoals Bed & Breakfast.'와 'the handle of a bathtub faucet was broken'에서 저, 즉 Ms. Panther가 Chiring Shoals Bed & Breakfast 부티크 호텔의 소유주이며 객실 욕조 수도꼭지의 손잡이가 부러졌다고 했고, 'I need to know whether you can have it sent to me by July 5.'와 'If you are unable to meet my shipping requirements, I will find other options.'에서 당신, 즉 Rustic Revival사가 7월 5일까지 그것, 즉 수도꼭지 손잡이를 보내줄 수 있는지 물으며 만약 배송 요구사항을 맞출 수 없다면, 다른 선택지를 찾을 것이라고 했다. 또한, 송장의 'Wellsworth Plumbing', 'Chiring Shoals Bed & Breakfast', 'July 4', 'new faucet'에서는 Rustic Revival사가 아닌, Wellsworth Plumbing사가 7월 4일에 Chiring Shoals Bed & Breakfast의 수도꼭지를 새로운 것으로 교체해주었다는 사실을 확인할 수 있다.
두 단서를 종합할 때, Rustic Revival사가 Ms. Panter의 배송 기한을 맞추지 못했다는 사실을 추론할 수 있다. 따라서 (B)가 정답이다.

어휘 alteration n. 수정, 변경 complimentary adj. 무료의

196-200번은 다음 웹페이지, 편지, 이메일에 관한 문제입니다.

www.magnumcruises.com
Magnum 크루즈사

홈	소개	보도	일자리

196-C저희는 현재 일 년 내내 운영하는 지역의 크루즈들에서 다음의 일자리들에 대한 지원자들을 받고 있습니다.

196-D남아프리카
고객 관리 담당자로서, Magnum Explorer에 탑승하여 10월부터 3월까지 손님들을 맞이하고, 활동을 준비하고, 고객 문제를 처리하는 일을 하십시오. 더 보기

196-D호주 & 태평양
오락 전문가로서, Magnum Endeavor에 탑승하여 11월부터 2월까지 오락 책임자의 감독 아래에서 창의적인 공연자로 일을 하십시오. 더 보기

196-D인도 & 스리랑카
배의 간호사로서, Magnum Adventure에 탑승하여 4월부터 7월까지 승객들의 그날그날의 건강을 보살피는 일을 하십시오. 더 보기

196-D동남아시아
198레스토랑 보조 매니저로서, Magnum Pacifica에 탑승하여 5월부터 9월까지 손님들에게 순조로운 식사, 서비스의 전달을 보장하는 일을 하십시오. 더 보기

지원하려면, 자기소개서와 함께, 당신의 이력서를 200100호, Capital 빌

딩, 65번지 Canal로, 싱가포르 049513에 있는 저희의 본사로 보내십시오. ¹⁹⁷오직 첫 심사를 통과한 지원자들만 연락받을 것입니다. 그들은 온라인 면접에 초청될 것입니다. 지원하실 때, 당신의 희망하는 직책을 명시해주십시오.

regional adj. 지역의, 지방의   operate v. 운영하다
address v. 처리하다, 다루다   aboard prep. 탑승한
supervision n. 감독, 관리   day-to-day adj. 그날그날의, 나날의
cover letter phr. 자기소개서   initial adj. 처음의   screening n. 심사
state v. 명시하다, 언급하다   desired adj. 희망하는

10월 22일
1245번지 Miller가
북시드니, 뉴사우스웨일스주 2060

관계자분께,

¹⁹⁸저는 레스토랑 보조 매니저 자리에 관심이 있습니다. 저는 제가 모든 자격 요건들을 충족할 수 있다고 확신합니다. 저는 식음료 관리에 학위를 가지고 있으며, 최근의 관련 업무 경험이 있고, 이전에 유람선에서 일한 적이 있습니다. 저는 또한 3개 국어를 할 수 있고, 면허증을 소지한 의사로부터 발급받은 양호한 건강을 나타내는 증명서를 가지고 있고, 유효한 모든 여행 서류들에 만반의 준비가 갖추어져 있습니다. 저는 이런 자격 요건들을 고려하여, 당신이 Magnum 크루즈사의 직책에 저를 진지하게 고려해주시기를 바랍니다.

Leo Manresa 드림

certificate n. 증명서, 증명   licensed adj. 면허증을 소지한, 허가받은
physician n. 의사   in order phr. 만반의 준비가 갖추어져
qualification n. 자격 요건, 조건   seriously adv. 진지하게, 심하게

¹⁹⁹수신: Leo Manresa <l.manresa@hypemail.com>
¹⁹⁹발신: Jessica Lewen <j.lewen@magnumcruises.com>
제목: 면접
날짜: 11월 11일

Mr. Manresa께,

Magnum 크루즈사의 일자리에 지원해주셔서 감사합니다. 저희는 당신이 당신의 지원을 계속 진행할 자격이 충분히 있다고 생각합니다. 이와 관련하여, 저희는 11월 15일 오전 10시에 있을 온라인 면접에 당신이 참석하도록 초청하고 싶습니다. 당신이 가능하다는 것을 확정하면 ¹⁹⁹세부적인 안내 사항이 제공될 것입니다. ²⁰⁰만약 합격한다면, 당신은 시즌 초에 당신의 일을 공식적으로 시작하기 전 2개월간의 훈련을 받기 위해 저희의 본사로 출장을 갈 것입니다.

Jessica Lewen 드림
채용 담당자
Magnum 크루즈사

sufficiently adv. 충분히   qualified adj. 자격이 있는
proceed with phr. ~을 계속 진행하다   in connection with phr. ~과 관련하여
confirm v. 확정하다, 확인하다   head office phr. 본사, 본점
undergo v. 받다, 겪다   officially adv. 공식적으로

196 Not/True 문제   중 ●●○

해석 Magnum 크루즈사에 대해 사실인 것은?
(A) 새로운 크루즈의 여행 일정표를 막 소개했다.
(B) 그것의 본사에 몇몇 빈자리가 있다.
(C) 서비스를 일 년 내내 제공한다.

(D) 유럽과 북아메리카의 도시들로 여행한다.

해설 웹페이지의 'We are currently taking applicants ~ on regional cruises operating throughout the year.'에서 저희, 즉 Magnum 크루즈사가 현재 일 년 내내 운영하는 지역의 크루즈들에서 지원자들을 받고 있다고 했으므로 (C)는 지문의 내용과 일치한다. 따라서 (C)가 정답이다. (A)와 (B)는 지문에 언급되지 않은 내용이다. (D)는 'Southern Africa', 'Australia & the Pacific', 'India & Sri Lanka', 'Southeast Asia'에서 남아프리카, 호주, 태평양, 인도, 스리랑카, 동남아시아에서 운항한다고 했으므로 지문의 내용과 일치하지 않는다.

어휘 itinerary n. 여행 일정표   opening n. 빈자리, 공석

패러프레이징

throughout the year 일 년 내내 → all year long 일 년 내내

197 추론 문제   중 ●●○

해석 광고되는 일자리들에 대해 암시되는 것은?
(A) 모든 지원자들이 회신을 받는 않을 것이다.
(B) 지원자들은 자격증이 있는 전문가여야 한다.
(C) 그것들은 이전의 크루즈 경험을 요구한다.
(D) 모든 것은 다른 사람들을 감독하는 것을 포함한다.

해설 웹페이지의 'Only applicants who make it through the initial screening process will be contacted.'에서 오직 첫 심사를 통과한 지원자들만 연락받을 것이라고 했으므로 모든 지원자들이 회신을 받는 않을 것이라는 사실을 추론할 수 있다. 따라서 (A)가 정답이다.

어휘 reply n. 회신   professional n. 전문가

198 육하원칙 문제   연계   중 ●●○

해석 Mr. Manresa는 어느 배에서 일하는 것에 지원하는가?
(A) Magnum Explorer
(B) Magnum Endeavor
(C) Magnum Adventure
(D) Magnum Pacifica

해설 이메일의 'I am interested in the position of assistant restaurant manager.'에서 저, 즉 Mr. Manresa는 레스토랑 보조 매니저 자리에 관심이 있다고 했다. 또한, 웹페이지의 'As an Assistant Restaurant Manager, work aboard the Magnum Pacifica'에서는 Magnum Pacifica에서 레스토랑 보조 매니저를 구한다는 사실을 확인할 수 있다.
두 단서를 종합할 때, Mr. Manresa는 Magnum Pacifica에서 일하는 것에 지원한다는 것을 알 수 있다. 따라서 (D)가 정답이다.

199 육하원칙 문제   하 ●○○

해석 Ms. Lewen은 Mr. Manresa에게 무엇을 제공할 것인가?
(A) 업무 목록
(B) 교육 계획서
(C) 비행기 티켓
(D) 일련의 안내 사항

해설 이메일의 'To: Leo Manresa', 'From: Jessica Lewen', 'Detailed instructions will be provided'에서 Ms. Lewen이 Mr. Manresa에게 세부적인 안내 사항이 제공될 것이라고 했으므로 (D)가 정답이다.

어휘 job duty phr. 업무   a set of phr. 일련의

해석   Mr. Manresa에 대해 추론될 수 있는 것은?

(A) 11월에 여행을 떠날 수도 있다.

(B) 싱가포르로 출장을 가야 할 수도 있다.

(C) 이전의 고용주에 의해 소개되었다.

(D) 인도와 스리랑카 근처의 배에서 일했다.

해설   이메일 의 'If successful, you will travel to our head office'에서 만약 합격한다면, 당신, 즉 Mr. Manresa는 저희, 즉 Magnum 크루즈사의 본사로 출장을 갈 것이라고 했다. 또한, 웹페이지 의 'our head office at ~, Singapore'에서는 Magnum 크루즈사의 본사가 싱가포르에 있다는 사실을 확인할 수 있다.

두 단서를 종합할 때, Mr. Manresa가 싱가포르로 출장을 가야 할 수도 있다는 사실을 추론할 수 있다. 따라서 (B)가 정답이다.

어휘   **depart** v. (여행을) 떠나다   **refer** v. 소개하다, 적용되다   **former** adj. 이전의 **employer** n. 고용주

PART 5

101 (B)	**102** (D)	**103** (D)	**104** (A)	**105** (C)
106 (B)	**107** (C)	**108** (C)	**109** (A)	**110** (A)
111 (D)	**112** (A)	**113** (C)	**114** (A)	**115** (D)
116 (D)	**117** (C)	**118** (B)	**119** (D)	**120** (D)
121 (D)	**122** (C)	**123** (C)	**124** (B)	**125** (D)
126 (A)	**127** (B)	**128** (A)	**129** (D)	**130** (A)

PART 6

131 (A)	**132** (D)	**133** (A)	**134** (D)	**135** (C)
136 (B)	**137** (D)	**138** (D)	**139** (A)	**140** (B)
141 (C)	**142** (A)	**143** (A)	**144** (A)	**145** (A)
146 (C)				

PART 7

147 (B)	**148** (B)	**149** (D)	**150** (C)	**151** (B)
152 (A)	**153** (B)	**154** (C)	**155** (D)	**156** (B)
157 (B)	**158** (C)	**159** (D)	**160** (A)	**161** (D)
162 (C)	**163** (A)	**164** (A)	**165** (A)	**166** (D)
167 (D)	**168** (D)	**169** (A)	**170** (A)	**171** (A)
172 (B)	**173** (C)	**174** (B)	**175** (A)	**176** (B)
177 (A)	**178** (D)	**179** (D)	**180** (D)	**181** (B)
182 (A)	**183** (D)	**184** (D)	**185** (B)	**186** (C)
187 (B)	**188** (D)	**189** (D)	**190** (D)	**191** (A)
192 (B)	**193** (A)	**194** (D)	**195** (C)	**196** (D)
197 (C)	**198** (B)	**199** (A)	**200** (A)	

PART 5

101 지시대명사/형용사 채우기 중 ●●○

해석 만약 비가 내린다면, 이 야외 활동들은 실내 활동들로 대체될 것이다.

해설 빈칸 뒤의 명사(events)를 꾸밀 수 있는 것은 형용사이므로 부정형용사 (A)와 (D), 지시형용사 (B)가 정답의 후보이다. 빈칸 뒤에 복수 명사(events)가 왔고, '이 야외 활동들은 실내 활동들로 대체될 것이다'라는 의미가 되어야 하므로 지시형용사 (B) these(이)가 정답이다. 부정형용사 (A)와 (D)는 단수 명사와 쓰여야 한다. 부정대명사 (C)는 형용사 자리에 올 수 없다.

어휘 outdoor adj. 야외의 substitute A with B phr. A를 B로 대체하다
indoor adj. 실내의 every adj. 모든 others n. 다른 사람들, 다른 것들
another adj. 또 다른

102 사람명사와 추상명사 구별하여 채우기 중 ●●○

해석 월간 회의들은 최근 새로이 전개된 사건들에 대해 설명을 하는 각 팀의 관리자에 의해 참석된다.

해설 전치사(by)의 목적어 자리에 오면서 소유격(each team's)의 꾸밈을 받을 수 있는 것은 명사이므로 명사 (B)와 (D)가 정답의 후보이다. 빈칸 뒤에 사람 명사를 선행사로 취하는 관계대명사 who가 왔고, '월간 회의들은 사건들에 대해 설명을 하는 각 팀의 관리자에 의해 참석된다'라는 의미가 되어야 자연스러우므로 사람명사 (D) supervisor(관리자)가 정답이다. 추상명사 (B) supervision(관리)을 쓸 경우 '월간 회의들은 사건들에 대해 설명을 하는 각 팀의 관리에 의해 참석된다'라는 어색한 문맥이 되며 관계대명사 who의 꾸밈을 받을 수 없다. 동사 또는 과거분사 (A)와 동사 (C)는 명사 자리에 올 수 없다.

어휘 attend v. 참석하다 rundown n. 설명
development n. 새로이 전개된 사건, 개발 supervise v. 관리하다, 감독하다

103 형용사 자리 채우기 중 ●●○

해석 구직 시장은 많은 최근의 졸업생들이 일자리를 찾기 시작하면서 경쟁적이게 되었다.

해설 2형식 동사 become의 보어 자리에 올 수 있는 것은 형용사이므로 형용사 (D) competitive(경쟁적인)가 정답이다. 동사 (A)와 (C), 부사 (B)는 보어 자리에 올 수 없다.

어휘 graduate n. 졸업생 look for phr. ~을 찾다 compete v. 경쟁하다
competitively adv. 경쟁적으로

104 동사 어휘 고르기 하 ●○○

해석 기술자들이 전력을 복구시키는 동안 주민들은 3시간을 기다려야 했다.

해설 빈칸은 조동사처럼 쓰이는 표현 have to(~해야 한다) 뒤에 오는 동사원형 자리이다. '전력을 복구시키는 동안 주민들은 3시간을 기다려야 했다'라는 문맥이므로 (A) wait(기다리다)가 정답이다.

어휘 resident n. 주민 technician n. 기술자 restore v. 복구시키다
practice v. 연습하다, 실행하다 grant v. 승인하다, 인정하다
agree v. 동의하다

105 가산 명사와 불가산 명사 구별하여 채우기 중 ●●○

해석 정치인들은 대통령의 경제 계획을 칭찬했는데, 특히 일자리 창출 및 안정에 관한 부분이었다.

해설 where로 시작되는 부사절(where ~ concerned)에서 주어 자리에 오면서 빈칸 앞의 명사(job)와 복합 명사를 만들 수 있는 것은 명사이므로 명사 (C)와 (D)가 정답의 후보이다. '일자리 창출 및 안정에 관한 것'이라는 의미가 되어야 하고, 명사(job) 앞에 관사가 없으므로 불가산 명사 (C) creation(창출)이 정답이다. 가산 명사 (D) creator(창조자)는 관사와 함께 쓰이거나 복수형으로 쓰여야 한다. 동사 (A)와 형용사 (B)는 주어 자리에 올 수 없다. 동사 (A)를 넣어 job create를 하나의 절로 보고 접속사 and가 또 다른 절 security are concerned를 연결하는 것으로 볼 경우, 가산명사 job 앞에 관사가 없고, 복수 동사 create와 함께 쓰일 수 없으며, 불가산 명사 security도 복수

TEST 6 해커스 토익 실전 1200제 READING

동사 are concerned와 함께 쓰일 수 없으므로 답이 될 수 없다. 참고로, 이 문장에서 where는 '~에 관한 한, ~한 경우에'라는 의미로 부사절을 이끄는 부사절 접속사로 쓰였음을 알아둔다.

어휘 praise v. 칭찬하다 security n. 안정 concerned adj. ~에 관한 create v. 창작하다, 창조하다 creative adj. 창의적인

106 동사 어휘 고르기 　　　　　　　　하 ●○○

해석 Tuscaloosa 공항은 휠체어 지원을 요청하는 승객들에게 그것을 제공한다.

해설 빈칸은 주격 관계대명사(who) 뒤에 오면서 목적어(it)를 취하는 동사 자리이다. '휠체어 지원을 요청하는 승객들'이라는 문맥이므로 (B) request(요청하다)가 정답이다.

어휘 provide v. 제공하다 assistance n. 지원, 보조 passenger n. 승객 touch v. 만지다 begin v. 시작하다 leave v. 남겨두다, 떠나다

107 형용사 자리 채우기 　　　　　　　　하 ●○○

해석 많은 호텔들이 그들의 객실들의 가격을 정할 때 수요의 계절적 변화를 고려한다.

해설 빈칸 뒤의 명사(changes)를 꾸밀 수 있는 것은 형용사이므로 형용사 (C)와 과거분사 (D)가 정답의 후보이다. '가격을 정할 때 계절적 변화를 고려하다'라는 의미가 되어야 하므로 형용사 (C) seasonal(계절적인)이 정답이다. 과거분사 (D)를 쓸 경우 '가격을 정할 때 길들여진 변화를 고려하다'라는 어색한 의미가 된다. 명사 또는 동사 (A)와 부사 (B)는 형용사 자리에 올 수 없다. 참고로, 동사 consider가 that이 생략된 명사절(the ___ ~ rooms)을 목적어로 취하는 것으로 보아, 명사로 쓰인 (A) seasons(계절들)를 명사절의 주어로 보고, changes를 '변화하다'라는 의미의 3인칭 단수 동사로 본다 해도, 복수 명사(seasons)와 단수 동사(changes)가 함께 쓰일 수 없고, '수요에 따라 계절이 변한다'라는 어색한 의미를 만든다.

어휘 consider v. 고려하다 price v. 가격을 정하다 season n. 계절; v. 양념하다 seasonally adv. 계절적으로, 정기적으로

108 부사 자리 채우기 　　　　　　　　중 ●●○

해석 공장 기계는 몇 주의 기간 동안 계속해서 작동할 것이다.

해설 동사(will operate)를 꾸밀 수 있는 것은 부사이므로 부사 (C) continuously(계속해서)가 정답이다. 동사 operate를 '(기계를) 가동하다'라는 의미의 타동사로 보고, 명사 (A) continuation(지속, 계속)을 목적어로 본다 해도, '공장 기계가 지속을 가동하다'라는 어색한 의미를 만든다. 참고로, 동사 operate는 자동사와 타동사로 모두 쓰임을 알아둔다. 동사 또는 과거분사 (B)와 형용사 (D)는 부사 자리에 올 수 없다.

어휘 factory n. 공장 equipment n. 기계, 장비 continue v. 계속하다, 계속되다 continuous adj. 계속되는, 지속되는

109 전치사 채우기 　　　　　　　　하 ●○○

해석 오로지 중요한 사실들만을 포함함으로써, 분석가들은 간결한 연구 보고서들을 작성할 수 있다.

해설 빈칸은 동명사구(including ~ facts)를 목적어로 취하는 전치사 자리이다. '오로지 중요한 사실들만을 포함함으로써, 간결한 연구 보고서들을 작성할 수 있다'라는 문맥이므로 방법이나 수단을 나타내는 전치사 (A) By(~함으로써)가 정답이다. 참고로, 전치사 by는 '~까지'라는 의미로 시점을, '~옆에'라는 의미로 위치를 나타내는 전치사로도 쓰일 수 있음을 알아둔다.

어휘 analyst n. 분석가 concise adj. 간결한 to prep. ~로 at prep. ~에서 beyond prep. ~ 저편에, ~ 너머

110 전치사 채우기 　　　　　　　　하 ●○○

해석 최고경영자는 오해가 없다는 것을 확실히 하기 위해 회사의 문제들에 대해 솔직하게 말했다.

해설 빈칸은 명사구(the company's problems)를 목적어로 취하는 전치사 자리이다. '최고경영자는 회사의 문제들에 대해 솔직하게 말했다'라는 의미가 되어야 하므로 (A) about(~에 대해)이 정답이다. 동사(speak)와 함께 '~을 대변하다, 대신 말하다'라는 의미의 어구 speak for를 만드는 (C) for (~의, ~위한)도 해석상 그럴듯해 보이지만, 전치사 for 뒤에 대변하는 대상인 사람 명사가 와야 한다.

어휘 frankly adv. 솔직하게 misunderstanding n. 오해, 착오 with prep. ~와 함께 in prep. ~에

111 부사 어휘 고르기 　　　　　　　　중 ●●○

해석 정부 건강 지침을 따르는 것은 식중독의 위험을 상당히 줄일 수 있다.

해설 빈칸은 동사(can reduce)를 꾸미는 부사 자리이다. '건강 지침을 따르는 것은 위험을 상당히 줄일 수 있다'라는 문맥이므로 (D) substantially(상당히)가 정답이다.

어휘 guideline n. 지침 reduce v. 줄이다 food poisoning phr. 식중독 optionally adv. 선택적으로 carefully adv. 조심스럽게 unexpectedly adv. 예상외로

112 명사 자리 채우기 　　　　　　　　하 ●○○

해석 마케팅 부서는 지난해의 홍보 활동에 돈을 너무 많이 지출했어서, 올해에는 삭감할 길을 찾고 있다.

해설 전치사(on)의 목적어 자리에 오면서 소유격(last year's)의 꾸밈을 받을 수 있는 것은 명사이므로 명사 (A) promotion(홍보 활동)이 정답이다. 동사 (B), 형용사 (C), 동사 또는 과거분사 (D)는 명사 자리에 올 수 없다.

어휘 be looking to do something phr. ~할 길을 찾고 있다 cutback n. 삭감 promote v. 홍보하다, 승진시키다 promotional adj. 홍보의, 판촉의

113 비교급 표현 채우기 　　　　　　　　중 ●●○

해석 Laurent Software사의 새로운 모바일 애플리케이션은 개발자들이 예상했던 것보다 더 높은 후기 평점을 얻었다.

해설 명사구(review score)를 꾸밀 수 있는 것은 형용사이므로 형용사 (A), (C), (D)가 정답의 후보이다. 빈칸 뒤에 than(~보다)이 왔으므로 함께 비교급 표현을 만드는 형용사 high(높은)의 비교급 (C) higher가 정답이다. 원급 (A)와 최상급 (D)는 비교급 표현 than과 함께 쓰일 수 없다. 부사 (B)는 형용사 자리에 올 수 없다.

어휘 earn v. 얻다 developer n. 개발자 anticipate v. 예상하다 highly adv. 매우

114 명사 관련 어구 채우기 　　　　　　　　하 ●○○

해석 한 달간의 교육 기간은 신입 직원들이 필수적인 기술들을 익히도록 의도되었다.

해설 빈칸은 빈칸 뒤의 명사(period)와 함께 복합 명사를 만들어 동사(is designed)의 주어 역할을 하는 명사 자리이다. '교육 기간은 필수적인 기술들을 익히도록 의도되었다'라는 의미이므로 빈칸 뒤의 명사 period(기간)와 함께 쓰여 '교육 기간'이라는 의미의 복합 명사 training period를 만드는 명사 (A) training(교육)이 정답이다.

어휘 design v. 의도하다, 설계하다 equip v. 익히게 하다, 갖추다

necessary adj. 필수적인 enrollment n. 등록 innovation n. 혁신
manufacturing n. 생산, 제조

115 접속부사 채우기 　중 ●●○

해석　Westgate 지하철역은 바로 지난달에 열렸지만, 그럼에도 불구하고 그것은 도시의 가장 붐비는 지하철역들 중 하나이다.

해설　첫 번째 절(Westgate Subway Station ~ month)과 등위접속사(but)로 연결된 두 번째 절(it ~ stops)이 주어와 동사를 갖춘 완전한 절이므로, 절과 절의 의미를 연결할 수 있는 접속부사 (B), (C), (D)가 정답의 후보이다. '바로 지난달에 열렸지만, 그럼에도 불구하고 도시의 가장 붐비는 지하철역들 중 하나이다'라는 의미가 되어야 하므로 앞뒤 절의 의미를 연결해주는 접속부사이면서 양보를 나타내는 (D) nonetheless(그럼에도 불구하고)가 정답이다. 접속사 (A) though(비록 ~이지만)는 이미 절 앞에 등위접속사 but이 있으므로 또 쓰일 수 없다. 참고로, 절과 절 사이에는 하나의 접속사만 올 수 있다.

어휘　instead adv. 대신에 therefore adv. 따라서, 그러므로

116 형용사 어휘 고르기　하 ●○○

해석　장차 통역사가 되려는 많은 사람들은 우리의 언어 수업들이 그들의 경력에 도움이 된다고 생각한다.

해설　빈칸은 5형식 동사 find의 목적격 보어 역할을 하는 형용사 자리이다. '언어 수업들이 경력에 도움이 된다고 생각하다'라는 문맥이므로 (D) helpful(도움이 되는)이 정답이다.

어휘　aspiring adj. (장차) ~가 되려는 interpreter n. 통역사
ambitious adj. 야망 있는 conservative adj. 보수적인
subtle adj. 미묘한

117 부사 자리 채우기　하 ●○○

해석　Sandy's Cantina사가 요즘 국내 패스트푸드 업계를 완전히 장악하고 있다.

해설　동사(dominates)를 꾸밀 수 있는 것은 부사이므로 부사 (C) completely(완전히, 충분히)가 정답이다. 형용사 또는 동사 (A), 형용사의 비교급 (B), 동명사 또는 현재분사 (D)는 부사 자리에 올 수 없다.

어휘　dominate v. 장악하다, 지배하다 these days phr. 요즘, 오늘날
complete adj. 완료된, 완전한; v. 완료하다

118 올바른 시제의 동사 채우기　하 ●○○

해석　Trinity Tablemates는 1년이 채 안 되게 영업해 왔지만, 이미 도시에서 최고의 식당으로서 지위를 차지한다.

해설　등위접속사(but)로 두 번째 절(already ~ town)과 연결된 첫 번째 절(Trinity Tablemates ~ year)에 주어(Trinity Tablemates)만 있고, 동사가 없으므로 동사 (A), (B), (C)가 정답의 후보이다. Trinity Tablemates가 도시에서 현재 최고의 식당으로서 지위를 차지한다고 했으므로 현재로부터 1년이 채 안 되는 과거에 시작하여 현재까지 영업을 해오고 있음을 알 수 있다. 따라서 현재 완료 시제 (B) has operated가 정답이다. 현재 시제 (A), 미래 시제 (C)는 과거부터 현재까지 계속된 일을 나타낼 수 없다. to 부정사 (D)는 동사 자리에 올 수 없다. 참고로, 현재 완료 시제는 과거에 시작된 일이 현재까지 계속되는 것을 나타낼 때뿐만 아니라, 방금 완료된 일이나 과거에 발생한 일이 현재까지 영향을 미치는 것을 표현한다.

어휘　rank v. (~로서) 지위를 차지하다, 평가되다 operate v. 영업하다, 가동하다

119 부사절 접속사 채우기 　중 ●●●

해석　Mr. Abrams는 그가 공급업체들과 거래하는 것에 대한 몇 가지 조언을 얻을 수 있도록 컨설팅 회사를 고용했다.

해설　이 문장은 주어(Mr. Abrams), 동사(hired), 목적어(a ~ firm)를 갖춘 완전한 절이므로, ___ ~ suppliers는 수식어 거품으로 보아야 한다. 이 수식어 거품은 동사(could get)가 있는 거품절이므로, 거품절을 이끌 수 있는 부사절 접속사 (A), (B), (C)가 정답의 후보이다. 'Mr. Abrams는 거래하는 것에 대한 조언을 얻을 수 있도록 컨설팅 회사를 고용했다'라는 의미가 되어야 하므로 목적을 나타내는 부사절 접속사 (A) so that(할 수 있도록)이 정답이다. 전치사 (D)는 거품절을 이끌 수 없다.

어휘　advice n. 조언 deal with phr. ~와 거래하다
in the event that phr. ~에 대비하여, ~의 경우 even if phr. 비록 ~이지만
regarding prep. ~에 관하여

120 관계부사 채우기 　중 ●●○

해석　주최자들은 그들이 200명의 손님들을 위한 행사를 열 수 있는 장소를 아직도 찾고 있다.

해설　문장은 주어(Organizers), 동사(are searching)를 갖춘 완전한 절이므로, ___ ~ guests는 수식어 거품으로 보아야 한다. 이 수식어 거품은 주어(they), 동사(can hold), 목적어(an event)를 갖춘 완전한 절이고, a venue를 선행사로 갖는 관계절이므로 장소를 나타내는 선행사와 함께 쓰일 수 있는 관계부사 (D) where가 정답이다. 관계대명사 (A)는 뒤에 주어나 목적어가 없는 불완전한 절이 와야 하며 앞에 사람 선행사가 와야 한다. 의문사 또는 관계대명사 (B)는 선행사를 가질 수 없다. 관계부사 (C)는 장소가 아닌 시간을 나타내는 관계부사이고, '~할 때'라는 의미의 부사절 접속사로 보더라도 '행사를 열 수 있는 장소를 찾을 때 아직 찾고 있다'라는 어색한 문맥이 된다.

어휘　organizer n. 주최자 venue n. 장소 hold v. 열다, 개최하다

121 부사 자리 채우기　하 ●○○

해석　비자 신청서는 지연을 방지하기 위해 기한을 엄수하여 제출되어야 한다.

해설　동사(must be submitted)를 꾸밀 수 있는 것은 부사이므로 부사 (D) punctually(기한을 엄수하여, 제시간에)가 정답이다. 형용사 (A), 동명사 또는 현재분사 (B), 명사 (C)는 동사를 꾸밀 수 없다.

어휘　application n. 신청(서) submit v. 제출하다 avoid v. 방지하다, 막다
delay n. 지연, 지체 punctual adj. 시간을 지키는
punctuate v. 간간이 끼어들다, 중단시키다 punctuation n. 구두점, 중단

122 형용사 어휘 고르기　하 ●○○

해석　새로운 기계에 투자하는 것은 돈이 많이 들지만, 장기적으로 그것은 이익이 된다.

해설　빈칸은 be동사(is)의 보어 역할을 하는 형용사 자리이다. '새로운 기계에 투자하는 것은 돈이 많이 들지만, 장기적으로 그것은 이익이 된다'라는 문맥이므로 (C) beneficial(이익이 되는, 이로운)이 정답이다.

어휘　machinery n. 기계 expensive adj. 돈이 많이 드는, 비싼
in the long run phr. 장기적으로 fortunate adj. 운 좋은
memorable adj. 기억에 남는 sudden adj. 갑작스러운

123 부정대명사/형용사 채우기 　중 ●●○

해석　비즈니스 좌석의 사람들은 먼저 비행기에 탑승할 수 있도록 허용될 것이다.

해설 문장에 동사(will be allowed)만 있고 주어가 없으므로 주어 역할을 할 수 있는 모든 보기가 정답의 후보이다. 전치사구(in business class)의 꾸밈을 받아 '비즈니스 좌석의 사람들은 먼저 비행기에 탑승할 수 있다'라는 문장을 만드는 부정대명사 (C) Those(~한 사람들)가 정답이다. 참고로, those는 이 문장에서 앞에 오는 명사를 대신하는 지시대명사가 아니라 막연히 '~한 사람들'이라는 의미의 부정대명사로 쓰였으며, those 뒤에는 반드시 관계절, 분사, 전치사구의 수식어가 온다는 것을 알아둔다. 주격 인칭대명사 (A)의 뒤에는 수식어가 올 수 없다. 지시대명사 (B) This는 '비즈니스 좌석의 이 사람은 먼저 탑승할 수 있도록 허용될 것이다'라는 의미로 해석상 그럴듯해 보이지만, 앞에 나온 단수 명사 또는 문장 전체를 대신하는 데 쓰이므로 답이 될 수 없다. 대명사 또는 형용사 (D) Either는 '둘 중 하나'라는 의미로 가리키는 대상이 두 개일 때 쓰인다.

어휘 board v. 탑승하다

124 부사 어휘 고르기 　　　　　중 ●●●○

해석 2주 후에, Prendit사는 그것의 사업 확장을 발표하기 위해 기자회견을 열 것이다.

해설 빈칸은 문장 전체(Prendit Corp. ~ expansion)를 꾸미는 부사 자리이다. 빈칸 앞의 시간 표현(Two weeks)과 함께 쓰여, '2주 후에 기자회견을 열 것이다'라는 의미가 되어야 하므로 시간 표현 바로 다음에 와서 '그 시간 이후에'라는 의미를 나타내는 시간 부사 (B) later(~ 후에, 나중에)가 정답이다. 참고로, later가 시간 표현 없이 오면 '지금 이후에(after now)'를 의미함을 알아둔다. 부사 (A) next(다음에)도 해석상 그럴듯해 보이지만, 시간 표현과 함께 쓰일 수 없다. 참고로, (A)를 형용사로 볼 경우 시간 표현(Two weeks)과 함께 쓸 수 있지만, 시간 표현 앞에 와야 하며 전치사 for나 in 등과 함께 쓰여, for/in next two weeks(다음 2주 동안/다음 2주 후에)의 형태가 되어야 한다.

어휘 hold v. 열다, 개최하다　press conference phr. 기자회견
announce v. 발표하다　usually adv. 주로　still adv. 여전히

125 동사 어휘 고르기 　　　　　중 ●●●○

해석 인사부장으로서, Ms. Goldfinch는 직원들을 모집하는 것을 담당한다.

해설 빈칸은 전치사(of) 뒤에서 목적어(staff)를 갖는 동명사 자리이다. '인사부장으로서 직원들을 모집하는 것을 담당한다'라는 문맥이므로 동사 recruit(모집하다)의 동명사 (D) recruiting이 정답이다. (C)의 manipulate(다루다, 조종하다)도 해석상 그럴듯해 보이지만, '다루다'라는 의미를 지닐 때는 사물 목적어가 와야 하며, 사람 목적어가 올 경우, 부정적인 의미로 사람을 조종한다는 의미가 되므로 답이 될 수 없다.

어휘 in charge of phr. ~을 담당하는　indicate v. 나타내다
compile v. 엮다, 편집하다

126 부사 자리 채우기 　　　　　중 ●●●○

해석 분기별 보너스는 영업팀의 모든 구성원이 몫을 받으며, 균등하게 분배된다.

해설 동사(is divided)를 꾸밀 수 있는 것은 부사이므로 부사 (A) equally(균등하게)가 정답이다. 형용사, 명사 또는 동사 (B), 명사 (C), 형용사의 비교급 (D)는 동사를 꾸밀 수 없다.

어휘 quarterly adj. 분기별의　divide v. 분배하다, 나누다
equal adj. 평등한; n. 동등한 것; v. ~와 같다　equality n. 평등, 균등

127 전치사 채우기 　　　　　중 ●●●○

해석 그 소프트웨어 학회는 업계의 개발자들 사이에 아이디어 나누는 것을 장려한다.

해설 빈칸은 명사(developers)를 목적어로 취하는 전치사 자리이다. '업계의 개발자들 사이에 아이디어 나누는 것'이라는 의미가 되어야 하므로 (B) among(~사이에)이 정답이다. (D) plus(~뿐만 아니라)도 해석상 그럴듯해 보이지만, 앞의 명사에 부가를 나타내는 전치사이므로 '아이디어뿐만 아니라 개발자들을 나누는 것'이라는 어색한 문맥을 만든다.

어휘 encourage v. 장려하다, 촉진하다　share v. 나누다, 공유하다
field n. 업계, 분야　above prep. ~보다 위로　into prep. ~ 안으로

128 형용사 어휘 고르기 　　　　　하 ●○○

해석 그 건물의 중심적인 위치는 그것을 몹시 매력적으로 만들며, 그것의 높은 임대료가 이것을 나타낸다.

해설 빈칸은 5형식 동사 make의 목적격 보어 역할을 하는 형용사 자리이다. '건물의 중심적인 위치는 그것을 몹시 매력적으로 만들며, 그것의 높은 임대료가 이것을 나타낸다'라는 의미가 되어야 하므로 (A) attractive(매력적인)가 정답이다.

어휘 central adj. 중심적인, 중앙의　extremely adv. 몹시, 극도로
rental price phr. 임대료　reflect v. 나타내다, 반영하다
actual adj. 실제의　attentive adj. 주의를 기울이는
complimentary adj. 무료의

129 재귀대명사 채우기 　　　　　하 ●○○

해석 Mr. Calderon은 동업자가 있었지만, 이제는 그 혼자서 회사를 운영한다.

해설 전치사(by)의 목적어 자리에 올 수 있는 재귀대명사 (A), 소유대명사 (B), 목적격 인칭대명사 (C)가 정답의 후보이다. 'Mr. Calderon은 동업자가 있었지만, 이제는 그 혼자서 회사를 운영한다'라는 의미가 되어야 하므로 전치사 by와 함께 쓰여 '혼자, 혼자 힘으로'라는 의미의 어구 by oneself를 만드는 재귀대명사 (A) himself가 정답이다. 소유대명사 (B)는 'Mr. Calderon은 동업자가 있었지만, 이제는 그의 것에 의해 회사를 운영한다'라는 어색한 문맥을 만든다. 목적격 인칭대명사 (C)는 'Mr. Calderon은 동업자가 있었지만, 이제는 그(Mr. Calderon이 아닌 다른 남성)에 의해 회사를 운영한다'라는 어색한 문맥이 되며, 목적격 인칭 대명사 him을 쓰기 위해서는 him이 의미하는 남성이 빈칸 앞에 등장해야 하는데, Mr. Calderon 외에 언급된 남성이 없으므로 답이 될 수 없다. 주격 인칭대명사 (D)는 전치사의 목적어 자리에 올 수 없다.

어휘 business partner phr. 동업자　run v. 운영하다

130 명사 어휘 고르기 　　　　　하 ●○○

해석 Mr. Parker는 낡은 갈색 소파를 치우고 그것을 창고에 두기로 결정했다.

해설 빈칸은 전치사(in)의 목적어 역할을 하는 명사 자리이다. '소파를 창고에 두다'라는 문맥이므로 (A) storage(창고)가 정답이다.

어휘 remove v. 치우다, 없애다　place v. 두다　solution n. 해결(책)
absence n. 부재, 결석　procedure n. 절차, 방법

PART 6

131-134번은 다음 이메일에 관한 문제입니다.

수신: Derrian Enterprises사 <info@derrianenterprises.com>
발신: Carlos Juarez <cjuar@jadeair.com>
제목: 문의 사항
날짜: 5월 9일

관계자분께:

저는 이전에 귀사의 서비스를 이용해 본 한 동료의 추천으로 글을 씁니다. 저는 Jade 항공사 마케팅 부서에서 일하고 있으며 저희는 저희의 20주년을 ¹³¹**기념하기 위해** 홍보 캠페인을 진행할 것입니다. 캠페인의 일환으로, 저희는 모든 승객들에게 무료 티셔츠를 나누어 줄 것입니다.

저는 당신이 제게 가격 ¹³²**견적서**를 줄 수 있기를 바랍니다. 저는 저희 로고가 전면에 인쇄된 붉은색 천으로 된 셔츠 4,000장을 받는 데 비용이 얼마나 들지 알고 싶습니다. ¹³³**뿐만 아니라,** 이 품목의 샘플 한 장을 제게 보내주실 수 있을까요? ¹³⁴**저는 그것이 입기 편하다는 것을 확실히 알고 싶습니다.** 샘플이 저희의 기준들을 충족하면, 저희는 주문을 진행할 것입니다.

감사합니다,

Carlos Juarez 드림
Jade 항공사

---

recommendation n. 추천 colleague n. 동료
anniversary n. ~주년 기념일 complimentary adj. 무료의
material n. 천, 소재 standard n. 기준 proceed with phr. ~을 진행하다

131 to 부정사 채우기   하 ●○○

해설 첫 번째 절(I ~ Jade Air)과 등위접속사(and)로 연결된 두 번째 절(we ~ anniversary)이 주어(we), 동사(are running), 목적어(a ~ campaign)를 갖춘 완전한 절이므로, ___ ~ anniversary는 수식어 거품으로 보아야 한다. 이 수식어 거품은 동사가 없는 거품구이므로, 거품구를 이끌 수 있는 to 부정사 (A)와 과거분사 (B)가 정답의 후보이다. 빈칸 뒤에 목적어(our 20th anniversary)가 있고 '20주년을 기념하기 위해 홍보 캠페인을 진행한다'라는 목적의 의미가 되어야 하므로, 목적어를 가질 수 있으면서 목적을 나타내는 to 부정사 (A) to celebrate가 정답이다. 과거분사 (B)는 빈칸 뒤에 목적어가 있으므로 답이 될 수 없다. 명사 (C)와 동사 (D)는 수식어 거품을 이끌 수 없다.

어휘 celebration n. 기념, 축하

132 명사 관련 어구 채우기   주변 문맥 파악   중 ●●○

해설 빈칸은 빈칸 앞의 명사(price)와 함께 복합 명사를 이루어 동사(give)의 직접 목적어 자리에 올 수 있는 명사 자리이다. '당신이 가격 ___를 줄 수 있기를 바란다'라는 문맥이므로 (A), (C), (D)가 정답의 후보이다. 뒤 문장에서 셔츠 4,000장을 받는 데 비용이 얼마나 들지 알고 싶다고 했으므로 가격 견적서를 받기 희망한다는 것을 알 수 있다. 따라서 (D) estimate(견적서)가 정답이다.

어휘 benefit n. 혜택 draft n. (아직 완성본이 아닌) 원고, 초안 analysis n. 분석

133 접속부사 채우기   주변 문맥 파악   중 ●●○

해설 앞 문장에서 로고가 인쇄된 셔츠 4,000장을 받는 데 비용이 얼마나 들지 알고 싶다고 했고, 빈칸이 있는 문장에서는 이 품목의 샘플 한 장을 보내줄 수 있냐고 했으므로, 앞 문장에서 언급된 내용, 즉 요청 사항에 추가로 덧붙일 때 사용되는 접속부사 (A) Furthermore(뿐만 아니라)가 정답이다.

어휘 for instance phr. 예를 들어 otherwise adv. 그렇지 않으면
after all phr. 결국에

134 알맞은 문장 고르기   중 ●●○

해석 (A) 그것은 저의 모든 명세 사항들을 충족시켰습니다.
(B) 그것은 정확히 제가 요청했던 것이 아니었습니다.

(C) 저는 그것이 언제 배송될 것인지 당신에게 알려 드릴 것입니다.
(D) 저는 그것이 입기 편하다는 것을 확실히 알고 싶습니다.

해설 앞부분에서 로고가 전면에 인쇄된 셔츠 4,000장을 받는 데 비용이 얼마나 드는지 알고 싶다고 한 후, 앞 문장 '(Furthermore), could you send me a sample for this item?'에서 이 품목의 샘플 한 장을 보내 달라고 요청했으므로 빈칸에는 샘플이 필요한 이유와 관련된 내용이 들어가야 함을 알 수 있다. 따라서 (D)가 정답이다.

어휘 satisfy v. 충족시키다 specification n. 명세 사항 notify v. 알리다
sure adj. 확실히 아는, 확신하는 comfortable adj. 편한, 편안한

135-138번은 다음 편지에 관한 문제입니다.

1월 18일

Lucinda Botello
소유주, Condesa 섬유회사
920번지 Cuevas가
멕시코시티, 멕시코 03100

Ms. Botello께,

저희는 당신을 우리 지역사회의 연례 기업가 정신 경연대회의 심사위원으로 초청하고 싶습니다. 매년, 지역 주민들은 그들의 사업 아이디어를 경험이 풍부한 ¹³⁵**전문가** 심사원단에 제시할 수 있습니다. 이러한 전문가들 중 한 명으로서, 당신은 선정된 기준에 근거하여 아이디어를 평가할 것입니다. ¹³⁶**그 발표들은 짧을 것입니다.** 각 ¹³⁷**참가자**는 그들의 제안을 공유하기 위해 오직 15분을 얻습니다.

당신이 기꺼이 수락한다면, 동봉된 양식을 우편으로 돌려보내 주십시오. 이 대회는 3월 6일 금요일 오전 10시부터 오전 11시 30분까지 저희의 시민 문화 회관에서 열릴 것입니다. 간단한 점심 식사가 ¹³⁸**이어질 것입니다.**

더 자세한 내용은 저희 웹사이트에서 찾을 수 있습니다.

Rafael Pedragon 드림
의장, 지역사회 기업가 정신 프로그램

---

judge n. 심사위원, 판사 entrepreneurship n. 기업가 정신
present v. 제시하다, 제출하다 panel n. 심사원단 expert n. 전문가
evaluate v. 평가하다 criteria n. 기준 proposal n. 제안, 제의
be willing to phr. 기꺼이 ~하다 enclosed adj. 동봉된
casual adj. 간단한, 우연한 chair n. 의장, 의자

135 명사 자리 채우기   중 ●●○

해설 전치사(of)의 목적이 자리에 오면서 빈칸 앞의 형용사(experienced)의 수식을 받을 수 있는 것은 명사이므로 명사 (C) specialists(전문가들)가 정답이다. 부사 (A), 동사 (B), 형용사 (D)는 명사 자리에 올 수 없다. (D) special을 '특별한 것, 특별한 사람'을 의미하는 명사로 본다 해도, 가산 명사이므로 복수형으로 쓰이거나 관사와 함께 쓰여야 한다.

어휘 specially adv. 특별하게 specialize v. 전문적으로 다루다, 전공하다
special adj. 특별한; n. 특별한 것, 특별한 사람

136 알맞은 문장 고르기   중 ●●○

해석 (A) 저희는 폭넓은 선택을 제공합니다.
(B) 그 발표들은 짧을 것입니다.
(C) 주제에 대한 제안들은 환영받습니다.
(D) 모든 참가자들은 상을 받을 것입니다.

해설 앞부분에서 지역 주민들이 사업 아이디어를 전문가 심사위원단에 제시한다고 했고, 뒤 문장 'Each (participant) gets only 15 minutes to share their proposal.'에서 각 참가자는 그들의 제안을 공유하기 위해 오직 15분을 얻는다고 했으므로 빈칸에는 발표 시간과 관련된 내용이 들어가야 함을 알 수 있다. 따라서 (B)가 정답이다.

어휘 selection n. 선택 brief adj. 짧은, 간단한 suggestion n. 제안
welcome adj. 환영받는, 좋은; v. 환영하다 contestant n. 참가자
prize n. 상

137 명사 어휘 고르기 전체 문맥 파악   하 ●○○

해설 빈칸은 동사(gets)의 주어 역할을 하는 명사 자리이다. '각 ____는 그들의 제안을 공유하기 위해 오직 15분을 얻는다'라는 문맥이므로 모든 보기가 정답의 후보이다. 앞부분에서 지역사회의 연례 기업가 정신 경영대회에 대해 언급하며, 지역 주민들은 그들의 사업 아이디어를 경험이 풍부한 전문가 심사원단에 제출할 수 있다고 했으므로, 각 참가자는 그들의 제안을 공유하기 위해 오직 15분을 얻는다는 것을 알 수 있다. 따라서 (D) participant(참가자)가 정답이다.

어휘 partner n. 동업자, 파트너 representative n. 대표, 대리인
spectator n. 관중

138 태에 맞는 동사 채우기   하 ●○○

해설 문장에 동사가 없으므로 동사 (A), (C), (D)가 정답의 후보이다. 빈칸 뒤에 수동태와 함께 쓰이는 by(~에 의해)가 있고 '그것(대회)이 간단한 점심 식사에 의해 뒤따라오다', 즉 대회 뒤에 간단한 점심 식사가 이어질 것이라는 수동의 의미이므로 수동태 (D) will be followed가 정답이다. 능동태 (A)와 (C)를 쓸 경우 각각 '그것(대회)이 간단한 점심 식사에 의해 다음에 오다/왔다'라는 어색한 문맥이 된다. 동명사 혹은 현재분사 (B)는 동사 자리에 올 수 없다.

139-142번은 다음 안내문에 관한 문제입니다.

9월 1일부로, *Canberra Post*지는 신문의 토요일 호를 발행하는 것을 중단할 것입니다. 이 결정은 주말 독자 수의 감소¹³⁹에 대응하여 이루어졌습니다. 이 인원수는 지난 3년간 약 50만 명에서 10만 명으로 ¹⁴⁰감소했습니다. 토요일 호를 중단함으로써, 저희는 저희의 평일 독자층에 집중할 수 있을 것입니다. 저희는 또한 저희의 평일 호에 몇몇 새로운 ¹⁴¹부문들을 추가할 것입니다. 이것들은 여행, 건강, 정원 가꾸기, 그리고 더 많은 것들을 포함할 것입니다. ¹⁴²그것들은 저희의 금요일 호에 나오기 시작할 것입니다.

publish v. 발행하다 edition n. 호, 판 decline n. 감소; v. 감소하다
discontinue v. 중단하다 focus on phr. ~에 집중하다
readership n. 독자층

139 전치사 표현 채우기   중 ●●●

해설 빈칸은 명사구(a decline ~ readers)를 목적어로 취하는 전치사 자리이다. '주말 독자 수의 감소에 대응하여'라는 의미가 되어야 하므로 빈칸 앞의 전치사구 in response와 함께 '~에 대응하여'라는 의미의 어구인 in response to를 만드는 전치사 (A) to가 정답이다.

어휘 of prep. ~의 by prep. ~에 의해 on prep. ~위에

140 시간 표현과 일치하는 시제의 동사 채우기   하 ●○○

해설 현재 완료 시제와 함께 쓰이는 시간 표현(over the past three years)이 있으므로 과거에 발생한 일이 현재까지 계속되거나, 과거에 발생한 일이 현

재까지 영향을 미치는 것을 표현할 때 사용되는 현재 완료 시제 (B) have decreased가 정답이다. 현재 진행 시제 (A), 과거 시제 (C), 현재 시제 (D)는 현재 완료를 나타내는 시간 표현과 함께 쓰일 수 없다.

어휘 decrease v. 감소하다, 감소시키다

141 명사 어휘 고르기 주변 문맥 파악   하 ●○○

해설 빈칸은 동사(will be adding)의 목적어 역할을 하는 명사 자리이다. '평일 호에 몇몇 새로운 ____을 추가할 것이다'라는 문맥이므로 모든 보기가 정답의 후보이다. 뒤 문장에서 이것들은 여행, 건강, 정원 가꾸기, 그리고 더 많은 것들을 포함할 것이라고 했으므로 평일 호에 몇몇 새로운 부문들을 추가할 것이라는 것을 알 수 있다. 따라서 (C) sections(부문들)가 정답이다.

어휘 method n. 방법 machine n. 기계 position n. 위치, 자리

142 알맞은 문장 고르기   하 ●○○

해석 (A) 그것들은 저희의 금요일 호에 나오기 시작할 것입니다.
(B) 환불에 관한 많은 문의들이 있었습니다.
(C) 저희는 저희 편집자의 미래에 행운을 빕니다.
(D) 하지만, 그것은 시 경계 내에서만 배달될 수 있습니다.

해설 앞 문장 'These will include Travel, Health, Gardening and more.'에서 이것들, 즉 새로운 부문들은 여행, 건강, 그리고 정원 가꾸기, 그리고 더 많은 것들을 포함할 것이라고 했으므로, 빈칸에는 신문에 새롭게 포함되는 부문들과 관련된 내용이 들어가야 함을 알 수 있다. 따라서 (A)가 정답이다.

어휘 appear v. 나오다, 발간되다 inquiry n. 문의 editor n. 편집자

143-146번은 다음 회람에 관한 문제입니다.

수신: 모든 콜 센터 직원들
발신: John Dooley, 고객 지원 전문가
제목: 정보 수집
날짜: 6월 22일

지난 6개월 동안, 전화를 건 사람들이 우리 직원들 중 한 명과 이야기하기 위해 기다린 시간의 양이 거의 두 배가 되었습니다. ¹⁴³이 시간은 5월에 7분이었으며, 현재 그것은 13분입니다. ¹⁴⁴고객들은 그들의 문제들을 해결하기 위한 다른 수단이 필요합니다. 따라서, 저는 우리 웹사이트에 새로운 페이지를 추가할 것입니다. 이것은 "자주 묻는 질문들"이라고 분류될 것이며, ¹⁴⁵포괄적인 답변을 담을 것입니다. 저는 여러분 각자가 우리 소프트웨어 프로그램들에 관해 여러분이 매일 ¹⁴⁶받는 가장 흔한 10가지 질문들의 목록을 제게 보내주시기를 바랍니다.

amount n. 양, 액수 representative n. 직원, 대표자
double v. 두 배가 되다, ~의 두 배이다
label v. ~을 분류하다, ~에 라벨을 붙이다 frequently adv. 자주, 빈번하게
contain v. 담다, 포함하다 common adj. 흔한, 보통의

143 지시대명사/지시형용사 채우기 주변 문맥 파악   중 ●●●

해설 명사(time)를 꾸밀 수 있는 것은 형용사이므로 지시형용사 (A)와 (C), 소유격 인칭대명사 (B)가 정답의 후보이다. 앞 문장에서 '전화를 건 사람들이 기다린 시간의 양이 거의 두 배가 되었다'라고 했고, 빈칸 뒤의 단수 명사(time)가 앞에서 언급한 시간을 가리키고 있으므로 '이 시간은 5월에 7분이었다'라는 문맥을 만드는 지시형용사 (A) This(이)가 정답이다. 소유격 인칭대명사 (B)는 '우리(콜 센터 직원들)의 시간은 5월에 7분이었다'라는 어색한 문맥이 된다. 참고로, 지시형용사 (C)는 복수 명사와 함께 쓰이며, 지시대명사로 쓰이는 경우 앞에 언급된 복수 명사를 대신할 때 쓰임을 알아둔다. 소유대명사

(D)는 형용사 자리에 올 수 없다.

144 알맞은 문장 고르기   상 ●●●

해석 **(A) 고객들은 그들의 문제들을 해결하기 위한 다른 수단이 필요합니다.**
(B) 새로운 초과근무 규정은 며칠 후에 시행될 것입니다.
(C) 우리 회사는 추가된 시간으로 인해 출시를 연기해야 했습니다.
(D) 우리의 전화 서비스가 일시적으로 연결이 끊어졌습니다.

해설 앞부분에서 지난 6개월 동안, 전화를 건 사람들이 직원과 이야기를 하기 위해 기다린 시간이 거의 두 배가 되었다고 했고, 뒤 문장 'Thus, I will add a new page to our Web site.'에서 따라서 웹사이트에 새로운 페이지를 추가할 것이라고 했으므로, 빈칸에는 이러한 문제를 해결하기 위해 전화 통화 외에 직원들과 연락할 수 있는 다른 방법이 필요하다는 것과 관련된 내용이 들어가야 함을 알 수 있다. 따라서 (A)가 정답이다.

어휘 means n. 수단   overtime n. 초과 근무
take effect phr. 시행되다, 적용되다   delay v. 연기하다
launch n. 출시; v. 출시하다   temporarily adv. 일시적으로
disconnect v. 연결을 끊다

145 형용사 자리 채우기   중 ●●○

해설 명사(answers)를 꾸밀 수 있는 것은 형용사이므로 형용사 (A)와 현재분사 (B)가 정답의 후보이다. '포괄적인 답변'이라는 의미가 되어야 하므로 형용사 (A) comprehensive(포괄적인, 종합적인)가 정답이다. 현재분사 (B)를 쓸 경우 '이것은 자주 묻는 질문들이라고 분류될 것이며, 이해하는 답변을 포함할 것이다'라는 어색한 의미가 된다. (B) comprehending을 동명사로 보고 명사 answers를 동명사의 목적어로 본다 해도, '이것은 자주 묻는 질문들이라고 분류될 것이며, 답변을 이해하는 것을 포함할 것이다'라는 어색한 의미가 된다. 부사 (C)와 명사 (D)는 형용사 자리에 올 수 없다.

어휘 comprehend v. 이해하다   comprehensively adv. 완전히, 철저히
comprehension n. 이해력

146 수, 태, 시제에 맞는 동사 채우기   중 ●●○

해설 명사 questions 다음에 나오는 목적격 관계대명사 that/which가 생략된 절 (you ~ programs)에 주어(you)만 있고 동사가 없으므로 동사인 (B), (C), (D)가 정답의 후보이다. 참고로, 선행사(questions)와 주어 사이에 목적격 관계대명사 which 또는 that이 생략되었음을 알아둔다. 동사 receive가 '~을 받다'라는 의미의 타동사로 쓰여 '여러분이 질문들을 받는다'라는 능동의 의미가 되어야 하고, 반복되는 동작을 나타내는 현재 시간 표현(each day)이 있으므로 현재 시제 능동태 (C) receive가 정답이다. 미래 시제 (B)는 미래 상황에 대한 추측이나 의지를 나타낸다. 현재 시제 수동태 (D)는 생략된 목적격 관계대명사를 목적어로 취할 수 없으므로 답이 될 수 없다. 동명사 또는 현재 분사 (A)는 동사 자리에 올 수 없다. 참고로, 현재 시제는 현재의 상태나 반복되는 동작, 일반적인 사실을 나타낼 수 있음을 알아둔다.

PART 7

147-148번은 다음 공고에 관한 문제입니다.

시청에서 제설 서비스를 필요로 함

[147]Brannethville은 시청 주변의 포장된 구역들에 있는 눈과 얼음의 제거에 대한 입찰을 구하고 있습니다. 제안서를 제출하기 전, 요구 조항들에 주의해 주십시오:

1. 모든 눈과 얼음이 매일 아침 7시까지 제거되어야 합니다.
2. 강설량이 보통에서 많은 날에는 계약자가 오전 7시부터 오후 5시까지 시간이 있어야 합니다.
3. [148]계약자는 모든 장비를 제공해야 합니다.
4. 계약은 제설 작업 필요 여부와는 관계없이, 12월 3일부터 5월 3일까지 6개월 동안 지속될 것입니다.

관심이 있으시다면, 당신의 제안서를 Brannethville 시청으로 보내주십시오. 자격을 얻으려면 입찰이 12월 1일까지 수령되어야 합니다.

---

removal n. 제거   seek v. 구하다, 찾다   bid n. 입찰
pave v. (도로를) 포장하다   proposal n. 제안(서)   contractor n. 계약자
snowfall n. 강설량   supply v. 제공하다   qualify v. 자격을 얻다

147 목적 찾기 문제   중 ●●○

해석 공고의 목적은 무엇인가?
(A) 새로운 규정을 발표하기 위해
(B) 계절성 작업에 대한 지원을 요청하기 위해
(C) 유용한 제설 관련 조언을 제공하기 위해
(D) 주민들에게 겨울에 대비할 것을 상기시키기 위해

해설 지문의 'Brannethville is seeking bids for the removal of snow and ice on paved areas'에서 Brannethville이 포장된 구역들에 있는 눈과 얼음의 제거에 대한 입찰을 구하고 있다고 했으므로 (B)가 정답이다.

어휘 regulation n. 규정, 규제   application n. 지원(서)   helpful adj. 유용한
remind v. 상기시키다

패러프레이징

> removal of snow and ice 눈과 얼음의 제거 → seasonal job 계절성 작업

148 육하원칙 문제   중 ●●○

해석 계약자들은 무엇을 하도록 요구되는가?
(A) 웹사이트에 등록한다
(B) 그들 소유의 장비를 제공한다
(C) 오직 밤에만 작업한다
(D) 12월까지 작업을 완료한다

해설 지문의 'The contractor must supply all equipment.'에서 계약자는 모든 장비를 제공해야 한다고 했으므로 (B)가 정답이다.

어휘 register v. 등록하다   complete v. 완료하다

패러프레이징

> supply ~ equipment 장비를 제공하나 → provide ~ equipment 장비를 제공한다

149-150번은 다음 이메일에 관한 문제입니다.

발신: Topline사 고객 서비스 <cs@topline.com>
수신: Chloe Schmidt <ch.sch@baltorco.org>
제목: 거래 종료
날짜: 6월 29일

Ms. Schmidt께,

[149]귀하께서 Topline사와 거래를 끊었다는 소식을 듣게 되어 유감입니다. 저희의 높은 통화 품질 및 고급 보안 기능들 때문에, Topline사는 전

세계 기업들에 선호되는 인터넷 전화 제공업체입니다. 한 달에 단 9.99달러로, Basic 상품 가입자들은 다른 Topline사 회원들과 인스턴트 메시지, 음성 통화, 그리고 화상 통화를 통해 의사소통을 할 수 있습니다. 한 달에 19.99달러로, Elite 상품 가입자들은 전 세계의 일반 전화 및 휴대전화로의 무제한 통화에 대한 추가적인 혜택을 받습니다.

¹⁴⁹그러니 다시 가입하시는 것은 어떠십니까? ¹⁵⁰새로운 Basic 또는 Elite 계정을 개설하시면, 저희는 귀하께 한 달의 무료 이용을 제공해드릴 것입니다. 귀하께서 결제 페이지에 도달하시면, 코드 142737을 입력하십시오.

Jerome Meyer 드림
고객 서비스 직원
Topline사

---

close an account with phr. ~와 거래를 끊다 advanced adj. 고급의
security n. 보안 prefer v. 선호하다 communicate v. 의사소통을 하다
unlimited adj. 무제한의 landline n. 일반 전화
complimentary adj. 무료의 usage n. 이용, 사용

149 목적 찾기 문제 하 ●○○

해석 이메일은 왜 쓰였는가?
(A) 서비스 문제에 대해 사과하기 위해
(B) 청구서의 납입을 요청하기 위해
(C) 새로운 제품을 광고하기 위해
(D) 고객에게 돌아오라고 설득하기 위해

해설 지문의 'We are sorry to hear that you closed your account with Topline.'에서 귀하가 Topline사와 거래를 끊었다는 소식을 듣게 되어 유감이라고 한 후, 'So why not join again?'에서 그러니 다시 가입하는 건 어떤지 물으며 다시 가입할 때 제공될 혜택에 대해 설명하고 있으므로 (D)가 정답이다.

어휘 apologize v. 사과하다 payment n. 납입, 지불 bill n. 청구서
persuade v. 설득하다

패러프레이징

join again 다시 가입하다 → return 돌아오다

150 육하원칙 문제 중 ●●○

해석 Ms. Schmidt는 어떻게 무료 서비스를 받을 수 있는가?
(A) 구독을 업그레이드함으로써
(B) 포인트를 현금으로 바꿈으로써
(C) 특정 숫자들을 입력함으로써
(D) 친구를 추천함으로써

해설 지문의 'Create a new ~ account, and we will give you one month of complimentary usage. When you reach the payment page, enter the code 142737.'에서 새로운 계정을 개설하면 귀하께 한 달의 무료 이용을 제공할 것이라고 했고, 결제 페이지에 도달하면 코드 142737을 입력하라고 했으므로 (C)가 정답이다.

어휘 redeem v. (현금으로) 바꾸다 refer v. 추천하다, 주목하게 하다

패러프레이징

free service 무료 서비스 → complimentary usage 무료 이용

151-152번은 다음 메시지 대화문에 관한 문제입니다.

Leo Henderson	오전 10시 48분

샌디에이고에서 출발하는 제 비행기가 5시간 동안 연착되었어요. 저는 오후 6시 30분까지 시카고에 도착하지 못할 거예요. 그래서 저는 오늘 오후 4시에 예정된 지역 관리자들의 회의에 참석하지 못할 거예요.

Shelly Summers	오전 10시 52분

¹⁵¹제가 지금 바로 이사님께 전화해서 그에게 알리겠습니다. 그는 일정을 변경하는 것을 원하실 수도 있습니다. 제가 확인해 보겠습니다.

Shelly Summers	오전 10시 59분

네, ¹⁵²그는 내일 아침 오전 8시 30분으로 일정을 변경하기를 원하십니다. 모든 지역 관리자들이 참석하길 원하십니다. 그것이 괜찮으시겠습니까?

Leo Henderson	오전 11시 2분

제가 재무 이사님과의 회의가 오전 9시 30분에 있지 않나요?

Shelly Summers	오전 11시 4분

네, 하지만 저희는 그것을 오후까지 연기할 수 있습니다. 당신은 오후 3시 이후에는 예정된 것이 아무것도 없습니다. 제가 재무 이사님과 확정하고 나면 당신에게 시간을 알려드리겠습니다. 즐거운 비행 되십시오!

---

miss v. (~에) 참석하지 못하다, 놓치다 scheduled adj. 예정된
inform v. 알리다 reschedule v. 일정을 변경하다
in attendance phr. 참석한 put off phr. 연기하다, 미루다
confirm v. 확정하다, 확인하다

151 의도 파악 문제 하 ●○○

해석 오전 10시 52분에, Ms. Summers가 "Let me check"라고 썼을 때 그녀가 의도한 것은?
(A) 비행기가 언제 도착할지 알아낼 것이다.
(B) 회사 이사에게 의견을 물을 것이다.
(C) 자동차와 운전기사가 이용 가능한지 알아볼 것이다.
(D) 지역 관리자들에게 연락할 것이다.

해설 지문의 'I'll call the director right now and inform him. He may want to reschedule.'에서 Ms. Summers가 지금 바로 이사님께 전화해서 그에게 알릴 것이고 그는 일정을 변경하는 것을 원할 수도 있다고 한 후, 'Let me check.'(제가 확인해 보겠습니다)라고 한 것을 통해, Ms. Summers가 회사 이사에게 의견을 물을 것임을 알 수 있다. 따라서 (B)가 정답이다.

어휘 determine v. 알아내다, 결정하다 consult v. 의견을 묻다, 상의하다

152 육하원칙 문제 하 ●○○

해석 Mr. Henderson은 내일 언제 지역 관리자 회의에 참석할 것인가?
(A) 오전 8시 30분에
(B) 오전 9시 30분에
(C) 오후 3시에
(D) 오후 6시 30분에

해설 지문의 'he wants to reschedule for tomorrow morning at 8:30 A.M. He would like all regional managers in attendance.'에서 그, 즉 회사 이사가 내일 아침 오전 8시 30분으로 일정을 변경하기를 원하며, 모든 지역 관리자들이 참석하길 원한다고 했으므로 (A)가 정답이다.

패러프레이징

attend 참석하다 → in attendance 참석한

153-154번은 다음 기사에 관한 문제입니다.

Ascott Foods사가 비닐봉지들에 작별을 고하다
Nicole Chase 작성

3월 20일—슈퍼마켓 체인인 ^{154-C}Ascott Foods사는 환경에 좋지 않은 일회용 비닐 쇼핑백을 더 이상 제공하지 않을 것이라고 발표했다. 그것은 Golden Supermarket사 이후로 그렇게 하는 두 번째 체인이 될 것이다. 하지만, Ascott사의 금지가 바로 시행되지는 않을 것이다. 회사 대표에 따르면, ¹⁵³재고품이 지속되는 동안은 각 상점이 비닐봉지 사용을 **계속할** 것이다.

앞으로 몇 주 후, ^{154-D}전국의 모든 166개의 Ascott Foods사 지점들이 재사용 가능한 캔버스 가방들을 제공하기 시작할 것이다. 고객들이 그것들을 사용하도록 장려하기 위해 ^{154-A}그것들은 3개월 동안 무료로 제공될 것이다. ^{154-B}그 회사는 자사의 농산물 포장에 플라스틱 사용을 막을 수 있는 방법들도 찾고 있다.

plastic bag phr. 비닐봉지 announce v. 발표하다
single-use adj. 일회용의 come into effect phr. 시행되다
supply n. 재고품 reusable adj. 재사용 가능한 avoid v. 막다, 방지하다
produce n. 농산물; v. 생산하다

153 동의어 찾기 문제 중 ●●○

해석 1문단 여덟 번째 줄의 단어 "keep"은 의미상 -와 가장 가깝다.
(A) 확보하다
(B) 계속하다
(C) 보류하다
(D) 보존하다

해설 keep을 포함한 구절 'each store will keep using plastic bags for as long as supplies last'에서 재고품이 지속되는 동안은 각 상점이 비닐봉지 사용을 계속할 것이라고 했으므로 keep은 '계속하다'라는 뜻으로 사용되었다. 따라서 '계속하다'라는 뜻을 지닌 (B) continue가 정답이다.

154 Not/True 문제 중 ●●○

해석 Ascott Foods사에 대해 사실이 아닌 것은?
(A) 3개월 동안 무료 쇼핑백들을 제공할 것이다.
(B) 과일 및 채소 상품들을 포함하도록 방침을 확장할 수도 있다.
(C) 일회용 봉지 사용을 중단하는 최초의 슈퍼마켓이 될 것이다.
(D) 전국에 많은 매장 지점들을 가지고 있다.

해설 지문의 'Ascott Foods ~ will no longer be providing single-use plastic shopping bags'와 'It will become the second chain to do so'에서 Ascott Foods사는 일회용 비닐 쇼핑백을 더이상 제공하지 않을 것이며, 그렇게 하는 두 번째 체인이 될 것이라고 했으므로 (C)는 지문의 내용과 일치하지 않는다. 따라서 (C)가 정답이다. (A)는 'They will come at no cost for three months'에서 그것들, 즉 재사용 가능한 캔버스 가방들이 3개월 동안 무료로 제공될 것이라고 했으므로 지문의 내용과 일치한다. (B)는 'The company is also looking for ways to avoid using plastic in its produce packaging.'에서 그 회사, 즉 Ascott Foods사는 자사의 농산물 포장에 플라스틱 사용을 막을 수 있는 방법들도 찾고 있다고 했으므로 지문의 내용과 일치한다. (D)는 'all 166 Ascott Foods locations across the country'에서 전국의 모든 166개의 Ascott Foods사 지점들이라고 했으므로 지문의 내용과 일치한다.

어휘 extend v. 확장하다, 연장하다 policy n. 방침, 정책
multiple adj. 많은, 다수의

패러프레이징

at no cost 무료로 → free 무료의
produce 농산물 → fruit and vegetable products 과일 및 채소 상품
166 ~ locations 166개의 지점들 → multiple store locations 많은 매장 지점들

155-157번은 다음 양식에 관한 문제입니다.

Cadigan사 경비 보고서

직원명: Cole Bradley
부서: 판매부
경비 목적: 고객 방문을 위한 출장
오늘의 날짜: 3월 28일

지출 날짜	설명	지출 분류	총액
3월 4일	Gateway 항공 — 토론토에서 포트로더데일로, 이코노미 좌석, 편도	이동	126.25달러
3월 4-6일	Julbee 자동차 대여점, 소형차, 하루당 50달러	이동	150.00달러
3월 4-5일	Bonneville 호텔, 1인용 객실, 1박당 90달러	숙박	180.00달러
3월 5일	Cowbell Grill, 4명	비즈니스 식사	270.00달러
¹⁵⁶3월 6일	Natura 항공 — 포트로더데일에서 토론토로, ¹⁵⁶비즈니스 좌석, 편도	이동	316.10달러
		총액	1,042.35달러

일반 지침:
· 모든 구매들은 지난 30일 이내에 발생했어야 한다.
· ^{155/157-B}모든 업무 관련 지출들에 대한 원본 영수증이 첨부되어야 하며, 그렇지 않을 경우 직원에 대한 환급이 거절될 것이다.
· 1인용 호텔 객실과 소형차 대여 비용뿐만 아니라, 이코노미 좌석의 이동 경비들도 전액 상환될 것이다. ¹⁵⁶비즈니스 좌석 항공권은 이코노미 좌석에 이용 가능한 좌석이 없을 때만 구매되어야 하며, 상황에 따라 **비용이 전액 상환되지 않을 수도 있다.** 출장을 위해 구입된 어떠한 개인 보험도 환급받을 수 없다.

expense n. 경비, 지출 trip n. 출장, 여행 compact car phr. 소형차
occur v. 발생하다, 일어나다 original adj. 원본의 attach v. 첨부하다
reimbursement n. 환급, 상환 deny v. 거절하다, 거부하다
pay back phr. 상환하다 reimbursable adj. 환급받을 수 있는

155 목적 찾기 문제 중 ●●○

해석 Mr. Bradley는 왜 양식을 작성했는가?
(A) 매출액을 밝히기 위해
(B) 견적서를 제공하기 위해
(C) 여행 일정을 제안하기 위해
(D) 보상을 요청하기 위해

해설 지문의 'Original receipts ~ must be attached or reimbursement to the employee will be denied.'에서 원본 영수증이 첨부되어야 하며, 그렇지 않을 경우 직원에 대한 환급이 거절될 것이라고 한 후, 환급 관련 지침에 대해 설명하고 있으므로 (D)가 정답이다.

어휘 reveal v. 밝히다, 드러내다 sales figure phr. 매출액
estimate n. 견적(서) itinerary n. 여행 일정
compensation n. 보상(금), 배상

패러프레이징

reimbursement 환급 → compensation 보상

156 추론 문제 　　　　　　　　　　상 ●●●

해석　Mr. Bradley에 대해 추론될 수 있는 것은?
　　　(A) 출장에서 법인 카드를 사용했다.
　　　(B) 항공편에 대해 전액 상환을 받지 못할 수도 있다.
　　　(C) 보고서를 제출하는 기한을 지키지 않았다.
　　　(D) 식사 비용에 허용되는 한도를 초과했다.

해설　지문의 'March 6', 'business class'에서 Mr. Bradley가 3월 6일에 비즈니스 좌석을 이용했다는 것을 알 수 있고, 'Business-class travel tickets ~ may not be paid back in full'에서 비즈니스 좌석 항공권은 전액 상환되지 않을 수도 있다고 했으므로 Mr. Bradley가 항공편에 대해 전액 상환을 받지 못할 수도 있음을 추론할 수 있다. 따라서 (B)가 정답이다.

어휘　corporate adj. 법인의, 기업의　repay v. 상환하다　exceed v. 초과하다
　　　acceptable adj. 허용되는, 용인되는

패러프레이징

be paid back in full 전액 상환되다 → be fully repaid 전액 상환되다

157 Not/True 문제 　　　　　　　　　중 ●●○

해석　Cadigan사에 대해 사실인 것은?
　　　(A) 최근 그것의 출장들에 관하여 규정을 바꿨다.
　　　(B) 몇몇 직원들로부터 지불 기록을 요구한다.
　　　(C) 그것의 본사를 토론토로 이전했다.
　　　(D) 몇몇 고객들에게 전액 환불을 제공한다.

해설　'Original receipts for all business-related expenses must be attached or reimbursement to the employee will be denied.'에서 모든 업무 관련 지출들에 대한 원본 영수증이 첨부되어야 하며, 그렇지 않을 경우 직원에 대한 환급이 거절될 것이라고 했다. 따라서 환급을 원하는 직원들은 원본 영수증을 첨부해야 함을 알 수 있으므로 (B)는 지문의 내용과 일치한다. 따라서 (B)가 정답이다. (A), (C), (D)는 지문에 언급되지 않은 내용이다.

어휘　relocate v. 이전하다, 이동하다　headquarters n. 본사

패러프레이징

original receipts 원본 영수증 → payment records 지불 기록

158-160번은 다음 이메일에 관한 문제입니다.

수신: 모든 트레이너들 <instructors@silvergym.com>
발신: Francesca Martinez <f.martinez@silvergym.com>
제목: 여러분 모두를 위한 최신 정보
날짜: 2월 1일

안녕하세요 여러분,

오늘부터, 헬스장 회원들은 우리의 새롭게 이용 가능한 Silver 헬스장 스마트폰 애플리케이션을 다운로드하여 그들의 회원 ID로 로그인할 수 있습니다. ¹⁵⁹⁻ᴮ/ᶜ이 애플리케이션은 사용자들이 우리 시설에서 기구를 사용하면서 그들이 체중을 얼마나 감량했는지에 대해 계속 파악하도록 도울 것입니다. ¹⁵⁸Silver 헬스장의 개인 트레이너로서, 여러분은 여러분이 함께하는 회원들이 가능한 한 이 서비스를 많이 이용하도록 권장해야 합니다. 이는 효과적이고 보람 있는 운동 프로그램을 보장하기 위함입니다.

또한, 이번 달에 우리는 특별 판촉 행사를 할 것입니다. ¹⁵⁹⁻ᴬ애플리케이션에 기록된 정해진 동작들을 따라 함으로써 최소 10파운드를 감량하는 모든 회원들은 그들이 선택하는 한 번의 무료 수업에 대한 쿠폰을 받을 수 있습니다. 이 제안에 관심 있는 사람들에게 ¹⁶⁰우리 수업들에 대한 세부 사항들이 입실 서명 프런트 옆의 게시판에 게시되어 있다는 것을 알려주시기 바랍니다.

이 활동에 대한 여러분의 협조에 감사드립니다!

Francesca Martinez 드림, 소유주, Silver 헬스장

keep track of phr. ~에 대해 계속 파악하다　equipment n. 기구, 장치
encourage v. 권장하다, 격려하다　effective adj. 효과적인
rewarding adj. 보람 있는　promotion n. 판촉(행사), 홍보
routine n. 정해진 동작, 일상　bulletin board phr. 게시판

158 목적 찾기 문제 　　　　　　　　하 ●○○

해석　이메일의 하나의 목적은 무엇인가?
　　　(A) 헬스장 회원들에게 요금 변경에 대해 알리기 위해
　　　(B) 고객들에게 규정에 대해 상기시키기 위해
　　　(C) 직원들에게 프로그램에 대해 알리기 위해
　　　(D) 사용자들에게 수업에 참여하도록 장려하기 위해

해설　지문의 'As the personal trainers at Silver Gym, you need to encourage the members you work with to use this service as much as possible.'에서 Silver 헬스장의 개인 트레이너로서, 여러분은 여러분이 함께하는 회원들이 가능한 한 이 서비스, 즉 스마트폰 애플리케이션을 많이 이용하도록 권장해야 한다고 했으므로 (C)가 정답이다.

어휘　notify v. 알리다, 공지하다　policy n. 규정, 정책

159 Not/True 문제 　　　　　　　　중 ●●○

해석　헬스장 회원들에 대해 언급되지 않은 것은?
　　　(A) 무료 수업을 받을 자격이 있다.
　　　(B) 애플리케이션을 사용하여 체중 감량을 관찰할 수 있다.
　　　(C) 헬스장에 있는 기구를 사용하여 운동할 수 있다.
　　　(D) 우편으로 혜택들에 대한 공지를 받을 것이다.

해설　지문에서 (D)는 언급되지 않은 내용이다. 따라서 (D)가 정답이다. (A)는 'Any member ~ can receive a voucher for one free class of their choice.'에서 회원들은 그들이 선택하는 한 번의 무료 수업에 대한 쿠폰을 받을 수 있다고 했으므로 지문의 내용과 일치한다. (B)와 (C)는 'The app will help users to keep track of how much weight they have lost using the equipment at our facility.'에서 이 애플리케이션은 사용자들이 자신들의 시설, 즉 헬스장에서 기구를 사용하면서 체중을 얼마나 감량했는지에 대해 계속 파악하도록 도울 것이라고 했으므로 지문의 내용과 일치한다.

어휘　eligible adj. ~할 자격이 있는　complimentary adj. 무료의
　　　monitor v. 관찰하다　notice n. 공지, 알림

패러프레이징

free class 무료 수업 → complimentary session 무료 수업
keep track of how much weight ~ lost 체중을 얼마나 감량했는지에 대해 계속 파악하다 → monitor weight loss 체중 감량을 관찰하다

160 육하원칙 문제 　　　　　　　　중 ●●○

해석　수업들에 대한 정보는 어디에서 볼 수 있는가?
　　　(A) 게시판에서

(B) 웹사이트에서
(C) 이메일에서
(D) 탈의실에서

해설 지문의 'details about our classes are posted on the bulletin board' 에서 수업들에 대한 세부 사항들이 게시판에 게시되어 있다고 했으므로 (A)가 정답이다.

어휘 notice board phr. 게시판 locker room phr. 탈의실

패러프레이징

information about classes 수업들에 대한 정보 → details about ~ classes 수업들에 대한 세부 사항들
bulletin board 게시판 → notice board 게시판

161-163번은 다음 안내문에 관한 문제입니다.

Gleason's Grill 종업원 교육 안내서

1단계
손님들이 자리에 앉자마자 그들에게 다가가서, 그들에게 호의적인 태도로 인사하세요. 일행의 각 구성원에게 충분한 메뉴판과 식기를 가져다주고 그들의 물컵을 채우세요. 163만약 당신이 새로운 손님들이 들어올 때 테이블을 응대하느라 바쁘다면, 큰 소리로 그들에게 인사하세요. — [1] —.

2단계
손님들에게 메뉴판을 살펴볼 시간을 주세요. — [2] —. 그들에게 우리의 일일 특선요리를 알려주고 메뉴 항목들에 대해 그들이 가지고 있는 모든 질문들에 답해주세요. 161손님이 특정 재료에 알레르기가 있어서 그들이 요리에 그것이 있는지에 관해 묻는 경우, 확신이 없다면 자리를 뜨는 것에 양해를 구하고 주방 직원으로부터 알아내세요. — [3] —. 162손님들이 주문할 준비가 되면, 누가 무엇을 주문했는지 적으면서, 당신의 메모지에 반드시 모든 것을 기록하세요. 그 다음, 실수가 일어나지 않았음을 확실히 하기 위해 그들에게 그들의 주문 내역들을 한 번 더 말하세요.

3단계
모든 것이 만족스러운지 알기 위해 음식을 가져다주고 몇 분 뒤에 손님들을 다시 확인해 보세요. 그들이 식사를 마치고 나면, 계산서를 가지고 오기 전에 디저트나 커피를 제안하세요. — [4] —.

seat v. 앉히다 friendly adj. 호의적인, 친근한 cutlery n. 식기
party n. 일행 acknowledge v. 인사하다, 아는체하다
loudly adv. 큰 소리로 go over phr. 살펴보다 inform v. 알리다
inquire v. 묻다 as to phr. ~에 관해 ingredient n. 재료
excuse v. (자리를 뜨는 것에 대해) 양해를 구하다
repeat v. 한 번 더 말하다, 반복하다 satisfactory adj. 만족스러운
bill n. 계산서, 고지서

---

161 육하원칙 문제 중 ●●○

해석 안내문에 따르면, 종업원들은 왜 주방 직원들과 대화해야 하는가?
(A) 음식이 얼마나 느리게 준비되고 있는지에 대해 불평하기 위해
(B) 아이들을 위한 더 작은 식사량을 요청하기 위해
(C) 그들에게 새롭게 추가된 메뉴 항목들을 알리기 위해
(D) 요리의 내용물에 대해 묻기 위해

해설 지문의 'In the event that a customer inquires as to whether a dish has a specific ingredient ~ find out from the kitchen staff'에서 손님들이 요리에 특정 재료가 있는지에 관해 문의하는 경우, 주방 직원으로부터 알아내라고 했으므로 (D)가 정답이다.

어휘 portion n. 양, 부분 added adj. 추가된

패러프레이징

ingredient 재료 → contents of a dish 요리의 내용물

---

162 육하원칙 문제 중 ●●○

해석 고객들의 주문을 받은 직후 종업원들은 무엇을 해야 하는가?
(A) 계산대에 메모지를 가져간다
(B) 추가적인 품목들을 추천한다
(C) 몇몇 선택된 것들을 확인한다
(D) 계산서에 각 항목을 추가한다

해설 지문의 'When the customers are ready to order, make sure to write everything down ~. Next, repeat their orders back to them to be certain that no mistakes have been made.'에서 고객들이 주문할 준비가 되면 반드시 모든 것을 기록하고, 그다음 실수가 일어나지 않았음을 확실히 하기 위해 그들에게 그들의 주문 내역들을 한 번 더 말하라고 했으므로 (C)가 정답이다.

어휘 notepad n. 메모지 additional adj. 추가적인
confirm v. 확인하다, 확정하다 selection n. 선택된 것

---

163 문장 위치 찾기 문제 하 ●○○

해석 [1], [2], [3], [4]로 표시된 위치 중, 다음 문장이 들어갈 곳으로 가장 적절한 것은?

"이것은 다른 직원들에게 그들이 식당에 들어왔다는 것을 알릴 것입니다."

(A) [1]
(B) [2]
(C) [3]
(D) [4]

해설 주어진 문장에서 이것이 다른 직원들에게 그들이 식당에 들어왔다는 것을 알릴 것이라고 했으므로, 이 문장이 직원들에게 사람들이 식당에 들어왔다는 것을 알려줄 수 있는 행동에 관한 내용이 제시된 부분에 들어가야 함을 알 수 있다. [1]의 앞 문장인 'If you are busy serving a table when new customers walk in, acknowledge them loudly.'에서 만약 당신이 새로운 손님들이 들어올 때 테이블을 응대하느라 바쁘다면, 큰 소리로 그들에게 인사하라고 했으므로, [1]에 주어진 문장이 들어가면 새로운 손님이 들어올 때 큰 소리로 그들에게 인사하면 이것이 다른 직원들에게 손님들이 식당에 들어왔다는 것을 알릴 것이라는 자연스러운 문맥이 된다는 것을 알 수 있다. 따라서 (A)가 정답이다.

어휘 alert v. 알리다, 의식하게 하다

164-167번은 다음 온라인 채팅 대화문에 관한 문제입니다.

Mimi Pearson [오후 3시 45분]
165새로운 문서 작성 소프트웨어로 문제를 겪고 있는 누구 다른 사람도 있나요?

Donald Platt [오후 3시 45분]
165저요. 제가 그것을 설치하려고 할 때마다, 제 화면이 멈춰요. 저는 IT 부서의 사람을 기다리고 있었어요.

Grace Helmsley [오후 3시 46분]
164-A한 IT 부서 직원이 제게 그들이 그 문제에 착수하고 있다고 말했어요. 164-B그들은 여기 2층을 방금 끝냈어요. Louis와 몇몇 다른 사람들도 문제들을 겪고 있었어요.

Louis Jones [오후 3시 46분]
맞아요. 제 소프트웨어는 이제 잘 작동하고 있어요. 165설치된 것이 작동하게 하려면 당신은 그저 운영 체제를 업데이트하기만 하면 돼요.

Mimi Pearson [오후 3시 47분]
그건 문제가 아니에요. 165저는 그것을 잘 설치할 수 있었어요. 저는 그 소프트웨어를 사용하는 방법을 알아내는 데 어려움을 겪고 있어요.

Donald Platt [오후 3시 48분]
Mimi, 회사 인트라넷에 사용자 설명서가 있어요. 당신이 원한다면 제가 당신에게 링크를 보내줄 수 있어요.

Grace Helmsley [오후 3시 48분]
당신은 도구 모음에서 자세한 설명들을 보기 위해 도움말 버튼을 클릭할 수도 있어요.

Mimi Pearson [오후 3시 49분]
저는 설명서가 있는지 몰랐어요. 166나중에 제가 그것들을 볼게요. Grace의 제안이 더 빠를 수도 있어서 저는 그것을 먼저 시도해볼게요, 그리고 제가 파일 하나를 당장 인쇄해야 해서요.

Louis Jones [오후 3시 50분]
회사는 우리에게 정말 교육을 제공해야 해요. 167제가 Mr. West와 얘기해 볼게요. 하지만 먼저 누가 그것을 필요하다고 생각하는지 알기 위해 이리저리 알아볼게요.

word processing phr. 문서 작성 install v. 설치하다 freeze v. 멈추다
work on phr. 착수하다, ~에 노력을 들이다 installation n. 설치된 것, 설치
figure out phr. 알아내다 manual n. 설명서 instruction n. 설명서
ask around phr. 이리저리 알아보다, 수소문하다

164 Not/True 문제
중 ●●○

해석 Ms. Helmsley에 대해 언급된 것은?
(A) IT 부서의 한 직원과 이야기했다.
(B) 건물의 3층에서 일한다.
(C) 운영체제 업데이트를 요청했다.
(D) 소프트웨어가 복잡하다고 생각한다.

해설 지문의 'An IT employee told me'에서 Ms. Helmsley가 한 IT 부서 직원이 자신에게 말했다고 했으므로 (A)는 지문의 내용과 일치한다. 따라서 (A)가 정답이다. (B)는 'They just finished here on the second floor.'에서 Ms. Helmsley가 그들, 즉 IT 부서 직원들이 여기 2층을 방금 끝냈다고 했으므로 지문의 내용과 일치하지 않는다. (C)와 (D)는 지문에 언급되지 않은 내용이다.

어휘 complicated adj. 복잡한

패러프레이징

An IT employee told me 한 IT 부서 직원이 자신에게 말했다 → spoke to a member of the IT department IT 부서의 한 직원과 이야기했다

165 의도 파악 문제
하 ●○○

해석 오후 3시 47분에, Ms. Pearson이 "That's not the problem"이라고 썼을 때, 그녀가 의도한 것은?
(A) 설명을 이해하지 못했다.
(B) 새로운 소프트웨어를 설치할 수 있었다.
(C) 문제가 해결되었다고 생각한다.
(D) IT 부서의 직원에게 연락할 수 없었다.

해설 지문의 'Anyone else having trouble with the new word processing software?'에서 Ms. Pearson이 새로운 문서 작성 소프트웨어로 문제를 겪고 있는 사람이 있는지 묻자, Mr. Platt이 'I am. Each time I try to install it, my screen freezes.'에서 자신이 그러하며 자신이 그것을 설치하려고 할 때마다 화면이 멈춘다고 했고, Mr. Jones가 'You just have to update your operating system for the installation to work.'에서 설치된 것이 작동하게 하려면 그저 운영 체제를 업데이트하기만 하면 된다고 하자, Ms. Pearson이 'That's not the problem.'(그건 문제가 아니에요)이라고 하면서 'I was able to install it just fine.'에서 자신은 그것을 잘 설치할 수 있었다고 한 것을 통해, Ms. Pearson은 새로운 소프트웨어를 설치할 수 있었다는 것을 알 수 있다. 따라서 (B)가 정답이다.

어휘 explanation n. 설명 issue n. 문제 resolve v. 해결하다

166 육하원칙 문제
중 ●●●

해석 Ms. Pearson은 왜 소프트웨어 설명서를 바로 보지 않기로 하는가?
(A) 그녀의 컴퓨터를 켤 수 없다.
(B) 그것들을 찾을 수 없다.
(C) Mr. Platt으로부터 멀리서 일한다.
(D) 시간이 많지 않아서 바쁘다.

해설 지문의 'I'll look at them later. I'll try Grace's suggestion first as it might be faster, and I need to print a file right away.'에서 Ms. Pearson이 나중에 그것들, 즉 설명서를 보겠다고 하며 파일 하나를 당장 인쇄해야 하고 Grace의 제안이 더 빠를 수도 있어서 그것을 먼저 시도할 것이라고 했다. 따라서 (D)가 정답이다.

어휘 in a hurry phr. (시간이 많지 않아서) 바쁜, 서둘러

167 추론 문제
중 ●●●

해석 Mr. Jones는 다음에 무엇을 할 것 같은가?
(A) 동료를 위해 문서를 인쇄한다
(B) 몇몇 2층 직원들에 관하여 문의한다
(C) Mr. West와 대화를 나눈다
(D) 직원들이 교육에 관심이 있는지 알아낸다

해설 지문의 'I'll talk to Mr. West. But first I'll ask around to see who feels they need it.'에서 Mr. Jones가 Mr. West와 얘기를 해볼 것이지만, 먼저 누가 그것, 즉 소프트웨어 사용에 대한 교육이 필요하다고 생각하는지 알기 위해 이리저리 알아보겠다고 했으므로 Mr. Jones는 직원들이 교육에 관심이 있는지 알아낼 것이라는 것을 추론할 수 있다. 따라서 (D)가 정답이다.

어휘 coworker n. 동료 find out phr. 알아내다

패러프레이징

ask around 이리저리 알아보다 → Find out 알아내다

168-171번은 다음 편지에 관한 문제입니다.

GALAXIS지

1월 7일

Dr. Frederick Simons
492번지 Lerner로, 901호
블룸필드 타운쉽, 마이애미주 48401

Dr. Simons께,

저희는 명왕성의 산들의 이야기에 대한 당신의 제안이 꽤 전도유망하다

고 생각했습니다. ¹⁷¹저희는 그것이 저희 독자들의 관심을 끌 것이라고 생각하며 당신이 ^{168-A/171}2,500에서 3,000단어의 기사를 작성해 ¹⁷¹주면 좋겠습니다. — [1] —. 이상적으로는, 저희는 이 기사가 명왕성의 지형 발견의 실마리가 되는 사건들에 초점을 맞추고 이것이 과학계에 얼마나 예기치 못한 일이었는지 강조하기를 바랍니다. — [2] —.

저희는 당신에게 그 기사에 대해 2,500달러를 제공할 수 있습니다. 하지만, ¹⁷⁰과거와 달리, 저희가 어떠한 이유로 당신의 작업물을 사용하지 않기로 결정할 경우, 저희가 당신에게 전액을 보상할 수 없을 것이라는 점을 유의하십시오. — [3] —. 그렇긴 하지만, 저희는 당신의 시간에 대해 당신에게 500달러를 지불할 것입니다. ^{168-C}저희는 그 기사를 저희의 5월호에 실을 예정이므로, 당신이 ^{168-B}3월 5일까지 당신의 초고를 제출해 주길 바랍니다. 저는 이 편지에 이 계약 조건들을 명시한 두 장의 계약서들을 함께 동봉했습니다. — [4] —. 만약 당신이 그것들에 동의한다면, ¹⁶⁹그 계약서들 중 하나에 서명을 하고 잡지사의 우편 주소를 사용하여 저희에게 돌려보내 주십시오. 나머지 하나는 당신의 기록을 위해 보관해 두십시오.

질문이나 우려 사항이 있다면, 주저하지 말고 제게 이메일로 연락하십시오. ¹⁷⁰저희는 당신과 다시 함께 일하기를 기대합니다.

Molly Hamilton 드림
수석 편집자, *Galaxis*지

---

proposal n. 제안 promising adj. 전도유망한, 조짐이 좋은
appeal v. 관심을 끌다, 호소하다 lead up to phr. ~의 실마리가 되다
discovery n. 발견 landform n. 지형 emphasize v. 강조하다
compensate v. 보상하다 intend to phr. ~할 예정이다, ~하려고 생각하다
enclose v. 동봉하다 state v. 명시하다, 기재하다 term n. (계약) 조건
hesitate v. 주저하다, 망설이다

168 Not/True 문제
중 ●●○

해석 Ms. Hamilton이 기사에 대한 정보로 언급하지 않은 것은?
(A) 단어 길이
(B) 마감일
(C) 발행 호
(D) 수정 과정

해설 지문에서 (D)는 언급되지 않은 내용이다. 따라서 (D)가 정답이다. (A)는 'write an article of 2,500 to 3,000 words'에서 2,500에서 3,000단어의 기사를 작성해 달라고 했으므로 지문의 내용과 일치한다. (B)는 'submit your first draft by March 5'에서 3월 5일까지 당신의 초고를 제출해 달라고 했으므로 지문의 내용과 일치한다. (C)는 'We intend to publish the article in our May issue'에서 그 기사를 5월호에 실을 예정이라고 했으므로 지문의 내용과 일치한다.

어휘 due date phr. 마감일, 만기일 revision n. 수정 process n. 과정

169 육하원칙 문제
중 ●●○

해석 Dr. Simons는 무엇을 하도록 요청받았는가?
(A) 계약서를 다시 우편으로 보낸다
(B) 몇몇 계약 조건들을 협상한다
(C) 몇몇 이메일 메시지들을 저장한다
(D) 기사를 다시 쓴다

해설 지문의 'please ~ return one of the contracts to us using the magazine's postal address'에서 그 계약서들 중 하나를 잡지사의 우편 주소를 사용하여 돌려보내 달라고 했으므로 (A)가 정답이다.

어휘 agreement n. 계약서 negotiate v. 협상하다

패러프레이징

return ~ contracts ~ using the ~ postal address 우편 주소를 사용하여 계약서를 돌려보내다 → Mail back an agreement 계약서를 다시 우편으로 보내다

170 추론 문제
중 ●●○

해석 *Galaxis*지에 대해 암시되는 것은?
(A) 구독자들은 온라인 콘텐츠를 수신하도록 선택할 수 있다.
(B) 몇몇 국가들에서 구매하는 것이 가능하다.
(C) Dr. Simons는 이전에 그것에 기사를 기고한 적이 있다.
(D) 그것의 프리랜서 작가들에게는 정규 직원보다 더 적은 급여를 지급한다.

해설 지문의 'unlike in the past, we will not be able to compensate you fully if we decide not to use your work for any reason'에서 과거와 달리, 자신들, 즉 *Galaxis*지가 어떠한 이유로 당신, 즉 Dr. Simons의 작업물을 사용하지 않기로 결정할 경우, 그에게 전액을 보상할 수 없을 것이라고 했고, 'We look forward to working with you again.'에서 당신, 즉 Dr. Simons와 다시 함께 일하기를 기대한다고 했으므로 Dr. Simons가 *Galaxis*지에 이전에 기사를 기고한 적이 있다는 것을 추론할 수 있다. 따라서 (C)가 정답이다.

어휘 contribute v. 기고하다, 공헌하다

171 문장 위치 찾기 문제
중 ●●○

해석 [1], [2], [3], [4]로 표시된 위치 중 다음 문장이 들어갈 곳으로 가장 적절한 것은?

"만약 그것이 이 양을 초과한다면, 저희는 그것을 실을 수 없을 것이라는 점을 유의해주십시오."

(A) [1]
(B) [2]
(C) [3]
(D) [4]

해설 주어진 문장에서 만약 그것이 이 양을 초과한다면, 저희는 그것을 실을 수 없을 것이라는 점을 유의해 달라고 했으므로, 이 문장이 실을 수 있는 양과 관련된 내용이 나오는 부분에 들어가야 함을 알 수 있다. [1]의 앞 문장인 'We ~ would like you to write an article of 2,500 to 3,000 words.'에서 저희는 당신이 2,500에서 3,000단어의 기사를 작성해 주면 좋겠다고 했으므로, [1]에 주어진 문장이 들어가면 2,500에서 3,000단어의 기사를 작성하길 원하며, 이 양을 초과할 경우 그것을 실을 수 없을 것이라는 자연스러운 문맥이 된다는 것을 알 수 있다. 따라서 (A)가 정답이다.

어휘 exceed v. 초과하다 amount n. 양, 총액 publish v. 싣다, 게재하다

172-175번은 다음 광고에 관한 문제입니다.

잊지 못할 경험을 위해 Galenus 여행사와 함께 멕시코의 Vallarta-Nayarit 지역을 방문하세요

¹⁷²Vallarta-Nayarit 지역은 제공할 것이 정말 많으며, 당신이 Galenus 여행사를 이용하여 여행을 예약하면, 당신은 당신의 여행 기간 동안 최대한의 지원을 받을 것입니다. 당신이 도착할 때 ¹⁷²당신을 맞이하기 위해 저희의 현지 지사의 직원들이 그곳에 가 있을 뿐만 아니라, 그들은 또한 당신이 관심을 가질 만한 어떠한 활동들이든 계획하는 데 도움을 줄 것입니다. 놓쳐서는 안 될 몇몇 지역들은 다음을 포함합니다:

Puerto Vallarta 시내
차량 통행이 금지된 산책로가 있는 이 도심 지역은 당신이 쇼핑하고, 식사

하고, 그리고 현지의 현대 미술관들을 방문하면서 관광할 수 있는 완벽한 장소입니다. 173주 광장은 길거리 공연자들과 작업 중인 예술가들로 항상 가득 차 있으므로 만약 당신이 아이들과 함께 여행한다면 이곳은 필수입니다.

Mismaloya
시내의 도보 거리 내에 있는 174이 지역은 가격이 적당한 숙박 시설들로 가득합니다. Mismaloya의 편안한 분위기는 돈을 너무 많이 쓰지 않고 해변에 더 가까이 있길 원하는 여행자들에게 이상적입니다. 인근 명소들은 Puerto Vallarta 동물원, Vallarta 식물원, 그리고 Las Animas 어드벤처 파크를 포함합니다.

Punta Mita
로맨틱한 휴가를 찾고 있으신가요? 신혼 여행객들, 유명 인사들, 그리고 관광객들 사이에서 인기 있는 이 마을은 백사장들, 외딴 휴양지들, 그리고 그림같이 아름다운 저녁노을들이 있는 휴식처입니다.

Riviera Nayarit
그것의 화려한 해변들로 유명한 175Riviera Nayarit은 골프장, 놀이공원, 그리고 모든 것이 포함된 5성급 호화 리조트들을 위해 가는 장소입니다. 생선 타코들과 다른 정통 별미들을 제공하는 해변 식당들은 이 지역의 200마일 구간의 도처에서 찾을 수 있습니다.

unforgettable adj. 잊지 못할 duration n. 기간 greet v. 맞이하다
land v. 도착하다 arrange v. (미리) 계획하다, 주선하다 miss v. 놓치다
boardwalk n. 산책로 dine v. 식사하다 contemporary adj. 현대의
must n. 필수, 꼭 보아야 하는 것 square n. 광장
at work phr. 작업 중인, 활동하는 affordable adj. (가격이) 적당한, 저렴한
accommodation n. 숙박 시설 botanical garden phr. 식물원
getaway n. 휴가 honeymooner n. 신혼 여행객 oasis n. 휴식처
isolated adj. 외딴 retreat n. 휴양지 picturesque adj. 그림같이 아름다운
sunset n. 저녁노을, 일몰 all-inclusive adj. 모두 포함된
authentic adj. 정통의, 진정한 delicacy n. 별미, 진미

172 추론 문제 상 ●●●

해석 Galenus 여행사에 대해 추론될 수 있는 것은?
(A) 현재 멕시코 여행에 대해 할인을 제공하고 있다.
(B) Vallarta-Nayarit 지역에 지점을 가지고 있다.
(C) 가족들을 위한 여행을 주선하는 것을 전문으로 한다.
(D) 모든 행선지들에 대해 여행 보험을 제공한다.

해설 지문의 'The Vallarta-Nayarit region has so much to offer'에서 Vallarta-Nayarit 지역은 제공할 것이 정말 많다고 했고, 'representatives from our local branch be there to greet you'에서 당신을 맞이하기 위해 저희의 현지 지사, 즉 Galenus 여행사의 Vallarta-Nayarit 지사 직원들이 그곳에 가 있을 것이라고 했으므로 Galenus 여행사가 Vallarta-Nayarit 지역에 지점을 가지고 있다는 사실을 추론할 수 있다. 따라서 (B)가 정답이다.

어휘 specialize in phr. ~을 전문으로 하다 destination n. 행선지

패러프레이징

local branch 현지 지사 → a location in ~ region 지역에 있는 지점

173 육하원칙 문제 중 ●●○

해석 광고에 따르면, Puerto Vallarta 시내는 왜 아이들을 데려오기 좋은 장소인가?
(A) 그곳의 도로들에는 차량이 들어올 수 없다.
(B) 많은 저렴한 식당들이 있다.
(C) 그곳에서 공개된 오락거리를 볼 수 있다.

(D) 해변에서 도보 거리 내에 있다.

해설 지문의 'It's a must if you're traveling with children as the main square is always full of street performers and artists at work.'에서 주 광장은 길거리 공연자들과 작업 중인 예술가들로 항상 가득 차 있으므로 만약 당신이 아이들과 함께 여행한다면 이곳, 즉 Puerto Vallarta 시내는 필수라고 했으므로 (C)가 정답이다.

어휘 allow v. 들어오게 하다 inexpensive adj. 저렴한, 비싸지 않은
public adj. 공개된, 공공의 entertainment n. 오락거리

패러프레이징

a good place to bring children 아이들을 데려오기 좋은 → a must if ~ traveling with children 아이들과 함께 여행한다면 필수

174 추론 문제 상 ●●●

해석 Mismaloya는 어느 집단의 흥미를 가장 많이 끌 것 같은가?
(A) 박물관 애호가들
(B) 알뜰한 여행자들
(C) 풍경 사진작가들
(D) 전문적인 예술가들

해설 지문의 'this area is full of affordable accommodations. ~ Mismaloya is ideal for travelers who want to be closer to the beach without spending too much money.'에서 이 지역, 즉 Mismaloya는 가격이 적당한 숙박 시설들로 가득하며, 돈을 너무 많이 쓰지 않고 해변에 더 가까이 있길 원하는 여행자들에게 이상적이라고 했으므로 Mismaloya는 알뜰한 여행자들의 흥미를 가장 많이 끌 것이라는 사실을 추론할 수 있다. 따라서 (B)가 정답이다.

어휘 lover n. 애호가 budget adj. 알뜰한, 검소한; n. 예산

175 추론 문제 중 ●●○

해석 Riviera Nayarit에 대해 암시되는 것은?
(A) 매우 비싼 숙박 시설 선택지들이 있다.
(B) 지역의 현대 미술 장소로 유명해지고 있다.
(C) 신혼부부들에게 인기 있는 행선지이다.
(D) 지난 10년간 크게 발전해왔다.

해설 지문의 'Riviera Nayarit is the place to go for ~ five-star luxury resorts'에서 Riviera Nayarit은 5성급 호화 리조트들을 위해 가는 장소라고 했으므로 Riviera Nayarit에 비싼 숙박 시설 선택지들이 있다는 사실을 추론할 수 있다. 따라서 (A)가 정답이다.

어휘 costly adj. 비싼 scene n. 장소, 분야 significantly adv. 크게, 상당히

패러프레이징

luxury resorts 호화 리조트들 → very costly accommodation 매우 비싼 숙박 시설

176-180번은 다음 회람과 이메일에 관한 문제입니다.

회람

수신: 모든 지점 관리자들
발신: Lori Morrison
제목: 재고 조사
날짜: 1월 5일

우리의 연간 재고 조사에 착수하기 위해 176/177-B우리는 모든 Super

Parties사 지점들에서 하루 동안의 휴업 일정을 잡아두었다는 것을 기억해 주십시오. ¹⁷⁶이 기간 동안, 모든 제품들은 손으로 세어져야 하며 우리의 컴퓨터 기록과 비교하여 대조되어야 합니다. 상세 내용은 아래에 있습니다.

지점	날짜
¹⁷⁷⁻ᴮ시카고, 일리노이	화요일, 2월 12일
¹⁷⁷⁻ᴮ포트웨인, 인디애나	수요일, 2월 13일
¹⁷⁷⁻ᴮ밀워키, 위스콘신	수요일, 2월 20일
¹⁷⁷⁻ᴮ/¹⁸⁰세인트루이스, ¹⁷⁷⁻ᴮ미주리	금요일, ¹⁸⁰2월 22일

여러분의 모든 직원들이 이러한 휴업들에 대해 알고 있고 그들이 도와줄 것을 요청받을 수 있다는 것을 확실히 하십시오. 덧붙여, ¹⁷⁷⁻ᴰ여러분의 고객들에게 위의 어떠한 날짜에든지 배송이 예정된 주문들은 영향을 받지 않을 것임을 알리십시오. 또한, 이 기간 동안 ¹⁷⁷⁻ᶜ그들은 우리 웹사이트를 통해 제품들을 계속 구매할 수 있습니다.

inventory n. 재고 조사, 물품 목록 schedule v. 예정이다
closure n. 휴업 undertake v. 착수하다 count v. (수를) 세다
verify v. 대조하다, 확인하다 against prep. ~과 비교하여, ~에 반대하여
aware adj. 알고 있는 advise v. 알리다, 조언하다 affect v. 영향을 미치다

---

¹⁷⁸수신: Adele Welch <a.welch@superparties.com>
발신: Brian Ledford <b.ledford@superparties.com>
제목: 추가 요청
날짜: 1월 6일

안녕하세요 Adele,

¹⁷⁸본사의 Amy Turner가 제가 요청했던 직원할인에 대한 당신의 승인을 요구하여서 당신께 연락을 드립니다. 그녀는 제게 ¹⁷⁸500달러가 넘는 모든 주문들은 지점 관리자의 승인을 받아야 한다고 말했습니다. 이전에 제가 말씀드렸듯이, ¹⁷⁹저는 다음 달에 있을 제 어린 사촌의 생일 파티를 위해 의상, 파티 게임들, 그리고 풍선들을 주문하길 원했으며, 그 총액은 600달러가 됩니다. 제가 양식을 가지고 언제 들르면 될지 제게 알려 주십시오.

저는 또한 ¹⁷⁹파티가 2월 23일에 인디애나에서 열릴 것이라는 점과, 지난 11월에 ¹⁷⁹/¹⁸⁰당신이 2월 21일부터 23일까지의 제 휴가 요청을 승인해 주셨다는 점을 상기시켜 드리고자 합니다. ¹⁸⁰저는 제가 저희 지점의 재고 조사에 참여할 수 없어서 매우 유감스럽습니다. 제가 없는 동안 저를 대신하도록 Lisa와 합의하였습니다.

감사합니다!

Brian

follow-up adj. 추가의; n. 후속 조치 acknowledgement n. 승인, 인정
approval n. 승인 stop by phr. 들르다 take place phr. 열리다
authorize v. 승인하다, 인가하다 take part in phr. ~에 참여하다
arrangement n. 합의, 준비 cover v. ~를 대신하다, 덮다

176 육하원칙 문제 중 ●●○

해석 Super Parties사는 왜 그것의 지점들의 문을 닫을 것인가?
(A) 재정적 손실을 줄이기 위해
(B) 상품 수를 세기 위해
(C) 시장 변화에 대처하기 위해
(D) 수리에 착수하기 위해

해설 회람의 'we have scheduled one-day closures at all Super Parties branches'와 'During this time, all products must be counted by hand'에서 모든 Super Parties사 지점들에서 하루 동안의 휴업 일정을 잡

아두었으며 이 기간 동안, 모든 제품들이 손으로 세어져야 한다고 했으므로 (B)가 정답이다.

어휘 financial loss phr. 재정적 손실 address v. ~에 대처하다, 해결하다

패러프레이징
> closing ~ branches 지점들의 문을 닫는 것 → closures at ~ branches 지점들에서 휴업
> products 상품들 → merchandise 상품

177 Not/True 문제 하 ●○○

해석 Super Parties사에 대해 언급되지 않은 것은?
(A) 물건들은 대여될 수 있다.
(B) 네 곳에 가게를 가지고 있다.
(C) 상품들은 온라인에서 구할 수 있다.
(D) 고객들에게 상품들을 배송한다.

해설 질문의 Super Parties사와 관련된 내용이 언급된 회람에서 (A)는 언급되지 않은 내용이다. 따라서 (A)가 정답이다. (B)는 'we have scheduled ~ closures at all Super Parties branches'에서 모든 Super Parties사 지점들에서 휴업 일정을 잡아두었다고 했고, 'Chicago, Illinois', 'Fort Wayne, Indiana', 'Milwaukee, Wisconsin', 'St. Louis, Missouri'에서 총 4개의 지점에서 휴업한다는 것을 알 수 있으므로 지문의 내용과 일치한다. (C)는 'they can still purchase products through our Web site'에서 그들, 즉 고객들은 우리, 즉 Super Parties사의 웹사이트를 통해 계속 제품들을 구매할 수 있다고 했으므로 지문의 내용과 일치한다. (D)는 'advise ~ customers that orders scheduled for delivery ~ will not be affected'에서 고객들, 즉 Super Parties사의 고객들에게 배송이 예정된 주문들은 영향을 받지 않을 것임을 알리라고 했으므로 지문의 내용과 일치한다.

어휘 rent v. 대여하다; n. 임대료 ship v. 배송하다

패러프레이징
> can ~ purchase products through ~ Web site 웹사이트를 통해 제품들을 구매할 수 있다 → merchandise is available online 상품들은 온라인에서 구할 수 있다
> orders scheduled for delivery 배송이 예정된 주문들 → ships products 상품들을 배송하다

178 추론 문제 중 ●●●

해석 Ms. Welch는 누구일 것 같은가?
(A) 최고 경영자
(B) 여행사 직원
(C) 지점장
(D) 수석 회계사

해설 이메일의 'To: Adele Welch'에서 이메일이 Ms. Welch에게 작성되었다는 것을 알 수 있고, 'Amy Turner ~ needs your acknowledgement'와 'any orders over $500 need to have a branch manager's approval'에서 Amy Turner가 당신, 즉 Ms. Welch의 승인을 요구하며, 500달러가 넘는 모든 주문들은 지점 관리자의 승인을 받아야 한다고 했으므로 Ms. Welch가 지점장이라는 사실을 추론할 수 있다. 따라서 (C)가 정답이다.

어휘 travel agent phr. 여행사 직원 accountant n. 회계사

패러프레이징
> branch manager 지점 관리자 → branch supervisor 지점장

해석   Mr. Ledford는 무엇을 할 계획인가?
(A) 새로운 도시로 이사한다
(B) 회사 세미나에 참석한다
(C) 교육 워크숍에 참석한다
(D) 가족들을 방문한다

해설   이메일의 'I was hoping to order costumes, party games, and balloons for my young cousin's birthday party next month'에서 저, 즉 Mr. Ledford가 다음 달에 있을 자신의 어린 사촌의 생일 파티를 위해 의상들, 파티 게임들, 그리고 풍선들을 주문하길 원했다고 했고, 'the party is taking place ~ on February 23'와 'you authorized my request for leave from February 21 to 23'에서 그 파티, 즉 어린 사촌의 생일 파티는 2월 23일에 열릴 것이며 2월 21일부터 23일까지의 Mr. Ledford의 휴가 요청이 승인되었다고 했으므로 (D)가 정답이다.

패러프레이징

> cousin 사촌 → family members 가족들

---

180 추론 문제   연계   중 ●●●

해석   Mr. Ledford는 어디에서 일할 것 같은가?
(A) 시카고에서
(B) 포트웨인에서
(C) 밀워키에서
(D) 세인트루이스에서

해설   이메일의 'you authorized my request for leave from February 21 to 23. I'm so sorry that I will be unavailable to take part in our branch's inventory.'에서 2월 21일부터 23일까지에 대한 자신, 즉 Mr. Ledford의 휴가 요청이 승인되었으며 이에 따라 자신의 지점의 재고 조사에 참여할 수 없어서 매우 유감스럽다고 했다. 또한, 회람의 'St. Louis', 'February 22'에서는 세인트루이스에서 재고 조사가 2월 22일에 열린다는 사실을 확인할 수 있다.
두 단서를 종합할 때, Mr. Ledford는 자신의 휴가 기간인 2월 21일부터 23일 사이에 재고 조사가 열리는 세인트루이스 지점에서 일하고 있다는 사실을 추론할 수 있다. 따라서 (D)가 정답이다.

181-185번은 다음 웹페이지와 이메일에 관한 문제입니다.

---

www.expressmovers.com

Express Movers사

소개		예약		위치

Express Movers사는 당신의 소지품을 운반하기 위한 최고의 회사입니다. ^{182-D}30년 넘게 장거리 이사 서비스를 전문으로 해온 저희 ¹⁸¹직원들은 당신의 물건이 포장된 직후와 똑같은 상태로 예정된 시간에 최종 목적지에 도착하도록 보장할 것입니다. ^{182-A}저희는 자동차, 트럭, 그리고 보트와 같은 탈것을 견인하기도 합니다.* 아래에 있는 저희의 저렴한 가격들을 확인하시고 수거 및 반환 시간을 정하시려면 **여기**를 클릭하십시오.

거리	가격
50마일 미만	300달러
50~200마일	500달러
201~500마일	750달러
¹⁸⁴500마일 초과	¹⁸⁴1,000달러

*거리에 상관없이, ^{182-A}차량당 500달러의 추가 요금이 있습니다.

---

transport v. 운반하다   belongings n. 소지품, 소유물
specialize v. 전문으로 하다   goods n. 물건, 소유물   destination n. 목적지
shape n. 상태   tow v. 견인하다   affordable adj. 저렴한
pickup n. 수거, 픽업   drop-off n. 반환   regardless of phr. ~에 상관없이

수신: 고객 서비스 <service@expressmovers.com>
발신: Jacqueline Gerard <jackieger39@tellmail.net>
제목: 이사 지원
날짜: 5월 23일
첨부: 아파트_정보.문서

안녕하세요,

저는 ¹⁸³롤리에 있는 저의 현재 아파트에서 가구와 가전제품들을 옮기는 것에 도움이 필요하여 이메일을 씁니다. ¹⁸³저는 최근 탬파에 있는 직장에 대한 제의를 받아들였으며 7월 1일인 제 시작일 전에 **그곳으로 이사를 해야 합니다.** 이상적으로는, 저는 제 소지품이 6월 29일에 수거되어 그 다음 날 배송되면 좋겠습니다.

첨부된 문서는 제가 옮겨야 할 물품들의 목록뿐만 아니라, 롤리 및 탬파의 아파트들의 위치에 관한 정보를 포함합니다. ¹⁸⁴이사의 대략적인 거리는 650마일이 될 것입니다. ¹⁸⁵저의 새로운 회사가 그들이 제게 저의 이사 비용을 상환해줄 것이라고 했으므로 저는 영수증이 필요할 것입니다.

더 자세한 정보를 위해서는 제게 연락해주십시오.

Jacqueline Gerard 드림

---

appliance n. 가전제품   accept v. 받아들이다, 수락하다
relocate v. 이사하다   approximate adj. 대략적인
reimburse v. 상환하다   expense n. 비용

---

181 육하원칙 문제   중 ●●○

해석   웹페이지에 따르면, 직원들은 무엇을 할 것인가?
(A) 도착지에서 물품들을 닦는다
(B) 물품들이 좋은 상태로 배송되도록 보장한다
(C) 거주지의 위치를 찾기 위해 내비게이션 시스템을 사용한다
(D) 미리 대금을 회수한다

해설   웹페이지의 'crew members will ensure that your goods arrive ~ in the same shape as they were upon being packed up'에서 직원들은 물건이 포장된 직후와 똑같은 상태로 도착하도록 보장할 것이라고 했으므로 (B)가 정답이다.

어휘   in good condition phr. 좋은 상태인   locate v. (위치를) 찾다
residence n. 거주지   in advance phr. 미리

패러프레이징

> shape 상태 → condition 상태

---

182 Not/True 문제   중 ●●●

해석   Express Movers사에 대해 언급된 것은?
(A) 추가 요금을 받고 자동차를 운반할 것이다.
(B) 최근 새로운 반환 센터를 열었다.
(C) 고객들을 위한 온라인 채팅 서비스를 제공한다.
(D) 10년 전에 설립되었다.

해설   웹페이지의 'We even tow vehicles, such as cars'에서 저희, 즉 Express Movers사가 자동차와 같은 탈것도 견인한다고 했고, 'There is an additional fee of $500 per vehicle'에서 이 서비스에는 차량당 500달러의 추가 요금이 있다고 했으므로 (A)는 지문의 내용과 일치한다. 따라서 (A)가 정답이다. (B)와 (C)는 지문에 언급되지 않은 내용이다. (D)는 'Having specialized in long-distance moving services for over 30 years'에서 30년 넘게 장거리 이사 서비스를 전문으로 해왔다고 했으므로 지문의 내용과 일치하지 않는다.

어휘 **automobile** n. 자동차 **establish** v. 설립하다 **decade** n. 10년

패러프레이징

tow ~ cars 자동차를 견인하다 → transport automobiles 자동차를 운반하다
additional fee 추가 요금 → extra charge 추가 요금

183 육하원칙 문제   중 ●●○

해석 Ms. Gerard는 왜 이사를 가는가?
(A) 몇몇 친척들 가까이에 살기 위해
(B) 대학 프로그램에 등록하기 위해
(C) 신규 프로젝트를 시작하기 위해
(D) 새로운 장소에서 일을 시작하기 위해

해설 이메일의 'my current apartment in Raleigh'에서 저, 즉 Ms. Gerard의 아파트는 현재 롤리에 있다고 했고, 'I've ~ accepted an offer for a job in Tampa and need to relocate there'에서 저, 즉 Ms. Gerard가 탬파에 있는 직장에 대한 제의를 받아들였으며 그곳으로 이사를 해야 한다고 했으므로 (D)가 정답이다.

어휘 **relative** n. 친척 **enroll** v. 등록하다 **take up** phr. (일 등을) 시작하다

184 추론 문제   연계   상 ●●●

해석 Ms. Gerard에 대해 추론될 수 있는 것은?
(A) 작은 아파트로 이사할 것이다.
(B) 곧 승진될 것이다.
(C) 창고에 몇몇 가구를 놓아둘 것이다.
(D) 서비스에 대해 최소 1,000달러를 지불할 것이다.

해설 이메일의 'The approximate distance of the move will be 650 miles.'에서 이사의 대략적인 거리가 650마일이 될 것이라고 했다. 또한, 웹페이지의 'more than 500 miles', '$1,000'에서는 이동 거리가 500마일 초과일 경우 1,000달러의 요금이 부과된다는 것을 알 수 있다.
두 단서를 종합할 때, Ms. Gerard의 이동 거리는 500마일 초과이므로 이사 비용으로 최소 1,000달러를 지불할 것임을 추론할 수 있다. 따라서 (D)가 정답이다.

어휘 **promote** v. 승진시키다, 홍보하다 **storage** n. 창고 **at least** phr. 최소한

185 육하원칙 문제   중 ●●○

해석 Ms. Gerard는 무엇을 요청했는가?
(A) 배송 일정
(B) 거래 기록
(C) 피드백 양식
(D) 계약서 사본

해설 이메일의 'I will need a receipt as my new company ~ would reimburse me for my relocation expenses.'에서 저, 즉 Ms. Gerard의 새로운 회사에서 본인의 이사 비용을 상환해줄 것이기 때문에 영수증이 필요할 것이라고 했으므로 (B)가 정답이다.

어휘 **transaction** n. 거래 **copy** n. 사본

패러프레이징

receipt 영수증 → transaction record 거래 기록

186-190번은 다음 이메일, 양식, 예정표에 관한 문제입니다.

수신: Jake Walker <j.walker@renewable.com>
발신: Luanne Wilkins <l.wilkins@urbanenergy.net>
제목: 제9회 도시 에너지 포럼
날짜: 2월 16일

Mr. Walker께,

제9회 도시 에너지 포럼에 대한 귀하의 문의에 감사드립니다. 이 행사는 스위스 베른에서 4월 26일부터 28일까지 개최될 것입니다. 전 세계의 도시들이 어떻게 효과적으로 재생 가능 에너지로 바꿀 수 있을지를 논의하기 위해 다양한 분야의 전문가들이 모일 것입니다.

186-C앞으로 계속 증가할 것으로 예상되는 도시 인구로 인해, 세계의 도시들이 충분하고, 깨끗하고, 그리고 지속 가능한 에너지 자원들을 개발해야 할 필요성이 시급해졌습니다. 도시 에너지 포럼은 참가자들에게 아이디어들을 만들어 내고 실질적인 해결책을 논의할 기회를 제공합니다.

귀하의 질문에 대해 답변 드리자면, 중앙 홀에서의 모든 발표들 및 토론들을 포함하는 일반 입장권은 2월 1일 이전에는 150유로이고 이후에는 185유로입니다. 188-C워크숍들은 회기당 35유로의 추가 비용으로 제공됩니다. 188-D후원 업체들의 구성원들에게는, 일반 입장료가 무료라는 것을 알아두시기 바랍니다. 더 자세한 정보를 위해 혹은 187디지털 서식으로 된 일정을 다운로드하시려면, www.urbanenergy.net/forum을 방문하십시오.

Luanne Wilkins 드림
도시 에너지 포럼

---

urban adj. 도시의 **inquiry** n. 문의 **sector** n. 분야 **gather** v. 모이다 **discuss** v. 논의하다, 토론하다 **shift** v. 바꾸다, 전환하다 **renewable energy** phr. 재생 가능 에너지 **population** n. 인구 **project** v. 예상하다, 추측하다 **sufficient** adj. 충분한 **sustainable** adj. 지속 가능한 **urgent** adj. 시급한, 다급한 **generate** v. 만들어 내다 **practical** adj. 실질적인 **solution** n. 해결책 **general** adj. 일반의 **admission** n. 입장 **sponsor** n. 후원 **program** n. 일정, 프로그램

제9회 도시 에너지 포럼
베른, 스위스·4월 26-28일

감사합니다! 귀하의 대금이 지불되었습니다. 당신의 기록을 위해 이 양식의 사본을 보관해주십시오. 어떠한 변경이라도 필요하시면, forum@urbanenergy.net으로 저희에게 연락해 주십시오.

주문 상세내역

188-D/189**이름**: Irwin Patel
189**회사(선택)**: Solar India사
주소: 75번지 Murti로, 뉴델리, 인도 110011
전화: 555-2390
이메일: i.patel@solarindia.com
티켓 수: 한 장(1)
지급 총액: 35,00유로
  – 188-D**입장료**: 0.00유로
  – 188-B/C**워크숍 비용**: 35,00유로

전액 환불을 받으시려면, 행사 시작 최소 3일 전에 저희에게 연락해 주십시오.

retain v. 보관하다 optional n. 선택(사항); adj. 선택적인

제9회 도시 에너지 포럼
베른, 스위스·4월 26-28일

¹⁹⁰⁻ᴰ**둘째 날 예정표**

오전 10시-11시 개회 발표
중앙 홀: 도시 에너지 포럼 의장 Kurt Bollinger가 재생 가능 에너지로의 전환을 가속화하는 것에 대해 이야기할 것입니다.

¹⁸⁸⁻ᴮ**오전 11시-오후 12시 ¹⁸⁸⁻ᴮ오전 워크숍**
¹⁸⁸⁻ᴮ**B홀:** "친환경 에너지에 자금 조달하기"
세계 에너지 투자 은행 최고 경영자 Eloisa Davide에 의해 발표됨

¹⁸⁸⁻ᶜ**C홀:** "정부가 어떻게 앞장설 수 있는가"
영국 에너지 계획 의장 Alan Holm에 의해 발표됨

오후 12시-2시 ¹⁹⁰⁻ᴮ점심 휴식

오후 2시-3시 30분 ¹⁸⁸⁻ᴮ오후 워크숍
¹⁸⁸⁻ᴮ**B홀:** "태양 에너지 사용하기"
남아시아 에너지 협회 창립자 ¹⁸⁹Lester Agarwal에 의해 발표됨(¹⁸⁹Solar India사 최고경영자)

¹⁸⁸⁻ᶜ**C홀:** "¹⁹⁰⁻ᴰ배터리 기술의 발전"
Queensland 대학교 공학 교수 Richard Liu에 의해 발표됨

오후 3시 30분-4시 30분 원탁 토론
중앙 홀: 도시 에너지 포럼의 일원인 Stephanie Bernard가 대중 매체에서 재생 가능 에너지를 홍보하는 것에 대한 토론을 진행할 것입니다.

agenda n. 예정표, 안건 accelerate v. 가속화하다 transition n. 전환
finance v. 자금을 조달하다; n. 자금
initiative n. (특정한 문제 해결·목적 달성을 위한 새로운) 계획
founder n. 창립자 advancement n. 발전 promote v. 홍보하다

---

186 Not/True 문제   중 ●●○

해석 이메일에 따르면, 도시들에 대해 사실인 것은?
(A) 각각 미래 포럼을 주최할 것이다.
(B) 더 나은 교통 시스템들이 필요하다.
(C) 더 붐벼질 것이다.
(D) 더 자주 정전을 겪을 수 있다.

해설 이메일의 'urban populations projected to continue growing in the future'에서 앞으로 계속 증가할 것으로 예상되는 도시 인구라고 했으므로 (C)는 지문의 내용과 일치한다. 따라서 (C)가 정답이다. (A), (B), (D)는 지문에 언급되지 않은 내용이다.

어휘 host v. 주최하다 crowded adj. 붐비는 suffer v. 겪다, 고통을 받다
power outage phr. 정전

패러프레이징

| populations ~ continue growing 인구가 계속 증가하다 → become more crowded 더 붐벼지다 |

---

187 육하원칙 문제   중 ●●○

해석 도시 에너지 포럼의 웹사이트에서 무엇이 이용 가능한가?

(A) 후원 신청서
(B) 일정 사본
(C) 환불 요청서
(D) 강연 필기록

해설 이메일의 'to download the program in digital format, visit www.urbanenergy.net/forum'에서 디지털 서식으로 된 일정을 다운로드하려면 웹사이트를 방문하라고 했으므로 (B)가 정답이다.

어휘 application n. 신청서 transcript n. 필기록 lecture n. 강연

---

188 Not/True 문제 연계   중 ●●●

해석 Mr. Patel에 대해 사실인 것은?
(A) 2월 1일 이전에 표를 구매했다.
(B) 그의 표는 그에게 중앙 홀에만 입장을 허가한다.
(C) 하나보다 더 많은 워크숍에 참가할 것이다.
(D) 그의 회사는 제9회 도시 에너지 포럼의 후원 업체이다.

해설 양식의 'Name: Irwin Patel', 'Admission fees: €0.00'에서 Irwin Patel의 입장가가 0.00유로라고 했다. 또한, 이메일의 'for members of sponsor organizations, general admission is free'에서는 후원 업체들의 구성원들에게는, 일반 입장료가 무료라는 것을 확인할 수 있다.
두 단서를 종합할 때, Mr. Patel이 제9회 도시 에너지 포럼의 후원 업체의 구성원임을 알 수 있으므로 (D)는 지문의 내용과 일치한다. 따라서 (D)가 정답이다. (A)는 지문에 언급되지 않은 내용이다. (B)는 양식의 'Workshop fees: €35.00'에서 Mr. Patel이 워크숍 비용으로 35유로를 지출했다고 했고, 예정표의 'Morning workshops', 'Hall B', 'Hall C'와 'Afternoon workshops', 'Hall B', 'Hall C'에서 워크숍들이 중앙 홀이 아닌 B홀 또는 C홀에서 진행됨을 알 수 있으므로 지문의 내용과 일치하지 않는다. (C)는 양식의 'Workshop fees: €35.00'에서 Mr. Patel이 워크숍 비용으로 35유로를 지출했다고 했고, 이메일의 'Workshops are offered at an additional cost of €35 per session.'에서 워크숍들은 회기당 35유로의 추가 비용으로 제공된다고 했으므로 Mr. Patel이 하나의 워크숍에 참여한다는 것을 알 수 있다. 따라서 지문의 내용과 일치하지 않는다.

어휘 grant v. 허가하다, 인정하다; n. 보조금 entry n. 입장

---

189 육하원칙 문제 연계   중 ●●○

해석 Mr. Patel은 어느 워크숍 진행자와 직업적인 관계를 맺고 있는가?
(A) Alan Holm
(B) Richard Liu
(C) Eloisa Davide
(D) Lester Agarwal

해설 양식의 'Name: Irwin Patel', 'Company (optional): Solar India'에서 Mr. Patel이 다니는 회사가 Solar India사임을 알 수 있다. 또한, 예정표의 'Lester Agarwal', 'CEO, Solar India'에서는 Lester Agarwal이 Solar India사 최고경영자라는 것을 확인할 수 있다.
두 단서를 종합할 때, Solar India사에 다니는 Mr. Patel이 Solar India사 최고경영자인 Lester Agarwal과 직업적인 관계를 맺고 있음을 알 수 있다. 따라서 (D)가 정답이다.

어휘 leader n. 진행자, 지도자

---

190 Not/True 문제   중 ●●●

해석 포럼의 둘째 날에 대해 언급된 것은?
(A) 몇몇 발표자들은 발표를 한 번보다 많이 할 것이다.
(B) 모든 참가자들에게는 1시간의 점심시간이 제공될 것이다.

(C) 텔레비전으로 방송되는 재생 가능 에너지에 대한 토론이 열릴 것이다.

(D) 배터리 기술에 대한 발표가 있을 것이다.

해설 예정표의 'Agenda for Day 2', 'Advancements in Battery Technology'에서 둘째 날 예정표에 배터리 기술의 발전에 대한 발표가 포함되어 있으므로 (D)는 지문의 내용과 일치한다. 따라서 (D)가 정답이다. (A)와 (C)는 지문에 언급되지 않은 내용이다. (B)는 '12:00-2:00 P.M.', 'Lunch break'에서 점심 휴식이 2시간임을 알 수 있으므로 지문의 내용과 일치하지 않는다.

어휘 televise v. 텔레비전으로 방송하다

191-195번은 다음 양식, 공고, 이메일에 관한 문제입니다.

Gumbo 식료품 회사 보상 프로그램
신청 양식

귀하의 지역 Gumbo사의 고객 서비스 카운터에 작성된 양식을 가져다주시거나 104번지 Jefferson가, 리치먼드, 버지니아주 23284에 있는 Gumbo 식료품 회사 보상 프로그램으로 우편을 보내주십시오. 귀하가 온라인 계정을 갖고 있다면, 귀하는 또한 www.shopgumbo.com에서 가입하실 수 있습니다.

이름: _____
주소: _____
전화: _____
이메일: _____

저희의 주간 소식지를 받고 할인 쿠폰이 귀하의 메일 수신함에 발송되도록 하려면 여기를 확인하세요.

프로그램 세부설명:

· 저희 매장 또는 온라인에서 귀하가 사용하는 1달러마다 1포인트를 받으세요. 식료품, 처방전, 잡지, 그리고 더 많은 것들에 대해 포인트를 받으세요!

· 191-C귀하가 받은 200포인트마다 귀하의 식료품 계산서에 더 큰 할인을 위해 사용될 수 있습니다.

· 가입할 191-A/195-C친구를 추천하여 즉시 100포인트를 받으세요.

---

reward n. 보상 drop off phr. 가져다주다 sign up phr. 가입하다
earn v. 받다, 얻다 grocery n. 식료품 medical prescription phr. 처방전
instantly adv. 즉시 refer v. 추천하다

저희 고객분들께 좋은 소식이 있습니다!

지역 Gumbo 식료품 회사와 Tiptop 가전제품 매장들에서 쇼핑함으로써 보상 포인트를 얻은 고객들은 이제 그들의 보상 포인트를 Fullerton사 주유소에서 기름을 채울 때 사용할 수 있게 될 것입니다. 191-A100포인트마다 당신의 연료 구매에 대해 1달러의 절약으로 교환될 수 있습니다.

193이 보상의 확대는 Gumbo사와 Tiptop사 쇼핑객들뿐만 아니라, Fullerton사의 고객들에게도 더 큰 가치와 절약을 전달할 것을 약속합니다.

192Fullerton사의 가스 보상 프로그램은 전국의 25개가 넘는 소매 회사들에서 이용 가능하며 전국적으로 수천 개의 주유소에서 사용될 수 있습니다. www.fullertongas.com에서 더 많이 알아보시거나 귀하의 지역의 Gumbo사 또는 Tiptop사에서 가스 보상을 위해 등록하는 것에 대해 문의하십시오.

---

fill up phr. 기름을 채우다 redeem v. 교환하다, 상환하다 fuel n. 연료
expansion n. 확대 promise v. 약속하다 saving n. 절약
nationwide adv. 전국적으로; adj. 전국의 register v. 등록하다

수신: Dale Wilson <d.wilson@okmail.com>
발신: Karen Sirling <k.sirling@shopgumbo.com>
제목: 보상 포인트

날짜: 4월 24일

Mr. Wilson께,

저희에게 연락해 주셔서 감사합니다. 194요청하신 대로 저는 귀하의 계좌 정보를 재확인했습니다. 지난주 귀하의 식료품점 방문에서 귀하가 얻은 64포인트를 귀하께 저희가 기입하지 않았던 것으로 보입니다. 방금 전에 제가 귀하의 정보를 수정하였습니다. 194다른 질문에 대해서는, 195-C지난달에 귀하께서 해주셨던 추천을 반영하도록 194/195-C귀하의 계정이 업데이트되었다194는 것을 제가 확인해드릴 수 있습니다. 모두 합쳐, 지난 2월에 회원이 되신 이후, 귀하께서는 350포인트를 얻으셨습니다.

저는 귀하께서 귀하의 포인트를 파악하고 저희 레시피 모음, 예산 편성 도구 등과 같은, 다른 제품들과 서비스들에 접근할 수 있도록 저희 웹사이트에 온라인 계정을 등록하시길 권장합니다.

거래해주셔서 감사합니다!

Karen Sirling 드림
고객 서비스 직원
Gumbo 식료품 회사

---

double-check v. 재확인하다 neglect v. (해야 할 일을) 하지 않다
credit v. (금액을) 기입하다; n. 신용 trip n. 방문, 여행
correct v. 수정하다; adj. 정확한 reflect v. 반영하다 referral n. 추천, 소개
altogether adv. 모두 합쳐, 총 keep track of phr. ~을 파악하다, 추적하다

최고난도 문제

191 Not/True 문제 연계 상 ●●●

해석 Gumbo 식료품 회사의 보상 프로그램에 대해 사실인 것은?

(A) 추천은 가스 할인을 위한 충분한 포인트를 얻게 한다.
(B) 온라인 구매가 가장 많은 포인트를 받을 자격을 얻는다.
(C) 얻어진 각각의 200포인트에 대해 쿠폰이 제공될 것이다.
(D) 처방전은 식료품보다 적은 포인트의 가치가 있다.

해설 양식의 'Instantly earn 100 points by referring a friend'에서 친구를 추천하여 즉시 100포인트를 받으라고 했다. 또한, 공고의 'Every 100 points can be redeemed for $1 in savings on ~ fuel purchase.'에서는 100포인트마다 연료 구매에 대해 1달러의 절약으로 교환될 수 있다는 것을 확인할 수 있다.
두 단서를 종합할 때, 추천을 통해 100포인트를 얻을 수 있으며 이는 연료 할인 1달러로 교환될 수 있다는 것을 알 수 있으므로 (A)는 지문의 내용과 일치한다. 따라서 (A)가 정답이다. (B)와 (D)는 지문에 언급되지 않은 내용이다. (C)는 양식의 'Every 200 points ~ can be used toward bigger discounts on your grocery bill.'에서 200포인트마다 귀하의 식료품 계산서에 더 큰 할인을 위해 사용될 수 있다고는 했지만 쿠폰이 제공된다고는 하지 않았으므로 지문의 내용과 일치하지 않는다.

어휘 qualify for phr. ~할 자격을 얻다

패러프레이징

savings on ~ fuel purchase 연료 구매에 대한 절약 → a discount on gas 가스 할인

최고난도 문제

192 추론 문제 상 ●●●

해석 Fullerton 가스 회사에 대해 암시되는 것은?

(A) 일부 소매점들에서 자동차 서비스를 제공할 것이다.
(B) 25개보다 많은 다른 회사들과 거래를 성사시켰다.
(C) 현재 그것의 주유소 지점들을 늘리는 중이다.
(D) 그것의 본사는 Gumbo 식료품 회사와 같은 건물에 있다.

해설   공고의 'Fullerton's Gas Rewards Program is available at over 25 retail firms across the country'에서 Fullerton사의 가스 보상 프로그램은 전국의 25개가 넘는 소매 회사들에서 이용 가능하다고 했으므로 Fullerton 가스 회사가 25개보다 많은 다른 회사들과 거래를 성사시켰다는 것을 추론할 수 있다. 따라서 (B)가 정답이다.

어휘   **automotive** adj. 자동차의   **deal** n. 거래
negotiate v. 성사시키다, 협의하다   **in the process of** phr. ~하는 중이다

193 동의어 찾기 문제   중 ●●○

해석   공고에서, 2문단 첫 번째 줄의 단어 "deliver"는 의미상 ─와 가장 가깝다.
(A) 전하다
(B) 수령하다
(C) 계속하다
(D) 탈퇴하다

해설   공고의 deliver를 포함한 구절 'This expansion of rewards promises to deliver greater value and savings'에서 이 보상의 확대는 더 큰 가치와 절약을 전달할 것을 약속한다고 했으므로 deliver는 '전달하다'라는 뜻으로 사용되었다. 따라서 '전하다'라는 뜻을 가진 (A) pass on이 정답이다.

194 목적 찾기 문제   중 ●●○

해석   Ms. Sirling은 왜 이메일을 썼는가?
(A) 최근의 주문을 확인하기 위해
(B) 특별 할인을 제공하기 위해
(C) 청구서 납부를 요청하기 위해
(D) 몇 가지의 문의 사항들을 다루기 위해

해설   이메일의 'I double-checked your account information as requested.'에서 요청한 대로 저, 즉 Ms. Sirling은 귀하, 즉 고객의 계좌 정보를 재확인했다고 했고, 'As for the other question, I can confirm that your account has been updated'에서 다른 질문에 대해서는, 고객의 계정이 업데이트되었다는 것을 확인해 줄 수 있다고 했으므로 (D)가 정답이다.

어휘   **verify** v. 확인하다, 입증하다   **offer** n. 할인
a couple of phr. 몇 가지의, 둘의

195 Not/True 문제 연계   상 ●●●

해석   Ms. Sirling이 Mr. Wilson에 대해 언급한 것은?
(A) 어떠한 포인트도 교환하지 않았다.
(B) 그의 회원 자격은 곧 만료될 것이다.
(C) 지난달에 최소 100포인트를 받았다.
(D) 그의 온라인 비밀번호가 최근에 바뀌었다.

해설   이메일의 'your account has been updated to reflect the referral that you made last month'에서 지난달에 귀하, 즉 Mr. Wilson이 했던 추천을 반영하기 위해 그의 계정이 업데이트되었다고 했다. 또한, 양식의 'Instantly earn 100 points by referring a friend'에서 친구를 추천하여 즉시 100포인트를 받으라고 한 것을 확인할 수 있다.
두 단서를 종합할 때, Mr. Wilson은 지난달에 친구 추천을 통해 즉시 100포인트를 받았다는 것을 알 수 있다. 따라서 (C)가 정답이다. (A), (B), (D)는 지문에 언급되지 않은 내용이다.

어휘   **expire** v. 만료되다

196-200번은 다음 웹페이지, 이메일, 직원 근무 시간 기록표에 관한 문제입니다.

Plumtree Nutritional Advice사

홈 | 블로그 | 질문과 답변 | 로그인

건강한 삶을 위한 조언들
[196]게시자: Brad Shear 수석 영양사

건강한 상태를 유지하는 것은 어려울 수 있지만, 저는 제 고객들이 계속해서 바르게 유지할 수 있도록 돕기 위해 아래의 목록을 종합했습니다:

반드시 하세요
· 하루에 최소 3잔의 물을 마신다
· [196]주 3회, 20분에서 30분 동안 운동을 한다
· 매일 밤 7시간의 수면을 취한다

하지 않도록 유의하세요
· 취침하기 1시간 이내에 저녁을 먹는다
· 한 번에 3시간 이상 앉아 있는다

더 알고 싶다면, 아래의 식단 및 운동 플랜 중 하나를 클릭하고 첫 상담을 잡으려면 제게 이메일을 보내십시오.

플랜	가격
[198]FreshStart	[198]30달러
[198]FreshUp	[198]35달러
[198]FreshPlus	[198]40달러
FreshPremium	45달러

tip n. 조언, 팁   **nutritionist** adj. 영양사   **fit** adj. 건강한, 날씬한
challenging adj. 어려운   **compile** v. 종합하다, 모으다
on track phr. 바르게, 순조롭게 나아가는   **set up** phr. (약속을) 잡다
initial adj. 처음의   **consultation** n. 상담

수신: Brad Shear <bshear@plumtreenutrition.com>
[197-C]발신: Madison Costa <maddiecosta77@rentmail.net>
날짜: 4월 28일
제목: 상담

Mr. Shear께,

저는 당신의 웹사이트에 있는 플랜들에 대해 상의하기 위해 당신과의 첫 예약을 잡고 싶어서 이메일을 씁니다. [197-C]당신은 제 동료들 중 한 명인 Kerry Franklin에 의해 제게 적극적으로 추천되었습니다. [197-C/198]그녀는 당신의 FreshPlus 플랜을 따르고 있으며 그것이 그녀의 건강을 크게 향상시켰다고 말합니다. 저는 당신의 새로운 고객이 되어 즐겁지만, [198]저는 그녀만큼 많이 돈을 지불하고 싶지는 않고 또한 가장 저렴한 플랜도 원하지 않습니다.

제 주된 문제는 제가 이전에 제 사무실에서 그랬던 것보다 더 늦은 근무 시간에 일하는 것으로 최근에 바뀌었다는 것이고, 저는 저의 수면과 식사 일정을 조절하는 것에 어려움을 겪고 있습니다. [199]제가 5월 4일에 제 회사와의 교육 활동을 위해 출장을 가야 하기 때문에, [200]저는 5월 2일 오전이나 5월 3일 오후 중 하나에 당신을 만나기를 희망하고 있습니다.

Madison Costa

appointment n. 예약, 약속   **coworker** n. 동료   **improve** v. 향상시키다
switch v. 바뀌다, 전환하다   **shift** n. (교대제의) 근무 시간
previously adv. 이전에   **adjust** v. 조절하다, 조정하다

Plumtree Nutritional Advice사 직원 근무 시간 기록표
[200]한 주의 매일마다 당신이 일한 시간을 기록하세요.
[200]직원명: Brad Shear

	5월 1일	[200]5월 2일	[200]5월 3일	5월 4일	5월 5일
[200]고객 상담 업무	4시간	[200]6시간	[200]0시간	6시간	4시간
행정 업무	0시간	1시간	0시간	1시간	2시간
교육 업무	0시간	0시간	6시간	0시간	0시간
총 시간	4시간	7시간	6시간	7시간	6시간

client n. 고객 administration n. 행정

196 육하원칙 문제 중 ●●○

해석 Mr. Shear는 그의 고객들에게 어떤 충고를 하는가?
(A) 하루에 최소 3끼 식사를 섭취한다
(B) 햇빛으로부터 피부를 보호한다
(C) 운동 경기들에 참가한다
(D) **규칙적인 신체 활동들에 참여한다**

해설 웹페이지의 'Posted by: Brad Shear', 'Exercise ~ three times per week'에서 Mr. Shear가 게시한 글에서 주 3회 운동을 하라고 했으므로 (D)가 정답이다.

어휘 protect v. 보호하다 athletic competition phr. 운동 경기
engage in phr. ~에 참여하다 regular adj. 규칙적인

패러프레이징

Exercise ~ three times per week 주 3회 운동하다 → Engage in regular physical activities 규칙적인 신체 활동들에 참여한다

197 Not/True 문제 중 ●●○

해석 FreshPlus 플랜에 대해 언급된 것은?
(A) Plumtree사의 웹사이트에 업데이트될 것이다.
(B) 곧 있을 회의에서 논의될 것이다.
(C) **Ms. Costa의 동료에 의해 이용되어 왔다.**
(D) 한정된 기간 동안 할인되었다.

해설 이메일의 'From: Madison Costa'에서 이메일이 Ms. Costa에 의해 작성된 것임을 알 수 있고 'You came ~ recommended to me by one of my coworkers, ~. She follows your FreshPlus plan'에서 자신, 즉 Ms. Costa의 동료들 중 한 명에 의해 당신, 즉 Mr. Shear가 추천되었으며 동료가 FreshPlus 플랜을 따르고 있다고 했으므로 (C)는 지문의 내용과 일치한다. 따라서 (C)가 정답이다. (A), (B), (D)는 지문에 언급되지 않은 내용이다.

어휘 upcoming adj. 곧 있을 colleague n. 동료

패러프레이징

one of ~ coworkers 동료들 중 한 명 → colleague 동료

198 육하원칙 문제 연계 중 ●●○

해석 Ms. Costa는 플랜에 대해 얼마를 지불할 의향이 있는가?
(A) 30달러
(B) **35달러**
(C) 40달러

(D) 45달러

해설 이메일의 'She follows your FreshPlus plan'에서 그녀, 즉 Ms. Franklin이 FreshPlus 플랜을 따르고 있다고 했고, 'I don't want to pay as much as she does and I also don't want the cheapest plan'에서 자신, 즉 Ms. Costa는 그녀, 즉 Ms. Franklin만큼 많이 돈을 지불하고 싶지는 않으며 가장 저렴한 플랜도 원하지 않는다고 했다. 또한, 웹페이지의 'FreshStart', '$30', 'FreshUp', '$35', 'FreshPlus', '$40'에서는 가격이 FreshPlus 플랜보다 낮으면서도 가장 저렴하지는 않은 플랜이 35달러의 FreshUp 플랜이라는 것을 확인할 수 있다.
두 단서를 종합할 때, Ms. Costa는 FreshUp 플랜을 선택하여 35달러를 지불할 의향이 있는 것임을 알 수 있다. 따라서 (B)가 정답이다.

199 육하원칙 문제 중 ●●○

해석 Ms. Costa는 5월에 무엇을 할 것인가?
(A) **회사 행사에 참석한다**
(B) 건강 보험을 신청한다
(C) 예약 시간을 변경한다
(D) 휴가로 하루를 쉰다

해설 이메일의 'I have to travel for a training activity with my company on May 4'에서 자신, 즉 Ms. Costa가 5월 4일에 회사와의 교육 활동을 위해 출장을 가야 한다고 했으므로 (A)가 정답이다.

어휘 attend v. 참석하다 corporate adj. 회사의, 기업의
take a day off phr. 하루를 쉬다

패러프레이징

training activity with ~ company 회사와의 교육 활동 → corporate event 회사 행사

200 추론 문제 연계 상 ●●●

해석 Ms. Costa가 언제 Mr. Shear를 만났을 것 같은가?
(A) **5월 2일에**
(B) 5월 3일에
(C) 5월 4일에
(D) 5월 5일에

해설 이메일의 'I'm hoping to meet with you either in the morning on May 2 or in the afternoon of May 3'에서 Ms. Costa가 5월 2일 오전이나 5월 3일 오후 중 하나에 Mr. Shear를 만나기를 희망하고 있다고 했다. 또한, 직원 근무 시간 기록표의 'Please enter the number of hours that you have worked for each day of the week.'에서는 한 주의 매일마다 일한 시간을 기록하라고 했고, 'Employee name: Brad Shear', 'Client consultation', 'May 2', '6h', 'May 3', '0h'에서는 Mr. Shear가 고객 상담 업무로 5월 2일에는 6시간, 5월 3일에는 0시간을 일했다는 것을 확인할 수 있다.
두 단서를 종합할 때, Ms. Costa는 Mr. Shear가 고객 상담 업무로 6시간을 일한 5월 2일에 Mr. Shear를 만났을 것임을 추론할 수 있다. 따라서 (A)가 정답이다.

PART 5

101 (C)	**102** (C)	**103** (B)	**104** (A)	**105** (A)
106 (C)	**107** (C)	**108** (C)	**109** (D)	**110** (C)
111 (B)	**112** (B)	**113** (C)	**114** (A)	**115** (C)
116 (A)	**117** (D)	**118** (A)	**119** (A)	**120** (D)
121 (C)	**122** (D)	**123** (B)	**124** (B)	**125** (B)
126 (B)	**127** (B)	**128** (C)	**129** (B)	**130** (D)

PART 6

131 (D)	**132** (C)	**133** (D)	**134** (B)	**135** (C)
136 (B)	**137** (D)	**138** (A)	**139** (B)	**140** (A)
141 (C)	**142** (D)	**143** (D)	**144** (B)	**145** (A)
146 (D)				

PART 7

147 (D)	**148** (C)	**149** (B)	**150** (C)	**151** (C)
152 (D)	**153** (B)	**154** (A)	**155** (C)	**156** (A)
157 (D)	**158** (B)	**159** (C)	**160** (B)	**161** (B)
162 (A)	**163** (C)	**164** (C)	**165** (C)	**166** (B)
167 (A)	**168** (B)	**169** (A)	**170** (D)	**171** (B)
172 (D)	**173** (A)	**174** (D)	**175** (C)	**176** (B)
177 (D)	**178** (A)	**179** (C)	**180** (A)	**181** (C)
182 (B)	**183** (B)	**184** (B)	**185** (A)	**186** (D)
187 (A)	**188** (B)	**189** (B)	**190** (D)	**191** (A)
192 (B)	**193** (C)	**194** (D)	**195** (D)	**196** (C)
197 (C)	**198** (C)	**199** (D)	**200** (D)	

PART 5

101 비교급 표현 채우기　　　하 ●○○

해석　세금 인상으로 인해 소기업들에게 있어 수익성을 달성하는 것은 이전보다 더 어렵다.

해설　빈칸 뒤에 than(~보다)이 왔으므로 함께 비교급 표현을 만드는 형용사 또는 부사의 비교급 (C) harder(더 어려운)가 정답이다. 형용사 또는 부사의 원급 (A)와 최상급 (D)는 비교급 표현과 함께 쓰일 수 없다. 부사 (B)는 be동사 (is)의 보어 자리에 올 수 없다.

어휘　attain v. 달성하다, 이루다　profitability n. 수익성　approved adj. 승인된

102 부사 자리 채우기　　　중 ●●○

해석　전동 공구들은 심각한 부상의 위험을 최소화하도록 조심스럽게 다루어져야

한다.

해설　빈칸 앞의 동사(should be handled)를 꾸밀 수 있는 것은 부사이므로 부사 (C) cautiously(조심스럽게)가 정답이다. 형용사 (A), 명사 또는 동사 (B), 형용사의 비교급 (D)는 동사를 꾸밀 수 없다.

어휘　power tool phr. 전동 공구　minimize v. 최소화하다　risk n. 위험 serious adj. 심각한　injury n. 부상　cautious adj. 조심스러운, 신중한 caution n. 주의, 경고; v. 주의를 주다

103 부사절 접속사 채우기　　　중 ●●○

해석　카드 소지자가 상품권을 온라인으로 활성화시키고 24시간 후에 그것은 사용될 수 있다.

해설　절(The gift card ~ 24 hours)과 절(the cardholder ~ online)을 연결할 수 있는 부사절 접속사 (B)와 (C)가 정답의 후보이다. '상품권을 온라인으로 활성화시키고 24시간 후에 그것은 사용될 수 있다'라는 의미가 되어야 하므로 시간을 나타내는 부사절 접속사 (B) after(~후에)가 정답이다. 부사절 접속사 (C)는 '상품권을 온라인으로 활성화시키는 동안 그것은 24시간 사용될 수 있다'라는 어색한 문맥을 만든다. 형용사 또는 부사 (A)와 부사 (D)는 절과 절을 연결할 수 없다.

어휘　gift card phr. 상품권　cardholder n. 카드 소지자 activate v. 활성화시키다, 작동시키다　later adv. 나중에 sometimes adv. 때때로, 가끔

104 동사 관련 어구 완성하기　　　중 ●●○

해석　그 회사의 많은 문제들은 적절한 리더십의 부족에 기인했다.

해설　빈칸은 be동사(were)와 함께 수동태를 만드는 p.p.형 자리이다. '많은 문제들은 적절한 리더십의 부족에 기인한다'라는 문맥에서 빈칸 앞의 be동사와 뒤의 전치사 to와 함께 '~은 -에 기인한다'라는 의미의 동사 어구 be attributed to를 만드는 동사 attribute(~에 기인하다)의 p.p.형 (A) attributed가 정답이다. 참고로, (B)의 rely(의지하다)는 전치사 on과 함께 rely on(~에 의지하다)의 형태로 자주 쓰임을 알아둔다.

어휘　a number of phr. 많은, 다수의　firm n. 회사　lack n. 부족 proper adj. 적절한, 제대로 된　rely v. 의지하다, 의존하다 mention v. 언급하다　determine v. 결정하다, 알아내다

최고난도 문제

105 전치사 표현 채우기　　　상 ●●●

해석　주민들의 요청에 의해, 의회는 Tyler 공원 주변에 가로등을 설치했다.

해설　빈칸은 명사구(the request of residents)를 목적어로 취하는 전치사 자리이다. '주민들의 요청에 의해, 의회는 가로등을 설치했다'라는 의미가 되어야 하므로 빈칸 뒤의 명사구 the request of와 함께 '~의 요청에 의해'라는 의미의 어구 at the request of를 만드는 전치사 (A) At(~에, ~에서)이 정답이다.

어휘　request n. 요청; v. 요청하다　resident n. 주민, 거주자　council n. 의회 install v. 설치하다　from prep. ~에서(부터)　under prep. ~아래에 among prep. (셋 이상의) 사이에

106 부사 어휘 고르기 　　　　　중 ●●○

해석 새로운 공장 장비의 자동화된 기능은 직원이 그것을 끊임없이 감시해야 할 필요성을 없앤다.

해설 빈칸은 to 부정사(to monitor)를 꾸미는 부사 자리이다. '자동화된 기능은 직원이 그것을 끊임없이 감시해야 할 필요성을 없앤다'라는 문맥이므로 (C) constantly(끊임없이, 계속해서)가 정답이다. (A) overly(지나치게)도 해석상 그럴듯해 보이지만, 정상적이고 필요한 것 이상임을 의미하며 일반적으로 형용사 앞에서 쓰인다.

어휘 automated adj. 자동화된, 자동의　feature n. 기능, 특징
equipment n. 장비, 장치　eliminate v. 없애다, 제거하다
personnel n. 직원, 사원　monitor v. 감시하다, 관찰하다
abruptly adv. 갑자기　immensely adv. 굉장히, 매우

107 가산 명사와 불가산 명사 구별하여 채우기 　　상 ●●●

해석 Mr. Zendaya는 마케팅에 개인적인 관심이 있는 유능한 직원이다.

해설 전치사(with)의 목적어 역할을 하면서 형용사(individual)의 꾸밈을 받을 수 있는 것은 명사이므로 명사 (B)와 (C)가 정답의 후보이다. 빈칸 앞에 부정관사(an)가 있으므로 단수 명사 (C) interest(관심)가 정답이다. 복수 명사 (B)는 부정관사와 함께 쓰일 수 없다. 동사 또는 과거분사 (A)와 동명사 또는 현재분사 (D)는 형용사의 꾸밈을 받을 수 없다. individual을 '개인'이라는 의미의 명사로 보고 과거분사 (A)와 현재분사 (D)가 이를 뒤에서 꾸미는 것으로 본다 해도, 각각 '마케팅에 관심이 있는/관심을 불러일으키는 개인과 함께하는 유능한 직원이다'라는 어색한 문맥이 된다.

어휘 competent adj. 유능한　individual adj. 개인적인; n. 개인

108 형용사 어휘 고르기 　　　　　중 ●●○

해석 그 오래된 다리는 구조적으로 불안정해졌고 수리되어야 한다.

해설 빈칸은 2형식 동사 become의 보어 역할을 하면서 부사(structurally)의 꾸밈을 받는 형용사 자리이다. '오래된 다리는 구조적으로 불안정해졌고 수리되어야 한다'라는 문맥이므로 (C) unstable(불안정한)이 정답이다.

어휘 structurally adv. 구조적으로　fix v. 수리하다　innovative adj. 혁신적인
temporary adj. 일시적인, 임시의　precise adj. 정확한

109 주어와 수 일치하는 동사 채우기 　　　중 ●●○

해석 Help-A-Neighbor 단체의 회원들은 다양한 지역 자선단체들을 후원한다.

해설 문장에 동사가 없으므로 동사 (B)와 (D)가 정답의 후보이다. 주어(The members)가 복수이므로 복수 동사 (D) support가 정답이다. 참고로, 주어(the members)와 동사 사이의 전치사구 of the Help-A-Neighbor Organization은 수식어 거품구이므로 동사의 수 결정에 아무런 영향을 주지 않는다. 단수 동사 (B)는 복수 주어와 함께 쓰일 수 없다. 형용사 (A)와 동명사 또는 현재분사 (C)는 동사 자리에 올 수 없다.

어휘 organization n. 단체, 기관　charitable adj. 자선의, 너그러운
supportive adj. 지지하는, 보완적인　support v. 후원하다, 지원하다

110 명사 자리 채우기 　　　　　하 ●○○

해석 젊은 사람들은 즐거움과 기회의 약속으로 인해 대도시들에 끌린다.

해설 전치사(of)의 목적어 자리에 올 수 있는 것은 명사이므로 명사 (C) excitement(즐거움)가 정답이다. 동사 (A), 동사 또는 형용사 (B), 형용사 (D)는 명사 자리에 올 수 없다.

어휘 draw v. 끌다, 유인하다　promise n. 약속, 공약　opportunity n. 기회

---

excite v. 흥분시키다　excited adj. 신이 난, 들뜬

최고난도 문제

111 명사 관련 어구 완성하기 　　　　상 ●●●

해석 Ms. Lawrence는 그것이 그들에게 적응할 충분한 시간을 줄 것이라고 생각하기 때문에 신입사원들을 3주 동안 훈련하는 것에 찬성한다.

해설 빈칸은 전치사(in)의 목적어 역할을 하면서 전치사구(of ~ employees)의 꾸밈을 받는 명사 자리이다. 'Ms. Lawrence는 신입사원들을 3주 동안 훈련하는 것에 찬성한다'라는 문맥이므로 빈칸 앞의 전치사 in과 뒤의 전치사 of와 함께 '~에 찬성하여'라는 의미의 어구 in favor of를 만드는 (B) favor(찬성, 호의)가 정답이다. (C) advance(진보, 발전)와 (D) order(순서)는 각각 in advance of(~보다 앞에)와 in order of(~의 순서로)라는 어구로 쓰이지만, 이 문장에서는 각각 'Ms. Lawrence는 신입사원들을 3주 동안 훈련하는 것보다 앞에 있다/신입사원들을 3주 동안 훈련하는 것의 순서이다'라는 어색한 문맥을 만든다. 참고로, (A) response(응답, 대답)는 in response to(~에 응하여)라는 어구로 자주 쓰인다.

어휘 adjust v. 적응하다, 조정하다

112 명사 관련 어구 완성하기 　　　　중 ●●○

해석 매달, 국가 삼림 단체는 기부자들에게 그것의 진행 중인 자연 환경 보호 활동들에 대해 최신 정보를 제공한다.

해설 빈칸은 빈칸 앞의 명사(conservation)와 복합 명사를 이루면서 전치사(on)의 목적어 역할을 하는 명사 자리이다. '단체는 진행 중인 자연 환경 보호 활동들에 대해 최신 정보를 제공한다'라는 문맥이므로 빈칸 앞의 명사 conservation(보호)과 함께 쓰여 '보호 활동'이라는 의미의 복합 명사 conservation efforts를 만드는 (B) efforts(활동, 노력)가 정답이다.

어휘 contributor n. 기부자　ongoing adj. 진행 중인
conservation n. (자연 환경) 보호, 보존　notice n. 공고　facility n. 시설
contact n. 연락, 접촉

113 전치사 표현 채우기 　　　　　중 ●●○

해석 BT사는 그것의 새롭게 임명된 최고경영자에게 경의를 표하여 저녁 만찬을 준비했다.

해설 빈칸은 명사구(its newly appointed CEO)를 목적어로 취하는 전치사 자리이다. '최고경영자에게 경의를 표하여 저녁 만찬을 준비했다'라는 의미가 되어야 하므로 빈칸 앞의 전치사구 in honor와 함께 '~에게 경의를 표하여'라는 의미의 어구 in honor of를 만드는 전치사 (C) of(~의)가 정답이다.

어휘 organize v. 준비하다, 조직하다　banquet n. 만찬, 연회
appoint v. 임명하다, 정하다　to prep. 로, ~쪽으로
toward prep. ~쪽으로, ~을 향하여　following prep. ~후에

114 시간 부사 채우기 　　　　　중 ●●○

해석 1년 간의 공사 이후에도 주택 개발은 완료되려면 아직 멀었다.

해설 빈칸은 동사구(is a long way from being completed)를 꾸미는 부사 자리이다. '주택 개발은 완료되려면 아직 멀었다'라는 의미가 되어야 하므로 시간을 나타내는 부사 (A) still(아직, 여전히)이 정답이다. (C) so(매우)도 해석상 그럴듯해 보이지만, 강조를 나타내는 부사로 형용사와 부사를 꾸민다. (D) far는 '훨씬'이라는 의미로 형용사를 꾸미거나, 부사 또는 전치사구와 함께 쓰여 '멀리'라는 의미를 나타낸다.

어휘 construction n. 공사, 건설　housing n. 주택, 주거　behind adv. 뒤에

115 부사절 접속사 채우기   중 ●●○

해석   다른 국가들이 손실을 입은 반면, 그 나라의 주식 시장은 이익을 달성했다.

해설   이 문장은 주어(The country's stock market), 동사(achieved), 목적어 (gains)를 갖춘 완전한 절이므로, ___ ~ losses는 수식어 거품으로 보아야 한다. 이 수식어 거품은 동사(suffered)가 있는 거품절이므로, 거품절을 이 끌 수 있는 부사절 접속사 (C) whereas(~한 반면에)가 정답이다. 접속부사 (A)는 수식어 거품을 이끌 수 없다. (B)는 접속부사일 경우 수식어 거품을 이 끌 수 없고, 전치사일 경우 거품절이 아닌 거품구를 이끈다. 전치사 (D)도 마 찬가지로 거품절이 아닌 거품구를 이끈다.

어휘   stock n. 주식, 재고   achieve v. 달성하다, 성취하다   gain n. 이익, 수익   nation n. 국가   suffer losses phr. 손실을 입다   thus adv. 따라서   besides adv. 게다가   concerning prep. ~에 관한

116 의문사 채우기   중 ●●●

해석   그 프로젝트 관리자는 누가 주말에 기꺼이 일할 것인지 알고 싶어한다.

해설   빈칸이 포함된 절(___ ~ weekend)이 to 부정사(to know)의 목적어 역할 을 하고 있으므로 문장 내에서 목적어로 쓰일 수 있는 명사절을 이끄는 명사 절 접속사 (A), (B), (C)가 정답의 후보이다. '누가 일할 것인지 알고 싶어 한 다'라는 의미가 되어야 하며 빈칸 뒤에 주어가 없는 불완전한 절이 왔으므로 의문대명사 (A) who(누가)가 정답이다. 의문대명사 (B)는 뒤에 목적어가 없 는 불완전한 절이 와야 한다. 의문부사 (C)는 뒤에 완전한 절이 와야 한다. 대 명사 (D)는 절을 이끌 수 없다.

어휘   be willing to phr. 기꺼이 ~하다

117 시간 표현과 일치하는 시제의 동사 채우기   중 ●●●

해석   지난 몇 달 동안, Ms. Saer는 그녀의 깊은 컴퓨터 공학 지식으로 동료들에게 깊은 인상을 주었다.

해설   문장에 동사가 없으므로 동사 (A)와 (D)가 정답의 후보이다. 현재 완료를 나 타내는 시간 표현(Over the past few months)이 왔으므로 과거에서 현재 까지 계속된 일을 표현하는 현재 완료 시제 (D) has impressed가 정답이 다. 현재 시제 (A)는 현재의 일을 나타낸다. 동명사 또는 현재분사 (B)와 형용 사 (C)는 동사 자리에 올 수 없다.

118 현재분사와 과거분사 구별하여 채우기   중 ●●●

해석   새로운 고객들을 유인하는 것은 현존하는 고객들을 유지하는 것보다 비용이 더 많이 든다.

해설   빈칸 뒤의 명사(ones)를 꾸밀 수 있는 것은 형용사이므로 현재분사 (A)와 과 거분사 (B)가 정답의 후보이다. 꾸밈을 받는 명사(ones)와 분사가 '현존하 는 고객들'이라는 의미의 능동 관계이므로 현재분사 (A) existing(현존하는, 기존의)이 정답이다. 과거분사 (B) existed를 쓸 경우 해석상 그럴듯해 보이 지만, 동사 exist(현존하다, 있다)는 자동사이므로 수동형인 과거분사로 쓰일 수 없다. 동사 (C)와 명사 (D)는 명사를 꾸밀 수 없다.

어휘   attract v. 유인하다, 끌어모으다   retain v. 유지하다   existence n. 존재

119 형용사 자리 채우기   중 ●●●

해석   금융 전문가들은 국제 경제가 불경기에서 빠져 나왔다는 확실한 징후를 보지 못했다.

해설   빈칸 뒤의 명사(indications)를 꾸밀 수 있는 것은 형용사이므로 형용사 (A) firm(확실한, 확고한)이 정답이다. 부사 (B), 명사 또는 동사 (C), 명사 (D)는 명사를 꾸밀 수 없다. 부사 (B)가 동사(have not seen)를 꾸미는 것

으로 본다 해도, '징후를 단호하게 보지 못했다'라는 어색한 문맥이 되며, 부 사가 동사를 꾸밀 때는 동사와 목적어 사이에 올 수 없고 '동사 + 목적어'의 앞이나 뒤에 와야 한다.

어휘   indication n. (~을 암시하는) 징후, 표시   recession n. 불경기, 후퇴   firm adj. 확실한, 확고한; n. 회사; v. 다지다, 안정되다   firmness n. 견고, 단단함

120 부사 자리 채우기   중 ●●●

해석   제조업체들은 운영비를 많이 낮출 방법들을 찾고 있다.

해설   to 부정사(to lower)를 꾸밀 수 있는 것은 부사이므로 부사 (D) considerably (많이, 상당히)가 정답이다. 명사 또는 현재분사 (A), 형용사 (B)와 (C)는 to 부정사를 꾸밀 수 없다. 참고로, 명사 way는 to 부정사를 취하는 명사이며, way to(~할 방법)를 관용구로 알아둔다.

어휘   manufacturer n. 제조업체   lower v. 낮추다; adj. 더 낮은   operating cost phr. 운영비, 경영비   consider v. 고려하다   considerate adj. 사려 깊은   considerable adj. 상당한

121 동사 어휘 고르기   상 ●●●

해석   그 집은 그것의 오래됨에 비해 좋은 상태이지만, 몇몇 바닥 타일들과 조명 기 구들은 교체되어야 할 수도 있다.

해설   빈칸은 be동사(be)와 함께 수동태를 만드는 p.p.형 자리이다. '몇몇 바 닥 타일들과 조명 기구들은 교체되어야 할 수도 있다'라는 문맥이므로 동 사 replace(교체하다)의 p.p.형 (C) replaced가 정답이다. (A)의 fill (채우다)도 해석상 그럴듯해 보이지만, 비어 있던 공간이나 내부가 채워지는 것을 의미하므로 답이 될 수 없다.

어휘   age n. 오래됨, 나이   lighting fixture phr. 조명 기구, 조명 장치   compare v. 비교하다   initiate v. 개시되게 하다

122 형용사 어휘 고르기   상 ●●●

해석   능력 있는 지도자들은 다른 사람들의 의견을 잘 받아들인다.

해설   빈칸은 be동사(are)의 보어 역할을 하는 형용사 자리이다. '능력 있는 지 도자들은 다른 사람들의 의견을 잘 받아들인다'라는 문맥이므로 형용사 (D) receptive(잘 받아들이는, 수용적인)가 정답이다. 참고로, be receptive to(~을 잘 받아들이다)를 관용구로 알아둔다.

어휘   capable adj. 능력 있는   informative adj. 유익한   successful adj. 성공적인   attractive adj. 매력적인

최고난도 문제

123 관계대명사 채우기   상 ●●●

해석   자신의 사진이 올해 잡지 표지로 선정된 사진작가는 10,000달러의 상금을 받 을 것이다.

해설   이 문장은 주어(The photographer), 동사(will be given), 목적어(a cash prize of $10,000)를 갖춘 완전한 절이므로, ___ ~ cover는 수식어 거품으 로 보아야 한다. 이 수식어 거품은 빈칸 앞의 사람 명사(The photographer) 를 선행사로 갖는 관계절이므로 사람 명사인 선행사와 함께 쓰일 수 있는 관 계대명사 (A)와 (C), 복합관계대명사 (D)가 정답의 후보이다. 관계절(___ ~ cover) 내에 주어(image)가 있으므로, 빈칸 뒤의 명사(image)를 꾸며서 함께 관계절 내의 주어가 될 수 있는 소유격 관계대명사 (C) whose(~의)가 정답이다. 주격 또는 목적격 관계대명사 (A)와 복합관계대명사 (D)는 관계 절 내에서 주어나 목적어 역할을 하기 때문에 다음에 주어나 목적어가 없는

불완전한 절이 와야 한다. 관계부사 (B)는 사람 명사(photographer)를 선행사로 가질 수 없으며 시간을 나타내는 선행사와 함께 쓰인다. (B)를 부사절 접속사로 본다 해도, 부사절 접속사는 주절의 앞이나 뒤에 와야 하며, 빈칸 뒤의 명사 image가 '사진'이라는 의미일 때는 가산 명사이므로 관사와 함께 쓰이거나 복수형으로 쓰여야 한다.

어휘 **cash prize** phr. 상금

124 명사 어휘 고르기 상 ●●●

해석 인턴들은 회사에만 전념을 할 것으로 기대된다.

해설 빈칸은 형용사(exclusive)의 꾸밈을 받는 명사 자리이다. '인턴들은 회사에만 전념을 할 것으로 기대된다'라는 문맥이므로 (B) commitment(참여, 헌신)가 정답이다.

어휘 **expect** v. 기대하다, 예상하다 **exclusive** adj. ~에만 한정된, ~에 한한
property n. 부동산, 건물 **negotiation** n. 협상, 절충
appreciation n. 감사, 감탄

최고난도 문제

125 복합관계부사 채우기 상 ●●●

해석 Mercura Auto사는 아무리 많은 비용이 들지라도 그것의 생산 시설을 멕시코로 옮길 것을 결정했다.

해설 이 문장은 주어(Mercura Auto), 동사(decided), 목적어(that ~ Mexico)를 갖춘 완전한 절이므로, ___ ~ is는 수식어 거품으로 보아야 한다. 이 수식어 거품은 동사(is)가 있는 거품절이다. 따라서, 빈칸 뒤의 절(___ ~ is)를 이끌어 수식어 거품 자리에 올 수 있는 거품절을 만들고, 'Mercura Auto사는 아무리 많은 비용이 들지라도 생산 시설을 옮기로 결정했다'라는 문맥을 만드는 복합관계부사 (B) however(아무리 ~할지라도)가 정답이다. 참고로, 복합관계부사 however는 'however + 형용사/부사 + 주어 + 동사'의 형태로 자주 쓰임을 알아둔다. 부사절 접속사 또는 부사 (A)와 부사절 접속사 (D)는 뒤에 '형용사 + 주어 + 동사' 형태가 올 수 없다. 강조 부사 (C)는 수식어 거품을 이끌 수 없다.

어휘 **production** n. 생산, 제작 **plant** n. 공장 **costly** adj. 많은 비용이 드는
once adv. 한 번; conj. ~하자마자 **very** adv. 매우 **just as** phr. 꼭 ~처럼

126 형용사 자리 채우기 중 ●●○

해석 주기적인 정비를 위해 웹 서버를 정지시키는 것은 이것이 시스템 오류를 방지할 수 있기 때문에 필수적이다.

해설 명사(maintenance)를 꾸밀 수 있는 것은 형용사이므로 형용사 (B) periodic (주기적인)이 정답이다. 명사 (A)와 (D), 부사 (C)는 형용사 자리에 올 수 없다. 참고로, (D)의 periodical은 '정기 간행의, 주기적인'이라는 의미의 형용사로 쓰일 수 있지만 복수를 나타내는 -s가 있으므로 '정기 간행물'이라는 의미의 명사로 쓰였음을 알아둔다.

어휘 **shut down** phr. 정지시키다, 폐쇄하다 **maintenance** n. 정비, 유지
vital adj. 필수적인 **period** n. 기간 **periodically** adv. 주기적으로

127 수량 표현 채우기 중 ●●○

해석 Mr. Tsai는 그가 이뤄내는 각 판매에 대해 10퍼센트의 수수료를 받는다.

해설 빈칸 뒤의 단수 가산 명사(sale)를 꾸밀 수 있는 수량 표현 (B) each(각)가 정답이다. 수량 표현 (A), (C), (D)는 복수 가산 명사와 함께 쓰인다.

어휘 **commission** n. 수수료, 위원회

128 동사 어휘 고르기 상 ●●●

해석 최근 방문객 설문조사의 긍정적인 결과는 훌륭한 관광지로서 스코츠데일의 명성을 강화한다.

해설 문장에 주어(The positive results of a recent visitor survey)만 있고 동사가 없으므로 빈칸은 동사 자리이다. '설문조사의 긍정적인 결과는 관광지로서의 명성을 강화한다'라는 문맥이므로 (C) reinforce(강화하다)가 정답이다.

어휘 **positive** adj. 긍정적인 **reputation** n. 명성, 평판
tourist destination phr. 관광지 **contradict** v. 반박하다, 부정하다
consult v. 상담하다 **permit** v. 허가하다, 용납하다

129 부사 어휘 고르기 상 ●●●

해석 Thornton & Jones사는 부정적인 평판을 피하기 위해 그것의 고객과의 의견 충돌을 은밀하게 해결했다.

해설 빈칸은 동사(settled)를 꾸미는 부사 자리이다. 'Thornton & Jones사는 부정적인 평판을 피하기 위해 의견 충돌을 은밀하게 해결했다'라는 문맥이므로 (B) confidentially(은밀하게)가 정답이다.

어휘 **settle** v. (문제 등을) 해결하다 **disagreement** n. 의견 충돌, 불일치
avoid v. 피하다, 자제하다 **negative** adj. 부정적인 **publicity** n. 평판, 홍보
wishfully adv. 갈망하여 **extensively** adv. 널리, 광범위하게
incrementally adv. 끊임없이, 증가하여

130 동명사와 명사 구별하여 채우기 중 ●●○

해석 학생들은 일상적인 학업 스트레스로부터 해방감을 제공하는 스포츠에 참여하기를 권장된다.

해설 동사(offers)의 목적어 자리에 올 수 있는 것은 명사이므로 동명사 (C)와 명사(D)가 정답의 후보이다. 부정관사(a) 다음에 올 수 있는 것은 명사이므로 명사 (D) release(해방감, 해방)가 정답이다. 동명사 (C)는 부정관사 다음에 올 수 없다. 형용사 (A), 동사 또는 과거분사 (B)는 명사 자리에 올 수 없다.

어휘 **encourage** v. 권장하다, 장려하다 **participate** v. 참여하다
offer v. 제공하다, 권하다 **release** n. 해방(감); v. 해방하다, 공개하다
releasable adj. 해방할 수 있는

PART 6

131-134번은 다음 공고에 관한 문제입니다.

모든 Diego사 직원들에게 알림

식원 구내식당은 해야 되는 몇 가지 작은 보수공사를 감안하여 6월 4일과 6월 7일 [131]**사이에** 이용할 수 없을 것입니다. 주요 개선점은 더 많은 햇빛이 들어오게 하기 위해 벽 중 하나에 창문을 추가하는 것이 될 것입니다. 게다가, 오래된 가전제품들은 최신의 것들로 교체될 것입니다. [132]**예를 들어**, 훨씬 더 큰 스테인리스제의 냉장고가 설치될 것입니다. 그 동안에, 여러분의 점심시간 동안에 회의실 1과 2를 [133]**이용하십시오.** [134]**두 공간들 모두 이 특정 목적을 위해 예약되어 있습니다.** 우리는 이 사안에 대한 여러분의 인내심과 이해에 감사드립니다.

inaccessible adj. 이용할 수 없는 **allow for** phr. ~을 감안하다
minor adj. 작은, 사소한 **renovation** n. 보수, 수리
primary adj. 주요한, 주된 **improvement** n. 개선(점)
appliance n. 가전제품, 기기 **substitute** v. 교체하다, 대신하다
in the meantime phr. 그 동안에

해커스 토익 실전 1200제 READING
TEST 7

131 전치사 채우기 중 ●●○

해설 빈칸은 명사구(June 4 and June 7)를 목적어로 취하는 전치사 자리이다. '구내식당은 6월 4일에서 6월 7일 사이에 이용할 수 없다'라는 의미가 되어야 하므로 등위접속사 and와 함께 쓰여 between A and B(A와 B 사이에) 구문을 만드는 전치사 (D) between(~ 사이에)이 정답이다.

어휘 since prep. ~부터 with prep. ~과 함께 into prep. ~안으로

132 접속부사 채우기 주변 문맥 파악 중 ●●○

해설 앞 문장에서 오래된 가전제품들은 최신의 것들로 교체될 것이라고 했고, 빈칸이 있는 문장에서는 훨씬 더 큰 스테인리스제의 냉장고가 설치될 것이라고 했으므로, 앞에서 말한 내용에 대한 예시를 언급하는 문장에서 사용되는 (C) For example(예를 들어)이 정답이다.

어휘 in case phr. ~한 경우에는 by all means phr. 물론, 반드시
on the whole phr. 전반적으로

133 명령문의 동사 자리 채우기 중 ●●○

해설 전치사구(In the meantime) 뒤에 나온 절이 주어가 없는 명령문이므로, 명령문의 동사로 사용되는 동사원형 (D) utilize(이용하다)가 정답이다. 3인칭 단수 동사 (A), 동명사 또는 현재분사 (B), 명사 (C)는 명령문의 동사 자리에 올 수 없다.

134 알맞은 문장 고르기 하 ●○○

해석 (A) 그 일정들은 문에도 게시되었습니다.
(B) 두 공간들 모두 이 특정 목적을 위해 예약되어 있습니다.
(C) 몇몇 직원들은 더 많은 시간을 요청했습니다.
(D) 휴식은 한 시간보다 적게 계속되기로 되어있었습니다.

해설 앞 문장 '(utilize) Conference Rooms 1 and 2 during your lunch breaks'에서 점심시간 동안에 회의실 1과 2를 이용하라고 했으므로 빈칸에는 두 개의 회의실 모두 점심시간 동안 사용될 목적으로 예약되어 있다는 내용이 들어가야 함을 알 수 있다. 따라서 (B)가 정답이다.

어휘 post v. 게시하다 reserve v. 예약하다 specific adj. 특정한
be supposed to phr. ~하기로 되어있다 last v. 계속되다, 지속되다

135-138번은 다음 편지에 관한 문제입니다.

Kendra Sampson
338번지 West Elm로
벌링턴시, 버몬트주 05402

Ms. Sampson께,

저희는 당신에게 당신의 *Literature Now*지의 구독이 6월 1일에 [135]**만료될** 것이라는 것을 알리기 위해 편지를 씁니다. 그 전에 당신이 당신의 구독이 끝나는 것을 방지하기 위해 그 어떠한 조치도 취하지 않는다면, 당신의 신용카드에 더 이상의 요금이 [136]**적용되지** 않을 것입니다. 하지만, 만약 당신이 당신의 구독을 연장하고 싶다면, 당신은 555-3922로 저희에게 연락함으로써 그렇게 할 수 있습니다.

[137]**상을 받은 저희의 출판물을 다시 구독할 많은 이유들이 있습니다.** 우선, 당신은 오늘날의 몇몇 최고 작가들의 단편 소설과 수필을 더 많이 즐길 수 있습니다. 당신은 또한 5월 갱신 할인으로 일 년 [138]**동안** 24달러를 절약할 수 있습니다. 저희는 당신이 *Literature Now*지를 계속해서 구독해주시기를 바랍니다.

*Literature Now*지 팀 드림

notify v. 알리다, 통지하다 subscription n. 구독, 가입
take action phr. 조치를 취하다 prevent v. 방지하다, 막다
charge n. 요금; v. 청구하다, 부과하다 for starters phr. 우선, 먼저
leading adj. 최고의, 선두적인 renewal n. 갱신

135 올바른 시제의 동사 채우기 주변 문맥 파악 중 ●●○

해설 that절(that ~ June 1)에 동사가 없으므로 동사 (A), (C), (D)가 정답의 후보이다. '당신의 구독이 6월 1일에 만료되다'라는 문맥인데, 뒤 문장에서 그 전에 당신이 구독이 끝나는 것을 방지하기 위해 어떠한 조치도 취하지 않는다면, 더 이상의 요금이 적용되지 않을 것이라고 했으므로 구독이 끝나는 시점이 미래임을 알 수 있다. 따라서 미래 시제 (C) will expire가 정답이다. 과거 시제 (A)는 이미 끝난 과거의 동작이나 상태를 나타내고, 현재 시제 (D)는 주로 반복적인 행동이나 습관을 나타낸다. 동명사 또는 현재분사 (B)는 동사 자리에 올 수 없다.

136 'be동사 + p.p.' 채우기 중 ●●○

해설 빈칸이 be동사(be) 다음에 왔으므로 진행형을 만드는 -ing형 (A)와 수동태를 만드는 p.p.형 (B)가 정답의 후보이다. '신용카드에 더 이상의 요금이 적용되지 않을 것이다'라는 수동의 의미가 되어야 하므로 빈칸 앞의 be동사와 함께 수동태를 만드는 p.p.형 (B) applied가 정답이다. -ing형 (A)는 미래 진행형을 만들어서 '요금이 적용되고 있는 중일 것이다'라는 어색한 문맥을 만든다. 3인칭 단수 동사 (C)와 동사원형 (D)는 be동사 다음에 올 수 없다.

137 알맞은 문장 고르기 상 ●●●

해석 (A) 시험 구독은 보통 6개월의 기간 동안 계속됩니다.
(B) 당신은 단 몇 주 안에 최신 호를 받을 것으로 기대할 수 있습니다.
(C) 저희의 기록은 당신이 2년 동안 *Literature Now*지의 구독자였다고 나타냅니다.
(D) 상을 받은 저희의 출판물을 다시 구독할 많은 이유들이 있습니다.

해설 뒤 문장 'For starters, you will be able to enjoy more short stories and essays from some of today's leading writers.'에서 우선, 오늘날의 몇몇 최고 작가들의 단편 소설과 에세이를 더 많이 즐길 수 있다고 한 후, 뒷부분에서 할인을 받아 금액도 절약할 수 있다고 했으므로 빈칸에는 출판물을 다시 구독할 많은 이유가 있다고 소개하는 내용이 들어가야 함을 알 수 있다. 따라서 (D)가 정답이다.

어휘 trial adj. 시험, 시험적인 typically adv. 보통, 일반적으로
latest adj. 최신의, 최근의 plenty of phr. 많은
award-winning adj. 상을 받은 publication n. 출판물, 출판

최고난도 문제

138 명사 관련 어구 완성하기 상 ●●●

해설 빈칸은 전치사(over)의 목적어 역할을 하는 명사 자리이다. '일 년 동안 24달러를 절약할 수 있다'라는 의미가 되어야 하므로, 빈칸 앞의 전치사 over와 뒤의 전치사 of와 함께 '~동안'이라는 의미의 어구 over the course of를 만드는 (A) course(경과, 과정)가 정답이다.

어휘 limit n. 한계 piece n. 조각 width n. 폭, 너비

139-142번은 다음 기사에 관한 문제입니다.

ALICE SPRINGS (8월 26일)— 다가오는 ¹³⁹에너지 프로젝트를 위해 Owler 사가 Alice Springs 시청에 의해 선정되었다. 그것은 모든 지역 공립 학교에 태양 전지판을 설치할 것이다. ¹⁴⁰몇몇 환경 단체들이 이 프로젝트에 대해 지지를 나타냈다. 이 프로젝트는 10월 1일에 Gillen 고등학교에서 시작되는데, ¹⁴¹이곳에는 225개의 전지판들이 갖춰질 것이다. 그 뒤에, Owler사는 East Side 초등학교와 Braitling 중학교로 넘어갈 것이다. 완료되면, 그 전지판들은 학교 이사회에 수천만 달러의 연간 ¹⁴²절약을 낳을 것으로 예상된다. "저희는 Owler사의 낮은 비용과 풍부한 경험 때문에 그것을 선택했습니다."라고 Alice Springs 시장 Tanya McCrindle이 말했다.

solar panel phr. 태양 전지판 be equipped with phr. ~을 갖추고 있다
board n. 이사회, 위원회 annual adj. 연간의, 연례의
a wealth of phr. 풍부한, 수많은

139 복합 명사 채우기 주변 문맥 파악 중 ●●●○

해설 빈칸이 명사(project) 앞에 있으므로 명사를 꾸미는 형용사 (A)와 과거분사 (C), 복합 명사를 만드는 명사 (B)가 정답의 후보이다. '___ 프로젝트를 위해 Owler사가 선정되었다'라는 문맥인데, 뒤 문장에서 회사는 모든 지역 공립 학교에 태양 전지판을 설치할 것이라고 했으므로 이 프로젝트가 에너지 관련 프로젝트임을 알 수 있다. 따라서 명사 project(프로젝트)와 함께 쓰여 '에너지 프로젝트'라는 의미의 복합 명사 energy project를 만드는 명사 (B) energy(에너지)가 정답이다. 부사 (D)는 명사를 꾸밀 수 없다.

어휘 energetic adj. 활기에 찬 energize v. 활기를 북돋우다
energetically adv. 활동적으로, 효과적으로

140 알맞은 문장 고르기 상 ●●●

해석 **(A) 몇몇 환경 단체들이 이 프로젝트에 대해 지지를 나타냈다.**
(B) 지역 주민들은 설치 작업을 수행하기 위해 자원했다.
(C) 그들은 추가적인 지연에 대해 부모들에게 사과했다.
(D) 계약을 따낸 사람은 익명으로 남을 것이다.

해설 앞 문장 'It will install solar panels at all local public schools.'에서 그것, 즉 Owler사가 모든 지역 공립 학교에 태양 전지판을 설치할 것이라고 했으므로 빈칸에는 이러한 환경 프로젝트에 대한 반응과 관련된 내용이 와야 함을 알 수 있다. 따라서 (A)가 정답이다.

어휘 indicate v. 나타내다 support n. 지지, 지원 volunteer v. 자원하다
apologize v. 사과하다 delay n. 지연, 지체; v. 연기하다
anonymous adj. 익명인

141 관계대명사 채우기 중 ●●●○

해설 이 문장은 주어(The project)와 동사(begins)를 모두 갖춘 완전한 절이므로, ___ ~ 225 panels는 수식어 거품으로 보아야 한다. 이 수식어 거품은 빈칸 앞의 장소 명사(Gillen High School)를 선행사로 갖는 관계절이며 관계절(___ ~ 225 panels) 내에 주어가 없으므로 주격 관계대명사 (C) which가 정답이다. 관계부사 (A)와 복합관계부사 (B) 뒤에는 완전한 절이 와야 한다. 명사절 접속사 (D)는 거품절을 이끌 수 없다.

142 명사 어휘 고르기 상 ●●●

해설 빈칸은 전치사(in)의 목적어 역할을 하면서 형용사(annual)의 꾸밈을 받는 명사 자리이다. '그 전지판들은 학교 이사회에 수천만 달러의 연간 절약을 낳을 것으로 예상된다'라는 문맥이므로 (D) savings(절약)가 정답이다. 참고로, (C) revenues(수익, 수입)는 학교가 태양 전지판을 통해 수익을 버는 것

이 아니므로 답이 될 수 없다.

어휘 subsidy n. 보조금 estimate n. 견적, 견적서; v. 추정하다

143-146번은 다음 이메일에 관한 문제입니다.

수신: Andrea Stinton <stinton.a@kuvarik.com>
발신: Leroy Wauters <wauters.l@kuvarik.com>
제목: 최근 점검
날짜: 11월 17일

Ms. Stinton께,

어제, 저는 도네츠크에 있는 Kuvarik사 생산 공장에 대한 의무 점검을 ¹⁴³실시했습니다. 체크리스트에 있는 많은 항목들이 만족스러웠지만, 저는 두 가지의 잠재적 ¹⁴⁴안전 문제들을 발견했습니다. 우선, 우리는 작년의 규제 변화로 인해 소화기 3대를 더 추가해야 합니다. ¹⁴⁵이것이 즉시 행해지지 않으면, 우리는 벌금을 부과 받을 것입니다. 두 번째로, 한 계단을 따라 몇몇 난간들이 없는 것을 발견했는데, ¹⁴⁶이것들은 긴급 상황이 발생할 경우에 필수적일 것입니다. 제가 새로운 난간들을 주문하기 전에, 저는 당신과 다양한 옵션들을 논의하고 싶습니다. 오늘 당신이 시간이 있을 때, 제 사무실에 들러주십시오.

Leroy Wauters 드림
시설 관리자

inspection n. 점검, 검사 mandatory adj. 의무적인, 필수의
satisfactory adj. 만족스러운 discover v. 발견하다, 깨닫다
potential adj. 잠재적인, 가능성이 있는 fire extinguisher phr. 소화기
regulation n. 규제, 규정 handrail n. 난간 stairway n. 계단
essential adj. 필수적인; n. 필수적인 것 emergency n. 긴급 상황
place an order phr. 주문하다 drop by phr. 들르다

143 동사 어휘 고르기 주변 문맥 파악 중 ●●●○

해설 빈칸은 문장에 주어(I)만 있고 동사가 없으므로 동사 자리이다. '어제, 나는 생산 공장에 대한 의무 점검을 ___했다'라는 문맥이므로 모든 보기가 정답의 후보이다. 뒤 문장에서 체크리스트에 있는 많은 항목들이 만족스러웠지만, 문제들을 발견했다고 했으므로 이메일의 작성자인 Mr. Wauters가 어제 점검을 실시했다는 것을 알 수 있다. 따라서 동사 conduct(실시하다)의 과거 시제 (D) conducted가 정답이다.

어휘 schedule v. ~을 예정에 넣다 postpone v. 연기하다 cancel v. 취소하다

144 명사 관련 어구 완성하기 전체 문맥 파악 중 ●●●○

해설 빈칸은 빈칸 뒤의 명사(issues)와 복합 명사를 이루어 동사(discovered)의 목적어 역할을 하는 명사 자리이다. '두 가지의 잠재적 ___ 문제들을 발견했다'라는 문맥이므로 모든 보기가 정답의 후보이다. 뒤 문장에서 작년의 규제 변화로 인해 소화기 3대를 더 추가해야 한다고 했고, 뒷부분에서 한 계단을 따라 몇몇 난간들이 없는 것을 발견했다고 했으므로 두 가지의 잠재적 안전 문제들을 발견했음을 알 수 있다. 따라서 빈칸 뒤의 명사 issues(문제들)와 함께 '안전 문제들'이라는 의미의 어구 safety issues를 만드는 (B) safety (안전)가 정답이다.

어휘 security n. 보안 personnel n. 인사

145 알맞은 문장 고르기 중 ●●●○

해석 **(A) 이것이 즉시 행해지지 않으면, 우리는 벌금을 부과 받을 것입니다.**
(B) 새로운 규제는 직원 안내서를 업데이트하기를 요구합니다.
(C) 신입 직원들은 소화기를 사용할 수 있도록 교육받았습니다.

(D) 예상했던 대로, 우리는 지난해 생산 할당량을 달성했습니다.

해설 앞 문장 'we need to add three more fire extinguishers due to a change in regulations last year'에서 작년의 규제 변화로 인해 소화기 3대를 더 추가해야 한다고 했으므로 빈칸에는 이것이 즉시 행해지지 않으면 벌금을 부과 받을 것이라는 내용이 들어가야 함을 알 수 있다. 따라서 (A)가 정답이다.

어휘 promptly adv. 즉시 issue v. (벌금을) 부과하다 fine n. 벌금 handbook n. 안내서, 입문서 meet v. 달성하다, 만나다 quota n. 할당량

146 명사와 수/인칭 일치하는 대명사 채우기 _{주변 문맥 파악} 상 ●●●

해설 and 다음의 절(___ ~ emergency)에 동사(would be)만 있고 주어가 없으므로 주어 자리에 올 수 있는 모든 보기가 정답의 후보이다. 앞 문장에서 한 계단을 따라 몇몇 난간들이 없는 것을 확인했다고 했으므로 몇몇 난간들(some handrails)을 가리키는 3인칭 복수 주격 인칭대명사 (D) they(그것들)가 정답이다. 3인칭 단수 주격 또는 목적격 인칭대명사 (A)와 지시대명사 (B)는 복수 명사를 가리킬 수 없다. 소유대명사 (C)는 '그들의 것은 긴급 상황이 발생할 경우 필수적일 것이다'라는 의미가 되는데, 앞 문장과 연결하면 '몇몇 난간들이 없는 것을 확인했는데, 그들의 것은 긴급 상황이 발생할 경우 필수적이다'라는 어색한 문맥을 만든다.

PART 7

147-148번은 다음 쿠폰에 관한 문제입니다.

BENISON HILLS
저희의 시즌 첫날입니다!
147각 입장권에 9.99달러
148-D3월 31일 오전 11시부터 오후 8시까지만 유효함

- 147/148-C유명한 Cliffdrop 롤러코스터를 포함하여, 모든 놀이기구에 사용 가능함
- Rocket Ship 시뮬레이션 상영관에는 유효하지 않음
- 5명까지 유효함
- 다른 그 어떤 할인과도 함께 사용될 수 없음

www.benisonhills.com / 555-6616
7554번지 Grand Ledge 고속도로, 선필드시, 마이애미주 48890

admission ticket phr. 입장권 ride n. 놀이기구
valid adj. 유효한, 정당한 offer n. 할인, 판매 상품

147 추론 문제 하 ●○○

해석 쿠폰은 어디에서 사용될 수 있을 것 같은가?
(A) 기차역에서
(B) 헬스장에서
(C) 음악실에서
(D) 놀이공원에서

해설 지문의 '$9.99 for each admission ticket'과 'Can be used for all rides, including ~ Roller Coaster'에서 각 입장권이 9.99달러이고 롤러코스터를 포함하여 모든 놀이기구에 사용 가능하다고 했으므로 쿠폰이 놀이공원에서 사용될 수 있다는 사실을 추론할 수 있다. 따라서 (D)가 정답이다.

어휘 amusement park phr. 놀이공원

148 Not/True 문제 하 ●○○

해석 Benison Hills에 대해 언급된 것은?

(A) 단체를 위한 특별 출입구가 있다.
(B) 그것의 식당 선택권으로 유명하다.
(C) 잘 알려진 놀이기구를 가지고 있다.
(D) 3월 내내 할인을 제공한다.

해설 지문의 'Can be used for ~ the famous Cliffdrop Roller Coaster'에서 유명한 Cliffdrop 롤러코스터에 사용 가능하다고 했으므로 (C)는 지문의 내용과 일치한다. 따라서 (C)가 정답이다. (A)와 (B)는 지문에 언급되지 않은 내용이다. (D)는 'Valid ~ on March 31 only'에서 3월 31일에만 유효하다고 했으므로 지문의 내용과 일치하지 않는다.

어휘 entrance n. 출입구, 입장 well-known adj. 잘 알려진, 유명한

패러프레이징

the famous ~ Roller Coaster 유명한 롤러코스터 → an attraction that is well-known 잘 알려진 놀이기구

149-150번은 다음 온라인 채팅 대화문에 관한 문제입니다.

Bastian Guthrie [오후 4시 35분] 저는 JEPN 제조사와 계속 함께 일하는 것이 우리에게 득이 된다고 생각하지 않아요.

Marie Holcomb [오후 4시 38분] 왜요? 문제가 있나요?

Bastian Guthrie [오후 4시 43분] 149많은 부품들이 결함이 있었기 때문에 그들의 지난번 주문은 반품되어야 했어요.

Marie Holcomb [오후 4시 44분] 그렇군요. 우리가 계약을 파기해야 할까요? 계약은 몇 달 동안 끝나지 않아요.

Bastian Guthrie [오후 4시 46분] 아니요. 하지만 저는 우리가 새로운 계약을 맺어야 한다고 생각하진 않아요. 150저는 당신이 대체 공급업체를 찾아 줬으면 해요.

Marie Holcomb [오후 4시 48분] 제가 처리할게요. 저는 제 컴퓨터에 제조업체들의 목록을 가지고 있어요. 하지만, 그들은 아마 JEPN사보다 비용을 더 많이 청구할 거예요.

Bastian Guthrie [오후 4시 49분] 괜찮아요. 우리는 더 적은 생산 지연을 겪어야 하고, 이는 장기적으로 우리가 돈을 절약하게 해줄 거예요.

in one's best interest phr. ~에게 득이 되는 order n. 주문, 주문서
component n. 부품, 요소 faulty adj. 결함 있는, 불완전한
break a contract phr. 계약을 파기하다 replacement n. 대체, 교체
supplier n. 공급업체, 공급자 see to phr. ~을 처리하다, 맡아 하다
manufacturer n. 제조업체 charge v. (비용을) 청구하다, 부과하다; n. 요금
delay n. 지연, 지체; v. 미루다, 연기하다

149 육하원칙 문제 하 ●○○

해석 Mr. Guthrie는 왜 JEPN 제조사를 교체하고 싶어하는가?
(A) 그것의 가격을 인상했다.
(B) 몇몇 결함이 있는 부품들을 보냈다.
(C) 그것의 제품을 판매하는 것을 지연시킨다.
(D) 구식의 기술을 사용한다.

해설 지문의 'Their last order had to be returned because many of the components were faulty.'에서 Mr. Guthrie가 많은 부품들이 결함이 있었기 때문에 그들, 즉 JEPN 제조사의 지난번 주문이 반품되어야 했다고 했으므로 (B)가 정답이다.

어휘 increase v. 인상하다, 증가시키다 defective adj. 결함이 있는
outdated adj. 구식의, 낡은

패러프레이징

components were faulty 부품들이 결함이 있었다 → defective parts 결함이 있는 부품들

150 의도 파악 문제   중 ●●○

해석 오후 4시 48분에, Ms. Holcomb이 "I will see to it"이라고 썼을 때 그녀가 의도한 것 같은 것은?
(A) 제조업체와 만날 것이다.
(B) 그녀의 컴퓨터에 몇몇 파일들을 다운로드할 것이다.
(C) 대체 공급업체를 찾을 것이다.
(D) 반드시 생산 기한을 맞출 것이다.

해설 지문의 'I'd like you to find a replacement supplier.'에서 Mr. Guthrie가 당신, 즉 Ms. Holcomb이 대체 공급업체를 찾아줬으면 한다고 하자, Ms. Holcomb이 'I will see to it.'(제가 처리할게요)이라고 한 것을 통해 Ms. Holcomb이 대체 공급업체를 찾을 것이라는 것을 알 수 있다. 따라서 (C)가 정답이다.

어휘 alternative adj. 대체의; n. 대안 meet a deadline phr. 기한을 맞추다

패러프레이징

a replacement supplier 대체 공급업체 → alternative suppliers 대체 공급업체

151-152번은 다음 이메일에 관한 문제입니다.

수신: Mobile Accessories사 <service@mobileaccessories.com>
발신: Naomi Clay <naomic@deftmail.com>
날짜: 1월 17일
제목: 주문 34928

관계자분께,

저는 오늘 아침에 귀사가 보낸 소포를 받았습니다. 유감스럽게도, ¹⁵¹그것은 제가 주문한 Athena 7의 휴대폰 케이스가 아니라 Athena 8의 휴대폰 케이스를 포함합니다. 올바른 상품이 제게 배송되면, 저는 제가 잘못 받은 것을 돌려보내겠습니다. 하지만, 이것은 귀사의 실수였으므로, ¹⁵²저는 귀사가 반품 배송 비용을 부담해야 한다고 생각합니다. 이것이 가능할지 제게 알려주시기 바랍니다.

Naomi Clay 드림

package n. 소포, 패키지 ship v. 배송하다, 운송하다; n. 선박
mistakenly adv. 잘못하여, 실수로 cover v. 부담하다, 보장하다
shipping n. 배송, 운송

151 목적 찾기 문제   하 ●○○

해석 Ms. Clay는 왜 이메일을 보냈는가?
(A) 소포를 받지 못했다.
(B) 서비스에 대한 금액이 너무 많이 청구되었다.
(C) 잘못된 물품을 배송받았다.
(D) 올바른 모델을 선택하지 않았다.

해설 지문의 'it includes a case for the Athena 8 phone rather than the one ~ that I ordered'에서 그것, 즉 소포가 Ms. Clay가 주문한 것이 아니라 Athena 8의 휴대폰 케이스를 포함한다고 했으므로 (C)가 정답이다.

어휘 overcharge v. (금액을 너무 많이) 청구하다

152 육하원칙 문제   하 ●○○

해석 Ms. Clay는 Mobile Accessories사가 무엇을 하기를 원하는가?
(A) 주소를 확인한다
(B) 환불을 제공한다
(C) 주문을 취소한다
(D) 비용을 부담한다

해설 지문의 'I think you should cover the cost of return shipping'에서 저, 즉 Ms. Clay는 귀사, 즉 Mobile Accessories사가 반품 배송 비용을 부담해야 한다고 생각한다고 했으므로 (D)가 정답이다.

어휘 confirm v. 확인하다 refund n. 환불

153-155번은 다음 회람에 관한 문제입니다.

회람

발신: ¹⁵⁵⁻ᴮSpencer Buffone, 건물 서비스 담당자
¹⁵³수신: Hylox 타워의 세입자들
날짜: 10월 4일
제목: ¹⁵⁵⁻ᴬ연례 창문 청소 일정

¹⁵⁵⁻ᴮ저는 다음 주 10월 10일부터 12일까지 작업자들이 Hylox 타워의 외부 창문을 청소하도록 준비했습니다. Hylox 타워의 장기 세입자들은 이미 이 과정에 대해 잘 알고 있습니다. 하지만, ¹⁵⁵⁻ᴰRazor Lee 연예기획사와 Wheatstock 출판사를 포함하여, 지난해에 이사 온 사업체들은 청소 당일에 창문들이 완전히 닫혀 있어야 한다는 점을 유의해 주시기 바랍니다. ¹⁵⁴입주자들은 또한 자신들의 사생활을 보장하기 위해 작업자들이 창문을 청소할 때 그들의 블라인드를 닫도록 권고됩니다.

창문 청소 일정은 다음과 같습니다:

건물의 북쪽	10월 10일 / 오전 10시-오후 5시
건물의 남동쪽	10월 11일 / 오전 8시-오후 3시
건물의 남서쪽	10월 12일 / 오후 12시-오후 7시

arrange v. 준비하다, 계획하다 exterior adj. 외부의 long-term adj. 장기의
tenant n. 세입자, 거주자 be familiar with phr. ~에 대해 잘 알다
ensure v. ~을 보장하다 privacy n. 사생활, 개인 정보

153 육하원칙 문제   하 ●○○

해석 누가 회람을 받을 것인가?
(A) 주차 안내원들
(B) 건물 입주자들
(C) 건설 작업자들
(D) 여행객 일원들

해설 지문의 'To: Tenants of Hylox Tower'에서 Hylox 타워의 세입자들이 수신인이라고 했으므로 (B)가 정답이다.

어휘 attendant n. 안내원, 종업원 occupant n. 입주자, 사용자

패러프레이징

Tenants 세입자들 → occupants 입주자들

154 육하원칙 문제   중 ●●○

해석 수신자들은 무엇을 하라고 당부받는가?
(A) 몇몇 창문들의 덮개를 닫는다

(B) Wheatstock 출판사 직원들을 환영한다

(C) 10월 12일 전에 선호도를 말한다

(D) 관리인의 도움을 위해 프런트 데스크에 전화한다

해설 지문의 'Occupants are ~ advised to close their blinds ~ when the workers are cleaning the windows.'에서 세입자들은 작업자들이 창문을 청소할 때 그들의 블라인드를 닫도록 권고된다고 했으므로 (A)가 정답이다.

어휘 **recipient** n. 수신자, 받는 사람 **be told to** phr. ~하라고 당부받다
covering n. 덮개 **state** v. 말하다, 명시하다
preference n. 선호(도), 애호 **janitorial** adj. 관리인의, 수위의

패러프레이징

blinds 블라인드 → coverings 덮개

155 추론 문제   중 ●●○

해석 Hylox 타워에 대해 암시되지 않는 것은?

(A) 외관은 일 년에 한 번 청소된다.

(B) 그것의 유지 관리는 Mr. Buffone에 의해 처리된다.

(C) 현재 임대를 위해 남겨진 몇몇 공간이 있다.

(D) 여러 사업체들에 의해 사용된다.

해설 지문에서 (C)는 추론할 수 없는 내용이다. 따라서 (C)가 정답이다. (A)는 'Annual Window Cleaning Schedule'에서 연례 창문 청소 일정이라고 했으므로 외관이 일 년에 한 번 청소된다는 사실을 추론할 수 있다. (B)는 'Spencer Buffone, Building Services Officer'와 'I have arranged for workers to clean the exterior windows of Hylox Tower'에서 건물 서비스 담당자인 Spencer Buffone이 작업자들이 Hylox 타워의 외부 창문을 청소하도록 준비했다고 했으므로 타워의 유지 관리는 Mr. Buffone에 의해 처리된다는 사실을 추론할 수 있다. (D)는 'businesses ~, including Razor Lee Entertainment and Wheatstock Publishing'에서 Razor Lee 연예기획사와 Wheatstock 출판사를 포함하는 사업체들이라고 했으므로 Hylox 타워가 여러 사업체들에 의해 사용된다는 사실을 추론할 수 있다.

어휘 **maintenance** n. 유지 관리, 보수 **occupy** v. (건물을) 사용하다, 차지하다

패러프레이징

Annual 연례의 → once a year 일 년에 한 번

156-157번은 다음 공고에 관한 문제입니다.

저희 이전합니다!

같은 장소에서의 25년 후에, Nickel Books는 3408번지 Polson가로 이전할 것입니다.* **156 그 이유는 현재 건물의 창고에 저희의 증가하는 재고를 위한 충분한 공간이 없다는 것입니다.** 새로운 가게는 4월 30일에 문을 열 것입니다. 축하하기 위해, 저희는 5월 1일부터 15일까지 모든 책과 잡지에 15퍼센트 할인을 제공할 것입니다. 게다가, **157-B25달러 이상 구매하시는 모든 분들은** 저희의 로고가 있는 **무료 손가방을 받을 것입니다.**

*Panhurst역의 5번 출구에서부터, 두 블록 정도 직진하세요. **157-D저희는** Color Kitchen이라는 식당 위에 위치해 있으며 그 건물의 이층과 삼층을 사용하고 있습니다.

storeroom n. 창고, 저장실 **growing** adj. 증가하는, 커지는
inventory n. 재고 **celebrate** v. 축하하다, 기념하다 **tote bag** phr. 손가방

156 육하원칙 문제   하 ●○○

해석 Nickel Books는 왜 새로운 장소로 이전할 것인가?

(A) 창고 공간이 부족하다.

(B) 건물 임대료가 상당히 올랐다.

(C) 주차 시설이 폐쇄되었다.

(D) 증가한 경쟁이 매출을 감소시켰다.

해설 지문의 'The reason is that the storeroom of our current building does not have enough space'에서 그 이유, 즉 Nickel Books가 이전하는 이유는 현재 건물의 창고에 충분한 공간이 없다는 것이라고 했으므로 (A)가 정답이다.

어휘 **storage** n. 창고, 보관소 **insufficient** adj. 부족한, 불충분한
property n. 건물, 부동산 **significantly** adv. 상당히, 심각하게

패러프레이징

storeroom ~ does not have enough space 창고에 충분한 공간이 없다
→ A storage area is insufficient 창고 공간이 부족하다

157 Not/True 문제   중 ●●○

해석 Nickel Books에 대해 언급된 것은?

(A) 신간과 중고 도서를 모두 판매할 것이다.

(B) 고객들에게 사은품의 선택권을 제공할 것이다.

(C) 이전보다 더 적은 직원들을 가질 것이다.

(D) 다른 사업체와 건물을 공유할 것이다.

해설 지문의 'We're located above a restaurant ~ and occupy the second and third floors of the building.'에서 우리, 즉 Nickel Books는 식당 위에 위치해 있으며 그 건물의 이층과 삼층을 사용하고 있다고 했으므로 식당, 즉 다른 사업체와 건물을 공유한다는 것을 알 수 있다. 따라서 (D)가 정답이다. (A)와 (C)는 지문에 언급되지 않은 내용이다. (B)는 'anyone making a purchase of $25 and over will receive a free tote bag'에서 25달러 이상 구매하는 모든 사람들은 무료 손가방을 받을 것이라고 했으므로 지문의 내용과 일치하지 않는다.

158-160번은 다음 기사에 관한 문제입니다.

Casa Bella사가 인도에 진출할 계획을 발표하다
Reena Singh 작성

158이탈리아 가구 소매업체인 Casa Bella사가 인도에 그것의 첫 지점을 열 계획을 발표했다. 회사는 뭄바이에 매장을 세울 계획이며, 개점은 잠정적으로 3월에 계획되어 있다. — [1] —. 그 매장은 Casa Bella사가 건설하는 데에 1천 8백만 달러의 비용이 들도록 할 것이고 이것의 다른 전 세계 지점들처럼 같은 제품과 서비스들을 제공할 것이다.

뭄바이 소매점에 더하여, **159-A다른 인도 도시들의 매장들도 계획되어 있다.** 회사 대표 Daniella Fieri에 따르면, **160인도 경제의 성장이 이 나라를 매력적인 대상으로 만들었다.** — [2] —. Ms. Fieri는 또한 **159-B회사가 이미 그것의 몇몇 제품 라인의 생산 공장을 인도에서 운영하고 있기** 때문에, 매장으로의 배송 비용이 낮을 것이라고 말했다. 가구 산업 전문가들은 높은 기대를 가지고 있으며, 매장 개업이 발표된 이후로 **159-D회사 주식의 가치가** 거의 10퍼센트만큼 **상승했다.** — [3] —.

159-C만약 인도의 소매판매점이 성공하면, Casa Bella사는 동남아시아로 확장할 것으로 보인다. 이 소매업체는 이미 유럽과 북아메리카에서 시장의 선두주자이다. — [4] —.

launch v. 진출하다; n. 진출   retailer n. 소매업체   branch n. 지점, 지사
tentatively adv. 잠정적으로   outlet n. 소매점   attractive adj. 매력적인
target n. 대상, 목표   expert n. 전문가, 전문 지식   expectation n. 기대, 예상
stock n. 주식

158 주제 찾기 문제   중 ●●○

해석   기사는 주로 무엇에 대한 것인가?

(A) 한 사업체에 대한 투자 기회

(B) 한 소매업체의 확장 계획

(C) 인도에 있는 두 회사 간의 합병

(D) 실적을 못 내는 제품 라인의 생산을 중단하려는 결정

해설   지문의 'Casa Bella, ~ retailer, has announced plans to open its first branch in India.'에서 소매업체인 Casa Bella사가 인도에 그것의 첫 지점을 열 계획을 발표했다고 한 후, Casa Bella사의 지점 확장 계획에 대해 설명하고 있으므로 (B)가 정답이다.

어휘   expansion n. 확장, 확대   discontinue v. (생산을) 중단하다, 그만두다   underperform v. 실적을 못 내다, 기량 발휘를 못하다

159 Not/True 문제   중 ●●○

해석   Casa Bella사에 대해 언급되지 않은 것은?

(A) 인도의 다양한 도시들에 소매판매점을 여는 것을 목표로 한다.

(B) 인도에서 몇몇 물품들을 생산한다.

(C) 동남아시아에서 사업을 시작했다.

(D) 주식 시장에서 가치가 상승했다.

해설   지문의 'Should the retail outlets in India be successful, Casa Bella will likely expand into Southeast Asia.'에서 만약 인도의 소매판매점이 성공하면, Casa Bella사는 동남아시아로 확장할 것으로 보인다고 했으므로 (C)는 지문의 내용과 일치하지 않는다. 따라서 (C)가 정답이다. (A)는 'stores in other Indian cities are planned'에서 다른 인도 도시들의 매장들도 계획되어 있다고 했으므로 지문의 내용과 일치한다. (B)는 'the company already operates a production plant for some of its product lines in India'에서 회사가 이미 그것의 몇몇 제품 라인의 생산 공장을 인도에서 운영하고 있다고 했으므로 지문의 내용과 일치한다. (D)는 'the value of the company's stock has gone up'에서 회사 주식의 가치가 상승했다고 했으므로 지문의 내용과 일치한다.

어휘   aim v. 목표로 하다, 겨냥하다   multiple adj. 다양한, 많은   manufacture v. 생산하다

패러프레이징

> operates a production plant for ~ product lines 제품 라인의 생산 공장을 운영한다 → manufactures some goods 몇몇 물품들을 생산한다

160 문장 위치 찾기 문제   중 ●●○

해석   [1], [2], [3], [4]로 표시된 위치 중, 다음 문장이 들어갈 곳으로 가장 적절한 것은?

"소비자들은 이제 집을 위한 물품들에 지출할 더 많은 소득을 가진다."

(A) [1]

(B) [2]

(C) [3]

(D) [4]

해설   주어진 문장에서 소비자들이 이제 집을 위한 물품들에 지출할 더 많은 소득을

가진다고 했으므로, 이 문장이 더 많아진 소득과 관련된 부분에 들어가야 함을 알 수 있다. [2]의 앞 문장인 'the growth of the Indian economy has made the country an attractive target'에서 인도 경제의 성장이 이 나라를 매력적인 대상으로 만들었다고 했으므로, [2]에 제시된 문장이 들어가면 인도의 경제 성장이 이 나라를 매력적인 대상으로 만들었으며 인도의 소비자들은 이제 집을 위한 물품들에 지출할 더 많은 소득을 가진다는 자연스러운 문맥이 된다는 것을 알 수 있다. 따라서 (B)가 정답이다.

161-164번은 다음 이메일에 관한 문제입니다.

수신: Anderson Roy <aroy@dauntelproperty.com>
발신: Elisa Kozlowski <elikoz@dauntelproperty.com>
제목: Foster가 기공식
날짜: 7월 8일

안녕하세요 Anderson,

저는 Parkersburg에 있는 소유지와 관련해서 당신과 연락하라고 전달받았습니다. 저는 Dauntel사가 이 부지를 그것의 가장 최근 연립주택 프로젝트인 Dalbo Homes의 부지로 선택했다는 것과 9월 4일에 건설의 시작을 ¹⁶²기공식으로 기념하길 원한다는 것을 알고 있습니다.

¹⁶¹그 지역의 영업 부장으로서, 당신이 그 행사를 담당할 것입니다. 제 일은 당신에게 지원을 제공하는 것입니다. 그 목적을 달성하기 위해서, 저는 ¹⁶²우리가 전국의 비슷한 행사들에 사용했던 것과 같은 패키지를 당신에게 보낼 것입니다. 그것은 기념식용 리본, 가위, 그리고 삽으로 구성되어 있습니다. 또한, ¹⁶³저는 당신이 직접 수정할 수 있는 마케팅 자료들을 제공할 것입니다. ¹⁶³Dalbo Homes와 관련된 정보를 포함하고 그것들을 필요에 따라 배부하는 것은 당신의 임무일 것입니다.

¹⁶⁴우리는 당신이 지역사회의 중요 유명인사들에게 행사에 참석하도록 요청하는 것을 추천합니다. 제가 당신에게 초대장 견본을 보내줄 수 있습니다. 당신은 또한 500달러의 음식 조달 예산을 받을 것입니다. 마지막으로, 우리가 지역 기자들과 연락할 수 있도록 그들의 연락처를 본사에 제공해주십시오.

그밖에 당신이 필요한 다른 어떤 것이 있다면, 555-4916으로 저에게 연락하실 수 있습니다.

Elisa Kozlowski 드림
마케팅 부장, Dauntel Property사

groundbreaking n. 기공(식); adj. 획기적인   instruct v. 전달하다
get in touch with phr. ~와 연락하다   property n. 소유지, 부동산, 건물
site n. 부지, 장소   celebrate v. 기념하다
be in charge of phr. ~을 담당하다, 책임지다
to that end phr. 그 목적을 달성하기 위해서   material n. 자료, 소재
distribute v. 배부하다   personality n. 유명인사, 성격
catering n. 음식 조달

161 목적 찾기 문제   중 ●●○

해석   이메일은 왜 보내졌는가?

(A) 소유지에 대해 문의하기 위해

(B) 동료에게 계획에 대해 알리기 위해

(C) 고객을 축하하기 위해

(D) 회의의 안건을 확정하기 위해

해설   지문의 'As the head of sales ~, you will be in charge of the event.'에서 영업 부장으로서, 당신이 그 행사를 담당할 것이라고 한 후, 행사 계획에 대해 설명하고 있으므로 (B)가 정답이다.

어휘 inquire v. 문의하다 inform v. 알리다, 통보하다 colleague n. 동료
confirm v. 확정하다, 확인하다 agenda n. 안건, 의제

162 추론 문제
상 ●●●

해석 Dauntel Property사에 대해 암시되는 것은?
(A) 전국에 건축물들을 짓는다.
(B) 상업 용지들을 관리하는 것을 전문으로 한다.
(C) 가격이 적당한 주택을 건설할 계획이다.
(D) 계약을 따기 위해 여러 경쟁자들을 이겼다.

해설 지문의 'a ground breaking ceremony'와 'the same package that
we have used for similar events across the country'에서 우리, 즉
Dauntel Property사가 전국의 비슷한 행사들, 즉 기공식과 비슷한 행사들
에 사용했던 것과 같은 패키지라고 했으므로 Dauntel Property사가 전국
에 건축물들을 짓는다는 사실을 추론할 수 있다. 따라서 (A)가 정답이다.

어휘 structure n. 건축물, 구조 specialize in phr. ~을 전문으로 하다
commercial property phr. 상업 용지 affordable adj. 가격이 적당한
beat v. 이기다

163 육하원칙 문제
중 ●●○

해석 Mr. Roy는 무엇을 담당할 것인가?
(A) 특별 행사를 위해 직원을 고용하는 것
(B) 건설 프로젝트를 감독하는 것
(C) 몇몇 홍보 자료들을 수정하는 것
(D) 서비스 계약서 초안을 작성하는 것

해설 지문의 'I will supply you with marketing materials that you can edit
yourself'와 'It will be your responsibility to include the relevant
information for Dalbo Homes'에서 당신 즉, Mr. Roy에게 직접 수정할
수 있는 마케팅 자료들을 제공할 것이고, Dalbo Homes와 관련한 정보를
포함하는 것은 당신, 즉 Mr. Roy의 임무일 것이라고 했으므로 (C)가 정답이
다.

어휘 supervise v. 감독하다, 지휘하다 revise v. 수정하다, 변경하다
promotional adj. 홍보의, 판촉의 draft v. 초안을 작성하다, 원고를 작성하다

패러프레이징

be responsible for ~을 담당하다 → be one's responsibility ~의 임무이다
marketing materials 마케팅 자료들 → promotional materials 홍보 자료들
edit 수정하다 → revising 수정하는 것

164 육하원칙 문제
중 ●●○

해석 Ms. Kozlowski는 Mr. Roy가 누구와 연락하기를 추천하는가?
(A) 인쇄소
(B) 지역 기자들
(C) 음식 공급 업체
(D) 지역사회 대표들

해설 지문의 'We recommend that you ask important personalities from
the community to attend the event.'에서 Ms. Kozlowski가 당신 즉,
Mr. Roy가 지역사회의 중요 유명인사들에게 행사에 참석하도록 요청하는
것을 추천한다고 했으므로 (D)가 정답이다.

패러프레이징

important personalities from the community 지역사회의 중요 유명인사들
→ Community representatives 지역사회 대표들

165-168번은 다음 온라인 채팅 대화문에 관한 문제입니다.

Aria Torrez [오후 2시 16분]
165여러분의 새로운 주차 자리에 문제가 있는 사람이 있나요? 저는 G구역
의 맨 안쪽에 있는 자리를 배정받았는데, 이곳은 사무실로부터 걸어서 먼
거리예요.

Mindy Summers [오후 2시 17분]
제 새로운 자리도 제 예전 자리보다 더 멀리 있어요. 하지만 166회사가 고객들
을 위해 더 가까운 공간을 필요로 하기 때문에, 저는 왜 그것이 저에게 배정
되었는지 이해해요.

Raymond Wells [오후 2시 17분]
167Aria, 당신은 우리 관리자와 이 문제를 얘기해보았나요? 어쩌면 회사가 당
신에게 좀 더 합당한 위치를 찾아줄 수도 있어요.

Aria Torrez [오후 2시 20분]
이전에 시도해봤어요. 그녀는 그녀가 해줄 수 있는 최선이 저를 대기 명단에 올
리는 것이라고 말했어요.

Carmen Salgado [오후 2시 20분]
168그냥 버스를 타는 건 어때요? 저는 Harrison가에서 내리는데, 거기서부
터 건물 입구까지 걸어서 짧은 거리예요. 여러 다른 버스들도 그곳에 서요.

Raymond Wells [오후 2시 23분]
아니면 저와 합승해도 돼요, Aria. 저는 건물의 뒷문 바로 앞에 주차해요.

Aria Torrez [오후 2시 24분]
제가 최근에 많은 추가 근무를 하고 있기 때문에 합승하는 것이 가능할지 저
는 잘 모르겠어요. 하지만, 저는 버스를 타는 방안을 확인해볼 거예요. 모두
들 고마워요!

assign v. 배정하다 bring up phr. (문제, 화제 등을) 얘기하다, 제기하다
reasonable adj. 합당한 carpool v. 합승하다 rear entrance phr. 뒷문
shift n. 교대 근무 (시간)

165 육하원칙 문제
중 ●●○

해석 Ms. Torrez는 어떤 문제가 있는가?
(A) 추가 근무가 배정되었다.
(B) 더 넓은 주차 공간이 필요하다.
(C) 사무실까지 너무 멀리 걸어야 한다.
(D) 회사에 이전보다 더 늦게 도착한다.

해설 지문의 'Do any of you have a problem with your new parking
spot? I was assigned one ~ in Lot G, which is a very long walk
from the office.'에서 Ms. Torrez가 새로운 주차 자리에 문제가 있는 사람
이 있는지 물으며 자신은 G구역에 있는 자리를 배정받았는데, 이곳이 사무실
로부터 걸어서 먼 거리라고 했으므로 (C)가 정답이다.

어휘 assign v. 배정하다 shift n. 근무

패러프레이징

a very long walk from the office 사무실로부터 걸어서 먼 거리 → walk too
far to the office 사무실까지 너무 멀리 걷다

166 추론 문제
중 ●●○

해석 주차 공간은 왜 재배정되었을 것 같은가?
(A) 직원들이 그들의 차량을 더 빠르게 가져오는 것을 허용하기 위해
(B) 건물에 대한 방문객 접근성을 향상 시키기 위해
(C) 주요 건설 작업을 위한 공간을 만들기 위해

(D) 경영진을 위한 더 많은 공간들을 따로 남겨두기 위해

해설 지문의 'the company needs the closer spaces for clients'에서 Ms. Summers가 회사가 고객들을 위해 더 가까운 공간을 필요로 한다고 했으므로 고객들의 건물 접근성을 향상시키기 위해 주차 공간이 재배정되었다는 사실을 추론할 수 있다. 따라서 (B)가 정답이다.

어휘 **reassign** v. 재배정하다, 새로 발령내다 **make room** phr. 공간을 만들다
reserve v. (자리 등을) 따로 남겨두다, 예약하다

167 의도 파악 문제   중 ●●○

해석 오후 2시 20분에, Ms. Torrez가 "I tried earlier"라고 썼을 때 그녀가 의도한 것 같은 것은?
(A) 관리자와 문제에 대해 논의했다.
(B) 다른 교통수단을 이용해보지 않았다.
(C) 팀 회의에서 문제를 제기했다.
(D) 제시간에 버스 정류장에 갈 수 없었다.

해설 지문의 'Aria, have you brought this up with our manager?'에서 Mr. Wells가 Ms. Torrez에게 관리자와 문제를 얘기해봤는지 묻자, Ms. Torrez가 'I tried earlier.'(이전에 시도해봤어요)라고 한 것을 통해, Ms. Torrez는 관리자와 이 문제에 대해 논의했음을 알 수 있다. 따라서 (A)가 정답이다.

패러프레이징

brought ~ up 문제를 얘기했다 → discussed an issue 문제에 대해 논의했다

168 추론 문제   중 ●●○

해석 Ms. Salgado에 대해 암시되는 것은?
(A) 그녀의 새로운 배정에 만족한다.
(B) 대중교통을 타고 출근한다.
(C) 회사를 위한 여행 준비를 다룬다.
(D) 주차 공간을 바꿀 의향이 있다.

해설 지문의 'Why don't you just take the bus? I get dropped off at Harrison Avenue, and it's a short walk to the building entrance from there.'에서 Ms. Salgado가 버스를 타는 게 어떤지 제안한 후, 본인은 Harrison가에서 내리는데, 거기서부터 건물 입구, 즉 회사 건물 입구까지 걸어서 짧은 거리라고 했으므로 Ms. Salgado는 대중교통을 타고 출근한다는 사실을 추론할 수 있다. 따라서 (B)가 정답이다.

어휘 **assignment** n. 배정, 배치 **handle** v. 다루다, 처리하다
trade v. 바꾸다, 교환하다

패러프레이징

bus 버스 → public transportation 대중교통

169-171번은 다음 공고에 관한 문제입니다.

169아이슬란드 문화유산 미술관에 들어오기 전에, 저희의 기본 규정들을 살펴봐 주십시오. 이것들은 모든 티켓 구매자들에게 적용됩니다. 이것들을 준수하는 것은 모든 방문객들이 즐거운 경험을 할 수 있도록 보장할 것입니다. — [1] —.

· 171당신은 어느 전시장 안에든 카메라를 가져갈 수 있지만, 몇몇 물품들은 사진이 찍힐 수 없다는 점을 알아두십시오. — [2] —. 이러한 물건들은 그에 따라 표시되어 있습니다.
· 큰 가방들은 로비 너머로 가져가질 수 없습니다. 당신은 가방과 다른 소지품들을 저희의 사물함들 중 하나에 보관할 수 있으며, 이것들은 저희

기념품 가게의 바로 맞은편에 있습니다.
· 170미술관 방문객들은 여름 달인 6월부터 8월 동안 정원을 거닐 수 있습니다. 1707월 10일에 연례 모금 행사가 예정되어 있기 때문에 그날에는 이것이 대중에게 개방되지 않는다는 점을 유의해 주십시오. — [3] —.
· 마감 시간 30분 전에 미술관 출구로 이동하기 시작해주시기를 권고 드립니다. — [4] —. 이때 안내 방송이 있을 것입니다.

어휘 **regulation** n. 규정, 단속 **comply with** phr. ~을 준수하다, 순응하다
ensure v. ~을 보장하다, 반드시 ~하게 하다 **aware** adj. 알고 있는
object n. 물건, 목표 **accordingly** adv. 그에 따라, 부응해서
belonging n. 소지품, 물건 **stroll** v. 거닐다, 산책하다; n. 산책
schedule v. 예정하다 **proceed** v. 이동하다, 진행하다

169 추론 문제   중 ●●○

해석 공고는 어디에서 볼 수 있을 것 같은가?
(A) 매표소 옆에서
(B) 영화 상영관 밖에서
(C) 행정실 옆에서
(D) 기념품 가게 안에서

해설 지문의 'Before entering the ~ Gallery, please review our basic regulations. These apply to all ticket holders.'에서 미술관에 들어오기 전에 기본 규정들을 살펴봐 달라고 한 후, 이것들은 모든 티켓 구매자들에게 적용된다고 했으므로 매표소 옆에서 찾을 수 있는 공고라는 사실을 추론할 수 있다. 따라서 (A)가 정답이다.

어휘 **administrative office** phr. 행정실, 총무부 **souvenir** n. 기념품

170 육하원칙 문제   중 ●●○

해석 7월 10일에 정원 입장이 왜 제한되는가?
(A) 정부 점검이 예정되어 있다.
(B) 보수 작업이 수행된다.
(C) 특별 전시가 계획되어 있다.
(D) 자선 행사가 열린다.

해설 지문의 'Gallery visitors may stroll around our garden'과 'it is closed to the public on July 10 as our annual fund-raiser is scheduled for that day'에서 갤러리 방문객들은 정원을 거닐 수 있으며 7월 10일에 연례 모금 행사가 예정되어 있기 때문에 그날에는 이것이 대중에게 개방되지 않는다고 했으므로 (D)가 정답이다.

어휘 **inspection** n. 점검, 검사 **maintenance** n. 보수, 유지 **exhibit** n. 전시
arrange v. 계획하다, 마련하다 **charity** n. 자선, 자선 단체

패러프레이징

fund-raiser 모금 행사 → charity event 자선 행사

171 문장 위치 찾기 문제   상 ●●●

해석 [1], [2], [3], [4]로 표시된 위치 중, 다음 문장이 들어갈 곳으로 가장 적절한 것은?
"이는 저희에게 작품을 빌려준 사람들의 요청에 따른 것입니다."
(A) [1]
(B) [2]
(C) [3]
(D) [4]

해설 주어진 문장에서 이는 작품을 빌려준 사람들의 요청에 따른 것이라고 했으

므로, 이 문장이 작품을 빌려준 사람들의 요청에 따른 결과와 관련된 부분에 들어가야 함을 알 수 있다. [2]의 앞 문장인 'You may bring a camera inside any of the display halls, but be aware that some items may not be photographed.'에서 어느 전시장 안에든 카메라를 가져갈 수 있지만, 몇몇 물품들은 사진이 찍힐 수 없다는 점을 알아두라고 했으므로, [2]에 제시된 문장이 들어가면 전시장 안의 몇몇 물품들은 사진이 찍힐 수 없는데, 이는 작품을 빌려준 사람들의 요청에 따른 것이라는 자연스러운 문맥이 된다는 것을 알 수 있다. 따라서 (B)가 정답이다.

172-175번은 다음 안내문에 관한 문제입니다.

Jade 항공사의 Easy Board 탑승 수속 서비스를 이용해보세요

당신의 1월 25일 무스카트에서 이스탄불까지의 항공편이 단 일주일 남았습니다. 당신의 탑승권을 받으려고 줄 서는 것을 피하기 위해, ¹⁷²**지희의 Easy Board 탑승 수속 서비스를 이용하시는 것이 어떨까요?** 당신이 Khalid 국제공항의 출발 구역에 들어오실 때, K구역 방향으로 가세요. ¹⁷³**저희의 탑승 수속 기계들은 출발과 도착을 나타내는 스크린과 가까운 그곳에 편리하게 위치되어 있습니다.** 먼저, 당신의 예약 번호를 입력하세요. 그다음 단계는 당신의 여권의 사진 페이지를 스캔하는 것입니다. 이후, 기계가 당신의 탑승권을 제공할 것입니다. 이 단계에서는, ¹⁷⁴**모든 부칠 짐들을 가지고 7번 데스크로 이동하세요.**

만약 당신이 저희의 Easy Board 탑승 수속 서비스를 이용하지 않는 것을 선호한다면, 당신은 저희의 일반 탑승 수속 카운터로 바로 이동할 수 있습니다. 하지만, ¹⁷⁵**저희가 4월 15일에는 디지털 탑승 수속 서비스로 완전히 전환할 것임을 유의해 주십시오.**

check-in n. 탑승 수속, 체크인 head v. ~ 방향으로 가다
adjacent adj. 가까운, 인접한 supply v. 제공하다, 공급하다
prefer v. 선호하다, 택하다 switch v. 전환하다, 바꾸다

172 목적 찾기 문제 중 ●●○

해석 안내문의 주 목적은 무엇인가?
(A) 상품이 이용될 것을 권하기 위해
(B) 시설의 배치가 변경되었다는 것이 알려지도록 하기 위해
(C) 항공편이 도착했다는 것을 알리기 위해
(D) 전자 서비스가 사용될 것을 제안하기 위해

해설 지문의 'why not use our Easy Board check-in service?'에서 Easy Board 탑승 수속 서비스를 이용하는 것이 어떤지 제안한 후, 기계를 이용하는 디지털 탑승 수속 서비스에 대해 설명하고 있으므로 (D)가 정답이다.

어휘 recommend v. 권하다, 추천하다 deal n. 상품, 거래; v. 다루다, 취급하다
take advantage of phr. ~을 이용하다 layout n. 배치, 설계, 레이아웃

173 육하원칙 문제 중 ●●○

해석 Jade 항공사의 탑승 수속 기계들은 어디에서 볼 수 있는가?
(A) 화면 옆에
(B) 라운지 내부에
(C) 입구에
(D) 엘리베이터 옆에

해설 지문의 'Our check-in machines are ~ adjacent to a screen'에서 탑승 수속 기계들이 스크린과 가까이 있다고 했으므로 (A)가 정답이다.

패러프레이징

adjacent to a screen 스크린 가까이 → Next to a display 화면 옆에

174 육하원칙 문제 중 ●●○

해석 탑승객들은 7번 데스크에서 무엇을 할 수 있는가?
(A) 탑승권을 검사 받는다
(B) 일련의 지침을 얻는다
(C) 인터넷 비밀번호를 받는다
(D) 일부 짐을 맡긴다

해설 지문의 'proceed with any check-in luggage to Desk 7'에서 모든 부칠 짐들을 가지고 7번 데스크로 이동하라고 했으므로 7번 데스크에서 짐을 맡긴다는 것을 알 수 있다. 따라서 (D)가 정답이다.

어휘 examine v. 검사하다, 조사하다 pick up phr. ~을 얻다

패러프레이징

luggage 짐 → baggage 짐

175 육하원칙 문제 하 ●○○

해석 4월 15일부터 무엇이 바뀔 것인가?
(A) 출발 시간
(B) 수하물 규제
(C) 수속 절차
(D) 환불 정책

해설 지문의 'we will be completely switching to a digital check-in service on April 15'에서 저희, 즉 Jade 항공사가 4월 15일에 디지털 탑승 수속 서비스로 완전히 전환할 것이라고 했으므로 (C)가 정답이다.

어휘 restriction n. 규제, 구속 policy n. 정책, 방침

176-180번은 다음 기사와 편지에 관한 문제입니다.

그린필드시가 새로운 시민회관 운영 시간을 도입하다

8월 10일—8월 4일에 발표된 보도 자료에서, 그린필드시 의회는 지방 정부에 의해 운영되는 시민회관의 운영 시간을 연장하려는 계획을 발표했다. 이 결정은 시의 서비스에 대한 주민들의 의견을 요청하기 위해 ¹⁷⁶**5월에 배포된 설문지의 답변**을 기반으로 한다. 보도 자료는 Oakwood 및 Selma 시민회관들이 오후 8시 30분까지 계속 열려있을 것인 반면, ¹⁷⁹**Belleville 및 Blanchard 시민회관들은 각각 오후 8시와 9시에 닫을 것임**을 명시했다. ¹⁷⁷**이 새로운 일정은 8월 15일에 시작할 것이다.** 공공서비스부 부장 Wilma Gomez는 8월 8일의 인터뷰에서 시민회관 운영 시간의 변경은 주민들을 위해 삶을 더 편리하게 만들고자 하는 시 정부의 진행 중인 노력의 일부라고 말했다.

press release phr. 보도 자료, 공식 발표 extend v. 연장하다, 확장하다
municipal government phr. 지방 정부 questionnaire n. 설문지
distribute v. 배포하다 solicit v. 요청하다 specify v. 명시하다
respectively adv. 각각, 각자 ongoing adj. 진행 중인; n. 진행

8월 12일

Wilma Gomez
공공서비스부
387번지 Paterson가
그린필드시, 매사추세츠주 02125

Ms. Gomez께,

저는 최근 발표된 우리 도시의 시민회관들의 운영 시간 변경과 관련하여 당신께 연락을 드립니다. 대체로, ¹⁷⁸**제가 작년에 은퇴한** 후로 다수의 프로그램

에 등록했기 때문에 저는 이 계획을 찬성합니다. 하지만, 저는 [179]제 아파트 건물에서 가장 가까운 시민회관은 오후 8시까지 추가적인 30분 동안만 열려 있을 것임을 알게 되어 실망했습니다. 다른 3개의 시설들은 평소보다 한 시간 더 늦게 문을 닫을 것이기 때문에 이것은 제게 불공평하다는 인상을 줍니다. [180]저는 당신의 부서가 이 결정을 재고하고 모든 시민회관이 동일한 시간만큼 연장된 그들의 운영 시간을 갖도록 보장할 것을 요청하고 싶습니다. 감사합니다.

Adam Ferris 드림

in favor of phr. ~을 찬성하여, 지지하여 **sign up for** phr. ~에 등록하다
a number of phr. 다수의, 많은 **disappoint** v. 실망시키다
strike v. 인상을 주다 **unfair** adj. 불공평한 **reconsider** v. 재고하다
ensure v. 보장하다, 보증하다

176 육하원칙 문제 　　　　　　　중 ●●○

해석 기사에 따르면, 5월에 무슨 일이 있었는가?
(A) 선거가 열렸다.
(B) 설문조사가 실시되었다.
(C) 발표가 났다.
(D) 서비스가 소개되었다.

해설 기사의 'questionnaires distributed in May'에서 5월에 배포된 설문지라고 했으므로 (B)가 정답이다.

어휘 **election** n. 선거, 선택 **conduct** v. 실시하다, 하다

패러프레이징

questionnaires 설문지 → A survey 설문조사

177 육하원칙 문제 　　　　　　　하 ●○○

해석 시민회관 운영 시간은 언제 연장될 것인가?
(A) 8월 4일에
(B) 8월 8일에
(C) 8월 10일에
(D) 8월 15일에

해설 기사의 'The new schedules will start on August 15.'에서 이 새로운 일정, 즉 시민회관의 연장된 운영 시간은 8월 15일에 시작할 것이라고 했으므로 (D)가 정답이다.

178 추론 문제 　　　　　　　중 ●●○

해석 Mr. Ferris에 대해 암시되는 것은?
(A) 현재 직장이 없다.
(B) 설문지를 작성했다.
(C) 최근 그린필드로 이사했다.
(D) 도시 시설의 자원봉사자다.

해설 편지의 'I retired last year'에서 Mr. Ferris가 작년에 은퇴했다고 했으므로 현재 직장이 없다는 사실을 추론할 수 있다. 따라서 (A)가 정답이다.

어휘 **unemployed** adj. 직장이 없는

179 육하원칙 문제 [연계] 　　　　　상 ●●●

해석 Mr. Ferris의 거주지에서 어떤 시민회관이 가장 가까운가?
(A) Oakwood 시민회관
(B) Selma 시민회관

(C) Belleville 시민회관
(D) Blanchard 시민회관

해설 편지의 'the community center nearest to my apartment building would ~ be staying open ~ until 8:00 P.M.'에서 저, 즉 Mr. Ferris의 아파트 건물에서 가장 가까운 시민회관은 오후 8시까지 열려 있을 것이라고 했다. 또한, 기사의 'the Belleville ~ centers will close at 8:00 ~ P.M.'에서는 Belleville 시민회관이 오후 8시에 닫을 것이라는 사실을 확인할 수 있다. 두 단서를 종합할 때, Mr. Ferris의 아파트 건물에서 가장 가까운 시민회관은 8시까지 열려 있을 Belleville 시민회관이라는 것을 알 수 있다. 따라서 (C)가 정답이다.

어휘 **residence** n. 거주지

패러프레이징

closest 가장 가까운 → nearest 가장 가까운
open until 8:00 P.M. 오후 8시까지 열다 → close at 8:00 ~ P.M. 오후 8시에 닫다

180 육하원칙 문제 　　　　　　　중 ●●○

해석 Mr. Ferris는 무엇을 요청하는가?
(A) 계획에 대한 수정
(B) 공무원과의 회의
(C) 제안에 대한 결정
(D) 일정 한 부

해설 편지의 'I would like to ask that your department reconsider this decision and ensure that all of the community centers have ~ operating hours extended'에서 당신의 부서가 시민회관 운영 시간에 대한 결정을 재고하고 모든 시민회관이 연장된 운영 시간을 갖도록 보장할 것을 요청하고 싶다고 했으므로 (A)가 정답이다.

어휘 **modification** n. 수정, 변경 **official** n. 공무원 **proposal** n. 제안, 제의

181-185번은 다음 일정표와 공고에 관한 문제입니다.

국립 우주 박물관
특별 전시 일정 ─ 여름

이름	설명	날짜
아폴로 프로그램	인간이 달을 방문하는 결과를 야기한 우주 프로그램에 대해 배워보세요.	[182-C]5월 26일-6월 15일
[184]위성으로 통신하기	현대 통신 위성들의 여러 역할들과 그것들이 어떻게 작동하는지 탐구해보세요.	[182-C/184]6월 16일-7월 5일
태양계 탐험하기	지구에서 우리 태양계 내의 다른 행성들로 보내진 다양한 우주선에 관한 전시를 살펴보세요.	[182-C]7월 6일-7월 25일
화성으로의 여행	계획된 유인 화성 탐사를 발견하고 그것들을 현실로 만들기 위해 극복되어야 하는 여러 문제들에 대해 알아보세요.	[182-C]7월 26일-8월 15일
[181]모든 특별 전시들은 Bergman홀에 **설치될** 것입니다. [182-B]이 전시들로의 입장은 일반 입장 요금에 포함되어 있지 않습니다. 추가 요금은 성인 11달러이고 학생 8달러입니다.		

satellite n. (인공)위성 **explore** v. 탐구하다, 탐험하다
function v. 작동하다, 기능하다; n. 기능 **examine** v. 살펴보다, 조사하다
manned adj. 유인의, 사람을 태운 **overcome** v. 극복하다, 이기다

admission n. 입장, 진입

모든 박물관 방문객들은 주목해주십시오

183박물관 2층 화재 스프링클러의 문제로 인해, 183/184Bergman홀에 침수 피해가 발생했습니다. 다행히도, 이 사고의 결과로 전시 중인 물품들 중 그 어느 것도 손상되지 않았습니다. 하지만, 1846월 25일부터 7월 2일까지 수리가 이뤄지는 동안 이 홀은 폐쇄될 것입니다. 184이 홀의 전시는 이 기간 동안 일시적으로 1층의 Sanderson홀로 옮겨질 것입니다. 저희는 이것이 야기할 수 있는 모든 불편함에 대해 사과드립니다. 185이전된 전시를 찾을 수 없는 방문객들은 저희 직원들 중 한 명에게 도움을 요청하셔야 합니다. 감사합니다.

occur v. 발생하다, 일어나다 fortunately adv. 다행히도
incident n. 사고, 사건 repair n. 수리, 보수
temporarily adv. 일시적으로, 임시로 cause v. 야기하다

181 동의어 찾기 문제 중 ●●○

해석 일정표에서, 1문단 첫 번째 줄의 표현 "set up"은 의미상 –와 가장 가깝다.
(A) 조정되다
(B) 개발되다
(C) 설치되다
(D) 작동되다

해설 일정표의 set up을 포함한 문장 'All special exhibits will be set up in Bergman Hall.'에서 모든 특별 전시들은 Bergman홀에 설치될 것이라고 했으므로 set up은 '설치되다'라는 뜻으로 사용되었다. 따라서 '설치되다'라는 뜻을 가진 (C) arranged가 정답이다.

182 Not/True 문제 중 ●●●

해석 국립 우주 박물관에 대해 사실인 것은?
(A) 일 년 중 일부 동안 닫는다.
(B) 몇몇 전시에 추가 요금을 청구한다.
(C) 여러 특별 전시를 동시에 주최한다.
(D) 다른 기관들로부터 빌려온 물품들을 포함한다.

해설 일정표의 'Access to these exhibits is not included in the regular admission price. The additional fee is $11 for adults and $8 for students.'에서 이 전시들, 즉 특별 전시로의 입장은 일반 입장 요금에 포함되어 있지 않으며, 추가 요금은 성인 11달러이고, 학생 8달러라고 했으므로 (B)는 지문의 내용과 일치한다. 따라서 (B)가 정답이다. (A)와 (D)는 지문에 언급되지 않은 내용이다. (C)는 'May 26-June 15', 'June 16-July 5', 'July 6-July 25', 'July 26-August 15'에서 여러 특별 전시들을 겹치는 날짜 없이 나눠서 전시하고 있다는 것을 알 수 있으므로 지문의 내용과 일치하지 않는다.

어휘 extra n. 추가 요금; adj. 추가의, 특별한 host v. 주최하다, 개최하다
at once phr. 동시에 feature v. (특별히) 포함하다 institution n. 기관, 시설

패러프레이징
additional fee 추가 비용 → charges extra 추가 요금을 청구하다

183 육하원칙 문제 중 ●●○

해석 공고에 따르면, 어떤 문제가 발생했는가?
(A) 물품이 잘못 배치되었다.
(B) 기기가 오작동하였다.
(C) 전시품이 분실되었다.

(D) 상자가 손상되었다.

해설 공고의 'Due to a problem with a fire sprinkler ~, water damage has occurred ~.'에서 화재 스프링클러의 문제로 인해, 침수 피해가 발생했다고 했으므로 (B)가 정답이다.

패러프레이징
a fire sprinkler 화재 스프링클러 → A device 기기

184 육하원칙 문제 연계 상 ●●●

해석 어느 전시가 Sanderson홀로 옮겨졌는가?
(A) 아폴로 프로그램
(B) 위성으로 통신하기
(C) 태양계 탐험하기
(D) 화성으로의 여행

해설 공고의 'water damage has occurred in Bergman Hall'과 'the hall will be closed from June 25 to July 2'와 'The exhibit in this hall will be ~ moved to Sanderson Hall ~ during this period.'에서 Bergman홀에 침수 피해가 발생했으며 6월 25일부터 7월 2일까지 이 홀, 즉 Bergman홀은 폐쇄될 것이므로 이 홀의 전시는 이 기간 동안 Sanderson홀로 옮겨질 것이라고 했다. 또한, 일정표의 'Communicating by Satellite', 'June 16-July 5'에서는 6월 16일부터 7월 5일까지 위성으로 통신하기가 전시되고 있다는 사실을 확인할 수 있다.
두 단서를 종합할 때, 6월 25일부터 7월 2일 사이에 진행되는 위성으로 통신하기 전시가 Sanderson홀로 옮겨질 것이라는 것을 알 수 있다. 따라서 (B)가 정답이다.

185 육하원칙 문제 중 ●●○

해석 몇몇 박물관 방문객들은 무엇을 하라고 지시받는가?
(A) 직원에게 말을 건다
(B) 다른 지점을 방문한다
(C) 티켓 환불을 요청한다
(D) 설문지를 작성한다

해설 공고의 'Visitors who are unable to find the relocated exhibit should ask one of our employees for assistance.'에서 이전된 전시를 찾을 수 없는 방문객들은 직원들 중 한 명에게 도움을 요청해야 한다고 했으므로 (A)가 정답이다.

패러프레이징
ask ~ employees for assistance 직원들에게 도움을 요청하다 → Talk to a staff member 직원에게 말을 걸다

186-190번은 다음 회람, 광고, 공고에 관한 문제입니다.

MEYERHOFFER 보험사
회람

수신: 전 직원
발신: James Loris, 인사 담당자
제목: 회사 야유회
날짜: 1월 11일

186만약 당신이 다음 달의 회사 야유회에 함께 갈 예정인지 아닌지 저에게 알려주지 않았다면, 이것이 이번 주말까지 이루어져야 한다는 것을 잊지 마세요. 190이것은 당일 여행일 것이고, 회사가 모든 음식, 교통, 그리고 오락 비용을 부담할 것입니다. 여러분들 각자 한 명의 동반자를 데리고 올 수 있습

니다. ¹⁹⁰야유회는 2월 22일 토요일에 열릴 것입니다. 우리는 Simon섬으로 이동하고 육지로 돌아오기 위해 Brunswick 페리를 이용할 것입니다. Simon섬은 아주 멋진 곳이어서, ¹⁸⁷저는 모든 지역 명소를 방문하는 것을 추천합니다. 여러분은 www.visitsimonisland.com에서 더 많이 알아볼 수 있습니다. 어쨌든, 당신이 참석하실 계획이라면 금요일까지 저에게 말해주세요. 감사합니다.

outing n. 야유회, 여행 come along phr. 함께 가다, 도착하다
cover v. 부담하다, 비용을 대다 companion n. 동반자, 동료
attraction n. 명소, 명물

Windward 호텔로 오세요

조지아의 Simon섬에 위치한 ¹⁸⁸⁻ᴮWindward 호텔은 대서양의 경치와 함께 웅장한 대지 위에 있습니다. 저희의 편안한 방들은 평면 텔레비전과 와이파이를 포함합니다. 바닷가 오두막집들 또한 하루 단위로 빌리는 것이 가능합니다. 손님들은 세계 최상급의 골프 코스, 헬스장, 수영장 그리고 회의실에 대한 이용 권한을 누릴 것입니다. 식사 선택권은 해산물 식당과 스테이크 전문 음식점을 포함합니다. ¹⁸⁷유명한 지역 명소는 역사적인 Fort Frederick 박물관과 Simon섬 등대 박물관을 포함합니다. 예약을 위해서는, 555-4081로 전화하시거나 www.windwardinn.com을 방문하세요.

sit v. ~에 있다 magnificent adj. 웅장한, 훌륭한 property n. 대지, 부동산

Brunswick 페리
승객들께 드리는 공고

봄 일정은 다음 달부터 적용될 것임을 알아 두십시오.

요금 (세금 포함 왕복 요금)

성인:	32달러
65세 이상 노인:	30달러
15세 이하 어린이:	22달러

¹⁸⁹⁻ᴮ**겨울 일정**
¹⁹⁰12월 1일 – 2월 28일 (¹⁸⁹⁻ᴮ주 5일, 목요일부터 월요일)

Brunswick 출발	Simon섬 도착	¹⁹⁰Simon섬 출발	¹⁹⁰Brunswick 도착
오전 8시 30분	오전 9시 15분	오전 9시 45분	오전 10시 30분
오전 11시	오전 11시 45분	¹⁹⁰오후 4시 15분	¹⁹⁰오후 5시

¹⁸⁹⁻ᴮ**봄 일정**
3월 1일 – 5월 31일 (¹⁸⁹⁻ᴮ주 7일)

Brunswick 출발	Simon섬 도착	Simon섬 출발	Brunswick 도착
오전 9시	오전 9시 45분	오전 10시 15분	오전 11시
오전 11시 30분	오후 12시 15분	오후 12시 45분	오후 1시 30분
오후 2시	오후 2시 15분	오후 5시	오후 5시 45분

Simon섬으로 떠나는 승객들은 최소 출발 45분 전까지 방문객 센터에서 탑승 수속을 해야 합니다. 놓친 출발에 대해서는 환불이 제공되지 않을 것입니다.

take effect phr. 적용되다 senior n. 노인, 고령자

---

186 목적 찾기 문제   중 ●●○

해석 회람의 목적은 무엇인가?
(A) 직원들에게 중요한 회의에 대해 알리기 위해
(B) 연례 야유회에 대한 제안을 요청하기 위해
(C) 직원 설문조사 참여를 확인하기 위해

(D) 직원들에게 확정 기한을 상기시키기 위해

해설 회람의 'If you haven't let me know whether you plan to come along ~, don't forget that this must be done by the end of the week.'에서 만약 당신이 함께 갈 예정인지 아닌지 자신, 즉 Mr. Loris에게 알려주지 않았다면, 이것이 이번 주말까지 이루어져야 한다는 것을 잊지 말라고 했으므로 (D)가 정답이다.

어휘 notify v. 알리다, 통지하다 verify v. 확인하다 remind v. 상기시키다
confirmation n. 확정, 확인

---

187 육하원칙 문제 연계   중 ●●●

해석 Mr. Loris는 몇몇 직원들에게 무엇을 할 것을 추천하는가?
(A) 박물관을 방문한다
(B) 가벼운 점심을 싼다
(C) 교통편을 준비한다
(D) 그들의 친척들을 초대한다

해설 회람의 'I would recommend visiting all of the local attractions'에서 Mr. Loris는 모든 지역 명소를 방문하는 것을 추천한다고 했다. 또한, 광고의 'Popular local attractions include the ~ Fort Frederick Museum and the Simon Island Lighthouse Museum.'에서는 유명한 지역 명소는 Fort Frederick 박물관과 Simon섬 등대 박물관을 포함한다는 사실을 확인할 수 있다.
두 단서를 종합할 때, Mr. Loris는 Simon섬의 모든 지역 명소를 방문하는 것을 추천했으므로 Simon섬의 명소 중 하나인 박물관 방문을 추천한다는 것을 알 수 있다. 따라서 (A)가 정답이다.

---

188 Not/True 문제   하 ●○○

해석 Windward 호텔에 대해 언급된 것은?
(A) 최소 이틀 숙박을 요구한다.
(B) 바다의 경치를 제공한다.
(C) 네 명 이상의 그룹을 위한 객실들이 있다.
(D) 무료 아침 식사를 제공한다.

해설 광고의 'the Windward Inn ~ with a view of the Atlantic Ocean'에서 Windward 호텔에 대서양의 경치가 있다고 했으므로 (B)는 지문의 내용과 일치한다. 따라서 정답은 (B)이다. (A), (C), (D)는 지문에 언급되지 않은 내용이다.

어휘 minimum adj. 최소의 complimentary adj. 무료의

---

189 Not/True 문제   중 ●●●

해석 Brunswick 페리에 대해 사실인 것은?
(A) 동시에 다수의 선박들을 운영한다.
(B) 겨울에 더 적은 항해를 한다.
(C) Simon섬으로 가는 길에 잠시 동안 멈춘다.
(D) 자동차가 이것의 배에 탈 수 있게 해준다.

해설 공고의 'WINTER SCHEDULE', '5 days a week', 'SPRING SCHEDULE', '7 days a week'에서 Brunswick 페리가 겨울에는 주 5일 운행하고, 봄에는 주 7일 운행한다는 것을 알 수 있으므로 (B)는 지문의 내용과 일치한다. 따라서 (B)가 정답이다. (A), (C), (D)는 지문에 언급되지 않은 내용이다.

어휘 multiple adj. 다수의, 많은 vessel n. 선박 simultaneously adv. 동시에
briefly adv. 잠시 동안, 간단히

190 추론 문제 연계 　　　　　　　　　　　상 ●●●

해석 회사 야유회에 참석하는 직원들에 대해 암시되는 것은?
(A) 그들 자신의 여객선 표를 사야 할 것이다.
(B) 오전 8시 30분까지 수속해야 한다.
(C) 출발을 놓치면 환불을 받을 수 있다.
(D) Brunswick에 5시 정각에 돌아올 것이다.

해설 회람의 'It will be a one-day trip'과 'The outing will take place on Saturday, February 22. We will use the Brunswick Ferry to travel to Simon island and return to the mainland.'에서 야유회는 당일 여행일 것이고 2월 22일 토요일에 열릴 것이며, Simon섬으로 이동하고 육지로 돌아오기 위해 Brunswick 페리를 이용할 것이라고 했다. 또한, 공고의 'December 1 – February 28', 'Leave Simon Island', '4:15 P.M.', 'Arrive Brunswick', '5:00 P.M.'에서는 12월 1일부터 2월 28일까지, Brunswick 페리가 오후 4시 15분에 Simon섬을 떠나서 Brunswick에 오후 5시 정각에 도착하는 것이 유일한 오후 시간대 일정이라는 것을 확인할 수 있다.
두 단서를 종합할 때, 2월 22일 토요일 Simon섬으로의 회사 야유회에 참석하는 직원들은 당일 여행을 한 뒤 그날의 유일한 오후 시간대 일정인 4시 15분 페리를 타고 Brunswick으로 오후 5시 정각에 돌아올 것이라는 사실을 추론할 수 있다. 따라서 (D)가 정답이다.

어휘 **obtain** v. 받다, 얻다

191-195번은 다음 안내문, 양식, 이메일에 관한 문제입니다.

Buzzchain은 어떻게 운영하나요?

191-A Buzzchain은 제품을 논평하고 온라인 마케팅에 대한 도움을 제공하는 소비자들의 네트워크입니다. 함께하기 위해서는, 가입하여 192-B 당신이 어떤 종류의 제품들에 관심이 있는지 저희에게 알려주세요. 저희는 후기를 위해 제품이 이용 가능할 때 당신에게 알려줄 것입니다. 당신은 무료 샘플 또는 가까운 상점에서 교환될 수 있는 상품권을 받게 될 것입니다.

191-C 회원으로서, 당신은 당신이 작성하는 모든 후기에 대해 포인트를 얻을 것입니다. 당신이 더 많은 활동을 할수록 당신은 각 후기에 대해 더 많은 포인트를 얻습니다. 저희의 파트너 웹사이트 www.linkchange.com에서 당신의 포인트를 제품 또는 서비스로 교환하세요.

활동	적립되는 포인트
설문조사에 답한다	10
최소 50단어의 후기를 작성한다	30
당신의 후기와 함께 사진 또는 영상을 업로드한다	50
소셜 미디어에 당신의 후기를 공유한다	60
당신의 공유된 콘텐츠에 25개 이상의 "좋아요"를 받는다	100
195 제품당 가능한 총 포인트	195 250

알림: 모든 제출물은 저희의 가이드라인을 충족시켜야 하며 평가의 대상이 됩니다.

---

consumer n. 소비자　**review** v. 논평하다, 검토하다; n. 후기
assistance n. 도움, 지원　**notify** v. (공식적으로) 알리다
voucher n. 상품권, 할인권　**exchange** v. 교환하다; n. 교환, 환전
earn v. 얻다, 벌다　**redeem** v. (쿠폰 등을 상품으로) 교환하다
submission n. 제출(물), 제시　**be subject to** phr. ~의 대상이 되는
evaluation n. 평가, 사정

192-B,C Buzzchain 후기 작성자:　　Buzzchain 후기 작성자 ID:
Sean Morgan　　　　　　　　M90746
제품명: Limba Air　　　　　　　192-E 카테고리: 가정 제품
첨부: 제품_사진.jpg

이 제품을 처음 사용하나요?
네.

당신은 일상 생활에서 비슷한 제품을 사용하나요?
아니요, 정기적으로 사용하지 않습니다. 하지만 192-A 저는 가끔 방향제를 구입합니다.

제품이 광고된 것처럼 기능했나요?
저는 처음에는 이것이 향기가 좋다고 생각했지만, 193-B 그 향기가 오래가진 못했습니다.

제품에 대한 당신의 전반적인 의견은 무엇인가요?
저는 Berry Fresh와 Crisp Sheets인 193-C 두 가지 향기의 상품을 받았습니다. 저는 첫 번째 것은 좋아하지 않았지만, 두 번째 것은 구입할 수도 있을 것 같습니다. 향기와 별개로, 저는 상품의 포장이 매력적이라고 생각했습니다.

이 제품을 친구들에게 추천할 것인가요?
저는 누가 제게 제 의견을 물어본다면 추천할 것 같습니다. 그렇지 않다면, 저는 잘 모르겠습니다.

---

household n. 가정, 가구　**air freshener** phr. 방향제
on occasion phr. 가끔　**overall** adj. 전반적인, 종합적인
packaging n. (상품의) 포장(재)　**attractive** adj. 매력적인

수신: Buzzchain 고객 서비스 <service@buzzchain.com>
발신: Sean Morgan <s.morgan@mynetmail.com>
제목: 문의
날짜: 5월 14일

관계자분께,

195 저는 최근에 제 첫 후기를 작성했으며, 저는 그것에 대해 최대치의 포인트를 받았습니다. 하지만, 제가 Linkchange 웹사이트를 방문했을 때, 저는 195 제가 원했던 비치 샌들을 위한 충분한 포인트가 없다는 것을 깨달았습니다. 194 후기를 작성할 더 많은 제품들을 가능한 빨리 저에게 보내줄 수 있나요? 저는 이달 말 여행을 위해 그 샌들을 갖고 싶습니다.

감사합니다.

Sean Morgan

---

maximum adj. 최대의

---

191 Not/True 문제 　　　　　　　　　　　중 ●●○

해석 Buzzchain에 대해 언급된 것은?
(A) 회사들이 그들의 제품을 판매하는 것을 도와준다.
(B) Linkchange로 고객들을 보내는 것에 대해 돈을 받는다.
(C) 온라인 활동들에 현금을 지급한다.
(D) 전국에 사무실을 유지한다.

해설 안내문의 'Buzzchain is a network of consumers who ~ provide assistance with online marketing.'에서 Buzzchain은 온라인 마케팅에 대한 도움을 제공하는 소비자들의 네트워크라고 했으므로 (A)는 지문의 내용과 일치한다. 따라서 (A)가 정답이다. (B)와 (D)는 지문에 언급되지 않은 내용이다. (C)는 'As a member, you will earn points for every review you complete.'에서 회원, 즉 Buzzchain의 회원으로서, 작성한 모든 후기에 대해 포인트를 얻을 수 있다고 했으므로 지문의 내용과 일치하지 않는다.

어휘 maintain v. 유지하다, 관리하다

패러프레이징

provide assistance with ~ marketing 마케팅에 도움을 주다 → helps ~ sell ~ products 제품을 판매하는 것을 도와주다

192 Not/True 문제 연계   중 ●●○

해석 Mr. Morgan에 대해 사실인 것은?
(A) 방향제의 단골 이용자이다.
(B) 가정용품에 관심을 표했다.
(C) 후기를 작성할 자격이 없다.
(D) 제품 포장을 디자인한다.

해설 양식의 'Buzzchain Reviewer: Sean Morgan', 'Category: Household products'에서 Sean Morgan이 가정 제품 카테고리의 제품에 대해 Buzzchain 후기를 작성했다고 했다. 또한, 안내문의 'let us know what kinds of products you are interested in'에서는 당신이 어떤 종류의 제품들에 관심이 있는지 저희, 즉 Buzzchain에게 알려달라고 한 사실을 확인할 수 있다.
두 단서를 종합할 때, Mr. Morgan이 가정용품에 관심을 표했다는 것을 알 수 있다. 따라서 (B)가 정답이다. (A)는 양식의 'I buy air fresheners on occasion'에서 Mr. Morgan이 가끔 방향제를 구입한다고 했으므로 지문의 내용과 일치하지 않는다. (C)는 양식의 'Buzzchain Reviewer: Sean Morgan'에서 Mr. Morgan이 Buzzchain 후기를 작성했다고 했으므로 지문의 내용과 일치하지 않는다. (D)는 지문에 언급되지 않은 내용이다.

어휘 frequent adj. 단골의, 잦은 household item phr. 가정용품
unqualified adj. 자격이 없는

193 Not/True 문제   중 ●●○

해석 Limba Air에 대해 언급된 것은?
(A) 하루 만에 배달될 수 있다.
(B) 몇 주 동안 지속되는 향기를 남긴다.
(C) 최소 두 가지 종류로 나온다.
(D) 웹사이트에서 구매될 수 있다.

해설 양식의 'I received a package of two scents'에서 두 가지 향기의 상품을 받았다고 했으므로 (C)는 지문의 내용과 일치한다. 따라서 (C)가 정답이다. (A)와 (D)는 지문에 언급되지 않은 내용이다. (B)는 'the scent didn't last long'에서 향기가 오래가지 못했다고 했으므로 지문의 내용과 일치하지 않는다.

어휘 variety n. 종류, 다양성

194 목적 찾기 문제   중 ●●○

해석 Mr. Morgan은 왜 이메일을 작성했는가?
(A) 그의 현재 포인트 총액을 확인하기 위해
(B) 그의 계정 정보를 업데이트하기 위해
(C) 제품의 품질에 대해 불만을 제기하기 위해
(D) 더 많은 후기를 작성하는 것에 대해 문의하기 위해

해설 이메일의 'Could you send me some more products to review as soon as possible?'에서 후기를 작성할 더 많은 제품들을 가능한 빨리 자신, 즉 Mr. Morgan에게 보내줄 수 있는지 물었으므로 (D)가 정답이다.

어휘 confirm v. 확인하다, 확정하다

195 추론 문제 연계   상 ●●●

해석 Mr. Morgan은 왜 그가 원했던 제품을 가질 수 없었을 것 같은가?
(A) 그는 몇몇 잘못된 정보를 제공했다.
(B) 제품이 부정적인 후기를 받았다.
(C) 그는 마감기한을 지나서 후기를 제출했다.
(D) 그 제품이 250포인트보다 더 비싸다.

해설 이메일의 'I recently completed my first review, and I received the maximum number of points for it.'에서 Mr. Morgan이 최근에 첫 후기를 작성했으며, 그것에 대해 최대치의 포인트를 받았다고 했고, 'I did not have enough points for the beach sandals I wanted'에서 Mr. Morgan이 원했던 비치 샌들을 위한 충분한 포인트가 없다고 했다. 또한, 안내문의 'Total possible points per product', '250'에서는 제품당 후기를 작성함으로써 가능한 총 포인트, 즉 최대치는 250점이라는 사실을 확인할 수 있다.
두 단서를 종합할 때, Mr. Morgan이 원했던 비치 샌들은 Mr. Morgan이 가지고 있는 250포인트보다 더 비싸다는 사실을 추론할 수 있다. 따라서 (D)가 정답이다.

어휘 negative adj. 부정적인, 나쁜 submit v. 제출하다, 항복하다

196-200번은 다음 이메일, 온라인 양식, 소식지에 관한 문제입니다.

수신: 모든 세입자들 <all@freshwater.com>
발신: Tom Phillips <t.phillips@freshwater.com>
제목: 요가 수업
날짜: 5월 24일

세입자분들께,

여러분 모두는 6월 2일 토요일 오후 5시부터 오후 6시까지의 Freshwater 아파트에서 요가 수업에 자유로이 참석할 수 있습니다. 196지역 헬스장 체인 Topflight Fitness의 강사 Janice Warren이 처음 요가를 하는 학생들과 경험이 많은 학생들 모두에게 조언을 하며 수업을 진행할 것입니다. 저희 건물의 세입자들만 참여할 수 있도록 허용되며, 총 수업 규모는 학생 30명으로 한정될 것이므로, 자리를 잡기 위해서는 꼭 빨리 등록하세요! 197이 수업에 참여하기 위한 비용은 1인당 10달러입니다.

200-D만약 수업 당일의 기상 상태가 좋다면, 이 수업은 저희의 앞쪽 잔디밭 야외에서 열릴 것입니다. 그렇지 않으면, 이것은 저희 건물 내의 헬스장에서 열릴 것입니다. 등록하려면 아파트 건물의 웹사이트에 접속하세요. 무엇이든 질문이 있다면 건물 관리자 Marcy Fried에게 555-3430으로 연락하세요.

Tom Phillips
건물 관리인
Freshwater 아파트

tenant n. 세입자, 거주자 welcome to phr. ~을 자유로이 할 수 있는
sign up phr. 등록하다, 신청하다 session n. 수업, 시간, 기간
favorable adj. 좋은, 호의적인 lawn n. 잔디밭
on-site adj. 건물 내의, 현장의 administrator n. 관리자, 행정관

Freshwater 아파트

홈	임대	세입자 페이지

197요가 수업, 6월 2일, 오후 5시 - 오후 6시
197등록 확인 페이지

197성명: Shawn Ewing
호수: 403

요가 경험: ¹⁹⁸⁻ᴬ저는 이전에 여러 요가 수업들을 들은 적이 있습니다. ¹⁹⁸⁻ᴰ저는 새로운 기술들을 배우는 것과 제 등을 튼튼하게 하는 것에 관심이 있습니다.

다른 참고 사항: ¹⁹⁸⁻ᴮ작년에, 저는 업무 현장 사고 중에 제 무릎을 다쳤습니다. 따라서, 저는 몇몇 자세들을 할 수 없을 수도 있습니다. 저는 추가적인 고통을 피할 수 있도록 제 동작을 조정하는 방법에 대해 강사가 저에게 조언해 줄 수 있기를 바랍니다.

반드시 당신의 개인 물병과 요가 매트를 수업에 가져와주십시오. 매트는 또한 2달러의 요금으로 대여하는 것이 가능합니다.

confirmation n. 확인, 확정 strengthen v. 튼튼하게 하다, 강화하다
workplace n. 업무 현장, 직장 adjust v. 조정하다, 적응하다
movement n. 동작, 움직임 avoid v. 피하다, 자제하다

Freshwater 아파트 월간 소식지

7월

이번 달, 모든 세입자들은 ¹⁹⁹우리 로비에 진행될 몇 가지 보수 공사에 대해 알고 있어야 합니다. 이 작업은 7월 20일부터 7월 31일까지 일어날 것으로 예상됩니다. ¹⁹⁹이 기간 동안, 저희의 건물의 정문은 막힐 것이고, 거주민들은 Grove가 근처의 출입구를 대신 사용해야 합니다.

7월 23일에, 저희의 정기 월례 모임이 3층 라운지에서 열릴 것입니다. 이는 건물의 다른 세입자들과 어울릴 수 있는 아주 좋은 기회가 될 것입니다. 게다가, 저희는 ²⁰⁰⁻ᴰ지난달 저희 건물 내의 헬스장에서 있었던 저희 요가 수업에서의 사진들을 보여드릴 것입니다.

renovation n. 보수, 수리 occur v. 일어나다, 발생하다
block off phr. (도로나 출입구를) 막다 gathering n. 모임, 수집품
socialize v. (사람들과) 어울리다, 교제하다

---

196 육하원칙 문제　하 ●○○

해석　Janice Warren은 누구인가?
(A) 건물 관리자
(B) 새로운 세입자
(C) 운동 강사
(D) 공사 작업자

해설　이메일의 'Instructor Janice Warren from local gym chain Topflight Fitness'에서 지역 헬스장 체인 Topflight Fitness의 강사 Janice Warren이라고 했으므로 (C)가 정답이다.

---

197 육하원칙 문제　연계　중 ●●○

해석　Mr. Ewing은 무엇을 해야 하는가?
(A) 헬스장 회원권에 가입한다
(B) 직접 Ms. Fried에게 말한다
(C) 10달러의 요금에 대해 비용을 지불한다
(D) 사진 공개 양식을 작성한다

해설　온라인 양식의 'Yoga Class', 'Signup Confirmation Page', 'Full Name: Shawn Ewing'에서 Mr. Ewing이 요가 수업을 신청했다는 것을 알 수 있다. 또한, 이메일의 'The cost to join the class is $10 per person.'에서는 이 수업, 즉 요가 수업에 참여하기 위한 비용이 1인당 10달러라는 사실을 확인할 수 있다.
두 단서를 종합할 때, Mr. Ewing은 요가 수업 참여 비용으로 10달러를 지불해야 한다는 것을 알 수 있다. 따라서 (C)가 정답이다.

어휘　in person phr. 직접 release n. 공개, (권리 등의) 양도

198 Not/True 문제　중 ●●○

해석　Mr. Ewing에 대해 언급되지 않은 것은?
(A) 이전에 요가 수업에 참여한 적이 있다.
(B) 지난 몇 년 이내에 부상을 당했다.
(C) 수업을 위해 매트를 대여할 것이다.
(D) 그의 등 힘을 향상시키고 싶어한다.

해설　질문의 Mr. Ewing과 관련된 내용이 언급된 온라인 양식에서 (C)는 언급되지 않은 내용이다. 따라서 (C)가 정답이다. (A)는 'I have taken several yoga classes before.'에서 이전에 여러 요가 수업을 들은 적이 있다고 했으므로 지문의 내용과 일치한다. (B)는 'Last year, I hurt my knee'에서 작년에 자신의 무릎을 다쳤다고 했으므로 지문의 내용과 일치한다. (D)는 'I am interested in ~ strengthening my back.'에서 자신의 등을 튼튼하게 하는 것에 관심이 있다고 했으므로 지문의 내용과 일치한다.

패러프레이징

have taken ~ yoga classes 요가 수업들을 들은 적이 있다 → has participated in a yoga class 요가 수업에 참여한 적이 있다
Last year 작년에 → within the past few years 지난 몇 년 이내에
hurt ~ knee 무릎을 다쳤다 → was injured 부상을 당했다
strengthening ~ back 등을 튼튼하게 하는 것 → improve strength in ~ back 등 힘을 향상시키다

---

199 육하원칙 문제　상 ●●●

해석　세입자들은 보수 기간 동안 무엇을 하라고 지시받는가?
(A) 3층에서 엘리베이터를 사용하는 것을 자제한다
(B) 앞쪽 잔디밭에 놓인 기구들을 조심한다
(C) Grove가에 있는 부지에 그들의 차를 주차한다
(D) 다른 입구를 통해 건물에 출입한다

해설　소식지의 'some renovation work that will be taking place in our lobby'와 'During this period, ~ residents should use the door near Grove Street instead.'에서 우리 로비, 즉 Freshwater 아파트의 로비에 진행될 몇 가지 보수 공사가 있을 것이라고 한 후, 이 기간 동안 거주민들은 Grove가 근처의 출입구를 대신 사용해야 한다고 했으므로 (D)가 정답이다.

어휘　alternate adj. 다른, 대안의

패러프레이징

door 출입구 → entryway 입구

---

200 Not/True 문제　연계　상 ●●●

해석　Freshwater 아파트의 요가 수업에 대해 언급된 것은?
(A) 라운지에서의 모임에 뒤이어 일어났다.
(B) 이것의 주최자는 몇몇 기술들을 시연했다.
(C) 이것의 강사는 첫 번째 수업의 일정을 변경했다.
(D) 좋지 않은 날씨로 인해 실내에서 진행되었다.

해설　이메일의 'If weather conditions ~ are favorable, the class will be held outdoors ~. Otherwise, it will take place in our on-site fitness center.'에서 기상 상태가 좋다면, 이 수업, 즉 요가 수업은 야외에서 열릴 것이고 그렇지 않으면, 건물 내의 헬스장에서 열릴 것이라고 했다. 또한, 소식지의 'our yoga class, which happened ~ in our on-site gym'에서는 요가 수업이 건물 내의 헬스장에서 있었다는 사실을 확인할 수 있다.

두 단서를 종합할 때, 요가 수업이 좋지 않은 날씨로 인해 야외가 아닌 건물 내의 헬스장에서 열렸다는 것을 알 수 있다. 따라서 (D)가 정답이다. (A), (B), (C)는 지문에 언급되지 않은 내용이다.

어휘 **follow** v. 뒤이어 일어나다, ~에 잇따르다   **demonstrate** v. 시연하다, 설명하다
reschedule v. 일정을 변경하다

패러프레이징

on-site fitness center 건물 내의 헬스장 → **indoors** 실내

PART 5

101 (D)	**102** (B)	**103** (C)	**104** (D)	**105** (D)
106 (C)	**107** (B)	**108** (A)	**109** (C)	**110** (A)
111 (B)	**112** (C)	**113** (B)	**114** (B)	**115** (D)
116 (C)	**117** (B)	**118** (A)	**119** (D)	**120** (C)
121 (C)	**122** (B)	**123** (D)	**124** (B)	**125** (A)
126 (D)	**127** (B)	**128** (C)	**129** (D)	**130** (B)

PART 6

131 (B)	**132** (D)	**133** (B)	**134** (A)	**135** (C)
136 (B)	**137** (B)	**138** (A)	**139** (C)	**140** (D)
141 (B)	**142** (A)	**143** (A)	**144** (C)	**145** (A)
146 (D)				

PART 7

147 (D)	**148** (B)	**149** (C)	**150** (B)	**151** (B)
152 (B)	**153** (A)	**154** (B)	**155** (A)	**156** (B)
157 (D)	**158** (C)	**159** (A)	**160** (B)	**161** (D)
162 (D)	**163** (C)	**164** (D)	**165** (B)	**166** (A)
167 (A)	**168** (B)	**169** (D)	**170** (D)	**171** (B)
172 (B)	**173** (D)	**174** (D)	**175** (D)	**176** (D)
177 (D)	**178** (B)	**179** (D)	**180** (D)	**181** (B)
182 (B)	**183** (A)	**184** (C)	**185** (B)	**186** (A)
187 (A)	**188** (D)	**189** (A)	**190** (D)	**191** (C)
192 (D)	**193** (B)	**194** (C)	**195** (C)	**196** (B)
197 (C)	**198** (B)	**199** (D)	**200** (D)	

PART 5

101 재귀대명사 채우기　하 ●○○

해석　Ms. Adams는 한국에서 온 Calterna Technology사의 직원들을 돕는 것에 직접 자원했다.

해설　'Ms. Adams는 직원들을 돕는 것에 직접 자원했다'라는 의미가 되어야 하므로 재귀대명사 (D) herself가 정답이다. 참고로, 재귀대명사는 목적어가 주어와 같은 사람이나 사물을 지칭할 때나, 주어나 목적어를 강조할 때 쓰임을 알아둔다. 주격 인칭대명사 (A)는 주어 자리에, 목적격 인칭대명사 (B)는 동사나 전치사의 목적어 자리에, 소유대명사 (C)는 주어, 목적어, 보어 자리에 온다.

어휘　volunteer v. 자원하다　assist v. 돕다　representative n. 직원, 대표

102 형용사 어휘 고르기　하 ●○○

해석　디자인 팀은 많은 유용한 아이디어들을 만들어낸 유익한 논의를 했다.

해설　빈칸은 명사(discussion)를 꾸미는 형용사 자리이다. '유용한 아이디어들을 만들어낸 유익한 논의'라는 문맥이므로 (B) valuable(유익한, 가치 있는)이 정답이다. 참고로, (D) generous(풍부한)도 해석상 그럴듯해 보이지만, '크기, 양 등이 풍부한'이라는 뜻으로 쓰임을 알아둔다.

어휘　discussion n. 논의, 토론　useful adj. 유용한　uncertain adj. 불확실한　redundant adj. 불필요한

103 부사 어휘 고르기　하 ●○○

해석　그 영화는 어떤 점에서는 책과 다르지만, 그것은 거의 같은 이야기를 한다.

해설　빈칸은 동사(tells)를 꾸미는 부사 자리이다. '그 영화는 책과 다르지만, 그것은 거의 같은 이야기를 한다'라는 문맥이므로 (C) nearly(거의)가 정답이다. (D) rarely(좀처럼 ~하지 않는)는 '그 영화는 책과 다르지만, 그것은 좀처럼 같은 이야기를 하지 않는다'라는 어색한 문맥을 만든다.

어휘　differ v. 다르다　eagerly adv. 열망하여, 간절히　previously adv. 이전에

104 명사 자리 채우기　하 ●○○

해석　Thurmond 철도사는 그것의 서비스 확장을 위한 충분한 자금을 가지고 있다.

해설　부정관사(an) 다음에 오면서 빈칸 앞 전치사(for)의 목적어 자리에 올 수 있는 것은 명사이므로 명사 (D) expansion(확장)이 정답이다. 동사 (A), 동사 또는 과거분사 (B), 형용사 (C)는 명사 자리에 올 수 없다.

어휘　capital n. 자금　expand v. 확장하다　expandable adj. 확장할 수 있는

105 부사 자리 채우기　상 ●●●

해석　많은 소매업체들이 국내에서 추가 비용 없이 상품들을 배송하는 반면, 그들은 해외 주문들에 대해서 높은 요금을 부과한다.

해설　동사(ship)를 꾸밀 수 있는 것은 부사이므로 부사 (D) domestically(국내에서)가 정답이다. 동사 (A), 동명사 또는 현재분사 (B), 형용사 또는 명사 (C)는 부사 자리에 올 수 없다. 현재분사 (B)가 빈칸 앞의 명사(items)를 꾸미는 구조로 본다 해도, '추가 비용 없이 길여지는 상품들을 배송하는 반면, 해외 주문들에 대해서 높은 요금을 부과한다'라는 어색한 문맥을 만든다.

어휘　retailer n. 소매업체　ship v. 배송하다; n. 배, 선박　additional adj. 추가의　charge v. (비용을) 부과하다　overseas adj. 해외의　domesticate v. (동물이) 길여지다, (동물을) 길들이다, (식물을) 재배하다　domestic adj. 국내의; n. 가사 도우미, 국산품

106 부사절 접속사 채우기　상 ●●●

해석　Fital Electronics사는 그것의 광고들이 더 많은 소비자들에게 관심을 끌기 시작하면서 더 많은 문의들을 받고 있다.

해설　절(Fital Electronics ~inquiries)과 절(its advertisements ~consumers)을 연결할 수 있는 관계대명사 또는 명사절 접속사 (A), 부사절 접속사 (B)와 (C)가 정답의 후보이다. '광고들이 더 많은 소비자들에게 관심을 끌기 시작

하면서 더 많은 문의들을 받고 있다'라는 의미가 되어야 하므로 부사절 접속사 (C) as(~하면서)가 정답이다. 관계대명사 또는 명사절 접속사 (A) which는 뒤에 주어, 목적어, 또는 보어가 없는 불완전한 절이 와야 하는데, 주어(its advertisements), 동사(have begun), 목적어(appealing)가 있는 완전한 절이 왔으므로 답이 될 수 없다. 부사 (D)는 절과 절을 연결할 수 없다.

어휘 appeal v. 관심을 끌다 although conj. 비록 ~이지만
gradually adv. 서서히

107 to 부정사 채우기 중 ●●○

해석 Ms. Goodman은 그녀가 믹서기를 구매했던 가게를 방문하기 위해 차를 몰고 패서디나로 갔다.

해설 빈칸 다음에 동사원형(visit)이 왔고 '가게를 방문하기 위해 차를 몰고 갔다'라는 의미가 되어야 하므로 목적을 나타내는 to 부정사를 만들 수 있는 (B) to가 정답이다. 전치사 (A), (C), (D)는 뒤에 명사가 와야 한다. 빈칸 뒤의 visit을 '방문'이라는 의미의 명사로 보고 전치사 (A), (C), (D)가 명사를 목적어로 취하는 형태로 볼 경우, 명사(visit)와 명사(the store)가 특별한 연결어 없이 나란히 오게 되므로 답이 될 수 없다.

어휘 purchase v. 구매하다 by prep. ~로, ~에 의하여 on prep. ~위에
due to phr. ~때문에

108 부사 어휘 고르기 중 ●●●

해석 Metrix사의 3D 스캐닝 소프트웨어는 경쟁 제품들보다 사진에 있는 물체들을 더 정확하게 식별할 수 있다.

해설 빈칸은 동사(can identify)를 꾸미는 부사 자리이다. '사진에 있는 물체들을 더 정확하게 식별할 수 있다'라는 문맥이므로 (A) accurately(정확하게)가 정답이다.

어휘 identify v. 식별하다, 발견하다 object n. 물체, 목표; v. 반대하다
originally adv. 원래, 본래 outwardly adv. 표면상으로, 겉으로
silently adv. 조용히

109 동사 어휘 고르기 상 ●●●

해석 Rexval Technologies사가 사용자 정보를 수집하긴 하지만, 그 회사는 이 정보를 절대 공개하지 않을 것이다.

해설 빈칸은 조동사(will) 뒤에 오는 동사원형 자리이다. '사용자 정보를 수집하긴 하지만, 이 정보를 공개하지 않을 것이다'라는 문맥이므로 (C) disclose(공개하다, 밝히다)가 정답이다. (B) oversee도 '감시하다, 단속하다'라는 의미로 그럴듯해 보이지만, 사람을 감시하거나 작업이나 활동이 제대로 이뤄지는지 단속하는 것을 나타내므로 답이 될 수 없다.

어휘 collect v. 수집하다 refuse v. 거절하다 exclude v. 제외하다, 배제하다

110 부사절 접속사 자리 채우기 중 ●●○

해석 만약 그 프레젠테이션이 더 많은 도표들을 포함한다면 그것은 더 효과적일 것이다.

해설 이 문장은 주어(The presentation), 동사(will be), 보어(more effective)를 갖춘 완전한 절이므로, ___ ~ charts는 수식어 거품으로 보아야 한다. 이 수식어 거품은 동사(includes)가 있는 거품절이므로, 거품절을 이끌 수 있는 부사절 접속사 (A) if(만약 ~한다면)가 정답이다. 전치사 또는 형용사 (B), 부사 (C), 형용사 또는 부사 (D)는 거품절을 이끌 수 없다.

어휘 effective adj. 효과적인 include v. 포함하다 chart n. 도표, 차트

unlike prep. ~과 달리; adj. 서로 다른 else adv. 또 다른
just adj. 공정한; adv. 단지

111 전치사 채우기 하 ●○○

해석 Coster 보안회사는 근무 시간 동안 개인적인 사유로 휴대폰의 사용을 허용하지 않는다.

해설 빈칸은 명사구(working hours)를 목적어로 취하는 전치사 자리이다. '근무 시간 동안 개인적인 사유로 휴대폰의 사용을 허용하지 않는다'라는 의미가 되어야 하므로 기간을 나타내는 전치사 (B) during(~ 동안)이 정답이다. (A) at(~에, ~에서), (C) around(~ 쯤), (D) since(~ 이래로, ~부터)도 해석상 그럴듯해 보이지만 뒤에 기간(working hours)이 아닌 시점을 나타내는 표현이 와야 하므로 답이 될 수 없다.

어휘 working hours phr. 근무 시간

112 명사 보어와 형용사 보어 구별하여 채우기 중 ●●●

해석 그 섬유는 열에 잘 견디는 물질로 구성되어 있다.

해설 be동사(is)의 보어 자리에 올 수 있는 형용사 (C)와 명사 (D)가 정답의 후보이다. '물질이 열에 잘 견딘다'라는 문맥이므로 빈칸 앞의 be동사(is)와 뒤의 전치사(to)와 함께 '~에 잘 견디다'라는 의미의 형용사 어구 be resistant to를 만드는 형용사 (C) resistant(잘 견디는)가 정답이다. 명사 (D) resistance(저항, 내성)를 쓸 경우 선행사(a substance)와 동격이 되어 '그 물질은 저항이다'라는 어색한 문맥이 된다. 동사 (A)와 (B)는 보어 자리에 올 수 없다.

어휘 textile n. 섬유, 직물 be made of phr. ~으로 구성되다
substance n. 물질, 실체 heat n. 열 resist v. 저항하다, 반대하다

113 시간 표현과 일치하는 시제의 동사 채우기 하 ●○○

해석 그 연구 보조원은 다음 주에 소비자 조사 자료를 검토할 것이다.

해설 문장에 주어(The ~ assistant)만 있고 동사가 없으므로 동사인 (B)와 (D)가 정답의 후보이다. 미래를 나타내는 시간 표현(next week)이 있으므로 미래 시제 (B) will review가 정답이다. 과거 시제 (D)는 미래를 나타내는 시간 표현과 함께 쓰일 수 없다. 명사 (A)와 동명사 또는 현재분사 (C)는 동사 자리에 올 수 없다. 현재분사 (C)를 빈칸 앞의 명사구(The ~ assistant)를 꾸미는 것으로 보고, survey를 '살피다, 점검하다'라는 의미의 동사로 본다 해도, 주어(The ~ assistant)가 3인칭 단수이므로 복수 동사(survey)와 함께 쓰일 수 없다.

어휘 assistant n. 보조원, 조수 reviewer n. 검토자, 논평가
review v. 검토하다; n. 검토

114 부사 어휘 고르기 하 ●○○

해석 방송국 스튜디오 관객들은 자주 소리 내어 웃으며 새로운 TV쇼에 긍정적으로 반응했다.

해설 빈칸은 동사(reacted)를 꾸미는 부사 자리이다. '관객들은 자주 소리 내어 웃으며 새로운 TV쇼에 긍정적으로 반응했다'라는 문맥이므로 (B) positively(긍정적으로)가 정답이다.

어휘 react v. 반응하다 frequently adv. 자주, 빈번히
suddenly adv. 갑자기, 불현듯 mutually adv. 서로 slowly adv. 천천히

115 복합관계대명사 채우기 중 ●●○

해석 Kractal Solutions사는 업무가 무엇이든 모든 직원들에게 각각 할당된 것을

완료하도록 요구한다.

해설 절(Kractal Solutions ~ job)과 절(it is)을 연결할 수 있는 등위접속사 (B)와 복합관계대명사 (D)가 정답의 후보이다. '업무가 무엇이든 모든 직원들에게 할당된 것을 완료하도록 요구한다'라는 의미가 되어야 하므로 복합관계대명사 (D) whatever(무엇이든)가 정답이다. 등위접속사 (B)는 '직원들에게 각각 할당된 업무를 완료하도록 요구하고 혹은 그것은 있다'라는 어색한 의미를 만든다. 대명사 (A)와 (C)는 절과 절을 연결할 수 없다.

어휘 require v. 요구하다 complete v. 완료하다 assigned adj. 할당된 anyone n. 누구나

116 부사 자리 채우기
중 ●●○

해석 Suntair Venture사의 이 프로젝트는 Fitan사 업무와 비교하여 꽤 어려울 것이다.

해설 형용사(difficult)를 꾸밀 수 있는 것은 부사이므로 부사 (C) moderately(꽤, 제법)가 정답이다. 형용사 또는 동사 (A), 동사 또는 과거분사 (B), 명사 (D)는 부사 자리에 올 수 없다. (B)를 빈칸 앞의 be동사(be)와 수동태를 만드는 p.p.형으로 본다 해도, 빈칸 뒤에 형용사가 있으므로 답이 될 수 없다. 참고로, 목적어와 목적격 보어를 모두 갖는 5형식 동사만 수동태 동사 다음에 목적격 보어로 쓰인 형용사를 취할 수 있음을 알아둔다.

어휘 task n. 업무 moderate adj. 보통의, 적당한; v. 완화하다 moderation n. 조정, 관리

117 전치사 채우기
상 ●●●

해석 변호사들은 Blade Lawncare사의 불공정한 거래 관행들에 관한 증거를 제출했다.

해설 빈칸은 명사구(Blade Lawncare's ~ practices)를 목적어로 취하는 전치사 자리이다 'Blade Lawncare사의 불공정한 거래 관행들에 관한 증거'라는 의미가 되어야 하므로 전치사 (B) concerning(~에 관한)이 정답이다.

어휘 present v. 제출하다, 제시하다 evidence n. 증거 unfair adj. 불공정한 practice n. 관행 along prep. ~을 따라 through prep. ~을 통해서 onto prep. ~쪽으로

118 동사 관련 어구 완성하기
중 ●●○

해석 스포츠 훈련 시설은 최신 운동 기구들을 갖추고 있다.

해설 빈칸은 be동사(is)와 함께 수동태를 만드는 p.p.형의 자리이다. '스포츠 훈련 시설은 최신 운동 기구들을 갖추고 있다'라는 문맥이므로 빈칸 앞의 be동사(is)와 뒤의 전치사 with와 함께 '~을 갖추고 있다'라는 의미의 동사 어구 be equipped with를 만드는 동사 equip(장비를 갖추다)의 p.p.형 (A) equipped가 정답이다. 참고로, (C)의 compose(구성하다)는 전치사 of와 함께 '~으로 구성되어 있다'라는 의미의 동사 어구 be composed of로 쓰임을 알아둔다.

어휘 facility n. 시설 latest adj. 최신의 target v. 목표로 삼다 obtain v. 획득하다

119 명사 자리 채우기
하 ●○○

해석 명단에 그들의 이름을 기록함으로써 사람들은 행사에 참여하려는 그들의 의사를 나타낼 수 있다.

해설 소유격 인칭대명사(their)의 꾸밈을 받으면서 동사(indicate)의 목적어 자리에 올 수 있는 것은 명사이므로 명사 (D) intention(의사)이 정답이다. 동사 (A)와 (C), 동사 또는 과거분사 (B)는 명사 자리에 올 수 없다.

어휘 indicate v. 나타내다 participate in phr. ~에 참여하다

---

register v. 기록하다, 등록하다 intend v. 의도하다

최고난도 문제

120 동사 어휘 고르기
상 ●●●

해석 경영 위원회는 남아메리카에서 회사의 활동을 안내할 전략적인 계획을 만들어 냈다.

해설 빈칸은 have동사(has)와 함께 현재 완료 시제를 만드는 p.p.형의 자리이다. '경영 위원회는 전략적인 계획을 만들어 냈다'라는 문맥이므로 동사 formulate(만들어 내다)의 p.p.형 (C) formulated가 정답이다. (B)의 nominate(정하다, 임명하다)도 해석상 그럴듯해 보이지만 일시를 정하거나 사람을 임명하는 것을 나타내므로 답이 될 수 없다.

어휘 committee n. 위원회 strategic adj. 전략적인 guide v. 안내하다, 이끌다 action n. 활동, 조치 recruit v. 고용하다 prevent v. 예방하다, 막다

최고난도 문제

121 사람명사와 사물/추상명사 구별하여 채우기
상 ●●●

해석 감자 부족의 결과로, Burger Bix는 감자튀김 1인분에 대한 가격을 20퍼센트만큼 인상할 것이다.

해설 전치사(for)의 목적어 자리에 오면서 형용사(single)의 꾸밈을 받을 수 있는 것은 명사이므로 명사 (A), (B), (C)가 정답의 후보이다. '감자튀김 1인분에 대한 가격을 인상할 것이다'라는 의미이므로 추상명사 (C) serving(1인분)이 정답이다. 사물명사 (A) service(서비스)와 사람명사 (B) server(서빙하는 사람)는 어색한 문맥을 만든다. 동사 (D)는 명사 자리에 올 수 없다. (D)를 '(테니스 등의) 서브'라는 의미의 명사로 본다 해도, 어색한 문맥을 만든다.

어휘 shortage n. 부족 single adj. 1인용의, 하나의; n. 한 개 serve v. 음식을 제공하다

최고난도 문제

122 명사 어휘 고르기
상 ●●●

해석 오디오 시스템의 설치는 끝났지만, 그 작업에 대한 송장은 아직 발송되지 않았다.

해설 빈칸은 관사(the)와 전치사(for) 사이에 올 수 있는 명사 자리이다. '오디오 시스템의 설치는 끝났지만, 그 작업에 대한 송장은 아직 발송되지 않았다'라는 문맥이므로 (B) invoice(송장)가 정답이다. (A) draft(초안)와 (C) proposal(제안)도 해석상 그럴듯해 보이지만, 설치가 끝난 후에 발송되는 것이 아니므로 문맥상 어울리지 않는다.

어휘 installation n. 설치 booking n. 예약, 장부 기입

123 to 부정사 채우기
중 ●●○

해석 Gishwa Music은 그것의 노래 모음을 사용자들이 무료로 검색할 수 있게 하는 매우 인기 있는 음악 스트리밍 프로그램이다.

해설 5형식 동사 allow의 목적격 보어 자리에 올 수 있는 to 부정사 (D) to browse가 정답이다. 동사 또는 과거분사 (A), 동사 또는 명사 (B)와 (C)는 allow의 목적격 보어 자리, 즉 to 부정사 자리에 올 수 없다. 빈칸 앞의 명사(users)를 3형식 동사의 목적어로 보고 과거분사 (A)를 목적어를 꾸미는 것으로 본다 해도, 과거분사 뒤에 목적어(its collection)를 취할 수 없으므로 답이 될 수 없다. (B)와 (C)를 '검색, 열람'이라는 의미의 명사로 보고, allow를 '주다, 지급하다'라는 의미의 4형식 동사로 보아, 'allow + 간접목적어

(users) + 직접목적어(browses/browse)' 형태를 만드는 것으로 본다 해도, 특별한 연결어 없이 빈칸 뒤의 명사구(its collection)와 나란히 올 수 없으므로 답이 될 수 없다.

어휘 allow v. ~할 수 있게 하다, 허용하다 collection n. (노래) 모음(집)
　　　browse v. 검색하다, 훑어보다; n. 검색, 열람

124 명사 관련 어구 완성하기 상 ●●●

해석 모든 직원들은 예외 없이, 다양한 개발 세미나에 참여할 것이다.

해설 빈칸은 관사(a)와 전치사(of) 사이에 온 명사 자리이다. '다양한 개발 세미나에 참여하다'라는 문맥이므로 빈칸 앞의 관사(a)와 뒤의 전치사(of)와 함께 '다양한'이라는 의미의 어구인 a range of를 만드는 명사 (B) range(다양성, 범위)가 정답이다. 참고로, (A) kind(종류)는 관사(a)와 전치사(of)와 함께 '일종의, ~같은'이라는 의미의 어구인 a kind of를 만들며 복수 명사(seminars)가 아닌 단수 명사와 함께 쓰임을 알아둔다.

어휘 exception n. 예외 participate in phr. ~에 참여하다
　　　development n. 개발, 발전 member n. 구성원, 일원 lack n. 부족

125 현재분사와 과거분사 구별하여 채우기 중 ●●○

해석 Ms. Thompkins가 Baird 대학교의 교수직을 수락하기 전에 그녀는 유명한 기자였다.

해설 명사(reporter)를 꾸밀 수 있는 것은 형용사이므로 과거분사 (A)와 현재분사 (C)가 정답의 후보이다. 수식 받는 명사(reporter)와 분사가 '유명한 기자'라는 의미이므로 과거분사 (A) distinguished(유명한, 성공한)가 정답이다. 현재분사 (C) distinguishing(구별하는)을 빈칸에 넣으면 '구별하는 기자(기자가 구별하다)'라는 어색한 의미가 되므로 답이 될 수 없다. 동사 (B)와 (D)는 형용사 자리에 올 수 없다.

어휘 accept v. 수락하다 faculty n. 교수(진) position n. 직, 일자리
　　　distinguish v. 구별하다, 식별하다

126 명사절 접속사 채우기 중 ●●○

해석 소셜 네트워크 사이트들의 출현과 함께, 대부분의 회사들은 그들이 광고하는 방법에 변화를 주었다.

해설 빈칸 이하(___ ~ advertise)는 전치사(in)의 목적어이므로, 목적어 자리에 올 수 있는 명사절을 이끄는 명사절 접속사 (D) how(~하는 방법)가 정답이다. 전치사 (A), 등위접속사 또는 부사 (B), 부사(C)는 명사절을 이끌 수 없다.

어휘 advent n. 출현 make a change phr. ~에 변화를 주다, 변경하다
　　　advertise v. 광고하다 about prep. ~에 대해 so conj. 그래서; adv. 정말
　　　thus adv. 따라서, 그러므로

127 'be동사 + p.p.' 채우기 중 ●●○

해석 지원서들의 처리 지연을 일으키는 오류는 즉시 처리되어야 한다.

해설 be동사(be) 다음에 올 수 있는 모든 보기가 정답의 후보이다. '오류가 처리되어야 한다'라는 수동의 의미가 되어야 하므로 빈칸 앞의 be동사(be)와 함께 수동태를 만드는 동사 address(처리하다, 다루다)의 p.p.형 (B) addressed가 정답이다. 명사 (A)와 (D)는 be동사 다음에 올 수는 있지만, 보어로서 주어와 동격 관계가 되어 '오류는 주소/주소들이 되어야 한다'라는 어색한 문맥을 만든다. -ing형 (C)를 쓸 경우 현재 진행형을 만드는데, 타동사이므로 뒤에 목적어가 와야 한다.

어휘 delay n. 지연 immediately adv. 즉시

128 부사절 접속사 자리 채우기 중 ●●○

해석 보상금 청구 신청이 부서에 의해 검토될 때까지는, 그 어떠한 대금도 보험가입자에게 지급될 수 없다.

해설 이 문장은 주어(No payments), 동사(can be made)를 갖춘 완전한 절이므로, ___ ~ the department는 수식어 거품으로 보아야 한다. 이 수식어 거품은 동사(has been examined)가 있는 거품절이므로, 거품절을 이끌 수 있는 부사절 접속사 (C) until(~할 때까지)이 정답이다. 부사 (A), 전치사 또는 부사 (B), 전치사 (D)는 거품절을 이끌 수 없다.

어휘 insurance subscriber phr. 보험가입자 claim n. (보상금에 대한) 청구 신청
　　　examine v. 검토하다 otherwise adv. 그렇지 않으면
　　　besides prep. ~외에; adv. 게다가, 뿐만 아니라
　　　despite prep. ~에도 불구하고

129 동사 관련 어구 완성하기 상 ●●●

해석 TotalMarket에서 판매되는 샐러드들에는 드레싱과 재활용 가능한 포크가 딸려 있다.

해설 빈칸은 주어(Salads)의 동사 자리이다. '샐러드들에는 드레싱과 포크가 딸려 있다'라는 문맥이므로 빈칸 뒤의 전치사(with)와 함께 '~이 딸려 있다'라는 의미의 동사 어구 come with를 만드는 동사 (D) come(나오다)이 정답이다. (A) contain(포함하다), (B) present(주다), (C) provide(제공하다)도 모두 해석상 그럴듯해 보이지만 타동사이므로 전치사 with와 함께 쓰일 수 없다. (C)를 '대비하다, 준비하다'라는 의미의 자동사로 볼 경우, '샐러드들은 포크와 함께 대비한다'라는 어색한 문맥을 만든다.

어휘 recyclable adj. 재활용 가능한

130 형용사 자리 채우기 중 ●●○

해석 우리의 기술자들에게 정확한 정보를 제공하지 않는 것은 부정확한 평가를 야기할 수 있다.

해설 명사(information)를 꾸밀 수 있는 것은 형용사이므로 형용사 (B) correct (정확한)가 정답이다. 동사 (A), 부사 (C), 명사 (D)는 형용사 자리에 올 수 없다. 참고로, 부사 (C)는 to 부정사(to give)와 목적어(information) 사이에는 오지 못하며, 'to 부정사 + 목적어'의 앞이나 뒤에 와야 한다.

어휘 failure n. ~하지 않음, 실패 technician n. 기술자
　　　inaccurate adj. 부정확한 assessment n. 평가
　　　correctly adv. 정확하게 corrector n. 교정자, 첨삭자

PART 6

131-134번은 다음 기사에 관한 문제입니다.

9월 9일, 멕시코시티—Compensa Solutions사는 그것의 최고 마케팅 책임자로서 Valeria Gomez의 ¹³¹임명을 발표했다. ¹³²그 발표는 어제 기자회견에서 이루어졌다. 기자들과 이야기하면서, 대변인 Thomas Walden은 Ms. Gomez를 회사의 고위 관리직에 훌륭한 추가 인력이라고 설명했다. "우리는 Ms. Gomez를 맞이하게 되어 ¹³³기쁘며, 그녀의 폭넓은 지식과 수년간의 경험을 통해 우리가 새로운 시장에 진출하도록 그녀가 도울 수 있기를 희망합니다."라고 그는 말했다. Ms. Gomez는 그녀가 이전에 이사직을 맡았던 적이 ¹³⁴없지만, 그녀는 다음의 도전에 대해 그녀가 준비되어있다고 장담했다.

announce v. 발표하다 describe v. 설명하다, 묘사하다 terrific adj. 훌륭한
addition n. 추가 인력, 추가 senior management phr. 고위 관리직

extensive adj. 폭넓은 give an assurance that phr. ~이라고 장담하다
challenge n. 도전

131 명사 어휘 고르기 주변 문맥 파악 중 ●●○

해설 빈칸은 동사(has announced)의 목적어 역할을 하는 명사 자리이다. 'Compensa Solutions사는 최고 마케팅 책임자로서 Valeria Gomez의 ____을 발표했다'라는 문맥이므로 모든 보기가 정답의 후보이다. 뒤 문장에서 대변인은 Ms. Gomez를 회사의 고위 관리직에 훌륭한 추가 인력이라고 설명했다고 했으므로 Compensa Solutions사가 최고 마케팅 책임자로 Ms. Gomez를 임명했음을 알 수 있다. 따라서 (B) appointment(임명)가 정답이다.

어휘 retirement n. 은퇴, 퇴직 investement n. 투자
accomplishment n. 업적

132 알맞은 문장 고르기 . 중 ●●○

해석 (A) 그들은 우수한 상품과 서비스를 제공한다.
(B) 회사의 매출은 1년 넘게 꾸준히 올랐다.
(C) 회사의 공석 목록은 웹사이트를 통해 접근 가능하다.
(D) 그 발표는 어제 기자 회견에서 이루어졌다.

해설 앞 문장의 'Compensa Solutions has announced the (appointment)'에서 Compensa Solutions사가 임명을 발표했다고 했고, 뒤 문장의 'Speaking to reporters'에서 기자들과 이야기했다고 했으므로 빈칸에는 발표가 기자들이 있는 자리에서 이루어졌다는 내용이 들어가야 함을 알 수 있다. 따라서 (D)가 정답이다.

어휘 superior adj. 우수한 climb v. 오르다 steadily adv. 꾸준히
open position phr. 공석 accessible adj. 접근 가능한
statement n. 발표, 성명 press conference phr. 기자 회견

133 현재분사와 과거분사 구별하여 채우기 하 ●○○

해설 be동사(are)의 보어 자리에 올 수 있는 과거분사 (B)와 현재분사 (D)가 정답의 후보이다. '우리는 Ms. Gomez를 맞이하게 되어 기쁘다'라는 의미로 주어(We)가 감정을 느끼는 주체이므로 동사 please(기쁘게 하다)의 과거분사 (B) pleased가 정답이다. 현재분사 (D)를 쓰면 '우리는 맞이하게 되어 기쁘게 한다'라는 어색한 문맥이 된다. 참고로, please와 같은 감정 동사의 현재분사와 과거분사를 구별할 때, 주어가 감정을 느끼면 과거분사, 주어가 감정의 원인이면 현재분사가 쓰임을 알아둔다. 동사 (A)와 (C)는 보어 자리에 올 수 없다.

134 부사절 접속사 자리 채우기 하 ●○○

해설 이 문장은 주어(she), 동사(gave), 목적어(assurances)를 갖춘 완전한 절이므로 ____ ~ previously는 수식어 거품으로 보아야 한다. 이 수식어 거품은 동사(has not held)가 있는 거품절이므로, 거품절을 이끌 수 있는 부사절 접속사 (A) While(~하지만; ~한 반면)이 정답이다. 전치사 (B), (C), (D)는 거품절을 이끌 수 없다.

어휘 in spite of phr. ~에도 불구하고 during prep. ~동안
because of phr. ~때문에

135-138번은 다음 안내문에 관한 문제입니다.

Middletown 사진 전시회에 참가하세요!

Middletown의 제8회 연례 사진 전시회가 8월 1일부터 14일까지 열릴

예정입니다. 지역 사진작가들이 참가하도록 [135]**요청됩니다.** 이 행사는 수많은 예술가들의 예술품을 포함할 것입니다. 예술 작품은 Emerson 갤러리와 시청에 [136]**전시될 것입니다.** 모든 예술품들은 이 2주간의 행사 후에 예술가들에게 돌려보내질 것입니다.

행사에 참여하기 위해서는, www.middletown.gov/photoexhibit을 방문하여 당신의 신청서를 제출하십시오. 저희는 1월 13일까지 행사에 [137]**선정된** 사람들에게 알려드릴 것입니다. 요건에 대한 추가 세부사항에 대해서는, 저희 웹사이트를 방문하십시오. [138]**또는 귀하께서 Middletown 예술 위원회 사무실에 들르셔도 됩니다.**

sign up for phr. ~에 참가하다 exhibition n. 전시회
participate v. 참가하다 feature v. (특별히) 포함하다
numerous adj. 수많은 artwork n. 예술품, 삽화 application n. 신청서
notify v. 알리다, 통지하다

135 'be동사 + p.p.' 채우기 중 ●●○

해설 빈칸이 be동사(are) 다음에 왔으므로 진행형을 만드는 -ing형 (B)와 수동태를 만드는 p.p.형 (C)가 정답의 후보이다. '사진작가들이 참가하도록 요청된다'라는 수동의 의미가 되어야 하므로 동사 invite(요청하다)의 p.p.형 (C) invited가 정답이다. -ing형 (B)는 능동 진행형을 만들 수 있지만, '사진작가들이 참석하기 위해서 초대하고 있다'라는 어색한 문맥이 된다. (B)를 '유혹적인'이라는 의미의 형용사로 보더라도 '지역 사진작가들은 참가하기에 유혹적이다'라는 어색한 문맥이 된다. 또한, (B)를 be동사(are)의 보어로서 '초대하는 것'이라는 의미의 동명사로 보더라도 주어(Local photographers)와 동격이 되어 '지역 사진작가들은 참가하기 위해서 초대하는 것이다'라는 어색한 문맥이 된다. 동사 (A)와 (D)는 be동사 다음에 올 수 없다.

136 명사 관련 어구 완성하기 주변 문맥 파악 중 ●●○

해설 빈칸은 전치사(on) 다음의 명사 자리이다. '예술품이 ____될 것이다'라는 문맥이므로 (B)와 (C)가 정답의 후보이다. 빈칸 뒤 문장에서 모든 예술품들은 이 2주간의 행사 후에 예술가들에게 돌려보내질 것이라고 했으므로 예술품이 2주 동안 전시될 것임을 알 수 있다. 따라서 빈칸 앞의 전치사 on과 함께 '전시된, 진열된'이라는 의미의 어구 on display를 만드는 명사 (B) display(전시, 진열)가 정답이다. 참고로, 명사 (A), (C), (D) 모두 전치사 on과 함께 쓰이지만, 각각 '근무 중인/판매되는/정각에'라는 의미로 쓰임을 알아둔다.

137 동사 어휘 고르기 중 ●●○

해설 빈칸은 명사(those)를 뒤에서 꾸미는 과거분사 자리이다. '행사에 선정된 사람들'이라는 문맥이므로 동사 select(선정하다)의 과거분사 (B) selected가 정답이다.

어휘 advise v. 조언하다 divide v. 분리하다 replace v. 교체하다

138 알맞은 문장 고르기 중 ●●○

해석 **(A) 또는 귀하께서 Middletown 예술 위원회 사무실에 들르셔도 됩니다.**
(B) 그것들은 저희의 모든 필수 기준을 따라야 합니다.
(C) 며칠 후에 발표가 있을 것입니다.
(D) 오직 소수의 참가자들만이 허용됩니다.

해설 앞 문장 'For further details on requirements, visit our Web site.'에서 요건에 대한 추가 세부사항에 대해서는, 웹사이트를 방문하라고 했으므로 빈칸에는 세부사항을 얻기 위한 또 다른 방법에 관한 내용이 들어가야 함을 알 수 있다. 따라서 (A)가 정답이다.

어휘 | drop by phr. 들르다 follow v. 따르다, 준수하다 necessary adj. 필수의 specification n. 기준, 설명서 entry n. 참가자 (수) permit v. 허용하다, 허가하다

139-142번은 다음 광고에 관한 문제입니다.

올가을, Edward Dormer사의 Winchester 캐주얼 재킷으로 당신의 옷장을 개선해보세요! 이 재킷은 브랜드의 상징적인 모습을 환기시키는데, [139]**이는** 1940년대에 인기가 있었습니다. 각 재킷은 내구성 있는[140]**재료들**로 수공되었습니다. 이것들은 고급 가죽과 알루미늄 지퍼를 포함합니다. 영국의 춥고 습한 기후에서 사용하도록 만들어졌기 때문에, 각각의 재킷을 내구성 있고 방수가 되도록 만들기 위해 특수한 코팅이 [141]**칠해져 있습니다.** [142]**따라서, 그것은 당신의 몸을 계속 따뜻하고, 건조하게 유지할 것입니다.** 온라인 및 전국의 저희 가게들에서 그것을 찾아보세요.

wardrobe n. 옷장 revive v. 환기시키다, 되살아나게 하다
iconic adj. 상징적인 handcraft v. 수공하다 durable adj. 내구성 있는
high-quality adj. 고급의 leather n. 가죽 climate n. 기후

139 관계대명사 채우기 하 ●○○

해설 | 이 문장은 주어(This jacket), 동사(revives), 목적어(the brand's ~ look)를 갖춘 완전한 절이므로, ___ ~ 1940s는 수식어 거품으로 보아야 한다. 이 수식어 거품은 동사(was)가 있으나 주어가 없는 불완전한 절이고, 빈칸 앞에 콤마가 있는 것으로 보아 빈칸 이하가 앞에 나온 사물 명사(the brand's look)에 대해 부가 설명을 해주는 계속적 용법으로 쓰였다는 것을 알 수 있다. 따라서 주격 사물 관계대명사 (C) which가 정답이다. 관계대명사 (A)는 사물 선행사를 가질 수 있지만, 콤마 바로 뒤에 올 수 없다. 관계대명사 (B)는 사람 선행사를 꾸민다. 부사절 접속사 또는 관계부사 (D)는 뒤에 완전한 절이 와야 한다.

140 명사 어휘 고르기 주변 문맥 파악 하 ●○○

해설 | 빈칸은 형용사(durable)의 꾸밈을 받으며 전치사(from)의 목적어 역할을 하는 명사 자리이다. '각 재킷은 내구성 있는 ___로 수공되었다'라는 문맥이므로 모든 보기가 정답의 후보이다. 뒤 문장에서는 고급 가죽과 알루미늄 지퍼를 포함한다고 했으므로 각 재킷은 내구성 있는 재료들로 수공되었음을 알 수 있다. 따라서 (D) materials(재료들, 소재들)가 정답이다.

어휘 | case n. 덮개, 용기 equipment n. 기구 shape n. 모양, 형태

141 올바른 시제의 동사 채우기 하 ●○○

해설 | 문장에 주어(a ~ coating)만 있고 동사가 없으므로 동사 (B)와 (C)가 정답의 후보이다. '영국의 춥고 습한 기후에서 사용하도록 만들어졌기 때문에 특수한 코팅이 칠해져 있다'라는 문맥이므로 현재의 상태를 나타내는 현재 시제 (B) is applied가 정답이다. 미래 시제 (C)는 현재의 상태를 나타낼 수 없다. 동명사 또는 현재분사 (A)와 to 부정사 (D)는 동사 자리에 올 수 없다.

어휘 | apply v. 칠하다, 적용하다

142 알맞은 문장 고르기 중 ●●○

해석 | (A) 따라서, 그것은 당신의 몸을 계속 따뜻하고, 건조하게 유지할 것입니다.
(B) 하지만, 이 재킷은 몇몇 사람들에게는 꽤 무거울 수 있습니다.
(C) 최초의 가죽 재킷들은 20세기 초에 등장했습니다.
(D) Mr. Dormer는 수년 동안 같은 재킷을 소유해왔습니다.

해설 | 앞 문장 'Designed for use in the UK's cold and wet climate, a

special coating (is applied) to make each jacket durable and waterproof.'에서 영국의 춥고 습한 기후에서의 사용하도록 만들어졌기 때문에, 각각의 재킷을 내구성 있고 방수가 되도록 만들기 위해 특수한 코팅이 칠해져 있다고 했으므로 빈칸에는 따라서 그것, 즉 재킷이 몸을 계속 따뜻하고, 건조하게 유지할 것이라는 내용이 들어가야 함을 알 수 있다. 따라서 (A)가 정답이다.

어휘 | appear v. 등장하다 own v. 소유하다

143-146번은 다음 공고에 관한 문제입니다.

Sortix 디지털 보안 자문 회사
긴급 공지

Zeno 운영체제의 제조업체인 Alephnet이 그것의 플랫폼의 이전 버전들에 대한 지원을 제공하는 것을 중단할 예정입니다. [143]**그 결과,** 그 회사는 Zeno-10의 소프트웨어 업그레이드를 더 이상 제공하지 않을 것입니다. 따라서, 빨리 Zeno-11로 업데이트하십시오. 이 조언을 [144]**무시하는 것**은 여러분의 컴퓨터들이 보안 위협에 취약한 상태가 되도록 할 수 있습니다. 전반적으로, Zeno-11은 [145]**이전의** 플랫폼인 Zeno-10에 비해 더 나은 보안을 제공합니다. 여러분 시스템의 안정성을 보장하기 위해, 저희는 여러분께 즉시 업데이트하는 것을 강력히 권고합니다. [146]**설치 지침 및 지원은 저희의 웹 사이트를 참고하십시오.** 추가 질문이 있는 경우에는, cs@sortix.com으로 저희에게 연락 주십시오.

support n. 지원 vulnerable adj. 취약한 threat n. 위협
stability n. 안정성 urge v. 권고하다, 촉구하다

143 접속부사 채우기 주변 문맥 파악 중 ●●○

해설 | 앞 문장에서 Zeno 운영체제의 제조업체가 그것의 플랫폼의 이전 버전들에 대한 지원을 제공하는 것을 중단할 것이라고 했고, 빈칸이 있는 문장에서는 그 회사가 Zeno-10의 소프트웨어 업그레이드를 더 이상 제공하지 않을 것이라고 했으므로, 앞에서 말한 내용에 따른 결과를 언급하는 내용의 문장에서 사용되는 (A) As a result(그 결과)가 정답이다.

어휘 | instead adv. 대신에 once adv. 한 번, 언젠가; conj. ~하자마자 however adv. 그러나

144 동사 어휘 고르기 주변 문맥 파악 중 ●●○

해설 | 빈칸은 동사(could leave)의 주어 역할을 하며 명사(this advice)를 목적어로 취할 수 있는 동명사 자리이다. '이 조언을 ___은 여러분의 컴퓨터들이 보안 위협에 취약한 상태가 되도록 할 수 있다'라는 문맥이므로 모든 보기가 정답의 후보이다. 앞 문장에서 빨리 Zeno-11로 업데이트하라고 했고, 뒤 문장에서 Zeno-11이 Zeno-10에 비해 더 나은 보안을 제공한다고 했으므로 더 나은 보안을 제공하는 Zeno-11로 업데이트하라는 이 조언을 무시하는 것은 컴퓨터들이 보안 위협에 취약한 상태가 되도록 할 수 있다는 것을 알 수 있다. 따라서 동사 ignore(무시하다)의 동명사 (C) Ignoring이 정답이다. (D)의 Avoid(피하다, 막다)도 해석상 그럴듯해 보이지만, 어떤 일이 일어나는 것을 미리 피하거나 막는 것을 의미하므로, 이미 발생한 조언과는 함께 쓸 수 없다.

어휘 | accept v. 받아들이다 obtain v. 취득하다

145 형용사 어휘 고르기 전체 문맥 파악 상 ●●●

해설 | 빈칸은 명사(platform)를 꾸미는 형용사 자리이다. 'Zeno-11은 ___ 플랫폼인 Zeno-10에 비해 더 나은 보안을 제공한다'라는 문맥이므로 모든 보기가 정답의 후보이다. 앞부분에서 Zeno-10의 소프트웨어 업그레이드를 더 이상 제공하지 않을 것이며, 빨리 Zeno-11로 업데이트하라고 했으므

로 Zeno-10은 Zeno-11의 이전의 플랫폼이라는 것을 알 수 있다. 따라서 (A) previous(이전의)가 정답이다.

어휘 clear adj. 명백한 standard adj. 표준의 popular adj. 인기 있는

146 알맞은 문장 고르기   중 ●●○

해석 (A) 이 특별 판촉이 끝나기 전에 지금 행동하십시오.
(B) 저희는 이용 가능해지는 즉시 여러분께 알림을 보내겠습니다.
(C) 현대의 사업 운영은 컴퓨터 기술에 달려있습니다.
(D) 설치 지침 및 지원은 저희의 웹사이트를 참고하십시오.

해설 앞 문장의 'we strongly urge you to update immediately'에서 즉시 업데이트하는 것을 강력히 권고한다고 한 뒤, 뒤 문장 'In case you have any additional questions, please contact us at cs@sortix.com.'에서 추가 질문이 있는 경우에는, 이메일로 연락하라고 했으므로 빈칸에는 업데이트에 대한 정보를 얻을 수 있는 방법과 관련된 내용이 들어가야 함을 알 수 있다. 따라서 (D)가 정답이다.

어휘 promotion n. 판촉, 홍보 expire v. 끝나다 available adj. 이용 가능한
reminder n. (상기 시켜 주는) 알림, 메모 operation n. 운영
depend on phr. ~에 달려있다, 의존하다 instruction n. 지침
refer to phr. 참고하다

PART 7

147-148번은 다음 영수증에 관한 문제입니다.

Ronson 가정용품사

167번지 Caldwell대로, 트윈 레이크스, 뉴멕시코주 86515
555-8863
— 날짜: 8월 8일 — 시각: 오후 5시 26분

¹⁴⁷⁻ᴰ이 영수증을 제시할 경우에만 환불이나 교환이 될 수 있습니다.

93432-B	선풍기	34.99달러
88822-F	HDMI 케이블	18.50달러
	소계	53.49달러
	5퍼센트 판매세	2.67달러
	총액	56.16달러
	현금	60.00달러
	거스름돈	3.84달러

Ronson 가정용품사를 방문해주셔서 감사합니다. www.ronsonhome.com에서 저희의 온라인 설문조사를 완료하시거나 고객센터에 555-9933으로 전화하셔서 ¹⁴⁸오늘 귀하의 쇼핑 경험에 대해 귀하께서 어떻게 생각하셨는지 저희에게 알려주십시오. 귀하는 자동으로 무료 태블릿 컴퓨터를 얻을 수 있는 추첨에 참여하게 될 것입니다.

---

refund n. 환불 exchange n. 교환 presentation n. 제시
complete v. 완료하다 automatically adv. 자동으로
enter into phr. 참여하다 draw n. 추첨

147 Not/True 문제   중 ●●●

해석 Ronson 가정용품사에 대해 언급된 것은?
(A) 밤늦게까지 영업을 한다.
(B) 현재 가전제품에 할인을 진행하고 있다.
(C) 신용카드 또는 직불카드를 받지 않는다.

(D) 반품된 상품을 받아 준다.

해설 지문의 'A refund or exchange may ~ be issued upon presentation of this receipt.'에서 이 영수증을 제시할 경우 환불이나 교환이 될 수 있다고 했으므로 (D)는 지문의 내용과 일치한다. 따라서 (D)가 정답이다. (A), (B), (C)는 지문에 언급되지 않은 내용이다.

어휘 appliance n. 가전제품 merchandise n. 상품

148 육하원칙 문제   하 ●○○

해석 고객들은 무엇을 하도록 요청받는가?
(A) 웹사이트에 회원으로 가입한다
(B) 상점에 대해 의견을 제공한다
(C) 쿠폰을 얻기 위해 서비스 센터에 전화한다
(D) 무료 기기를 얻기 위해 추첨식 복권을 구매한다

해설 지문의 'Please tell us what you thought of your shopping experience today'에서 오늘 귀하의 쇼핑 경험에 대해 귀하가 어떻게 생각했는지 알려달라고 했으므로 (B)가 정답이다.

어휘 sign up phr. 가입하다 provide v. 제공하다
raffle ticket phr. 추첨식 복권 device n. 기기, 장치

패러프레이징

tell ~ what you thought 어떻게 생각했는지 알려주다 → Provide feedback 의견을 제공하다

149-150번은 다음 온라인 고객 서비스 채팅 대화문에 관한 문제입니다.

Robert Patton   [오후 1시 3분]
안녕하세요. 제가 두 달 전에 이사했는데도, 저는 제 새 주소지로 은행 명세서를 하나도 받지 못했어요.

RMF 은행   [오후 1시 5분]
그렇군요, Mr. Patton. 귀하께서는 아마도 저희 온라인 은행 서비스를 이용하여 귀하의 연락처를 업데이트해야 할 것 같습니다. 귀하께서 이렇게 한 후에, 귀하의 신원을 확인하기 위해 귀하의 전화기로 ¹⁴⁹⁻ᴮ**암호가 전송될 것입니다.** 변경 사항들이 적용되려면 ¹⁴⁹⁻ᶜ**귀하께서는 20초 이내에 그것을 입력해야 할 것입니다.**

Robert Patton   [오후 1시 6분]
사실, 저는 이미 그것을 했어요.

RMF 은행   [오후 1시 7분]
음, 그렇다면 ¹⁵⁰**저희 웹사이트에서 선호 연락 수단 설정을 확인해보세요.** 만약 귀하께서 전자 옵션을 선택하셨다면, 귀하의 명세서가 귀하께 이메일로 발송되었을 것입니다. ¹⁵⁰**출력된 자료가 귀하께 발송되도록 하기 위해서는 문서 옵션을 선택하셔야 합니다.**

Robert Patton   [오후 1시 10분]
잠시만요... 네, 했어요. 도움 주셔서 감사해요.

---

statement n. 명세서 contact information phr. 연락처
confirm v. 확인하다 identity n. 신원 take effect phr. 적용되다
hard copy phr. 출력된 자료

149 Not/True 문제   중 ●●○

해석 암호에 대해 언급된 것은?
(A) Mr. Patton에 의해 선정될 것이다.
(B) 직원에게 제시되어야 한다.

(C) 즉시 입력되어야 한다.

(D) 이름을 바탕으로 할 것이다.

해설 지문의 'a code will be sent'와 'You'll have to type it in within 20 seconds'에서 암호가 전송될 것이며 당신, 즉 Mr. Patton은 20초 안에 그 것, 즉 암호를 입력해야 한다고 했으므로 (C)는 지문의 내용과 일치한다. 따라서 (C)가 정답이다. (A), (B), (D)는 지문에 언급되지 않은 내용이다.

어휘 select v. 선정하다 enter v. 입력하다, 들어가다

패러프레이징

within 20 seconds 20초 이내 → right away 즉시

150 의도 파악 문제 상 ●●●

해석 오후 1시 10분에, Mr. Patton이 "OK, done"이라고 썼을 때, 그가 의도한 것 같은 것은?

(A) 그의 연락처를 업데이트했다.

(B) 온라인 설정을 변경했다.

(C) 은행 거래를 완료했다.

(D) 금융 관련 서류를 인쇄했다.

해설 지문의 'check the Communication Preferences setting at our Web site'에서 RMF 은행이 자신들의 웹사이트에서 선호 연락 수단 설정을 확인 해보라고 한 뒤, 'You need to select the Paper option to get hard copies sent to you.'에서 출력된 자료가 당신, 즉 Mr. Patton에게 발송되 도록 하기 위해서는 문서 옵션을 선택해야 한다고 하자, Mr. Patton이 'OK, done.'(네, 했어요)이라고 한 것을 통해, Mr. Patton이 웹사이트에서 설정을 변경했음을 알 수 있다. 따라서 (B)가 정답이다.

어휘 transaction n. 거래 financial adj. 금융의

패러프레이징

setting at ~ Web site 웹사이트에서의 설정 → online setting 온라인 설정

151-153번은 다음 이메일에 관한 문제입니다.

수신: 모든 지점 직원들
발신: Oliver Harwood <oliverh@centuriarealtors.com>
날짜: 4월 5일
제목: 발표

안녕하세요 여러분,

151저는 여러분 모두에게 이곳 우리 지사에서의 몇몇 변경 사항들을 알려드리고자 합니다.

우선, 151/152-B우리 지역 영업 책임자인 Cathy Kane이 이달 말에 151그녀의 자리에서 물러날 것입니다. Ms. Kane은 거의 20년 동안 Centuria 부동산 중개소와 함께 한 후 은퇴할 예정입니다. 저는 여러분이 그녀에게 행운을 빌어 주길 바랍니다. 우리는 이달 말에 그녀를 위한 기념 만찬을 준비할 것입니다. 자세한 내용은 곧 여러분에게 이메일로 보내질 것입니다.

151우리는 또한 Alex Chen을 이곳 포틀랜드에 있는 우리 지사로 맞이하게 되어 기쁩니다. 152-BMr. Chen은 Ms. Kane의 역할을 대신할 것입니다. 그는 이전에 Karma 부동산 중개소에서 동일한 역할을 수행했으며 15년 이상 의 업계 경험이 있습니다. 152-A/DMr. Chen은 이번 주에 Ms. Kane 아래에 서 교육을 시작할 것입니다.

마지막으로, 저는 여러분에게 Jennifer Wagner가 지역 영업 부책임자로 승진 되었다는 것을 알려드리게 되어 기쁩니다. 우리는 지역 시장에 대한 그녀의

전문 지식이 우리 모두에게 자산이 되리라 생각합니다. 그녀는 다음 주에 그 역할을 맡을 것입니다. 153그녀의 팀원들은 우리의 다음 직원회의에서 발표될 것입니다.

모두 감사합니다!

Oliver Harwood 드림

inform v. 알리다, 통지하다 step down phr. 물러나다, 사임하다
celebratory adj. 기념하는 step into phr. 대신하다, 시작하다
capacity n. 역할, 능력 promote v. 승진시키다, 장려하다
associate adj. 부-, 준-; n. 동료 expertise n. 전문 지식
assume v. 맡다, 가정하다

151 목적 찾기 문제 하 ●○○

해석 이메일의 목적은 무엇인가?

(A) 정책에 대한 의견을 요청하기 위해

(B) 직원들에게 직원 배치 변경을 알리기 위해

(C) 비어 있는 직책들을 알리기 위해

(D) 채용 절차에 대한 변경을 설명하기 위해

해설 지문의 'I would like to inform ~ a few changes here at our branch.' 에서 이곳 지사에서의 몇몇 변경 사항들을 알려주겠다고 한 후, 'our district sales manager ~ will be stepping down from her position'에서 자 신들의 지역 영업 책임자가 그녀의 자리에서 물러날 것이라고 했고, 'We are also pleased to welcome Alex Chen to our branch'에서 Alex Chen 을 자신들의 지사로 맞이하게 되어 기쁘다고 했으므로 (B)가 정답이다.

어휘 opinion n. 의견 staffing n. 직원 배치 available adj. 비어 있는
modification n. 변경 procedure n. 절차

152 Not/True 문제 중 ●●○

해석 Mr. Chen에 대해 언급된 것은?

(A) Jennifer Wagner를 교육해달라고 요청받았다.

(B) 이전에 지역 영업 책임자로 일했다.

(C) Ms. Kane의 자리를 일시적으로 인계받을 것이다.

(D) 4월 말에 중개소 사무실에 올 것이다.

해설 지문의 'our district sales manager, Cathy Kane'에서 Cathy Kane 이 지역 영업 책임자라고 했고, 'Mr. Chen will be stepping into Ms. Kane's role. He previously served in the same capacity'에서 Mr. Chen이 Ms. Kane의 역할을 대신할 것이며 그가 이전에 동일한 역할을 수행했다고 했으므로 (B)는 지문의 내용과 일치한다. 따라서 (B)가 정답이 다. (A)와 (D)는 'Mr. Chen will begin training under Ms. Kane this week.'에서 Mr. Chen은 이번 주에 Ms. Kane 아래에서 교육을 시작할 것 이라고 했으므로 지문의 내용과 일치하지 않는다. (C)는 지문에 언급되지 않 은 내용이다.

어휘 temporarily adv. 일시적으로 take over phr. 인계받다, 인수하다

153 육하원칙 문제 하 ●○○

해석 다음 직원회의에서 무엇이 일어날 것인가?

(A) Ms. Wagner의 팀원들이 발표될 것이다.

(B) 은퇴를 기념하기 위해 선물이 주어질 것이다.

(C) 신입사원들이 소개될 것이다.

(D) Mr. Harwood와의 교육이 진행될 것이다.

해설 지문의 'Her team's members will be announced at our next staff

TEST 8

해커스 토익 실전 1200제 READING

meeting.'에서 그녀, 즉 Ms. Wagner의 팀원들이 다음 직원회의에서 발표될 것이라고 했으므로 (A)가 정답이다.

어휘 celebrate v. 기념하다, 축하하다　introduce v. 소개하다
　　 conduct v. 진행하다

154-157번은 다음 이메일에 관한 문제입니다.

수신: Reggie Bartlett <regbart@somepost.com>
발신: 고객서비스 <custservice@forteelectric.com>
제목: 대금 청구서
　　첨부: 5월 청구서
날짜: 6월 1일

Mr. Bartlett께,

¹⁵⁴첨부된 것은 귀하의 5월 전기 요금 고지서입니다. 정확성을 보장하기 위해 금액을 확인하시고 6월 10일까지 귀하의 요금을 지불해주십시오. 귀하는 www.forteelectric.com/payments에서 은행 송금 혹은 신용카드로 그것을 하실 수 있습니다. 만약 귀하께서 그것을 선호하신다면, ¹⁵⁵귀하는 저희 사이트에서 자동 납부를 설정하실 수도 있습니다. 이것은 월별 요금을 납부하는 시간을 절약하는 데 도움이 될 것입니다!

¹⁵⁷⁻ᴬ만약 귀하께서 귀하의 고지서나 저희 서비스에 관해 문의 사항이 있으시다면, 555-0022로 저희 고객 서비스 담당자 중 한 명에게 연락하십시오. ¹⁵⁶귀하의 청구서에 인쇄된 계좌 번호를 알려주시면, 저희 직원 중 한 명이 귀하를 도와드릴 것입니다.

¹⁵⁷⁻ᴮ만약 귀하께서 정전을 겪고 계신다면, www.forteelectric.com/outages를 방문하여 저희 서비스의 상태를 확인하실 수 있습니다. 이 사이트는 현재 서비스 상태에 대한 정보를 제공할 것이며, 서비스 복구에 드는 예상 시간을 귀하께 제공할 것입니다.

¹⁵⁷⁻ᶜ귀하께서는 귀하의 휴대폰으로 Forte Electric사 애플리케이션을 다운로드하실 수도 있습니다! 정전에 관해 알아보고, 귀하의 계정 잔액을 확인하며, 대금까지 지불하세요. 새 청구서가 유효할 때 귀하는 알림을 받을 것입니다.

귀하의 지속적인 거래에 감사드립니다.

Forte Electric사, 고객 서비스 드림

electricity bill phr. 전기 요금 고지서　ensure v. 보장하다
accuracy n. 정확성　transfer n. 송금　set up phr. 설정하다
automatic adj. 자동의　regarding prep. ~에 관해
agent n. 담당자, 대리인　account number phr. 계좌 번호
representative n. 직원, 대표　assist v. 돕다　power outage phr. 정전
status n. 상태　recovery n. 복구　balance n. 잔액, 잔고
notification n. 알림

154　목적 찾기 문제　　중 ●●●

해석 이메일의 주 목적은 무엇인가?
　　(A) 서비스 재활성화를 요청하기 위해
　　(B) 공과금 고지서를 제공하기 위해
　　(C) 새로운 애플리케이션 서비스를 알리기 위해
　　(D) 부정확한 요금을 보고하기 위해

해설 지문의 'Attached is your monthly electricity bill for May.'에서 첨

부된 것은 5월 전기 요금 고지서라고 한 후, 고지서 납부 방법에 대해 안내하고 있으므로 (B)가 정답이다. (C)는 'You may ~ download the ~ application'에서 애플리케이션을 다운로드할 수 있다고는 했지만 새로운 애플리케이션인지는 알 수 없고, 지문 뒷부분에서 한 문장으로만 등장했으므로 답이 될 수 없다.

어휘 reactivation n. 재활성화　utility fee phr. 공과금
　　 inaccurate adj. 부정확한　charge n. 요금

155　육하원칙 문제　　중 ●●●

해석 Forte Electric사의 웹사이트에서 고객들은 무엇을 할 수 있는가?
　　(A) 자동 납부를 설정한다
　　(B) 시간에 따른 그들의 사용량을 추적한다
　　(C) 서비스를 취소한다
　　(D) 주소 변경을 알린다

해설 지문의 'you may ~ set up automatic payments on our site'에서 저희, 즉 Forte Electric사의 사이트에서 자동 납부를 설정할 수 있다고 했으므로 (A)가 정답이다.

어휘 track v. 추적하다　usage n. 사용(량)　address n. 주소; v. 처리하다

156　육하원칙 문제　　중 ●●●

해석 이메일에 따르면, 요금 청구서에는 무엇이 포함되어 있는가?
　　(A) 선호하는 납부 방법
　　(B) 고객 계좌 번호
　　(C) 은행명
　　(D) 고객 서비스 전화번호

해설 지문의 'the account number printed on your bill'에서 귀하, 즉 고객의 청구서에 계좌 번호가 인쇄되어 있다고 했으므로 (B)가 정답이다.

어휘 banking institution phr. 은행, 금융기관

157　Not/True 문제　　중 ●●●

해석 전기 서비스를 확인하는 방법으로 언급되지 않은 것은?
　　(A) 회사 직원에게 전화하는 것
　　(B) 웹사이트의 최신 정보를 확인하는 것
　　(C) 휴대전화 애플리케이션을 여는 것
　　(D) 문자 메시지 알림을 보내는 것

해설 (D)는 지문에 언급되지 않은 내용이다. 따라서 (D)가 정답이다. (A)는 'If you have any questions regarding ~ services, contact one of our customer service agents at 555-0022.'에서 만약 서비스에 관해 문의 사항이 있다면 전화로 고객 서비스 담당자 중 한 명에게 연락하라고 했으므로 지문의 내용과 일치한다. (B)는 'If you are experiencing a power outage, you may check on the status of our services by going to www.forteelectric.com/outages.'에서 만약 정전을 겪고 있다면, 웹사이트를 방문하여 서비스의 상태를 확인할 수 있다고 했으므로 지문의 내용과 일치한다. (C)는 'You may also download the ~ application on your mobile phone! Find out about outages'에서 휴대폰으로 애플리케이션을 다운로드할 수도 있으며, 전기 서비스에 관련된 정전에 관해 알아보라고 했으므로 지문의 내용과 일치한다.

어휘 review v. 확인하다, 논평하다

158-159번은 다음 광고에 관한 문제입니다.

> **제35회 ^{158-B}연례 캐나다 서부 빈티지 자동차 쇼**
> ¹⁵⁹금요일과 토요일, ^{158-A}7월 7일-8일, 오전 10시-오후 9시
>
> 400대가 넘는 차량이 전시된 ^{158-C}올해의 빈티지 자동차 쇼를 보기 위해 Vernon 시내를 방문하세요!
>
> ^{158-D}입장료는 무료이며, 기념품은 수많은 판매자들로부터 구입할 수 있을 것입니다. 핫도그, 햄버거, 감자튀김, 청량음료, 그리고 더 많은 것들을 스낵과 음료 부스에서 확인해보세요!
>
> ¹⁵⁹유료 주차는 금요일에 시내에서 이용 가능하지만, 주말에는 대중에게 무료입니다. 그리고 빈티지 스포츠카를 얻을 수 있는 저희의 추첨에 참여하는 것을 잊지 마세요! 두 날 모두 박람회 안내 데스크에서 추첨을 신청하세요. 더 많은 정보를 위해서는, www.wcvintageautoshow.com을 방문하세요.

vehicle n. 자동차, 탈것　on view phr. 전시된　admission n. 입장료
souvenir n. 기념품　numerous adj. 수많은　beverage n. 음료
public n. 대중, 사람들　raffle n. 추첨　sign up for phr. 신청하다
draw n. 추첨

158 Not/True 문제　　중 ●●●○

해석　자동차 쇼에 대해 언급되지 않은 것은?
(A) 이틀의 기간 동안 진행될 것이다.
(B) 12개월마다 한 번 개최된다.
(C) 교외에 있는 장소에서 개최된다.
(D) 참석에 대해서는 요금을 부과하지 않는다.

해설　(C)는 'Visit downtown ~ for ~ auto show'에서 자동차 쇼를 보기 위해 시내를 방문하라고 했으므로 지문의 내용과 일치하지 않는다. 따라서 (C)가 정답이다. (A)는 'July 7-8'에서 자동차 쇼가 7월 7일과 7월 8일 이틀에 걸쳐 진행된다는 것을 알 수 있으므로 지문의 내용과 일치한다. (B)는 'Annual ~ Auto Show'에서 연례 자동차 쇼라고 했으므로 지문의 내용과 일치한다. (D)는 'Admission is free'에서 입장료는 무료라고 했으므로 지문의 내용과 일치한다.

어휘　venue n. 장소　suburbs n. 교외(도심지를 벗어난 주택 지역)
attendance n. 참석

159 육하원칙 문제　　중 ●●●○

해석　토요일에만 방문객들에게 무엇이 이용 가능한가?
(A) 무료 주차
(B) 음식 및 음료 샘플
(C) 경품 추첨 참여
(D) 대중교통 이용

해설　지문의 'Friday and Saturday'에서 방문객들이 금요일과 토요일에 자동차 쇼를 방문할 것이라는 것을 알 수 있고, 'Paid parking is available ~ on Friday, but is free to the public on weekends.'에서 유료 주차는 금요일에 이용 가능하지만, 주말에는 대중에게 무료라고 했으므로 (A)가 정답이다.

어휘　complimentary adj. 무료의, 칭찬하는　participation n. 참여
access n. 이용, 접근

패러프레이징

> free 무료의 → complimentary 무료의

160-162번은 다음 기사에 관한 문제입니다.

> 7월 14일— ¹⁶⁰St. Louis 식당 협회는 8월 1일부터 월 이용 플랜을 제공하기 시작할 것이다. — [1] —. 목적은 이 도시의 잘 알려지지 않은 식당들을 홍보하는 것이다. "우리 단체에 속한 많은 점포들은 지난 6개월 이내에 문을 열어서, 그들은 아직 단골손님들이 많지 않습니다."라고 현 협회장 Martha Hale은 말했다. — [2] —.
>
> 사람들이 가입할 때, ¹⁶¹그들은 그들이 선호하는 음식의 종류를 표시하도록 요구받을 것이다. — [3] —. 그들은 St. Louis 식당 협회의 웹사이트에 로그인하여 그들의 정보를 업데이트함으로써 언제든지 이것을 바꿀 수 있다. ¹⁶²가입자들은 매월 다른 식당에서의 두 개의 메인 요리 쿠폰을 받게 될 것이며, 월 요금 20달러만이 청구될 것이다. — [4] —. St. Louis 식당 협회는 이 이용 모델이 회원들을 위한 전반적인 고객 증가로 이어질 것이라고 낙관하고 있다.

subscription n. 이용, 가입, 구독　promote v. 홍보하다
establishment n. 점포, 시설　regular customer phr. 단골손님
sign up phr. 가입하다　indicate v. 표시하다, 나타내다
voucher n. 쿠폰　entrée n. (스테이크를 제외한) 메인 요리
optimistic adj. 낙관하는　overall adj. 전반적인

160 주제 찾기 문제　　중 ●●●○

해석　기사는 주로 무엇에 관한 것인가?
(A) 지역의 요리 방식들을 기념하는 행사
(B) 지역 사업체들을 홍보하는 서비스
(C) 8월에 개업할 사업체
(D) 식당들에서 사용될 상품

해설　지문의 'The St. Louis Restaurant Association will begin offering a monthly subscription plan ~. The goal is to promote the city's little-known restaurants.'에서 St. Louis 식당 협회가 월 이용 플랜을 제공하기 시작할 것이며, 이것의 목적은 이 도시의 잘 알려지지 않은 식당들을 홍보하는 것이라고 했으므로 (B)가 정답이다.

어휘　celebrate v. 기념하다, 축하하다

패러프레이징

> the city's ~ restaurants 이 도시의 식당들 → local businesses 지역 사업체들

161 육하원칙 문제　　중 ●●●○

해석　가입자들은 그들의 음식 선호도를 어떻게 변경할 수 있는가?
(A) 협회에 이메일을 보냄으로써
(B) 월 이용을 갱신함으로써
(C) 고객 센터에 양식을 보냄으로써
(D) 온라인 계정에 접속함으로써

해설　지문의 'they will be asked to indicate their preferred types of foods. They can change this ~ by logging in to the St. Louis Restaurant Association's Web site'에서 그들, 즉 가입자들은 그들이 선호하는 음식의 종류를 표시하도록 요구받을 것이고, St. Louis 식당 협회의 웹사이트에 로그인하여 이것을 바꿀 수 있다고 했으므로 (D)가 정답이다.

어휘　renew v. 갱신하다　account n. 계정, 계좌

패러프레이징

> logging in 로그인하는 것 → accessing an online account 온라인 계정에 접속하는 것

162 문장 위치 찾기 문제 중 ●●○

해석 [1], [2], [3], [4]로 표시된 위치 중, 다음 문장이 들어갈 곳으로 가장 적절한 것은?

"이 금액은 2인분 식사의 정가보다 훨씬 더 적습니다."

(A) [1]
(B) [2]
(C) [3]
(D) [4]

해설 주어진 문장에서 이 금액은 2인분 식사의 정가보다 훨씬 더 적다고 했으므로, 이 문장이 식사의 금액과 관련된 내용이 나오는 부분에 들어가야 함을 알 수 있다. [4]의 앞 문장인 'Subscribers will receive a voucher for two entrées ~ and will be billed a monthly fee of only $20.'에서 가입자들은 두 개의 메인 요리 쿠폰을 받게 될 것이며, 월 요금 20달러만이 청구될 것이라고 했으므로 [4]에 제시된 문장이 들어가면 두 개의 메인 요리 쿠폰에 대해 월 20달러만이 청구될 것인데, 이 금액은 2인분 식사의 정가보다 훨씬 더 적다는 자연스러운 문맥이 된다는 것을 알 수 있다. 따라서 (D)가 정답이다.

어휘 **amount** n. 금액, 양 **significantly** adv. 훨씬, 상당히
regular price phr. 정가 **meal** n. 식사

163-166번은 다음 메시지 대화문에 관한 문제입니다.

¹⁶⁶5월 3일 금요일

Allan McDonald [오후 1시 35분]
지난주에 우리는 이곳 BYR사 팀장들의 리더십 기술을 향상시키는 것에 대해 이야기했었죠. 저는 이런 종류의 기업 교육을 전문으로 하는 Rework Pro라는 회사를 발견했어요.

Julianne Nash [오후 1시 37분]
좋아요. ¹⁶³우리 월별 직원 설문조사 결과는 우리 직원들이 그들의 직속 상사들로부터 더 효과적인 지도를 원한다는 것을 보여줘요. 저는 다른 회사에 직원을 빼앗기지 않도록 보장하기 위해 우리가 이 문제를 즉시 다루어야 한다고 생각해요.

Mallory Smithers [오후 1시 38분]
Rework Pro사는 어떤 종류의 서비스를 제공하죠?

Allan McDonald [오후 1시 41분]
¹⁶⁴그들은 우리를 위한 맞춤 워크숍을 기획해줄 거예요. 이것들은 Rework Pro사 강사에 의해 실시될 거예요.

Julianne Nash [오후 1시 42분]
그것으로 충분할까요? ¹⁶⁴우리가 정기적으로 워크숍을 직접 열고 있지만, 우리는 여전히 이 문제를 가지고 있어요.

Allan McDonald [오후 1시 45분]
자격을 갖춘 강사가 있는 것은 큰 차이를 만들 거예요.

Mallory Smithers [오후 1시 46분]
저도 동의해요. 하지만, ¹⁶⁵저는 일정 계획에 대해 걱정스러워요. 우리는 6월에 몇몇 프로젝트 마감일이 있고, 우리의 많은 직원들이 8월에 그들의 여름 휴가를 갈 거예요.

Allan McDonald [오후 1시 46분]
¹⁶⁵제가 그것을 이미 확인했어요. Rework Pro사 직원이 워크숍이 7월에 진행될 수 있다고 말했어요.

Julianne Nash [오후 1시 48분]
그렇다면 남아 있는 단 한 가지 문제는 이 프로그램이 우리의 예산 내에

맞을 것인지의 여부일 것 같네요.

Allan McDonald [오후 1시 49분]
¹⁶⁶Rework Pro사가 3일 후에 제게 견적서를 보낼 거예요. 우리의 수요일 회의에서 그것을 논의할 수 있도록, 두 분 모두에게 사본을 이메일로 보낼게요.

specialize in phr. ~을 전문으로 하다 **corporate** adj. 기업의
effective adj. 효과적인 **guidance** n. 지도, 지침
immediate supervisor phr. 직속 상사 **address** v. 다루다
immediately adv. 즉시 **ensure** v. 보장하다, 확실히 하다
lose v. 빼앗기다 **custom** adj. 맞춤의 **conduct** v. 실시하다
sufficient adj. 충분한 **instructor** n. 강사 **concerned** adj. 걱정스러운
remaining adj. 남아 있는 **budget** n. 예산 **quote** n. 견적서

---

163 추론 문제 하 ●○○

해석 BYR사에 대해 암시되는 것은?
(A) 몇몇 직원들을 관리직으로 승진시켰다.
(B) 상사들에게 혜택을 제공한다.
(C) 직원들로부터 주기적인 피드백을 요청한다.
(D) 작년에 다른 회사들에 직원들을 빼앗겼다.

해설 지문의 'The results from our monthly employee survey'에서 우리, 즉 BYR사의 월별 직원 설문조사 결과에 대해 언급했으므로 BYR사가 매월 직원들에게 설문조사를 실시한다는 것을 추론할 수 있다. 따라서 (C)가 정답이다.

어휘 **promote** v. 승진시키다 **periodic** adj. 주기적인
feedback n. 피드백, 의견

패러프레이징

monthly 월별 → periodic 주기적인

---

164 의도 파악 문제 중 ●●●

해석 오후 1시 42분에, Ms. Nash가 "Will that be sufficient"라고 썼을 때, 그녀가 의도한 것 같은 것은?
(A) 워크숍이 빨리 준비될 수 있다.
(B) 직원 채용 문제가 계속 해결되지 않을 것이다.
(C) 관리자들이 더 긴 훈련 기간이 필요하다.
(D) 교육 방식이 효과적이지 않다.

해설 지문의 'They will design custom workshops for us.'에서 Mr. McDonald가 그들, 즉 Rework Pro사가 우리, 즉 BYR사를 위한 맞춤 워크숍을 기획해줄 것이라고 하자, Ms. Nash가 'Will that be sufficient?'(그것으로 충분할까요?)라고 한 후, 'We regularly hold workshops ourselves, but we still have this issue.'에서 우리가 정기적으로 워크숍을 직접 열고 있지만, 여전히 이 문제를 가지고 있다고 한 것을 통해, Ms. Nash는 현재의 워크숍이 문제를 해결하는데 효과적이지 않다고 생각한다는 것을 알 수 있다. 따라서 (D)가 정답이다.

어휘 **staffing** n. 직원 채용 **unresolved** adj. 해결되지 않은
instructional adj. 교육의 **ineffective** adj. 효과적이지 않은

패러프레이징

workshops 워크숍 → instructional method 교육 방식

---

165 육하원칙 문제 중 ●●○

해석 Mr. McDonald는 그가 이미 무엇을 했다고 말하는가?

(A) 직원 휴가 일자를 확인했다
(B) 일정 관련 정보를 요청했다
(C) 워크숍 참석자들의 이름을 제공했다
(D) 장소의 이용 가능 여부를 확인했다

해설 지문의 'I'm concerned about scheduling'에서 Ms. Smithers가 일정 계획이 걱정스럽다고 하자, 'I already checked that. The Rework Pro representative said that the workshops could be done in July.'에서 Mr. McDonald가 이미 자신이 그것, 즉 일정 계획을 확인했으며 Rework Pro사 직원이 워크숍이 7월에 진행될 수 있다고 말했다고 했으므로 (B)가 정답이다.

어휘 **request** v. 요청하다 **attendee** n. 참석자 **confirm** v. 확인하다
venue n. 장소 **availability** n. 이용 가능 여부, 유용성

166 추론 문제
중 ●●○

해석 다음 주에 무슨 일이 일어날 것 같은가?
(A) Rework Pro사가 가격 견적서를 제시할 것이다.
(B) Mr. McDonald가 강사를 만날 것이다.
(C) Ms. Smithers가 예산안을 제출할 것이다.
(D) BYR사가 프로젝트 마감일을 변경할 것이다.

해설 지문의 'May 3 Friday'에서 대화가 5월 3일 금요일에 이루어졌다는 것을 알 수 있고, 'Rework Pro is sending me a quote in three days.'에서 Rework Pro사가 3일 후에 견적서를 보낼 것이라고 했으므로 Rework Pro사가 3일 후인 다음 주 월요일에 가격 견적서를 제시할 것임을 추론할 수 있다. 따라서 (A)가 정답이다.

어휘 **submit** v. 제시하다, 제출하다 **estimate** n. 견적(서) **present** v. 제출하다
budget proposal phr. 예산안

패러프레이징

> is sending ~ a quote 견적서를 보낼 것이다 → will submit a price estimate 가격 견적서를 제시할 것이다

167-168번은 다음 공고에 관한 문제입니다.

도서 기증

7월 20일부터 8월 20일까지, Willpoint 공공도서관은 사람들로부터 도서 기증을 받을 것이며, 저희는 현재 ¹⁶⁷기증된 물품들의 분류를 도와줄 자원봉사자들을 찾고 있습니다. 만약 당신이 18세 이상이라면, 직접 도서관에서 신청하세요. 당신은 하루에 최소 2시간 동안 시간을 내어야 할 것입니다.

¹⁶⁸⁻ᴮ도서를 기증하길 원하는 사람들은 저희 도서관을 방문하시면 됩니다. 도서들은 ¹⁶⁸⁻ᴬ평일 오전 9시부터 오후 11시까지, 주말 오전 9시부터 오후 6시까지의 저희의 정규 운영 시간 동안 도서관에 가져올 수 있습니다. ¹⁶⁸⁻ᴮ당신은 또한 시청에 있는 저희 기증 상자에 그것들을 둘 수 있으며, 이것은 월요일에서 금요일까지 오전 9시부터 오후 5시까지 열려 있습니다.

donation n. 기증, 기부 **seek** v. 찾다 **volunteer** n. 자원봉사자
sorting n. 분류, 구분 **in person** phr. 직접, 몸소 **minimum** n. 최소
regular adj. 정규의 **operating hours** phr. 운영 시간

167 육하원칙 문제
중 ●●○

해석 공고에 따르면, 자원봉사자들은 무엇을 할 것인가?
(A) 도서관에 기부된 물품들을 정리한다
(B) 아이들을 지도하는 것을 돕는다
(C) 방문객들이 서비스를 신청하는 것을 돕는다

(D) 배송을 위한 책들을 준비한다

해설 지문의 'volunteers to help with the sorting of donated items'에서 기증된 물품들의 분류를 도와줄 자원봉사자들이라고 했으므로 (A)가 정답이다.

어휘 **organize** v. 정리하다, 체계화하다 **give** v. 기부하다, 주다
supervise v. 지도하다, 감독하다 **apply for** phr. 신청하다, 지원하다
shipment n. 배송

패러프레이징

> sorting 분류 → organize 정리하다

168 Not/True 문제
중 ●●○

해석 Willpoint 공공도서관에 대해 사실인 것은?
(A) 토요일과 일요일에는 더 늦게 문을 닫는다.
(B) 여러 장소들에서 기증품을 받는다.
(C) 8월에 그것의 운영 시간을 연장할 것이다.
(D) 그것의 시설들 중 몇 개를 수리하고 있다.

해설 지문의 'Those who want to donate their books can visit our library.'에서 도서를 기증하길 원하는 사람들은 저희, 즉 Willpoint 공공도서관을 방문하면 된다고 했고, 'You can also leave them in our donation box at City Hall'에서 또한 시청에 있는 자신의 기증 상자에 그것들을 둘 수 있다고 했으므로 (B)는 지문의 내용과 일치한다. 따라서 (B)가 정답이다. (A)는 'our regular operating hours of 9:00 A.M. to 11:00 P.M. on weekdays and from 9:00 A.M. to 6:00 P.M. on weekends'에서 평일은 오전 9시부터 오후 11시까지, 주말은 오전 9시부터 오후 6시까지가 정규 운영 시간이라고 했으므로 지문의 내용과 일치하지 않는다. (C)와 (D)는 지문에 언급되지 않은 내용이다.

어휘 **multiple** adj. 여러, 다수의 **extend** v. 연장하다, 확대하다
renovate v. 수리하다, 개조하다 **facility** n. 시설, 설비

169-171번은 다음 이메일에 관한 문제입니다.

수신: Adriana Cole <ad.cole@scribeofficesupplies.com>
발신: Owen Fender <owenfender@jesterenterprises.com>
제목: 구매 주문
날짜: 4월 15일

Ms. Cole께,

저희 회사에 의해 내려진 최근의 결정에 관해 귀하께 연락을 드립니다. ― [1] ―. 더욱 환경친화적으로 되기 위해, ¹⁷⁰저희는 복사기 및 프린터의 종이 사용을 줄일 계획입니다. ¹⁷¹저희는 5월 1일부터 저희 문서들의 대부분을 컴퓨터로 저장하기 시작할 것입니다. ― [2] ―. ¹⁷⁰따라서, ¹⁶⁹/¹⁷⁰저희의 월 주문을 네 상자에서 두 상자로 줄이고자 합니다. ― [3] ―. 게다가, 저희는 이제부터는 재생 용지만 구매하고자 합니다. 이것이 비용이 얼마나 들지 제게 알려 주십시오. ¹⁷⁰저는 저희가 현재 장기 고객으로서 자격이 있는 할인을 저희가 귀사의 재활용 종이 제품들을 구매할 때 받을 수 있기를 바랍니다. ― [4] ―. 감사드리며, 앞으로도 저희가 귀사와 계속 거래하기를 바랍니다.

Owen Fender 드림
구매 담당자, Jester사

cut down phr. 줄이다 **store** v. 저장하다, 보관하다
electronically adv. 컴퓨터로, 전자적으로 **recycled paper** phr. 재생 용지
qualify v. 자격이 있다 **long-term** adj. 장기의, 장기적인

169 목적 찾기 문제　중 ●●○

해석　이메일은 왜 쓰였는가?

(A) 공급업체에 주문 조정을 알리기 위해

(B) 신상품에 대해 문의하기 위해

(C) 정책에 대한 불만 사항을 제출하기 위해

(D) 더 높은 할인율을 요구하기 위해

해설　지문의 'we would like to reduce our monthly order'에서 월 주문을 줄이고자 한다고 했으므로 (A)가 정답이다. 참고로, (D)도 지문에서 할인을 받을 수 있길 바란다는 내용이 언급되어 정답이 될 것 같지만, 더 높은 할인율을 요구하는 내용은 언급되지 않았으므로 답이 될 수 없다.

어휘　**supplier** n. 공급업체, 공급자　**adjustment** n. 조정
complaint n. 불만 사항, 불평

패러프레이징

reduce ~ order 주문을 줄이다 → order adjustment 주문 조정

170 추론 문제　상 ●●●

해석　Jester사에 대해 암시되는 것은?

(A) 관리자가 경영 비용을 줄이기로 결정했다.

(B) 현재의 복사기와 프린터를 유지하지 않을 것이다.

(C) 환경과 관련된 노력이 긍정적인 주목을 받았다.

(D) 용지에 대해 정가를 지불하지 않아 왔다.

해설　'we plan to cut down on our use of paper'와 'Therefore, we would like to reduce ~ order'에서 자신들, 즉 Jester사가 종이 사용을 줄일 계획이며, 따라서 주문을 줄이고자 한다고 했고, 'I hope we will receive the discount we currently qualify for ~ when we purchase ~ recycled paper products.'에서 현재 자신들이 자격이 있는 할인을 자신들이 재활용 종이 제품들을 구매할 때 받을 수 있기를 바란다고 했으므로 Jester사가 종이 관련 주문에 대해 할인을 받아왔다는 사실을 추론할 수 있다. 따라서 (D)가 정답이다. 참고로, (C)는 Jester사가 더욱 환경친화적으로 되기 위한 노력을 하고 있다고 했지만, 이것이 긍정적인 주목을 받았는지는 알 수 없으므로 답이 될 수 없다.

어휘　**operating expense** phr. 경영 비용　**publicity** n. 주목, 평판
regular price phr. 정가, 정상 가격

171 문장 위치 찾기 문제　중 ●●○

해석　[1], [2], [3], [4]로 표시된 위치 중, 다음 문장이 들어갈 곳으로 가장 적절한 것은?

"하지만, 저희는 다양한 목적들을 위해 용지 공급이 여전히 필요할 것입니다."

(A) [1]

(B) [2]

(C) [3]

(D) [4]

해설　주어진 문장에서 하지만 다양한 목적들을 위한 용지 공급이 여전히 필요할 것이라고 했으므로, 이 문장이 용지 공급과 관련된 내용이 나오는 부분에 들어가야 함을 알 수 있다. [2]의 앞 문장인 'We will begin storing most of our documents electronically on May 1.'에서 5월 1일부터 자신들의 문서들의 대부분을 컴퓨터로 저장하기 시작할 것이라고 했으므로, [2]에 제시된 문장이 들어가면 문서들의 대부분을 컴퓨터로 저장하기 시작할 것이지만 다양한 목적들을 위해 용지 공급이 여전히 필요할 것이라는 자연스러운 문맥이 된다는 것을 알 수 있다. 따라서 (B)가 정답이다.

어휘　**supply** n. 공급　**various** adj. 다양한

172-175번은 다음 기사에 관한 문제입니다.

LiteraLegends가 새로운 작가들에게 출판 기회를 제공하다

자신의 작품이 출판되도록 노력하는 작가들에게 희망을 주는 것이 있다! ¹⁷²**단 5년 전에 설립된**, LiteraLegends는 작가들에게 그들의 소설, 단편 소설, 시, 그리고 비소설 작품들을 출판할 기회를 제공하는 웹사이트이다. 작가들은 그들의 작품을 사이트에 간단히 업로드하고, 회원들은 그들의 읽는 즐거움을 위해 그것들을 다운로드할 수 있다.

LiteraLegends의 최고경영자 Sam Ashoka는 "글을 처음 써본 작가들은 대개 자신의 작품을 무료로 제공합니다. ^{173-D}**회원들은 그들이 읽은 것이 마음에 든다면, 그들은 긍정적인 후기를 남깁니다.**"라고 말했다. 만약 한 작품이 인기를 얻게 되면, 그 작가는 그때 회원들에게 다운로드에 대한 요금을 부과할 수 있는 선택권을 갖게 된다. 그 가격은 2.99달러만큼 낮을 수도 있고 35.99달러만큼 높을 수도 있다. ¹⁷⁴**LiteraLegends는 모든 판매들에 20퍼센트의 수수료를 청구하며**, 또한 작가들이 주류 출판사로 판로를 넓히도록 돕는다.

¹⁷⁵*The Belivers*의 유명한 작가 Meridiana Chase는 LiteraLegends에서 그녀의 작품에 대한 상당한 독자층을 키운 후 한 출판사에 의해 발견되었다. "일부 작품들은 100만회가 넘게 다운로드되었습니다"라고 Ashoka는 또한 말했다. "유명한 비디오 콘텐츠 사이트가 연기자들에게 가져다준 것과 같은 수준의 성공을 LiteraLegends가 작가들에게 가져다주기를 희망합니다."

author n. 작가, 저자　**publication** n. 출판　**found** v. 설립하다
novel n. 소설　**non-fiction** n. 비소설　**simply** adv. 간단히, 단지
option n. 선택(권)　**charge** v. 요금을 부과하다　**commission** n. 수수료
promote v. 판로를 넓히다, 홍보하다　**mainstream** adj. 주류의
discover v. 발견하다　**publishing house** phr. 출판사
significant adj. 상당한　**readership** n. 독자(층)　**performer** n. 연기자

172 동의어 찾기 문제　중 ●●○

해석　1문단 첫 번째 줄의 단어 "Founded"는 의미상 -와 가장 가깝다.

(A) 발견된

(B) 설립된

(C) 찾아진

(D) 밝혀진

해설　Founded를 포함한 구절 'Founded just five years ago'에서 단 5년 전에 설립되었다고 했으므로 founded는 '설립된'이라는 뜻으로 사용되었다. 따라서 '설립된'이라는 뜻을 가진 (B) Established가 정답이다.

173 Not/True 문제　중 ●●○

해석　LiteraLegends에 대해 언급된 것은?

(A) 다른 웹사이트들에서 서비스를 제공한다.

(B) 고객들이 미리 비용을 지불할 것을 요구한다.

(C) 다른 회사들과 제휴를 맺고 있다.

(D) 사용자들이 의견을 제공하도록 허용한다.

해설　지문의 'If members like what they read, they leave a positive review.'에서 회원들은 그들이 읽은 것이 마음에 든다면 긍정적인 후기를 남긴다고 했으므로 (D)는 지문의 내용과 일치한다. 따라서 (D)가 정답이다. (A), (B), (C)는 지문에 언급되지 않은 내용이다.

어휘　**in advance** phr. 미리　**form** v. 맺다, 형성하다　**partnership** n. 제휴, 협력

패러프레이징

leave a ~ review 후기를 남기다 → provide feedback 의견을 제공하다

174 육하원칙 문제 　중 ●●○

해석　LiteraLegends는 어떻게 수익을 만들어내는가?
(A) 회원권에 대해 요금을 부과함으로써
(B) 판매 수수료를 가져감으로써
(C) 구독료를 받음으로써
(D) 광고를 냄으로써

해설　지문의 'LiteraLegends charges a 20 percent commission fee on all sales'에서 LiteraLegends가 모든 판매들에 20퍼센트의 수수료를 청구한다고 했으므로 (B)가 정답이다.

어휘　collect v. (급료 따위)를 받다　subscription fee phr. 구독료

패러프레이징

charges ~ commission fee on ~ sales 판매들에 수수료를 청구하다
→ taking a sales commission 판매 수수료를 가져가는 것

175 육하원칙 문제 　하 ●○○

해석　Meridiana Chase는 누구인가?
(A) 출판사 대변인
(B) 문학 평론가
(C) 인기 작가
(D) 마케팅 전문가

해설　지문의 'Well-known author of *The Belivers*, Meridiana Chase'에서 Meridiana Chase가 *The Belivers*의 유명한 작가라고 했으므로 (C)가 정답이다.

어휘　spokesperson n. 대변인　literary adj. 문학의　critic n. 평론가, 비평가　expert n. 전문가

패러프레이징

Well-known 유명한 → popular 인기 있는

176-180번은 다음 웹페이지와 편지에 관한 문제입니다.

www.csjobsglobal.com
CS JOBS GLOBAL사

| 홈 | **구인 목록** | 로그인 | 연락처 | 도움말 |

Talle Centrum 콜센터
인도, 스리랑카, 그리고 방글라데시에 있는 사무실들을 가진, [176]저희는 20년 넘게 세계 기업들을 위한 콜센터 서비스의 선두적인 제공 업체입니다. 저희는 고객 서비스 직원들로 이뤄진 팀에 합류하는 것에 관심있는 사람들을 찾고 있습니다.

[177-C]**책무**
· 기업 고객들을 위한 고객 서비스 전화 응대하기
· 고객 정보 수집 및 관리하기
· 필요에 따라 해결책 및 서비스 권하기
· [177-C]정기적인 교육 워크숍 및 회의 참석하기

[176/177-A/D]**자격 요건**
· 최소 2년제 대학이 요구됨
· [177-A]탄력적 근무 시간제로 기꺼이 일하려 해야 함
· [177-D]이전 경험이 선호됨
· [176]영어, 독일어, 또는 프랑스어에 뛰어난 서면 및 구두 의사소통 능력

[178-B]**보상**

· [178-B]시간당 12.50달러에 더하여 실적 보너스
· 건강 보험
· 주택 및 교통 보조금

지원 마감일은 7월 10일입니다.

leading adj. 선두적인　provider n. 제공 업체　handle v. 응대하다, 다루다
gather v. 수집하다　maintain v. 관리하다, 유지하다
recommend v. 권하다, 추천하다　periodic adj. 정기적인, 주기적인
minimum n. 최소　willing adj. 기꺼이 ~하는
flexible hours phr. 탄력적 근무 시간제　prefer v. 선호하다
verbal adj. 구두의　subsidy n. 보조금, 장려금　application n. 지원, 신청

[178-B]**Talle Centrum 콜센터**
www.tallecentrum.com

8월 16일

Angela Lakmal
22 Weerangula로
모렌나, 스리랑카

Ms. Lakmal께,

귀하의 고용에 대해 논의하기 위해 8월 10일에 들려주셔서 감사합니다. 합의된 것처럼, [178-B]귀하는 이곳 콜롬보의 저희 센터에서 **고객 서비스 정규 직원 직무를 맡게 될 것입니다.** 귀하께서는 한 주에 최소 40시간을 일하게 될 것입니다. 보상은 광고된 대로일 것입니다. [180]**귀하께서 다르게 명시하지 않는다면, 귀하의 시작일은 9월 15일이 될 것입니다.** 저희는 귀하가 저희 팀에 오는 것을 기대하고 있습니다!

[179]**만약 해결되지 않은 문제가 있다면,** 555-2795로 제게 **전화해 주십시오.** 그렇지 않다면, 귀하의 첫 출근 날에 귀하를 만나길 기다리고 있겠습니다.

Dennis Carlsen 드림
인사부 관리자

employment n. 고용, 채용　take on phr. ~을 맡다　specify v. 명시하다
look forward phr. ~을 기대하다, ~을 기다리다

176 추론 문제 　하 ●○○

해석　Talle Centrum 콜센터에 대해 암시되는 것은?
(A) 스리랑카에서 시작되었다.
(B) 새로운 지사를 열 것이다.
(C) 현재 소프트웨어 제품을 개발하고 있다.
(D) 여러 가지 언어로 서비스를 제공한다.

해설　웹페이지의 'we have been a leading provider of contact center services for global companies ~. We are seeking individuals interested in joining our team of customer service agents.'에서 저희, 즉 Talle Centrum 콜센터는 세계 기업들을 위한 콜센터 서비스의 선두적인 제공 업체이며, 고객 서비스 직원들로 이뤄진 팀에 합류하는 것에 관심 있는 사람들을 찾고 있다고 했고, 'QUALIFICATIONS', 'Excellent written and verbal communication skills in English, German, or French'에서 자격 요건에 영어, 독일어, 또는 프랑스어에 뛰어난 서면 및 구두 의사소통 능력이 있으므로, Talle Centrum 콜센터가 여러 가지 언어로 콜센터 서비스를 제공한다는 사실을 추론할 수 있다. 따라서 (D)가 정답이다.

어휘　originate v. 시작되다　develop v. 개발하다

177 Not/True 문제 중 ●●○

해석 광고된 직책에 대해 언급된 것은?
(A) 고정된 업무 일정을 포함한다.
(B) 해외 출장 기회들을 제공한다.
(C) 정기적인 교육을 수반한다.
(D) 이전 업무 경험을 필요로 한다.

해설 웹페이지의 'RESPONSIBILITIES', 'Participating in periodic training workshops'에서 책무에 정기적인 교육 워크숍 참석하기가 있으므로 (C)는 지문의 내용과 일치한다. 따라서 (C)가 정답이다. (A)는 'QUALIFICATIONS', 'Must be willing to work flexible hours'에서 자격 요건에 탄력적 근무 시간제로 기꺼이 일하려 해야 한다는 것이 있으므로 지문의 내용과 일치하지 않는다. (B)는 지문에 언급되지 않은 내용이다. (D)는 'QUALIFICATIONS', 'Previous experience preferred'에서 자격 요건에 이전 경험이 선호된다고는 했지만, 꼭 필요로 한다고 하지 않았으므로 지문의 내용과 일치하지 않는다.

어휘 **overseas** adj. 해외의, 외국의 **travel** n. 출장, 이동, 여행
involve v. 수반하다 **prior** adj. 이전의

패러프레이징

periodic training workshops 정기적인 교육 워크숍 → regular training sessions 정기적인 교육

178 Not/True 문제 연계 중 ●●●

해석 Ms. Lakmal에 대해 언급된 것은?
(A) 모든 판매에 대해 보너스를 받을 것이다.
(B) 잘한 일에 대해서는 추가 보수를 받을 것이다.
(C) 전문 자격증을 취득해야 할 것이다.
(D) 주로 밤에 일할 것이다.

해설 편지의 'Talle Centrum Contact Center', 'you will be taking on the role of a ~ customer service agent'에서 Talle Centrum 콜센터에서 보낸 편지의 수신자인 Ms. Lakmal이 고객 서비스 직원 직무를 맡게 될 것이라고 했다. 또한, 웹페이지의 'Talle Centrum Contact Center', 'COMPENSATION', '$12.50 per hour plus performance bonuses'에서는 Talle Centrum 콜센터에서 보상으로 시간당 12.50달러에 더하여 실적 보너스를 준다는 것을 확인할 수 있다.
두 단서를 종합할 때, Ms. Lakmal은 Talle Centrum 콜센터의 고객 서비스 직원으로 근무하며 잘한 일에 대해서는 추가 보수를 받을 것임을 알 수 있으므로 (B)는 지문의 내용과 일치한다. 따라서 (B)가 정답이다. (A), (C), (D)는 지문에 언급되지 않은 내용이다.

어휘 **earn** v. 취득하다, 획득하다 **certificate** n. 자격증
mostly adv. 주로, 일반적으로

패러프레이징

bonus 보너스 → extra pay 추가 보수

최고난도 문제

179 동의어 찾기 문제 상 ●●●

해석 편지에서, 2문단 첫 번째 줄의 단어 "addressed"는 의미상 -와 가장 가깝다.
(A) 전달된
(B) 제기된
(C) 기록된
(D) 해결된

해설 편지의 addressed를 포함한 문장 'If you have any concerns that have not been addressed, please call'에서 만약 해결되지 않은 문제가 있다면 전화해 달라고 했으므로 addressed는 '해결된'이라는 뜻으로 사용되었다. 따라서 '해결된'이라는 뜻을 가진 (D) dealt with가 정답이다.

180 추론 문제 중 ●●○

해석 Ms. Lakmal은 언제 그녀의 근무를 시작할 것 같은가?
(A) 8월 10일
(B) 8월 17일
(C) 9월 1일
(D) 9월 15일

해설 편지의 'Your start date, unless you specify otherwise, will be on September 15.'에서 귀하, 즉 Ms. Lakmal가 다르게 명시하지 않는 나면 그녀의 시작일, 즉 근무 시작일은 9월 15일이 될 것이라고 했으므로 Ms. Lakmal이 그녀의 근무를 9월 15일에 시작할 것임을 추론할 수 있다. 따라서 (D)가 정답이다.

어휘 **employment** n. 근무, 고용

181-185번은 다음 편지와 일정표에 관한 문제입니다.

Dawn Taylor
42번지 Coote로
블러프힐, 네이피어 4110
뉴질랜드

Ms. Taylor께,

뉴질랜드 요트 타기 협회(NZSS)의 100주년을 기념하는 [182]2월에 있을 [181/182]행사에서 제가 연설해달라는 당신의 요청에 대해 영광스럽게 생각합니다. NZSS의 전 회장으로서, 저는 이 동호회의 역사를 잘 알고 있습니다. 그리고 제가 지도자직에서 물러난 이후 몇 년 동안 그것이 발전해나가는 것을 지켜보는 것은 기쁨이었습니다.

[182]유감스럽게도, 제가 같은 날에 요트 타기 경주에 참가할 예정이기 때문에, [181/182]저는 참가할 수 없습니다. 저 대신에, 저는 요트 타기에 열성적인 사람이자 뛰어난 대중 연설가인 Brenda Wilson을 추천하고 싶습니다. [183]또다른 좋은 대안은 Ling Zhang일 것인데, 그녀는 단독 요트 타기에서 세계 기록을 경신했습니다. Alison Scott 또한 머릿속에 떠오릅니다. 그녀의 할아버지가 NZSS의 초기 구성원이었기 때문에, 그녀는 협회의 초창기에 관한 흥미로운 이야기들을 가지고 있습니다. [183]만약 이 사람들 중 한 명이 행사에서 연설하기에 적합해 보인다면 제게 알려주십시오. 그러면 제가 그 사람의 이메일 주소를 당신에게 드리겠습니다.

Patrick Patel 드림

mark v. 기념하다, 나타내다 **acquainted with** phr. ~을 알고 있는
please v. 기쁘게하다 **take part in** phr. ~에 참가하다
enthusiast n. 열성적인 사람 **accomplished** adj. 뛰어난, 성취된
original adj. 초기의, 원래의 **suitable** adj. 적합한

순조로운 요트 타기의 100주년 행사에 대한 일정:
뉴질랜드 요트 타기 협회의 기념일 축하

장소: Walter Donahue 클럽 회관
날짜: 2월 28일

시간	행사	[183]연설자
오후 5시-5시 20분	[185-D]개회사 - "요트를 조종하는 동지들을 환영합니다"	Dominika Gladstone
오후 5시 20분-5시 50분	주요 연설 - "왜 요트 타기가 중요한가"	[183]Ling Zhang
오후 6시-7시 30분	Ketch실에서의 저녁 연회	
오후 7시 30분-8시	[185-C]슬라이드쇼 - "수년 동안의 NZSS"	Winny Baxter
[184]오후 8시-8시 30분	우승자에게는 상품이 있는 [184]NZSS 관련 일반상식 퀴즈 놀이	David Young
오후 8시 40분-9시	[185-A]Breakwater 항구 위로의 불꽃놀이	

anniversary n. 기념일 fellow adj. 동료의; n. 동지, 동료
sailor n. 요트를 조종하는 사람 address n. 연설 banquet n. 연회, 만찬
trivia quiz phr. 일반상식 퀴즈

181 목적 찾기 문제 중 ●●○

해석 편지의 주 목적은 무엇인가?
(A) 행사를 여는 것을 제안하기 위해
(B) 초대를 거절하기 위해
(C) 몇몇 자격 요건을 검토하기 위해
(D) 날짜 변경을 요청하기 위해

해설 편지의 'I am honored by your request that I speak at the event'에서 행사에서 연설해달라는 당신의 요청에 대해 영광스럽게 생각한다고 한 후, 'I am unable to join'에서 자신은 참가할 수 없다고 했으므로 (B)가 정답이다.

어휘 hold v. 열다, 개최하다 turn down phr. 거절하다 invitation n. 초대(장)
qualification n. 자격 (요건)

182 육하원칙 문제 하 ●○○

해석 편지에 따르면, Mr. Patel은 2월에 무엇으로 바쁠 것인가?
(A) 회원 명부를 만드는 것
(B) 대회에 참가하는 것
(C) 전시회를 준비하는 것
(D) 지역 선거에 출마하는 것

해설 이메일의 'I am honored by your request that I speak at the event in February'에서 2월에 있을 행사에서 자신, 즉 Mr. Patel이 연설해달라는 당신의 요청에 대해 영광스럽게 생각한다고 했고, 'Regrettably, I am unable to join because I will be taking part in a sailing race on the same day.'에서 유감스럽게도, 같은 날에 요트 타기 경주에 참가할 예정이기 때문에, 자신은 참가할 수 없다고 했으므로 (B)가 정답이다.

어휘 occupied adj. 바쁜, 사용 중인 directory n. 명부 exhibition n. 전시회
run v. 출마하다 election n. 선거

패러프레이징

taking part in a ~ race 경주에 참가하는 것 → Participating in a competition 대회에 참가하는 것

【최고난도 문제】

183 추론 문제 연계 상 ●●●

해석 Mr. Patel은 무엇을 했을 것 같은가?

(A) Mr. Zhang의 연락처를 행사 주최자에게 보냈다
(B) Ms. Taylor에게 강의에 적합한 주제를 제공했다
(C) Ms. Scott의 배경에 대해 연설했다
(D) Mr. Zhang에게 요트 타는 법을 가르쳤다

해설 이메일의 'Another good choice would be Ling Zhang'에서 또다른 좋은 대안, 즉 이메일 작성인인 Mr. Patel 대신에 연설을 할 사람으로 Mr. Zhang이 또 다른 좋은 대안이라고 했고, 'Let me know if one of these people seems suitable to speak at the event. Then I will provide you with that person's e-mail address.'에서 만약 이 사람들, 즉 Mr. Patel이 추천한 사람들 중 한 명이 행사에서 연설하기에 적합해 보인다면 자신에게 알려달라고 하며, 그 사람의 이메일 주소를 주겠다고 했다. 또한, 일정표의 'Speaker', 'Ling Zhang'에서는 Mr. Zhang이 연설을 했음을 확인할 수 있다.

두 단서를 종합할 때, Mr. Patel이 Mr. Zhang의 연락처를 행사 주최자에게 보냈다는 사실을 추론할 수 있다. 따라서 (A)가 정답이다.

어휘 contact details phr. 연락처 organizer n. 주최자
background n. (사회, 성장) 배경

패러프레이징

e-mail address 이메일 주소 → contact details 연락처

184 육하원칙 문제 중 ●●○

해석 일정표에 따르면, 참석자들은 언제 게임을 할 것인가?
(A) 오후 5시
(B) 오후 6시
(C) 오후 8시
(D) 오후 8시 40분

해설 일정표의 '8:00-8:30 P.M.', 'NZSS trivia quiz'에서 오후 8시부터 8시 30분까지 NZSS 관련 일반상식 퀴즈 놀이가 진행된다고 했으므로 (C)가 정답이다.

어휘 attendee n. 참석자

패러프레이징

game 게임 → quiz 퀴즈 놀이

185 Not/True 문제 중 ●●○

해석 순조로운 요트 타기의 100주년에 무엇이 일어나지 않을 것인가?
(A) 야외 쇼
(B) 제품 시연
(C) 시청각 발표
(D) 개회사

해설 질문의 100 Years of Smooth Sailing과 관련된 내용이 언급된 일정표에서 (B)는 언급되지 않은 내용이다. 따라서 (B)가 정답이다. (A)는 'Fireworks display over Breakwater Harbor'에서 Breakwater 항구 위로의 불꽃놀이가 있으므로 지문의 내용과 일치한다. (C)는 'Slideshow'에서 슬라이드쇼가 있으므로 지문의 내용과 일치한다. (D)는 'Opening speech'에서 개회사가 있으므로 지문의 내용과 일치한다.

어휘 outdoor adj. 야외의 demonstration n. 시연, 설명 visual adj. 시청각의

패러프레이징

Slideshow 슬라이드쇼 → visual presentation 시청각 발표
Opening speech 개회사 → opening talk 개회사

발신: Claude Symonds <cs100@edgeattire.com>
수신: Sheila Bryant <bryant@edgeattire.com>
날짜: 8월 6일
제목: Fredericton 스타일 박람회의 사전 준비
첨부: 변경사항.xls

안녕하세요 Sheila,

저는 Fredericton 스타일 박람회의 조직 위원회로부터 다시 연락을 받았습니다. 그들은 우리가 9월 10일에 있을 우리의 패션쇼를 연장할 수 있다고 말했습니다. 또한, 비록 모델들에 대한 우리의 최종 선택이 확정된 것 같았지만, Leila Vinch는 결국 참석할 수 없습니다. 그래서, ¹⁸⁶저는 이번 주말까지 당신이 대신할 사람을 구했으면 합니다. ¹⁸⁷부스에 관해서는, 어서 이 행사의 전체 기간 동안 사용할 하나를 빌려주세요. 우리가 패션쇼를 위해 사용할 옷과 액세서리를 수용할 보관 공간을 빌릴 수 있는 가능성에 대해서도 꼭 물어봐 주세요.

Claude 드림

lead-up n. (~의) 사전 준비 alteration n. 변경사항 extend v. 연장하다
confirm v. 확정하다 replacement n. 대신할 사람, 대체물
entire adj. 전체의 duration n. 기간, 지속 possibility n. 가능성
storage n. 보관

Fredericton 스타일 박람회

대여자: Edge 의류사
연락처: Sheila Bryant, 555-4096

부스 크기: 4×4 (평방미터)
¹⁸⁷**대여 비용:** 320달러 (일일 대여료 80달러×4일)
보증금: 45달러

이용약관: ^{188-A/B/C}부스 대여는 행사 티켓 4장, 테이블 1개, 의자 2개, 콘센트 1개, 조명 1세트, 일반 표지판 1개를 포함합니다. ^{188-D}다음은 추가 요금으로 이용 가능합니다:

추가 콘센트, 테이블, 의자: 하루 20달러
맞춤 표지판: 50달러의 설치 비용
¹⁸⁹와이파이 이용: 하루 10달러
^{188-D}보관소 대여: 하루 15달러

renter n. 대여자 deposit n. 보증금 electrical outlet phr. 콘센트
custom adj. 맞춤의, 주문의 installation n. 설치 access n. 이용, 접근

9월 27일

Fredericton 스타일 박람회
5번지 Bulkley가
셀번, 노바스코샤 B0T 1W0

Fredericton 스타일 박람회께,

저희 회사는 귀사의 최근 행사에 출품 회사로서 참여했습니다. 저희는 일반 부스와 저희의 패션쇼에 사용되는 물품들을 위한 보관 사물함을 요청했습니다. 하지만, 제가 저희의 최종 청구서를 확인했을 때, ¹⁸⁹저는 저희에게 인터넷 이용에 대한 비용 또한 청구되었다는 것을 알아차렸습니다. ^{189/190}저희에게 잘못 청구된 금액을 가능한 한 빨리 제게 환불해주십시오. ¹⁹⁰저는 또한 이것이 완료되었을 때 제게 누군가가 알려주길 원합니다. 귀하께서는 555-3938로 제게 연락하실 수 있습니다. 감사합니다.

Claude Symonds 드림
Edge 의류사

exhibitor n. 출품 회사, 출품자 bill n. 청구서 notice v. 알아차리다
charge v. (비용을) 청구하다 mistakenly adv. 잘못하여

186 목적 찾기 문제 하 ●○○

해석 이메일의 목적은 무엇인가?
(A) 몇몇 업무를 맡기기 위해
(B) 가격 견적서를 요청하기 위해
(C) 몇몇 항의를 하기 위해
(D) 다가오는 행사를 연기하기 위해

해설 이메일의 'I'll need you to find a replacement by the end of this week'에서 이번 주말까지 당신이 대신할 사람을 구했으면 한다고 한 뒤 부스를 빌리는 것과 관련한 여러 업무들을 요청하고 있으므로 (A)가 정답이다.

어휘 assign v. 맡기다, 배정하다 price estimate phr. 가격 견적서
postpone v. 연기하다 upcoming adj. 다가오는, 곧 있을

187 추론 문제 연계 상 ●●●

해석 Fredericton 스타일 박람회에 대해 추론될 수 있는 것은?
(A) 총 4일 동안 지속되었다.
(B) 늦게 문을 여는 출품 회사들에게 벌금을 부과한다.
(C) 모델들이 패션 업계에서 일을 찾도록 도와준다.
(D) 그것의 웹사이트에서 출품 회사들의 상품을 홍보했다.

해설 이메일의 'As for a booth, ~ rent one for the entire duration of the event.'에서 부스에 관해서는 이 행사, 즉 Fredericton 스타일 박람회의 전체 기간 동안 사용할 하나를 빌려 달라고 했다. 또한, 송장의 'Rental charge: $320 ($80 daily rental×4 days)'에서는 부스 대여 비용이 총 320달러로 일일 대여료 80달러를 총 4일간 지불했음을 확인할 수 있다.
두 단서를 종합할 때, Fredericton 스타일 박람회 행사의 전체 기간이 총 4일이었다는 사실을 추론할 수 있다. 따라서 (A)가 정답이다.

어휘 last v. 지속되다 penalty n. 벌금, 불이익

188 Not/True 문제 중 ●●○

해석 모든 부스 대여에 포함되지 않는 것은?
(A) 박람회 티켓
(B) 가구
(C) 전등
(D) 보관 공간

해설 질문의 booth rental과 관련된 내용이 언급된 송장의 'The following are available for an extra fee:', 'Storage rental: $15 per day'에서 추가 요금으로 이용 가능한 목록에 하루 15달러 요금의 보관소 대여가 있으므로 보관소 대여가 모든 부스 대여에 포함되지 않는다는 것을 알 수 있다. 따라서 (D)가 정답이다. 'Booth rentals include ~ event tickets, ~ table, ~ chairs, ~ lighting'에서 부스 대여는 행사 티켓, 테이블, 의자, 그리고 조명을 포함한다고 했으므로 (A), (B), (C)는 지문의 내용과 일치한다.

패러프레이징

table, ~ chairs 테이블, 의자 → furniture 가구
lighting 조명 → lights 전등

189 추론 문제 연계   중 ●●○

해석   Mr. Symonds는 행사의 각 날에 얼마를 과잉 청구받았을 것 같은가?

(A) 10달러
(B) 15달러
(C) 20달러
(D) 50달러

해설   편지의 'I noticed that we were also charged for access to the Internet. Please refund me the amount ~ mistakenly charged'에서 편지의 발신자인 Mr. Symonds가 자신들에게 인터넷 이용에 대한 비용 또한 청구되었다는 것을 알아차렸으며, 잘못 청구된 금액을 자신에게 환불해 달라고 했다. 또한, 송장의 'Wi-Fi access: $10 per day'에서는 와이파이 이용에 대한 비용이 하루 10달러임을 확인할 수 있다.

두 단서를 종합할 때, Mr. Symonds는 인터넷 이용에 대한 비용, 즉 하루 10달러씩을 행사 각 날에 과잉 청구받았다는 사실을 추론할 수 있다. 따라서 (A)가 정답이다.

어휘   overcharge v. 과잉 청구하다

190 육하원칙 문제   중 ●●○

해석   Mr. Symonds는 왜 Fredericton 스타일 박람회의 직원이 그에게 연락할 것을 요청하는가?

(A) 청구서가 부정확했던 이유를 설명하기 위해
(B) 환불이 완료되었음을 그에게 알려주기 위해
(C) 환불을 요청하는 방법을 설명하기 위해
(D) 어디서 대금이 지불될 수 있는지 그에게 알려주기 위해

해설   편지의 'Please refund me the amount ~ mistakenly charged'와 'I would also like someone to let me know when this has been done.'에서 잘못 청구된 금액을 자신 즉, Mr. Symonds에게 환불해달라고 하며, 이것이 완료되었을 때 누군가, 즉 Fredericton 스타일 박람회 직원이 자신에게 알려주길 원한다고 했으므로 (B)가 정답이다.

어휘   inaccurate adj. 부정확한

191-195번은 다음 후기, 이메일, 그리고 건물 목록에 관한 문제입니다.

www.cityrank.com
홈 | 순위 | **후기** | 소개 | 연락처
당신은 여기에 있습니다: 후기 > 미네소타 > 미니애폴리스

전반적으로 멋진 도시!
2월 16일에 Randy S.에 의해 게시됨

저는 지난 12년 동안 여기에서 살았고, 저는 이곳을 사랑합니다. 이곳은 소도시의 느낌을 지닌 대도시입니다. 주민들은 주로 젊고, 세련되며, 대부분의 사람들은 꽤 따뜻하고 친절합니다. 저는 192-C취업 시장이 호전되고 있다는 것도 들었습니다. 192-A많은 소비재 상품에 대한 세금과 가격은 전국의 평균보다 더 높을 수 있지만, 이 도시는 신뢰할 수 있는 공공 서비스들을 제공합니다. 집들도 알맞은 가격이며, 볼 것과 할 것들이 정말 많습니다. 191그것의 훌륭한 미술관들, 극장들, 공원들, 소매점들, 그리고 식당들과 함께, 미니애폴리스는 모든 것이 다루어져 있습니다. 게다가 192-B/193이 도시는 매우 편리한 철도 및 버스 시스템을 갖추고 있어서, 193개인 차량 없이 돌아다니는 것을 수월하게 합니다. 192-D제가 생각할 수 있는 유일한 나쁜 점은 겨울 동안의 매서운 추위입니다. 이사를 고려하는 누구에게나, 저는 미니애폴리스를 당신의 집으로 만들라고 말합니다!

population n. 주민, 사람들, 인구   predominantly adv. 주로

---

sophisticated adj. 세련된   improve v. 호전되다, 개선되다
consumer goods phr. 소비재 상품   average n. 평균; adj. 평균의
dependable adj. 신뢰할 수 있는   affordable adj. 알맞은 가격의
retail outlet phr. 소매점   convenient adj. 편리한
personal adj. 개인의, 사적인   severe adj. 매서운, 혹독한
consider v. 고려하다, 숙고하다   move n. 이사

수신: Linda Hamdi <l.hamdi@archerrealty.com>
발신: Mitch Myers <m.myers@minimail.com>
제목: 문의
날짜: 5월 3일

안녕하세요 Linda,

저는 Bio-link Resources사의 Ethel Johnston에 의해 당신을 소개받았습니다. 저는 최근에 그들과 함께 하는 일을 맡았고, 그녀가 미니애폴리스에서 임차할 장소에 대해서 제가 당신에게 연락할 것을 제안했습니다. 저는 현재 이곳 시카고에 있는 방 두 개짜리 아파트에 대해 1,800달러를 지불하고 있습니다. 저는 1,400달러 이내로 비슷한 것을 원합니다. 그리고 193제가 차를 가지고 있지 않을 것이기 때문에, 저는 그것이 제 사무실에서 걸어갈 수 있는 거리 내에 있으면 좋겠습니다. 또한, 제 아내와 저는 야외에서 있는 것을 좋아해서, 195공원과 가까운 것이 최고일 것입니다. 저희의 예정 도착일은 6월 초입니다. 가능한 한 빨리 연락을 주시면 고맙겠습니다. 감사합니다!

Mitch Myers 드림

refer v. 소개하다, 참고하다   no more than phr. ~이내의
distance n. 거리   outdoors adv. 야외에서   arrival n. 도착

Archer 부동산
www.archerrealty.com

건물 목록들
5월 4일에 Linda Hamdi에 의해 작성됨

고객명: Mr. Mitch Myers
연락처: 555-2934
이메일: m.myers@minimail.com
194-A**예정 전입일**: 6월 3일

2615번지 Logan가 — 1,350달러
· 견목 바닥, 체육관, 비즈니스 센터, 194-C침실 2개 포함
· 194-B최소 2년 임대

1611번지 Plymouth가 — 1,050달러
· 애완동물 허용, 지정 주차, Plymouth 쇼핑센터에 가까움, 194-C침실 2개
· 194-B최소 6개월 임대

195**1311번지 N 17번가 — 1,220달러**
· 충분한 주차 공간, 195North Commons 공원에 가까움, 194-C침실 2개
· 194-B최소 1년 임대

2020번지 Golden Valley로 — 1,300달러
· Golden Valley 기차역 및 Sacred 심장 병원에 가까움, 194-C침실 2개
· 194-B최소 1년 임대

property n. 건물, 부동산   feature v. (특별히) 포함하다
reserved adj. 지정된, 예약된   ample adj. 충분한

191 동의어 찾기 문제   중 ●●○

해석 후기에서, 1문단 여섯 번째 줄의 단어 "covered"는 의미상 ―와 가장 가깝다.
(A) 차지된
(B) 보고된
(C) 처리된
(D) 기대된

해설 후기의 covered를 포함한 문장 'With its great galleries, theaters, ~ Minneapolis has everything covered.'에서 훌륭한 미술관들, 극장들과 함께 미니애폴리스는 모든 것이 다루어져 있다고 했으므로 covered는 '다뤄진'이라는 뜻으로 사용되었다. 따라서 '처리된'이라는 뜻을 가진 (C) taken care of가 정답이다.

192 Not/True 문제   하 ●○○

해석 미니애폴리스에 대해 언급된 것은?
(A) 다른 도시들보다 더 낮은 세금을 가지고 있다.
(B) 대중교통에 대한 선택권이 거의 없다.
(C) 높은 실업률을 가지고 있다.
(D) 매우 추운 날씨를 가지고 있다.

해설 후기의 'The only negative thing ~ is the severe cold during winter.'에서 유일한 나쁜 점은 겨울 동안의 매서운 추위라고 했으므로 (D)가 지문의 내용과 일치한다. 따라서 (D)가 정답이다. (A)는 'Taxes ~ for many consumer goods may be higher than the national average'에서 많은 소비재 상품에 대한 세금이 전국의 평균보다 더 높을 수 있다고 했으므로 지문의 내용과 일치하지 않는다. (B)는 'the city has a very convenient rail and bus system'에서 이 도시가 매우 편리한 철도 및 버스 시스템을 갖추고 있다고 했으므로 지문의 내용과 일치하지 않는다. (C)는 'the job market is improving'에서 취업 시장이 호전되고 있다고 했으므로 지문의 내용과 일치하지 않는다.

어휘 unemployment n. 실업(률)

패러프레이징

severe cold 매서운 추위 → extremely cold weather 매우 추운 날씨

최고난도 문제

193 추론 문제 연계   상 ●●●

해석 미니애폴리스의 어떤 측면이 Mr. Myers의 흥미를 끌 것 같은가?
(A) 호화로운 주택들
(B) 편리한 대중교통
(C) 호전되는 취업 시장
(D) 최신 유행의 소매점들

해설 이메일의 'I won't have a car'에서 자신, 즉 Mr. Myers가 차를 가지고 있지 않을 것이라고 했다. 또한, 후기의 'the city has a very convenient rail and bus system, making it easy to get around without a personal vehicle'에서는 이 도시, 즉 미니애폴리스는 매우 편리한 철도 및 버스 시스템을 갖추고 있어서, 개인 차량 없이도 수월하게 돌아다닐 수 있다고 했다. 두 단서를 종합할 때, Mr. Myers는 차를 가지고 있지 않으므로 개인 차량 없이도 수월하게 돌아다닐 수 있게 해주는 편리한 대중교통 시스템에 흥미를 가질 것이라는 사실을 추론할 수 있다. 따라서 (B)가 정답이다.

어휘 luxury adj. 호화로운   trendy adj. 최신 유행의, 유행을 쫓는

패러프레이징

rail and bus system 철도 및 버스 시스템 → public transportation 대중교통

194 Not/True 문제   상 ●●●

해석 Ms. Hamdi에 의해 열거된 건물들에 대해 암시되지 않는 것은?
(A) 6월 초에 이용 가능할 것이다.
(B) 임대 계약을 요구한다.
(C) 한 개 이상의 침실을 가지고 있다.
(D) 도시의 남쪽에 위치해 있다.

해설 질문의 properties listed by Ms. Hamdi와 관련된 내용이 언급된 건물 목록에서 (D)는 언급되지 않은 내용이다. 따라서 (D)가 정답이다. (A)는 'Expected move-in: June 3'에서 6월 3일이 예정 전입일이므로 이때 열거된 건물들이 이용 가능하다는 것을 알 수 있으므로 지문의 내용과 일치한다. (B)는 'Minimum two-year lease', 'Minimum six-month lease', 'Minimum one-year lease', 'Minimum one-year lease'에서 열거된 건물들이 최소 6개월에서 2년까지의 임대 계약을 요구하므로 지문의 내용과 일치한다. (C)는 'two bedrooms'에서 모든 열거된 건물들이 침실 2개를 포함하고 있으므로 지문의 내용과 일치한다.

패러프레이징

two bedrooms 침실 2개 → more than one bedroom 한 개 이상의 침실

195 추론 문제 연계   상 ●●●

해석 Mr. Myers는 어느 장소에 관심이 있을 것 같은가?
(A) 2615번지 Logan가
(B) 1611번지 Plymouth가
(C) 1311번지 N 17번가
(D) 2020번지 Golden Valley로

해설 이메일의 'something close to a park would be best'에서 Mr. Myers가 공원과 가까운 것이 최고일 것이라고 했다. 또한, 건물 목록의 '1311 N 17th Avenue', 'convenient to North Commons Park'에서는 1311번지 N 17번가가 North Commons 공원에서 가깝다는 것을 확인할 수 있다. 두 단서를 종합할 때, Mr. Myers는 North Commons 공원에서 가까운 1311번지 N 17번가에 관심이 있을 것이라는 사실을 추론할 수 있다. 따라서 (C)가 정답이다.

196-200번은 다음 웹페이지, 이메일, 그리고 후기에 관한 문제입니다.

La Mesa		
소개	예약	연락처

30년이 넘게, La Mesa는 정통 스페인 요리를 즐기는 시애틀 주민들에 의해 선택되는 식당이었습니다. 주인인 ¹⁹⁶⁻ᴮJose Garcia 셰프는 스페인의 안달루시아 지역의 요리 방식을 전문으로 하는데, 이곳은 그가 태어나고 자란 곳입니다. 비록 그가 준비하는 모든 음식이 훌륭하지만, 사람들은 ²⁰⁰그의 네 가지 가장 유명한 요리를 맛보기 위해 먼 지역들에서 옵니다:

가스파초: 식초와 다양한 채소를 포함하는 상쾌한 차가운 수프. 더운 여름날에 최고!

푸체로: 쇠고기, 감자, 그리고 계절 채소로 만든 푸짐한 스튜. 집에서 만든 빵과 함께 제공.

토르티야 데 파타타스: 계란, 양파, 그리고 감자가 매운 소시지와 혼합되어 완벽한 오믈렛을 만듦.

²⁰⁰페스카이토 프리토: 시장에서 갓 들어와서 완벽하게 튀겨진 생선.

resident n. 주민   authentic adj. 정통의   cuisine n. 요리

specialize in phr. ~을 전문으로 하다
signature dish phr. 요리사의 가장 유명한 요리 refreshing adj. 상쾌한
vinegar n. 식초 seasonal adj. 계절의 combine v. 혼합시키다

발신: Sally Mendez < s.mendez@lamesa.com>
수신: Kyle Graves <k.graves@aceair.com>
제목: 서비스 요청
날짜: 8월 2일

Mr. Graves께,

저희 식당의 에어컨 중 하나가 제대로 작동하지 않고 있습니다. [197]귀사의 직원이 지난달에 수리한 부엌에 있는 에어컨은 괜찮으나, 이제는 프라이빗 다이닝룸에 있는 에어컨이 완전히 작동을 멈췄습니다. [198]이 문제를 해결하기 위해 다른 기술자를 식당으로 보내주실 수 있나요? 저희는 매일 오전 11시 30분에 문을 열기 때문에, 귀사의 기술자가 아침 일찍 올 수 있다면 좋겠습니다.

저는 가능한 한 빨리 이것이 해결되길 원합니다. [199]메인 다이닝룸의 테이블 중 어느 것도 충분히 크지 않기 때문에, 이 프라이빗 다이닝룸은 저희가 15명 이상의 단체를 수용할 수 있는 유일한 선택지입니다. 저 방에 있는 에어컨이 작동하지 않아서 예약을 취소해야 하는 것은 막을 수 있으면 좋겠습니다. 감사합니다.

Sally Mendez 드림
총지배인, La Mesa

properly adv. 제대로 completely adv. 완전히 technician n. 기술자
accommodate v. 수용하다 avoid v. 피하다 reservation n. 예약

식당: La Mesa
후기 작성자: David Porter
날짜: 8월 5일
점수: 4/5

저는 저희 회사 최고경영자의 퇴직 기념 파티를 8월 4일에 La Mesa에서 열도록 준비했습니다. 전반적으로, 모든 사람들이 이 식당에 깊은 인상을 받았습니다. 식당은 깨끗하고 편안했으며, 인테리어는 매우 편안한 분위기를 만들어냈습니다. 게다가, 특히 [199]우리 일행에 18명이 있었다는 것을 고려하면 서비스는 훌륭했습니다. 저희에게 배정된 웨이터는 친절하고 유능했습니다. 음식에 관해서는, 우리 대부분이 우리가 주문했던 요리에 매우 만족했습니다. 저는 셰프가 확실히 정통 스페인 요리법과 양념들을 사용하려고 했다는 것이 특히 마음에 들었습니다. 하지만, [200]저는 셰프의 가장 유명한 요리 중 하나인 해산물 요리를 먹었는데, 그것은 약간 너무 구워졌었습니다.

retirement n. 퇴직, 은퇴 decor n. 인테리어, 실내장식
atmosphere n. 분위기 assign v. 배정하다 obviously adv. 확실히
seasoning n. 양념 overcooked adj. 너무 구워진

196 Not/True 문제 중 ●●○

해석 Mr. Garcia에 대해 언급된 것은?
(A) 몇몇 식당들을 운영한다.
(B) 스페인에서 태어났다.
(C) 최근에 시애틀로 이사했다.
(D) 요리학교에 다닌 적이 있다.

해설 웹페이지의 'Chef Jose Garcia, specializes in the cooking style of the Andalusia region of Spain, which is where he was born and raised'에서 셰프인 Mr. Garcia는 스페인의 안달루시아 지역의 요리 방식

을 전문으로 하며 이곳이 그가 태어나고 자란 곳이라고 했으므로 (B)가 정답이다. (A), (C), (D)는 지문에 언급되지 않은 내용이다.

어휘 operate v. 운영하다 relocate v. 이사하다, 이동하다
attend school phr. 학교에 다니다 culinary adj. 요리의

197 육하원칙 문제 하 ●○○

해석 이메일에 따르면, 지난달에 무슨 일이 있었는가?
(A) 부엌이 개조되었다.
(B) 직원이 승진되었다.
(C) 기기가 수리되었다.
(D) 메뉴가 업데이트되었다.

해설 이메일의 'The air conditioner in the kitchen ~ fixed last month is fine'에서 지난달에 수리한 부엌에 있는 에어컨은 괜찮다고 했으므로 (C)가 정답이다.

어휘 remodel v. 개조하다 promote v. 승진시키다
appliance n. 기기, 가전제품 repair v. 수리하다

패러프레이징

air conditioner 에어컨 → appliance 기기

198 육하원칙 문제 중 ●●○

해석 Ms. Mendez는 Mr. Graves에게 무엇을 해달라고 요청하는가?
(A) 몇몇 장비를 주문한다
(B) 작업자를 보낸다
(C) 몇몇 가구를 수리한다
(D) 예약을 확정한다

해설 이메일의 'Would you be able to send another technician to the restaurant to deal with this problem?'에서 이메일 작성자인 Ms. Mendez가 이메일 수신자인 Mr. Graves에게 이 문제를 해결하기 위해 다른 기술자를 식당으로 보내줄 수 있는지 물었으므로 (B)가 정답이다.

어휘 equipment n. 장비, 기구 confirm v. 확정하다, 확인하다

패러프레이징

send ~ technician 기술자를 보내다 → Send a worker 작업자를 보내다

199 추론 문제 연계 상 ●●●

해석 Mr. Porter에 대해 암시되는 것은?
(A) 그의 동료들과 함께 다른 행사를 준비하고 있다.
(B) La Mesa에서 디저트 식사를 하지 않기로 결심했다.
(C) 머지않아 그의 회사에서 은퇴할 것이다.
(D) 식당의 메인 구역에 앉지 않았다.

해설 후기의 'there were 18 people in our party'에서 우리, 즉 Mr. Porter가 속한 일행에 18명이 있었다고 했다. 또한, 이메일의 'The private dining room is the only option we have to accommodate groups of 15 or more, as none of the tables in the main dining room are large enough.'에서는 메인 다이닝룸의 테이블 중 어느 것도 충분히 크지 않기 때문에, 이 프라이빗 다이닝룸이 식당이 15명 이상의 단체를 수용할 수 있는 유일한 선택지라는 사실을 확인할 수 있다.
두 단서를 종합할 때, Mr. Porter가 속한 일행은 15명 이상인 18명이었으므로 메인 다이닝룸이 아닌 프라이빗 다이닝룸에서 식사를 했다는 것을 추론할 수 있다. 따라서 (D)가 정답이다.

어휘 coworker n. 동료 retire v. 은퇴하다, 퇴직하다

해석   Mr. Porter가 어느 요리를 시켰을 것 같은가?
      (A) 가스파초
      (B) 푸체로
      (C) 토르티야 데 파타타스
      (D) 페스카이토 프리토

해설   후기의 'I had the seafood dish, one of the chef's signature dish'에서 저, 즉 Mr. Porter가 셰프의 가장 유명한 요리 중 하나인 해산물 요리를 먹었다고 했다. 또한, 웹페이지의 'his four signature dishes'와 '*Pescaito Frito*: Fish ~ fried to perfection.'에서는 셰프의 가장 유명한 요리 중에 완벽하게 튀겨진 생선인 페스카이토 프리토가 있음을 확인할 수 있다.
      두 단서를 종합할 때, Mr. Porter가 해산물 요리를 시켰으므로 셰프의 가장 유명한 요리 중 유일한 해산물 요리인 *페스카이토 프리토*를 시켰다는 것을 추론할 수 있다. 따라서 (D)가 정답이다.

TEST 9

PART 5

101 (B)	102 (D)	103 (B)	104 (A)	105 (B)
106 (C)	107 (B)	108 (C)	109 (B)	110 (C)
111 (D)	112 (C)	113 (C)	114 (C)	115 (C)
116 (B)	117 (B)	118 (C)	119 (B)	120 (C)
121 (C)	122 (B)	123 (A)	124 (C)	125 (D)
126 (C)	127 (C)	128 (B)	129 (D)	130 (B)

PART 6

131 (B)	132 (D)	133 (D)	134 (A)	135 (C)
136 (D)	137 (D)	138 (A)	139 (A)	140 (C)
141 (B)	142 (A)	143 (A)	144 (A)	145 (D)
146 (A)				

PART 7

147 (C)	148 (D)	149 (C)	150 (C)	151 (C)
152 (D)	153 (B)	154 (C)	155 (D)	156 (A)
157 (B)	158 (D)	159 (C)	160 (C)	161 (B)
162 (A)	163 (B)	164 (B)	165 (D)	166 (A)
167 (B)	168 (C)	169 (B)	170 (B)	171 (B)
172 (B)	173 (C)	174 (C)	175 (C)	176 (D)
177 (B)	178 (C)	179 (A)	180 (D)	181 (D)
182 (C)	183 (A)	184 (C)	185 (D)	186 (C)
187 (D)	188 (B)	189 (B)	190 (D)	191 (D)
192 (B)	193 (D)	194 (D)	195 (B)	196 (C)
197 (C)	198 (A)	199 (C)	200 (B)	

PART 5

101 부사 자리 채우기 · 하 ●○○

해석 해외에서 수입된 농산물들은 일반적으로 높은 가격에 판매된다.

해설 동사(are sold)를 꾸밀 수 있는 것은 부사이므로 부사 (B) generally (일반적으로, 대체로)가 정답이다. 형용사 또는 명사 (A), 동사 또는 과거분사 (C), 명사 (D)는 부사 자리에 올 수 없다. 명사 (A)와 (D)를 be동사(are)의 보어로 보고 sold ~ prices가 명사를 꾸미는 것으로 본다 해도, '농산물들은 높은 가격에 판매되는 육군 대장/보편성이다'라는 어색한 문맥을 만든다.

어휘 agricultural product phr. 농산물 import v. 수입하다 overseas n. 해외, 외국; adv. 해외로 general adj. 일반적인; n. (육군) 대장 generalize v. 일반화하다

102 5형식 동사의 수동태 · 상 ●●●

해석 Erin Costa는 독일에 있는 Biogant사의 연구부서장으로 임명되었으며, 가을에 그곳으로 이동할 것이다.

해설 첫 번째 절(Erin Costa ~ Germany)에 동사가 없으므로 동사인 모든 보기가 정답의 후보이다. 보기의 동사 name(임명하다)은 목적어와 목적격 보어를 갖는 5형식 동사인데, 빈칸 뒤에 목적격 보어(head of Biogant's research department)만 있고, 'Erin Costa는 연구부서장으로 임명되었다'라는 수동의 의미가 되어야 하므로 수동태 (D) has been named가 정답이다. 능동태 (A), (B), (C)를 쓸 경우 동사 다음에 목적어와 목적격 보어가 모두 와야 한다. 참고로, 이 문장은 동사 name이 수동태로 쓰이면서 목적어(Erin Costa)가 주어 자리에 오고 목적격 보어(head of Biogant's research department)가 동사 뒤에 남은 형태임을 알아둔다.

103 부사절 접속사 채우기 · 상 ●●●

해석 만일 연사가 제시간에 강의를 마친다면, 6시에 축하 연회가 열릴 것이다.

해설 이 문장은 주어(The reception)와 동사(will take place)를 갖춘 완전한 절이므로 ___ ~ time은 수식어 거품으로 보아야 한다. 이 수식어 거품은 동사(finishes)가 있는 거품절이므로, 거품절을 이끌 수 있는 부사절 접속사 (A), (B), (C)가 정답의 후보이다. '만일 연사가 제시간에 강의를 마친다면, 6시에 축하 연회가 열릴 것이다'라는 문맥이므로 (B) provided(만일 ~이라면)가 정답이다. 접속부사 (D)는 수식어 거품을 이끌 수 없다.

어휘 reception n. (축하) 연회 take place phr. 열리다 on time phr. 제시간에 so that phr. ~할 수 있도록 as if phr. 마치 ~처럼 otherwise adv. 그렇지 않으면

104 명사 어휘 고르기 · 중 ●●○

해석 Quora 카페의 주인들은 그들의 새로운 메뉴를 광고하는 안내문을 마을 곳곳에 게시했다.

해설 빈칸은 동사(posted)의 목적어 역할을 하는 명사 자리이다. '카페의 주인들은 새로운 메뉴를 광고하는 안내문을 게시했다'라는 문맥이므로 (A) notices(안내문, 공고문)가 정답이다.

어휘 post v. 게시하다, 공고하다 measure n. 수단, 조치; v. 측정하다 record n. 기록; v. 기록하다 contract n. 계약(서); v. 계약하다, 줄어들다

105 수, 태, 시제에 맞는 동사 채우기 · 상 ●●●

해석 모든 회의 참석자들은 많은 유용한 정보를 배운 것에 대해 만족을 표했다.

해설 문장에 동사가 없으므로 동사 (A), (B), (D)가 정답의 후보이다. 빈칸 뒤에 목적어(satisfaction)가 있고, 주어(All of the conference attendees)가 복수이므로 능동태 복수 동사 (B) expressed가 정답이다. 수동태 (A)는 목적어를 취할 수 없다. 단수 동사 (D)는 단수 주어와 함께 쓰여야 한다. 동명사 또는 현재분사 (C)는 동사 자리에 올 수 없다.

어휘 conference n. 회의 attendee n. 참석자 useful adj. 유용한 express v. 표하다, 나타내다

106 명사 자리 채우기 하 ●○○

해석 Elevai 유람선 회사의 최신 배들은 다양한 식당과 오락 선택권을 특징으로 한다.

해설 타동사(feature)의 목적어 자리에 오면서 형용사(large)의 꾸밈을 받을 수 있는 것은 명사이므로 명사 (C) selection(선택, 선정)이 정답이다. 동사 또는 과거분사 (A), 형용사 (B), 동사 또는 형용사 (D)는 명사 자리에 올 수 없다. 참고로, a large[wide] selection of(다양한)를 관용구로 알아둔다.

어휘 feature v. ~을 특징으로 하다 dining n. 식당
entertainment n. 오락(거리) selective adj. 선택적인, 선별적인
select v. 선택하다; adj. 엄선된

107 형용사 어휘 고르기 중 ●●○

해석 전문가들에 따르면, 엄격한 규제가 시행되지 않으면 대기 오염이 악화될 수 있다.

해설 빈칸은 명사(regulations)를 꾸미는 형용사 자리이다. '엄격한 규제가 시행되지 않으면 대기 오염이 악화될 수 있다'라는 문맥이므로 (B) strict(엄격한)가 정답이다.

어휘 pollution n. 오염 worsen v. 악화되다 unless conj. ~하지 않으면
regulation n. 규제 enforce v. 시행하다 curious adj. 호기심 많은
equal adj. 동등한 hazardous adj. 위험한

108 명사절 접속사 채우기 중 ●●○

해석 그 책은 당신이 가지고 있는 식물이 어느 것이든 간에 당신에게 어떻게 그것을 보살필지에 대한 조언들을 줄 수 있다.

해설 to 부정사구(to care for)의 목적어 자리에 온 명사절(___ ~ have)의 명사(plants)를 꾸밀 수 있는 것은 형용사이므로, 형용사 역할을 할 수 있는 의문형용사 (B)와 복합관계형용사 (C)가 정답의 후보이다. '그 책은 당신이 가지고 있는 식물이 어느 것이든 간에 당신에게 조언들을 줄 수 있다'라는 의미가 되어야 하므로 복합관계형용사 (C) whichever(어느 것이든 간에)가 정답이다. 의문형용사 (B)는 '어떤 식물을 가지고 있는지를 보살핀다'라는 어색한 문맥을 만든다. 관계부사 (A)와 복합관계대명사 (D)는 명사를 꾸밀 수 없다.

어휘 tip n. 조언, 팁 care for phr. ~을 보살피다 whoever n. 누구든 ~하는 사람

109 명사 관련 어구 완성하기 상 ●●●

해석 Piercent Cosmetics사는 외국 고객들을 상대할 영업사원을 구하고 있다.

해설 빈칸은 명사(sales)와 복합 명사를 이루어 전치사(for)의 목적어 역할을 하는 명사 자리이다. '외국 고객들을 상대할 영업사원'이라는 의미이므로 빈칸 앞의 명사 sales와 함께 쓰여 '영업사원'이라는 의미의 어구 sales associate를 만드는 (B) associate(사원)가 정답이다. (A) character도 '사람, 인물'이라는 의미로 해석상 그럴듯해 보이지만, 성질을 나타내는 형용사 뒤에 와서 '~한 사람'이라는 의미를 나타낸다.

어휘 look for phr. ~을 찾다 deal with phr. ~을 상대하다
foreign adj. 외국의 proprietor n. 소유주 attribute n. 속성, 자질

110 강조 부사 채우기 중 ●●○

해석 그 식당은 무료 디저트에 더하여 심지어 20퍼센트 할인까지 제공한다.

해설 '식당은 무료 디저트에 더하여 심지어 20퍼센트 할인까지 제공한다'라는 의미가 되어야 하므로 단어나 구를 앞에서 강조하는 강조 부사 (C) even(심지어)이 정답이다.

어휘 in addition to phr. ~에 더하여 yet adv. 아직 quite adv. 꽤

far adv. 훨씬

111 상관접속사 채우기 상 ●●●

해석 경영진의 목표는 협업뿐만 아니라, 혁신에 도움이 되는 분위기를 조성하는 것이다.

해설 단어(innovation)와 단어(collaboration)를 연결할 수 있고, '경영진의 목표는 협업뿐만 아니라, 혁신에 도움이 되는 분위기를 조성하는 것이다'라는 문맥이므로 상관접속사 (D) as well as(~뿐만 아니라)가 정답이다. 상관접속사 (A)는 or와 함께 either A or B(A 또는 B 중 하나)의 형태로 쓰인다. 전치사 (B)는 빈칸 뒤의 명사(collaboration)를 목적어로 취하는 수식어 거품구로 볼 수 있으나, '경영진의 목표는 협업에도 불구하고, 혁신에 도움이 되는 분위기를 조성하는 것이다'라는 어색한 문맥을 만든다. 접속부사 (C)는 단어와 단어를 연결할 수 없다.

어휘 administration n. 경영진 atmosphere n. 분위기
conducive to phr. ~에 도움이 되는 innovation n. 혁신

112 명사 어휘 고르기 상 ●●●

해석 채용 담당자들은 마케팅 부서 내 몇몇 공석에 대한 지원서들을 검토할 것이다.

해설 빈칸은 전치사(for)의 목적어 역할을 하면서 형용사(several)의 꾸밈을 받는 명사 자리이다. '채용 담당자들은 몇몇 공석에 대한 지원서들을 검토할 것이다'라는 문맥이므로 (C) openings(공석)가 정답이다.

어휘 application n. 지원서 document n. 서류
description n. 설명서, 설명 issue n. 문제, 사안

113 전치사 채우기 하 ●○○

해석 비용을 아끼기 위해 금요일 대신에 목요일에 회의가 열렸다.

해설 빈칸은 명사(Friday)를 목적어로 취하는 전치사 자리이다. '비용을 아끼기 위해 금요일 대신에 목요일에 회의가 열렸다'라는 의미가 되어야 하므로 (C) instead of(~ 대신에)가 정답이다.

어휘 save v. 아끼다 such as phr. ~과 같은 due to phr. ~ 때문에
regardless of phr. ~에 상관없이

114 동사 어휘 고르기 중 ●●○

해석 그 워크숍은 장차 기업인이 될 사람들에게 다양한 필수적인 사업 기능들을 수행하는 방법을 가르친다.

해설 빈칸은 빈칸 앞의 to와 함께 to 부정사를 만드는 동사원형 자리이다. '다양한 필수적인 사업 기능들을 수행하는 방법'이라는 문맥이므로 (C) perform(수행하다, 해내다)이 정답이다.

어휘 aspiring adj. 장차 ~이 될 entrepreneur n. 기업인
essential adj. 필수적인 function n. 기능 impress v. 깊은 인상을 주다
convene v. 소집하다 affect v. ~에 영향을 미치다

115 부사 어휘 고르기 중 ●●○

해석 Mr. Branson은 Turnbull 국제공항의 직원이 그에게 연락한 후 즉시 그의 수하물을 찾아오기 위해 떠났다.

해설 빈칸은 동사(left)를 꾸미는 부사 자리이다. '직원이 그에게 연락한 후 즉시 그의 수하물을 찾아오기 위해 떠났다'라는 문맥이므로 (C) instantly(즉시)가 정답이다.

어휘 luggage n. 수하물, 짐 representative n. 직원 firstly adv. 첫째로
closely adv. 면밀히, 가까이 expertly adv. 전문적으로, 훌륭하게

116 동사 관련 어구 완성하기 중 ●●○

해석 사용하지 않는 땅을 개발하는 것에 앞서, Kinsport 부동산은 시와 합의에 도달해야 한다.

해설 빈칸은 조동사(must) 뒤에 오는 동사원형 자리이다. 'Kinsport 부동산은 시와 합의에 도달해야 한다'라는 문맥이므로 빈칸 뒤의 명사 agreement(합의)와 함께 '합의에 도달하다'라는 의미의 어구 reach an agreement를 만드는 (B) reach(도달하다)가 정답이다.

어휘 prior to phr. ~에 앞서 unused adj. 사용하지 않는 occupy v. 차지하다 reserve v. 예약하다, 유보하다 alert v. 경계시키다; adj. 경계하는

117 동사 어휘 고르기 중 ●●○

해석 직원들은 상사의 승인을 받기 위해 금요일까지 제안서를 제출해야 한다.

해설 빈칸은 조동사(should) 뒤에 오는 동사원형 자리이다. '직원들은 제안서를 제출해야 한다'라는 문맥이므로 (B) submit(제출하다)이 정답이다.

어휘 proposal n. 제안(서) supervisor n. 상사, 감독관 approval n. 승인 resign v. 사임하다 compel v. 강요하다 command v. 명령하다

최고난도 문제

118 부사 자리 채우기 상 ●●●

해석 그 도시가 새로운 정책을 채택한 이후 그것이 모아온 세금의 액수는 확실히 증가했다.

해설 동사(has grown)를 꾸밀 수 있는 것은 부사이므로 부사 (C) reliably(확실히)가 정답이다. 형용사 (A), 명사 (B)와 (D)는 부사 자리에 올 수 없다. 동사 grow를 '기르다, 사육하다'라는 의미의 타동사로 보고 명사 (B)와 (D)를 목적어로 보면 각각 '세금의 액수가 의존/신뢰도를 길렀다'라는 의미로 해석상 그럴듯해 보이지만, 타동사 grow는 식물이나 동물 등을 기르는 것을 나타내므로 답이 될 수 없다.

어휘 collect v. 모으다 adopt v. 채택하다 reliable adj. 신뢰할 수 있는

최고난도 문제

119 보어 자리 채우기 상 ●●●

해석 Ms. Orville은 그녀의 고객들이 그녀의 작업물에 만족되도록 하기 위해 항상 열심히 노력한다.

해설 사역동사 make의 목적격 보어 자리에는 원형 부정사나 p.p.형이 올 수 있으므로 p.p.형 (B)와 원형 부정사 (D)가 정답의 후보이다. 동사 make의 목적어(her clients)와 목적격 보어가 '고객들이 만족되다'라는 의미의 수동 관계이므로 p.p.형 (B) satisfied가 정답이다. 원형 부정사 (D)는 능동의 의미를 나타내므로 답이 될 수 없다. 명사 (A)를 빈칸 앞의 명사(clients)와 함께 복합 명사를 만드는 것으로 볼 경우 해석상 그럴듯해 보이지만, 복합 명사가 되기 위해서는 첫 번째 단어인 clients가 단수형이어야 한다. 동명사 또는 현재분사 (C)는 사역동사 make의 목적격 보어 자리에 올 수 없다.

어휘 try v. 노력하다 hard adv. 열심히 satisfaction n. 만족

120 동명사와 명사 구별하여 채우기 중 ●●○

해석 Phoenix 재단은 수요일에 자연을 보호하는 것에 대한 발표를 할 것이다.

해설 전치사(about)의 목적어 자리에 올 수 있는 것은 명사이므로 명사 (B)와 동명사 (C)가 정답의 후보이다. 명사(nature)를 목적어로 취하면서 전치사의 목적어 자리에 올 수 있는 것은 동명사이므로 동명사 (C) protecting (보호하는 것)이 정답이다. 명사 (B)는 명사 앞에 다른 명사가 연결되거나 전치

사 없이 바로 올 수 없으므로 답이 될 수 없다. 동사 (A)와 형용사 (D)는 전치사의 목적어 자리에 올 수 없다. 형용사 (D)가 명사(nature)를 꾸미는 것으로 본다 해도, '보호하는 자연(자연이 보호하다)'이라는 어색한 문맥을 만든다.

어휘 protection n. 보호

최고난도 문제

121 가산 명사와 불가산 명사 구별하여 채우기 상 ●●●

해석 Sam Park는 그의 팟캐스트 *Money Talk*에서, 금융 시장에 대해 정기적인 논평을 제공한다.

해설 타동사(provides)의 목적어 자리에 오면서 형용사(regular)의 꾸밈을 받을 수 있는 것은 명사이므로 명사 (A), (C), (D)가 정답의 후보이다. 빈칸 앞에 관사가 없으므로 불가산 명사 (C) commentary(논평)가 정답이다. 사람명사 (A) commenter(논평자, 주석자)와 (D) commentator(해설자)는 가산 명사로 관사와 함께 쓰이거나 복수형으로 쓰여야 한다. 동사 또는 과거분사 (B)는 명사 자리에 올 수 없다.

어휘 podcast n. 팟캐스트 comment v. 논평하다; n. 논평

최고난도 문제

122 부사절 접속사 채우기 상 ●●●

해석 그녀의 일에 집중하기 위해서, Ms. Heinz는 근무하는 동안 그녀의 휴대 전화를 사용하지 않는다.

해설 이 문장은 주어(Ms. Heinz), 동사(does not use), 목적어(her cell phone)를 갖춘 완전한 절이므로, ___ on duty는 수식어 거품으로 보아야 한다. 따라서 수식어 거품을 이끌 수 있는 현재분사 (A), 부사절 접속사 (B)와 (D)가 정답의 후보이다. '일에 집중하기 위해 근무하는 동안 휴대 전화를 사용하지 않는다'라는 의미가 되어야 하므로 부사절 접속사 (B) while (~하는 동안)이 정답이다. 참고로, 이 수식어 거품은 주어(Ms. Heinz)와 be동사(is)가 생략된 분사구문이다. 현재분사 (A) conducting(수행하는)도 해석상 그럴듯해 보이지만, conduct가 타동사이므로 뒤에 전치사(on) 없이 바로 목적어가 와야 한다. 부사절 접속사 (D) after(~한 후)는 뒤에 분사구문이 올 경우, 주어와 be동사가 생략된 분사구문은 올 수 없고, 주어는 생략 가능하지만 be동사가 being(being on duty) 형태로 남아야 한다. 참고로, '주어 + be동사'가 생략된 분사구문을 이끌 수 없는 부사절 접속사로는 after, before, since가 있다. 부사 (C)는 수식어 거품을 이끌 수 없다. 부사 (C) scarcely (거의 ~ 않는)가 동사 use를 수식하는 것으로 본다 해도, '일에 집중하기 위해서, 근무하는 동안 휴대전화를 거의 사용하지 않는다'라는 어색한 문맥을 만들고, 부정의 뜻을 담고 있어, 부정어 not과 함께 쓸 수 없다.

어휘 focus on phr. ~에 집중하다 cell phone phr. 휴대전화 on duty phr. 근무 중인

123 명사 자리 채우기 상 ●●●

해석 직원들은 공장 자동화가 실업으로 이어질 수 있기 때문에 그것에 대한 제안에 반대했다.

해설 전치사(to)의 목적어 자리에 올 수 있는 것은 명사이므로 명사 (A) proposals (제안, 제의)가 정답이다. 참고로, object to(~에 반대하다)를 관용구로 알아둔다. 동사 또는 과거분사 (B), 동사 (C)와 (D)는 전치사의 목적어 자리에 올 수 없다. 동사원형 (C)가 빈칸 앞의 to와 함께 to 부정사를 만드는 것으로 본다 해도, 직원들은 '공장 자동화가 실업으로 이어질 수 있기 때문에 그것을 제안하기 위해서 반대했다'라는 어색한 문맥을 만든다.

어휘 factory n. 공장 automation n. 자동화 lead to phr. ~으로 이어지다 propose v. 제안하다, 제시하다

124 동사 어휘 고르기 　　　　　상 ●●●

해석 고객들은 그들이 가지고 있는 어떠한 불만 사항이라도 우리 서비스 데스크로
보낼 수 있다.

해설 빈칸은 조동사(may) 뒤에 오는 동사원형 자리이다. '고객들은 어떠한 불만
사항이라도 서비스 데스크로 보낼 수 있다'라는 문맥이므로 (C) direct(보내
다)가 정답이다.

어휘 complaint n. 불만 사항, 불평　demand v. 요구하다
accept v. 받아들이다　engage v. 사로잡다, 고용하다

125 형용사 어휘 고르기 　　　　　상 ●●●

해석 Glenmark 밴드는 그것의 멤버들 중 한 명이 병에 걸린 후에 그것의 임박한 콘
서트를 연기했다.

해설 빈칸은 명사(concert)를 꾸미는 형용사 자리이다. '멤버들 중 한 명이 병에 걸
린 후에 그것의 임박한 콘서트를 연기했다'라는 문맥이므로 (D) impending
(임박한)이 정답이다.

어휘 fall ill phr. 병에 걸리다　postpone v. 연기하다, 미루다
instinctive adj. 본능적인　former adj. 이전의
eventful adj. 다사다난한, 파란만장한

126 가정법 동사 채우기 　　　　　상 ●●●

해석 만약 Mr. Vines가 배송이 보통 일주일 이상 걸린다는 것을 알았다면, 그는 그
의 주문을 취소했을 것이다.

해설 If절(If ~ a week)의 동사가 과거 완료 시제(had known)이고 '만약
Mr. Vines가 배송이 보통 일주일 이상 걸린다는 것을 알았다면, 그는 그
의 주문을 취소했을 것이다'라는 의미로 과거 사실의 반대를 가정하고 있
으므로 가정법 과거 완료 문장임을 알 수 있다. 따라서 가정법 과거 완료의
주절의 동사 자리에 올 수 있는 'would/could/might/should have p.p.'인
(C) would have canceled가 정답이다. 현재 완료 시제 (A)와 (B), 미래 시
제 (D)는 가정법 과거 완료의 주절의 동사 자리에 올 수 없다.

어휘 order n. 주문, 질서　cancel v. 취소하다

127 전치사 채우기 　　　　　중 ●●○

해석 스키장들은 지난 시즌에 11월 말부터 4월 중순까지 영업을 했다.

해설 이 문장은 주어(Ski resorts), 동사(were), 보어(open)를 갖춘 완전한 절이
므로, ___ ~ season은 수식어 거품으로 보아야 한다. 이 수식어 거품은 동
사가 없는 거품구이므로, 거품구를 이끌 수 있는 전치사 (A), (C), (D)가 정답
의 후보이다. '스키장들은 11월 말부터 4월 중순까지 영업을 했다'라는 의미
가 되어야 하므로 (C) from(~부터)이 정답이다. 부사절 접속사 (B)는 거품구
가 아닌 거품절을 이끈다.

어휘 ski resort phr. 스키장　open adj. 영업을 하는　late adj. 말의; adv. 늦게
into prep. ~안으로　within prep. ~이내에

128 부정대명사/형용사 채우기 　　　　　중 ●●○

해석 그 도서관의 웹사이트는 그것의 바뀐 운영 시간에 대해 아무것도 언급하지 않
았다.

해설 이 문장은 not이 있는 부정문이고, '그 도서관의 웹사이트는 그것의 바뀐
운영 시간에 대해 아무것도 언급하지 않았다'라는 문맥이므로 부정대명사
(B) anything(아무것)이 정답이다. 부정대명사 (A)와 (C)는 긍정문에 쓰인
다. 부정대명사 (D)는 '그 도서관의 웹사이트는 그것의 바뀐 운영 시간에 대
해 둘 다 언급하지 않았다'라는 어색한 문맥을 만든다.

어휘 operating hours phr. 운영 시간　some n. 몇 개, 일부; adj. 조금의, 어떤
someone n. 어떤 사람, 누구

129 전치사 채우기 　　　　　중 ●●○

해석 신입사원들은 그들의 경력 및 능력에 따라 다른 팀들에 배치될 것이다.

해설 이 문장은 주어(The new employees)와 동사(will be assigned)를 갖춘
완전한 절이므로, ___ ~ abilities는 수식어 거품으로 보아야 한다. 이 수식
어 거품은 동사가 없는 거품구이므로, 거품구를 이끌 수 있는 과거분사 (B)와
전치사구 (D)가 정답의 후보이다. 빈칸 뒤에 목적어(their ~ abilities)가 있
고 '신입사원들은 경력 및 능력에 따라 다른 팀들에 배치될 것이다'라는 의미
가 되어야 하므로 전치사구 (D) depending on(~에 따라)이 정답이다. 과거
분사 (B)는 뒤에 목적어를 취할 수 없다. 형용사 (A)와 동사 (C)는 수식어 거
품을 이끌 수 없다.

어휘 assign v. 배치하다　dependable adj. 신뢰할 수 있는
depend v. ~에 달려 있다, 신뢰하다

130 부사절 접속사 채우기 　　　　　중 ●●○

해석 Mr. Cruise는 시간이 넉넉했음에도 불구하고 그의 업무를 제시간에 완료할
수 없었다.

해설 이 문장은 주어(Mr. Cruise), 동사(was), 보어(not able)를 갖춘 완전한
절이므로, ___ ~ day는 수식어 거품으로 보아야 한다. 이 수식어 거품은
동사(had)가 있는 거품절이므로, 거품절을 이끌 수 있는 부사절 접속사 (B)
와 (C)가 정답의 후보이다. '시간이 넉넉했음에도 불구하고 그의 업무를 제시
간에 완료할 수 없었다'라는 문맥이므로 (B) even though(~에도 불구하고)
가 정답이다. 부사절 접속사 (C)는 '시간이 넉넉하자마자 그의 업무를 제시간
에 완료할 수 없었다'라는 어색한 문맥을 만든다. 전치사 (A)와 전치사 또는
접속부사 (D)는 거품절을 이끌 수 없다.

어휘 task n. 업무　have all day phr. 시간이 넉넉하다
in spite of phr. ~에도 불구하고　besides prep. ~외에; adv. 게다가

PART 6

131-134번은 다음 이메일에 관한 문제입니다.

수신: Raymond Ashburn <ray.ash@insta-flux.com>
발신: Gail Stromboli <stromboli@insta-flux.com>
날짜: 11월 13일
제목: 수석 프로그램 분석가

Raymond께,

당신은 아마 우리의 수석 프로그램 분석가인 Heidi Birt가 5주 후에
Insta-Flux사를 떠날 것이라는 것을 들었을 것입니다. 저는 그녀의 후임자를
고용하는 것을 담당하고 있으며 당신에게 몇 가지 ¹³¹**의견**을 요청하고 싶습니
다. 첫째로, 당신은 여기 우리 피닉스 지사에 있는 프로그래머들 중 누군가가
그 자리를 채울 만큼 충분히 ¹³²**숙련되어** 있다고 생각하십니까? ¹³³**그렇지 않
다면, 다른 지점에 있는 누군가를 추천해 주십시오.** 적합한 내부 후보자를 찾
을 수 없다면, 저는 그 일자리에 대해 광고를 내야 합니다. 하지만, 저는 이 과
정을 ¹³⁴**피하는** 것을 선호합니다.

당신으로부터 연락을 기다리겠습니다.

Gail Stromboli 드림
인사부장

senior adj. 수석의, 고위의 analyst n. 분석가
in charge of phr. ~을 담당하는 replacement n. 후임자
suitable adj. 적합한 internal adj. 내부의

131 명사 어휘 고르기 전체 문맥 파악 중 ●●○

해설 빈칸은 전치사(for)의 목적어 역할을 하면서 한정사(some)의 꾸밈을 받는 명사 자리이다. '당신에게 몇 가지 ___을 요청하고 싶다'라는 문맥이므로 모든 보기가 정답의 후보이다. 뒤 문장에서 우리 피닉스 지사에 있는 프로그래머들 중 누군가가 그 자리를 채울 만큼 충분히 (숙련되어) 있다고 생각하는지에 대해 물었고, 뒷부분에서 적합한 내부 후보자를 찾을 수 없다면, 광고를 내야 한다고 했으므로 의견을 요청하고 싶다는 것을 알 수 있다. 따라서 (B) suggestions(의견)가 정답이다.

어휘 report n. 보고서 explanation n. 설명 assurance n. 확인, 장담

132 'be동사 + p.p.' 채우기 중 ●●●

해설 빈칸이 be동사(are) 다음에 왔으므로 모든 보기가 정답의 후보이다. '누군가가 그 자리를 채울 만큼 충분히 숙련되어 있다'라는 수동의 의미가 되어야 하므로 be동사(are)와 함께 수동태를 만드는 p.p.형 (D) experienced (숙련되다)가 정답이다. 명사 (A)와 (C)는 보어로서 주어와 동격 관계가 되어 각각 '누군가가 경험/경험들이다'라는 어색한 문맥을 만든다. -ing형 (B) experiencing을 쓰면 '누군가가 그 자리를 채울 만큼 충분히 ~을 경험하고 있는 중이다'라는 능동의 의미로 동사 뒤에 목적어가 와야 한다.

133 알맞은 문장 고르기 중 ●●○

해석 (A) 저는 그녀가 뛰어난 부서장이 될 것이라고 생각합니다.
(B) 게다가, 당신은 퇴직 위로금을 받을 것입니다.
(C) 직업소개소가 이와 관련하여 매우 도움이 되었습니다.
(D) 그렇지 않다면, 다른 지점에 있는 누군가를 추천해 주십시오.

해설 앞 문장 'do you think that any of the programmers here at our Phoenix branch are (experienced) enough to fill the position?'에서 여기 우리 피닉스 지사에 있는 프로그래머들 중 누군가가 그 자리를 채울 만큼 충분히 숙련되어 있다고 생각하는지 물었으므로 빈칸에는 자리를 채울 누군가를 추천해달라는 내용이 들어가야 함을 알 수 있다. 따라서 (D)가 정답이다.

어휘 make v. ~이 되다 furthermore adv. 게다가
retirement bonus phr. 퇴직 위로금
employment agency phr. 직업소개소
in this regard phr. 이와 관련하여, 이러한 점에서 recommend v. 추천하다

134 동명사 채우기 중 ●●○

해설 타동사 prefer의 목적어 자리에는 to 부정사나 동명사가 올 수 있으므로 동명사 (A) avoiding(피하는 것)이 정답이다. 'to + 동명사' 형태 (B), 동사 (C), 동사 또는 과거분사 (D)는 prefer의 목적어 자리에 올 수 없다.

어휘 avoid v. 피하다, 막다

135-138번은 다음 공고에 관한 문제입니다.

호텔 투숙객분들은 주목해주십시오:

저희는 최근에 저희 시설에서의 수리를 완료하였으며, 호텔의 새로운 특징들을 소개하게 되어 기쁩니다!

첫째로, 저희 수영장 시설들은 135확장되었고, 이제 어린이들을 위한 새로운 구역을 포함합니다. 136저희는 또한 여러분의 편의를 위해 새 탈의실을 설치했습니다. 게다가, 저희 호텔 프런트가 열대 지방의 모습을 갖도록 다시 꾸며졌습니다. 여러분은 저희의 공공 구역에서 예술작품을 137보고 로비에 있는 새 소파에서 휴식을 취할 수 있습니다.

여러분이 배가 고플 때는, 저희의 가장 최신 식당을 시도해보십시오! 그곳에서 여러분은 음료수 목록138과 함께, 다양한 인기 있는 바비큐 요리를 발견할 수 있습니다. 그 식당은 저희 호텔 프런트 옆에 위치해 있습니다.

renovation n. 수리, 수선 facility n. 시설 feature n. 특징
furthermore adv. 게다가 reception desk phr. (호텔의) 프런트
tropical adj. 열대 지방의 check out phr. 보다, 확인하다
relax v. 휴식을 취하다 a variety of phr. 다양한 dish n. 요리, 접시
beverage n. 음료수

135 수, 태, 시제에 맞는 동사 채우기 주변 문맥 파악 상 ●●●

해설 and 앞의 절(our swimming pool facilities ___)에 동사가 없고 '수영장 시설이 확장되다'라는 수동의 의미가 되어야 하므로 수동태 동사 (A)와 (C)가 정답의 후보이다. 앞 문장에서 최근에 시설에서의 수리를 완료했다고 했으므로 수영장 시설이 확장된 것이 과거에 시작하여 방금 완료된 일임을 알 수 있다. 따라서 과거에 발생한 일이 현재까지 영향을 미치거나 방금 완료된 것을 표현할 때 쓰이는 현재 완료 시제 수동태 (C) have been expanded가 정답이다. 미래 시제 (A)는 이미 완료된 일을 나타낼 수 없다. 능동태 (B)와 (D)는 수동의 의미를 나타낼 수 없다.

어휘 expand v. 확장하다

136 알맞은 문장 고르기 중 ●●○

해석 (A) 그러한 물품들을 수영장 구역 안에 들이지 않도록 해주십시오.
(B) 여러분은 그것들을 로비에 있는 직원에게 요청할 수 있습니다.
(C) 그 수업들은 유명한 강사에 의해 가르쳐졌습니다.
(D) 저희는 또한 여러분의 편의를 위해 새 탈의실을 설치했습니다.

해설 앞 문장에서 'our swimming pool facilities (have been expanded), and now included a new area for children'에서 저희 수영장 시설들이 확장되었고, 이제 어린이들을 위한 새로운 구역을 포함한다고 했으므로 빈칸에는 새로운 어린이 구역 외의 수영장 시설 확장에 관한 내용이 들어가야 함을 알 수 있다. 따라서 (D)가 정답이다.

어휘 keep ~ out of phr. ~을 안에 들이지 않다 well-known adj. 유명한
instructor n. 강사 changing room phr. 탈의실 convenience n. 편의

137 능위접속사 채우기 상 ●●●

해설 동사구(check out ~ public areas)와 동사구(relax ~ the lobby)를 연결할 수 있는 등위접속사 (B)와 (D)가 정답의 후보이다. '공공 구역에서 예술작품을 보고 로비에 있는 새 소파에서 휴식을 취할 수 있다'라는 의미가 되어야 하므로 등위접속사 (D) and(그리고)가 정답이다. 등위접속사 (B)는 '예술작품을 보지만 휴식을 취할 수 있다'라는 어색한 문맥을 만든다. 접속사 (C)도 등위접속사로 쓰일 수는 있으나, 오직 절과 절만 연결할 수 있고 단어나 구는 연결하지 못한다. 참고로, 등위접속사로 연결된 구나 절에서 서로 중복된 단어는 생략될 수 있는데, 이 문장의 경우 두 번째 절(relax ~ the lobby)에서 중복되는 주어(You)와 조동사(can)가 생략된 것으로 볼 수 있지만, 접속사 (C)가 절과 절을 연결한 것으로 볼 경우 '공공 구역에서 예술 작품을 봐서 로비에서 휴식을 취할 수 있다'라는 어색한 문맥을 만든다. 부사절 접속사 (A)는 구와 구를 연결할 수 없고, 절과 절을 연결할 때는 중복되는 단어를 생략할

수 없다.

어휘 until conj. ~할 때까지 yet conj. 하지만 so conj. 그래서

138 전치사 채우기 중 ●●○

해설 빈칸은 명사구(a list of beverages)를 목적어로 취하는 전치사 자리이다. '음료수 목록과 함께, 다양한 인기 있는 바비큐 요리를 발견할 수 있다'라는 의미가 되어야 하므로, 부가를 나타내는 전치사 (A) along with(~과 함께)가 정답이다. 참고로, (B) between은 '~ 사이에'라는 의미로 두 개의 대상 사이의 관계나 위치, 또는 시간을 나타낸다는 것을 알아둔다.

어휘 towards prep. ~ 쪽으로, ~을 향하여 such as phr. ~과 같은

139-142번은 다음 회람에 관한 문제입니다.

수신: Ludwig Flooring사 직원들
발신: Sylvia Kerry, 인사부장
제목: 연례 성과 검토
날짜: 6월 10일

다시 한번 우리의 연례 성과 평가를 할 시간입니다. 여러분의 관리자가 회의 일정을 잡기 위해 여러분에게 ¹³⁹곧 연락할 것입니다.

이 평가들은 여러분이 여러분의 관리자와 여러분의 기대 및 우려 사항을 논의할 수 있게 해줄 것입니다. 그것들은 또한 당신의 강점 및 약점을 검토할 ¹⁴⁰기회를 제공합니다. 만약 개선이 필요한 경우, 여러분은 직원 개발 교육과정에 참여하도록 요구될 것입니다. ¹⁴¹**이러한 경우 교육이 의무적일 것임을 명심하십시오.**

평가가 시작될 수 있기 전에, 여러분은 6월 13일까지 여러분의 성과에 대한 자체 평가를 완료해야 합니다. 논의 전에 이것을 진행하는 것이 지난번 평가에서 더 나은 결과를 ¹⁴²낳았습니다. 모든 성과 평가는 7월 1일까지 완료되어야 합니다.

annual adj. 연례의, 연간의 evaluation n. 평가
expectation n. 기대, 예상 strength n. 강점 weakness n. 약점
improvement n. 개선, 향상 participate v. 참여하다
self-assessment n. 자체 평가 prior to phr. ~ 전에, 앞서

139 부사 어휘 고르기 중 ●●○

해설 빈칸은 동사(will contact)를 꾸미는 부사 자리이다. '관리자가 회의 일정을 잡기 위해 여러분에게 곧 연락할 것이다'라는 문맥이므로 (A) shortly(곧)가 정답이다.

어휘 rarely adv. 거의 ~하지 않다 typically adv. 보통, 일반적으로
hopefully adv. 바라건대, 희망을 갖고

140 명사 어휘 고르기 주변 문맥 파악 중 ●●○

해설 빈칸은 동사(provide)의 목적어 역할을 하는 명사 자리이다. '그것들은 또한 당신의 강점 및 약점을 검토할 ＿＿를 제공한다'라는 문맥이므로 모든 보기가 정답의 후보이다. 앞 문장에서 이 평가들은 여러분의 기대 및 우려 사항을 여러분의 관리자와 논의할 수 있게 해줄 것이라고 했으므로 이 평가들은 또한 강점 및 약점을 검토할 기회를 제공한다는 것을 알 수 있다. 따라서 (C) opportunity(기회)가 정답이다.

어휘 rehearsal n. 리허설, 예행연습 authority n. 지휘권, 권한
designation n. 지명, 명칭

141 알맞은 문장 고르기 중 ●●○

해설 (A) 혁신적인 상품 개발은 우리의 성공에 중요합니다.
(B) 이러한 경우 교육이 의무적일 것임을 명심하십시오.
(C) 신입 직원들을 위한 오리엔테이션이 월요일에 예정되어 있습니다.
(D) 최고 판매실적 달성자들은 보상으로 상여금을 받습니다.

해설 앞 문장 'If improvement is needed, you will be asked to participate in staff development courses.'에서 만약 개선이 필요한 경우, 직원 개발 교육과정에 참여하도록 요구될 것이라고 했으므로 빈칸에는 이러한 경우 교육이 의무적일 것이라는 내용이 들어가야 함을 알 수 있다. 따라서 (B)가 정답이다.

어휘 innovative adj. 혁신적인 crucial adj. 중요한 obligatory adj. 의무적인
reward v. (보상으로) ~을 주다

142 시간 표현과 일치하는 시제의 동사 채우기 중 ●●○

해설 문장에 주어(Doing this prior to the discussion)만 있고 동사가 없으므로 동사 (A), (C), (D)가 정답의 후보이다. 과거를 나타내는 시간 표현(in the last evaluation)이 있으므로 과거 시제 (A) produced가 정답이다. 현재 시제 (C)와 미래 시제 (D)는 과거에 발생한 일을 나타낼 수 없다. to 부정사 (B)는 동사 자리에 올 수 없다.

143-146번은 다음 기사에 관한 문제입니다.

(6월 3일)—최근 신문 ¹⁴³**보도**에 따르면, 병에 든 생수 회사 IcyBrook사는 이 것의 이름을 Juniper Food & Bev사로 바꿀 계획입니다. 이 결정은 3월에 있었던 회사의 주스 회사 Berry Crush사의 인수 이후에 내려졌다. ¹⁴⁴**이것은 1년 간의 협상 끝에 그 회사를 인수했다.**

"저희는 이제 더 다양한 제품을 판매할 것입니다. 저희의 원래 이름은 더 이상 저희 브랜드를 ¹⁴⁵**완전히** 나타내지 못합니다."라고 최고경영자 Charles Shah 는 말했다. 결과적으로 ¹⁴⁶**추가적인** 변화들이 있을 것이다. 이것들 중 하나는 새로운 로고가 될 것이다. 세부사항은 다가오는 몇 주에 걸쳐 발표될 것이다.

bottled adj. 병에 든 acquisition n. 인수, 습득 original adj. 원래의
represent v. 나타내다, 대표하다 coming adj. 다가오는, 다음의

최고난도 문제

143 복합 명사 채우기 상 ●●●

해설 빈칸이 명사(news) 뒤에 있으므로 복합 명사를 만드는 명사 (A), (B), (D) 가 정답의 후보이다. '최근 신문 보도에 따르면'이라는 문맥이므로 빈칸 앞의 명사 news(뉴스)와 함께 쓰여 '신문 보도'라는 의미의 복합 명사 news coverage를 만드는 명사 (A) coverage(보도)가 정답이다. 명사 (B)와 (D) 를 쓰면 각각 '신문 표지들/표지에 따르면'이라는 어색한 의미가 된다. 형용사 (C)는 명사를 뒤에서 수식할 수 없다.

어휘 coverable adj. 덮을 수 있는

144 알맞은 문장 고르기 중 ●●●

해설 **(A) 이것은 1년간의 협상 끝에 그 회사를 인수했다.**
(B) 따라서, 그 음료는 소비자들 사이에서 인기가 없었다.
(C) 또 다른 직위 임명이 곧 발표될 예정이다.
(D) 전 직원이 대회에 참가하도록 권장된다.

해설 앞 문장 'The decision was made after the company's acquisition of the juice company Berry Crush in March.'에서 이 결정은 3월에 있

었던 회사의 주스 회사 Berry Crush사의 인수 이후에 내려졌다고 했으므로 빈칸에는 이 회사의 인수와 관련된 내용이 들어가야 함을 알 수 있다. 따라서 (A)가 정답이다.

어휘 take over phr. 인수하다 negotiation n. 협상
appointment n. 임명, 약속 encourage v. 권장하다
take part in phr. ~에 참가하다, 참여하다 contest n. 대회

145 부사 자리 채우기   하 ●○○

해설 동사(represents)를 꾸밀 수 있는 것은 부사이므로 부사 (D) fully(완전히)가 정답이다. 형용사 (A), 형용사의 최상급 (B), 명사 (C)는 동사를 꾸밀 수 없다. full을 '충분히, 족히'라는 의미의 부사로 보고 (A)와 (D)를 각각 부사의 원급과 최상급으로 본다 해도, full이 부사로 쓰이는 경우 동사를 뒤에서만 꾸밀 수 있으므로 답이 될 수 없다.

어휘 fullness n. 풍부함, 완벽함

146 형용사 어휘 고르기   주변 문맥 파악   중 ●●○

해설 빈칸은 명사(changes)를 꾸미는 형용사 자리이다. '결과적으로 ___ 변화들이 있을 것이다'라는 문맥이므로 모든 보기가 정답의 후보이다. 앞 문장에서 회사의 원래 이름은 더 이상 자신들의 브랜드를 (완전히) 나타내지 못한다고 했고, 뒤 문장에서 이것들 중 하나는 새로운 로고가 될 것이라고 했으므로 회사 이름 변경의 결과로 새로운 로고를 비롯해 추가적인 변화들이 있을 것임을 알 수 있다. 따라서 (A) further(추가적인)가 정답이다.

어휘 regulatory adj. 규제력을 지닌 slow adj. 느린 confidential adj. 비밀의

PART 7

147-148번은 다음 공고에 관한 문제입니다.

노인 승객들은 주목해주십시오

Harrisburg 대중교통 시스템(HMTS)의 승객들은 버스표가 판매되는 어느 곳에서든 노인용 통행권을 구입할 수 있음을 알아두십시오. [147]당신의 노인용 통행권을 구입하기 위해서는, 다음 단계들을 완료하기만 하면 됩니다:

- 아무 매표 장소를 방문하여 당신이 65세 혹은 그 이상임을 보여주는 사진이 있는 유효한 신분증을 제시하십시오.
- 당신의 현재 주소와 전화번호를 포함하여 신청서를 작성하십시오.
- 46달러의 월간 이용료 또는 단 420달러의 연간 요금(12개월 전체에 대한)을 지불하십시오.

당신의 카드는 당신이 기다리는 동안 처리될 것입니다. 그 후, 어떤 HMTS 버스에 탑승할 때라도 이 카드를 제시하기만 하면 됩니다. [148]만약 당신의 카드가 분실되었다면, 대체품은 5달러의 비용이 들 것입니다.

---

senior n. 노인, 고령자 pass n. 통행권 present v. 제시하다
valid adj. 유효한 identification n. 신분증
registration form phr. 신청서 board v. 탑승하다
replacement n. 대체품, 교체, 후임자

147 주제 찾기 문제   하 ●○○

해설 공고는 주로 무엇에 대한 것인가?
(A) 교통카드 구매를 위한 장소
(B) 버스 운전자들에 대한 규정

(C) 교통 통행권 구입에 대한 설명
(D) 시스템 이용료의 증가

해설 지문의 'To get your senior pass, simply complete the following steps'에서 노인용 통행권을 구입하기 위해서는, 다음 단계들을 완료하기만 하면 된다고 한 후, 통행권 구입 방법을 설명하고 있으므로 (C)가 정답이다.

어휘 regulation n. 규정 operator n. 운전자 transit n. 교통, 수송

148 추론 문제   하 ●○○

해설 승객들은 왜 5달러의 요금을 낼 것 같은가?
(A) 카드 유효성을 1개월 연장하기 위해
(B) 처음으로 가입하기 위해
(C) 일일 통행권을 구매하기 위해
(D) 분실된 물품을 대체하기 위해

해설 지문의 'If your card is lost, a replacement will cost $5.'에서 카드가 분실되었다면, 대체품은 5달러의 비용이 들 것이라고 했으므로 승객들은 분실된 카드를 대체하기 위해 5달러의 요금을 낼 것이라는 사실을 추론할 수 있다. 따라서 (D)가 정답이다.

어휘 extend v. 연장하다 validity n. 유효성

패러프레이징

lost 분실된 → missing 분실된

149-150번은 다음 메시지 대화문에 관한 문제입니다.

Ellen Greenburg [오후 5시 14분]
[149]저는 Cromwell Electronics사의 곧 있을 광고를 위한 대본이 정말 마음에 들어요. 우리 작가들이 대단히 훌륭하게 해냈어요.

Kelsey Chenoweth [오후 5시 15분]
저도 동의해요. 그런데, 한 가지가 있어요. [149]Marian Ellis는 오늘 리허설 동안 그다지 활기차지 않았어요. 다음 주에 우리가 광고를 녹음할 때 그녀가 그렇게 소리를 낸다면 Cromwell Electronics사는 만족하지 않을 거예요. 어쩌면 우리는 다른 성우를 찾는 것을 고려해야 해요. 우리에게는 다른 사람을 고용할 예산이 충분히 남아 있어요.

Ellen Greenburg [오후 5시 18분]
저도 그걸 알아챘어요. 우리는 열정적이고 표현력이 있는 사람이 필요해요. 그렇지 않으면, [150-C]이 광고가 라디오에서 재생될 때 이것은 소비자들의 관심을 사로잡지 못할 거예요. 그녀에게 한 번 더 기회를 주기로 해요. 만약 그녀가 나아지지 않는다면, 우리는 대신할 사람을 찾을 거예요.

---

script n. 대본 commercial n. 광고 superb adj. 훌륭한
lively adj. 활기찬 voice actor phr. 성우 budget n. 예산
enthusiastic adj. 열정적인 expressive adj. 표현력 있는
capture v. (관심 등을) 사로잡다

149 의도 파악 문제   중 ●●○

해설 오후 5시 15분에, Mr. Chenoweth가 "There is one thing, though"라고 썼을 때 그가 의도한 것 같은 것은?
(A) 작가가 대본을 변경해야 한다고 생각한다.
(B) 광고 프로젝트의 예산에 대해 걱정이 된다.
(C) 한 사람의 연기에 문제가 있음을 발견했다.
(D) 광고의 공개일이 연기되어야 한다고 생각한다.

해설 지문의 'I really like the script for Cromwell Electronics' upcoming commercial. Our writers did a superb job.'에서 Ms. Greenburg가

Cromwell Electronics사의 곧 있을 공고를 위한 대본이 정말 마음에 들며, 작가들이 대단히 훌륭하게 해냈다고 하자, Mr. Chenoweth가 'There is one thing, though.'(그런데, 한 가지가 있어요)라고 한 후, 'Marian Ellis wasn't very lively during the rehearsal today. Cromwell Electronics isn't going to be happy if she sounds like that when we record the advertisement next week.'에서 Marian Ellis가 오늘 리허설 동안 그다지 활기차지 않았으며, 다음 주에 우리가 광고를 녹음할 때 그녀가 그렇게 소리를 낸다면 Cromwell Electronics사는 만족하지 않을 것이라고 한 것을 통해, Mr. Chenoweth가 Ms. Ellis의 연기에 문제가 있음을 발견했다는 것을 알 수 있다. 따라서 (C)가 정답이다.

어휘 **identify** v. 발견하다 **performance** n. 연기, 수행, 실행
release n. 공개, 출시 **postpone** v. 연기하다

150 Not/True 문제   중 ●●○

해석 Cromwell Electronics사에 대해 언급된 것은?
(A) 그것의 전자제품의 범위를 확장하고 있다.
(B) 더 많은 마케팅 인력을 채용하려고 계획하고 있다.
(C) 그것의 상품을 라디오에서 홍보할 것이다.
(D) 과거에 Marian Ellis를 고용한 적이 있다.

해설 지문의 'the commercial ~ when it is played over the radio'에서 이 광고, 즉 Cromwell Electronics사의 광고가 라디오에서 재생될 때라고 했으므로 (C)는 지문의 내용과 일치한다. 따라서 (C)가 정답이다. (A), (B), (D)는 지문에 언급되지 않은 내용이다.

어휘 **expand** v. 확장하다 **range** n. 범위, 다양성 **promote** v. 홍보하다
employ v. 고용하다

151-152번은 다음 웹페이지에 관한 문제입니다.

---

www.sterlingstaffingsolutions.com/staffing_services

Sterling Staffing Solutions사
인력 서비스

당신이 어떤 산업에 종사하든 ¹⁵¹⁻ᶜSterling Staffing Solutions사는 당신이 단기 일자리를 채울 적임자를 찾는 데 도움을 줄 수 있습니다. 당신의 요구사항에 대한 설명과 함께 저희에게 연락 주시기만 하면, 저희는 당신에게 가장 적합한 직원을 찾기 위해 수천 개의 구직자 이력서가 있는 저희의 데이터베이스를 찾아볼 것입니다. 저희는 당신이 선택을 할 때까지 적격인 사람들을 선별하고 당신의 회사가 그들을 위한 면접 시간을 정하는 데 도움을 줄 것입니다. ¹⁵²하지만 다수의 저희 경쟁자들과 달리, 저희는 거기에서 멈추지 않을 것입니다. 저희는 기대가 충족되고 있는지 확실히 하기 위해 **당신의 새로운 근로자의 고용 기간 동안 당신과 정기적인 연락을 유지할 것입니다.** 당신의 직원 채용 절차는 Sterling Staffing Solutions사와 함께 훨씬 더 쉬워질 것입니다.

---

short-term adj. 단기의 **description** n. 설명 **consult** v. 찾아보다
jobseeker n. 구직자 **appropriate** adj. 적합한 **screen** v. 선발하다
qualified adj. 적격인 **majority** n. 다수
keep in contact with phr. ~와 연락을 유지하다 **duration** n. 기간
expectation n. 기대, 예상 **staffing** n. 직원 채용

151 Not/True 문제   상 ●●●

해석 Sterling Staffing Solutions사에 대해 언급된 것은?
(A) 기업이 승진을 위해 근로자들을 교육하는 것을 돕는다.
(B) 직원 배치에 관해 최종적인 결정을 한다.
(C) 기업들을 위한 임시 직원을 채용한다.

(D) 전국적으로 위치한 수많은 사무실을 가지고 있다.

해설 지문의 'Sterling Staffing Solutions can help you find the right people to fill short-term positions'에서 Sterling Staffing Solutions사는 단기 일자리를 채울 적임자를 찾는 데 도움을 줄 수 있다고 했으므로 (C)는 지문의 내용과 일치한다. 따라서 (C)가 정답이다. (A), (B), (D)는 지문에 언급되지 않은 내용이다.

어휘 **train** v. 교육하다 **promotion** n. 승진, 홍보 **placement** n. 배치
recruit v. 채용하다 **numerous** adj. 수많은

패러프레이징

short-term 단기의 → temporary 임시의

152 추론 문제   중 ●●○

해석 Sterling Staffing Solutions사의 사업 경쟁자들에 대해 암시되는 것은?
(A) 한정적인 이용 가능한 구직자 인력을 가지고 있다.
(B) 후보들을 철저하게 평가하지 않는다.
(C) 그들의 서비스에 대해 요금을 더 많이 청구한다.
(D) 계속되는 지원을 제공하지 않는다.

해설 지문의 'But unlike the majority of our competitors, we won't stop there. We will keep in regular contact with you for the duration of your new worker's employment'에서 하지만 다수의 경쟁자들과 달리, 저희, 즉 Sterling Staffing Solutions사는 거기에서, 즉 사람들을 선별하고 면접 시간을 정하는 데 도움을 주는 것에서 멈추지 않고 새로운 근로자의 고용 기간 동안 당신, 즉 고객과 정기적인 연락을 유지할 것이라고 했으므로, Sterling Staffing Solutions사와 달리 다른 사업 경쟁자들은 고용 이후에 계속되는 지원을 제공하지 않는다는 사실을 추론할 수 있다. 따라서 (D)가 정답이다.

어휘 **pool** n. 이용 가능 인력 **thoroughly** adv. 철저하게
evaluate v. 평가하다 **candidate** n. 후보
ongoing adj. 계속되는, 진행 중인 **support** n. 지원

패러프레이징

rivals 경쟁자들 → competitors 경쟁자들
keep in regular contact 정기적인 연락을 유지하다 → provide ongoing support 계속되는 지원을 제공하다

153-154번은 다음 이메일에 관한 문제입니다.

수신: Jonas Bianchi <jbianchi@adomosuits.com>
발신: Valeria Lugo <vallugo@vsells.com>
제목: 인사말
날짜: 8월 10일

Mr. Bianchi께,

저는 귀사의 오랜 팬이며, 저는 소셜 미디어에서 귀하의 회사의 블로그 최신 정보를 정기적으로 읽습니다. 저는 당신이 당신의 브랜드를 오늘날의 모습으로 만든 방법을 정말 존경합니다. 저는 언젠가 같은 일을 할 수 있기를 희망하는 사업가입니다. 저는 서로가 아는 지인인 Naila Zane으로부터 당신의 이메일 주소를 받았는데, 그녀는 당신이 제게 올바른 방향을 알려줄 수도 있다고 말했습니다. ¹⁵³제 제품을 홍보하기 위해 제가 사용하는 블로그를 당신이 방문하여 그것에 대해 당신이 어떻게 생각하는지 알려줄 의향이 있다면, 저는 매우 감사할 것입니다. 그 주소는 www.icglyblog.com/V_sells입니다.

또한, ¹⁵⁴저는 당신의 고객층을 키우기 위해 당신이 소셜 미디어 웹사이트에서 광고 공간을 구입한 적이 있는지, 만약 당신이 구입했다면 그것이 그럴만한 가치가 있었는지 궁금했습니다.

시간을 내주셔서 감사드리며, 곧 연락 주시기 바랍니다.

Valeria Lugo
소유주, V Sells사

---

follower n. 팬, 추종자 admire v. 존경하다 entrepreneur n. 사업가
mutual acquaintance phr. 서로가 아는 지인, 상호 지인
point v. 알려주다, 가리키다 grateful adj. 감사하는
customer base phr. 고객층 worth adj. ~할 가치가 있는

---

153 목적 찾기 문제 　　　　　중 ●●○

해석 이메일의 목적은 무엇인가?
(A) 블로그에 있는 게시물에 대해 문의하기 위해
(B) 웹페이지에 대한 의견을 받기 위해
(C) 회사의 일자리에 지원하기 위해
(D) 제품에 대한 감탄을 표현하기 위해

해설 지문의 'If you are willing to visit the blog ~ and let me know what you think of it, I would be very grateful.'에서 자신의 블로그를 방문하여 그것에 대해 당신이 어떻게 생각하는지 알려줄 의향이 있다면, 매우 감사할 것이라고 했으므로 (B)가 정답이다.

어휘 inquire v. 문의하다 post n. 게시물 admiration n. 감탄, 존경

패러프레이징

blog 블로그 → Web page 웹페이지
what you think 당신이 어떻게 생각하는지 → feedback 의견

---

154 추론 문제 　　　　　중 ●●○

해석 Ms. Lugo가 무엇을 고려하고 있는 것 같은가?
(A) 새로운 웹사이트를 시작하는 것
(B) 마케팅 보조원을 고용하는 것
(C) 온라인으로 상품을 홍보하는 것
(D) 회원 할인을 제공하는 것

해설 지문의 'I was wondering if you ever purchased advertising space on social media Web sites to grow your customer base, and whether it was worth it if you did'에서 저, 즉 Ms. Lugo는 당신, 즉 Mr. Bianchi가 그의 고객층을 키우기 위해 소셜 미디어 웹사이트에서 광고 공간을 구입한 적이 있는지, 만약 구입했다면 그것이 그럴만한 가치가 있었는지 궁금했다고 했으므로 Ms. Lugo가 소셜 미디어 웹사이트, 즉 온라인에서 홍보하는 것을 고려하고 있다는 사실을 추론할 수 있다. 따라서 (C)가 정답이다.

어휘 launch v. 시작하나, 술시하다 goods n. 상품

패러프레이징

on social media Web sites 소셜 미디어 웹사이트에서 → online 온라인으로

155-157번은 다음 회람에 관한 문제입니다.

회람: 전 영업 직원, Battista 백화점
발신: Andreas Nielsen, 매장 관리자
¹⁵⁵날짜: 10월 22일

영업 직원분들께,

최근 직원회의 동안의 여러분의 의견에 근거하여, 경영진은 유니폼을 착용하도록 하는 요건을 없애기로 결정했습니다. 하지만, 우리가 우리

고객들에게 전문적인 이미지를 보여주는 것은 여전히 중요합니다. 그런 점에서, ¹⁵⁵영업 직원들은 매장의 새로운 복장 규정을 따르도록 요구될 것인데, 이는 아래에 설명되어 있습니다. ¹⁵⁵이러한 변경 사항들은 다음 달 초에 시행될 것입니다.

¹⁵⁶여성 직원들의 경우, 여러분은 흰색 상의와 함께 검은색 치마나 바지를 입어야 합니다. ¹⁵⁶신발은 더 이상 굽이 높을 필요는 없지만, 모든 신발은 검은색 가죽이어야 하며 발끝이 트여있어서는 안 됩니다. 수수한 장신구는 허용됩니다. 헤어 스타일은 직원의 재량에 달려있지만, 자연스럽지 않은 색은 허용되지 않습니다.

^{157-B}남성 직원들의 경우, ^{157-C}여러분은 흰색 칼라 셔츠와 함께 검은색 바지를 입어야 합니다. ^{157-A}신발은 검은색 가죽이어야 합니다. ^{157-D}남성에게도 수수한 장신구는 허용됩니다. 여러분은 자신의 헤어 스타일을 선택할 수 있으며, 깔끔하게 유지되는 한 ^{157-B}턱수염과 콧수염도 허용됩니다.

매장의 복장 규정에 대해 추가 정보가 필요하다면, 여러분의 부서 관리자와 이야기하십시오.

---

eliminate v. 없애다 professional adj. 전문적인
dress code phr. 복장 규정 go into effect phr. 시행되다
female adj. 여성의 top n. 상의 high-heeled adj. 굽 높은
footwear n. 신발 open-toed adj. 발끝이 트인
modest adj. 수수한, 보통의 permit v. 허용하다 discretion n. 재량
male adj. 남성의 trouser n. 바지 acceptable adj. 허용되는
beard n. 턱수염 moustache n. 콧수염 tidy adj. 깔끔한

---

155 육하원칙 문제 　　　　　상 ●●●

해석 11월 초에 무슨 일이 일어날 것인가?
(A) 새 유니폼이 직원들에게 배포될 것이다.
(B) 복장 규정을 논의하기 위한 회의가 개최될 것이다.
(C) 관리자들이 새로운 규정의 목록을 배포할 것이다.
(D) 새로운 정책이 시행될 것이다.

해설 지문의 'Date: October 22'에서 회람이 10월 22일에 작성된 것을 알 수 있고, 'sales staff will be required to follow the store's new dress code'와 'These changes go into effect at the beginning of next month.'에서 영업 직원들은 매장의 새로운 복장 규정을 따르도록 요구될 것이며, 이러한 변경사항들은 다음 달 초, 즉 11월 초에 시행될 것이라고 했으므로 (D)가 정답이다.

어휘 distribute v. 배포하다 hand out phr. 배포하다 regulation n. 규정

패러프레이징

new dress code 새로운 복장 규정 → new policy 새로운 정책

---

156 추론 문제 　　　　　중 ●●○

해석 Battista 백화점의 여성 영업 직원들에 대해 암시되는 것은?
(A) 현재 굽 높은 신발을 신도록 요구된다.
(B) 헤어스타일에 관한 지침이 있다.
(C) 검은색 유니폼을 입는다.
(D) 어떤 장신구든 착용하는 것을 삼가도록 요청받는다.

해설 지문의 'For female staff members'와 'Shoes no longer have to be high-heeled'에서 여성 직원들의 경우 신발은 더 이상 굽이 높을 필요는 없다고 했으므로 현재 Battista 백화점의 여성 직원들의 신발은 굽이 높아야 한다는 사실을 추론할 수 있다. 따라서 (A)가 정답이다.

어휘 guideline n. 지침 refrain from phr. ~을 삼가다, 자제하다

157 Not/True 문제
하 ●○○

해석 남성 직원들의 복장 규정의 일부가 아닌 것은?
(A) 가죽 신발이 신어져야 한다.
(B) 수염은 허용되지 않는다.
(C) 칼라 셔츠가 요구된다.
(D) 장신구는 허용된다.

해설 지문의 'For Male employees'와 'beards and moustaches are permitted'에서 남성 직원들의 경우 턱수염과 콧수염이 허용된다고 했으므로 (B)는 지문의 내용과 일치하지 않는다. 따라서 (B)가 정답이다. (A)는 'Shoes must be black leather.'에서 남성 직원은 신발이 검은색 가죽이어야 한다고 했으므로 지문의 내용과 일치한다. (C)는 'you have to wear ~ collared shirt'에서 칼라 셔츠를 입어야 한다고 했으므로 지문의 내용과 일치한다. (D)는 'Modest jewelry is also acceptable for men.'에서 남성에게도 수수한 장신구는 허용된다고 했으므로 지문의 내용과 일치한다.

패러프레이징
beards and moustaches 턱수염과 콧수염 → Facial hair 수염
shoes 신발 → footwear 신발
acceptable 허용되는 → permitted 허용되는

158-160번은 다음 기사에 관한 문제입니다.

Shire 극단의 연극
Andrew Craft 작성

런던의 오락 지구에 위치한 Shire 극단은 [158]그것의 현재 연극인 *The West Wind*가 원래 계획되었던 대로 7월에 상연을 끝내지 않을 것이라고 발표했다. ─ [1] ─. [158]대신에, 그것은 최소 한 시즌 더 계속할 것이다. ─ [2] ─. [159]이는 그 연극의 매진된 공연들로 인해 티켓을 살 수 없었던 연극 팬들에게 반가운 소식이다. ─ [3] ─. Julie Fielding에 의해 쓰인 *The West Wind*는 현재 Noah Wilson을 주연으로 한다. ─ [4] ─. Shire 극단은 그가 이 작품을 계속할 것인지 아닌지는 아직 밝히지 않았다. 하지만, 이 극단은 여자 주인공으로서 Fiona O'Rourke의 복귀를 공식화했다. [160-B]그녀의 연기력은 비평가들로부터 격찬을 받아왔다. 이 극단은 무대 장치와 의상을 개선하기 위해 두 달의 휴식을 가질 것이라고 말했다. 그 공연의 다음 시즌은 올해 9월에 초연을 할 것으로 예상된다.

situated adj. 위치한, 놓여 있는   district n. 지구, 지역   current adj. 현재의   run n. 상연   originally adv. 원래   unable adj. ~할 수 없는   sold-out adj. 매진된   performance n. 공연, 연기   star v. ~를 주연으로 하다   disclose v. 밝히다   production n. (상연) 작품, (연극의) 상연   company n. 극단   confirm v. 공식화하다, 확정하다   lead n. 주인공   acclaim v. 격찬하다   critic n. 비평가   premiere v. 초연을 하다

최고난도 문제

158 주제 찾기 문제
상 ●●●

해석 기사는 주로 무엇에 대한 것인가?
(A) 유명한 작가에 의해 쓰인 새로운 연극
(B) 연극 비평가의 의견
(C) 연극의 이전 출연진
(D) 연극 상연의 연장

해설 지문의 'its ~ play, *The West Wind*, will not end its run ~ as originally planned'와 'Instead, it will continue for at least one more season.'에서 연극 *The West Wind*가 원래 계획되었던 대로 상연을 끝내지 않을 것

이며 대신에, 그것은 최소 한 시즌 더 계속할 것이라고 했으므로 (D)가 정답이다.

어휘 former adj. 이전의   extension n. 연장, 확대

---

159 문장 위치 찾기 문제
하 ●○○

해석 [1], [2], [3], [4]로 표시된 위치 중, 다음 문장이 들어갈 곳으로 가장 적절한 것은?

"그들 중 많은 이들은 그들이 이 연극을 볼 기회를 얻지 못할 것을 걱정했다."

(A) [1]
(B) [2]
(C) [3]
(D) [4]

해설 주어진 문장에서 그들 중 많은 이들은 그들이 이 연극을 볼 기회를 얻지 못할 것을 걱정했다고 했으므로, 이 문장이 연극을 볼 기회를 얻지 못하는 것과 관련된 내용이 나오는 부분에 들어가야 함을 알 수 있다. [3]의 앞 문장인 'This comes as great news to the theater fans who have been unable to buy tickets for the play's sold-out performances.'에서 이는 그 연극의 매진된 공연들로 인해 티켓을 살 수 없었던 연극 팬들에게 반가운 소식이라고 했으므로, [3]에 제시된 문장이 들어가면 매진된 공연들로 인해 연극 팬들이 티켓을 살 수 없었으며, 그들 중 많은 이들이 이 연극을 볼 기회를 얻지 못할 것을 걱정했다는 자연스러운 문맥이 된다는 것을 알 수 있다. 따라서 (C)가 정답이다.

어휘 concern v. 걱정하다

---

160 Not/True 문제
중 ●●○

해석 Fiona O'Rourke에 대해 언급된 것은?
(A) 같은 역할을 계속 연기하지 않을 것이다.
(B) 긍정적인 평가를 받아왔다.
(C) 이전에 Noah Wilson과 함께 일한 적이 없다.
(D) 9월 중에 휴가를 낼 것이다.

해설 지문의 'Her acting skills have been acclaimed by critics.'에서 그녀, 즉 Fiona O'Rourke의 연기력은 비평가들로부터 격찬을 받아왔다고 했으므로 (B)는 지문의 내용과 일치한다. 따라서 (B)가 정답이다. (A), (C), (D)는 지문에 언급되지 않은 내용이다.

어휘 positive adj. 긍정적인   take time off phr. 휴가를 내다

패러프레이징
have been acclaimed 격찬을 받아왔다 → has received positive reviews 긍정적인 평가를 받아왔다

161-163번은 다음 공고에 관한 문제입니다.

[161]Boyle Regency 호텔
분실물 보관소 물품들

분실물 보관소 물품들에 대한 다음 정보를 꼼꼼히 읽어주십시오.

호텔 로비, 행사장, 화장실, 그리고 라운지에서 발견된 물품들은 메인 프런트로 반납될 것입니다. 만약 당신이 그 구역들에서 무언가를 잃어버렸다면, 프런트로 가서 근무 중인 관리자와 이야기하십시오.

[162]저희 식당, 카페, 그리고 뷔페 식사 구역에서 발견된 소지품은 Bates가에 있는 호텔 뒷문의 두 번째 프런트로 반납될 것입니다. 근무 중인 관리자에게 그 구역들에서 분실된 물품들에 대해 문의하세요.

만약 당신이 저희 체육관, 스파, 또는 수영 시설에서 무언가를 잊어버린다면, 스파의 프런트 데스크로 가십시오. 저희 접수 담당자들 중 한 명이 당신을 도와드릴 것입니다.

[161]당신이 묵었던 방에서 당신이 무언가를 잊어버린다면, 메인 프런트에서 확인하십시오. 만약 당신이 이미 떠났다면, 555-3009로 전화하십시오. 저희 시설관리과 직원들 중 한 명이 당신의 물건이 반납되었는지 확인할 것입니다.

[163]상당히 값비싼 분실물들은 90일 동안 보관되는데, 그 이후에 그것들은 지역 자선단체를 위해 경매로 처분됩니다. 값이 덜 나가는 분실물들은 한 달의 기간 동안 보관되고 난 후에 버려집니다.

lost and found phr. 분실물 보관소 reception desk phr. 프런트, 접수처
on-duty adj. 근무 중인, 당직의 belonging n. 소지품
secondary adj. 두 번째의, 2차적인 rear adj. 뒤쪽의
depart v. 떠나다, 출발하다 housekeeping n. 시설관리과
of value phr. 값비싼, 귀중한 valuable adj. 값이 나가는, 귀중한
auction off phr. 경매로 처분하다 charity n. 자선단체

161 추론 문제 중 ●●●○

해석 공고는 누구를 대상으로 하는 것 같은가?
(A) 프런트 직원들
(B) 숙박시설에 있는 손님들
(C) 호텔에서 일하는 관리자들
(D) 홀을 예약하는 행사 주최자들

해설 지문의 'Boyle Regency Hotel'에서 호텔에서 작성한 공고임을 알 수 있고 'Should you forget something in the room you stayed in, check at the main reception desk.'에서 당신이 묵었던 방에서 당신이 무언가를 잊어버린다면, 메인 프런트에서 확인하라고 했으므로 숙박시설에 머무르는 손님들을 대상으로 하는 공고라는 사실을 추론할 수 있다. 따라서 (B)가 정답이다.

어휘 accommodation n. 숙박 organizer n. 주최자

162 육하원칙 문제 중 ●●○

해석 뷔페 구역에서 방문객들이 물건을 잃어버린다면 그들은 누구에게 이야기해야 하는가?
(A) 두 번째 프런트에 있는 관리자
(B) 호텔 정문에 있는 직원
(C) 식당의 관리자
(D) 시설관리과 직원

해설 지문의 'Belongings found in ~ buffet dining area will be turned in to the secondary reception desk ~. Ask the manager ~ about items lost in those areas.'에서 뷔페 식사 구역에서 발견된 소지품들은 두 번째 프런트로 반납될 것이며, 관리자에게 그 구역들에서 분실된 물품들에 대해 문의하라고 했으므로 (A)가 정답이다.

패러프레이징

an item 물건 → Belongings 소지품

163 육하원칙 문제 중 ●●○

해석 90일 후에도 주인이 나타나지 않는 몇몇 소지품들에는 무슨 일이 일어나는가?
(A) 직원들에게 나눠진다.
(B) 자선단체를 위해 판매된다.
(C) 중고품 가게에 기증된다.

(D) 창고 시설로 보내진다.

해설 지문의 'Lost items of significant value are stored for 90 days, after which they are auctioned off for local charities.'에서 상당히 값비싼 분실물들은 90일 동안 보관되는데, 그 이후, 즉 90일 후에 그것들은 지역 자선단체를 위해 경매로 처분된다고 했으므로 (B)가 정답이다.

어휘 distribute v. 나누다, 분배하다 used-goods n. 중고품
storage facility phr. 창고 시설

패러프레이징

auctioned off for ~ charities 자선단체를 위해 경매로 처분되다 → sold for charity groups 자선단체를 위해 판매되다

164-167번은 다음 소식지 기사에 관한 문제입니다.

Lundus사 소식지
12월호

Lundus사가 자신감 있게 한 해를 마무리하다

11월부터, Lundus사의 주가는 Erco 플라자 사업과 향후 프로젝트들의 유망한 라인업 덕분에 사상 최고였다. "Erco 플라자를 위해, 저희는 요하네스버그 바로 외곽에 적당한 가격의 작은 땅을 구입할 수 있었습니다. 그리고 [165]저희는 그곳에 쇼핑몰에 대한 높은 수요가 있을 것이라고 정확하게 예측했습니다." 라고 [164]회사 최고경영자인 Mia Jenkins는 말했다. 쇼핑몰 내의 모든 상점들은 그것들이 이용 가능하기 시작했던 것과 같은 달인 8월 말에 모두 팔렸다.

"[166]Erco 플라자 프로젝트에서의 그들의 역할로 특히 칭찬을 받을 만한 두 명의 직원들은 선임 토지 인수 관리자인 Declan Chetty와 건설 프로젝트 관리자인 Aimee Joubert입니다."라고 Ms. Jenkins가 언급했다.

[164]회사의 다음 계획은 현대식 아파트 타워로 [164/167-C]교체될 노후 주택 단지인 Brakpan Glade의 재개발이다. 내년에, [167-D]Lundus사는 Redruth 산업단지에 대규모의 대지를 인수하기를 희망한다. 만약 모든 것이 순조롭게 진행된다면, [167-A]그것은 그 다음에 그곳에 Basin Rock Components사를 위해서 생산 시설을 지을 것이다.

confidently adv. 자신감 있게 as of phr. ~부터
all-time adj. 사상 (최고의[최저의]) high n. 최고(수준/수치)
venture n. 사업 promising adj. 유망한 affordable adj. 적당한 가격의
plot n. 작은 땅, 대지 point out phr. 언급하다 agenda n. 계획, 안건
redevelopment n. 재개발 housing complex phr. 주택 단지
on behalf of phr. ~을 위해서, ~을 대표하여

164 추론 문제 중 ●●○

해석 Ms. Jenkins는 누구일 것 같은가?
(A) 시 위원회의 일원
(B) 개발 회사의 대표
(C) 투자 회사의 설립자
(D) 디자인 대행사의 임원

해설 지문의 'company CEO Mia Jenkins'에서 Ms. Jenkins가 회사 최고경영자라고 했고, 'Next on the company's agenda is the redevelopment of ~ an aging housing complex that will be replaced'에서 이 회사의 다음 계획은 교체될 노후 주택 단지의 재개발이라고 했으므로 Ms. Jenkins가 개발 회사의 대표라는 사실을 추론할 수 있다. 따라서 (B)가 정답이다.

어휘 municipal adj. 시의 committee n. 위원회 founder n. 설립자
executive n. 임원

패러프레이징

company CEO 회사 최고경영자 → head of a ~ company 회사의 대표

165 동의어 찾기 문제   중 ●●○

해석 1문단 세 번째 줄의 단어 "predicted"는 의미상 –와 가장 가깝다.
(A) 숙고했다
(B) 조사했다
(C) 예상했다
(D) 받아들였다

해설 predicted를 포함한 구절 'we correctly predicted that there would be high demand for a mall there'에서 저희는 그곳에 쇼핑몰에 대한 높은 수요가 있을 것이라고 정확하게 예측했다고 했으므로 predicted는 '예측했다'라는 뜻으로 사용되었다. 따라서 '예상했다'라는 뜻을 가진 (C) forecasted 가 정답이다.

166 추론 문제   중 ●●○

해석 Ms. Joubert에 대해 암시되는 것은?
(A) Erco 플라자 프로젝트에 참여했다.
(B) 요하네스버그에서 직업 교육을 받았다.
(C) 8월에 기업체를 운영하기 시작했다.
(D) Mr. Chetty에 의해 전달된 지시를 따랐다.

해설 지문의 'Two employees especially deserving of praise for their roles in the Erco Plaza project are ~ Aimee Joubert'에서 Erco 플라자 프로젝트에서의 그들의 역할로 특히 칭찬을 받을 만한 두 명의 직원들 중 한 명이 Aimee Joubert라고 했으므로 Ms. Joubert가 Erco 플라자 프로젝트에 참여했다는 사실을 추론할 수 있다. 따라서 (A)가 정답이다.

어휘 professional training phr. 직업 교육
business enterprise phr. 기업(체)   follow v. 따르다

167 Not/True 문제   상 ●●●

해석 Lundus사의 목표가 아닌 것은?
(A) 고객을 위한 프로젝트를 수행하는 것
(B) 자체 제품을 제작하는 것
(C) 몇몇 오래된 건설물을 교체하는 것
(D) 일부 토지에 대한 소유권을 획득하는 것

해설 지문에서 (B)는 언급되지 않은 내용이다. 따라서 (B)가 정답이다. (A)는 'it will ~ build a production facility there on behalf of Basin Rock Components'에서 그것, 즉 Lundus사는 Basin Rock Components사, 즉 고객을 위해서 생산 시설을 지을 것이라고 했으므로 지문의 내용과 일치한다. (C)는 'the redevelopment of Brakpan Glade, an aging housing complex that will be replaced'에서 교체될 노후 주택 단지인 Brakpan Glade의 재개발을 할 것이라고 했으므로 지문의 내용과 일치한다. (D)는 'Lundus Incorporated hopes to acquire a large plot'에서 Lundus사가 대규모의 대지를 인수하기를 희망한다고 했으므로 지문의 내용과 일치한다.

어휘 carry out phr. 수행하다   manufacture v. 제작하다
structure n. 건설물   possession n. 소유권

168-171번은 다음 메시지 대화문에 관한 문제입니다.

Fatima Shiraz (오후 7시 40분)
168당신은 5월에 방콕에서 열리는 섬유 박람회에 갈 계획인가요?

Stefano Alto (오후 7시 43분)
네. 저는 아마 3일 동안 갈 것 같아요.

Fatima Shiraz (오후 7시 43분)
당신은 비행편을 이미 예매했나요? 저는 우리가 함께 이동할 수 있다고 생각했어요.

Stefano Alto (오후 7시 45분)
저도 그게 좋아요. 169저는 5월 12일 오전 8시 20분으로 Royal Siam 항공사의 표를 예매했어요. 저는 며칠 전에 막 표를 구했는데, 좌석이 많이 남아 있었어요.

Fatima Shiraz (오후 7시 46분)
좋아요! 169제가 몇몇 여행 웹사이트들을 확인해 보고, 169/170우리가 함께 갈 수 있을지 당신에게 알려줄게요.

Fatima Shiraz (오후 7시 59분)
170모든 준비가 끝났어요!

Stefano Alto (오후 8시 4분)
좋아요. 170제가 오전 5시 30분에 당신을 데리러 갈게요. 저는 공항의 장기 주차장에 제 차를 두고 갈 계획이에요.

Fatima Shiraz (오후 8시 5분)
고마워요! 좋은 생각이에요. 어쨌든, 저는 지금 가봐야 해요. 171저의 팀장이 Dresden Fashion사에 대해 이야기하기 위해 제가 그의 사무실에 들르길 원해요. 그들은 우리가 지난달에 그들에게 보냈던 직물에 문제를 겪고 있어요.

---

textile n. 섬유, 직물   fair n. 박람회   book v. 예매하다, 예약하다
vehicle n. 차, 차량   long-term adj. 장기의, 장기적인   stop by phr. 들르다
fabric n. 직물   ship v. 보내다

168 주제 찾기 문제   하 ●○○

해석 주로 논의되는 것은 무엇인가?
(A) 지점을 여는 것
(B) 생산 시설을 견학하는 것
(C) 산업 박람회에 참석하는 것
(D) 휴가를 가는 것

해설 지문의 'Are you planning to go to the textile fair ~?'에서 Ms. Shiraz 가 섬유 박람회에 갈 계획인지 물은 후, 박람회 참석과 관련된 내용에 대해 이야기하고 있으므로 (C)가 정답이다.

어휘 branch n. 지점   tour v. 견학하다, 여행하다   attend v. 참석하다

패러프레이징

go to the textile fair 섬유 박람회에 가다 → Attending a trade fair 산업 박람회에 참석하는 것

169 의도 파악 문제   상 ●●●

해석 오후 7시 59분에, Ms. Shiraz가 "All set"이라고 썼을 때 그녀가 의도한 것은?
(A) 3일간의 휴가 신청서를 제출했다.
(B) Mr. Alto와 같은 비행기를 탈 것이다.
(C) Mr. Alto를 위해 항공권을 구입했다.

(D) 업데이트된 여행 일정표를 보낼 것이다.

해설 지문의 'I booked a ticket on Royal Siam Airlines'에서 Mr. Alto가 Royal Siam 항공사의 표를 예매했다고 하자, 'Let me check some travel Web sites, and I'll let you know if we can go together.'에서 Ms. Shiraz가 몇몇 여행 웹사이트들을 확인해 보고, 우리, 즉 Mr. Alto와 Ms. Shiraz가 함께 갈 수 있을지 알려주겠다고 한 후, 'All set!'(모든 준비가 끝났어요!)이라고 한 것을 통해 Ms. Shiraz가 Mr. Alto와 같은 항공권을 예매했다는 것을 알 수 있다. 따라서 (B)가 정답이다.

어휘 submit v. 제출하다   leave n. 휴가; v. 떠나다
catch v. (버스, 기차 등을) 타다   itinerary n. 여행 일정표

170 육하원칙 문제 　　　　　　　　　　 중 ●●○

해석 Mr. Alto는 Ms. Shiraz를 위해 무엇을 하겠다고 제안하는가?
(A) 호텔을 예약한다
(B) 그녀를 공항까지 태워준다
(C) 여행사에 연락한다
(D) 소포를 가지러 간다

해설 지문의 'I'll let you know if we can go together'와 'All set!'에서 Ms. Shiraz가 우리, 즉 Mr. Alto와 Ms. Shiraz가 함께 갈 수 있을지, 즉 같은 비행편을 탈 수 있을지 알려주겠다고 한 후, 같이 갈 모든 준비가 끝났다고 했고 'I'll pick you up at 5:30 A.M. I plan on leaving my vehicle ~ at the airport.'에서 Mr. Alto가 오전 5시 30분에 당신, 즉 Ms. Shiraz를 데리러 갈 것이며, 공항에 그의 차를 두고 갈 계획이라고 했으므로 (B)가 정답이다.

어휘 reservation n. 예약   give ~ a ride phr. ~를 태워주다
travel agent phr. 여행사 (직원)   parcel n. 소포

최고난도 문제

171 육하원칙 문제 　　　　　　　　　　 상 ●●●

해석 Ms. Shiraz는 왜 그녀의 상사와 만날 것인가?
(A) 수송이 늦어진 이유를 설명할 것이다.
(B) 고객 불만 사항에 대해 논의할 것이다.
(C) 사무실 전근을 요청할 것이다.
(D) 업무가 완료되었음을 확인할 것이다.

해설 지문의 'My team manager wants ~ to talk about Dresden Fashion. They have a problem with the fabric we shipped them'에서 Ms. Shiraz가 자신의 팀장이 Dresden Fashion사에 대해 이야기하길 원하며, Dresden Fashion사는 자신들, 즉 Ms. Shiraz의 회사가 그들에게 보냈던 직물에 문제를 겪고 있다고 했으므로 (B)가 정답이다.

어휘 shipment n. 수송   complaint n. 불만 사항   transfer n. 전근
confirm v. 확인하다   task n. 업무

패러프레이징

supervisor 상사 → team manager 팀장
talk about ~ a problem 문제에 대해 이야기하다 → discuss a ~ complaint 불만 사항에 대해 논의하다

172-175번은 다음 기사에 관한 문제입니다.

5월 15일

172 17개국에서 운영되는 국제 호텔 체인인 Westwood Lodge는 곧 있을 Gold Rewards의 이용 가능성을 발표했다. 회원제에 가입하는 손님들

은 어느 Westwood Lodge 지점에서나 포인트를 적립할 수 있을 것이다.
— [1] —.

이 새로운 계획은 173-C 단 두 달 전 Westwood Lodge의 최고경영자로 승진된 Dianna Keyes의 공으로 여겨진다. 그녀는 "기존 고객 유지가 저희 사업 전략의 핵심 부분이어야 합니다."라고 최근 Travel Magazine지와의 인터뷰에서 말했다. — [2] —. "저희의 경쟁사들이 이런 종류의 시스템을 개발했으므로, 저희 또한 저희의 손님들에게 그것에 대한 이용 기회를 제공해야 합니다."라고 말했다.

175 Gold Rewards 계정을 가진 사람들은 방값을 지불하는 대신에 그들의 포인트를 사용할 수 있을 것이다. — [3] —. 포인트는 다양한 다른 서비스들에도 적용될 수 있다. 예를 들어, 174-A/D 이곳 마이애미의 Westwood Lodge에 묵고 있는 손님들은 해변을 내려다보는 테라스에서의 촛불 켠 저녁식사 혹은 최신식 헬스장에서 트레이너들 중 한 명과의 개인 수업을 예약할 수 있을 것이다. — [4] —. 174-B 그들은 로비에 있는 가게에서 기념품을 살 수도 있다. 그리고 174-C 호텔이 스파 건설 공사를 완료하면, 손님들은 포인트를 마사지 및 미용 관리로 교환할 수 있을 것이다.

upcoming adj. 곧 있을, 다가오는   sign up for phr. ~에 가입하다
accumulate v. 적립하다   location n. 지점   initiative n. 계획
credit to phr. ~의 공으로 여기다   retention n. 유지   existing adj. 기존의
in lieu of phr. ~ 대신에   patio n. (옥외) 테라스   overlook v. ~을 내려다보다
session n. 수업   state-of-the-art adj. 최신식의   souvenir n. 기념품
redeem v. 교환하다   treatment n. 관리

172 주제 찾기 문제 　　　　　　　　　　 중 ●●●

해석 기사의 주요 주제는 무엇인가?
(A) 기업의 해외로의 확장
(B) 회원제 프로그램의 시작
(C) 신규 호텔 지점의 개관식
(D) 오락 시설의 건설

해설 지문의 'Westwood Lodge ~ has announced the upcoming availability of Gold Rewards. Guests who sign up for a membership will be able to accumulate points at any Westwood Lodge location.'에서 Westwood Lodge가 곧 있을 Gold Rewards의 이용 가능성을 발표했으며, 회원제에 가입하는 손님들은 어느 Westwood Lodge 지점에서나 포인트를 적립할 수 있을 것이라고 한 후, 이 회원제 프로그램에 관한 설명을 하고 있으므로 (B)가 정답이다.

어휘 expansion n. 확장, 확대   overseas adv. 해외로   launch n. 시작, 출시

173 Not/True 문제 　　　　　　　　　　 중 ●●○

해석 Ms. Keyes에 대해 언급된 것은?
(A) 두 달 전에 정책 변경을 시행했다.
(B) Westwood Lodge의 경쟁사에 의해 고용되었다.
(C) 회사에서 최근에 대표직 자리를 맡았다.
(D) 지역 TV 쇼에서 인터뷰를 했다.

해설 지문의 'Dianna Keyes, who was promoted to CEO of Westwood Lodge just two months ago'에서 단 두 달 전 Westwood Lodge의 최고경영자로 승진된 Dianna Keyes라고 했으므로 (C)는 지문의 내용과 일치한다. 따라서 (C)가 정답이다. (A), (B), (D)는 지문에 언급되지 않은 내용이다.

어휘 implement v. 시행하다   take on phr. ~을 맡다

패러프레이징

> was promoted to CEO 최고경영자로 승진되었다 → took on a leadership role 대표직 자리를 맡았다

174 Not/True 문제

상 ●●●

해석 마이애미에 있는 Westwood Lodge의 현재 특징이 아닌 것은?
(A) 헬스장
(B) 선물 가게
(C) 스파
(D) 야외 식당

해설 지문의 'once the hotel completes construction of its spa, guests will be able to redeem points for massages and beauty treatments'에서 호텔, 즉 마이애미의 Westwood Lodge가 스파 건설 공사를 완료하면, 손님들이 포인트를 마사지 및 미용 관리로 교환할 수 있을 것이라고 했으므로 현재는 스파가 없다는 것을 알 수 있다. 따라서 (C)가 정답이다. (A)와 (D)는 'guests staying at the Westwood Lodge here in Miami will be able to book a candlelight dinner on the patio ~ or a private session ~ at the ~ gym'에서 이곳 마이애미의 Westwood Lodge에 묵고 있는 손님들은 테라스에서의 촛불 켠 저녁 식사 혹은 헬스장에서의 개인 수업을 예약할 수 있을 것이라고 했으므로 지문의 내용과 일치한다. (B)는 'They can even purchase souvenirs at the store'에서 그들, 즉 묵고 있는 손님들은 가게에서 기념품을 살 수도 있다고 했으므로 지문의 내용과 일치한다.

패러프레이징

> gym 헬스장 → fitness center 헬스장
> souvenirs 기념품 → gift 선물
> on the patio 테라스에서의 → outdoor 야외의

175 문장 위치 찾기 문제

중 ●●○

해석 [1], [2], [3], [4]로 표시된 위치 중, 다음 문장이 들어갈 곳으로 가장 적절한 것은?

"하지만, 여행 성수기 동안에는 무료 숙박과 관련하여 약간의 제한이 있을 것입니다."

(A) [1]
(B) [2]
(C) [3]
(D) [4]

해설 주어진 문장에서 하지만, 여행 성수기 동안에는 무료 숙박과 관련하여 약간의 제한이 있을 것이라고 했으므로, 이 문장이 무료 숙박 관련 내용이 나오는 부분에 들어가야 함을 알 수 있다. [3]의 앞 문장인 'Individuals with a Gold Rewards account will be able to use their points in lieu of paying for a room.'에서 Gold Rewards 계정을 가진 사람들은 방값을 지불하는 대신에 그들의 포인트를 사용할 수 있을 것이라고 했으므로, [3]에 제시된 문장이 들어가면 Gold Rewards 계정을 가진 사람들은 방값을 지불하는 대신에 그들의 포인트를 사용할 수 있을 것이지만, 여행 성수기 동안에는 무료 숙박과 관련하여 약간의 제한이 있을 것이라는 자연스러운 문맥이 된다는 것을 알 수 있다. 따라서 (C)가 정답이다.

어휘 complimentary adj. 무료의, 칭찬의 peak season phr. 성수기

176-180번은 다음 두 이메일에 관한 문제입니다.

¹⁷⁸수신: David Horton <d.horton@admin.simpsonuniversity.edu>
발신: Patricia Wheeler <p.wheeler@ims.com>
제목: 연구 프로젝트
날짜: 3월 4일
첨부: 팸플릿.이미지

Mr. Horton께,

저는 미디어 연구소의 연구원입니다. ^{176-D}제 동료들과 저는 소셜 미디어 사용이 학업 성적에 미치는 영향에 대해 연구하고 있습니다. ¹⁷⁹저희는 그들의 소셜 미디어 습관에 대한 설문조사에 참여할 200명의 대학생들을 찾고 있습니다. 유일한 조건은 그들이 올해 졸업을 해야 한다는 것입니다.

학생 참여를 장려하기 위해, ¹⁷⁷설문지를 작성하는 사람은 누구나 Feldman 서점의 20달러 쿠폰을 받을 것입니다. 그리고, 물론, 서희는 참가자들의 비밀을 존중할 것이며, 저희 연구가 발표될 때 학생을 식별할 수 있는 그 어떠한 정보도 포함되지 않을 것입니다. 참여를 희망하는 학생들은 이메일로 제게 연락해야 합니다.

첨부된 것은 프로젝트에 관한 더 많은 정보를 포함하고 있는 팸플릿입니다. ¹⁷⁸제 기관이 당신의 캠퍼스에 복사본들을 배포하는 것이 허용될지 제게 알려주십시오. 문의 사항이나 우려 사항이 있으시면, 언제든지 제게 이메일로 연락하거나 555-9383으로 전화해 주십시오.

Patricia Wheeler 드림

academic adj. 학업의 look for phr. ~을 찾다 habit n. 습관
encourage v. 장려하다 complete v. 작성하다, 완료하다
questionnaire n. 설문지 voucher n. 쿠폰, 상품권
confidentiality n. 비밀, 기밀성 identify v. 식별하다
acceptable adj. 허용되는, 괜찮은 distribute v. 배포하다

수신: Patricia Wheeler <p.wheeler@ims.com>
발신: Scott Mendoza <s.mendoza@heymail.com>
제목: 설문조사
날짜: 3월 19일

Ms. Wheeler께,

¹⁷⁸저는 오늘 제 대학교인 Simpson 대학교에서 당신의 팸플릿들 중 하나를 받았습니다. 당신의 프로젝트는 매우 흥미로운 것 같고, ¹⁷⁹저는 설문조사를 작성하고 싶습니다. 저는 팸플릿에 언급된 참여를 위한 요건을 충족합니다.

어떻게 진행해야 하는지 제게 알려주십시오. 가능하다면, 저는 이번 주에 설문지를 작성하고 싶습니다. ¹⁸⁰저는 대학 농구팀의 일원이며, 저희는 다음 주 토요일 주 챔피언십 결승전에서 경기를 할 것입니다. 다음 주에는 저희 코치님께서 몇 번의 연습 일정을 잡으셔서, 제게 자유시간이 없을 것입니다.

Scott Mendoza 드림

requirement n. 요건, 조건 proceed v. 진행하다 fill out phr. 작성하다
free time phr. 자유시간

176 Not/True 문제

중 ●●○

해석 Ms. Wheeler에 대해 언급된 것은?
(A) 학생 단체의 장이다.
(B) 교육 기관에서 교수이다.
(C) 소셜 미디어 애플리케이션을 개발하고 있다.
(D) 동료들과 프로젝트를 진행하고 있다.

해설 이메일1의 'My colleagues and I are studying the effects of social media use on academic performance.'에서 제 동료들과 저, 즉 Ms. Wheeler의 동료들과 Ms. Wheeler가 소셜 미디어 사용이 학업 성적에 미치는 영향에 대해 연구하고 있다고 했으므로 (D)는 지문의 내용과 일치한다. 따라서 (D)가 정답이다. (A), (B), (C)는 지문에 언급되지 않은 내용이다.

어휘 head n. 장, 우두머리 organization n. 단체 develop v. 개발하다
associate n. 동료

패러프레이징

colleagues 동료들 → associates 동료들

177 육하원칙 문제   중 ●●○

해석 설문조사의 참가자들은 무엇을 받을 것인가?
(A) 20달러의 현금 지급
(B) 소매판매점의 쿠폰
(C) 대학 행사를 위한 입장권
(D) 인기 작가가 쓴 책

해설 이메일1의 'anyone who completes the questionnaire will receive a $20 voucher for Feldman Bookstore'에서 설문지를 작성하는 사람은 누구나 Feldman 서점의 20달러 쿠폰을 받을 것이라고 했으므로 (B)가 정답이다.

어휘 payment n. 지급 retail outlet phr. 소매판매점 author n. 작가

패러프레이징

a ~ voucher for ~ Bookstore 서점의 쿠폰 → A coupon for a retail outlet 소매판매점의 쿠폰

178 추론 문제 연계   상 ●●●

해석 Mr. Horton은 무엇을 했을 것 같은가?
(A) 미리 설문조사 한 부를 요청했다.
(B) 몇 가지 추가 질문들과 함께 Ms. Wheeler에게 전화했다.
(C) 문서가 배포되도록 허락했다.
(D) 연구 과제에 참여할 학생들을 선발했다.

해설 이메일1의 'To: David Horton <d.horton@admin.simpsonuniversity.edu>'에서 Mr. Horton의 이메일 주소를 통해 그가 Simpon 대학 관련자임을 알 수 있고, 'Please let me know if it would be acceptable ~ to distribute copies on your campus.'에서는 당신, 즉 Mr. Horton의 캠퍼스에서 복사본들, 즉 프로젝트 관련 팸플릿을 배포하는 것이 허용될지 자신, 즉 Ms. Wheeler에게 알려달라고 했다. 또한, 이메일2의 'I was given ~ your pamphlets at my school, Simpson University.'에서는 Mr. Mendoza가 Simpson 대학교에서 당신, 즉 Ms. Wheeler의 팸플릿을 받았다는 것을 알 수 있다.
두 단서를 종합할 때, Mr. Horton은 Ms. Wheeler가 Mr. Horton이 관련되어 있는 Simpson 대학교에서 팸플릿을 배포하는 것을 허락했고 이에 따라 Mr. Mendoza가 Simpson 대학에서 Ms. Wheeler의 팸플릿을 받았다는 사실을 추론할 수 있다. 따라서 (C)가 정답이다.

어휘 in advance phr. 미리 follow-up adj. 추가의, 후속의
permission n. 허락 hand out phr. 배포하다

패러프레이징

distribute copies 사본을 배포하다 → document ~ be handed out 문서가 배포되다

179 추론 문제 연계   중 ●●○

해석 Mr. Mendoza에 대해 암시되는 것은?
(A) 그의 대학의 마지막 학년에 있다.
(B) 최근에 Simpson 대학으로 편입했다.
(C) 이전에 Ms. Wheeler에게 연락한 적이 있다.
(D) 학교 도서관에서 시간제로 일한다.

해설 이메일2의 'I'd like to complete the survey. I meet the requirement for participation that was mentioned in the pamphlet.'에서 저, 즉 Mr. Mendoza는 설문 조사를 작성하고 싶다고 하며 자신이 팸플릿에 언급된 참여를 위한 요건을 충족한다고 했다. 또한, 이메일1의 'We are looking for ~ university students to participate in a survey ~. The only condition is that they must be graduating this year.'에서는 설문조사에 참여할 대학생들을 찾고 있으며 유일한 조건은 그들이 올해 졸업을 해야 한다는 것임을 알 수 있다.
두 단서를 종합할 때, Mr. Mendoza는 올해 졸업을 해야 한다는 설문조사의 요건을 만족하므로 그가 대학의 마지막 학년에 있다는 사실을 추론할 수 있다. 따라서 (A)가 정답이다.

어휘 transfer v. 편입하다, 이동하다 part-time adv. 시간제로; adj. 시간제의

180 육하원칙 문제   중 ●●○

해석 Mr. Mendoza는 왜 다음 주에 시간이 나지 않을 것인가?
(A) 다른 주로 여행을 갈 것이다.
(B) 스포츠 경기를 위해 준비할 것이다.
(C) 기말고사를 위해 공부할 것이다.
(D) 프로팀에 지원할 것이다.

해설 이메일2의 'I am a member of the university's basketball team, and we are playing in the state championship final ~. Our coach has scheduled ~ practices next week, so I will not have any free time.'에서 저, 즉 Mr. Mendoza는 대학 농구팀의 일원이며 주 챔피언십 결승전에서 경기를 할 것이고, 다음 주에는 팀의 코치가 연습 일정을 잡아서 자신에게 자유시간이 없을 것이라고 했으므로 (B)가 정답이다.

어휘 final exam phr. 기말고사
try out phr. (팀원·배역 선발 등을 위한 경쟁에) 지원하다

패러프레이징

unavailable 시간이 나지 않는 → not have any free time 자유시간이 없다
basketball ~ championship final 농구 챔피언십 결승전 → sports event 스포츠 경기

181-185번은 다음 이메일과 기사에 관한 문제입니다.

수신: Melinda Landry <mell@konect.com>
발신: Donald Patterson <dp10@konect.com>
날짜: 12월 30일
제목: 새로운 직책

Melinda께,

인사부 부국장인 Tessa Fischer가 제게 이번 봄에 신설될 새로운 관리직에 대한 몇몇 추천을 제안해 달라고 요청했습니다. [181]저는 4명의 쟁쟁한 후보자들을 떠올릴 수 있었지만, 가능하다면 저는 당신이 두 명을 더 제안해주면 좋겠습니다. [182]Tessa에 따르면, 나이와 경험은 적응력보다 덜 중요합니다.

[183]제가 승진을 제안할 계획인 직원들은 우리 휴스턴 생산 공장의 감독

관인 Winston Bonham, 우리 인사부 과장인 Abel Marquez, 우리 마케팅 팀장인 Daisy Roberts, 그리고 우리 연구소의 수석 엔지니어인 Griselda Todson입니다.

당신의 선택을 제안할 때, ¹⁸³임명된 사람은 우리의 새로운 고온 부서를 운영할 것이라는 점을 명심해야 하는데, 이 부서는 열에 잘 견디는 개스킷을 개발하는 것에 주력할 것입니다.

Donald Patterson 드림
전무 이사
Konect사

deputy director phr. 부국장 personnel n. 인사부, 직원
put forward phr. 제안하다, 내다 strong adj. 쟁쟁한, 실력 있는
adaptability n. 적응력 promotion n. 승진, 홍보 supervisor n. 감독관
plant n. 공장 chief adj. 수석의, 주된; n. 장 appointee n. 임명된 사람
focus on phr. ~에 주력하다
gasket n. 개스킷(파이프나 엔진 등의 사이에 끼우는 마개)
resistant adj. ~에 잘 견디는

Konect사가 운영을 확장하여, 시장 점유율을 회복하다

오스틴 (3월 17일)—텍사스에 본사를 둔 회사 ¹⁸⁴Konect사는 10여 년 만에 처음으로 북미에서 개스킷 시장 점유율의 절반 이상을 차지했다. 이것의 최근 성공은 극한의 열을 견딜 수 있는 합성 소재로 만들어진 개스킷인 일련의 신제품들로 인한 결과이다.

전무 이사 Donald Patterson에 따르면, Konect사는 오랫동안 고무 및 금속 개스킷의 선도적인 생산업체였지만, ¹⁸⁴그것은 최근 몇 년간 이곳에서 인도 회사인 Suraja Industries사와 경쟁하기 위해 고군분투해왔다. "¹⁸³하지만, 저희의 고온 부서의 출범과 함께, 저희는 더 경쟁력 있게 되었습니다." 라고 Patterson은 말했다. "그리고 ¹⁸³그 공로의 대부분은 그 부서장에게 돌려질 수 있을 것인데, 그의 제조 관련 배경지식이 높은 품질 기준의 성취로 이어졌습니다."

¹⁸⁵Konect사의 주가는 지난 분기에 15퍼센트 상승했으며, 분석가 Benedict Tink는 가까운 미래에 그것이 꾸준히 상승할 것으로 예측한다.

expand v. 확장하다 operation n. 운영 regain v. 회복하다, 되찾다
market share phr. 시장 점유율 capture v. 차지하다, 점유하다
synthetic material phr. 합성 소재 withstand v. 견디다
extreme adj. 극한의, 극도의 leading adj. 선도적인 rubber n. 고무
struggle v. 고군분투하다 compete against phr. ~와 경쟁하다
competitive adj. 경쟁력 있는 credit n. 공로 background n. 배경지식
achievement n. 성취, 달성 standard n. 기준, 표준
stock price phr. 주가 steadily adv. 꾸준히

181 목적 찾기 문제   중 ●●○

해석 Mr. Patterson은 왜 Ms. Landry에게 연락했는가?
(A) 회사에 대한 그녀의 공헌을 칭찬하기 위해
(B) 그녀가 신청서를 제출하도록 장려하기 위해
(C) 그녀가 몇몇 동료들과 연락을 하도록 하기 위해
(D) 그녀에게 몇 가지 제안사항들을 제공해달라고 요청하기 위해

해설 이메일의 'I have been able to think of ~ candidates, but I would like you to propose two more'에서 저, 즉 Mr. Patterson이 후보자들을 떠올릴 수 있었지만, 당신, 즉 Ms. Landry가 두 명을 더 제안해주면 좋겠다고 했으므로 (D)가 정답이다.

어휘 praise v. 칭찬하다 contribution n. 공헌 in touch phr. 연락하는

---

coworker n. 동료

182 육하원칙 문제   중 ●●○

해석 Ms. Fischer는 직원을 선정하는 동안 무엇에 중점을 두었는가?
(A) 중요한 기한을 맞추는 능력
(B) 기술 발전에 대한 친숙도
(C) 변화에 대처하는 능력
(D) 조직 전략에 대한 지식

해설 이메일의 'According to Tessa, age and experience are less important than adaptability.'에서 Tessa, 즉 Ms. Fischer에 따르면, 나이와 경험은 적응력보다 덜 중요하다고 했으므로 (C)가 정답이다.

어휘 ability n. 능력 deadline n. 기한 familiarity n. 친숙도
deal with phr. 대처하다, 대응하다 organizational adj. 조직의

최고난도 문제

183 추론 문제 연계   상 ●●●

해석 어느 직원이 승진을 했을 것 같은가?
(A) Winston Bonham
(B) Abel Marquez
(C) Daisy Roberts
(D) Griselda Todson

해설 이메일의 'The personnel I ~ suggest for promotion are Winston Bonham, a supervisor at our Houston production plant'와 'the appointee will be running our new High Temperature Division'에서는 승진을 제안할 직원들 중에 휴스턴 생산 공장의 감독관인 Winston Bonham이 포함되어 있으며, 임명된 사람, 즉 승진자는 우리, 즉 Konect사의 새로운 고온 부서를 운영할 것이라고 했다. 또한, 기사의 'We've become more competitive, ~ with the launch of our High Temperature Division'과 'much of the credit can be given to the head of that division, whose manufacturing background has led to the achievement'에서는 우리, 즉 Konect사는 고온 부서의 출범과 함께 더 경쟁력 있게 되었으며, 그 공로의 대부분은 그 부서장에게 돌려질 수 있을 것인데, 그의 제조 관련 배경지식이 성취로 이어졌다고 한 사실 확인할 수 있다.
두 단서를 종합할 때, 생산 공장의 감독관이었기 때문에 제조 관련 배경지식이 있는 Winston Bonham이 고온 부서의 부서장으로 승진했다는 사실을 추론할 수 있다. 따라서 (A)가 정답이다.

184 추론 문제   상 ●●●

해석 Suraja Industries사에 대해 추론될 수 있는 것은?
(A) 오스틴에 생산 공장을 설립하려고 시도하고 있다.
(B) 다른 회사와 계약을 체결했다.
(C) 북미 시장에서 상품을 판매한다.
(D) 광범위한 종류의 개스킷에 대한 특허권을 구매했다.

해설 기사의 'Konect has captured more than half of the market share for gaskets in North America'에서 Konect사가 북미에서 개스킷 시장 점유율의 절반 이상을 차지했다고 했고, 'it has struggled ~ to compete here against ~ Suraja Industries'에서 그것, 즉 Konect사가 이곳, 즉 북미에서 Suraja Industries사와 경쟁하기 위해 고군분투해왔다고 했으므로 Suraja Industries사가 북미 시장에서 개스킷을 판매한다는 사실을 추론할 수 있다. 따라서 (C)가 정답이다.

어휘 **attempt** v. 시도하다 **set up** phr. 설립하다
sign an agreement phr. 계약을 체결하다 **goods** n. 상품
patent n. 특허(권) **a wide assortment of** phr. 광범위한 종류의

185 육하원칙 문제 중 ●●○

해석 기사에 따르면, Mr. Tink는 무슨 일이 일어날 것이라고 생각하는가?
(A) 한 발명품은 환경 안전성을 개선하는 데 사용될 것이다.
(B) 한 회사 임원이 합병을 제안할 것이다.
(C) 한 제조업체는 상업 대출을 승인 받을 것이다.
(D) 한 회사의 주식 가치가 증가할 것이다.

해설 기사의 'Konect's stock price increased ~ last quarter, and analyst Benedict Tink predicts that it will rise steadily in the near future.'에서 Konect사의 주가가 지난 분기에 상승했으며, 분석가 Benedict Tink는 가까운 미래에 그것이 꾸준히 상승할 것으로 예측한다고 했으므로 (D)가 정답이다.

어휘 **invention** n. 발명(품) **environmental** adj. 환경의
executive n. 임원, 경영진 **merger** n. 합병 **grant** v. 승인하다
commercial loan phr. 상업 대출

패러프레이징

rise 상승하다 → increase 증가하다

186-190번은 다음 이메일, 후기, 문자 메시지에 관한 문제입니다.

발신: Marielle DuBois <m.dubois@starmaxfilms.com>
186수신: Brian O'Reilly <b.oreilly@starmaxfilms.com>
제목: *Hollow Lives* 시사회
날짜: 3월 13일

안녕하세요 Brian,

저는 186우리 스튜디오의 최신 영화인 *Hollow Lives*에 대해 당신이 현재 하고 있는 편집이 상당히 걱정된다는 것을 당신에게 알려주고 싶습니다. 이 영화는 4월 1일에 처음으로 상영될 예정입니다. 그리고 당신이 며칠 전에 편집이 예상보다 오래 걸리고 있다고 말했기 때문에, 저는 우리가 그 전까지 모든 것이 다 준비하지 못할까 봐 걱정됩니다

게다가, 188만약 우리가 그곳에서 시사회를 개최하지 않으면, 저는 제가 예약한 장소인 Hibiscus 극장에 대해 취소 수수료를 물게 될 것입니다. 이것은 이 영화의 예산에 큰 타격을 줄 것인데, 정확히 말하면 5,000달러입니다. 필요하다면 제가 시사회 일정을 변경하기 위한 준비를 할 수 있도록 187매일 제게 상황 보고를 보내주십시오.

Marielle DuBois 드림
감독, Starmax 영화 스튜디오

premiere n. 시사회; v. 처음으로 상영하다, 개봉하다 **editing** n. 편집
be set to phr. ~할 예정이다 **concerned** adj. 걱정하는
cancellation n. 취소 **venue** n. 장소 **hit** n. 타격 **exact** adj. 정확한
status n. (진행 과정상의) 상황 **arrangement** n. 준비, 마련
reschedule v. 일정을 변경하다

MovieBuzz.com
당신의 좋아하는 영화들에 대한 온라인 후기들!

Hollow Lives ★★★★★
게시글 작성자: Christopher White

저는 188지난주 Crosswood 극장에서의 Starmax 영화 스튜디오의 *Hollow Lives* 시사회에 참석할 정도로 충분히 운이 좋았으며, 그것은 확실한 큰 기쁨이었습니다! 저는 Marielle DuBois 감독이 여전히 그녀의 영화 줄거리에 실험을 하려고 한다는 것을 보게 되어 기뻤습니다. 여기서, 그녀는 성공적인 할리우드 제작자가 되기 위해 고군분투하는 한 여성의 매혹적인 이야기를 들려줍니다.

190-DDiana를 연기한 주연 여배우 Nancy Hyland는 그녀의 첫 연기에서 환상적으로 잘 해냅니다. 예를 들어, 189-B이 영화는 Diana가 직면하는 도전들이 점차 그녀의 성격에 극적인 변화를 일으키는 30년의 기간을 다룹니다. Ms. Hyland는 이 변화를 완벽히 연기합니다.

절대로 *Hollow Lives*를 놓치지 마십시오. 이것은 당신의 가슴에 진정으로 와 닿을 영화입니다!

catch v. 참석하다, 잡다 **treat** n. 큰 기쁨 **delighted** adj. 기쁜
plot n. 줄거리 **captivating** adj. 매혹적인 **struggle** v. 고군분투하다
performance n. 연기, 수행 **face** v. 직면하다 **dramatic** adj. 극적인
portray v. 연기하다 **flawlessly** adv. 완벽히, 나무랄 데 없이
touch one's heart phr. 가슴에 와 닿다

받은 날짜: 9월 4일
받은 시간: 오전 10시 2분

안녕하세요, Marielle. 아시다시피, 190-D저는 *Hollow Lives*에서 맡은 Diana로서의 제 역할로 인해 Greenfield 영화제의 여우주연상 후보로 지명되었습니다. 저는 10월 1일의 이 영화제 시상식에 3장의 초대장을 받았습니다. 하지만, 저는 그것들 중 두 장만 사용하면 됩니다. 만약 당신이 추가 손님을 데리고 오고 싶으시다면, 저에게 알려만 주시면 저는 제 여분의 초대장을 당신에게 드릴 것입니다. 190-B거기에서 당신을 만나기를 기대합니다.

nominate v. 후보로 지명하다 **extra** adj. 여분의, 추가의

186 추론 문제 중 ●●○

해석 Mr. O'Reilly는 누구일 것 같은가?
(A) 제작자
(B) 배우
(C) 편집자
(D) 감독

해설 이메일의 'To: Brian O'Reilly', 'the editing you are currently doing for ~ studio's latest movie'에서 이메일의 수신자가 Brian O'Reilly임을 확인할 수 있고, 스튜디오의 최신 영화에 대해 당신, 즉 Mr. O'Reilly가 현재 하고 있는 편집이라고 했으므로 Mr. O'Reilly가 영화 편집자라는 사실을 추론할 수 있다. 따라서 (C)가 정답이다.

187 육하원칙 문제 중 ●●○

해석 Ms. DuBois는 Mr. O'Reilly에게 무엇을 제공해달라고 요청하는가?
(A) 새롭게 고용된 주연들을 위한 대본
(B) 제작에 대한 예산 보고서
(C) 유망한 연기자의 이력서

(D) 일일 진행 상황 업데이트

해설 이메일의 'Please send me status reports every day'에서 매일 저, 즉 Ms. DuBois에게 상황 보고를 보내달라고 했으므로 (D)가 정답이다.

어휘 **script** n. 대본 **budget** n. 예산 **production** n. (영화) 제작
prospective adj. 유망한 **talent** n. 연기자, 재능 **progress** n. 진행 상황

패러프레이징

send ~ status reports every day 매일 상황 보고를 보내다 → Updates on daily progress 일일 진행 상황 업데이트

188 육하원칙 문제 연계 　　　　상 ●●●

해석 Ms. DuBois는 *Hollow Lives*의 시사회 전에 무엇을 해야 했는가?
(A) 장면 간의 전환을 확인한다
(B) 5,000달러의 금액을 지불한다
(C) 스튜디오의 추가 보조자를 모집한다
(D) 축하 행사를 준비한다

해설 이메일의 'I will be charged a cancellation fee for ~ Hibiscus Theater, if we don't hold the premiere there. This will be ~ $5,000'에서 만약 우리가 Hibiscus 극장에서 시사회를 개최하지 않으면, 저, 즉 Ms. DuBois는 그곳에 대해 취소 수수료를 물게 될 것이며 이것은 5,000달러라고 했다. 또한, 후기의 'the premiere of ~ Hollow Lives ~ at the Crosswood Theater'에서는 *Hollow Lives* 시사회가 Crosswood 극장에서 열렸다는 사실을 확인할 수 있다.
두 단서를 종합할 때, *Hollow Lives*의 시사회를 Hibiscus 극장이 아닌 Crosswood 극장에서 진행했으므로 Ms. DuBois가 시사회 전에 Hibiscus 극장에 대해 취소 수수료 5,000달러를 지불해야 했음을 알 수 있다. 따라서 (B)가 정답이다.

어휘 **transition** n. 전환 **recruit** v. 모집하다 **assistant** n. 보조자
arrange for phr. ~을 준비하다 **celebratory** adj. 축하의

189 Not/True 문제 　　　　중 ●●○

해석 *Hollow Lives*에 대해 언급된 것은?
(A) 경험이 없는 감독의 창작품이었다.
(B) 수십 년의 기간 동안 일어난다.
(C) 인기 영화 잡지에서 비판을 받았다.
(D) 다양한 주요 도시들에서 촬영된 장면들을 포함한다.

해설 후기의 'the film covers a 30-year period'에서 이 영화, 즉 *Hollow Lives*가 30년의 기간을 다룬다고 했으므로 (B)는 지문의 내용과 일치한다. 따라서 (B)가 정답이다. (A), (C), (D)는 지문에 언급되지 않은 내용이다.

어휘 **creation** n. 창작품 **inexperienced** adj. 경험이 없는
take place phr. 일어나다 **criticize** v. 비판하다, 비난하다
shoot v. 촬영하다, 쏘다 **major** adj. 주요한

패러프레이징

a 30-year period 30년의 기간 → a period of several decades 수십 년의 기간

최고난도 문제

190 Not/True 문제 연계 　　　　상 ●●●

해석 Ms. Hyland에 대해 언급된 것은?
(A) 곧 나올 영화에 출연하기로 계약되었다.
(B) Ms. DuBois와 9월 4일에 직접 만날 것이다.

(C) 그녀의 동료들 중 한 명과 저녁 식사 일정을 잡았다.
(D) 그녀의 가장 첫 번째 연기로 상을 받을지도 모른다.

해설 후기의 'Lead actress Nancy Hyland, who played Diana, does a fantastic job in her first performance.'에서 Diana를 연기한 주연 여배우 Nancy Hyland는 그녀의 첫 연기에서 환상적으로 잘 해냈다고 했다. 또한, 문자 메시지의 'I have been nominated for the Greenfield Film Festival's Best Actress Award for my role as Diana in *Hollow Lives*'에서는 저, 즉 Ms. Hyland가 *Hollow Lives*에서 맡은 Diana로서의 자신의 역할로 인해 Greenfield 영화제의 여우주연상 후보로 지명되었다는 사실을 확인할 수 있다.
두 단서를 종합할 때, Diana를 연기한 Ms. Hyland가 그녀의 첫 연기로 여우주연상 후보로 지명되었음을 알 수 있다. 따라서 (D)가 정답이다. (A)와 (C)는 지문에 언급되지 않은 내용이다. (B)는 문자 메시지의 'I look forward to seeing you there.'에서 Ms. Hyland가 거기에서, 즉 10월 1일의 Greenfield 영화제에서 당신, 즉 Ms. DuBois를 만나기를 기대한다고 했으므로 지문의 내용과 일치하지 않는다.

어휘 **contract** v. 계약하다 **upcoming** adj. 곧 나올, 다가오는
in person phr. 직접 **colleague** n. 동료

패러프레이징

have been nominated for ~ Award 수상 후보에 올랐다 → might receive an award 상을 받을지도 모른다

191-195번은 다음 견적서, 이메일, 웹페이지에 관한 문제입니다.

191-D **Hilltop AC사**
191-D **25년 넘게 스카츠데일에 서비스를 제공하고 있습니다!**

191-B **수령인: Brent 회계사무소**	**날짜:** 5월 21일
연락처: Jeremy Watson	191-B **주소:**
전화번호: 555-7264	Flanders 건물
이메일: j.watson@brentacc.com	1509번지 Greene 로터리
	스카츠데일시, 애리조나주 85254

설명	금액
Becool Glacier 에어컨 한 대 설치	150달러
192 **Becool Alpine 에어컨 한 대 수리**	192 **300달러**
Becool Frost 에어컨 한 대 수리	400달러
Becool Frost 에어컨 한 대 청소	125달러
	총액 975달러

예약을 하려면, 555-3209로 전화하거나 service@hilltop.com으로 이메일을 보내십시오. 저희의 고객 서비스 책임자인 Judith Hawkins가 기꺼이 당신을 도울 것입니다. 191-A/194 **Hilltop AC사의 기술자들은 월요일부터 토요일, 오전 8시부터 오후 5시까지 서비스 요청을 수행할 수 있습니다.**

accounting n. 회계사무소 **install** v. 설치하다 **repair** v. 수리하다
book an appointment phr. 예약하다

수신: Judith Hawkins <service@hilltop.com>
발신: Jeremy Watson <j.watson@brentacc.com>
제목: 청구서 오류
193 **날짜:** 6월 3일

Ms. Hawkins께,

저는 지난주에 귀사의 기술자가 제 사무실에서 한 작업에 대한 청구서를 받았습니다. 유감스럽게도, 그것은 오류를 포함합니다. 당신이 제게 처음 ↻

견적서를 보내준 후에 저희가 논의했듯이, ¹⁹²제 건물의 정비 담당자가 Becool Alpine 에어컨에 대한 문제를 해결할 수 있었습니다. 따라서, 귀사의 기술자는 그것에 대해 어떠한 작업도 수행할 필요가 없었습니다. 수정된 청구서를 제게 보내 주시겠습니까? 이것을 해주시면, 저는 전액을 지불할 것입니다. 저는 국세청에 의해 주최되는 ¹⁹³세금 세미나에 참석하기 때문에 저는 오늘 오후 내내 사무실에 없을 것입니다. 하지만, 궁금한 점이 있으시면, ¹⁹³내일 제게 전화로 연락하실 수 있습니다. 감사합니다.

Jeremy Watson 드림
총관리자
Brent 회계사무소

billing n. 청구서 bill n. 청구서 technician n. 기술자
unfortunately adv. 유감스럽게도 initial adj. 처음의 estimate n. 견적서
maintenance manager phr. 정비 담당자 resolve v. 해결하다
revised adj. 수정된, 변경된 out of phr. ~에 없는 host v. 주최하다

---

www.hilltopac.com/customer_testimonials

J. Watson에 의해 6월 7일에 게시됨

전반적으로, 저는 Hilltop AC사에 대해 매우 긍정적인 경험을 했습니다. ¹⁹⁴기술자는 제가 요청한 대로 오후 6시에 시간을 엄수하여 도착했고, 그는 매우 정중하고 효율적이었습니다. ¹⁹⁵저는 또한 그가 설치한 신형 에어컨의 다양한 기능을 제게 보여주는 것에 그가 시간을 들인 것이 고마웠습니다. 저의 유일한 불만 사항은 제 청구서에 오류가 있었다는 것이지만, 고객 서비스 책임자가 이 문제를 신속하게 처리해주었습니다. 저는 누구에게나 Hilltop AC사를 강력하게 추천할 것입니다.

overall adv. 전반적으로 positive adj. 긍정적인
promptly adv. 시간을 엄수하여, 정확히 제시간에 polite adj. 정중한
efficient adj. 효율적인 appreciate v. 고마워하다, 인정하다, 이해하다
recommend v. 추천하다

191 Not/True 문제

상 ●●●

해석 Hilltop AC사에 대해 언급된 것은?
(A) 서비스를 주 7일 제공한다.
(B) Flanders 건물에 위치해 있다.
(C) 스카츠데일에 두 번째 지점을 열었다.
(D) 20년보다 더 전에 설립되었다.

해설 견적서의 'Hilltop AC', 'Serving Scottsdale for over 25 years!'에서 Hilltop AC사가 25년 넘게 스카츠데일에 서비스를 제공하고 있다고 했으므로 (D)는 지문의 내용과 일치한다. 따라서 (D)가 정답이다. (A)는 'Hilltop AC technicians are available ~ Monday to Saturday ~.'에서 Hilltop AC사의 기술자들은 월요일부터 토요일 즉, 주 6일 동안 가능하다고 했으므로 지문의 내용과 일치하지 않는다. (B)는 'Prepared for: Brent Accounting', 'Address: Flanders Building'에서 견적서의 수령인이 Brent 회계사무소이고 그 주소가 Flanders 건물이라고 했으나 Hilltop AC사의 위치는 언급되지 않았으므로 지문의 내용과 일치하지 않는다. (C)는 지문에 언급되지 않은 내용이다.

어휘 establish v. 설립하다

패러프레이징

over 25 years 25년 넘게 → over two decades 20년 넘게

---

192 육하원칙 문제 연계

상 ●●●

해석 Mr. Watson은 어느 금액을 지불할 필요가 없었는가?
(A) 150달러
(B) 300달러
(C) 400달러
(D) 125달러

해설 이메일의 'the maintenance manager in my building was able to resolve the issue with the Becool Alpine air conditioner. Therefore, the technician from your company did not need to do any work on it.'에서 제 건물, 즉 Mr. Watson의 건물의 정비 담당자가 Becool Alpine 에어컨에 대한 문제를 해결할 수 있었으므로 귀사의 기술자는 그것에 대해 어떠한 작업도 수행할 필요가 없었다고 했다. 또한, 견적서의 'Repair one Becool Alpine air conditioner', '$300.00'에서는 Becool Alpine 에어컨 한 대의 수리 견적이 300달러임을 확인할 수 있다.
두 단서를 종합할 때, Mr. Watson은 Becool Alpine 에어컨을 수리한 비용 300달러에 대해 금액을 지불할 필요가 없었다는 것을 알 수 있다. 따라서 (B)가 정답이다.

193 육하원칙 문제

상 ●●●

해석 Mr. Watson은 왜 6월 3일에 전화를 받을 수 없었는가?
(A) 그의 회사의 다른 지사를 방문하고 있었다.
(B) 정부 기관에 불만 사항을 제출하고 있었다.
(C) 그의 고객의 세금 서류를 검토하고 있었다.
(D) 정보를 제공하는 회의에 참여하고 있었다.

해설 이메일의 'Date: June 3'에서 이메일이 6월 3일에 작성되었다고 했고, 'I will be out of the office all afternoon today as I am attending a tax seminar'에서 저, 즉 Mr. Watson이 세금 세미나에 참석하기 때문에 오늘, 즉 6월 3일 오후 내내 사무실에 없을 것이라고 한 후, 'you can contact me by phone tomorrow'에서 내일은 자신에게 전화로 연락할 수 있다고 했으므로 (D)가 정답이다.

어휘 informational adj. 정보를 제공하는, 정보의 session n. 회의

패러프레이징

seminar 세미나 → informational session 정보를 제공하는 회의

194 육하원칙 문제 연계

상 ●●●

해석 Hilltop AC사는 무엇을 하기로 동의했는가?
(A) 막판에 예약을 변경한다
(B) 청소 중 손상된 기기를 교체한다
(C) 추가 요금에 대해 할인을 제공한다
(D) 정규 근무 시간의 범위를 넘어서 작업자를 보낸다

해설 견적서의 'Hilltop AC technicians are available to perform service calls ~, 8 A.M. to 5 P.M.'에서 Hilltop AC사의 기술자들은 오전 8시부터 오후 5시까지 서비스 요청을 수행할 수 있다고 했다. 또한, 웹페이지의 'The technician arrived promptly at 6 P.M.'에서는 기술자가 오후 6시에 시간을 엄수하여 도착했다는 것을 확인할 수 있다.
두 단서를 종합할 때, Hilltop AC사가 기술자를 정규 근무 시간인 오후 5시 이후에 보냈다는 것을 알 수 있다. 따라서 (D)가 정답이다.

어휘 at the last minute phr. 막판에, 마지막 순간에 appliance n. 기기
damage v. 손상시키다 outside of phr. ~의 범위를 넘어서

regular hours phr. 정상 근무 시간

195 육하원칙 문제   중 ●●○

해석   Mr. Watson이 그의 사무실을 방문한 기술자에 대해 말하는 것은?
(A) 정비 담당자와 상의했다.
(B) 기기 작동에 대해 설명했다.
(C) 저렴한 모델을 추천했다.
(D) 예정된 시간 이후에 도착했다.

해설   웹페이지의 'I ~ appreciated that he took the time to show me the various functions of the new air conditioner he installed.'에서 저, 즉, Mr. Watson은 그, 즉 기술자가 자신이 설치한 신형 에어컨의 다양한 기능을 보여주는 것에 시간을 들인 것이 고마웠다고 했으므로 (B)가 정답이다.

어휘   consult v. 상의하다, 상담하다   operation n. 작동
inexpensive adj. 저렴한

패러프레이징

show ~ functions of the ~ air conditioner 에어컨의 기능을 보여주다
→ explained the operation of a device 기기 작동에 대해 설명했다

196-200번은 다음 프레젠테이션 슬라이드와 두 이메일에 관한 문제입니다.

ESTEBAN 부동산 – 교육 계획

주거용에서 상업용 부동산 임대업으로의 전환을 용이하게 위해, 우리 직원들은 다음 사항을 이해해야 할 것입니다:

– 196-A도시 구역법 (일부 사업체들은 도시의 특정 구역 내에서 영업하도록 허용되지 않음)
– 196-B상업용 임대 계약 (상업용 세입자들을 위한 임대차 계약들은 거주용 세입자들을 위한 것들보다 더 복잡함)
– 196-D건물 보안 (사업체들은 많은 귀중한 물건들을 가지고 있는 경향이 있고, 이는 건물을 제대로 안전하게 지키는 것이 중요하도록 만듦)

이 문제들 등을 해결하기 위한 교육 수업이 연말에 예정될 것입니다.

*199슬라이드는 *Sandra Williams*에 의해 준비됨*

reality n. 부동산   facilitate v. 용이하게 하다   transition n. 전환
residential adj. 주거용의   commercial adj. 상업용의
real estate phr. 부동산   zoning n. 구역(제)
operate v. 영업하다, 작동하다   tenant n. 세입자   complex adj. 복잡한
tend to phr. (~하는) 경향이 있다   of value phr. 귀중한, 가치 있는
properly adv. 제대로   secure v. 안전하게 지키다   address v. 해결하다

수신: 지점 관리자들 <branchmanagers@estebanrealty.com>
197발신: George Esteban <g.esteban@estebanrealty.com>
제목: 교육
날짜: 10월 14일

여러분 모두 알다시피, 우리 회사는 내년부터 상업용 부동산 관리에 초점을 두기로 결정했습니다. 197이 전략은 수익에서의 엄청난 증가로 이어질 것으로 기대됩니다. 하지만, 우리가 그것을 실행할 수 있기 전에, 우리 직원들은 교육을 받아야 할 것입니다.
198-B제가 여러분의 각 지점들에서 워크숍들이 열리도록 준비했습니다.

198-A/C이것들은 전국부동산협회의 전문가들에 의해 이끌어질 것이며 11월과 12월에 열릴 것입니다. 저는 다음 주에 여러분에게 구체적인 시간과 날짜를 제공해 드릴 것입니다.

200패서디나와 샌타바버라 지점의 경우, 저는 각 교육 수업에 최소 9명이 참가하길 바랍니다. 롱비치와 샌디에이고 지점은 현재 인원이 부족하기 때문에, 6명만 참석해야 합니다. 이 사람들은 그다음 그들이 습득한 지식을 그들 각자의 사무실에 있는 다른 직원들에게 전달할 수 있습니다.

George Esteban 드림
회장
Esteban 부동산

focus on phr. ~에 초점을 두다   significant adj. 상당한
boost n. 증가, 부양책   earning n. 수익   implement v. 실행하다
undergo v. 받다, 겪다   arrange v. 준비하다
understaffed adj. 인원이 부족한   pass along phr. 전달하다
acquire v. 습득하다, 얻다   respective adj. 각자의

수신: George Esteban <g.esteban@estebanrealty.com>
발신: Sandra Williams <s.williams@estebanrealty.com>
제목: 교육 최신 정보
날짜: 11월 2일

Mr. Esteban께,

저는 그저 귀하께 교육에 대한 최신 정보를 제공해드리고 싶었습니다. 내일 1차 워크숍이 시작될 것입니다. 어제 롱비치 지점에서 화재 스프링클러 시스템이 오작동한 사소한 문제가 하나 있었으므로 회의실은 이용할 수 없습니다. 하지만, 팀장들 중 한 명인 Sam Weber가 근처 회의장에 회의실을 마련했으므로, 워크숍은 예정대로 진행될 것입니다. 귀하께서 요청하신 대로, 각 지점에서 첫 번째 수업에 참석할 직원들의 수는 여기 있습니다:

– 샌타바버라: 직원 10명
– 200패서디나: 직원 8명
– 롱비치: 직원 6명
– 샌디에이고: 직원 6명

질문 사항이나 염려 사항이 있으면 제게 알려주십시오.

199Sandra Williams 드림
199인사부장
Esteban 부동산

update n. 최신 정보   minor adj. 사소한   malfunction v. 오작동하다
nearby adj. 근처의   conference n. 회의   proceed v. 진행되다
on schedule phr. 예정대로

196 Not/True 문제   상 ●●●

해석   프레젠테이션 슬라이드에 따르면, Esteban 부동산 직원들은 무엇에 대한 교육을 받지 않을 것인가?
(A) 시 규정
(B) 법적 계약
(C) 건물 유지관리
(D) 건물 보호

해설   프레젠테이션 슬라이드에서 (C)는 언급되지 않은 내용이다. 따라서 (C)가 정답이다. (A)는 'City Zoning Laws'에서 도시 구역법에 대해 배운다고 했으므로 지문의 내용과 일치한다. (B)는 'Commercial Lease Agreements'에서 상업용 임대 계약에 대해서 배운다고 했으므로 지문의 내용과 일치한다.

(D)는 'Building Security'에서 건물 보안에 대해 배운다고 했으므로 지문의 내용과 일치한다.

어휘 municipal adj. 시의 regulation n. 규정 legal adj. 법적인
maintenance n. 유지관리 property n. 건물, 부동산

패러프레이징

City ~ Laws 도시 법 → Municipal regulations 시 규정
Agreements 계약 → contracts 계약
Building Security 건물 보안 → Property protection 건물 보호

197 육하원칙 문제 상 ●●●

해석 Mr. Esteban은 새로운 전략으로 무엇을 달성하기를 바라는가?
(A) 감소된 고객 불만
(B) 개선된 직원 특전
(C) 증가된 회사 수익
(D) 감소된 운영비

해설 이메일1의 'From: George Esteban', 'It is hoped that this strategy will lead to a significant boost in earnings.'에서 Mr. Esteban은 이 전략이 수익에서의 엄청난 증가로 이어질 것으로 기대된다고 했으므로 (C)가 정답이다.

어휘 benefit n. 특전, 수당 profit n. 수익, 이익

패러프레이징

a significant boost in earnings 수익에서의 엄청난 증가 → Increased ~ profits 증가된 수익

198 Not/True 문제 상 ●●●

해석 워크숍들에 대해 언급된 것은?
(A) 외부 전문가에 의해 실시될 것이다.
(B) 회사 본사에서 열릴 것이다.
(C) 두 달 넘게 열릴 것이다.
(D) 모든 참가자들에 대해 시험을 포함할 것이다.

해설 이메일1의 'These will be led by specialists from the National Realtors Association ~.'에서 이것들, 즉 Esteban 부동산의 워크숍들은 전국부동산협회의 전문가들에 의해 이끌어질 것이라고 했으므로 (A)는 자문의 내용과 일치한다. 따라서 (A)가 정답이다. (B)는 'I have arranged for workshops to be held at each of your branches.'에서 각 지점들에서 워크숍들이 열리도록 준비했다고 했으므로 지문의 내용과 일치하지 않는다. (C)는 'These ~ will take place in November and December.'에서 이것들, 즉 워크숍들은 11월과 12월에 열릴 것이라고 했으므로 지문의 내용과 일치하지 않는다. (D)는 지문에 언급되지 않은 내용이다.

어휘 conduct v. 실시하다 headquarters n. 본사
take place phr. 열리다, 일어나다 participant n. 참가자

패러프레이징

specialists 전문가들 → experts 전문가들

199 육하원칙 문제 연계 중 ●●○

해석 프레젠테이션 슬라이드는 누가 준비했는가?
(A) 회사 사장
(B) 부동산 중개인
(C) 부서장

(D) 지점장

해설 의 'Slide prepared by Sandra Williams'에서 슬라이드가 Sandra Williams에 의해 준비되었다고 했다. 또한, 의 'Sandra Williams', 'Human Resources Manager'에서는 Sandra Williams가 인사부장이라는 것을 확인할 수 있다.
두 단서를 종합할 때, 프레젠테이션 슬라이드는 인사부장인 Sandra Williams에 의해 준비되었다는 것을 알 수 있다. 따라서 (C)가 정답이다.

패러프레이징

Human Resources Manager 인사부장 → department head 부서장

200 육하원칙 문제 연계 상 ●●●

해석 어느 사무실이 Mr. Esteban의 요구사항을 충족하지 않았는가?
(A) 샌타바버라
(B) 패서디나
(C) 롱비치
(D) 샌디에이고

해설 의 'For the Pasadena ~ branches, I would like at least nine people to participate in ~ training session.'에서 패서디나 지점의 경우, 저, 즉 Mr. Esteban은 교육 수업에 최소 9명이 참가하길 바란다고 했다. 또한, 의 'Pasadena: 8 staff members'에서는 패서디나 지점에서 직원 8명이 참석한다는 것을 확인할 수 있다.
두 단서를 종합할 때, Mr. Esteban이 패서디나 사무실에서 최소 9명이 참석할 것을 요구했으나 8명의 직원이 참석할 것이므로 패서디나 사무실이 Mr. Esteban의 요구사항을 충족하지 않았음을 알 수 있다. 따라서 (B)가 정답이다.

TEST 10

p 293

PART 5

101 등위접속사 채우기　　　　　중 ●●○

해석　이코노미석에는 남은 좌석이 없지만, 비즈니스석에는 몇 개가 남아 있다.

해설　절(There ~ class)과 절(several ~ business)을 연결할 수 있는 것은 접속사이므로 모든 보기가 정답의 후보이다. '이코노미석에는 남은 좌석이 없지만, 비즈니스석에는 몇 개가 남아 있다'라는 의미가 되어야 하므로 상반되는 내용의 단어와 단어, 구와 구, 절과 절을 연결하는 등위접속사 (A) but(하지만)이 정답이다. (B)는 명사절 접속사일 경우 that이 이끄는 명사절이 문장 내에서 주어, 목적어, 보어 역할을 하는데 빈칸 앞의 절(There ~ class)이 주어(There), 동사(are), 보어(seats)를 모두 갖춘 완전한 절이므로 빈칸에 올 수 없다. 관계대명사일 경우 콤마 바로 뒤에 올 수 없다. 접속사 (C)는 콤마 뒤에서 쓰일 수 없으며 형용사나 부사의 비교급과 함께 쓰여야 한다. 참고로, 접속사 (D)는 부사 neither와 함께 상관접속사 neither A nor B(A도 B

도 아닌)의 형태로 자주 쓰임을 알아둔다.

어휘　remain v. 남아 있다　than conj. ~보다

102 격에 맞는 인칭대명사 채우기　　　　　중 ●●○

해석　Mr. Gaviria는 그의 직원들 중 아무도 시간이 없어서 Mr. Horne의 직원들에게 도움을 요청했다.

해설　전치사(of)의 목적어 자리에 올 수 있는 목적격 인칭대명사 (B), 소유대명사 (C), 재귀대명사 (D)가 정답의 후보이다. '그의 것(직원들) 중에 아무도 시간이 없어서 Mr. Horne의 직원들에게 도움을 요청했다'라는 의미가 되어야 하므로 소유대명사 (C) his가 정답이다. 목적격 인칭대명사 (B)와 재귀대명사 (D)를 쓸 경우 각각 '그(Mr. Gaviria) 중에/그(Mr. Gaviria) 자신 중에 아무도 시간이 없어서 Mr. Horne의 직원들에게 도움을 요청했다'라는 어색한 문맥이 된다. 주격 인칭 대명사 (A)는 목적어 자리에 올 수 없다.

어휘　assistance n. 도움, 지원

103 명사 자리 채우기　　　　　하 ●○○

해석　Brinity 전자회사의 최신 냉장고는 그것의 이전 모델과 비교하여 에너지 사용에서의 상당한 감소를 보여준다.

해설　동사(shows)의 목적어 자리에 오면서 형용사(significant)의 꾸밈을 받을 수 있는 것은 명사이므로 명사 (A) reduction(감소)이 정답이다. 동사 또는 과거분사 (B), 동사 (C)와 (D)는 명사 자리에 올 수 없다.

어휘　latest adj. 최신의　significant adj. 상당한, 중요한
predecessor n. 이전 모델, 전임자　reduce v. 줄이다, 축소하다

104 부사 자리 채우기　　　　　하 ●○○

해석　배달 중에, 부서지기 쉬운 물건들이 들어 있는 소포들은 조심스럽게 다루어져야 한다.

해설　동사(must ~ handled)를 꾸밀 수 있는 것은 부사이므로 부사 (D) cautiously(조심스럽게)가 정답이다. 명사 또는 동사 (A)와 (C), 형용사 (B)는 동사를 꾸밀 수 없다. 참고로, handled를 복수 명사 (C) cautions(경고들)를 꾸미는 과거분사로 본다 해도, '소포들은 다루어진 경고들이 되어야 한다'라는 어색한 문맥이 된다.

어휘　contain v. ~이 들어 있다, 포함하다　delicate adj. 부서지기 쉬운, 섬세한
handle v. 다루다, 처리하다　cautious adj. 조심스러운

105 현재분사와 과거분사 구별하여 채우기　　　　　상 ●●●

해석　회사의 재정적인 어려움에 관한 의견을 말하면서, Mr. Sawyer는 모든 부서장들에게 경비를 줄이도록 요청했다.

해설　이 문장은 주어(Mr. Sawyer), 동사(asked), 목적어(all ~ managers), 목적격 보어(to cut expenses)를 갖춘 완전한 절이므로 ___ on ~ difficulties는 수식어 거품으로 보아야 한다. 따라서 수식어 거품이 될 수 있는 현재분사 (A)와 과거분사 (C)가 정답의 후보이다. 주절의 주어(Mr. Sawyer)와 분사가 'Mr. Sawyer가 회사의 재정적인 어려움에 관한 의견을 말하다'라는 의미의 능동 관계이므로 현재분사 (A) Remarking(말하다)이 정답이다. 과거분사 (C)를 쓸 경우 'Mr. Sawyer가 회사의 재정적

인 어려움에 관한 의견을 말해지다'라는 어색한 문맥이 된다. 참고로, 동사 remark는 자동사와 타동사 모두로 쓰임을 알아둔다. 명사 또는 동사 (B)와 (D)는 수식어 거품을 이끌 수 없다.

어휘 department manager phr. 부서장 cut v. 줄이다, 단축하다
expense n. 경비 remark v. (의견을) 말하다; n. 의견, 논평

106 주어와 수 일치하는 동사 채우기 중 ●●○

해석 Terta사의 서비스 센터들은 고객 불만을 추적하는 전문적인 소프트웨어를 이용한다.

해설 문장에 동사가 없으므로 동사인 (A), (B), (D)가 정답의 후보이다. 주어 (The service centers)가 복수이므로 복수 동사 (A) employ가 정답이다. 참고로, 주어(The service centers)와 동사 사이의 전치사구 of Terta Corporation은 수식어 거품구이므로 동사의 수 결정에 아무런 영향을 주지 않는다. 단수 동사 (B)와 (D)는 복수 주어의 동사 자리에 올 수 없다. 현재분사 또는 동명사 (C)는 동사 자리에 올 수 없다. Specialized가 이 문장의 동사이고 현재분사 (C)가 빈칸 앞의 명사구(The service ~ Corporation)를 꾸미는 것이라면, '이용하는/고용하는 Terta사의 서비스 센터들은 고객 불만을 추적하는 전문적인 소프트웨어를 상세히 설명한다'라는 어색한 문맥이 되고 분사는 목적어나 전치사구를 동반하지 않고 단독으로 쓰일 경우 주로 명사 앞에서 명사를 꾸미기 때문에 (C)는 답이 될 수 없다.

어휘 specialized adj. 전문적인 track v. 추적하다; n. 선로
employ v. 이용하다, 고용하다

107 동사 어휘 고르기 상 ●●●

해석 임원들은 아시아 국가들로 제조업을 옮김으로써 더 가격이 적당한 노동력을 얻기를 기대한다.

해설 빈칸은 전치사(by)의 목적어 역할을 하는 동명사 자리이다. '아시아 국가들로 제조업을 옮김으로써 더 가격이 적당한 노동력을 얻기를 기대한다'라는 문맥이므로 동사 shift(옮기다, 이전하다)의 동명사 (C) shifting이 정답이다. (B)의 substitute(대체하다)와 (D)의 transform(바꾸다, 변형시키다)도 해석상 그럴듯해 보이지만, 제조업체를 아시아 국가들의 제조업체로 대체하거나 바꾼다는 의미가 아니라, '제조업 그 자체를 아시아 국가들로 대체하다/바꾸다'라는 어색한 의미가 되므로 답이 될 수 없다. 참고로, (B)의 substitute는 substitute A for B(B를 A로 대체하다)의 형태로 자주 쓰임을 알아둔다. 또한, (D)의 transform은 into/to와 함께 '바꾸다, 전환하다'라는 의미로 쓰이지만, 성질, 기능, 용도 등을 바꾸는 것을 나타낸다.

어휘 board member phr. 임원, 이사 gain v. 얻다, 늘리다
affordable adj. (가격이) 적당한 manufacturing n. 제조업, 제조
invert v. 뒤집다, 거꾸로 하다

108 부사 어휘 고르기 중 ●●○

해석 때때로, Godsal 가전제품사는 직원들을 위한 세미나를 실시하며, 이는 효과적인 교육 프로그램으로 입증되었다.

해설 빈칸은 문장 전체를 꾸미는 부사 자리이다. '때때로, 직원들을 위한 세미나를 실시한다'라는 문맥이므로 (C) Occasionally(때때로, 가끔)가 정답이다. (A) Potentially(잠재적으로)도 해석상 그럴듯해 보이지만, 지금은 그러하지 않지만 앞으로 그럴 수 있다는 가능성을 나타내므로 현재 세미나를 실시하고 있다는 문맥과는 어울리지 않는다.

어휘 prove v. 입증하다, 드러내다 effective adj. 효과적인
questionably adv. 의심스럽게 unanimously adv. 만장일치로

109 부정대명사/형용사 채우기 중 ●●○

해석 뉴욕시는 주차 규정을 위반하여 적발된 어떤 운전자들에게라도 25달러의 벌금을 부과할 것이다.

해설 복수 명사(drivers)와 함께 쓰일 수 있는 부정형용사 (A)와 수량 형용사 (B)가 정답의 후보이다. '적발된 어떤 운전자들에게라도 25달러의 벌금을 부과할 것이다'라는 의미이므로 (A) any(어떤 ~라도)가 정답이다. 수량 형용사 (B) few(거의 없는)를 쓸 경우 '거의 없는 운전자들에게 벌금을 부과할 것이다'라는 어색한 문맥이 된다. 수량 형용사 (C)는 가산 단수 명사를, 수량 형용사 (D)는 불가산 명사를 꾸민다. 참고로, few와 a few(몇몇의)를 구별하여 알아둔다.

어휘 impose v. 부과하다, 도입하다 fine n. 벌금
in violation of phr. ~을 위반하여 policy n. 규정, 정책
each adj. 각각의 much adj. 많은

110 부사 자리 채우기 중 ●●○

해석 인터넷 접속이 끊어질 때마다 간단히 재설정 버튼만 누르면, 그 문제는 즉시 고쳐질 것이다.

해설 동사(push)를 꾸밀 수 있는 것은 부사이므로 부사 (B) Simply(간단히)가 정답이다. 형용사 (A), 명사 (C), 동사 (D)는 동사를 꾸밀 수 없다. (C)를 동사(push)의 주어 자리에 온 명사로 본다 해도, 불가산 명사이므로 복수 동사(push)와 함께 쓸 수 없다. 참고로, 첫 번째 절(Simply push ~ button)은 주어(you)가 생략된 명령문임을 알아둔다.

어휘 disconnect v. (접속이) 끊어지다, 끊다 simple adj. 간단한
simplicity n. 간단함 simplify v. 간단하게 하다

111 동명사와 명사 구별하여 채우기 중 ●●○

해석 연간 마케팅 계획을 세우는 것은 Ms. Hurley와 그녀의 팀의 책임이었다.

해설 문장에 동사(has been)만 있고 주어가 없으므로 주어 자리에 올 수 있는 명사 (A)와 (D), 동명사 (C)가 정답의 후보이다. 빈칸 뒤의 명사구(the yearly ~ plan)를 목적어로 취할 수 있는 것은 동명사이므로 (C) Producing(세우는 것, 만들어내는 것)이 정답이다. 명사 (A)와 (D)는 목적어(the yearly ~ plan)를 취할 수 없다. 동사 또는 과거분사 (B)는 주어 자리에 올 수 없다. 과거분사 (B)를 빈칸 뒤의 명사구(the yearly ~ plan)를 꾸미는 것으로 본다 해도, 과거분사는 관사(the) 다음에 와야 하므로 답이 될 수 없다.

어휘 yearly adj. 연간의 responsibility n. 책임, 의무
produce n. 농산물; v. 생산하다 production n. 생산, 생산량

112 명사 보어와 형용사 보어 구별하여 채우기 상 ●●●

해석 HynaCorp사의 최신 화학 공장은 분기 말까지 완전히 정상 가동될 것이다.

해설 be동사(be)의 보어 자리에 올 수 있는 명사 (A)와 (D), 형용사 (B)가 정답의 후보이다. 부사(fully)의 꾸밈을 받고 있고, 보어가 주어(HynaCorp's ~ plant)의 상태를 설명하고 있으므로 형용사 (B) functional(가동되는)이 정답이다. 명사 (A)와 (D)를 쓸 경우 주어(HynaCorp's ~ plant)와 동격이 되어 각각 '공장이 완전히 기능/기능들일 것이다'라는 어색한 문맥이 된다. 부사 (C)는 보어 자리에 올 수 없다.

어휘 plant n. 공장 fully adv. 완전히, 충분히 quarter n. 분기
function n. 기능; v. 기능하다 functionally adv. 기능상, 함수적으로

113 형용사 어휘 고르기 중 ●●○

해석 대부분의 휴가 패키지들이 선택 관광을 포함하고 있기 때문에, 관광객들은 수

월하게 여행을 원하는 대로 만들 수 있다.

해설 빈칸은 명사(tours)를 꾸미는 형용사 자리이다. '대부분의 휴가 패키지들이 선택 관광을 포함하고 있기 때문에 여행을 원하는 대로 만들 수 있다'라는 문맥이므로 (B) optional(선택적인)이 정답이다.

어휘 customize v. 원하는 대로 만들다, 주문제작하다 scheduled adj. 예정된
affluent adj. 부유한, 돈이 많은 reliable adj. 신뢰할 수 있는

114 전치사 표현 채우기 중 ●●○

해석 건물의 로비에 위치한 카페는 모든 세입자들에게 할인을 제공한다.

해설 빈칸은 명사구(the lobby ~ building)를 목적어로 취하는 전치사 자리이다. '건물의 로비에 위치한 카페'라는 의미가 되어야 하므로 빈칸 앞의 과거분사 located와 함께 '~에 위치하다'라는 의미의 어구인 located in을 만드는 전치사 (D) in(~에)이 정답이다. (A)와 (C)도 해석상 그럴듯해 보이지만 (A)는 셋 이상의 대상 사이에 있는 것을 나타내고, (C)는 표면 위나, 무언가에 접해서 가까이 있는 것을 나타낸다.

어휘 discount n. 할인; v. 할인하다 tenant n. 세입자, 임차인
from prep. ~부터, ~에서

115 동사 어휘 고르기 상 ●●●

해석 위원회가 Mr. Souko의 사업 제안서를 검토하자마자, 그것은 그에게 상당한 보조금을 수여 했다.

해설 빈칸은 주어(it)의 동사 자리이다. '그것(위원회)은 그에게 상당한 보조금을 수여 했다'라는 문맥이므로 (B) awarded(수여 했다)가 정답이다. (D)의 donate(기부하다)도 해석상 그럴듯해 보이지만, donate는 사람명사가 아닌 기부하는 금액이나 물품을 목적어로 취하므로 답이 될 수 없다.

어휘 committee n. 위원회 review v. 검토하다 proposal n. 제안(서)
considerable adj. 상당한 subsidy n. 보조금, 장려금
charge v. 청구하다 access v. 접근하다

116 시간 표현과 일치하는 시제의 동사 채우기 하 ●○○

해석 Hightower 은행의 웨스트코비나 지점은 지난달 초에 엘몬티로 옮겼다.

해설 과거 시제와 함께 쓰이는 시간 표현(last month)이 있으므로 과거 시제 (B) moved가 정답이다. 현재 시제 (A), 현재 완료 시제 (C), 미래 시제 (D)는 과거를 나타내는 시간 표현과 함께 쓰일 수 없다.

어휘 branch n. 지점

117 전치사 채우기 상 ●●●

해석 Kerner 재단은 정부로부터 지원을 받으며, 기업 후원자들을 통해서도 기금을 받는다.

해설 빈칸은 명사구(corporate sponsors)를 목적어로 취하는 전치사 자리이다. '기업 후원자들을 통해 기금을 받는다'라는 의미가 되어야 하므로 (C) through(~을 통해)가 정답이다. (A) over도 '~을 통해'라는 의미를 가지지만, 전화, 라디오, TV, 컴퓨터 등의 방송 매체를 통하는 것을 의미한다.

어휘 support v. 지원하다 government n. 정부 funding n. 기금
corporate adj. 기업의 along prep. ~을 따라 across prep. ~을 가로질러

118 수량 표현 채우기 중 ●●○

해석 비록 대부분의 설문조사들에서 Hamada사의 SUV가 Sunza사의 것보다 더 높은 순위를 차지하지만, 두 회사의 차량들 모두 믿을 수 있다고 알려져 있다.

해설 빈칸 뒤의 복수 가산 명사(vehicles)를 꾸밀 수 있는 것은 형용사이므로 수량 형용사 (B)와 (D)가 정답의 후보이다. 'Hamada사의 SUV가 Sunza사의 것보다 더 높은 순위를 차지하지만, 두 회사의 차량들 모두 믿을 수 있다고 알려져 있다'라는 의미가 되어야 하므로 (B) both(둘 다, 모두)가 정답이다. (D) several(몇몇의)을 쓸 경우, 'Hamada사의 SUV가 Sunza사의 것보다 더 높은 순위를 차지하지만, 몇몇 차량들은 믿을 수 있다고 알려져 있다'라는 어색한 문맥이 된다. 등위 접속사 (A)는 접속사(Although)로 이미 연결된 절을 연결할 수 없다. 한정사 (C)는 두 가지 대상 중 하나를 가리킬 때 사용되며 단수 명사와 쓰인다. 참고로, either는 or(또는)와 함께 상관접속사 either A or B(A 또는 B 중 하나)의 형태로 쓰일 수 있음을 알아둔다.

어휘 rank v. (높은 순위를) 차지하다 vehicle n. 차량, 차
dependable adj. 믿을 수 있는, 신뢰할 만한

119 형용사 어휘 고르기 중 ●●○

해석 지금은 공적 생활에서 은퇴한, Ms. Hicks는 휴스턴 시장으로서의 그녀의 임기 동안 중요한 인물이었다.

해설 빈칸은 명사(figure)를 꾸미는 형용사 자리이다. 'Ms. Hicks는 임기 동안 중요한 인물이었다'라는 문맥이므로 (D) prominent(중요한)가 정답이다.

어휘 public life phr. 공적 생활, 공유 figure n. 인물 term n. 임기, 용어
previous adj. 이전의 private adj. 사적인 numerous adj. 무수한

120 형용사 어휘 고르기 중 ●●○

해석 예산 삭감으로 인해, 이제부터 시 위생 검사관들은 1년에 오직 두 번만 식당들에 정기 방문을 할 것이다.

해설 빈칸은 명사(visits)를 꾸미는 형용사 자리이다. '1년에 오직 두 번만 정기 방문을 할 것이다'라는 문맥이므로 (D) routine(정기적인)이 정답이다. (C) industrious(근면한, 부지런한)도 해석상 그럴듯해 보이지만, 사람이 근면하거나 부지런한 것을 의미하므로 답이 될 수 없다.

어휘 due to phr. ~로 인해 budget n. 예산 cut n. 삭감; v. 자르다
inspector n. 검사관 frequent adj. 빈번한, 잦은
impressive adj. 인상적인

121 동명사와 명사 구별하여 채우기 중 ●●○

해석 심각한 오류들의 발행을 방지하기 위해 웹사이트에 기사를 업로드하기 전에 그것을 철저히 확인하십시오.

해설 전치사(before)의 목적어 자리에 올 수 있는 명사 (A)와 동명사 (C)가 정답의 후보이다. 빈칸 다음에 온 목적어(it)를 취할 수 있는 것은 동명사이므로 동명사 (C) uploading(업로드하는 것)이 정답이다. 명사 (A)는 목적어를 가질 수 없다. 동사 또는 과거분사(B)와 to 부정사 (D)는 전치사의 목적어 자리에 올 수 없다.

어휘 check v. 확인하다 thoroughly adv. 철저히
prevent v. 방지하다, 예방하다 publication n. 발행, 출간
serious adj. 심각한

122 전치사 채우기 상 ●●●

해석 자선 경매 후에, 지역 밴드들은 Brighton 홀에서 무료 콘서트를 열 것이다.

해설 이 문장은 주어(local bands), 동사(will hold), 목적어(a ~ concert)를 갖춘 완전한 절이므로, ___ the charity auction은 수식어 거품으로 보아야 한다. 이 수식어 거품은 동사가 없는 거품구이므로 거품구를 이끌 수 있는 전치사 (A), (B), (D)가 정답의 후보이다. '자선 경매 후에 무료 콘서트를 열 것이다'라는 의미가 되어야 하므로 (D) Following(~후에)이 정답이다. (B)

Upon(~의 직후에)도 해석상 그럴듯해 보이지만, '~의 직후에'라는 의미로 쓰이기 위해서는 동명사나 delivery(배달), arrival(도착) 등 동작을 나타내는 명사와 함께 쓰여야 한다. 참고로, upon이 '~일 때, ~에'라는 의미로 쓰이기 위해서는 시간 표현과 함께 쓰여야 하며, 따라서 upon the event가 아닌, upon the start of the event(행사가 시작할 때)와 같이 쓰여야 한다. 접속사 (C)는 거품구를 이끌 수 없다.

어휘 charity auction phr. 자선 경매 toward prep. ~쪽으로, ~을 향하여
whereas conj. ~에 반해서, 반면

123 지시대명사/지시형용사 채우기   상 ●●●

해석 항공사 마일리지들은 보통 일정 기간 후에 만료됨에도 불구하고, Leisure Plans사에 의해 제공되는 것들은 그렇지 않다.

해설 주절(___ ~ do not)에 동사(do)만 있고, 주어가 없으므로 주어 자리에 올 수 있는 주격 인칭대명사 (A), 지시대명사 (C), 가짜주어로 쓰이는 (D)가 정답의 후보이다. 빈칸이 과거분사(offered)의 꾸밈을 받고 있고, 'Leisure Plans사에 의해 제공되는 것들은 그렇지 않다'라는 의미가 되어야 하므로 앞에 나온 복수 명사(airline miles)를 대신하는 지시대명사 (C) those(그것들)가 정답이다. 주격 인칭대명사 (A)는 수식어의 꾸밈을 받을 수 없고, (D)는 '~이 있다'를 나타내며 'there + 동사(be, remain, exist) + 진짜주어'의 형태로 쓰인다. 목적격 인칭대명사 (B)는 주어 자리에 올 수 없다.

어휘 expire v. 만료되다 offer v. 제공하다, 제안하다

124 명사 어휘 고르기   중 ●●○

해석 직원들은 다른 프로젝트 마감일들에 대해 내부 전산망에 있는 일정표를 참고할 수 있다.

해설 빈칸은 전치사(to)의 목적어 역할을 하는 명사 자리이다. '마감일들에 대해 내부 전산망에 있는 일정표를 참고할 수 있다'라는 문맥이므로 (D) timetable(일정표, 시간표)이 정답이다.

어휘 refer to phr. ~을 참고하다 intranet n. 내부 전산망
catalog n. 목록, 카탈로그 category n. 범주 formation n. 형성

125 형용사 자리 채우기   상 ●●●

해석 일본과 인도 사이의 무역 협정은 소매업 부문에서 이례적인 경제 성장을 촉진시켰다.

해설 명사구(economic growth)를 꾸밀 수 있는 것은 형용사이므로 형용사 (D) exceptional(이례적인)이 정답이다. 전치사 (A) except(~을 제외하고)도 '그 무역 협정은 소매업 부분에서의 경제 성장을 제외하고 촉진시켰다'라는 의미로 해석상 그럴듯해 보이지만, facilitate(~을 촉진시키다)는 타동사이므로 뒤에 목적어가 와야 한다. 명사 (B)와 동사 (C)는 형용사 자리에 올 수 없다.

어휘 trade agreement phr. 무역 협정 facilitate v. 촉진시키다
retail sector phr. 소매업 부문 except prep. ~을 제외하고; v. 제외하다
exception n. 예외, 이례

126 복합 명사 채우기   상 ●●●

해석 Qartman사의 공장 직원들은 더 나은 복지혜택들뿐만 아니라 상당한 급료 인상을 바라고 있다.

해설 전치사(for)의 목적어 역할을 하면서 형용사(sizable)의 꾸밈을 받을 수 있

는 것은 명사이므로 빈칸 앞의 명사 pay(급료, 보수)와 함께 쓰여 '급료 인상'이라는 의미의 복합 명사 pay raise를 만드는 (A)와 (B)가 정답의 후보이다. raise는 가산 명사이므로 복수형 (B) raises가 정답이다. 단수 명사 (A)는 관사와 함께 쓰여야 하는데 빈칸 앞에 관사가 없으므로 답이 될 수 없다. 과거분사 (C)와 현재분사 (D)는 명사 자리에 올 수 없다. 분사가 빈칸 앞의 명사 (pay)를 꾸미는 것으로 본다 해도, 분사가 목적어나 전치사구를 동반하지 않고 단독으로 쓰일 경우, 명사(pay) 앞에 와야 하므로 답이 될 수 없다.

어휘 sizable adj. 상당한

127 형용사 자리 채우기   상 ●●●

해석 지원자는 면접에서 매우 긍정적인 인상을 주어서 그는 즉시 고용되었다.

해설 부정관사(a) 앞에 와서 명사(impression)를 꾸밀 수 있어야 하므로 형용사 (D) such(매우)가 정답이다. 참고로, such는 뒤에 온 that절과 연결되어 '매우 ~여서 -하다'는 의미를 가지고, 'such + a + 형용사 + 명사'의 형태로 쓰인다. 부사 (A), (B), (C)는 부정관사(a) 앞에 와서 명사를 꾸밀 수 없다.

어휘 candidate n. 지원자, 후보자 impression n. 인상, 감명
immediately adv. 즉시 so adv. 매우 too adv. 너무

128 동사 어휘 고르기   중 ●●○

해석 Venus 의류사는 그것의 텔레비전 캠페인에 성공하지 못해서 그것의 제품들을 광고하기 위해 소셜 미디어로 방향을 바꿨다.

해설 빈칸은 to 부정사를 만드는 동사원형 자리이다. '텔레비전 캠페인에 성공하지 못해서 제품들을 광고하기 위해 소셜 미디어로 방향을 바꿨다'라는 문맥이므로 (C) market(광고하다, 시장에 내놓다)이 정답이다.

어휘 unsuccessful adj. 성공하지 못한 generate v. 발생시키다, 만들어 내다
exchange v. 교환하다 contribute v. 기여하다

129 형용사 자리 채우기   상 ●●●

해석 직원들은 고객들이 반드시 가게 바깥에 질서 있는 태도로 줄을 서게 할 것이다.

해설 관사(an) 뒤에 와서 명사(manner)를 꾸밀 수 있는 것은 형용사이므로 형용사 (C)와 현재분사 (D)가 정답의 후보이다. '질서 있는 태도로 줄을 서게 하다'라는 문맥이므로 형용사 (C) orderly(질서 있는, 정돈된)가 정답이다. 현재분사 (D)는 '고객들이 명령을 내리는/주문하는 태도로 줄을 서게 하다'라는 어색한 문맥을 만든다. 명사 또는 동사 (A)와 (B)는 형용사 자리에 올 수 없다.

어휘 ensure v. 반드시 ~하게 하다, 보장하다 line up phr. 줄을 서다
manner n. 태도, 방식 order n. 명령, 순서; v. 명령하다, 주문하다

130 동명사와 명사 구별하여 채우기   중 ●●○

해석 Electa사의 최고 경영자로서 Jonas Meier를 대신한 이후로, Ms. Harris는 그 회사의 미래에 대한 낙관을 표했다.

해설 전치사(Since)의 목적어가 될 수 있는 동명사 (A)와 명사 (D)가 정답의 후보이다. 빈칸 뒤의 명사(Jonas Meier)를 목적어로 취할 수 있는 것은 동명사이므로 (A) replacing(대신하는 것)이 정답이다. 명사 (D)는 연결어 없이 빈칸 뒤의 명사와 나란히 올 수 없다. 동사 또는 과거분사 (B)와 동사 (C)는 전치사의 목적어 자리에 올 수 없다. 과거분사 (B)가 명사 Jonas Meier를 꾸미는 것으로 보더라도 since 뒤에는 과거의 시간이나 사건을 나타내는 표현이 와야 하므로 답이 될 수 없다.

어휘 express v. 표하다, 나타내다 optimism n. 낙관(론)
replace v. 대신하다, 대체하다

PART 6

131-134번은 다음 광고지에 관한 문제입니다.

> **Forge가 문을 열다!**
>
> Lodz 공과 대학(LTI)이 Forge를 자랑스럽게 소개합니다. Forge는 창작자들의 공동체에 의해 운영되는 ¹³¹작업공간입니다. 이곳은 아마추어 발명가들이 그들의 프로젝트들을 개발할 수 있는 장소입니다. 당신의 관심사가 전자 기기, 목공품, 혹은 금속세공에 ¹³²있든 아니든, Forge는 당신이 당신의 창의적인 상상을 실현하도록 도와줄 수 있습니다. 이것은 3D 프린터, 레이저 절단기, 그리고 그 이상의 것들과 같은 다양한 설비들에 대한 ¹³³공유된 이용을 제공합니다. 모든 LTI 학생들은 대학 정상 운영 시간 동안 이 장비를 자유롭게 사용할 수 있습니다. 기계는 무료로 사용될 수 있고, 재료들은 필요 시 저렴한 가격에 제공됩니다. ¹³⁴저희는 심지어 당신이 필요할 수 있는 무엇이든지 주문하도록 도와줄 수 있습니다. 더 많은 정보를 위해서는 Kaminski 건물에 들르거나, www.lodz.edu/forge를 방문하십시오.

proudly adv. 자랑스럽게 **lie** v. 있다, 위치해 있다 **electronic** n. 전자 기기
carpentry n. 목공품 **metalworking** n. 금속세공
realize v. (목표를) 실현하다, 알아차리다 **vision** n. 상상, 시력
a range of phr. 다양한 **facility** n. 설비, 시설
laser cutter phr. 레이저 절단기 **equipment** n. 장비 **machinery** n. 기계
material n. 재료, 물질 **stop by** phr. ~에 (잠시) 들르다

---

131 명사 어휘 고르기 주변 문맥 파악 하 ●○○

해설 빈칸은 be동사(is)의 주격 보어 역할을 하는 명사 자리이다. 'Forge는 창작자들의 공동체에 의해 운영되는 ___이다'라는 문맥이므로 모든 보기가 정답의 후보이다. 뒤 문장에서 이곳은 아마추어 발명가들이 그들의 프로젝트들을 개발할 수 있는 장소라고 했으므로 Forge가 발명가들이 작업을 할 수 있는 장소임을 알 수 있다. 따라서 (C) workspace(작업공간)가 정답이다.

어휘 **group** n. 집단 **course** n. 과정, 강의 **discussion** n. 논의, 상의

---

132 부사절 접속사 채우기 주변 문맥 파악 중 ●●○

해설 이 문장은 주어(the Forge), 동사(can help), 목적어(you), 목적격 보어(realize ~ vision)를 갖춘 완전한 절이므로, ___ ~ metalworking은 수식어 거품으로 보아야 한다. 이 수식어 거품은 동사(lies)가 있는 거품절이므로, 거품절을 이끌 수 있는 부사절 접속사인 모든 보기가 정답의 후보이다. 뒤 문장에서 3D 프린터, 레이저 절단기와 같은 다양한 설비들에 대한 이용을 제공한다고 했으므로 빈칸이 있는 문장에는 그러한 기계들을 필요로 하는 어떤 분야든지 도움을 줄 수 있다는 내용이 와야 한다. 따라서 양보를 나타내서 '당신의 관심사가 전자 기기, 목공품, 혹은 금속세공에 있든 아니든'이라는 의미를 만드는 부사절 접속사 (A) Whether(~이든 아니든)가 정답이다. 참고로, whether는 '~인지 아닌지'라는 의미의 명사절 접속사로도 쓰일 수 있으며, 이때 whether가 이끄는 명사절은 문장에서 주어, 보어, 목적어로 쓰일 수 있음을 알아둔다.

어휘 **unless** conj. ~하지 않는 한 **although** conj. 비록 ~일지라도
whereas conj. ~한 반면에

최고난도 문제

133 동사 어휘 고르기 전체 문맥 파악 상 ●●●

해설 빈칸은 명사(access)를 꾸미는 형용사 역할을 하는 과거분사 자리이다. '다양한 설비들에 대한 ___ 이용을 제공한다'라는 문맥이므로 모든 보기가 정답

의 후보이다. 앞부분에서 Forge는 발명가들이 프로젝트들을 개발할 수 있는 장소라고 한 후, 뒤 문장에서 모든 LTI 학생들은 이 장비를 자유롭게 사용할 수 있다고 했으므로, 학생들이 시설 이용을 공유한다는 것을 알 수 있다. 따라서 (B) shared(공유된)가 정답이다. 참고로, (A) paid(지불된)도 그럴듯해 보이지만, 뒷부분에서 기계는 무료로 사용될 수 있다고 했으므로 답이 될 수 없다.

어휘 **supervise** v. 감독하다, 지도하다 **finish** v. 끝나다, 완료하다

---

134 알맞은 문장 고르기 상 ●●●

해석 (A) 저희는 모든 사용자들에게 무료 배송을 제공합니다.
(B) 기부를 위한 물품들은 사무실에 놓여질 수 있습니다.
(C) 저희는 심지어 당신이 필요할 수 있는 무엇이든지 주문하도록 도와줄 수 있습니다.
(D) 회원권 요금은 매달 미리 지불되어야 합니다.

해설 앞 문장 'materials are provided at a low cost when required'에서 재료들은 필요 시 저렴한 가격에 제공된다고 했으므로 빈칸에는 필요한 재료의 제공과 관련된 내용이 들어가야 함을 알 수 있다. 따라서 (C)가 정답이다.

어휘 **shipping** n. 배송 **donation** n. 기부 **drop off** phr. ~에 놓다, 맡기다
even adv. 심지어 **in advance** phr. 미리, 사전에

135-138번은 다음 기사에 관한 문제입니다.

> **Stelly의 신작이 매진되다**
>
> 뉴올리언스 (4월 24일)— 지역 작가 Maria Stelly는 그녀의 소설 *Mystery Street*를 ¹³⁵쓰기 위해 거의 10년을 보냈다. 하지만 이 책이 월요일에 마침내 발간되었을 때, 그것은 2시간 만에 매진되었다. 그것은 뉴올리언스 전역에 있는 17개 서점들에 ¹³⁶배포되었다.
>
> "비록 저의 첫 번째 출판물이 제법 성공하긴 했지만, 저는 *Mystery Street*의 인기에 놀랐으며, 저의 모든 팬들에게 감사드립니다."라고 Stelly가 말했다. 그녀는 그 책의 인기에 대해 획기적인 마케팅이 부분적으로 원인이 된다고 생각한다. ¹³⁷이것은 소셜 미디어에서 활발한 독자들을 겨냥하는 것을 수반했다. Stelly의 새로운 책의 추가 부수들은 4월 30일에 구입할 수 ¹³⁸있게 될 것이다.

sell out phr. 매진되다 **local** adj. 지역의 **decade** n. 10년 **novel** n. 소설
release v. 발간하다, 공개하다 **throughout** prep. 전역에, 도처에
publication n. 출판(물) **moderately** adv. 제법, 적절하게
popularity n. 인기 **innovative** adj. 획기적인, 혁신적인
responsible adj. 원인이 되는, 책임이 있는 **available** adj. 구입할 수 있는

---

135 to 부정사 채우기 중 ●●○

해설 이 문장은 주어(Local writer Maria Stelly), 동사(spent), 목적어(a decade)를 갖춘 완전한 절이므로, ___ ~ Mystery Street는 수식어 거품으로 보아야 한다. 이 수식어 거품은 동사가 없는 거품구이므로, 거품구를 이끌며 '쓰기 위해'라는 의미의 목적을 나타내는 to 부정사 (C) to write가 정답이다. 동사 (A)와 (B), 명사 (D)는 수식어 거품을 이끌 수 없다.

---

136 동사 어휘 고르기 주변 문맥 파악 중 ●●○

해설 빈칸은 be동사(was)와 함께 쓰여 수동태를 만드는 p.p.형의 자리이다. '그것은 뉴올리언스 전역에 있는 17개 서점들에 ___되었다'라는 문맥이므로 모든 보기가 정답의 후보이다. 앞 문장에서 이 책이 발간되었을 때, 2시간 만에 매진되었다고 했으므로 서점에 이 책이 배포되었다는 것을 알 수 있다. 따라서 동사 distribute(배포하다)의 p.p.형 (A) distributed가 정답이다.

어휘 report v. 알리다 connect v. 연결하다 compare v. 비교하다

137 알맞은 문장 고르기 중 ●●○

해석 (A) 이것은 소셜 미디어에서 활발한 독자들을 겨냥하는 것을 수반했다.
(B) 뉴올리언스는 이전에 이 행사를 주최해본 적이 없었다.
(C) 그렇지만 Stelly는 오직 1년 전에 소설 쓰는 것을 시작했다.
(D) Stelly의 첫 번째 소설은 농장에서 자란 한 어린 소녀에 관한 것이었다.

해설 앞 문장 'innovative marketing is partially responsible for the book's popularity'에서 그 책의 인기에 대해 획기적인 마케팅이 부분적으로 원인이 된다고 했으므로 빈칸에는 마케팅 방식과 관련된 내용이 들어가야 함을 알 수 있다. 따라서 (A)가 정답이다.

어휘 involve v. 수반하다, 포함하다 target v. 겨냥하다 active adj. 활발한 host v. 주최하다 ceremony n. 행사, 의식 fiction n. 소설

138 올바른 시제의 동사 채우기 전체 문맥 파악 중 ●●●

해설 '추가 부수들은 4월 30일에 구입할 수 있다'라는 문맥인데, 이 경우 빈칸이 있는 문장만으로 올바른 시제의 동사를 고를 수 없으므로 주변 문맥이나 전체 문맥을 파악한다. 지문 처음의 'April 24'에서 이 기사가 4월 24일자 기사라고 언급되었고 앞부분에서 책이 매진되었다고 했으므로, 4월 24일을 기준으로 보았을 때 책이 다시 입고되는 4월 30일은 미래임을 알 수 있다. 따라서 미래 시제 (D) will become이 정답이다. 과거 시제 (A), 현재 완료 시제 (B), 과거 진행 시제 (C)는 미래를 나타낼 수 없다.

어휘 become v. ~이 되다, ~해지다

139-142번은 다음 이메일에 관한 문제입니다.

수신: Joe Hamlin <joe.ham@homeready.com>
발신: Caroline Quigley <car.qui@homeready.com>
제목: 판매 관리자
날짜: 8월 9일

Mr. Hamlin께,

저는 우리의 판매 관리자들 중 한 명인, Deborah Watson이 8월 16일에 우리의 생산 시설에 139방문할 것임을 당신께 알려드리기 위해 글을 씁니다. Ms. Watson은 우리 회사에 새로 들어왔습니다. 140그러므로, 공장을 둘러보고 어떻게 우리의 청소 기기들이 만들어지는지 배우는 것이 그녀에게 중요합니다.

공장의 보조 감독관으로서, 저는 당신이 Ms. Watson을 조립 라인에 데려가면 좋겠습니다. 우리가 우리의 제품을 생산하는 방식에 대해 그녀가 익숙해질 수 있도록 생산 시설의 주변을 그녀와 141동행하십시오. 142동시에 우리의 최신 모델 라인에 특별한 주의를 기울여 주십시오. 또한, 그녀가 질문을 하고 우리의 직원들 중 일부와 이야기를 나누도록 장려하십시오.

Caroline Quigley 드림
최고 감독관, Home Ready사 생산 공장

manufacturing facility phr. 생산 시설 appliance n. 기기, 기구
assistant adj. 보조의; n. 보조 assembly n. 조립, 의회
familiar adj. 익숙한 encourage v. 장려하다, 권장하다

139 동사 어휘 고르기 전체 문맥 파악 상 ●●●

해설 빈칸은 be동사(be)와 함께 쓰여 진행형을 만드는 -ing형의 자리이다. 'Deborah Watson이 8월16일에 생산 시설에 ___할 것이다'라는 문맥이

므로 모든 보기가 정답의 후보이다. 뒤 문장에서 Ms. Watson이 우리 회사에 새로 들어왔다고 한 후, 지문 뒷부분에서 공장을 둘러보고 어떻게 자신들의 청소 기기들이 만들어지는지 배우는 것이 그녀에게 중요하다고 했으므로 Ms. Watson이 생산 시설에 방문할 것임을 알 수 있다. 따라서 동사 visit(방문하다)의 -ing형 (C) visiting이 정답이다.

어휘 evaluate v. 평가하다 leave v. 떠나다 suspend v. 중단하다

140 접속부사 채우기 주변 문맥 파악 하 ●○○

해설 빈칸은 콤마와 함께 문장의 맨 앞에 온 접속부사 자리이다. 앞 문장에서 Ms. Watson이 회사에 새로 들어왔다고 했고, 빈칸이 있는 문장에서는 공장을 둘러보고 생산 과정을 배우는 것이 그녀에게 중요할 것이라고 했으므로, 앞 문장의 상황에 대한 결과를 나타낼 때 사용되는 접속부사 (D) Accordingly (그러므로)가 정답이다.

어휘 that is phr. 즉 in contrast phr. 대조적으로
unusually adv. 평소와 달리, 특이하게

141 동사 어휘 고르기 중 ●●●

해설 Please로 시작하는 절(Please ~ facility)은 주어 없이 시작되는 명령문으로 빈칸은 동사 자리이다. '생산 시설의 주변을 그녀와 동행하십시오'라는 문맥이 되어야 하므로 (B) accompany(동행하다)가 정답이다. (D) demonstrate도 '설명하다'라는 의미로 해석상 그럴듯해 보이지만, demonstrate A to B(B에게 A를 설명하다)의 형태로 쓰이므로 목적어로 사람이 아닌 무엇을 설명하려는지가 와야 한다.

어휘 promote v. 승진시키다, 홍보하다 recruit v. 모집하다, 뽑다

142 알맞은 문장 고르기 상 ●●●

해석 (A) 그 방문 후에 만약 당신이 그녀가 고용되어야 한다고 생각한다면 저에게 알려주십시오.
(B) 생산 전에 이 결함을 제거하는 것이 가능할 수 있습니다.
(C) 당신의 여행의 모든 비용이 8월까지 환불될 것입니다.
(D) 동시에 우리의 최신 모델 라인에 특별한 주의를 기울여 주십시오.

해설 앞 문장 'Please (accompany) her around the manufacturing facility so that she can become familiar with how we produce our merchandise.'에서 우리가 우리의 제품을 생산하는 방식에 대해 그녀가 익숙해질 수 있도록 생산 시설의 주변을 그녀와 동행하라고 했으므로 빈칸에는 제품 관련 생산 시설을 둘러보는 것과 관련된 내용이 들어가야 함을 알 수 있다. 따라서 (D)가 정답이다.

어휘 hire v. 고용하다 eliminate v. 제거하다 defect n. 결함
reimburse v. 환급하다, 배상하다 attention n. 주의, 주목

143-146번은 다음 회람에 관한 문제입니다.

수신: Brentwood사의 전 직원
발신: Dale Rosen, 인사부 부장
날짜: 2월 26일
제목: 사무실 내에서의 휴대폰

지난 한 달 동안, 몇몇 부서장들은 휴대폰 사용에 관한 걱정을 표현했습니다. 특히, 회의들의 143생산성이 상당히 감소하였습니다. 따라서, Brentwood사는 새로운 규정을 시작하기로 144결정했습니다. 이제부터, 휴대폰들은 회의실 내에 가져오는 것 대신 직원들의 책상 위에 놓여 있어야 합니다. 이것은 145방해

들을 막기 위한 것입니다. 논의되고 있는 주제들에 직원들이 더 잘 집중할 수 있게 되는 것이 저희의 바람입니다. ¹⁴⁶우리는 이 회사 규정에 한 가지 예외를 허용할 것입니다. 만약 긴급한 전화나 메시지가 예상된다면, 휴대폰은 무음 모드로 안에 가져올 수 있습니다.

---

concern n. 걱정, 관심 in particular phr. 특히, 특별히
decrease v. 감소하다 significantly adv. 상당히
launch v. 시작하다, 개시하다 policy n. 규정, 정책 conference n. 회의
prevent v. 막다, 예방하다 concentrate v. 집중하다 urgent adj. 긴급한
silent mode phr. 무음 모드

최고난도 문제

143 명사 어휘 고르기 전체 문맥 파악 상 ●●●

해설 빈칸은 정관사(the)와 전치사(of) 사이에 올 수 있는 명사 자리이다. '회의들의 ___이 상당히 감소했다'라는 문맥이므로 모든 보기가 정답의 후보이다. 앞 문장에서 부서장들은 휴대폰 사용에 관한 걱정을 표했다고 했고, 뒷부분에서 휴대폰들은 회의실 내에 가져오는 것 대신 책상 위에 놓여 있어야 하고 이를 통해 직원들이 더 잘 집중할 수 있길 바란다고 했으므로 휴대폰 사용이 회의들의 생산성을 떨어뜨렸음을 알 수 있다. 따라서 (C) productivity(생산성)가 정답이다.

어휘 duration n. 지속, 기간 attendance n. 출석 number n. 개수, 수

144 올바른 시제의 동사 채우기 주변 문맥 파악 중 ●●○

해설 문장에 주어(Brentwood Corp.)만 있고 동사가 없으므로 동사인 (B), (C), (D)가 정답의 후보이다. 뒤 문장에서 이제부터 휴대폰들은 회의실 내에 가져오는 것 대신 직원들의 책상 위에 놓여 있어야 한다고 했으므로 새로운 규정을 시작하기로 결정이 내려졌다는 것을 알 수 있다. 따라서 과거에 시작되어 방금 완료되었거나 과거에 발생한 일이 현재까지 영향을 미칠 때 사용되는 현재 완료 시제 (D) has decided가 정답이다. 과거 진행 시제 (B)는 특정한 과거 시점에 진행되고 있던 일을 나타내고, 현재 시제 (C)는 현재의 상태, 반복적인 행동이나 습관을 나타낼 때 사용된다. 현재분사 또는 동명사 (A)는 동사 자리에 올 수 없다.

145 명사 어휘 고르기 주변 문맥 파악 상 ●●●

해설 빈칸은 동사(prevent)의 목적어 역할을 하는 명사 자리이다. '이것은 ___을 막기 위한 것이다'라는 문맥이므로 (A), (B), (D)가 정답의 후보이다. 뒤 문장에서 논의되고 있는 주제들에 직원들이 더 잘 집중할 수 있게 되는 것을 바란다고 했으므로 회의에 집중하는 것의 방해들을 막기 위해 새로운 규정을 시작한다는 것을 알 수 있다. 따라서 (D) interruptions(방해들)가 정답이다.

어휘 error n. 오류 charge n. 요금 regulation n. 규정

146 알맞은 문장 고르기 중 ●●○

해석 (A) 개인용 기기들은 회사에 의해 제공될 것입니다.
(B) 당신은 필요에 따라 당신의 휴대폰을 통해 인터넷에 접속할 수 있습니다.
(C) 시청각 시스템은 사전에 예약되어야 합니다.
(D) 우리는 이 회사 규정에 한 가지 예외를 허용할 것입니다.

해설 앞부분에서 이제부터 회의실 내에 휴대폰을 가져올 수 없다고 했고, 뒤 문장 'If an urgent call or message is expected, a phone may be brought inside on silent mode.'에서 만약 긴급한 전화나 메시지가 예상된다면, 휴대폰은 무음 모드로 안에 가져올 수 있다고 했으므로 빈칸에는 회의실 내에 휴대폰을 가져갈 수 있는 예외 사항에 관한 내용이 들어가야 함을

알 수 있다. 따라서 (D)가 정답이다.

어휘 audiovisual adj. 시청각의 reserve v. 예약하다
in advance phr. 사전에 exception n. 예외

PART 7

147-148번은 다음 설명서에 관한 문제입니다.

Deena 정수기 관리 설명서

¹⁴⁷당신의 새로운 Deena 정수기가 수년간 지속되도록 보장하기 위해서, 다음의 간단한 관리 설명서를 반드시 따라주십시오:

· 필터를 설치하고 난 후, 모든 먼지를 씻어내고 필터를 사용할 수 있도록 준비하기 위해 아무 수도꼭지를 틀어서 최소 2분 동안 물이 그것을 통과하여 흐르도록 하십시오.
· ¹⁴⁸6개월마다 각 장치 내의 필터를 교체하십시오. 물에서 제거된 물질들의 축적은 흐름을 막는 것을 야기할 수 있습니다. 세제를 사용하는 것은 필터를 손상시키고 그것이 제대로 작동하는 것을 막을 수 있기 때문에 시도하지 마십시오.
· 장마철 동안에는, 필터들이 더 자주 교체되어야 할 수도 있다는 것을 명심하십시오.

---

water filtration system phr. 정수기 maintenance n. 관리, 유지
ensure v. 보장하다, 확보하다 install v. 설치하다 faucet n. 수도꼭지
buildup n. 축적 substance n. 물질 blockage n. (흐름을) 막는 것, 폐색
attempt v. 시도하다 prevent v. 막다 function v. 작동하다, 기능하다
properly adv. 제대로, 적절히 rainy season phr. 장마철, 우기
frequently adv. 자주, 빈번하게

147 목적 찾기 문제 중 ●●●

해석 설명서의 목적은 무엇인가?
(A) 적합한 모델을 선택하는 과정을 설명하기 위해
(B) 시스템의 이점들을 설명하기 위해
(C) 수리 절차에 대해 기술자들을 교육시키기 위해
(D) 고객들이 제품의 수명을 연장하도록 돕기 위해

해설 지문의 'To ensure your new Deena Water Filtration System lasts for years, be sure to follow ~ instructions:'에서 당신의 새로운 Deena 정수기가 수년간 지속되도록 보장하기 위해서, 설명서를 반드시 따르라고 했으므로 (D)가 정답이다.

어휘 suitable adj. 적합한 illustrate v. 설명하다 technician n. 기술자
procedure n. 절차, 과정 extend v. 연장하다, 확대하다

148 육하원칙 문제 하 ●○○

해석 사용자들은 무엇을 정기적으로 해야 하는가?
(A) 점검 일정을 잡는다
(B) 부품을 교체한다
(C) 수질을 확인한다
(D) 필터 세제를 바른다

해설 지문의 'Change the filter in each device every six months.'에서 6개월마다 각 장치 내의 필터를 교체하라고 했으므로 (B)가 정답이다.

어휘 inspection n. 점검, 검사 replace v. 교체하다
component n. 부품, 요소 apply v. 바르다, 적용하다

149-150번은 다음 이메일에 관한 문제입니다.

발신: 관리팀 <admin@mtelecom.com>
수신: Vince Dantley <dantley_v@centercourt.com>
제목: 당신의 Myer 통신사 비밀번호
날짜: 3월 11일

Vince Dantley께,

¹⁴⁹당신은 현재 Myer 통신사의 무료 와이파이 서비스를 사용할 수 있게 되는 것에서 한 단계만이 남아 있습니다. 당신은 등록 페이지에서 다음의 비밀번호를 입력하기만 하면 됩니다:

g7z33xyu1g4

이것은 다음 10분 이내로 행해져야 한다는 것에 유의하십시오. 그렇지 않으면, 당신은 등록 절차를 처음부터 다시 시작해야 할 것이며 새로운 비밀번호를 받아야 할 것입니다. ¹⁵⁰⁻ᴰ당신이 성공적으로 등록하고 나면, 당신은 당신의 장치를 사용할 때마다 자동으로 로그인될 것입니다.

¹⁵⁰⁻ᴮMyer 통신사의 와이파이 서비스는 중앙철도역, Burnett 공항, 그리고 Estuary 광장을 포함하여, 윌밍턴 주변에 있는 12개 이상의 장소들에서 제공됩니다. ¹⁵⁰⁻ᴬ사용자들은 일주일에 20시간을 할당받습니다.

Myer 통신사 드림

input v. 입력하다 registration n. 등록 successfully adv. 성공적으로
automatically adv. 자동으로 dozen n. 12개 location n. 장소
plaza n. 광장 allot v. 할당하다

149 추론 문제   중 ●●○

해석 Mr. Dantley에 대해 추론될 수 있는 것은?
(A) 등록 절차를 완료하지 않았다.
(B) 비밀번호를 기억할 수 없었다.
(C) 휴대폰 애플리케이션에 대해 돈을 지불했다.
(D) 최근에 윌밍턴으로 이사했다.

해설 지문의 'You are now just one step away from being able to use ~ service. All you need to do is input the following password on the registration page:'에서 당신, 즉 Mr. Dantley는 현재 서비스를 사용할 수 있게 되는 것에서 한 단계만이 남아 있다고 하며 등록 페이지에서 다음의 비밀번호를 입력하기만 하면 된다고 했으므로, Mr. Dantley가 아직 등록 절차를 진행 중이라는 사실을 추론할 수 있다. 따라서 (A)가 정답이다.

어휘 relocate v. 이사하다, 이동하다

150 Not/True 문제   중 ●●○

해석 Myer 통신사의 와이파이 서비스에 대해 사실이 아닌 것은?
(A) 제한된 시간 동안 사용될 수 있다.
(B) 몇몇 교통 시설들에서 이용할 수 있다.
(C) 출시된 지 일 년이 채 되지 않는다.
(D) 등록된 사용자들에게는 자동으로 연결된다.

해설 지문에서 (C)는 언급되지 않은 내용이다. 따라서 (C)가 정답이다. (A)는

'Users are allotted 20 hours per week.'에서 사용자들은 일주일에 20시간을 할당받는다고 했으므로 지문의 내용과 일치한다. (B)는 'Myer Telecom's Wi-Fi service is offered in ~ locations ~, including Central Rail Station, Burnett Airport, ~.'에서 Myer 통신사의 와이파이 서비스는 중앙철도역과 Burnett 공항을 포함하는 장소들에서 제공된다고 했으므로 지문의 내용과 일치한다. (D)는 'Once you have successfully registered, you will be logged in automatically every time you use your device.'에서 당신이 성공적으로 등록하고 나면, 당신은 당신의 장치를 사용할 때마다 자동으로 로그인될 것이라고 했으므로 지문의 내용과 일치한다.

어휘 limited adj. 제한된 available adj. 이용할 수 있는
transportation n. 교통 facility n. 시설 launch v. 출시하다

151-153번은 다음 기사에 관한 문제입니다.

Faber Medical and Dental의 개조가 완료되다

6월 24일—¹⁵¹Wallberg Health Group사는 내일 Doeville에 있는 Faber Medical and Dental의 새롭게 개조된 3층을 다시 열 예정이다. 이제 14개의 진료실들을 포함하는 그 공간이 의료진들이 진찰에 더 많은 시간을 쏠 수 있도록 하는 동시에 환자 대기 시간을 줄이는 데 도움이 될 것으로 예상된다. Wallberg Health Group사 대표 Joan Bronson에 따르면, Faber Medical and Dental로의 방문은 작년에만 거의 22퍼센트가 증가했다. "¹⁵²Doeville의 거주자들은 점점 더 나이가 들고 있고, 이는 의사의 진찰을 받아야 하는 더 많은 환자들을 낳았습니다. 지금까지, Faber Medical and Dental은 이러한 환자들에게 그들이 받아야 마땅한 치료를 제공하기 위한 자원들이 부족했습니다."

증가하는 수요를 따라가기 위해, Faber Medical and Dental은 또한 9명의 추가적인 공인된 간호사들과 2명의 전임 일반의들을 고용했다. ¹⁵³그 층이 행정실로 쓰였을 때 그것을 이전에 사용했던 25명의 직원들은 그들의 이전 업무들을 재개하기 위해 그곳으로 돌아올 것이다. 거의 140만 달러가 드는 6개월짜리의 재건축이 시작되었을 때, 그들은 Wallberg Health Group사의 Sharaton 및 McCollough 지점들로 보내졌었다.

renovation n. 개조, 보수 reopen v. 다시 열다, 재개하다
feature v. (특별히) 포함하다 examination room phr. 진료실
consultation n. 진찰, 상담 representative n. 대표, 직원
result in phr. (결과를) 낳다, 야기하다 resource n. 자원 lack v. 부족하다
attontion n. 치료, 보살핌 deserve v. ~을 받아야 마땅하다
keep up with phr. ~을 따라가다 registered adj. 공인된, 등록한
general practitioner phr. 일반의 formerly adv. 이전에
occupy v. 사용하다, 차지하다 administrative office phr. 행정실
resume v. 재개하다, 다시 시작하다 duty n. 업무, 의무 location n. 지점
reconstruction n. 재건축

151 목적 찾기 문제   중 ●●○

해석 기사의 목적은 무엇인가?
(A) 병원의 경영진 변화를 발표하기 위해
(B) 이용 가능한 의료진의 부족에 대해 항의하기 위해
(C) 시설이 곧 이용할 수 있음을 알리기 위해
(D) 의사들을 고용하는 과정을 설명하기 위해

해설 지문의 'Wallberg Health Group will be reopening its newly renovated third floor ~ tomorrow.'에서 Wallberg Health Group사는 내일 새롭게 개조된 3층을 다시 열 예정이라고 했으므로 (C)가 정답이다.

어휘   announce v. 발표하다, 알리다   complain v. 항의하다, 불평하다
report v. 알리다, 보고하다   accessible adj. 이용할 수 있는

패러프레이징

> will be reopening ~ tomorrow 내일 다시 열 예정이다 → will soon be
> accessible 곧 이용할 수 있을 것이다

152   육하원칙 문제   중 ●●○

해석   무엇이 Faber Medical and Dental의 수요가 증가하도록 했는가?
(A) 향상된 서비스들
(B) 한 병원의 폐업
(C) 노령화 인구
(D) 무료 진찰

해설   지문의 'The residents ~ are getting older, which has resulted in more patients needing to see a doctor.'에서 거주자들이 점점 더 나이가 들고 있고, 이는 의사의 진찰을 받아야 하는 더 많은 환자들을 낳았다고 했으므로 (C)가 정답이다.

어휘   improved adj. 향상된, 개선된   closure n. 폐업, 폐쇄
aging population phr. 노령화 인구

패러프레이징

> The residents ~ are getting older 거주자들이 점점 더 나이가 들고 있다
> → aging population 노령화 인구

153   추론 문제   상 ●●●

해석   행정 직원들에 대해 암시되는 것은?
(A) 그들의 새로운 직책들에 대한 교육을 받을 것이다.
(B) 임시로 다른 지점들에 새로 발령을 받았다.
(C) 단기 휴가를 갈 것을 요청받았다.
(D) 새로 건설된 건물로 이동되었다.

해설   지문의 'The ~ staff that formerly occupied ~ an administrative office will return ~. They were sent to Wallberg Health Group's Sharaton and McCollough locations when the six-month ~ reconstruction began.'에서 이전에 행정실을 사용했던 직원들이 돌아올 것이며, 6개월짜리의 재건축이 시작되었을 때 그들은 Wallberg Health Group사의 Sharaton 및 McCollough 지점들로 보내졌다고 했으므로 행정 직원들이 재건축 기간 동안 잠시 다른 지점으로 발령을 받았다는 사실을 추론할 수 있다. 따라서 (B)가 정답이다.

어휘   temporarily adv. 임시로, 일시적으로   reassign v. 새로 발령하다
short-term adj. 단기의   leave of absence phr. 휴가

패러프레이징

> administrative staff 행정 직원 → staff that ~ occupied ~ an
> administrative office 행정실을 사용했던 직원
> sent to ~ locations 지점들로 보내진 → reassigned to ~ locations 지점들에 새로 발령을 받은

154-155번은 다음 메시지 대화문에 관한 문제입니다.

Dan Hummel (오후 8시 19분)
저는 Natalia Manco의 유럽 순회공연에 관해 몇 가지 안 좋은 소식들

을 접했어요. ¹⁵⁴우리는 추가적인 공지 전까지 그녀의 남은 콘서트들을 연기해야 할 거예요.

Phoebe Fiscella (오후 8시 21분)
정말이에요? 우리는 이미 그 공연들에 대해 많은 티켓들을 판매했어요.

Dan Hummel (오후 8시 24분)
저도 알지만, ¹⁵⁴그녀가 매우 아파서, 그녀가 금방 노래를 할 수 있을 가능성이 없어요. 제가 언론을 위한 성명서 작업을 시작할게요. 우리는 또한 그녀가 공연하기로 예정되어 있었던 공연장들에게 이 상황에 대해 알려야 해요. ¹⁵⁵그것을 지금 해줄 수 있나요?

Phoebe Fiscella (오후 8시 25분)
아마도요. ¹⁵⁵지금은 꽤 늦은 저녁이라서, 저는 모든 관리자들이 시간이 될지 잘 모르겠어요. 하지만 내일은 제가 확실하게 이것을 할 수 있을 거예요.

postpone v. 연기하다, 미루다   further adj. 추가적인, 더 이상의   ill adj. 아픈
chance n. 가능성, 기회   any time soon phr. 금방, 곧
statement n. 성명서, 진술서   media n. 언론, 매체   perform v. 공연하다
available adj. 시간이 되는, 구할 수 있는   definitely adv. 확실하게

154   육하원칙 문제   중 ●●○

해석   일부 순회공연은 왜 연기되었는가?
(A) 공연들이 좋은 평가를 받지 못했다.
(B) 공연자에게 일정 문제가 있다.
(C) 가수에게 건강 문제가 있다.
(D) 티켓들이 잘 팔리지 않았다.

해설   지문의 'We're going to have to postpone the rest of her concerts'에서 Mr. Hummel이 그녀 즉, Ms. Manco의 남은 콘서트들을 연기해야 할 것이라고 한 후, 'she is very ill, so there is no chance that she will be able to sing any time soon'에서 그녀가 매우 아파서 그녀가 금방 노래를 할 수 있을 가능성이 없다고 했으므로 (C)가 정답이다.

어휘   review n. 평가, 검토   conflict n. 문제, 충돌

패러프레이징

> ill 아픈 → has a health issue 건강 문제가 있다

155   의도 파악 문제   중 ●●○

해석   오후 8시 25분에, Ms. Fiscella가 "Possibly"라고 썼을 때 그녀가 의도한 것은?
(A) Ms. Manco의 콘서트들이 매진될 것인지 확신할 수 없다.
(B) 내일 언론사 대표와 만날 수도 있다.
(C) 아마 티켓들을 구매했던 사람들에게 환불을 제공할 것이다.
(D) Mr. Hummel의 요청을 즉시 수행하지 못할 수도 있다.

해설   지문의 'Could you do that now?'에서 Mr. Hummel이 그것, 즉 공연장들에게 이 상황에 대해 알리는 것을 지금 해줄 수 있는지 묻자, Ms. Fiscella가 'Possibly.'(아마도요)라고 한 후, 'It's pretty late in the evening, so I don't know if all of the managers will be available. But I will definitely be able to do this tomorrow.'에서 지금은 꽤 늦은 저녁이라서, 모든 관리자들이 시간이 될지는 잘 모르겠지만, 내일은 자신이 확실하게 이것을 할 수 있을 것이라고 한 것을 통해, Ms. Fiscella가 Mr. Hummel의 요청을 즉시 수행하지 못할 수도 있다는 것을 알 수 있다. 따라서 (D)가 정답이다.

어휘   confirm v. 확신하다   sell out phr. 매진되다   likely adv. 아마
refund n. 환불   fulfill v. 수행하다

156-157번은 다음 공고에 관한 문제입니다.

Annenberg 카운티 지역사회 채용 박람회

화요일, 6월 15일, 오후 1시에서 오후 5시까지
Annenberg 컨벤션 센터에서 — Seaview 대연회장, 2층

일자리가 필요하신가요?
다음을 포함하는 다양한 지역 회사들의 직원들을 와서 만나보세요:
- Wender 호텔 서비스사
- Porter 의료 센터
- Gelec사
- Renew 제조회사
- Annenberg 운송회사
- Oarfield 기술회사

이 행사는 무료로 참석할 수 있지만, 자리가 제한적입니다. 그러므로, ¹⁵⁶참가자들은 www.annenbergcounty.com/events에서 사전에 신청해야 합니다. 신청 마감기한은 6월 5일입니다. 채용 박람회 당일에, 나누어줄 당신의 이력서와 자기소개서의 사본들을 가져오고, 전문적으로 옷을 입고, 현장 인터뷰에 대비하십시오. ^{157-A}Annenberg 컨벤션 센터는 Gibbs역 6번 출구에서 도보 2분 거리이고, 컨벤션 센터 주차장은 시간당 10달러에 이용할 수 있습니다.

---

community n. 지역사회, 공동체 various adj. 다양한 attend v. 참석하다
register v. 신청하다 in advance phr. 사전에 résumé n. 이력서
cover letter phr. 자기소개서 hand out phr. 나누어주다, 배포하다
professionally adv. 전문적으로 on-the-spot adj. 현장의

---

156 육하원칙 문제 중 ●●○

해석 채용 박람회에 참석하는 것에 관심 있는 사람들은 6월 5일까지 무엇을 해야 하는가?
(A) 온라인으로 금액을 지불한다
(B) 신청 부스를 방문한다
(C) 웹페이지에서 신청한다
(D) 거주 증명서를 제출한다

해설 지문의 'participants must register in advance at www.annenbergcounty.com/events. The deadline for registration is June 5.'에서 참가자들은 웹사이트에서 사전에 신청해야 하며, 신청 마감기한은 6월 5일이라고 했으므로 (C)가 정답이다.

어휘 make payment phr. (금액을) 지불하다 sign up phr. 신청하다
proof n. 증명(서), 증거(물) residency n. 거주

패러프레이징

must ~ do by ~까지 해야 한다 → deadline ~ is 마감기한이 ~이다
register 신청하다 → Sign up 신청하다

---

157 Not/True 문제 중 ●●○

해석 Annenberg 컨벤션 센터에 대해 언급된 것은?
(A) 대중교통을 통해 접근할 수 있다.
(B) 얼마 안 되는 주차 공간들이 있다.
(C) 평일 아침에는 문을 닫는다.
(D) 유명한 호텔에 인접해 있다.

해설 지문의 'Annenberg Convention Center is a two-minute walk from ~ Gibbs Station'에서 Annenberg 컨벤션 센터는 Gibbs역에서 도보 2분 거리라고 했으므로 (A)는 지문의 내용과 일치한다. 따라서 (A)가 정답이다.

(B), (C), (D)는 지문에 언급되지 않은 내용이다.

어휘 accessible adj. 접근할 수 있는 public transportation phr. 대중교통
adjacent adj. 인접한, 가까운 well-known adj. 유명한, 잘 알려진

158-161번은 다음 온라인 채팅 대화문에 관한 문제입니다.

Neil Webb [오후 4시 20분]
안녕하세요, 여러분. ¹⁵⁸저는 우리 부서 팀장인, Mr. Tate를 오늘 아침에 만났고, 그는 제게 전국 슈퍼마켓 체인 Vatusi Foods사의 광고를 만들 팀을 조직해달라고 요청했어요. Elsa, 당신은 시간이 되나요?

Elsa Moss [오후 4시 23분]
저도 도와드리고 싶지만, 저는 현재 Dresden 의류사 캠페인을 작업 중이에요. 저는 두 프로젝트 모두를 동시에 할 수 없을 거예요.

Neil Webb [오후 4시 23분]
제가 그것을 잊고 있었네요. Courtney, 당신이 그 캠페인의 팀장이지요. Elsa를 몇 주 동안 넘겨줄 수 있나요? ^{159-D}우리가 작년에 제작했던 Vatusi Foods사 광고를 그녀가 작업했어서, 이번 건에 그녀가 포함되어야 해요.

Courtney McGuire [오후 4시 24분]
만약 그것이 정말로 필수적이라면, 저는 그녀를 당신의 팀으로 이동시킬 수 있어요. 하지만 그것은 제 마감일을 맞추는 것을 어렵게 만들 거예요.

Neil Webb [오후 4시 25분]
¹⁶⁰Elsa의 결손을 만회하기 위해 당신의 프로젝트에 두 명의 보조 마케팅 직원들을 배정해달라고 제가 Mr. Tate에게 요청하는 것은 어떨까요?

Courtney McGuire [오후 4시 26분]
그러면 고맙겠어요. ¹⁶⁰그렇지 않으면, 저는 Dresden 의류사에 기간 연장을 요청해야 할 수도 있어요. Elsa, 당신은 이번 주말부터 Vatusi Foods사 캠페인을 시작할 수 있어요.

Elsa Moss [오후 4시 27분]
알겠어요. Neil, ¹⁶¹당신은 팀이 이 프로젝트에 대해 논의하기 위해 언제 다 같이 모일 것인지 알고 있나요?

Neil Webb [오후 4시 30분]
¹⁶¹금요일 아침이요. 저희는 오전 10시에 2층 회의실에서 만날 거예요. 제가 당신에게 안건이 담긴 이메일을 보내줄게요.

---

organize v. 조직하다 chain n. 체인(점) help out phr. 도와주다
spare v. 넘겨주다, 내어주다 involve v. 포함하다, 수반하다
absolutely adv. 정말로, 전적으로 necessary adj. 필수적인
transfer v. 이동시키다 assign v. 배정하다, 맡기다
make up for phr. ~을 만회하다 loss n. 결손, 손실
extension n. (기간의) 연장, 확장 get together phr. (다 같이) 모이다
discuss v. 논의하다 agenda n. 안건

---

158 육하원칙 문제 중 ●●○

해석 Mr. Tate는 오늘 아침에 무엇을 했는가?
(A) 새로운 팀원을 소개했다
(B) 부하 직원에게 업무를 맡겼다
(C) 부서장에게 이야기했다
(D) 광고에 대한 의견을 제공했다

해설 지문의 'I met with our department manager, Mr. Tate, this morning, and he asked me to organize a team'에서 Mr. Webb이 자신의 부서 팀장인 Mr. Tate를 오늘 아침에 만났으며, 그가 자신에게 팀을 조직할 것을 요청했다고 했으므로 (B)가 정답이다.

어휘 subordinate n. 부하 직원

159 Not/True 문제   중 ●●○

해석 Vatusi Foods사에 대해 언급된 것은?
(A) 최근에 추가적인 직원들을 고용했다.
(B) 지역 소유의 회사이다.
(C) 광고 방송 아이디어를 싫어했다.
(D) 이전에 Ms. Moss와 일한 적이 있다.

해설 지문의 'She worked on the Vatusi Foods advertisement ~ last year'에서 Mr. Webb이 그녀, 즉 Ms. Moss가 작년에 Vatusi Foods사 광고를 작업했다고 했으므로 (D)는 지문의 내용과 일치한다. 따라서 (D)가 정답이다. (A), (B), (C)는 지문에 언급되지 않은 내용이다.

어휘 dislike v. 싫어하다 commercial adj 광고 방송의, 상업적인

160 의도 파악 문제   중 ●●●

해석 오후 4시 26분에, Ms. McGuire가 "I'd appreciate that"이라고 썼을 때 그녀가 의도한 것 같은 것은?
(A) 직원이 새로 발령되면 안 된다고 생각한다.
(B) 프로젝트 마감일의 연장이 필요하다.
(C) 캠페인이 발표되면 안 된다고 생각한다.
(D) 더 많은 직원들이 그녀의 팀에 추가되길 원한다.

해설 지문의 'Why don't I ask Mr. Tate to assign two ~ staff to your project to make up for the loss of Elsa?'에서 Mr. Webb이 자신이 Mr. Tate에게 Elsa의 결손을 만회하기 위해 당신, 즉 Ms. McGuire의 프로젝트에 두 명의 직원들을 배정해달라고 요청하는 것은 어떨지 묻자, Ms. McGuire가 'I'd appreciate that.'(그러면 고맙겠어요)이라고 한 후 'Otherwise, I might have to ask Dresden Apparel for an extension.'에서 그렇지 않으면, 자신이 Dresden 의류사에 기간 연장을 요청해야 할 수도 있다고 한 것을 통해, Ms. McGuire는 더 많은 직원들이 그녀의 팀에 추가되길 원한다는 것을 알 수 있다. 따라서 (D)가 정답이다.

어휘 release v. 발표하다, 공개하다

161 추론 문제   중 ●●●

해석 Ms. Moss는 금요일에 무엇을 할 것 같은가?
(A) 몇몇 직원들의 성과를 평가한다
(B) 새로운 팀원들과의 회의에 참석한다
(C) 회사의 이전 고객에게 이메일을 보낸다
(D) Dresden 의류사에 대한 발표를 한다

해설 지문의 'do you know when the team will get together to discuss this project?'에서 Ms. Moss가 Mr. Webb에게 그 팀, 즉 원래 있던 Dresden 의류사 프로젝트팀이 아닌 새롭게 합류하게 된 Vatusi Foods사 프로젝트팀이 이 프로젝트에 대해 논의하기 위해 언제 다 같이 모일 것인지 알고 있는지 묻자, 'Friday morning.'에서 Mr. Webb이 금요일 아침이라고 답했으므로 Ms. Moss가 금요일 아침에 새로운 팀과 프로젝트에 대해 논의하는 회의에 참석할 것임을 추론할 수 있다. 따라서 (B)가 정답이다.

어휘 evaluate v. 평가하다 performance n. 성과, 수행
participate in phr. ~에 참석하다, 참가하다 former adj. 이전의

162-164번은 다음 광고에 관한 문제입니다.

QUEENSBORO 피자

¹⁶²⁻ᴬ저희는 하트포드의 모든 지역 주민들에게 무료로 배달해드립니다!*

---

¹⁶³⁻ᴰ지금부터 6월 30일까지, 다음 항목들 중 어떤 것이든 세 가지로 구성된 19.99달러 Queen's Combo를 주문하세요:

¹⁶²⁻ᶜ미디엄 치즈피자 1개
미트 소스 ¹⁶²⁻ᴮ스파게티 1개
구운 닭고기 ¹⁶²⁻ᴮ시저 샐러드 1개
버터 바른 ¹⁶²⁻ᴮ막대 빵 6개
매운 ¹⁶²⁻ᴮ닭 날개 10개

또한, 여름 내내, ¹⁶⁴프리미엄 토핑이 있는 아무 ¹⁶²⁻ᶜ/¹⁶⁴라지 피자를 주문하고 ¹⁶⁴라지 치즈 피자를 완전 무료로 받으세요!

프리미엄 토핑은 다음을 포함합니다:
아티초크
햇볕에 말린 토마토
구운 고추

¹⁶²⁻ᴰ저희의 새로운 스마트폰 애플리케이션을 이용하면 주문이 빠르고 쉽습니다! 애플리케이션을 다운로드하고 시작하기 위해 당신의 개인 정보와 결제 정보를 등록하기만 하면 됩니다. 당신의 첫 주문에 대해 20퍼센트 할인을 받기 위해 결제창에 홍보용 코드 4SUMR을 입력하세요.

*하트포드 시외에서 2킬로미터까지 떨어진 지역에 대해서는, 5달러의 추가 요금이 있습니다.

---

neighborhood n. 지역 주민, 이웃 consist of phr. ~(으)로 구성되다
grilled adj. 구운 breadstick n. 막대 빵 absolutely adv. 완전
sun-dried adj. 햇볕에 말린 roasted adj. 구운 checkout n. 결제창, 계산
up to phr. ~까지 charge n. 요금

162 Not/True 문제   중 ●●○

해석 Queensboro 피자에 대해 사실이 아닌 것은?
(A) 모든 배달에 대해 요금을 청구한다.
(B) 피자 외에 다른 품목들도 제공한다.
(C) 최소 두 가지 크기의 피자를 만든다.
(D) 모바일 애플리케이션을 통해 주문을 받는다.

해설 지문의 'We deliver free to all neighborhoods in Hartford!'에서 자신들, 즉 Queensboro 피자는 하트포드의 모든 지역 주민들에게 무료로 배달해준다고 했으므로 (A)는 지문의 내용과 일치하지 않는다. 따라서 (A)가 정답이다. (B)는 'spaghetti', 'Caesar salad', 'breadsticks', 'chicken wings'에서 스파게티, 시저 샐러드, 막대 빵, 닭 날개가 있다고 했으므로 지문의 내용과 일치한다. (C)는 'medium ~ pizza'와 'buy ~ large pizza'에서 미디엄 피자를 언급하고 라지 피자를 주문하라고 했으므로 지문의 내용과 일치한다. (D)는 'Ordering is quick and easy using our new smartphone application!'에서 저희의 새로운 스마트폰 애플리케이션을 이용하면 주문이 빠르고 쉽다고 했으므로 지문의 내용과 일치한다.

어휘 fee n. 요금 serve v. (음식을) 제공하다 besides prep. ~ 외에
at least phr. 최소 through prep. ~을 통해

163 Not/True 문제   중 ●●○

해석 Queen's Combo에 대해 언급된 것은?
(A) 무료 사이드 샐러드를 포함한다.
(B) 최근에 가격이 인하되었다.
(C) 다음 달에 선택 사항들이 바뀔 것이다.
(D) 제한된 기간 동안만 이용할 수 있다.

해설 지문의 'From now until June 30, order a ~ Queen's Combo'에서 지

금부터 6월 30일까지, Queen's Combo를 주문하라고 했으므로 (D)는 지문의 내용과 일치한다. 따라서 (D)가 정답이다. (A), (B), (C)는 지문에 언급되지 않은 내용이다.

어휘 **complimentary** adj. 무료의 **option** n. 선택(사항)

From now until 지금부터 ~까지 → for a limited time 제한된 기간 동안

164 육하원칙 문제 하 ●○○

해석 고객들은 어떻게 무료 피자를 받을 수 있는가?
(A) 결제하기 위해 신용카드를 사용함으로써
(B) 여름 경품 추첨에 참여함으로써
(C) 특정한 재료가 있는 품목을 주문함으로써
(D) 식당에서 상품권을 제시함으로써

해설 지문의 'buy ~ pizza with premium toppings and receive ~ cheese pizza absolutely free'에서 프리미엄 토핑이 있는 피자를 주문하고 치즈 피자를 완전 무료로 받으라고 했으므로 (C)가 정답이다.

어휘 **enter** v. 참여하다, 들어가다 **prize draw** phr. 경품 추첨
voucher n. 상품권

패러프레이징

pizza with premium toppings 프리미엄 토핑이 있는 피자 → item with special ingredients 특정한 재료가 있는 품목

165-167번은 다음 회람에 관한 문제입니다.

회람

수신: 전 직원
발신: Patricia Diaz, 최고경영자, BestSnack사
제목: 신나는 소식
날짜: 3월 18일

¹⁶⁵저는 우리의 BestSnack 자판기가 다음 주 월요일부터 전국 1,000개의 테스트 장소들에서 **출시될 것임을** 모두에게 **알리게 되어 기쁩니다.** 여러분 모두 알다시피, BestSnack은 터치스크린 기술이 있는 우리의 자판기입니다. — [1] —. 이것은 사용자들이 범주들을 바탕으로 물품들을 선택함으로써 그들의 영양상의 필요에 따라 맞춰진 음료들과 간식들을 선택할 수 있게 합니다. 제로 칼로리, 저탄수화물, 그리고 무가당의 선택 사항들이 있습니다. — [2] —. ¹⁶⁶/¹⁶⁷마케팅팀은 현재 ¹⁶⁷BestSnack에 대해 ¹⁶⁶/¹⁶⁷전국 언론 매체들에 알리는 언론 보도자료를 제작하는 중입니다. — [3] —. 직원으로서, 여러분은 이 기계들에서 제품들을 구매함으로써 테스트 과정에 참여하도록 요청됩니다. — [4] —. 기계의 위치들과 물품 가격들에 대한 세부사항은 이번 주에 여러분에게 제공될 것입니다.

delighted adj. 기쁜 **vending machine** phr. 자판기
launch v. 출시하다, 시작하다 **nationwide** adj. 전국의
beverage n. 음료 **tailor** v. 맞추다 **nutritional** adj. 영양상의
low-carbohydrate adj. 저탄수화물의 **sugar-free** adj. 무가당의
be in the process of phr. ~하는 중이다
press release phr. 언론 보도자료 **inform** v. 알리다
news outlet phr. 언론 매체, 방송국 **participate in** phr. ~에 참여하다

165 목적 찾기 문제 중 ●●○

해석 회람의 하나의 목적은 무엇인가?

(A) 회사 정책 변화를 알리기 위해
(B) 제품 출시에 대한 정보를 제공하기 위해
(C) 회사 구내식당에 추가된 것을 알리기 위해
(D) 직원들에게 이용 가능한 새로운 혜택을 소개하기 위해

해설 지문의 'I'm delighted to announce ~ that our BestSnack Vending Machine will be launched'에서 우리의 BestSnack 자판기가 출시될 것임을 알리게 되어 기쁘다고 했으므로 (B)가 정답이다.

어휘 **policy** n. 정책, 규정 **release** n. 출시 **addition** n. 추가된 것, 부가물
benefit n. 혜택, 이득

패러프레이징

announce 알리다 → provide information 정보를 제공하다
Vending Machine will be launched 자판기가 출시될 것이다 → product release 제품 출시

166 육하원칙 문제 중 ●●○

해석 Ms. Diaz는 마케팅 직원들이 무엇을 하고 있다고 말하는가?
(A) 사람들의 식사 습관에 대한 설문조사를 완료하는 것
(B) 언론사들을 위한 공식 성명서를 만들어 내는 것
(C) 회사의 공급업체들과의 회의를 준비하는 것
(D) 가까운 장래의 캠페인 행사를 계획하는 것

해설 지문의 'The marketing team is currently in the process of creating press releases informing national news outlets'에서 마케팅팀은 현재 전국 언론 매체들에 알리는 언론 보도자료를 제작하는 중이라고 했으므로 (B)가 정답이다.

어휘 **complete** v. 완료하다 **statement** n. 성명서, 진술서
supplier n. 공급업체 **arrange** v. 준비하다

패러프레이징

creating 제작하는 것 → Developing 만들어 내는 것
press releases informing ~ news outlets 언론 매체들에 알리는 언론 보도자료 → official statements for media companies 언론사들을 위한 공식 성명서

167 문장 위치 찾기 문제 중 ●●○

해석 [1], [2], [3], [4]로 표시된 위치 중, 다음 문장이 들어갈 곳으로 가장 적절한 것은?

"우리는 우리의 웹사이트에도 메시지를 게시할 것입니다."

(A) [1]
(B) [2]
(C) [3]
(D) [4]

해설 주어진 문장에서 우리는 우리의 웹사이트에도 메시지를 게시할 것이라고 했으므로, 이 문장이 메시지와 관련된 내용이 나오는 부분에 들어가야 함을 알 수 있다. [3]의 앞 문장인 'The marketing team is currently in the process of creating press releases informing national news outlets about the BestSnack.'에서 마케팅팀이 현재 BestSnack에 대해 전국 언론 매체들에 알리는 언론 보도자료를 제작하는 중이라고 했으므로, [3]에 제시된 문장이 들어가면 마케팅팀이 현재 언론 보도자료를 제작하고 있고 이 메시지는 웹사이트에도 게시될 것이라는 자연스러운 문맥이 된다는 것을 알 수 있다. 따라서 (C)가 정답이다.

어휘 **post** v. 게시하다

168-171번은 다음 광고에 관한 문제입니다.

> **Freewater 라벤더 농장**
>
> 이번 여름 특별한 경험을 찾고 있으신가요? Lewiston시 바로 외곽의 821번지 Corkscrew로에 있는 168Freewater 라벤더 농장에 방문하세요! 168이 농장의 그림 같은 장소와 아름다운 풍경은 이곳을 휴식을 취하기에 이상적인 공간으로 만듭니다.
>
> 저희의 향기로운 라벤더 들판 사이를 산책하거나 169모두 농장의 가장 질 좋은 라벤더로 완벽하게 맛을 낸 170-A레모네이드, 차, 케이크, 그리고 쿠키와 같은 집에서 직접 만든 즐거움들을 Freewater 카페에서 시식해보세요. 비누, 로션, 향유를 포함하여 라벤더를 함유한 제품들을 위해 170-C저희의 기념품점에 들르세요. 저희는 또한 지역 장인들의 수공예품과 지역 농부들의 잼, 꿀, 피클, 그리고 치즈를 취급합니다.
>
> 이 카페는 강과 산의 경관과 함께 앉을 수 있는 야외 공간을 특별히 포함합니다. Freewater 라벤더 농장은 또한 소풍 단체들을 환영하며, 탁자와 벤치가 있는 170-B아름다운 야외 식사 공간을 가지고 있습니다.
>
> 그리고 당연히, 농장으로의 여행은 아름답고 향기로운 라벤더꽃의 구매 없이는 완성되지 않을 것입니다! 171저희의 수확 부스에 잠깐 들려서 단 12달러에 말린 혹은 싱싱한 라벤더 한 다발을 사세요. 저희의 운영과 서비스들에 대한 추가적인 세부사항을 위해서는, 오늘 www.freewaterlavender.com을 방문하세요!

picturesque adj. 그림 같은, 생생한 **landscape** n. 풍경
ideal adj. 이상적인 **stroll** v. 산책하다 **fragrant** adj. 향기로운
sample v. 시식하다, 맛보다; n. 견본품 **delight** n. 즐거움, 기쁨
flavor v. 맛을 내다 **carry** v. 취급하다 **handicraft** n. 수공예품
artisan n. 장인 **feature** v. (특별히) 포함하다
naturally adv. 당연히, 자연히 **drop by** phr. ~에 잠깐 들르다
harvest n. 수확 **pick up** phr. ~을 사다, 얻다 **bunch** n. 다발

168 주제 찾기 문제   중 ●●○

해석   광고는 주로 무엇에 대한 것인가?
(A) 농업 시설의 볼거리들
(B) 지역 농장의 새로운 제품들
(C) 자연식품의 건강상의 이점들
(D) 장인들을 위한 지역 공예 박람회

해설   지문의 'Visit the Freewater Lavender Farm'과 'The farm's picturesque location and beautiful landscape make it an ideal place to relax.'에서 Freewater 라벤더 농장에 방문하라고 했고, 이 농장의 그림 같은 장소와 아름다운 풍경은 이곳을 휴식을 취하기에 이상적인 공간으로 만든다고 한 후, 농장에 있는 카페, 기념품점, 수확 부스 등 여러 볼거리들을 소개하고 있으므로 (A)가 정답이다. (B)도 지문에서 농장의 여러 제품들을 소개하고 있어 답이 될 것 같지만, 새로운 제품인지는 알 수 없으므로 답이 될 수 없다.

어휘   **attraction** n. 볼거리, 명소 **agricultural** adj. 농업의 **craft** n. 공예, 기술

패러프레이징

> Lavender Farm 라벤더 농장 → agricultural facility 농업 시설

169 동의어 찾기 문제   중 ●●●

해석   2문단 두 번째 줄의 단어 "finest"는 의미상 -와 가장 가깝다.
(A) 최고의
(B) 가장 부드러운

(C) 가장 흔한
(D) 가장 비싼

해설   지문의 finest를 포함한 구절 'all perfectly flavored with the farm's finest lavender'에서 모두 농장의 가장 질 좋은 라벤더로 완벽하게 맛을 냈다고 했으므로 finest는 '가장 질 좋은'이라는 뜻으로 사용되었다. 따라서 '최고의'라는 뜻을 가진 (A) best가 정답이다.

170 Not/True 문제   중 ●●○

해석   Freewater 라벤더 농장의 특징이 아닌 것은?
(A) 집에서 직접 만든 제품들을 제공하는 식사 시설
(B) 야외 식사를 하기 위한 공간
(C) 다양한 지역 상품들을 파는 가게
(D) 지역 예술가들의 작품을 포함하는 미술관

해설   지문에서 (D)는 언급되지 않은 내용이다. 따라서 (D)가 정답이다. (A)는 'sample homemade delights such as lemonade, teas ~ at the Freewater Café'에서 레모네이드, 차와 같은 집에서 직접 만든 즐거움들을 Freewater 카페에서 시식해보라고 했으므로 지문의 내용과 일치한다. (B)는 'a beautiful outdoor dining area'에서 아름다운 야외 식사 공간이 있다고 했으므로 지문의 내용과 일치한다. (C)는 'Stop by our gift shop'과 'We also carry handicrafts from local artisans and jams, honey, pickles, and cheeses from local farmers.'에서 기념품점에 들르라고 하며 지역 장인들의 수공예품과 지역 농부들의 잼, 꿀, 피클, 그리고 치즈를 취급한다고 했으므로 지문의 내용과 일치한다.

어휘   **dining establishment** phr. 식사 시설, 식당 **serve** v. 제공하다, 내다
meal n. 식사 **a variety of** phr. 다양한

패러프레이징

> Café 카페 → dining establishment 식사 시설
> outdoor dining area 야외 식사 공간 → area for having outdoor meals 야외 식사를 하기 위한 공간

171 육하원칙 문제   하 ●○○

해석   방문객들은 농장의 부스에서 무엇을 할 수 있는가?
(A) 특별 행사를 주최하기 위해 등록한다
(B) 몇몇 꽃들을 구매한다
(C) 제품들의 견본품을 써 본다
(D) 입장권을 구매한다

해설   지문의 'Drop by our harvest booth and pick up a bunch of ~ lavender'에서 저희, 즉 농장의 수확 부스에 잠깐 들려서 라벤더 한 다발을 사라고 했으므로 (B)가 정답이다.

어휘   **function** n. 행사, 기능 **admission ticket** phr. 입장권

패러프레이징

> pick up a bunch of ~ lavender 라벤더 한 다발을 사다 → buy some flowers 몇몇 꽃들을 구매하다

172-175번은 다음 웹페이지에 관한 문제입니다.

> www.clearyfoods.com
> **Cleary Foods**
>
> | 홈 | 상점 | 위치 | 보상 프로그램 | 소식 | 연락처 |
> | --- | --- | --- | --- | --- | --- |
>
> 쇼핑객들께:

Cleary Foods는 단순히 높은 품질의 식료품이나 가정 필수품보다 제공할 것이 훨씬 더 많습니다.

1. 저희의 신선육 구역의 정육점 주인들은 기꺼이 당신의 고기를 조각들로 잘라주고 지방을 제거해줍니다. ¹⁷²그들은 또한 당신을 위해 당신의 요리용 칼들을 날카롭게 갈아줄 것입니다. — [1] —. 만약 그들이 주문을 받느라 바쁘다면, 그저 당신의 칼들을 지정된 칼 두는 곳에 놓아두고 당신이 쇼핑을 다 끝낸 후에 그것들을 되찾으세요.
2. 날씨가 따뜻할 때, ^{174-D}저희의 직원에게 집에 가는 길에 냉동 제품들이 녹지 않도록 그것들을 드라이아이스와 함께 포장해달라고 요청하는 것을 기억하세요. — [2] —. 또한, ^{174-B}만약 당신이 냉장 보관되지 않은 음료들을 구매한다면 와인 구역에 있는 저희의 완전 새로운 급속 음료 냉장 장치를 사용해보세요.
3. ^{173-D}저희는 가게에 없는 특별한 제품들을 저희의 판매업체들이 가지고 있는 한 당신을 위해 그것들을 주문할 것입니다. ^{173-D/174-C}계산대에서 신청서를 작성하고 ^{174-C}그것을 계산대 직원에게 주십시오. — [3] —.

¹⁷⁵당신의 다음 Cleary Foods 방문에서는 이러한 서비스들을 반드시 이용해 보세요. — [4] —. ¹⁷⁵참여하는 가게들의 전체 목록을 위해 여기를 클릭하세요.

grocery n. 식료품 household n. 가정 necessity n. 필수품
butcher n. 정육점 주인 trim away phr. 제거하다
sharpen v. 날카롭게 갈다 drop off phr. 놓아두다
designated adj. 지정된 station n. 두는 곳, 장소 retrieve v. 되찾다
brand new phr. 완전 새로운 rapid adj. 급속의, 빠른 chiller n. 냉장 장치
unrefrigerated adj. 냉장 보관되지 않은
stock v. (판매할 상품을 갖추 두고) 있다; n. 재고품 vendor n. 판매업체
request form phr. 신청서 checkout counter phr. 계산대
complete adj. 전체의, 완전한

172 추론 문제   상 ●●●

해석 Cleary Foods의 정육점 주인들에 대해 암시되는 것은?
(A) 기꺼이 특별한 양념들로 구입품에 풍미를 더한다.
(B) 고객들에게 고기 준비에 대한 조언을 제공한다.
(C) 다양한 상품들에 대해 매일 할인을 제공한다.
(D) 서비스를 곧바로 행하지 못할 수 있다.

해설 지문의 'They will ~ sharpen your cooking knives for you'와 'If they are busy taking orders, just drop your knives off ~ and retrieve them when you're done shopping.'에서 그들, 즉 Cleary Foods의 정육점 주인들은 요리용 칼들을 날카롭게 갈아줄 것이며 만약 그들이 주문을 받느라 바쁘다면, 그냥 당신의 칼들을 놓아두고 당신이 쇼핑을 다 끝낸 후에 그것들을 되찾아가라고 했으므로, 정육점 주인들이 곧바로 칼을 갈아주지 못할 수도 있다는 사실을 추론할 수 있다. 따라서 (D)가 정답이다.

어휘 glad adj. 기꺼이 ~하는, 기쁜 purchase n. 구입품, 구입; v. 구입하다
seasoning n. 양념 preparation n. 준비

173 Not/True 문제   상 ●●●

해석 특별 주문들에 대해 사실인 것은?
(A) 프로그램의 회원들만이 이용 가능하다.
(B) 고객들은 선불로 지불하도록 요구된다.
(C) 추가 요금을 내면 집 주소로 배달될 수도 있다.
(D) 신청서들은 가게의 계산대에 놓여있을 수도 있다.

해설 지문의 'We will order special products ~ as long as our vendors carry them. Just fill out a request form at the checkout counter'에

서 우리, 즉 Cleary Foods는 특별한 제품들을 자신들의 판매업체들이 가지고 있는 한 주문할 것이라고 하며 계산대에서 신청서를 작성하라고 했으므로 (D)는 지문의 내용과 일치한다. 따라서 (D)가 정답이다. (A), (B), (C)는 지문에 언급되지 않은 내용이다.

어휘 in advance phr. 선불로, 미리 charge n. 요금 place v. 놓다, 두다

174 Not/True 문제   중 ●●○

해석 Cleary Foods의 새로운 장비에 대해 언급된 것은?
(A) 꽃 통로에 위치해 있다.
(B) 음료들을 빨리 차갑게 한다.
(C) 특별 신청서들을 처리한다.
(D) 장바구니를 위한 드라이아이스를 만든다.

해설 지문의 'try our brand new rapid beverage chiller ~ if you're purchasing unrefrigerated drinks'에서 만약 당신이 냉장 보관되지 않은 음료들을 구매한다면 우리, 즉 Cleary Foods의 완전 새로운 급속 음료 냉각 장치를 사용해보라고 했으므로 (B)는 지문의 내용과 일치한다. 따라서 (B)가 정답이다. (A)는 지문에 언급되지 않은 내용이다. (C)는 'Just fill out a request form ~ and give it to the cashier.'에서 신청서를 작성하고 계산대 직원에게 그것을 주라고는 했으나 새로운 장비가 신청서를 처리한다고는 하지 않았으므로 지문의 내용과 일치하지 않는다. (D)는 'ask our staff to package frozen items with dry ice'에서 직원에게 냉동 제품들을 드라이아이스와 함께 포장해달라고 요청하라고는 했으나 새로운 장비가 드라이아이스를 만든다고는 하지 않았으므로 지문의 내용과 일치하지 않는다.

어휘 aisle n. 통로 cool v. 차갑게 하다; adj. 서늘한
process v. 처리하다; n. 과정, 절차 grocery bag phr. 장바구니

패러프레이징

try ~ rapid beverage chiller 급속 음료 냉각 장치를 사용하다 → cools beverages quickly 음료들을 빨리 차갑게 하다

175 문장 위치 찾기 문제   상 ●●●

해석 [1], [2], [3], [4]로 표시된 위치 중, 다음 문장이 들어갈 곳으로 가장 적절한 것은?

"그것들은 현재 전국의 선택된 지점들에서 이용할 수 있습니다."

(A) [1]
(B) [2]
(C) [3]
(D) [4]

해설 주어진 문장에서 그것들은 현재 전국의 선택된 지점들에서 이용할 수 있다고 했으므로, 이 문장이 현재 이용 가능한 것들과 관련된 내용이 나오는 부분에 늘어가야 함을 알 수 있다. [4]의 앞 문장인 'Make sure to take advantage of these services on your next visit to Cleary Foods.'에서 당신의 다음 Cleary Foods 방문에서는 이러한 서비스들을 반드시 이용해보라고 했고, 뒤 문장인 'Click here for a complete list of participating stores.'에서 참여하는 가게들의 전체 목록을 위해서는 링크를 클릭하라고 했으므로 [4]에 제시된 문장이 들어가면 다음 방문에 이러한 서비스들을 반드시 이용해보고, 이러한 것들은 현재 전국의 선택된 지점들에서 이용 가능하며, 서비스들을 제공하는 가게들의 전체 목록을 위해서는 링크를 클릭하라는 자연스러운 문맥이 된다는 것을 알 수 있다. 따라서 (D)가 정답이다.

어휘 currently adv. 현재, 지금 select adj. 선택된, 엄선된; v. 선택하다
location n. 지점

176-180번은 다음 공고와 회람에 관한 문제입니다.

자선 자동차 경매
6월 25일 Metropolitan 공원에서

¹⁷⁹제21회 연례 자선 자동차 경매가 6월 25일에 Metropolitan 공원에서 열릴 것입니다. ¹⁷⁶이 연례 활동은 몇몇 주요 자동차 제조업체들로부터 후원을 받으며 주 전역의 아동 자선 단체들을 위한 기금을 모읍니다.

공원은 오전 10시에 대중에게 개방될 것입니다. 경매는 오후 1시에 시작되며 오후 6시 혹은 모든 자동차들이 팔렸을 때 끝납니다. 상업용 차량들을 포함하여, 자동차와 트럭들에 대한 좋은 거래들을 찾으세요. 가족을 데려와 야외에서 재미있는 하루를 즐기세요. 경매에 더하여, ¹⁷⁸빈티지 자동차 전시회, 음식 부스, 놀이 공간, 그리고 다양한 자동차 관련 제품들을 판매하는 노점상들이 있을 것입니다. 이 행사의 티켓은 1인당 5달러입니다.

문의가 있으시다면, 555-3403으로 전화주시고 혹은 ¹⁷⁷판매될 차량들의 미리 보기를 위해서는 www.charitycarauction.org를 방문하세요.

charity n. 자선, 자선 사업   sponsor v. 후원하다   major adj. 주요한
automobile n. 자동차   manufacturer n. 제조업체   raise v. 모으다
commercial adj. 상업용의   exhibit n. 전시(물)   vendor n. 노점상, 행상인
inquiry n. 문의   preview n. 미리 보기, 시사회

회람

6월 15일

¹⁷⁹수신: 모든 Metropolitan 공원 직원들
발신: Joel Gage, 공원 서비스 책임자
제목: 행사 준비

¹⁷⁹제21회 연례 자선 자동차 경매의 준비로, 저는 모든 분들께 몇 가지를 상기시켜드리고자 합니다. ¹⁷⁹행사 하루 전날, ¹⁷⁸/¹⁷⁹우리는 ¹⁷⁹경매 및 예정된 전시를 위한 차량들의 ¹⁷⁸/¹⁷⁹배달을 받을 것입니다. ¹⁷⁸나머지는 북쪽 출입구를 통해 안으로 들여질 반면 판매될 차량들은 우리의 안전한 주차장에 그대로 있을 것입니다.

행사 당일에, 남쪽 출입구는 보행자들에게 개방될 것이고, 동쪽 출입구는 공원 및 행사 직원들을 위해 따로 남겨두어 질 것이고, 서쪽 출입구는 구급요원 용일 것입니다. ¹⁸⁰시의 경찰서로부터 교통 및 군중 관리에 대한 지원이 제공될 것입니다.

여러분이 어떠한 질문이라도 있으시다면, 망설이지 말고 전화해주시거나 공원 내 있는 제 사무실에 들러주십시오. ¹⁷⁹저는 회의에 참석하기 위해 시카고로 출장을 갈 예정이기 때문에 다음 주에는 저를 만날 수 없다는 것을 유의해 주십시오. 저는 배달일에 여러분 모두를 뵙도록 하겠습니다.

in preparation for phr. ~의 준비로   secure adj. 안전한
pedestrian n. 보행자   reserve v. 따로 남겨두다, 예약하다
emergency personnel phr. 구급요원   assistance n. 지원
traffic n. 교통, 차량   crowd n. 군중   hesitate v. 망설이다, 주저하다
unavailable adj. 만날 수 없는, 이용할 수 없는

176 주제 찾기 문제   중 ●●○

해석 공고는 주로 무엇에 대한 것인가?
(A) 제품 출시
(B) 야외 콘서트
(C) 모금 활동
(D) 스포츠 행사

해설 공고의 'This yearly activity ~ raises money for children's charities around the state.'에서 이 연례 활동은 주 전역의 아동 자선 단체들을 위한 기금을 모은다고 했으므로 (C)가 정답이다.

어휘 launch n. 출시   fund-raising n. 모금

패러프레이징

activity ~ raises money for ~ charities 활동은 자선 단체들을 위한 기금을 모은다 → A fund-raising activity 모금 활동

177 육하원칙 문제   하 ●○○

해석 독자들은 왜 웹사이트를 방문해야 하는가?
(A) 부스 공간을 예약하기 위해
(B) 향후 행사들을 위한 제안서들을 제출하기 위해
(C) 몇몇 판매 상품들을 미리 보기 위해
(D) 단체를 위한 티켓들을 구매하기 위해

해설 공고의 'visit www.charitycarauction.org to get a preview of the cars for sale'에서 판매될 차량들의 미리 보기를 위해서는 웹사이트를 방문하라고 했으므로 (C)가 정답이다.

어휘 submit v. 제출하다   proposal n. 제안서   offering n. 판매 상품, 제공하는 것

패러프레이징

get a preview of ~을 미리 보다 → see ~ in advance 미리 보다
cars for sale 판매될 차량들 → offerings 판매 상품들

178 추론 문제   연계   상 ●●●

해석 빈티지 자동차들에 대해 암시되는 것은?
(A) 추첨에서 경품으로 제공될 것이다.
(B) 행사 마지막 날에 판매될 것이다.
(C) 북쪽 출입구를 통해 운반될 것이다.
(D) 안전한 주차장에 주차될 것이다.

해설 공고의 'there will be a vintage car exhibit'에서 빈티지 자동차 전시회가 있을 것이라고 했다. 또한, 회람의 'we will be receiving deliveries of vehicles for the auction and the planned display. The cars for sale will stay in our secure parking lot while the rest will be brought inside through the north entrance.'에서는 경매 및 예정된 전시를 위한 차량들의 배달을 받을 것이라고 하며 나머지는 북쪽 출입구를 통해 안으로 들여질 반면 판매될 차량들은 안전한 주차장에 그대로 있을 것임을 확인할 수 있다.
두 단서를 종합할 때, 나머지, 즉 판매될 차량들이 아닌 전시를 위한 빈티지 자동차들은 북쪽 출입구를 통해 운반될 것임을 추론할 수 있다. 따라서 (C)가 정답이다.

어휘 draw n. 추첨; v. 그리다, 끌다

179 추론 문제   연계   상 ●●●

해석 Mr. Gage에 대해 추론될 수 있는 것은?
(A) 6월 25일 전에 출장에서 돌아올 것이다.
(B) 구급 팀원들을 도와줄 자원봉사자들을 찾고 있다.
(C) 월말에 새로운 사무실로 이동할 것이다.
(D) 다음 주에 시카고에서 휴가를 보낼 계획을 하고 있다.

해설 공고의 'The 21st Annual Charity Car Auction will be held on June 25 at Metropolitan Park.'에서 제21회 연례 자선 자동차 경매가 6월 25일에 Metropolitan 공원에서 열린다고 했다. 또한, 회람의 'To: All

Metropolitan Park staff'에서는 회람이 Metropolitan 공원 직원들에게 보내진 것임을 알 수 있고, 'In preparation for the 21st Annual Charity Car Auction', 'One day before the event, we will be receiving deliveries'에서는 제21회 연례 자선 자동차 경매의 준비라며 행사 하루 전날에 배달을 받을 것이라고 한 후, 'I will be unavailable next week as I will be traveling ~ to attend a conference. I will see all of you on the day of the deliveries.'에서는 자신, 즉 Mr. Gage가 회의에 참석하기 위해 출장을 갈 예정이기 때문에 다음 주에는 자신을 만날 수 없으며 여러분 모두를 배송일에 보겠다고 한 사실을 확인할 수 있다.

두 단서를 종합할 때, Mr. Gage는 6월 25일 전에 출장에서 돌아올 것임을 추론할 수 있다. 따라서 (A)가 정답이다.

어휘 seek v. 찾다, 구하다   assist v. 돕다   crew n. 팀원, 팀
take a vacation phr. 휴가를 보내다

180 동의어 찾기 문제   중 ●●○

해석 회람에서, 2문단 세 번째 줄의 단어 "management"는 의미상 ~와 가장 가깝다.

(A) 관리
(B) 권한
(C) 경영진
(D) 운영

해설 회람에서 management를 포함한 문장 'Assistance with traffic and crowd management will be provided by the city's police department.'에서 시의 경찰서로부터 교통 및 군중 관리에 대한 지원이 제공될 것이라고 했으므로 management는 '관리'라는 뜻으로 사용되었다. 따라서 '관리, 통제'라는 뜻을 가진 (A) control이 정답이다.

181-185번은 다음 보도 자료와 이메일에 관한 문제입니다.

2월 14일—181-C Larcorn 개발사는 포틀랜드 지역에 두 개의 새로운 주거 건물들을 발표하게 되어 기쁘다. City View 181-C 아파트는 올해 5월 10일에 완공될 것이고 30가구를 포함할 것이다. 182-C 상업 지역에 있는 이것의 편리한 위치는 이것을 젊은 전문직 종사자들 사이에서 인기 있도록 만들 것임이 확실하다. 183 건물은 또한 주민들에 의해 무료로 이용될 수 있는 운동 센터와 오락 라운지와 같은 생활 편의 시설들을 포함할 것이다. 181-C Larcorn사는 또한 Park로에 있는 Star 분양 아파트도 완공할 예정이다. 182-B 이 20층의 건물은 40개의 호화로운 방들과 여러 가지의 고급 상점들과 식당들을 포함할 것이다. 182-A 이 프로젝트의 완공일은 7월 28일이다. 두 건물 모두에 대한 더 많은 정보를 위해서는, www.larcorn.com을 방문하면 된다.

residential adj. 주거의, 거주의   property n. 건물, 부동산
unit n. 가구, 세대   business district phr. 상업 지역   sure adj. 확실한
professional n. 전문 종사자; adj. 전문적인   feature v. (특별히) 포함하다
amenity n. 생활 편의 시설   resident n. 주민   story n. (건물의) 층, 이야기
an assortment of phr. 여러 가지의   high-end adj. 고급의
completion date phr. 완공일

수신: Sheila Bridges <s.bridges@mailranger.com>
발신: Victor Marino <v.marino@topspeedmovers.com>
제목: 183 이사
날짜: 7월 22일
첨부: 송장.doc

Ms. Bridges께,

저는 그저 다음 주 일정을 확인하고자 했습니다. 저희의 운송업자들은

8월 1일 오전 7시 30분에 당신의 현재 거주지에 도착할 것입니다. 저희는 183 당신의 소지품들을 포장하고 그것들을 트럭에 싣는 것에 대략 3시간이 걸릴 것으로 예상하는데, 이것은 저희가 City View 아파트에 오전 11시 30분까지 도착할 것을 의미합니다. 184 주택 관리자에게 그 시간에 저희가 세대에 접근하는 것을 허락하도록 다시 한번 말해 주십시오.

저는 또한 당신이 7월 14일에 받은 송장에 오류가 있다는 것을 알려드리고자 했습니다. 당신이 883달러가 청구되었어야 했을 때, 실수로 당신은 980달러가 청구되었습니다. 185 당신이 제시한 쿠폰은 당신이 10퍼센트의 가격 공제를 받을 자격이 있도록 하는데, 그러나 이것이 포함되지 않았습니다. 제가 정정된 송장을 이 이메일에 첨부했습니다. 저희의 실수가 야기했을 수 있는 모든 불편에 대해 사과드립니다.

Victor Marino 드림
부팀장, Topspeed Movers사

invoice n. 송장   confirm v. 확인하다   residence n. 거주지, 주택
approximately adv. 대략, 거의   pack v. 포장하다   belonging n. 소지품
load v. 싣다; n. 짐, 화물   remind v. 다시 한번 말하다, 상기시키다
grant v. 허락하다, 승인하다   mistakenly adv. 실수로   deduction n. 공제
attach v. 첨부하다   corrected adj. 정정된   inconvenience n. 불편

181 Not/True 문제   상 ●●●

해석 Larcorn 개발사에 대해 사실인 것은?
(A) 오피스 타워를 건설하는 경쟁 입찰에서 이겼다.
(B) 특정 날짜에 예정된 축하 행사가 있다.
(C) 두 개의 프로젝트들을 완공하는 과정에 있다.
(D) 구매자들이 보는 것이 가능한 모델 세대들이 있다.

해설 보도 자료의 'Larcorn Development is pleased to announce two new residential properties'에서 Larcorn 개발사는 두 개의 새로운 주거 건물들을 발표하게 되어 기쁘다고 했고, 'Apartments will be completed on May 10 of this year', 'Larcorn will also be finishing ~ Condominiums'에서 아파트는 올해 5월 10일에 완공될 것이며 Larcorn사는 분양 아파트도 완공할 예정이라고 했으므로 (C)는 지문의 내용과 일치한다. 따라서 (C)가 정답이다. (A), (B), (D)는 지문에 언급되지 않은 내용이다.

어휘 competitive adj. 경쟁의   bid n. 입찰; v. 값을 부르다
celebration n. 축하 행사, 기념 행사   specific adj. 특정한, 구체적인

182 Not/True 문제   상 ●●●

해석 Star 분양 아파트에 대해 언급된 것은?
(A) 5월 10일에 완성될 것이다.
(B) 상업 공간들을 포함할 것이다.
(C) 상업 지역에 위치할 것이다.
(D) 도시공원을 내려다볼 것이다.

해설 보도 자료의 'This ~ building will include ~ an assortment of high-end shops and restaurants.'에서 이 건물, 즉 Star 분양 아파트는 여러 가지의 고급 상점들과 식당들을 포함할 것이라고 했으므로 (B)는 지문의 내용과 일치한다. 따라서 (B)가 정답이다. (A)는 'The completion date for this project is July 28.'에서 이 프로젝트, 즉 Star 분양 아파트의 개발 프로젝트의 완공일은 7월 28일이라고 했으므로 지문의 내용과 일치하지 않는다. (C)는 'Its convenient location in the business district'에서 상업 지역에 있는 이것, 즉 City View 아파트의 편리한 위치라고 했으므로 지문의 내용과 일치하지 않는다. (D)는 지문에 언급되지 않은 내용이다.

어휘 commercial adj. 상업의, 상업적인   overlook v. 내려다보다, 간과하다

최고난도 문제

183 추론 문제 연계   상 ●●●

해석   Ms. Bridges에 대해 암시되는 것은?

(A) 매달 관리비를 지불할 것이다.

(B) 체육관에 무료로 출입할 수 있을 것이다.

(C) 부분적인 환불을 받을 것이다.

(D) 이삿짐 운송 회사의 사무실을 방문할 것이다.

해설   이메일이 'Move'에서 이사가 일어난다는 것을 알 수 있고, 'it will take ~ three hours to pack your belongings and load them onto the truck, ~ we should arrive at City View Apartments'에서 당신, 즉 Ms. Bridges의 소지품들을 포장하고 그것들을 트럭에 싣는 것에 3시간이 걸릴 것이며, City View 아파트에 도착할 것이라고 했다. 또한, 보도 자료의 'The building will also feature ~ a fitness center ~ that can be used without charge by residents.'에서는 건물, 즉 City View 아파트는 또한 주민들에 의해 무료로 이용될 수 있는 운동 센터를 포함할 것임을 확인할 수 있다.

두 단서를 종합할 때, Ms. Bridges는 이사하여 City View 아파트의 주민이 될 것이므로, 운동센터를 무료로 출입 및 이용할 수 있을 것이라는 사실을 추론할 수 있다. 따라서 (B)가 정답이다.

어휘   maintenance fee phr. 관리비
have access to phr. ~에 출입(접근)할 수 있다   partial adj. 부분적인
refund n. 환불; v. 환불하다   moving company phr. 이삿짐 운송 회사

패러프레이징

fitness center 운동 센터 → gym 체육관
can be used without charge 무료로 이용될 수 있다 → have free access 무료로 출입할 수 있다

184 육하원칙 문제   상 ●●●

해석   Ms. Bridges는 무엇을 하도록 요청되는가?

(A) 배달 시간을 확정한다

(B) 건물 관리인에게 연락한다

(C) 추가적인 지불금을 낸다

(D) 이전의 이메일에 답한다

해설   이메일의 'Please remind the residence manager to grant us access to the unit at that time.'에서 이메일 수신자인 Ms. Bridges에게 주택 관리자에게 그 시간에 자신들, 즉 Topspeed Movers사가 세대에 접근하는 것을 허락하도록 다시 한번 말해달라고 했으므로 (B)가 정답이다.

어휘   reply to phr. ~에 답하다   previous adj. 이전의

패러프레이징

remind the residence manager 주택 관리자에게 다시 한번 말하다
→ Contact a building manager 건물 관리인에게 연락한다

185 육하원칙 문제   상 ●●●

해석   Mr. Marino는 어떤 문제를 언급하는가?

(A) 송장이 발송되지 않았다.

(B) 아파트에 접근할 수 없다.

(C) 예약은 변경될 수 없다.

(D) 할인이 적용되지 않았다.

해설   이메일의 'The coupon ~ qualifies you for a ~ price deduction, but this was not included.'에서 이메일 발신자인 Mr. Marino가 쿠폰은 당신, 즉 Ms. Bridges가 가격 공제를 받을 자격이 있도록 하는데, 그러나 이것이 포함되지 않았다고 했으므로 (D)가 정답이다.

어휘   appointment n. 예약, 약속   discount n. 할인

패러프레이징

price deduction ~ was not included 가격 공제가 포함되지 않았다
→ A discount was not applied 할인이 적용되지 않았다

186-190번은 다음 두 이메일과 일정표에 관한 문제입니다.

수신: Maureen Chapman <maureen@lovetts.com>
발신: Rodney Tucker <rt77@exchanger.com>
제목: 더 많은 시간에 대한 요청
날짜: 4월 10일

Ms. Chapman께,

Lovett's 백화점에서의 정규직 근무를 제안해주신 것에 감사드립니다. 저는 제가 계산대 직원으로서 일을 잘하고 있다고 느끼며, 제 동료들과 함께 일하는 것을 즐겨왔습니다. 유감스럽게도, 저는 이 제안을 거절해야 합니다. 저는 현재 소프트웨어 회사에 고용되는 동안 학점을 얻게 해주는 저의 학교 컴퓨터학과의 여름 직무 프로그램에 고려되고 있습니다. ¹⁸⁶이 프로그램은 6월부터 8월까지 계속됩니다. 만약 제가 이 프로그램에 받아들여진다면, 저는 시간제 직무를 할 시간조차 없을 것입니다. 그렇지 않으면, ¹⁸⁶/¹⁹⁰올해 12월에 제가 졸업할 때까지 저는 기꺼이 Lovett's 백화점에서 계속 일할 것입니다. ¹⁹⁰그 후에, 저는 제 삼촌이 소유하고 있는 보험회사에서 일할 계획입니다.

Rodney Tucker 드림

full-time adj. 정규직의   checkout n. 계산대   colleague n. 동료
unfortunately adv. 유감스럽게도   turn down phr. ~을 거절하다
course credit phr. 학점   admit v. 받아들이다, 허가하다
part-time adj. 시간제의   position n. 직무, 직책   insurance n. 보험

전자제품 구역, Lovett's 백화점
¹⁸⁶/¹⁸⁸6월 둘째 주의 일정표

	6월 9일	6월 10일	6월 11일	6월 12일	¹⁸⁷6월 13일
오전 8시 -오후 12시	· Hazel Gates · Annie Montrose	· Dion Kirk · Hazel Gates	· Annie Montrose · Chico Benavidez	· Hazel Gates · Rodney Tucker	· Chico Benavidez · Rodney Tucker
오후 12시 -오후 3시	· Annie Montrose	· Hazel Gates	· Chico Benavidez	· Rodney Tucker	· Dion Kirk
¹⁸⁷오후 3시 -오후 7시	· Rodney Tucker	· Chico Benavidez · Rodney Tucker	· Chico Benavidez · Rodney Tucker	· Chico Benavidez	· ¹⁸⁷Annie Montrose · ¹⁸⁷Dion Kirk

¹⁸⁶/¹⁸⁸정규직 직원들: Chico Benavidez (23시간), Rodney Tucker (23시간)

¹⁸⁷시간제 직원들: Hazel Gates (12시간), Dion Kirk (11시간), Annie Montrose (15시간)

electronics n. 전자제품

수신: 전 직원 <staff@lovetts.com>
발신: Maureen Chapman <maureen@lovetts.com>
제목: 직원 사임
¹⁹⁰날짜: 12월 3일

직원분들께,

저는 ¹⁹⁰저희의 가장 소중한 직원들 중 한 명인, Rodney Tucker가 Lovett's 백화점을 떠날 것이라는 것을 모든 분들께 알리고자 합니다. Mr. Tucker는 저희 조직의 중요한 구성원이었습니다. 그는 시간제 직원으로 시작한 후에 구역 관리자직으로 승진되었습니다. 그를 위해 송별회가 12월 5일 오후 8시에서 9시에 직원실에서 열릴 것입니다. ¹⁸⁹Rodney가 지난 한 해 동안 관리했던 가전제품 구역의 직원들은 확실히 참석하도록 요구됩니다. 하지만, 모든 분들이 이 모임에 함께 하도록 장려됩니다. 저는 여러분을 그곳에서 만나길 바랍니다.

Maureen Chapman 드림
인사부장, Lovett's 백화점

---

resignation n. 사임, 사직 valued adj. 소중한, 높이 평가되는
promote v. 승진하다, 홍보하다 farewell party phr. 송별회
appliance n. 가전제품 obviously adv. 확실히, 분명히
join v. 함께 하다, 가입하다 gathering n. 모임

---

186 추론 문제 연계 상 ●●●

해석 Mr. Tucker에 대해 암시되는 것은?
(A) 그가 원했던 일자리를 얻지 못했다.
(B) 소매점을 위한 컴퓨터 프로그램을 설계했다.
(C) 주로 여름 휴가 동안 여행을 간다.
(D) 초과 근무 수당을 받을 기회를 받지 못했다.

해설 이메일1의 'The program runs from June through August. If I'm admitted into the program, I will not even have time for a part-time position. Otherwise, I would be happy to keep working for Lovett's Department Store until ~ in December of this year.'에서 프로그램, 즉 여름 직무 프로그램은 6월부터 8월까지 계속되며, 만약 자신, 즉 Mr. Tucker가 그 프로그램에 받아들여진다면 시간제 직무를 할 시간조차 없을 것이라고 했고, 그렇지 않으면 올해 12월까지 기꺼이 Lovett's 백화점에서 계속 일할 것이라고 했다. 또한, 일정표의 'Schedule for the second week of June'과 'Full-time staff: ~ Rodney Tucker ~'에서는 6월 둘째 주의 일정표의 정규직 직원들 목록에 Mr. Tucker의 이름이 있다는 것을 확인할 수 있다.
두 단서를 종합할 때, Mr. Tucker는 여름 직무 프로그램에 받아들여지지 못했고, 따라서 6월에도 계속 Lovett's 백화점에서 정규직으로 일했다는 사실을 추론할 수 있다. 따라서 (A)가 정답이다.

어휘 design v. 설계하다, 디자인하다 retail store phr. 소매점
opportunity n. 기회 overtime pay phr. 초과 근무 수당

187 육하원칙 문제 중 ●●○

해석 몇몇 시간제 근무 직원들은 언제 저녁에 함께 일했는가?
(A) 6월 8일
(B) 6월 10일
(C) 6월 12일

(D) 6월 13일

해설 일정표의 'Part-time staff: ~ Dion Kirk ~, Annie Montrose'에서 Mr. Kirk와 Ms. Montrose가 시간제 직원들임을 알 수 있고 'June 13', '3:00 P.M.-7:00 P.M.', 'Annie Montrose', 'Dion Kirk'에서 Ms. Montrose와 Mr. Kirk가 6월 13일에 오후 3시부터 오후 7시까지 함께 근무했음을 알 수 있으므로 (D)가 정답이다.

패러프레이징

part-timer 시간제 근무 직원 → Part-time staff 시간제 직원

188 추론 문제 상 ●●●

해석 Lovett's 백화점에 대해 추론될 수 있는 것은?
(A) 지점들은 모두 동일한 운영 시간을 가진다.
(B) 정규직 직원들은 일주일에 23시간씩 일한다.
(C) 직원들을 위한 관리 교육 프로그램을 운영한다.
(D) 최근에서야 컴퓨터를 판매하기 시작했다.

해설 일정표의 'Schedule for the second week of June', 'Full-time staff: Chico Benavidez (23 hours), Rodney Tucker (23 hours)'에서 정규직 직원들인 Mr. Benavidez와 Mr. Tucker가 23시간을 근무한다는 것을 알 수 있으므로 정규직 직원들은 일주일에 23시간씩 일할 것임을 추론할 수 있다. 따라서 (B)가 정답이다.

어휘 branch n. 지점 operation n. 운영, 작업

189 육하원칙 문제 중 ●●○

해석 두 번째 이메일에 따르면, 누가 송별회에 초대되었는가?
(A) 보상 프로그램의 회원들
(B) 단체의 기금모금 행사의 기부자들
(C) 가전제품 구역의 공급업체들
(D) 특정 구역에 배치된 직원들

해설 이메일2의 'Members of the Appliances Section ~ are obviously expected to attend.'에서 가전제품 구역의 직원들은 확실히 참석하도록 요구된다고 했으므로 (D)가 정답이다.

어휘 contributor n. 기부자, 기여자 fund-raiser n. 기금모금 행사, 기금 모금자
supplier n. 공급업체, 공급 회사 station v. ~을 배치하다; n. 역, 정거장
certain adj. 특정한, 확실한

패러프레이징

Members of the Appliances Section 가전제품 구역의 직원들 → Staff stationed in a certain area 특정 구역에 배치된 직원들

190 추론 문제 연계 상 ●●●

해석 Mr. Tucker가 왜 Lovett's 백화점을 떠나는 것 같은가?
(A) 몇 가지 자격 요건을 충족시키는 데 실패했다.
(B) 그의 가족 사업을 확장할 계획이다.
(C) 다른 도시로 이사하는 것을 준비하고 있다.
(D) 친척의 회사에서 직책을 맡을 것이다.

해설 이메일2의 'Date: December 3', 'Rodney Tucker ~ will be leaving Lovett's Department Store'에서 이메일이 작성된 날짜가 12월 3일이고, Mr. Tucker가 Lovett's 백화점을 떠날 것이라고 했다. 또한, 이메일1의 'I would be happy to keep working for Lovett's Department Store until ~ December of this year. After that, I plan to work at the insurance firm my uncle owns.'에서는 올해 12월까지 자신, 즉

TEST 10
해커스 토익 실전 1200제 READING

Mr. Tucker는 기꺼이 Lovett's 백화점에서 계속 일할 것이며, 그 후에 자신의 삼촌이 소유하고 있는 보험회사에서 일할 계획이라는 사실을 확인할 수 있다.

두 단서를 종합할 때, Mr. Tucker가 올해 12월 이후로 삼촌의 보험회사에서 일하기 위해 Lovett's 백화점을 떠난다는 사실을 추론할 수 있다. 따라서 (D)가 정답이다.

어휘 **fail** v. 실패하다 **satisfy** v. 충족시키다 **requirement** n. 자격 요건
expand v. 확장하다 **relocate** v. 이사하다 **relative** n. 친척

패러프레이징

> firm ~ uncle owns 삼촌이 소유하고 있는 회사 → relative's company 친척의 회사

191-195번은 다음 지도와 두 이메일에 관한 문제입니다.

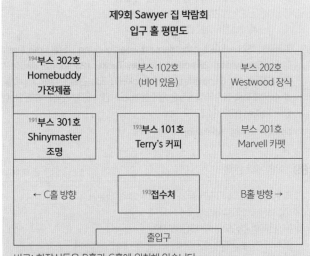

제9회 Sawyer 집 박람회
입구 홀 평면도

[194]부스 302호 Homebuddy 가전제품	부스 102호 (비어 있음)	부스 202호 Westwood 장식
[191]부스 301호 Shinymaster 조명	[193]부스 101호 Terry's 커피	부스 201호 Marvell 카펫
← C홀 방향	[193]접수처	B홀 방향 →
	출입구	

비고: 화장실들은 B홀과 C홀에 위치해 있습니다.

floor plan phr. 평면도 **vacant** adj. 비어 있는 **decor** n. 장식
carpeting n. 카펫(류) **entrance** n. 출입구

수신: Carl Takata <c.takata@sawyerhome.org>
발신: Molly Manzotti <m.manzotti@sawyerhome.org>
제목: 변경 사항들
날짜: 5월 26일

Carl,

저는 입구 홀에 부스 배정의 변경 사항에 대한 몇 가지 요청들을 받았습니다. 우선, [193]우리는 [193/192-A]우리의 주요 후원 업체인 Delta 은행[193]을 접수처 뒤에 있는 부스에 배치해야 합니다. 이렇게 하여, 참가자들은 그들이 입구를 통과하여 들어올 때 그것을 즉시 볼 수 있을 것입니다. [193]그곳에 지금 우리가 누구를 배치했든 현재 비어 있는 곳으로 옮겨져야 할 것입니다.

또한, [192-C]Westwood 장식은 그것의 가구 제품들을 위한 더 많은 공간이 필요하므로, [192-B]우리는 그들을 Marvell사와 자리를 바꾸도록 할 것입니다. 저는 지금 다른 회의에 가는 길입니다. 후에 추가적인 변경사항들이 있으면 제가 당신께 알려드리겠습니다. 감사합니다!

Molly

assignment n. 배정, 배치 **primary** adj. 주요한 **sponsor** n. 후원 업체
immediately adv. 즉시, 즉각 **empty** adj. 비어 있는 **switch** v. 바꾸다

수신: [195]Carl Takata <c.takata@sawyerhome.org>
발신: Molly Manzotti <m.manzotti@sawyerhome.org>
제목: 최신 정보
날짜: 5월 26일

안녕하세요 Carl,

당신에게 더 일찍 연락하지 못해 정말 미안합니다. 저는 고객들과 가격 및 부스 배정에 대해 협상하느라 바빴는데, 오늘 아침 이후로 추가적인 변경사항이 생겼습니다. [194]기획 위원회는 비슷한 제품들을 파는 회사들을 가능한 한 서로 가까이 위치시키고 싶어 합니다. 그것은 우리가 부스 302호의 사용자를 C홀로 이동시킬 것임을 의미합니다. [195]저는 아직 부스 배정이 필요한 판매 회사들의 긴 목록을 가지고 있습니다. 저는 내일 오전 9시쯤 그 장소에 잠시 들를 때 그것을 가져갈 것입니다. 제가 가는 길에 당신을 위해 가져갈 것이 있다면 제게 알려주십시오. 또 뵙겠습니다.

Molly

negotiate v. 협상하다 **additional** adj. 추가적인
planning committee phr. 기획 위원회 **occupant** n. 사용자, 입주자
vendor n. 판매 회사 **stop by** phr. 잠시 들르다 **venue** n. 장소

191 추론 문제
중 ●●●○

해석 고객들은 어디에서 조명 기구들을 찾을 수 있겠는가?
(A) 부스 101호
(B) 부스 201호
(C) 부스 301호
(D) 부스 302호

해설 지도의 'Booth 301 Shinymaster Lighting'에서 부스 301호에 배치된 판매업체가 Shinymaster 조명이라고 했으므로 고객들이 부스 301호에서 조명 관련 상품을 찾을 수 있을 것임을 추론할 수 있다. 따라서 (C)가 정답이다.

어휘 **light fixture** phr. 조명 기구

패러프레이징

> light fixtures 조명 기구들 → Lighting 조명

192 Not/True 문제
중 ●●●○

해석 Westwood 장식에 대해 언급된 것은?
(A) 주요 행사 후원 업체이다.
(B) 다른 홀로 이동될 것이다.
(C) 그것의 상품을 위한 더 많은 공간을 필요로 한다.
(D) Marvell 카펫 뒤의 부스를 요청했다.

해설 이메일1의 'Westwood Decor needs more space for its furniture items'에서 Westwood 장식은 그것의 가구 제품들을 위한 더 많은 공간을 필요로 한다고 했으므로 (C)는 지문의 내용과 일치한다. 따라서 (C)가 정답이다. (A)는 'our primary sponsor, Delta Bank'에서 자신들, 즉 박람회 행사의 주요 후원 업체가 Delta 은행이라고 했으므로 지문의 내용과 일치하지 않는다. (B)는 'we're going to have them switch places with Marvell'에서 그들, 즉 Westwood 장식을 Marvell사와 자리를 바꾸도록 할 것이라고 했는데, Marvell사는 Westwood와 같은 홀에 있으므로 지문의 내용과 일치하지 않는다. (D)는 Westwood 장식이 Marvell 카펫 뒤의 부스에 위치해 있다고는 했지만, Westwood 장식이 그것을 요청했는지는 언급되지 않았다.

어휘 **merchandise** n. 상품, 물품

furniture items 가구 제품들 → merchandise 상품

193 육하원칙 문제 연계 　　　　　　　상 ●●●

해석　Delta 은행은 누구의 부스를 대체하는가?
(A) Marvell 카펫
(B) Westwood 장식
(C) Terry's 커피
(D) Shinymaster 조명

해설　이메일1의 'we need to place ~ Delta Bank, in the booth behind the registration desk', 'Whoever we have there now will need to be moved'에서 Delta 은행을 접수처 뒤에 있는 부스에 배치해야 하며, 그곳에 지금 누구를 배치했든 옮겨져야 한다고 했다. 또한, 지도의 'Registration Desk', 'Booth 101 Terry's Coffee'에서는 접수처 뒤에 위치한 부스 101호에 현재 Terry's 커피가 배치되어 있음을 확인할 수 있다.
두 단서를 종합할 때, Delta 은행은 접수처 뒤에 있는 부스에 배치되어 있던 Terry's 커피를 대체할 것임을 알 수 있다. 따라서 (C)가 정답이다.

어휘　replace v. 대체하다, 교체하다

최고난도 문제

194 추론 문제 연계 　　　　　　　상 ●●●

해석　C홀에 대해 추론될 수 있는 것은?
(A) 낮은 가격의 부스들이 있다.
(B) 화장실이 하나도 없다.
(C) 모든 가전제품 판매자들을 수용할 것이다.
(D) 더 많은 판매 회사들을 수용하기 위해 추가되었다.

해설　이메일2의 'The planning committee wants to keep companies that sell similar items located as close to each other as possible. That means we'll be moving the ~ booth 302 into Hall C.'에서 기획위원회는 비슷한 제품들을 파는 회사들을 가능한 한 서로 가까이 위치시키고 싶어 하며, 그것은 우리가 부스 302호를 C홀로 이동시킬 것임을 의미한다고 했다. 또한, 지도의 'Booth 302 Homebuddy Appliances'에서는 부스 302호에 배치된 판매업체가 Homebuddy 가전제품이라는 것을 확인할 수 있다.
두 단서를 종합할 때, C홀에는 가전제품을 판매하는 업체들이 배치될 것임을 추론할 수 있다. 따라서 (C)가 정답이다.

어휘　lower-priced adj. 낮은 가격의　accommodate v. 수용하다

195 육하원칙 문제 　　　　　　　중 ●●○

해석　Ms. Manzotti는 그녀가 Mr. Takata에게 무엇을 가져갈 것이라고 하는가?
(A) 평면도
(B) 음식 주문
(C) 판매업체 목록
(D) 행사 달력

해설　이메일2의 'To: Carl Takata', 'I still have a long list of vendors ~. I'll bring it tomorrow'에서 이메일 수신자인 Mr. Tanaka에게 자신, 즉 Ms. Manzotti가 판매 회사들의 긴 목록을 가지고 있으며 내일 그것을 가져갈 것이라고 했으므로 (C)가 정답이다.

196-200번은 다음 편지, 브로슈어, 안내문에 관한 문제입니다.

9월 20일

Arapali Express사
Nichi 건물, Lalmati
자발푸르, 마디야 프라데시 482002

담당자분께,

저는 Arapali Express사의 9월 7일 AE010 항공편 승객으로서 196저의 경험에 대해 말씀드리고 싶습니다. 전반적으로, 그것은 만족스러웠습니다. 197저는 몇몇 다른 사람들보다 먼저 탑승할 수 있었던 것과 우리 항공편이 제시간에 출발했던 것을 높이 평가합니다. 하지만, 저는 거의 즉시 제 영상 모니터에 문제가 생겼고, 승무원의 도움에도 불구하고, 그것을 작동시키지 못했습니다. 게다가, 197저는 제 신용카드의 문제 때문에 온라인으로 접속할 수 없었습니다. 다행히도, 비행이 그리 길지는 않았습니다. 그렇지 않았다면, 저는 매우 불만스러웠을 것입니다. 저는 귀사가 향후에는 모든 기내 기기들이 제대로 작동하는지 확실하게 하는 조치를 취하기를 바랍니다.

Sandra Bulsara 드림

passenger n. 승객　satisfactory adj. 만족스러운　board v. 탑승하다
depart v. 출발하다　assistance n. 도움　extremely adv. 매우
frustrated adj. 불만스러운　take steps phr. 조치를 취하다
ensure v. 확실하게 하다, 보장하다　onboard adj. 기내의, 선상의

Arapali Express사 객실 등급 및 편의시설

196퍼스트 클래스
· 증가된 수하물 허용량
· 무료 와이파이
· 무료 고급 간식과 음료가 있는 고급 식사 서비스
· 휴대용 장치가 있는 특대형 좌석 등받이 모니터
· 196무료 고급 피부 관리 키트
· 우선 체크인 및 탑승

199-C비즈니스 클래스
· 증가된 수하물 허용량
· 무료 와이파이
· 무료 고급 간식과 음료가 있는 예정된 식사 서비스
· 199-C터치스크린을 사용할 수 있는 대형 좌석 등받이 모니터
· 우선 체크인 및 탑승

197/200프리미엄 이코노미 클래스 200(국제선 전용)
· 증가된 수하물 허용량
· 197유료 와이파이 이용
· 예정된 식사 서비스
· 일반 좌석 등받이 모니터
· 197우선 탑승

이코노미 클래스
· 예정된 식사 서비스
· 유료 와이파이 이용
· 일반 좌석 등받이 모니터

amenity n. 편의시설　baggage n. 수하물, 짐　allowance n. 허용량, 비용
complimentary adj. 무료의　gourmet adj. 고급의
extra-large adj. 특대형의　handheld adj. 휴대용의, 손에 쥘 수 있는
priority n. 우선(권)　regular adj. 일반의, 보통의

*Arapali Express*사 기내 잡지

이달의 새 영화들:

영화를 보기 위해, 당신의 영상 모니터 전원을 켜고 화면을 조종하기 위해 이용 가능한 제어 장치를 사용하십시오. 헤드폰은 무료로 제공됩니다. 도움을 원하시면, 기내 승무원을 부르십시오.

²⁰⁰경로:	²⁰⁰영화:	장르:	길이:
²⁰⁰**인도 국내**	²⁰⁰*Mr. Matchbox*	전기물	83분
인도에서 아프리카로	*Tabla in Heaven*	드라마	112분
인도에서 동남아시아로	*Boman Verma's Fantastic Adventures*	코미디	98분
인도에서 중동으로	*Bride from Nagpur*	로맨스	121분
인도에서 유럽으로	*Tiger that Roams the City*	스릴러	105분

참고:
1. ¹⁹⁹⁻ᶜP360과 P380 항공기만 터치스크린과 휴대용 장치를 갖추고 있습니다.
2. P110과 P120를 제외한 모든 항공기에서 와이파이는 이용 가능합니다.
3. 몇몇 영화들은 국내선들에서 이용 불가능할 수 있습니다.

switch on phr. 전원을 켜다 **control** n. 제어 장치, 통제
navigate v. 조종하다, 항해하다 **free of charge** phr. 무료로
in-flight adj. 기내의 **crew** n. 승무원 **biopic** n. 전기물
domestic adj. 국내의

196 목적 찾기 문제 하 ●○○

해석 편지는 왜 쓰였는가?
(A) 보상을 신청하기 위해
(B) 비행 일정을 취소하기 위해
(C) 규정 위반을 보고하기 위해
(D) 몇 가지 의견을 전달하기 위해

해설 편지의 'I wish to tell you about my experience'에서 자신의 경험에 대해 말하고 싶다고 한 후 자신의 비행 경험에 대해 느낀 점을 말하고 있으므로 (D)가 정답이다.

어휘 **compensation** n. 보상 **itinerary** n. 일정(표) **policy** n. 규정, 정책
violation n. 위반, 방해 **convey** v. 전달하다

197 추론 문제 연계 중 ●●○

해석 Ms. Bulsara는 어떤 등급에 앉았을 것 같은가?
(A) 퍼스트 클래스
(B) 비즈니스 클래스
(C) 프리미엄 이코노미 클래스
(D) 이코노미 클래스

해설 편지의 'I appreciated being able to board before some of the others'와 'I could not get online access because of a problem with my credit card'에서 자신, 즉 Ms. Bulsara는 몇몇 다른 사람들보다 먼저 탑승할 수 있었던 것을 높이 평가한다고 했고, 자신의 신용카드의 문제 때문에 온라인으로 접속할 수 없었다고 했다. 또한, 브로슈어의 'Premium Economy Class', 'Paid Wi-Fi access', 'Priority boarding'에서는 프리미엄 이코노미 클래스가 유료 와이파이 이용과 우선 탑승권을 포함한다는 것을 확인할 수 있다.

두 단서를 종합할 때, Ms. Bulsara는 우선 탑승권과 유료 와이파이 이용이 가능한 프리미엄 이코노미 클래스에 앉았다는 사실을 추론할 수 있다. 따라서 (C)가 정답이다.

패러프레이징

board before ~ others 다른 사람들보다 먼저 탑승하다 → Priority boarding 우선 탑승권

get online access ~ with ~ credit card 신용카드 온라인으로 접속하다 → Paid Wi-Fi access 유료 와이파이 이용

198 육하원칙 문제 중 ●●○

해석 퍼스트 클래스의 승객들에게는 무엇이 독점적으로 이용 가능한가?
(A) 보너스 항공사 마일리지
(B) 더 큰 수하물 허용량
(C) 이른 탑승 특권
(D) 피부 관리 제품들

해설 브로슈어의 'First Class', 'Complimentary luxury skin care kit'에서 퍼스트 클래스만 무료 고급 피부 관리 키트를 포함한다는 것을 확인할 수 있으므로 (D)가 정답이다. 참고로, (A)는 언급되지 않았고 (B)와 (C)는 비즈니스 클래스 및 프리미엄 이코노미 클래스 승객들에게도 이용 가능하므로 답이 될 수 없다.

어휘 **exclusively** adv. 독점적으로 **privilege** n. 특권

패러프레이징

skin care kit 피부 관리 키트 → Skin care products 피부 관리 제품들

199 Not/True 문제 연계 상 ●●●

해석 비즈니스 클래스의 영상 제어 장치에 대해 언급된 것은?
(A) 국제선들에는 제공되지 않는다.
(B) 사전에 구체적으로 요청되어야 한다.
(C) 몇몇 항공기 모델들에는 설치되지 않았다.
(D) 사용하기 위해 약간의 추가 요금이 든다.

해설 브로슈어의 'Business Class', 'Large seatback monitor with touch-screen access'에서 비즈니스 클래스가 터치스크린을 사용할 수 있는 대형 좌석 등받이 모니터를 포함한다고 했다. 또한, 안내문의 'Only P360 and P380 aircraft are equipped with touch screens'에서는 P360과 P380 항공기만 터치스크린을 갖췄다는 것을 확인할 수 있다.

두 단서를 종합할 때, 비즈니스 클래스의 영상 제어 장치인 터치스크린 모니터가 P360과 P380 항공기에만 설치된 장치임을 알 수 있으므로 (C)는 지문의 내용과 일치한다. 따라서 (C)가 정답이다. (A), (B), (D)는 지문에 언급되지 않은 내용이다.

어휘 **specifically** adv. 구체적으로 **ahead of time** phr. 사전에

패러프레이징

video controls 영상 제어 장치 → touch screens 터치스크린

최고난도 문제

200 추론 문제 연계 상 ●●●

해석 영화 *Mr. Matchbox*에 대해 암시되는 것은?
(A) 모든 등급에서 무료로 제공되는 유일한 것이다.
(B) 프리미엄 이코노미 승객들에게는 보이지 않을 수도 있다.
(C) 항공사의 선택물에 추가된 최신 영화이다.
(D) 추후 국제노선에서는 보이지 않을 수도 있다.

해설 안내문의 'Route: Within India', 'Movie: *Mr. Matchbox*'에서 경로가 인도 국내일 때 영화 *Mr. Matchbox*를 볼 수 있다고 했다. 또한, 브로슈어의

'Premium Economy Class (international flights only)'에서는 프리미엄 이코노미 클래스는 국제선 전용임을 확인할 수 있다.

두 단서를 종합할 때, 인도 국내선의 상영 영화 *Mr. Matchbox*는 국제선 전용인 프리미엄 이코노미 클래스 승객들에게는 보이지 않을 수도 있다는 사실을 추론할 수 있다. 따라서 (B)가 정답이다. (C)도 안내문에서 이달의 새 영화들이라고 소개하고 있어 답이 될 것 같지만, 최신 영화인지는 알 수 없으므로 답이 될 수 없다.

어휘   view v. 보다, 생각하다   latest adj. 최신의, (가장) 최근의
selection n. 선택물, 선택

PART 5

101 (C)	102 (D)	103 (B)	104 (D)	105 (B)
106 (A)	107 (C)	108 (B)	109 (C)	110 (C)
111 (B)	112 (B)	113 (C)	114 (B)	115 (C)
116 (B)	117 (B)	118 (C)	119 (C)	120 (C)
121 (C)	122 (B)	123 (A)	124 (C)	125 (C)
126 (D)	127 (D)	128 (D)	129 (B)	130 (D)

PART 6

131 (A)	132 (C)	133 (C)	134 (A)	135 (A)
136 (D)	137 (C)	138 (C)	139 (D)	140 (B)
141 (A)	142 (A)	143 (B)	144 (C)	145 (A)
146 (A)				

PART 7

147 (D)	148 (C)	149 (B)	150 (D)	151 (D)
152 (C)	153 (B)	154 (A)	155 (C)	156 (C)
157 (C)	158 (B)	159 (C)	160 (A)	161 (C)
162 (B)	163 (A)	164 (C)	165 (C)	166 (A)
167 (C)	168 (D)	169 (C)	170 (B)	171 (D)
172 (C)	173 (B)	174 (C)	175 (D)	176 (A)
177 (D)	178 (C)	179 (A)	180 (D)	181 (A)
182 (B)	183 (B)	184 (C)	185 (C)	186 (B)
187 (A)	188 (B)	189 (D)	190 (C)	191 (B)
192 (C)	193 (B)	194 (D)	195 (A)	196 (C)
197 (C)	198 (B)	199 (C)	200 (A)	

PART 5

101 형용사 어휘 고르기 　　　　　　　중 ●●○

해석　사업체가 연말까지 그것의 수익성을 향상시킬 것이라는 점이 분명해졌다.

해설　빈칸은 2형식 동사 become의 보어 역할을 하는 형용사 자리이다. '수익성을 향상시킬 것이라는 점이 분명해지다'라는 문맥이므로 (C) obvious(분명한, 명백한)가 정답이다.

어휘　profitability n. 수익성, 수익　attractive adj. 매력적인, 멋진
honest adj. 정직한, 솔직한　inclusive adj. 포함된

102 'be동사 + p.p.' 채우기 　　　　　　　상 ●●●

해석　만약 대금 결제일이 놓쳐지면, 체육관 회원들은 그들의 계좌를 직접 정산해야 한다.

해설　빈칸이 be동사(is) 다음에 왔으므로 모든 보기가 정답의 후보이다. '대금 결제일이 놓쳐지다'라는 수동의 의미가 되어야 하므로 be동사와 함께 수동태를 만드는 p.p.형 (D) missed(놓쳐지다)가 정답이다. 명사 (A)와 (B)는 보어로서 주어와 동격이 되어 각각 '대금 결제일은 실수/실수들이다'라는 어색한 문맥을 만든다. -ing형 (C)는 '대금 결제일이 놓치고 있다'라는 어색한 문맥을 만들며, (C) missing을 '없어진, 사라진'이라는 의미의 형용사로 본다 해도, '대금 결제일이 없어진다면'이라는 어색한 문맥을 만든다.

어휘　payment deadline phr. 대금 결제일　settle v. 정산하다
account n. 계좌　in person phr. 직접, 몸소

103 전치사 채우기 　　　　　　　중 ●●○

해석　관리자가 막 떠나고 있었을 때 직원들이 사무실 안으로 들어갔다.

해설　빈칸은 명사(the office)를 목적어로 취하는 전치사 자리이므로 전치사 (A), (B), (C)가 정답의 후보이다. '사무실 안으로 들어갔다'라는 의미가 되어야 하므로 방향을 나타내는 전치사 (B) into(~안으로, ~로)가 정답이다. 빈도 부사 (D) often(자주, 흔히)은 일반 동사(came) 앞에 와야 한다.

어휘　above prep. ~보다 위에, 위로　throughout prep. 도처에, 내내

104 명사 어휘 고르기 　　　　　　　상 ●●●

해석　급여 인상의 가능성은 Ms. Farina가 그녀의 실적을 향상시키도록 적절한 금전적 동기부여를 제공했다.

해설　빈칸은 형용사(financial)의 꾸밈을 받는 명사 자리이다. '급여 인상의 가능성이 실적을 향상시키도록 금전적 동기부여를 제공하다'라는 문맥이므로 (D) motivation(동기부여, 자극)이 정답이다.

어휘　possibility n. 가능성　adequate adj. 적절한
performance n. 실적, 수행, 연기　contribution n. 기여, 공헌
discussion n. 논의　decision n. 결정

105 형용사 어휘 고르기 　　　　　　　중 ●●○

해석　Primordial Technologies사는 네 달 동안 50,000달러를 사용하였으며, 이는 그것의 그해 전체 광고 예산의 절반이다.

해설　빈칸은 명사구(advertising budget)를 꾸미는 형용사 자리이다. '이것의 그해 전체 광고 예산의 절반이다'라는 문맥이므로 (B) entire(전체의)가 정답이다.

어휘　advertising n. 광고　eager adj. 열성적인, 열망하는
reliant adj. 의존하는, 의지하는　adjacent adj. 인접한

106 전치사 표현 채우기 　　　　　　　상 ●●●

해석　Ms. Brooks는 고객 불만을 다룰 수 있는 것으로 임원에 의해 인정받았다.

해설　빈칸은 동명사구(being ~ complaints)를 목적어로 취하는 전치사 자리이다. '고객 불만을 다룰 수 있는 것으로 인정받다'라는 의미가 되어야 하므로 빈칸 앞의 동사 was recognized와 함께 '~으로 인정받다'라는 의미의 어구인 be recognized for를 만드는 전치사 (A) for(~으로, ~에 대해)가 정답이다. (B) about(~에 대해)도 해석상 그럴듯해 보이지만, be recognized about의 형태로 쓰일 수 없다.

어휘 recognize v. 인정하다 handle v. 다루다 within prep. ~이내에
between prep. ~사이에

107 부사 어휘 고르기 중 ●●○

해석 알맞은 가격의 주택의 부족과 높은 실업률은 인구 밀도가 높은 도시들의 몇 가지 문제들이다.

해설 빈칸은 과거분사(populated)를 꾸미는 부사 자리이다. '주택의 부족과 높은 실업률은 인구 밀도가 높은 도시들의 문제들이다'라는 문맥이 되어야 하므로 (C) heavily(많이, 심하게)가 정답이다. 참고로, heavily[densely] populated(인구 밀도가 높은)를 관용구로 알아둔다.

어휘 affordable adj. 알맞은 가격의 housing n. 주택
unemployment n. 실업(률) solely adv. 단독으로, 오로지
evenly adv. 고르게, 균등하게 nearly adv. 거의

108 명사 자리 채우기 상 ●●●

해석 그 보조 관리자는 Greene 재단의 프로젝트들 중 하나를 감독하기 위한 권한을 부여받았다.

해설 빈칸 앞에 목적어를 두 개 가지는 4형식 동사 give(~에게 -을 주다)가 수동태로 쓰여 간접 목적어(The assistant administrator)가 주어 자리에 왔으므로, 빈칸은 직접 목적어 자리이다. 따라서 목적어 자리에 올 수 있는 명사 (B) authority(권한)가 정답이다. 부사 (A), 동사 (C), 형용사 (D)는 명사 자리에 올 수 없다. 동사 give를 목적어를 한 개만 갖는 3형식 동사로 보고 부사 (A)가 동사(was given)를 꾸미는 것으로 본다 해도, '보조 관리자가 위압적으로 주어졌다'라는 어색한 문맥을 만든다.

어휘 assistant adj. 보조의 administrator n. 관리자
oversee v. 감독하다 authoritatively adv. 위압적으로
authorize v. 권한을 부여하다 authoritative adj. 권위적인

109 명사 관련 어구 완성하기 중 ●●○

해석 대출 담당 직원은 은행의 단골 고객들과의 견고한 관계를 발전시켰다.

해설 빈칸은 형용사(strong)의 꾸밈을 받는 명사 자리이다. '단골 고객들과의 견고한 관계를 발전시켰다'라는 문맥이므로 빈칸 뒤의 전치사 with와 함께 '~와의 관계'라는 의미의 어구인 connection with를 만드는 (C) connection (관계)이 정답이다. (D) agreement(동의)도 해석상 그럴듯해 보이지만, agreement는 주로 conclude(체결하다, 끝내다), reach(이르다, 도달하다) 등의 동사와 함께 쓰인다.

어휘 loan officer phr. 대출 담당 직원 regular client phr. 단골 고객
conversion n. 전환 knowledge n. 지식

110 부사 어휘 고르기 중 ●●○

해석 직원 안내서는 연장된 휴가를 요청하는 과정을 명확하게 설명한다.

해설 빈칸은 동사(describes)를 꾸미는 부사 자리이다. '직원 안내서는 과정을 명확하게 설명한다'라는 문맥이 되어야 하므로 (C) specifically(명확하게)가 정답이다.

어휘 manual n. 안내서 extended adj. 연장된 leave of absence phr. 휴가
extremely adv. 극도로 immediately adv. 즉시
accidentally adv. 우연히

111 동사 어휘 고르기 중 ●●○

해석 기술자들은 주요 펌프의 고장이 손상된 전선에서 야기되었다고 추측한다.

해설 빈칸은 주절의 주어(Engineers) 뒤에 오면서 that절(that ~ wiring)을 목적어로 취하는 동사 자리이다. '고장이 손상된 전선에서 야기되었다고 추측한다'라는 문맥이므로 (B) suspect(추측하다)가 정답이다.

어휘 engineer n. 기술자 breakdown n. 고장 damaged adj. 손상된
electrical wiring phr. 전선 admire v. 감탄하다 resume v. 재개하다
implement v. 실행하다

112 동사 어휘 고르기 상 ●●●

해석 발표를 할 때, 연구원들은 주제에 대한 철저한 이해를 보여주어야 한다.

해설 빈칸은 '~해야 한다'라는 뜻의 조동사처럼 쓰이는 표현 have to 뒤에 오는 동사원형 자리이다. '발표를 할 때, 연구원들은 철저한 이해를 보여주어야 한다'라는 문맥이므로 (B) demonstrate(보여주다)가 정답이다.

어휘 presentation n. 발표 thorough adj. 철저한 subject matter phr. 주제
arrange v. 마련하다, 준비하다 initiate v. 시작하다, 일으키다
substitute v. 대체하다

113 수, 태, 시제에 맞는 동사 채우기 상 ●●●

해석 봉사자들은 곧 있을 세미나의 마지막에 모든 참가자들에게 간식을 제공할 것이다.

해설 문장에 동사가 없으므로 동사인 모든 보기가 정답의 후보이다. 주어(Volunteers)와 동사(serve)가 '봉사자들은 간식을 제공할 것이다'라는 능동의 의미가 되어야 하고 미래를 나타내는 시간 표현(upcoming)이 있으므로 미래 시제 능동태 (C) will be serving이 정답이다. 수동태 (A)와 (D)는 각각 '봉사자들은 모든 참가자들에게 간식을 제공받을 것이다/받았다'라는 어색한 문맥을 만들고, 'A에게 B를 제공하다'라는 의미의 serve B to A가 수동태로 바뀌면 B be served to A가 되어 served 뒤에 목적어가 없어야 하므로 빈칸 뒤의 명사(refreshments)를 목적어로 취할 수 없다. 단수 동사 (B)는 복수 명사와 함께 쓰일 수 없다.

어휘 volunteer n. 봉사자 refreshment n. 간식 attendee n. 참석자
upcoming adj. 곧 있을, 다가오는

114 부사절 접속사 채우기 상 ●●●

해석 메인 서버가 고장 나는 경우에 대비하여 회사는 기록의 사본을 포함하는 예비 서버를 가지고 있다.

해설 이 문장은 주어(The firm), 동사(has), 목적어(a backup ~ records)를 갖춘 완전한 절이므로, ___ ~fail은 수식어 거품으로 보아야 한다. 이 수식어 거품은 동사(should fail)가 있는 거품절이므로, 거품절을 이끌 수 있는 부사절 접속사 (B), (C), (D)가 정답의 후보이다. '메인 서버가 고장 나는 경우에 대비하여 예비 서버를 가지고 있다'라는 문맥이므로 부사절 접속사 (B) in the event that (~에 대비하여)가 정답이다. 전치사구 (A)는 거품절이 아닌 거품구를 이끈다.

어휘 backup adj. 예비의 contain v. 포함하다 duplicate adj. 사본의
records n. 기록 fail v. 고장 나다 because of phr. ~ 때문에
as long as phr. ~하는 한 now that phr. ~이니까

115 형용사 자리 채우기 중 ●●○

해석 만약 Falconia사가 그것의 주문 규모를 늘린다면 Nimble Dynamics사는 계약한 배송비를 기꺼이 낮추고자 한다.

해설 명사구(shipping price)를 꾸밀 수 있는 것은 형용사이므로 과거분사 (C) contracted(계약한)가 정답이다. 명사 (A)와 (B), 부사 (D)는 형용사

자리에 올 수 없다.

어휘 **willing to** phr. 기꺼이 ~하고자 하는 **shipping price** phr. 배송비
contractibility n. 수축, 수축성 **contraction** n. 수축
contractually adv. 계약상(으로)

116 동사 어휘 고르기 · 상 ●●●

해석 기업가들이 소규모 사업을 시작하는 것이 장려될 수 있도록 시의회는 보조금을 확대하는 것에 찬성한다.

해설 빈칸은 타동사(favors)의 목적어 역할을 하는 동명사 자리이다. 소규모 사업을 시작하는 것이 장려될 수 있도록 보조금을 확대하는 것에 찬성한다는 의미가 되어야 하므로 동사 enlarge(확대하다)의 동명사 (B) enlarging이 정답이다.

어휘 **city council** phr. 시의회 **favor** v. 찬성하다 **subsidy** n. 보조금
encourage v. 장려하다 **entrepreneur** n. 기업가 **envelop** v. 동봉하다
relieve v. 줄이다, 경감하다 **constrain** v. 제한하다

117 도치 구문 채우기 · 상 ●●●

해석 지난해에 X300 노트북은 Magnet사의 가장 인기 있는 모델도, 가장 인기가 없는 것도 아니었다.

해설 빈칸 뒤의 주어(it)와 동사(was)가 도치되어 있으므로 부정어(not)가 있는 절 뒤에서 도치된 절을 이끌 수 있는 부정어 (B) nor(~도 아니다)가 정답이다. 등위접속사 (A), (C), (D)는 도치된 절을 이끌 수 없다.

어휘 **but** conj. 그러나 **and** conj. 그리고 **yet** conj. 그렇지만; adv. 아직

118 관계대명사 채우기 · 중 ●●○

해석 손님들은 Enterprise Seminars 앞으로 작성된 수표로 지불해달라고 요청받는다.

해설 선행사(checks)가 사물이며, 빈칸에 들어갈 관계대명사가 관계절(___ ~ Enterprise Seminars)에서 주어 역할을 해야 한다. 따라서 사물/사람 선행사에 쓰는 주격 관계대명사 (C) that이 정답이다. 명사절 접속사 (A)는 형용사 역할을 하는 관계절을 이끌 수 없다. 관계대명사 (B)와 (D)는 선행사가 사람일 때 쓰일 수 있다. 참고로, that절(___ ~ Enterprise Seminars)이 선행사(checks)를 꾸미는 관계절임을 알아둔다.

어휘 **check** n. 수표 **make out** phr. (문서 등을) 작성하다

119 명사 관련 어구 완성하기 · 상 ●●●

해석 개정된 정책 아래, 모든 외국인 노동자들은 3년 유효기간의 허가증을 발급받게 될 것이다.

해설 빈칸은 빈칸 뒤의 명사(dates)와 복합 명사를 이루어 전치사(with)의 목적어 역할을 하는 명사 자리이다. '모든 외국인 노동자들은 3년 유효기간의 허가증을 발급받게 될 것이다'라는 문맥이므로 빈칸 뒤의 명사 dates(기간, 날짜)와 함께 쓰여 '유효기간'이라는 의미의 어구인 validity dates를 만드는 (C) validity(유효)가 정답이다.

어휘 **revised** adj. 개정된 **policy** n. 정책 **permit** n. 허가증
productivity n. 생산성 **partnership** n. 동업 **symbol** n. 상징

120 형용사 어휘 고르기 · 상 ●●●

해석 참가자들은 계속 상을 탈 자격이 있기 위해 항상 대회의 규칙을 준수해야 한다.

해설 빈칸은 2형식 동사 remain의 보어 역할을 하는 형용사 자리이다. '계속 상을 탈 자격이 있기 위해 대회의 규칙을 준수해야 한다'라는 문맥이므로 (C) eligible(자격이 있는)이 정답이다.

어휘 **participant** n. 참가자 **observe** v. (법률·규칙 등을) 준수하다, 관찰하다
remain v. 계속 ~이다 **compatible** adj. 양립될 수 있는
responsive adj. 즉각 반응하는 **privileged** adj. 특권을 가진

121 형용사 어휘 고르기 · 중 ●●○

해석 BioPharmin사에 의해 만들어진 항생제는 전염병에 효과적인 치료제임이 드러났다.

해설 빈칸은 명사(treatment)를 꾸미는 형용사 자리이다. '항생제가 전염병에 효과적인 치료제임이 드러나다'라는 문맥이므로 (C) effective(효과적인)이 정답이다.

어휘 **antibiotic** n. 항생제 **prove** v. ~임이 드러나다, 판명되다
treatment n. 치료제 **infectious disease** phr. 전염병
assembled adj. 모인, 집합된 **eternal** adj. 영원한 **intimate** adj. 친밀한

122 부사 자리 채우기 · 중 ●●○

해석 화재로 인해, 몇몇 농산물들은 상점에서 비교적 찾기 어려워졌다.

해설 빈칸 뒤의 형용사(hard)를 꾸밀 수 있는 것은 부사이므로 부사 (B) relatively(비교적)가 정답이다. 동사 (A), 형용사 또는 명사 (C), 명사 (D)는 형용사를 꾸밀 수 없다.

어휘 **agricultural product** phr. 농산물 **relate** v. 관련시키다
relative adj. 관련된; n. 친척 **relativity** n. 상대성

123 제안·요청·의무의 주절을 뒤따르는 that절에 '동사원형' 채우기 · · · 상 ●●●

해석 주최자는 발표자들이 그들의 연설을 15분 이하로 유지할 것을 권장한다.

해설 that절(that ~ less)에 동사가 없고 주절(The organizer recommends)에 제안을 나타내는 동사(recommends)가 왔으므로 that절의 동사 자리에는 동사원형이 와야 한다. 따라서 동사원형 (A) keep(유지하다)이 정답이다. 3인칭 단수 동사 (B), 미래 시제 (C)와 현재 진행 시제 (D)는 동사원형 자리에 올 수 없다. 참고로, recommend(권하다), request(요청하다), suggest(제안하다), demand(요구하다)처럼 제안·요청·의무를 나타내는 동사의 목적어 자리에 온 that절에는 동사원형이 온다는 것을 알아둔다.

어휘 **organizer** n. 주최자 **presenter** n. 발표자, 진행자 **speech** n. 연설

124 부사 어휘 고르기 · 중 ●●○

해석 Queensland Holdings사는 지난 십 년 동안 꾸준히 긍정적인 수익을 만들어냄으로써 그것의 투자자들을 만족시켰다.

해설 빈칸은 동명사(generating)를 꾸미는 부사 자리이다. '십 년 동안 꾸준히 긍정적인 수익을 만들어냄으로써 투자자들을 만족시켰다'라는 문맥이므로 (C) consistently(꾸준히)가 정답이다.

어휘 **generate** v. 만들어내다, 발생시키다 **return** n. 수익
automatically adv. 자동적으로 **hopefully** adv. 바라건대
temporarily adv. 일시적으로

125 형용사 자리 채우기　중 ●●○

해석　분석가들은 국가의 경제가 회복의 길에 있다는 것을 암시하는 충분한 양의 증거를 발견했다.

해설　명사(amount)를 꾸밀 수 있는 것은 형용사이므로 형용사 (C) sufficient (충분한)가 정답이다. 동사 (A), 명사 (B), 부사 (D)는 형용사 자리에 올 수 없다.

어휘　analyst n. 분석가　evidence n. 증거　recovery n. 회복

126 격에 맞는 인칭대명사 채우기　중 ●●○

해석　운전자들은 사고에서 그들이 보호되는 것을 보장하기 위해 그들의 자동차 보험을 갱신해야 한다.

해설　동사(are protected)의 주어 자리에 올 수 있는 인칭대명사가 필요하므로 주격 인칭대명사 (D) they가 정답이다. 재귀대명사 (A), 목적격 인칭대명사 (B), 소유격 인칭대명사 (C)는 주어 자리에 올 수 없다.

어휘　renew v. 갱신하다　ensure v. 보장하다

최고난도 문제

127 전치사 표현 채우기　상 ●●●

해석　Sanjay Medhi는 9월 1일부로 Deacon 의과 대학의 동문회장이 되었다.

해설　빈칸은 전치사(as)와 함께 전치사구를 이루어 명사구(September 1)를 목적어로 취하는 전치사 자리이다. '9월 1일부로 동문회장이 되었다'라는 의미가 되어야 하므로 빈칸 앞의 전치사 as와 함께 '~부로'라는 의미의 전치사구 as of를 만드는 전치사 (D) of(~의)가 정답이다.

어휘　alumni association phr. 동문회　on prep. ~에　until prep. ~까지　upon prep. ~에

128 사람명사 추상명사 구별하여 채우기　중 ●●○

해석　그 실험실은 그것의 자금에 삶을 변화시키는 혁신들의 발전을 위한 상당한 할당량을 가지고 있다.

해설　형용사(significant)의 꾸밈을 받을 수 있는 것은 명사이므로 명사 (B)와 (D)가 정답의 후보이다. '자금에 상당한 할당량을 가지고 있다'라는 문맥이므로 추상명사 (D) allocation(할당량, 할당)이 정답이다. 명사 (B)는 '자금에 상당한 할당자를 가지고 있다'라는 어색한 문맥을 만든다. 동사 (A)는 명사 자리에 올 수 없다. 동명사 또는 현재분사 (C)는 형용사가 아닌 부사의 꾸밈을 받는다.

어휘　laboratory n. 실험실　significant adj. 상당한　funding n. 자금, 기금　advancement n. 발전, 진보　life-changing adj. 삶을 변화시키는　innovation n. 혁신　allocate v. 할당하다

129 부사 자리 채우기　상 ●●●

해석　회의 동안, 관리자는 직원들에게 어떤 회사 규정 위반이라도 이에 따른 부정적인 결과가 있을 것이라고 반복적으로 상기시켰다.

해설　주절의 동사(reminded)를 꾸밀 수 있는 것은 부사이므로 부사 (B) repeatedly(반복적으로)가 정답이다. 동사 (A), 동사 또는 과거분사 (C), 명사 (D)는 동사를 꾸밀 수 없다.

어휘　supervisor n. 관리자　remind v. 상기시키다　violation n. 위반　consequence n. (발생한 일의) 결과　repeat v. 되풀이하다　repetition n. 반복

130 태에 맞는 동사 채우기　상 ●●●

해석　새로운 게임 *Battle Planet*이 출시된 이후로 많은 팬들은 활발하게 온라인 토론들에 참여해오고 있다.

해설　종속절(since ~ ___)에 동사가 없으므로 동사인 모든 보기가 정답의 후보이다. 주어(the new game *Battle Planet*)와 동사(release)가 '새로운 게임 *Battle Planet*이 출시되었다'라는 수동의 의미를 가지므로 수동태 (D) was released가 정답이다. 능동태 (A), (B), (C)는 답이 될 수 없다. 명사 (A) releases가 빈칸 앞의 명사 the new game *Battle Planet*과 복합명사를 이루어 전치사 since의 목적어 자리에 온 것으로 본다 해도, release가 '출시'라는 의미로 쓰일 때는 불가산 명사이므로 복수형으로 쓰일 수 없다. release가 '방출, 유출'이라는 의미로 쓰일 때 가산 명사와 불가산 명사 모두에 해당되며 해석상 그럴듯해 보이지만, 가스·화학 물질 등의 방출, 유출을 의미하므로 답이 될 수 없다.

어휘　numerous adj. 많은, 무수한　engage v. 참여하다

PART 6

131-134번은 다음 후기에 관한 문제입니다.

CAMPFIRE사 STARLIGHT DREAM 2

우리는 한때 Campfire사의 초기 Starlight Dream을 "돈으로 구매할 수 있는 최고의 디지털 리더기"라고 불렀습니다. 여러분들 중 많은 이들이 분명히 동의했습니다. 그것의 눈부신 화면, 날렵한 디자인, 그리고 긴 배터리 수명 때문에 이것이 출시되었을 때에 이것은 **¹³¹인기가 있었습니다.** 그렇다면, 완전히 새로운 Starlight Dream 2는 더 나아졌지만, 그것을 살 가치가 있을까요? 비록 전반적으로 처음의 **¹³²것**보다는 싸지만, 기본 장치는 여전히 250달러에 팔리고 있습니다. 두 개 모두의 일반적인 기능들을 비교해봅시다. **¹³³몇 개의 미묘하지만 중요한 차이들이 있습니다.** Dream 2는 더 얇고, 당신의 손에 더 편안하게 맞습니다. 약간 더 큰 화면은 30퍼센트의 더 많은 단어들을 보여주지만, 그것은 60그램 더 무겁습니다. 또한 그 새로운 **¹³⁴장치**는 견고하지만 우아한 알루미늄 본체를 드러냅니다.

original adj. 초기의　evidently adv. 분명히, 눈에 띄게　dazzling adj. 눈부신　display n. 화면; v. 보여주다　release v. 출시하다　all-new phr. 완전히 새로운　overall adv. 전반적으로　initial adj. 처음의　unit n. 장치　feature n. 기능　slightly adv. 약간　exhibit v. 드러내다, 전시하다　sturdy adj. 견고한　elegant n. 우아한

131 형용사 어휘 고르기　전체 문맥 파악　하 ●○○

해설　빈칸은 be동사(was)의 보어 역할을 하는 형용사 자리이다. '이것이 출시되었을 때에 이것은 ___다'라는 문맥이므로 모든 보기가 정답의 후보이다. 앞부분에서 초기 Starlight Dream을 돈으로 구매할 수 있는 최고의 디지털 리더기라고 불렀다고 했으며, 앞 문장에서 많은 이들이 동의했다고 했으므로 출시되었을 때 인기가 있었음을 알 수 있다. 따라서 (A) popular(인기 있는)가 정답이다.

어휘　predictable adj. 예상할 수 있는　unavailable adj. 이용할 수 없는　durable adj. 내구성 있는

132 부정대명사/형용사 채우기　중 ●●○

해설　'비록 전반적으로 처음의 것보다는 싸지만'이라는 의미가 되어야 하고, 빈칸이 형용사(initial)의 꾸밈을 받고 있으므로 정해지지 않은 단수 가산 명사를 대신하는 부정대명사 (C) one(~것)이 정답이다. 참고로, one은 앞에서 언급

TEST 11 해커스 토익 실전 1200제 READING

된 Starlight Dream 리더기를 지칭하고 있음을 알아둔다. 인칭대명사 (A)와 지시대명사 (B)는 앞의 명사를 대신하는 경우 형용사의 꾸밈을 받을 수 없다. 부정대명사 (D)도 형용사의 꾸밈을 받을 수 없다.

133 알맞은 문장 고르기　　중 ●●○

해석　(A) 이전의 모델은 다른 모든 것들을 모든 면에서 능가합니다.
　　　(B) 프리미엄 버전은 모바일 인터넷 연결을 제공합니다.
　　　(C) 몇 개의 미묘하지만 중요한 차이들이 있습니다.
　　　(D) Campfire사는 제품 출시에 앞서 선주문을 받습니다.

해설　앞 문장 'Let's compare the ~ features on both.'에서 두 개 모두의 기능들을 비교해보자고 했으므로, 빈칸에는 기능상 몇 개의 미묘하지만 중요한 차이들이 있다는 내용이 들어가야 함을 알 수 있다. 따라서 (C)가 정답이다.

어휘　surpass v. 능가하다　connectivity n. 연결　subtle adj. 미묘한　important adj. 중요한　pre-order n. 선주문　launch n. 출시

134 명사 어휘 고르기　　하 ●○○

해설　빈칸은 형용사(new)의 꾸밈을 받는 명사 자리이다. '새로운 장치는 견고하지만 우아한 알루미늄 본체를 드러낸다'라는 문맥이므로 (A) device(장치)가 정답이다.

어휘　service n. 서비스　order n. 주문　bundle n. 꾸러미, 묶음

135-138번은 다음 공고에 관한 문제입니다.

주주들을 위한 공고

Orbitall사는 그것의 예정된 주주 회의의 장소를 변경하였습니다. 그것은 12월 5일 오후 4시 30분에 JadeLink 센터 대신 Rudalle 호텔 연회장에서 135**열릴 것입니다.**

또한, 저희는 또 하나의 변경을 했습니다. 136**저희는 이제 참석하기 위한 사전 신청을 요구합니다.** 여러분들은 지금쯤 올해의 보고서와 함께 주주 성명서 양식을 받으셨을 것입니다. 그것을 작성하셔서 10월 31일까지 다시 보내주십시오. 저희는 여러분의 이름이 손님 목록에 추가되면 이메일 137**확인**을 보내드릴 것입니다.

결의안에 투표를 하시기 위해 여러분이 138**참석할** 필요는 없다는 것을 알고 계시기 바랍니다. Orbitall사의 웹사이트 www.orbitall.com/vote를 통해 투표하는 것 또한 가능합니다.

---
shareholder n. 주주　venue n. 장소　banquet hall phr. 연회장　statement n. 성명서　vote v. 투표하다　resolution n. 결의안, 해결책

135 올바른 시제의 동사 채우기　주변 문맥 파악　중 ●●○

해설　문장에 동사가 없으므로 동사인 모든 보기가 정답의 후보이다. '그것은 12월 5일 오후 4시 30분에 Rudalle 호텔 연회장에서 열린다'라는 문장인데, 앞 문장에서 예정된 주주 회의의 장소를 변경했다고 했으므로 주주 회의가 열리는 시점은 미래임을 알 수 있다. 따라서 미래 시제 (A) will take place가 정답이다. 현재 완료 시제 (B), 과거 시제 (C), 과거 완료 시제 (D)는 미래의 일을 나타낼 수 없다.

136 알맞은 문장 고르기　　상 ●●●

해석　(A) 그러나, 모임은 다음 해에 틀림없이 일어날 것입니다.
　　　(B) 이사회는 새로운 대표 이사를 임명했습니다.

(C) 발표는 보통 기자 회견에서 이뤄집니다.
(D) 저희는 이제 참석하기 위한 사전 신청을 요구합니다.

해설　앞 문장 'In addition, we have made another change.'에서 또 하나의 변경을 했다고 했고, 뒷부분에서 주주 성명서 양식을 작성해서 보낸 후, 손님 목록에 추가되면 이메일을 보낼 것이라고 했으므로, 빈칸에는 참석하기 위한 사전 신청을 요구한다는 내용이 들어가야 함을 알 수 있다. 따라서 (D)가 정답이다.

어휘　gathering n. 모임　board n. 이사회　company director phr. 대표 이사　press conference phr. 기자 회견　advance adj. 사전의　registration n. 신청

137 복합 명사 채우기　　상 ●●●

해설　빈칸이 명사(e-mail) 뒤에 있고 '이름이 손님 목록에 추가되면, 이메일 확인을 보낼 것이다'라는 문맥이므로 빈칸 앞의 명사 e-mail(이메일)과 함께 쓰여 '이메일 확인'이라는 의미의 복합 명사 e-mail confirmation을 만드는 명사 (C) confirmation(확인)이 정답이다. 동사 (A)와 (D)는 명사를 꾸밀 수 없고 형용사 (B)는 명사를 뒤에서 꾸밀 수 없다.

어휘　confirm v. 확인하다, 사실임을 보여주다　confirmable adj. 확인할 수 있는

138 형용사 어휘 고르기　주변 문맥 파악　중 ●●○

해설　빈칸은 be동사(be)의 보어 역할을 하는 형용사 자리이다. '투표를 하기 위해 여러분이 ＿＿할 필요는 없다'라는 문맥이므로 모든 보기가 정답의 후보이다. 뒤 문장에서 Orbitall사의 웹사이트를 통해 투표하는 것 또한 가능하다고 했으므로 회의에 참석할 필요는 없다는 것을 알 수 있다. 따라서 (C) present (참석한)가 정답이다.

어휘　licensed adj. 허가를 받은　selective adj. 선택적인　knowledgeable adj. 아는 것이 많은

139-142번은 다음 이메일에 관한 문제입니다.

수신: Ron Winkle <r.winkle@gotmail.com>
발신: TG 지하철 고객 서비스 <cs@tgmetro.com>
제목: 보고된 문제
날짜: 3월 19일
첨부: 10달러 승차권

Mr. Winkle께,

TG 지하철은 귀하가 3월 14일에 겪으신 문제에 대해 사과드리고 싶습니다. 139**저희는 귀하의 불만을 확실히 이해할 수 있습니다.** 짧은 지연조차도 바쁜 일정을 틀어지게 만들기에 충분합니다. 승객들이 반드시 그들의 목적지에 항상 정각에 도착하도록 하는 것이 저희의 목표임을 보장해 드립니다. 유감스럽게도, 이번 경우에는, 나뭇가지가 저희의 노선 중 하나에 140**떨어졌고**, 이는 지연을 일으켰습니다. 이 상황을 해결하는 데에는 한 시간보다 적게 걸렸습니다. 여전히, 저희는 앞으로의 141**재발**을 피하고자 노력하고 있습니다. 철도 위에 걸려 있는 나뭇가지들은 다가오는 몇 주 동안 손질될 것입니다. 첨부된 10달러 상당의 전자 승차권을 받아주십시오. 귀하가 그것을 저희의 사과의 표시142**로써** 여겨주시길 바랍니다. 만약 귀하가 추가적인 도움이 필요하시다면, 귀하께서는 언제든지 저희에게 이메일을 보내주시면 됩니다.

Shane Costa 드림
고객 서비스 직원

---
pass n. 승차권　apologize v. 사과하다　delay n. 지연　upset v. (계획·상황 등이) 틀어지게 만들다　assure v. 보장하다, 확신하다

destination n. 목적지 on time phr. 정각에
unfortunately adv. 유감스럽게도 overhang v. ~ 위에 걸리다
trim v. 다듬다, 손질하다 token n. 표시 apology n. 사과
assistance n. 도움

139 알맞은 문장 고르기 상 ●●●

해석 (A) 귀하의 불만은 고객 서비스 직원에 의해 처리되었습니다.
(B) 저희 직원들은 이 문제가 발생했던 것을 알지 못했습니다.
(C) 저희는 귀하의 예약을 기꺼이 변경해드리겠습니다.
(D) 저희는 귀하의 불만을 확실히 이해할 수 있습니다.

해설 빈칸 앞 문장 'TG Metro would like to apologize for the problem'에서 TG 지하철은 문제에 대해 사과하고 싶다고 했고, 뒤 문장 'Even a short delay is enough to upset a busy schedule.'에서 짧은 지연조차도 바쁜 일정을 틀어지게 만들기에 충분하다고 했으므로, 빈칸에는 고객의 불만을 이해할 수 있다는 내용이 들어가야 함을 알 수 있다. 따라서 (D)가 정답이다.

어휘 complaint n. 불만 address v. 처리하다, 다루다
unaware adj. 알지 못하는 occur v. 발생하다 frustration n. 불만, 좌절

140 올바른 시제의 동사 채우기 주변 문맥 파악 상 ●●●

해설 '이번 경우에는, 나뭇가지가 노선들 중 하나에 떨어지고, 이는 지연을 일으켰다'라는 문맥인데, 뒤 문장에서 이 상황을 해결하는 데 한 시간보다 적게 걸렸다고 했으므로 나뭇가지가 노선들 중 하나에 떨어진 시점은 과거임을 알 수 있다. 따라서 과거 시제 (B) fell이 정답이다. 현재 시제 (A)는 과거의 일을 나타낼 수 없고, 미래 시제 (C)와 현재 완료 진행 시제 (D)는 이미 완료된 과거의 일을 나타낼 수 없다.

141 명사 어휘 고르기 전체 문맥 파악 중 ●●○

해설 빈칸은 부정관사(a) 다음에 올 수 있는 명사 자리이다. '저희는 앞으로의 ___을 피하고자 노력하고 있다'라는 문맥이므로 모든 보기가 정답의 후보이다. 앞부분에서 나뭇가지가 노선들 중 하나에 떨어져 지연을 일으켰다고 했고, 뒤 문장에서 철도 위에 걸려 있는 나뭇가지들은 다가오는 몇 주 동안 손질될 것이라고 했으므로 나뭇가지로 인해 발생한 문제와 관련하여 앞으로의 재발을 피하고자 노력하고 있음을 알 수 있다. 따라서 (A) recurrence(재발)가 정답이다.

어휘 malfunction n. 고장 violation n. 위반 termination n. 종료

142 전치사 표현 채우기 상 ●●●

해설 빈칸은 명사구(a token of our apology)를 목적어로 취하는 전치사 자리이다. '저희의 사과의 표시로써'라는 의미가 되어야 하므로 빈칸 뒤의 명사구 a token of와 함께 '~의 표시로써'라는 의미의 어구인 as a token of를 만드는 전치사 (A) as(~로써)가 정답이다. (D) with는 '~와 함께'라는 의미로 빈칸에 쓸 경우 '사과의 표시와 함께 그것을 여겨주길 바란다'라는 어색한 문맥이 된다.

어휘 to prep. ~에 along prep. ~을 따라

143-146번은 다음 공고에 관한 문제입니다.

Demair International이 더 친환경적으로 되고 있다

Demair International은 최근 143**환경적으로** 지속가능한 실천들에 참여하기 위해 노력하는 호텔과 게스트하우스의 단체인 Green Stay Network

(GSN)에 가입하였습니다. GSN의 회원으로서 그것의 의무들을 이행하기 위해, Demair International은 모든 스위트룸에 144**교육용** 소책자를 놓아둡니다. 이것들은 저희 호텔에 머무는 동안 물과 에너지를 보존하는 방법을 간단한 용어들로 설명합니다. 게다가, Demair International은 이제 모든 직원들에게 숙박 산업에서의 지속가능한 실천에 대한 교육용 영상을 145**볼 것을** 요구합니다. 또한 더 큰 개선이 계획되어 있습니다. 146**앞으로의 조치는 태양열 전지판의 설치를 포함할 것입니다.**

join v. 가입하다 engage in phr. 참여하다 sustainable adj. 지속가능한
practice n. 실천, 관행 suite n. 스위트룸 accommodation n. 숙박
improvement n. 개선 as well phr. 또한

143 부사 자리 채우기 중 ●●○

해설 형용사(sustainable)를 꾸밀 수 있는 것은 부사이므로 부사 (B) environmentally (환경적으로)가 정답이다. 형용사 (A), 명사 (C)와 (D)는 형용사를 꾸밀 수 없다.

어휘 environmental adj. 환경의 environment n. 환경
environmentalist n. 환경운동가

144 형용사 어휘 고르기 주변 문맥 파악 중 ●●○

해설 빈칸은 명사(brochures)를 꾸미는 형용사 자리이다. '모든 스위트룸에 ___ 소책자를 놓아둔다'라는 문맥이므로 모든 보기가 정답의 후보이다. 뒤 문장에서 이것들은 우리 호텔에 머무는 동안 물과 에너지를 보존하는 방법을 간단한 용어로 설명한다고 했으므로 물과 에너지를 보존할 수 있는 방법에 대한 교육용 소책자를 놓아둔다는 것을 알 수 있다. 따라서 (C) instructional(교육용의)이 정답이다.

어휘 controversial adj. 논란의, 논란이 많은 difficult adj. 어려운
entertaining adj. 재미있는, 즐거움을 주는

145 제안·요청·의무의 주절을 뒤따르는 that절에 '동사원형' 채우기 상 ●●●

해설 that절(that ~ industry)에 동사가 없고 주절(Demair International ~ requires)에 요청을 나타내는 동사(requires)가 왔으므로 that절의 동사 자리에는 동사원형이 와야 한다. 따라서 동사원형 (A) watch가 정답이다. 동명사 또는 현재분사 (B), 3인칭 단수 동사 (C), to 부정사 (D)는 동사원형 자리에 올 수 없다.

146 알맞은 문장 고르기 중 ●●○

해석 **(A) 앞으로의 조치는 태양열 전지판의 설치를 포함할 것입니다.**
(B) 투어를 신청하시려면, 안내 데스크의 직원에게 이야기하십시오.
(C) 이번 주 후반에 다양한 장소에서 촬영될 것입니다.
(D) 보상 포인트는 객실 업그레이드를 위해 전환될 수 있습니다.

해설 앞부분에서 호텔의 환경적으로 지속가능한 실천들을 이행하기 위해 달라진 점들을 소개하고 있고, 앞 문장 'Bigger improvements are planned as well.'에서 또한 더 큰 개선이 계획되어 있다고 했으므로 빈칸에는 앞으로의 조치에 관한 내용이 들어가야 함을 알 수 있다. 따라서 (A)가 정답이다.

어휘 measure n. 조치 installation n. 설치 solar panel phr. 태양열 전지판
sign up for phr. ~을 신청하다 reward point phr. 보상 포인트
redeem v. 전환하다, 바꾸다

PART 7

147-148번은 다음 메시지 대화문에 관한 문제입니다.

Erika Raimond [오전 11시 46분]
우리가 지난달 주문했던 주문 제작 펜들이 방금 배달되었어요. 안타깝게도, 우리 회사의 이름이 철자가 잘못 쓰여 있어요. ¹⁴⁷제가 우리를 위해 그것들을 만든 회사에 전화했지만, 그들이 이 상황을 해결하는 데에 최소 3일이 걸릴 거예요.

Jayce Vills [오전 11시 48분]
이런. ¹⁴⁸우리는 내일 세미나에서 나누어줄 것이 아무것도 없을 거예요.

Erika Raimond [오전 11시 50분]
¹⁴⁸사실, 우리는 우리의 로고가 새겨져 있는 몇 개의 메모지를 창고에 가지고 있어요. 저는 우리가 그것들을 사용해도 아무도 신경 쓸 것 같지는 않아요.

Jayce Vills [오전 11시 55분]
당신 말이 맞아요. 우선은 그것들을 사용하기로 하지만, 우리는 또한 이 펜들이 수정될 수 있도록 그것들을 돌려보내야 해요.

custom adj. 주문 제작의 unfortunately adv. 안타깝게도
at least phr. 최소한 resolve v. 해결하다 hand out phr. 나누어주다
storage n. 창고 mind v. 신경 쓰다, 꺼리다 for now phr. 우선은

147 육하원칙 문제   중 ●●○

해석 Ms. Raimond는 오늘 아침에 무엇을 했는가?
(A) 세미나에 참석했다
(B) 약속을 잡았다
(C) 소포를 부쳤다
(D) 공급회사에 연락했다

해설 지문의 'I called the company that made them for us'에서 Ms. Raimond가 우리를 위해 그것들, 즉 펜들을 만든 회사에 전화했다고 했으므로 (D)가 정답이다.

어휘 mail v. 부치다, 보내다 package n. 소포 supplier n. 공급회사, 공급자

패러프레이징

called the company that made them 그것들을 만든 회사에 전화했다
→ Contacted a supplier 공급회사에 연락했다

148 의도 파악 문제   중 ●●○

해석 오전 11시 55분에, Mr. Vills가 "You have a point"라고 썼을 때 그가 의도한 것 같은 것은?
(A) 주문이 환불되어야 한다.
(B) 활동이 연기되어야 한다.
(C) 몇몇 문구류가 행사에 사용될 수 있다.
(D) 몇몇 상품들이 창고에 두어져야 한다.

해설 지문의 'We won't have anything to hand out at ~ seminar.'에서 Mr. Vills가 세미나에서 나누어줄 것이 아무것도 없을 것이라고 했고, 'Actually, we have some notepads ~ in storage. I don't think anyone will mind if we use them.'에서 Ms. Raimond가 사실, 우리는 몇 개의 메모지를 창고에 가지고 있으며 우리가 그것들을 사용해도 아무도 신경 쓸 것 같지는 않다고 하자, Mr. Vills가 'You have a point.'(당신 말이 맞아요)라고 한 것을 통해, 몇몇 문구류, 즉 메모지가 행사에 사용될 수 있음을 알 수 있다. 따라서 (C)가 정답이다.

어휘 postpone v. 연기하다 stationery n. 문구류

패러프레이징

notepads 메모지들 → stationery 문구류

149-150번은 다음 공고에 관한 문제입니다.

공고

¹⁴⁹보통 직원들과 장비를 이동시키기 위해 업무용 승강기로 이용되는 4호 승강기가 다음 주 6월 27일부터 29일까지 잠시 이용할 수 없을 것이라는 점을 숙지해주십시오. 기술자들이 정기 보수를 시행할 것입니다. 그 동안에, 3호 승강기가 업무용 승강기로 사용될 것입니다. ¹⁵⁰세입자들의 통행증은 그 승강기에서 작동하지 않을 것이므로, 1호 또는 2호 승강기를 사용해주십시오. 저희는 이것이 야기할 수 있는 모든 불편들에 대해 사과드립니다. 추가 문의사항이 있으시면 건물의 관리사무실로 언제든 연락해주십시오.

Parker Residential 타워 관리진

transport v. 나르다, 옮기다 equipment n. 장비 briefly adv. 잠시
unavailable adj. 이용할 수 없는 routine maintenance phr. 정기 보수
in the meantime phr. 그 동안에 tenant n. 세입자
pass card phr. 통행증 inconvenience n. 불편

149 목적 찾기 문제   상 ●●●

해석 공고의 목적은 무엇인가?
(A) 로비의 예정된 보수를 알리기 위해
(B) 주민들에게 일시적인 변경을 알리기 위해
(C) 세입자들에게 새로운 건물 방침을 알리기 위해
(D) 기술자들에게 지침을 제공하기 위해

해설 지문의 'Be advised that elevator 4 ~ will be briefly unavailable'에서 4호 승강기가 잠시 이용할 수 없을 것이라는 점을 숙지해달라고 한 후, 승강기 이용에 관한 일시적인 변경에 대해 안내하고 있으므로 (B)가 정답이다.

어휘 renovation n. 보수 temporary adj. 일시적인 policy n. 방침, 정책

패러프레이징

be briefly unavailable 잠시 이용할 수 없다 → a temporary change 일시적인 변경

150 추론 문제   상 ●●●

해석 건물 세입자들에 대해 암시되는 것은?
(A) 방문객 규정에 대해서 불평을 했다.
(B) 관리사무실을 방문해야 할 것이다.
(C) 직원들과 모든 승강기를 공유할 것이다.
(D) 승강기를 사용하기 위해 통행증이 필요하다.

해설 지문의 'Tenants' pass cards will not function in that elevator, so please use either elevators 1 or 2.'에서 세입자들의 통행증은 그 승강기, 즉 업무용 승강기에서는 작동하지 않을 것이므로, 1호 또는 2호 승강기를 사용해달라고 했으므로 세입자들은 승강기를 사용하기 위해 통행증이 필요하다는 사실을 추론할 수 있다. 따라서 (D)가 정답이다.

151-154번은 다음 기사에 관한 문제입니다.

발표가 Tatkraft사의 주가를 증가시키다

6월 13일—¹⁵¹독일의 전기자동차 제조회사인 Tatkraft사의 주식이 최고 경영자 Johannes Schneider의 회사 **실적** 발표 후에 급격히 상승했다. ¹⁵²지난주, Mr. Schneider는 Tatkraft사가 지난해 2억 1천 2백만 달러의 수익을 냈으며 올해 50만대 이상의 새로운 자동차를 판매할 것으로 예상한다고 발표했다. 긍정적인 재정적 결과를 계속해서 내놓는 Tatkraft사의 능력에 대한 투자자들의 강한 확신을 드러내며, 회사의 주가는 그 후에 한 주당 567달러에서 601달러까지 상승하였다. ¹⁵³작년 이전에는, 수요를 따라가는 것에 지속적으로 실패한 생산량으로 인해 그 회사는 투자자들에게 그것의 성장 잠재력을 확신시키는 데 어려움을 겪었다. ¹⁵⁴자동차 산업 전문가 Elias Muller의 고용 후 시행된 개선들 덕분에, 회사는 그것의 제조과정을 간소화하였고 자동차를 더욱 효율적으로 생산하고 있다. 현재, Tatkraft사는 1천억 달러 이상의 가치가 있다고 평가된다.

share n. 주식 manufacturer n. 제조회사 profit n. 수익
stock price phr. 주가 subsequently adv. 그 후에, 나중에
reveal v. 드러내다 prior to phr. 이전에 struggle v. 어려움을 겪다
convince v. 확신시키다, 설득하다 capacity n. 잠재력
consistently adv. 지속적으로 keep up with phr. 따라가다
improvement n. 개선 implement v. 시행하다
automotive adj. 자동차의 veteran n. 전문가 efficiently adv. 효율적으로

151 동의어 찾기 문제 중 ●●○

해석 1문단 두 번째 줄의 단어 "performance"는 의미상 –와 가장 가깝다.
(A) 일상
(B) 외관
(C) 발표
(D) 성취

해설 performance를 포함한 문장 'Shares ~ increased sharply following ~ announcement of the company's performance.'에서 주식이 회사의 실적 발표 후에 급격히 상승했다고 했으므로 performance는 '실적'이라는 뜻으로 사용되었다. 따라서 '성취, 업적'이라는 뜻을 가진 (D) achievement가 정답이다.

152 육하원칙 문제 중 ●●○

해석 Mr. Schneider는 그 전주에 무엇을 했는가?
(A) 상업용 부지를 매입했다.
(B) 새로운 고위 간부를 임명했다.
(C) 예상되는 판매량에 대한 정보를 제공했다.
(D) 주주들 사이에서 수익을 분배했다.

해설 지문의 'Last week, Mr. Schneider announced that Tatkraft ~ expects to sell over half a million new cars this year.'에서 지난주, Mr. Schneider는 Tatkraft사가 올해 50만대 이상의 새로운 자동차를 판매할 것으로 예상한다고 발표했다고 했으므로 (C)가 정답이다.

어휘 property n. 부지 appoint v. 임명하다 top executive phr. 고위 간부
anticipated adj. 예상되는 distribute v. 분배하다

패러프레이징

expects to sell half a million ~ cars 50만대 이상의 자동차를 판매할 것으로 예상하다 → anticipated sales 예상되는 판매량

해석 Tatkraft사의 투자자들에 대해 암시되는 것은?
(A) 새해에 차량을 주문했다.
(B) 회사의 가능성에 대해 의심을 품었다.
(C) 2년 전에 그들의 투자를 늘렸다.
(D) 회사가 불공평하게 평가되었다고 생각한다.

해설 지문의 'Prior to last year, the company struggled to convince investors of its capacity for growth'에서 작년 이전에는, 그 회사, 즉 Tatkraft사가 투자자들에게 그것의 성장 잠재력을 확신시키는 데 어려움을 겪었다고 했으므로 투자자들이 회사의 가능성에 대해 의심을 품었다는 사실을 추론할 수 있다. 따라서 (B)가 정답이다.

어휘 place an order phr. 주문하다 vehicle n. 차량 doubt n. 의심
unfairly adv. 불공평하게

패러프레이징

capacity for growth 성장 잠재력 → potential 가능성

154 추론 문제 상 ●●●

해석 Mr. Muller는 주로 무엇을 담당하는 것 같은가?
(A) 생산 목표를 달성하는 것
(B) 판매 전략을 개발하는 것
(C) 재정 결과를 분석하는 것
(D) 고객 불만 사항을 해결하는 것

해설 지문의 'after the hiring of Elias Muller ~, the company ~ is producing cars more efficiently'에서 Elias Muller의 고용 후 회사는 자동차를 더욱 효율적으로 생산하고 있다고 했으므로 Mr. Muller가 주로 생산 목표를 달성하는 것을 담당하고 있다는 사실을 추론할 수 있다. 따라서 (A)가 정답이다.

어휘 meet v. 달성하다 analyze v. 분석하다 resolve v. 해결하다

155-156번은 다음 웹페이지에 관한 문제입니다.

www.twilighttheater.com
TWILIGHT 극장

| 홈 | 소개 | 공연 | 후원 업체 | 참여하기 | 연락하기 |

^{155-A/B}53년 전 조용한 시골길의 농가에 설립된 Twilight 극장은 연극, 마술 공연, 희극, 그리고 뮤지컬 형식의 오락으로 또 다른 즐거운 여름을 제공하게 되어 기쁩니다. 저희는 250명의 좌석 수, 다양한 유형의 공연에 적응할 수 있는 무대, 그리고 아래층에 맞고 잊을 수 없는 식사를 제공하는 훌륭한 식당을 가지고 있습니다. 공연을 보러 오셔서 왜 ^{156-C}*The National Gazette*지가 지난 12년 동안 저희를 꾸준히 지역의 최고 소규모 공연 극장으로 평가해왔는지 알아보세요.

^{155-D}저희의 매력적인 시설은 또한 개인 파티, 가족 모임, 결혼식, 그리고 기념일을 위해 예약하는 것이 가능합니다. 더 많은 정보를 원하신다면 <u>저희에게 연락해주세요.</u>

farmhouse n. 농가 seating capacity phr. 좌석 수
adaptable adj. 적응할 수 있는 serve v. 제공하다
unforgettable adj. 잊을 수 없는 consistently adv. 꾸준히
rate v. 평가하다 charming adj. 매력적인 reunion n. 모임, 상봉

155 Not/True 문제　　　　　　　　　중 ●●○

해석　Twilight 극장에 대해 언급되지 않은 것은?
(A) 이전 농가 건물을 사용한다.
(B) 다양한 공연들을 제공한다.
(C) 그것의 좌석 수를 확장했다.
(D) 특별한 행사들을 위해 예약될 수 있다.

해설　지문에서 (C)는 언급되지 않은 내용이다. 따라서 (C)가 정답이다. (A)와 (B)는 'Established in a farmhouse ~, the Twilight Theater is pleased to offer ~ plays, magic shows, comedy acts, and musicals.'에서 농가에 설립된 Twilight 극장이 연극, 마술 공연, 희극, 그리고 뮤지컬을 제공하게 되어 기쁘다고 했으므로 지문의 내용과 일치한다. (D)는 'Our ~ facility is ~ available to book for private parties, family reunions, weddings, and anniversaries.'에서 시설, 즉 Twilight 극장은 개인 파티, 가족 모임, 결혼식, 그리고 기념일을 위해 예약하는 것이 가능하다고 했으므로 지문의 내용과 일치한다.

어휘　occupy v. (공간을) 사용하다, 차지하다　expand v. 확장하다

패러프레이징

> farmhouse 농가 → farm building 농가 건물
> plays, magic shows, comedy acts, and musicals 연극, 마술 공연, 희극, 그리고 뮤지컬 → a variety of shows 다양한 공연들
> is ~ available to book 예약이 가능하다 → can be reserved 예약될 수 있다
> private parties, family reunions, weddings, and anniversaries 개인 파티, 가족 모임, 결혼식, 그리고 기념일 → special events 특별한 행사들

156 Not/True 문제　　　　　　　　　상 ●●●

해석　*The National Gazette*지에 대해 언급된 것은?
(A) 후원 업체로서 Twilight 극장을 지원한다.
(B) 지역 극장들에 대한 그것의 첫 번째 호를 발행했다.
(C) Twilight 극장을 여러 차례 칭찬해왔다.
(D) 최근 그것의 12주년을 축하했다.

해설　지문의 '*The National Gazette* has consistently rated us the region's best ~ playhouse for the last 12 years'에서 *The National Gazette*지가 지난 12년 동안 저희, 즉 Twilight 극장을 꾸준히 지역의 최고 극장으로 평가해왔다고 했으므로 (C)는 지문의 내용과 일치한다. 따라서 (C)가 정답이다. (A), (B), (D)는 지문에 언급되지 않은 내용이다.

어휘　regional adj. 지역의　repeatedly adv. 여러 차례　commend v. 칭찬하다

패러프레이징

> has consistently rated ~ the ~ best 꾸준히 최고로 평가해왔다 → has repeatedly commended 여러 차례 칭찬해왔다

157-158번은 다음 광고에 관한 문제입니다.

¹⁵⁷광고 판매원

영국의 일간 그리고 주간 신문의 선두적인 출판사인 Emerald 출판사가 그것의 런던 사무실에서 일할 지원자를 찾고 있습니다. 이 직무는 할당된 지구들 내의 회사들에 전화로 회사의 출판물 포트폴리오를 홍보하는 것을 포함합니다.

¹⁵⁷**주요 책무:**
· 문의에 답변하는 것
· 광고 지면을 예약하는 것
· 고객 기록 유지하는 것

· ¹⁵⁷수익 목표를 달성하는 것

자격 요건:
· 고객들과 협상하는 능력
· 훌륭한 전화 의사소통 능력
· 최소 1년의 미디어 판매 경험이 선호됨
· 사무용 소프트웨어에 정통함

이것은 ¹⁵⁸⁻ᴮ20,000파운드에서 24,000파운드(경험에 비례하여)의 연간 기본 급여와 건강 보험, 퇴직금 그리고 유급 휴가와 같은 복지들을 **제공하는** 정규직입니다.

지원하시려면 여기를 클릭하세요.

sales executive phr. 판매원　leading adj. 선두적인
candidate n. 지원자　promote v. 홍보하다　assigned adj. 할당된
sector n. 지구　primary adj. 주요한　revenue target phr. 수익 목표
qualification n. 자격 요건　negotiate v. 협상하다　familiarity n. 정통함
compensation n. 급여, 보상　relative adj. 비례하는
retirement savings phr. 퇴직금　paid time off phr. 유급 휴가

157 추론 문제　　　　　　　　　상 ●●●

해석　Emerald 출판사에 대해 암시되는 것은?
(A) 여러 국가들에서 신문들을 소유한다.
(B) 최근에 새로운 사무실로 이전했다.
(C) 그것의 직원에게 재정적인 목표를 부과한다.
(D) 몇몇 다른 웹사이트들을 유지한다.

해설　지문의 'Advertising Sales Executive', 'Primary responsibilities:', 'Meeting revenue targets'에서 Emerald 출판사 광고 판매원의 주요 책무에 수익 목표를 달성하는 것이 있음을 알 수 있으므로 직원에게 재정적인 목표를 부과한다는 사실을 추론할 수 있다. 따라서 (C)가 정답이다.

패러프레이징

> revenue targets 수익 목표 → financial goals 재정적인 목표

158 Not/True 문제　　　　　　　　　중 ●●○

해석　광고된 일자리에 대해 언급된 것은?
(A) 학위를 가진 지원자를 필요로 한다.
(B) 이력에 기반하여 급여를 지급할 것이다.
(C) 가끔의 출장을 수반할 것이다.
(D) 소프트웨어 사용 교육을 제공한다.

해설　지문의 'offering annual base compensation of £20,000 to £24,000 (relative to experience)'에서 경험에 비례하여 20,000파운드에서 24,000파운드의 연간 기본 급여를 제공한다고 했으므로 (B)는 지문의 내용과 일치한다. 따라서 (B)가 정답이다. (A), (C), (D)는 지문에 언급되지 않은 내용이다.

어휘　degree n. 학위　work history phr. 이력　occasional adj. 가끔의

패러프레이징

> relative to experience 경험에 비례하여 → based on work history 이력에 기반하여

159-161번은 다음 편지에 관한 문제입니다.

8월 24일

Leanna Murillo
111번지 Fort가, 바스테르
세인트키츠 네비스, 세인트키츠 네비스 1201

Ms. Murillo께,

159Carpenters United는 그것의 제5회 학술 토론회를 계획하는 것을 시작했는데, 이것은 2월 20일부터 23일까지 싱가포르의 장소에서 세계 각지의 구성원들을 함께 모을 것입니다. 이전의 행사들처럼, **160-B목표는 우리 분야의 최신 기술 발전을 논의하는 것이 될 것입니다.** ─ [1] ─. **160-C그것은 또한 구성원들이 인맥을 만들 기회가 될 것입니다.**

이번에, **160-D우리는 지속가능한 건축 자재에 대한 홍보 캠페인을 계획하는 추가적인 일을 가질 것입니다.** ─ [2] ─. **160-D이 캠페인은 새로운 자재들로 바꾸는 것의 환경적인 이점들뿐만 아니라 목공에서 그것들이 할 수 있는 역할에 대한 인식을 확산시킬 것입니다. 161우리는 이 캠페인을 소셜 미디어, 공개 행사, 또는 전통적인 광고를 통해 수행할 것인지 결정해야 할 것입니다.** ─ [3] ─.

학술회는 다음 3년의 우리 대표직 위원회의 구성원들을 결정하기 위한 투표로 마무리 지을 것입니다.

우리는 우리 협회의 주요 구성원으로서 당신이 참석할 수 있기를 바랍니다. ─ [4] ─.

Danton Spritz
회장, Carpenters United

symposium n. 학술 토론회 venue n. 장소 as with phr. ~처럼
aim n. 목표 discuss v. 논의하다 connection n. 인맥, 연줄
publicity campaign phr. 홍보 캠페인 sustainable adj. 지속가능한
material n. 자재 awareness n. 인식 carpentry n. 목공
switch v. 바꾸다 carry out phr. 수행하다 determine v. 결정하다
leadership n. 대표직 committee n. 위원회 association n. 협회

159 목적 찾기 문제 상 ●●●

해석 편지의 목적은 무엇인가?
(A) 행사의 참석을 확인하기 위해
(B) 대표직의 변화를 알리기 위해
(C) 정기적인 모임을 알리기 위해
(D) 일련의 규칙들을 강조하기 위해

해설 지문의 'Carpenters United has begun planning its fifth symposium'에서 Carpenters United가 그것의 제5회 학술 토론회를 계획하는 것을 시작했다고 한 후, 학술 토론회에 대한 정보를 제공하고 있으므로 (C)가 정답이다.

어휘 confirm v. 확인하다 gathering n. 모임 a set of phr. 일련의

패러프레이징

fifth symposium 제5회 학술회 → a regular gathering 정기 모임

160 Not/True 문제 중 ●●○

해석 편지에 따르면, 참석자들은 무엇을 하지 않을 것인가?
(A) 성공적인 회사들에 상을 준다
(B) 업계 혁신들에 대해 논의한다

(C) 내부의 인적 네트워크를 형성하는 것에 참여한다
(D) 대중의 인식 활동을 계획한다

해설 지문에서 (A)는 언급되지 않은 내용이다. 따라서 (A)가 정답이다. (B)는 'the aim will be to discuss the latest ~ developments in ~ field'에서 목표는 분야의 최신 발전을 논의하는 것이 될 것이라고 했으므로 지문의 내용과 일치한다. (C)는 'It will ~ be an opportunity for members to form connections.'에서 그것, 즉 학술 토론회는 구성원들이 인맥을 만들 기회가 될 것이라고 했으므로 지문의 내용과 일치한다. (D)는 'we will have the ~ task of planning a publicity campaign'과 'The campaign will spread awareness about the role that new materials can play in carpentry'에서 홍보 캠페인을 계획하는 일을 가질 것이며 이 캠페인은 목공에서 그것들, 즉 새로운 자재들이 할 수 있는 역할에 대한 인식을 확산시킬 것이라고 했으므로 지문의 내용과 일치한다.

어휘 innovation n. 혁신 engage in phr. ~에 참여하다

패러프레이징

discuss the latest ~ developments in ~ field 분야의 최신 발전을 논의하다
→ Talk about industry innovations 업계 혁신들에 대해 논의하다
form connections 인맥을 만들다 → Engage in ~ networking 인적 네트워크를 형성하는 것에 참여하다

161 문장 위치 찾기 문제 중 ●●●

해석 [1], [2], [3], [4]로 표시된 위치 중, 다음 문장이 들어갈 곳으로 가장 적절한 것은?

"우리의 선택은 아마 그때 이용 가능한 자금에 달려있을 것입니다."

(A) [1]
(B) [2]
(C) [3]
(D) [4]

해설 주어진 문장에서 우리의 선택은 아마 그때 이용 가능한 자금에 달려있을 것이라고 했으므로, 이 문장이 선택과 관련된 내용이 나오는 부분에 들어가야 함을 알 수 있다. [3]의 앞 문장인 'We will need to decide whether to carry out this campaign through social media, public events, or traditional advertising.'에서 우리는 이 캠페인을 소셜 미디어, 공개 행사, 또는 전통적인 광고를 통해 수행할 것인지 결정해야 할 것이라고 했으므로, [3]에 주어진 문장이 들어가면 어떤 방법으로 캠페인을 수행할 것인지에 대한 선택은 아마 그때 이용 가능한 자금에 달려있을 것이라는 자연스러운 문맥이 된다는 것을 알 수 있다. 따라서 (C)가 정답이다.

어휘 funding n. 자금

162-164번은 다음 회의록에 관한 문제입니다.

FINTRAD사

7월 8일의 회의록

참석자: Sherilyn Mitchell, Dan Gregory, Marva Jackson
결석: Harvey Fleck
요약
· **162/163-AMr. Fleck은 상하이의 패션 산업 박람회에서 우리의 상점 체인을 대표하고 있기 때문에 그는 참석하지 않았으며** 7월 15일까지 돌아오지 않을 것입니다.
· 지난 분기의 홍보 행사가 판매량에 대한 그것의 효과를 포함하여 논의되었으며, 이것은 이전 분기와 비교하여 3퍼센트 상승했습니다.

- Ms. Jackson은 9월의 밀라노 패션 위크 행사에서의 남성들을 위한 ¹⁶²Fintrad사의 새로운 의류 라인 출시에 관해 물었습니다. Ms. Mitchell은 상세한 계획에 대해 Fintrad사의 글로벌 마케팅부장에게 연락하기로 했습니다.
- 7월 16일의 다음 회의에서 최종 승인될 사항들은 팀 구성원들의 역할을 포함합니다. ¹⁶⁴Mr. Gregory와 Ms. Jackson이 각각 보도 자료와 인터넷 홍보를 다루는 것에 자원한 반면, Mr. Fleck의 역할은 추후 결정될 것입니다.

represent v. 대표하다 quarter n. 분기 item n. 사항, 항목
finalize v. 최종 승인하다 volunteer v. 자원하다 handle v. 다루다
press release phr. 보도 자료 respectively adv. 각각
determine v. 결정하다

162 추론 문제 중 ●●○

해석 Fintrad사는 무엇일 것 같은가?
(A) 회의 주최업체
(B) 의류 소매업체
(C) 금융 서비스 회사
(D) 마케팅 대행사

해설 지문의 'Mr. Fleck ~ is representing our store chain at the Fashion Industry Fair in Shanghai'와 'the launch of Fintrad's new clothing line'에서 Mr. Fleck이 상하이의 패션 산업 박람회에서 우리, 즉 Fintrad사의 상점 체인을 대표하고 있다고 했고, Fintrad사의 새로운 의류 라인 출시라고 했으므로 Fintrad사가 의류 소매업체라는 사실을 추론할 수 있다. 따라서 (B)가 정답이다.

어휘 conference n. 회의 agency n. 대행사

163 Not/True 문제 중 ●●○

해석 Mr. Fleck에 대해 언급된 것은?
(A) 현재 출장 중이다.
(B) 최근에 주요한 거래를 체결했다.
(C) 판매량 증가를 책임지고 있었다.
(D) 보통 본사에서 근무한다.

해설 지문의 'Mr. Fleck did not participate because he is representing our store chain at the Fashion Industry Fair in Shanghai'에서 Mr. Fleck은 상하이의 패션 산업 박람회에서 우리의 상점 체인을 대표하고 있기 때문에 그는 참석하지 않았다고 했으므로 (A)는 지문의 내용과 일치한다. 따라서 (A)가 정답이다. (B), (C), (D)는 지문에 언급되지 않은 내용이다.

어휘 conclude v. 체결하다 head office phr. 본사

164 추론 문제 중 ●●○

해석 온라인 활동을 담당하는 것에 누가 배치될 것 같은가?
(A) Sherilyn Mitchell
(B) Dan Gregory
(C) Marva Jackson
(D) Harvey Fleck

해설 지문의 'Mr. Gregory and Ms. Jackson volunteered to handle press releases and Internet promotions, respectively'에서 Mr. Gregory와 Ms. Jackson이 각각 보도 자료와 인터넷 홍보를 다루는 것에 자원했다고 했으므로 Ms. Jackson이 온라인 활동을 담당하는 것에 배치될 것이라는 사실을 추론할 수 있다. 따라서 (C)가 정답이다.

어휘 place v. 배치하다, 두다 in charge of phr. ~을 담당하는

패러프레이징

online activities 온라인 활동 → Internet promotions 인터넷 홍보

165-167번은 다음 이메일에 관한 문제입니다.

수신: Evan Kensington <evkens44@nearmail.net>
발신: Madison Garcia <m.garcia@fosteracademy.com>
제목: 비즈니스 작문 온라인 강좌
날짜: 2월 18일

Mr. Kensington께,

Foster 학원의 온라인 비즈니스 작문 수업에 등록해주셔서 감사드립니다. 저는 당신이 저희와 함께하게 되어 기쁩니다! ¹⁶⁷⁻ᴬ이 강좌는 총 4주 동안 계속될 것입니다. 수료와 동시에, 당신은 편지, 보고서, 계약서 등과 같은 중요한 문서들을 어떻게 작성하는지 알게 될 것입니다.

¹⁶⁵/¹⁶⁶수업의 첫날인 2월 27일 전에, 당신이 완료해야 할 몇 가지 과제가 있습니다. ¹⁶⁶무엇보다 먼저, 당신의 Foster 학원 온라인 계정에 로그인하여 '과제들'을 클릭하세요. 당신은 그 링크에 이미 올라온 몇 가지 읽기 과제들을 발견할 것입니다. 가능한 한 빨리 이것들을 꼭 검토하십시오.

또한, 당신이 www.fosteracademy.com/programs에서 TeachViewer 소프트웨어를 다운받고 그 애플리케이션이 당신의 컴퓨터에서 성공적으로 작동하는지 빨리 확인하는 것이 매우 중요합니다. ¹⁶⁷⁻ᴮ/ᴰ이 프로그램은 다른 강좌 참가자들과 함께하는 수업 토론 포럼에서 게시글을 작성하는 수단으로 자주 사용될 것입니다.

시작할 때 행운을 빌며, 어떤 질문이나 우려 사항이 있다면 제게 이메일을 보내주십시오.

Madison Garcia 드림, Foster 학원의 강사

register v. 등록하다 run v. 계속되다 in total phr. 총
completion n. 수료 first and foremost phr. 무엇보다 먼저
account n. 계정 assignment n. 과제 frequently adv. 자주
means n. 수단, 방법 discussion n. 토론

165 목적 찾기 문제 중 ●●○

해석 이메일의 주 목적은 무엇인가?
(A) 몇몇 서류들의 제출을 요청하기 위해
(B) 등록 과정을 설명하기 위해
(C) 학생이 수업에 대한 준비를 하도록 하기 위해
(D) 수료증서를 제공하기 위해

해설 지문의 'Before ~ the first day of the class—there are a few tasks ~ to complete.'에서 수업의 첫날 전에, 완료해야 할 몇 가지 과제가 있다고 한 후, 수업을 듣기 전 준비해야 할 사항을 설명하고 있으므로 (C)가 정답이다.

어휘 submission n. 제출 get ready (for) phr. (~에 대한) 준비를 하다
certificate n. 증서

166 육하원칙 문제 중 ●●○

해석 Mr. Kensington은 2월 27일 전에 무엇을 해달라고 요청받는가?
(A) 온라인 페이지를 탐색한다
(B) 웹사이트에 댓글을 게시한다
(C) 강좌 일정표를 인쇄한다
(D) 몇몇 출판물을 다운로드한다

해설 지문의 'Before February 27 ~ there are few tasks ~ to complete. First and foremost, log on to your Foster Academy online account and click on 'Assignments'.'에서 수업의 첫날인 2월 27일 전에 완료해야 할 몇 가지 과제가 있으며 무엇보다 먼저, Foster 학원 온라인 계정에 로그인하여 '과제들'을 클릭하라고 했으므로 (A)가 정답이다.

어휘 navigate v. 탐색하다, 항해하다 comment n. 댓글
publication n. 출판물

167 Not/True 문제   중 ●●○

해석 비즈니스 작문 강좌에 대해 언급되지 않은 것은?
(A) 몇 주에 걸쳐 열릴 것이다.
(B) 소프트웨어의 사용을 요구한다.
(C) 성적이 매겨지는 글쓰기 과제와 함께 끝날 것이다.
(D) 동급생들 사이의 의사소통을 수반한다.

해설 지문에서 (C)는 언급되지 않은 내용이다. 따라서 (C)가 정답이다. (A)는 'This course will run for four weeks in total.'에서 이 강좌는 총 4주 동안 계속될 것이라고 했으므로 지문의 내용과 일치한다. (B)와 (D)는 'This program will be used ~ as a means of making posts on a class discussion forum with other course participants.'에서 이 프로그램, 즉 TeachViewer 소프트웨어가 다른 강좌 참가자들과 함께하는 수업 토론 포럼에서 게시글을 작성하는 수단으로 사용될 것이라고 했으므로 지문의 내용과 일치한다.

어휘 take place phr. 열리다, 발생하다 grade v. 성적을 매기다
involve v. 수반하다, 포함하다 classmate n. 동급생, 급우

패러프레이징

run for four weeks 4주 동안 계속되다 → take place over several weeks 몇 주에 걸쳐 열리다
program will be used 프로그램이 사용될 것이다 → the use of ~ software 소프트웨어의 사용
a class discussion ~ with other course participants 다른 강좌 참가자들과 함께하는 수업 토론 → communication among classmates 동급생들 사이의 의사소통

168-171번은 다음 온라인 채팅 대화문에 관한 문제입니다.

| Fran Jenkins | [오전 11시 40분] |

안녕하세요, 팀원들. ¹⁶⁸제가 논의하고 싶은 것이 있어요. 여러분 모두가 바쁜 것은 알지만, ¹⁶⁸우리는 이번 여름 사무실의 친목 활동으로 무엇을 할지 생각해야 해요. 저는 해변 여행에 관해 생각해 보았어요. 아이디어가 있는 사람 있나요?

| Harriet Tibbs | [오전 11시 43분] |

수영을 하기에는 물이 너무 차가울 것이라고 생각하지 않나요? 스포츠 센터에 있는 수영장은 어때요?

| Gary Franklin | [오전 11시 43분] |

또는 지역 공원에서의 소풍은요? 우리는 한동안 그것을 못했잖아요.

| Fran Jenkins | [오전 11시 45분] |

저도 당신에게 동의해요, Harriet. 그리고 저는 스포츠 시설이 수영장에서 음식물을 허용할지 잘 모르겠지만, 소풍 아이디어는 마음에 들어요.

| Gary Franklin | [오전 11시 47분] |

¹⁶⁹⁻ᶜHenderson 공원에 좋은 소풍 장소가 있어요. 그곳에는 큰 운동장과 많은 주차 공간이 있어요.

| Harriet Tibbs | [오전 11시 48분] |

그곳이 좋긴 하지만, ¹⁶⁹⁻ᶜ그곳은 혼잡해질 수 있어요. Gold Ridge 공원은 보통 그만큼 많은 사람들이 없고 우리가 바비큐도 할 수 있기 때문에 이곳이 더 나을 수도 있어요.

| Fran Jenkins | [오전 11시 49분] |

샐러드, 수박, 그리고 많은 음료들과 함께, 바비큐는 완벽할 거예요. ¹⁷⁰우리의 식비 예산은 올해 1,200달러로 더 많아요.

| Gary Franklin | [오전 11시 50분] |

좋아요! ¹⁷¹우리는 그 금액이면 출장 요식업자도 고용할 수 있어요. 저는 Ruth Bernard라는 괜찮은 사람을 알고 있어요. 그녀는 제 형제의 결혼식에 음식을 공급했어요. 저는 그녀로부터 견적서를 받을 수 있어요.

| Fran Jenkins | [오전 11시 52분] |

그렇게 해주세요. 대략 60명의 사람들에 대해서 그녀가 얼마나 청구하는지 알아봐주세요. 그럼 우리의 계획들을 마무리 짓기 위해 금요일에 다시 만납시다.

figure out phr. 생각해내다 social adj. 친목의, 사교적인
in a while phr. 한동안 crowded adj. 혼잡한 budget n. 예산
caterer n. 출장 요식업자 estimate n. 견적서 charge v. 청구하다
finalize v. 마무리 짓다

168 육하원칙 문제   중 ●●○

해석 Ms. Jenkins는 그녀의 팀과 무엇을 논의하고 싶어 하는가?
(A) 회의 안건을 마무리 짓는 것
(B) 여행 일정표를 확정하는 것
(C) 행사를 위한 자원봉사자를 모으는 것
(D) 야유회에 대한 아이디어들을 진전시키는 것

해설 지문의 'There's something I'd like to discuss.'와 'we need to figure out what to do for the office's social activity'에서 Ms. Jenkins가 자신이 논의하고 싶은 것이 있다고 하며 사무실의 친목 활동으로 무엇을 할지 생각해내야 한다고 했으므로 (D)가 정답이다.

어휘 agenda n. 안건 confirm v. 확정하다 travel itinerary phr. 여행 일정표
gather v. 모으다 develop v. 진전시키다, 발전시키다 outing n. 야유회

169 Not/True 문제   중 ●●○

해석 Henderson 공원에 대해 언급된 것은?
(A) 사무실에 가장 가까운 곳이다.
(B) 방문객들이 그들의 애완동물을 가져오는 것을 허용한다.
(C) 많은 사람들을 끌어들이는 편이다.
(D) 대여를 위한 실내 공간이 있다.

해설 지문의 'Henderson Park has a nice picnic area.'에서 Mr. Franklin이 Henderson 공원에 좋은 소풍 장소가 있다고 하자, 'it can get crowded'에서 Ms. Tibbs가 그곳, 즉 Henderson 공원은 혼잡해질 수 있다고 했으므로 (C)는 지문의 내용과 일치한다. 따라서 (C)가 정답이다. (A), (B), (D)는 지문에 언급되지 않은 내용이다.

어휘 attract v. 끌어들이다 indoor adj. 실내의

패러프레이징

get crowded 혼잡해지다 → attract large crowds 많은 사람들을 끌어들이다

해커스 토익 실전 1200제 READING

170 의도 파악 문제 중 ●●○

해석 오전 11시 50분에, Mr. Franklin이 "Fantastic"이라고 썼을 때 그가 의도한 것은?
(A) 매우 많은 사람이 온다는 것에 기쁘다.
(B) 예산이 그가 생각했던 것보다 많았다.
(C) 출장 음식 서비스의 높은 가격에 놀랐다.
(D) 장소 임대료가 그가 생각했던 것보다 더 비싸다.

해설 지문의 'Our food budget is higher this year at $1,200.'에서 Ms. Jenkins가 식비 예산이 올해 1,200달러로 더 많다고 하자, Ms. Franklin이 'Fantastic!'(좋아요!)이라고 한 것을 통해, Mr. Franklin이 생각했던 것보다 예산이 많았음을 알 수 있다. 따라서 (B)가 정답이다.

어휘 realize v. 생각하다, 인식하다

171 육하원칙 문제 중 ●●○

해석 Mr. Franklin은 무엇을 추천하는가?
(A) 행사를 직원들로 제한시키는 것
(B) 야외 바비큐를 주최하는 것
(C) 샐러드와 과일을 제공하는 것
(D) Ruth Bernard를 고용하는 것

해설 지문의 'We could even hire a caterer ~. I know a good one named Ruth Bernard.'에서 Mr. Franklin이 우리는 출장 요식업자도 고용할 수 있다며 Ruth Bernard라는 괜찮은 사람을 알고 있다고 했으므로 (D)가 정답이다.

어휘 host v. 주최하다 serve v. 제공하다

172-175번은 다음 이메일에 관한 문제입니다.

수신: Lauren Bisson <laurenb@junomail.com>
발신: Jaleela Attar <j_attar@geladatech.com>
제목: 회신: 질문
날짜: 2월 8일

Ms. Bisson께,

¹⁷²저는 당신이 Gelada Technologies사에서 일을 시작하는 것에 대해 조금 긴장감을 느낄 수도 있다는 것을 이해하며 당신이 가능한 한 준비가 되길 원한다는 것에 기쁩니다. 당신이 저희 건물에 도착하면 무엇을 해야 하는지에 대한 당신의 질문에 응하여, 일 층의 안내 데스크에서 멈추어 주십시오. — [1] —. 그곳의 직원이 당신을 기다리고 있을 것입니다. ¹⁷³⁻ᴮ비록 당신의 정규 근무는 오전 9시에 시작되지만, ¹⁷³⁻ᴮ/¹⁷⁴당신과 다른 신입 직원들은 처음 이틀 동안 오리엔테이션 세션에 참여할 것입니다. ¹⁷³⁻ᴮ이날들에는 당신이 반드시 오전 8시에 도착하도록 하십시오. — [2] —.

오리엔테이션 세션은 당신의 일상 업무와 Gelada Technologies사의 규정들을 다룰 것입니다. ¹⁷⁵당신은 또한 당신이 직접 익숙해져야 하는 몇 개의 소프트웨어 애플리케이션이 설치된 노트북 컴퓨터를 지급받을 것입니다. — [3] —. ¹⁷⁴교육을 받는 날 동안에는 점심이 제공될 것이므로 그것을 가져올 필요가 없습니다. 마지막으로, 저희는 직원들이 일할 때 편안함을 느끼도록 캐주얼 복장 규정을 지키고 있으니, 이에 따라 옷을 입어주시기 바랍니다. — [4] —.

저는 이 정보가 당신의 질문들을 다루고 있기를 바랍니다. 다음 주에 뵙겠습니다.

Jaleela Attar 드림
인사부 관리자, Gelada Technologies사

---

cover v. 다루다 day-to-day adj. 일상의, 그날그날의 issue v. 지급하다 familiarize v. 익숙하게 하다 maintain v. 지키다, 유지하다 accordingly adv. 이에 따라

172 목적 찾기 문제 중 ●●○

해석 Ms. Attar는 왜 이메일을 썼는가?
(A) 수습직원에게 몇 가지 문서들을 제출하도록 상기시키기 위해
(B) 구직 면접에 관한 질문에 답하기 위해
(C) 교육 워크숍에 대한 의견을 요청하기 위해
(D) 출근 첫날에 대해 직원을 준비시키기 위해

해설 지문의 'I understand that you may be ~ nervous about starting work ~ and am glad that you want to be as prepared as possible.'에서 저, 즉 Ms. Attar는 당신이 일을 시작하는 것에 대해 긴장할 수도 있다는 것을 이해하며 당신이 가능한 한 준비가 되길 원한다는 것에 기쁘다고 한 후, 출근 첫날에 진행될 일들을 안내하고 있으므로 (D)가 정답이다.

어휘 remind v. 상기시키다 trainee n. 수습직원 submit v. 제출하다

173 Not/True 문제 중 ●●○

해석 교육 세션에 대해 사실인 것은?
(A) 견학 후에 즉시 시작할 것이다.
(B) 참가자들이 평소보다 더 일찍 도착하도록 요구한다.
(C) 두 개의 다른 그룹을 위해 따로따로 열릴 것이다.
(D) 보통 건물의 1층에서 열린다.

해설 지문의 'Although your normal workday begins at 9:00 A.M., ~ new staff members will be participating in orientation sessions on the first two days. Make sure you arrive at 8:00 A.M. on these days.'에서 비록 정규 근무는 오전 9시에 시작되지만, 신입 직원들은 처음 이틀 동안 오리엔테이션 세션에 참여할 것이라고 하며, 이날들에는 반드시 오전 8시에 도착하도록 하라고 했으므로 (B)는 지문의 내용과 일치한다. 따라서 (B)가 정답이다. (A), (C), (D)는 지문에 언급되지 않은 내용이다.

어휘 immediately adv. 즉시 separately adv. 따로따로

174 추론 문제 상 ●●●

해석 Gelada Technologies사에 대해 암시되는 것은?
(A) 몇몇 직원들이 재택근무를 하도록 허용한다.
(B) 직원들에 의해 사용되는 소프트웨어를 업데이트했다.
(C) 신입 직원들을 위해 두 끼의 식사를 준비할 것이다.
(D) 최근에 그것의 사무실 복장 규정을 바꿨다.

해설 지문의 'new staff members will be participating in orientation sessions on the first two days'에서 신입 직원들은 처음 이틀 동안의 오리엔테이션 세션에 참석할 것이라고 했고, 'lunch ~ will be provided on the days you are training'에서 교육을 받는 날 동안에는 점심이 제공될 것이라고 했으므로 Gelada Technologies사가 신입 직원들을 위해 이틀 동안의 점심, 즉 총 두 끼의 식사를 준비할 것이라는 사실을 추론할 수 있다. 따라서 (C)가 정답이다.

어휘 arrange v. 준비하다

패러프레이징

lunch 점심 → meals 식사

175 문장 위치 찾기 문제   상 ●●●

해석 [1], [2], [3], [4]로 표시된 위치 중, 다음 문장이 들어갈 곳으로 가장 적절한 것은?

"이것들에 대한 상세한 설명이 교육 자료에 포함되어 있습니다."

(A) [1]
(B) [2]
(C) [3]
(D) [4]

해설 주어진 문장에서 이것들에 대한 상세한 설명이 교육 자료에 포함되어 있다고 했으므로, 이 문장이 상세한 설명이 제공되어야 하는 것과 관련된 내용이 나오는 부분에 들어가야 함을 알 수 있다. [3]의 앞 문장인 'You will also be issued a laptop with several software applications installed that you must familiarize yourself with.'에서 당신은 또한 당신이 직접 익숙해져야 하는 몇 개의 소프트웨어 애플리케이션이 설치된 노트북 컴퓨터를 지급받을 것이라고 했으므로, [3]에 주어진 문장이 들어가면 직접 익숙해져야 하는 몇 개의 소프트웨어 애플리케이션에 대한 상세한 설명이 교육 자료에 포함되어 있다는 자연스러운 문맥이 된다는 것을 알 수 있다. 따라서 (C)가 정답이다.

어휘 instruction n. 설명   material n. 자료

176-180번은 다음 양식과 이메일에 관한 문제입니다.

Migoi 항공사

분실 수하물 신고

도착 구역의 수하물 서비스 창구에서 작성되어야 함

저희는 귀하의 수하물을 찾아내고 돌려드리기 위해 저희의 최선을 다할 것입니다. ¹⁷⁸그러나, 만약 그것이 15일 후에 발견되지 않는다면, 그것은 공식적으로 분실되었다고 공표될 것이며, 배상이 지급될 것입니다.

승객 성명	Jane Rubenstein
전화번호	555-6090
이메일 주소	rube@otomail.net
¹⁷⁶다음 달 동안의 주소	Snow Treasure 리조트, ¹⁷⁶Yuksom, 시킴주 737113, 인도
체류 기간	11일
¹⁷⁷⁻ᶜ영구 주소지	47570번지 ¹⁷⁷⁻ᶜEast Harry가, Wichita, 캔자스주 67230, 미국
출발 공항	Kansas City 공항
도착 공항	Gangtok 공항
¹⁷⁷⁻ᴰ항공편 번호	¹⁷⁷⁻ᴮMA882

분실 수하물 정보

유형	여행 가방
색상	분홍색
상표	Regem
설명	알루미늄으로 만들어짐; 사각형 모양; 측면에 한 개의 손잡이와 뒷면에 한 개의 손잡이; 앞면에 자메이카 국기 스티커
¹⁷⁷⁻ᴬ수하물 수취 번호	¹⁷⁷⁻ᴬAJ8727TP

저는 제가 아는 한 위 세부사항이 완전하고 정확함을 선서합니다.

서명 Jane Rubenstein   날짜: 11월 28일

baggage n. 수하물   utmost n. 최선; adj. 최대한   locate v. 찾아내다
declare v. 공표하다   reimbursement n. 배상   issue v. 지급하다

---

duration n. 기간   permanent address phr. 영구 주소지, 본적
departure n. 출발   suitcase n. 여행 가방   description n. 설명

발신: Jane Rubenstein <rube@otomail.net>
수신: Anand Bedi <a.bedi@migoiair.com>
제목: 수하물 수취 AJ8727TP번에 대한 후속 조치
날짜: 12월 16일

Mr. Bedi께,

¹⁷⁹제 Regem 여행 가방의 상태에 대한 정보를 제게 계속 제공해주셔서 감사드립니다. ¹⁷⁶그것이 이제 공식적으로 분실되었다고 분류되었으므로, 저는 우리가 이전의 이메일에서 논의했던 보상을 받고 싶습니다. 이것뿐만 아니라, 저는 당신이 제 여행 가방이 분실되었음을 진술하는 서류와 당신이 제게 지불할 정확한 금액을 명시한 서류를 보내주시기를 바랍니다. 이것은 ¹⁸⁰제가 제 여행 보험 제공업체인 Expedition Enhancers에게 이차적인 보상을 청구할 것이기 때문인데, 저는 서류가 제공될 경우에만 그렇게 할 수 있습니다.

Jane Rubenstein 드림

---

status n. 상태   classify v. 분류하다   compensation n. 보상
previous adj. 이전의   specify v. 명시하다   precise adj. 정확한
secondary adj. 이차적인   coverage n. 보상

---

176 육하원칙 문제   중 ●●○

해석 Ms. Rubenstein은 그녀의 여행 동안 어디에서 머무를 것인가?

(A) Yuksom에서
(B) Wichita에서
(C) Kansas City에서
(D) Gangtok에서

해설 양식의 'Address during the next month', 'Yuksom'에서 다음 달 동안의 주소가 Yuksom이라고 했으므로 (A)가 정답이다.

---

177 Not/True 문제   중 ●●○

해석 Ms. Rubenstein에 대해 사실이 아닌 것은?
(A) 수하물 수취 코드를 받았다.
(B) MA882 항공편의 승객이었다.
(C) East Harry가에 거주한다.
(D) 항공사로부터 보상 마일리지를 받는다.

해설 질문의 Ms. Rubenstein과 관련된 내용이 언급된 양식에서 (D)는 언급되지 않은 내용이다. 따라서 (D)가 정답이다. (A)는 'Baggage claim number', 'AJ8727TP'에서 수하물 수취 번호가 AJ8727TP임을 알 수 있으므로 지문의 내용과 일치한다. (B)는 'Flight number', 'MA882'에서 항공편 번호가 MA882임을 알 수 있으므로 지문의 내용과 일치한다. (C)는 'Permanent address', 'East Harry Street'에서 영구 주소지가 East Harry가에 있음을 알 수 있으므로 지문의 내용과 일치한다.

어휘 reside v. 거주하다, 살다   earn v. 받다, 얻다

패러프레이징

claim number 수취 번호 → claim code 수취 코드
Permanent address 영구 주소지 → resides on ~에 거주하다

---

178 추론 문제 연계   중 ●●○

해석 Ms. Rubenstein의 여행 가방에 대해 암시되는 것은?

(A) 출발 공항에 맡겨졌다.
(B) 제품 견본이 들어 있다.
(C) 15일 넘게 분실되었다.
(D) 개인 정보가 있는 이름표가 있다.

해설 ㅣ양식ㅣ의 'If ~ it has not been found after 15 days, it will be officially declared lost'에서 그것, 즉 수하물이 15일 후에 발견되지 않는다면, 공식적으로 분실되었다고 공표될 것이라고 했다. 또한, ㅣ이메일ㅣ의 'it is ~ officially classified as lost'에서는 그것, 즉 Ms. Rubenstein의 여행 가방이 공식적으로 분실되었다고 분류되었다고 했다.
두 단서를 종합할 때, Ms. Rubenstein의 여행 가방이 15일이 넘게 분실되었다는 사실을 추론할 수 있다. 따라서 (C)가 정답이다.

어휘 ㅣ **personal detail** phr. 개인정보

179 육하원칙 문제 상 ●●●

해석 ㅣ이메일에 따르면, Migoi 항공사는 무엇을 제공했는가?
(A) 정기적인 상태 업데이트
(B) 전용 라운지 출입
(C) 스캔된 금융 서류
(D) 숙박시설 상품권

해설 ㅣ이메일의 'Thank you for keeping me informed about the status of my ~ suitcase.'에서 여행 가방의 상태에 대한 정보를 계속 제공해주어서 감사하다고 했으므로 (A)가 정답이다.

어휘 ㅣ **regular** adj. 정기적인 **entry** n. 출입 **exclusive** adj. 전용의 **accommodation** n. 숙박시설 **voucher** n. 상품권

패러프레이징

keeping ~ informed about the status 상태에 대한 정보를 계속 제공하는 것
→ Regular status updates 정기적인 상태 업데이트

180 육하원칙 문제 중 ●●○

해석 ㅣ Ms. Rubenstein은 그녀가 무엇을 할 것이라고 말하는가?
(A) 다른 회사로부터 보상을 청구한다
(B) 분실된 물품들의 목록을 제공한다
(C) 공무원에게 불만을 제기한다
(D) 여행 가방의 설명서를 보낸다

해설 ㅣ이메일의 'I will be claiming secondary coverage from my travel insurance provider'에서 저, 즉 Ms. Rubenstein이 여행 보험 제공업체에게 이차적인 보상을 청구할 것이라고 했으므로 (A)가 정답이다.

어휘 ㅣ **ask for** phr. 청구하다 **payment** n. 보상, 지급 **government official** phr. 공무원 **luggage** n. 여행 가방, 수하물

181-185번은 다음 이메일과 영수증에 관한 문제입니다.

수신: Andrew Quintanar <a.quintanar@baudmail.com>
발신: Lynn Choi <l.choi@makerfoods.com>
제목: 불만 사항
날짜: 5월 1일
¹⁸³첨부: 상품권 a592900g

Mr. Quintanar께,

¹⁸¹/¹⁸²저는 귀하께서 Maker Foods사의 모바일 애플리케이션을 사용하여 제출하신 불만사항을 읽고 걱정을 하였습니다. 저희는 신뢰할 수 있는 포장 공정을 가지고 있으며, ¹⁸¹구매된 과자봉지가 거의 전부 공기로

가득찬 것으로 발견된 귀하의 것과 같은 경우들은, 정말 흔치 않습니다. 이 문제는 기계 결함에 의해 야기되었을 것이라고 예상됩니다.

귀하께 보상하기 위해, 저는 다양한 저희 회사의 제품들을 포함하는 소포를 보내드리고 싶습니다. 저희가 그것을 보낼 수 있는 주소를 제공해주십시오. 뿐만 아니라, 저는 ¹⁸³⁻ᴮ귀하께서 구매하셨던 상품인 Curly 감자칩으로 교환될 수 있는 상품권을 첨부했습니다. 그것은 또한 Fruit Chunks, Diet Puffs, 그리고 Galaxy Munchies를 포함한 저희의 다른 몇몇 상품에도 유효합니다. 비록 이 상품권에 유효기간은 없지만, ¹⁸³⁻ᴮ이것은 Shop Rich Group사의 소매망에 속한 가게에서만 받아들여질 것입니다.

Lynn Choi 드림
고객 서비스 직원

voucher n. 상품권 **concerned** adj. 걱정하는 **submit** v. 제출하다 **dependable** adj. 신뢰할 수 있는 **process** n. 공정 **unusual** adj. 흔치 않은 **likely** adv. ~할 것으로 예상되는 **compensate** v. 보상하다 **contain** v. 포함하다 **redeem** v. 교환하다, 상환하다 **good** adj. 유효한 **expiration date** phr. 유효기간 **belong** v. 속하다

¹⁸³⁻ᴮ**Gordon's Grocers**
당신의 부엌을 알맞은 가격으로 채우세요.
99구획, Bessell로
Baudin Beach, 사우스 오스트레일리아주 5222
+61 8 5553 6885

닭 날개 (2킬로그램)	5.78달러
아보카도 (680그램)	6.40달러
¹⁸³⁻ᴮCurly 감자칩 (1봉지)	¹⁸³⁻ᴮ무료 **상품권 a592900g**
참치 통조림 (4세트)	3.79달러
¹⁸⁴정상가격:	*3.99달러*
¹⁸⁴당신은 절약함:	*0.20달러*
소계:	15.97달러
세금:	1.76달러
합계:	17.73달러

5월 7일 오후 7시 48분
¹⁸⁵www.gordonsgrocers.au에 방문하셔서서
저희의 식료품 배달 서비스를 이용해보세요.
남은 하루 즐겁게 보내세요!

stock v. 채우다 **no charge** phr. 무료 **drop-off** n. 배달

181 육하원칙 문제 중 ●●○

해석 ㅣ Ms. Choi는 무엇에 대해 걱정하는가?
(A) 고객의 상품 관련 경험
(B) 쇼핑 애플리케이션의 인기
(C) 제조 과정의 감독
(D) 포장에 인쇄된 유효기간

해설 ㅣ이메일의 'I was concerned to read the complaint you submitted ~.'에서 저, 즉 Ms. Choi는 귀하, 즉 고객이 제출한 불만 사항을 읽고 걱정을 했다고 했고, 'cases like yours, where a purchased bag of snacks is ~ entirely full of air'에서 구매된 과자봉지가 전부 공기로 가득 찬 귀하의 것과 같은 경우들이라고 했으므로 (A)가 정답이다.

어휘 ㅣ **popularity** n. 인기 **supervision** n. 감독 **manufacturing** n. 제조

182 추론 문제   중 ●●●○

해석 Mr. Quintanar는 어떻게 문제를 알렸을 것 같은가?

(A) 고객 서비스 센터에 전화함으로써

(B) 온라인 양식을 작성함으로써

(C) 의견 카드를 제출함으로써

(D) 안내 데스크에 방문함으로써

해설 이메일의 'I ~ read the complaint you submitted using ~ mobile application.'에서 귀하 즉, Mr. Quintanar가 모바일 애플리케이션을 사용하여 제출한 불만 사항을 읽었다고 했으므로 Mr. Quintanar가 온라인 양식을 작성함으로써 문제를 알렸을 것이라는 사실을 추론할 수 있다. 따라서 (B)가 정답이다.

어휘 complete v. 작성하다, 완료하다

183 Not/True 문제 연계   상 ●●●

해석 Gordon's Grocers에 대해 언급된 것은?

(A) 다수의 지점을 설립했다.

(B) Shop Rich Group사의 일부이다.

(C) 주말에는 오후 8시에 문을 닫는다.

(D) Maker Foods사의 간식을 홍보하고 있다.

해설 영수증의 'Gordon's Grocers', 'Curly Chips (1 bag)', 'no charge **voucher a592900g**'에서 상품권 a592900g가 Gordon's Grocers에서 Curly 감자칩 1봉지를 구매하는 데 사용되었다고 했다. 또한, 이메일의 'Attachment: voucher a592900g'와 'a voucher that may be redeemed for ~, Curly Chips'에서 Curly 감자칩으로 교환될 수 있는 상품권 a592900g라고 했고, 'it will only be accepted by a store that belongs to the retail network Shop Rich Group'에서 이것, 즉 상품권이 Shop Rich Group사의 소매망에 속한 가게에서만 받아들여질 것이라고 했음을 확인할 수 있다.

두 단서를 종합할 때, Gordon's Grocers가 Shop Rich Group사의 소매망에 속하는 일부임을 알 수 있다. 따라서 (B)가 정답이다. (A), (C), (D)는 지문에 언급되지 않은 내용이다.

어휘 establish v. 설립하다 multiple adj. 다수의 branch n. 지점

패러프레이징

belongs to ~에 속하다 → is part of ~의 일부이다

184 육하원칙 문제   중 ●●○

해석 거래 동안 무엇이 일어났는가?

(A) 상품권이 음료로 교환되었다.

(B) 신용카드가 지불을 위해 사용되었다.

(C) 상품에 할인이 적용되었다.

(D) 판매세가 잘못 계산되었다.

해설 영수증의 'Normal price: $3.99', 'You save: $0.20'에서 정상가격이 3.99달러이고 절약한 금액이 0.20달러라고 했으므로 (C)가 정답이다.

어휘 transaction n. 거래, 처리 exchange v. 교환하다 apply v. 적용하다
sales tax phr. 판매세 incorrectly adv. 잘못

패러프레이징

save 절약하다 → discount 할인

185 육하원칙 문제   중 ●●○

해석 영수증에 따르면, 쇼핑객들은 Gordon's Grocers 웹사이트에서 무엇을 할 수

있는가?

(A) 가게의 역사에 대해 배운다

(B) 일자리를 찾는다

(C) 가정 배달 일정을 잡는다

(D) 홍보 상품들을 훑어본다

해설 영수증의 'Visit www.gordonsgrocers.au to use our grocery drop-off service.'에서 웹사이트에 방문하여 식료품 배달 서비스를 이용해보라고 했으므로 (C)가 정답이다.

어휘 job vacancy phr. 일자리 schedule v. 일정을 잡다
browse v. 훑어보다 promotional adj. 홍보의

패러프레이징

use ~ drop-off service 배달 서비스를 이용하다 → Schedule a home delivery 가정 배달 일정을 잡다

186-190번은 다음 웹사이트, 이메일, 회람에 관한 문제입니다.

www.oakbaycenter.com

Oak Bay 레크리에이션 센터

| 홈 | 소개 | 시설 | 수업 | 예약 |

6월 15일부터 7월 20일까지, 저희는 모든 수준의 학생들에게 수영 수업을 제공할 것입니다.

수업	설명	강사	일정
[187]파랑	[187]완전한 초보자들이 기본적인 수영 기술을 배울 것입니다.	Beth Park	화요일 / 목요일 오후 6시-오후 7시
초록	중급 수영을 하는 사람들이 자유형과 배영을 연습할 것입니다.	Brett Harford	토요일 / 일요일 오전 9시-오전 10시
노랑	평영과 같은 중상급 기술들이 가르쳐질 것입니다.	Denise Porter	월요일 / 수요일 오후 3시-오후 4시
빨강	숙련된 수영을 하는 사람들이 그들의 기술을 향상시킬 수 있는 기회	[189]Carl Hong	[189]토요일 / 일요일 오후 6시 30분-오후 7시 30분

등록하시기 위해서는, 안내 데스크를 방문하셔서 신청 양식을 작성해주십시오. 문의 사항이 있으시면, 당신은 프로그램 진행자 David Williams에게 555-0398로 연락하시거나 d.williams@oakbaycenter.com으로 이메일을 보내주실 수 있습니다.

complete adj. 완전한 low-intermediate adj. 중급의
high-intermediate adj. 중상급의 skilled adj. 숙련된
inquiry n. 문의 사항

발신: Hanna Donaldson <h.donaldson@digital.com>
수신: David Williams <d.williams@oakbaycenter.com>
날짜: 6월 1일
제목: 수영 수업

Mr. Williams께,

제가 수업을 등록하는 것을 도와주셔서 감사드립니다. 저는 몇 가지 후속 질문들이 있습니다. 물품 보관함의 대여 비용이 요금에 포함되어 있나요? [186]저는 제 사무실에서 수영장으로 곧바로 갈 예정이기 때문에, 저는 제 소지품들을 보관할 수 있는 장소가 필요합니다. 또한, 저는 개인 수업을 예약하는 것이 가능한지 궁금합니다. 제 가족은 8월에 해변으로 여행을 갈 것입니다. [187]저는 이전에 수영을 한 번도 해본 적이 없기 때문에, 저는 제가 등록

한 수업이 바다에서 수영하는 것에 대해 저를 준비시키기에 충분하지 않을까 봐 걱정이 됩니다. 감사합니다.

Hanna Donaldson 드림

register v. 등록하다 follow-up adj. 후속의 straight adv. 곧바로
belonging n. 소지품 arrange v. 예약하다 prepare v. 준비시키다

회람

수신: 전 직원
발신: Maria Gomez
날짜: 5월 25일
제목: 운영 시간

Oak Bay 레크리에이션 센터의 ¹⁸⁸운영 시간은 여름 동안 연장될 것입니다. 6월 10일부터 8월 31까지, 저희는 매일 1시간 늦게 문을 닫을 예정입니다:

월요일에서 화요일: 오전 8시 30분 – 오후 8시
금요일: 오전 8시 30분 – 오후 9시 30분
토요일: 오전 8시 – 오후 10시
¹⁸⁸일요일: 오전 8시 – 오후 9시

¹⁸⁸이 기간 동안 있는 국가공휴일의 경우, 저희는 일요일 일정을 따를 것입니다. 또한, ¹⁸⁹토요일과 일요일 저녁의 수업이 원래 계획된 것보다 1시간 늦게 시작할 것이라는 것을 유의해 주십시오. 이러한 변화를 그들에게 알리기 위해 ¹⁹⁰다음 주 월요일에 등록된 모든 학생에게 이메일이 보내질 것입니다.

operation n. 운영 extend v. 연장하다
national holiday phr. 국가 공휴일 occur v. 있다, 발생하다

186 추론 문제 중 ●●○

해석 Ms. Donaldson에 대해 암시되는 것은?
(A) 바다 근처에 산다.
(B) 현재 고용된 상태이다.
(C) 물품 보관함을 대여하였다.
(D) Mr. Williams에게 전화를 할 것이다.

해설 이메일의 'I will be coming to the pool straight from my office'에서 저, 즉 Ms. Donaldson이 자신의 사무실에서 수영장으로 곧바로 갈 예정이라고 했으므로 Ms. Donaldson이 현재 고용된 상태라는 사실을 추론할 수 있다. 따라서 (B)가 정답이다.

187 추론 문제 연계 중 ●●○

해석 Ms. Donaldson은 어떤 수업을 등록했을 것 같은가?
(A) 파랑
(B) 초록
(C) 노랑
(D) 빨강

해설 이메일의 'I've never tried swimming before'에서 저, 즉 Ms. Donaldson은 이전에 수영을 한 번도 해본 적이 없다고 했다. 또한, 웹사이트의 'Blue', 'Complete beginners'에서는 파랑 수업이 완전한 초보자들을 대상으로 한다고 했다.
두 단서를 종합할 때, Ms. Donaldson은 파랑 수업을 등록했을 것이라는 사실을 추론할 수 있다. 따라서 (A)가 정답이다.

패러프레이징

never tried 한 번도 해본 적이 없다 → complete beginners 완전한 초보자들

188 육하원칙 문제 상 ●●●

해석 여름 동안 국가공휴일에 수영장은 어떤 시간에 닫을 것인가?
(A) 오후 8시에
(B) 오후 9시에
(C) 오후 9시 30분에
(D) 오후 10시에

해설 회람의 'hours of operation will be extended for the summer'와 'Sunday: 8:00 A.M. – 9:00 P.M.'에서 운영 시간이 여름 동안 연장될 것이며 일요일에는 오전 8시부터 오후 9시까지 운영한다고 했고, 'For national holidays ~ during this period, we will follow the Sunday schedule.'에서 이 기간, 즉 여름 동안의 국가 공휴일의 경우, 일요일 일정을 따를 것이라고 했으므로 (B)가 정답이다.

최고난도 문제

189 육하원칙 문제 연계 상 ●●●

해석 어느 강사의 수업 일정이 변경되었는가?
(A) Beth Park의 것
(B) Brett Harford의 것
(C) Denise Porter의 것
(D) Carl Hong의 것

해설 회람의 'classes on Saturday and Sunday evenings will start one hour later than originally planned'에서 토요일과 일요일 저녁의 수업이 원래 계획된 것보다 1시간 늦게 시작할 것이라고 했다. 또한, 웹사이트의 'Carl Hong', 'Saturdays / Sundays 6:30 P.M. – 7:30 P.M'에서는 Carl Hong 강사의 수업이 토요일과 일요일 저녁에 진행된다는 사실을 확인할 수 있다.
두 단서를 종합할 때, 토요일과 일요일 저녁의 수업인 Carl Hong 강사의 수업 일정이 변경되었다는 것을 알 수 있다. 따라서 (D)가 정답이다.

패러프레이징

has been rescheduled 일정이 변경되었다 → will start one hour later than originally planned 원래 계획된 것보다 1시간 늦게 시작할 것이다

190 육하원칙 문제 상 ●●●

해석 회람에 따르면, 다음 주에 무슨 일이 일어날 것인가?
(A) 일정이 갱신될 것이다.
(B) 강사들이 배정될 것이다.
(C) 학생들이 연락을 받을 것이다.
(D) 시설이 점검될 것이다.

해설 회람의 'An e-mail will be sent to all registered students next Monday'에서 다음 주 월요일에 등록된 모든 학생들에게 이메일이 보내질 것이라고 했으므로 (C)가 정답이다.

어휘 update v. 갱신하다 assign v. 배정하다 inspect v. 점검하다

패러프레이징

An e-mail will be sent to ~ students 학생들에게 이메일이 보내질 것이다
→ Students will be contacted 학생들이 연락을 받을 것이다

수신: Windfield 미술관 직원 <staff@windfieldart.com>
발신: Martina Klancy <m.klancy@windfieldart.com>
제목: 조각품들을 다루는 것
날짜: 11월 23일

안녕하세요, 여러분.

우리 미술관이 다음 달 다수의 조각품들을 전시할 것이기 때문에, 모두가 어떻게 이러한 유형의 미술품을 다루는지에 대해 아는 것이 중요합니다. 다음 지시사항을 주목해주시기 바랍니다:

1. 어떤 조각품이든 다루기 전에 보호용 천 장갑을 착용해주십시오.
2. 관리 벽장에 보관된 청소용 스프레이를 사용하여 조각된 작품들의 밑 부분을 닦아 주십시오. 이것은 목요일 오후에 완료되어야 합니다. 미술관 방문자들에게 예술작품이 청소되거나 닦이는 동안에는 이것이 보여질 수 없다고 알려주십시오.
3. ¹⁹¹무게가 15킬로그램 이상 나가는 모든 작품들은 미술관을 통과하여 **이동되기 전에 손수레 위에 놓여야 합니다.** 더 가벼운 예술 작품들은 장갑이 착용되어 있는 한 손으로 옮겨질 수 있습니다.
4. ¹⁹⁵Fragile Hands와 같이 매우 귀중한 작품들은 유리 상자 안에 넣어져야 합니다. 이 상자들은 미술관이 가장 덜 바쁜 때인 **목요일 아침에 닦여야 합니다.**

만약 질문이 있으면, 주저 말고 언제든지 제 사무실로 방문해주십시오.

Martina Klancy 드림
소유주, Windfield 미술관

handle v. 다루다 sculpture n. 조각품 exhibit v. 전시하다
protective adj. 보호용의 wipe down phr. ~을 닦다 base n. 밑 부분
maintenance n. 관리, 유지 dust v. 닦다 transport v. 옮기다
relocate v. 옮기다 valuable adj. 귀중한 enclose v. 넣다

Windfield 미술관

미술관 방문객들은 저희 건물이 내일 11월 25일부터 11월 29일 금요일까지 문을 닫을 것임을 아셔야 합니다. 이번 폐쇄는 ¹⁹²**최근 나이지리아로부터 우리의 시설에 도착한 Kali Adisa에 의해 만들어진 조각품들의 설치를 수용하기** 위해 일어나는 것입니다. 저희가 준비를 완료하는 동안 여러분들의 인내심에 감사드립니다.

이 기간 동안, 저희는 저희의 고객들이 Ms. Adisa의 12월 전시회에 대한 정보를 저희의 모바일 애플리케이션에서 보는 것을 권장드립니다. ¹⁹⁴**예매권은 오직 애플리케이션을 통해서만 할인된 가격에 이용 가능합니다.** ¹⁹³저희 미술관의 겨울 전시회에 대한 팸플릿도 미술관 정문에 부착된 투입구에서 가져가실 수 있습니다.

¹⁹⁴Martina Klancy
소유주, Windfield 미술관

closure n. 폐쇄 accommodate v. 수용하다 installation n. 설치
facility n. 시설 arrangement n. 준비 patron n. 고객, 후원자
exhibition n. 전시 advance ticket phr. 예매권
exclusively adv. 오직 slot n. 투입구 attached adj. 부착된

수신: Martina Klancy <m.klancy@windfieldart.com>
발신: Joshua Nero <j.nero@brexfordmuseum.org>
제목: 지난주의 방문
날짜: 12월 16일

Ms. Klancy께,

저는 지난주 당신의 미술관에서의 Kali Adisa 전시회의 성공에 대해 축하하고 싶습니다. 저는 ¹⁹⁴**제가 할인된 가격에 전시 티켓을 구매하라는 당신의 권유를 받아들인 것**이 기뻤습니다. 전반적으로, 저는 Ms. Adisa의 작품에 감명을 받았습니다. 그것들은 현대 나이지리아 예술의 훌륭한 표현입니다.

그러나, 저는 비평가들로부터 들었던 한 작품인 ¹⁹⁵Fragile Hands가 제가 방문한 날 그것의 상자가 닦이고 있어서 이용 가능하지 않았다는 것에 실망했습니다. 다행히, 제가 구매한 티켓이 며칠 동안의 입장을 포함하고 있어서, 나중에 다시 와서 그 작품을 보는 것을 계획할 것입니다.

다시 한번 더 축하드리며, 저는 다음 주 금요일 저희의 기금 모금 행사에서 당신을 뵙길 기대합니다.

Joshua Nero 드림
큐레이터, Brexford 미술관

delighted adj. 기쁜 recommendation n. 권유 representation n. 표현
contemporary adj. 현대의 critic n. 비평가 luckily adv. 다행히
admission n. 입장 fund-raiser n. 기금 모금 행사

---

191 육하원칙 문제   중 ●●○

해석 직원들은 무게가 15킬로그램이 넘는 조각상들에 대해 무엇을 해야 하는가?
(A) 미술관의 바닥에 그것들을 둔다
(B) 그것들을 옮기기 위해 장비를 사용한다
(C) 2주에 한 번 청소용 스프레이를 바른다
(D) 손으로 그것들을 들어 올릴 때 장갑을 착용한다

해설 이메일1의 'Any pieces weighing more than 15 kilograms must be placed on a cart before being transported'에서 무게가 15킬로그램 이상 나가는 모든 작품들은 이동되기 전에 손수레 위에 놓여야 한다고 했으므로 (B)가 정답이다.

어휘 apply v. 바르다 lift v. 들어 올리다

패러프레이징

cart 손수레 → equipment 장비
being transported 이동되는 것 → move 옮기다

---

192 육하원칙 문제   상 ●●●

해석 공고에 따르면, 최근에 무슨 일이 있었는가?
(A) 몇몇 기능들이 모바일 애플리케이션에 추가되었다.
(B) 조각가가 전시에 대한 일련의 강의를 하였다.
(C) 몇몇 작품들이 다른 나라로부터 전달되었다.
(D) 미술관이 고객들에게 영구적인 폐쇄를 알렸다.

해설 공고의 'sculptures ~ recently arrived at our facility from Nigeria'에서 최근 나이지리아로부터 우리의 시설에 조각품들이 도착했다고 했으므로 (C)가 정답이다.

어휘 feature n. 기능 a series of phr. 일련의 lecture n. 강의
permanent adj. 영구적인 closure n. 폐쇄

패러프레이징

sculptures 조각품들 → works 작품들
arrived at ~ facility from Nigeria 나이지리아로부터 시설에 도착했다 → were delivered from another country 다른 나라로부터 전달되었다

193 육하원칙 문제　　　　　　　　　　중 ●●○

해석　Windfield 미술관의 정문에서 무엇이 이용 가능한가?
　　　(A) 할인 쿠폰
　　　(B) 정보 소책자
　　　(C) 미술품 사진
　　　(D) 예매권

해설　공고의 'Pamphlets about ~ exhibitions can ~ be picked up from the slot attached to our gallery's front door.'에서 전시회에 대한 팸플릿이 미술관 정문에 부착된 투입구에서 가져가질 수 있다고 했으므로 (B)가 정답이다.

어휘　print n. 사진

패러프레이징

Pamphlets about ~ exhibitions 전시회에 대한 팸플릿 → Informational booklets 정보 소책자

194 육하원칙 문제　연계　　　　　　　상 ●●●

해석　Ms. Klancy는 Mr. Nero에게 무엇을 권유했는가?
　　　(A) 더 적은 사람들이 있는 날에 시설을 방문하는 것
　　　(B) 인기 있는 조각품들의 몇몇 사진을 찍는 것
　　　(C) 전시회에 관해 몇몇 예술 비평가들과 이야기를 하는 것
　　　(D) 입장권을 구매하기 위해 모바일 애플리케이션을 사용하는 것

해설　이메일2의 'I took your recommendation to purchase tickets ~ at a reduced price'에서 저, 즉 Mr. Nero가 할인된 가격에 전시 티켓을 구매하라는 당신, 즉 Ms. Klancy의 권유를 받아들였다고 했다. 또한, 공고의 'Advance tickets are available at a discounted rate exclusively through the application.'과 'Martina Klancy'에서는 예매권은 오직 애플리케이션을 통해서만 할인된 가격에 이용 가능하다고 알리는 공고를 Ms. Klancy가 작성했음을 알 수 있다.
　　　두 단서를 종합할 때, Ms. Klancy는 Mr. Nero에게 모바일 애플리케이션을 사용하여 입장권을 구매하는 것을 추천했음을 알 수 있다. 따라서 (D)가 정답이다.

어휘　pass n. 입장권

최고난도 문제

195 추론 문제　연계　　　　　　　　상 ●●●

해석　Mr. Nero는 언제 Kali Adisa 전시회를 봤을 것 같은가?
　　　(A) 목요일 아침에
　　　(B) 목요일 오후에
　　　(C) 금요일 아침에
　　　(D) 금요일 오후에

해설　이메일2의 'Fragile Hands—was not available on the day I visited because its case was being dusted off'에서 Mr. Nero가 방문한 날 Fragile Hands가 그것의 상자가 닦이고 있어서 이용 가능하지 않았다고 했다. 또한, 이메일1의 'Highly valuable pieces, such as Fragile Hands, need to be enclosed in glass cases. These cases must be dusted on Thursday mornings'에서는 Fragile Hands와 같이 매우 귀중한 작품들은 유리 상자 안에 넣어져야 하며 목요일 아침에 닦여야 한다고 한 사실을 확인할 수 있다.
　　　두 단서를 종합할 때, Mr. Nero는 Fragile Hands의 상자가 닦였던 목요일 아침에 Kali Adisa 전시회를 봤다는 사실을 추론할 수 있다. 따라서 (A)가 정답이다.

196-200번은 다음 두 이메일과 소식지 기사에 관한 문제입니다.

[198]수신: Leroy Stark <l.stark@realtouchphotography.com>
발신: Amanda Verona <a.verona@realtouchphotography.com>
[196]날짜: 5월 17일
제목: 질문

안녕하세요 Leroy,

저는 [196]RealTouch 사진 스튜디오에서 제가 어제 막 일하기 시작했다는 것을 알지만, 저는 한 고객으로부터 벌써 예약을 받았습니다! 제가 사진 촬영을 할 행사는 6월 2일의 CiteBook 출판회사의 제15회 연례 직원 시상식입니다. 제가 당신에게 이메일을 보내는 이유는 제가 이 작업에 대해 CiteBook 사에 얼마를 청구해야 하는지 알기 위해서입니다. 당신은 어느 정도가 적절할 것인지 아십니까?

[197]이 행사는 네 시간 동안 진행될 것이지만, CiteBook사의 최고경영자는 제가 마지막 두 시간 동안만 사진을 찍어주면 된다고 합니다. 또한, [198]당신이 작년에 이 행사에서 촬영을 했고 이것이 같은 장소에서 열릴 것이기 때문에, 당신은 그 장소가 제가 현장에서 필요할 모든 적절한 조명과 장비들을 갖추고 있는지 아십니까?

Amanda 드림

shoot a photo phr. 촬영을 하다　bill v. 청구하다
appropriate adj. 적절한　venue n. 장소　lighting n. 조명

수신: Amanda Verona <a.verona@realtouchphotography.com>
[200]발신: Patrick Chen <pat_chen@citebook.com>
제목: 다음 주의 행사
[200]날짜: 5월 25일

[200]Ms. Verona께,

[200]저희의 다가오는 직원 시상식에서 사진을 찍는 것에 동의해주셔서 감사드립니다. 저는 당신께 단지 몇 가지만 상기시켜 드리고 싶습니다. 첫 번째로, [199]반드시 오후 6시에 도착해서 촬영을 위해 예약된 장소를 준비하는 것을 시작해주십시오. 저는 당신이 오후 7시부터 9시까지만 촬영을 할 것임을 알지만, 저희는 오후 7시에 신속하게 저희의 경영진들을 촬영하고 싶기 때문에 저는 당신이 예정보다 일찍 그곳에 있을 것을 확실하게 하고 싶습니다.

또한, [198]당신이 필요할 조명과 장비들은 Rosewood홀에 모두 설치되어야 합니다. 추가적인 무엇이든지 들고 오는 것에 대해 걱정하지 마십시오. 행사 동안 질문이 있으시다면, 제가 이 행사의 모든 것을 감독하는 것을 담당하고 있으므로, 제 핸드폰으로 555-9233으로 문자 메시지를 보내주십시오.

[200]6월 2일에 뵙기를 기대하겠습니다.

Patrick Chen 드림
행사 계획자
CiteBook사

upcoming adj. 다가오는　reserved adj. 예약된
ahead of time phr. 예정보다 일찍　executive n. 경영진
promptly adv. 신속하게　ensure v. 확실하게 하다　set up v. 설치하다
in charge of phr. 담당하다

CiteBook사 소식지

직원 시상식이 성공적이었다
Fiona Walsh 작성

7월 1일 — 지난달의 연례 직원 시상식은 대성공이었습니다. 최고경영자가 몇몇 직원들에게 지난 겨울의 전자책 소셜미디어 캠페인 작업에 대해 메달을 나누어주는 것과 함께 무수한 상들이 수여되었습니다.

²⁰⁰행사 계획자 Patrick Chen 또한 5월에 원래 그가 예약했던 사람이 아파서 마지막 순간에 대체 사진사를 찾으며, 훌륭하게 일을 해냈습니다. 그 사진사는 각 부서의 직원들뿐만 아니라 우리의 경영진들의 훌륭한 사진을 촬영했습니다. 행사의 사진들을 보시려면, 회사 네트워크로 여기 링크를 따라가십시오.

countless adj. 무수한 distribute v. 나누어주다
at the last minute phr. 마지막 순간에 originally adv. 원래

196 추론 문제 · 상 ●●●

해석 RealTouch 사진 스튜디오에 대해 암시되는 것은?
(A) 소셜 미디어 페이지를 게시했다.
(B) 올해 기념행사를 개최할 것이다.
(C) 5월에 새로운 직원을 고용했다.
(D) 다시 이용하는 고객들에게 할인을 제공한다.

해설 이메일1의 'Date: May 17'에서 이메일이 5월 17일에 쓰였음을 알 수 있고, 'I just started working at RealTouch Photography Studio yesterday'에서 저, 즉 Ms. Verona가 RealTouch 사진 스튜디오에서 어제 막 일하기 시작했다고 했으므로 RealTouch 사진 스튜디오가 5월에 새로운 직원을 고용했다는 사실을 추론할 수 있다. 따라서 (C)가 정답이다.

어휘 launch v. 개시하다 anniversary adj. 기념의 discount n. 할인

197 육하원칙 문제 · 중 ●●○

해석 CiteBook사 시상식은 얼마 동안 지속할 것인가?
(A) 2시간 동안
(B) 3시간 동안
(C) 4시간 동안
(D) 5시간 동안

해설 이메일1의 'The event will last for four hours'에서 이 행사 즉, CiteBook사 시상식은 네 시간 동안 진행될 것이라고 했으므로 (C)가 정답이다.

패러프레이징

ceremony 시상식 → event 행사

198 추론 문제 연계 · 상 ●●●

해석 Mr. Stark에 대해 암시되는 것은?
(A) 장소에 몇몇 조명 장비를 가지고 올 것이다.
(B) 작년에 Rosewood 홀에서 몇몇 사진을 찍었다.
(C) Ms. Verona의 교육을 맡고 있다.
(D) CiteBook사의 전자책 상품들과 익숙하다.

해설 이메일1의 'To: Leroy Stark'에서 이메일의 수신자가 Mr. Stark임을 알 수 있고, 'you shot photos at this event last year and it's being held in the same venue'에서 당신, 즉 Mr. Stark가 작년에 이 행사에서 촬영을 했고 이것이 같은 장소에서 열릴 것이라고 했다. 또한, 이메일2의 'the lighting ~ you'll need should be all set up in Rosewood Hall'에서는 당신, 즉 Ms. Verona가 사진 촬영에 필요할 조명은 Rosewood홀에 모두 설치되어야 한다고 했다.
두 단서를 종합할 때, Mr. Stark가 작년에 이번 행사와 동일한 장소인 Rosewood홀에서 사진을 찍었다는 사실을 추론할 수 있다. 따라서 (B)가 정답이다.

어휘 be responsible for phr. ~을 맡고 있다

패러프레이징

shot photos 촬영을 했다 → took some pictures 사진을 찍었다

199 동의어 찾기 문제 · 상 ●●●

해석 두 번째 이메일에서, 1문단 두 번째 줄의 표현 "show up"은 의미상 –와 가장 가깝다.
(A) 안내하다
(B) 전시하다
(C) 도착하다
(D) 감명을 주다

해설 이메일2의 show up을 포함한 구절 'please ~ show up and start preparing ~ at 6 P.M.'에서 오후 6시에 도착해서 준비하는 것을 시작해달라고 했으므로 show up은 '도착하다'라는 뜻으로 사용되었다. 따라서 '도착하다'라는 뜻을 가진 (C) arrive가 정답이다.

최고난도 문제

200 육하원칙 문제 연계 · 상 ●●●

해석 기사에 따르면, 6월 2일에 무슨 일이 있었는가?
(A) Ms. Verona가 병으로 작업할 수가 없었다.
(B) 마케팅 직원들이 향후의 캠페인을 공개했다.
(C) Mr. Chen이 오후 7시에 경영진들과 사진 촬영을 했다.
(D) CiteBook사의 최고경영자가 직원들에게 상금을 나누어주었다.

해설 이메일2의 'FROM: Patrick Chen', 'DATE: May 25', 'Dear Ms. Verona', 'Thank you for agreeing to take some photographs at our upcoming staff awards ceremony.'에서 5월 25일에 쓰인 이메일에서 이메일 수신자인 Ms. Verona가 직원 시상식에 사진을 찍어주는 것에 동의해주어 이메일 발신자인 Mr. Chen이 감사하다고 했고, 'I look forward to seeing you on June 2.'에서 6월 2일에 Ms. Verona를 보기를 기대하겠다고 했다. 또한, 소식지 기사의 'Event planner Patrick Chen ~ finding a replacement photographer at the last minute because the one he had originally booked back in May was sick.'에서는 행사 계획자인 Mr. Chen이 5월에 원래 예약했던 사람이 아파서 마지막 순간에 대체 사진사를 찾았다는 사실을 확인할 수 있다.
두 단서를 종합할 때, Mr. Chen이 5월에 예약했던 Ms. Verona가 6월 2일에 병으로 작업할 수가 없었다는 것을 알 수 있다. 따라서 (A)가 정답이다.

어휘 due to phr. ~으로, 때문에 illness n. 병 unveil v. 공개하다
cash prize phr. 상금

PART 5

101 (A)	102 (D)	103 (C)	104 (B)	105 (B)
106 (D)	107 (B)	108 (C)	109 (B)	110 (C)
111 (C)	112 (D)	113 (B)	114 (B)	115 (D)
116 (B)	117 (D)	118 (B)	119 (D)	120 (D)
121 (B)	122 (D)	123 (D)	124 (B)	125 (C)
126 (A)	127 (C)	128 (C)	129 (C)	130 (D)

PART 6

131 (D)	132 (A)	133 (A)	134 (C)	135 (D)
136 (D)	137 (D)	138 (B)	139 (C)	140 (C)
141 (C)	142 (C)	143 (C)	144 (D)	145 (D)
146 (A)				

PART 7

147 (C)	148 (B)	149 (D)	150 (D)	151 (D)
152 (C)	153 (B)	154 (B)	155 (D)	156 (B)
157 (D)	158 (C)	159 (B)	160 (D)	161 (C)
162 (C)	163 (A)	164 (A)	165 (C)	166 (B)
167 (D)	168 (B)	169 (D)	170 (C)	171 (B)
172 (D)	173 (A)	174 (B)	175 (B)	176 (B)
177 (A)	178 (D)	179 (B)	180 (D)	181 (D)
182 (B)	183 (C)	184 (A)	185 (D)	186 (D)
187 (A)	188 (D)	189 (D)	190 (A)	191 (B)
192 (A)	193 (B)	194 (D)	195 (A)	196 (B)
197 (B)	198 (A)	199 (B)	200 (D)	

PART 5

101 조동사 다음에 동사원형 채우기   중 ●●○

해석 훌륭한 발표자들은 대개 사람들의 기분을 감지할 수 있고 그에 따라 그들의 말투를 바꿀 수 있다.

해설 조동사(can) 다음에 올 수 있는 것은 동사원형이므로 동사원형 (A) sense가 정답이다. 동사 또는 과거분사 (B), 동명사 또는 현재분사 (C), 부사 (D)는 조동사 다음의 동사원형 자리에 올 수 없다.

어휘 mood n. 기분, 분위기 tone n. 말투, 어조 accordingly adv. 그에 따라
sense v. 감지하다; n. 감각 sensibly adv. 현명하게, 현저히

102 격에 맞는 인칭대명사 채우기   하 ●○○

해석 Ms. Paget의 항공편은 월요일 밤이 되어서야 도착해서, 그녀는 회의를 옮기

는 것을 요청했다.

해설 so로 시작하는 절(so ~ moved)에 동사(asked)만 있고 주어가 없으므로 주어 자리에 올 수 있는 소유대명사 (C)와 주격 인칭대명사 (D)가 정답의 후보이다. '그녀는 회의를 옮기는 것을 요청했다'라는 문맥이므로 주격 인칭대명사 (D) she(그녀)가 정답이다. 소유대명사 (C)를 쓸 경우 '그녀의 것은 회의를 옮기는 것을 요청했다'라는 어색한 문맥이 된다. 목적격 인칭대명사 (A)와 재귀대명사 (B)는 주어 자리에 올 수 없다.

어휘 flight n. 항공편, 비행

103 to 부정사의 in order to 채우기   중 ●●●

해석 Hartman Motors사는 경쟁력을 유지하기 위해 그것의 가격들을 상당히 낮추었다.

해설 이 문장은 주어(Hartman Motors), 동사(lowered), 목적어(its prices)를 갖춘 완전한 절이므로, ___ ~ competitive는 수식어 거품으로 보아야 한다. 따라서 수식어 거품을 이끌 수 있는 모든 보기가 정답의 후보이다. 이 수식어 거품은 동사(stay)만 있고 주어가 없으며 '경쟁력을 유지하기 위해'라는 의미가 되어야 하므로, 목적을 나타내는 to 부정사를 만들기 위해 동사원형(stay) 앞에 to가 와야 한다. 따라서 목적을 나타내는 to 부정사 대신 쓸 수 있는 (C) in order to(~하기 위해)가 정답이다. 부사절 접속사 (A)는 뒤에 주어와 동사를 갖춘 완전한 절이 와야 한다. 전치사 (B)와 (D)는 뒤에 명사가 와야 한다. 참고로, to 부정사가 목적을 나타낼 때는 to 대신 in order to나 so as to를 쓸 수 있음을 알아둔다.

어휘 lower v. 낮추다 significantly adv. 상당히 now that phr. ~이므로
on account of phr. ~때문에 in spite of phr. ~에도 불구하고

104 형용사 어휘 고르기   중 ●●○

해석 냉동실은 고기의 신선도를 보존하는 이상적인 보관 상태를 유지한다.

해설 빈칸은 복합 명사(storage conditions)를 꾸미는 형용사 자리이다. '냉동실은 신선도를 보존하는 이상적인 보관 상태를 유지한다'라는 문맥이므로 (B) ideal(이상적인)이 정답이다.

어휘 freezer n. 냉동실 maintain v. 유지하다
storage condition phr. 보관 상태 low adj. 낮은 visible adj. 보이는
sincere adj. 성실한

105 시간 표현과 일치하는 시제의 동사 채우기   중 ●●○

해석 합병은 지난 2년 동안 협상 중에 있어 왔지만, 곧 완료될 것 같다.

해설 but 앞의 절(The merger ~ years)에 주어(The merger)만 있고 동사가 없으므로 동사 (B), (C), (D)가 정답의 후보이다. 현재 완료를 나타내는 시간 표현(for the past two years)이 있으므로 과거에 발생한 일이 현재까지 영향을 미치거나 방금 완료된 것을 표현할 때 사용되는 현재 완료 시제 (B) has been이 정답이다. 미래 시제 (C)와 현재 진행 시제 (D)는 현재 완료 시간 표현과 함께 쓰일 수 없다. to 부정사 (A)는 동사 자리에 올 수 없다.

어휘 merger n. 합병 negotiation n. 협상
close to phr. 곧 ~할 것 같은, ~에 가까운 conclude v. 완료하다

106 수, 태, 시제가 맞는 동사 채우기   중 ●●○

해석   Greenvale 병원의 많은 자선 프로그램들은 넉넉한 보조금으로 지원되고 있다.

해설   문장에 동사가 없으므로, 동사 (A)와 (D)가 정답의 후보이다. 주어(Many of ~ programs)가 복수이고, 동사 support(지원하다, 지지하다)가 타동사인데 빈칸 뒤에 목적어가 없으므로 복수 동사이면서 수동태인 (D) are being supported가 정답이다. 단수 동사 (A)는 복수 주어와 함께 쓰일 수 없다. to 부정사 (B)와 동명사 또는 현재분사 (C)는 동사 자리에 올 수 없다.

어휘   charitable adj. 자선의, 자선을 베푸는   generous adj. 넉넉한, 관대한
grant n. 보조금

107 전치사 채우기   중 ●●○

해석   수송품은 그것의 품질을 확인하기 위해 창고 직원들에 의해 검사되고 있다.

해설   빈칸은 명사구(warehouse personnel)를 목적어로 취하는 전치사 자리이다. '창고 직원들에 의해 검사되고 있다'라는 의미가 되어야 하므로 전치사 (B) by(~에 의해)가 정답이다.

어휘   shipment n. 수송품, 발송   examine v. 검사하다, 조사하다
warehouse n. 창고   personnel n. 직원들   quality n. 품질
in prep. ~에   at prep. ~에서   over prep. ~위에, ~너머로

108 명사 관련 어구 완성하기   중 ●●○

해석   Fit Trend사의 건강 추적 장치는 의심 없이 시장 내 같은 종류 중에서 가장 유능한 기기이다.

해설   빈칸은 전치사(without)의 목적어 자리에 올 수 있는 명사 자리이다. '건강 추적 장치는 의심 없이 가장 유능한 기기이다'라는 문맥이므로 빈칸 앞의 전치사 without과 함께 '의심 없이, 이의 없이'라는 의미의 어구 without question을 만드는 명사 (C) question(의심)이 정답이다.

어휘   fitness n. 건강, 신체 단련   tracker n. 추적 장치, 추적자
capable adj. 유능한, ~을 할 수 있는   trust n. 신뢰, 신임
means n. 수단, 방법   value n. 가치

109 부사 어휘 고르기   상 ●●●

해석   각 지점장은 그 지역의 관리자 및 다른 지점장들에게 고객들의 불평사항들을 즉시 보고해야 한다.

해설   빈칸은 동사(should report)를 꾸미는 부사 자리이다. '각 지점장은 지역의 관리자 및 다른 지점장들에게 고객들의 불평사항들을 즉시 보고해야 한다'라는 문맥이므로 (B) directly(즉시, 바로)가 정답이다. (C) upwardly(위쪽으로)도 해석상 그럴듯해 보이지만, 주어인 각 지점장(Each branch manager)과 보고의 대상 중 하나인 다른 지점장들(other branch managers)은 상하관계가 아닌 대등한 관계이므로 답이 될 수 없다.

어휘   branch manager phr. 지점장   report v. 보고하다, 알리다
complaint n. 불평사항, 항의   regional adj. 지역의   supervisor n. 관리자
lately adv. 최근에   abruptly adv. 갑자기

110 명사 자리 채우기   중 ●●○

해석   Haxpa사가 Brava Holdings사를 인수할 때 위원회는 순조로운 변화를 보장했다.

해설   부정관사(a) 다음에 올 수 있으면서 형용사(smooth)의 꾸밈을 받을 수 있는 것은 명사이므로 명사 (C) transition(변화)이 정답이다. (A)는 동명사일 경우 부정관사(a) 다음에 올 수 없고, 현재분사일 경우 명사 자리에 올 수 없다.

형용사 (B)와 (D)는 명사 자리에 올 수 없다.

어휘   committee n. 위원회   ensure v. 보장하다   smooth adj. 순조로운, 매끄러운
take control of phr. 인수하다, 장악하다   transit v. 통과하다, 수송하다; n. 수송
transitory adj. 일시적인   transitional adj. 변천하는, 과도기의

111 격에 맞는 인칭대명사 채우기   하 ●○○

해석   마케팅 교육생들에게 팀 프로젝트를 위해 그들의 파트너들을 결정하도록 몇 분이 주어졌다.

해설   명사(partners) 앞에서 형용사처럼 명사를 꾸밀 수 있는 인칭대명사는 소유격이므로 소유격 인칭대명사 (C) their가 정답이다. 주격 인칭대명사 (A), 목적격 인칭대명사 (B), 재귀대명사 (D)는 명사를 꾸밀 수 없다. 참고로, 빈칸을 전치사(on) 다음의 목적어 자리로 생각하여 목적격 인칭대명사 (B)와 재귀대명사 (D)를 선택하지 않도록 주의한다.

어휘   trainee n. 교육생, 훈련생

112 부사 자리 채우기   중 ●●○

해석   많이 홍보된 영화치고, *Origin of Hope*는 주말 박스 오피스 동안 놀랄 만큼 저조했다.

해설   부사(poorly)를 꾸밀 수 있는 것은 부사이므로 부사 (D) surprisingly(놀랄 만큼, 대단히)가 정답이다. 동사 또는 명사 (A), 동사 또는 과거분사 (B), 동명사 또는 현재분사 (C)는 부사를 꾸밀 수 없다. 동사 did를 '~을 하다'라는 의미의 타동사로 보고 명사 (A)와 동명사 (C)를 타동사의 목적어로 본다 해도, 각각 '박스 오피스 동안 놀라운 일을 저조하게 하다/놀라게 하는 것을 저조하게 하다'라는 어색한 문맥을 만든다. 또한, 명사 (A)가 '놀라운 일'을 나타낼 때는 가산 명사이므로 관사와 함께 쓰이거나 복수 명사로 쓰여야 한다. did를 동사를 강조하는 조동사로 보고 동사 (A)를 주절(*Origin of Hope* ~ office)의 동사로 본다 해도, surprise(~를 놀라게 하다)는 타동사이므로 뒤에 목적어가 와야 한다.

어휘   promotion n. 홍보   poorly adv. 저조하게, 형편없이

113 관계대명사 채우기   하 ●○○

해석   Laura Baker는 그 새로운 인턴을 교육하는 것을 담당하며, 그는 이번 여름에 고용될 것이다.

해설   이 문장은 주어(Laura Baker), 동사(is)를 갖춘 완전한 절이므로, ___ ~ summer는 수식어 거품으로 보아야 한다. 이 수식어 거품은 동사(will be employed)만 있고 주어가 없는 불완전한 절이며 빈칸 앞의 명사구(the ~ intern)를 선행사로 갖는 관계절이므로 관계절을 이끄는 관계대명사 (A), (B), (D)가 정답의 후보이다. 선행사(the ~ intern)가 사람이므로, 선행사가 사람일 때 사용되는 주격 관계대명사 (B) who가 정답이다. 주격 또는 목적격 관계대명사 (A)는 선행사가 사물일 때 쓰인다. 주격 또는 목적격 관계대명사 (D)는 관계대명사일 때 전치사나 콤마 바로 뒤에 올 수 없다. 부정대명사 (C)는 거품절을 이끌 수 없다.

어휘   in charge of phr. ~을 담당하는   instruct v. 교육하다   employ v. 고용하다

114 명사 어휘 고르기   중 ●●○

해석   *The Manchester Post*지는 한 달의 시험 구독을 무료로 제공함으로써 독자들을 끌어들였다.

해설   빈칸은 동명사(offering)의 목적어 역할을 하는 명사 자리이다. '시험 구독을 무료로 제공함으로써 독자들을 끌어들였다'라는 문맥이므로 (B) subscription(구독)이 정답이다. 참고로, 이 문장은 명사 subscription이 명사 trial(시험)과 함께 쓰여 '시험 구독'이라는 의미의 복합 명사를 만들고,

형용사(one-month)의 꾸밈을 받는 구조임을 알아둔다.

어휘 attract v. 끌어들이다 trial n. 시험, 재판; adj. 시험의, 시험적인
introduction n. 도입, 소개 section n. 부분, 구획 information n. 정보

115 전치사 채우기　　　　　　　　　　　　　중 ●●○

해석 시간제 근로자들의 것들을 포함하여 모든 급여는 매달 10일에 지급될 것이다.

해설 이 문장은 주어(All salaries), 동사(will be paid)를 갖춘 완전한 절이므로,
___ ~ employees는 수식어 거품으로 보아야 한다. 이 수식어 거품은 동사
가 없는 거품구이므로, 거품구를 이끌 수 있는 전치사 (B), (C), (D)가 정답의
후보이다. '시간제 근로자들의 것들을 포함하여'라는 의미가 되어야 하므로
전치사 (D) including(~을 포함하여)이 정답이다. 부사절 접속사 (A)는 거품
구가 아닌 거품절을 이끈다.

어휘 salary n. 급여, 봉급 while conj ~하는 동안, ~이긴 하지만
into prep. ~안으로 throughout prep. ~동안, 내내

116 태에 맞는 동사 채우기　　　　　　　　　중 ●●○

해석 인도에 그들의 차들을 주차된 채로 두는 차량 소유주들에게는 115달러의 벌
금이 부과된다.

해설 문장에 주어(A fine of $115)만 있고 동사가 없으므로 동사인 모든 보기가
정답의 후보이다. 주어(A fine of $115)와 동사(impose)가 '115달러의 벌
금이 부과되다'라는 수동의 의미를 가지므로 수동태 동사 (B) is imposed
가 정답이다. (A), (C), (D)는 능동태이므로 답이 될 수 없다. parked를 '주
차했다'라는 의미의 동사로 보고 과거분사 (A)가 빈칸 앞의 명사구(A fine of
$115)를 꾸미는 구조로 본다 해도, '115달러의 벌금이 주차했다'라는 어색
한 문맥이 된다.

어휘 fine n. 벌금 vehicle n. 차량 sidewalk n. 인도
impose v. 부과하다, 도입하다

117 전치사 채우기　　　　　　　　　　　　　중 ●●○

해석 Dr. Chauncey의 면접 동안 그의 이전 업무 경험이 논해졌다.

해설 이 문장은 주어(Dr. Chauncey's ~ experience)와 동사(was discussed)
를 갖춘 완전한 절이므로, ___ ~ interview는 수식어 거품으로 보아야 한
다. 이 수식어 거품은 동사가 없는 거품구이므로, 거품구를 이끌 수 있는 전치
사 (A), (C), (D)가 정답의 후보이다. 'Dr. Chauncey의 면접 동안 그의 업
무 경험이 논해졌다'라는 의미가 되어야 하므로 기간을 나타내는 전치사 (D)
during(~동안)이 정답이다. 부사 또는 명사 (B)는 수식어 거품을 이끌 수
없다.

어휘 previous adj. 이전의 discuss v. 논하다, 상의하다
about prep. ~에 대한 aside adv. 한쪽으로, ~외에는; n. 방백
along prep. ~을 따라

118 형용사 자리 채우기　　　　　　　　　　중 ●●○

해석 제품 디자인에 사려 깊은 접근법을 취하는 것은 Hyde Enterprises사가 성공
할 수 있게 했다.

해설 명사(approaches)를 꾸밀 수 있는 것은 형용사이므로 형용사 (B)
thoughtful(사려 깊은)이 정답이다. 명사 또는 동사 (A), 명사 (C), 부사 (D)
는 형용사 자리에 올 수 없다.

어휘 adopt v. 채택하다 approach n. 접근법; v. 접근하다 thought n. 생각
think v. 생각하다 thoughtfulness n. 사려 깊음
thoughtfully adv. 생각이 깊게

119 부사 자리 채우기　　　　　　　　　　　중 ●●○

해석 Tyne 의류회사는 일 년 내내 홍보 활동을 자주 함으로써 새로운 쇼핑객들을
더 잘 끌어모을 수 있었다.

해설 동명사(holding)를 꾸밀 수 있는 것은 부사이므로 부사 (D) frequently(자
주)가 정답이다. 형용사 또는 동사 (A), 명사 (B), 동명사 또는 현재분사 (C)
는 동명사를 꾸밀 수 없다. 참고로, 동명사는 명사 역할을 하지만 부사의 꾸밈
을 받는다는 것을 알아둔다.

어휘 attract v. 끌어모으다 promotion n. 홍보 활동, 승진
throughout prep. 내내, 도처에 frequent adj. 잦은; v. 자주 다니다
frequency n. 빈도

120 부사절 접속사 채우기　　　　　　　　　중 ●●○

해석 비록 Ms. Nielsen은 준비들에 도움이 필요하지만 그녀는 발표를 진행하는 것
에 동의했다.

해설 이 문장은 주어(Ms. Nielsen), 동사(has agreed)를 갖춘 완전한 절이므로
___ ~ preparations는 수식어 거품으로 보아야 한다. 이 수식어 거품은 동
사(needs)가 있는 거품절이므로, 거품절을 이끌 수 있는 부사절 접속사인 모
든 보기가 정답의 후보이다. '비록 그녀는 도움이 필요하지만 발표를 진행하
는 것에 동의했다'라는 의미가 되어야 하므로 양보를 나타내는 부사절 접속사
(D) although(비록 ~이지만)가 정답이다.

어휘 lead v. 진행하다, 이끌다 presentation n. 발표 after conj. ~한 이후에
since conj. ~때문에, ~이후로 unless conj. ~이 아니라면

121 명사 어휘 고르기　　　　　　　　　　　중 ●●○

해석 신입 직책에 있는 사람들은 숙련된 동료들의 지도 아래에서 성장한다.

해설 빈칸은 전치사(under)의 목적어 역할을 하는 명사 자리이다. '신입 직책에 있
는 사람들은 숙련된 동료들의 지도 아래에서 성장한다'라는 문맥이므로 (B)
guidance(지도, 안내)가 정답이다.

어휘 entry-level adj. 신입의, 말단인 thrive v. 성장하다, 번창하다
experienced adj. 숙련된, 경험 있는 coworker n. (직장) 동료
familiarity n. 친근함, 익숙함 confirmation n. 확인
invitation n. 초대, 초청

122 부사 어휘 고르기　　　　　　　　　　　중 ●●○

해석 Ms. Wyman은 3년 전에 사직했지만, 여전히 이전 동료들을 만나기 위해 가
끔 들른다.

해설 빈칸은 동사구(stops by)를 꾸미는 부사 자리이다. 'Ms. Wyman은 여전히
이전 동료들을 만나기 위해 가끔 들른다'라는 문맥이므로 (D) occasionally
(가끔)가 정답이다. (B) recently(최근에)도 해석상 그럴듯해 보이지만, 주로
과거 또는 현재 완료 시제와 함께 쓰이며 현재 시제와는 함께 쓰일 수 없다.

어휘 resign v. 사직하다, 물러나다 stop by phr. 들르다
catch up with phr. ~을 만나다, 따라잡다 former adj. 이전의
colleague n. 동료 jointly adv. 공동으로
gradually adv. 서서히, 점진적으로

123 형용사 자리 채우기　　　　　　　　　　중 ●●○

해석 무역 박람회는 판매 회사들을 전 세계의 유망한 구매자들과 연결해줄 것을 약
속한다.

해설 명사(buyers)를 꾸밀 수 있는 것은 형용사이므로 과거분사 (B)와 형용사
(D)가 정답의 후보이다. '유망한 구매자들과 연결해줄 것을 약속한다'라는 의

미가 되어야 하므로 형용사 (D) prospective(유망한)가 정답이다. 과거분사 (B)를 쓸 경우 '답사되는 구매자들'이라는 어색한 의미가 된다. 동사 또는 명사 (A)와 명사 (C)는 형용사 자리에 올 수 없다.

trade show phr. 무역 박람회 **vendor** n. 판매 회사, 노점상
prospect v. (금 등을 찾아서) 답사하다; n. 가망, 가능성
prospector n. 탐사자, 탐광자

124 동사 어휘 고르기 상 ●●●

해석 교통 공무원들은 지하철 노선 폐쇄의 영향을 줄이기 위해 추가 버스들을 보냈다.

해설 빈칸은 to 부정사를 만드는 동사원형 자리이다. '지하철 노선 폐쇄의 영향을 줄이기 위해 추가 버스들을 보냈다'라는 문맥이므로 (B) diminish(줄이다)가 정답이다.

어휘 **transport** n. 교통; v. 수송하다 **official** n. 공무원; adj. 공식적인
send out phr. 보내다, 파견하다 **extra** adj. 추가의 **impact** n. 영향, 충격
assess v. 재다, 평가하다 **intensify** v. 심화시키다
dismiss v. 해고하다, 해산시키다

125 현재분사와 과거분사 구별하여 채우기 상 ●●●

해석 알맞은 도구들을 공급받으면, 수리 팀은 몇 주가 아니라 며칠 안에 업무를 끝낼 수 있다.

해설 이 문장은 주어(the repair crew), 동사(can finish), 목적어(the job)를 갖춘 완전한 절이므로 ___ ~ tools는 수식어 거품으로 보아야 한다. 따라서 수식어 거품을 이끌 수 있는 과거분사 (C)와 현재분사 (D)가 정답의 후보이다. 주절의 주어(the repair crew)와 분사구문이 '수리 팀이 알맞은 도구들을 공급받다'라는 의미의 수동 관계이므로 동사 supply(공급하다)의 과거분사 (C) Supplied가 정답이다. 현재분사 (D)는 능동의 의미를 나타내므로 답이 될 수 없다. 명사 (A)와 명사 또는 동사 (B)는 수식어 거품을 이끌 수 없다.

어휘 **repair** n. 수리 **crew** n. 팀 **rather than** phr. ~가 아니라, ~ 보다는
supplier n. 공급자, 공급 회사 **supply** n. 공급; v. 공급하다

126 부사절 접속사 채우기 상 ●●●

해석 만약 영화가 팬들로부터 좋은 평가를 받는다면, 이르면 내년에 속편이 제작을 시작할 수 있다.

해설 이 문장은 주어(a sequel), 동사(could start), 목적어(production)를 갖춘 완전한 절이므로 ___ ~ by fans는 수식어 거품으로 보아야 한다. 이 수식어 거품은 동사(is received)가 있는 거품절이므로, 거품절을 이끌 수 있는 부사절 접속사 (A)와 (D)가 정답의 후보이다. '만약 영화가 좋은 평가를 받는다면, 속편이 제작을 시작할 수 있다'라는 문맥이므로 (A) Providing(만약 ~한다면)이 정답이다. 부사 (B)는 거품절을 이끌 수 없다. 전치사 (C)는 거품절이 아닌 거품구를 이끈다.

어휘 **receive** v. 받다, 받아들이다 **sequel** n. 속편 **production** n. 제작, 생산
likewise adv. 똑같이, 또한 **due to** phr. ~ 때문에
even if phr. 비록 ~일지라도

127 to 부정사 채우기 중 ●●○

해석 인턴십 프로그램은 학생들이 다른 직업들에서 일하는 것이 어떤지를 탐구할 수 있게 했다.

해설 5형식 동사 allow의 목적격 보어 자리에 올 수 있는 것은 to 부정사이므로 to 부정사 (C) to explore가 정답이다. 동사 (A), 동사 또는 과거분사 (B), 형용

사 (D)는 동사 allow의 목적격 보어 자리에 올 수 없다. 동사 allow를 목적어만을 취하는 3형식 동사로 보고 과거분사 (B)가 빈칸 앞의 명사 students를 수식하는 것으로 본다 해도, '탐구된 학생들'이라는 어색한 의미를 만들며, 과거분사는 빈칸 뒤에 온 명사절(what ~ jobs)을 목적어로 취할 수 없다.

어휘 **explore** v. 탐구하다 **exploratory** adj. 탐사의, 탐구의

128 명사 관련 어구 완성하기 상 ●●●

해석 Puff 제과점은 여러 가지의 맛으로 채워진 컵케이크 선물 상자들을 판매한다.

해설 빈칸은 전치사(with)의 목적어 역할을 하는 명사 자리이다. '여러 가지의 맛으로 채워진 컵케이크 선물 상자'라는 문맥이므로 빈칸 앞의 부정관사 an과 빈칸 뒤의 전치사 of와 함께 '여러 가지의'라는 의미의 어구 an assortment of를 만드는 (C) assortment(여러 가지, 모음)가 정답이다. (B)의 an amount of도 '상당한'이라는 의미로 해석상 그럴듯해 보이지만, 양이 상당한 것을 의미하며, 불가산 명사와 함께 쓰인다.

어휘 **flavor** n. 맛, 풍미 **acquisition** n. 습득, 인수 **availability** n. 유효성, 유용성

129 사람명사와 추상명사 구별하여 채우기 상 ●●●

해석 Baxter사는 그것의 전문적인 교육 강좌들을 감독해줄 조력자들을 찾고 있다.

해설 전치사(for)의 뒤에 올 수 있는 것은 명사이므로 명사 (C)와 (D)가 정답의 후보이다. '교육 강좌들을 감독해줄 조력자들을 찾고 있다'라는 의미가 되어야 하므로 사람명사 (C) facilitators(조력자)가 정답이다. 추상명사 (D) facilitation(편리화)은 '교육 강좌들을 감독해줄 편리화를 찾고 있다'라는 어색한 문맥을 만든다. 동사 (A)와 (B)는 명사 자리에 올 수 없다.

어휘 **oversee** v. 감독하다, 목격하다 **professional** adj. 전문적인
facilitate v. 가능하게 하다

130 태에 맞는 동사 채우기 중 ●●○

해석 기술자들이 오류들로 인해 메인 서버를 확인하는 동안 회사 자료는 대체 서버에 저장될 것이다.

해설 주절(The firm's data ~ server)에 주어(The firm's data)만 있고 동사가 없으므로 동사 (A), (B), (D)가 정답의 후보이다. 동사 store가 '저장하다'라는 의미의 타동사인데 빈칸 뒤에 목적어가 없고 '회사 자료는 대체 서버에 저장될 것이다'라는 수동의 의미이므로 수동태 (D) will be stored가 정답이다. 능동태 (A)와 (B)는 답이 될 수 없다. to 부정사 (C)는 동사 자리에 올 수 없다.

어휘 **alternate** adj. 대체의; v. 번갈아 나오게 만들다 **technician** n. 기술자

PART 6

131-134번은 다음 이메일에 관한 문제입니다.

발신: Gail Rossey <g.rossey@quailcooling.com>
수신: Peter Edmonds <pe880@tmail.net>
제목: 회신: 제품 불만
날짜: 3월 22일

Mr. Edmonds께,

3월 21일 자 귀하의 이메일은 귀하의 Quail Cooling사 에어컨이 귀하가 그것을 켤 때마다 큰 소음을 ¹³¹**일으킨다**고 말했습니다. ¹³²**이 문제는 아마 결함이 있는 부품에 의해 발생되는 것 같습니다.**

귀하는 그 제품을 귀하가 그것을 구매했던 가게로 다시 가져가야 하는지 여부에 대해 문의했습니다. ¹³³대신에, 저는 귀하께서 그것을 Quail Cooling사의 서비스 센터로 가져오시길 권장합니다. 귀하의 집에서 가장 가까운 곳은 147번지 Field가에 있습니다. 기다려야 하는 것을 피하기 위해, 귀하께서는 555-2827로 전화하여 사전에 예약을 할 수도 있습니다.

기술자가 현장에서 귀하의 에어컨을 수리해줄 것입니다. ¹³⁴서비스 요금은 청구되지 않을 것입니다.

Gail Rossey 드림
고객 서비스 직원, Quail Cooling사

indicate v. 말하다, 명시하다 recommend v. 권장하다, 추천하다
avoid v. 피하다 appointment n. 예약, 일정 in advance phr. 사전에, 미리
on the spot phr. 현장에서 fee n. 요금 charge v. 청구하다

최고난도 문제

131 시간 표현과 일치하는 시제의 동사 채우기 상 ●●●

해설 that절(that ~ on)에 동사가 없으므로 동사 (A)와 (D)가 정답의 후보이다. 반복적 행위를 나타내는 시간 표현(every time)이 있고 이와 함께 현재 시제 동사(turn on)가 왔으므로 현재 시제 (D) makes가 정답이다. 과거 시제 (A)는 반복적인 행위를 나타내는 시간 표현과 함께 쓰일 수 없다. 동명사 또는 현재분사 (B)와 to 부정사 (C)는 동사 자리에 올 수 없다.

132 알맞은 문장 고르기 중 ●●○

해석 (A) 이 문제는 아마 결함이 있는 부품에 의해 발생되는 것 같습니다.
(B) 수리공이 귀하의 집을 방문할 예정입니다.
(C) 귀하께서 귀하의 영수증을 제시하는 한 저는 귀하를 도울 수 있습니다.
(D) 사용자 설명서의 지시를 따르십시오.

해설 앞 문장 'Your e-mail ~ indicated that your Quail Cooling air conditioner (makes) a loud noise every time you turn it on.'에서 귀하의 이메일은 귀하의 Quail Cooling사의 에어컨이 귀하가 그것을 켤 때마다 큰 소음을 일으킨다고 말했다고 한 후, 뒷부분에서 수리를 위한 서비스 센터 방문 방법에 관한 세부 사항을 설명하고 있으므로 빈칸에는 에어컨의 문제와 관련된 내용이 들어가야 함을 알 수 있다. 따라서 (A)가 정답이다.

어휘 faulty adj. 결함이 있는 schedule v. 예정하다, 일정을 잡다
as long as phr. ~하는 한 present v. 제시하다; adj. 현재의
direction n. 지시, 방향

133 접속부사 채우기 주변 문맥 파악 중 ●●○

해설 빈칸은 콤마와 함께 문장의 맨 앞에 온 접속부사 자리이다. 앞 문장에서 귀하가 그 제품을 구매했던 가게로 다시 가져가야 하는지 여부에 대해 문의했다고 했고, 빈칸이 있는 문장에서는 귀하가 그것을 Quail Cooling사의 서비스 센터로 가져오길 권장한다고 했으므로, 앞에 언급된 내용과 다른 새로운 내용을 언급할 때 사용되는 접속부사 (A) Instead(대신에)가 정답이다.

어휘 furthermore adv. 더욱이 nonetheless adv. 그럼에도 불구하고
therefore adv. 그러므로

134 명사 관련 어구 채우기 주변 문맥 파악 중 ●●○

해설 명사(fee) 앞에서 복합 명사를 만들 수 있는 명사 (A), (C), (D)와 명사를 꾸밀 수 있는 형용사 (B)가 모두 정답의 후보이다. '___ 요금은 청구되지 않을 것이다'라는 문맥인데, 앞 문장에서 기술자가 현장에서 에어컨을 수리해 줄

것이라고 한 후, 빈칸이 있는 문장에서는 요금이 청구되지 않을 것이라고 했으므로 수리 서비스에 대한 요금이 청구되지 않을 것임을 알 수 있다. 따라서 빈칸 뒤의 명사 fee(요금)와 함께 쓰여 '서비스 요금'이라는 의미의 복합 명사 service fee를 만드는 명사 (C) service(서비스)가 정답이다.

어휘 shipping n. 운송(료) monthly adj. 매월의 transfer n. 이동; v. 이동하다

135-138번은 다음 초대장에 관한 문제입니다.

Blackpool 실내악 협회가
자랑스럽게 그것의 봄 콘서트를 선보입니다
5월 3일에

Greenfield 강당에서 ¹³⁵다시 열리게 될 Blackpool 실내악 협회의 봄 콘서트에 당신을 정중히 초대합니다. 작년에 처음 사용된, 이 장소는 최대 300명의 사람들을 앉힐 수 있습니다. 이 콘서트는 현악 4중주와 피아노 3중주의 공연들을 포함할 것입니다. 연회의 밤은 오후 7시에 시작해 오후 9시까지 ¹³⁶계속될 것입니다.

콘서트 당일 밤에, 티켓은 출입구에서 20달러에 판매될 것입니다. 시즌권을 가지고 있는 사람들은 건물에 무료로 들어갈 수 있을 뿐만 아니라, 마지막 리허설과 파티 후에 열리는 사교 모임에 참석할 수 있을 것입니다. 이것들은 각각 5월 2일과 4일에 ¹³⁷일어날 것입니다. ¹³⁸두 가지 모두 오후 5시에 열릴 예정입니다. 더 자세한 내용을 위해, 저희의 웹사이트를 방문하십시오.

chamber music phr. 실내악 society n. 협회 cordially adv. 정중히
auditorium n. 강당 venue n. 장소 entrance n. 출입구
after-party n. 파티 후에 열리는 사교 모임 respectively adv. 각각

135 부사 어휘 고르기 주변 문맥 파악 중 ●●○

해설 빈칸은 동사(will be held)를 꾸미는 부사 자리이다. 'Greenfield 강당에서 ___ 열리게 될 것이다'라는 문맥이므로 모든 보기가 정답의 후보이다. 뒤 문장에서 이 장소는 작년에 처음 사용되었다고 했으므로 작년에 이어 이번에도 Greenfield 강당이 사용될 것임을 알 수 있다. 따라서 (D) again(다시, 한 번 더)이 정답이다.

어휘 weekly adv. 매주의 effectively adv. 효과적으로, 사실상
last adv. 마지막으로

136 병치 구문 채우기 중 ●●○

해설 '연회의 밤은 오후 7시에 시작해 오후 9시까지 계속될 것이다'라는 의미가 되어야 하고, 등위접속사(and)가 동사(start)와 또 다른 동사인 빈칸을 연결하고 있음을 알 수 있다. 앞의 동사(start)가 조동사(will) 뒤에 오는 동사원형이므로 그와 같은 형태인 동사원형 (D) continue(계속되다)가 정답이다. 명사 (A), 부사 (B), 동명사 또는 현재분사 (C)는 동사 자리에 올 수 없다.

어휘 continuation n. 계속, 연속 continually adv. 계속해서, 끊임없이

137 동사 어휘 고르기 주변 문맥 파악 중 ●●○

해설 빈칸은 조동사(will) 다음에 오는 동사원형 자리이다. '이것들은 각각, 5월 2일과 4일에 ___ 것이다'라는 문맥이므로 모든 보기가 정답의 후보이다. 앞 문장에서 시즌권을 가지고 있는 사람들은 마지막 리허설과 파티 후에 열리는 작은 사교 모임에 참석할 수 있다고 했으므로, 리허설과 파티 후에 열리는 사교 모임은 각각 5월 2일과 4일에 일어날 것임을 알 수 있다. 따라서 (D) occur (일어나다, 발생하다)가 정답이다.

어휘 resume v. 재개하다 broadcast v. 방송하다 expire v. 만료되다

해석　(A) 4월 20일에 예약이 확정되었습니다.

　　　(B) 두 가지 모두 오후 5시에 열릴 예정입니다.

　　　(C) 당신의 기부금은 유용하게 사용될 것입니다.

　　　(D) 그것은 연회를 하기에 적절한 장소였습니다.

해설　앞 문장 'These will (occur) on May 2 and 4, respectively.'에서 이것
들은 각각 5월 2일과 4일에 일어날 것이라고 했으므로 빈칸에는 두 행사와
관련된 내용이 들어가야 함을 알 수 있다. 따라서 (B)가 정답이다.

어휘　reservation n. 예약　confirm v. 확정하다　donation n. 기부금
put to good use phr. ~을 유용하게 사용하다, ~을 잘 활용하다
suitable adj. 적절한, 알맞은　banquet n. 연회, 만찬

139-142번은 다음 후기에 관한 문제입니다.

Emerald Island 리조트, 호주 ★★★★★
2월 12일에 Agatha Henriksen에 의해 게시된 후기

제 남편과 저는 저희의 한 달 동안의 휴가를 마무리하기 위해 139**조용히 있을
수 있는** 휴가지를 찾고 있었습니다. Emerald Island 리조트는 이것을 위한
가장 적절한 장소로 보였습니다. 외딴 해양 공원에 위치해 있는, 이 리조트는
그들만의 수영장이 딸린 독립된 저택들이 특징입니다. 이 리조트는 또한 최고
의 서비스로 유명합니다. 이것이 그것이 또한 비쌀 수 있는 이유입니다. 140**다
행히**, 저희는 적당한 가격에 상품을 확보했습니다. 1일 무료 숙박권 외에, 이
할인은 와인 시음과 마사지를 포함했습니다. 인상적인 환경에서부터 최고의
고객 서비스까지, Emerald Island 리조트는 141**모든** 예상을 뛰어넘었습니다.
가고 싶은 이들을 위해, 이 리조트는 케언스에서 비행기로 90분이 걸립니다.
142**배를 통해 그것에 도착하는 것도 가능합니다.**

getaway n. 휴가지, 도주　month-long adj. 한 달 동안의
suitable adj. 적절한　situate v. 위치시키다　remote adj. 외딴, 먼
marine park phr. 해양 공원　feature v. ~이 특징이다, ~을 특징으로 삼다
detached adj. 독립된　have a reputation for phr. ~으로 유명하다
top-notch adj. 최고의, 일류의　secure v. 확보하다, 획득하다
affordable adj. (가격이) 적당한　apart from phr. ~ 외에, ~은 제외하고
offer n. 할인, 제안　surroundings n. 환경　superb adj. 최고의
surpass v. 뛰어넘다, 능가하다　expectation n. 예상, 기대

최고난도 문제

해설　빈칸은 명사(getaway)를 꾸미는 형용사 자리이다. '한 달 동안의 휴가를 마무
리하기 위해 ____한 휴가지를 찾고 있었나'라는 문맥이므로 모든 보기가 정답
의 후보이다. 뒷 부분에서 이 리조트는 외딴 해양 공원에 위치해 있고, 독립된
저택들이 특징이라고 했으므로, Emerald Island 리조트가 조용한 휴가지임
을 알 수 있다. 따라서 (C) private(조용히 있을 수 있는, 사적인)가 정답이다.

어휘　traditional adj. 전통적인　bargain adj. 헐값의　popular adj. 인기 있는

해설　빈칸은 콤마와 함께 문장의 맨 앞에 온 접속부사 자리이다. 앞 문장에서 최고
의 서비스가 그것, 즉 Emeral Island 리조트가 또한 비쌀 수 있는 이유라고
했고, 빈칸이 있는 문장에서는 적당한 가격에 상품을 확보했다고 했으므로 앞
문장보다 긍정적인 상황을 나타낼 때 사용되는 접속부사 (C) Fortunately
(다행히)가 정답이다.

어휘　once adv. 언젠가, 한 번　nearly adv. 거의　additionally adv. 게다가

해설　빈칸 뒤의 단수 가산 명사(expectation)를 꾸밀 수 있는 한정사 (B)와 수량
표현 (C)가 정답의 후보이다. '인상적인 환경에서부터 최고의 고객 서비스까
지, 리조트는 ____ 예상을 뛰어넘었다'라는 문맥이므로 리조트의 많은 부분이
만족스러웠다는 것을 알 수 있다. 따라서 (C) every(모든)가 정답이다. 한정
사 (B)를 쓸 경우 '인상적인 환경에서부터 최고의 고객 서비스까지, 리조트는
어떤 예상도 뛰어넘지 않았다'라는 어색한 의미가 되며 문맥상 어울리지 않는
다. 지시형용사 (A)와 한정사 (D)는 복수 가산 명사와 함께 쓰인다.

해석　(A) 그 도시는 야외활동 애호가들에게 아주 좋습니다.

　　　(B) 저는 기꺼이 당신의 예약을 해드릴 것입니다.

　　　(C) 배를 통해 그것에 도착하는 것도 가능합니다.

　　　(D) 덴마크로 돌아오는 저희의 항공편이 지연되었습니다.

해설　앞 문장 'For those wishing to go, the resort is 90 minutes by plane
from Cairns.'에서 가고 싶은 이들을 위해, 이 리조트는 케언스에서 비행기
로 90분이 걸린다고 했으므로 빈칸에는 Emerald Island 리조트에 가는 방
법과 관련된 내용이 들어가야 함을 알 수 있다. 따라서 (C)가 정답이다.

어휘　outdoor adj. 야외(활동)의　enthusiast n. 애호가, 열렬한 팬
reach v. 도착하다, 도달하다　delay v. 지연하다, 연기하다

143-146번은 다음 설명서에 관한 문제입니다.

Delux Home Brewer (DHB)로 당신의 첫 번째 커피 한 잔을 만들기 전에,
기기는 143**세척되어야** 합니다. 이것은 기기 내 모든 잔여물을 제거합니다. 위
에 있는 뚜껑을 열고 안에 물을 부음으로써 시작하십시오. 그 양은 가득이라
고 표시된 선에 닿아야 하지만, 초과해서는 안 됩니다. 144**다음으로**, 뚜껑을 닫
고 DHB의 플러그를 콘센트에 꽂으십시오. 커피포트가 내부 트레이에 얹혀 있
는 것을 확인하십시오. 이제, 간단히 청소 버튼을 누르고 모든 물이 DHB를 통
해 순환할 때까지 기다리십시오. 145**이 물은 배수구에 흘려 보내져야 합니다.**

당신은 이제 당신의 첫 번째 한 회분의 커피를 만들 준비가 되었습니다. 이 과정
에 대한 146**정확한** 안내를 위해 이 설명서의 7쪽을 참고하십시오.

eliminate v. 제거하다, 없애다　residue n. 잔여물　lid n. 뚜껑
pour v. 붓다　reach v. ~에 닿다, 도달하다　exceed v. 넘다, 초과하다
marked adj. 표시된, 뚜렷한　plug v. (전기 기구)의 플러그를 꽂다; n. 플러그
electronic outlet phr. 콘센트　rest on phr. ~에 얹혀 있다
circulate v. 순환하다　batch n. 한 회분

해설　빈칸은 be동사(be) 다음에 와서 수동태를 만드는 p.p.형의 자리이다. '기
기는 ____되어야 한다'라는 문맥이므로 모든 보기가 정답의 후보이다. 뒤 문
장에서 이것이 기기 내 모든 잔여물을 제거한다고 했고 뒷부분에서 물을 붓
고 청소 버튼을 눌러 물이 순환할 때까지 기다리라고 했으므로, 기기가 세척
되어야 한다는 것을 알 수 있다. 따라서 동사 wash(세척하다)의 p.p.형 (C)
washed가 정답이다. 참고로, (B)의 check(점검하다)도 해석상 그럴듯해 보
이지만, 기기를 점검하는 행위 자체가 기기 내 모든 잔여물을 제거할 수는 없
으므로 답이 될 수 없다.

어휘　take v. 가져가다　shake v. 흔들다

해설　빈칸은 콤마와 함께 문장의 맨 앞에 온 접속부사 자리이다. 앞 문장에서 기기

내 물의 양이 표시된 선을 초과해서는 안 된다고 했고, 빈칸이 있는 문장에서는 뚜껑을 닫고 플러그를 콘센트에 꽂으라고 했으므로, 앞에서 말한 내용과 다음 단계로 이어지는 내용의 문장에서 사용되는 접속부사 (D) Next(다음으로)가 정답이다.

어휘 alternatively adv. 그 대신에 likewise adv. 비슷하게
eventually adv. 결국

145 알맞은 문장 고르기 중 ●●○

해석 (A) 그 필터는 그러한 목적으로 만들어지지 않았습니다.
(B) 최대 네 가지 다른 옵션들이 선택될 수 있습니다.
(C) 표준 1회 제공량은 10온스로 구성됩니다.
(D) 이 물은 배수관을 따라 흘려 보내져야 합니다.

해설 앞 문장 'Now, simply press the Clean button and wait until all the water has circulated through the DHB.'에서 이제, 간단히 청소 버튼을 누르고 모든 물이 DHB를 통해 순환할 때까지 기다리라고 했으므로 빈칸에는 청소를 위해 사용된 물과 관련된 내용이 들어가야 함을 알 수 있다. 따라서 (D)가 정답이다.

어휘 standard adj. 표준의 serving n. 1회 제공량, 1인분
consist of phr. ~으로 구성되다 drain n. 배수관; v. 물을 빼내다

146 형용사 자리 채우기 중 ●●○

해설 빈칸 뒤의 명사(directions)를 꾸밀 수 있는 것은 형용사이므로 형용사 (A) precise(정확한)가 정답이다. 부사 (B), 명사 (C)와 (D)는 형용사 자리에 올 수 없다.

어휘 precisely adv. 정확하게 precision n. 정확, 정밀
preciseness n. 명확함, 정확성

PART 7

147-148번은 다음 광고에 관한 문제입니다.

Fiona's Garden!
147당신의 꽃과 식물에 필요한 물건을 위해 Fiona's Garden에 방문하세요!
폭넓은 품종에서 선택하세요!

· 결혼식과 다른 특별한 행사들을 위한 모든 사이즈의 주문 제작된 꽃꽂이들.
· 147다양한 실내 식물들과 나무들.
· 148시내 전 지역에 대한 배달 서비스. 100달러 이상 주문 시 무료.

가격과 상품을 상의하시려면 555-3049로 저희에게 전화하세요. Fiona's Garden은 Orlando 시내에 938번지 Colonial로에 위치해 있습니다. 저희의 운영 시간은 월요일부터 금요일까지, 오전 10시부터 오후 7시까지입니다.

variety n. 품종, 다양성 customized adj. 주문 제작된, 개개인의 요구에 맞춘
floral arrangement phr. 꽃꽂이 occasion n. 행사, 경우
a range of phr. 다양한 indoor adj. 실내의
discuss v. 상의하다, 논의하다 operation n. 운영

147 육하원칙 문제 하 ●○○

해석 Fiona's Garden은 어떤 종류의 사업체인가?
(A) 특별한 행사들을 위한 행사 기획 업체
(B) 개인 또는 기업 행사를 위한 장소
(C) 식물과 꽃들의 공급 업체

(D) 가정과 사업체를 위한 조경 업체

해설 지문의 'Visit Fiona's Garden for all of your flower and plant needs!'와 'A range of indoor plants and trees.'에서 꽃과 식물에 필요한 물건을 위해 Fiona's Garden에 방문하라고 하며, 다양한 실내 식물들과 나무들이 있다고 했으므로, Fiona's Garden이 꽃과 식물을 판매한다는 사실을 알 수 있다. 따라서 (C)가 정답이다.

어휘 venue n. 장소 function n. 행사, 기능 supplier n. 공급업체
landscaper n. 조경 업체, 정원사

148 육하원칙 문제 중 ●●○

해석 고객들은 어떻게 무료 배달을 받을 자격이 있게 될 수 있는가?
(A) 새로운 제품을 주문함으로써
(B) 일정 금액을 지불함으로써
(C) 전화로 주문함으로써
(D) 시내 지역에 주소지를 가짐으로써

해설 지문의 'Delivery services to all locations within city limits. Free for orders of $100 or more.'에서 시내 전 지역에 대한 배달 서비스가 제공되며, 100달러 이상 주문 시 무료라고 했으므로 (B)가 정답이다. 참고로, 시내 지역에 배달이 제공되는 것은 맞지만, 100달러 이상을 주문해야 무료라고 했으므로 (D)는 정답이 될 수 없다.

어휘 eligible adj. ~할 자격이 있는 specific adj. 일정의, 특정한

패러프레이징

orders of $100 or more 100달러 이상 주문 → spending a specific amount 일정 금액을 지불하는 것

149-150번은 다음 회람에 관한 문제입니다.

회람

수신: 공장 운영 부서, Cready Power사
발신: Millie Wickens, 공장 부팀장
날짜: 월요일, 9월 14일
제목: 출입 시스템

이번 주 수요일, 공장 운영실에 입장하는 시스템이 바뀔 것입니다. 149이것은 우리가 현재 사용하고 있는 플라스틱 카드들이 분실 혹은 손상으로 인해 자주 재발급되기 때문입니다. 카드 리더기 대신에, 우리는 지문 인식기를 사용하기 시작할 것입니다. 하지만, 수리공이 오전 11시쯤까지 도착하지 않을 것이기 때문에 150여러분은 여전히 수요일에 여러분의 출입 카드를 가져와야 합니다. 여러분 모두가 오후 1시에 여러분의 지문을 등록하도록 요구될 것이기 때문에 점심을 먹고 그 시간 전에 돌아오십시오.

plant n. 공장, 시설 gain entry phr. 입장하다 reissue v. 재발급하다
fingerprint n. 지문 register v. 등록하다

149 육하원칙 문제 중 ●●○

해석 현재의 보안 시스템은 왜 변화될 것인가?
(A) 민감한 정보가 보호되어야 한다.
(B) 몇몇 기계가 손상되었다.
(C) 몇몇 추가적인 직원들이 고용되었다.
(D) 몇몇 물품들이 자주 교체되어야 한다.

해설 지문의 'This is because the plastic cards ~ often need to be reissued'에서 이것, 즉 입장하는 시스템이 바뀌는 것은 플라스틱 카드들이

자주 재발급되기 때문이라고 했으므로 (D)가 정답이다.

어휘 security n. 보안 sensitive adj. 민감한, 세심한
replace v. 교체하다, 대체하다 frequently adv. 자주

패러프레이징

often need to be reissued 자주 재발급되어야 하다 → must be replaced
frequently 자주 교체되어야 하다

150 육하원칙 문제 중 ●●○

해석 공장 운영 부서의 직원들은 수요일 오후 1시에 무엇을 할 것인가?
(A) 고객을 만난다
(B) 설문지를 작성한다
(C) 교육을 실시한다
(D) 정보를 제공한다

해설 지문의 'you still should bring your access card on Wednesday'와
'Please return ~ before 1 P.M. because all of you will be required
to register your fingerprints at that time.'에서 여러분, 즉 공장 운영 부
서의 직원들은 수요일에 여전히 출입 카드를 가져와야 하며, 오후 1시에 지문
을 등록하도록 요구되기 때문에 그 시간 전에 돌아와야 한다고 했으므로, 수
요일 오후 1시에 공장 운영 부서의 직원들은 지문 등록을 할 것임을 알 수 있
다. 따라서 (D)가 정답이다.

어휘 questionnaire n. 설문지

패러프레이징

register ~ fingerprints 지문을 등록하다 → Provide ~ data 정보를 제공하다

151-152번은 다음 메시지 대화문에 관한 문제입니다.

Marcus Jones 오전 10시 3분
안녕하세요, Ms. Girard. 저는 Assure Technology사의 Marcus입니다. 저
는 당신의 소포를 가지고 방금 도착했어요. ¹⁵¹저는 내부 통화 장치 시스템을
시도해보았지만, 응답을 받지 못했습니다. 제가 당신의 아파트에 이것을 가
져갈 수 있도록 저를 들어가게 해주시겠어요?

Helen Girard 오전 10시 4분
오, 죄송해요, 하지만 지금 저는 제 사무실에 있어요. ¹⁵²대신 그것을 건물 관
리인에게 맡겨주세요. 그에게 연락하려면 내부 통화 장치에 101을 입력하기
만 하면 돼요.

Marcus Jones 오전 10시 5분
그럴 수 있으면 좋겠네요. ¹⁵²하지만 이것이 귀중한 컴퓨터 부품들을 포함
하고 있기 때문에 당신은 이 소포에 서명을 하기 위해 이곳에 있어야 해요.

Helen Girard 오전 10시 5분
알겠어요. 그렇다면, 오후 5시 30분에 아파트로 다시 와주실 수 있나요? 그때
쯤에는 제가 집에 있을 거예요.

intercom n. 내부 통화 장치 contain v. 포함하다
valuable adj. 귀중한, 값비싼

151 추론 문제 상 ●●●

해석 Mr. Jones에 대해 추론될 수 있는 것은?
(A) 사무실로 소포를 가져왔다.
(B) 주소의 위치를 알아낼 수 없다.
(C) 관리자로부터 도움을 요청했다.

(D) 건물에 들어갈 수 없다.

해설 지문의 'I tried the intercom system, but I didn't get a reply. Could
you please let me in so that I can bring it up to your apartment
unit?'에서 Mr. Jones가 자신은 내부 통화 장치 시스템을 시도했지만, 응답
을 받지 못했고 당신, 즉 Ms. Girard의 아파트에 이것, 즉 소포를 가져갈 수
있도록 들어가게 해달라고 했으므로 (D)가 정답이다.

어휘 locate v. ~의 위치를 알아내다 residence n. 주소, 거주지
assistance n. 도움, 지원

152 의도 파악 문제 중 ●●○

해석 오전 10시 5분에, Mr. Jones가 "I wish I could"라고 썼을 때 그가 의도한
것은?
(A) 몇몇 장비가 운반되기에 너무 무겁다.
(B) 회사는 앞으로의 수송을 급히 처리할 수 없다.
(C) 몇몇 물품들은 고객에게 직접 전달되어야 한다.
(D) 관리소는 현재 열려 있지 않다.

해설 지문의 'Please leave it with the building manager instead.'에서
Ms. Girard가 대신 그것을 건물 관리인에게 맡겨달라고 하자 Mr. Jones
가 'I wish I could.'(그럴 수 있으면 좋겠네요)라고 한 후, 'But you must
be here to sign for this package, as it contains valuable computer
parts.'에서 이 소포가 귀중한 컴퓨터 부품들을 포함하고 있기 때문에
Ms. Girard가 그것에 서명을 하기 위해 이곳에 있어야 한다고 한 것을 통해
Mr. Jones가 컴퓨터 부품들을 포함한 소포를 고객에게 직접 전달해야 함을
알 수 있다. 따라서 (C)가 정답이다.

어휘 rush v. 급히 처리하다, 서두르다 upcoming adj. 앞으로의
shipment n. 수송 directly adv. 직접

패러프레이징

computer parts 컴퓨터 부품들 → items 물품들

153-155번은 다음 이메일에 관한 문제입니다.

수신: Galina Kusnetsov <galinakus@postamail.com>
발신: Jovin 의료 센터 <admin@jmc.com>
제목: 저희의 새로운 모바일 애플리케이션
날짜: 9월 18일

Ms. Kusnetsov께,

당신은 ¹⁵⁴⁻ᴰJovin 의료 센터가 지난주에 환자들이 예약을 관리하고 질문을
하기 위해 사용할 수 있는 모바일 애플리케이션을 출시했다는 것을 알게 되어
흥미로울 수도 있습니다. 저희는 서의의 전화가 자주 통화 중이기 때문에 근무
시간 동안 병원 직원에게 전화해야 하는 것이 불편할 수 있다는 것을 알고 있습
니다. — [1] —. ¹⁵³따라서 저희는 저희 환자들의 대부분이 항상 접속 가능한
이 애플리케이션을 사용하여 저희에게 급하게 연락해야 하는 사람들을 위해
저희의 전화를 비워줄 수 있기를 바랍니다.

일단 당신이 Jovin 의료 센터 애플리케이션을 다운로드했다면, 당신의 의료 센
터 ID 번호를 사용하여 가입하십시오. — [2] —. 당신의 환자 프로필은 당신
의 다가오는 예약들을 나열하고 취소 또는 변경을 요청할 수 있는 선택권을 제
공할 것입니다. ¹⁵⁵또한 채팅 시스템은 진료 과정에 대한 당신의 질문에 대해
답을 얻을 수 있게 합니다. — [3] —. ¹⁵⁴⁻ᴮ애플리케이션이 현재는 이러한 기
능들로 제한되어 있지만, 저희는 환자들이 건강 검진 결과와 같은, 다른 정
보에 접근하는 것을 가능하도록 만들 계획입니다. 애플리케이션에 관한 문의
사항이 있다면, 이 이메일에 답장하거나 저희의 웹사이트에 업데이트된 자주
묻는 질문 페이지를 읽어주십시오. — [4] —.

Jovin 의료 센터

launch v. 출시하다 appointment n. 예약, 약속 inquiry n. 질문, 문의
clinic n. 병원 inconvenient adj. 불편한 accessible adj. 접속 가능한
urgently adv. 급하게 reach v. 연락하다 cancellation n. 취소
modification n. 변경, 수정 procedure n. 과정, 절차

153 육하원칙 문제 중 ●●○

해석 이메일에 따르면, 애플리케이션의 목적은 무엇인가?
(A) 정규 진료 환자들에게 추가 조언을 제공하기 위해
(B) 병원으로의 통화량을 줄이기 위해
(C) 예약 취소 횟수를 줄이기 위해
(D) 환자들이 인근 병원들의 위치를 찾도록 하기 위해

해설 지문의 'We ~ hope that most of our patients will use the application,
~ and free up our phone lines'에서 저희 즉, Jovin 의료 센터는 환자들
의 대부분이 애플리케이션을 사용하고, 자신들의 전화를 비워줄 수 있기를 바
란다고 했으므로 (B)가 정답이다.

어휘 follow-up adj. 추가의, 후속의 volume n. 양, 부피
nearby adj. 인근의; adv. 인근에

패러프레이징

free up ~ phone lines 전화를 비우다 → reduce the volume of calls 통
화량을 줄이다

154 Not/True 문제 상 ●●●

해석 Jovin 의료 센터 애플리케이션에 대해 사실인 것은?
(A) 의사들과 간호사들에게 직접 연락하는 데에 사용될 수 있다.
(B) 의료 기록들을 표시하도록 업데이트될 수도 있다.
(C) 소액의 비용을 지불한 후에 설치될 수 있다.
(D) 현재 약 한 달 동안 작동해왔다.

해설 지문의 'While the application is currently limited ~, we plan to
make it possible for patients to access other information, such
as the results of medical tests.'에서 애플리케이션, 즉 Jovin 의료 센
터 애플리케이션이 현재는 제한되어 있지만, 환자들이 건강 검진 결과와 같
은, 다른 정보에 접근하는 것을 가능하도록 만들 계획이라고 했으므로 (B)는
지문의 내용과 일치한다. 따라서 (B)가 정답이다. (A)와 (C)는 지문에 언급
되지 않은 내용이다. (D)는 'Jovin Medical Center launched a mobile
application last week'에서 Jovin 의료 센터가 지난주에 모바일 애플리케
이션을 출시했다고 했으므로 지문의 내용과 일치하지 않는다.

어휘 display v. 표시하다, 보여주다 record n. 기록
functional adj. 작동하는 approximately adv. 약, 대략

패러프레이징

access ~ the results of medical tests 건강 검진 결과에 접근하다
→ display medical records 의료 기록을 표시하다

155 문장 위치 찾기 문제 상 ●●●

해석 [1], [2], [3], [4]로 표시된 위치 중, 다음 문장이 들어갈 곳으로 가장 적절한
것은?

"당신은 새로운 예약을 하고 당신이 가질 수 있는 어떤 질문들이든 묻기 위해
이 기능을 사용할 수 있습니다."

(A) [1]

(B) [2]
(C) [3]
(D) [4]

해설 주어진 문장에서 당신은 새로운 예약을 하고 당신이 가질 수 있는 어떤 질문
들이든 묻기 위해 이 기능을 사용할 수 있다고 했으므로, 이 문장이 예약 및
문의를 할 수 있는 기능과 관련된 내용이 나오는 부분에 들어가야 함을 알 수
있다. [3]의 앞 문장인 'A chat system ~ allows you to get answers to
your questions about clinic procedures.'에서 채팅 시스템은 진료 과
정에 대한 당신의 질문들에 대해 답을 얻을 수 있게 해준다고 했으므로, [3]에
제시된 문장이 들어가면 채팅 시스템은 진료 과정들에 대한 질문들에 대해 답
을 얻을 수 있게 하며, 새로운 예약을 하고 어떤 질문들이든 묻기 위해 이 기
능, 즉 채팅 시스템을 사용할 수 있다는 자연스러운 문맥이 된다는 것을 알 수
있다. 따라서 (C)가 정답이다.

어휘 feature n. 기능, 특징

156-158번은 다음 웹페이지에 관한 문제입니다.

www.organifresh.com
Organi Fresh사 – 식사 시간을 쉽게 만들다

소개 | 메뉴 | 주문 | 자주 묻는 질문 | 연락처

Organi Fresh사는 당신을 위해 일을 해줌으로써 음식을 사고 건강한 식사
를 준비하는 것으로부터 걱정을 덜어 드립니다. ¹⁵⁶당신이 Organi Fresh사
식사 배달을 주문하면, 당신은 저희의 매우 숙련된 전문 요리사들에 의해 준
비된 일주일 치의 맛있는 음식을 받게 될 것입니다. 저희의 모든 음식은 제
철 유기농 농작물과 천연 재료들을 사용해 만들어집니다. 저희는 절대 방부제
를 사용하지 않으며, 저희는 기름, 설탕, 그리고 소금의 사용을 최소한도로 유
지합니다.

¹⁵⁷⁻ᴬ아시아, 지중해, 그리고 남미 요리의 조합을 포함하는 저희의 메뉴를 간
단히 한 번 본 다음, 당신이 일주일 동안 원하는 식사를 고르세요. ¹⁵⁷⁻ᴮ저희의
표준 플랜으로, 당신은 하루 28달러의 비용으로 일주일 동안 하루에 세 끼
의 식사를 받게 될 것입니다. 또는, 단돈 22.50달러의 비용으로 일주일 동안
하루에 두 끼의 식사를 받을 수 있도록 저희의 점심 & 저녁 플랜을 주문하세
요. ¹⁵⁷⁻ᶜ이 모든 가격들은 배송비를 포함합니다!

마지막으로, 저희의 모든 식사들은 전자레인지 조리와 오븐 사용이 둘 다 가
능한 용기들로 포장됩니다. ¹⁵⁶/¹⁵⁸⁻ᶜ당신의 일주일 치 주문은 얼음과 함께 냉
장 박스에 포장되어 매주 금요일에 신선하게 배송될 것입니다. 저희를 한 번
만 이용해보시면, 저희는 당신이 더 많은 것을 위해 다시 돌아올 것이라 확신
합니다!

take the hassle out phr. 걱정을 덜어주다 meal n. 식사, 끼니
seasonal adj. 제철의 produce n. 농작물 preservative n. 방부제
minimum n. 최소한도 Mediterranean adj. 지중해의
cuisine n. 요리 pack v. 포장하다 container n. 용기
microwavable adj. 전자레인지로 조리할 수 있는
ovenproof adj. 오븐에 사용할 수 있는 cooler n. 냉장 박스, 냉장고

156 주제 찾기 문제 하 ●○○

해석 웹페이지의 주제는 무엇인가?
(A) 유기농 식당
(B) 사전 포장된 식사 서비스
(C) 출장 음식 공급업체
(D) 새로운 다이어트 프로그램

해설 지문의 'When you order an Organi Fresh meal delivery, you'll get

~ delicious food prepared'에서 Organi Fresh 식사 배달을 주문하면, 준비된 맛있는 음식을 받게 될 것이라고 했고, 'Your order for the week will be shipped ~ in a cooler packed with ice ~.'에서 일주일 치 주문이 얼음과 함께 냉장 박스에 포장되어 배송될 것이라고 했으므로 (B)가 정답이다.

어휘 organic adj. 유기농의 pre-packed adj. 사전 포장된
catering n. 출장 음식 공급 diet n. 다이어트, 식단

157 Not/True 문제   상 ●●●

해석 웹페이지에 언급되지 않은 정보는?
(A) 요리 종류
(B) 주문 옵션
(C) 배달 비용
(D) 보관 조언

해설 지문에서 (D)는 언급되지 않은 내용이다. 따라서 (D)가 정답이다. (A)는 'our menu, which includes a mix of Asian, Mediterranean, and South American cuisine'에서 아시아, 지중해, 그리고 남미 요리의 조합을 포함한 메뉴라고 했으므로 지문의 내용과 일치한다. (B)는 'With our Standard Plan, you'll get three meals a day ~ at a cost of $28 per day. Or, order our Lunch & Dinner Plan to receive two meals a day ~ at a cost of just $22.50 per day.'에서 표준 플랜과 함께, 하루 28달러의 비용으로 하루에 세 끼의 식사를 받게 될 것이며, 단돈 22.50달러의 비용으로 하루에 두 끼의 식사를 받을 수 있도록 자신들의 점심 & 저녁 플랜을 주문하라고 했으므로 지문의 내용과 일치한다. (C)는 'All of these prices include the cost of shipping!'에서 모든 가격들은 배송비를 포함한다고 했으므로 지문의 내용과 일치한다.

어휘 storage n. 보관, 저장 suggestion n. 제안

158 Not/True 문제   중 ●●○

해석 식사 주문에 대해 사실인 것은?
(A) 바로 먹어져야 한다.
(B) 전화로 주문될 수 있다.
(C) 매주 같은 날에 배송된다.
(D) 재사용 가능한 용기와 함께 온다.

해설 지문의 'Your order for the week will be shipped ~ every Friday.'에서 당신의 일주일 치 주문은 매주 금요일에 배송될 것이라고 했으므로 (C)는 지문의 내용과 일치한다. 따라서 (C)가 정답이다. (A), (B), (D)는 지문에 언급되지 않은 내용이다.

어휘 consume v. 먹다, 소모하다 reusable adj. 재사용 가능한

패러프레이징

shipped ~ every Friday 매주 금요일에 배송되다 → delivered on the same day each week 매주 같은 날에 배송되다

159-161번은 다음 기사에 관한 문제입니다.

Wave Technologies사가 Uptron사 인수를 확정하다

12월 8일—전자회사 Wave Technologies사는 가전제품 제조업체인 Uptron사를 인수했다. ¹⁵⁹이 움직임은 수익성이 높은 주방가전 시장에서 그것의 존재감을 높이려는 Wave Technologies사의 전념의 증거로 보인다. 이미 텔레비전과 같은 가전제품의 선도적인 생산업체로서 자사를 확고히 한 ¹⁶⁰⁻ᴰWave Technologies사는 2년 전에 Bolton 백화점 체인과 식기

세척기와 냉장고를 공급하는 계약을 체결했다.

"Uptron사 인수는 저희가 저희의 제품 범위를 확장하고 저희의 기존 고객들에게 더 나은 서비스를 제공할 수 있도록 할 것입니다"라고 Wave Technologies사의 최고 사업전략가인 Karen Fowler가 말했다. ¹⁶¹이번 매입은 Wave Technologies사에게 Uptron사의 12,000제곱미터의 오하이오주 공장에 대한 접근권을 제공하며, 이는 제품 안전성에 대한 국제 기준들을 충족시킨다. 하지만, Wave Technologies사는 계속해서 인디애나주에 기반을 둘 것이다.

acquisition n. 인수, 매입 acquire v. 인수하다, 획득하다
appliance n. 가전제품 manufacturer n. 제조업체
demonstration n. 증거, 입증 commitment n. 전념, 헌신
presence n. 존재감, 영향력 lucrative adj. 수익성이 높은
establish v. 확고히 하다, 설립하다 agreement n. 계약, 합의
dishwasher n. 식기세척기 chain n. (상점·호텔 등의) 체인
expand v. 확장하다, 확대하다 serve v. 서비스를 제공하다
purchase n. 매입, 구매 base v. 기반을 두다, 본거지를 두다

159 육하원칙 문제   중 ●●○

해석 Wave Technologies사는 왜 Uptron사를 인수했는가?
(A) 경쟁사가 제품을 출시하는 것을 막기 위해
(B) 시장 내 점유율을 더욱 확대하기 위해
(C) 주요 고객과 계약을 맺기 위해
(D) 다른 나라에서 가게들을 열기 위해

해설 지문의 'The move is seen as a demonstration of Wave Technologies' commitment to increasing its presence in the ~ market.'에서 이 움직임, 즉 Uptron사 인수는 시장에서 존재감을 높이려는 Wave Technologies사의 전념의 증거로 보인다고 했으므로 (B)가 정답이다.

어휘 competitor n. 경쟁사, 경쟁자 further adv. 더욱 share n. 점유율, 지분

패러프레이징

increasing ~ presence in the ~ market 시장에서 존재감을 높이는 것
→ expand ~ share of a market 시장 내 점유율을 확대하다

160 Not/True 문제   중 ●●○

해석 Bolton 백화점에 대해 언급된 것은?
(A) 12월에 그것의 제품 라인의 폭을 넓힐 것이다.
(B) Uptron사와 제휴 관계를 맺었었다.
(C) 약 2년 전에 설립되었다.
(D) Wave Technologies사에 의해 만들어진 제품들을 판매한다.

해설 지문의 'Wave Technologies entered into an agreement with the Bolton Department Store chain two years ago to provide dishwashers and refrigerators.'에서 Wave Technologies사는 2년 전에 Bolton 백화점 체인과 식기세척기와 냉장고를 공급하는 계약을 체결했다고 했으므로 (D)는 지문의 내용과 일치한다. 따라서 (D)가 정답이다. (A), (B), (C)는 지문에 언급되지 않은 내용이다.

어휘 approximately adv. 약, 대략

161 추론 문제   상 ●●●

해석 Wave Technologies사에 대해 암시되는 것은?
(A) 최근에 그것의 제품 안정성 기준을 변경했다.
(B) 오하이오주로 제조 장비를 옮길 것이다.

(C) 생산 능력을 크게 늘렸다.

(D) 인디애나주의 직원 규모를 줄였다.

해설 지문의 'The purchase provides Wave Technologies with access to Uptron's 12,000-square-meter Ohio plant'에서 이번 매입은 Wave Technologies사에게 Uptron사의 12,000제곱미터의 오하이오주 공장에 대한 접근권을 제공한다고 했으므로, 그것의 생산 능력이 크게 늘어났다는 것을 추론할 수 있다. 따라서 (C)가 정답이다.

어휘 production capacity phr. 생산 능력 significantly adv. 크게, 상당히 reduce v. 줄이다 workforce n. 직원, 노동력

162-163번은 다음 송장에 관한 문제입니다.

> **Joyful Home Housekeeping Services사**
> *3948번지 Beechnut가, 레스브리지, 앨버타주 T1H-0L6*
>
> 송장 번호: 394827
> ¹⁶²송장 날짜: 2월 28일
> ¹⁶²고객: Severson 회계사무소
> 583번지 South Parkside로, 사무실 12호
> 레스브리지, 앨버타주 T1H-0L4
>
> 제공 서비스:
> | | | |
> |---|---|---|
> | 2월 18일 | 바닥 청소 및 진공청소기로 청소 | 380.00달러 |
> | 2월 21일 | 실내 및 실외 창문 세척 | 260.00달러 |
> | 2월 22일 | ¹⁶³소파와 의자들의 스팀 청소 | 130.00달러 |
>
> 소계: 770.00달러
>
> 세금: 92.40달러
>
> 총 지불액: 862.40달러　　　　납부 기한: 3월 7일

invoice n. 송장 accounting firm phr. 회계사무소 vacuum v. 진공청소기로 청소하다 interior adj. 실내의 exterior adj. 실외의

162 추론 문제
중 ●●●○

해석 2월 28일에 무엇이 일어났을 것 같은가?
(A) 사무실 실외 창문이 세척되었다.
(B) 고객이 직원에 대해 항의를 했다.
(C) 고객을 위한 대금 청구서가 마련되었다.
(D) 직원이 건물 내 카펫을 진공청소기로 청소했다.

해설 지문의 'DATE OF INVOICE: February 28', 'CLIENT: Severson Accounting Firm'에서 송장 날짜가 2월 28일이며, 고객인 Severson 회계사무소에 발송된 것임을 확인할 수 있으므로 2월 28일에 고객을 위한 대금 청구서가 마련되었다는 것을 추론할 수 있다. 따라서 (C)가 정답이다.

패러프레이징
INVOICE 송장 → billing statement 대금 청구서

163 육하원칙 문제
중 ●●●○

해석 Severson 회계사무소는 가구 청소 서비스에 대해 얼마를 지불해야 할 것인가?
(A) 130.00달러
(B) 260.00달러
(C) 380.00달러

(D) 770.00달러

해설 지문의 'Steam-cleaning of sofa and chairs $130.00'에서 가구인 소파와 의자들의 스팀 청소가 130달러임을 알 수 있으므로 (A)가 정답이다.

어휘 furniture n. 가구

패러프레이징
furniture cleaning services 가구 청소 서비스 → Steam-cleaning of sofa and chairs 소파와 의자들의 스팀 청소

164-167번은 다음 온라인 채팅 대화문에 관한 문제입니다.

> **Zelda Coe**　　　　　　　오후 3시 15분
> ¹⁶⁴저는 저의 직원들이 원격으로 근무하도록 허용할지 고민해오고 있어요. 이건 그냥 생각일 뿐이에요. ¹⁶⁴어떻게 생각하세요?
>
> **Stuart Ojeda**　　　　　　오후 3시 15분
> 음, ¹⁶⁵그것은 멀리 떨어져 사는 직원들에게는 이상적일 수 있겠지만, 몇몇은 필요한 장비가 없을 수도 있어요.
>
> **Libby Schuster**　　　　　오후 3시 16분
> ¹⁶⁵맞아요. 그들의 집에 있는 컴퓨터들은 저희가 사용하는 그래픽 디자인 소프트웨어를 실행하기에 충분히 강력하지 않을 수 있어요.
>
> **Zelda Coe**　　　　　　　오후 3시 16분
> 알겠어요. 만약 제가 이 선택권을 적합한 컴퓨터를 가지고 있으면서 재택 근무하기를 선호하는 사람에게 제공한다면요?
>
> **Stuart Ojeda**　　　　　　오후 3시 17분
> 잘 모르겠어요. ¹⁶⁶제 예전 직장에서, 저는 집에서 일한 직원들은 회의 중에 더 적게 기여했다는 것을 발견했어요.
>
> **Libby Schuster**　　　　　오후 3시 17분
> 또한, 만약 그들이 동료들을 정기적으로 만나지 않으면 그들은 배제되었다고 느낄 수 있어요. 어쨌든, 사무실에 오는 것은 직원들이 일하기에 좋은 마음가짐을 갖게 해요.
>
> **Zelda Coe**　　　　　　　오후 3시 18분
> 여러분 모두의 의견들에 감사해요. ^{167-D}제가 조사를 좀 해보고 이것에 대해 더 철저히 살펴볼게요.

consider v. 고민하다, 고려하다 remotely adv. 원격으로 ideal adj. 이상적인 suitable adj. 적합한, 적절한 prefer v. 선호하다 telecommute v. 재택 근무하다 contribute v. 기여하다, 공헌하다 excluded adj. 배제되는 coworker n. (직장) 동료 regularly adv. 정기적으로 thoroughly adv. 철저히

164 의도 파악 문제
중 ●●●○

해석 오후 3시 15분에, Ms. Coe가 "It's just an idea"라고 썼을 때 그녀가 의도한 것은?
(A) 결정이 아직 내려지지 않았다.
(B) 구체적인 답변을 원한다.
(C) 문제가 해결되었다.
(D) 계획을 발전시킬 시간이 없었다.

해설 지문의 'I've been considering allowing my staff to work remotely.'에서 Ms. Coe가 직원들이 원격으로 근무하도록 허용할지 고민해오고 있다고 한 후, 'It's just an idea.'(이건 그냥 생각일 뿐이에요)라고 하며, 'What do you think?'에서 동료들에게 어떻게 생각하는지 질문한 것을 통해, Ms. Coe가 아직 결정을 내리지 않았다는 것을 알 수 있다. 따라서 (A)가

정답이다.

어휘 decision n. 결정 specific adj. 구체적인, 특정한 resolve v. 해결하다
develop v. 발전시키다

165 육하원칙 문제 　　중 ●●○

해석 Mr. Ojeda와 Ms. Schuster는 무엇에 동의하는가?
(A) 집에서 일하는 사람들은 팀의 일원처럼 느껴지지 않는다.
(B) 사무실에 출근하는 직원들은 자주 늦는다.
**(C) 직원들은 원격으로 근무하기 위해 필요한 것을 가지고 있지 않을 수도
있다.**
(D) 사무실 밖에서 일하는 사람들은 신뢰할 수 없다.

해설 지문의 'it could be ideal for employees who live far away, but
some might not have the necessary equipment'에서 Mr. Ojeda
가 그것, 즉 원격으로 근무하는 것이 멀리 떨어져 사는 직원들에게는 이상
적일 수 있겠지만, 몇몇은 필요한 장비가 없을 수도 있다고 하자, 'Right.
Their home computers might not be powerful enough to run the
graphic design software we use.'에서 Ms. Schuster가 맞다고 동의
하며 그들의, 즉 몇몇 직원들의 집에 있는 컴퓨터들은 자신이 사용하는 그
래픽 디자인 소프트웨어를 실행하기에 충분히 강력하지 않을 수 있다고 했으
므로 (C)가 정답이다.

어휘 commute v. 통근하다 unreliable adj. 신뢰할 수 없는

166 추론 문제 　　중 ●●○

해석 Mr. Ojeda에 대해 암시되는 것은?
(A) 업무능력 평가를 실시하는 것이 필요하다고 생각한다.
(B) 재택근무가 선택지였던 사무실에서 일한 적이 있다.
(C) 몇몇 직원들이 급여 인상을 받아야 한다고 생각한다.
(D) 최근에 관리직으로 승진되었다.

해설 지문의 'At my old job, I found that employees who worked from
home contributed less during meetings.'에서 Mr. Ojeda가 예전 직
장에서, 집에서 일한 직원들이 회의 중에 더 적게 기여했다는 것을 발견했다
고 했으므로 그가 이전에 재택근무를 할 수 있는 회사에서 일했다는 사실을
추론할 수 있다. 따라서 (B)가 정답이다.

어휘 promote v. 승진시키다, 홍보하다

패러프레이징

worked from home 집에서 일했다 → telecommuting 재택근무

167 Not/True 문제 　　중 ●●○

해석 Ms. Coe가 그녀가 할 것이라고 언급한 것은?
(A) 제안서를 작성한다
(B) 직원들로부터 피드백을 요청한다
(C) 상사에게 신청서를 제출한다
(D) 사안에 대해 신중하게 생각한다

해설 지문의 'I'm going to do some research and look into this more
thoroughly.'에서 Ms. Coe가 자신이 조사를 좀 해보고 이것에 대해 더 철
저히 살펴볼 것이라고 했으므로 (D)는 지문의 내용과 일치한다. 따라서 (D)
가 정답이다. (A), (B), (C)는 지문에 언급되지 않은 내용이다.

어휘 presentation n. 제안서, 발표 submit v. 제출하다 request n. 신청(서)
superior n. 상사; adj. 뛰어난, 상급의 carefully adv. 신중하게

패러프레이징

look into ~ thoroughly 철저히 살펴보다 → Consider ~ carefully 신중하
게 생각하다

168-171번은 다음 편지에 관한 문제입니다.

Cost Smart사 고객님들께,

들으셨을지도 모르겠지만, 전국의 몇몇 다른 대형 소매점들은 이번 주 초에
사이버 범죄자들의 표적이 되었습니다. 이것은 개인 정보 및 지불 내역을 포
함한, 고객 정보의 절도를 야기했을 수 있습니다. — [1] —. 저희는 여러분을
소중하게 여기고 여러분의 정보에 대한 승인되지 않은 접근이 얼마나 위협이
될 수 있는지 알고 있기 때문에, [168]저희는 Cost Smart사의 시스템을 유사
한 공격으로부터 보호하기 위해 저희가 할 수 있는 모든 것을 할 것이라고
약속드립니다.

[171]저희는 이미 저희의 보안 및 암호화 소프트웨어를 업그레이드했습니다.
— [2] —. 저희는 또한 직원들에게 그들이 취해야 할 예방 조치를 알도록 추가
적인 교육을 제공할 계획입니다. 저희의 조치들이 사이버 범죄자들을 막는 데
에 효과적일 것으로 생각하지만, Cost Smart사 고객으로서, [168]저희는 여러
분에게도 주의할 것을 요청드립니다.

[169]저희는 절대 여러분께 개인 정보를 요청하기 위해 전화로 연락하지 않
을 것이라는 점을 유의하십시오. — [3] —. [169]만약 여러분이 자신을 Cost
Smart사 고객 서비스 직원으로 소개하는 발신자들로부터 문자 메시지를
받는다면, 즉시 그것들을 삭제하십시오. — [4] —. 또한, [170]이메일들의 링크
를 클릭하기 보다는 항상 곧바로 저희의 웹사이트를 방문하십시오. 여러분
에게 안내된 그 웹사이트는 저희 것과 똑같이 보이도록 제작된 것일 수도 있
습니다. 이것은 여러분을 속여서 여러분의 비밀번호를 입력하게 하는 것이고,
그렇게 함으로써 그것을 그 사이트 관리자에게 보여주는 것입니다.

여러분의 신의에 감사드립니다. 질문이 있으시면, 555-8897로 저희에게 전
화 주십시오.

Florence Stoddard
Cost Smart사 회장 드림

retail store phr. 소매점 target v. 표적(목표)으로 삼다, 겨냥하다
theft n. 절도, 도둑질 threat n. 위험, 위협 unauthorized adj. 승인되지 않은
safeguard v. 보호하다 attack n. 공격 encryption n. 암호화
aware adj. 아는 precaution n. 예방 조치, 사전 대책
deter v. 막다, 저지하다 cautious adj. 주의 깊은, 신중한
direct v. 안내하다, 향하다 thereby adv. 그렇게 함으로써
reveal v. 보이다, 드러내다 operator n. 관리자, 경영자

168 목적 찾기 문제 　　상 ●●●

해석 편지의 목적은 무엇인가?
(A) 온라인 쇼핑을 피해야 한다는 것을 제안하기 위해
(B) 몇몇 예방책들을 설명하기 위해
(C) 범죄자들이 어떻게 도용된 정보를 사용하는지 설명하기 위해
(D) 고객 정보의 손실에 대해 사과하기 위해

해설 지문의 'we promise to do everything we can to safeguard ~
system'에서 저희, 즉 Cost Smart사는 시스템을 보호하기 위해 자신들
이 할 수 있는 모든 것을 할 것이라고 약속한다고 했고, 'we ask you to be
cautious as well'에서 여러분, 즉 고객들도 주의할 것을 요청한다고 한 후
보호를 위한 방법들을 설명하고 있으므로 (B)가 정답이다.

어휘 preventive measure phr. 예방책 stolen adj. 도용된, 훔친

169 추론 문제 중 ●●○

해석 편지에서 언급된 문자 메시지에 대해 암시되는 것은?
(A) 고객이 주문들을 확정하도록 한다.
(B) 다가오는 판매 행사들을 광고한다.
(C) 정규 업무 시간 중에는 수신되지 않는다.
(D) 가게 직원들에 의해 발송되지 않는다.

해설 지문의 'we will never contact you over the phone'과 'If you receive text messages from senders representing themselves as Cost Smart customer service associates, delete them immediately.'에서 저희, 즉 Cost Smart사는 절대 고객들에게 전화로 연락하지 않을 것이며 만약 여러분, 즉 고객들이 자신을 Cost Smart사 고객 서비스 직원으로 소개하는 발신자들로부터 문자 메시지를 받는다면, 즉시 그것들을 삭제하라고 했으므로 문자 메시지의 발신자가 Cost Smart사의 고객 서비스 직원이 아니라는 사실을 추론할 수 있다. 따라서 (D)가 정답이다.

어휘 confirm v. 확정하다 upcoming adj. 다가오는

170 육하원칙 문제 중 ●●○

해석 편지에 따르면, 고객들은 왜 이메일 링크를 클릭하면 안 되는가?
(A) 컴퓨터를 바이러스로 감염시킬 수 있다.
(B) 보안 프로그램들을 손상시킬 것이다.
(C) 가짜 웹페이지로 연결될 수 있다.
(D) 중요한 정보를 삭제할 것이다.

해설 지문의 'always visit our Web site directly rather than clicking on links in e-mails. The Web sites you are directed to may be designed to look exactly like ours.'에서 이메일들의 링크를 클릭하기보다는 항상 곧바로 저희, 즉 Cost Smart사의 웹사이트에 방문하도록 하며, 여러분, 즉 고객들에게 안내된 웹사이트는 Cost Smart사의 것과 똑같이 보이도록 제작된 것일 수도 있다고 했으므로 (C)가 정답이다.

어휘 infect v. 감염시키다 disable v. 손상시키다 lead v. 연결되다

171 문장 위치 찾기 문제 중 ●●○

해석 [1], [2], [3], [4]로 표시된 위치 중, 다음 문장이 들어갈 곳으로 가장 적절한 것은?

"저희는 이러한 개선들이 여러분의 정보가 저희의 시스템에서 불법적으로 빠져나가는 것을 예방하도록 도울 것이라고 확신합니다."

(A) [1]
(B) [2]
(C) [3]
(D) [4]

해설 주어진 문장에서 이러한 개선들이 여러분의 정보가 저희의 시스템에서 불법적으로 빠져나가는 것을 예방하도록 도울 것이라고 확신한다고 했으므로, 이 문장이 보안 시스템 개선에 관련된 내용이 나오는 부분에 들어가야 함을 알 수 있다. [2]의 앞 문장인 'We have already upgraded our security and encryption software.'에서 저희, 즉 Cost Smart사는 이미 보안 및 암호화 소프트웨어를 업그레이드했다고 했으므로, [2]에 제시된 문장이 들어가면 Cost Smart사는 보안 및 암호화 소프트웨어 업그레이드와 같은 개선들이 고객의 정보가 시스템에서 불법적으로 빠져나가는 것을 예방하도록 도울 것이라고 확신한다는 자연스러운 문맥이 된다는 것을 알 수 있다. 따라서 (B)가 정답이다.

어휘 confident adj. 확신하는, 자신감이 있는 prevent v. 예방하다, 막다

172-175번은 다음 이메일에 관한 문제입니다.

수신: Christina Meister <chrismeister@gomail.com>
발신: 175Martin Jedlika <mjedlikakey@translations.com>
제목: 회신: 문서 번역
날짜: 7월 8일

Ms. Meister께,

Key 번역 회사에 당신의 영어-그리스어 문서 번역의 필요에 관해 연락해 주셔서 감사합니다. 저희는 당신이 보낸 파일을 검토했고 저희가 그 작업을 완료하는 데 약 10시간이 걸릴 것으로 예상합니다. 172당신은 아래에서 저희의 최초 견적을 확인할 수 있습니다:

페이지	페이지당 40달러로 책정된 4페이지
기간	10시간
번역	160달러
173-A최초 고객 10퍼센트 할인	173-A-16달러
총액	144달러

저희는 또한 번역의 보증된 출력물을 제공할 수 있습니다. 이것은 번역가의 이름과 서명, 그리고 번역의 정확성을 확인하는 문구가 포함할 것입니다. 저희는 아래와 같은 요금으로 택배를 통해 당신에게 그것을 보내드릴 수 있습니다:

국내 표준 (2-3일)	16달러
174국내 특송 (1일)	17422달러
국제 표준 (5-8일)	25달러
국제 특송 (3-4일)	33달러

175만약 당신이 보증된 출력물을 필요로 한다면, 당신이 어떤 택배 옵션을 선호하는지 명시한 답장을 보내주십시오, 그러면 저희는 그에 맞춰 견적을 수정할 것입니다. 그렇지 않다면, 저희의 웹사이트의 계좌 정보를 이용해 간단히 계좌 이체를 하십시오. 당신의 지불액을 받자마자, 저희는 이 프로젝트에 착수할 것입니다.

172저희는 당신의 답변을 기다립니다!

Martin Jedlika 드림
프로젝트 담당자, Key 번역회사

---

translation n. 번역 contact v. 연락하다 estimate v. 예상하다
approximately adv. 약, 거의 initial adj. 최초의, 첫 번째 quote n. 견적
duration n. 기간 certified adj. 보증된, 증명된 hard copy phr. 출력물
signature n. 서명 statement n. 문구, 성명 affirm v. 확인하다
accuracy n. 정확성 courier n. 택배, 배달원 accordingly adv. 그에 맞춰
bank transfer phr. 계좌 이체 proceed v. 착수하다, 시작하다

172 목적 찾기 문제 중 ●●○

해석 이메일은 왜 쓰였는가?
(A) 프로젝트가 진행 중이라는 것을 입증하기 위해
(B) 문서 번역을 요청하기 위해
(C) 프로젝트 연기에 대해 설명하기 위해
(D) 잠재적인 고객에게 가격을 명시하기 위해

해설 지문의 'You can find our initial quote below:'에서 아래에서 자신들, 즉 Key 번역 회사의 최초 견적을 확인할 수 있다고 했고, 'We look forward to your reply!'에서 당신의 답변을 기다린다고 했으므로 잠재적인 고객에게 견적을 발송했다는 사실을 확인할 수 있다. 따라서 (D)가 정답이다.

어휘 verify v. 입증하다, 확인하다 in progress phr. 진행 중인

potential adj. 잠재적인

173 Not/True 문제   중 ●●○

해석 Ms. Meister에 대해 언급된 것은?
(A) Key 번역회사와 거래해본 적이 없다.
(B) 많은 회사들의 견적들을 비교하고 있다.
(C) 7월에 그리스로 여행을 갈 것이다.
(D) 그녀의 이메일에 정확한 파일을 포함시키지 않았다.

해설 지문의 '10% first-time customer discount', '-$16'에서 최초 고객 10퍼센트 할인에서 Ms. Meister가 16달러를 할인받았음을 알 수 있으므로 (A)는 지문의 내용과 일치한다. 따라서 (A)가 정답이다. (B), (C), (D)는 지문에 언급되지 않은 내용이다.

어휘 compare v. 비교하다 a number of phr. 많은, 다수의

174 육하원칙 문제   하 ●○○

해석 문서의 당일 배송에는 얼마나 비용이 드는가?
(A) 16달러
(B) 22달러
(C) 25달러
(D) 33달러

해설 지문의 'Domestic Express (1 day)', '$22'에서 국내 특송 (1일)이 22달러임을 알 수 있으므로 (B)가 정답이다.

어휘 one-day n. 당일

175 육하원칙 문제   중 ●●○

해석 Mr. Jedlika에 따르면, Ms. Meister는 왜 이메일에 답장해야 하는가?
(A) 번역이 정확하다는 것을 확인하기 위해
(B) 추가적인 서비스를 이용하기 위해
(C) 은행 계좌에 대한 정보를 제공하기 위해
(D) 파일에 대한 수정을 승인하기 위해

해설 지문의 'Martin Jedlika', 'If you require a certified hard copy, please send a reply'에서 이메일의 발신자인 Mr. Jedlika가 만약 당신, 즉 Ms. Meister가 보증된 출력물을 필요로 한다면, 답장을 보내달라고 했으므로 (B)가 정답이다.

어휘 confirm v. 확인하다

176-180번은 다음 이메일과 온라인 양식에 관한 문제입니다.

수신: Contigo 여행사 <service@contigotours.com>
발신: Jason Lambert <jlamb63@howmail.net>
제목: 몬테비데오 관광

날짜: 3월 20일

안녕하세요,

저는 ¹⁷⁶⁻ᴮ이번 주 초에 당신의 여행사 웹페이지에 게시된 몬테비데오 여행 중 하나를 예약하는 것에 관심이 있어서 이 이메일을 씁니다. 저는 ¹⁷⁹당신이 당신의 관광에 3박과 5박 호텔 숙박 선택권 둘 다를 가지고 있다는 것을 알고 있습니다. 하지만, 5박 호텔 숙박 선택권이 푼타델에스테로의 추가적인 여행을 포함한다는 것 외에, ¹⁷⁷저는 그 두 가지 선택권 간의 차이점이 무엇인지 확실히 알지 못합니다. 각 관광에 대한 몇 가지 상세한 정보를 제게 보내주시겠습니까?

또한, 저는 혼자서 답사를 좀 하기 위해 차를 빌리고 싶습니다. 저는 이것을 제가 준비하도록 당신이 도와줄 수 있기를 바라고 있었습니다. ¹⁷⁹만약 제가 5박 관광을 간다면, 저는 6월 15일에 차를 반납하고 싶습니다. 이것은 제가 시카고에서 6월 16일에 참석하는 회의를 위해 그곳으로 돌아가야 하기 때문입니다. ¹⁷⁹그렇지 않으면, 저는 차를 더 일찍 반납할 것입니다.

Jason Lambert 드림

book v. 예약하다 post v. 게시하다, 발송하다 stay n. 숙박; v. 머무르다
in-depth adj. 상세한, 심층의 explore v. 답사하다, 탐험하다
arrange v. 준비하다 drop off phr. 반납하다, 되돌려주다
conference n. 회의 attend v. 참석하다

Sunway Car Rentals사
확인 페이지

¹⁷⁹Jason Lambert, 아래 귀하의 대여 차량에 대한 예약 상세정보를 검토해주십시오.

차량 모델: Trekker V70 컨버터블
¹⁷⁸이 모델은 어떤 모바일 기기와도 연결이 가능한 내장 터치스크린이 있는 GPS가 이것의 계기판에 딸려있습니다.

¹⁷⁹대여 기간: 6월 10일-6월 13일
¹⁸⁰당신의 차량을 저희의 공항 지점이 아닌 Sunway사의 16번지 Maria로 사무실에 반납할 것을 명심하십시오.

지불 총액: 350달러
이 총액은 50달러의 보험 보증금을 포함합니다.

지불 방법: Surefire 신용카드 번호 4553-1002-2023-9099

review v. 검토하다, 확인하다 built-in adj. 내장된, 붙박이의
dashboard n. 계기판 location n. 지점 deposit n. 보증금, 예금

176 Not/True 문제   중 ●●○

해석 Contigo 여행사에 대해 언급된 것은?
(A) 시카고에 사무실을 열었다.
(B) 웹사이트를 최근에 업데이트했다.
(C) 계획된 주말여행을 취소했다.
(D) 지불 절차를 바꿨다.

해설 이메일의 'the tours to Montevideo ~ was posted on your travel agency's Web page earlier this week'에서 이번 주 초에 당신의 여행사 웹페이지에 몬테비데오 여행이 게시되었다고 했으므로 (B)는 지문의 내용과 일치한다. 따라서 (B)가 정답이다. (A), (C), (D)는 지문에 언급되지 않은 내용이다.

어휘 recently adv. 최근에 cancel v. 취소하다

177 육하원칙 문제   상 ●●●

해석 Mr. Lambert가 무엇을 요청하는가?
(A) 여행 선택권에 대한 세부 사항
(B) 항공편 출발 날짜
(C) 관리자에 대한 연락처 정보
(D) 숙박 선택권에 대한 추천

해설 이메일의 'I'm not entirely sure what the difference is between the two options. Could you please send me some in-depth information about each tour?'에서 자신, 즉 Mr. Lambert가 그 두 가지 선택권, 즉 여행에 관련된 선택권 간의 차이점이 무엇인지 확실히 알지 못하며, 각 관광에 대해 몇 가지 상세한 정보를 보내 달라고 요청했으므로 (A)가 정답이다.

어휘 detail n. 세부사항 supervisor n. 관리자 lodging n. 숙박, 숙소

178 동의어 찾기 문제   중 ●●○

해석 양식에서, 2문단 2번째 줄의 단어 "connect"는 의미상 -와 가장 가깝다.
(A) 대화하다
(B) 매다
(C) 배정하다
(D) 연결하다

해설 온라인 양식의 connect를 포함한 문장 'This model comes with ~ GPS ~ that is able to connect to any mobile device.'에서 이 모델은 어떤 모바일 기기와도 연결이 가능한 GPS가 딸려있다고 했으므로 connect는 '연결하다'라는 뜻으로 사용되었다. 따라서 '연결하다'라는 뜻을 가진 (D) link가 정답이다.

179 추론 문제 연계   중 ●●○

해석 Mr. Lambert에 대해 암시되는 것은?
(A) 시카고에서의 그의 약속에 늦을 것이다.
(B) 몬테비데오에 3박 동안 머무를 것이다.
(C) 6월 10일에 환불을 받을 것이다.
(D) 폰타델에스테에 있는 친구를 방문할 것이다.

해설 온라인 양식의 'Jason Lambert, please review the booking details for your rental vehicle below.'에서 Mr. Lambert에게 아래 그의 대여 차량에 대한 예약 상세정보를 검토해달라고 했고, 'Rental Period: June 10—June 13'에서 대여 기간이 6월 10일에서 6월 13일까지임을 알 수 있다. 또한, 이메일의 'you have both three-night and five-night hotel stay options for your tours'에서는 당신, 즉 Contigo 여행사가 관광에 3박과 5박 호텔 숙박 선택권 둘 다를 가지고 있다고 했고, 'If I go with the five-night tour, I'd prefer to drop off the car on June 15.'과 'Otherwise, I'll return the car earlier.'에서는 만약 자신, 즉 Mr. Lambert가 5박 관광을 간다면 6월 15일에 차를 반납하고 싶고, 그렇지 않으면 차를 더 일찍 반납할 것이라고 했다.
두 단서를 종합할 때, Mr. Lambert는 차량을 6월 10일에서 6월 13일까지 대여했고 6월 15일보다 일찍 반납했으므로 두 가지 호텔 숙박 선택권 중 3박을 선택했다는 사실을 추론할 수 있다. 따라서 (B)가 정답이다.

어휘 appointment n. 약속 receive v. 받다 refund n. 환불

180 추론 문제   중 ●●○

해석 Sunway Car Rentals사에 대해 추론될 수 있는 것은?
(A) 최근에 추가적인 차량들을 구매했다.
(B) 여행 잡지에 실렸다.
(C) 6월 15일에 영업을 하지 않을 것이다.
(D) 하나 이상의 지점을 운영한다.

해설 온라인 양식의 'Please be sure to drop off your vehicle at Sunway's 16 Maria Way office—not our airport location.'에서 당신의 차량을 자신들의 공항 지점이 아닌 Sunway사의 16번지 Maria로 사무실에 반납할 것을 명심하라고 했으므로 Sunway Car Rentals사는 하나 이상의 지점을 운영한다는 것을 추론할 수 있다. 따라서 (D)가 정답이다.

어휘 additional adj. 추가적인 operate v. 운영하다 branch n. 지점

181-185번은 다음 기사와 광고에 관한 문제입니다.

DesignChic Magazine지
여름을 위한 최고의 테라스 가구
작성: Darrell Cruz

[183]5월 10일—따뜻한 여름밤을 당신의 테라스에서 쉬면서 보내는 것보다 나은 것은 없다. [181]당신의 테라스에 적절한 가구를 찾는 것은 당신의 집의 야외 공간을 당신만의 것으로 만드는 것의 비결이다. 수많은 가구 소매업체들이 이번 시즌에 인기 있는 테라스 세트들을 가지고 있지만, Diamond Home사보다 더 좋다고 여겨지는 것은 아무것도 없다.

[184-A]그것의 설립 이후 변함없이 높은 소비자 평가와 함께, Diamond Home사는 이번 여름에 멋진 테라스 컬렉션을 가지고 있다. 현대적인 의자들, 탁자들, 그리고 다른 상품들로 채워진 [182-B]Diamond Home사의 여름 야외 라인은 전적으로 환경에 해를 끼치지 않는 유기농 재료들로 만들어진다. 회사의 최고경영자, [183]Nina Roman은 심지어 이번 달에 우리 간행물과의 인터뷰에서 이 컬렉션은 이미 회사의 단골 고객들로부터 극찬의 평가를 받았다고 말했다. 이 라인 내 몇몇 가구들을 보려면, 여기를 클릭하면 된다.

---

patio n. 테라스, 안뜰   beat v. 더 낫다, ~을 능가하다
outdoor adj. 야외의, 옥외의   numerous adj. 수많은
retailer n. 소매업체   regard v. ~으로 여기다, 간주하다
consumer n. 소비자   rating n. 평가   modern adj. 현대적인
entirely adv. 전적으로   organic adj. 유기농의   material n. 재료
harm v. 해를 끼치다   publication n. 간행물   rave adj. 극찬의, 호의적인
loyal customer phr. 단골 고객

Diamond Home사의 볼티모어 지점
개업 기념 특별 할인!

'당신 집의 디자인을 새롭게 단장할 방법을 찾고 있습니까? 그렇다면 6월 10일부터 11일까지, Diamond Home사의 아주 새로운 볼티모어 지점에서의 개업 기념 특별 할인을 놓치지 마십시오. [184-A]10년도 더 전에 설립된 Diamond Home사는 고객들에게 양질의 가구를 가져다주는 데 전념하고 있습니다. 그리고 이제 여러분은 이 놀라운 가구들 중 일부를 살 수 있고 추가적인 혜택을 받을 수 있습니다! 이번 주말 세일에서 아래의 놀라운 혜택들을 꼭 확인해 보십시오.

[185]제품	[185]혜택
[185]테라스 의자	[185]한 개를 사고, 한 개를 공짜로 얻으세요
[184-C]식탁	구매 시 무료 그릇 세트
[184-C]컴퓨터 책상	당신의 다음 구매를 위한 50퍼센트 할인 쿠폰

할인에 포함된 구체적인 제품들에 대한 더 많은 세부사항은
www.diamondhome.com/baltimorestore에서 찾을 수 있습니다.

---

freshen up phr. 새롭게 단장하다 **brand-new** adj. 아주 새로운
commit v. 전념하다, 헌신하다 **quality** adj. 양질의, 고급의
check out phr. 확인하다

181 추론 문제
상 ●●●

해석 기사는 누구를 대상으로 하는 것 같은가?
(A) 회사 임원들
(B) 가구 제조업체들
(C) 웹 디자이너들
(D) 주택 소유자들

해설 기사의 'Finding the right furniture ~ is the key to making the
outdoor space at your house your own.'에서 적절한 가구를 찾는 것은
당신의 집의 야외공간을 당신만의 것으로 만드는 것의 비결이라고 했으므로
자신의 집을 소유한 사람들을 대상으로 하는 기사임을 추론할 수 있다. 따라
서 (D)가 정답이다.

어휘 **executive** n. 임원, 간부 **manufacturer** n. 제조업체

182 Not/True 문제
중 ●●○

해석 Diamond Home사의 여름 컬렉션에 대해 언급된 것은?
(A) 유명인의 주택에서 촬영되었다.
(B) 환경친화적인 재료로 만들어졌다.
(C) 해외에 위치한 공장에서 생산되었다.
(D) 텔레비전의 광고 캠페인에서 특집으로 다루어졌다.

해설 기사의 'the Diamond Home summer outdoor line is made ~ of
organic materials that do not harm the environment'에서 Diamond
Home사의 여름 야외 라인은 환경에 해를 끼치지 않는 유기농 재료로 만들
어진다고 했으므로 (B)는 지문의 내용과 일치한다. 따라서 (B)가 정답이다.
(A), (C), (D)는 지문에 언급되지 않은 내용이다.

어휘 **celebrity** n. 유명인 **residence** n. 주택, 거주지
environmentally friendly phr. 환경친화적인
overseas adv. 해외에; adj. 해외의
feature v. 특집으로 다루다, 특별히 포함하다

패러프레이징

made ~ of organic materials that do not harm the environment 환경
에 해를 끼치지 않는 유기농 재료들로 구성된 → created with environmentally
friendly materials 환경친화석인 새료로 민들어진

183 육하원칙 문제
중 ●●○

해석 Ms. Roman은 5월에 무엇을 했는가?
(A) 고객 만족도 조사를 실시했다
(B) 그녀 소유의 라이프스타일 잡지를 출시했다
(C) 간행물을 위한 몇몇 질문에 대답했다
(D) 업계 무역 박람회에 참석했다

해설 기사의 'May 10', 'Nina Roman, ~ said in an interview this month
with our publication'에서 기사가 작성된 것이 5월 10일이고 Ms. Roman
이 이번 달에 간행물과의 인터뷰에서 말했다고 했으므로 (C)가 정답이다.

어휘 **conduct** v. 실시하다, 실행하다 **launch** v. 출시하다, 착수하다
trade fair phr. 무역 박람회

패러프레이징

said in an interview 인터뷰에서 말했다 → Answered some questions 몇
몇 질문에 대답했다

184 Not/True 문제 연계
상 ●●●

해석 Diamond Home사에 대해 언급된 것은?
(A) 10년 이상 동안 높이 평가받았다.
(B) 백화점에서 그것의 제품들을 판매한다.
(C) 야외 가구의 생산을 전문으로 한다.
(D) 이번 여름에 몇몇 새로운 가게들을 열 것이다.

해설 광고의 'Founded over 10 years ago, Diamond Home'에서
Diamond Home사가 10년도 더 전에 설립되었다고 했다. 또한, 기사의
'With constantly high consumer ratings since its founding'에서는
그것, 즉 Diamond Home사의 설립 이후 그것은 변함없이 높은 소비자 평
가를 받았다는 사실을 확인할 수 있다.
두 단서를 종합할 때, Diamond Home사는 10년도 더 전에 설립된 이후 변
함없이 높은 소비자 평가를 받아왔다는 것을 알 수 있다. 따라서 (A)가 정답
이다. (C)는 광고의 'Kitchen tables', 'Computer desks'에서 식탁과 컴
퓨터 책상도 판매하고 있다는 것을 알 수 있으므로 지문의 내용과 일치하지
않는다. (B)와 (D)는 지문에 언급되지 않은 내용이다.

어휘 **highly** adv. 높이 **rate** v. 평가하다 **specialize in** phr. ~을 전문으로 하다

패러프레이징

high consumer ratings 높은 소비자 평가 → highly rated 높이 평가받은
over 10 years 10년도 더 → more than a decade 10년 이상

185 육하원칙 문제
중 ●●○

해석 야외 가구에 대해 무슨 혜택이 제공되는가?
(A) 무료 제품 견본들
(B) 제품의 반값 할인 쿠폰
(C) 무료 주방용품 한 세트
(D) 하나의 가격에 두 개의 제품

해설 광고의 'Item', 'Patio chairs', 'Deal', 'Buy one, get one free'에서 제품
에 대한 혜택으로 야외 가구인 테라스 의자를 구매할 경우 한 개를 사면, 한 개
는 공짜로 얻는다고 했으므로 (D)가 정답이다.

어휘 **complimentary** adj. 무료의 **kitchenware** n. 주방용품

패러프레이징

Buy one, get one free 한 개를 사고, 한 개를 공짜로 얻는다 → Two items for
the price of one 하나의 가격에 두 개의 제품

186-190번은 다음 구인 광고, 편지, 이메일에 관한 문제입니다.

여러 지원 가능한 일자리 - Quadra 부동산

당신은 로스앤젤레스에서 가장 큰 상업용 부동산 중개소에서 일하는 것에 관
심 있으십니까? Quadra 부동산은 그것의 모든 직원들에게 후한 보상과 복지
혜택을 제공하는 성장하는 기업입니다. 저희는 현재 다음과 같은 일자리를 채
워줄 사람들을 찾고 있습니다:

[187]회계사 / Fairfax 지점
[187]요건: 회계학 학사 학위 및 3년의 관련 경력

부동산 중개인 / Huntington 지점

요건: 부동산 중개인 자격증 및 4년의 관련 경력

접수원 / San Pedro 지점
요건: 고등학교 졸업장 및 2년의 관련 경력

부팀장 / Forest Grove 지점
요건: 경영학 학사 학위 및 6년의 관련 경력

¹⁸⁶이 일자리들에 관한 더 많은 정보와 지원하는 방법에 관한 설명을 위해, 저희의 홈페이지인 www.quadrarealty.com에 방문해주십시오.

realty n. 부동산 commercial adj. 상업용의 real estate phr. 부동산
generous adj. 후한, 너그러운 compensation n. 보상
benefits package phr. 복지 혜택 accountant n. 회계사
bachelor n. 학사 accounting n. 회계학 realtor n. 부동산 중개인
diploma n. 졸업장

7월 15일
David Reynolds Quadra 부동산
1602번지 Delta가
로스앤젤레스, 캘리포니아주 90293

Mr. Reynolds께,

Quadra 부동산의 직원이 되는 것에 저의 관심을 표하고자 합니다. ¹⁸⁷저는 제가 명단에 기재된 일자리에 아주 적합하다고 생각합니다. 비록 저는 이전에 부동산 중개업소에서 일한 적은 없지만, ¹⁸⁷저는 대학에서 회계학을 전공했습니다. ¹⁸⁷/¹⁸⁸⁻ᴰ또한, 저는 지난 4년간 Blackwood 건설회사의 회계부서에서 근무했습니다. 저는 ¹⁸⁸⁻ᴰ제 회사가 오클랜드로 이전할 계획이기 때문에 지금 새로운 고용 기회를 찾고 있고, 저는 로스앤젤레스 지역에 남길 원합니다.

당신은 질문이 있으시면 제게 555-0393으로 전화 혹은 j.quayle@digiquest.com으로 이메일을 통해 연락할 수 있습니다. 유감스럽게도, ¹⁸⁹저는 저의 현재 근무 일정 때문에 평일 아침에만 면접을 볼 수 있습니다. 제 지원서를 고려해주셔서 감사합니다.

Jenna Quayle 드림

suited adj. 적합한 listed adj. (명단에) 기재된 previously adv. 이전에
major in phr. ~을 전공하다 relocate v. 이전하다 remain v. 남다
reach v. 연락하다 unfortunately adv. 유감스럽게도

수신: Doug Stevens <d.stevens@quadra.com>, Laura Meyers <l.meyers@quadra.com>, Jeff Kim <j.kim@quadra.com>, Pauline Greer <p.greer@quadra.com>
발신: Brett Reynolds <b.reynolds@quadra.com>
제목: 고용 현황
날짜: 9월 8일

안녕하세요 여러분,

저는 모든 지점 매니저들에게 고용 절차에 관해 최신 정보를 알려주고 싶었습니다. 현시점에서, 저희는 공석들에 대한 몇몇 유망한 지원자들이 있습니다. ¹⁸⁹면접들은 다음의 날들에 이루어질 것입니다:

월요일, 9월 15일 (오후 2시)
¹⁸⁹수요일, 9월 17일 (오전 10시)
목요일, 9월 18일 (오후 4시)
토요일, 9월 20일 (오전 11시)

¹⁹⁰만약 당신에게 제가 지원자들에게 묻길 바라는 구체적인 질문들이 있

다면, 저에게 그것들을 보내주십시오. 저는 지원자들과의 제 첫 번째 만남을 준비할 시간을 가질 수 있도록 9월 10일까지 이 정보가 필요할 것입니다. 면접이 완료되면, 저는 가장 적합한 지원자들에 대한 요약 보고서들을 만들 것입니다. 이것들은 당신이 검토할 수 있도록 9월 24일에 이메일로 발송될 것입니다.

Brett Reynolds 드림
인사부장, Quadra 부동산

update v. 최신 정보를 알려주다, 갱신하다 branch manager phr. 지점장
promising adj. 유망한 candidate n. 지원자, 후보자
take place phr. 이루어지다, 일어나다 applicant n. 지원자
suitable adj. 적합한

---

186 육하원칙 문제 하 ●○○

해석 지원자들은 어떻게 지원 가능한 일자리들에 대해 더 알아낼 수 있는가?
(A) 채용 대행사에 이메일을 보냄으로써
(B) 지역 사무실에 잠시 들름으로써
(C) 지점장에게 전화함으로써
(D) 회사 웹사이트를 방문함으로써

해설 구인 광고의 'Please go to our homepage, ~ for more information about these positions and instructions on how to apply.'에서 이 일자리들에 관한 더 많은 정보와 지원하는 방법에 관한 설명을 위해, 자신들, 즉 Quadra 부동산의 홈페이지에 방문하라고 했으므로 (D)가 정답이다.

어휘 recruitment n. 채용 stop by phr. 잠시 들르다

---

187 육하원칙 문제 연계 중 ●●○

해석 Ms. Quayle은 어느 지점의 일자리에 지원했는가?
(A) Fairfax 지점
(B) Huntington 지점
(C) San Pedro 지점
(D) Forest Grove 지점

해설 이메일의 'I believe that I am well suited for the listed position.'에서 저, 즉 Ms. Quayle은 자신이 명단에 기재된 일자리에 아주 적합하다고 생각한다고 했고, 'I majored in accounting in university. In addition, I have spent the last four years in the accounting department ~.'에서는 대학에서 회계학을 전공했으며 지난 4년간 회계부서에서 근무했다고 했다. 또한, 구인 광고의 'Accountant / Fairfax Branch', 'Requirements: Bachelor's degree in accounting and three years' related experience'에서는 Fairfax 지점의 회계사 일자리의 요건이 회계학 학사 학위 및 3년의 관련 경력이라는 것을 확인할 수 있다.
두 단서를 종합할 때, Ms. Quayle은 Fairfax 지점의 회계사 일자리에 지원했다는 것을 알 수 있다. 따라서 (A)가 정답이다.

---

188 Not/True 문제 상 ●●●

해석 Blackwood 건설회사에 대해 언급된 것은?
(A) 몇몇 사무실들을 닫을 것이다.
(B) 새로운 건축 프로젝트를 시작할 것이다.
(C) 더 많은 직원들을 고용할 것이다.
(D) 다른 도시로 이동할 것이다.

해설 편지의 'In addition, I have spent the last four years in ~ Blackwood Construction.'과 'my company is planning to relocate to Oakland, and I wish to remain in the Los Angeles area'에서 또한, 저, 즉 Ms. Quayle이 지난 4년간 Blackwood 건설회사에서 근무했고, 자신의 회사

가 오클랜드로 이전할 계획이며 자신은 로스앤젤레스 지역에 남길 원한다고 했으므로 (D)는 지문의 내용과 일치한다. 따라서 (D)가 정답이다. (A), (B), (C)는 지문에 언급되지 않은 내용이다.

어휘 building n. 건축, 건물

패러프레이징

is planning to relocate to Oakland 오클랜드로 이전할 계획이다
→ will move to a different city 다른 도시로 이동할 것이다

최고난도 문제

189 추론 문제 연계   상 ●●●

해석 Ms. Quayle은 언제 면접을 볼 것 같은가?
(A) 9월 15일에
(B) 9월 17일에
(C) 9월 18일에
(D) 9월 20일에

해설 편지의 'I am only available to interview on weekday mornings'에서 자신, 즉 Ms. Quayle은 평일 아침에만 면접을 볼 수 있다고 했다. 또한, 이메일의 'The interviews will take place on the following days:'와 'Wednesday, September 17 (10 A.M.)'에서는 면접이 9월 17일 수요일 오전 10시에 이루어진다는 것을 확인할 수 있다.
두 단서를 종합할 때, Ms. Quayle은 평일 아침 9월 17일에 면접을 볼 것이라는 것을 추론할 수 있다. 따라서 (B)가 정답이다.

190 추론 문제   중 ●●○

해석 Mr. Reynolds에 대해 암시되는 것은?
(A) 직접 면접을 진행할 것이다.
(B) 이미 지원자에게 제안을 했다.
(C) 일자리가 아직 채용 가능한지 확신할 수 없다.
(D) 신입 직원들의 교육을 담당하고 있다.

해설 이메일의 'If you have any specific questions you would like me to ask the applicants, please send them to me.'와 'I will ~ prepare for my first meetings with the candidates'에서 만약 자신, 즉 Mr. Reynolds가 지원자들에게 묻길 바라는 구체적인 질문이 있다면, 자신에게 그것들을 보내 달라고 했고, 지원자들과의 첫 번째 만남을 준비할 것이라고 했으므로 Mr. Reynolds가 직접 면접을 진행할 것이라는 사실을 추론할 수 있다. 따라서 (A)가 정답이다.

어휘 personally adv. 직접, 개인적으로   uncertain adj. 확신이 없는, 잘 모르는   in charge of phr. ~을 남낭하는

191-195번은 다음 소식지 기사, 영수증, 설문지에 관한 문제입니다.

Bath Vitals사 직원 소식지
3월 9일

경품을 타기 위해 설문조사를 하는 고객
Vincent Heidecker 작성

올해 초, ¹⁹²Bath Vitals사의 이사회는 고객 만족도를 높이기 위해서, 쇼핑객들이 조사될 필요가 있다는 결론을 내렸다. ¹⁹¹고객들이 우리 웹사이트를 방문하고 설문조사를 완료하도록 독려하기 위해, 그들은 200달러의 상품권을 받을 수 있는 기회를 제공받을 것이다. 매달, 우리는 온라인 설문조사를 완료한 두 명의 고객들에게 우리의 모든 지점들에서 교환할 수 있는 상품권을 수여할 것이다. 마케팅부장 Cassandra Jo가 설문조사 작성을 담당하는 동안,

정보 분석가 Joshua Gooding은 응답들을 처리하는 것을 담당할 것이다.

어휘 executive board phr. 이사회   gift certificate phr. 상품권
award v. 수여하다; n. 상   redeemable adj. 교환할 수 있는
in charge of phr. ~을 담당하는   process v. 처리하다   response n. 응답

Bath Vitals사
89번지 West Sinto가
스포캔, 워싱턴주
(509) 555 9889

월요일, 5월 12일, 오후 12시 30분

수량	제품	가격
1	¹⁹⁵Charmy 비누 (여섯 묶음)	¹⁹⁵6.89달러
1	Brilliant Fiber 손수건	12.19달러
1	Mayor's Choice 샴푸	3.49달러
1	Grandi & Corto 샤워 커튼	34.99달러

소계	57.56달러
세금	4.03달러
총액	61.59달러
현금	65.00달러
거스름돈	3.41달러

^{193-B}단골 쇼핑객 카드 소지자   ^{193-B}Lindsey Brant
새롭게 누적된 포인트   17
총 포인트   211

당신은 저희의 모든 지점들에서 교환 가능한 200달러 상품권에 당첨되실 수 있습니다. 자격을 얻으려면, ¹⁹²www.bathvitals.com/feedback에 방문하여 오늘 당신의 쇼핑 경험에 대한 짧은 설문조사를 완료하거나 고객 서비스 카운터에서 간단히 설문지를 손으로 작성하세요.

어휘 accumulated adj. 누적된, 축적된   qualify v. 자격을 얻다
questionnaire n. 설문지

www.bathvitals.com/feedback

다음 질문들에 답변한 후, 계속 진행하기 위해 "다음" 버튼을 누르세요.

¹⁹⁵**당신의 이름:** Lindsey Brant   **방문한 지점:** 스포캔   **방문 일자:** 5월 12일

저희의 고객 서비스는 어떠셨습니까?
¹⁹⁴점원이 제가 필요한 것이 있는지 물어봤지만 어떤 욕실 슬리퍼가 가장 편한지 제게 말해주지 못했습니다.

저희의 선택권을 어떻게 평가하시겠습니까?
저는 선택할 수 있는 많은 브랜드와 제품들이 있어서 좋았습니다.

당신은 저희의 가격에 만족하셨습니까?
네. 당신의 가격들은 Ted's Toiletries사의 것들보다 5에서 10퍼센트 저렴했습니다.

가게의 진열이 편리하다고 생각하셨나요?
그렇지 않아요. ¹⁹⁵저는 7번 통로에서 Charmy사에 의해 만들어진 비누를 찾을 것이라고 예상했지만, 그것은 방향제와 샤워 꼭지 사이의 4번 통로에 있었습니다.

다음 ▷

rate v. 평가하다 layout n. 진열, 배치 convenient adj. 편리한
air freshener phr. 방향제 showerhead n. 샤워 꼭지

191 주제 찾기 문제   상 ●●●

해석 소식지 기사의 주요 주제는 무엇인가?
(A) 회사의 확장
(B) 고객들을 위한 장려책
(C) 설문조사 결과
(D) 경영진들의 여행

해설 소식지 기사의 'To encourage customers to visit ~ Web site and complete the survey, they will be offered ~ a $200 gift certificate.'에서 고객들이 웹사이트를 방문하고 설문조사를 완료하도록 독려하기 위해, 그들은 200달러의 상품권을 받을 것이라고 했으므로 (B)가 정답이다.

어휘 expansion n. 확장 incentive n. 장려책, 우대책
excursion n. 여행, 나들이 executive n. 경영진, 간부

192 추론 문제 연계   중 ●●○

해석 Bath Vitals사는 소식지를 발행한 후 무엇을 하기로 결정했을 것 같은가?
(A) 피드백을 모으기 위한 또 다른 방법을 사용한다
(B) 컨설팅 회사로부터 도움을 요청한다
(C) 웹사이트 내용을 바꾼다
(D) 지점들 중 몇몇을 보수한다

해설 소식지 기사의 'the Bath Vitals executive board concluded that ~ shoppers need to be surveyed'에서 Bath Vitals사의 이사회가 쇼핑객들이 조사될 필요가 있다는 결론을 내렸다고 했다. 또한, 영수증의 'visit www.bathvitals.com/feedback and complete a short survey ~ or simply fill out a questionnaire ~ at our customer service counter'에서는 고객들에게 웹사이트에 방문하여 짧은 설문조사를 완료하거나 고객 서비스 카운터에서 간단히 설문지를 작성하라고 한 것을 확인할 수 있다.
두 단서를 종합할 때, 고객들을 조사하기 위해 온라인 설문조사 방식과 함께 고객 서비스 카운터에서 설문지를 작성하는 방법을 제공하기로 결정했다는 사실을 추론할 수 있다. 따라서 (A)가 정답이다.

어휘 method n. 방법 gather v. 모으다 renovate v. 보수하다

193 Not/True 문제   상 ●●●

해석 영수증에 따르면, Bath Vitals사에 대해 사실인 것은?
(A) 새로운 지점을 열 계획이다.
(B) 고객 보상 프로그램을 운영한다.
(C) 평일 저녁에 계속해서 열려있다.
(D) 추가적인 직원들을 고용할 생각이다.

해설 영수증의 'Frequent Shopper Cardholder', 'Lindsey Brant', 'New Points Accumulated', '17', 'Total Points', '211'에서 단골 쇼핑객 카드 소지자인 Ms. Brant가 구매한 제품들에 대해 새롭게 누적된 포인트 17점을 얻었고, 총 포인트가 211점임을 알 수 있으므로 (B)는 지문의 내용과 일치한다. 따라서 (B)가 정답이다. (A), (C), (D)는 지문에 언급되지 않은 내용이다.

어휘 run v. 운영하다, 경영하다 remain v. 계속해서 ~하다, ~채로 남아 있다

194 육하원칙 문제   상 ●●●

해석 Ms. Brant는 직원에게 무엇을 요청했는가?
(A) 최저가격 보증
(B) 매장 배치도

(C) 제품 추천
(D) 선물 포장 서비스

해설 설문지의 'A sales clerk ~ couldn't tell me which bathroom slippers were the most comfortable.'에서 점원은 어떤 욕실 슬리퍼가 가장 편한지 저, 즉 Ms. Brant에게 말해주지 못했다고 했으므로 (C)가 정답이다.

어휘 recommendation n. 추천 gift-wrapping n. 선물 포장

패러프레이징

tell ~ which ~ slippers were the most comfortable 어떤 슬리퍼가 가장 편한지 말하다 → A product recommendation 제품 추천

195 육하원칙 문제 연계   중 ●●○

해석 4번 통로에서 Ms. Brant가 구매한 것의 가격은 얼마인가?
(A) 6.89달러
(B) 12.19달러
(C) 3.49달러
(D) 34.99달러

해설 설문지의 'Your name: Lindsey Brant', 'I expected to find the soap made by Charmy in Aisle 7, but it was in Aisle 4'에서 Ms. Brant는 자신이 7번 통로에서 Charmy사에 의해 만들어진 비누를 찾을 것이라고 예상했지만, 그것은 4번 통로에 있었다고 했다. 또한, 영수증의 'Charmy soap (six-pack)', '$6.89'에서는 Charmy 비누 (여섯 묶음)가 6.89달러라는 것을 확인할 수 있다.
두 단서를 종합할 때, Ms. Brant가 4번 통로에서 구매한 것은 Charmy사의 비누이며 그것의 가격은 6.89 달러임을 확인할 수 있다. 따라서 (A)가 정답이다.

196-200번은 다음 웹페이지와 두 이메일에 관한 문제입니다.

	Park 호텔		
소개	예약	장소	연락

196-B Olympia 시내의 Dawson 컨벤션 센터 옆에 편리하게 위치한, Park 호텔은 출장 여행객들과 관광객들 모두에게 이상적입니다. 저희의 최근에 개조된 건물은 197-C 최첨단 피트니스 센터, 197-A 선물 가게, 그리고 197-D 최고급 식당을 포함합니다. 그리고 저희는 이번 여름에 손님들을 위한 여러 가지 특별 할인 요금이 있습니다:

• 단체 요금: 친구들 혹은 동료들과 여행하시나요? 당신의 일행이 4개 이상의 객실들을 예약할 때 하룻밤에 110달러만 지불하세요.
• 200 평일 요금: 만약 당신의 숙박이 금요일, 토요일, 혹은 일요일을 포함하지 않는다면, 당신은 하룻밤에 130달러만 청구될 것입니다.
• 198-A 장기 숙박 요금: 만약 당신이 저희와 7일 이상 숙박할 계획이라면, 당신은 하룻밤에 115달러로 객실을 예약할 수 있습니다.
• 회원 요금: 저희 Park 호텔 보상 프로그램의 회원들은 하룻밤에 120달러만 청구됩니다.

이 요금들은 8월 31일까지 유효하고 고급 객실에만 적용됩니다.
198-C 예약할 때 전액이 지불되어야 합니다.

ideal adj. 이상적인 alike adv. 모두, 똑같이 renovate v. 개조하다, 보수하다
state-of-the-art adj. 최첨단의, 최신의 rate n. 요금, 가격
party n. 일행, 정당 extended stay phr. 장기 숙박
valid adj. 적용되는, 유효한 deluxe adj. 고급의

수신: Park 호텔 고객 서비스 <customerservice@parkhotel.com>
발신: Beth Davidson <b.davidson@westmail.com>
제목: 예약 83478
날짜: 6월 15일

저는 귀하께 제가 6월 12일에 한 예약에 관해 연락합니다. 저는 오늘 아침에 우연히 제 온라인 신용카드 명세서를 확인했고, 저는 제가 과잉 청구되었다는 것을 알게 되었습니다. ¹⁹⁸⁻ᴬ저는 장기 숙박 요금에 대한 자격이 있어야 했습니다. 귀하의 호텔의 누군가가 이 문제를 해결하기 위해 제게 가능한 빨리 연락해주면 감사하겠습니다. 또한, ¹⁹⁹귀사의 셔틀버스는 매일 밤 언제 운영을 중단하나요? 저는 제 항공편이 오후 11시 30분에 도착하기 때문에 문의합니다. 만약 귀사의 셔틀버스가 이렇게 늦게 운영하지 않는다면, 저는 그냥 택시를 잡아 탈 것입니다.

Beth Davidson 드림

notice v. 알다, 주목하다 overcharge v. 과잉 청구하다
qualify for phr. ~에 대한 자격이 있다 resolve v. 해결하다
issue n. 문제, 사안 flight n. 항공편, 항공 arrive v. 도착하다
operate v. 운영하다

수신: Beth Davidson <b.davidson@westmail.com>
발신: Joseph Hong <j.hong@parkhotel.com>
제목: 예약 83478
날짜: 6월 16일
첨부 파일: 셔틀_시간표.doc

Ms. Davidson께,

저는 귀하의 예약과 관련해 생긴 실수에 대해 사과드리고자 합니다. 저희의 온라인 예약 시스템의 오류로 인해 ²⁰⁰귀하는 평일 요금으로 청구된 것 같습니다. 귀하가 초과 지불한 금액은 당신의 신용카드로 늦어도 6월 18일까지 지불 거절될 것입니다. 귀하의 문의 사항에 관해서는, 저희의 셔틀 서비스는 매일 오전 1시까지 이용 가능하므로, 귀하는 어떤 문제도 없을 것입니다. 제가 이 이메일에 시간표를 포함했습니다. 귀하는 필요한 다른 도움이 있으시면 제게 알려주십시오.

Joseph Hong 드림

appear v. ~인 것 같아 보이다, 나타나다 bill v. 청구하다
amount n. 금액, 액수 overpay v. 초과 지불하다
with regard to phr. ~에 관해서는 available adj. 이용 가능한

최고난도 문제

196 Not/True 문제　　　상 ●●●

해석　Park 호텔에 대해 언급된 것은?
(A) 여름에 재단장될 것이다.
(B) 행사 장소 근처에 위치해 있다.
(C) 총회를 개최할 것이다.
(D) 새로운 객실 종류를 도입하고 있다.

해설　웹페이지의 'Conveniently located next to the Dawson Convention Center ~, the Park Hotel'에서 Park 호텔은 Dawson 컨벤션 센터 옆에 편리하게 위치해 있다고 했으므로 (B)는 지문의 내용과 일치한다. 따라서 (B)가 정답이다. (A), (C), (D)는 지문에 언급되지 않은 내용이다.

어휘　refurbish v. 재단장하다, 새로 꾸미다 situate v. 위치시키다, 두다
convention n. 총회, 대회 introduce v. 도입하다, 소개하다

패러프레이징

Conveniently located next to the ~ Convention Center 컨벤션 센터 옆에 편리하게 위치한 → situated near an event venue 행사 장소 근처에 위치한

197 Not/True 문제　　　중 ●●○

해석　Park 호텔에서 이용 가능하지 않은 것은?
(A) 상점
(B) 비즈니스 센터
(C) 체육관
(D) 식사 공간

해설　질문의 Park 호텔과 관련된 내용이 언급된 웹페이지에서 (B)는 언급되지 않은 내용이다. 따라서 (B)가 정답이다. (A)는 'a gift shop'에서 선물 가게를 포함한다고 했으므로 지문의 내용과 일치한다. (C)는 'a state-of-the-art fitness center'에서 최첨단 피트니스 센터를 포함한다고 했으므로 지문의 내용과 일치한다. (D)는 'a five-star restaurant'에서 최고급 식당을 포함한다고 했으므로 지문의 내용과 일치한다.

패러프레이징

shop 가게 → store 상점
fitness center 피트니스 센터 → gym 체육관
restaurant 식당 → dining area 식사 공간

198 Not/True 문제 연계　　　상 ●●●

해석　Ms. Davidson에 대해 언급된 것은?
(A) 호텔에 최소 일주일 동안 머무를 것이다.
(B) 관광에 대한 환불을 받을 것이다.
(C) 체크인할 때 그녀의 객실에 대해 지불할 것이다.
(D) 그녀의 동료 몇 명과 함께 여행할 것이다.

해설　이메일1의 'I should have qualified for the Extended Stay Rate.'에서 저, 즉 Ms. Davidson은 장기 숙박 요금에 대한 자격이 있어야 했다고 했다. 또한, 웹페이지의 'Extended Stay Rate: If you ~ stay with us for seven days or more, you can reserve a room for $115 per night.'에서는 장기 숙박 요금은 만약 당신, 즉 고객이 저희, 즉 Park 호텔에 7일 이상 숙박한다면 하룻밤에 115달러로 객실을 예약할 수 있다고 했다. 두 단서를 종합할 때, Ms. Davidson은 장기 숙박 요금에 대한 자격이 있으므로 최소 7일을 숙박할 것임을 알 수 있다. 따라서 (A)가 정답이다. (B)와 (D)는 지문에 언급되지 않은 내용이다. (C)는 웹페이지의 'Payment must be made in full at the time of booking.'에서 예약할 때 전액이 지불되어야 한다고 했으므로 지문의 내용과 일치하지 않는다.

어휘　at least phr. 최소한 coworker n. (직장) 동료

패러프레이징

stay with us for seven days or more 저희와 7일 이상 숙박한다 → stay at the hotel for at least a week 최소 일주일 동안 호텔에 머무른다

199 육하원칙 문제　　　중 ●●○

해석　Ms. Davidson은 왜 셔틀 서비스에 대해 문의하는가?
(A) 택시가 이용 가능할지 여부를 잘 모른다.
(B) 늦은 밤에 공항에 도착할 것이다.
(C) 온라인 시간표가 오류를 포함하고 있다고 생각한다.
(D) 그것이 더 이상 제공되지 않는다고 들었다.

해설　이메일1의 'when does your shuttle bus stop running each night?

I'm asking because my flight arrives at 11:30 P.M. If your shuttle bus does not operate this late, I will just catch a taxi.'에서 귀사, 즉 Park 호텔의 셔틀버스가 매일 밤 언제 운영을 중단하는지 물은 후, 저, 즉 Ms. Davidson의 항공편이 오후 11시 30분에 도착하기 때문에 문의하며 만약 귀사의 셔틀버스가 이렇게 늦게 운영하지 않는다면, 그냥 택시를 잡아탈 것이라고 했으므로 (B)가 정답이다.

어휘 inquire v. 문의하다, 알아보다   uncertain adj. 잘 모르는

200 육하원칙 문제 연계   중 ●●○

해석 Ms. Davidson은 원래 하룻밤에 얼마가 청구되었는가?
(A) 110달러
(B) 115달러
(C) 120달러
(D) 130달러

해설 이메일2의 'you were billed the Weekday Rate'에서는 당신, 즉 Ms. Davidson은 평일 요금으로 청구되었다고 했다. 또한, 웹페이지의 'Weekday Rate: ~ $130 per night.'에서는 평일 요금이 하룻밤에 130달러라는 사실을 확인할 수 있다.
두 단서를 종합할 때, Ms. Davidson이 원래 평일 요금으로 청구되었으므로 130달러를 지불했다는 것을 알 수 있다. 따라서 (D)가 정답이다.

어휘 originally adv. 원래, 본래

물토익부터 **불토익**까지, **1200제**로 토익 졸업!

해커스 토익

실전 1200제
READING RC

초판 8쇄 발행 2024년 7월 22일
초판 1쇄 발행 2020년 7월 1일

지은이	해커스 어학연구소
펴낸곳	(주)해커스 어학연구소
펴낸이	해커스 어학연구소 출판팀

주소	서울특별시 서초구 강남대로61길 23 (주)해커스 어학연구소
고객센터	02-537-5000
교재 관련 문의	publishing@hackers.com
동영상강의	HackersIngang.com

ISBN	978-89-6542-373-7 (13740)
Serial Number	01-08-01

영어 전문 포털, 해커스토익
Hackers.co.kr

해커스토익

· 매일 실전 RC/LC 문제 및 토익 보카 TEST 등 **다양한 무료 학습 컨텐츠**
· 매월 무료 적중예상특강 및 실시간 토익시험 정답확인/해설강의

외국어인강 1위, 해커스인강
HackersIngang.com

해커스인강

· 취약 문제 유형을 분석해주는 인공지능 시스템 **해커스토익 '빅플' 어플**(교재 내 이용권 수록)
· **무료 단어암기장&단어암기 MP3 및 정답녹음 MP3**
· 토익 스타강사의 고득점 전략이 담긴 **본 교재 인강**

[외국어인강 1위] 헤럴드 선정 2018 대학생 선호브랜드 대상 '대학생이 선정한 외국어인강' 부문 1위

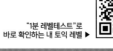

"1분 레벨테스트"로
바로 확인하는 내 토익 레벨 ▶

토익 교재 시리즈

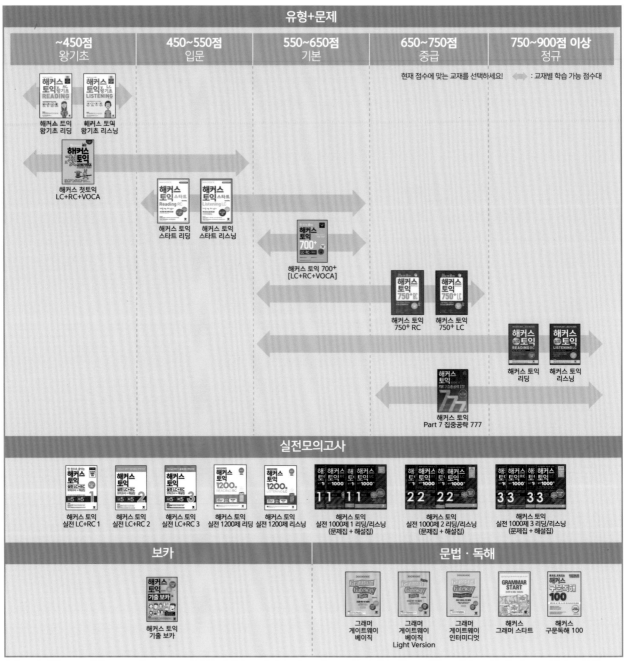

유형+문제

~450점 왕기초	450~550점 입문	550~650점 기본	650~750점 중급	750~900점 이상 정규

현재 점수에 맞는 교재를 선택하세요! ⇢ : 교재별 학습 가능 점수대

해커스 토익 왕기초 리딩 / 해커스 토익 왕기초 리스닝

해커스 첫토익 LC+RC+VOCA

해커스 토익 스타트 리딩 / 해커스 토익 스타트 리스닝

해커스 토익 700+ [LC+RC+VOCA]

해커스 토익 750+ RC / 해커스 토익 750+ LC

해커스 토익 리딩 / 해커스 토익 리스닝

해커스 토익 Part 7 집중공략 777

실전모의고사

해커스 토익 실전 LC+RC 1 / 해커스 토익 실전 LC+RC 2 / 해커스 토익 실전 LC+RC 3 / 해커스 토익 실전 1200제 리딩 / 해커스 토익 실전 1200제 리스닝 / 해커스 토익 실전 1000제 1 리딩/리스닝 (문제집 + 해설집) / 해커스 토익 실전 1000제 2 리딩/리스닝 (문제집 + 해설집) / 해커스 토익 실전 1000제 3 리딩/리스닝 (문제집 + 해설집)

보카 | 문법 · 독해

해커스 토익 기출 보카

그래머 게이트웨이 베이직 / 그래머 게이트웨이 베이직 Light Version / 그래머 게이트웨이 인터미디엇 / 해커스 그래머 스타트 / 해커스 구문독해 100

토익스피킹 교재 시리즈

해커스 토익스피킹 스타트 / 만능 템플릿과 위기탈출 표현으로 해커스 토익스피킹 5일 완성 / 해커스 토익스피킹 / 해커스 토익스피킹 실전모의고사 15회

오픽 교재 시리즈

해커스 오픽 스타트 [Intermediate 공략] / 서베이부터 실전까지 해커스 오픽 매뉴얼 / 해커스 오픽 [Advanced 공략]